# CHAMBERS
# BOOK OF FACTS

# CHAMBERS BOOK OF FACTS

*Editor*
Melanie Parry

*with the assistance of*
Trevor Anderson
*and*
Una McGovern

CHAMBERS

CHAMBERS
An imprint of Chambers Harrap Publishers Ltd
7 Hopetoun Crescent
Edinburgh EH7 4AY



First edition 1992
This edition first published Chambers 1998
Revised edition 2000
Revised edition 2002



British Library Cataloguing in Publication Data for this book is available from the British Library.

ISBN 0550 10057 1

Designed and typeset in Great Britain by Chambers Harrap Publishers Ltd
Printed and bound in France by Aubin

# CONTRIBUTORS

*Senior Editor*
Melanie Parry

*Editors*
Trevor Anderson
Una McGovern

*Contributors*
Russell Eberst
Olwen Fowler
Satpal Kaushal
Min Lee
Sandy Mullay
Melanie Sinker

*Proof-readers*
Jennifer Gibb
Virginia Klein
Jane Pollock
Martin Mellor

*Keyer*
David Wood

*Prepress*
Helen Bleck
Paula McCulloch

# ABBREVIATIONS

Used in *Book of Facts*

| | |
|---|---|
| AD | Anno Domini |
| admin | administration |
| BC | Before Christ |
| c | century |
| c. | circa |
| C | Celsius (Centigrade) |
| cc | cubic centimetre(s) |
| Chin | Chinese |
| CIS | Commonwealth of Independent States |
| cm | centimetre(s) |
| Co | County |
| cont. | continued |
| cu | cubic |
| cwt | hundredweight |
| e | estimate |
| E | east(ern) |
| eg | for example |
| Eng | English |
| F | Fahrenheit |
| fl oz | fluid ounce(s) |
| fl | flourished (floruit) |
| Fr | French |
| ft | foot (feet) |
| g | gram(s) |
| gal | gallons |
| Ger | German |
| Gr | Greek |
| h | hour(s) |
| ha | hectare(s) |
| Hung | Hungarian |
| I(s) | Island(s) |
| ie | that is (id est) |
| in | inch(es) |
| Ir | Irish |
| Ital | Italian |
| Jap | Japanese |
| K | Kelvin |
| kg | kilogram(s) |
| kJ | kilojoules |
| l | litre(s) |
| L | Lake |
| Lat | Latin |
| lb | pound(s) |
| l y | light year(s) |
| m | metre(s) |
| min | minute(s) |
| mi | mile(s) |
| mm | millimetre(s) |
| Mt | Mount(ain) |
| Mts | Mountains |
| N | north(ern) |
| no. | number |
| oz | ounce(s) |
| p(p) | page(s) |
| pop | population |
| Port | Portuguese |
| pt | pint(s) |
| r. | reigned |
| R | River |
| Russ | Russian |
| S | south(ern) |
| sec | second(s) |
| Span | Spanish |
| sq | square |
| St | Saint |
| Sta | Santa |
| Ste | Sainte |
| Swed | Swedish |
| TV | television |
| UT | Unified Team |
| v. | versus |
| vols. | volumes |
| W | west(ern) |
| yd | yard(s) |

**See also**

Common abbreviations pp315–21
National holiday abbreviations p67
Currency abbreviations pp260–70
Chemistry abbreviations pp383–5
International organizations pp294, 296

**Other conventions**

Months are abbreviated to the first three letters (3 Jan 1817)

# CONTENTS

## SPACE



## EARTH



## CLIMATE AND ENVIRONMENT

## TIME



## NATURAL HISTORY



## HUMAN LIFE



## HISTORY

## SOCIAL STRUCTURE



## COMMUNICATION

## SCIENCE, ENGINEERING AND MEASUREMENT



## ARTS AND CULTURE

## SPORT AND GAMES



## THOUGHT AND BELIEF

## Planetary data

| Planet | Distance from Sun (million km/mi) Maximum | | Minimum | | Sidereal period | Axial rotation period (equatorial) | Diameter (equatorial) km | mi |
|---|---|---|---|---|---|---|---|---|
| **Mercury** | 69.4 | 43.0 | 46.8 | 29.0 | 88 d | 58 d 16 h | 4 878 | 3 031 |
| **Venus** | 109.0 | 67.6 | 107.6 | 66.7 | 224.7 d | 243 d | 12 104 | 7 521 |
| **Earth** | 152.6 | 94.6 | 147.4 | 91.4 | 365.256 d | 23 h 56 m | 12 756 | 7 927 |
| **Mars** | 249.2 | 154.5 | 207.3 | 128.5 | 687 d | 24 h 37 m 23 s | 6 794 | 4 222 |
| **Jupiter** | 817.4 | 506.8 | 741.6 | 459.8 | 11.86 y | 9 h 50 m 30 s | 142 800 | 88 700 |
| **Saturn** | 1 512 | 937.6 | 1 346 | 834.6 | 29.46 y | 10 h 14 m | 120 536 | 74 900 |
| **Uranus** | 3 011 | 1 867 | 2 740 | 1 699 | 84.01 y | 16–28 h[1] | 51 118 | 31 765 |
| **Neptune** | 4 543 | 2 817 | 4 466 | 2 769 | 164.79 y | 18–20 h[1] | 49 492 | 30 754 |
| **Pluto** | 7 364 | 4 566 | 4 461 | 2 766 | 247.7 y | 6 d 9 h | 2 300 | 1 429 |

y: years d: days h: hours m: minutes s: seconds km: kilometres mi: miles

[1]Different latitudes rotate at different speeds.

## Planetary satellites

| | Year discovered | Distance from planet km | mi | Diameter km | mi |
|---|---|---|---|---|---|
| **Earth** | | | | | |
| Moon | — | 384 000 | 239 000 | 3 476 | 2 160 |
| **Mars** | | | | | |
| Phobos | 1877 | 9 380 | 5 830 | 27 | 17 |
| Deimos | 1877 | 23 460 | 14 580 | 15 | 9 |
| **Jupiter** | | | | | |
| Metis | 1979 | 128 000 | 80 000 | 40 | 25 |
| Adrastea | 1979 | 129 000 | 80 000 | 24 | 15 |
| Amalthea | 1892 | 181 000 | 112 000 | 270 | 170 |
| Thebe | 1979 | 222 000 | 138 000 | 100 | 62 |
| Io | 1610 | 422 000 | 262 000 | 3 630 | 2 260 |
| Europa | 1610 | 671 000 | 417 000 | 3 138 | 1 950 |
| Ganymede | 1610 | 1 070 000 | 665 000 | 5 260 | 3 270 |
| Callisto | 1610 | 1 883 000 | 1 170 000 | 4 800 | 3 000 |
| Leda | 1974 | 11 100 000 | 6 900 000 | 20 | 12 |
| Himalia | 1904 | 11 480 000 | 7 134 000 | 180 | 110 |
| Lysithea | 1938 | 11 720 000 | 7 283 000 | 40 | 25 |
| Elara | 1905 | 11 740 000 | 7 295 000 | 80 | 50 |
| Ananke | 1951 | 21 200 000 | 13 174 000 | 30 | 19 |
| Carme | 1938 | 22 600 000 | 14 044 000 | 40 | 25 |
| Pasiphae | 1908 | 23 500 000 | 14 603 000 | 50 | 31 |
| Sinope | 1914 | 23 700 000 | 14 727 000 | 40 | 25 |
| **Saturn** | | | | | |
| Pan | 1990 | 134 000 | 83 000 | 20 | 12 |
| Atlas | 1980 | 138 000 | 86 000 | 40 | 25 |
| Prometheus | 1980 | 139 000 | 86 000 | 100 | 62 |

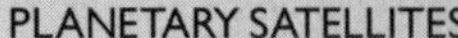





| | Year discovered | Distance from planet km | mi | Diameter km | mi |
|---|---|---|---|---|---|
| Pandora | 1980 | 142 000 | 88 000 | 100 | 62 |
| Epimetheus | 1980 | 151 000 | 94 000 | 140 | 87 |
| Janus | 1980 | 151 000 | 94 000 | 200 | 120 |
| Mimas | 1789 | 186 000 | 116 000 | 390 | 240 |
| Enceladus | 1789 | 238 000 | 148 000 | 500 | 310 |
| Calypso | 1980 | 295 000 | 183 000 | 30 | 19 |
| Telesto | 1980 | 295 000 | 183 000 | 24 | 15 |
| Tethys | 1684 | 295 000 | 183 000 | 1 050 | 650 |
| Dione | 1684 | 377 000 | 234 000 | 1 120 | 700 |
| Helene | 1982 | 378 000 | 235 000 | 35 | 22 |
| Rhea | 1672 | 527 000 | 327 000 | 1 530 | 950 |
| Titan | 1655 | 1 222 000 | 759 000 | 5 150 | 3 200 |
| Hyperion | 1848 | 1 481 000 | 920 000 | 300 | 190 |
| Iapetus | 1671 | 3 560 000 | 2 212 000 | 1 460 | 900 |
| Phoebe | 1898 | 12 950 000 | 8 047 000 | 220 | 135 |
| **Uranus** | | | | | |
| Miranda | 1948 | 130 000 | 81 000 | 470 | 290 |
| Ariel | 1851 | 191 000 | 119 000 | 1 160 | 720 |
| Umbriel | 1851 | 266 000 | 165 000 | 1 170 | 725 |
| Titania | 1787 | 436 000 | 271 000 | 1 580 | 980 |
| Oberon | 1787 | 583 000 | 362 000 | 1 520 | 945 |
| Cordelia | 1986 | 49 300 | 31 000 | 15 | 9 |
| Ophelia | 1986 | 53 800 | 33 000 | 20 | 12 |
| Bianca | 1986 | 59 100 | 37 000 | 50 | 31 |
| Cressida | 1986 | 61 750 | 38 000 | 70 | 43 |
| Desdemona | 1986 | 62 700 | 39 000 | 50 | 31 |
| Juliet | 1986 | 64 350 | 40 000 | 70 | 43 |
| Portia | 1986 | 66 090 | 41 000 | 90 | 56 |
| Rosalind | 1986 | 69 920 | 43 000 | 50 | 31 |
| Belinda | 1986 | 75 100 | 47 000 | 50 | 31 |
| Puck | 1986 | 85 890 | 53 000 | 170 | 110 |
| 1997U1 | 1997 | 7 200 000 | 4 475 000 | 60 | 37 |
| 1997U2 | 1997 | 12 200 000 | 7 580 000 | 120 | 75 |
| **Neptune** | | | | | |
| Triton | 1846 | 355 000 | 221 000 | 2 700 | 1 675 |
| Nereid | 1949 | 5 515 000 | 3 427 000 | 340 | 210 |
| Naiad | 1989 | 48 200 | 30 000 | 50 | 31 |
| Thalassa | 1989 | 50 000 | 31 000 | 80 | 50 |
| Despina | 1989 | 52 500 | 33 000 | 150 | 93 |
| Galatea | 1989 | 62 000 | 39 000 | 180 | 112 |
| Larissa | 1989 | 73 600 | 46 000 | 190 | 118 |
| Proteus | 1989 | 117 600 | 73 000 | 400 | 249 |
| **Pluto** | | | | | |
| Charon | 1978 | 19 700 | 12 240 | 1 200 | 750 |

## Comets

The solid nucleus of a comet is usually several kilometres in diameter; it consists of ice, dust and solid particles like a large, dirty snowball. When the comet passes close to the Sun, a cloud of gas and dust is ejected from the nucleus, forming a huge head or coma, many thousands of kilometres in diameter. The radiations from the Sun elongate the gas and dust to form one or more tails, often extending millions of kilometres in space. These tails point away from the Sun, but as the comet recedes, the tail will decrease in length until the comet returns to its latent dirty snowball state.

| Comet | First seen | Period of orbit (years) | Comet | First seen | Period of orbit (years) |
|---|---|---|---|---|---|
| Halley | 240BC | 75 | Daylight Comet | 1910 | *not known* |
| Tycho | 1577 | *not known* | Schwassmann-Wachmann 1 | 1925 | 15 |
| Kirch[1] | 1680 | 8 814 | Arend-Roland | 1957 | *not known* |
| De Chéseaux | 1744 | *not known* | Mrkos | 1957 | *not known* |
| Lexell | 1770 | 5.6 | Humason | 1961 | 3 000 |
| Encke | 1786 | 3.3 | Seki-Lines | 1962 | *not known* |
| Flauergues | 1811 | 3 094 | Ikeya-Seki | 1965 | 880 |
| Pons-Winnecke | 1819 | 6.34 | Tago-Sato-Kosaka | 1969 | 420 000 |
| Great Comet | 1843 | 512.6 | Bennett | 1970 | 1 680 |
| Donati | 1858 | 1 950 | Kohoutek | 1973 | 75 000 |
| Tebbutt | 1861 | 409.1 | West | 1975 | 500 000 |
| Swift-Tuttle | 1862 | 125 | IRAS-Araki-Alcock | 1983 | *not known* |
| Cruls | 1882 | 758.4 | Hale-Bopp | 1995 | 2 400 |
| Wolf | 1884 | 8.4 | Hyakutake | 1996 | 18 000 |
| Morehouse | 1908 | *not known* | | | |

[1]Kirch also known as Newton.

## Annual meteor showers

Meteors appear to radiate from named star region.

| Shower | Dates | Maximum activity | Notes |
|---|---|---|---|
| Quadrantids | 1–6 Jan | 3–4 Jan | swift |
| Lyrids | 19–25 Apr | 22 Apr | |
| Alpha-Scorpiids | 20 Apr–19 May | 28 Apr–10 May | S Hemisphere |
| Eta Aquariids | 1–8 May | 5 May | |
| Delta Aquariids | 15 Jul–10 Aug | 28 Jul–5 Aug | S Hemisphere |
| Perseids | 27 Jul–17 Aug | 11–14 Aug | very reliable |
| Orionids | 15–25 Oct | 21 Oct | |
| Taurids | 25 Oct–25 Nov | 4–14 Nov | |
| Leonids | 14–20 Nov | 17–18 Nov | many in 1998–9 |
| Geminids | 8–14 Dec | 13–14 Dec | very reliable |
| Ursids | 19–24 Dec | 22–23 Dec | |

## Sun data

**Physical characteristics of the Sun**

Diameter 1 392 530km; Volume $1.414 \times 10^{18}$ km$^3$; Mass $1.9891 \times 10^{30}$ kg

**Density (water = 1)**

| | |
|---|---|
| Mean density of entire Sun | 1.410g cm$^{-3}$ |
| Interior (centre of Sun) | 150g cm$^{-3}$ |
| Surface (photosphere) | $10^{-3}$g cm$^{-3}$ |
| Chromosphere | $10^{-6}$ g cm$^{-3}$ |
| Low corona | $1.7 \times 10^{-16}$ g cm$^{-3}$ |

**Temperature**

| | |
|---|---|
| Interior (centre) | 15 000 000K |
| Surface (photosphere) | 6 050K |
| Sunspot umbra (typical) | 4 240K |
| Penumbra (typical) | 5 680K |
| Chromosphere | 4 300 to 50 000K |
| Corona | 800 000 to 5 000 000K |

**Rotation (as seen from Earth)**

| | |
|---|---|
| Of solar equator | 26.8 days |
| At solar latitude 30° | 28.2 days |
| At solar latitude 60° | 30.8 days |
| At solar latitude 75° | 31.8 days |

**Chemical composition of photosphere**

| Element | % weight |
|---|---|
| Hydrogen | 73.46 |
| Helium | 24.85 |
| Oxygen | 0.77 |
| Carbon | 0.29 |
| Iron | 0.16 |
| Neon | 0.12 |
| Nitrogen | 0.09 |
| Silicon | 0.07 |
| Magnesium | 0.05 |
| Sulphur | 0.04 |
| Other | 0.10 |

## Solar system

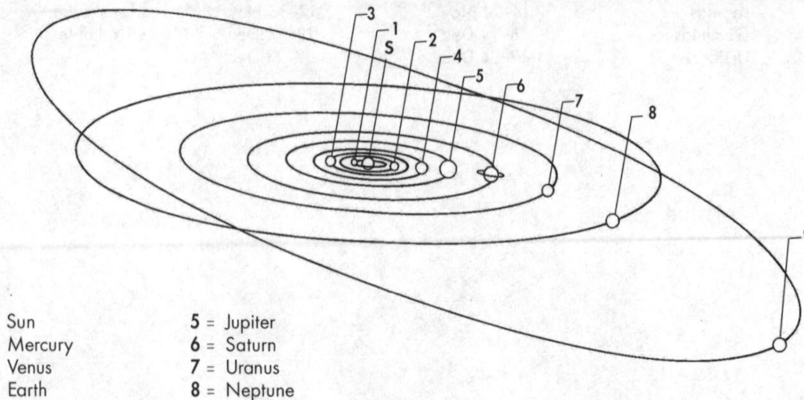


**S** = Sun
**1** = Mercury
**2** = Venus
**3** = Earth
**4** = Mars
**5** = Jupiter
**6** = Saturn
**7** = Uranus
**8** = Neptune
**9** = Pluto

## Total and annular solar eclipses 1991–2020

The eclipse begins in the first country named. In an annular eclipse, part of the Sun remains visible.

| Date | Type of eclipse | Visibility path |
|---|---|---|
| 15 Jan 1991 | Annular | S Pacific, New Zealand, S Australia |
| 11 Jul 1991 | Total | Mid-Pacific, C and S America |
| 4–5 Jan 1992 | Annular | N American coast, Mid-Pacific |
| 30 Jun 1992 | Total | S American coast, S Atlantic |
| 10 May 1994 | Annular | Mid-Pacific, N America, N Africa |
| 3 Nov 1994 | Total | Indian Ocean, S Atlantic, S America, Mid-Pacific |
| 29 Apr 1995 | Annular | S Pacific, S America |
| 24 Oct 1995 | Total | Middle East, S Asia, S Pacific |
| 9 Mar 1997 | Total | C and N Asia, Arctic |
| 26 Feb 1998 | Total | Mid-Pacific, C America, N Atlantic |
| 22 Aug 1998 | Annular | Indonesia, S Pacific, Indian Ocean |
| 16 Feb 1999 | Annular | Indian Ocean, Australia |
| 11 Aug 1999 | Total | N Atlantic, N Europe, Middle East, N India |
| 21 Jun 2001 | Total | S Atlantic, S Africa, Madagascar |
| 14 Dec 2001 | Annular | Pacific, C America |
| 10 Jun 2002 | Annular | Indonesia, Pacific, Mexico |
| 4 Dec 2002 | Total | S Africa, Indian Ocean, Australia |
| 31 May 2003 | Annular | Iceland, Greenland |
| 23 Nov 2003 | Total | Antarctic |
| 8 Apr 2005 | Annular/Total | Pacific, Panama, Venezuela |
| 3 Oct 2005 | Annular | Atlantic, Spain, Libya, Indian Ocean |
| 29 Mar 2006 | Total | Atlantic, Libya, Turkey, Russia |
| 22 Sep 2006 | Annular | Guyana, Atlantic, Indian Ocean |
| 7 Feb 2008 | Annular | Antarctic |
| 1 Aug 2008 | Total | Arctic, Siberia, China |
| 26 Jan 2009 | Annular | S Atlantic, Indian Ocean, Borneo |
| 22 Jul 2009 | Total | India, China, Pacific |
| 15 Jan 2010 | Annular | Africa, Indian Ocean, China |
| 11 Jul 2010 | Total | Pacific, S Chile |
| 20–21 May 2012 | Annular | China, N Pacific, N America |
| 13 Nov 2012 | Total | N Australia, Pacific |
| 9–10 May 2013 | Annular | Australia, Pacific |
| 3 Nov 2013 | Total | Atlantic, C Africa, Ethiopia |
| 20 Mar 2015 | Total | N Atlantic, Arctic |
| 9 Mar 2016 | Total | Indonesia, Pacific |
| 1 Sep 2016 | Annular | Atlantic, Africa, Madagascar, Indian Ocean |
| 26 Feb 2017 | Annular | Pacific, S America, Atlantic, Africa |
| 21 Aug 2017 | Total | Pacific, N America, Atlantic |
| 2 Jul 2019 | Total | Pacific, S America |
| 26 Dec 2019 | Annular | Middle East, Sri Lanka, Indonesia, Pacific |
| 21 Jun 2020 | Annular | Africa, Middle East, China, Pacific |
| 12 Dec 2020 | Total | Pacific, S America, Atlantic |

## Lunar eclipses 1991–2020

| Date | Type of eclipse | Time of mid-eclipse UT[1] | Where visible |
|---|---|---|---|
| 21 Dec 1991 | Partial | 10.34 | Pacific, N America (W Coast), Japan, Australia |
| 15 Jun 1992 | Partial | 04.58 | N, C and S America, W Africa |
| 9–10 Dec 1992 | Total | 23.45 | Africa, Europe, Middle East, part of S America |
| 4 Jun 1993 | Total | 13.02 | Pacific, Australia, SE Asia |
| 29 Nov 1993 | Total | 06.26 | N and S America |
| 25 May 1994 | Partial | 03.32 | C and S America, part of N America, W Africa |
| 15 Apr 1995 | Partial | 12.19 | Pacific, Australia, SE Asia |
| 4 Apr 1996 | Total | 00.11 | Africa, SE Europe, S America |
| 27 Sep 1996 | Total | 02.55 | C and S America, part of N America, W Africa |
| 24 Mar 1997 | Partial | 04.41 | C and S America, part of N America, W Africa |
| 16 Sep 1997 | Total | 18.47 | S Africa, E Africa, Australia |
| 28 Jul 1999 | Partial | 11.34 | Pacific, Australia, SE Asia |
| 21 Jan 2000 | Total | 04.45 | N America, part of S America, SW Europe, W Africa |
| 16 Jul 2000 | Total | 13.57 | Pacific, Australia, SE Asia |
| 9 Jan 2001 | Total | 20.22 | Europe, Asia, Africa |
| 5 Jul 2001 | Partial | 14.57 | Asia, Australia, Pacific |
| 16 May 2003 | Total | 03.41 | Americas, Europe, Africa |
| 9 Nov 2003 | Total | 01.20 | Americas, Europe, Africa, W Asia |
| 4 May 2004 | Total | 20.32 | Europe, Africa, Asia |
| 28 Oct 2004 | Total | 03.05 | Americas, Europe, Africa |
| 17 Oct 2005 | Partial | 12.05 | E Asia, Pacific, N America |
| 7 Sep 2006 | Partial | 18.53 | Australia, Asia, E Africa |
| 3 Mar 2007 | Total | 23.22 | Europe, Asia, Africa |
| 28 Aug 2007 | Total | 10.39 | Australia, Pacific, part of N America |
| 21 Feb 2008 | Total | 03.27 | Americas, Europe, Africa |
| 16 Aug 2008 | Partial | 21.12 | Europe, Africa, W Asia |
| 31 Dec 2009 | Partial | 19.23 | Asia, Africa, Europe |
| 26 Jun 2010 | Partial | 11.39 | Pacific Rim |
| 21 Dec 2010 | Total | 08.17 | N and S America |
| 15 Jun 2011 | Total | 20.12 | Asia, Africa, Europe |
| 10 Dec 2011 | Total | 14.32 | Pacific, Australia, E Asia |
| 4 Jun 2012 | Partial | 11.03 | Pacific, Australasia |
| 25 Apr 2013 | Partial | 20.09 | Asia, Africa, Europe |
| 14 Apr 2014 | Total | 07.47 | N and S America |
| 8 Oct 2014 | Total | 10.54 | Pacific, Australia, W Americas |
| 4 Apr 2015 | Partial | 12.01 | Pacific, Australasia |
| 28 Sep 2015 | Total | 02.47 | Africa, Europe, Americas |
| 7 Aug 2017 | Partial | 18.21 | Asia, Africa, Australia |
| 31 Jan 2018 | Total | 13.30 | Pacific, Australia, Asia |
| 27 Jul 2018 | Total | 20.22 | Asia, Africa, part of Europe |
| 21 Jan 2019 | Total | 05.12 | Americas, part of Europe |
| 16 Jul 2019 | Partial | 21.31 | Asia, Africa, Europe |

[1]Universal Time, equivalent to Greenwich Mean Time (GMT).

## The lunar 'seas'

| Latin name | English name | Latin name | English name |
|---|---|---|---|
| Lacus Mortis | Lake of Death | Mare Serenitatis | Sea of Serenity |
| Lacus Somniorum | Lake of Dreams | Mare Smythii | Smyth's Sea |
| Mare Australe | Southern Sea | Mare Spumans | Foaming Sea |
| Mare Crisium | Sea of Crises | Mare Tranquillitatis | Sea of Tranquility |
| Mare Fecunditatis | Sea of Fertility | Mare Undarum | Sea of Waves |
| Mare Frigoris | Sea of Cold | Mare Vaporum | Sea of Vapours |
| Mare Humboldtianum | Humboldt's Sea | Oceanus Procellarum | Ocean of Storms |
| Mare Humorum | Sea of Moisture | Palus Epidemiarum | Marsh of Epidemics |
| Mare Imbrium | Sea of Showers | Palus Nebularum | Marsh of Mists |
| Mare Ingenii | Sea of Geniuses | Palus Putredinis | Marsh of Decay |
| Mare Marginis | Marginal Sea | Palus Somnii | Marsh of Sleep |
| Mare Moscoviense | Moscow Sea | Sinus Aestuum | Bay of Heats |
| Mare Nectaris | Sea of Nectar | Sinus Iridum | Bay of Rainbows |
| Mare Nubium | Sea of Clouds | Sinus Medii | Central Bay |
| Mare Orientale | Eastern Sea | Sinus Roris | Bay of Dew |

## The constellations

| Latin name | English name | Latin name | English name | Latin name | English name |
|---|---|---|---|---|---|
| Andromeda | Andromeda | Cygnus | Swan | Pavo | Peacock |
| Antlia | Air Pump | Delphinus | Dolphin | Pegasus | Winged Horse |
| Apus | Bird of Paradise | Dorado | Swordfish | Perseus | Perseus |
| Aquarius | Water Bearer | Draco | Dragon | Phoenix | Phoenix |
| Aquila | Eagle | Equuleus | Little Horse | Pictor | Easel |
| Ara | Altar | Eridanus | River Eridanus | Pisces | Fishes |
| Aries | Ram | Fornax | Furnace | Piscis Austrinus | Southern Fish |
| Auriga | Charioteer | Gemini | Twins | Puppis | Ship's Stern |
| Boötes | Herdsman | Grus | Crane | Pyxis | Mariner's Compass |
| Caelum | Chisel | Hercules | Hercules | Reticulum | Net |
| Camelopardalis | Giraffe | Horologium | Clock | Sagitta | Arrow |
| Cancer | Crab | Hydra | Sea Serpent | Sagittarius | Archer |
| Canes Venatici | Hunting Dogs | Hydrus | Water Snake | Scorpius | Scorpion |
| Canis Major | Great Dog | Indus | Indian | Sculptor | Sculptor |
| Canis Minor | Little Dog | Lacerta | Lizard | Scutum | Shield |
| Capricornus | Sea Goat | Leo | Lion | Serpens | Serpent |
| Carina | Keel | Leo Minor | Little Lion | Sextans | Sextant |
| Cassiopeia | Cassiopeia | Lepus | Hare | Taurus | Bull |
| Centaurus | Centaur | Libra | Scales | Telescopium | Telescope |
| Cepheus | Cepheus | Lupus | Wolf | Triangulum | Triangle |
| Cetus | Whale | Lynx | Lynx | Triangulum Australe | Southern Triangle |
| Chamaeleon | Chameleon | Lyra | Harp | Tucana | Toucan |
| Circinus | Compasses | Mensa | Table | Ursa Major | Great Bear |
| Columba | Dove | Microscopium | Microscope | Ursa Minor | Little Bear |
| Coma Berenices | Berenice's Hair | Monoceros | Unicorn | Vela | Sails |
| Corona Australis | Southern Crown | Musca | Fly | Virgo | Virgin |
| Corona Borealis | Northern Crown | Norma | Level | Volans | Flying Fish |
| Corvus | Crow | Octans | Octant | Vulpecula | Fox |
| Crater | Cup | Ophiuchus | Serpent Bearer | | |
| Crux | Southern Cross | Orion | Orion | | |

## The 20 brightest stars

The apparent brightness of a star is represented by a number called its magnitude. The larger the number, the fainter the star. The faintest stars visible to the naked eye are slightly fainter than magnitude 6. Only about 6 000 of the billions of stars in the sky are visible to the naked eye.

| Star name | Distance (light years) | Apparent magnitude | Absolute magnitude |
|---|---|---|---|
| Sirius A | 8.6 | -1.46 | +1.4 |
| Canopus | 98 | -0.72 | -8.5 |
| Arcturus | 36 | -0.06 | -0.3 |
| Alpha Centauri A | 4.3 | -0.01 | +4.4 |
| Vega | 26.5 | +0.04 | +0.5 |
| Capella | 45 | +0.05 | -0.7 |
| Rigel | 900 | +0.14 | -6.8 |
| Procyon A | 11.2 | +0.37 | +2.6 |
| Betelgeuse | 520 | +0.41 | -5.5 |
| Achernar | 118 | +0.51 | -1.0 |
| Beta Centauri | 490 | +0.63 | -5.1 |
| Altair | 16.5 | +0.77 | +2.2 |
| Aldebaran | 68 | +0.86 | -0.2 |
| Spica | 220 | +0.91 | -3.6 |
| Antares | 520 | +0.92 | -4.5 |
| Pollux | 35 | +1.16 | +0.8 |
| Fomalhaut | 22.6 | +1.19 | +2.0 |
| Deneb | 1 500 | +1.26 | -6.9 |
| Beta Crucis | 490 | +1.28 | -4.6 |
| Alpha Crucis | 120 | +0.83 | -4.0 |

## The 20 nearest stars

| Star name | Distance (light years) | Apparent magnitude | Absolute magnitude |
|---|---|---|---|
| Proxima Centauri | 4.3 | +11.05 | +15.5 |
| Alpha Centauri A | 4.3 | -0.01 | +4.4 |
| Alpha Centauri B | 4.3 | +1.33 | +5.7 |
| Barnard's Star | 5.9 | +9.54 | +13.3 |
| Wolf 359 | 7.6 | +13.53 | +16.7 |
| Lalande 21185 | 8.1 | +7.50 | +10.5 |
| Sirius A | 8.6 | -1.46 | +1.4 |
| Sirius B | 8.6 | +8.68 | +11.6 |
| Luyten 726-8A | 8.9 | +12.45 | +15.3 |
| UV 726-8B | 8.9 | +12.95 | +15.3 |
| Ross 154 | 9.4 | +10.60 | +13.3 |
| Ross 248 | 10.3 | +12.29 | +14.8 |
| Epsilon Eridani | 10.8 | +3.73 | +6.1 |
| Ross 128 | 10.8 | +11.10 | +13.5 |
| Luyten 789-6 | 10.8 | +12.18 | +14.6 |
| 61 Cygni A | 11.1 | +5.22 | +7.6 |
| 61 Cygni B | 11.1 | +6.03 | +8.4 |
| Epsilon Indi | 11.2 | +4.68 | +7.0 |
| Procyon A | 11.2 | +0.37 | +2.7 |
| Procyon B | 11.2 | +10.70 | +13.0 |

## Largest ground-based telescopes

| Telescope name | Type | Observatory | Site (altitude m/ft) | Mirror/dish size | Founded |
|---|---|---|---|---|---|
| Anglo-Australian Telescope (AAT) | optical | Anglo-Australian Observatory | Siding Spring Mountain, NSW, Australia (1 165m/3 820ft) | 3.9m | 1974 |
| Arecibo Telescope | radio | National Astronomy and Ionosphere Centre | Puerto Rico (496m/1 625ft) | 304.8m | 1963 |
| Australia Telescope | radio | Commonwealth Scientific and Industrial Research Organization | Throughout NSW, Australia | 7 × 22m, 1 × 64m | 1990 |
| Bol'shoi Teleskop Azimutal'nyi | optical | Special Astrophysical Observatory | Mt Pastukhov, Zelenchukskaya, Russia (2 100m/6 900ft) | 6m | 1976 |
| — | optical | Byurakan Astrophysical Observatory | Mt Aragatz, Armenia (1 500m/5 000ft) | 2.6m | 1976 |
| C Donald Shane Telescope | optical | Lick Observatory | Mt Hamilton, California, USA (1 277m/4 190ft) | 3.05m | 1959 |
| California Submillimetre Observatory | submilli-metre | California Institute of Technology | Mauna Kea, Hawaii, USA (4 160m/13 650ft) | 10.4m | 1986 |
| Canada-France-Hawaii Telescope (CFHT) | optical | Canada-France-Hawaii Telescope Corporation | Mauna Kea, Hawaii, USA (4 180m/13 720ft) | 3.6m | 1979 |
| — | optical | Cerro Tololo Inter-American Observatory | Cerro Tololo, Chile (2 160m/7 100ft) | 4m | 1976 |
| Effelsberg Radio Telescope | radio | Max Planck Institut für Radioastronomie | Effelsberg, nr Bonn, Germany | 100m | 1971 |
| ESO New Technology Telescope | optical | European Southern Observatory | Cerro Tololo, Chile (2 160m/7 100ft) | 3.6m | 1990 |
| ESO 3.6m | optical | European Southern Observatory | Cerro La Silla, Chile (2 400m/7 850ft) | 3.6m | 1976 |
| — | radio | Five College Radio Astronomy | New Salem, Massachusetts, USA | 14m | 1969 |
| Gemini North Telescope, Gemini South Telescope | optical/ infrared | various | Mauna Kea, Hawaii, USA (4 160m/13 650ft) Cerro Pachón, Chile (2 715m/8 907ft) | 2 × 8.1m | 1999 |
| George Ellery Hale Telescope | optical | Palomar Observatory | Palomar Mountain, California, USA (1 700m/ 5 600ft) | 5.08m | 1948 |
| — | optical | German-Spanish Astronomical Centre | Calar Alto, Spain (2 160m/7 100ft) | 3.5m | 1985 |
| Harlan J Smith Telescope | optical | McDonald Observatory | Mt Locke, Texas, USA (2 070m/6 791ft) | 2.7m | 1968 |
| Hobby-Eberly Telescope | optical | McDonald Observatory | Mt Fowlkes, Texas, USA (2 100m/6 900ft) | 11m | 1997 |
| Irénée du Pont Telescope | optical | Mt Wilson and Las Campanas Observatories | Cerro Las Campanas, Chile (2 510m/8 235ft) | 2.57m | 1977 |
| IRAM Array | milli-metre | Institut de Radio Astronomie Millimétrique | Plateau de Bure, France (2 552m/8 373ft) | 4 × 15m | 1979 |
| Isaac Newton Telescope | optical | Observatory Roque de los Muchachos | La Palma, Canary Is (2 336m/7 660ft) | 2.54m | 1984 |
| James Clerk Maxwell Telescope (JCMT) | submilli-metre | Royal Observatory, Edinburgh | Mauna Kea, Hawaii, USA (4 160m/13 650ft) | 15m | 1987 |
| Keck Telescope | optical/ infrared | California Association for Research and Astronomy (CARA) | Mauna Kea, Hawaii, USA (4 160m/13 650ft) | 2 × 10m | 1990 |

## LARGEST GROUND-BASED TELESCOPES

| Telescope name | Type | Observatory | Site (altitude m/ft) | Mirror/dish size | Founded |
|---|---|---|---|---|---|
| Lovell Telescope | radio | Nuffield Radio Astronomy Laboratory (Jodrell Bank), University of Manchester | Jodrell Bank, Cheshire, UK | 76m | 1957 |
| MERLIN (Multi-Element Radio-Linked Interferometer Network) | radio | Nuffield Radio Astronomy Laboratory (Jodrell Bank), University of Manchester | UK (Midlands and Wales) | 5 × 25m, 1 × 32m, 1 × 76m | 1980 |
| Multiple Mirror Telescope | optical | Whipple Observatory | Mt Hopkins, Arizona, USA (2 606m/8 550ft) | 4.5m | 1979 |
| NASA Infrared Telescope Facility (IRTF) | infrared | NASA | Mauna Kea, Hawaii, USA (4 160m/13 650ft) | 3m | 1979 |
| — | milli-metre | National Radio Astronomy Observatory (NRAO) | Kitt Peak, Arizona, USA (1 920m/6 300ft) | 12m | 1982 |
| Nicholas U Mayall Telescope | optical | Kitt Peak National Observatory | Kitt Peak, Arizona, USA (2 100m/6 900ft) | 4m | 1973 |
| Nobeyama Millimetre Array | milli-metre | Nobeyama Radio Observatory | Nobeyama, Japan (1 300m/4 265ft) | 5 × 10m | 1986 |
| Nobeyama Radio Telescope | radio | Nobeyama Radio Observatory | Nobeyama, Japan (1 300m/4 265ft) | 45m | 1970 |
| Parkes Radio Telescope | radio | Australian National Radio Observatory | Nr Parkes, NSW, Australia (392m/1 285ft) | 64m | 1961 |
| Shajin Telescope | optical | Crimean Astrophysical Observatory | Simeis, Ukraine (680m/2 230ft) | 2.6m | 1961 |
| Subaru Telescope | optical/ infrared | National Astronomical Observatory of Japan | Mauna Kea, Hawaii, USA (4 160m/13 650ft) | 8m | 1999 |
| Swedish/European Submillimetre Telescope | submilli-metre | European Southern Observatory | Cerro Tololo, Chile (2 160m/7 100ft) | 10m | 1987 |
| United Kingdom Infrared Telescope (UKIRT) | infrared | Royal Observatory, Edinburgh | Mauna Kea, Hawaii, USA (4 180m/13 720ft) | 3.8m | 1979 |
| Very Large Array (VLA) | radio | National Radio Astronomy Observatories | Socorro, New Mexico, USA | 27 × 25m | 1980–1 |
| William Herschel Telescope | optical | Observatory Roque de los Muchachos | La Palma, Canary Is (2 332m/7 650ft) | 4.2 m | 1987 |

## Significant space missions

| Mission | Nation/ Agency | Launch date | Event description |
|---|---|---|---|
| Sputnik 1 | USSR | 4 Oct 57 | Earth satellite |
| Sputnik 2 | USSR | 3 Nov 57 | Dog Laika |
| Explorer 1 | USA | 1 Feb 58 | Discovered radiation belt (Van Allen) |
| Luna 1 | USSR | 2 Jan 59 | Escaped Earth gravity |
| Vanguard 2 | USA | 17 Feb 59 | Earth photo |
| Luna 2 | USSR | 12 Sept 59 | Lunar impact |
| Luna 3 | USSR | 4 Oct 59 | Lunar photo (far side) |
| TIROS 1 | USA | 1 Apr 60 | Weather satellite |
| Transit 1B | USA | 13 Apr 60 | Navigation satellite |
| ECHO 1 | USA | 12 Aug 60 | Communications satellite |
| Sputnik 5 | USSR | 19 Aug 60 | Two dogs recovered alive |
| Vostok 1 | USSR | 12 Apr 61 | Manned orbital flight |
| Mariner 2 | USA | 26 Aug 62 | Venus flyby |
| Vostok 6 | USSR | 16 Jun 63 | Woman in orbit |
| Ranger VII | USA | 28 Jul 64 | Close-up television pictures of the Moon |
| Mariner 4 | USA | 28 Nov 64 | Mars flyby pictures |
| Early Bird | USA | 6 Apr 65 | Commercial geostationary communications satellite |
| Venera 3 | USSR | 16 Nov 65 | Venus impact |
| A-1 Asterix | France | 26 Nov 65 | French launched satellite |
| Gemini 7 | USA | 4 Dec 65 | Manned rendezvous |
| Gemini 6 | USA | 15 Dec 65 | Manned rendezvous |
| Luna 9 | USSR | 31 Jan 66 | Lunar soft landing |
| Gemini 8 | USA | 16 Mar 66 | Manned docking |
| Luna 10 | USSR | 31 Mar 66 | Lunar orbiter |
| Surveyor 1 | USA | 30 May 66 | US soft landing on Moon |
| Lunar Orbiter 1 | USA | 10 Aug 66 | US lunar orbiter |
| Cosmos 186/188 | USSR | 22–28 Oct 67 | Automatic docking |
| WRESAT | Australia | 29 Nov 67 | Australian launched satellite |
| Zond 5 | USSR | 14 Sep 68 | Animals around the Moon |
| Apollo VIII | USA | 21 Dec 68 | Manned lunar orbit |
| Soyuz 4 | USSR | 14 Jan 69 | Transfer of crews |
| Soyuz 5 | USSR | 15 Jan 69 | Transfer of crews |
| Apollo XI | USA | 16 Jul 69 | Manned lunar landing |
| Oshumi | Japan | 11 Feb 70 | Japanese launched satellite |
| Long March | China | 24 Apr 70 | Chinese launched satellite |
| Venera 7 | USSR | 17 Aug 70 | Venus soft landing |
| Luna 16 | USSR | 12 Sep 70 | Unmanned sample return |
| Luna 17 | USSR | 10 Nov 70 | Unmanned Moon rover |
| Mars 2 | USSR | 19 May 71 | Mars orbit |
| Mars 3 | USSR | 28 May 71 | Mars soft landing, no data returned |
| Mariner 9 | USA | 30 May 71 | Mars orbit |
| Prospero | UK | 28 Oct 71 | UK launched satellite |
| Pioneer 10 | USA | 3 Mar 72 | Jupiter flyby; Crossed Pluto orbit; Escaped solar system |
| Pioneer 11 | USA | 6 Apr 73 | Jupiter flyby; Saturn flyby |
| Mariner 10 | USA | 3 Nov 73 | Venus flyby; Three Mercury flybys |
| Venera 9 | USSR | 8 Jun 75 | Venus orbit |
| Apollo/Soyuz | USA/USSR | 15 Jul 75 | Manned international co-operative mission |
| Viking 1 | USA | 20 Aug 75 | Spacecraft operations on Mars surface |
| Voyager 2 | USA | 20 Aug 77 | Jupiter flyby; Saturn flyby; Uranus flyby; Neptune flyby |
| Voyager 1 | USA | 5 Sep 77 | Jupiter flyby; Saturn flyby |
| ISEE-C | USA | 12 Aug 78 | Comet intercept |
| Ariane/CAT | ESA | 24 Dec 79 | European launcher |
| Rohini | India | 18 Jul 80 | Indian launched satellite |
| STS 1 | USA | 12 Apr 81 | Space shuttle flight |

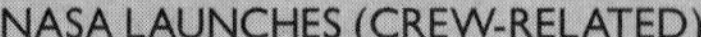

## NASA LAUNCHES (CREW-RELATED)

| Mission | Nation/ Agency | Launch date | Event description |
|---|---|---|---|
| STS 2 | USA | 12 Nov 81 | Launch vehicle re-use |
| Soyuz T9 | USSR | 27 Jun 83 | Construction in space |
| STS 51A | USA | 8 Nov 84 | Satellite retrieval |
| Vega 1 | USSR | 15 Dec 84 | Halley flyby |
| Giotto | ESA | 2 Jul 85 | Close-up of comet Halley |
| Soyuz T15 | USSR | 13 Mar 86 | Ferry between space stations |
| Soyuz TM4/6 | USSR | 21 Dec 87 | Year-long flight |
| Phobos 2 | USSR | 12 Jan 88 | Phobos rendezvous |
| Buran | USSR | 15 Nov 88 | Unmanned space shuttle |
| Galileo | USA | 18 Oct 89 | Close-up photographs of an asteroid |
| Muses-A | Japan | 24 Jan 90 | Moon orbiter |
| HST | USA/ESA | 24 Apr 90 | Large space telescope |
| Soyuz TM11 | USSR | 2 Dec 90 | Paying passenger flight |
| Pegsat | USA | 5 Apr 90 | First airborne launch |
| Lacrosse 2 | USA | 8 Mar 91 | Radar surveillance |
| Almaz 1 | Russia | 30 Mar 91 | Survey mapping |
| CGRO | USA | 5 Apr 91 | Gamma-ray astronomy |
| Topex/Poseidon | ESA | 10 Aug 92 | Geodetic mapping |
| Endeavour | USA | 12 Sep 92 | 50th Space shuttle flight |
| Clementine | USA | 25 Jan 94 | Lunar/asteroid exploration |
| P. 91 (STEP 2) | USA | 19 May 94 | Explosion scatters space debris |
| ISO | ESA | 17 Nov 95 | Infrared space observatory |
| SOHO | USA | 2 Dec 95 | Monitoring solar activity |
| NEAR | USA | 17 Feb 96 | Asteroid rendezvous |
| MGS | USA | 7 Nov 96 | Mars global survey |
| MPF | USA | 4 Dec 96 | Mars Pathfinder explored surface |
| Haruka | Japan | 12 Feb 97 | Radio astronomy |
| Iridium | USA | 5 May 97 | Communication constellation |
| Cassini/Huygens | USA | 15 Oct 97 | Saturn/Titan study in 2004 |
| Deep space 1 | USA | 24 Oct 98 | Ion propulsion spacecraft |
| STS 95 | USA | 29 Oct 98 | John Glenn's return to space |
| Zarya | USA/Russia/ESA/ Canada/Japan | 20 Nov98 | First launch in International Space Station assembly |
| MCO | USA | 11 Dec 98 | Mars climate survey |
| MPL | USA | 3 Jan 99 | Mars surface investigation |
| STS 92 | USA | 11 Oct 00 | 100th space shuttle flight |
| Expedition 1 | USA/Russia/ESA/ Canada/Japan | 31 Oct 00 | First residents of International Space Station |

## NASA launches (Crew-related)

| Mission | Launch | Duration[1] | Crew | Comment |
|---|---|---|---|---|
| Mercury MR3 (Freedom 7) | 5 May 61 | 0:15 | Shepard | First US manned suborbital flight |
| Mercury MR4 (Liberty Bell 7) | 21 Jul 61 | 0:16 | Grissom | Suborbital flight |
| Mercury MA5 | 29 Nov 61 | 3:16 | Enos | Chimpanzee |
| Mercury MA6 (Friendship 7) | 20 Feb 62 | 4:55 | Glenn | First US manned orbital flight |
| Mercury MA7 (Aurora 7) | 24 May 62 | 4:56 | Carpenter | Orbital flight; manual re-entry |
| Mercury MA8 (Sigma 7) | 3 Oct 62 | 9:13 | Schirra | 6 orbits |
| Mercury MA9 (Faith 7) | 15–16 May 62 | 34:20 | Cooper | 22 orbits; last Mercury flight |
| Gemini I | 8 Apr 64 | | | Test of launch vehicle compatability |
| Gemini II | 19 Jan 65 | | | Unmanned suborbital test flight |
| Gemini III | 23 Mar 65 | 4:53 | Grissom/Young | First manned Gemini flight |

| Mission | Launch | Duration[1] | Crew | Comment |
|---|---|---|---|---|
| Gemini IV | 3–7 Jun 65 | 97:56 | McDivitt/White | First spacewalk (by White, 36 min) |
| Gemini V | 21–29 Aug 65 | 190:56 | Cooper/Conrad | Simulated rendezvous manoeuvres |
| Gemini VI | 25 Oct 65 | | | Orbit not achieved |
| Gemini VII | 4–18 Dec 65 | 330:35 | Borman/Lovell | Part of mission without spacesuits |
| Gemini VII-A | 15–16 Dec 65 | 25:51 | Schirra/Stafford | First space rendezvous (with Gemini VII) |
| Gemini VIII | 16–17 Mar 66 | 10:42 | Armstrong/Scott | Rendezvous/docking with Agena target vehicle |
| Gemini IX-A | 3–6 Jun 66 | 72:21 | Stafford/Cernan | Docking not achieved |
| Gemini X | 18–21 Jul 66 | 70:47 | Young/Collins | First docked vehicle manoeuvres and spacewalks |
| Gemini XI | 12–15 Sep 66 | 71:17 | Conrad/Gordon | Rendezvous/docking and spacewalks |
| Gemini XII | 11–15 Nov 66 | 94:35 | Lovell/Aldrin | Rendezvous/docking and spacewalks |
| Apollo I | 27 Jan 67 | | Grissom/White/Chaffee | Astronauts killed in command module in fire at launch site |
| Apollo IV | 9 Nov 67 | | | First launch by Saturn V rocket; successful launch of unmanned module |
| Apollo V | 22–24 Jan 68 | | | Flight test of lunar module in Earth orbit |
| Apollo VII | 11–22 Oct 68 | 260:09 | Schirra/Eisele/Cunningham | First manned Apollo flight in Earth orbit |
| Apollo VIII | 21–27 Dec 68 | 147:01 | Borman/Lovell/Anders | First manned orbit of Moon (10 orbits) |
| Apollo IX | 3–13 Mar 69 | 241:01 | McDivitt/Scott/Schweickart | First manned lunar module flight in Earth orbit |
| Apollo X | 18–26 May 69 | 192:03 | Stafford/Young/Cernan | First lunar module orbit of Moon |
| Apollo XI | 16–24 Jul 69 | 195:18 | Armstrong[2]/Aldrin[2]/Collins | First men on Moon, 20 Jul, Sea of Tranquility |
| Apollo XII | 14–24 Nov 69 | 244:36 | Conrad[2]/Bean[2]/Gordon | Moon landing, 19 Nov, Ocean of Storms |
| Apollo XIII | 11–17 Apr 70 | 142:54 | Lovell/Swigert/Haise | Mission aborted, ruptured oxygen tank |
| Apollo XIV | 31 Jan–9 Feb 71 | 216:02 | Shepard[2]/Mitchell[2]/Roosa | Moon landing, 5 Feb, Fra Mauro area |
| Apollo XV | 26 Jul–7 Aug 71 | 295:12 | Scott[2]/Irwin[2]/Worden | Moon landing, 30 Jul, Hadley Rille; Lunar Roving Vehicle used |
| Apollo XVI | 16–27 Apr 72 | 265:51 | Young[2]/Duke[2]/Mattingly | Moon landing, 20 Apr, Descartes |
| Apollo XVII | 7–19 Dec 72 | 301:52 | Cernan[2]/Schmitt[2]/Evans | Longest Apollo mission, 11 Dec, Taurus-Littrow |
| Skylab 1 | 14 May 73 | | Unmanned space station | Launched unmanned, uncontrolled re-entry 1979 |
| Skylab 2 | 25 May 73 | 672:50 | Conrad/Kerwin/Weitz | Repairs in orbit, duration record (28 days) |
| Skylab 3 | 28 Jul 73 | 1427:09 | Bean/Garriott/Lousma | New duration record (59 days) |
| Skylab 4 | 16 Nov 73 | 2017:15 | Carr/Gibson/Pogue | Final visit (84 days) |
| Apollo-Soyuz Test Project | 15–24 Jul 75 | 217:28 | Stafford/Brand/Slayton | Rendezvous/docking with Soyuz 19 (► p16) |

[1] (h:min).
[2] Astronauts who landed on the Moon; the remaining astronaut was the pilot of the command module.

## Shuttle flights 1985–2000

| Flight/Name | Launch | Landing | Commander/Pilot/ Number of other crew | Payload |
|---|---|---|---|---|
| STS 51-C (D) | 24 Jan 85 | 27 Jan 85 | Mattingly/Shriver/3 | USA 8 |
| STS 51-D (D) | 12 Apr 85 | 19 Apr 85 | Bobko/Williams/5 | Telesat 9, Leasat 3 |
| STS 51-B (Ch) | 29 Apr 85 | 6 May 85 | Overmyer/Gregory/5 | Nusat, Spacelab 3[1] |
| STS 51-G (D) | 17 Jun 85 | 24 Jun 85 | Brandenstein/Creighton/5 | Morelos 1, Arabsat 1B, Telstar 3D, Spartan 1 |
| STS 51-F (Ch) | 29 Jul 85 | 6 Aug 85 | Fullerton/Bridges/5 | PDP |
| STS 51-I (D) | 27 Aug 85 | 3 Sep 85 | Engle/Covey/3 | Aussat 1, ASC 1, Leasat 4 |
| STS 51-J (A) | 3 Oct 85 | 7 Oct 85 | Bobko/Grabe/3 | USA 11, USA 12 |
| STS 61-A (Ch) | 30 Oct 85 | 6 Nov 85 | Hartsfield/Nagel/6 | GLOMR, Spacelab D1[1] |
| STS 61-B (A) | 26 Nov 85 | 3 Dec 85 | Shaw/O'Connor/5 | Morelos 2, Aussat 2, OEX, RCA Satcom K2 |
| STS 61-C (C) | 12 Jan 86 | 18 Jan 86 | Gibson/Bolden/5 | RCA Satcom K1, Hitchhiker G1[1] |
| STS 51-L (Ch) | 28 Jan 86 | exploded | Scobee/Smith/5 | TDRS |
| STS 26 (D) | 29 Sep 88 | 3 Oct 88 | Hauck/Covey/3 | TDRS 3 |
| STS 27 (A) | 2 Dec 88 | 6 Dec 88 | Gibson/Gardner/3 | USA 34 (Lacrosse 1) |
| STS 29 (D) | 13 Mar 89 | 18 Mar 89 | Coates/Blaha/3 | TDRS |
| STS 30 (A) | 4 May 89 | 8 May 89 | Walker/Grabe/3 | Magellan |
| STS 28 (C) | 8 Aug 89 | 13 Aug 89 | Shaw/Richards/3 | Dept of Defense |
| STS 34 (A) | 18 Oct 89 | 23 Oct 89 | Williams/McCulley/3 | Galileo |
| STS 33 (D) | 23 Nov 89 | 28 Nov 89 | Gregory/Blaha/3 | Dept of Defense |
| STS 32 (C) | 9 Jan 90 | 20 Jan 90 | Brandenstein/Wetherbee/3 | LDEF |
| STS 36 (A) | 28 Feb 90 | 4 Mar 90 | Creighton/Casper/3 | Dept of Defense |
| STS 31 (D) | 25 Apr 90 | 29 Apr 90 | Shriver/Bolden/3 | HST |
| STS 41 (D) | 6 Oct 90 | 10 Oct 90 | Richards/Cabana/3 | Ulysses |
| STS 38 (A) | 16 Nov 90 | 20 Nov 90 | Covey/Culbertson/3 | Dept of Defense |
| STS 35 (C) | 3 Dec 90 | 10 Dec 90 | Brand/Gardner/3 | Astro-1 |
| STS 37 (A) | 5 Apr 91 | 11 Apr 91 | Nagel/Cameron/3 | GRO |
| STS 40 (C) | 5 Jun 91 | 14 Jun 91 | O'Connor/Gutierrez/5 | Spacelab Life Sciences 1 |
| STS 43 (A) | 2 Aug 91 | 11 Aug 91 | Blaha/Baker/3 | TDRS-E |
| STS 48 (D) | 13 Sep 91 | 18 Sep 91 | Creighton/Reightler/3 | UARS |
| STS 44 (A) | 24 Nov 91 | 1 Dec 91 | Gregory/Henricks/4 | Dept of Defense |
| STS 42 (D) | 22 Jan 92 | 30 Jan 92 | Grabe/Oswald/5 | International microgravity laboratory[1] |
| STS 45 (A) | 24 Mar 92 | 2 Apr 92 | Bolden/Duffy/5 | ATLAS[1] (Earth observation) |
| STS 49 (E) | 7 May 92 | 16 May 92 | Brandenstein/Chilton/5 | satellite reorientation |
| STS 50 (C) | 25 Jun 92 | 9 Jul 92 | Richards/Bowersox/5 | Spacelab USML 1 |
| STS 46 (A) | 31 Jul 92 | 8 Aug 92 | Shriver/Allen/5 | Eureca, TSS 1 |
| STS 47 (E) | 12 Sep 92 | 20 Sep 92 | Gibson/Brown/5 | Spacelab |
| STS 52 (C) | 22 Oct 92 | 1 Nov 92 | Wetherbee/Baker/4 | Lageos 2 |
| STS 53 (D) | 2 Dec 92 | 9 Dec 92 | Walker/Cabana/3 | USA 87, ODERACS |
| STS 54 (E) | 13 Jan 93 | 19 Jan 93 | Casper/McMonagle/3 | TDRS 6 |
| STS 56 (D) | 8 Apr 93 | 17 Apr 93 | Cameron/Oswald/3 | ATLAS 2, Spartan 201 |
| STS 55 (C) | 26 Apr 93 | 6 May 93 | Nagel/Henricks/5 | Spacelab D2 |
| STS 57 (E) | 21 Jun 93 | 1 Jul 93 | Grabe/Duffy/4 | Spacehab, Eureca retrieval |
| STS 51 (D) | 12 Sep 93 | 22 Sep 93 | Culbertson/Readdy/3 | ACTS, Orfeus-SPAS |
| STS 58 (C) | 18 Oct 93 | 1 Nov 93 | Blaha/Searfoss/5 | Spacelab Life Sciences 2 |
| STS 61 (E) | 2 Dec 93 | 13 Dec 93 | Covey/Bowersox/5 | Hubble Telescope refurbishment |
| STS 60 (D) | 3 Feb 94 | 11 Feb 94 | Bolden/Reightler/4 | Spacehab 2, WSF, Bremsat, ODERACS |
| STS 62 (C) | 4 Mar 94 | 18 Mar 94 | Casper/Allen/3 | OAST 2, USMP 2 |
| STS 59 (E) | 9 Apr 94 | 20 Apr 94 | Gutierrez/Chilton/4 | SRL 1 |
| STS 65 (C) | 8 Jul 94 | 23 Jul 94 | Cabana/Halsell/5 | Spacelab IML-2 |
| STS 64 (D) | 9 Sep 94 | 20 Sep 94 | Richards/Hammond/4 | Spartan 201, SAFER, LITE |
| STS 68 (E) | 30 Sep 94 | 11 Oct 94 | Baker/Wilcutt/4 | SRL 2 |
| STS 66 (A) | 3 Nov 94 | 14 Nov 94 | McMonagle/Brown/4 | Atlas, CRISTA-SPAS |

| Flight/Name | Launch | Landing | Commander/Pilot/ Number of other crew | Payload |
|---|---|---|---|---|
| STS 63 (D) | 3 Feb 95 | 11 Feb 95 | Wetherbee/Collins/4 | Spartan, Spacehab, MIR formation |
| STS 67 (E) | 2 Mar 95 | 18 Mar 95 | Oswald/Gregory/5 | Astro 2 |
| STS 71 (A) | 27 Jun 95 | 7 Jul 95 | Gibson/Precourt/5-6 | MIR docking, Spacelab |
| STS 70 (D) | 13 Jul 95 | 22 Jul 95 | Henricks/Kregel/3 | TDRS-7 |
| STS 69 (E) | 7 Sep 95 | 18 Sep 95 | Walker/Cockrell/3 | Spartan, Wake Shield Facility 2 |
| STS 73 (C) | 20 Oct 95 | 5 Nov 95 | Bowersox/Rominger/5 | Spacelab, USML 2 |
| STS 74 (A) | 12 Nov 95 | 20 Nov 95 | Cameron/Halsell/3 | MIR docking |
| STS 72 (E) | 11 Jan 96 | 20 Jan 96 | Duffy/Jett/4 | Spartan 206, OAST, SFU retrieval |
| STS 75 (C) | 22 Feb 96 | 9 Mar 96 | Allen/Horowitz/5 | USMP 3, TSS 1R |
| STS 76 (A) | 22 Mar 96 | 31 Mar 96 | Chilton/Searfoss/4 | MIR docking |
| STS 77 (E) | 19 May 96 | 29 May 96 | Casper/Brown/4 | Spacehab, Spartan 207 |
| STS 78 (C) | 20 Jun 96 | 7 Jul 96 | Henricks/Kregel/5 | LMS 1, Spacelab |
| STS 79 (A) | 16 Sep 96 | 26 Sep 96 | Readdy/Wilcutt/4 | MIR docking, Spacehab |
| STS 80 (C) | 19 Nov 96 | 7 Dec 96 | Cockrell/Rominger/3 | Wake Shield 3, Orfeus-SPAS |
| STS 81 (A) | 12 Jan 97 | 22 Jan 97 | Baker/Jett/4 | MIR docking |
| STS 82 (D) | 11 Feb 97 | 21 Feb 97 | Bowersox/Horowitz/5 | Hubble Telescope refurbishment |
| STS 83 (C) | 4 Apr 97 | 8 Apr 97 | Halsell/Still/5 | Microgravity Science Lab-1 |
| STS 84 (A) | 15 May 97 | 24 May 97 | Precourt/Collins/5 | MIR docking |
| STS 94 (C) | 1 Jul 97 | 17 Jul 97 | Halsell/Still/5 | Microgravity Science Lab-1 reflight |
| STS 85 (D) | 7 Aug 97 | 19 Aug 97 | Brown/Rominger/4 | MPESS, CRISTA-SPAS |
| STS 86 (A) | 26 Sep 97 | 6 Oct 97 | Wetherbee/Bloomfield/5 | MIR docking |
| STS 87 (C) | 19 Nov 97 | 5 Dec 97 | Kregel/Lindsey/4 | Spartan 201/USMP 4 |
| STS 89 (E) | 22 Jan 98 | 31 Jan 98 | Wilcutt/Edwards/5 | MIR docking |
| STS 90 (C) | 17 Apr 98 | 3 May 98 | Searfoss/Altman/5 | Neurolab, GAS |
| STS 91 (D) | 2 Jun 98 | 12 Jun 98 | Precourt/Pudwill/Gorie/4 | MIR docking, Spacehab |
| STS 95 (D) | 29 Oct 98 | 7 Nov 98 | Brown/Lindsey/5 | Spacehab, Spartan 201 |
| STS 88 (E) | 4 Dec 98 | 15 Dec 98 | Cabana/Sturckow/4 | International Space Station assembly |
| STS 96 (D) | 27 May 99 | 6 Jun 99 | Rominger/Husband/5 | International Space Station assembly |
| STS 93 (C) | 23 July 99 | 27 July 99 | Collins/Ashby/3 | AXAF, MSX |
| STS 103 (D) | 19 Dec 99 | 27 Dec 99 | Brown/Kelly/5 | Hubble servicing |
| STS 99 (E) | 11 Feb 00 | 22 Feb 00 | Kregell/Pudwill/Gorie/4 | SRTM, EarthKAM |
| STS 101 (A) | 19 May 00 | 29 May 00 | Halsell/Horowitz/5 | International Space Station assembly |
| STS 106 (A) | 8 Sep 00 | 19 Sep 00 | Wilcutt/Altman/5 | International Space Station assembly |
| STS 92 (D) | 11 Oct 00 | 24 Oct 00 | Duffy/Melroy/5 | International Space Station assembly |

A: Atlantis Ch: Challenger C: Columbia D: Discovery E: Endeavour

[1]Not separated from shuttle.

## Major Russian launches (Crew-related) [1]

| Mission | Launch | Duration [2] | Crew | Comment |
|---|---|---|---|---|
| Vostok 1 | 12 Apr 61 | 01:48 | Gagarin | First space flight (1 orbit) |
| Vostok 2 | 6 Aug 61 | 25:18 | Titov | Day-long mission |
| Vostok 3 | 11 Aug 62 | 94:22 | Nikolayev | First dual mission |
| Vostok 4 | 12 Aug 62 | 71:00 | Popovich | First dual mission |
| Vostok 6 | 16 Jun 63 | 70:50 | Tereshkova | First woman in space |
| Voshkod 1 | 12 Oct 64 | 24:17 | Komarov/Feoktistov/ Yegorov | Three man flight |
| Voshkod 2 | 18 Mar 65 | 26:02 | Belyayev/Leonov | First spacewalk (EVA) |

## MAJOR RUSSIAN LAUNCHES (CREW-RELATED)

| Mission | Launch | Duration[2] | Crew | Comment |
|---|---|---|---|---|
| Soyuz 1 | 23 Apr 67 | 27:00 | Komarov | Cosmonaut killed on re-entry |
| Soyuz 4 | 14 Jan 69 | 71:14 | Shatalov | Khrunov and Yeliseyev transferred from Soyuz 5 |
| Soyuz 5 | 15 Jan 69 | 72:46 | Volynov/Khrunov/Yeliseyev | Docked with Soyuz 4 |
| Soyuz 10 | 22 Apr 71 | 48:00 | Shatalov/Yeliseyev/ Rukavishnikov | Docked with Salyut 1 space station but did not enter for undisclosed reason |
| Soyuz 11 | 6 Jun 71 | 23 days | Dobrovolsky/Volkov/ Patsayev | Docked with Salyut 1; crew killed on re-entry |
| Salyut 3 | 25 Jun 74 | 214 days | Soyuz 14 | Operational military space station |
| Soyuz 14 | 4 Jul 74 | 16 days | Popovich/Artyukhin | Docked with Salyut 3 |
| Salyut 4 | 26 Dec 74 | 769 days | Soyuz 17/Soyuz 18/Soyuz 20 | Space station; re-entered 2 Feb 77 |
| Soyuz 17 | 9 Jan 75 | 30 days | Gubarev/Grechko | Docked with Salyut 4 |
| Soyuz 19 (Apollo-Soyuz Test Project) | 15 Jul 75 | 6 days | Kubasov/Leonov | First international space mission with USA; crew transfer |
| Salyut 5 | 22 Jun 76 | 412 days | Soyuz 21/Soyuz 24 | Space station; re-entered 8 Aug 77 |
| Soyuz 21 | 6 Jul 76 | 49 days | Volynov/Zholobov | Docked with Salyut 5 |
| Soyuz 23 | 14 Oct 76 | 2 days | Zudov/Rozhdestivensky | Attempted docking with Salyut 5 |
| Soyuz 24 | 7 Feb 77 | 18 days | Gorbatko/Glazkov | Docked with Salyut 5 |
| Salyut 6 | 29 Sep 77 | 1 764 days | Soyuz 25 through Soyuz 40 | Space station; re-entered 29 Jul 82 |
| Soyuz 26 | 10 Dec 77 | 96 days | Romanenko/Grechko | First prime crew Salyut 6; broke endurance record |
| Soyuz 27 | 10 Jan 78 | 65 days | Dzhanibekov/Makarov | First visiting crew to Salyut 6 |
| Soyuz 28 | 2 Mar 78 | 8 days | Gubarev/Remek | Second visiting crew to Salyut 6 |
| Soyuz 29 | 15 Jun 78 | 140 days | Kovalenok/Ivanchenko | Second prime crew of Salyut 6 |
| Soyuz 32 | 25 Feb 79 | 108 days | Lyakhov/Ryumin | Third prime crew of Salyut 6; broke endurance record |
| Soyuz T1 | 16 Dec 79 | 100 days | | Redesigned Soyuz craft |
| Soyuz T4 | 12 Mar 81 | 75 days | Kovalenok/Savinykh | Last prime crew of Salyut 6 |
| Soyuz 39 | 22 Mar 81 | 8 days | Dzhanibekov/Gurragcha | Mongolian cosmonaut |
| Soyuz 40 | 14 May 81 | 8 days | Popov/Prunariu | Last visiting crew to Salyut 6 |
| Salyut 7 | 19 Apr 82 | 9 years | Soyuz T5 through Soyuz T15 | Space station; re-entered 7 Feb 91 |
| Soyuz T5 | 14 May 82 | 106 days | Berezovoy/Ledebev | Crew broke endurance record |
| Soyuz T7 | 19 Aug 82 | 113 days | Popov/Serebrov/Savitskaya | Savitskaya, second woman in space |
| Soyuz T9 | 27 Jun 83 | 149 days | Lyakhov/Alexandrov | Docked with Salyut 7 |
| Soyuz T10-1 | 27 Sep 83 | | Titov/Strekalov | Exploded on launch pad; crew safe |
| Soyuz T10 | 8 Feb 84 | 263 days | Kizim/Solovyov/Atkov | Crew broke endurance record |
| Soyuz T12 | 17 Jul 84 | 12 days | Dzhanibekov/Savitskaya/ Volk | Docked with Salyut 7; first female EVA |
| Soyuz T14 | 17 Sep 85 | 65 days | Vasyutin/Volkov/Grechko | Docked with Salyut 7; mission terminated when Vasyutin fell ill |
| MIR 1 | 19 Feb 86 | Projected 13 years | Soyuz T15 onwards | Space station; designed for orbit; modular construction |
| Soyuz T15 | 13 Mar 86 | 125 days | Kizim/Solovyov | Docked with both MIR and Salyut 7 |

| Mission | Launch | Duration[2] | Crew | Comment |
|---|---|---|---|---|
| Soyuz TM1 | 21 May 86 | 9 days | | Redesigned Soyuz T craft |
| Kvant 1 | 31 Mar 87 | in orbit | | Astrophysical module attached to MIR |
| Soyuz TM3 | 22 Jul 87 | 160 days | Viktorenko/Alexandrov/Faris | Docked with MIR |
| Soyuz TM4 | 21 Dec 87 | 179 days | Titov/Manarov/Levchenko | Docked with MIR; Titov and Manarov completed 365-day flight |
| Kvant 2 | 26 Nov 89 | in orbit | | Module attached to MIR on 6 Dec 89 |
| Kristall | 31 May 90 | in orbit | | Material processing module added to MIR |
| Soyuz TM11 | 2 Dec 90 | 175 days | Afanasyev/Manarov/Akiyama | Docked with MIR; Japanese journalist on board |
| Soyuz TM12 | 18 May 91 | | Artsebarsky/Krikalev/Sharman | Docked with MIR; first British cosmonaut |
| Soyuz TM13 | 2 Oct 91 | | Volkov/Aubakirov/Vietiboeck (Austria) | Docked with MIR; partial crew rotation (Artsebarsky down) |
| Soyuz TM14 | 17 Mar 92 | 146 days | Viktorenko/Kaleri/Flade (Germany) | Docked with MIR; crew rotation (Volkov, Krikalev down) |
| Soyuz TM15 | 27 Jul 92 | 189 days | A Solovyov/Avdeyev | [3] |
| Soyuz TM16 | 24 Jan 93 | 179 days | Manakov/Poleshchuk | [3] |
| Soyuz TM17 | 1 Jul 93 | 197 days | Tsibliev/Serebrov | [3] |
| Soyuz TM18 | 8 Jan 94 | 182 days | Afanasyev/Usachyov/Polyakov | [3] |
| Soyuz TM19 | 1 Jul 94 | 126 days | Malenchenko/Musabayev | [3] |
| Soyuz TM20 | 3 Oct 94 | 170 days | Viktorenko/Kondakova/Merbold | [3] |
| Soyuz TM21 | 14 Mar 95 | 181 days | Dezhurov/Strekalov/Thagard | [3] |
| Spektr Module | 20 May 95 | | | Module attached to MIR |
| Soyuz TM22 | 3 Sep 95 | 179 days | Gidzenko/Avdeyev/Reiter | [3] |
| Soyuz TM23 | 21 Feb 96 | 194 days | Onufrienko/Usachyov | [3] |
| Priroda Module | 23 Apr 96 | | | Module attached to MIR |
| Soyuz TM24 | 17 Aug 96 | 197 days | Korzun/Kaleri | [3] |
| Soyuz TM25 | 10 Feb 97 | 185 days | Tsibliev/Lazutkin/Ewald | [3] |
| Soyuz TM26 | 5 Aug 97 | 197 days | A Solovyov/Vinogradov | [3] |
| Soyuz TM27 | 29 Jan 98 | 207 days | Musbayev/Budarin/Eyharts | [3] |
| Soyuz TM28 | 13 Aug 98 | 198 days | Padalka/Avdeyev/Baturin | [3] |
| Soyuz TM29 | 20 Feb 99 | 188 days | Afanasyev/Haignere/Bella | [3] |
| Soyuz TM30 | 6 Apr 00 | 71 days | Zalyotin/Kaleri | MIR maintenance |

[1]USSR until 1990.

[2] (h:min).

[3] The purpose was basically the same for all the Soyuz spacecraft: they were all 'ferry' craft which were used to take crews to and from MIR, acting as 'lifeboats' in case of emergencies.

## Some satellites in geostationary orbit (1965–92)

| Satellites | Years of Launch | Satellites | Years of Launch | Satellites | Years of Launch |
|---|---|---|---|---|---|
| Anik | 1972–91 | Eutelsat | 1990–1 | Meteosat | 1977–88 |
| Apple 1 | 1981 | Fleetsatcom 1–8 | 1978–89 | MOP 1–2 | 1989–91 |
| Arabsat 1A, 1B | 1985 | Galaxy 1, 2, 3, 6 | 1983–90 | Morelos 1–2 | 1985 |
| Asiasat 1 | 1990 | GMS 1–4 | 1977–89 | NATO 1–4A | 1970–91 |
| Astra | 1988–91 | GOES 1–7 | 1975–87 | Palapa | 1976–90 |
| Aurora 2 | 1991 | Gorizont 1–24 | 1978–91 | Panamsat | 1988 |
| Aussat 1–3 | 1985–7 | Gstar 1–4 | 1985–90 | Raduga 1–28 | 1975–91 |
| Ayama 1–2 | 1979–80 | Himawari 1–3 | 1977–84 | RCA Satcom | 1975–90 |
| Brasilsat 1–2 | 1985–6 | IMEWS | 1970–87 | Sakura 2, 3 | 1983–8 |
| China 15, 18, 22 | 1984–8 | Inmarsat 2 | 1990–1 | SBS 1–6 | 1980–90 |
| China 25–6 | 1988–90 | Insat 1A, B, C, D | 1982–90 | Skynet 1A–4C | 1969–90 |
| Comstar 1 | 1976–81 | Intelsat 1–2 | 1965–7 | SMS 1–3 | 1974–5 |
| Cosmos | 1987–91 | Intelsat 3 | 1968–70 | Superbird 1 | 1989 |
| CS-2, CS-3 | 1983–8 | Intelsat 4 | 1971–5 | Symphonie 1–2 | 1974–5 |
| DFS-Kopernicus | 1989–90 | Intelsat 4A | 1975–8 | Tactical comsat | 1969 |
| DSCS 1–16 | 1971–82 | Intelsat 5 | 1980–9 | TDF | 1988–90 |
| DSCS-3 | 1985 | Intelsat 5A | 1985–9 | TDRS 1, 3, 4, 5 | 1983–91 |
| DSP | 1990–2 | Intelsat 6 | 1989–91 | Telecom 1A–2A | 1984–91 |
| Early Bird | 1965 | JCSat 1–2 | 1989–90 | Telesat 1–9 | 1972–85 |
| ECS 1–2 | 1979–80 | Leasat 1–5 | 1984–90 | Telstar 3A, C, D | 1983–5 |
| ECS 1–5 | 1983–8 | LES 6, 8, 9 | 1968–76 | TV-Sat 1–2 | 1987–9 |
| Ekran 1–19 | 1976–88 | Marcopolo 1 | 1989 | USA 7, 11, 12, 20, 28, 48 | 1984–8 |
| ESA GEOS 2 | 1978 | Marecs 1–2 | 1981–4 | Westar 1–5 | 1974–82 |
| ETS 2, 3, 5 | 1977–87 | Marisat 1–3 | 1976 | Yuri 3A | 1990 |

## Some satellites in geostationary orbit (1992–2000)

| Satellite | Launch date | Satellite | Launch date | Satellite | Launch date |
|---|---|---|---|---|---|
| USA 78 | 10 Feb 1992 | Hispasat 1B | 22 Jul 1993 | Turksat 1B | 10 Aug 1994 |
| Superbird B1 | 27 Feb 1992 | Insat 2B | 22 Jul 1993 | USA 105 | 27 Aug 1994 |
| Arabsat 1C | 27 Feb 1992 | ACTS | 12 Sep 1993 | Optus B3 | 27 Aug 1994 |
| Galaxy 5 | 14 Mar 1992 | Raduga 30 | 30 Sep 1993 | Cosmos 2291 | 21 Sep 1994 |
| Gorizont 25 | 2 Apr 1992 | Intelsat 7F1 | 22 Oct 1993 | Intelsat 703 | 6 Oct 1994 |
| Telecom 2B | 15 Apr 1992 | Gorizont 28 | 28 Oct 1993 | Solidaridad 2 | 8 Oct 1994 |
| Inmarsat 2 F-4 | 15 Apr 1992 | Gorizont 29 | 18 Nov 1993 | Thaicom 2 | 8 Oct 1994 |
| Palapa 7 | 18 May 1992 | Meteosat 6 | 20 Nov 1993 | Ekspress | 13 Oct 1994 |
| Intelsat K | 10 Jun 1992 | Solidaridad 1 | 20 Nov 1993 | Elektro | 31 Oct 1994 |
| USA 82 | 2 Jul 1992 | USA 97 | 28 Nov 1993 | Astra 1D | 1 Nov 1994 |
| Insat 2A | 9 Jul 1992 | Nato 4B | 8 Dec 1993 | Orion 1 | 29 Nov 1994 |
| Eutelsat 2 F-4 | 9 Jul 1992 | Telstar 401 | 16 Dec 1993 | DFH 3 | 29 Nov 1994 |
| Gorizont 26 | 14 Jul 1992 | DBS 1 | 18 Dec 1993 | Luch | 16 Dec 1994 |
| Aussat B1 | 13 Aug 1992 | Thaicom 1 | 18 Dec 1993 | DSP F17 | 22 Dec 1994 |
| Satcom C4 | 31 Aug1992 | Gals 1 | 20 Jan 1994 | Raduga 32 | 28 Dec 1994 |
| Cosmos 2209 | 10 Sep 1992 | Raduga 1-3 | 5 Feb 1994 | Intelsat 704 | 10 Jan 1995 |
| Hispasat 1A | 10 Sep 1992 | Milstar DFS 1 | 7 Feb 1994 | UHF FO 4 | 29 Jan 1995 |
| Satcom C3 | 10 Sep1992 | Raduga 31 | 18 Feb 1994 | SFU | 17 Mar 1995 |
| DFS 3 | 12 Oct 1992 | Galaxy 7 | 19 Feb 1994 | GMS | 17 Mar 1995 |
| Galaxy 7 | 28 Oct 1992 | GOES 8 | 13 Apr 1994 | Intelsat 705 | 22 Mar 1995 |
| Ekran 20 | 30 Oct 1992 | Gorizont 30 | 19 May 1994 | Brasilsat B2 | 28 Mar 1995 |
| Gorizont 27 | 27 Nov 1992 | Intelsat 702 | 17 Jun 1994 | Hot Bird 1 | 28 Mar 1995 |
| Superbird A1 | 1 Dec 1992 | UHF FO 3 | 24 Jun 1994 | AMSC-1 | 7 Apr 1995 |
| Cosmos 2224 | 17 Dec 1992 | Cosmos 2282 | 6 Jul 1994 | USA 110 | 4 May 1995 |
| TDRS 6 | 13 Jan 1993 | PAS 2 | 8 Jul 1994 | Intelsat 706 | 17 May 1995 |
| Raduga 29 | 25 Mar 1993 | BS-3N | 8 Jul 1994 | GOES 9 | 23 May 1995 |
| Astra 1C | 12 May 1993 | Apstar 1 | 21 Jul 1994 | UHF FO 5 | 31 May 1995 |
| Galaxy 4 | 25 Jun 1993 | Brasilsat B1 | 10 Aug 1994 | DBS 3 | 10 Jun 1995 |

## SOME SATELLITES IN GEOSTATIONARY ORBIT (1992–2000)



| Satellite | Launch date |
|---|---|
| TDRS 7 | 13 Jul 1995 |
| DSCS III-9 | 31 Jul 1995 |
| PAS 4 | 3 Aug 1995 |
| Mugunghwa | 5 Aug 1995 |
| JCSat 3 | 29 Aug 1995 |
| N-Star a | 29 Aug 1995 |
| Cosmos 2319 | 30 Aug 1995 |
| Telstar 402 | 24 Sep 1995 |
| Luch | 11 Oct 1995 |
| Astra 1E | 19 Oct 1995 |
| UHF FO 6 | 22 Oct 1995 |
| Milstar DFS 2 | 6 Nov 1995 |
| Gals 2 | 17 Nov 1995 |
| Asiasat 2 | 28 Nov 1995 |
| Telecom 2C | 6 Dec 1995 |
| Insat 2C | 6 Dec 1995 |
| Galaxy 3R | 15 Dec 1995 |
| Echostar 1 | 28 Dec 1995 |
| Panamsat 3R | 2 Jan 1996 |
| Measat 1 | 12 Jan 1996 |
| Koreasat 2 | 14 Jan 1996 |
| Gorizont 31 | 25 Jan 1996 |
| Palapa C-1 | 1 Feb 1996 |
| N-Star b | 5 Feb 1996 |
| Intelsat 707 | 14 Mar 1996 |
| Inmarsat 3F-1 | 3 Apr 1996 |
| Astra 1F | 8 Apr 1996 |
| MSAT 1 | 20 Apr 1996 |
| USA 118 | 24 Apr 1996 |
| Palapa | 6 May 1996 |
| AMOS | 6 May 1996 |
| Galaxy 9 | 24 May 1996 |
| Gorizont 32 | 25 May 1996 |
| Intelsat 709 | 15 Jun 1996 |
| Apstar 1A | 3 Jul 1996 |
| Arabsat 2A | 9 Jul 1996 |
| Turksat 1C | 9 Jul 1996 |
| UHF FO 7 | 25 Jul 1996 |
| Italsat 2 | 8 Aug 1996 |
| Telecom 2D | 8 Aug 1996 |
| Inmarsat 3 | 6 Sep 1996 |
| GE-1 | 8 Sep 1996 |
| Echostar 2 | 11 Sep 1996 |
| Ekspress | 26 Sep 1996 |
| Arabsat 2B | 13 Nov 1996 |
| Measat 2 | 13 Nov 1996 |
| Hot Bird 2 | 21 Nov 1996 |
| Inmarsat | 18 Dec 1996 |
| GE-2 | 30 Jan 1997 |
| Nahuelsat | 30 Jan 1997 |
| JCSat 4 | 17 Feb 1997 |
| USA 130 | 23 Feb1997 |
| Intelsat 801 | 1 Mar 1997 |
| Tempo | 8 Mar 1997 |
| Thaicom 3 | 16 Apr 1997 |
| B-Sat 1A | 16 Apr 1997 |
| GOES 10 | 25 Apr 1997 |
| DFH 3 | 11 May 1997 |
| Thor 2 | 21 May 1997 |
| Telstar 5 | 24 May 1997 |
| Inmarsat 3F-4 | 3 Jun 1997 |
| Insat 2D | 3 Jun 1997 |
| Feng Yung | 10 Jun 1997 |
| Intelsat 802 | 25 Jun 1997 |
| Superbird 3 | 28 Jul 1997 |
| Panamsat 6 | 8 Aug 1997 |
| Cosmos 2345 | 14 Aug 1997 |
| Agila 2 | 19 Aug 1997 |
| Panamsat 5 | 28 Aug 1997 |
| Hot Bird 3 | 2 Sep 1997 |
| Meteosat 7 | 2 Sep 1997 |
| Intelsat 803 | 23 Sep 1997 |
| Echostar 3 | 5 Oct 1997 |
| Apstar 2R | 16 Oct 1997 |
| DSCS III B-13 | 25 Oct 1997 |
| Kupon | 12 Nov 1997 |
| Sirius 2 | 12 Nov 1997 |
| Cakrawarta | 12 Nov 1997 |
| JCSat 5 | 2 Dec 1997 |
| Astra 1G | 2 Dec 1997 |
| Galaxy 8i | 8 Dec 1997 |
| Intelsat 804 | 21 Dec 1997 |
| Skynet 4D | 10 Jan 1998 |
| Brasilsat B3 | 4 Feb 1998 |
| Inmarsat 3F-5 | 4 Feb 1998 |
| Hot Bird 4 | 27 Feb 1998 |
| Intelsat 806 | 28 Feb 1998 |
| UHF FO 8 | 16 Mar 1998 |
| B-Sat 1B | 28 Apr 1998 |
| Nilesat 1 | 28 Apr 1998 |
| Cosmos 2350 | 29 Apr 1998 |
| Echostar 4 | 7 May 1998 |
| Zhongwei 1 | 30 May 1998 |
| Thor 3 | 10 Jun 1998 |
| Intelsat 805 | 18 Jun 1998 |
| Sinosat | 18 Jul 1998 |
| ST-1 | 25 Aug 1998 |
| Astra 2A | 30 Aug 1998 |
| Panamsat 7 | 16 Sep 1998 |
| Sirius 3 | 5 Oct 1998 |
| Eutelsat W2 | 5 Oct 1998 |
| Hot Bird 5 | 9 Oct 1998 |
| UHF FO 9 | 20 Oct 1998 |
| Afristar | 28 Oct 1998 |
| GE-5 | 28 Oct 1998 |
| PAS 8 | 4 Nov 1998 |
| BONUM-1 | 22 Nov 1998 |
| SatMex 5 | 6 Dec 1998 |
| PAS 6B | 22 Dec 1998 |
| Telstar 6 | 15 Feb 1999 |
| JCSAT 6 | 16 Feb 1999 |
| Arabsat 3A | 26 Feb 1999 |
| Skynet 4E | 26 Feb 1999 |
| Raduga-1 | 28 Feb 1999 |
| Asiasat 3S | 21 Mar 1999 |
| Insat 2E | 2 April 1999 |
| Nimiq 1 | 20 May 1999 |
| Telkom 1 | 12 Aug 1999 |
| Koreasat 3 | 4 Sep 1999 |
| Yamal 101 | 6 Sep 1999 |
| Yamal 102 | 6 Sep 1999 |
| Telstar 7 | 25 Sep 1999 |
| Orion 2 | 19 Oct 1999 |
| GE-4 | 13 Nov 1999 |
| Galaxy XI | 21 Dec 1999 |
| Galaxy XR | 24 Jan 2000 |
| Superbird 4 | 17 Feb 2000 |
| Asiastar | 21 Mar 2000 |
| Galaxy IVR | 18 Apr 2000 |
| Echostar 6 | 14 Jul 2000 |
| PAS 9 | 27 Jul 2000 |

There are no universally agreed estimates of the natural phenomena given in this section. Surveys make use of different criteria for identifying natural boundaries, and use different techniques of measurement. The sizes of continents, oceans, seas, deserts, and rivers are particularly subject to variation.

**Age** 4 500 000 000 years (accurate to within a very small percentage of possible error)
**Area** 509 600 000 sq km/197 000 000 sq mi
**Mass** 5 976 × $10^{27}$ grams
**Land surface** 148 000 000 sq km/57 000 000 sq mi (c.29% of total area)
**Water surface** 361 600 000 sq km/140 000 000 sq mi (c.71% of total area)
**Circumference at equator** 40 076km/24 902mi
**Circumference of meridian** 40 000km/24 860mi

## Continents

| Name | Area sq km | Area sq mi | | Lowest point below sea level | m | ft | Highest elevation | m | ft |
|---|---|---|---|---|---|---|---|---|---|
| Africa | 30 293 000 | 11 696 000 | (20.2%) | Lake Assal, Djibouti | 156 | 512 | Mt Kilimanjaro, Tanzania | 5 895 | 19 340 |
| Antarctica | 13 975 000 | 5 396 000 | (9.3%) | Bently subglacial trench | 2 538 | 8 327 | Vinson Massif | 5 140 | 16 864 |
| Asia | 44 493 000 | 17 179 000 | (29.6%) | Dead Sea, Israel/Jordan | 400 | 1 312 | Mt Everest, China-Nepal | 8 848 | 29 028 |
| Oceania | 8 945 000 | 3 454 000 | (6%) | Lake Eyre, S Australia | 15 | 49 | Puncak Jaya (Ngga Pulu) | 5 030 | 16 500 |
| Europe[1] | 10 245 000 | 3 956 000 | (6.8%) | Caspian Sea, SW Asia | 29 | 94 | Mt El'brus, Russia | 5 642 | 18 510 |
| North America | 24 454 000 | 9 442 000 | (16.3%) | Death Valley, California | 86 | 282 | Mt McKinley, Alaska | 6 194 | 20 320 |
| South America | 17 838 000 | 6 887 000 | (11.9%) | Peninsular Valdez, Argentina | 40 | 131 | Aconcagua, Argentina | 6 960 | 22 831 |

[1]Including the former western USSR.

## Largest islands

| Name | Area[1] sq km | Area[1] sq mi | Name | Area[1] sq km | Area[1] sq mi |
|---|---|---|---|---|---|
| Australia | 7 692 300 | 2 970 000 | Java | 129 000 | 49 800 |
| Greenland | 2 175 600 | 840 000 | North I, New Zealand | 114 000 | 44 000 |
| New Guinea | 790 000 | 305 000 | Cuba | 110 900 | 42 800 |
| Borneo | 737 000 | 285 000 | Newfoundland | 109 000 | 42 100 |
| Madagascar | 587 000 | 226 600 | Luzon | 105 000 | 40 500 |
| Baffin | 507 000 | 195 800 | Iceland | 103 000 | 39 800 |
| Sumatra | 425 000 | 164 100 | Mindanao | 94 600 | 36 500 |
| Honshu (Hondo) | 228 000 | 88 000 | Novaya Zemlya (two islands) | 90 600 | 35 000 |
| Great Britain | 219 000 | 84 600 | Ireland | 84 100 | 32 500 |
| Victoria, Canada | 217 300 | 83 900 | Hokkaido | 78 500 | 30 300 |
| Ellesmere, Canada | 196 000 | 75 700 | Hispaniola | 77 200 | 29 800 |
| Celebes | 174 000 | 67 200 | Sakhalin | 75 100 | 29 000 |
| South I, New Zealand | 151 000 | 58 300 | Tierra del Fuego | 71 200 | 27 500 |

[1]Areas are rounded to the nearest 100 sq km/sq mi.

## Major island groups

| Name | Country | Sea/Ocean | Constituent islands |
|---|---|---|---|
| Aeolian | Italy | Mediterranean | Stromboli, Lipari, Vulcano, Salina |
| Åland | Finland | Gulf of Bothnia | Ahvenanmaa, Eckero, Lemland, Lumparland, Vardo |
| Aleutian | USA | Pacific | Andreanof, Adak, Atka, Fox, Umnak, Unalaska, Unimak, Near, Attu, Rat, Kiska, Amchitka |
| Alexander | Canada | Pacific | Baranof, Prince of Wales |
| Antilles, Greater | — | Caribbean | Cuba, Jamaica, Haiti and the Dominican Republic, Puerto Rico |
| Antilles, Lesser | — | Caribbean | Windward, Leeward, Netherlands Antilles |
| Andaman | India | Bay of Bengal | over 300 islands including N Andaman, S Andaman, Middle Andaman, Little Andaman |
| Azores | Portugal | Atlantic | nine main islands: Flores, Corvo, Terceira, Graciosa, São Jorge, Faial, Pico, Santa Maria, Formigar, São Miguel |
| Bahamas, The | The Bahamas | Atlantic | 700 islands including Great Abaco, Acklins, Andros, Berry, Cat, Cay, Crooked, Exuma, Grand Bahama, Inagua, Long, Mayaguana, New Providence, Ragged |
| Balearic | Spain | Mediterranean | Ibiza, Majorca, Menorca, Formentera, Cabrera |
| Bay | Honduras | Caribbean | Utila, Roatan, Guanja |
| Bismarck Archipelago | Papua New Guinea | Pacific | c.200 islands including New Britain, New Ireland, Admiralty, Lavonga, New Hanover |
| Bissagos | Guinea-Bissau | Atlantic | 15 islands including Orango, Formosa, Caravela, Roxa |
| Canadian Arctic Archipelago | Canada | Arctic | main islands: Baffin, Victoria, Queen Elizabeth, Banks |
| Canary | Spain | Atlantic | Tenerife, Gomera, Las Palmas, Hierro, Lanzarote, Fuerteventura, Gran Canaria |
| Cape Verde | Cape Verde | Atlantic | 10 islands divided into 1. Barlavento (windward) group: Santo Antão, São Vicente, Santa Luzia, São Nicolau, Boa Vista, Sal and 2. Sotavento (leeward) group: São Tiago, Maio Fogo, Brava |
| Caroline | USA | Pacific | c.680 islands including Yop, Ponape, Truk, Kusac, Palau |
| Chagos | UK | Indian | Diego Garcia, Peros, Banhos, Salomon |
| Channel | UK | English | Jersey, Guernsey, Alderney, Sark |
| Chonos Archipelago | Chile | Pacific | main islands: Chaffers, Benjamin, James, Melchior, Victoria, Luz |
| Commander | Russia | Bering Sea | main islands: Bering, Medny |
| Comoros | Comoros (excluding French Mayotte) | Mozambique Channel | Grand Comore, Anjouan, Mohéli, Mayotte |
| Cook | New Zealand | Pacific | main islands: Rarotonga, Palmerston, Mangaia |
| Cyclades | Greece | Aegean | c.220 islands including Andros, Mikonos, Milos, Naxos, Paros, Kithnos, Sérifos, Tinos, Siros |
| Denmark | Denmark | Baltic | main islands: Zealand, Fyn, Lolland, Falster, Bornholm |
| Desolation | France | Indian | Kerguélen, Grande Terre, and 300 islets |
| Dodecanese | Greece | Aegean | 12 islands including Kásos, Kárpathos, Rhodes, Sámos, Khalki, Tilos, Simi, Astipalaia, Kós, Kálimnos, Léros, Pátmos |
| Ellice | Tuvalu | Pacific | main islands: Funafuti, Nukefetau, Nukulailai, Nanumea |
| Falkland | UK | Atlantic | over 200 islands including W Falkland, E Falkland, S Georgia, S Sandwich |
| Faroe | Denmark | Atlantic | 22 islands including Stromo, Ostero |

## MAJOR ISLAND GROUPS

| Name | Country | Sea/Ocean | Constituent islands |
|---|---|---|---|
| Fiji | Fiji | Pacific | main islands: Viti Levu, Vanua Levu |
| Frisian, East | Germany and Denmark | North Sea | main islands: Borkum, Juist, Norderney, Langeoog, Spiekeroog, Wangerooge |
| Frisian, North | Germany and Denmark | North Sea | main islands: (German) Sylt, Föhr, Nordstrand, Pellworm, Amrum; (Danish) Rømø, Fanø, Mandø |
| Frisian, West | Netherlands | North Sea | main islands: Texel, Vlieland, Terschelling, Ameland, Schiermonnikoog |
| Galapagos | Ecuador | Pacific | main islands: San Cristóbal, Santa Cruz, Isabela, Floreana, Santiago, Fernandina |
| Gilbert | Kiribati | Pacific | main islands: Tarawa, Makin, Abaiang, Abemama, Tabiteuea, Nonouti, Beru |
| Gotland | Sweden | Baltic | main islands: Gotland, Fårö, Karlsö |
| Greenland | Denmark | N Atlantic/Arctic | main islands: Greenland, Disko |
| Hawaiian | USA | Pacific | 8 main islands: Hawaii, Oahu, Maui, Lanai, Kauai, Molokai, Kahoolawe, Niihau |
| Hebrides, Inner | UK | Atlantic | main islands: Skye, Eigg, Coll, Tiree, Mull, Iona, Staffa, Jura, Islay |
| Hebrides, Outer | UK | Atlantic | Lewis, Harris, N and S Uist, Benbecula, Barra |
| Indonesia | Indonesia | Pacific | 13 677 islets and islands including Java, Sumatra, Kalimantau, Celebes, Lesser Sundas, Moluccas, Irian Jaya |
| Ionian | Greece | Aegean | Kerkira, Kefalliniá, Zakinthos, Levkas |
| Japan | Japan | Pacific | main islands: Hokkaido, Honshu, Shikoku, Kyushu, Ryuku |
| Juan Fernandez | Chile | Pacific | Más á Tierra, Más Afuera, Santa Clara |
| Kuril | Russia | Pacific | 56 islands including Shumsu, Iturup, Urup, Paramushir, Onekotan, Shiaskhotan, Shikotanto, Kunashir, Shimushir |
| Laccadive | India | Arabian Sea | 27 islands including Amindivi, Laccadive, Minicoy, Androth, Kavaratti |
| Line | Kiribati | Pacific | main islands: Christmas, Fanning, Washington |
| Lofoten | Norway | Norwegian Sea | main islands: Hinnøy, Austvågøy, Vestvågøy, Moskenes |
| Madeira | Portugal | Atlantic | Madeira, Ilha do Porto Santo, Ilhas Desertas, Ilhas Selvagens |
| Malay Archipelago | Indonesia, Malaysia, Philippines | Pacific/Indian | main islands: Borneo, Celebes, Java, Luzon, Mindanao, New Guinea, Sumatra |
| Maldives | Maldives | Indian | 19 clusters, main island: Male |
| Malta | Malta | Mediterranean | main islands: Malta, Gozo, Comino |
| Mariana | Mariana Islands | Pacific | 14 islands including Saipan, Tinian, Rota, Pagan, Guguan |
| Marquesas | France | Pacific | 10 islands including Nukultiva, Ua Pu, Ua Huka, Hiva Oa, Tahuata, Fatu Hiva, Eïao, Hatutu |
| Marshall | Marshall Islands | Pacific | main islands: Bikini, Wotha, Kwajalein, Eniwetok, Maiura, Jalut, Rogelap |
| Mascarenes | — | Indian | main islands: Réunion, Mauritius, Rodrigues |
| Melanesia | — | Pacific | main groups of islands: Solomon Islands, Bismarck Archipelago, New Caledonia, Papua New Guinea, Fiji, Vanuatu |
| Micronesia | — | Pacific | main groups of islands: Caroline, Gilberts, Marianas, Marshalls, Guam, Kiribati, Nauru |
| New Hebrides | Vanuatu | Pacific | main islands: Espíritu Santo, Malekula, Efate, Ambrim, Eromanga, Tanna, Epi, Pentecost, Aurora |
| New Siberian | Russia | Arctic | main islands: Kotelny, Faddeyevski |
| Newfoundland | Canada | Atlantic | Prince Edward, Anticosti |
| Nicobar | India | Bay of Bengal | main islands: Great Nicobar, Camorta with Nancowry, Car Nicobar, Teressa, Little Nicobar |

| Name | Country | Sea/Ocean | Constituent islands |
|---|---|---|---|
| Northern Land | Russia | Arctic | main islands: Komsomolets, Bolshevik, October Revolution |
| Novaya Zemlya | Russia | Arctic | 2 main islands: North, South |
| Orkney | UK | North Sea | main islands: Mainland, South Ronaldsay, Sanday, Westray, Hoy, Stronsay, Shapinsay, Rousay |
| Pelagian | Italy | Mediterrannean | Lampedusa, Linosa, Lampione |
| Philippines | Philippines | Pacific | over 7 100 islands and islets including Luzon, Mindanao, Samar, Palawan, Mindoro, Panay, Negros, Cebu, Leyte, Masbate, Bohol |
| Polynesia | — | Pacific | main groups of islands: New Zealand, French Polynesia, Phoenix Islands, Hawaii, Line, Cook Islands, Pitcairn, Tokelau, Tonga, Society, Easter, Samoa, Kiribati, Ellice |
| Queen Charlotte | Canada | Pacific | 150 islands including Prince Rupert, Graham, Moresby, Louise, Lyell, Kunghit |
| São Tomé and Príncipe | São Tomé and Príncipe | Atlantic | main islands: São Tomé, Príncipe |
| Scilly | UK | English Channel | c.150 islands including St Mary's, St Martin's, Tresco, St Agnes, Bryher |
| Seychelles | Seychelles | Indian | 115 islands including Praslin, La Digue, Silhouette, Mahé, Bird |
| Shetland | UK | North Sea | 100 islands including Mainland, Unst, Yell, Whalsay, West Burra |
| Society | France | Pacific | island groups: Windward, Leeward; main island: Tahiti |
| Solomon | Solomon Islands | Pacific | main islands: Choiseul, Guadalcanal, Malaita, New Georgia, San Cristóbal, Santa Isabel |
| South Orkney | UK | Atlantic | main islands: Coronation, Signy, Laurie, Inaccessible |
| South Shetland | UK | Atlantic | main islands: King George, Elephant, Clarence, Gibbs, Nelson, Livingstone, Greenwich, Snow, Deception, Smith |
| Sri Lanka | Sri Lanka | Indian | main islands: Sri Lanka, Mannar |
| Taiwan | Taiwan | China Sea/Pacific | main islands: Taiwan, Lan Hsü, Lü Tao, Quemoy, the Pescadores |
| Tasmania | Australia | Tasman Sea | main islands: Tasmania, King, Flinders, Bruny |
| Tierra del Fuego | Argentina/Chile | Pacific | main islands: Tierra del Fuego, Isla de los Estados, Hoste, Navarino, Wallaston, Diego Ramírez, Desolación, Santa Inés, Clarence, Dawson |
| Tres Marías | Mexico | Pacific | María Madre, María Magdalena, María Cleofás, San Juanito |
| Tristan da Cunha | UK | Atlantic | 5 islands including Tristan da Cunha, Gough, Inaccessible, Nightingale |
| Tuamotu Archipelago | France | Pacific | c.80 islands including Makatea, Fakarava, Rangiroa, Anaa, Hao, Reao, Gambiev, Duke of Gloucester |
| Vesterålen | Norway | Norwegian Sea | main islands: Hinnøy, Langøya, Andøya, Hadseløy |
| Virgin | USA | Caribbean | over 50 islands including St Croix, St Thomas, St John |
| Virgin | UK | Caribbean | main islands: Tortola, Virgin Gorda, Anegada, Jost Van Dyke |
| Zanzibar | Tanzania | Indian | main islands: Zanzibar, Tumbatu, Kwale |
| Zemlya Frantsa-Iosifa | Russia | Arctic | c.167 islands including Graham Bell, Wilczekland, Georgeland, Hooker, Zemlya Aleksandry, Ostrov Rudol'fa |

## Oceans

| Name | Area sq km | sq mi | | Greatest depth | m | ft | Average depth | m | ft |
|---|---|---|---|---|---|---|---|---|---|
| Arctic | 13 986 000 | 5 400 000 | (3%) | Eurasia Basin | 5 122 | 16 804 | Arctic | 1 330 | 4 400 |
| Atlantic | 82 217 000 | 31 700 000 | (24%) | Puerto Rico Trench | 8 648 | 28 372 | Atlantic | 3 700 | 12 100 |
| Indian | 73 426 000 | 28 350 000 | (20%) | Java Trench | 7 725 | 25 344 | Indian | 3 900 | 12 800 |
| Pacific | 181 300 000 | 70 000 000 | (46%) | Mariana Trench | 11 040 | 36 220 | Pacific | 4 300 | 14 100 |

## Largest seas

| Name | Area[1] sq km | sq mi | Name | Area[1] sq km | sq mi |
|---|---|---|---|---|---|
| Coral Sea | 4 791 000 | 1 850 000 | Arafura Sea | 1 037 000 | 400 000 |
| Arabian Sea | 3 863 000 | 1 492 000 | Philippine Sea | 1 036 000 | 400 000 |
| S China (Nan) Sea | 3 685 000 | 1 423 000 | Sea of Japan | 978 000 | 378 000 |
| Mediterranean Sea | 2 516 000 | 971 000 | E Siberian Sea | 901 000 | 348 000 |
| Bering Sea | 2 304 000 | 890 000 | Kara Sea | 883 000 | 341 000 |
| Bay of Bengal | 2 172 000 | 839 000 | E China Sea | 664 000 | 256 000 |
| Sea of Okhotsk | 1 590 000 | 614 000 | Andaman Sea | 565 000 | 218 000 |
| Gulf of Mexico | 1 543 000 | 596 000 | North Sea | 520 000 | 201 000 |
| Gulf of Guinea | 1 533 000 | 592 000 | Black Sea | 508 000 | 196 000 |
| Barents Sea | 1 405 000 | 542 000 | Red Sea | 453 000 | 175 000 |
| Norwegian Sea | 1 383 000 | 534 000 | Baltic Sea | 414 000 | 160 000 |
| Gulf of Alaska | 1 327 000 | 512 000 | Arabian Gulf | 239 000 | 92 000 |
| Hudson Bay | 1 232 000 | 476 000 | St Lawrence Gulf | 238 000 | 92 000 |
| Greenland Sea | 1 205 000 | 465 000 | | | |

Oceans are excluded.

[1]Areas are rounded to the nearest 1 000 sq km/sq mi.

## Largest lakes

| Name/Location | Area[1] sq km | sq mi | Name/Location | Area[1] sq km | sq mi |
|---|---|---|---|---|---|
| Caspian Sea, Iran/Russia/ Turkmenistan/Kazakhstan/ Azerbaijan | 371 000 | 143 240 [2] | Winnipeg, Canada | 24 390 | 9 420 |
| Superior, USA/Canada | 82 260 | 31 760 [3] | Malawi/Nyasa, E Africa | 22 490 | 8 680 |
| Aral Sea, Uzbekistan/ Kazakhstan | 64 500 | 24 900 [2] | Balkhash, Kazakhstan | 17 000–22 000 | 6 560–8 490[2] |
| Victoria, E Africa | 62 940 | 24 300 | Ontario, Canada | 19 270 | 7 440[3] |
| Huron, USA/Canada | 59 580 | 23 000[3] | Ladoga, Russia | 18 130 | 7 000 |
| Michigan, USA | 58 020 | 22 400 | Chad, W Africa | 10 000–26 000 | 3 860–10 040 |
| Tanganyika, E Africa | 32 000 | 12 360 | Maracaibo, Venezuela | 13 010 | 5 020[4] |
| Baikal, Russia | 31 500 | 12 160 | Patos, Brazil | 10 140 | 3 920[4] |
| Great Bear, Canada | 31 330 | 12 100 | Onega, Russia | 9 800 | 3 780 |
| Great Slave, Canada | 28 570 | 11 030 | Rudolf, E Africa | 9 100 | 3 510 |
| Erie, USA/Canada | 25 710 | 9 930[3] | Eyre, Australia | 8 800 | 3 400[4] |
| | | | Titicaca, Peru | 8 300 | 3 200 |

The Caspian and Aral Seas, being entirely surrounded by land, are classified as lakes.

[1]Areas are rounded to the nearest 10 sq km/sq mi.
[2] Salt lakes.
[3] Average of areas given by Canada and USA.
[4] Salt lagoons.

## Longest rivers

| Name | Outflow | Length[1] km | mi |
|---|---|---|---|
| Nile-Kagera-Ruvuvu-Ruvusu-Luvironza | Mediterranean Sea (Egypt) | 6 690 | 4 160 |
| Amazon-Ucayali-Tambo-Ene-Apurimac | Atlantic Ocean (Brazil) | 6 570 | 4 080 |
| Mississippi-Missouri-Jefferson-Beaverhead-Red Rock | Gulf of Mexico (USA) | 6 020 | 3 740 |
| Chang Jiang (Yangtze) | E China Sea (China) | 5 980 | 3 720 |
| Yenisey-Angara-Selenga-Ider | Kara Sea (Russia) | 5 870 | 3 650 |
| Amur-Argun-Kerulen | Tartar Strait (Russia) | 5 780 | 3 590 |
| Ob-Irtysh | Gulf of Ob, Kara Sea (Russia) | 5 410 | 3 360 |
| Plata-Parana-Grande | Atlantic Ocean (Argentina-Uruguay) | 4 880 | 3 030 |
| Huang He (Yellow) | Yellow Sea (China) | 4 840 | 3 010 |
| Congo-Lualaba | S Atlantic Ocean (Angola-Democratic Republic of Congo) | 4 630 | 2 880 |
| Lena | Laptev Sea (Russia) | 4 400 | 2 730 |
| Mackenzie-Slave-Peace-Finlay | Beaufort Sea (Canada) | 4 240 | 2 630 |
| Mekong | S China Sea (Vietnam) | 4 180 | 2 600 |
| Niger | Gulf of Guinea (Nigeria) | 4 100 | 2 550 |

[1]Lengths are given to the nearest 10km/mi, and include the river plus tributaries comprising the longest watercourse.

## Largest deserts

| Name/Location | Area[1] sq km | sq mi |
|---|---|---|
| Sahara, N Africa | 8 600 000 | 3 320 000 |
| Arabian, SW Asia | 2 330 000 | 900 000 |
| Gobi, Mongolia and NE China | 1 166 000 | 450 000 |
| Patagonian, Argentina | 673 000 | 260 000 |
| Great Victoria, SW Australia | 647 000 | 250 000 |
| Great Basin, SW USA | 492 000 | 190 000 |
| Chihuahuan, Mexico | 450 000 | 174 000 |
| Great Sandy, NW Australia | 400 000 | 154 000 |
| Sonoran, SW USA | 310 000 | 120 000 |
| Kyzyl Kum, Kazakhstan | 300 000 | 116 000 |
| Takla Makan, N China | 270 000 | 104 000 |
| Kalahari, SW Africa | 260 000 | 100 000 |
| Kara Kum, Turkmenistan | 260 000 | 100 000 |
| Kavir, Iran | 260 000 | 100 000 |
| Syrian, Saudi Arabia/Jordan/Syria/Iraq | 260 000 | 100 000 |
| Nubian, Sudan | 260 000 | 100 000 |
| Thar, India/Pakistan | 200 000 | 77 000 |
| Ust'-Urt, Kazakhstan | 160 000 | 62 000 |
| Bet-Pak-Dala, S Kazakhstan | 155 000 | 60 000 |
| Simpson, C Australia | 145 000 | 56 000 |
| Dzungaria, China | 142 000 | 55 000 |
| Atacama, Chile | 140 000 | 54 000 |
| Namib, SE Africa | 134 000 | 52 000 |
| Sturt, SE Australia | 130 000 | 50 000 |
| Bolson de Mapimi, Mexico | 130 000 | 50 000 |
| Ordos, China | 130 000 | 50 000 |
| Alashan, China | 116 000 | 45 000 |

[1]Desert areas are very approximate, because clear physical boundaries may not occur.

## Highest waterfalls

| Name | Height[1] m | ft | Name | Height[1] m | ft |
|---|---|---|---|---|---|
| Angel (upper fall), Venezuela | 807 | 2 648 | Pilao, Brazil | 524 | 1 719 |
| Itatinga, Brazil | 628 | 2 060 | Ribbon, USA | 491 | 1 611 |
| Cuquenán, Guyana-Venezuela | 610 | 2 001 | Vestre Mardola, Norway | 468 | 1 535 |
| Ormeli, Norway | 563 | 1 847 | Kaieteur, Guyana | 457 | 1 500 |
| Tysse, Norway | 533 | 1 749 | Cleve-Garth, New Zealand | 450 | 1 476 |

[1]Height denotes individual leaps.

## Deepest caves

| Name/Location | Depth m | ft | Name/Location | Depth m | ft |
|---|---|---|---|---|---|
| Jean Bernard, France | 1 494 | 4 902 | Dachstein-Mammuthöhle, Austria | 1 174 | 3 852 |
| Snezhnaya, Caucasus | 1 340 | 4 396 | Zitu, Spain | 1 139 | 3 737 |
| Puertas de Illamina, Spain | 1 338 | 4 390 | Badalona, Spain | 1 130 | 3 707 |
| Pierre-Saint-Martin, France | 1 321 | 4 334 | Batmanhöhle, Austria | 1 105 | 3 625 |
| Sistema Huautla, Mexico | 1 240 | 4 068 | Schneeloch, Austria | 1 101 | 3 612 |
| Berger, France | 1 198 | 3 930 | G E S Malaga, Spain | 1 070 | 3 510 |
| Vqerdi, Spain | 1 195 | 3 921 | Lamprechstofen, Austria | 1 024 | 3 360 |

## Highest mountains

| Name | Height[1] m | ft | Location |
|---|---|---|---|
| Everest | 8 850 | 29 030 | China-Nepal |
| K2 | 8 610 | 28 250 | Kashmir-Jammu |
| Kangchenjunga | 8 590 | 28 170 | India-Nepal |
| Lhotse | 8 500 | 27 890 | China-Nepal |
| Kangchenjunga S Peak | 8 470 | 27 800 | India-Nepal |
| Makalu I | 8 470 | 27 800 | China-Nepal |
| Kangchenjunga W Peak | 8 420 | 27 620 | India-Nepal |
| Lhotse E Peak | 8 380 | 27 500 | China-Nepal |
| Dhaulagiri | 8 170 | 26 810 | Nepal |
| Cho Oyu | 8 150 | 26 750 | China-Nepal |
| Manaslu | 8 130 | 26 660 | Nepal |
| Nanga Parbat | 8 130 | 26 660 | Kashmir-Jammu |
| Annapurna I | 8 080 | 26 500 | Nepal |
| Gasherbrum I | 8 070 | 26 470 | Kashmir-Jammu |
| Broad Peak I | 8 050 | 26 400 | Kashmir-Jammu |
| Gasherbrum II | 8 030 | 26 360 | Kashmir-Jammu |
| Gosainthan | 8 010 | 26 290 | China |
| Broad Peak Central | 8 000 | 26 250 | Kashmir-Jammu |
| Gasherbrum III | 7 950 | 26 090 | Kashmir-Jammu |
| Annapurna II | 7 940 | 26 040 | Nepal |
| Nanda Devi | 7 820 | 25 660 | India |
| Rakaposhi | 7 790 | 25 560 | Kashmir |
| Kamet | 7 760 | 25 450 | India |
| Ulugh Muztagh | 7 720 | 25 340 | Tibet |
| Tirich Mir | 7 690 | 25 230 | Pakistan |
| Muz Tag Ata | 7 550 | 24 760 | China |
| Communism Peak | 7 490 | 24 590 | Tajikistan |
| Pobedy Peak | 7 440 | 24 410 | China-Kyrgyzstan |
| Aconcagua | 6 960 | 22 830 | Argentina |
| Ojos del Salado | 6 910 | 22 660 | Argentina-Chile |

[1]Heights are given to the nearest 10 m/ft.

## Major volcanoes

| Name | Height m | ft | Major eruptions (years) | Last eruption (year) |
|---|---|---|---|---|
| Aconcagua (Argentina) | 6 959 | 22 831 | extinct | — |
| Ararat (Turkey) | 5 137 | 16 853 | extinct | — |
| Awu (Sangihe Is, Indonesia) | 1 327 | 4 355 | 1711, 1856, 1892, 1968 | 1992 |
| Bezymianny (Russia) | 2 800 | 9 186 | 1955–6, 1981 | 1997 |
| Coseguina (Nicaragua) | 847 | 2 779 | 1835 | 1835 |
| Cotopaxi (Ecuador) | 5 897 | 19 347 | 1877 | 1975 |
| El Chichón (Mexico) | 1 350 | 4 430 | 1982 | 1982 |
| Erebus (Antarctica) | 4 023 | 13 200 | 1947, 1972, 1980, 1986, 1991 | 1995 |
| Etna (Italy) | 3 239 | 10 625 | 122, 1169, 1329, 1536, 1669, 1928, 1964, 1971, 1981, 1986, 1992, 1994 | 2001 |
| Fuji (Japan) | 3 776 | 12 388 | 1707 | 1707 |
| Galunggung (Java) | 2 181 | 7 155 | 1822, 1918 | 1984 |
| Hekla (Iceland) | 1 500 | 4 920 | 1693, 1845, 1947–8, 1970, 1981, 1991 | 2000 |
| Helgafell (Iceland) | 215 | 706 | 1973 | 1973 |
| Hudson (Chile) | 1 750 | 5 742 | 1971, 1973 | 1991 |
| Jurullo (Mexico) | 1 330 | 4 255 | 1759–74 | 1774 |
| Katmai (Alaska) | 2 047 | 6 715 | 1912, 1920, 1921, 1931, 1962 | 1974 |
| Kilauea (Hawaii) | 1 250 | 4 100 | 1823–1924, 1952, 1955, 1960, 1967–8, 1968–74, 1983–7, 1988, 1991, 1992, 1994 | 2001 |
| Kilimanjaro (Tanzania) | 5 928 | 19 450 | extinct | Pleistocene |
| Klyuchevskoy (Russia) | 4 850 | 15 910 | 1700–1966, 1984, 1985, 1993 | 2001 |
| Krakatoa (Sumatra) | 818 | 2 685 | 1680, 1883, 1927, 1952–3, 1969, 1980, 1995, 1999 | 2001 |
| La Soufrière (St Vincent) | 1 234 | 4 048 | 1718, 1812, 1902, 1971–2 | 1997 |
| Laki (Iceland) | 500 | 1 642 | 1783, 1784, 1938 | 1996 |
| Lamington (Papua New Guinea) | 1 781 | 5 844 | 1951 | 1956 |
| Lassen Peak (USA) | 3 186 | 10 453 | 1914–15 | 1921 |
| Mauna Loa (Hawaii) | 4 171 | 13 685 | 1750, 1859, 1880, 1887, 1919, 1950, 1984 | 1987 |
| Mayon (Philippines) | 2 464 | 8 084 | 1616, 1766, 1814, 1897, 1968, 1978, 1993 | 2000 |
| Nyamuragira (Congo, Democratic Republic of) | 3 056 | 10 026 | 1884, 1921–38, 1971, 1980, 1984, 1988, 1995 | 2000 |
| Paricutín (Mexico) | 3 188 | 10 460 | 1943–52 | 1952 |
| Pelée, Mont (Martinique) | 1 397 | 4 584 | 1902, 1929–32 | 1932 |
| Pinatubo, Mt (Philippines) | 1 759 | 5 770 | 1391, 1991 | 1992 |
| Popocatèpetl (Mexico) | 5 483 | 17 990 | 1347, 1920, 1998, 2000 | 2001 |
| Rainier, Mt (USA) | 4 394 | 14 416 | 1st-cBC, 1820, 1825 | 1882 |
| Ruapehu (New Zealand) | 2 797 | 9 175 | 1945, 1953, 1969, 1975, 1986 | 1995 |
| St Helens, Mt (USA) | 2 549 | 8 364 | 1800, 1831, 1835, 1842–3, 1857, 1980, 1982, 1987 | 1991 |
| Santoriní/Thíra (Greece) | 566 | 1 857 | 1470BC, 197BC, AD46, 1570–3, 1707–11, 1866–70, 1950 | 1950 |
| Soufrière Hills (Montserrat) | | | 1995– | 2000 |
| Stromboli (Italy) | 931 | 3 055 | 1768, 1882, 1889, 1907, 1930, 1936, 1941, 1950, 1952, 1975, 1986, 1990 | 1996 |
| Surtsey (Iceland) | 174 | 570 | 1963–7 | 1967 |
| Taal (Philippines) | 1 448 | 4 752 | 1906, 1911, 1965, 1969, 1977 | 1988 |
| Tambora (Sumbawa, Indonesia) | 2 868 | 9 410 | 1815 | 1880 |
| Tarawera (New Zealand) | 1 149 | 3 770 | 1886 | 1973 |
| Unzen (Japan) | 1 360 | 4 461 | 1360, 1791, 1991 | 1996 |
| Vesuvius (Italy) | 1 289 | 4 230 | 79, 472, 1036, 1631, 1779, 1906 | 1944 |
| Vulcano (Italy) | 503 | 1 650 | antiquity, 1444, 1730–40, 1786, 1873, 1888–90 | 1890 |

EARTH

## Major tsunamis

Tsunamis are long-period ocean waves associated with earthquakes, volcanic explosions, or landslides. They are also referred to as *seismic sea waves* and popularly, but incorrectly, as *tidal waves*.

| Location of source | Year | Height m | ft | Location of deaths/damage | Deaths |
|---|---|---|---|---|---|
| Papua New Guinea | 1998 | 10 | 33 | Papua New Guinea | 2 200 + |
| Peru | 1996 | 4.9 | 16 | Peru | 12 |
| Irian Jaya, Indonesia | 1996 | 7 | 23 | Indonesia | 161 |
| Makassar Straits, Indonesia | 1996 | 4.9 | 16 | Indonesia | 9 |
| Skagway, Alaska[1] | 1994 | 11 | 36 | Skagway, Alaska | 1 |
| Java trench (Indian Ocean) | 1994 | 11 | 36 | Java | 223 |
| Sea of Japan | 1993 | 30.5 | 100 | Japan, Russia | 202 |
| Flores I (Indonesia) | 1992 | 26 | 85 | Indonesia | 400 |
| Nicaragua | 1992 | 9 | 30 | Nicaragua | 167 |
| Sea of Japan | 1983 | 15 | 49 | Japan, Korea | 103 |
| Indonesia | 1979 | 9.8 | 32 | Indonesia | 187 |
| Celebes Sea | 1976 | 30 | 98 | Philippines | 5 000 |
| Alaska | 1964 | 32 | 105 | Alaska, Aleutian Is, California | 122 |
| Chile | 1960 | 25 | 82 | Chile, Hawaii, Japan | 1 260 |
| Aleutian Is | 1957 | 15.9 | 52 | Hawaii, Japan | 0 |
| Kamchatka | 1952 | 18.3 | 60 | Kamchatka, Kuril Is, Hawaii | many |
| Aleutian Is | 1946 | 32 | 105 | Aleutian Is, Hawaii, California | 165 |
| Nankaido (Japan) | 1946 | 6.1 | 20 | Japan | 1 997 |
| Kii (Japan) | 1944 | 7.6 | 25 | Japan | 998 |
| Sanriku (Japan) | 1933 | 28.3 | 93 | Japan, Hawaii | 3 000 |
| E Kamchatka | 1923 | 20.1 | 66 | Kamchatka, Hawaii | 3 |
| S Kuril Is | 1918 | 11.9 | 39 | Kuril Is, Russia, Japan, Hawaii | 23 |
| Sanriku (Japan) | 1896 | 29.9 | 98 | Japan | 27 122 |
| Sunda Strait | 1883 | 35.1 | 115 | Java, Sumatra | 36 000 |
| Chile | 1877 | 22.9 | 75 | Chile, Hawaii | many |
| Chile | 1868 | 21 | 69 | Chile, Hawaii | 25 000 |
| Hawaii | 1868 | 20.1 | 66 | Hawaii | 81 |
| Japan | 1854 | 6.1 | 20 | Japan | 3 000 |
| Flores Sea | 1800 | 24.1 | 79 | Indonesia | 400–500 |
| Ariake Sea | 1792 | 9.1 | 30 | Japan | 9 745 |
| Italy | 1783 | ? | ? | Italy | 30 000 |
| Ryukyu Is | 1771 | 11.9 | 39 | Ryukyu Is | 11 941 |
| Portugal | 1775 | 15.8 | 52 | W Europe, Morocco, W Indies | 60 000 |
| Peru | 1746 | 24.1 | 79 | Peru | 5 000 |
| Japan | 1741 | 9 | 30 | Japan | 1 000 + |
| SE Kamchatka | 1737 | 29.9 | 98 | Kamchatka, Kuril Is | ? |
| Peru | 1724 | 24.1 | 79 | Peru | ? |
| Japan | 1707 | 11.6 | 38 | Japan | 30 000 |
| W Indies | 1692 | ? | ? | Jamaica | 2 000 |
| Banda Is | 1629 | 14.9 | 49 | Indonesia | ? |
| Sanriku (Japan) | 1611 | 25 | 82 | Japan | 5 000 |
| Japan | 1605 | ? | ? | Japan | 4 000 |
| Kii (Japan) | 1498 | ? | ? | Japan | 5 000 |

[1]Tsunami caused by the dock collapsing into the sea.

## Major earthquakes

All magnitudes on the Richter scale. The energy released by earthquakes is measured on the logarithmic Richter scale. Thus

2 Barely perceptible; 5 Rather strong; 7+ Very strong

| Location | Year | Magnitude | Deaths |
|---|---|---|---|
| Vanuatu | 2002 | 7.2 | — |
| El Salvador | 2001 | 6.6 | 300+ |
| Gujurat (India) | 2001 | 7.9 | 19 000+ |
| El Salvador | 2001 | 7.7 | 675+ |
| Bengkulu (Sumatra) | 2000 | 7.9 | 115+ |
| Armenia (Colombia) | 1999 | 6.0 | 1 100+ |
| Izmit (NW Turkey) | 1999 | 7.4 | 17 000+ |
| Nantou Province (Taiwan) | 1999 | 7.6 | 2 400+ |
| Badakhshan Province (Afghanistan) | 1998 | 7.1 | 5 000+ |
| Rustaq, Afghanistan | 1998 | 6.1 | 4 000+ |
| Qayen (E Iran) | 1997 | 7.1 | 2 400 |
| Ardabil (NW Iran) | 1997 | 5.5 | 965+ |
| Xinjiang Region (China) | 1996 | 6.9 | 26 |
| Biak I (Indonesia) | 1996 | 7.9 | 108 |
| Flores Sea (near Indonesia) | 1996 | 7.9 | — |
| Samar (Philippines) | 1996 | 7.9 | — |
| Andreanof Is (off Alaskan coast) | 1996 | 7.9 | — |
| Lijiang, Yunan Province (China) | 1996 | 7.0 | 304 |
| Kuril Is (Russia) | 1995 | 7.9 | 0 |
| Dinar (Turkey) | 1995 | 6.0 | 71+ |
| Manzanillo (Mexico) | 1995 | 7.6 | 66 |
| Sungai Penuh, S Sumatra (Indonesia) | 1995 | 6.7 | 84 |
| S Mexico | 1995 | 7.3 | — |
| Egion, Gulf of Corinth (Greece) | 1995 | 6.1 | 20+ |
| Neftegorsk, Sakhalin I (E Russia) | 1995 | 7.5 | 2 000 |
| W Colombia | 1995 | 6.4 | 31 |
| Kobe (Japan) | 1995 | 7.2 | 6 300 |
| Mindoro I (Philippines) | 1994 | * | 60 |
| Hokkaido I (Japan) and Kuril Is (Russia) (undersea) | 1994 | 8.2 | 16+ |
| NW Algeria | 1994 | 5.6 | 171+ |
| Bolivia (617km underground) | 1994 | 8.2 | 5 |
| Paez River Valley (SW Colombia) | 1994 | 6.8 | 269 |
| Java (Indonesia) | 1994 | 7.7 | 200 |
| Sumatra I (Indonesia) | 1994 | 7.2 | 215 |
| Halmahera I (Indonesia) | 1994 | 6.8 | 7+ |
| Los Angeles, California (USA) | 1994 | 6.8 | 61 |
| Maharashtra State (India) | 1993 | 6.5 | 22 000 |
| Guam (Mariana Is) | 1993 | 8.1 | — |
| Okushiri and Hokkaido Is (N Japan) | 1993 | 7.8 | 185 |
| Papua New Guinea | 1993 | 6.8 | 60 |
| Maumere, Flores I (Indonesia) | 1992 | 7.5 | 1 232 |
| Cairo (Egypt) | 1992 | 5.9 | 552 |
| Joshua Tree and Yucca Valley, California (USA) | 1992 | 7.4 | 2 |
| Kyrgyzstan | 1992 | * | 50+ |
| Erzincan (Turkey) | 1992 | 6.8 | 500 |
| Nusa Tenggara Is (Indonesia) | 1992 | 6.8 | 2 500 |
| Uttar Pradesh (India) | 1991 | 6.1 | 1 000 |
| Costa Rica/Panama | 1991 | 7.5 | 80 |
| Georgia | 1991 | 7.2 | 100 |
| Afghanistan | 1991 | 6.8 | 1 000 |
| Pakistan | 1991 | 6.8 | 300 |
| Cabanatuan City (Philippines) | 1990 | 7.7 | 1 653 |
| NW Iran | 1990 | 7.5 | 40 000 |
| N Peru | 1990 | 5.8 | 200 |
| Romania | 1990 | 6.6 | 70 |
| Philippines | 1990 | 7.7 | 1 600 |
| San Francisco (USA) | 1989 | 6.9 | 100 |
| Armenia | 1988 | 7.0 | 25 000 |
| SW China | 1988 | 7.6 | 1 000 |
| Nepal/India | 1988 | 6.9 | 900 |
| Mexico City (Mexico) | 1985 | 8.1 | 7 200 |
| N Yemen | 1982 | 6.0 | 2 800 |
| S Italy | 1980 | 7.2 | 4 500 |
| El Asnam (Algeria) | 1980 | 7.3 | 5 000 |
| NE Iran | 1978 | 7.7 | 25 000 |
| Tangshan (China) | 1976 | 8.2 | 242 000 |
| Guatemala City (Guatemala) | 1976 | 7.5 | 22 778 |
| Kashmir (India) | 1974 | 6.3 | 5 200 |
| Managua (Nicaragua) | 1972 | 6.2 | 5 000 |
| S Iran | 1972 | 6.9 | 5 000 |
| Chimbote (Peru) | 1970 | 7.7 | 66 000 |
| NE Iran | 1968 | 7.4 | 11 600 |
| Anchorage (USA) | 1964 | 8.5 | 131 |
| NW Iran | 1962 | 7.1 | 12 000 |
| Agadir (Morocco) | 1960 | 5.8 | 12 000 |
| Erzincan (Turkey) | 1939 | 7.9 | 23 000 |
| Chillan (Chile) | 1939 | 7.8 | 30 000 |
| Quetta (India) | 1935 | 7.5 | 60 000 |
| Gansu (China) | 1932 | 7.6 | 70 000 |
| Nan-shan (China) | 1927 | 8.3 | 200 000 |
| Kwanto (Japan) | 1923 | 8.3 | 143 000 |
| Gansu (China) | 1920 | 8.6 | 180 000 |
| Avezzano (Italy) | 1915 | 7.5 | 30 000 |
| Messina (Italy) | 1908 | 7.5 | 120 000 |
| Valparaiso (Chile) | 1906 | 8.6 | 20 000 |
| San Francisco (USA) | 1906 | 8.3 | 500 |
| Ecuador/Colombia | 1868 | * | 70 000 |
| Calabria (Italy) | 1783 | * | 50 000 |
| Lisbon (Portugal) | 1755 | * | 70 000 |
| Calcutta (India) | 1737 | * | 300 000 |
| Hokkaido (Japan) | 1730 | * | 137 000 |
| Catania (Italy) | 1693 | * | 60 000 |
| Caucasia (Caucasus) | 1667 | * | 80 000 |

| Location | Year | Magnitude | Deaths | Location | Year | Magnitude | Deaths |
|---|---|---|---|---|---|---|---|
| Shensi (China) | 1556 | * | 830 000 | Corinth (Greece) | 856 | * | 45 000 |
| Chihli (China) | 1290 | * | 100 000 | Antioch (Turkey) | 526 | * | 250 000 |
| Silicia (Asia Minor) | 1268 | * | 60 000 | | | | |

*Magnitude not available

## Earthquake severity measurement

Modified Mercalli intensity scale (1956 Revision)

| Intensity value | Description |
|---|---|
| I | Not felt; marginal and long-period effects of large earthquakes. |
| II | Felt by persons at rest, on upper floors or favourably placed. |
| III | Felt indoors; hanging objects swing; vibration like passing of light trucks; duration estimated; may not be recognized as an earthquake. |
| IV | Hanging objects swing; vibration like passing of heavy trucks, or sensation of a jolt like a heavy ball striking the walls; standing cars rock; windows, dishes, doors rattle; glasses clink; crockery clashes; in the upper range of IV, wooden walls and frames creak. |
| V | Felt outdoors; direction estimated; sleepers awoken; liquids disturbed, some spilled; small unstable objects displaced or upset; doors swing, close, open; shutters, pictures move; pendulum clocks stop, start, change rate. |
| VI | Felt by all; many frightened and run outdoors; persons walk unsteadily; windows, dishes, glassware break; knick-knacks, books, etc, fall off shelves; pictures off walls; furniture moves or overturns; weak plaster and masonry D crack; small bells ring (church, school); trees, bushes shake visibly, or heard to rustle. |
| VII | Difficult to stand; noticed by drivers; hanging objects quiver; furniture breaks; damage to masonry D, including cracks; weak chimneys broken at roof line; fall of plaster, loose bricks, stones, tiles, cornices, also unbraced parapets and architectural ornaments; some cracks in masonry C; waves on ponds, water turbid with mud; small slides and caving in along sand or gravel banks; large bells ring; concrete irrigation ditches damaged. |
| VIII | Steering of cars affected; damage to masonry C and partial collapse; some damage to masonry B; none to masonry A; fall of stucco and some masonry walls; twisting, fall of chimneys, factory stacks, monuments, towers, elevated tanks; frame houses move on foundations if not bolted down; loose panel walls thrown out; decayed piling broken off; branches broken from trees; changes in flow or temperature of springs and wells; cracks in wet ground and on steep slopes. |
| IX | General panic; masonry D destroyed; masonry C heavily damaged, sometimes with complete collapse; masonry B seriously damaged; general damage to foundations; frame structures, if not bolted, shift off foundations; frames racked; serious damage to reservoirs; underground pipes break; conspicuous cracks in ground; in alluviated areas sand and mud ejected, earthquake fountains, sand craters. |
| X | Most masonry and frame structures destroyed with their foundations; some well-built wooden structures and bridges destroyed; serious damage to dams, dykes, embankments; large landslides; water thrown on banks of canals, rivers, lakes, etc; sand and mud shifted horizontally on beaches and flat land; rails bent slightly. |
| XI | Rails bent greatly; underground pipelines completely out of service. |
| XII | Damage nearly total; large rock masses displaced; lines of sight and level distorted; objects thrown into the air. |

Notes:

| | |
|---|---|
| Masonry A | Good workmanship, mortar and design; reinforced, especially laterally, and bound together by using steel, concrete etc; designed to resist lateral forces. |
| Masonry B | Good workmanship and mortar; reinforced, but not designed in detail to resist lateral forces. |
| Masonry C | Ordinary workmanship and mortar; no extreme weakness like failing to tie in at corners, but neither reinforced nor designed against horizontal forces. |
| Masonry D | Weak materials, such as adobe; poor mortar; low standards of workmanship; weak horizontally. |

## Properties of common minerals

| Name | Type | Hard-ness | Specific gravity | Crystal | Optical | Fracture |
|---|---|---|---|---|---|---|
| Talc | Silicate | 1 | 2.6–2.8 | Monoclinic | Pale green or grey, pearly lustre | Uneven |
| Graphite | Element | 1–2 | 2.1–2.3 | Trigonal/ hexagonal | Grey metallic lustre | Perfect basal cleavage |
| Gypsum | Sulphate | 2 | 2.32 | Monoclinic | White to transparent | Splintery |
| Calcite | Carbonate | 3 | 2.71 | Trigonal/ hexagonal | Double refraction | Perfect rhombic cleavage |
| Barytes | Sulphate | 3–3.5 | 4.5 | Orthorhombic | Pale, translucent | Perfect cleavage |
| Aragonite | Carbonate | 3.5–4 | 2.95 | Orthorhombic | Translucent white streak | Subconchoidal |
| Dolomite | Carbonate | 3.5–4 | 2.85 | Trigonal/ hexagonal | Pale, translucent | Rhombohedral cleavage |
| Fluorite | Halide | 4 | 3.18 | Cubic | Many colours, fluorescent | Perfect octahedral cleavage |
| Apatite | Phosphate | 5 | 3.1–3.2 | Trigonal/ hexagonal | Usually green | Uneven |
| Sodalite | Silicate | 5.5–6 | 2.2–2.4 | Cubic | Blue | Uneven |
| Pyrite | Sulphide | 6–6.5 | 5.0 | Cubic | 'Fool's Gold' | Uneven |
| Quartz | Oxide | 7 | 2.65 | Trigonal/ hexagonal | Translucent, also microcrystalline | Uneven |
| Garnet | Silicate | 7 | 3.5–4.3 | Cubic | Various forms, often plum red | Uneven |
| Tourmaline | Silicate | 7–7.5 | 3.0–3.2 | Trigonal/ hexagonal | Often pink or green | Uneven |
| Zircon | Silicate | 7.5 | 4.3 | Tetragonal | Often brown | Uneven |
| Beryl | Silicate | 7–8 | 2.6–2.9 | Trigonal/ hexagonal | Many colours, emerald green | Uneven |
| Spinel | Oxide | 7.5–8 | 3.5–4.1 | Cubic | Many colours, vitreous lustre | Uneven |
| Corundum | Oxide | 9 | 4.0–4.1 | Trigonal/ hexagonal | Various forms including ruby and sapphire | Uneven |
| Diamond | Element | 10 | 3.52 | Cubic | Transparent, sparkles if cut | Octahedral cleavage |

## Mohs' hardness scale

The relative hardness of solids can be expressed using a scale of numbers from 1 to 10, each relating to a mineral (1 representing talc, 10 representing diamond). The method was devised by Friedrich Mohs (1773–1839), a German mineralogist. Sets of hardness pencils are used to test specimens to see what will scratch them; other useful instruments include: fingernail (2.5), copper coin (3.5), steel knife (5.5), glass (6.0).

| | | | | | | | | | |
|---|---|---|---|---|---|---|---|---|---|
| Talc | 1 | Calcite | 3 | Apatite | 5 | Quartz | 7 | Corundum | 9 |
| Gypsum | 2 | Fluorite | 4 | Orthoclase | 6 | Topaz | 8 | Diamond | 10 |

## Classification of sedimentary rocks

Sedimentary rocks result from the deposition of materials transported by water, wind or ice. Clastic rocks are the eroded remnants of earlier rocks; chemical sediments are formed from precipitation out of solution; organic sediments are formed from living material.

| **Clastic** | |
|---|---|
| Conglomerate | Large, rounded, cemented |
| Breccia | Coarse, angular, cemented |
| Gritstone | Coarse |
| Sandstone | Medium |
| Greensand | With glauconite |
| Greywacke | Deep ocean sediments |
| Siltstone | Fine, with more quartz than shale |
| Loess | Fine, angular particles |
| Marl | Fine silt or clay with limestone cement |
| Shale | Very fine laminated clay and detritus |
| Mudstone | Clay and very fine grains cemented with iron or calcite |
| Clay | Very fine; absorbs water |
| **Chemical** | |
| Limestone | Calcium carbonate |
| Chalk | Soft white limestone, mostly microfossils |
| Tufa | Calcium carbonate; precipitated from fresh water |
| Dolomite | Calcium and magnesium carbonate |
| Ironstone | Limestone or chert enriched in iron, often Pre-Cambrian |
| Chert and flint | Hard silicatious nodules or sheets in chalk or limestone |
| **Organic** | |
| Peat | Plant material |
| Lignite | Soft, carbonaceous |
| Coal | Hard, brittle, carbonaceous |
| Jet | Hard, black, coal-like |

## Principal metamorphic rocks

Metamorphic rocks are produced when pressure and heat cause changes in existing rocks.

| Name | Texture | Origin |
|---|---|---|
| Slate | Aligned minerals produce perfect cleavage; not necessarily aligned with bedding | Sedimentary shale and clay |
| Phyllite | As slate, but coarser, with small-scale folding | Medium grain sediments |
| Schist | Flaky minerals such as mica give glittery, foliated texture | Sediments buried deep in mountain belts, eg siltstones |
| Gneiss | Medium/coarse grain; quartz, feldspar and mica with darker layers or lines | High pressure and temperature, from sediment or granite; abundant deep under continents |
| Migmatite | Mixture of dark schist and light granitic rock; highly folded | Extensive deep metamorphism of sediments |
| Eclogite | Coarse grain; mostly green pyroxene and red garnet | Very high temperature and pressure close to mantle |
| Amphibolite | Coarse grain; often foliated; mostly hornblende | Highly metamorphosed igneous dolorite |
| Marble | Crystalline, soft and sugary; made of calcium carbonate | Limestone heated by igneous intrusion |
| Hornfels | Fine grain; dark coloured with quartz, mica and pyroxene | Sediments closest to hot igneous intrusion |
| Quartzite | Medium grain; of even texture with fused quartz crystals; very hard | Sandy sediment heated by intrusion or regional metamorphism |
| Serpentenite | Coarse grain; green serpentine minerals | Intense metamorphism of olivine-rich rock |

## Principal igneous rocks

Igneous rocks result from volcanic activity in the Earth's crust and upper mantle.

| Rock | Texture | Type | Composition | Origin | Features | Varieties |
|---|---|---|---|---|---|---|
| Granite | Coarse | Acid | >20% quartz, K-feldspars, mica | Intrusive batholiths | Occasional phenocrysts | Pink, white and microgranite |
| Pegmatite | Coarse | Acid | >20% quartz, mica and feldspar | Deep batholiths and dykes | Very large crystals | Occasional rare minerals |
| Diorite | Coarse | Intermediate | Plagioclase feldspar and hornblende | Dykes associated with granite | Biotite and pyroxene | Granodiorite with quartz |
| Syenite | Coarse | Intermediate | Little or no quartz, otherwise like granite | Dykes and sills near granite | Often pink | Nepheline syenite, quartz syenite |
| Gabbro | Coarse | Basic | Plagioclase, pyroxene and olivine | Large layered intrusions | Layers of magnetite | Olivine gabbro |
| Larvikite | Coarse | Intermediate | Feldspar crystals with pyroxene, mica and amphibolite banks | Small sills | Popular for cladding banks | None |
| Anorthosite | Coarse | Basic | >90% plagioclase feldspar | Layered intrusions, on Moon | Aligned mineral grains | Can include olivine and pyroxene |
| Dolerite | Medium | Basic | <10% quartz with plagioclase and pyroxene | Dykes and sills near basalt | Dark colour | None |
| Dunite | Medium | Ultrabasic | Almost entirely olivine | Deep sourced intrusions | Can contain chromite | None |
| Kimberlite | Coarse | Ultrabasic | Dense ferro-magnesian minerals | Pipes of deep ancient volcanoes | Sometimes contains diamonds | None |
| Peridotite | Coarse | Ultrabasic | No quartz or feldspar, mostly olivine and garnet | Caught up in intrusions | Possibly derived from mantle | With pyroxene and hornblende |
| Rhyolite | Fine | Acid | As granite | Explosive volcanic eruptions | Phenocrysts and gas bubbles | Banded form |
| Obsidian | Glassy | Acid | Silica-rich glass | Rapid cooling of acid lava | Black, glassy | Snowflake obsidian |
| Lamprophyre | Medium | Acid to basic | Amphibole pyroxene and biotite | Dykes and sills around granite | Phenocrysts of biotite and hornblende | None |
| Andesite | Fine | Intermediate | Mainly plagioclase | Volcanoes above subduction zones | Dark with white phenocrysts | With vesicles of zeolite |
| Trachyte | Fine | Intermediate | <10% quartz, rich in alkali feldspar | Lava flows, dykes and sills | Not many | Sometimes porphyritic |
| Basalt | Fine | Basic | Plagioclase and pyroxene | Volcanic eruptions | Dark — the commonest lava | Bubbles and vesicles |
| Tuff | Fine | Acid to basic | Consolidated volcanic fragments | Thrown out by volcanic vents | Variable | Tuff-breccia, lapilli-tuff |
| Pumice | Fine | Acid to basic | Glass and minute silicate crystals | Rapidly quenched frothy lava | Can sometimes float | Bubbles and vesicles |

## Geological time scale

| Eon | Era | Period | Epoch | Million years before present | Geological events | Sea life | Land life |
|---|---|---|---|---|---|---|---|
| Phanerozoic | Cenozoic | Quaternary | Holocene | 0.01 | Glaciers recede. Sea level rises. Climate becomes more equable. | As now. | Forests flourish again. Humans acquire agriculture and technology. |
| | | | Pleistocene | 2.0 | Widespread glaciers melt periodically causing seas to rise and fall. | As now. | Many plant forms perish. Small mammals abundant. Primitive humans established. |
| | | Tertiary | Pliocene | 5.1 | Continents and oceans adopting their present form. Present climatic distribution established. Ice caps develop. | Giant sharks extinct. Many fish varieties. | Some plants and mammals die out. Primates flourish. |
| | | | Miocene | 24.6 | Seas recede further. European and Asian land masses join. Heavy rain causes massive erosion. Red Sea opens. | Bony fish common. Giant sharks. | Grasses widespread. Grazing mammals become common. |
| | | | Oligocene | 38.0 | Seas recede. Extensive movements of earth's crust produce new mountains (eg Alpine-Himalayan chain). | Crabs, mussels, and snails evolve. | Forests diminish. Grasses appear. Pachyderms, canines and felines develop. |
| | | | Eocene | 54.9 | Mountain formation continues. Glaciers common in high mountain ranges. Greenland separates. Australia separates. | Whales adapt to sea. | Large tropical jungles. Primitive forms of modern mammals established. |
| | | | Palaeocene | 65 | Widespread subsidence of land. Seas advance again. Considerable volcanic activity. Europe emerges. | Many reptiles become extinct. | Flowering plants widespread. First primates. Giant reptiles extinct. |
| | Mesozoic | Cretaceous | Late<br>Early | 97.5<br>144 | Swamps widespread. Massive alluvial deposition. Continuing limestone formation. S America separates from Africa. India, Africa and Antarctica separate. | Turtles, rays, and now-common fish appear. | Flowering plants established. Dinosaurs become extinct. |
| | | Jurassic | Malm<br>Dogger<br>Lias | 163<br>188<br>213 | Seas advance. Much river formation. High mountains eroded. Limestone formation. N America separates from Africa. Central Atlantic begins to open. | Reptiles dominant. | Early flowers. Dinosaurs dominant. Mammals still primitive. First birds. |
| | | Triassic | Late<br>Middle<br>Early | 231<br>243<br>248 | Desert conditions widespread. Hot climate gradually becomes warm and wet. Break up of Gondwanaland into continents. | Ichthyosaurs, flying fish and crustaceans appear. | Ferns and conifers thrive. First mammals, dinosaurs, and flies. |

| | | | | | | | |
|---|---|---|---|---|---|---|---|
| Phanerozoic | Palaeozoic | Permian | Late<br>Early | 258<br>286 | Some sea areas cut off to form lakes. Earth movements form mountains. Glaciation in southern hemisphere. | Some shelled fish become extinct. | Deciduous plants. Reptiles dominant. Many insect varieties. |
| | | Carboniferous | Pennsylvanian<br>Mississippian | 320<br>360 | Sea-beds rise to form new land areas. Enormous swamps. Partly-rotted vegetation forms coal. | Amphibians and sharks abundant. | Extensive evergreen forests. Reptiles breed on land. Some insects develop wings. |
| | | Devonian | Late<br>Middle<br>Early | 374<br>387<br>408 | Collision of continents causing mountain formation (Appalachians, Caledonides and Urals). Sea deeper but narrower. Climatic zones forming. Iapetus ocean closed. | Fish abundant. Primitive sharks. First amphibians. | Leafy plants. Some invertebrates adapt to land. First insects. |
| | | Silurian | Pridoli<br>Ludlow<br>Wenlock<br>Llandovery | 414<br>421<br>428<br>438 | New mountain ranges form. Sea level varies periodically. Extensive shallow sea over the Sahara. | Large vertebrates. | First leafless land plants. |
| | | Ordovician | Ashgill<br>Caradoc<br>Llandeilo<br>Llanvirn<br>Arenig<br>Tremadoc | 448<br>458<br>468<br>478<br>488<br>505 | Shore lines still quite variable. Increasing sedimentation. Europe and N America moving together. | First vertebrates. Coral reefs develop. | None |
| | | | Merioneth<br>St David's<br>Caerfai | 525<br>540<br>590 | Much volcanic activity, and long periods of marine sedimentation. | Shelled invertebrates. Trilobites. | None |
| Proterozoic | Precambrian | Vendian | | 650 | Shallow seas advance and retreat over land areas. Atmosphere uniformly warm. | Seaweed. Algae and invertebrates. | None |
| | | Riphean | Late<br>Middle<br>Early | 900<br>1300<br>1600 | Intense deformation and metamorphism. | Earliest marine life and fossils. | None |
| | | Early Proterozoic | | 2500 | Shallow shelf seas. Formation of carbonate sediments and 'red beds'. | First appearance of stromatolites. | None |
| Arch-aean | | Archaean (Azoic) | | 4600 | Banded iron formations. Formation of the earth's crust and oceans. | None | None |

# CLIMATE AND ENVIRONMENT

## Climatic zones

The earth may be divided into zones, approximating to zones of latitude, such that each zone possesses a distinct type of climate.

The principal zones are:

❑ **Tropical** One zone of wet climate near the equator (either constantly wet or monsoonal with wet and dry seasons, tropical savannah with dry winters); the average temperature is not below 18°C;
Amazon forest
Malaysia
S Vietnam
India
Africa
Congo Basin
Indonesia
S E Asia
Australia

❑ **Subtropical** Two zones of steppe and desert climate (transition through semi-arid to arid);
Sahara
Central Asia
Mexico
Australia
Kalahari

❑ **Mediterranean** Zones of rainy climate with mild winters; coolest month above 0°C but below 18°C;
California
S Africa
S Europe
parts of Chile
SW Australia

❑ **Temperate** Rainy climate (includes areas of temperate woodland, mountain forests, and plains with no dry season; influenced by seas — rainfall all year, small temperate changes); average temperature between 3°C and 18°C;
Most of Europe
Eastern Asia
NW/NE USA
New Zealand
Southern Chile

❑ **Boreal** Climate with a great range of temperature in the northern hemisphere (in some areas the most humid month is in summer and there is ten times more precipitation than the driest part of winter. In other areas the most humid month is in winter and there is ten times more precipitation than in the driest part of summer); in the coldest period temperatures do not exceed 3°C and in the hottest do not go below 10°C;
Prairies of USA
parts of S Africa
parts of Russia
parts of Australia

❑ **Polar caps** Snowy climate (tundra and ice-cap) with little or no precipitation. There is permafrost in the tundra and vegetation includes lichen and moss all year, and grass in the summer; the highest annual temperature in the polar region is below 0°C and in the tundra the average temperature is 10°C;
Arctic regions of Russia and N America
Antarctica

## Great ice ages

**Precambrian era** Early Proterozoic
**Precambrian era** Upper Proterozoic
**Palaeozoic era** Upper Carboniferous
**Cenozoic era** Pleistocene[1]
(Last 4 periods of glaciation)
Günz (Nebraskan or Jerseyan) 520 000–490 000 years ago
Mindel (Kansan) 430 000–370 000 years ago
Riss (Illinoian) 130 000–100 000 years ago
Würm (Wisconsin and Iowan) 40 000–18 000 years ago

[1]The Pleistocene epoch is synonymous with 'The Ice Age'.

## Wind force and sea disturbance

| Beaufort number | m/sec | Wind speed kph | Wind speed mph | Wind name | Observable wind characteristics | Sea disturbance number | Average wave ht. m | Average wave ht. ft | Observable sea characteristics |
|---|---|---|---|---|---|---|---|---|---|
| 0 | 1 | <1 | <1 | Calm | Smoke rises vertically | 0 | 0 | 0 | Sea like a mirror |
| 1 | 1 | 1–5 | 1–3 | Light air | Wind direction shown by smoke drift, but not by wind vanes | 0 | 0 | 0 | Ripples like scales, without foam crests |
| 2 | 2 | 6–11 | 4–7 | Light breeze | Wind felt on face; leaves rustle; vanes moved by wind | 1 | 0.3 | 0–1 | More definite wavelets, but crests do not break |
| 3 | 4 | 12–19 | 8–12 | Gentle breeze | Leaves and small twigs in constant motion; wind extends light flag | 2 | 0.3–0.6 | 1–2 | Large wavelets; crests begin to break; scattered white horses |
| 4 | 7 | 20–28 | 13–18 | Moderate | Raises dust, loose paper; small branches moved | 3 | 0.6–1.2 | 2–4 | Small waves become longer; fairly frequent white horses |
| 5 | 10 | 29–38 | 19–24 | Fresh | Small trees in leaf begin to sway; crested wavelets on inland waters | 4 | 1.2–2.4 | 4–8 | Moderate waves with a more definite long form; many white horses; some spray possible |
| 6 | 12 | 39–49 | 25–31 | Strong | Large branches in motion; difficult to use umbrellas; whistling heard in telegraph wires | 5 | 2.4–4 | 8–13 | Large waves form; more extensive white foam crests; some spray probable |
| 7 | 15 | 50–61 | 32–38 | Near gale | Whole treees in motion; inconvenience walking against wind | 6 | 4–6 | 13–20 | Sea heaps up; streaks of white foam blown along |
| 8 | 18 | 62–74 | 39–46 | Gale | Breaks twigs off trees; impedes progress | 6 | 4–6 | 13–20 | Moderately high waves of greater length; well-marked streaks of foam |
| 9 | 20 | 75–88 | 47–54 | Strong gale | Slight structural damage occurs | 6 | 4–6 | 13–20 | High waves; dense streaks of foam; sea begins to roll; spray affects visibility |
| 10 | 26 | 89–102 | 55–63 | Storm | Trees uprooted; considerable damage occurs | 7 | 6–9 | 20–30 | Very high waves with long overhanging crests; dense streaks of foam blown along; generally white appearance of surface; heavy rolling |
| 11 | 30 | 103–17 | 64–72 | Violent storm | Widespread damage | 8 | 9–14 | 30–45 | Exceptionally high waves; long white patches of foam; poor visibility; ships lost to view behind waves |
| 12–17 | ⩾33 | ⩾118 | ⩾73 | Hurricane | | 9 | 14 | >45 | Air filled with foam and spray; sea completely white; very poor visibility |

## Windstorms

A **cyclone** is a circulation of winds in the atmosphere which rotates anticlockwise round a depression in the northern hemisphere and clockwise in the southern.
A **hurricane** is a windstorm originating over tropical oceans in the N hemisphere, with winds in excess of 74mph. Hurricanes are named by the National Hurricane Center, USA, in alphabetical sequence as they occur each year. Since 1978 names given have been alternately male/female. In the N Pacific they are known as **typhoons**. Abbrev H. and T.
A **tornado** is a column of air rotating rapidly around a very low pressure centre.

| Name | Location | Year | Deaths | Damage in US $ million[1] |
|---|---|---|---|---|
| C. Gloria | Madagascar, Mozambique | 2000 | * | * |
| C. Eline | Madagascar, Mozambique | 2000 | * | * |
| Cyclone | Orissa | 1999 | 10 000+ | 2 300 |
| H. Floyd | Florida, N Carolina, The Bahamas | 1999 | 57 | 3 000–6 000 |
| H. Mitch | C America (Honduras, Nicaragua), Florida | 1998 | 10 000+ | 5 500 |
| H. Georges | NE Caribbean, Mississippi | 1998 | 602 | 5 900 |
| T. Linda | Vietnam, Thailand | 1997 | 453 | 400 |
| H. Fran | N Carolina | 1996 | 34 | 3 200 |
| H. Opal | NW Florida | 1995 | 19 | 3 000 |
| H. Marilyn | Virgin Is, Puerto Rico | 1995 | 9 | 1 500 |
| H. Gordon | Florida, Alabama | 1994 | 4 | 400 |
| H. Andrew | S Florida, The Bahamas | 1992 | 88 | 26 500 |
| H. Iniki | Kauai, Hawaii | 1992 | 3 | 1 800 |
| H. Bob | NE USA | 1991 | 17 | 1 500 |
| Cyclone | Bangladesh | 1991 | 200 000 | — |
| H. Hugo | S Carolina | 1989 | 49 | 7 000 |
| H. Gilbert | Caribbean, Mexico | 1988 | 318 | 5 000 |
| H. Joan | Caribbean | 1988 | 216 | — |
| Winter Storm | S England, NW France | 1987 | 17 | 1 700 |
| T. Vera | Korea, Democratic People's Republic of (North Korea) | 1986 | — | 40 |
| H. Juan | Louisiana | 1985 | 12 | 1 500 |
| H. Elena | Mississippi, Alabama, NW Florida | 1985 | 2 | 1 250 |
| H. Gloria | E USA | 1985 | 15 | 900 |
| H. Kate | Florida (Keys), NW Florida | 1985 | 16 | 300 |
| Cyclone | Bangladesh | 1985 | 11 000 | — |
| Ts. Ike and June | Philippines (Mindanao) | 1984 | 1 000 | 220 |
| H. Alicia | N Texas | 1983 | 18 | 2 000 |
| H. Allen | S Texas | 1980 | 235 | 300 |
| H. David | Florida, E USA | 1979 | 2 400 | 320 |
| H. Frederic | Alabama, Mississippi | 1979 | 31 | 2 300 |
| H. Eloise | NW Florida | 1975 | 100 | 490 |
| H. Carmen | Louisiana | 1974 | 1 | 150 |
| Tornadoes | C USA | 1974 | 322 | 1 000 |
| H. Fifi | C America (Honduras) | 1974 | 10 000 | 1 000 |
| C. Tracy | Australia (Darwin) | 1974 | 65 | 1 000 |
| H. Agnes | E Coast, USA | 1972 | 122 | 2 100 |
| Cyclone | Bangladesh | 1970 | 300 000 | 86 |
| H. Camille | Mississippi, Louisiana | 1969 | 256 | 1 420.7 |
| H. Beulah | S Texas | 1967 | 15 | 200 |
| H. Betsy | SE Florida, SE Louisiana, Mississippi | 1965 | 75 | 1 420.5 |
| T. Louise | Philippines (Mindanao) | 1964 | 58 | 600 |
| H. Hilda | C Louisiana | 1964 | 38 | 125 |
| H. Dora | NE Florida | 1964 | 5 | 250 |
| H. Cleo | SE Florida | 1964 | 154 | 128.5 |
| H. Flora | Haiti, Cuba, Dominican Republic | 1963 | 7 000 | 625 |
| H. Carla | Texas | 1961 | 46 | 408 |
| H. Donna | Florida, E USA | 1960 | 50 | 387 |
| T. Vera | Ise Bay, Japan | 1959 | 5 098 | 600 |

| Name | Location | Year | Deaths | Damage in US $ million[1] |
|---|---|---|---|---|
| H. Audrey | Louisiana, N Texas | 1957 | 390 | 150 |
| H. Diane | NE USA | 1955 | 184 | 831.7 |
| H. Hazel | S Carolina, N Carolina | 1954 | 95 | 281 |
| H. Carol | NE USA | 1954 | 60 | 461 |
| Typhoon | Japan (Toyama, N Honshu) | 1954 | 3 000 | — |
| Hurricane | SE Florida, Louisiana, Mississippi | 1947 | 51 | 110 |
| Typhoon | Japan (Makurazaki) | 1945 | 3 756 | 400 |
| Hurricane | NE USA | 1944 | 390 | 100 |
| Cyclone | Bangladesh | 1942 | 61 000 | — |
| Hurricane | Georgia, S Carolina, N Carolina | 1940 | 50 | 5 |
| Hurricane | New England | 1938 | 600 | 306 |
| Hurricane | Florida (Keys) | 1935 | 408 | 12 |
| Hurricane | S Texas | 1933 | 40 | — |
| Hurricane | Texas (Freeport) | 1932 | 40 | — |
| Hurricane | Cuba | 1932 | 2 500 | — |
| Hurricane | Belize | 1931 | 2 000 | — |
| Hurricane | San Zenon, Santo Domingo, Dominican Republic | 1930 | 2 000 | 60 |
| Hurricane | Florida (Lake Okeechobee) | 1928 | 1 836 | 25 |
| Hurricane | Florida (Miami) | 1926 | 243 | 112 |
| Typhoon | China (Shantou) | 1922 | 28 000 | — |
| Hurricane | Florida (Keys), S Texas | 1919 | 600–900 | 22 |
| Typhoon | Japan (Honshu) | 1917 | 4 000 | 50 |
| Hurricane | N Texas (Galveston), Louisiana (New Orleans) | 1915 | 550 | 63 |
| Tornado | Ohio, Indiana | 1913 | 700 | 200 |
| Typhoon | China (Wenchang) | 1912 | 50 000 | — |
| Hurricane | Louisiana (Grand Isle) | 1909 | 350 | — |
| Typhoon | Hong Kong | 1906 | 10 000 | 20 |
| Hurricane | SE Florida | 1906 | 164 | — |
| Hurricane | Mississippi, Alabama, Florida (Pensacola) | 1906 | 134 | — |
| Hurricane | N Texas (Galveston) | 1900 | 6 000 | 30 |
| Hurricane | San Ciriaco | 1899 | 3 369 | 20 |
| Typhoon | Philippines (Leyte) | 1897 | 10 000 | 10 |
| Hurricane | S Carolina, Georgia | 1893 | 1 000 | — |
| Typhoon | W Coast, Japan | 1884 | 2 000 | — |
| Cyclone | India (Bombay) | 1882 | 100 000 | — |
| Typhoon | China | 1881 | 300 000 | — |
| Cyclone | Bangladesh (Bakarganj) | 1876 | 215 000 | — |
| Cyclone | India (Calcutta) | 1864 | 50 000 | — |
| Cyclone | Bangladesh (Bakarganj) | 1822 | 50 000 | — |
| Hurricane | Cuba | 1791 | 3 000 | — |
| Hurricane | West Indies, Barbados, Martinique, St Vincent, Guadeloupe | 1780 | 24 000 | — |
| Cyclone | India (Calcutta) | 1737 | 300 000 | — |
| Winter Storm | UK (sinking of the Spanish Armada) | 1588 | 20 000 | — |

[1]No adjustment has been made for inflation.

## Meteorological extremes

The hottest place is Dallol, Ethiopia, at 34.4°C/93.9°F (annual mean temperature).

The highest recorded temperature in the shade is 58°C/136.4°F, at al'Aziziyah, Libya, on 13 September 1922.

The coldest place is Pole of Cold, Antarctica, at -57.8°C/-72°F (annual mean temperature).

The driest place is the Atacama desert near Calama, Chile, where no rainfall was recorded in over 400 years to 1972.

The most rain to fall in 24 hours was 1 870mm/74in, which fell on Cilaos, Réunion, in the Indian Ocean, on 15–16 March 1952.

The wettest place is Tutunendo, Colombia, where the rainfall is 11 770mm/464in (annual average).

The greatest amount of snow to fall in 12 months was 31 102mm/1 225in, at Paradise, Mt Rainier, in Washington, USA, in 1971–2.

The most rainy days in a year are the c.350 experienced on Mt Waialeale, Kauai, Hawaii, USA.

The least sunshine occurs at the North and South Poles, where the Sun does not rise for 182 days of winter.

The greatest amount of sunshine occurs in the eastern Sahara: more than 4 300 hours a year (97% of daylight hours).

The highest recorded surface wind speed is 371kph/231mph, at Mt Washington, New Hampshire, USA, on 12 April 1934.

## Acid rain

A term generally used for polluted rainfall associated with the burning of fossil fuels. It is implicated in damage to forests and the stonework of buildings, and increases the acid content of soils and lakes, harming crops and fish.

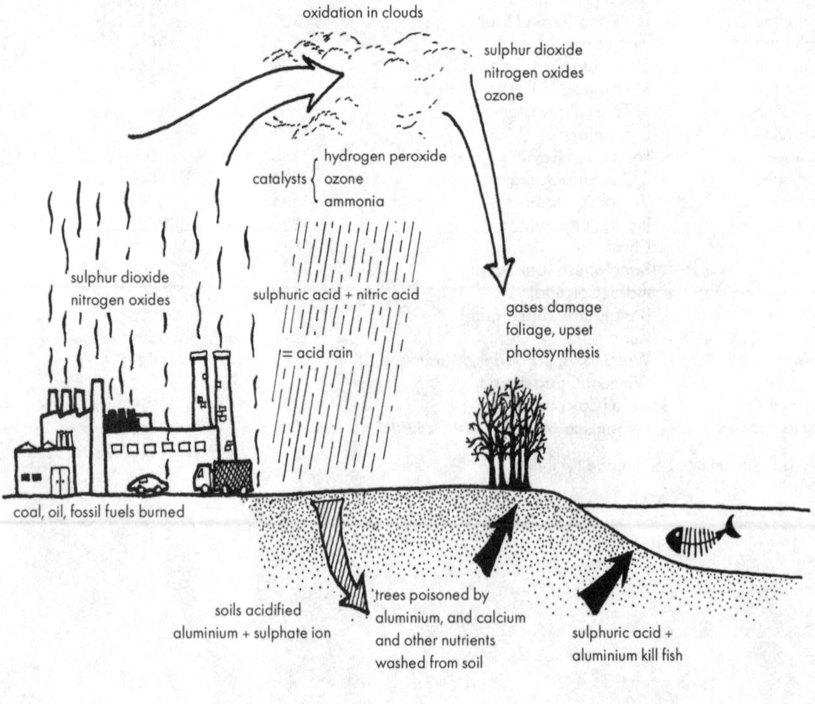

oxidation in clouds
sulphur dioxide
nitrogen oxides
ozone
catalysts { hydrogen peroxide, ozone, ammonia
sulphur dioxide
nitrogen oxides
sulphuric acid + nitric acid
= acid rain
gases damage foliage, upset photosynthesis
coal, oil, fossil fuels burned
soils acidified
aluminium + sulphate ion
trees poisoned by aluminium, and calcium and other nutrients washed from soil
sulphuric acid + aluminium kill fish

## Environmental disasters on land

| Location | Event | Date | Consequence |
|---|---|---|---|
| Basle, Switzerland | Fire in Sandoz factory warehouse resulted in major chemical spill. | Nov 1980 | River Rhine rendered lifeless for 200km/124mi. |
| Beirut | Toxic waste dumped by Italian company. | Jul–Sep 1988 | Italy forced to take back its poison drums. |
| Bhopal, India | Toxic gas leaked from a Union Carbide pesticide plant and enveloped a nearby slum area housing 200 000 people. | Dec 1984 | Possibly 10 000 people died (officially 2 352). Survivors suffer ravaged lungs and/or blindness. $100km^2/39mi^2$ affected by the gas. |
| Camelford, Cornwall | 20 tonnes of aluminium sulphate were flushed down local rivers after an accident at a water treatment works. | Jul 1988 | 60 000 fish killed. Local people suffered from vomiting, diarrhoea, blisters, mouth ulcers, rashes and memory loss. |
| Chernobyl, Ukraine | Nuclear reactor exploded, releasing a radioactive cloud over Europe. | Apr 1986 | Fewer than 50 people were killed, but the radioactive cloud spread as far as Britain, contaminating farmland. 100 000 Soviet citizens may die of radiation-induced cancer, a further 30 000 fatalities are possible worldwide. 250 000 people evacuated from the area in five years. |
| Cubatão, Brazil | Uncontrolled pollution from nuclear industry. | 1980s | Local population suffer serious ailments and genetic deformities. 30% of deaths are caused by pollution-related diseases and damage to respiratory systems. |
| Cumbria, England | Fire in Windscale plutonium production reactor burned for 24 hours and ignited 3 tonnes of uranium. | Oct 1957 | Radioactive material spread throughout the countryside. In 1983 the British government said 39 people probably died of cancer as a result. Unofficial sources say 1 000. |
| Decatur, Alabama, USA | Fire at Browns Ferry reactor caused by a technician checking for air leaks with a lighted candle. | Mar 1975 | $100 million damage. Electrical controls burned out, lowering cooling water to dangerous levels. |
| Detroit, Michigan, USA | Malfunction in sodium cooling system at the Enrico Fermi demonstration breeder reactor. | Oct 1966 | Partial core meltdown. Radiation was contained. |
| Erwin, Tennessee, USA | Highly enriched uranium released from top-secret nuclear fuel plant. | Aug 1979 | 1 000 people contaminated (with up to 5 times as much radiation as would normally be received in a year). |
| Flixborough, England | Container of cyclohexane exploded. | June 1974 | 28 people died. |
| Goiânia, Brazil | Major radioactive contamination incident involving an abandoned radiotherapy unit containing radioactive caesium chloride salts. | Sep–Oct 1987 | People evacuated; homes demolished; 249 people affected by sickness or death. |
| Gore, Oklahoma, USA | A cylinder of nuclear material burst after being improperly heated at Kerr-McGee plant. | Jan 1986 | 1 worker died, 100 hospitalized. |
| Idaho Falls, Idaho, USA | Accident at experiment reactor. | Jan 1961 | 3 workers killed. Damage contained, despite high radiation levels at the plant. |

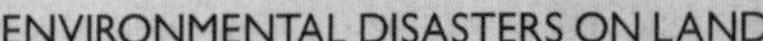



| Location | Event | Date | Consequence |
|---|---|---|---|
| Kasli, Russia | Chemical explosion in tanks containing nuclear waste. | 1957 | Radioactive material spread. Major evacuation of area. |
| Kuwait | Iraqi forces set alight 600 oil wells. | Feb 1991 | Air pollution consisted of clouds of soot and oil particles which obscured the sun and fell as 'black rain'. Threat that it would turn into sulphur dioxide and fall as acid rain. Incidence of fatal bronchitis expected to increase. Possible serious contamination of agricultural land and water supplies particularly in Iraq's Tigris and Euphrates valleys. |
| Love Canal, near Niagara Falls, New York, USA | Dumping of drums containing hazardous waste at Love Canal, which by the 1970s were leaking toxic chemicals. | 1940s to 1952 | More than 240 families evacuated, countryside contaminated. |
| Lucens Vad, Switzerland | Coolant malfunction in an experimental underground reactor. | Jan 1969 | Large amount of radiation released into cavern, which was then sealed. |
| Minimata Bay, Japan | Dumping of chemicals, including methyl mercury. | 1953 | Minimata disease, characterized by cerebral palsy, had killed more than 300 people by 1983. Thousands more suffered genetic abnormalities, brain disease and nervous disorders. |
| Monongahela River, Pennsylvania, USA | Storage tank ruptured and spilled 3 800 000 gallons of diesel oil into the Monongahela river. | Jan 1988 | Water supply to 23 000 residents of Pittsburgh cut off. Oil slick spread into W Virginia, growing to 77km/48mi, and reached Steubenville, Ohio. |
| Monticello, Minnesota, USA | Water-storage space at Northern States Power Company's reactor overflowed. | Nov 1971 | 50 000 gallons of radioactive waste water dumped in Mississippi River. St Paul water system contaminated. |
| Rochester, New York, USA | Steam-generator pipe broke at the Rochester Gas & Electric Company's plant. | Jan 1982 | Small amounts of radioactive steam escaped. |
| Seveso, N Italy | Leak of toxic TCDD gas containing the poison dioxin. | Jul 1976 | Local population still suffering; in worst contaminated area, topsoil had to be removed and buried in a giant plastic-coated pit. |
| Tennessee, USA | 100 000 gallons of radioactive coolant leaked into the containment building of the TVA's Sequoyah 1 plant. | Feb 1981 | 8 workers contaminated. |
| Three Mile Island, Harrisburg, Pennsylvania, USA | Water pump broke down releasing radioactive steam. | Mar 1979 | Pollution by radioactive gases. Some authorities claimed regional cancer, child deformity. Massive clean-up operation resulted in 150 tonnes of radioactive rubble and 250 000 gallons of radioactive water. |
| Tsuruga, Japan | Accident during repairs of a nuclear plant. | Apr 1981 | 100 workers exposed to radioactive material. |

## Oil spills at sea

| Name | Location | Date | Consequence |
|---|---|---|---|
| *Amoco Cadiz*, Cyprus-registered tanker, grounded and spilled 65 562 000 gallons | near Portshall, France | Mar 1978 | marine pollution; 160km/99mi of French coast polluted. |
| *Aragon* spilled 7 350 000 gallons | off Madeira Is | Dec 1989 – Jan 1990 | marine pollution |
| *Atlantic Empress* and *Aegean Captain*; collision between tankers caused spillage of 88 200 000 gallons | off Trinidad and Tobago | Jul 1979 | marine pollution |
| *Burmah Agate* collided and spilled 10 700 000 gallons | Galveston Bay, Texas | Nov 1979 | marine pollution |
| *Castillo de Beliver* tanker; fire caused spillage of 73 500 000 gallons | off Cape Town, South Africa | Aug 1983 | marine pollution |
| *Diamond Grace*, Panamanian-registered tanker, grounded and spilled 4 000 000 gallons | off Yokohama, Japan | Jul 1997 | marine pollution |
| *Ekofisk* oil field; blow-out caused spillage of 8 200 000 gallons | North Sea | Apr 1977 | marine pollution |
| *Exxon Valdez*, US tanker, grounded on Bligh Reef and spilled 10 080 000 gallons | Prince William Sound, Alaska | Mar 1989 | 1 770km/1 162mi of Alaskan coastline polluted. More than 3 600 sq km/1 390 sq mi of water fouled. Thousands of animals killed. |
| *Gulf*; Iraq pumped oil at a rate of 4 200 000 gallons a day into the sea | 10mi off coast near Kuwait City | Jan–Feb 1991 | Threat to desalination plants and therefore to water supply. Devastating effect on all areas of marine environment. |
| *Ixtoc* oil well; blow-out caused spillage of 176 400 000 gallons | Gulf of Mexico | Jun 1979 | marine pollution |
| *Hawaiian Patrol*; fire caused spillage of 29 106 000 gallons | N Pacific | Feb 1977 | marine pollution |
| *Keo*; hull failure caused spillage of 88 200 000 gallons | off Massachusetts, USA | Nov 1969 | marine pollution |
| *Kharg 5*, Iranian supertanker, spilled 19 000 000 gallons of light crude oil after an explosion in its hull | 700km/435mi N of the Canary Is, Atlantic Ocean | Dec 1989 | 370km/230mi oil slick almost reached Morocco. About 40% evaporated and much sank to ocean floor, endangering fish and oysters. |
| *Kirki*, Greek tanker, broke up and spilled 5 880 000 gallons of light crude oil | off Cervantes, W Australia | Jul 1991 | Pollution of conservation zones and lobster fishery. |
| *Nowruz* oil field; blow-out caused spillage of about 176 400 000 gallons | Persian Gulf | Feb 1983 | marine pollution |
| *Othello* collided and spilled 17 640 000–29 400 000 gallons | Tralhavet Bay, Sweden | Mar 1970 | marine pollution |
| *Sea Star* collided and spilled 33 810 000 gallons | Gulf of Oman | Dec 1972 | marine pollution |
| *Sewaren* storage tank rupture caused spillage of 8 400 000 gallons | New Jersey | Nov 1969 | marine pollution |
| *Torrey Canyon* grounded and spilled 34 986 000 gallons | off Land's End, England | Mar 1967 | marine pollution |
| *Urquiola* grounded and spilled 29 400 000 gallons | La Coruña, Spain | May 1976 | marine pollution |
| *World Glory*; hull failure caused spillage of 13 524 000 gallons | off South Africa | Jun 1968 | marine pollution |

## World Heritage sites

This list is up-to-date to December 1998. It comprises the 552 sites in 113 countries selected by UNESCO as being of such outstanding natural, environmental or cultural importance that they merit exceptional international efforts to make them more widely known and to save them from damage and destruction.

❑ **Albania**
Butrinti

❑ **Algeria**
Algiers (Casbah)
Al Qal'a of Beni Hammad
Djémila (Roman ruins)
M'Zab Valley
Tassili N'Ajjer
Timgad (Roman ruins)
Tipasa (archaeological site)

❑ **Argentina**
Iguazú National Park
Jesuit Missions of the Guaranis (shared with Brazil)
Los Glaciares National Park

❑ **Armenia**
Haghpat Monastery

❑ **Australia**
Central Eastern Australian Rainforest
Fraser I
Great Barrier Reef
Heard and McDonald Is
Kakadu National Park
Lord Howe I
Macquarie I
Queensland (wet tropics)
Riversleigh/Naracoorte (mammal fossil sites)
Shark Bay
Tasmanian Wilderness
Uluru-Kata Tjuta National Park
Willandra Lakes region

❑ **Austria**
Hallstatt-Dachstein Salzkammergut cultural landscape
Salzburg (historic city centre)
Schönbrunn palace and gardens

❑ **Bangladesh**
Bagerhat (historic mosque city)
Paharpur (ruins of the Buddhist Vihara)
Sundarbans (mangrove forest)

❑ **Belarus**
Belovezhskaya Pushcha/Bialowieza Forest (shared with Poland)

❑ **Belize**
Barrier Reef Reserve System

❑ **Benin**
Dahomey (royal palaces)

❑ **Bolivia**
Jesuit Missions of the Chiquitos
Potosi (mining town)
Sucre (historic city)

❑ **Brazil**
Bom Jesus do Congonhas (sanctuary)
Brasilia
Iguaçu National Park
Jesuit Missions of the Guaranis (shared with Argentina)
Olinda (historic centre)
Ouro Preto (historic town)
Salvador da Bahia (historic centre)
São Luis (historic centre)
Serra da Capivara National Park

❑ **Bulgaria**
Boyana Church
Ivanovo rock-hewn churches
Kazanlak (Thracian tomb)
Madara Rider
Nessebar (old city)
Pirin National Park
Rila Monastery
Srebarna Nature Reserve
Sveshtari (Thracian tomb)

❑ **Cambodia**
Angkor

❑ **Cameroon**
Dja Faunal Reserve

❑ **Canada**
Anthony I
Canadian Rocky Mountain Parks
Dinosaur Provincial Park
Gros Morne National Park
Head-Smashed-In Buffalo Jump complex
L'Anse aux Meadows Historic Park
Lunenburg (old city)
Nahanni National Park
Quebec (historic area)
Tatshenshini-Alsek, Kluane National Park, Wrangell St Elias National Park and Reserve, and Glacier Bay National Park (shared with USA)
Waterton Glacier International Peace Park (shared with USA)
Wood Buffalo National Park

❑ **Central African Republic**
Manovo-Gounda St Floris National Park

❑ **Chile**
Rapa Nui National Park (Easter I)

❑ **China**
Beijing (Imperial Palace of the Ming and Qing dynasties)
Chengde (mountain resort and outlying temples)
Mt Emei scenic area including Leshan giant Buddha scenic area
Great Wall
Huanglong area
Mt Huangshan
Jiuzhaigou Valley area

Lhasa (Potala Palace)
Lijiang (old town)
Lushan National Park
Mausoleum of the first Qin emperor
Mogao caves
Mt Taishan
Ping Yao (ancient city)
Qufu (temple and cemetery of Confucius and the K'ung family mansion)
Suzhou (classical gardens)
Wudang mountains (ancient building complex)
Wulingyuan area
Zhoukoudian (Peking Man site)

❑ **Colombia**
Cartagena (port, fortress and monuments)
Los Katios National Park
San Agustín Archaeological Park
Santa Cruz de Mompox (historic centre)
Tierradentro National Archaeological Park

❑ **Congo, Democratic Republic of (Zaïre)**
Garamba National Park
Kahuzi-Biega National Park
Okapi Faunal Reserve
Salonga National Park
Virunga National Park

❑ **Costa Rica**
Cocos I National Park
La Amistad National Park (shared with Panama)

❑ **Côte d'Ivoire**
Comoé National Park
Mt Nimba Nature Reserve (shared with Guinea)
Taï National Park

❑ **Croatia**
Dubrovnik (old city)
Plitvice Lakes National Park
Porec (episcopal complex of the Euphrasian basilica in the historic centre)
Split (historic centre with Diocletian's Palace)
Trogir (historic city)

❑ **Cuba**
Old Havana and its fortifications
Santiago de Cuba, San Pedro de la Roca Castle
Trinidad and the Valley de los Ingenios

❑ **Cyprus**
Paphos (archaeological site)
Troödos region (painted churches)

❑ **Czech Republic**
Cesky Krumlov (historic centre)
Kutna Hora (historic centre) with Church of St Barbara and the Cathedral of Our Lady at Sedlec
Lednice-Valtice cultural landscape
Prague (historic centre)
Telc (historic centre)
Zelena Hora (pilgrimage church of St John of Nepomuk)

❑ **Denmark**
Jelling (mounds, runic stones and church)
Roskilde Cathedral

❑ **Dominica**
Morne Trois Pitons National Park

❑ **Dominican Republic**
Santo Domingo

❑ **Ecuador**
Galapagos Is National Park
Quito (old city)
Sangay National Park

❑ **Egypt**
Abu Mena (Christian ruins)
Abu Simbel to Philae (Nubian monuments)
Cairo (Islamic sector)
Memphis and its Necropolis with the Pyramid fields
Thebes and its Necropolis

❑ **El Salvador**
Joya de Cerén (archaeological site)

❑ **Estonia**
Tallinn (historic centre, old town)

❑ **Ethiopia**
Aksum (archaeological site)
Awash Lower Valley
Fasil Ghebbi and Gondar monuments
Lalibela rock-hewn churches
Omo Lower Valley
Simien National Park
Tiya (carved steles)

❑ **Finland**
Old Rauma
Petäjävesi (old church)
Suomenlinna (fortress)
Verla groundwood and board mill

❑ **France**
Amiens Cathedral
Arc-et-Senans (Royal saltworks)
Arles (Roman and Romanesque monuments)
Avignon (historic centre)
Bourges Cathedral
Canal du Midi
Carcassonne (historic fortified city)
Chambord (château and estate)
Chartres Cathedral
Corsica (Cape Girolata, Cape Porto, Scandola Natural Reserve and the Piana Calanches)
Fontainebleau (palace and park)
Fontenay (Cistercian abbey)
Mont St Michel and its bay
Nancy (Place Stanislas, Place de la Carrière and Place d'Alliance)
Orange (Roman theatre and triumphal arch)
Paris (banks of the Seine)
Pont du Gard (Roman aqueduct)
Pyrenees, Mt Perdu landscape (shared with Spain)
Rheims (Cathedral of Notre-Dame, St Remy Abbey and Palace of Tau)
St Savin-sur-Gartempe (church)
Strasbourg (Grande Île)
Versailles (palace and park)
Vézelay (basilica and hill)
Vézère (decorated caves)

❑ **Georgia**
Bagrati Cathedral and Gelati Monastery
Mtskheta (historic church ensemble)
Upper Svaneti

❑ **Germany**
Aachen Cathedral
Bamberg
Bauhaus and its sites in Weimar and Dessau
Brühl (Augustusburg and Falkenlust castles)
Cologne Cathedral
Eisleben and Wittenberg, the Luther memorials
Hildesheim (St Mary's Cathedral and St Michael's Church)
Lorsch (abbey and Altenmünster)
Lübeck (Hanseatic city)
Maulbronn (monastery)
Messel Pit (fossil site)
Potsdam and Berlin palaces and parks
Quedlinburg (collegiate church, castle and old town)
Rammelsberg mines and historic town of Goslar
Speyer Cathedral
Trier (Roman monuments, cathedral and Liebfrauen church)
Völklingen ironworks
Wies (pilgrimage church)
Würzburg Residence

❑ **Ghana**
Ashante traditional buildings
Forts and castles of Ghana

❑ **Greece**
Athens (Acropolis)
Bassae (temple of Apollo Epicurius)
Daphni, Hossios Luckas and Nea Moni of Chios monasteries
Delos
Delphi (archaeological site)
Epidaurus (archaeological site)
Meteora
Mt Athos
Mystras
Olympia (archaeological site)
Rhodes (medieval city)
Samos (Pythagoreion and Heraion)
Thessalonika (Paleochristian and Byzantine monuments)
Vergina (archaeological site)

❑ **Guatemala**
Antigua Guatemala
Quirigua (archaeological site and ruins)
Tikal National Park

❑ **Guinea**
Mt Nimba Nature Reserve (shared with Côte d'Ivoire)

❑ **Haiti**
Citadel, Sans-Souci and site of Ramiers National Historic Park and Palace

❑ **Honduras**
Maya ruins of Copan
Río Plátano Biosphere Reserve

❑ **Hungary**
Aggtelek caves and the Slovak Karst (shared with Slovakia)
Budapest (banks of the Danube and the Buda Castle quarter)
Hollókö (traditional village)
Pannonhalma, Millenary Benedictine Abbey and its natural environment

❑ **India**
Agra Fort
Ajanta caves
Elephanta caves
Ellora caves
Fatehpur Sikri (Moghul city)
Goa (churches and convents)
Hampi (monuments)
Humayun's Tomb
Kaziranga National Park
Keoladeo National Park
Khajuraho (monuments)
Konarak (Sun Temple)
Mahabalipuram (monuments)
Manas Wildlife Sanctuary
Nanda Devi National Park
Pattadakal (monuments)
Qutb Minar
Sanchi Buddhist monuments
Sundarbans National Park
Taj Mahal
Thanjavur (Brihadisvara Temple)

❑ **Indonesia**
Borobudur Temple compounds
Komodo National Park
Prambanan Temple compounds
Sangiran (early man site)
Ujung Kulon National Park

❑ **Iran**
Esfahan (Meidan Emam)
Persepolis
Tchogha Zanbil Ziggurat and complex

❑ **Iraq**
Hatra

❑ **Ireland**
Skellig Michael
Valley of the Boyne

❑ **Israel**
Jerusalem (old city and its walls)

❑ **Italy**
Agrigento (archaeological area)
Alberobello (the trulli)
Amalfi (the coast)
Barumini, Sardinia (the nuraghi)
Casale (Villa Romana)
Caserta (18th-c palace, park, aqueduct of Vanvitelli and the San Leucio complex)
Castel del Monte
Crespi d'Adda
Ferrara (Renaissance city)
Florence (historic centre)
I Sassi di Matera

Modena (cathedral, Torre Civica and Piazza Grande)
Naples (historic centre)
Padua (botanical garden)
Pienza (historic city centre)
Pisa (Piazza del Duomo)
Pompeii, with Herculaneum and Torre Annunziata archaeological areas
Portovenere, Cinque Terre and the islands of Palmaria, Tino and Tinetto
Ravenna, early Christian monuments and mosaics
Rome (historic centre)
San Gimignano (historic centre)
Santa Maria delle Grazie with *The Last Supper* by Leonardo da Vinci
Siena (historic centre)
Turin (royal houses of Savoy)
Valcamonica (rock drawings)
Venice and its lagoon
Vicenza (city and Palladian villas of the Veneto)

❑ **Japan**
Ancient Kyoto (Kyoto, Uji and Otsu cities)
Himeji-jo
Hiroshima Peace Memorial (Genbaku Dome)
Horyu-ji (Buddhist monuments)
Itsukushima Shinto shrine
Shirakami-Sanchi
Shirakawa-go and Gokayama (historic villages)
Yakushima

❑ **Jordan**
Petra
Quseir Amra

❑ **Kenya**
Mt Kenya (national park and natural forest)
Sibiloi and Central I national parks

❑ **Korea, Republic of (South Korea)**
Ch'angdokkung Palace complex
Chongmyo Shrine
Haeinsa Temple, including woodblocks of the Tripitaka Koreana
Hwasong Fortress
Sokkuram Grotto

❑ **Laos**
Luang Prabang

❑ **Latvia**
Riga (historic centre)

❑ **Lebanon**
Anjar (archaeological site)
Baalbek
Byblos
Tyre (archaeological site)

❑ **Libya**
Cyrene (archaeological site)
Ghadamès (old town)
Leptis Magna (archaeological site)
Sabratha (archaeological site)
Tadrart Acacus (rock-art sites)

❑ **Lithuania**
Vilnius (historic centre)

❑ **Luxembourg**
City of Luxembourg, old quarters and fortifications

❑ **Macedonia**
Ohrid and its lake

❑ **Madagascar**
Tsingy Bemaraha Nature Reserve

❑ **Malawi**
Lake Malawi National Park

❑ **Mali**
Cliffs of Bandiagara (land of the Dogons)
Djenné (old towns)
Timbuktu

❑ **Malta**
Hal Saflieni Hypogeum
Megalithic temples
Valetta (old city)

❑ **Mauritania**
Ancient ksour of Ouadane, Chinguetti, Tichitt and Oualata
Banc d'Arguin National Park

❑ **Mexico**
Chichen Itza (pre-Hispanic city)
El Tajin (pre-Hispanic city)
El Vizcaino Whale Sanctuary
Guadalajara (hospicio Cabañas)
Guanajuato (historic town) and adjacent mines
Mexico City (historic centre and Xochimilco)
Morelia (historic centre)
Oaxaca (historic zone) and Monte Alban (archaeological site)
Palenque (pre-Hispanic city and national park)
Popocatepetl (16th-c monasteries on the slopes)
Puebla (historic centre)
Queretaro historic monuments zone
Sian Ka'an (Biosphere reserve)
Sierra de San Francisco (rock paintings)
Teotihuacán (pre-Hispanic city)
Uxmal (pre-Hispanic town)
Zacatecas (historic centre)

❑ **Morocco**
Aït-Ben-Haddou (fortified village)
Fez (Medina)
Marrakesh (Medina)
Meknes (historic city)
Tétouan (Medina)
Volubilis (archaeological site)

❑ **Mozambique**
Island of Mozambique

❑ **Nepal**
Chitwan National Park
Kathmandu Valley
Lumbini (birthplace of Lord Buddha)
Sagarmatha National Park

❑ **The Netherlands**
Amsterdam defence line
Kinderdijk-Elshout (mill network)
Schokland and its surroundings
Willemstad (historic area, inner city and harbour)

❑ **New Zealand**
Te Wahipounamu
Tongariro National Park

❑ **Niger**
Air and Ténéré (nature reserves)
'W' National Park

❑ **Norway**
Alta (rock drawings)
Bergen (Bryggen area)
Røros (mining town)
Urnes Stave Church

❑ **Oman**
Arabian Oryx Sanctuary
Bahla Fort
Bat, Al-Khutm and Al-Ayn (archaeological sites)

❑ **Pakistan**
Lahore (fort and Shalamar gardens)
Mohenjo Daro (archaeological site)
Rohtas Fort
Takht-i-Bahi Buddhist ruins
Taxila (archaeological remains)
Thatta (historical monuments)

❑ **Panama**
Darien National Park
La Amistad National Park (shared with Costa Rica)
Panama (historic district, with Salón Bolívar)
Portobelo and San Lorenzo fortifications

❑ **Paraguay**
Jesuit Missions

❑ **Peru**
Chan Chan (archaeological site)
Chavin (archaeological site)
Cuzco (old city)
Huascarán National Park
Lima (historic centre)
Machu Picchu (historic sanctuary)
Manu National Park
Nasca and Pampas de Jumana (lines and geoglyphs)
Rio Abiseo National Park

❑ **Philippines**
Baroque churches of the Philippines
Rice terraces of the Philippine Cordilleras
Tubbataha Reef Marine Park

❑ **Poland**
Auschwitz concentration camp
Belovezhskaya Pushcha/Bialowieza Forest (shared with Belarus)
Cracow (historic centre)
Malbork (castle of the Teutonic order)
Torun (medieval town)
Warsaw (historic centre)
Wieliczka saltmines
Zamosc (old city)

❑ **Portugal**
Alcobaça (monastery)
Angra do Heroismo (Azores)
Batalha (monastery)
Belém (tower) and Monastery of the Hieronymites
Evora (historic centre)
Oporto (historic centre)
Sintra (cultural landscape)
Tomar (Convent of Christ)

❑ **Romania**
Biertan
Danube Delta
Horezu Monastery
Painted churches of northern Moldavia

❑ **Russian Federation**
Kamchatka volcanic region
Kizhi Pogost
Kolomenskoye (Church of the Ascension)
L Baikal
Moscow (Kremlin and Red Square)
Novgorod (historic monuments)
St Petersburg (historic centre)
Sergiev Posad
Solovetsky Is
Virgin Komi forests
Vladimir and Suzdal monuments

❑ **Senegal**
Djoudj Bird Sanctuary
Gorée I
Niokolo-Koba National Park

❑ **Seychelles**
Aldabra Atoll
Vallée de Mai Nature Reserve

❑ **Slovakia**
Aggtelek caves and the Slovak Karst (shared with Hungary)
Banska Stiavnica
Spissky Hrad
Vlkolinec

❑ **Slovenia**
Skocjan caves

❑ **Spain**
Altamira Cave
Avila (old town) with its Extra-Muros churches
Barcelona (Parque and Palacio Güell, Casa Milá, Palau de la Musica Catalana and Hospital de Sant Pau)
Burgos Cathedral
Caceres (old town)
Córdoba (historic centre)
Cuenca (historic walled town)
Doñana National Park
El Escurial (monastery and site)
Garajonay National Park (Canary Is)
Granada (Alhambra, Generalife and Albayzin)
Kingdom of Asturias (its churches)
Las Médulas
Mérida
Poblet Monastery
Pyrenees, Mt Perdu landscape (shared with France)
Salamanca (old city)
San Millán Yuso and Suso monasteries
Santa Maria de Guadalupe (royal monastery)
Santiago de Compostela (old town and route)

Segovia (old town and its aqueduct)
Seville (cathedral, Alcazar and Archivo de Indias)
Teruel (Mudejar architecture)
Toledo (historic city)
Valencia, 'La Lonja de la Seda'

❑ **Sri Lanka**
Anuradhapura (sacred city)
Dambulla (Golden Rock Temple)
Galle (old town and its fortifications)
Kandy (sacred city)
Polonnaruwa (ancient city)
Sigiriya (ancient city)
Sinharaja Forest Reserve

❑ **Sweden**
Birka and Hovgården
Drottningholm Palace
Engelsberg ironworks
Gammelstad (church town)
Laponian area
Skogskyrkogården
Tanum (rock carvings)
Visby (Hanseatic town)

❑ **Switzerland**
Berne (old city)
Müstair (Benedictine convent)
St Gall (convent)

❑ **Syria**
Aleppo (old city)
Bosra (ancient city)
Damascus (old city)
Palmyra (archaeological site)

❑ **Tanzania**
Kilimanjaro National Park
Kilwa Kisiwani and Songa Mnara ruins
Ngorongoro area
Selous Game Reserve
Serengeti National Park

❑ **Thailand**
Ayutthaya (historic city) and associated towns
Ban Chiang (archaeological site)
Sukhothai (historic city) and associated towns
Thungyai-Huai Kha Khaeng (wildlife sanctuaries)

❑ **Tunisia**
Carthage (archaeological site)
Dougga/Thugga
El Djem (amphitheatre)
Ichkeul National Park
Kairouan
Kerkuane (Punic town and necropolis)
Sousse (Medina)
Tunis (Medina)

❑ **Turkey**
Divrigi (Great Mosque and hospital)
Göreme National Park and rock sites of Cappadocia
Hattusha (Hittite city)
Hierapolis-Pamukkale
Istanbul (historic areas)
Nemrut Dag (archaeological site)
Safranbolu (old city)
Xanthos-Letoon

❑ **Uganda**
Bwindi Impenetrable National Park
Rwenzori Mountains National Park

❑ **Ukraine**
St Sophia and Lavra of Kiev-Pechersk

❑ **UK**
Bath
Blenheim Palace
Canterbury Cathedral, St Augustine's Abbey and St Martin's Church
Durham (castle and cathedral)
Edinburgh (old town and new town)
Giant's Causeway and its coast
Gough Island Wildlife Reserve (South Atlantic Ocean)
Greenwich (maritime buildings and park)
Gwynedd (castles and towns of King Edward I)
Hadrian's Wall
Henderson I (Pacific Ocean)
Ironbridge Gorge
St Kilda I
Stonehenge, Avebury and related megalithic sites
Studley Royal Park and the ruins of Fountains Abbey
Tower of London
Westminster (palace and abbey) and St Margaret's Church

❑ **USA**
Cahokia Mounds site
Carlsbad Caverns National Park
Chaco Culture National Historical Park
Everglades National Park
Grand Canyon National Park
Great Smoky Mountains National Park
Hawaii Volcanoes National Park
Independence Hall, Philadelphia
Mammoth Cave National Park
Mesa Verde National Park
Monticello and the University of Virginia in Charlottesville
Olympic National Park
Pueblo de Taos
Puerto Rico (La Fortaleza and San Juan historic site)
Redwood National Park
Statue of Liberty
Tatshenshini-Alsek, Kluane National Park, Wrangell St Elias National Park and Reserve, and Glacier Bay National Park (shared with Canada)
Waterton Glacier International Peace Park (shared with Canada)
Yellowstone National Park
Yosemite National Park

❑ **Uruguay**
Colonia del Sacramento (historic quarter)

❑ **Uzbekistan**
Bukhara
Itchan Kala (historic city)

❑ **Vatican City**
Vatican City

❑ **Venezuela**
Canaima National Park
Coro and its port

❑ **Vietnam**
Ha Long Bay
Hué (complex of monuments)

❑ **Yemen**
Sana'a (old city)
Shibam (old walled city)
Zabid (historic town)

❑ **Yugoslavia**
Durmitor National Park
Kotor and its gulf
Stari Ras and Sopocani
Studenica Monastery

❑ **Zambia**
Victoria Falls/Mosi-oa-Tunya (shared with Zimbabwe)

❑ **Zimbabwe**
Khami ruins
Great Zimbabwe National Monument
Mana Pools, National Park and Sapi and Chewore safari areas
Victoria Falls/Mosi-oa-Tunya (shared with Zambia)

## National parks and nature reserves

The first national park was Yellowstone, Wyoming, which was obtained by the US government during the 1870s for the use and enjoyment of the people. By the late 1980s there were more than 3 000 national parks and wildlife reserves scattered around the world. All together, they covered approximately 4 million km$^2$/1.5 million mi$^2$. Below is a selection of the best known.

| Name | Country | Area (km$^2$) [1] | Special features |
|---|---|---|---|
| Altos de Campana | Panama | 48 | Great variety of plant zones |
| Amazonia | Brazil | 9940 | Rainforest |
| Badlands | USA | 985 | Prehistoric fossils; dramatically eroded hills |
| Banff | Canada | 6640 | Spectacular glaciated scenery; hot springs |
| Beinn Eighe | UK | 48 | Original Scottish pine forest |
| Bialowieski | Poland | 53 | Largest remnant of primeval forest; European bison |
| Burren | Ireland | 15 | Limestone pavement with remarkable plants |
| Camargue | France | 131 | Wetland; many rare birds, especially flamingoes |
| Canaima | Venezuela | 30000 | World's highest waterfall, Angel Falls |
| Canyonlands | USA | 1365 | Deep gorges, colourful rock, spectacular landforms |
| Carlsbad Caverns | USA | 189 | Huge limestone caverns with millions of bats |
| Carnarvon | Australia | 2980 | Bush-tailed rock wallabies; aboriginal cave paintings |
| Chitwan | Nepal | 932 | Royal Bengal tigers, gavials (type of Indian crocodile), Gangetic dolphins |
| Corbett | India | 520 | Indian tigers; gavials, muggers (both types of Indian crocodile) |
| Dartmoor | UK | 954 | Wild ponies |
| Death Valley | USA | 8368 | Lowest point in W hemisphere; unique flora, fauna |
| Doñana | Spain | 507 | Wetland; rare birds and mammals; Spanish lynx |
| Everglades | USA | 5929 | Swamp, mangrove; subtropical wildlife refuge |
| Etosha | Namibia | 22270 | Swampland and bush; rare and abundant wildlife |
| Fiordland | New Zealand | 12570 | Kiwis, keas, wekas, takahe, kakapo (all flightless birds, except for the kea) |
| Fuji-Hakone-Izu | Japan | 1232 | Mt Fuji; varied animal and plant life |
| Galápagos Islands | Ecuador | 6937 | Giant iguanas, giant tortoises |
| Gemsbok | Botswana | 24305 | Desert, grassland; lions and large herds of game |
| Gir | India | 258 | Asiatic lions |
| Glacier | USA | 4102 | Virgin coniferous forest; glaciers |
| Gran Paradiso | Italy | 702 | Alpine scenery; chamois, ibex |

| Name | Country | Area (km²) [1] | Special features |
|---|---|---|---|
| Grand Canyon | USA | 4 834 | Mile-deep canyon, colourful walls; many life zones |
| Great Smoky Mountains | USA | 2 094 | Varied wildlife including wild turkey, black bear |
| Hardangervidda | Norway | 3 422 | Plateau of ancient rock; large wild reindeer herd |
| Hawaii Volcanoes | USA | 920 | Active volcanoes, rare plants and animals |
| Heron Island | Australia | 0.17 | Part of Great Barrier Reef; corals, invertebrates, fish |
| Hoge Veluwe | Netherlands | 54 | Largely stabilized dunes; wet and dry heath |
| Iguazú/Iguaçu | Argentina/Brazil | 6 900 | Iguazú/Iguaçu Falls |
| Ixtacihuatl-Popocatépetl | Mexico | 257 | Snow-capped volcanoes |
| Kafue | Zambia | 22 400 | Numerous animals and birds; black rhinoceros refuge |
| Kakadu | Australia | 20 277 | Aboriginal rock art; crocodiles, water birds |
| Kaziranga | India | 430 | Indian one-horned rhinoceros, swamp deer |
| Khao Yai | Thailand | 2 169 | Large caves and waterfalls; many bird species |
| Kilimanjaro | Tanzania | 756 | Africa's highest peak, Mt Kilimanjaro; colobus monkeys |
| Kinabalu | Malaysia | 754 | Orchids; South-East Asia's highest peak, Mt Kinabalu |
| Kosciusko | Australia | 6 469 | Australia's highest peak, Mt Kosciusko; mountain pygmy possum |
| Kruger | South Africa | 19 485 | Wide range of animals and birds; rare white rhinoceros |
| Lainzer Tiergarten | Austria | 25 | Ancient forest and meadow; wild boar, deer, moufflon (wild sheep) |
| Lake District | UK | 2 292 | Lake and mountain scenery |
| Los Glaciares | Argentina/Chile | 1 618 | Glacial landforms |
| Manu | Peru | 15 328 | Small mammals, birds; Amazon/Andean ecosystems |
| Mercantour | France | 685 | Alpine scenery and flora |
| Mt Apo | Philippines | 728 | Volcanoes; monkey-eating eagles |
| Mt Cook | New Zealand | 699 | New Zealand's highest peak, Mt Cook |
| Mt Olympus | Greece | 40 | Maquis and forest; wild mountain goats |
| Muddus | Sweden | 493 | Glaciated area with forest and tundra; Lapp pasture |
| Namib Desert/Naukluft | Namibia | 23 400 | Only true desert in southern Africa |
| Ngorongoro | Tanzania | 21 475 | Huge volcanic crater |
| Olympic | USA | 3 712 | Rugged peaks, glaciers, dense forest; Roosevelt elk |
| Petrified Forest | USA | 379 | Tree-trunks millions of years old; colourful sands |
| Pfälzerwald | Germany | 1 793 | Forest; European bison, moufflon (wild sheep), mountain goats |
| Phu Rua | Thailand | 120 | Mountain forest zones from tropical to pine. |
| Redwood | USA | 442 | Virgin redwood; Roosevelt elk |
| Royal | Australia | 150 | World's second-oldest national park (1879) |
| Ruwenzori | Uganda | 995 | Hippopotamuses, chimpanzees, baboons, colobus monkeys |
| Sagarmatha | Nepal | 1 148 | Mt Everest; impeyan pheasant, Himalayan tahr (wild goat) |
| Sarek | Sweden | 1 970 | Lapland; herds of reindeer |
| Serengeti | Tanzania | 14 763 | Huge animal migrations at start of dry season |
| Snowdonia | UK | 2 142 | Glaciated mountain scenery; varied flora and fauna |
| Swiss | Switzerland | 169 | Alpine forests and flora; reintroduced ibex |
| Tatra | Czech Republic/ Poland | 712 | Bears, lynxes, marmots; mountain scenery |

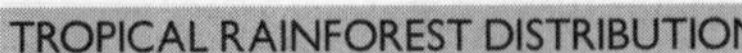


| Name | Country | Area (km²)[1] | Special features |
|---|---|---|---|
| Tikal | Guatemala | 574 | Mayan ruins; rainforest animals |
| Toubkal | Morocco | 360 | Barbary apes, porcupines, hyenas, bald ibis |
| Tsavo | Kenya | 20 812 | Vast range of wildlife |
| Ujung-Kulon | Indonesia | 1 229 | Low-relief forest; Javan tiger, Javan rhinoceros |
| Uluru | Australia | 1 326 | Desert; Uluru (Ayers Rock) and the Olgas |
| Victoria Falls | Zimbabwe/ Zambia | 190 | Spectacular waterfall |
| Virunga | Congo, Democratic Republic of | 7 800 | Mountain gorillas; active volcanoes |
| Waterton Lakes | Canada | 526 | Varied flora and fauna |
| Waza | Cameroon | 1 700 | Giraffes, elephants, ostriches, waterbuck |
| Wolong | China | 2 000 | Giant pandas; also golden langurs, snow leopards |
| Wood Buffalo | Canada | 44 800 | Refuge for American buffalo (bison), whooping crane |
| Yellowstone | USA | 8 991 | World's greatest geyser area; bears, deer, elk, bison |
| Yosemite | USA | 3 080 | High waterfalls; varied flora and fauna; giant sequoias |

[1]To convert km² to mi², multiply by 0.386.

## Tropical rainforest distribution

For information on the rate of destruction of tropical rainforests, see p53

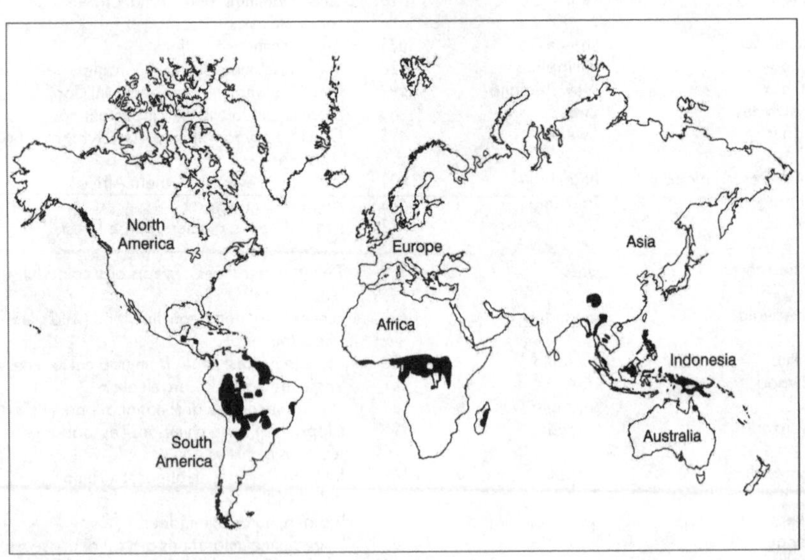

## Tropical rainforests (rate of destruction)

The destruction of the world's rainforests has taken place largely as a result of economic pressures for more agricultural land and products. This destruction has led to a huge increase in the amount of carbon dioxide being released into the atmosphere. It also causes the degradation and erosion of top-soil, increasing the risk of rivers silting up and flooding. Rainforests are home to half the world's plant and animal species, many of which are now in imminent danger of extinction. The following data are 1997 FAO estimates for 87 tropical countries, taken from *State of the World's Forests 1997* published by the Food and Agriculture Organization of the United Nations.

| Region | Forest area 1995 (1 000 ha)[1] | Annual forest loss 1990–5 (1 000 ha) | Annual rate of destruction (%) |
|---|---|---|---|
| **Africa** | | | |
| West Sahelian Africa | 39 827 | 295 | 0.7 |
| East Sahelian Africa | 57 542 | 420 | 0.7 |
| West Moist Africa | 46 324 | 492 | 1 |
| Central Africa | 204 677 | 1 201 | 0.6 |
| Tropical Southern Africa | 141 311 | 1 158 | 0.8 |
| Insular East Africa | 15 220 | 131 | 0.8 |
| *Total Tropical Africa* | *504 901* | *3 695* | *0.7* |
| **Asia** | | | |
| South Asia | 77 137 | 141 | 0.2 |
| Continental Southeast Asia | 70 163 | 1 164 | 1.6 |
| Insular Southeast Asia | 132 466 | 1 750 | 1.3 |
| *Total Tropical Asia* | *279 766* | *3 055* | *1.1* |
| **North and Central America** | | | |
| Central America and Mexico | 75 018 | 959 | 1.2 |
| Caribbean | 4 425 | 78 | 1.7 |
| *Total Tropical North and Central America* | *79 443* | *1 037* | *1.3* |
| **South America** | 827 946 | 4 655 | 0.6 |
| **Oceania** | 41 903 | 151 | 0.4 |
| **TOTAL** | **1 733 959** | **12 593** | **0.7** |

[1]One hectare (ha) = 10 000 sq m. To convert ha to sq km, divide by 100; to convert ha to sq mi, multiply by 0.003861.

## Map of shipping forecast areas

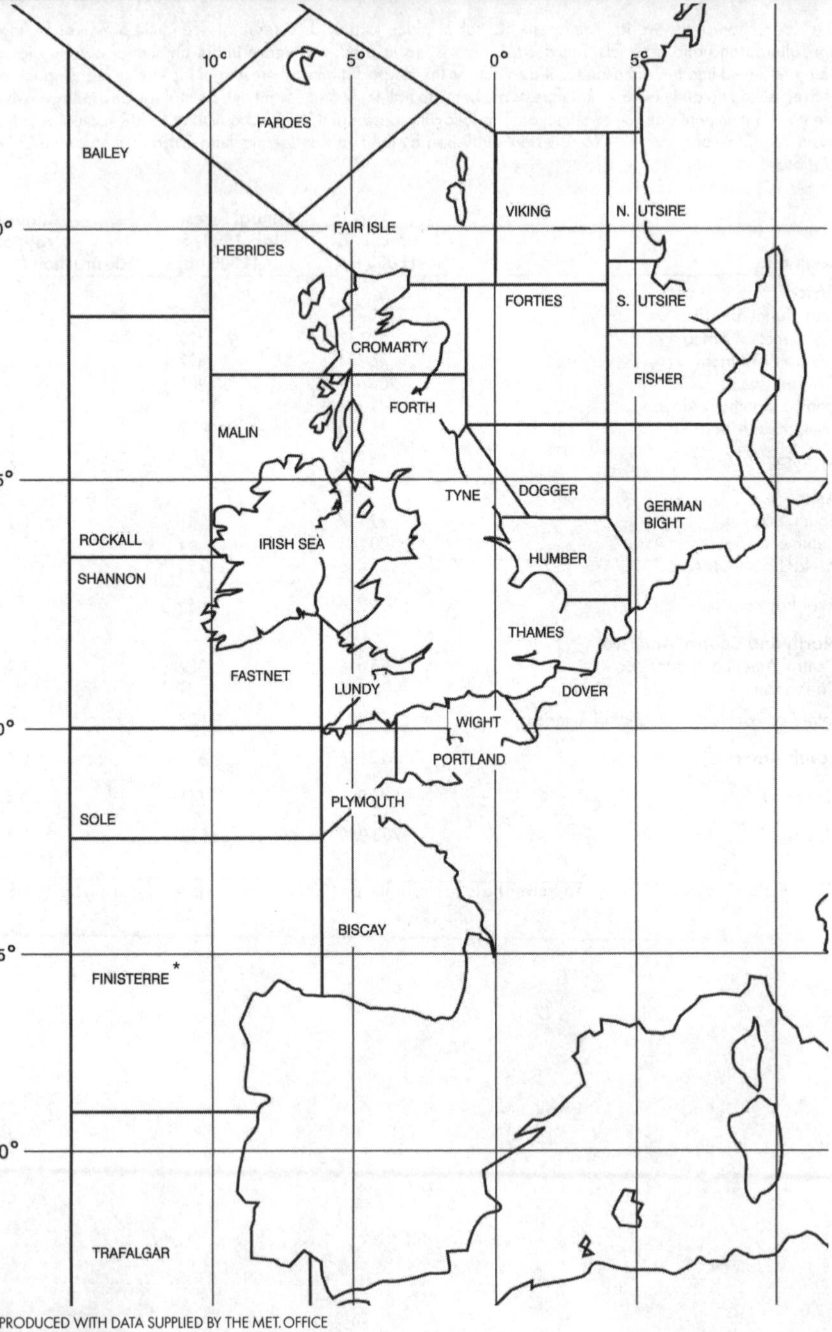

10°
5°
0°
5°
FAROES
BAILEY
VIKING
N. UTSIRE
60°
FAIR ISLE
HEBRIDES
FORTIES
S. UTSIRE
CROMARTY
FISHER
FORTH
MALIN
55°
TYNE
DOGGER
GERMAN BIGHT
ROCKALL
IRISH SEA
SHANNON
HUMBER
THAMES
FASTNET
LUNDY
DOVER
50°
WIGHT
PORTLAND
PLYMOUTH
SOLE
BISCAY
45°
FINISTERRE *
40°
TRAFALGAR

REPRODUCED WITH DATA SUPPLIED BY THE MET. OFFICE

* Renamed FitzRoy 2002

## Perpetual calendar 1801–2040

The calendar for each year is given under the corresponding letter below.

| | | | | | | | | | |
|---|---|---|---|---|---|---|---|---|---|
| 1801 | I | 1849 | C | 1897 | K | 1945 | C | 1993 | K |
| 1802 | K | 1850 | E | 1898 | M | 1946 | E | 1994 | M |
| 1803 | M | 1851 | G | 1899 | A | 1947 | G | 1995 | A |
| 1804 | B | 1852 | J | 1900 | C | 1948 | J | 1996 | D |
| 1805 | E | 1853 | M | 1901 | E | 1949 | M | 1997 | G |
| 1806 | G | 1854 | A | 1902 | G | 1950 | A | 1998 | I |
| 1807 | I | 1855 | C | 1903 | I | 1951 | C | 1999 | K |
| 1808 | L | 1856 | F | 1904 | L | 1952 | F | 2000 | N |
| 1809 | A | 1857 | I | 1905 | A | 1953 | I | 2001 | C |
| 1810 | C | 1858 | K | 1906 | C | 1954 | K | 2002 | E |
| 1811 | E | 1859 | M | 1907 | E | 1955 | M | 2003 | G |
| 1812 | H | 1860 | B | 1908 | H | 1956 | B | 2004 | J |
| 1813 | K | 1861 | E | 1909 | K | 1957 | E | 2005 | M |
| 1814 | M | 1862 | G | 1910 | M | 1958 | G | 2006 | A |
| 1815 | A | 1863 | I | 1911 | A | 1959 | I | 2007 | C |
| 1816 | D | 1864 | L | 1912 | D | 1960 | L | 2008 | F |
| 1817 | G | 1865 | A | 1913 | G | 1961 | A | 2009 | I |
| 1818 | I | 1866 | C | 1914 | I | 1962 | C | 2010 | K |
| 1819 | K | 1867 | E | 1915 | K | 1963 | E | 2011 | M |
| 1820 | N | 1868 | H | 1916 | N | 1964 | H | 2012 | B |
| 1821 | C | 1869 | K | 1917 | C | 1965 | K | 2013 | E |
| 1822 | E | 1870 | M | 1918 | E | 1966 | M | 2014 | G |
| 1823 | G | 1871 | A | 1919 | G | 1967 | A | 2015 | I |
| 1824 | J | 1872 | D | 1920 | J | 1968 | D | 2016 | L |
| 1825 | M | 1873 | G | 1921 | M | 1969 | G | 2017 | A |
| 1826 | A | 1874 | I | 1922 | A | 1970 | I | 2018 | C |
| 1827 | C | 1875 | K | 1923 | C | 1971 | K | 2019 | E |
| 1828 | F | 1876 | N | 1924 | F | 1972 | N | 2020 | H |
| 1829 | I | 1877 | C | 1925 | I | 1973 | C | 2021 | K |
| 1830 | K | 1878 | E | 1926 | K | 1974 | E | 2022 | M |
| 1831 | M | 1879 | G | 1927 | M | 1975 | G | 2023 | A |
| 1832 | B | 1880 | J | 1928 | B | 1976 | J | 2024 | D |
| 1833 | E | 1881 | M | 1929 | E | 1977 | M | 2025 | G |
| 1834 | G | 1882 | A | 1930 | G | 1978 | A | 2026 | I |
| 1835 | I | 1883 | C | 1931 | I | 1979 | C | 2027 | K |
| 1836 | L | 1884 | F | 1932 | L | 1980 | F | 2028 | N |
| 1837 | A | 1885 | I | 1933 | A | 1981 | I | 2029 | C |
| 1838 | C | 1886 | K | 1934 | C | 1982 | K | 2030 | E |
| 1839 | E | 1887 | M | 1935 | E | 1983 | M | 2031 | G |
| 1840 | H | 1888 | B | 1936 | H | 1984 | B | 2032 | J |
| 1841 | K | 1889 | E | 1937 | K | 1985 | E | 2033 | M |
| 1842 | M | 1890 | G | 1938 | M | 1986 | G | 2034 | A |
| 1843 | A | 1891 | I | 1939 | A | 1987 | I | 2035 | C |
| 1844 | D | 1892 | L | 1940 | D | 1988 | L | 2036 | F |
| 1845 | G | 1893 | A | 1941 | G | 1989 | A | 2037 | I |
| 1846 | I | 1894 | C | 1942 | I | 1990 | C | 2038 | K |
| 1847 | K | 1895 | E | 1943 | K | 1991 | E | 2039 | M |
| 1848 | N | 1896 | H | 1944 | N | 1992 | H | 2040 | B |

# PERPETUAL CALENDAR

## A

**January**

| S | M | T | W | T | F | S |
|---|---|---|---|---|---|---|
| 1 | 2 | 3 | 4 | 5 | 6 | 7 |
| 8 | 9 | 10 | 11 | 12 | 13 | 14 |
| 15 | 16 | 17 | 18 | 19 | 20 | 21 |
| 22 | 23 | 24 | 25 | 26 | 27 | 28 |
| 29 | 30 | 31 | | | | |

**February**

| S | M | T | W | T | F | S |
|---|---|---|---|---|---|---|
| | | | 1 | 2 | 3 | 4 |
| 5 | 6 | 7 | 8 | 9 | 10 | 11 |
| 12 | 13 | 14 | 15 | 16 | 17 | 18 |
| 19 | 20 | 21 | 22 | 23 | 24 | 25 |
| 26 | 27 | 28 | | | | |

**March**

| S | M | T | W | T | F | S |
|---|---|---|---|---|---|---|
| | | | 1 | 2 | 3 | 4 |
| 5 | 6 | 7 | 8 | 9 | 10 | 11 |
| 12 | 13 | 14 | 15 | 16 | 17 | 18 |
| 19 | 20 | 21 | 22 | 23 | 24 | 25 |
| 26 | 27 | 28 | 29 | 30 | 31 | |

**April**

| S | M | T | W | T | F | S |
|---|---|---|---|---|---|---|
| | | | | | | 1 |
| 2 | 3 | 4 | 5 | 6 | 7 | 8 |
| 9 | 10 | 11 | 12 | 13 | 14 | 15 |
| 16 | 17 | 18 | 19 | 20 | 21 | 22 |
| 23 | 24 | 25 | 26 | 27 | 28 | 29 |
| 30 | | | | | | |

**May**

| S | M | T | W | T | F | S |
|---|---|---|---|---|---|---|
| | 1 | 2 | 3 | 4 | 5 | 6 |
| 7 | 8 | 9 | 10 | 11 | 12 | 13 |
| 14 | 15 | 16 | 17 | 18 | 19 | 20 |
| 21 | 22 | 23 | 24 | 25 | 26 | 27 |
| 28 | 29 | 30 | 31 | | | |

**June**

| S | M | T | W | T | F | S |
|---|---|---|---|---|---|---|
| | | | | 1 | 2 | 3 |
| 4 | 5 | 6 | 7 | 8 | 9 | 10 |
| 11 | 12 | 13 | 14 | 15 | 16 | 17 |
| 18 | 19 | 20 | 21 | 22 | 23 | 24 |
| 25 | 26 | 27 | 28 | 29 | 30 | |

**July**

| S | M | T | W | T | F | S |
|---|---|---|---|---|---|---|
| | | | | | | 1 |
| 2 | 3 | 4 | 5 | 6 | 7 | 8 |
| 9 | 10 | 11 | 12 | 13 | 14 | 15 |
| 16 | 17 | 18 | 19 | 20 | 21 | 22 |
| 23 | 24 | 25 | 26 | 27 | 28 | 29 |
| 30 | 31 | | | | | |

**August**

| S | M | T | W | T | F | S |
|---|---|---|---|---|---|---|
| | | 1 | 2 | 3 | 4 | 5 |
| 6 | 7 | 8 | 9 | 10 | 11 | 12 |
| 13 | 14 | 15 | 16 | 17 | 18 | 19 |
| 20 | 21 | 22 | 23 | 24 | 25 | 26 |
| 27 | 28 | 29 | 30 | 31 | | |

**September**

| S | M | T | W | T | F | S |
|---|---|---|---|---|---|---|
| | | | | | 1 | 2 |
| 3 | 4 | 5 | 6 | 7 | 8 | 9 |
| 10 | 11 | 12 | 13 | 14 | 15 | 16 |
| 17 | 18 | 19 | 20 | 21 | 22 | 23 |
| 24 | 25 | 26 | 27 | 28 | 29 | 30 |

**October**

| S | M | T | W | T | F | S |
|---|---|---|---|---|---|---|
| 1 | 2 | 3 | 4 | 5 | 6 | 7 |
| 8 | 9 | 10 | 11 | 12 | 13 | 14 |
| 15 | 16 | 17 | 18 | 19 | 20 | 21 |
| 22 | 23 | 24 | 25 | 26 | 27 | 28 |
| 29 | 30 | 31 | | | | |

**November**

| S | M | T | W | T | F | S |
|---|---|---|---|---|---|---|
| | | | 1 | 2 | 3 | 4 |
| 5 | 6 | 7 | 8 | 9 | 10 | 11 |
| 12 | 13 | 14 | 15 | 16 | 17 | 18 |
| 19 | 20 | 21 | 22 | 23 | 24 | 25 |
| 26 | 27 | 28 | 29 | 30 | | |

**December**

| S | M | T | W | T | F | S |
|---|---|---|---|---|---|---|
| | | | | | 1 | 2 |
| 3 | 4 | 5 | 6 | 7 | 8 | 9 |
| 10 | 11 | 12 | 13 | 14 | 15 | 16 |
| 17 | 18 | 19 | 20 | 21 | 22 | 23 |
| 24 | 25 | 26 | 27 | 28 | 29 | 30 |
| 31 | | | | | | |

## B (leap year)

**January**

| S | M | T | W | T | F | S |
|---|---|---|---|---|---|---|
| 1 | 2 | 3 | 4 | 5 | 6 | 7 |
| 8 | 9 | 10 | 11 | 12 | 13 | 14 |
| 15 | 16 | 17 | 18 | 19 | 20 | 21 |
| 22 | 23 | 24 | 25 | 26 | 27 | 28 |
| 29 | 30 | 31 | | | | |

**February**

| S | M | T | W | T | F | S |
|---|---|---|---|---|---|---|
| | | | 1 | 2 | 3 | 4 |
| 5 | 6 | 7 | 8 | 9 | 10 | 11 |
| 12 | 13 | 14 | 15 | 16 | 17 | 18 |
| 19 | 20 | 21 | 22 | 23 | 24 | 25 |
| 26 | 27 | 28 | 29 | | | |

**March**

| S | M | T | W | T | F | S |
|---|---|---|---|---|---|---|
| | | | | 1 | 2 | 3 |
| 4 | 5 | 6 | 7 | 8 | 9 | 10 |
| 11 | 12 | 13 | 14 | 15 | 16 | 17 |
| 18 | 19 | 20 | 21 | 22 | 23 | 24 |
| 25 | 26 | 27 | 28 | 29 | 30 | 31 |

**April**

| S | M | T | W | T | F | S |
|---|---|---|---|---|---|---|
| 1 | 2 | 3 | 4 | 5 | 6 | 7 |
| 8 | 9 | 10 | 11 | 12 | 13 | 14 |
| 15 | 16 | 17 | 18 | 19 | 20 | 21 |
| 22 | 23 | 24 | 25 | 26 | 27 | 28 |
| 29 | 30 | | | | | |

**May**

| S | M | T | W | T | F | S |
|---|---|---|---|---|---|---|
| | | 1 | 2 | 3 | 4 | 5 |
| 6 | 7 | 8 | 9 | 10 | 11 | 12 |
| 13 | 14 | 15 | 16 | 17 | 18 | 19 |
| 20 | 21 | 22 | 23 | 24 | 25 | 26 |
| 27 | 28 | 29 | 30 | 31 | | |

**June**

| S | M | T | W | T | F | S |
|---|---|---|---|---|---|---|
| | | | | | 1 | 2 |
| 3 | 4 | 5 | 6 | 7 | 8 | 9 |
| 10 | 11 | 12 | 13 | 14 | 15 | 16 |
| 17 | 18 | 19 | 20 | 21 | 22 | 23 |
| 24 | 25 | 26 | 27 | 28 | 29 | 30 |

**July**

| S | M | T | W | T | F | S |
|---|---|---|---|---|---|---|
| 1 | 2 | 3 | 4 | 5 | 6 | 7 |
| 8 | 9 | 10 | 11 | 12 | 13 | 14 |
| 15 | 16 | 17 | 18 | 19 | 20 | 21 |
| 22 | 23 | 24 | 25 | 26 | 27 | 28 |
| 29 | 30 | 31 | | | | |

**August**

| S | M | T | W | T | F | S |
|---|---|---|---|---|---|---|
| | | | 1 | 2 | 3 | 4 |
| 5 | 6 | 7 | 8 | 9 | 10 | 11 |
| 12 | 13 | 14 | 15 | 16 | 17 | 18 |
| 19 | 20 | 21 | 22 | 23 | 24 | 25 |
| 26 | 27 | 28 | 29 | 30 | 31 | |

**September**

| S | M | T | W | T | F | S |
|---|---|---|---|---|---|---|
| | | | | | | 1 |
| 2 | 3 | 4 | 5 | 6 | 7 | 8 |
| 9 | 10 | 11 | 12 | 13 | 14 | 15 |
| 16 | 17 | 18 | 19 | 20 | 21 | 22 |
| 23 | 24 | 25 | 26 | 27 | 28 | 29 |
| 30 | | | | | | |

**October**

| S | M | T | W | T | F | S |
|---|---|---|---|---|---|---|
| | 1 | 2 | 3 | 4 | 5 | 6 |
| 7 | 8 | 9 | 10 | 11 | 12 | 13 |
| 14 | 15 | 16 | 17 | 18 | 19 | 20 |
| 21 | 22 | 23 | 24 | 25 | 26 | 27 |
| 28 | 29 | 30 | 31 | | | |

**November**

| S | M | T | W | T | F | S |
|---|---|---|---|---|---|---|
| | | | | 1 | 2 | 3 |
| 4 | 5 | 6 | 7 | 8 | 9 | 10 |
| 11 | 12 | 13 | 14 | 15 | 16 | 17 |
| 18 | 19 | 20 | 21 | 22 | 23 | 24 |
| 25 | 26 | 27 | 28 | 29 | 30 | |

**December**

| S | M | T | W | T | F | S |
|---|---|---|---|---|---|---|
| | | | | | | 1 |
| 2 | 3 | 4 | 5 | 6 | 7 | 8 |
| 9 | 10 | 11 | 12 | 13 | 14 | 15 |
| 16 | 17 | 18 | 19 | 20 | 21 | 22 |
| 23 | 24 | 25 | 26 | 27 | 28 | 29 |
| 30 | 31 | | | | | |

## C

**January**

| S | M | T | W | T | F | S |
|---|---|---|---|---|---|---|
| | 1 | 2 | 3 | 4 | 5 | 6 |
| 7 | 8 | 9 | 10 | 11 | 12 | 13 |
| 14 | 15 | 16 | 17 | 18 | 19 | 20 |
| 21 | 22 | 23 | 24 | 25 | 26 | 27 |
| 28 | 29 | 30 | 31 | | | |

**February**

| S | M | T | W | T | F | S |
|---|---|---|---|---|---|---|
| | | | | 1 | 2 | 3 |
| 4 | 5 | 6 | 7 | 8 | 9 | 10 |
| 11 | 12 | 13 | 14 | 15 | 16 | 17 |
| 18 | 19 | 20 | 21 | 22 | 23 | 24 |
| 25 | 26 | 27 | 28 | | | |

**March**

| S | M | T | W | T | F | S |
|---|---|---|---|---|---|---|
| | | | | 1 | 2 | 3 |
| 4 | 5 | 6 | 7 | 8 | 9 | 10 |
| 11 | 12 | 13 | 14 | 15 | 16 | 17 |
| 18 | 19 | 20 | 21 | 22 | 23 | 24 |
| 25 | 26 | 27 | 28 | 29 | 30 | 31 |

**April**

| S | M | T | W | T | F | S |
|---|---|---|---|---|---|---|
| 1 | 2 | 3 | 4 | 5 | 6 | 7 |
| 8 | 9 | 10 | 11 | 12 | 13 | 14 |
| 15 | 16 | 17 | 18 | 19 | 20 | 21 |
| 22 | 23 | 24 | 25 | 26 | 27 | 28 |
| 29 | 30 | | | | | |

**May**

| | | | | | | |
|---|---|---|---|---|---|---|
| | | 1 | 2 | 3 | 4 | 5 |
| 6 | 7 | 8 | 9 | 10 | 11 | 12 |
| 13 | 14 | 15 | 16 | 17 | 18 | 19 |
| 20 | 21 | 22 | 23 | 24 | 25 | 26 |
| 27 | 28 | 29 | 30 | 31 | | |

**June**

| | | | | | | |
|---|---|---|---|---|---|---|
| | | | | | 1 | 2 |
| 3 | 4 | 5 | 6 | 7 | 8 | 9 |
| 10 | 11 | 12 | 13 | 14 | 15 | 16 |
| 17 | 18 | 19 | 20 | 21 | 22 | 23 |
| 24 | 25 | 26 | 27 | 28 | 29 | 30 |

**July**

| | | | | | | |
|---|---|---|---|---|---|---|
| 1 | 2 | 3 | 4 | 5 | 6 | 7 |
| 8 | 9 | 10 | 11 | 12 | 13 | 14 |
| 15 | 16 | 17 | 18 | 19 | 20 | 21 |
| 22 | 23 | 24 | 25 | 26 | 27 | 28 |
| 29 | 30 | 31 | | | | |

**August**

| | | | | | | |
|---|---|---|---|---|---|---|
| | | | 1 | 2 | 3 | 4 |
| 5 | 6 | 7 | 8 | 9 | 10 | 11 |
| 12 | 13 | 14 | 15 | 16 | 17 | 18 |
| 19 | 20 | 21 | 22 | 23 | 24 | 25 |
| 26 | 27 | 28 | 29 | 30 | 31 | |

**September**

| | | | | | | |
|---|---|---|---|---|---|---|
| | | | | | | 1 |
| 2 | 3 | 4 | 5 | 6 | 7 | 8 |
| 9 | 10 | 11 | 12 | 13 | 14 | 15 |
| 16 | 17 | 18 | 19 | 20 | 21 | 22 |
| 23 | 24 | 25 | 26 | 27 | 28 | 29 |
| 30 | | | | | | |

**October**

| | | | | | | |
|---|---|---|---|---|---|---|
| | 1 | 2 | 3 | 4 | 5 | 6 |
| 7 | 8 | 9 | 10 | 11 | 12 | 13 |
| 14 | 15 | 16 | 17 | 18 | 19 | 20 |
| 21 | 22 | 23 | 24 | 25 | 26 | 27 |
| 28 | 29 | 30 | 31 | | | |

**November**

| | | | | | | |
|---|---|---|---|---|---|---|
| | | | | 1 | 2 | 3 |
| 4 | 5 | 6 | 7 | 8 | 9 | 10 |
| 11 | 12 | 13 | 14 | 15 | 16 | 17 |
| 18 | 19 | 20 | 21 | 22 | 23 | 24 |
| 25 | 26 | 27 | 28 | 29 | 30 | |

**December**

| | | | | | | |
|---|---|---|---|---|---|---|
| | | | | | | 1 |
| 2 | 3 | 4 | 5 | 6 | 7 | 8 |
| 9 | 10 | 11 | 12 | 13 | 14 | 15 |
| 16 | 17 | 18 | 19 | 20 | 21 | 22 |
| 23 | 24 | 25 | 26 | 27 | 28 | 29 |
| 30 | 31 | | | | | |

## D (leap year)

**January**

| S | M | T | W | T | F | S |
|---|---|---|---|---|---|---|
| | 1 | 2 | 3 | 4 | 5 | 6 |
| 7 | 8 | 9 | 10 | 11 | 12 | 13 |
| 14 | 15 | 16 | 17 | 18 | 19 | 20 |
| 21 | 22 | 23 | 24 | 25 | 26 | 27 |
| 28 | 29 | 30 | 31 | | | |

**February**

| S | M | T | W | T | F | S |
|---|---|---|---|---|---|---|
| | | | | 1 | 2 | 3 |
| 4 | 5 | 6 | 7 | 8 | 9 | 10 |
| 11 | 12 | 13 | 14 | 15 | 16 | 17 |
| 18 | 19 | 20 | 21 | 22 | 23 | 24 |
| 25 | 26 | 27 | 28 | 29 | | |

**March**

| S | M | T | W | T | F | S |
|---|---|---|---|---|---|---|
| | | | | | 1 | 2 |
| 3 | 4 | 5 | 6 | 7 | 8 | 9 |
| 10 | 11 | 12 | 13 | 14 | 15 | 16 |
| 17 | 18 | 19 | 20 | 21 | 22 | 23 |
| 24 | 25 | 26 | 27 | 28 | 29 | 30 |
| 31 | | | | | | |

**April**

| S | M | T | W | T | F | S |
|---|---|---|---|---|---|---|
| | 1 | 2 | 3 | 4 | 5 | 6 |
| 7 | 8 | 9 | 10 | 11 | 12 | 13 |
| 14 | 15 | 16 | 17 | 18 | 19 | 20 |
| 21 | 22 | 23 | 24 | 25 | 26 | 27 |
| 28 | 29 | 30 | | | | |

**May**

| | | | | | | |
|---|---|---|---|---|---|---|
| | | | 1 | 2 | 3 | 4 |
| 5 | 6 | 7 | 8 | 9 | 10 | 11 |
| 12 | 13 | 14 | 15 | 16 | 17 | 18 |
| 19 | 20 | 21 | 22 | 23 | 24 | 25 |
| 26 | 27 | 28 | 29 | 30 | 31 | |

**June**

| | | | | | | |
|---|---|---|---|---|---|---|
| | | | | | | 1 |
| 2 | 3 | 4 | 5 | 6 | 7 | 8 |
| 9 | 10 | 11 | 12 | 13 | 14 | 15 |
| 16 | 17 | 18 | 19 | 20 | 21 | 22 |
| 23 | 24 | 25 | 26 | 27 | 28 | 29 |
| 30 | | | | | | |

**July**

| | | | | | | |
|---|---|---|---|---|---|---|
| | 1 | 2 | 3 | 4 | 5 | 6 |
| 7 | 8 | 9 | 10 | 11 | 12 | 13 |
| 14 | 15 | 16 | 17 | 18 | 19 | 20 |
| 21 | 22 | 23 | 24 | 25 | 26 | 27 |
| 28 | 29 | 30 | 31 | | | |

**August**

| | | | | | | |
|---|---|---|---|---|---|---|
| | | | | 1 | 2 | 3 |
| 4 | 5 | 6 | 7 | 8 | 9 | 10 |
| 11 | 12 | 13 | 14 | 15 | 16 | 17 |
| 18 | 19 | 20 | 21 | 22 | 23 | 24 |
| 25 | 26 | 27 | 28 | 29 | 30 | 31 |

**September**

| | | | | | | |
|---|---|---|---|---|---|---|
| 1 | 2 | 3 | 4 | 5 | 6 | 7 |
| 8 | 9 | 10 | 11 | 12 | 13 | 14 |
| 15 | 16 | 17 | 18 | 19 | 20 | 21 |
| 22 | 23 | 24 | 25 | 26 | 27 | 28 |
| 29 | 30 | | | | | |

**October**

| | | | | | | |
|---|---|---|---|---|---|---|
| | | 1 | 2 | 3 | 4 | 5 |
| 6 | 7 | 8 | 9 | 10 | 11 | 12 |
| 13 | 14 | 15 | 16 | 17 | 18 | 19 |
| 20 | 21 | 22 | 23 | 24 | 25 | 26 |
| 27 | 28 | 29 | 30 | 31 | | |

**November**

| | | | | | | |
|---|---|---|---|---|---|---|
| | | | | | 1 | 2 |
| 3 | 4 | 5 | 6 | 7 | 8 | 9 |
| 10 | 11 | 12 | 13 | 14 | 15 | 16 |
| 17 | 18 | 19 | 20 | 21 | 22 | 23 |
| 24 | 25 | 26 | 27 | 28 | 29 | 30 |

**December**

| | | | | | | |
|---|---|---|---|---|---|---|
| 1 | 2 | 3 | 4 | 5 | 6 | 7 |
| 8 | 9 | 10 | 11 | 12 | 13 | 14 |
| 15 | 16 | 17 | 18 | 19 | 20 | 21 |
| 22 | 23 | 24 | 25 | 26 | 27 | 28 |
| 29 | 30 | 31 | | | | |

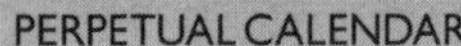

## E

**January**

| S | M | T | W | T | F | S |
|---|---|---|---|---|---|---|
| | | 1 | 2 | 3 | 4 | 5 |
| 6 | 7 | 8 | 9 | 10 | 11 | 12 |
| 13 | 14 | 15 | 16 | 17 | 18 | 19 |
| 20 | 21 | 22 | 23 | 24 | 25 | 26 |
| 27 | 28 | 29 | 30 | 31 | | |

**February**

| S | M | T | W | T | F | S |
|---|---|---|---|---|---|---|
| | | | | | 1 | 2 |
| 3 | 4 | 5 | 6 | 7 | 8 | 9 |
| 10 | 11 | 12 | 13 | 14 | 15 | 16 |
| 17 | 18 | 19 | 20 | 21 | 22 | 23 |
| 24 | 25 | 26 | 27 | 28 | | |

**March**

| S | M | T | W | T | F | S |
|---|---|---|---|---|---|---|
| | | | | | 1 | 2 |
| 3 | 4 | 5 | 6 | 7 | 8 | 9 |
| 10 | 11 | 12 | 13 | 14 | 15 | 16 |
| 17 | 18 | 19 | 20 | 21 | 22 | 23 |
| 24 | 25 | 26 | 27 | 28 | 29 | 30 |
| 31 | | | | | | |

**April**

| S | M | T | W | T | F | S |
|---|---|---|---|---|---|---|
| | 1 | 2 | 3 | 4 | 5 | 6 |
| 7 | 8 | 9 | 10 | 11 | 12 | 13 |
| 14 | 15 | 16 | 17 | 18 | 19 | 20 |
| 21 | 22 | 23 | 24 | 25 | 26 | 27 |
| 28 | 29 | 30 | | | | |

**May**

| S | M | T | W | T | F | S |
|---|---|---|---|---|---|---|
| | | | 1 | 2 | 3 | 4 |
| 5 | 6 | 7 | 8 | 9 | 10 | 11 |
| 12 | 13 | 14 | 15 | 16 | 17 | 18 |
| 19 | 20 | 21 | 22 | 23 | 24 | 25 |
| 26 | 27 | 28 | 29 | 30 | 31 | |

**June**

| S | M | T | W | T | F | S |
|---|---|---|---|---|---|---|
| | | | | | | 1 |
| 2 | 3 | 4 | 5 | 6 | 7 | 8 |
| 9 | 10 | 11 | 12 | 13 | 14 | 15 |
| 16 | 17 | 18 | 19 | 20 | 21 | 22 |
| 23 | 24 | 25 | 26 | 27 | 28 | 29 |
| 30 | | | | | | |

**July**

| S | M | T | W | T | F | S |
|---|---|---|---|---|---|---|
| | 1 | 2 | 3 | 4 | 5 | 6 |
| 7 | 8 | 9 | 10 | 11 | 12 | 13 |
| 14 | 15 | 16 | 17 | 18 | 19 | 20 |
| 21 | 22 | 23 | 24 | 25 | 26 | 27 |
| 28 | 29 | 30 | 31 | | | |

**August**

| S | M | T | W | T | F | S |
|---|---|---|---|---|---|---|
| | | | | 1 | 2 | 3 |
| 4 | 5 | 6 | 7 | 8 | 9 | 10 |
| 11 | 12 | 13 | 14 | 15 | 16 | 17 |
| 18 | 19 | 20 | 21 | 22 | 23 | 24 |
| 25 | 26 | 27 | 28 | 29 | 30 | 31 |

**September**

| S | M | T | W | T | F | S |
|---|---|---|---|---|---|---|
| 1 | 2 | 3 | 4 | 5 | 6 | 7 |
| 8 | 9 | 10 | 11 | 12 | 13 | 14 |
| 15 | 16 | 17 | 18 | 19 | 20 | 21 |
| 22 | 23 | 24 | 25 | 26 | 27 | 28 |
| 29 | 30 | | | | | |

**October**

| S | M | T | W | T | F | S |
|---|---|---|---|---|---|---|
| | | 1 | 2 | 3 | 4 | 5 |
| 6 | 7 | 8 | 9 | 10 | 11 | 12 |
| 13 | 14 | 15 | 16 | 17 | 18 | 19 |
| 20 | 21 | 22 | 23 | 24 | 25 | 26 |
| 27 | 28 | 29 | 30 | 31 | | |

**November**

| S | M | T | W | T | F | S |
|---|---|---|---|---|---|---|
| | | | | | 1 | 2 |
| 3 | 4 | 5 | 6 | 7 | 8 | 9 |
| 10 | 11 | 12 | 13 | 14 | 15 | 16 |
| 17 | 18 | 19 | 20 | 21 | 22 | 23 |
| 24 | 25 | 26 | 27 | 28 | 29 | 30 |

**December**

| S | M | T | W | T | F | S |
|---|---|---|---|---|---|---|
| 1 | 2 | 3 | 4 | 5 | 6 | 7 |
| 8 | 9 | 10 | 11 | 12 | 13 | 14 |
| 15 | 16 | 17 | 18 | 19 | 20 | 21 |
| 22 | 23 | 24 | 25 | 26 | 27 | 28 |
| 29 | 30 | 31 | | | | |

## F (leap year)

**January**

| S | M | T | W | T | F | S |
|---|---|---|---|---|---|---|
| | | 1 | 2 | 3 | 4 | 5 |
| 6 | 7 | 8 | 9 | 10 | 11 | 12 |
| 13 | 14 | 15 | 16 | 17 | 18 | 19 |
| 20 | 21 | 22 | 23 | 24 | 25 | 26 |
| 27 | 28 | 29 | 30 | 31 | | |

**February**

| S | M | T | W | T | F | S |
|---|---|---|---|---|---|---|
| | | | | | 1 | 2 |
| 3 | 4 | 5 | 6 | 7 | 8 | 9 |
| 10 | 11 | 12 | 13 | 14 | 15 | 16 |
| 17 | 18 | 19 | 20 | 21 | 22 | 23 |
| 24 | 25 | 26 | 27 | 28 | 29 | |

**March**

| S | M | T | W | T | F | S |
|---|---|---|---|---|---|---|
| | | | | | | 1 |
| 2 | 3 | 4 | 5 | 6 | 7 | 8 |
| 9 | 10 | 11 | 12 | 13 | 14 | 15 |
| 16 | 17 | 18 | 19 | 20 | 21 | 22 |
| 23 | 24 | 25 | 26 | 27 | 28 | 29 |
| 30 | 31 | | | | | |

**April**

| S | M | T | W | T | F | S |
|---|---|---|---|---|---|---|
| | | 1 | 2 | 3 | 4 | 5 |
| 6 | 7 | 8 | 9 | 10 | 11 | 12 |
| 13 | 14 | 15 | 16 | 17 | 18 | 19 |
| 20 | 21 | 22 | 23 | 24 | 25 | 26 |
| 27 | 28 | 29 | 30 | | | |

**May**

| S | M | T | W | T | F | S |
|---|---|---|---|---|---|---|
| | | | | 1 | 2 | 3 |
| 4 | 5 | 6 | 7 | 8 | 9 | 10 |
| 11 | 12 | 13 | 14 | 15 | 16 | 17 |
| 18 | 19 | 20 | 21 | 22 | 23 | 24 |
| 25 | 26 | 27 | 28 | 29 | 30 | 31 |

**June**

| S | M | T | W | T | F | S |
|---|---|---|---|---|---|---|
| 1 | 2 | 3 | 4 | 5 | 6 | 7 |
| 8 | 9 | 10 | 11 | 12 | 13 | 14 |
| 15 | 16 | 17 | 18 | 19 | 20 | 21 |
| 22 | 23 | 24 | 25 | 26 | 27 | 28 |
| 29 | 30 | | | | | |

**July**

| S | M | T | W | T | F | S |
|---|---|---|---|---|---|---|
| | | 1 | 2 | 3 | 4 | 5 |
| 6 | 7 | 8 | 9 | 10 | 11 | 12 |
| 13 | 14 | 15 | 16 | 17 | 18 | 19 |
| 20 | 21 | 22 | 23 | 24 | 25 | 26 |
| 27 | 28 | 29 | 30 | 31 | | |

**August**

| S | M | T | W | T | F | S |
|---|---|---|---|---|---|---|
| | | | | | 1 | 2 |
| 3 | 4 | 5 | 6 | 7 | 8 | 9 |
| 10 | 11 | 12 | 13 | 14 | 15 | 16 |
| 17 | 18 | 19 | 20 | 21 | 22 | 23 |
| 24 | 25 | 26 | 27 | 28 | 29 | 30 |
| 31 | | | | | | |

**September**

| S | M | T | W | T | F | S |
|---|---|---|---|---|---|---|
| | 1 | 2 | 3 | 4 | 5 | 6 |
| 7 | 8 | 9 | 10 | 11 | 12 | 13 |
| 14 | 15 | 16 | 17 | 18 | 19 | 20 |
| 21 | 22 | 23 | 24 | 25 | 26 | 27 |
| 28 | 29 | 30 | | | | |

**October**

| S | M | T | W | T | F | S |
|---|---|---|---|---|---|---|
| | | | 1 | 2 | 3 | 4 |
| 5 | 6 | 7 | 8 | 9 | 10 | 11 |
| 12 | 13 | 14 | 15 | 16 | 17 | 18 |
| 19 | 20 | 21 | 22 | 23 | 24 | 25 |
| 26 | 27 | 28 | 29 | 30 | 31 | |

**November**

| S | M | T | W | T | F | S |
|---|---|---|---|---|---|---|
| | | | | | | 1 |
| 2 | 3 | 4 | 5 | 6 | 7 | 8 |
| 9 | 10 | 11 | 12 | 13 | 14 | 15 |
| 16 | 17 | 18 | 19 | 20 | 21 | 22 |
| 23 | 24 | 25 | 26 | 27 | 28 | 29 |
| 30 | | | | | | |

**December**

| S | M | T | W | T | F | S |
|---|---|---|---|---|---|---|
| | 1 | 2 | 3 | 4 | 5 | 6 |
| 7 | 8 | 9 | 10 | 11 | 12 | 13 |
| 14 | 15 | 16 | 17 | 18 | 19 | 20 |
| 21 | 22 | 23 | 24 | 25 | 26 | 27 |
| 28 | 29 | 30 | 31 | | | |

## G

**January**

| S | M | T | W | T | F | S |
|---|---|---|---|---|---|---|
| | | | 1 | 2 | 3 | 4 |
| 5 | 6 | 7 | 8 | 9 | 10 | 11 |
| 12 | 13 | 14 | 15 | 16 | 17 | 18 |
| 19 | 20 | 21 | 22 | 23 | 24 | 25 |
| 26 | 27 | 28 | 29 | 30 | 31 | |

**February**

| S | M | T | W | T | F | S |
|---|---|---|---|---|---|---|
| | | | | | | 1 |
| 2 | 3 | 4 | 5 | 6 | 7 | 8 |
| 9 | 10 | 11 | 12 | 13 | 14 | 15 |
| 16 | 17 | 18 | 19 | 20 | 21 | 22 |
| 23 | 24 | 25 | 26 | 27 | 28 | |

**March**

| S | M | T | W | T | F | S |
|---|---|---|---|---|---|---|
| | | | | | | 1 |
| 2 | 3 | 4 | 5 | 6 | 7 | 8 |
| 9 | 10 | 11 | 12 | 13 | 14 | 15 |
| 16 | 17 | 18 | 19 | 20 | 21 | 22 |
| 23 | 24 | 25 | 26 | 27 | 28 | 29 |
| 30 | 31 | | | | | |

**April**

| S | M | T | W | T | F | S |
|---|---|---|---|---|---|---|
| | | 1 | 2 | 3 | 4 | 5 |
| 6 | 7 | 8 | 9 | 10 | 11 | 12 |
| 13 | 14 | 15 | 16 | 17 | 18 | 19 |
| 20 | 21 | 22 | 23 | 24 | 25 | 26 |
| 27 | 28 | 29 | 30 | | | |

**May**

| S | M | T | W | T | F | S |
|---|---|---|---|---|---|---|
| | | | | 1 | 2 | 3 |
| 4 | 5 | 6 | 7 | 8 | 9 | 10 |
| 11 | 12 | 13 | 14 | 15 | 16 | 17 |
| 18 | 19 | 20 | 21 | 22 | 23 | 24 |
| 25 | 26 | 27 | 28 | 29 | 30 | 31 |

**June**

| S | M | T | W | T | F | S |
|---|---|---|---|---|---|---|
| 1 | 2 | 3 | 4 | 5 | 6 | 7 |
| 8 | 9 | 10 | 11 | 12 | 13 | 14 |
| 15 | 16 | 17 | 18 | 19 | 20 | 21 |
| 22 | 23 | 24 | 25 | 26 | 27 | 28 |
| 29 | 30 | | | | | |

**July**

| S | M | T | W | T | F | S |
|---|---|---|---|---|---|---|
| | | 1 | 2 | 3 | 4 | 5 |
| 6 | 7 | 8 | 9 | 10 | 11 | 12 |
| 13 | 14 | 15 | 16 | 17 | 18 | 19 |
| 20 | 21 | 22 | 23 | 24 | 25 | 26 |
| 27 | 28 | 29 | 30 | 31 | | |

**August**

| S | M | T | W | T | F | S |
|---|---|---|---|---|---|---|
| | | | | | 1 | 2 |
| 3 | 4 | 5 | 6 | 7 | 8 | 9 |
| 10 | 11 | 12 | 13 | 14 | 15 | 16 |
| 17 | 18 | 19 | 20 | 21 | 22 | 23 |
| 24 | 25 | 26 | 27 | 28 | 29 | 30 |
| 31 | | | | | | |

**September**

| S | M | T | W | T | F | S |
|---|---|---|---|---|---|---|
| | 1 | 2 | 3 | 4 | 5 | 6 |
| 7 | 8 | 9 | 10 | 11 | 12 | 13 |
| 14 | 15 | 16 | 17 | 18 | 19 | 20 |
| 21 | 22 | 23 | 24 | 25 | 26 | 27 |
| 28 | 29 | 30 | | | | |

**October**

| S | M | T | W | T | F | S |
|---|---|---|---|---|---|---|
| | | | 1 | 2 | 3 | 4 |
| 5 | 6 | 7 | 8 | 9 | 10 | 11 |
| 12 | 13 | 14 | 15 | 16 | 17 | 18 |
| 19 | 20 | 21 | 22 | 23 | 24 | 25 |
| 26 | 27 | 28 | 29 | 30 | 31 | |

**November**

| S | M | T | W | T | F | S |
|---|---|---|---|---|---|---|
| | | | | | | 1 |
| 2 | 3 | 4 | 5 | 6 | 7 | 8 |
| 9 | 10 | 11 | 12 | 13 | 14 | 15 |
| 16 | 17 | 18 | 19 | 20 | 21 | 22 |
| 23 | 24 | 25 | 26 | 27 | 28 | 29 |
| 30 | | | | | | |

**December**

| S | M | T | W | T | F | S |
|---|---|---|---|---|---|---|
| | 1 | 2 | 3 | 4 | 5 | 6 |
| 7 | 8 | 9 | 10 | 11 | 12 | 13 |
| 14 | 15 | 16 | 17 | 18 | 19 | 20 |
| 21 | 22 | 23 | 24 | 25 | 26 | 27 |
| 28 | 29 | 30 | 31 | | | |

## H (leap year)

**January**

| S | M | T | W | T | F | S |
|---|---|---|---|---|---|---|
| | | | 1 | 2 | 3 | 4 |
| 5 | 6 | 7 | 8 | 9 | 10 | 11 |
| 12 | 13 | 14 | 15 | 16 | 17 | 18 |
| 19 | 20 | 21 | 22 | 23 | 24 | 25 |
| 26 | 27 | 28 | 29 | 30 | 31 | |

**February**

| S | M | T | W | T | F | S |
|---|---|---|---|---|---|---|
| | | | | | | 1 |
| 2 | 3 | 4 | 5 | 6 | 7 | 8 |
| 9 | 10 | 11 | 12 | 13 | 14 | 15 |
| 16 | 17 | 18 | 19 | 20 | 21 | 22 |
| 23 | 24 | 25 | 26 | 27 | 28 | 29 |

**March**

| S | M | T | W | T | F | S |
|---|---|---|---|---|---|---|
| 1 | 2 | 3 | 4 | 5 | 6 | 7 |
| 8 | 9 | 10 | 11 | 12 | 13 | 14 |
| 15 | 16 | 17 | 18 | 19 | 20 | 21 |
| 22 | 23 | 24 | 25 | 26 | 27 | 28 |
| 29 | 30 | 31 | | | | |

**April**

| S | M | T | W | T | F | S |
|---|---|---|---|---|---|---|
| | | | 1 | 2 | 3 | 4 |
| 5 | 6 | 7 | 8 | 9 | 10 | 11 |
| 12 | 13 | 14 | 15 | 16 | 17 | 18 |
| 19 | 20 | 21 | 22 | 23 | 24 | 25 |
| 26 | 27 | 28 | 29 | 30 | | |

**May**

| S | M | T | W | T | F | S |
|---|---|---|---|---|---|---|
| | | | | | 1 | 2 |
| 3 | 4 | 5 | 6 | 7 | 8 | 9 |
| 10 | 11 | 12 | 13 | 14 | 15 | 16 |
| 17 | 18 | 19 | 20 | 21 | 22 | 23 |
| 24 | 25 | 26 | 27 | 28 | 29 | 30 |
| 31 | | | | | | |

**June**

| S | M | T | W | T | F | S |
|---|---|---|---|---|---|---|
| | 1 | 2 | 3 | 4 | 5 | 6 |
| 7 | 8 | 9 | 10 | 11 | 12 | 13 |
| 14 | 15 | 16 | 17 | 18 | 19 | 20 |
| 21 | 22 | 23 | 24 | 25 | 26 | 27 |
| 28 | 29 | 30 | | | | |

**July**

| S | M | T | W | T | F | S |
|---|---|---|---|---|---|---|
| | | | 1 | 2 | 3 | 4 |
| 5 | 6 | 7 | 8 | 9 | 10 | 11 |
| 12 | 13 | 14 | 15 | 16 | 17 | 18 |
| 19 | 20 | 21 | 22 | 23 | 24 | 25 |
| 26 | 27 | 28 | 29 | 30 | 31 | |

**August**

| S | M | T | W | T | F | S |
|---|---|---|---|---|---|---|
| | | | | | | 1 |
| 2 | 3 | 4 | 5 | 6 | 7 | 8 |
| 9 | 10 | 11 | 12 | 13 | 14 | 15 |
| 16 | 17 | 18 | 19 | 20 | 21 | 22 |
| 23 | 24 | 25 | 26 | 27 | 28 | 29 |
| 30 | 31 | | | | | |

**September**

| S | M | T | W | T | F | S |
|---|---|---|---|---|---|---|
| | | 1 | 2 | 3 | 4 | 5 |
| 6 | 7 | 8 | 9 | 10 | 11 | 12 |
| 13 | 14 | 15 | 16 | 17 | 18 | 19 |
| 20 | 21 | 22 | 23 | 24 | 25 | 26 |
| 27 | 28 | 29 | 30 | | | |

**October**

| S | M | T | W | T | F | S |
|---|---|---|---|---|---|---|
| | | | | 1 | 2 | 3 |
| 4 | 5 | 6 | 7 | 8 | 9 | 10 |
| 11 | 12 | 13 | 14 | 15 | 16 | 17 |
| 18 | 19 | 20 | 21 | 22 | 23 | 24 |
| 25 | 26 | 27 | 28 | 29 | 30 | 31 |

**November**

| S | M | T | W | T | F | S |
|---|---|---|---|---|---|---|
| 1 | 2 | 3 | 4 | 5 | 6 | 7 |
| 8 | 9 | 10 | 11 | 12 | 13 | 14 |
| 15 | 16 | 17 | 18 | 19 | 20 | 21 |
| 22 | 23 | 24 | 25 | 26 | 27 | 28 |
| 29 | 30 | | | | | |

**December**

| S | M | T | W | T | F | S |
|---|---|---|---|---|---|---|
| | | 1 | 2 | 3 | 4 | 5 |
| 6 | 7 | 8 | 9 | 10 | 11 | 12 |
| 13 | 14 | 15 | 16 | 17 | 18 | 19 |
| 20 | 21 | 22 | 23 | 24 | 25 | 26 |
| 27 | 28 | 29 | 30 | 31 | | |

## PERPETUAL CALENDAR

### I

**January**

| S | M | T | W | T | F | S |
|---|---|---|---|---|---|---|
| | | | | 1 | 2 | 3 |
| 4 | 5 | 6 | 7 | 8 | 9 | 10 |
| 11 | 12 | 13 | 14 | 15 | 16 | 17 |
| 18 | 19 | 20 | 21 | 22 | 23 | 24 |
| 25 | 26 | 27 | 28 | 29 | 30 | 31 |

**February**

| S | M | T | W | T | F | S |
|---|---|---|---|---|---|---|
| 1 | 2 | 3 | 4 | 5 | 6 | 7 |
| 8 | 9 | 10 | 11 | 12 | 13 | 14 |
| 15 | 16 | 17 | 18 | 19 | 20 | 21 |
| 22 | 23 | 24 | 25 | 26 | 27 | 28 |

**March**

| S | M | T | W | T | F | S |
|---|---|---|---|---|---|---|
| 1 | 2 | 3 | 4 | 5 | 6 | 7 |
| 8 | 9 | 10 | 11 | 12 | 13 | 14 |
| 15 | 16 | 17 | 18 | 19 | 20 | 21 |
| 22 | 23 | 24 | 25 | 26 | 27 | 28 |
| 29 | 30 | 31 | | | | |

**April**

| S | M | T | W | T | F | S |
|---|---|---|---|---|---|---|
| | | | 1 | 2 | 3 | 4 |
| 5 | 6 | 7 | 8 | 9 | 10 | 11 |
| 12 | 13 | 14 | 15 | 16 | 17 | 18 |
| 19 | 20 | 21 | 22 | 23 | 24 | 25 |
| 26 | 27 | 28 | 29 | 30 | | |

**May**

| S | M | T | W | T | F | S |
|---|---|---|---|---|---|---|
| | | | | | 1 | 2 |
| 3 | 4 | 5 | 6 | 7 | 8 | 9 |
| 10 | 11 | 12 | 13 | 14 | 15 | 16 |
| 17 | 18 | 19 | 20 | 21 | 22 | 23 |
| 24 | 25 | 26 | 27 | 28 | 29 | 30 |
| 31 | | | | | | |

**June**

| S | M | T | W | T | F | S |
|---|---|---|---|---|---|---|
| | 1 | 2 | 3 | 4 | 5 | 6 |
| 7 | 8 | 9 | 10 | 11 | 12 | 13 |
| 14 | 15 | 16 | 17 | 18 | 19 | 20 |
| 21 | 22 | 23 | 24 | 25 | 26 | 27 |
| 28 | 29 | 30 | | | | |

**July**

| S | M | T | W | T | F | S |
|---|---|---|---|---|---|---|
| | | | 1 | 2 | 3 | 4 |
| 5 | 6 | 7 | 8 | 9 | 10 | 11 |
| 12 | 13 | 14 | 15 | 16 | 17 | 18 |
| 19 | 20 | 21 | 22 | 23 | 24 | 25 |
| 26 | 27 | 28 | 29 | 30 | 31 | |

**August**

| S | M | T | W | T | F | S |
|---|---|---|---|---|---|---|
| | | | | | | 1 |
| 2 | 3 | 4 | 5 | 6 | 7 | 8 |
| 9 | 10 | 11 | 12 | 13 | 14 | 15 |
| 16 | 17 | 18 | 19 | 20 | 21 | 22 |
| 23 | 24 | 25 | 26 | 27 | 28 | 29 |
| 30 | 31 | | | | | |

**September**

| S | M | T | W | T | F | S |
|---|---|---|---|---|---|---|
| | | 1 | 2 | 3 | 4 | 5 |
| 6 | 7 | 8 | 9 | 10 | 11 | 12 |
| 13 | 14 | 15 | 16 | 17 | 18 | 19 |
| 20 | 21 | 22 | 23 | 24 | 25 | 26 |
| 27 | 28 | 29 | 30 | | | |

**October**

| S | M | T | W | T | F | S |
|---|---|---|---|---|---|---|
| | | | | 1 | 2 | 3 |
| 4 | 5 | 6 | 7 | 8 | 9 | 10 |
| 11 | 12 | 13 | 14 | 15 | 16 | 17 |
| 18 | 19 | 20 | 21 | 22 | 23 | 24 |
| 25 | 26 | 27 | 28 | 29 | 30 | 31 |

**November**

| S | M | T | W | T | F | S |
|---|---|---|---|---|---|---|
| 1 | 2 | 3 | 4 | 5 | 6 | 7 |
| 8 | 9 | 10 | 11 | 12 | 13 | 14 |
| 15 | 16 | 17 | 18 | 19 | 20 | 21 |
| 22 | 23 | 24 | 25 | 26 | 27 | 28 |
| 29 | 30 | | | | | |

**December**

| S | M | T | W | T | F | S |
|---|---|---|---|---|---|---|
| | | 1 | 2 | 3 | 4 | 5 |
| 6 | 7 | 8 | 9 | 10 | 11 | 12 |
| 13 | 14 | 15 | 16 | 17 | 18 | 19 |
| 20 | 21 | 22 | 23 | 24 | 25 | 26 |
| 27 | 28 | 29 | 30 | 31 | | |

### J (leap year)

**January**

| S | M | T | W | T | F | S |
|---|---|---|---|---|---|---|
| | | | | 1 | 2 | 3 |
| 4 | 5 | 6 | 7 | 8 | 9 | 10 |
| 11 | 12 | 13 | 14 | 15 | 16 | 17 |
| 18 | 19 | 20 | 21 | 22 | 23 | 24 |
| 25 | 26 | 27 | 28 | 29 | 30 | 31 |

**February**

| S | M | T | W | T | F | S |
|---|---|---|---|---|---|---|
| 1 | 2 | 3 | 4 | 5 | 6 | 7 |
| 8 | 9 | 10 | 11 | 12 | 13 | 14 |
| 15 | 16 | 17 | 18 | 19 | 20 | 21 |
| 22 | 23 | 24 | 25 | 26 | 27 | 28 |
| 29 | | | | | | |

**March**

| S | M | T | W | T | F | S |
|---|---|---|---|---|---|---|
| | 1 | 2 | 3 | 4 | 5 | 6 |
| 7 | 8 | 9 | 10 | 11 | 12 | 13 |
| 14 | 15 | 16 | 17 | 18 | 19 | 20 |
| 21 | 22 | 23 | 24 | 25 | 26 | 27 |
| 28 | 29 | 30 | 31 | | | |

**April**

| S | M | T | W | T | F | S |
|---|---|---|---|---|---|---|
| | | | | 1 | 2 | 3 |
| 4 | 5 | 6 | 7 | 8 | 9 | 10 |
| 11 | 12 | 13 | 14 | 15 | 16 | 17 |
| 18 | 19 | 20 | 21 | 22 | 23 | 24 |
| 25 | 26 | 27 | 28 | 29 | 30 | |

**May**

| S | M | T | W | T | F | S |
|---|---|---|---|---|---|---|
| | | | | | | 1 |
| 2 | 3 | 4 | 5 | 6 | 7 | 8 |
| 9 | 10 | 11 | 12 | 13 | 14 | 15 |
| 16 | 17 | 18 | 19 | 20 | 21 | 22 |
| 23 | 24 | 25 | 26 | 27 | 28 | 29 |
| 30 | 31 | | | | | |

**June**

| S | M | T | W | T | F | S |
|---|---|---|---|---|---|---|
| | | 1 | 2 | 3 | 4 | 5 |
| 6 | 7 | 8 | 9 | 10 | 11 | 12 |
| 13 | 14 | 15 | 16 | 17 | 18 | 19 |
| 20 | 21 | 22 | 23 | 24 | 25 | 26 |
| 27 | 28 | 29 | 30 | | | |

**July**

| S | M | T | W | T | F | S |
|---|---|---|---|---|---|---|
| | | | | 1 | 2 | 3 |
| 4 | 5 | 6 | 7 | 8 | 9 | 10 |
| 11 | 12 | 13 | 14 | 15 | 16 | 17 |
| 18 | 19 | 20 | 21 | 22 | 23 | 24 |
| 25 | 26 | 27 | 28 | 29 | 30 | 31 |

**August**

| S | M | T | W | T | F | S |
|---|---|---|---|---|---|---|
| 1 | 2 | 3 | 4 | 5 | 6 | 7 |
| 8 | 9 | 10 | 11 | 12 | 13 | 14 |
| 15 | 16 | 17 | 18 | 19 | 20 | 21 |
| 22 | 23 | 24 | 25 | 26 | 27 | 28 |
| 29 | 30 | 31 | | | | |

**September**

| S | M | T | W | T | F | S |
|---|---|---|---|---|---|---|
| | | | 1 | 2 | 3 | 4 |
| 5 | 6 | 7 | 8 | 9 | 10 | 11 |
| 12 | 13 | 14 | 15 | 16 | 17 | 18 |
| 19 | 20 | 21 | 22 | 23 | 24 | 25 |
| 26 | 27 | 28 | 29 | 30 | | |

**October**

| S | M | T | W | T | F | S |
|---|---|---|---|---|---|---|
| | | | | | 1 | 2 |
| 3 | 4 | 5 | 6 | 7 | 8 | 9 |
| 10 | 11 | 12 | 13 | 14 | 15 | 16 |
| 17 | 18 | 19 | 20 | 21 | 22 | 23 |
| 24 | 25 | 26 | 27 | 28 | 29 | 30 |
| 31 | | | | | | |

**November**

| S | M | T | W | T | F | S |
|---|---|---|---|---|---|---|
| | 1 | 2 | 3 | 4 | 5 | 6 |
| 7 | 8 | 9 | 10 | 11 | 12 | 13 |
| 14 | 15 | 16 | 17 | 18 | 19 | 20 |
| 21 | 22 | 23 | 24 | 25 | 26 | 27 |
| 28 | 29 | 30 | | | | |

**December**

| S | M | T | W | T | F | S |
|---|---|---|---|---|---|---|
| | | | 1 | 2 | 3 | 4 |
| 5 | 6 | 7 | 8 | 9 | 10 | 11 |
| 12 | 13 | 14 | 15 | 16 | 17 | 18 |
| 19 | 20 | 21 | 22 | 23 | 24 | 25 |
| 26 | 27 | 28 | 29 | 30 | 31 | |

## K

**January**

| S | M | T | W | T | F | S |
|---|---|---|---|---|---|---|
| | | | | | 1 | 2 |
| 3 | 4 | 5 | 6 | 7 | 8 | 9 |
| 10 | 11 | 12 | 13 | 14 | 15 | 16 |
| 17 | 18 | 19 | 20 | 21 | 22 | 23 |
| 24 | 25 | 26 | 27 | 28 | 29 | 30 |
| 31 | | | | | | |

**February**

| S | M | T | W | T | F | S |
|---|---|---|---|---|---|---|
| | 1 | 2 | 3 | 4 | 5 | 6 |
| 7 | 8 | 9 | 10 | 11 | 12 | 13 |
| 14 | 15 | 16 | 17 | 18 | 19 | 20 |
| 21 | 22 | 23 | 24 | 25 | 26 | 27 |
| 28 | | | | | | |

**March**

| S | M | T | W | T | F | S |
|---|---|---|---|---|---|---|
| | 1 | 2 | 3 | 4 | 5 | 6 |
| 7 | 8 | 9 | 10 | 11 | 12 | 13 |
| 14 | 15 | 16 | 17 | 18 | 19 | 20 |
| 21 | 22 | 23 | 24 | 25 | 26 | 27 |
| 28 | 29 | 30 | 31 | | | |

**April**

| S | M | T | W | T | F | S |
|---|---|---|---|---|---|---|
| | | | | 1 | 2 | 3 |
| 4 | 5 | 6 | 7 | 8 | 9 | 10 |
| 11 | 12 | 13 | 14 | 15 | 16 | 17 |
| 18 | 19 | 20 | 21 | 22 | 23 | 24 |
| 25 | 26 | 27 | 28 | 29 | 30 | |

**May**

| S | M | T | W | T | F | S |
|---|---|---|---|---|---|---|
| | | | | | | 1 |
| 2 | 3 | 4 | 5 | 6 | 7 | 8 |
| 9 | 10 | 11 | 12 | 13 | 14 | 15 |
| 16 | 17 | 18 | 19 | 20 | 21 | 22 |
| 23 | 24 | 25 | 26 | 27 | 28 | 29 |
| 30 | 31 | | | | | |

**June**

| S | M | T | W | T | F | S |
|---|---|---|---|---|---|---|
| | | 1 | 2 | 3 | 4 | 5 |
| 6 | 7 | 8 | 9 | 10 | 11 | 12 |
| 13 | 14 | 15 | 16 | 17 | 18 | 19 |
| 20 | 21 | 22 | 23 | 24 | 25 | 26 |
| 27 | 28 | 29 | 30 | | | |

**July**

| S | M | T | W | T | F | S |
|---|---|---|---|---|---|---|
| | | | | 1 | 2 | 3 |
| 4 | 5 | 6 | 7 | 8 | 9 | 10 |
| 11 | 12 | 13 | 14 | 15 | 16 | 17 |
| 18 | 19 | 20 | 21 | 22 | 23 | 24 |
| 25 | 26 | 27 | 28 | 29 | 30 | 31 |

**August**

| S | M | T | W | T | F | S |
|---|---|---|---|---|---|---|
| 1 | 2 | 3 | 4 | 5 | 6 | 7 |
| 8 | 9 | 10 | 11 | 12 | 13 | 14 |
| 15 | 16 | 17 | 18 | 19 | 20 | 21 |
| 22 | 23 | 24 | 25 | 26 | 27 | 28 |
| 29 | 30 | 31 | | | | |

**September**

| S | M | T | W | T | F | S |
|---|---|---|---|---|---|---|
| | | | 1 | 2 | 3 | 4 |
| 5 | 6 | 7 | 8 | 9 | 10 | 11 |
| 12 | 13 | 14 | 15 | 16 | 17 | 18 |
| 19 | 20 | 21 | 22 | 23 | 24 | 25 |
| 26 | 27 | 28 | 29 | 30 | | |

**October**

| S | M | T | W | T | F | S |
|---|---|---|---|---|---|---|
| | | | | | 1 | 2 |
| 3 | 4 | 5 | 6 | 7 | 8 | 9 |
| 10 | 11 | 12 | 13 | 14 | 15 | 16 |
| 17 | 18 | 19 | 20 | 21 | 22 | 23 |
| 24 | 25 | 26 | 27 | 28 | 29 | 30 |
| 31 | | | | | | |

**November**

| S | M | T | W | T | F | S |
|---|---|---|---|---|---|---|
| | 1 | 2 | 3 | 4 | 5 | 6 |
| 7 | 8 | 9 | 10 | 11 | 12 | 13 |
| 14 | 15 | 16 | 17 | 18 | 19 | 20 |
| 21 | 22 | 23 | 24 | 25 | 26 | 27 |
| 28 | 29 | 30 | | | | |

**December**

| S | M | T | W | T | F | S |
|---|---|---|---|---|---|---|
| | | | 1 | 2 | 3 | 4 |
| 5 | 6 | 7 | 8 | 9 | 10 | 11 |
| 12 | 13 | 14 | 15 | 16 | 17 | 18 |
| 19 | 20 | 21 | 22 | 23 | 24 | 25 |
| 26 | 27 | 28 | 29 | 30 | 31 | |

## L (leap year)

**January**

| S | M | T | W | T | F | S |
|---|---|---|---|---|---|---|
| | | | | | 1 | 2 |
| 3 | 4 | 5 | 6 | 7 | 8 | 9 |
| 10 | 11 | 12 | 13 | 14 | 15 | 16 |
| 17 | 18 | 19 | 20 | 21 | 22 | 23 |
| 24 | 25 | 26 | 27 | 28 | 29 | 30 |
| 31 | | | | | | |

**February**

| S | M | T | W | T | F | S |
|---|---|---|---|---|---|---|
| | 1 | 2 | 3 | 4 | 5 | 6 |
| 7 | 8 | 9 | 10 | 11 | 12 | 13 |
| 14 | 15 | 16 | 17 | 18 | 19 | 20 |
| 21 | 22 | 23 | 24 | 25 | 26 | 27 |
| 28 | 29 | | | | | |

**March**

| S | M | T | W | T | F | S |
|---|---|---|---|---|---|---|
| | | 1 | 2 | 3 | 4 | 5 |
| 6 | 7 | 8 | 9 | 10 | 11 | 12 |
| 13 | 14 | 15 | 16 | 17 | 18 | 19 |
| 20 | 21 | 22 | 23 | 24 | 25 | 26 |
| 27 | 28 | 29 | 30 | 31 | | |

**April**

| S | M | T | W | T | F | S |
|---|---|---|---|---|---|---|
| | | | | | 1 | 2 |
| 3 | 4 | 5 | 6 | 7 | 8 | 9 |
| 10 | 11 | 12 | 13 | 14 | 15 | 16 |
| 17 | 18 | 19 | 20 | 21 | 22 | 23 |
| 24 | 25 | 26 | 27 | 28 | 29 | 30 |

**May**

| S | M | T | W | T | F | S |
|---|---|---|---|---|---|---|
| 1 | 2 | 3 | 4 | 5 | 6 | 7 |
| 8 | 9 | 10 | 11 | 12 | 13 | 14 |
| 15 | 16 | 17 | 18 | 19 | 20 | 21 |
| 22 | 23 | 24 | 25 | 26 | 27 | 28 |
| 29 | 30 | 31 | | | | |

**June**

| S | M | T | W | T | F | S |
|---|---|---|---|---|---|---|
| | | | 1 | 2 | 3 | 4 |
| 5 | 6 | 7 | 8 | 9 | 10 | 11 |
| 12 | 13 | 14 | 15 | 16 | 17 | 18 |
| 19 | 20 | 21 | 22 | 23 | 24 | 25 |
| 26 | 27 | 28 | 29 | 30 | | |

**July**

| S | M | T | W | T | F | S |
|---|---|---|---|---|---|---|
| | | | | | 1 | 2 |
| 3 | 4 | 5 | 6 | 7 | 8 | 9 |
| 10 | 11 | 12 | 13 | 14 | 15 | 16 |
| 17 | 18 | 19 | 20 | 21 | 22 | 23 |
| 24 | 25 | 26 | 27 | 28 | 29 | 30 |
| 31 | | | | | | |

**August**

| S | M | T | W | T | F | S |
|---|---|---|---|---|---|---|
| | 1 | 2 | 3 | 4 | 5 | 6 |
| 7 | 8 | 9 | 10 | 11 | 12 | 13 |
| 14 | 15 | 16 | 17 | 18 | 19 | 20 |
| 21 | 22 | 23 | 24 | 25 | 26 | 27 |
| 28 | 29 | 30 | 31 | | | |

**September**

| S | M | T | W | T | F | S |
|---|---|---|---|---|---|---|
| | | | | 1 | 2 | 3 |
| 4 | 5 | 6 | 7 | 8 | 9 | 10 |
| 11 | 12 | 13 | 14 | 15 | 16 | 17 |
| 18 | 19 | 20 | 21 | 22 | 23 | 24 |
| 25 | 26 | 27 | 28 | 29 | 30 | |

**October**

| S | M | T | W | T | F | S |
|---|---|---|---|---|---|---|
| | | | | | | 1 |
| 2 | 3 | 4 | 5 | 6 | 7 | 8 |
| 9 | 10 | 11 | 12 | 13 | 14 | 15 |
| 16 | 17 | 18 | 19 | 20 | 21 | 22 |
| 23 | 24 | 25 | 26 | 27 | 28 | 29 |
| 30 | 31 | | | | | |

**November**

| S | M | T | W | T | F | S |
|---|---|---|---|---|---|---|
| | | 1 | 2 | 3 | 4 | 5 |
| 6 | 7 | 8 | 9 | 10 | 11 | 12 |
| 13 | 14 | 15 | 16 | 17 | 18 | 19 |
| 20 | 21 | 22 | 23 | 24 | 25 | 26 |
| 27 | 28 | 29 | 30 | | | |

**December**

| S | M | T | W | T | F | S |
|---|---|---|---|---|---|---|
| | | | | 1 | 2 | 3 |
| 4 | 5 | 6 | 7 | 8 | 9 | 10 |
| 11 | 12 | 13 | 14 | 15 | 16 | 17 |
| 18 | 19 | 20 | 21 | 22 | 23 | 24 |
| 25 | 26 | 27 | 28 | 29 | 30 | 31 |

## PERPETUAL CALENDAR

### M

**January**

| S | M | T | W | T | F | S |
|---|---|---|---|---|---|---|
| | | | | | | 1 |
| 2 | 3 | 4 | 5 | 6 | 7 | 8 |
| 9 | 10 | 11 | 12 | 13 | 14 | 15 |
| 16 | 17 | 18 | 19 | 20 | 21 | 22 |
| 23 | 24 | 25 | 26 | 27 | 28 | 29 |
| 30 | 31 | | | | | |

**February**

| S | M | T | W | T | F | S |
|---|---|---|---|---|---|---|
| | | 1 | 2 | 3 | 4 | 5 |
| 6 | 7 | 8 | 9 | 10 | 11 | 12 |
| 13 | 14 | 15 | 16 | 17 | 18 | 19 |
| 20 | 21 | 22 | 23 | 24 | 25 | 26 |
| 27 | 28 | | | | | |

**March**

| S | M | T | W | T | F | S |
|---|---|---|---|---|---|---|
| | | 1 | 2 | 3 | 4 | 5 |
| 6 | 7 | 8 | 9 | 10 | 11 | 12 |
| 13 | 14 | 15 | 16 | 17 | 18 | 19 |
| 20 | 21 | 22 | 23 | 24 | 25 | 26 |
| 27 | 28 | 29 | 30 | 31 | | |

**April**

| S | M | T | W | T | F | S |
|---|---|---|---|---|---|---|
| | | | | | 1 | 2 |
| 3 | 4 | 5 | 6 | 7 | 8 | 9 |
| 10 | 11 | 12 | 13 | 14 | 15 | 16 |
| 17 | 18 | 19 | 20 | 21 | 22 | 23 |
| 24 | 25 | 26 | 27 | 28 | 29 | 30 |

**May**

| | | | | | | |
|---|---|---|---|---|---|---|
| 1 | 2 | 3 | 4 | 5 | 6 | 7 |
| 8 | 9 | 10 | 11 | 12 | 13 | 14 |
| 15 | 16 | 17 | 18 | 19 | 20 | 21 |
| 22 | 23 | 24 | 25 | 26 | 27 | 28 |
| 29 | 30 | 31 | | | | |

**June**

| | | | | | | |
|---|---|---|---|---|---|---|
| | | | 1 | 2 | 3 | 4 |
| 5 | 6 | 7 | 8 | 9 | 10 | 11 |
| 12 | 13 | 14 | 15 | 16 | 17 | 18 |
| 19 | 20 | 21 | 22 | 23 | 24 | 25 |
| 26 | 27 | 28 | 29 | 30 | | |

**July**

| | | | | | | |
|---|---|---|---|---|---|---|
| | | | | | 1 | 2 |
| 3 | 4 | 5 | 6 | 7 | 8 | 9 |
| 10 | 11 | 12 | 13 | 14 | 15 | 16 |
| 17 | 18 | 19 | 20 | 21 | 22 | 23 |
| 24 | 25 | 26 | 27 | 28 | 29 | 30 |
| 31 | | | | | | |

**August**

| | | | | | | |
|---|---|---|---|---|---|---|
| | 1 | 2 | 3 | 4 | 5 | 6 |
| 7 | 8 | 9 | 10 | 11 | 12 | 13 |
| 14 | 15 | 16 | 17 | 18 | 19 | 20 |
| 21 | 22 | 23 | 24 | 25 | 26 | 27 |
| 28 | 29 | 30 | 31 | | | |

**September**

| | | | | | | |
|---|---|---|---|---|---|---|
| | | | | 1 | 2 | 3 |
| 4 | 5 | 6 | 7 | 8 | 9 | 10 |
| 11 | 12 | 13 | 14 | 15 | 16 | 17 |
| 18 | 19 | 20 | 21 | 22 | 23 | 24 |
| 25 | 26 | 27 | 28 | 29 | 30 | |

**October**

| | | | | | | |
|---|---|---|---|---|---|---|
| | | | | | | 1 |
| 2 | 3 | 4 | 5 | 6 | 7 | 8 |
| 9 | 10 | 11 | 12 | 13 | 14 | 15 |
| 16 | 17 | 18 | 19 | 20 | 21 | 22 |
| 23 | 24 | 25 | 26 | 27 | 28 | 29 |
| 30 | 31 | | | | | |

**November**

| | | | | | | |
|---|---|---|---|---|---|---|
| | | 1 | 2 | 3 | 4 | 5 |
| 6 | 7 | 8 | 9 | 10 | 11 | 12 |
| 13 | 14 | 15 | 16 | 17 | 18 | 19 |
| 20 | 21 | 22 | 23 | 24 | 25 | 26 |
| 27 | 28 | 29 | 30 | | | |

**December**

| | | | | | | |
|---|---|---|---|---|---|---|
| | | | | 1 | 2 | 3 |
| 4 | 5 | 6 | 7 | 8 | 9 | 10 |
| 11 | 12 | 13 | 14 | 15 | 16 | 17 |
| 18 | 19 | 20 | 21 | 22 | 23 | 24 |
| 25 | 26 | 27 | 28 | 29 | 30 | 31 |

### N (leap year)

**January**

| S | M | T | W | T | F | S |
|---|---|---|---|---|---|---|
| | | | | | | 1 |
| 2 | 3 | 4 | 5 | 6 | 7 | 8 |
| 9 | 10 | 11 | 12 | 13 | 14 | 15 |
| 16 | 17 | 18 | 19 | 20 | 21 | 22 |
| 23 | 24 | 25 | 26 | 27 | 28 | 29 |
| 30 | 31 | | | | | |

**February**

| S | M | T | W | T | F | S |
|---|---|---|---|---|---|---|
| | | 1 | 2 | 3 | 4 | 5 |
| 6 | 7 | 8 | 9 | 10 | 11 | 12 |
| 13 | 14 | 15 | 16 | 17 | 18 | 19 |
| 20 | 21 | 22 | 23 | 24 | 25 | 26 |
| 27 | 28 | 29 | | | | |

**March**

| S | M | T | W | T | F | S |
|---|---|---|---|---|---|---|
| | | | 1 | 2 | 3 | 4 |
| 5 | 6 | 7 | 8 | 9 | 10 | 11 |
| 12 | 13 | 14 | 15 | 16 | 17 | 18 |
| 19 | 20 | 21 | 22 | 23 | 24 | 25 |
| 26 | 27 | 28 | 29 | 30 | 31 | |

**April**

| S | M | T | W | T | F | S |
|---|---|---|---|---|---|---|
| | | | | | | 1 |
| 2 | 3 | 4 | 5 | 6 | 7 | 8 |
| 9 | 10 | 11 | 12 | 13 | 14 | 15 |
| 16 | 17 | 18 | 19 | 20 | 21 | 22 |
| 23 | 24 | 25 | 26 | 27 | 28 | 29 |
| 30 | | | | | | |

**May**

| | | | | | | |
|---|---|---|---|---|---|---|
| | 1 | 2 | 3 | 4 | 5 | 6 |
| 7 | 8 | 9 | 10 | 11 | 12 | 13 |
| 14 | 15 | 16 | 17 | 18 | 19 | 20 |
| 21 | 22 | 23 | 24 | 25 | 26 | 27 |
| 28 | 29 | 30 | 31 | | | |

**June**

| | | | | | | |
|---|---|---|---|---|---|---|
| | | | | 1 | 2 | 3 |
| 4 | 5 | 6 | 7 | 8 | 9 | 10 |
| 11 | 12 | 13 | 14 | 15 | 16 | 17 |
| 18 | 19 | 20 | 21 | 22 | 23 | 24 |
| 25 | 26 | 27 | 28 | 29 | 30 | |

**July**

| | | | | | | |
|---|---|---|---|---|---|---|
| | | | | | | 1 |
| 2 | 3 | 4 | 5 | 6 | 7 | 8 |
| 9 | 10 | 11 | 12 | 13 | 14 | 15 |
| 16 | 17 | 18 | 19 | 20 | 21 | 22 |
| 23 | 24 | 25 | 26 | 27 | 28 | 29 |
| 30 | 31 | | | | | |

**August**

| | | | | | | |
|---|---|---|---|---|---|---|
| | | 1 | 2 | 3 | 4 | 5 |
| 6 | 7 | 8 | 9 | 10 | 11 | 12 |
| 13 | 14 | 15 | 16 | 17 | 18 | 19 |
| 20 | 21 | 22 | 23 | 24 | 25 | 26 |
| 27 | 28 | 29 | 30 | 31 | | |

**September**

| | | | | | | |
|---|---|---|---|---|---|---|
| | | | | | 1 | 2 |
| 3 | 4 | 5 | 6 | 7 | 8 | 9 |
| 10 | 11 | 12 | 13 | 14 | 15 | 16 |
| 17 | 18 | 19 | 20 | 21 | 22 | 23 |
| 24 | 25 | 26 | 27 | 28 | 29 | 30 |

**October**

| | | | | | | |
|---|---|---|---|---|---|---|
| 1 | 2 | 3 | 4 | 5 | 6 | 7 |
| 8 | 9 | 10 | 11 | 12 | 13 | 14 |
| 15 | 16 | 17 | 18 | 19 | 20 | 21 |
| 22 | 23 | 24 | 25 | 26 | 27 | 28 |
| 29 | 30 | 31 | | | | |

**November**

| | | | | | | |
|---|---|---|---|---|---|---|
| | | | 1 | 2 | 3 | 4 |
| 5 | 6 | 7 | 8 | 9 | 10 | 11 |
| 12 | 13 | 14 | 15 | 16 | 17 | 18 |
| 19 | 20 | 21 | 22 | 23 | 24 | 25 |
| 26 | 27 | 28 | 29 | 30 | | |

**December**

| | | | | | | |
|---|---|---|---|---|---|---|
| | | | | | 1 | 2 |
| 3 | 4 | 5 | 6 | 7 | 8 | 9 |
| 10 | 11 | 12 | 13 | 14 | 15 | 16 |
| 17 | 18 | 19 | 20 | 21 | 22 | 23 |
| 24 | 25 | 26 | 27 | 28 | 29 | 30 |
| 31 | | | | | | |

## International time differences

The time zones of the world are conventionally measured from longitude 0° at Greenwich Observatory (Greenwich Mean Time, GMT).

Each 15° of longitude east of this point is one hour ahead of GMT (eg when it is 2pm in London it is 3pm or later in time zones to the east). Hours ahead of GMT are shown by a plus sign, eg + 3, + 4/8.

Each 15° west of this point is one hour behind GMT (eg 2pm in London would be 1pm or earlier in time zones to the west). Hours behind GMT are shown by a minus sign, eg - 3, - 4/8.

Some countries adopt time zones that vary from standard time. Also, during the summer, several countries adopt Daylight Saving Time (or Summer Time), which is one hour ahead of the times shown below.

| Country | Time difference |
|---|---|
| Afghanistan | $+4\frac{1}{2}$ |
| Albania | +1 |
| Algeria | +1 |
| Andorra | +1 |
| Angola | +1 |
| Antigua and Barbuda | -4 |
| Argentina | -3 |
| Armenia | +4 |
| Australia | $+8/10\frac{1}{2}$ |
| Austria | +1 |
| Azerbaijan | +4 |
| Bahamas, The | -5 |
| Bahrain | +3 |
| Bangladesh | +6 |
| Barbados | -4 |
| Belarus | +2 |
| Belgium | +1 |
| Belize | -6 |
| Benin | +1 |
| Bermuda | -4 |
| Bhutan | +6 |
| Bolivia | -4 |
| Bosnia-Herzegovina | +1 |
| Botswana | +2 |
| Brazil | -2/5 |
| Brunei | +8 |
| Bulgaria | +2 |
| Burkina Faso | 0 |
| Burundi | +2 |
| Cambodia | +7 |
| Cameroon | +1 |
| Canada | $-3\frac{1}{2}/8$ |
| Cape Verde | -1 |
| Central African Republic | +1 |
| Chad | +1 |
| Chile | -4 |
| China | +8 |
| Colombia | -5 |
| Comoros | +3 |
| Congo | +1 |
| Congo, Democratic Republic of | +1/2 |
| Costa Rica | -6 |
| Côte d'Ivoire | 0 |
| Croatia | +1 |
| Cuba | -5 |
| Cyprus | +2 |
| Czech Republic | +1 |
| Denmark | +1 |
| Djibouti | +3 |
| Dominica | -4 |
| Dominican Republic | -4 |
| Ecuador | -5 |
| Egypt | +2 |
| El Salvador | -6 |
| Equatorial Guinea | +1 |
| Eritrea | +3 |
| Estonia | +2 |
| Ethiopia | +3 |
| Falkland Is | -4 |
| Fiji | +12 |
| Finland | +2 |
| France | +1 |
| Gabon | +1 |
| Gambia, The | 0 |
| Georgia | +4 |
| Germany | +1 |
| Ghana | 0 |
| Gibraltar | +1 |
| Greece | +2 |
| Greenland | -3 |
| Grenada | -4 |
| Guatemala | -6 |
| Guinea | 0 |
| Guinea-Bissau | 0 |
| Guyana | -4 |
| Haiti | -5 |
| Honduras | -6 |
| Hong Kong | +8 |
| Hungary | +1 |
| Iceland | 0 |
| India | $+5\frac{1}{2}$ |
| Indonesia | +7/9 |
| Iran | $+3\frac{1}{2}$ |
| Iraq | +3 |
| Ireland | 0 |
| Israel | +2 |
| Italy | +1 |
| Jamaica | -5 |
| Japan | +9 |
| Jordan | +2 |
| Kazakhstan | +4/6 |
| Kenya | +3 |
| Kiribati | +12 |
| Korea, Democratic People's Republic of (North Korea) | +9 |
| Korea, Republic of (South Korea) | +9 |
| Kuwait | +3 |
| Kyrgyzstan | +5 |
| Laos | +7 |
| Latvia | +2 |
| Lebanon | +2 |
| Lesotho | +2 |
| Liberia | 0 |
| Libya | +1 |
| Liechtenstein | +1 |
| Lithuania | +2 |
| Luxembourg | +1 |
| Macedonia | +1 |
| Madagascar | +3 |
| Malawi | +2 |
| Malaysia | +8 |
| Maldives | +5 |
| Mali | 0 |
| Malta | +1 |
| Marshall Is | +12 |
| Mauritania | 0 |
| Mauritius | +4 |
| Mexico | -6/8 |
| Moldova | +2 |
| Monaco | +1 |
| Morocco | 0 |
| Mozambique | +2 |
| Myanmar (Burma) | $+6\frac{1}{2}$ |
| Namibia | +1 |
| Nauru | +12 |
| Nepal | $+5\frac{3}{4}$ |
| Netherlands | +1 |
| New Zealand | +12 |
| Nicaragua | -6 |
| Niger | +1 |
| Nigeria | +1 |
| Norway | +1 |
| Oman | +4 |
| Pakistan | +5 |
| Panama | -5 |
| Papua New Guinea | +10 |
| Paraguay | -4 |
| Peru | -5 |
| Philippines | +8 |
| Poland | +1 |
| Portugal | 0 |
| Qatar | +3 |
| Romania | +2 |
| Russia | +2/12 |
| Rwanda | +2 |
| St Kitts and Nevis | -4 |
| St Lucia | -4 |
| St Vincent and the Grenadines | -4 |
| Samoa | -11 |
| San Marino | +1 |
| São Tomé and Príncipe | 0 |
| Saudi Arabia | +3 |
| Senegal | 0 |
| Seychelles | +4 |
| Sierra Leone | 0 |
| Singapore | +8 |
| Slovakia | +1 |
| Slovenia | +1 |
| Solomon Is | +11 |
| Somalia | +3 |
| South Africa | +2 |
| Spain | +1 |
| Sri Lanka | $+5\frac{1}{2}$ |
| Sudan, The | +2 |
| Suriname | -3 |
| Swaziland | +2 |
| Sweden | +1 |
| Switzerland | +1 |
| Syria | +2 |
| Taiwan | +8 |
| Tajikistan | +5 |
| Tanzania | +3 |
| Thailand | +7 |
| Togo | 0 |
| Tonga | +13 |
| Trinidad and Tobago | -4 |
| Tunisia | +1 |
| Turkey | +2 |
| Turkmenistan | +5 |
| Tuvalu | +12 |
| Uganda | +3 |
| Ukraine | +2 |
| United Arab Emirates | +4 |
| UK | 0 |
| Uruguay | -3 |
| USA | -5/10 |
| Uzbekistan | +5 |
| Vanuatu | +11 |
| Venezuela | -4 |
| Vietnam | +7 |
| Yemen | +3 |
| Yugoslavia, Federal Republic of | +1 |
| Zambia | +2 |
| Zimbabwe | +2 |

# Year equivalents

## Jewish[1] (AM)

| | |
|---|---|
| 5756 | (25 Sep 1995–13 Sep 1996) |
| 5757 | (14 Sep 1996–1 Oct 1997) |
| 5758 | (2 Oct 1997–20 Sep 1998) |
| 5759 | (21 Sep 1998–10 Sep 1999) |
| 5760 | (11 Sep 1999–29 Sep 2000) |
| 5761 | (30 Sep 2000–17 Sep 2001) |
| 5762 | (18 Sep 2001–6 Sep 2002) |
| 5763 | (7 Sep 2002–26 Sep 2003) |
| 5764 | (27 Sep 2003–15 Sep 2004) |
| 5765 | (16 Sep 2004–3 Oct 2005) |
| 5766 | (4 Oct 2005–22 Sep 2006) |
| 5767 | (23 Sep 2006–12 Sep 2007) |
| 5768 | (13 Sep 2007–29 Sep 2008) |
| 5769 | (30 Sep 2008–18 Sep 2009) |
| 5770 | (19 Sep 2009–8 Sep 2010) |
| 5771 | (9 Sep 2010–28 Sep 2011) |
| 5772 | (29 Sep 2011–16 Sep 2012) |
| 5773 | (17 Sep 2012–4 Sep 2013) |
| 5774 | (5 Sep 2013–24 Sep 2014) |
| 5775 | (25 Sep 2014–13 Sep 2015) |
| 5776 | (14 Sep 2015–2 Oct 2016) |
| 5777 | (3 Oct 2016–20 Sep 2017) |
| 5778 | (21 Sep 2017–9 Sep 2018) |
| 5779 | (10 Sep 2018–29 Sep 2019) |
| 5780 | (30 Sep 2019–18 Sep 2020) |

## Islamic[2] (H)

| | |
|---|---|
| 1416 | (31 May 1995–18 May 1996) |
| 1417 | (19 May 1996–8 May 1997) |
| 1418 | (9 May 1997–27 Apr 1998) |
| 1419 | (28 Apr 1998–16 Apr 1999) |
| 1420 | (17 Apr 1999–5 Apr 2000) |
| 1421 | (6 Apr 2000–25 Mar 2001) |
| 1422 | (26 Mar 2001–14 Mar 2002) |
| 1423 | (15 Mar 2002–3 Mar 2003) |
| 1424 | (4 Mar 2003–21 Feb 2004) |
| 1425 | (22 Feb 2004–9 Feb 2005) |
| 1426 | (10 Feb 2005–30 Jan 2006) |
| 1427 | (31 Jan 2006–20 Jan 2007) |
| 1428 | (21 Jan 2007–9 Jan 2008) |
| 1429 | (10 Jan 2008–28 Dec 2008) |
| 1430 | (29 Dec 2008–17 Dec 2009) |
| 1431 | (18 Dec 2009–6 Dec 2010) |
| 1432 | (7 Dec 2010–26 Nov 2011) |
| 1433 | (27 Nov 2011–14 Nov 2012) |
| 1434 | (15 Nov 2012–4 Nov 2013) |
| 1435 | (5 Nov 2013–24 Oct 2014) |
| 1436 | (25 Oct 2014–13 Oct 2015) |
| 1437 | (14 Oct 2015–1 Oct 2016) |
| 1438 | (2 Oct 2016–21 Sep 2017) |
| 1439 | (22 Sep 2017–10 Sep 2018) |
| 1440 | (11 Sep 2018–31 Aug 2019) |
| 1441 | (1 Sep 2019–19 Aug 2020) |

## Hindu[3] (SE)

| | |
|---|---|
| 1917 | (22 Mar 1995–20 Mar 1996) |
| 1918 | (21 Mar 1996–21 Mar 1997) |
| 1919 | (22 Mar 1997–21 Mar 1998) |
| 1920 | (22 Mar 1998–21 Mar 1999) |
| 1921 | (22 Mar 1999–20 Mar 2000) |
| 1922 | (21 Mar 2000–21 Mar 2001) |
| 1923 | (22 Mar 2001–21 Mar 2002) |
| 1924 | (22 Mar 2002–21 Mar 2003) |
| 1925 | (22 Mar 2003–20 Mar 2004) |
| 1926 | (21 Mar 2004–21 Mar 2005) |
| 1927 | (22 Mar 2005–21 Mar 2006) |
| 1928 | (22 Mar 2006–21 Mar 2007) |
| 1929 | (22 Mar 2007–20 Mar 2008) |
| 1930 | (21 Mar 2008–21 Mar 2009) |
| 1931 | (22 Mar 2009–21 Mar 2010) |
| 1932 | (22 Mar 2010–21 Mar 2011) |
| 1933 | (22 Mar 2011–20 Mar 2012) |
| 1934 | (21 Mar 2012–21 Mar 2013) |
| 1935 | (22 Mar 2013–21 Mar 2014) |
| 1936 | (22 Mar 2014–21 Mar 2015) |
| 1937 | (22 Mar 2015–20 Mar 2016) |
| 1938 | (21 Mar 2016–21 Mar 2017) |
| 1939 | (22 Mar 2017–21 Mar 2018) |
| 1940 | (22 Mar 2018–21 Mar 2019) |
| 1941 | (22 Mar 2019–20 Mar 2020) |

### Hindu[4] (VE)

| | |
|---|---|
| 2052 | (14 Mar 1995–13 Mar 1996) |
| 2053 | (14 Mar 1996–13 Mar 1997) |
| 2054 | (14 Mar 1997–13 Mar 1998) |
| 2055 | (14 Mar 1998–13 Mar 1999) |
| 2056 | (14 Mar 1999–13 Mar 2000) |
| 2057 | (14 Mar 2000–13 Mar 2001) |
| 2058 | (14 Mar 2001–13 Mar 2002) |
| 2059 | (14 Mar 2002–13 Mar 2003) |
| 2060 | (14 Mar 2003–13 Mar 2004) |
| 2061 | (14 Mar 2004–13 Mar 2005) |
| 2062 | (14 Mar 2005–13 Mar 2006) |
| 2063 | (14 Mar 2006–13 Mar 2007) |
| 2064 | (14 Mar 2007–13 Mar 2008) |
| 2065 | (14 Mar 2008–13 Mar 2009) |
| 2066 | (14 Mar 2009–13 Mar 2010) |
| 2067 | (14 Mar 2010–13 Mar 2011) |
| 2068 | (14 Mar 2011–13 Mar 2012) |
| 2069 | (14 Mar 2012–13 Mar 2013) |
| 2070 | (14 Mar 2013–13 Mar 2014) |
| 2071 | (14 Mar 2014–13 Mar 2015) |
| 2072 | (14 Mar 2015–13 Mar 2016) |
| 2073 | (14 Mar 2016–13 Mar 2017) |
| 2074 | (14 Mar 2017–13 Mar 2018) |
| 2075 | (14 Mar 2018–13 Mar 2019) |
| 2076 | (14 Mar 2019–13 Mar 2020) |

Gregorian equivalents are given in parentheses and are AD (= Anno Domini, also called CE, Common Era).

[1] Calculated from 3761BC (= Before Christ, also called BCE, Before Common Era), said to be the year of the creation of the world. AM = Anno Mundi.

[2] Calculated from AD622, the year in which the Prophet went from Mecca to Medina. H = Hegira.

[3] Calculated from AD78, the beginning of the Saka era (SE), used alongside Gregorian dates in Government of India publications since 22 Mar 1957.

[4] Calculated from 58BC, the beginning of the Vikrama era (VE). Other important Hindu eras include: Kalacuri era (AD248), Gupta era (AD320), and Harsa era (AD606).

## Month equivalents

Gregorian equivalents to other calendars are given in parentheses; the figures refer to the number of solar days in each month.

### Gregorian

(Basis: Sun)
January (31)
February (28 or 29)
March (31)
April (30)
May (31)
June (30)
July (31)
August (31)
September (30)
October (31)
November (30)
December (31)

### Jewish

(Basis: Moon)
Tishri (Sep – Oct) (30)
Heshvan (Oct – Nov) (29 or 30)
Kislev (Nov – Dec) (29 or 30)
Tevet (Dec – Jan) (29)
Shevat (Jan – Feb) (30)
Adar (Feb – Mar) (29 or 30)
Adar Sheni (*leap years only*)
Nisan (Mar – Apr) (30)
Iyar (Apr – May) (29)
Sivan (May – Jun) (30)
Tammuz (Jun – Jul) (29)
Av (Jul – Aug) (30)
Elul (Aug – Sep) (29)

### Islamic

(Basis: Moon)
Muharram (Sep – Oct) (30)
Safar (Oct – Nov) (29)
Rabi I (Nov – Dec) (30)
Rabi II (Dec – Jan) (29)
Jumada I (Jan – Feb) (30)
Jumada II (Feb – Mar) (29)
Rajab (Mar – Apr) (30)
Shaban (Apr – May) (29)
Ramadan (May – Jun) (30)
Shawwal (Jun – Jul) (29)
Dhu al-Qadah (Jul – Aug) (30)
Dhu al-Hijjah (Aug – Sep) (29 or 30)

### Hindu

(Basis: Moon)
Chaitra (Mar – Apr) (29 or 30)
Vaisakha (Apr – May) (29 or 30)
Jyaistha (May – Jun) (29 or 30)
Asadha (Jun – Jul) (29 or 30)
Dvitiya Asadha (*certain leap years*)
Sravana (Jul – Aug) (29 or 30)
Dvitiya Sravana (*certain leap years*)
Bhadrapada (Aug – Sep) (29 or 30)
Asvina (Sep – Oct) (29 or 30)
Karttika (Oct – Nov) (29 or 30)
Margasirsa (Nov – Dec) (29 or 30)
Pausa (Dec – Jan) (29 or 30)
Magha (Jan – Feb) (29 or 30)
Phalguna (Feb – Mar) (29 or 30)

## The seasons

| N Hemisphere | S Hemisphere | Duration |
|---|---|---|
| Spring | Autumn | From vernal/autumnal equinox (c.21 Mar) to summer/winter solstice (c.21 Jun) |
| Summer | Winter | From summer/winter solstice (c.21 Jun) to autumnal/spring equinox (c.23 Sep) |
| Autumn | Spring | From autumnal/spring equinox (c.23 Sep) to winter/summer solstice (c.21 Dec) |
| Winter | Summer | From winter/summer solstice (c.21 Dec) to vernal/autumnal equinox (c.21 Mar) |

## Months (Associations of gems and flowers)

In many Western countries, the months are traditionally associated with gemstones and flowers. There is considerable variation between countries. The following combinations are widely recognized in North America and the UK.

| Month | Gemstone | Flower |
|---|---|---|
| January | Garnet | Carnation, Snowdrop |
| February | Amethyst | Primrose, Violet |
| March | Aquamarine, Bloodstone | Jonquil, Violet |
| April | Diamond | Daisy, Sweet Pea |
| May | Emerald | Hawthorn, Lily of the Valley |
| June | Alexandrite, Moonstone, Pearl | Honeysuckle, Rose |
| July | Ruby | Larkspur, Water Lily |
| August | Peridot, Sardonyx | Gladiolus, Poppy |
| September | Sapphire | Aster, Morning Glory |
| October | Opal, Tourmaline | Calendula, Cosmos |
| November | Topaz | Chrysanthemum |
| December | Turquoise, Zircon | Holly, Narcissus, Poinsettia |

## Wedding anniversaries

In many Western countries, different wedding anniversaries have become associated with gifts of different materials. There is some variation between countries.

| | | | | | | | | | |
|---|---|---|---|---|---|---|---|---|---|
| 1st | Cotton, Paper | 6th | Sugar | 11th | Steel | 20th | China | 45th | Sapphire |
| 2nd | Paper, Cotton | 7th | Copper, Wool | 12th | Silk, Linen | 25th | Silver | 50th | Gold |
| 3rd | Leather | 8th | Bronze, Pottery | 13th | Lace | 30th | Pearl | 55th | Emerald |
| 4th | Fruit, Flowers | 9th | Pottery, Willow | 14th | Ivory | 35th | Coral | 60th | Diamond |
| 5th | Wood | 10th | Tin | 15th | Crystal | 40th | Ruby | 70th | Platinum |

## Chinese animal years and times 1960–2019

| Chinese | English | Years | | | | | Time of day (hours) |
|---|---|---|---|---|---|---|---|
| Shu | Rat | 1960 | 1972 | 1984 | 1996 | 2008 | 2300–0100 |
| Niu | Ox | 1961 | 1973 | 1985 | 1997 | 2009 | 0100–0300 |
| Hu | Tiger | 1962 | 1974 | 1986 | 1998 | 2010 | 0300–0500 |
| Tu | Hare | 1963 | 1975 | 1987 | 1999 | 2011 | 0500–0700 |
| Long | Dragon | 1964 | 1976 | 1988 | 2000 | 2012 | 0700–0900 |
| She | Serpent | 1965 | 1977 | 1989 | 2001 | 2013 | 0900–1100 |
| Ma | Horse | 1966 | 1978 | 1990 | 2002 | 2014 | 1100–1300 |
| Yang | Sheep | 1967 | 1979 | 1991 | 2003 | 2015 | 1300–1500 |
| Hou | Monkey | 1968 | 1980 | 1992 | 2004 | 2016 | 1500–1700 |
| Ji | Cock | 1969 | 1981 | 1993 | 2005 | 2017 | 1700–1900 |
| Gou | Dog | 1970 | 1982 | 1994 | 2006 | 2018 | 1900–2100 |
| Zhu | Boar | 1971 | 1983 | 1995 | 2007 | 2019 | 2100–2300 |

## National holidays

The first part of each listing gives the holidays that occur on fixed dates (though it should be noted that holidays often vary according to local circumstances and the day of the week on which they fall). Most dates are accompanied by an indication of the purpose of the day, eg Independence = Independence Day; dates which have no gloss are either fixed dates within the Christian calendar (for which see below) or bank holidays.

The second part of the listing gives holidays that vary, usually depending on religious factors. The most common of these are given in abbreviated form (see list below).

A number in brackets such as (Independence) (2) refers to the number of days devoted to the holiday.

The listings do not include holidays that affect only certain parts of a country, half-day holidays, or Sundays.

The following abbreviations are used for variable religious feast-days:

**A** Ascension Thursday
**Ad** Id-ul-Adha (also found with other spellings — especially Eid-ul-Adha; various names relating to this occasion are used in different countries, such as Tabaski, Id el-Kebir, Hari Raja Haji)
**Ar** Arafa
**As** Ashora (found with various spellings)
**C** Carnival (immediately before Christian Lent, unless specified)
**CC** Corpus Christi
**D** Diwali, Deepavali
**EM** Easter Monday
**ER** End of Ramadan (known generally as Id/Eid-ul-Fitr, but various names relating to this occasion are used in different countries, such as Karite, Hari Raja Puasa)
**ES** Easter Sunday
**GF** Good Friday
**HS** Holy Saturday
**HT** Holy Thursday
**NY** New Year
**PB** Prophet's Birthday (known generally as Maul-id-al-Nabi in various forms and spellings)
**R** First day of Ramadan
**WM** Whit Monday

The following fixed dates are shown without gloss:

**Jan 1** New Year's Day
**Jan 6** Epiphany
**May 1** Labour Day (often known by a different name, such as Workers' Day)
**Aug 15** Assumption of Our Lady
**Nov 1** All Saints' Day
**Nov 2** All Souls' Day
**Dec 8** Immaculate Conception
**Dec 24** Christmas Eve
**Dec 25** Christmas Day
**Dec 26** Boxing Day/St Stephen's Day
**Dec 31** New Year's Eve

**Afghanistan** Apr 27 (Sawr Revolution), May 1, Aug 19 (Independence); Ad (3), Ar, As, ER (3), NY (Hindu), PB, R

**Albania** Jan 1, 11 (Republic), May 1, Nov 28 (Independence), 29 (Liberation)

**Algeria** Jan 1, May 1, Jun 19 (Righting), Jul 5 (Independence), Nov 1 (Revolution); Ad, As, ER, NY (Muslim), PB

**Andorra** Jan 1, 6, Mar 19 (St Joseph), May 1, Jun 24 (St John), Aug 15, Sep 8 (Our Lady of Meritxell), Nov 1, 4 (St Charles), Dec 8, 25, 26; A, C, CC, EM, GF, WM

**Angola** Jan 1, Feb 4 (Commencement of the Armed Struggle), May 1, Sep 17 (National Hero), Nov 11 (Independence), Dec 10 (MPLA Foundation), 25 (Family)

**Antigua and Barbuda** Jan 1, May 1, Nov 1 (Independence), Dec 25, 26; EM, GF, WM; Jul (CARICOM), Carnival (1st week in Aug) (2)

**Argentina** Jan 1, May 1, 25 (National), Jun 10 (Malvinas Islands Memorial), 20 (Flag), Jul 9 (Independence), Aug 17 (Death of General San Martin), Oct 12 (Columbus), Dec 8, 25, 31; GF, HT

**Armenia** Jan 1, 6 (Armenian Christmas), Apr 24 (Day of Remembrance of the Victims of the Genocide), May 28 (Declaration of the First Armenian Republic, 1918), Dec 7 (Day of Remembrance of the Victims of the Earthquake); EM, ES, GF, HS; Sep Holiday

**Australia** Jan 1, Apr 25 (Anzac), Dec 25, 26 (*except South Australia*); Australia (Jan), EM, GF, HS; *additional days vary between states*

**Austria** Jan 1, 6, May 1, Aug 15, Oct 26 (National), Nov 1, Dec 8, 24, 25, 26; A, CC, EM, WM

**Azerbaijan** Jan 1, 20 (Sorrow), 8 Mar (Women), May 28 (Republic), Oct 9 (Armed Services), 18 (Statehood), Nov 17 (National Survival), Dec 31 (Day of Azerbaijani Solidarity Worldwide); Ad

**Bahamas, The** Jan 1, Jul 10 (Independence), Dec 25, 26; EM, GF, WM; Labour (Jun), Emancipation (Aug), Discovery (Oct)

**Bahrain** Jan 1, Dec 16 (National); Ad (3), As (2), ER (3), NY (Muslim), PB

**Bangladesh** Feb 21 (Shaheed), Mar 26 (Independence), May 1, Jul 1, Nov 7 (National Revolution), Dec 16 (Victory), 25, 31; Ad (3), ER (3), NY (Bengali), NY (Muslim), PB, Shab-e-Barat (Apr), Buddah Purnima (Apr/May), Shab-I-Qadr (May), Jumat-ul-Wida (May), Durga Puza (Oct)

**Barbados** Jan 1, Nov 30 (Independence), Dec 25, 26; EM, GF, WM, Kadooment (Aug), May Holiday, United Nations (Oct)

**Belarus** Jan 1, 7 (Russian Orthodox Christmas), Mar 8 (Women), May 1, 9 (Victory), Jul 27 (Independence), Nov 2 (Dsiady/Day of Commemoration), Dec 25; GF, HS, ES, EM, Russian Orthodox Easter (2)

**Belgium** Jan 1, May 1, Jul 21 (National), Aug 15, Nov 1, 11 (Armistice), Dec 25; A, EM, WM; May, Aug, Nov Bank Holidays; Regional Holiday (Jul *in N*, Sep *in S*)

**Belize** Jan 1, Mar 9 (Baron Bliss), May 1, 24 (Commonwealth), Sep 10 (National), 21 (Independence), Oct 12 (Columbus), Nov 19 (Garifuna Settlement), Dec 25, 26; EM, GF, HS

**Benin** Jan 1, 16 (Martyrs), Apr 1 (Youth), May 1, Oct 26 (Armed Forces), Nov 30 (National), Dec 25, 31 (Feed Yourself); Ad, ER

**Bhutan** May 2 (Birthday of Jigme Dorji Wangchuk), Jun 2 (Coronation of Fourth Hereditary King), Jul 21 (First Sermon of Lord Buddha, Death of Jigme Dorji Wangchuk), Nov 11–13 (Birthday of HM Jigme Singye Wangchuk), Dec 17 (National)

**Bolivia** Jan 1, May 1, Aug 6 (Independence), Nov 1, Dec 25; C (2), CC, GF

**Botswana** Jan 1, 2, Sep 30 (Botswana), Dec 25, 26; A, EM, GF, HS, President's Day (Jul); Jul, Oct Public Holidays

**Brazil** Jan 1, Apr 21 (Independence Hero Tiradentes), May 1, Sep 7 (Independence), Oct 12, Nov 2 (Memorial), 15 (Proclamation of the Republic), Dec 25; C (2), CC, GF, HS, HT

**Brunei** Jan 1, Feb 23 (National), May 31 (Royal Brunei Malay Regiment), Jul 15 (Sultan's Birthday), Dec 25; Ad, ER (2), GF, NY (Chinese), NY (Muslim), PB, R, Meraj (Mar–Apr), Revelation of the Koran (May)

**Bulgaria** Jan 1, May 1 (2), 24 (Slav Literature, Bulgarian Education and Culture), Sep 9 (National), Nov 7 (October Revolution)

**Burkina Faso** Jan 1, 3 (1966 Revolution), May 1, Aug 4, 15, Nov 1, Dec 25; A, Ad, EM, ER, PB, WM

**Burma** ► **Myanmar**

**Burundi** Jan 1, May 1, Jul 1 (Independence), Aug 15, Sep 18 (Victory of Uprona), Nov 1, Dec 25; A

**Cambodia** Jan 9 (National), Apr 17 (Victory over American Imperialism), May 1, 20 (Day of Hatred), Sep 22 (Feast of the Ancestors); Cambodian New Year (Apr)

**Cameroon** Jan 1, Feb 11 (Youth), May 1, 20 (National), Aug 15, Dec 25; A, Ad, ER, GF

**Canada** Jan 1, Jul 1 (Canada) (*except Newfoundland*), Nov 11 (Remembrance) Dec 25, 26; EM, GF, Labour (Sep), Thanksgiving (Oct), Victoria (May); *additional days vary between states*

**Cape Verde** Jan 1, 20 (National Heroes), Mar 8 (Women), May 1, Jun 1 (Children), Sep 12 (National), Dec 24, 25; GF

**Central African Republic** Jan 1, Mar 29 (Death of President Boganda), May 1, Jun 1 (Mothers), Aug 13 (Independence), 15, Sep 1 (Arrival of the Military Committee for National Recovery), Nov 1, Dec 1 (Republic), 25; A, EM, WM

**Chad** Jan 1, May 1, 25 (Liberation of Africa), Jun 7 (Liberation), Aug 11 (Independence), Nov 1, 28 (Republic), Dec 25; Ad, EM, ER, PB

**Chile** Jan 1, May 1, 21 (Battle of Iquique), Jun 29 (Sts Peter and Paul), Aug 15, Sep 11 (National Liberation), 18 (Independence), 19 (Armed Forces), Oct 12 (Day of the Race), Nov 1, Dec 8, 25, 31; GF, HS

**China** Jan 1, May 1, Oct 1 (National) (2); Spring Festival (4) (Jan/Feb)

**Colombia** Jan 1, 6, May 1, Jun 29 (Sts Peter and Paul), Jul 20 (Independence), Aug 7 (National), 15, Oct 12 (Columbus), Nov 1, 15 (Independence of Cartagena), Dec 8, 25, 30, 31; A, CC, GF, HT, St Joseph (Mar), Sacred Heart (Jun)

**Comoros** May 9 (Islamic New Year), 18 (Ashoura), Jul 6 (Independence), 18 (Mouloud/Prophet's Birthday), Nov 17 (President Abdallah's Assassination), 28 (Leilat al-Meiraj/Ascension of the Prophet); Ad, ER, R

**Congo** Jan 1, Mar 18 (Day of the Supreme Sacrifice), May 1, Jul 31 (Revolution), Aug 13–15 (The Three Glorious Days), Nov 1 (Day of the Dead), Dec 25 (Children), 31 (Foundation of the Party and People's Republic)

**Congo, Democratic Republic of (Zaïre)** Jan 1, 4 (Martyrs of Independence), May 1, 20 (Mouvement Populaire de la Révolution), Jun 24 (Anniversary of Currency, Promulgation of the 1967 Constitution, and Day of the Fishermen), 30 (Independence), Dec 25

**Costa Rica** Jan 1, Mar 19 (St Joseph), Apr 11 (National Heroes), May 1, Jun 29 (Sts Peter and Paul), Jul 25 (Annexation of Guanacaste), Aug 2 (Our Lady of the Angels), 15 (Mothers), Sep 15 (Independence), Oct 12 (Day of the Race), Dec 8, 25; CC, GF, HS, HT

**Côte d'Ivoire** Jan 1, May 1, Aug 15, Nov 1, Dec 7 (Independence), 24, 25, 31; A, Ad, EM, ER, GF, WM

**Croatia** Jan 1, 6, May 1, 30 (Republic), Jun 22, Aug 5 (Independence), 15 (Assumption), Nov 1, Dec 25, 26; EM, GF

**Cuba** Jan 1 (Day of Liberation), May 1, Jul 25 (National Rebellion) (2), Oct 10 (Beginning of the Independence Wars)

**Cyprus** Jan 1, 6, Mar 25 (Greek Independence), May 1, Oct 28 (Greek National), 29 (Turkish National), Dec 25, 26; Ad, EM, ER, GF, HS, PB

**Czech Republic** Jan 1, 2, May 1, Jul 5 (Sts Cyril and Methodius), 6 (Martyrdom of Jan Hus), Oct 28 (Independence), Dec 24, 25, 26; EM

**Denmark** Jan 1, Jun 5 (Constitution), Dec 24, 25, 26; A, EM, GF, HT, WM, General Prayer (Apr/May)

**Djibouti** Jan 1, May 1, Jun 27 (Independence) (2), Dec 25; Ad (2), ER (2), NY (Muslim), PB, Al-Isra Wal-Mira'age (Mar–Apr)

**Dominica** Jan 1, May 1, Nov 3 (Independence), 4 (Community Service), Dec 25, 26; C (2), EM, GF, WM, August Monday

**Dominican Republic** Jan 1, 6, 21 (Our Lady of Altagracia), 26 (Duarte), Feb 27 (Independence), May 1, Aug 16 (Restoration of the Republic), Sep 24 (Our Lady of Mercy), Dec 25; CC, GF

**Ecuador** Jan 1, May 1, 24 (Independence Battle), Jun 30, Jul 24 (Bolivar), Aug 10 (Independence), Oct 9 (Independence of Guayaquil), 12 (Columbus), Nov 2, 3 (Independence of Cuenca), Dec 6 (Foundation of Quito), 25, 31; C (2), GF, HT

**Egypt** Jan 7 (Eastern Orthodox Christmas), Apr 25 (Sinai Liberation), May 1, Jun 18 (Evacuation), Jul 1, 23 (Revolution Anniversary), Oct 6 (Armed Forces); Ad (2), Ar, ER (2), NY (Muslim), PB, Palm Sunday and Easter Sunday (Eastern Orthodox), Sham El-Nessim (Apr–May)

**Eire ▸ Ireland, Republic of**

**El Salvador** Jan 1, May 1, Jun 29, 30, Sep 15 (Independence), Oct 12 (Columbus), Nov 2, 5 (First Cry of Independence), Dec 24, 25, 30, 31; GF, HT, Ash Wednesday, San Salvador (4)

**England and Wales** Jan 1, Dec 25, 26; EM, GF, Early May, Late May and Summer (Aug) Bank Holidays

**Equatorial Guinea** Jan 1, May 1, Jun 5 (President's Birthday), Aug 3 (Armed Forces), Oct 12 (Independence), Dec 10 (Human Rights), 25; CC, GF, Constitution (Aug)

**Eritrea** Jan 1, 6 , May 24 (Independence), Jun 20 (Martyrs'), Sep 1 (Beginning of the Armed Struggle), Dec 25; ER, Ad

**Estonia** Jan 1, Feb 24 (Independence), May 1 (Spring), Jun 23 (Victory/Anniversary of the Battle of Vönnu), 24 (St John), Dec 25, 26; GF, HS, ES, EM, Whit Sunday

**Ethiopia** Jan 7 (Ethiopian Christmas), 19 (Ethiopian Epiphany), Mar 2 (Victory of Adwa), Apr 6 (Patriots), May 1, Sep 12 (Revolution), 27 (Finding of the True Cross); Ad, ER, NY (Ethiopian, Sep), PB, Ethiopian Good Friday and Easter

**Fiji** Jan 1, Oct 12 (Fiji), Dec 25, 26; D, EM, GF, HS, PB, August Bank Holiday, Queen's Birthday (Jun), Prince Charles's Birthday (Nov)

**Finland** Jan 1, May 1, Oct 31 (All Saints Observance), Nov 1, Dec 6 (Independence), 24, 25, 26, 31; A, EM, GF, Midsummer Eve and Day (Jun), Twelfthtide (Jan), Whitsuntide (May–Jun)

**France** Jan 1, May 1, 8 (Armistice), Jul 14 (Bastille), Aug 14 (Assumption Eve), 15, Oct 31 (All Saints' Eve), Nov 1, 11 (Armistice), Dec 24, 25, 31; A, EM, GF, HS, WM, Ascension Eve, Whit Holiday Eve, Law of 20 Dec 1906, Law of 23 Dec 1904

**Gabon** Jan 1, Mar 12 (Anniversary of Renewal), May 1, Aug 17 (Independence), Nov 1, Dec 25; Ad, EM, ER, WM

**Gambia, The** Jan 1, Feb 18 (Independence), May 1, Aug 15 (St Mary), Dec 25; Ad, As, ER (2), GF, PB

**Georgia** Jan 6 (Eastern Orthodox Christmas), May 26 (Independence), Dec 31; GF, HS, ES, EM

**Germany** Jan 1, May 1, Jun 17 (National), Oct 3 (Unity), Dec 24, 25, 26; A, EM, GF, WM, Day of Penance (Nov)

**Ghana** Jan 1, Mar 6 (Independence), May 1, Jun 4 (June 4 Revolution), Jul 1 (Republic), Dec 25, 26, 31 (Revolution); EM, GF, HS

**Greece** Jan 1, 6, Mar 25 (National), May 1, Aug 15, Oct 28 (National), Dec 25, 26; GF, EM, WM, Monday in Lent

**Grenada** Jan 1–2, Feb 7 (Independence), May 1, Aug 3–4 (Emancipation), Oct 25 (Thanksgiving), Dec 25, 26; CC, EM, GF, WM

**Guatemala** Jan 1, May 1, Jun 30 (Army), Jul 1, Sep 15 (Independence), Oct 12 (Day of the Race), 20 (1944 Revolution), Nov 1, Dec 24, 25, 31; GF, HS, HT

**Guinea** Jan 1, Apr 3 (Second Republic), May 1, Aug 15, Oct 2 (Independence), Nov 1 (Army), Dec 25; Ad, EM, ER, PB

**Guinea-Bissau** Jan 1, 20 (National Heroes), Feb 8 (BNG Anniversary and Monetary Reform), Mar 8 (Women), May 1, Aug 3 (Martyrs of Colonialism), Sep 12 (National), 24 (Establishment of the Republic), Nov 14 (Readjustment), Dec 25

**Guyana** Jan 1, Feb 23 (Republic), May 1, Aug 1 (Freedom), Dec 25, 26; Ad, D, EM, GF, PB, Phagwah (Mar), Caribbean (Jul)

**Haiti** Jan 1 (Independence), 2 (Ancestry), Apr 14 (Americas), May 1, Aug 15, Oct 17 (Dessalines), 24 (United Nations), Nov 1, 2, 18 (Vertières), Dec 5 (Discovery), 25; A, C, CC, GF

**Honduras** Jan 1, Apr 14 (Pan American), May 1, Sep 15 (Independence), Oct 3 (Francisco Morazán's Birthday), 12 (America's Discovery), 21 (Armed Forces), Dec 25, 31; GF, HT

**Hungary** Jan 1, Apr 4 (Liberation), May 1, Aug 20 (Constitution), Nov 7 (October Socialist Revolution), Dec 25, 26; EM

**Iceland** Jan 1, May 1, Jun 17 (Independence), Dec 25, 26; A, EM, GF, HT, WM, First Day of Summer, August Holiday Monday

**India** Jan 1 (*some states*), 26 (Republic), May 1 (*some states*), Jun 30, Aug 15 (Independence), Oct 2 (Mahatma Ghandi's Birthday), Dec 25, 31; NY (Parsi, Aug, *some states*)

**Indonesia** Jan 1, Aug 17 (Independence), Dec 25; A, Ad, ER (2), GF, NY (Icaka, Mar), NY (Muslim), PB, Ascension of the Prophet (Mar/Apr), Waisak (May)

**Iran** Feb 11 (Revolution), Mar 20 (Oil), 21 (Now Rooz) (4), Apr 1 (Islamic Republic), 2 (13th of Farvardin), Jun 5 (15th Khordad Uprising); Ad, As, ER, PB, Prophet's Mission (Apr), Birth of the Twelfth Imam (Apr/May), Martyrdom of Imam Ali (May), Death of Imam Jaffar Sadegh (Jun/Jul), Birth of Imam Reza (Jul), Id-E-Ghadir (Aug), Death of the Prophet and Martyrdom of Imam Hassan (Oct/Nov)

**Iraq** Jan 1, 6 (Army), Feb 8 (8th February Revolution), Mar 21 (Spring), May 1, Jul 14 (14th July Revolution), 17 (17th July Revolution); Ad (4), As, ER (3), NY (Muslim), PB

**Ireland** Jan 1, Mar 17 (St Patrick), Dec 25, 26; EM, GF, June Holiday, August Holiday, October Holiday, Christmas Holiday

**Ireland, Northern ► Northern Ireland**

**Israel** Jan 1, May 14 (Independence); NY (Jewish, Sep/Oct), Purim (Mar), First Day of Passover (Apr), Last Day of Passover (Apr), Pentecost (Jun), Fast of Av (Aug), Day of Atonement (Oct), Feast of Tabernacles (Oct) (2)

**Italy** Jan 1, 6, Apr 25 (Liberation), May 1, Aug 14 (Mid-August Holiday) (2), Nov 1, Dec 8, 25, 26; EM

**Jamaica** Jan 1, May 23 (Labour), Aug 5 (Independence), Oct 20 (National Heroes), Dec 25, 26; Ash Wednesday, EM, GF

**Japan** Jan 1, 2, 3, 15 (Adults), Feb 11 (National Founding), Mar 21 (Vernal Equinox), Apr 29 (Emperor's Birthday), May 3 (Constitution Memorial), 5 (Children), Sep 15 (Respect for the Aged), 23 (Autumn Equinox), Oct 10 (Health-Sports), Nov 3 (Culture), 23 (Labour Thanksgiving)

**Jordan** Jan 1, May 1, 25 (Independence), Jun 10 (Great Arab Revolt and Army), Aug 11 (Accession of King Hussein), Nov 14 (King Hussein's Birthday), Dec 25; Ad (4), R, ER (4), NY (Muslim), PB

**Kazakhstan** Jan 1, Mar 8 (Women), 22 (Nauryz Meyrami/Kazakh New Year), May 1, 9 (Victory), Aug 30 (Constitution), Oct 25 (State Sovereignty), Dec 16 (Independence), 31

**Kenya** Jan 1, May 1, Jun 1 (Madaraka), Oct 20 (Kenyatta), Dec 12 (Independence), 25, 26; EM, GF, ER (3)

**Kiribati** Jan 1, Jul 12 (Independence) (3), Dec 25, 26; GF, HS, EM, Youth (Aug)

**Korea, Democratic People's Republic of (North Korea)** Jan 1, Feb 16 (Kim Jong Il's Birthday) (2), Mar 8 (Women), Apr 15 (Kim-Il Sung's Birthday), May 1 (May Day), Aug 15 (Liberation), Sep 9 (Independence), Oct 10 (Foundation of the Korean Workers' Party), Dec 27 (Constitution)

**Korea, Republic of (South Korea)** Jan 1–3, Mar 1 (Independence Movement), 10 (Labour), Apr 5 (Arbor), May 5 (Children), Jun 6 (Memorial), Jul 17 (Constitution), Aug 15 (Liberation), Oct 1 (Armed Forces), 3 (National Foundation), 9 (Korean Alphabet), Dec 25; NY (Chinese, Jan/Feb), Lord Buddha's Birthday (May), Moon Festival (Sep/Oct)

**Kuwait** Jan 1, Feb 25 (National) (3); Ad (3), ER (3), NY (Muslim), PB, Ascension of the Prophet (Mar/Apr), Standing on Mt Arafat (Aug)

**Kyrgyzstan** Jan 1, 7 (Russian Orthodox Christmas), Feb 9 (Orozo Ait), Mar 8 (Women), 21 (Nooruz/Lunar New Year), Apr 18 (Kurban Ait), May 1, 9 (Victory), Aug 31 (Independence)

**Laos** Jan 24 (Army), May 1, Dec 2 (National); Lao New Year/Water Festival (3) (Mid-April)

**Latvia** Jan 1, May 1, Jun 23 (St John), 24 (Midsummer Festival), Nov 18 (National/Proclamation of the Republic), Dec 24, 25, 26; GF

**Lebanon** Jan 1, Feb 9 (St Maron), May 1, Aug 15, Nov 1, 22 (Independence), Dec 25; Ad (3), As, EM, GF, ER (3), NY (Muslim), PB

**Lesotho** Jan 1, Mar 12 (Moshoeshoe's Day), 21 (National Tree Planting), May 2 (King's Birthday), Oct 4 (Independence), Dec 25, 26; A, EM, GF, Family (Jul), National Sports (Oct)

**Liberia** Jan 1, Feb 11 (Armed Forces), Mar 15 (J J Roberts), Apr 12 (Redemption), May 14 (National Unification), Jul 26 (Independence), Aug 24 (National Flag), Nov 29 (President Tubman's Birthday), Dec 25; Decoration (Mar), National Fast and Prayer (Apr), Thanksgiving (Nov)

**Libya** Mar 2 (Declaration of Establishment of Authority of People), 8 (National), 28 (Evacuation of British Troops), Jun 11 (Evacuation of US Troops), Jul 23 (National), Sep 1 (National), Oct 7 (Evacuation of Italian Fascists); Ad (4), ER (3), PB

**Liechtenstein** Jan 1, 6, Feb 2 (Candlemas), Mar 19 (St Joseph), May 1, Aug 15, Nov 1, Dec 8, 24, 25, 26, 31; A, C, CC, EM, GF, WM

**Lithuania** Jan 1, Feb 16 (Independence), May 1, Jun 14 (Mourning and Hope), Jul 6 (Anniversary of the Coronation of Grand Duke Mindaugas), Nov 1, Dec 25, 26; GF, EM; Mothers Day (May)

**Luxembourg** Jan 1, May 1, Jun 23 (National), Aug 15, Nov 1, 2, Dec 25, 26, 31; A, EM, WM, Shrove Monday

**Macedonia** Jan 1, 2, May 1 (2); Aug, Oct Bank Holidays

**Madagascar** Jan 1, Mar 29 (Memorial), May 1, Jun 26 (Independence), Aug 15, Nov 1, Dec 25, 30 (National); A, EM, GF, WM

**Malawi** Jan 1, Mar 3 (Martyrs), May 14 (Kamuzu), Jul 6 (Republic), Oct 17 (Mothers), Dec 22 (Tree Planting), 25, 26; EM, GF, HS

**Malaysia** Jan 1 (*some states*), May 1, Jun 3 (Head of State's Birthday), Aug 31 (National), Dec 25; Ad, D (*most states*), ER (2), NY (Chinese, Jan/Feb, *most states*), NY (Muslim), PB, Wesak (*most states*); *several local festivals*

**Maldives** Jan 1, Jul 26 (Independence) (2), Nov 11 (Republic) (2); Ad (4), ER (3), NY (Muslim), PB, R (2), Huravee (Feb), Martyrs (Apr), National (Oct/Nov) (2)

**Mali** Jan 1, 20 (Army), May 1, 25 (Africa), Sep 22 (National), Nov 19 (Liberation), Dec 25; Ad, ER, PB, Prophet's Baptism (Nov)

**Malta** Jan 1, Mar 31 (National), May 1, Aug 15, Dec 13 (Republic), 25; GF

**Mauritania** Jan 1, May 1, 25 (Africa), Jul 10 (Armed Forces), Nov 28 (Independence); Ad, ER, NY (Muslim), PB

**Mauritius** Jan 1, 2, Mar 12 (Independence), May 1, Nov 1, Dec 25; Ad, D, ER, PB, Chinese Spring Festival (Jan/Feb)

**Mexico** Jan 1, Feb 5 (Constitution), Mar 21 (Birthday of Benito Juárez), May 1, 5 (Puebla Battle), Sep 1 (Presidential Report), 16 (Independence), Oct 12 (Columbus), Nov 2, 20 (Mexican Revolution), Dec 12 (Our Lady of Guadaloupe), 25, 31; HT, GF

**Moldova** Jan 1, 7 (Moldovan Christmas) (2), Mar 8 (Women), May 1, 9 (Victory and Commemoration), Aug 27 (Independence), 31 (Limba Noastra/National Language); GF, EM; Mertsishor/Spring Festival (1st week in Mar)

**Monaco** Jan 1, 27 (St Devote), May 1, 8 (Armistice, 1945), Jul 14 (National), Aug 15, Sep 3 (Liberation), Nov 1, 11 (Armistice, 1918), 19 (Prince of Monaco), Dec 8, 25; EM, WM

**Mongolia** Jan 1, 2, Mar 8 (Women), May 1, Jul 10 (People's Revolution) (3), Nov 7 (October Revolution)

**Morocco** Jan 1, Mar 3 (Throne), May 1, 23 (Fête Nationale), Jul 9 (Youth), Aug 14 (Qued-ed-Dahab), Nov 6 (Al-Massira), 18 (Independence); Ad (2), ER (2), NY (Muslim), PB

**Mozambique** Jan 1, Feb 3 (Heroes), Apr 7 (Mozambican Women), May 1, Jun 25 (Independence), Sep 7 (Victory), 25 (Armed Forces), Dec 25

**Myanmar (Burma)** Jan 4 (Independence), Feb 12 (Union), Mar 2 (Peasants), 27 (Resistance), Apr 1, May 1, Jul 19 (Martyrs), Oct 1, Dec 25; NY (Burmese), Thingyan (Apr) (4), End of Buddhist Lent (Oct), Full Moon days

**Namibia** Jan 1, Mar 21 (Independence), May 1, 4 (Casinga), May 25 (Africa/Anniversary of the OAU's Foundation), Aug 26 (Heroes), Dec 10 (Human Rights), Dec 25, 26; GF, HS, ES, EM, A

**Nauru** Jan 1, 31 (Independence), May 17 (Constitution), Jul 1 (Takeover), Oct 27 (Angam), Dec 25, 26; GF, EM (2)

**Nepal** Jan 11 (King Prithvi Memorial), Feb 19 (Late King Tribhuvan Memorial and Democracy), Nov 8 (Queen's Birthday), Dec 16 (King Mahendra Memorial and Constitution), 29 (King's Birthday); NY (Sinhala/Tamil, Apr), Maha Shivarata (Feb/Mar)

**Netherlands** Jan 1, Apr 30 (Queen's Birthday), May 5 (Liberation), Dec 25, 26; A, EM, GF, WM

**New Zealand** Jan 1, 2, Feb 6 (Waitangi), Apr 25 (Anzac), Dec 25, 26; EM, GF, Queen's Birthday (Jun), Labour (Oct)

**Nicaragua** Jan 1, May 1, Jul 19 (Sandinista Revolution), Sep 14 (Battle of San Jacinto), 15 (Independence), Dec 8, 25; GF, HT

**Niger** Jan 1, Apr 15 (Assumption of Power by Supreme Military Council), May 1, Aug 3 (Independence), Dec 18 (National), 25; Ad, ER, PB

**Nigeria** Jan 1, May 1, Oct 1 (National), Dec 25, 26; Ad (2), EM, ER (2), GF, PB

**Northern Ireland** Jan 1, Mar 17 (St Patrick, *not general*), Dec 25, 26, 29; GF, EM, Early May, Late May, July Bank Holiday, Summer Bank Holiday (Aug)

**Norway** Jan 1, May 1, 17 (Constitution), Dec 25, 26; A, EM, GF, HT, WM

**Oman** Nov 18 (National) (2), Dec 31; Ad (5), ER (4), NY (Muslim), PB, Lailat al-Miraj (Mar/Apr)

**Pakistan** Mar 23 (Pakistan), May 1, Jul 1, Aug 14 (Independence), Sep 6 (Defence of Pakistan), 11 (Death of Quaid-e-Azam), Nov 9 (Iqbal), Dec 25 (Christmas/Birthday of Quaid-e-Azam), 31; Ad (3), As (2), ER (3), PB, R

**Panama** Jan 1, 9 (National Mourning), May 1, Oct 11 (Revolution), 12 (Dia de la Hispanidad), Nov 3 (Independence from Colombia), 4 (Flag), 28 (Independence from Spain), Dec 8 (Mothers), 25; C (2), GF

**Papua New Guinea** Jan 1, Aug 15 (National Constitution), Sep 16 (Independence), Dec 25, 26; EM, GF, HS, Queen's Birthday (Jun), Remembrance (Jul)

**Paraguay** Jan 1, Feb 3 (St Blás), Mar 1 (Heroes), May 1, 14 (National Flag), 15 (Independence), Jun 12 (Peace with Bolivia), Aug 15, 25 (Constitution), Sep 29 (Battle of Boqueron), Oct 12 (Day of the Race), Nov 1, Dec 8, 25, 31; CC, GF, HT

**Peru** Jan 1, May 1, Jun 29 (Sts Peter and Paul), 30, Jul 28 (Independence) (2), Aug 30 (St Rose of Lima), Oct 8 (Combat of Angamos), Nov 1, Dec 8, 25, 31; GF, HT

**Philippines** Jan 1, May 1, Jun 12 (Independence), Jul 4 (Philippine–American Friendship), Nov 1, 30 (National Heroes), Dec 25, 30 (Rizal), 31; GF, HT

**Poland** Jan 1, May 1, Jul 22 (National Liberation), Nov 1, Dec 25, 26; CC, EM

**Portugal** Jan 1, Apr 25 (Liberty), May 1, Jun 10 (Portugal), Aug 15, Oct 5 (Republic), Nov 1, Dec 1 (Independence Restoration), Dec 8, 24, 25; C, CC, GF

**Qatar** Sep 3 (Independence), Dec 31; Ad (4), ER (4)

**Romania** Jan 1, 2, May 1(2), Aug 23 (National)

**Russia** Jan 1, 7 (Russian Orthoox Christmas) (2), Mar 8 (Women), Apr 2 (Unity of the Peoples), May 1 (Spring and Labour) (2), 9 (Victory in Europe), Jun 12 (Russian Independence), Aug 22 (Anniversary of 1991 Restoration and National Flag Day), 31 (Language), Nov 7 (October Revolution); Spring Festival (1st week in Mar), Russian Orthodox Easter (Apr)

**Rwanda** Jan 1, 28 (Democracy), May 1, Jul 1 (Independence), 5 (Peace), Aug 1 (Harvest), 15, Sep 25 (Referendum), Oct 26 (Armed Forces), Nov 1, Dec 25; A, EM, WM

**St Kitts and Nevis** Jan 1, Sep 19 (Independence), Dec 25, 26, 31; EM, GF, WM, Labour (May), Queen's Birthday (Jun), August Monday

**St Lucia** Jan 1, 2, Feb 22 (Independence), May 1, Dec 13 (St Lucia), Dec 25, 26; C, CC, EM, GF, WM, Emancipation (Aug), Thanksgiving (Oct)

**St Vincent and the Grenadines** Jan 1, 22 (Discovery), Oct 27 (Independence), Dec 25, 26; C (Jul), EM, GF, WM, Labour (May), Caricom (Jul), Emancipation (Aug)

**Samoa** Jan 1, 2, Apr 25 (Anzac), Jun 1 (Independence) (3), Oct 12 (Lotu-o-Tamai), Dec 25, 26; EM, GF, HS

**San Marino** Jan 1, 6, Feb 5 (Liberation and St Agatha), Mar 25 (Arengo), Apr 1 (Captains Regents' Ceremony), May 1, Jul 28 (Fall of Fascism), Aug 15, Sep 3 (San Marino and Republic), Oct 1 (Investiture of the New Captains Regent), Nov 1, 2 (Commemoration of the Dead), Dec 8, 25, 26

**São Tomé and Príncipe** Jan 1, Feb 3 (Liberty Heroes), May 1, Jul 12 (National Independence), Sep 6 (Armed Forces), 30 (Agricultural Reform), Dec 21 (Power of the People), 25 (Family)

**Saudi Arabia** Sep 23 (National); Ad (7), ER (4)

**Scotland** Jan 1, 2, Dec 25, 26; GF, Early May, Late May, Summer Bank Holiday (Aug)

**Senegal** Jan 1, Feb 1 (Senegambia), Apr 4 (National), May 1, Aug 15, Nov 1, Dec 25; Ad, EM, ER, NY (Muslim), PB, WM

**Seychelles** Jan 1, 2, May 1, Jun 5 (Liberation), 29 (Independence), Aug 15, Nov 1, Dec 8, 25; CC, GF, HS

**Sierra Leone** Jan 1, Apr 19 (Republic), Dec 25, 26; Ad, EM, ER, GF, PB

**Singapore** Jan 1, May 1, Aug 9 (National), Dec 25; Ad, D, ER, GF, NY (Chinese, Jan/Feb) (2), Vesak

**Slovakia** Jan 1 (New Year and Independence), 6, May 1, 8 (Liberation of the Republic), Jul 5 (Sts Cyril and Methodius), Aug 19 (Slovak National Uprising), Sep 1 (Constitution of the Slovak Republic), 15 (Our Lady of the Seven Sorrows), Nov 1, Dec 24, 25; GF, EM

**Solomon Islands** Jan 1, Jul 7 (Independence), Dec 25, 26; EM, GF, HS, WM, Queen's Birthday (Jun)

**Somalia** Jan 1, May 1, Jun 26 (Independence), Jul 1 (Union), Oct 21 (Revolution) (2); Ad (2), ER (2), PB

**South Africa** Jan 1, Apr 6 (Founders), May 31 (Republic), Oct 10 (Kruger), Dec 16 (Vow), 25, 26; A, GF, Family (Mar/Apr)

**Spain** Jan 1, 6, Mar 19 (*most areas*), May 1, Aug 15, Oct 12 (Hispanity), Nov 1, Dec 6 (Constitution), 8, 25; CC, GF, HS, HT

**Sri Lanka** Jan 14 (Tamil Thai Pongal), Feb 4 (Independence), May 1, 22 (National Heroes), Jun 30, Dec 25, 31; Ad, D, ER, GF, NY (Sinhala/Tamil, Apr), PB, Maha Sivarathri (Feb/Mar), Full Moon (*monthly*)

**Sudan, The** Jan 1 (Independence), Mar 3 (Unity), Apr 6 (Revolution), Dec 25; Ad (5), ER (5), NY (Muslim), PB, Sham al-Naseem (Apr/May)

**Suriname** Jan 1, Feb 25 (Revolution), May 1, Jul 1 (Freedom), Nov 25 (Independence), Dec 25, 26; EM, ER, GF, Holi (Mar)

**Swaziland** Jan 1, Apr 25 (National Flag), Jul 22 (King's Birthday), Sep 6 (Independence), Oct 24 (United Nations), Dec 25, 26; A, EM, GF, Commonwealth (Mar)

**Sweden** Jan 1, 6, May 1, Nov 1, Dec 24, 25, 26, 31; A, EM, GF, WM, Midsummer Eve and Day (Jun)

**Switzerland** Jan 1, Aug 1 (National), Aug 15 (*many cantons*), Nov 1 (*many cantons*), Dec 24, 25, 26; A, CC (*many cantons*), EM, GF, WM; *several local holidays*

**Syria** Jan 1, Mar 8 (Revolution), Apr 17 (Evacuation), May 1, 6 (Martyrs), Jul 23 (Egyptian Revolution), Sep 1 (Libyan Unity), Oct 6 (Liberation), Dec 25; Ad (3), ER (4), ES, NY (Muslim), PB

**Tajikistan** Jan 1, Mar 8 (Women), 21 (Navrus), May 9 (Victory), Sep 9 (Independence), Oct 14 (Formation of the Tajik Republic); ER

**Taiwan** Jan 1, 2, 3, Mar 29 (Youth), Apr 5 (Ching Ming), Jul 1, Sep 28 (Birthday of Confucius), Oct 10 (National), 25 (Taiwan Restoration), 31 (Birthday of Chiang Kai-Shek), Nov 12 (Birthday of Dr Sun Yat Sen), Dec 25 (Constitution); NY (Chinese, Jan/Feb) (3), Dragon Boat Festival (Jun), Mid-Autumn Festival (Sep/Oct)

**Tanzania** Jan 1, 12 (Zanzibar Revolution), Feb 5 (Chama Cha Mapinduzi and Arusha Declaration), May 1, Jul 7 (Saba Saba Peasants), Dec 9 (Independence/Republic), 25; Ad, EM, ER (2), GF, PB

**Thailand** Jan 1, Apr 6 (Chakri), 13 (Songkran), May 1, 5 (Coronation), Jul 1 (Mid-Year), Aug 12 (Queen's Birthday), Oct 23 (King Chulalongkorn), Dec 5 (King's Birthday), 10 (Constitution), 31; ER, Makha Bucha (Feb), Visakha Bucha (May), Buddhist Lent (Jul)

**Togo** Jan 1, 13 (Liberation), 24 (Economic Liberation), Apr 24 (Victory), 27 (National), May 1, Aug 15, Nov 1, Dec 25; A, Ad, ER

**Tonga** Jan 1, Apr 25 (Anzac), May 5 (Birthday of Crown Prince Tupouto'a), Jun 4 (Emancipation), Jul 4 (Birthday and Coronation of King Taufa'ahau Tupou IV), Nov 4 (Constitution), Dec 4 (King Tupou I), 25, 26; EM, GF

**Trinidad and Tobago** Jan 1, Jun 19 (Labour), Aug 1 (Discovery), 31 (Independence), Sep 24 (Republic), Dec 25, 26; CC, EM, GF, WM

**Tunisia** Jan 1, 18 (Revolution), Mar 20 (Independence), Apr 9 (Martyrs), May 1, Jun 1 (Victory), 2 (Youth), Jul 25 (Republic), Aug 3 (President's Birthday), 13 (Women), Sep 3 (3 Sep 1934), Oct 15 (Evacuation); Ad (2), ER (2), NY (Muslim), PB

**Turkey** Jan 1, Apr 23 (National Sovereignty and Children), May 19 (Youth and Sports), Aug 30 (Victory), Oct 29 (Republic); Ad (4), ER (3)

**Turkmenistan** Jan 1, 12 (Remembrance/Anniversary of the Battle of Geok-Tepe), Feb 19 (Birthday of Turkem President Sapurmurat Turkmenbashi), Mar 8 (Women), May 9 (Victory); Navrus Bayram (Feb), Gurban Bayram (Apr), Day of Revival and Unity (May), Independence (Oct)

**Tuvalu** Jan 2, Mar 3 (Commonwealth), Jun 14 (Queen's Official Birthday), Aug 14 (Children), Oct 1 (Tuvalu/ Independence) (2), Nov 14 (Prince of Wales's Birthday), Dec 25, 26; EM, ES, GF, HS

**Uganda** Jan 1, Apr 1 (Liberation), May 1, Oct 9 (Independence), Dec 25, 26; EM, ER, GF, HS

**UK ▸ England and Wales; Northern Ireland; Scotland**

**Ukraine** Jan 1, 7 (Eastern Orthodox Christmas) (2), Mar 8 (Women), May 1, 2, 9 (Victory), Aug 24 (Independence) (3), 7 November (Revolution) (2); EM, GF, HT

**United Arab Emirates** Jan 1, Aug 6 (Accession of Ruler), Dec 2 (National) (2); Ad (3), ER (4), NY (Muslim), PB, Lailat al-Miraj (Mar/Apr)

**Uruguay** Jan 1, Apr 19 (Landing of the 33 Orientales), May 1, 18 (Las Piedras Battle), Jun 19 (Artigas), Jul 18 (Constitution), Aug 25 (Independence), Oct 12 (Columbus), Nov 2, Dec 25; C (2), GF, HT, Mon–Wed of Holy Week

**USA** Jan 1, third Monday in January (Martin Luther King's Birthday) (*not all states*), Jul 4 (Independence), Nov 11 (Veterans), Dec 25; Washington's Birthday (3rd Mon in Feb), Memorial (last Mon in May), Labor (1st Mon in Sep), Discoverers' (2nd Mon in Oct), Thanksgiving (last Thurs in Nov); *much local variation*

**Uzbekistan** Jan 1, 2, Mar 8 (Women), 21 (Navrus), Sep 1 (Independence), Dec 8 (Constitution)

**Vanuatu** Jan 1, Mar 5 (Chiefs), May 1, Jul 30 (Independence), Aug 15, Dec 25, 26; A, EM, GF, Constitution (Oct), Unity (Nov)

**Venezuela** Jan 1, 6, Mar 19 (St Joseph), Apr 19 (Constitution), May 1, Jun 24 (Battle of Carabobo), 29 (Sts Peter and Paul), Jul 5 (Independence), 24 (Bolivar), Aug 15, Oct 12 (Columbus), Nov 1, Dec 8, 25; A, C (2), CC, GF, HT

**Vietnam** Jan 1, May 1, Sep 2 (Independence)

**Yemen** Jan 1, Mar 8 (Women), May 1, 22 (National), Jun 22 (Corrective Move), Sep 26 (Revolution, *N area*), Oct 14 (Revolution), Nov 30 (Independence); Ad (3), ER (2), NY (Muslim), PB

**Zaïre ▸ Congo, Democratic Republic of**

**Zambia** Jan 1, May 1, 25 (Africa Freedom), Oct 24 (Independence), Dec 25; GF, HS, Youth (Mar), Heroes (Jul), Unity (Jul), Farmers (Aug)

**Zimbabwe** Jan 1, Apr 18 (Independence), 19 (Defence Forces), May 1, 25 (Africa), Aug 11 (Heroes) (2), Dec 25, 26; EM, G

# NATURAL HISTORY

## Cereals

| English name | Species | Area of origin | English name | Species | Area of origin |
|---|---|---|---|---|---|
| barley | *Hordeum vulgare* | Middle East | oats | *Avena sativa* | Mediterranean basin |
| maize (or corn, sweet corn, Indian corn) | *Zea mays* | C America | rice | *Oryza sativa* | Asia |
| millet, common | *Panicum miliaceum* | tropics, warm temperate regions | rye | *Secale cereale* | Mediterranean, SW Asia |
| millet, foxtail (or Italian millet) | *Setaria italica* | as common millet | sorghum (or Kaffir corn) | *Sorghum bicolor* | Africa, Asia |
| millet, bulrush | *Pennisetum americanum* | as common millet | wheat | Genus *Triticum*, 20 species | Mediterranean, W Asia |

## Edible fruits (Temperate and Mediterranean)

| English name | Species | Colour | Area of origin |
|---|---|---|---|
| apple | *Malus pumila* | green, yellow, red | temperate regions |
| apricot | *Prunus armeniaca* | yellow, orange | Asia |
| bilberry | *Vaccinium myrtillus* | blue, black | Europe, N Asia |
| blackberry (or bramble) | *Rubus fruticosus* | purple, black | N hemisphere |
| blackcurrant | *Ribes nigrum* | black | Europe, Asia, Africa |
| blueberry | *Vaccinium corymbosum* | blue, purple, black | America, Europe |
| Cape gooseberry ► physalis | | | |
| cherry (sour) | *Prunus cerasus* | red | temperate regions |
| cherry (sweet) | *Prunus avium* | purple, red | temperate regions |
| clementine | *Citrus reticulata* | orange | W Mediterranean |
| cranberry | *Vaccinium oxycoccus* | red | N America |
| damson | *Prunus damascena* | purple | temperate regions |
| date | *Phoenix dactylifera* | yellow, red, brown | Persian Gulf |
| date-plum ► persimmon | | | |
| fig | *Ficus carica* | white, black, purple, green | W Asia |
| gooseberry | *Ribes grossularia* | green, red | Europe |
| grape | *Vitis vinifera* | green, purple, black | Asia |
| grapefruit | *Citrus × paradisi* | yellow | W Indies |
| greengage | *Prunus italica* | green | temperate regions |
| kiwi fruit | *Actinidia chinensis* | brown skin, green flesh | China |
| kumquat | *Fortunella margarita* | orange | China |
| lemon | *Citrus limon* | yellow | India, S Asia |
| lime | *Citrus aurantifolia* | green | SE Asia |
| loganberry | *Rubus loganobaccus* | red | America |
| loquat | *Eriobotrya japonica* | yellow | China, Japan |
| lychee | *Litchi chinensis* | reddish-brown skin, white flesh | China |
| mandarin (or tangerine) | *Citrus reticulata* | orange | China |
| medlar | *Mespilus germanica* | russet brown | SE Europe, Asia |
| melon | *Cucumis melo* | green, yellow | Egypt |
| minneola ► tangelo | | | |

| English name | Species | Colour | Area of origin |
|---|---|---|---|
| mulberry | *Morus nigra* | purple, red | W Asia |
| nectarine | *Prunus persica nectarina* | orange, red | China |
| orange | *Citrus sinensis* | orange | China |
| peach | *Prunus persica* var. *nectarina* | yellow, red | China |
| pear | *Pyrus communis* | yellow | Middle East, E Europe |
| persimmon (or date-plum) | *Diospyros kaki* | yellow, orange | E Asia |
| physalis (or Cape gooseberry) | *Physalis alkekengi* | yellow | S America |
| plum | *Prunus domestica* | red, yellow, purple, orange | temperate regions |
| pomegranate | *Punica granatum* | red, yellow | Persia |
| pomelo | *Citrus maxima* | yellow | Malaysia |
| quince | *Cydonia oblonga* | golden | Iran |
| raspberry | *Rubus idaeus* | red, crimson | N hemisphere |
| redcurrant | *Ribes rubrum* | red | Europe, Asia, Africa |
| rhubarb | *Rheum rhaponticum* | red, green, pink | Asia |
| satsuma | *Citrus reticulata* | orange | Japan |
| strawberry | *Fragaria ananassa* | red | Europe, Asia |
| tangelo (or mineola, or ugli) | *Citrus × tangelo* | orange, yellow | N America |
| tangerine ► mandarin | | | |
| ugli ► tangelo | | | |
| water melon | *Citrullus vulgaris* | green, yellow | Africa |
| white currant | *Ribes rubrum* cv. | white | W Europe |

## Edible fruits (Tropical)

| English name | Species | Colour | Area of origin |
|---|---|---|---|
| acerola | *Malpighia glabra* | yellow, red | America |
| avocado | *Persea americana* | green, purple | C America |
| banana | *Musa acuminita* | yellow | India, S Asia |
| breadfruit | *Artocarpus altilis* | greenish brown, yellow | Malaysia |
| carambola | *Averrhoa carambola* | yellow, green | S China |
| cherimoya | *Annona cherimola* | green skin, white flesh | Peru |
| guava | *Psidium guajava* | green, yellow | S America |
| mango | *Mangifera indica* | green, yellow, orange, red, purple | S Asia |
| papaya (or pawpaw) | *Carica papaya* | green, yellow, orange | tropics |
| passion fruit | *Passiflora edulis* | purple, yellow, brown | S America |
| pineapple | *Ananas comosus* | green, yellow | S America |
| sapodilla plum | *Manilkara zapota* | brown | C America |
| soursop | *Anona muricata* | green | America |
| tamarind | *Tamarindus indica* | brown | Africa, S Asia |

## Herbs

Herbs may be used for medicinal, cosmetic or culinary purposes. Any part of those marked * may be poisonous when ingested.

| English name | Species | Origin | Part of plant used |
|---|---|---|---|
| aconite* (or monkshood or winter aconite) | *Aconitum napellus* | Europe, NW Asia | tuber |
| agrimony | *Agrimonia eupatoria* | Europe | flowers |
| alecost (or costmary) | *Balsimata major* | E Mediterranean | leaves, flowers |
| aloe | *Aloe vera* | Africa | leaves |
| aniseed | *Pimpinella anisum* | Asia | fruits (seed heads) |
| basil | *Ocimum basilicum* | tropics | leaves, flowering shoots |
| borage | *Borago officinalis* | Mediterranean | leaves, flowers |

| English name | Species | Origin | Part of plant used |
|---|---|---|---|
| celandine | *Chelidonium majus* | Europe | buds |
| celery | *Apium graveolens* | Europe | roots, stems, leaves |
| chamomile | *Anthemis nobilis* | Europe, Asia | flowers |
| chervil | *Anthriscus cerefolium* | Europe, Asia | leaves |
| chicory | *Cichorium intybus* | Europe | leaves, roots |
| chives | *Allium schoenoprasum* | Europe, America | leaves |
| coriander | *Coriandrum sativum* | N Africa, W Asia | leaves, fruits |
| dandelion | *Taraxacum officinalis* | Europe | leaves, roots |
| deadly nightshade* | *Atropa belladonna* | Europe, Asia | root |
| dill | *Anethum graveolens* | S Europe | leaves, fruits (seeds) |
| elderberry | *Sambucus nigra* | Europe | flowers, fruits |
| epazote | *Chenopodium ambrosioides* | C and S America | leaves |
| fennel, Florentine | *Foeniculum vulgare* var. *azoricum* | Mediterranean | leaves, stems, fruits (seeds) |
| feverfew | *Tanacetum parthenium* | SE Europe, W Asia | leaves, flowers |
| foxglove* | *Digitalis purpurea* | Europe | leaves |
| garlic | *Allium sativum* | Asia | bulbs |
| gentian | *Gentiana lutea* | Europe | rhizomes, roots |
| ginseng | *Panax pseudo-ginseng* | China | roots |
| guaiacum | *Guaiacum officinale* | Caribbean | leaves |
| heartsease (or wild pansy) | *Viola tricolor* | Europe | flowers |
| hemlock* | *Conium maculatum* | Europe | all parts |
| hemp (or ganja or cannabis or marijuana) | *Cannabis sativa* | Asia | leaves, flowers |
| henbane | *Hyoscyamus niger* | Europe, W Asia, N Africa | leaves, fruits (seeds) |
| henna | *Lawsonia inermis* | Asia, Africa | leaves |
| horseradish | *Armoracia rusticana* | SE Europe, W Asia | roots, flowering shoots, leaves |
| hyssop | *Hyssopus officinalis* | S Europe | leaves, flowers |
| juniper | *Juniperus communis* | Mediterranean | fruits (berries), wood |
| lavender | *Lavandula vera* | Mediterranean | flowers, stems |
| leek | *Allium porrum* | Europe | stem, leaves |
| lemon | *Citrus limon* | Asia | fruits |
| lemon balm | *Melissa officinalis* | S Europe | leaves |
| lily of the valley | *Convallaria majalis* | Europe, N America | leaves, flowers |
| lime | *Tilia cordata* | Europe | flowers |
| liquorice | *Glycyrrhiza glabra* | Europe | roots |
| lovage | *Levisticum officinale* | W Asia | leaves, shoots, stems, roots |
| mandrake | *Mandragora officinarum* | Himalayas, SE Europe, W Asia | roots |
| marjoram | *Oreganum majorana* | Africa, Mediterranean, Asia | leaves, shoots, stems |
| marsh mallow | *Althaea officinalis* | Europe, Asia | leaves, roots |
| maté | *Ilex paraguariensis* | S America | leaves |
| milfoil ► yarrow | | | |
| monkshood ► aconite | | | |
| mugwort | *Artemesia vulgaris* | Europe, Asia | leaves |
| myrrh | *Commiphora myrrha* | Arabia, Africa | resin |
| myrtle | *Myrtus communis* | Asia, Mediterranean | leaves, flower heads, fruits (berries) |
| nasturtium | *Tropaeolom majus* | Peru | leaves, flowers, fruits |
| onion | *Allium cepa* | Asia | bulbs |
| oregano | *Origanum vulgare* | Mediterranean | leaves, shoots, stems |
| parsley | *Petroselinum crispum* | Mediterranean | leaves, stems |
| peony | *Paeonia officinalis* | Europe, Asia, N America | roots, seeds |
| peppermint | *Mentha × piperita* | Europe | leaves |
| poppy, opium* | *Papaver somniferum* | Asia | fruits, seeds |
| purslane | *Portulaca oleracea* | Europe | leaves |
| rosemary | *Rosmarinus officinalis* | Mediterranean | leaves |
| rue | *Ruta graveolens* | Mediterranean | leaves, stems, flowers |

| English name | Species | Origin | Part of plant used |
|---|---|---|---|
| saffron | *Crocus sativus* | Asia Minor | flowers |
| sage | *Salvia officinalis* | N Mediterranean | leaves |
| sorrel | *Rumex acetosa* | Europe | leaves |
| spearmint | *Mentha spicata* | Europe | leaves |
| tansy | *Tanacetum vulgare* | Asia | leaves, flowers |
| tarragon, French | *Artemesia dracunculus* | Asia, E Europe | leaves, stems |
| thyme | *Thymus vulgaris* | Mediterranean | leaves, stems, flowers |
| valerian | *Valeriana officinalis* | Europe, Asia | rhizomes, roots |
| vervain | *Verbena officinalis* | Europe, Asia, N Africa | leaves, flowers |
| watercress | *Nasturtium officinale* | Europe, Asia | leaves, shoots, stems |
| witch hazel | *Hamamelis virginiana* | N America, E Asia | leaves, shoots, bark |
| wormwood | *Artemesia absinthium* | Europe | leaves, flowering shoots |
| yarrow (or milfoil) | *Achillea millefolium* | Europe, W Asia | flower heads, leaves |

## Spices

| English name | Species | Origin | Part of plant used |
|---|---|---|---|
| allspice | *Pimenta dioica* | America, W Indies | fruits |
| annatto | *Bixa orellana* | S America, W Indies | seeds |
| asafoetida | *Ferula assa-foetida* | W Asia | sap |
| bay | *Laurus nobilis* | Mediterranean, Asia Minor | leaves |
| caper | *Capparis spinosa* | Europe | flower buds |
| caraway | *Carum carvi* | Europe, Asia | seeds |
| cardamom | *Elettaria cardamomum* | SE Asia | seeds |
| cayenne | *Capsicum annuum* | America, Africa | fruit pods |
| chilli pepper | *Capsicum frutescens* | America | fruit pods |
| cinnamon | *Cinnamomum zeylanicum* | India | bark |
| cloves | *Eugenia caryophyllus* | Moluccas | buds |
| cocoa | *Theobroma cacoa* | S America | seeds (beans) |
| coconut | *Cocus nucifera* | Polynesia | fruits |
| coriander | *Coriandrum sativum* | S Europe | fruits |
| cumin | *Cuminum cyminum* | Mediterranean | fruits (seed heads) |
| curry leaf | *Murraya koenigi* | India | leaves |
| fennel | *Foeniculum vulgare* | S Europe | fruits |
| fenugreek | *Trigonella foenum-graecum* | India, S Europe | seeds |
| horseradish | *Armoracia rusticana* | E Europe | roots |
| ginger | *Zingiber officinale* | SE Asia | rhizomes |
| mace | *Myristica fragrans* | Moluccas | seeds |
| mustard, black | *Brassica nigra* | Europe, Africa, Asia, America | seeds |
| mustard, white | *Sinapis alba* | Europe, Asia | seeds |
| nutmeg | *Myristica fragrans* | Indonesia | seeds |
| paprika | *Capsicum annuum* | S America | fruit pods |
| pepper | *Piper nigrum* | India | seeds |
| sandalwood | *Santalum album* | India, Indonesia, Australia | heartwood, roots |
| sassafras | *Sassafras albidum* | N America | root bark |
| sesame | *Sesamum indicum* | tropics | seeds |
| soya | *Glycine max* | China | fruit (beans) |
| tamarind | *Tamarindus indica* | Africa | fruits |
| turmeric | *Curcuma longa* | SE Asia | rhizomes |
| vanilla | *Vanilla planifolia* | C America | fruit pods |

## Vegetables

| English name | Species | Part eaten | Colour | Area of origin |
|---|---|---|---|---|
| artichoke, Chinese | *Stachys affinis* | tuber | white | China |
| artichoke, globe | *Cynara scolymus* | buds | green, purple | Mediterranean |
| artichoke, Jerusalem | *Helianthus tuberosus* | tuber | white | N America |
| asparagus | *Asparagus officinalis* | young shoots | green, white | Europe, Asia |
| aubergine (or eggplant) | *Solanum melongena* | fruit | purple, white | Asia, Africa |
| avocado | *Persea americana* | fruit | green, purple | C America |
| bean sprout | *Vigna radiata* | shoots | white, pale brown | China |
| bean, blackeyed | *Vigna unguiculata* | seeds | white/black | India, Iran |
| bean, borlotti (or Boston bean or pinto bean) | *Phaseolus vulgaris* | seeds | pink/brown | America |
| bean, broad | *Vicia faba* | seeds and pods | white | Africa, Europe |
| bean, flageolet | *Phaseolus vulgaris* | seeds | white, pale green | America |
| bean, French | *Phaseolus vulgaris* | pods | green | America |
| bean, haricot | *Phaseolus vulgaris* | seeds | white | America |
| bean, kidney | *Phaseolus vulgaris* | seeds | red | America |
| beans, runner | *Phaseolus coccineus* | pods | green | America |
| bean, soya | *Glycine max* | seeds | green | E Asia |
| beetroot | *Beta vulgaris* | root | white, dark red | Mediterranean |
| broccoli | *Brassica oleracea* | buds and leaves | green, purple | Europe |
| Brussels sprout | *Brassica oleracea (gemmifera)* | buds | green | N Europe |
| cabbage | *Brassica oleracea* | leaves | green, red, white | Europe, W Asia |
| cardoon | *Cynara cardunculus* | inner stalks and flower heads | white, green | Mediterranean |
| carrot | *Daucus carota* | root | orange | Asia |
| cauliflower | *Brassica oleracea* (Botrytis) | flower buds | white, green | Middle East |
| celeriac | *Apium graveolens var. rapaceum* | root | white | Mediterranean |
| celery | *Apium graveolens var. dulce* | stalks | white, green | Europe, N Africa, America |
| chayote (or chocho) | *Sechium edule* | fruit | white, green | America |
| chick-pea | *Cicer arietinum* | seeds | beige, golden, dark brown | W Asia |
| chicory | *Cichorium intybus* | leaves | red, green | Europe, W Asia |
| chinese leaf | *Brassica pekinensis* | leaf stalks | white, green | E Asia, China |
| chives | *Allium schoenoprasum* | leaves | green, white | Europe, N America |
| courgette (or zucchini) | *Cucurbita pepo* | fruit | green | S America, Africa |
| cucumber | *Cucumus sativus* | fruit | green | S Asia |
| eggplant ► aubergine | | | | |
| endive | *Cichorium endivia* | leaves | yellow, green | S Europe, E Indies, Africa |
| fennel, Florentine | *Foeniculum vulgare var. dulce* | leaf stalks | white, green | Europe |
| kale (or borecole) | *Brassica oleracea* (Acephala) | leaves | green | Europe |
| kohlrabi | *Brassica oleracea* (Gongylodes) | stems | white | Europe |
| laver | *Porphyra leucosticta, P. umbilicalis* | leaves and stems | purple-pink | Europe |
| leek | *Allium porrum* | leaves and stems | green, white | Europe, N Africa |
| lentil | *Lens culinaris* | seeds | white, green, pink, red | S Asia |
| lettuce | *Lactuca sativa* | leaves | green, white | Middle East |
| marrow | *Cucurbita pepo* | fruit | green | America |
| mooli | *Raphanus sativus* | root | white | E Africa |
| mushroom | *Agaricus campestris* | fruiting body | brown, white | worldwide |

| English name | Species | Part eaten | Colour | Area of origin |
|---|---|---|---|---|
| okra | *Abelmoschus esculentus* | pods and seeds | green, white | Africa |
| onion | *Allium cepa* | bulb | white, pink | C Asia |
| parsnip | *Pastinaca sativa* | root | white, yellow | Europe |
| pea | *Pisum sativum* | pods and seeds | green | Asia, Europe |
| pepper | *Capsicum annuum* | fruit | red, green, yellow | S America |
| potato | *Solanum tuberosum* | tuber | white | S America |
| pumpkin | *Cucurbita pepo* | fruit | yellow, orange | S America |
| radish | *Raphanus sativus* | root | red, white | China, Japan |
| salsify | *Tragopogon porrifolius* | root | white | S Europe |
| sorrel | *Rumex acetosa* | leaves | green | Europe |
| spinach | *Spinacea oleracea* | leaves | green | Asia |
| squash, winter | *Cucurbita maxima* | fruit | green, yellow, orange | America |
| squash, summer | *Cucurbita pepo* | fruit | yellow, orange, green | America |
| swede | *Brassica napus* (Napobrassica) | root | yellow, white | Europe |
| sweet potato | *Ipomoea batatas* | tuber | white, yellow, red to purple | C America |
| swiss chard | *Beta vulgaris* subsp. *cicla* | leaves and stems | green, white | Europe |
| tomato | *Lycopersicon esculentum* | fruit | red | S America |
| turnip | *Brassica rapa* | root | white | Middle East |
| watercress | *Nasturtium officinale* | leaves and stems | green | Europe, Asia |
| yam | Genus *Dioscorea* 60 species | tuber | white, orange | tropics |
| zucchini ► courgette | | | | |

## Flowers (Bulbs, corms, rhizomes and tubers)

| English name | Genus/Family | Colour | Country/Continent of origin |
|---|---|---|---|
| acidanthera | *Acidanthera* | white | NE Africa |
| African lily (or lily-of-the-Nile) | *Agapanthus* | white, purple | S Africa |
| agapanthus | *Agapanthus* | blue, white | S Africa |
| allium | *Allium* | blue, lilac, white, rose | Asia, Europe |
| amaryllis (or belladonna lily) | *Amaryllis* | rose-pink | S Africa, tropical America |
| anemone | *Anemone* | white, lilac, blue | Mediterranean, Asia, Europe |
| belladonna lily ► amaryllis | | | |
| bluebell | *Hyacinthoides* | blue | Europe |
| camassia | *Camassia* | white, cream, blue, purple | N America |
| chionodoxa (or glory of the snow) | *Chionodoxa* | blue, white, pink | Greece, Turkey |
| crinum | *Crinum* | rose-pink, white | S Africa |
| crocosmia | *Crocosmia* | orange | S Africa |
| crocus | *Crocus* | purple, rose, yellow, pink, orange | Mediterranean, Asia, Africa |
| crown imperial | *Fritillaria* | orange | N India |
| curtonus | *Curtonus* | orange | S Africa |
| cyclamen | *Cyclamen* | white, pink, red | Asia, Mediterranean |
| daffodil (or narcissus) | *Narcissus* | white, yellow, orange | Mediterranean, Europe |
| dog's tooth violet ► erythronium | | | |
| erythronium (or dog's tooth violet) | *Erythronium* | purple, pink, white, yellow | Europe, Asia |
| fritillaria | *Fritillaria* | red, yellow | Europe, Asia, N America |
| galtonia | *Galtonia* | white | S Africa |

| English name | Genus/Family | Colour | Country/Continent of origin |
|---|---|---|---|
| gladiolus | *Gladiolus* | purple, yellow | Europe, Asia |
| glory of the snow ► chionodoxa | | | |
| harebell | *Campanula* | blue | N temperate regions |
| hippeastrum | *Hippeastrum* | pink, white, red | tropical America |
| hyacinth | *Hyacinthus* | blue, white, red | S Europe, Asia |
| hyacinth, grape | *Muscari* | blue | Europe, Mediterranean |
| hyacinth, wild | *Scilla* | blue, purple, pink, white | Asia, S Europe |
| iris | *Iris* | purple, white, yellow | N temperate regions |
| Ithuriel's spear | *Brodiaea* | white, pink, blue | N America |
| lapeirousia | *Lapeirousia* | red | S Africa |
| lily | *Lilium* | white, pink, crimson, yellow, orange, red | China, Europe, America |
| lily-of-the-Nile ► African lily | | | |
| lily-of-the-valley | *Convallaria* | white | Europe, Asia, America |
| naked ladies | *Colchicum* | white, pink, purple | Asia, Europe |
| nerine | *Nerine* | pink, salmon | S Africa |
| ornithogalum | *Ornithogalum* | white, yellow | S Africa |
| peacock (or tiger flower) | *Tigridia* | white, orange, red, yellow | Asia |
| rouge, giant | *Tigridia* | white, yellow, red, lilac | Mexico |
| snake's head | *Fritillaria* | purple, white | Europe |
| snowdrop | *Galanthus* | white | Europe |
| snowflake | *Leucojum* | white, green | S Europe |
| solfaterre | *Crocosmia × crocosmiflora* | orange, red | S Africa |
| Solomon's seal | *Polygonatum* | white | Europe, Asia |
| squill | *Scilla* | blue, purple | Europe, Asia, S Africa |
| sternbergia | *Sternbergia* | yellow | Europe |
| striped squill | *Puschkinia* | bluish-white | Asia |
| tiger flower ► peacock | | | |
| tiger lily | *Lilium* | orange | Asia |
| tulip | *Tulipa* | orange, red, pink, white, crimson, lilac | Europe, Asia |
| wand flower | *Dierama* | white, pink, mauve, purple | S Africa |
| winter aconite | *Eranthis* | yellow | Greece, Turkey |

## Flowers (Herbaceous)

| English name | Genus/Family | Colour | Country/Continent of origin |
|---|---|---|---|
| acanthus | *Acanthus* | white, rose, purple | Europe |
| African violet | *Saintpaulia* | violet, white, pink | Africa |
| alum root | *Heuchera* | rose, pink, red | N America |
| alyssum | *Alyssum* | white, yellow, pink | S Europe |
| anchusa | *Anchusa* | blue | Asia, S Europe |
| anemone | *Hepatica* | white, red-pink, blue | Europe, Caucasus |
| asphodel | *Asphodelus* | white, yellow | S Europe |
| aster | *Aster* | white, blue, purple, pink | Europe, Asia, N America |
| astilbe | *Astilbe* | white, pink, red | Asia |
| aubrietia | *Aubrieta* | purple | SE Europe |
| begonia | *Begonia* | pink | S America, the Pacific |
| bellflower | *Campanula* | blue, white | N temperate regions |
| bergamot | *Monarda* | white, pink, red, purple | N America |
| bistort | *Polygonum* | rose-pink | Japan, Himalayas |
| bleeding heart | *Dicentra* | pink, white, red | China, Japan, N America |
| bugbane | *Cimicifuga* | white | N America, Japan |
| busy lizzie | *Impatiens* | crimson, pink, white | tropics |
| buttercup | *Ranunculus* | yellow | temperate regions |
| carnation | *Dianthus* | white, pink, red | temperate regions |
| catmint | *Nepeta* | blue, mauve | Europe, Asia |

| English name | Genus/Family | Colour | Country/Continent of origin |
|---|---|---|---|
| celandine, giant | *Ranunculus* | white, copper-orange | Europe |
| Christmas rose | *Helleborus* | white, pink | Europe |
| chrysanthemum | *Chrysanthemum* | yellow, white | China |
| cinquefoil | *Potentilla* | orange, red, yellow | Europe, Asia |
| columbine (or granny's bonnet) | *Aquilegia* | purple, dark blue, pink, yellow | Europe |
| Cupid's dart | *Catananche* | blue, white | Europe |
| dahlia | *Dahlia* | red, yellow, white | Mexico |
| daisy | *Bellis* | white, yellow, pink | Europe |
| delphinium | *Delphinium* | white, mauve, pink, blue | Europe, N America |
| echinacea | *Echinacea* | rose-red, purple | N America |
| edelweiss | *Leontopodium* | yellow, white | Europe, Asia |
| evening primrose | *Oenothera* | yellow | N America |
| everlasting flower (or immortelle) | *Helichrysum bracteatum* | yellow | Australia |
| everlasting flower, pearly | *Anaphalis* | white | N America, Himalayas |
| fleabane | *Erigeron* | white, pink, blue, violet | Australia |
| forget-me-not | *Myosotis* | blue | Europe |
| foxglove | *Digitalis* | white, yellow, pink, red | Europe, Asia |
| fraxinella | *Dictamnus* | white, mauve | Europe, Asia |
| gentian | *Gentiana* | blue, yellow, white, red | temperate regions |
| geranium | *Pelargonium* | scarlet, pink, white | temperate regions, subtropics |
| geum | *Geum* | orange, red, yellow | S Europe, N America |
| goat's beard | *Aruncus* | white | N Europe |
| golden rod | *Solidago* | yellow | Europe |
| granny's bonnet ► columbine | | | |
| gypsophila | *Gypsophila* | white, pink | Europe, Asia |
| Hattie's pincushion (or the melancholy gentleman) | *Astrantia* | white, pink | Europe |
| heliopsis | *Heliopsis* | orange-yellow | N America |
| hellebore | *Helleborus* | plum-purple, white | Asia, Greece |
| herb Christopher | *Actaea* | white | N America |
| hollyhock | *Alcaea* | white, yellow, pink, red, maroon | Europe, China |
| hosta | *Hosta* | violet, white | China, Japan |
| immortelle ► everlasting flower | | | |
| kaffir lily | *Schizostylis* | red, pink | S Africa |
| kirengeshoma | *Kirengeshoma* | yellow | Japan |
| liatris | *Liatris* | heather-purple | N America |
| lobelia | *Lobelia* | white, red, blue, purple | Africa, N America, Australia |
| loosestrife | *Lysimachia* | rose-pink, purple | Europe |
| lotus | *Lotus* | yellow, pink, white | Asia, America |
| lupin | *Lupinus* | blue, yellow, pink, red | N America |
| marigold, African (or French marigold) | *Tagetes* | yellow, orange | Mexico |
| marigold, pot | *Calendula* | orange, apricot, cream | unknown |
| meadow rue | *Thalictrum* | yellow-white | Europe, Asia |
| mullein | *Verbascum* | yellow, white, pink, purple | Europe, Asia |
| nasturtium | *Tropaeolum* | yellow, red, orange | S America, Mexico |
| orchid | *Orchidaea* | red, purple, white, violet, green, brown, yellow, pink | tropics |
| ox-eye | *Buphthalmum* | yellow | Europe |
| pansy | *Viola* | white, yellow | temperate regions |
| peony | *Paeonia* | white, yellow, pink, red | Asia, Europe |
| Peruvian lily | *Alstroemeria* | cream, pink, yellow, orange, red | S America |
| petunia | *Petunia* | blue, violet, purple, white, pink | S America |
| phlox | *Phlox* | blue, white, purple, red | America |
| poppy | *Papaver* | red, orange, white, yellow, lilac | N temperate regions |
| primrose | *Primula* | yellow | N temperate regions |
| primula | *Primula* | white, pink, yellow, blue, purple | N temperate regions |

| English name | Genus/Family | Colour | Country/Continent of origin |
|---|---|---|---|
| red-hot poker | *Kniiphofia* | white, yellow, orange, red | S Africa |
| salvia | *Salvia* | red, yellow, blue | S America, Europe, Asia |
| sea holly | *Eryngium* | blue, green-grey, white | Europe, S America |
| sidalcea | *Sidalcea* | lilac, pink, rose | N America |
| snapdragon | *Antirrhinum* | white, yellow, pink, red, maroon | Europe, Asia, S America |
| speedwell | *Veronica* | blue, white | Europe, Asia |
| spiderwort | *Tradescantia* | white, blue, pink, red, purple | N America |
| stokesia | *Stokesia* | white, blue, purple | N America |
| sunflower | *Helianthus* | yellow | N America |
| sweet pea | *Lathyrus* | purple, pink, white, red | Mediterranean |
| sweet william | *Dianthus* | white, pink, red, purple | S Europe |
| thistle, globe | *Echinops* | blue, white-grey | Europe, Asia |
| thistle, Scotch (or cotton thistle) | *Onopordum* | purple | Europe |
| violet | *Viola* | mauve, blue | N temperate regions |
| water chestnut | *Trapa* | white, lilac | Asia |
| water lily | *Nymphaea* | white, blue, red, yellow | worldwide |
| wolfsbane | *Aconitum* | blue, white, rose, yellow | Europe, Asia |
| yarrow | *Achillea* | white, cream | Europe, W Asia |

## Flowers (Shrubs)

| English name | Genus/Family | Colour | Country/Continent of origin |
|---|---|---|---|
| abelia | *Abelia* | white, rose-purple | Asia, China, Mexico |
| abutilon | *Abutilon* | lavender-blue | S America |
| acacia (or mimosa or wattle) | *Acacia* | yellow | Australia, tropical Africa, tropical America |
| almond, dwarf | *Prunus* | white, crimson, rose-pink | Asia, Europe |
| ampelopsis | *Ampelopsis* | green (blue-black fruit) | Far East |
| anthyllis | *Anthyllis* | yellow | Europe |
| azalea | *Rhododendron* | pink, purple, white, yellow, crimson | N hemisphere |
| berberis | *Berberis* | yellow, orange | Asia, America, Europe |
| bottle brush | *Callistemon* | red | Australia |
| bougainvillea | *Bougainvillea* | lilac, pink, purple, red, orange, white | S America |
| broom | *Cytisus* | yellow | Europe |
| buckthorn | *Rhamnus* | red, black | N hemisphere |
| buddleia | *Buddleja* | purple, yellow, white | China, S America |
| cactus | *Cactaceae* | red, purple, orange, yellow, white | America |
| calico bush (or mountain laurel) | *Kalmia* | white, pink | China |
| camellia | *Camellia* | white, pink, red | Asia |
| caryopteris | *Caryopteris* | blue, violet | Asia |
| ceanothus | *Ceanothus* | pink, blue, purple | N America |
| ceratostigma | *Ceratostigma* | purple-blue | China |
| Chinese lantern | *Physalis* | orange, red | Japan |
| cistus | *Cistus* | white, pink | Europe |
| clematis | *Clematis* | white, purple, violet, blue, pink, yellow | N temperate regions |
| clerodendron | *Clerodendron* | white, purple-red | China |
| colquhounia | *Colquhounia* | scarlet, yellow | Himalayas |
| cornelian cherry | *Cornus* | yellow | Europe |
| coronilla | *Coronilla* | yellow | S Europe |
| corylopsis | *Corylopsis* | yellow | China, Japan |
| cotoneaster | *Cotoneaster* | white (red fruit) | Asia |
| currant, flowering | *Ribes* | red, white, pink | N America |

## FLOWERS (SHRUBS)

| English name | Genus/Family | Colour | Country/Continent of origin |
|---|---|---|---|
| Desfontainia | *Desfontainia* | scarlet-gold | S America |
| deutzia | *Deutzia* | white, pink | Asia |
| diplera | *Diplera* | pale pink | China |
| dogwood | *Cornus* | white | Europe, SW Asia |
| embothrium | *Embothrium* | scarlet | S America |
| escallonia | *Escallonia* | white, pink | S America |
| euchryphia | *Euchryphia* | white | Chile, Australasia |
| euryops | *Euryops* | yellow | S Africa |
| fabiana | *Fabiana* | white, mauve | S America |
| firethorn | *Pyracantha* | white (red, orange, yellow fruits) | China |
| forsythia | *Forsythia* | yellow | China |
| frangipani | *Plumeria* | white, pink, yellow | tropical America |
| fuchsia | *Fuchsia* | red, pink, white | C and S America, New Zealand |
| gardenia | *Gardenia* | white | tropics |
| garland flower | *Daphne* | pink, crimson, white, purple | Europe, Asia |
| garrya | *Garrya* | green | California and Oregon |
| gorse (or furze or whin) | *Ulex* | yellow | Europe, Britain |
| hawthorn | *Crataegus* | white (orange-red berries) | N America, Europe, N Africa |
| heath, winter-flowering | *Erica* | white, pink, red | Africa, Europe |
| heather | *Calluna* | pink, purple, white | Europe, W Asia |
| hebe | *Hebe* | blue-white | New Zealand |
| helichrysum | *Helichrysum* | yellow | Australia, S Africa |
| hibiscus | *Hibiscus* | pink, mauve, purple, white, red | China, India |
| honeysuckle | *Lonicera* | white, yellow, pink, red | temperate regions |
| hydrangea | *Hydrangea* | white, pink, blue | Asia, America |
| hyssop | *Hyssopus* | bluish-purple | S Europe, W Asia |
| indigofera | *Indigofera* | rose-purple | Himalayas |
| ipomoea (or morning glory) | *Ipomoea* | white, red, blue | tropical America |
| japonica | *Chaenomeles* | white, pink, orange, red, yellow | N Asia |
| jasmine | *Jasminum* | white, yellow, red | Asia |
| Jerusalem sage | *Phlomis* | yellow | Europe |
| kerria | *Kerria* | yellow | China |
| kolkwitzia | *Kolkwitzia* | pink | China |
| laburnum | *Laburnum* | yellow | Europe, Asia |
| lavender | *Lavandula* | purple | Europe |
| leptospermum | *Leptospermum* | red, white | Australasia |
| lespedeza | *Lespedeza* | rose-purple | China, Japan |
| leycesteria | *Leycesteria* | claret | Himalayas |
| lilac (or syringa) | *Syringa* | purple, pink, white | Balkans |
| lion's tail | *Leonotis* | red | S Africa |
| magnolia | *Magnolia* | yellow, white, rose, purple | China, Japan |
| mahonia | *Mahonia* | yellow | Japan |
| malus | *Malus* | white, pink, red | N America, Asia |
| menziesa | *Menziesa* | wine-red | Japan |
| mimosa ► acacia | | | |
| mimulus | *Mimulus* | cream, orange, red | N America |
| mock orange | *Philadelphus* | white | Europe, Asia, N America |
| moltkia | *Moltkia* | voilet-blue | Greece |
| morning glory ► ipomoea | | | |
| mother-of-pearl | *Symphoricarpus* | pink, white, red fruit | N America |
| mountain ash ► rowan | | | |
| myrtle | *Myrtus* | pink, white | Europe |
| oleander | *Nerium* | white, pink, purple, red | Mediterranean |
| olearia | *Olearia* | white, yellow | New Zealand |
| oleaster | *Elaeagnus* | yellow | Europe, Asia, N America |

| English name | Genus/Family | Colour | Country/Continent of origin |
|---|---|---|---|
| osmanthus | *Osmanthus* | white | China |
| pearl bush | *Exochorda* | white | China |
| peony | *Paeonia* | pink, red, white, yellow | Europe, Asia, N America |
| pieris | *Pieris* | white | China |
| poinsettia | *Euphorbia* | scarlet | Mexico |
| potentilla | *Potentilla* | yellow, red, orange | Asia |
| rhododendron | *Rhododendron* | red, purple, pink, white | S Asia |
| rhus | *Rhus* | foliage grey, purple, red | Europe, N America |
| ribbon woods | *Hoheria* | white | New Zealand |
| robinia | *Robinia* | rose-pink | N America |
| rock rose (or sun rose) | *Helianthemum* | white, yellow, pink, orange, red | Europe |
| rose | *Rosa* | pink, red, white, cream, yellow | N temperate regions |
| rosemary | *Rosmarinus* | violet | Europe, Asia |
| rowan (or mountain ash) | *Sorbus* | white (red, yellow berries) | Europe, Asia |
| sage, common | *Salvia* | green, white, yellow, reddish purple | S Europe |
| St John's wort | *Hypericum* | yellow | Europe, Asia |
| sea buckthorn | *Hippophae* | silver, orange | SW Europe |
| senecio | *Senecio* | yellow | New Zealand |
| skimmia | *Skimmia* | white | Japan, China |
| snowberry | *Symphoricarpos* | pink, white | N America |
| spiraea | *Spiraea* | white, pink, crimson | China, Japan |
| stachyurus | *Stachyurus* | pale yellow | China |
| staphylea | *Staphylea* | rose-pink | Europe, Asia |
| sun rose ► rock rose | | | |
| syringa ► lilac | | | |
| tamarisk | *Tamarix* | pink, white | Europe |
| thyme | *Thymus* | purple, white, pink | Europe |
| veronica | *Veronica* | white, pink, lilac, purple | New Zealand |
| viburnum | *Viburnum* | white, pink | Europe, Asia, Africa |
| Virginia creeper | *Parthenocissus* | foliage orange, red (blue-black fruits) | N America |
| wattle ► acacia | | | |
| weigela | *Weigela* | pink, red | N China |
| winter sweet | *Chimonanthus* | yellow | China |
| wisteria | *Wisteria* | mauve, white, pink | China, Japan |
| witch-hazel | *Hamamelis* | red, yellow | China, Japan |

## Fungi

| English name | Species | Colour | Edibility |
|---|---|---|---|
| base toadstool (or ugly toadstool) | *Lactarius necator* | green, brown | poisonous |
| beautiful clavaria | *Ramaria formosa* | yellow, ochre, red, purple | poisonous |
| beefsteak fungus | *Fistulina hepatica* | red | edible |
| blusher | *Amanita fubescens* | red, brown | poisonous (raw) or edible (cooked) |
| brain mushroom | *Gyromitra esculenta* | chestnut, dark brown | poisonous |
| buckler agaric | *Entoloma clypeatum* | grey, brown | edible |
| Caesar's mushroom | *Amanita Caesarea* | red, yellow | edible |
| chanterelle | *Cantharellus cibarius* | yellow, ochre | excellent |
| clean mycena | *Mycena pura* | purple | poisonous |
| clouded agaric | *Lepista nebularis* | grey, brown | poisonous |
| common earthball | *Scleroderma aurantium* | ochre, yellow, brown | poisonous |
| common grisette | *Amanita vaginita* | grey, yellow | edible |
| common morel | *Morchella esculenta* | light brown, black | edible |
| common puffball | *Lycoperdon perlatum* | white, cream, brown | edible |

## FUNGI

| English name | Species | Colour | Edibility |
|---|---|---|---|
| common stinkhorn | *Phallus impudicus* | white, green | edible |
| death cap | *Amanita phalloides* | grey, green, yellow, brown | deadly |
| deceiver, common laccaria | *Laccaria laccata* | purple, pink, orange | edible |
| destroying angel | *Amanita virosa* | white, brown | deadly |
| dingy agaric | *Tricholoma portentosum* | grey, black, yellow, lilac | edible |
| dryad's saddle | *Polyporus squamosus* | yellow, brown | edible |
| fairies bonnets | *Coprinus disseminatus* | grey, purple | worthless |
| fairy ring champignon | *Marasmius oreades* | beige, ochre, red, brown | edible |
| field mushroom | *Agaricus campestris* | white, brown | excellent |
| firwood agaric | *Tricholoma auratum* | green, yellow, brown | edible |
| fly agaric | *Amanita muscaria* | red, orange, white | poisonous |
| garlic marosmius | *Marosmius scorodonius* | red, brown | edible |
| gypsy mushroom | *Rozites caperata* | yellow, ochre | edible |
| hedgehog mushroom | *Hydnum repandum* | white, beige, yellow | edible |
| honey fungus | *Armillaria mellea* | honey, brown, red | inedible |
| horn of plenty (or trumpet of the dead) | *Craterellus cornucopiodes* | brown, black | very good |
| horse mushroom | *Agaricus arvensis* | white, yellow, ochre | very good |
| Jew's ear fungus | *Auricularia auricula judae* | yellow, brown | worthless |
| larch boletus | *Suillus grevillei* | yellow | edible |
| liberty cap (or 'magic mushroom') | *Psilocybe semilanceata* | brown | poisonous |
| lurid boletus | *Boletus luridus* | olive, brown, yellow | poisonous (raw) or edible (cooked) |
| morel | *Morchella* | brown | good |
| naked mushroom | *Lepista nuda* | purple, brown | edible |
| old man of the woods | *Strobilomyces floccopus* | brown, black | edible |
| orange-peel fungus | *Aleuria aurantia* | orange, red | edible |
| oyster mushroom | *Pleurotus ostreatus* | brown, black, grey, blue, purple | edible |
| panther cap (or false blusher) | *Amanita pantherina* | brown, ochre, grey, white | poisonous |
| parasol mushroom | *Macrolepiota procera* | beige, ochre, brown | excellent |
| penny-bun fungus | *Boletus edulis* | chestnut brown | excellent |
| périgord truffle | *Tuber melanosporum* | black, red-brown | excellent |
| Piedmont truffle | *Tuber magnatum* | white | edible |
| purple blewit | *Tricholomopsis rutilans* | yellow, red | edible |
| saffron milk cap | *Lactorius delicioses* | orange, red | poisonous (raw) or edible (cooked) |
| St George's mushroom | *Calocybe gambosa* | white, cream | edible |
| Satan's boletus | *Boletus satanus* | grey | poisonous (raw) or edible (cooked) |
| scarlet-stemmed boletus | *Boletus calopus* | grey, brown | poisonous |
| shaggy ink cap (or lawyer's wig) | *Coprinus comatus* | white, ochre | edible |
| sickener (or emetic russala) | *Russula emetica* | pink, red | poisonous |
| stinkhorn | *Phallus impudicus* | olive, green | inedible |
| stinking russula | *Russula foetens* | ochre, brown | poisonous |
| stout agaric | *Amanita spissa* | grey, brown | edible |
| strong scented garlic | *Tricholoma saponaceum* | grey, green, brown | poisonous |
| sulphur tuft (or clustered woodlover) | *Hypholoma fasciculare* | yellow, red, brown | poisonous |
| summer truffle | *Tuber aestivum* | dark brown | very good |
| white truffle | *Tuber magnatum* | cream, pale brown | excellent |
| winter fungus (or velvet shank) | *Flammulina velutipes* | yellow, brown, ochre | edible |
| wood agaric | *Collybia dryophila* | yellow, brown, rust | edible |
| wood mushroom | *Agaricus sylvaticus* | grey, red, brown | edible |
| woolly milk-cap (or griping toadstool) | *Lactarius torminosus* | pink, brown | poisonous |
| yellow stainer | *Agaricus xanthodermus* | white, yellow, grey | poisonous |
| yellow-brown boletus (or slippery jack) | *Suillus luteus* | yellow, brown | edible |

## Trees (Europe and N America)

| English name | Species | Deciduous/ Evergreen | Continent of origin |
|---|---|---|---|
| alder, common | *Alnus glutinosa* | deciduous | Europe |
| almond | *Prunus dulcis* | deciduous | W Asia, N Africa |
| apple | *Malus pumila* | deciduous | Europe, W Africa |
| apple, crab | *Malus sylvestris* | deciduous | Europe, Asia |
| ash, common | *Fraxinus exzcelsior* | deciduous | Europe |
| aspen | *Populus tremula* | deciduous | Europe |
| bean tree, Red Indian | *Catalpa bignonioides* | deciduous | America, E Asia |
| beech, common | *Fagus sylvatica* | deciduous | Europe |
| beech, copper | *Fagus purpurea* ('Atropunicea') | deciduous | Europe |
| beech, noble | *Nothofagus obliqua* | deciduous | S America |
| birch, silver | *Betula pendula* | deciduous | Europe, America, Asia |
| box | *Buxus sempervirens* | evergreen | Europe, N Africa |
| Brazil nut | *Bertholletia excelsa* | evergreen | S America |
| camellia, deciduous | *Stewartia pseudo-camellia* | deciduous | Asia |
| castor-oil tree, prickly | *Eleutherococcus pictus* | deciduous | tropics |
| cedar of Lebanon | *Cedrus libani* | evergreen | Asia |
| cedar, smooth Tasmanian | *Athrotaxis cupressoides* | evergreen | Australia |
| cedar, white | *Thuja occidentalis* | evergreen | America |
| cherry, morello (or sour cherry) | *Prunus cerasus* | deciduous | Europe, Asia |
| cherry, wild (or gean) | *Prunus avium* | deciduous | Europe |
| chestnut, horse | *Aesculus hippocastanum* | deciduous | Asia, SW Europe |
| chestnut, sweet (or Spanish chestnut) | *Castanea sativa* | deciduous | Europe, Africa, Asia |
| cypress, Lawson | *Chamaecyparis lawsoniana* | evergreen | America |
| deodar | *Cedrus deodara* | evergreen | Asia |
| dogwood, common | *Cornus sanguinea* | deciduous | Europe |
| elm, Dutch | *Ulmus × hollandica* | deciduous | Europe |
| elm, English | *Ulmus procera* | deciduous | Europe |
| elm, wych | *Ulmus glabra* | deciduous | Europe |
| fig | *Ficus carica* | evergreen | Asia |
| fir, Douglas | *Pseudotsuga menziesii* | evergreen | America |
| fir, red | *Abies magnifica* | evergreen | America |
| ginkgo | *Ginkgo biloba* | deciduous | Asia |
| grapefruit | *Citrus × paradisi* | evergreen | Asia |
| gum, blue | *Eucalyptus globulus* | evergreen | Australia |
| gum, cider | *Eucalyptus gunnii* | evergreen | Australia |
| gum, snow | *Eucalyptus panciflora* | evergreen | Australia |
| gutta-percha tree | *Eucommia ulmoides* | deciduous | China |
| hawthorn | *Crataegus monogyna* | deciduous | Europe |
| hazel, common | *Corylus avellana* | deciduous | Europe, W Asia, N Africa |
| hemlock, Western | *Tsuga heterophylla* | evergreen | America |
| holly | *Ilex aquifolium* | evergreen | Europe, N Africa, W Asia |
| hornbeam | *Carpinus betulus* | deciduous | Europe, Asia |
| Joshua-tree | *Yucca brevifolia* | evergreen | America |
| Judas-tree | *Cercis siliquastrum* | deciduous | S Europe, Asia |
| juniper, common | *Juniperus communis* | evergreen | Europe, Asia |
| laburnum, common | *Laburnum anagyroides* | deciduous | Europe |
| larch, European | *Larix decidua* | deciduous | Europe |
| larch, golden | *Pseudolarix kaempferi* | deciduous | E Asia |
| leatherwood | *Eucryphia lucida* | evergreen | Australia |
| lemon | *Citrus limon* | evergreen | Asia |
| lime | *Citrus aurantiifolia* | evergreen | Asia |
| lime, small-leafed | *Tilia cordata* | deciduous | Europe |
| locust tree | *Robinia pseudoacacia* | deciduous | America |
| magnolia (or white laurel) | *Magnolia virginiana* | evergreen | America |
| maple, field (or common maple) | *Acer campestre* | deciduous | Europe |

## TREES (EUROPE AND N AMERICA)

| English name | Species | Deciduous/ Evergreen | Continent of origin |
|---|---|---|---|
| maple, sugar | *Acer saccharum* | deciduous | America |
| medlar | *Mespilus germanica* | deciduous | Europe |
| mimosa | *Acacia dealbata* | deciduous | Australia, Europe |
| mockernut | *Carya tomentosa* | deciduous | America |
| monkey puzzle | *Araucaria araucana* | evergreen | S America |
| mountain ash ► rowan | | | |
| mulberry, common | *Morus nigra* | deciduous | Asia |
| mulberry, white | *Morus alba* | deciduous | Asia |
| myrtle, orange bark | *Myrtus apiculata* | evergreen | S America |
| nutmeg, California | *Torreya californica* | evergreen | America |
| oak, California live | *Quercus agrifolia* | deciduous | America |
| oak, cork | *Quercus suber* | evergreen | S Europe, N Africa |
| oak, English (or common oak) | *Quercus robur* | deciduous | Europe, Asia, Africa |
| oak, red | *Quercus rubra* | deciduous | America |
| olive | *Olea europaea* | evergreen | S Europe |
| orange, sweet | *Citrus sinensis* | evergreen | Asia |
| pagoda-tree | *Sophora japonica* | deciduous | China, Japan |
| pear | *Pyrus communis* | deciduous | Europe, W Asia |
| pine, Austrian | *Pinus nigra* subsp. *nigra* | evergreen | Europe, Asia |
| pine, Corsican | *Pinus nigra* subsp. *laricio* | evergreen | Europe |
| pine, Monterey | *Pinus radiata* | evergreen | America |
| pine, Scots | *Pinus sylvestris* | evergreen | Europe |
| plane, London | *Platanus × hispanica* | deciduous | Europe |
| plane, Oriental | *Platanus orientalis* | deciduous | SE Europe, Asia |
| plum | *Prunus domestica* | deciduous | Europe, Asia |
| poplar, balsam | *Populus balsamifera* | deciduous | America, Asia |
| poplar, black | *Populus nigra* | deciduous | Europe, Asia |
| poplar, Lombardy | *Populus nigra* 'Italica' | deciduous | Europe |
| poplar, white | *Populus alba* | deciduous | Europe |
| quince | *Cydonia oblonga* | deciduous | Asia |
| raoul | *Nothofagus procera* | deciduous | S America |
| rowan (or mountain ash) | *Sorbus aucuparia* | deciduous | Europe |
| sassafras, American | *Sassafras albidum* | deciduous | America |
| service tree, true | *Sorbus domestica* | deciduous | Europe |
| silver fir, common | *Abies alba* | evergreen | Europe |
| spruce, Norway | *Picea abies* | evergreen | Europe |
| spruce, sitka | *Picea sitchensis* | evergreen | America, Europe |
| strawberry tree | *Arbutus unedo* | evergreen | Europe |
| sycamore ('plane') | *Acer pseudoplatanus* | deciduous | Europe, W Asia |
| tamarack | *Larix laricina* | deciduous | N America |
| tree of heaven | *Ailanthus altissima* | deciduous | China |
| tulip tree | *Liriodendron tulipfera* | deciduous | America |
| walnut, black | *Juglans nigra* | deciduous | America |
| walnut, common | *Juglans regia* | deciduous | Europe, Asia |
| whitebeam | *Sorbus aria* | deciduous | Europe |
| willow, pussy (or goat willow or sallow willow) | *Salix caprea* | deciduous | Europe, Asia |
| willow, weeping | *Salix babylonica* | deciduous | Asia |
| willow, white | *Salix alba* | deciduous | Europe |
| yew, common | *Taxus baccata* | evergreen | N temperate regions |

## Trees (Tropical)

| Name | Species | Deciduous/ Evergreen | Continent of origin |
|---|---|---|---|
| African tulip tree | *Spathodea campanulata* | evergreen | Africa |
| almond, tropical | *Terminalia catappa* | deciduous | Asia |
| angel's trumpet | *Brugmansia × candida* | deciduous | S America |
| autograph tree | *Clusia rosea* | evergreen | Asia |
| avocado | *Persea americana* | evergreen | America |
| bamboo | *Schizostachyum glauchifolium* | deciduous | America |
| banana | *Musa × paradisiaca* | plant dies after fruiting | Asia |
| banyan | *Ficus benghalensis* | evergreen | Asia |
| baobab (or dead rat's tree) | *Adansonia digitata* | deciduous | Africa |
| beach heliotrope | *Argusia argentea* | evergreen | S America |
| bo tree | *Ficus religiosa* | deciduous | Asia |
| bombax | *Bombax ceiba* | deciduous | Asia |
| bottle brush | *Callistemon citrinus* | evergreen | Australia |
| breadfruit | *Artocarpus altilis* | evergreen | Asia |
| brownea | *Brownea macrophylla* | evergreen | C America |
| calabash | *Crescentia cujete* | evergreen | America |
| candlenut | *Aleurites moluccana* | evergreen | Asia |
| cannonball | *Courouptia guianensis* | evergreen | S America |
| chinaberry (or bead tree) | *Melia azedarach* | deciduous | Asia |
| Christmas-berry | *Schinus terebinthifolius* | evergreen | America |
| coconut palm | *Cocus nucifera* | evergreen | Asia |
| coffee tree | *Coffea liberica* | evergreen | Africa |
| Cook pine | *Araucaria columnaris* | evergreen | America |
| coral tree | *Erythrina coralloides* | deciduous | C America |
| coral shower | *Cassia grandis* | deciduous | Asia |
| cotton, wild | *Cochlospermum vitifolium* | deciduous | C and S America |
| crape myrtle | *Lagerstroemia indica* | deciduous | Asia |
| date palm | *Phoenix dactylifera* | evergreen | Asia and Africa |
| dragon tree | *Dracaena draco* | evergreen | Africa (Canary Is) |
| durian | *Durio zibethinus* | evergreen | Asia |
| ebony | *Diospyros ebenum* | evergreen | Asia |
| elephant's ear | *Enderolobium cyclocarpum* | deciduous | S America |
| flame tree | *Delonix regia* | deciduous | Africa (Madagascar) |
| gold tree | *Cybistax donnell-smithii* | deciduous | Asia |
| golden rain | *Koelreuteria paniculata* | deciduous | Asia |
| golden shower | *Cassia fistula* | deciduous | Asia |
| guava | *Psidium guajeva* | evergreen | S America |
| ironwood (or casuarina) | *Casuarina equisetifolia* | deciduous | Australia and Asia |
| jacaranda | *Jacaranda mimosifolia* | deciduous | S America |
| jackfruit (or jack) | *Artocarpus heterophyllus* | evergreen | Asia |
| kapok tree | *Ceiba pentandra* | deciduous | Old and New World tropics |
| koa | *Acacia koa* | evergreen | Oceania (Hawaii) |
| lipstick tree | *Bixa orellanna* | evergreen | America |
| lychee | *Litchi chinensis* | evergreen | China |
| macadamia nut | *Macadamia integrifolia* | evergreen | Australia |
| mahogany | *Swietenia mahogoni* | evergreen | S America |
| mango | *Mangifera indica* | evergreen | Asia |
| mesquite | *Prosopis pallida* | evergreen | America |
| monkeypod (or rain tree) | *Albizia saman* | evergreen | S America |
| Norfolk island pine | *Araucaria heterophylla* | evergreen | Oceania (Norfolk I) |
| octopus tree | *Schefflera actinophylla* | evergreen | Australia |
| ohi' a lehua | *Metrosideros collina* | evergreen | Oceania (Hawaii) |
| pandanus (or screw pine) | *Pandanus tectorius* | evergreen | Oceania |
| paperbark tree | *Melaleuca quinquenervia* | evergreen | Australia |

| Name | Species | Deciduous/ Evergreen | Continent of origin |
|---|---|---|---|
| powderpuff | *Calliandra haematocephala* | evergreen | S America |
| royal palm | *Roystonea regia* | evergreen | America (Cuba) |
| sandalwood | *Santalum album* | deciduous | Asia |
| sand-box tree | *Hura crepitans* | deciduous | Americas |
| sausage tree | *Kigelia pinnata* | evergreen | Africa |
| scrambled egg tree | *Cassia glauca* | evergreen | Americas |
| Surinam cherry | *Eugenia uniflora* | evergreen | S America |
| teak tree | *Tectona grandis* | evergreen | Asia |
| tiger's claw | *Erythrina variegata* | deciduous | Asia |
| yellow oleander | *Thevetia peruviana* | evergreen | Americas (W Indies) |

## Fish — Record holders

**Fastest** — Over short distances, the sailfish can reach a speed of 110kph/68mph; however marlins are the fastest over longer distances, and can reach a burst speed of 68–80kph/40–50mph.

**Largest** — The whale shark (*Rhincodon typus*) is said to reach over 18m/59ft, with the largest on record being 12.65m/41ft 6in, weighing an estimated 21.5 tonnes.

**Smallest** — The dwarf pygmy goby (*Pandaka pygmaea*), found in the streams and rivers of Luzon in the Philippines, measures 7.5–9.9mm and weighs 4–5mg.

**Smallest in British waters** — Guillet's goby (*Lebetus guilleti*) reaches a maximum length of 24mm.

**Most widespread** — The distribution of the bristlemouths of genus *Cyclothone* is worldwide excluding the Arctic.

**Most restricted** — The devil's hole pupfish (*Cyprinodon diabolis*) inhabits only a small area of water above a rock shelf in a spring-fed pool in Ash Meadows, Nevada, USA.

**Deepest dweller** — In 1970 a brotulid *Bassogigas profundissimus* was recovered from a depth of 8 299m/27 230ft, making it the deepest living vertebrate.

**Largest fish ever caught on a rod** — In 1959 a great white shark measuring 5.13m/16ft 10in and weighing 1 208kg/2 664 lb was caught off S Australia.

**Largest freshwater fish found in Britain and Ireland** — Reportedly, in 1815 a pike (*Esox lucius*) was taken from the River Shannon in Ireland weighing 41.7kg/92 lb; however there is evidence of a pike weighing 32.7kg/72 lb having been caught on Loch Ken, Scotland, in 1774.

**Largest saltwater fish caught by anglers in the UK** — In 1933 a tunny weighing 385.989kg/851lb was caught near Whitby, Yorkshire.

**Longest-lived species** — Some specimens of the sturgeon are thought to be over 80 years old.

**Shortest-lived species** — Tooth carp of the suborder *Cyprinodontidae* live for only 8 months in the wild.

**Greatest distance covered by a migrating fish** — A bluefin tuna was tagged in 1958 off California and caught in 1963 in Japan; it had covered a distance of 9 335km/5 800mi.

## Birds — Record holders

**Highest flier** — Ruppell's griffon, a vulture, has been measured at 11 275m (about 7mi) above sea level.

**Furthest migrator** — The arctic tern travels up to 36 000km/22 400mi each year, flying from the Arctic to the Antarctic and back again.

**Fastest flier** — The peregrine falcon can dive through the air at speeds up to 185kph/115mph. The fastest bird in level flight is the eider duck, which can reach 80kph/50mph.

**Fastest animal on two legs** — The ostrich can maintain a speed of 50kph/31mph for 15 minutes or more, and it may reach 65–70kph/40–43mph in short bursts, eg when escaping from predators.

| | |
|---|---|
| **Smallest** | The bee hummingbird of Cuba is under 6cm/2.4in long and weighs 3g/0.1oz. |
| **Greatest wingspan** | The wandering albatross can reach 3.65m/12ft. |
| **Heaviest flying bird** | The great bustard and the kori bustard both weigh up to 18kg/40 lb, with swans not far behind at about 16kg/35 lb. |
| **Deepest diver** | The emperor penguin can reach a depth of 265m/870ft. The great northern diver or loon can dive to about 80m/262ft — deeper than any other flying bird. |
| **Most abundant** | Africa's red-billed quelea is the most numerous wild bird, with an estimated population of about 1 500 million. The domestic chicken is the most abundant of all birds, numbering over 4 000 million. |
| **Most feathers** | The greatest number of feathers counted on a bird was 25 216, on a swan. |

## Mammals — Record holders

| | |
|---|---|
| **Largest** | The blue whale, up to 30m/98ft long and weighing up to 150 tonnes, is the largest known mammal. The largest existing land mammal is the male African elephant, standing up to 3.3m/11ft at the shoulder and weighing up to 7 tonnes. |
| **Tallest** | The giraffe stands up to 5.5m/18ft high. |
| **Smallest** | The pygmy white-toothed shrew, also called the Etruscan shrew, has a body about 5cm/2in long and weighs up to 2.5g/0.1oz. Some bats weigh even less. |
| **Fastest on land** | The cheetah can reach 100kph/62mph, but only in short bursts. The pronghorn can maintain speeds of 50kph/31mph for several kilometres. |
| **Most prolific breeder** | A North American meadow mouse produced 17 litters in a single year (4–9 babies per litter). |
| **Most widespread** | Humans are the most widely distributed mammals, closely followed by the house mouse, which has accompanied humans to all parts of the world. |

## Mammals

Mammals are the group of animals to which humans belong. They are characterized by the presence of mammary glands in the female which produce milk on which the young can be nourished. They are divided into monotremes or egg-laying mammals; marsupials in which the young are born at an early stage of development and then grow outside the mother's womb, often in a pouch; placental mammals in which the young are nourished in the womb by the mother's blood and are born at a late stage of development. A crucial aspect of mammals is the fact that their hair and skin glands allow them to regulate their temperatures from within, ie they are endothermic (warm-blooded). This confers on them a greater adaptability to more varied environments than that of reptiles. There are over 4 000 species of mammals, most of which are terrestrial, the exceptions being species of bat which have developed the ability to fly, and the whale which leads an aquatic existence.

| Name | Family/Species | Size (cm)[1] | Distribution | Food | Special features |
|---|---|---|---|---|---|
| ❑ **Monotremes** | | | | | |
| echidna, long-beaked | Species *Zaglossus bruijni* | 45–90 | New Guinea | earthworms | prominent beak; short spines scattered among fur |
| echidna, short-beaked | Species *Tachyglossidae aculeatus* | 30–45 | Australia, Tasmania and New Guinea | ants, termites | fur covered in protective spines; known to live up to 50 years in captivity |
| platypus | Family *Ornithorhynchidae* | 45–60 | E Australia and Tasmania | invertebrates, larvae | noted for its duck-like snout |
| ❑ **Marsupials** | | | | | |
| bandicoot | Family *Peramelidae* | 15–56 | Australia and New Guinea | insectivorous and omnivorous | highest reproductive rate of all marsupials |
| kangaroo | Family *Macropodidae* | to 165 | Australia and New Guinea | grasses, plants | most popularly known of Australian mammals, noted for its bounding motion and prominent female pouch; includes all species of wallaby |
| kangaroo, rat | Family *Macropodidae* | 28.4–30 | Australia and New Guinea | grasses, plants | rabbit-sized version of its larger namesake |
| koala | Family *Phascolarctidae* | 78 | E Australia | eucalyptus leaves | marsupial with popular reputation; intensive management has significantly revived population numbers which at one time seemed threatened with extinction |
| mole, marsupial | Family *Notoryctidae* | 13–15 | Australia | insects, larvae | only Australian mammal that has specialized in burrowing |
| oppossum | Family *Didelphidae* | 7–55 | C and S America | earthworms, fruit, insects, small vertebrates, crustaceans, fish, frogs, reptiles | generally known for its dreadful smell |
| possum, brushtail | Family *Phalangeridae* | 34–70 | Australia, New Guinea, Solomon Is and New Zealand | leaves, fruit, bark, eggs, invertebrates | the most commonly encountered of all Australian mammals |

| Name | Family/Species | Size (cm)[1] | Distribution | Food | Special features |
|---|---|---|---|---|---|
| wallaby ▸ kangaroo | | | | | |
| wombat | Family *Vombatidae* | 870–115 | SE Australia and Tasmania | grasses | poor eyesight compensated by keen senses of smell and hearing |
| ❑ **Placental mammals** | | | | | |
| aardvark | Family *Orycteropodidae* | 105–130 | Africa S of the Sahara | ants, termites | secretive, nocturnal creature; characterized by its long, tubular snout |
| anteater | Family *Myrmecophagidae* | 16–22 | C and S America | ants and sometimes termites | noted, particularly the giant anteater, for its long, elongated snout |
| antelope, dwarf | Tribe *Neotragini* | 45–55 | Africa | leaves, grass, fruit, buds | unusual among hoofed mammals in that the female is larger than the male |
| armadillo | Family *Dasypodidae* | 12.5–100 | southern N America, C and S America | vertebrates, insects, fungi, tubers, fruit, carrion | noted, particularly the giant armadillo, for its protective suit of armour |
| ass | Subgenus *Asinus* | 200–210 | Africa and Asia | grass, leaves | renowned as a beast of burden |
| baboon and mandrill | Genus *Papio* | 56–80 | Africa | fruit, plants, insects, small mammals | able to walk over long distances |
| badger | Family *Mustelidae* | 50–100 | Africa, Europe, Asia and N America | vertebrates, invertebrates, fruit, roots, earthworms | mainly nocturnal; European species characterized by its distinctive black and white markings |
| bat | Order *Chiroptera* | 15–200 (wingspan) | worldwide except for the Arctic and Antarctic | insects, vertebrates, fish, fruit | the only vertebrate, except for birds, capable of sustained flight; noted for its powers of echo location and tendency to cluster in large numbers |
| bear, black | Species *Ursus americanus* | 1.3–1.8 m | N America | omnivorous | smaller and more secretive than the brown or grizzly bear, its greater ability to adapt has helped it to survive in greater numbers |
| bear, grizzly (or brown bear) | Species *Ursus arctos* | 200–280 | NW America and former USSR | omnivorous | noted for its size (up to half a ton); much reduced population due to hunting, loss of natural habitat |
| beaver | Genus *Castor* | 80–120 | N America, Asia and Europe | plants, wood | renowned for its industry and ability to construct dams and lodges in streams and ponds |
| beaver, mountain | Family *Aplondontidae* | 30–41 | Pacific Coast of Canada and USA | leaves, plant materials | land-dwelling and burrowing animal; causes great damage to forest areas |
| bison, American | Species *Bison bison* | to 380 | N America | grazing fodder | once numbered in millions in the prairies of N America, now survives only in parks and refuges |
| bison, European | Species *Bison bonasus* | to 290 | former USSR | grazing fodder | became extinct in the wild in 1919, but has now been re-established in parts of the former USSR |
| boar | Family *Suidae* | 58–210 | Europe, Africa and Asia | plants, larvae, frogs, mice, earthworms | wild pig; characteristically ugly appearance; intelligent and highly adaptable; includes species of warthog |
| buffalo, wild water | Species *Bubalus arnee* | 240–280 | SE Asia | grazing fodder | adept at moving through the muddy areas which they inhabit |

| Name | Family/Species | Size (cm)[1] | Distribution | Food | Special features |
|---|---|---|---|---|---|
| bush baby | Subfamily *Galaginae* | 12–32 | Africa and S Asia | insects, fruit, gum | highly agile, arboreal creature |
| bushbuck | Species *Tragelaphus scriptus* | 110–145 | Africa S of the Sahara | grazing fodder | occupies habitats with dense cover; dark brown or chestnut coat with white markings |
| camel | Species *Camelus bactrianus* | 190–230 (height of hump) | Mongolia | plants, vegetation | two humps |
| capybara | Family *Hydrochoeridae* | 106–134 | S America | grass | largest living rodent, lives in groups by the edge of water; traditionally hunted for its meat and skin |
| cat | Family *Felidae* | 20–400 | worldwide | carnivorous | acute sense of vision and smell |
| cattle | Family *Bovidae* | 180–200 | worldwide | grass | agricultural animal existing in both long-horned and polled or hornless breeds |
| chamois | Species *Rupicapra rupicapra* | 125–135 | Europe and Asia | grass, leaves, lichen | has adapted to alpine and subalpine conditions and to life on snowy mountains; part of its defence mechanism in fighting is its evasive running and dodging movement |
| cheetah | Family *Felidae* | 112–135 | Africa | hoofed animals up to 40kg, such as gazelles, impala, wildebeest calves | the fastest of all land animals, reaching speeds of 100kph/62mph |
| chimpanzee | Genus *Pan* | 70–85 | W and C Africa | fruit, leaves, seeds, insects, small mammals | most intelligent of the great apes; recent studies suggest that adults teach their offspring how to use tools |
| chinchilla | Family *Chinchillidae* | 25 | S America | grazing fodder | widely hunted as food and for its valuable fur |
| civet | Family *Viverridae* | 33–84 | Africa and Asia | fruit, small mammals, birds, rodents, insects, small reptiles | cat-like carnivore; nocturnal hunter; economic source of civet oil |
| colugo | Genus *Cynocephalus* | 33–42 | SE Asia | leaves, shoots, buds, flowers | also known as flying lemur, a reference to the membrane which stretches from its neck to the tips of its fingers, toes and tail, allowing it to glide from tree to tree |
| coyote | Species *Canis latrans* | 70–97 | N America | squirrels, rabbits, mice, antelope, deer, mountain sheep | makes unique howling sound; regarded as agricultural pest for its attacks on farm animals, but also kills agricultural vermin |
| coypu | Species *Myocastor coypu* | 50 | S America | freshwater plants | highly aquatic rodent; burrows into banks; beaver-like qualities |

| Name | Family/Species | Size (cm)[1] | Distribution | Food | Special features |
|---|---|---|---|---|---|
| deer | Family *Cervidae* | 41–152 | N and S America, Europe and Asia | grass, shoots, twigs, leaves, flowers, fruit | distinguished in the male by the presence of antlers most characteristically used to attack other males during the rutting period; species include red deer, reindeer, waipiti, and the moose or elk |
| dingo | Species *Canis dingo* | 150 | Australasia | rabbits, lizards, grasshoppers, wild pigs, kangaroos | history of the dingo in Australia dates back 8 000 years; descendant of the wolf; lives in packs |
| dog | Species *Canis familiaris* | 20–75 | worldwide | carnivorous | first animal to be domesticated; c.400 domestic breeds |
| dolphin | Family *Delphinidae* | 120–400 | worldwide | fish, squid | renowned for grace, agility, intelligence; highly developed social organization and communication systems |
| dolphin, river | Family *Platanistidae* | 210–260 | SE Asia and S America | fish, shrimp, squid, octopus | virtually blind, but with highly sensitive system of echo location |
| dormouse | Family *Gliridae* | 6–19 | Europe, Africa, Turkey, Asia and Japan | omnivorous | halfway between mouse and squirrel both in form and behaviour |
| dromedary | Species *Camelus dromedarius* | 190–230 (height of hump) | SW Asia, N Africa and Australia | plants, vegetation | domesticated camel with one hump; important as a beast of burden, and source of wool and milk |
| duiker | Subfamily *Cephalophinae* | 55–72 | Africa S of the Sahara | leaves, fruit, shoots, buds, seeds, bark, small birds, rodents | named after its habit of diving into cover when disturbed |
| eland | Genus *Taurotragus* | 250–350 | Africa | grazing fodder | elegant and highly mobile spiral horned antelope; experiments in the agricultural domestication of the common eland have taken place in Africa |
| elephant, African | Species *Loxodonta africana* | 600–750 | Africa S of the Sahara | grass, plants, leaves, twigs, flowers, fruit | largest living mammal, with distinctive trunk and large tusks and ears; drastically reduced population |
| fox | Family *Canidae* | 24–100 | N and S America, Europe, Asia and Africa | rodents, birds, invertebrates, fruit, fish, rabbits, hares, earthworms | justified reputation for cunning, intelligence and resourcefulness |
| gazelle | Genus *Gazella* | 122–166 | Africa | leaves, grass, fruit | birth peaks adapted to coincide with abundance of feeding vegetation during the spring and early rains |
| gerbil | Subfamily *Gerbillinae* | 6–7.5 | Africa and Asia | seeds, fruits, leaves, stems, roots, bulbs, insects, snails | defence mechanisms include colour of skin closely allied to the environment for hiding purposes, wide field of vision, and the ability to hear low frequency sounds such as the beating of owls' wings; domesticated form is the Mongolian gerbil often kept as a pet |

| Name | Family/Species | Size (cm) [1] | Distribution | Food | Special features |
|---|---|---|---|---|---|
| gerenuk | Genus *Litocranius* | 140–160 | Africa | leaves, shoots, flowers, fruit | graceful, delicate creature; rises on hind legs in order to extend its reach when feeding on the leaves of tall shrubs and bushes |
| gibbon | Family *Hylobatidae* | 45–65 | SE Asia | fruit, leaves, invertebrates | renowned for spectacular ability to move among trees using swinging movements of arms; loud and sophisticated voice |
| giraffe | Species *Giraffa camelopardalis* | 380–470 | Africa S of the Sahara | leaves, shoots, herbs, flowers, fruit, seeds | distinguished by its mottled coat and the length of its neck which allows it to feed on foliage which is out of the reach of smaller mammals |
| gnu | Genus *Connochaetes* | 194–209 | Africa | grazing fodder | characterized by massive head and mane, bearded throat, tail which reaches almost to the ground |
| goat, mountain | Species *Oreamnos americanus* | to 175 | N America | grazing fodder | large, ponderous rock climber, adapted to living in snowy mountains of N America |
| goat, wild | Species *Capra aegagrus* | 130–140 | S Europe, Middle East and Asia | grazing fodder | subspecies includes domestic goat |
| gopher | Family *Geomyidae* | 12–22.5 | N America | plant materials | highly adapted to its burrowing and subterranean existence |
| gorilla | Genus *Gorilla* | 150–170 | C Africa | leaves and stems | largest living primate; the most intelligent of land animals (after humans); unjustified reputation for ferocity, perhaps based on its size, and habit of beating its chest in a show of aggression |
| guinea pig | Genus *Cavia* | 28 | S America | herbs, grasses | tailless rodent; domesticated form is the *Cavia porcellus* |
| hamster | Subfamily *Cricetinae* | 5.3–10.2 | Europe, Middle East, former USSR and China | mainly seeds, shoots, root vegetables | familiar western pet, but aggressive towards own species in the wild |
| hare | Genus *Lepus* | 40–76 | N and S America, Africa, Europe, Asia and Arctic | grass, herbs, plants, bark, twigs | well-developed ability to run from predators; species include jack-rabbits and the Arctic hare |
| hare, Patagonian | Genus *Dolichotis* | 45 | S America | grasses, herbs | unusual characteristic in a mammal of being strictly monogamous |
| hartebeest | Genus *Alcelaphus* | 195–200 | Africa | grass, vegetation | distinctive long face, sloping back |
| hedgehog | Subfamily *Erinaceinae* | 10–15 | Europe, Asia and Africa | earthworms, beetles, slugs, earwigs, caterpillars | ability to curl up and use prickly, spined back as protection |
| hippopotamus | Family *Hippopotamidae* | 150–345 | Africa | terrestrial vegetation | large, heavy and barrel-shaped with short stumpy legs; wallows in water |

| Name | Family/Species | Size (cm)[1] | Distribution | Food | Special features |
|---|---|---|---|---|---|
| horse | Subgenus *Equus* | 200–210 | worldwide in domesticated form; Asia, N and S America and Australia in the wild | grass, leaves | historically useful as a beast of burden and means of transport, and for agricultural, military and recreational purposes |
| hyena | Family *Hyaeninae* | 85–140 | Africa and Asia | carrion, mammals, insects, small vertebrates, eggs, fruit, vegetables | scavenger and hunter, with highly developed systems of communication; family includes the aardwolf |
| ibex | Species *Capra ibex* | 85–143 | C Europe, Asia and Africa | grazing fodder | large horned creature saved from extinction in C Europe |
| impala | Genus *Aepyceros* | 128–142 | Africa | grass, leaves, flowers, fruit, seeds | attractive, graceful creature with fawn and mahogany coat; females and young gather in large herds; male has a lyre-shaped horn |
| jackal | Genus *Canis* | 65–106 | Africa, SE Europe and Asia | fruit, invertebrates, reptiles, birds, small mammals, carrion | unfair reputation as cowardly scavenger |
| jaguar | Species *Panthera onca* | 112–185 | C and S America | deer, monkeys, sloths, birds, turtles, frogs, fish , small rodents | only cat to be found in the Americas |
| jerboa | Family *Dipodidae* | 4–26 | N Africa, Turkey, Middle East and C Asia | seeds, vegetation, insects | long hind legs allow movement by hopping and jumping |
| lemming | Tribe *Lemmini* | 10–11 | N America and Eurasia | plants, bulbs, roots, mosses | Norway lemming is noted for its mass migration which sometimes results in drowning |
| lemur | Family *Lemuridae* | 12–70 | Madagascar | flowers, leaves, bamboo shoots | mainly nocturnal and arboreal |
| lemur, flying ► colugo | | | | | |
| leopard | Species *Panthera pardus* | 100–190 | Africa and Asia | mainly small mammals, birds | opportunistic, nocturnal hunter; adept at climbing trees |
| lion | Species *Panthera leo* | 240–300 | Africa | meat of animals which weigh 50–500 kg | known as the 'King of Beasts'; the most socially organized of the cat family |
| llama | Species *Lama glama* | 230–400 | S America | plants and vegetation | S American beast of burden |
| lynx | Species *Felis lynx* | 67–110 | Europe and N America | rodents, small hoofed mammals | lives in cold northern latitudes; well adapted to travelling through deep snow |
| macaque | Genus *Macaca* | 38–70 | Asia and N Africa | mainly fruit, insects, leaves, crops, small animals | heavily built and partly terrestrial genus of monkey; includes the Rhesus monkey adapted to life in the Himalayas, and the Barbary apes imported into Gibraltar in the 18c |
| marmoset | Family *Callitrichidae* | 17.5–40 | S America | fruit, flowers, nectar, gum, frogs, snails, lizards, spiders, insects | small, colourful, squirrel-like monkeys; includes species of tamarins |

| Name | Family/Species | Size (cm)[1] | Distribution | Food | Special features |
|---|---|---|---|---|---|
| marten | Genus *Martes* | 30–75 | N America, Europe and Asia | mice, squirrels, rabbits, grouse, fruit, nuts | one species, the fisher, unique for its ability to penetrate the quilled defences of the porcupine |
| mole | Family *Talpidae* | 2.4–7.5 | Europe, Asia and N America | earthworms, insect larvae, slugs | almost exclusively subterranean existence |
| mongoose | Family *Viverridae* | 24–58 | Africa, S Asia and SW Europe | vertebrates, insects, fruit, snakes | some species live in social groups; often seen in the tripod position, ie standing up on hind legs and tail |
| monkey, capuchin | Family *Cebidae* | 25–63 | S America | insects, fruit, leaves, seeds, other small mammals | mainly lives in social groupings for the purposes of defence, foraging for food, and rearing young |
| mouse ► rat | | | | | |
| narwhal | Species *Monodon monceros* | 400–500 | former USSR, N America and Greenland | shrimp, cod, flounder | distinctive single tusk in the male can reach lengths of up to 3m |
| okapi | Species *Okapia johnstoni* | 190–200 | C Africa | mainly leaves and shoots | secretive and elusive creature; strange-looking mixture of giraffe and zebra |
| orang-utan | Species *Pongo pygmaeus* | 150 | forests of N Sumatra and Borneo | fruit, leaves, insects | sparse covering of long red-brown hair; adults have large naked fatty folds around face; life span of 35 years in the wild; much diminished population |
| otter | Subfamily *Lutrinae* | 40–123 | N and S America, Europe, Asia and Africa | frogs, crabs, fish, aquatic birds | only truly amphibious members of the general weasel family; greatly reduced population due to persecution, loss of natural habitat |
| panda, giant | Species *Ailuropoda melanoleuca* | 130–150 | China | bamboo | rare; poor breeder; the success rate of breeding in captivity has been extremely low |
| polar bear | Species *Ursus maritimus* | 250–300 | N polar regions | mainly seals, carcasses of large marine animals | unique for its large size, white coat and adaptation to aquatic living |
| porcupine (New World) | Family *Erethizontidae* | 30–86 | N and S America | bark, roots, shoots, leaves, berries, seeds, nuts, flowers | arboreal version of Old World porcupine; excellent climber |
| porcupine (Old World) | Family *Hystricidae* | 37–47 | Africa and Asia | roots, bulbs, fruit, berries | heavily quilled and spiny body |
| porpoise | Family *Phocoenidae* | 120–150 | N temperate zone, W Indo-Pacific, temperate and sub-antarctic waters of S America and Auckland Islands | fish, squid, crustaceans | large range of sounds for the purpose of echo location |
| puma | Species *Felis concolor* | 105–196 | N and S America | deer, rodents | wide-ranging hunter; includes subspecies cougar |
| rabbit, European | Genus *Oryctolagus* | 38–58 | Europe, Africa, Australia, New Zealand and S America | grass, herbs, roots, plants, bark | burrowing creature; opportunistic animal in widespread environment; noted for its breeding capacity; domesticated rabbits descended from this genus |

| Name | Family/Species | Size (cm) [1] | Distribution | Food | Special features |
|---|---|---|---|---|---|
| racoon | Genus *Procyon* | 55 | N, S and C America | frogs, fish, birds, eggs, fruit, nuts, small rodents, insects, corn | black masked face; distinctive ringed tail; reputation for mischief |
| rat (New World) | Subfamily *Hesperomyinae* | 5–8 | N and S America | seeds, grain, plants, nuts, fruit, fungi, insects, crustaceans, fish | numerous species adapted to living in all possible forms of habitat |
| rat (Old World) | Subfamily *Murinae* | 4.5–8.2 | Europe, Asia, Africa and Australia | omnivorous | large number of species; one of the most successful mammals at adapting to any form of environment |
| reedbuck | Genus *Redunca* | 110–176 | Africa | grass, leaves, crops | graceful, elegant animal; distinctive whistling sounds, leaping movements |
| rhinoceros | Family *Rhinocerotidae* | 250–400 | Africa and tropical Asia | plant foliage | name derives from horn growing from snout; use of the horn for commercial purposes has brought the animal to the verge of extinction |
| seal | Family *Phocidae* | 117–490 | mainly polar, subpolar and temperate seas | fish, squid, crustaceans | graceful swimmer and diver; some species have been the object of controversial culling procedures |
| sheep, American bighorn | Species *Ovis canadensis* | 168–186 | N America | grazing fodder | large horns and body similar to an ibex; clings to the vicinity of cliffs |
| sheep, barbary | Genus *Ammotragus* | 155–165 | N Africa | grazing fodder | large head and horns up to 84cm in length |
| sheep, blue | Genus *Pseudois* | 91 (shoulder height) | Asia | grazing fodder | blue coat; curved horns |
| shrew | Family *Soricidae* | 3.5–4.8 | Europe, Asia, Africa, N America and northern S America | insects, earthworms | generally poor eyesight compensated for by acute sense of smell and hearing |
| shrew, elephant- | Order *Macroscelidea* | 10.4–29.4 | Africa | invertebrates, plants, fruit, seeds | distinctive creature with beady eyes, long, pointed snout and short legs |
| skunk | Subfamily *Mephitinae* | 40–68 | N and S America | insects, small mammals, eggs, fruit | evil-smelling defence mechanism; major carrier of rabies |
| sloth, three-toed | Family *Bradypodidae* | 56–60 | S America | leaves | smaller version of the two-toed sloth; slightly more active both by day and night |
| sloth, two-toed | Family *Megalonychidae* | 58–70 | S America | leaves | arboreal, nocturnal creature noted for the slowness of its movement |
| springbuck | Genus *Antidorcas* | 96–115 | S Africa | mainly grass | gregarious creature which migrates in herds of tens of thousands |
| springhare | Family *Pedetidae* | 36–43 | S Africa | grass and soil | burrowing creature like a miniature kangaroo; moves usually by hopping; hunted by humans as a source of food and for its skin |

| Name | Family/Species | Size (cm)[1] | Distribution | Food | Special features |
|---|---|---|---|---|---|
| squirrel | Family *Sciuridae* | 6.6–10 | N and S America, Europe, Africa and Asia | nuts, seeds, plants, insects | large number of species living in a variety of environments and including arboreal, burrowing and flying creatures; species include the marmot and chipmunk, grey squirrel noted for its ability to strip bark and damage young trees |
| tapir | Genus *Tapirus* | 180–250 | C and S America and SE Asia | grass, leaves, vegetation, buds, fruit, shoots | strange-looking, nocturnal mammal with distinctive snout; all species exist in vastly reduced numbers |
| tarsier | Genus *Tarsius* | 11–14 | islands of SE Asia | insects, lizards, bats, birds, snakes | proportionally large eyes; extraordinary ability to rotate neck |
| tiger | Species *Panthera tigris* | 220–360 | India, Manchuria, China and Indonesia | hoofed animals, eg deer and wild pigs | solitary hunters, stalk for prey |
| vole | Tribe *Microtini* | 10–11 | N America, Europe, Asia and the Arctic | grasses, seeds, aquatic plants, insects | population fluctuates in regular patterns or cycles |
| walrus | Species *Odobenus rosmarus* | 250–320 | Arctic seas | marine molluscs and invertebrates | characterized by its thick folds of skin, twin tusks |
| waterbuck | Species *Kobus ellipsiprymnus* | 177–235 | Africa | grasses, reeds, rushes, aquatic vegetation | shaggy coat and heavy gait; gives off an oily, detectable secretion on its coat |
| weasel | Subfamily *Mustelinae* | 15–55 | Arctic, N and S America, Europe, Asia and Africa | rodents, rabbits, birds, insects, lizards, frogs | certain species have been exploited for their fur, eg mink, ermine; includes species of ferret and polecat |
| whale, beaked | Family *Ziphiidae* | 400–1 280 | worldwide | mainly squid | named after its distinctive, protuberant, dolphin-like beak |
| whale, blue | Species *Balaenoptera musculus* | to 3 000 | Arctic and subtropics | krill | largest animal that has ever lived |
| whale, grey | Species *Eschrichtius robustus* | 1 190–1 520 | N Pacific | fish, crustaceans, ocean floor molluscs | long migration to breed, from the Arctic to the subtropics; one of the most heavily barnacled of the whale species |
| whale, humpback | Species *Megaptera novaeangliae* | 1 600 | worldwide | mainly fish, krill | highly acrobatic, with wide range of sounds; migrates between Arctic and mid-Pacific |
| whale, killer | Species *Orcinus orca* | 900–1 000 | worldwide in cool coastal waters | fish, squid, birds, and other marine mammals | toothed whale; dorsal fin narrow and vertical; co-operative and highly co-ordinated hunter, with triangular fins and distinctive white and black colouring, not generally a threat to humans |
| whale, long-finned pilot | Species *Globicephala melaena* | 600 | temperate waters of the N Atlantic | cuttlefish, squid | best known for mysterious mass strandings on beaches |
| whale, sperm | Species *Physeter catodon* | to 2 070 | widespread in temperate and tropical waters | mainly squid | largest of the toothed whales; prodigious deep sea diver |

| Name | Family/Species | Size (cm)[1] | Distribution | Food | Special features |
|---|---|---|---|---|---|
| whale, white | Species *Delphinaptems leucas* | 300–500 | N Russia, N America and Greenland | crustaceans, worms, molluscs | distinctive white skin; wide range of bodily, facial and vocal expressions |
| wild cat | Species *Felis silvestris* | 50–80 | Europe, India and Africa | small mammals, birds | domestic cat may be descended from the African wild cat |
| wolf, grey | Species *Canis lupus* | 100–150 | N America, Europe, Asia and Middle East | moose, deer, caribou | noted for hunting in packs |
| wolverine | Species *Gulo gulo* | to 83 | Arctic and subarctic regions | small mammals, deer, caribou, birds, plants, carrion | heavily built; long, dark coat of fur; adapted for hunting in soft, deep snow |
| zebra | Subgenus *Hippotigris* | 215–230 | Africa | grass, leaves | famous for black and white stripes |

[1]To convert cm to inches, multiply by 0.3937; generally, size denotes length from head to tip of tail.

## Birds

Birds are warm-blooded, egg-laying, and, in the case of adults, feathered vertebrates of the class Aves; there are approximately 8 600 species classified into 29 Orders and 181 Families. Birds are constructed for flight. The body is streamlined to reduce air resistance, the fore-limbs are modified as feathered wings, and the skeletal structure, heart and wing muscles, centre of gravity, and lung capacity are all designed for the act of flying. Two exceptions to this are the ratites or flightless birds which have become too large to be capable of sustained flight, eg the ostrich, kiwi and emu, and the penguin which has evolved into a highly aquatic creature. Birds are thought to have evolved from reptiles, their closest living relative being the crocodile.

| Name | Family | Size (cm)[1] | Distribution | Food | Special features |
|---|---|---|---|---|---|
| **❑ Flightless birds** | | | | | |
| cassowary | *Casauriidae* | 150 | Australia and New Guinea | fruit, plants, insects | claws capable of inflicting fatal wounds on humans |
| emu | *Dromaiidae* | 160–190 | Australia | plants, fruit, flowers, insects | highly mobile, nomadic population |
| kiwi | *Apterygidae* | 35–55 | New Zealand | earthworms, insects, seeds, berries | smallest of the Ratitae order; nocturnal |
| ostrich | *Struthonidae* | 275 | dry areas of Africa | mainly leaves, flowers, seeds of plants | fastest animal on two legs |
| rhea | *Rheidae* | 100–150 | grasslands of S America | leaves, roots, seeds, insects, small vertebrates | lives in flocks |
| tinamou | *Tinamidae* | 15–49 | C and S America | seeds, fruit, insects, small animals | sustains flight over short distances |
| **❑ Birds of prey** | | | | | |
| buzzard | *Accipitridae* | 80 | worldwide except Australasia and Malaysia | small mammals | spends much time perching; kills prey on ground |

| Name | Family | Size (cm)[1] | Distribution | Food | Special features |
|---|---|---|---|---|---|
| condor | *Cathartidae* | 60–100 | the Americas | carrion | Andean condor has largest wingspan of any living bird (up to 3m) |
| eagle, bald | *Accipitridae* | 80–100 | N America | fish, birds, mammals | name refers to white plumage on head and neck; national symbol of USA |
| eagle, golden | *Accipitridae* | 80–100 | N hemisphere | rabbits, hares, carrion | kills with talons; most numerous large eagle |
| eagle, harpy | *Accipitridae* | 90 | C America to Argentina | some birds, tree-dwelling mammals | the world's largest eagle; black, white and grey; large feet |
| eagle, sea | *Accipitridae* | 70–120 | coastline worldwide | fish | breeds on sea cliffs |
| falcon | *Falconidae* | 15–60 | worldwide | birds, carrion, large insects, small mammals | remarkable powers of flight and sight |
| harrier | *Accipitridae* | 50 | worldwide | small mammals, birds | hunts by flying low in regular search pattern |
| kite | *Accipitridae* | 52–58 | worldwide | insects, snails, small vertebrates, carrion | most varied and diverse group of hawks |
| osprey | *Pandionidae* | 55–58 | worldwide | fish | feet specially adapted for catching fish |
| owl | *Strigidae* | 12–73 | worldwide | mainly small mammals | acute sight and hearing; swallows prey whole; nocturnal |
| owl, barn | *Tytonidae* | 30–45 | worldwide | small vertebrates | feathered legs; nests high above ground |
| secretary bird | *Sagittaridae* | 100 | Africa | rodents, reptiles, large beetles, grasshoppers | walks up to 30km/20mi per day |
| sparrowhawk | *Accipitridae* | to 27 (male), to 38 (female) | Eurasia, NW Africa, C and S America | small birds | long tail, small round wings |
| vulture (New World) | *Cathartidae* | 60–100 | the Americas | carrion, carcasses | lives in colonies; locates food mainly by sight; head often lacking long feathers |
| vulture (Old World) | *Accipitridae* | 150–270 (wingspan) | worldwide except the Americas | carrion | no sense of smell |
| ❑ **Songbirds** | | | | | |
| accentor | *Prunellidae* | 14–18 | Palaearctic | insects, seeds | complex social organization and mating systems |
| bird of paradise | *Paradisaeidae* | 12.5–100 | New Guinea, Moluccas and Eastern Australia | frogs, nestling birds, insects, fruit, plants | brilliantly ornate plumage; elaborate courtship displays |
| bowerbird | *Ptilinorhynchidae* | 25–37 | Australia and New Guinea | mainly fruit, vegetable matter | male builds bowers to attract female for mating |
| bulbul | *Pycnonotidae* | 13–23 | Africa, Madagascar, S Asia and the Philippines | fruits, berries, insects | several species renowned for powerful, beautiful singing voice |
| bunting | *Emberizidae* | 15–20 | worldwide | seeds, crustaceans, insects | large family including species of sparrow, finch, and cardinals |
| butcherbird | *Cracticidae* | 26–58 | Australia, New Guinea and New Zealand | large insects, crustaceans, reptiles, small mammals, young birds | highly aggressive; sings loudly at dawn, thus has alternative name of 'bushman's clock' |

| Name | Family | Size (cm)[1] | Distribution | Food | Special features |
|---|---|---|---|---|---|
| chaffinch | *Fringillidae* | 11–19 | Europe, N and S America, Africa and Asia | seeds | strong bill; melodious singing voice |
| cowbird | *Icteridae* | 17–54 | N and S America | fruit, seeds, crustaceans, insects | forages for food using distinctive gaping movements of the bill |
| crow | *Corvidae* | 20–66 | worldwide, except New Zealand | omnivorous | adaptable, intelligent; with complex social systems |
| dipper | *Cinclidae* | 17–20 | Europe, S Asia and W regions of N and S America | water insects, molluscs, crustaceans, worms, tadpoles, small fish | strong legs and toes allow mobility to walk under water |
| drongo | *Dicruridae* | 18–38 | S Asia and Africa | insects, lizards, small birds | pugnacious |
| flowerpecker | *Dicaeidae* | 8–20 | SE Asia and Australasia | berries, nectar, insects | short tongue specially adapted for feeding on nectar |
| flycatcher (Old World) | *Muscicapidae* | 9–27 | worldwide except N and S America | insects | tropical species brightly coloured; feeds on the wing |
| flycatcher, silky | *Ptilogonidae* | to 14 | N and S America | insects | feeds on the wing |
| honeycreeper, Hawaiian | *Drepanididae* | 10–20 | Hawaiian Is | nectar, fruit, seeds, insects | widely varying bills between species adapted to different environments |
| honeyeater | *Meliphagidae* | 10–32 | Australasia, Pacific Is, Hawaii and S Africa | nectar, insects, fruits, berries | brush tongue adapted for nectar feeding |
| lark | *Alaudidae* | 11–19 | worldwide | seeds, flowers, leaves, insects | ground-dwelling; elaborate singing displays |
| leafbird | *Irenidae* | 12–24 | S Asia | insects, fruit | forest dwellers; ability to mimic sounds of other birds |
| magpie-lark | *Grallinidae* | 19–50 | Australasia and New Guinea | insects, tadpoles, seeds, fruit | adaptation to urban surroundings makes it amongst the best-known birds in Australia |
| mockingbird | *Mimidae* | 20–33 | N and S America | invertebrates, fruit | great ability to mimic sounds |
| nuthatch | *Sittidae* | 14–20 | worldwide except S America and New Zealand | insects, invertebrates, seeds, nuts | name reflects ability of the European species to break open nuts |
| oriole | *Oriolidae* | 18–30 | Europe, Asia, Philippines, Malaysia, New Guinea and Australia | insects, fruit | melodious singing voice |
| palmchat | *Dulidae* | 18 | Hispaniola and W Indies | berries, flowers and plants | communal nesting with individual compartments for each nesting pair |
| robin | *Turdinae* | 13 | worldwide except New Zealand | worms, snails, fruit, insects | territorial, uses song to deter intruders |
| shrike | *Laniidae* | 15–35 | Africa, N America, Asia and New Guinea | mainly insects | noted for its sharply hooked bill |
| shrike, cuckoo- | *Campephagidae* | 14–40 | Africa, S Asia | mainly insects, caterpillars | peculiar courtship display; family includes colourful minivets |
| shrike, vanga | *Vangidae* | 12–30 | Madagascar | insects, frogs, small reptiles | dwindling numbers of population; some endangered species |

| Name | Family | Size (cm)[1] | Distribution | Food | Special features |
|---|---|---|---|---|---|
| sparrow | *Ploceidae* | 10–20 | African tropics in origin, now worldwide | seeds, insects, bread, household scraps | some species renowned for having adapted to an urban environment |
| starling | *Sturnidae* | 16–45 | Europe, Asia and Africa | fruit, insects, pollen, nectar, seeds | gregarious; nests in colonies, roosts communally |
| sunbird | *Nectariniidae* | 8–16 | Africa, SE Asia and Australasia | insects, nectar | named for its bright plumage |
| swallow | *Hirundinidae* | 12–23 | worldwide | insects | noted for strong and agile flight |
| thrush | *Turdinae* | 12–26 | worldwide, except New Zealand | worms, snails, fruit | loud and varied singing voice |
| tit | *Paridae* | 11–14 | N America, Europe, Asia and Africa | insects, seeds, vegetable matter, nuts | nests in holes, wide range of singing voice |
| tree-creeper | *Certhiidae* | 12–15 | N hemisphere and S Africa | insects, seeds | forages on trees for food |
| tree-creeper, Australian | *Climacteridae* | 15 | Australia and New Guinea | mainly ants | forages for food on the trunks and limbs of trees |
| vireo | *Vireonidae* | 10–17 | N and S America | insects, fruit | distinctive thick and slightly hooked bill |
| wagtail | *Motacillidae* | 14–17 | worldwide, although rare in Australia | insects, seeds | spectacular song in flight |
| warbler, American | *Parulidae* | 10–16 | N and S America | insects, berries, vegetable matter | well developed and often complex songs |
| wattle-bird | *Callaeidae* | 25–53 | New Zealand | insects, fruit, invertebrates | distinctive fleshy fold of skin at base of bill |
| waxbill | *Estrildidae* | 9–13.5 | Africa, SE Asia and Australasia | mainly seeds, grain | several species drink by sucking, in the manner of pigeons and doves |
| waxwing | *Bombycillidae* | 18 | W hemisphere | fruit, berries, insects | wax-like, red tips on secondary flight feathers |
| white-eye | *Zosteropidae* | 12 | Africa, SE Asia and Australasia | insects, spiders, nectar, fruit | distinctive ring of tiny white feathers formed round the eyes |
| wood-swallow | *Artamidae* | 15–20 | tropical Asia and Australasia | insects | tends to huddle together in small groups on branches of trees; elegant flyer and glider; highly aggressive towards other birds |
| wren | *Troglodytidae* | 8–15 | N and S America, Europe and Asia | invertebrates | nests play ceremonial role in courtship |
| ❑ **Waterfowl** | | | | | |
| diver ► loon | | | | | |
| duck | *Anatidae* | wide range | worldwide | vegetation | gregarious; migratory |
| flamingo | *Phoenicopterides* | 90–180 | tropics, N America, S Europe | minute organisms | red/pink colour of plumage caused by diet |
| goose | *Anatidae* | wide range | N hemisphere | grass, underwater plants | migratory |
| great northern diver ► loon | | | | | |
| grebe | *Podicipedidae* | 22–60 | worldwide | insects, crustaceans, fish | highly aquatic, adapted for swimming and diving under water |

| Name | Family | Size (cm)[1] | Distribution | Food | Special features |
|---|---|---|---|---|---|
| hammerhead | *Scopidae* | 56 | Africa S of the Sahara, Madagascar, and S Arabia | mainly frogs and tadpoles, also small fish, shrimps, insects | builds a remarkably elaborate nest with entrance tunnel and internal chamber |
| heron | *Ardeidae* | 30–140 | worldwide | carnivorous; aquatic prey | mainly a wading bird |
| ibis | *Threskiornithidae* | 50–100 | warmer regions of all continents | crustaceans, insects, larvae, small fish, frogs, small reptiles | family also includes species of spoonbill named for shape of bill |
| loon or diver | *Gaviidae* | 66–95 | high latitudes of the N hemisphere, migrating to temperate zones | mainly fish | highly territorial and aggressive; loud warning calls; also known as diver; includes great northern diver which can dive deeper than any other flying bird |
| screamer | *Anhimidae* | 69–90 | warmer parts of S America | herbivorous | highly vocal, trumpet-like alarm calls give it its name |
| shoebill | *Balaenicipitidae* | 120 | E Africa | fish, aquatic prey | also known as the whale-headed stork because it has a large head on a short neck |
| stork | *Ciconiidae* | 60–120 | S America, Asia, Africa and Australia | fish, insects, frogs, snakes, mice, lizards | known for its long bill and long neck |
| swan | *Anatidae* | 100–160 | worldwide, freshwater, sheltered shores and estuaries | underwater plants | very long neck |
| **❑ Shorebirds** | | | | | |
| auk | *Alcidae* | 16–76 | cold waters of the N hemisphere | fish, plankton | same family as the extinct and flightless great auk; species include varieties of puffin and guillemot |
| avocet | *Recurvirostridae* | 29–48 | worldwide, except high latitudes | insects, larvae | particularly graceful walk; long slender legs give rise to alternative name of stilt |
| courser | *Glareolidae* | 15–25 | Africa, S Europe, Asia and Australia | insects | inhabits dry, flat savanna, grassland and the shores of large rivers |
| curlew, stone- | *Burhinidae* | 36–52 | Africa, Europe, Asia, Australia and parts of S America | eggs, insects, worms, molluscs, crustaceans, small vertebrates, amphibians | leg joints give alternative name of thickknee |
| gull | *Laridae* | 31–76 | worldwide, scarce in the tropics | fish, marine invertebrates | highly gregarious with elaborate systems of communication |
| jacana | *Jacanidae* | 17–53 | tropics | insects, frogs, fish, invertebrates | ability to walk on floating vegetation gives alternative name of lily trotter |
| oystercatcher | *Haematopididae* | 40–45 | tropical and temperate coastlines, except tropical Africa and S Asia | shellfish, worms, insects | powerful bill for breaking shells; despite the name, they do not eat oysters |
| phalarope | *Phalaropidae* | 19–25 | high latitudes of the N hemisphere | insects, crabs, shrimps | wading bird which also regularly swims |
| plover | *Charadriidae* | 15–40 | worldwide | shellfish, insects | swift runner; strong flier |
| plover, crab | *Dromadidae* | 38 | coasts of E Africa, India, Persian Gulf, Sri Lanka and Madagascar | crabs | single species with mainly white and black plumage |

| Name | Family | Size (cm)[1] | Distribution | Food | Special features |
|---|---|---|---|---|---|
| sandpiper | *Scolopacidae* | 12–60 | worldwide | invertebrates, insects, berries | spectacular flight patterns |
| seedsnipe | *Thinocoridae* | 17–28 | W coast of S America | seeds, leaves | named after its diet |
| sheathbill | *Chionididae* | 35–43 | sub-Antarctic and E coast of S America | plankton, algae, carcasses, offal | scavenger of a communal and quarrelsome nature |
| skimmer | *Rhynchopidae* | 37–51 | tropics and subtropics of N and S America, Africa and S Asia | fish, shrimps | uniquely shaped bill aids capture of prey in shallow waters |
| skua | *Stercorariidae* | 43–61 | mainly high latitudes of the N hemisphere | fish, small sea birds, insects, eggs | known for chasing other seabirds until they disgorge their food |
| snipe, painted | *Rostratulidae* | 19–24 | S America, Africa, S Asia and Australia | molluscs, earthworms, seeds | spectacular female plumage; distinctive running action with lowered head |
| stilt ► avocet | | | | | |
| ❑ **Seabirds** | | | | | |
| albatross | *Diomedidae* | 70–140 | S hemisphere | fish | noted for its size and power of flight |
| cormorant (or shag) | *Phalacrocoracidae* | 50–100 | worldwide | fish and crustaceans | marine equivalent of falcons, used in fishing |
| darter | *Anhingidae* | 80–100 | tropical, subtropical, temperate regions | fish, insects | distinctive swimming action occasions name of snake-bird |
| frigatebird | *Fregatidae* | 70–110 | tropical oceans | fish, young birds | enormous wings; adept at flying; forces other birds to disgorge their food |
| fulmar | *Procellariidae* | to 60 | N and S oceans | fish | comes to land only to breed; can eject foul-smelling vomit to deter predators |
| gannet | *Sulidae* | up to 90 | worldwide | fish, squid | complex behaviour during mating |
| guillemot | *Alcidae* | 38–42 | N hemisphere | fish, crustaceans, worms | eggs shaped so they do not roll off cliff ledge |
| pelican | *Pelecanidae* | 140–180 | tropics and subtropics | fish, crustaceans | known for its long bill |
| penguin | *Spheniscidae* | 40–115 | S hemisphere | fish, crustaceans, squid | flightless: wings modified as flippers; feathers waterproof; highly social |
| petrel, diving | *Pelecanoididae* | 16–25 | S hemisphere | fish | great resemblance to the auk |
| petrel, storm- | *Hydrobatidae* | 12–25 | high latitudes of N and S hemispheres | fish, other marine organisms | considerable powers of migration |
| puffin | *Alcidae* | 28–32 | N hemisphere | fish and crustaceans | nests in burrows in very large colonies |
| shag ► cormorant | | | | | |
| shearwater | *Procellariidae* | 28–91 | subantarctic and subtropical zones | fish, plankton | many species known for long migrations |
| tropicbird | *Phaethontidae* | 25–45 | tropical seas | small fish and squid | elongated central tail feathers produce distinctive flight pattern |

| Name | Family | Size (cm)[1] | Distribution | Food | Special features |
|---|---|---|---|---|---|
| **❑ Arboreal birds** | | | | | |
| barbet | *Capitonidae* | 9–32 | tropics, except Australasia | mainly fruits, berries, buds, insects | nests in holes made in rotten timber or sand banks |
| bee-eater | *Meropidae* | 15–38 | Africa, Asia and Australia | insects | colourful plumage |
| cuckoo | *Cuculidae* | 15–90 | worldwide | insects, especially caterpillars | some species lay eggs in the nests of other birds and rely on foster parents to feed the young |
| cuckoo-roller | *Leptosomatidae* | 38–43 | Madagascar and Comoros Is | large insects, chameleons | diminishing population due to destruction of natural habitat |
| honeyguide | *Indicatoridae* | 10–20 | Africa and S Asia | insects, beeswax | named for peculiar habit of eating the wax of honeycombs |
| hoopoe | *Upupidae* | 31 | Africa, SE Asia and S Europe | mainly small insects | named after its distinctive 'hoo hoo' call |
| hornbill | *Bucerotidae* | 38–126 | tropics of Africa and Australasia | fruit, insects, small animals | noted for its long, heavy bill |
| jacamar | *Galbulidae* | 13–30 | tropical America | insects | long, slender bill; attractive, green, metallic plumage |
| kingfisher | *Alcedinidae* | 10–46 | worldwide | insects, shrimps, frogs, lizards, crabs, snails, worms | colourful plumage, strong bill; characteristic diving movements to catch prey |
| motmot | *Momotidae* | 20–50 | tropical America | insects, frogs, small reptiles, fruit | typically attractive, with distinctive long tail feathers |
| mousebird | *Coliidae* | 30–35 | Africa S of the Sahara | leaves, fruit, seeds, nectar | distinguished by its crest and long tail |
| parrot | *Psittacidae* | 10–100 | mainly tropics of S hemisphere | seeds, nuts, berries, fruit, insects | mainly sedentary; unmelodic voice, not known to mimic sounds outside captivity |
| pigeon | *Columbidae* | 17–90 | worldwide, except high latitudes | seeds, flowers, fruit, berries, leaves, small snails | large family including species of dove, known for its distinctive cooing sound |
| puffbird | *Bucconidae* | 14–32 | tropical America | insects, lizards | named after its stout, puffy appearance |
| roller | *Coraciidae* | 27–38 | Africa, Europe, Asia, Australia | insects, frogs, fruit | named after its courtship display of diving from great heights in a rolling motion |
| sandgrouse | *Pteroclididae* | 25–48 | Africa, S Europe and S Asia | seeds, berries, insects | mainly terrestrial birds |
| tody | *Todidae* | 10–12 | Greater Antilles | mainly insects, seeds | captures its insect prey from the underside of leaves and twigs |
| toucan | *Ramphastidae* | 34–66 | S America | seeds, berries, fruits, insects, small animals | known for its bright plumage and immense bill |
| trogon | *Trogonidae* | 25–35 | tropics, except Australasia | mainly insects, fruit | colourful, attractive plumage |
| turaco | *Musophagidae* | 35–76 | Africa S of the Sahara | mainly fruit | noted for its loud and resounding call |
| woodhoopoe | *Phoeniculidae* | 21–43 | Africa S of the Sahara | insects, fruit | long graduated tail; strongly hooked bill; some species also called scimitar bill |
| woodpecker | *Picidae* | 10–58 | worldwide, except Australasia and Antarctica | insects, fruit, nuts | named after its manner of excavating wood and tree bark for food |

| Name | Family | Size (cm)[1] | Distribution | Food | Special features |
|---|---|---|---|---|---|
| **❑ Aerial feeders** | | | | | |
| frogmouth | *Podargidae* | 23–53 | SE Asia and Australasia | beetles, scorpions, centipedes, frogs, snails, mice, small birds, fruit | distinctively shaped bill with extremely wide gape |
| hummingbird | *Trochilidae* | 6–22 | N and S America | nectar, insects | the humming sound is made by the wings when hovering |
| nightjar | *Caprimulgidae* | 19–29 | worldwide | mainly insects | nocturnal |
| nightjar, owlet- | *Aegothelidae* | 23–44 | Australasia | insects, small vertebrates | perches in upright owl-like way |
| oilbird | *Steatornithidae* | 53 | tropical S America | fruit | the only nocturnal, fruit-eating bird |
| potoo | *Nyctibiidae* | 23–51 | tropical C and S America | insects | nocturnal bird, also known as 'tree-nighthawk' |
| swift | *Apodidae* | 10–25 | worldwide | insects | lands only on near-vertical surfaces; spends most of life flying |
| swift, crested | *Hemiprocnidae* | 17–33 | SE Asia and New Guinea | insects | named after the prominent crest on its head |
| **❑ Passerines**[2] | | | | | |
| antbird | *Formicariidae* | 8–36 | parts of S America and W Indies | small insects, spiders, lizards, frogs | named after the habit some species have of following armies of ants to prey |
| bellbird | *Cotingidae* | 9–45 | C and S America | fruit | long, metallic sounding display call |
| broadbill | *Eurylaimidae* | 13–28 | tropical Africa and Asia, and the Philippines | mainly insects | noted for its colourful broad bill |
| false sunbird | *Philepittidae* | 15 | Madagascar | fruit | noted for the bright blue and emerald wattle which develops around the eyes of the male during breeding season |
| flycatcher (New World) | *Tyrannidae* | 9–27 | N and S America | insects | feeds on wing |
| flycatcher, tyrant | *Tyrannidae* | 5–14 | N and S America, W Indies and Galapagos Is | insects, fish, fruit | many species known for spectacular aerial courtship display |
| gnateater | *Conopophagidae* | 14 | parts of S America | insects | long thin legs; short tail |
| lyrebird | *Menuridae* | 80–90 | SE Australia | invertebrates | named after its extravagant tail which resembles a Greek lyre |
| manakin | *Pipridae* | 9–15 | C and S America | fruit, insects | highly elaborate courtship display |
| ovenbird | *Furnariidae* | to 25 | S America | mainly insects | one species, the true ovenbird, builds substantial nests like mud-ovens |
| pitta | *Pittidae* | 15–28 | Africa, SE Asia and Australasia | mainly insects, spiders, worms, snails | long legs; short tail; colourful plumage |
| plantcutter | *Phytotomidae* | 18–19 | western S America | buds, shoots, leaves, fruit | bill is ideally adapted for feeding on fruit and plants; regarded as a horticultural and agricultural pest |
| scrub-bird | *Atrichornithidae* | 16–21 | E and SW Australia | insects, small lizards, frogs | small terrestrial bird; long graduated tail |
| tapaculo | *Rhinocryptidae* | 8–25 | S and C America | insects, larvae, spiders | distinctive moveable flap covers the nostril |

| Name | Family | Size (cm)[1] | Distribution | Food | Special features |
|---|---|---|---|---|---|
| woodcreeper | *Dendrocolaptidae* | 20–37 | S America and W Indies | insects, frogs, lizards | stiff tail feathers used as support in climbing trees, foraging for food |
| wren, New Zealand | *Xenicidae* | 8–10 | New Zealand | insects | bird family thought to have colonized the islands in the Tertiary Period[3] |
| **❑ Game-birds and cranes** | | | | | |
| bustard | *Otitidae* | 37–132 | Africa, S Europe, Asia and Australia | plants, leaves, seeds, berries, insects, small reptiles and mammals, birds' eggs, nestlings | characterized by its frequent pauses during walking to observe its surroundings |
| coot | *Rallidae* | 14–51 | worldwide | small animals, vegetable food | conspicuous for its loud harsh vocal strains at night |
| crane | *Gruidae* | 80–150 | worldwide, except S America and Antarctica | omnivorous | characterized by its long legs |
| currasow | *Cracidae* | 75–112 | Southern N America and S America | leaves, insects, frogs | noted for agility in running along branches before taking flight |
| finfoot | *Heliornithidae* | 30–62 | tropics of America, Africa and SE Asia | mainly insects | long, slender neck; agile on land and in water |
| grouse | *Tetraonidae* | 30–90 | N hemisphere | leaves, buds, berries, fruit, insects | many species threatened by hunting and use of pesticides |
| guinea fowl | *Numididae* | 45–60 | Africa | mainly insects, bulbs | virtually unfeathered head and neck; often domesticated |
| hoatzin | *Opisthocomidae* | 60 | tropical S America | leaves, fruit and flowers of the white mangrove, fish, crabs | musky odour; top-heavy, retarded flight; unique digestive system |
| kagu | *Rhynochetidae* | 56 | New Caledonia | earthworms | sole species; forest dwelling |
| limpkin | *Aramidae* | 60–70 | C and S America | large snails | sole species; noted for its wailing voice |
| mesite | *Mesoenatidae* | 25–27 | Madagascar | fruit, insects | highly terrestrial, sedentary; endemic to Madagascar |
| pheasant | *Phasianidae* | 40–235 | worldwide | seeds, shoots, berries, insects | elaborate courtship display |
| plains wanderer | *Pedionomidae* | 16 | SE Australia | insects, seeds, vegetable substances | male incubates the eggs and raises the young |
| quail, button | *Turnicidae* | 11–19 | Africa, S Asia and Australia | insects, seeds, plants | secretive; terrestrial; only three toes, hind toe absent |
| seriema | *Cariamidae* | 75–90 | S America | omniverous, especially small snakes | heavily feathered head and crest |
| sunbittern | *Eurypygidae* | 46 | forest swamps of C and S America | insects, crustacea, minnows | complex markings |
| trumpeter | *Psophiidae* | 43–53 | tropical S America | berries, fruit, insects | named after its trumpeting call of warning or alarm |
| turkey | *Meleagrididae* | 90–110 | N America | fruit, seeds, vegetation, invertebrates | characterized by male's distinctive strutting displays during breeding |

[1]To convert cm to inches, multiply by 0.3937.
[2] Any bird of the worldwide order *Passeriformes* ('perching birds'), which comprises more than half the living species of birds; landbirds.
[3] See Geological time scale pp34–5.

## Reptiles

Reptiles are egg-laying vertebrates of the class Reptilia, having evolved from primitive amphibians; there are 6 547 species divided into Squamata (lizards and snakes), Chelonia (tortoises and turtles), Crocodylia (crocodiles and alligators) and Rhynococephalia (the tuatara).

Most reptiles live on the land, breathe with lungs, and have horny or plated skins. Reptiles require the rays of the sun to maintain their body temperature, ie they are cold-blooded or ectothermic. This confines them to warm, tropical and subtropical regions, but does allow some species to exist in particularly hot desert environments in which mammals and birds would find it impossible to sustain life. Extinct species of reptile include the dinosaur and pterodactyl.

| Name | Family | Size (cm) [1] | Distribution | Food | Special features |
|---|---|---|---|---|---|
| alligator | *Alligatoridae* | 200–550 | S USA, C and S America and E China | fish, birds, mammals, amphibians, reptiles | able to inflict fatalities on humans but attacks rare; only the American alligator is currently free from being an endangered species, noted for its longevity in protected environments |
| anguid | *Anguidae* | 6–30 | N and S America, Europe, Asia and NW Africa | small lizards, mice, birds' eggs, tadpoles, earthworms, spiders, scorpions, grasshoppers, moths, wasps, larvae | distinctive bony-plated scales which reach round the underside giving the creature a rigid appearance |
| boa | *Boidae* | 200–400 | Western N America, S America, Africa, Madagascar, Asia, Fiji, Solomon Is and New Guinea | birds, mammals | famous constricting snake, includes within its family species of anaconda |
| chameleon | *Chamaeleontidae* | 2–28 | Africa outwith the Sahara, Madagascar, Middle East, S Spain, S Arabian peninsula, Sri Lanka, Crete, India and Pakistan | insects, spiders, scorpions, small birds, mammals | noted for its ability to change colour and blend into its environment |
| crocodile | *Crocodylidae* | 150–750 | pantropical and some temperate regions of Africa | vertebrates | distinguished from the alligator by the visible fourth tooth in the lower jaw; famous for its huge jaws, fierce appearance, and violent hunting and ambush techniques when capturing prey; populations have been decimated by the demand for luxury leather and several species are endangered |
| gecko | *Gekkonidae* | 1.5–24 | N and S America, Africa, S Europe, Asia and Australia | mainly insects | noted for its vocalization and ability to climb; able to shed its tail as a defence mechanism against predators |
| iguana | *Iguanidae* | to 200 | C and S America, Madagascar, Fiji and Tonga | mainly insects | terrestrial and tree-dwelling lizard; active by day, able to survive in exceptionally high temperatures |
| lizard, beaded | *Helodermatidae* | 33–45 | SW USA, W Mexico to Guatemala | small mammals, birds, lizards, frogs, birds, eggs insects, earthworms, carrion | possesses a mildly venomous bite |

| Name | Family | Size (cm)[1] | Distribution | Food | Special features |
|---|---|---|---|---|---|
| lizard, blind | *Dibamidae* | 12–16.5 | SE Asia | insects | so-named because the eyes are concealed within the skin |
| lizard, Bornean earless | *Lanthanotidae* | to 20 | Borneo | fish, earthworms, birds' eggs | lacks an external ear opening; partly aquatic and a good swimmer; capable of short, rapid movements on land |
| lizard, chisel-tooth | *Agamidae* | 4–35 | Africa, Asia and Australia | insects, fruit, plants, eggs | named after its distinctive teeth; family includes the flying dragon which is able to glide from perch to perch |
| lizard, girdle-tailed | *Cordylidae* | 5–27.5 | Africa S of the Sahara, Madagascar | mainly insectivorous and carnivorous | terrestrial; active by day; adapted to arid environments |
| lizard, monitor | *Varanidae* | 12–150 | Africa, S Asia, Indo-Australian archipelago, Philippines, New Guinea and Australia | carrion, large snails, grasshoppers, beetles, scorpions, crocodiles' and birds' eggs, fish, lizards, snakes, birds, shrews, squirrels | consumes its prey whole in the manner of snakes; includes the Komodo dragon, the largest living lizard which has a prodigious appetite and is capable of killing pigs and small deer |
| lizard, night | *Xantisiidae* | 3.5–12 | C America | mainly insects | most species active by night, secretive by day |
| lizard, snake | *Pygopodidae* | 6.5–31 | New Guinea and Australia | mainly insects | snake-like appearance; broad but highly extensible tongue |
| lizard, wall and sand | *Lacertidae* | 4–22 | Europe, Africa, Asia and Indo-Australian archipelago | mainly insects, snails, worms | highly conspicuous lizard living in open and sandy environments; terrestrial, active by day |
| lizard, worm | *Amphisbaenidae* | 15–35 | subtropical regions of N and S America, Africa, Middle East, Asia and Europe | mainly insects, snails, worms | worm-like, burrowing reptile; some of the species have the rare ability to move backwards and forwards |
| pipesnake | *Aniliidae* | <100 | S America, SE Asia | snakes, eels | tail has brilliantly coloured red underside; burrows in swampy regions and feeds on other snakes |
| python | *Pythonidae* | 100–1 000 | tropical and subtropical Africa, SE Asia, Australia, Mexico and C America | birds, mammals | capable of killing humans, especially children, by constriction |
| skink | *Scincidae* | 2.8–35 | tropical and temperate regions | crabs, insects, seeds | family of terrestrial, tree-dwelling or burrowing species, including highly adept swimmers and those able to swim through sand |
| snake, dawn blind | *Anomalepidae* | 11–30 | C and S America | ants, termites | short tail, indistinct head, one or two teeth in the lower jaw |
| snake, front fanged | *Elapidae* | 38–560 | worldwide in warm regions | frogs, snakes, eels, rodents, lizards, and other vertebrates | highly venomous family with short fangs; responsible for numerous human fatalities; includes the mamba, the adder and the cobra with its famous broad, hooded head |

| Name | Family | Size (cm)[1] | Distribution | Food | Special features |
|---|---|---|---|---|---|
| snake, harmless | *Colubridae* | 13–350 | worldwide | wide variety of vertebrates | large family which includes terrestrial, burrowing, arboreal and aquatic species; called harmless because of the inability of most species to inject or produce venomous saliva |
| snake, shieldtail | *Uropeltidae* | 20–50 | S India and Sri Lanka | earthworms and insects | small burrowing snake, with tiny eyes, so-called because the tail ends abruptly and forms a rough cylindrical shield |
| snake, thread | *Leptotyphlopidae* | 15–90 | C and S America, Africa and Asia | ants and termites | small and exceptionally slender burrowing snake |
| snake, typical blind | *Typhlopidae* | 15–90 | C and S America, Africa S of the Sahara, SE Europe, S Asia, Taiwan and Australia | ants, termites, larvae | burrowing snake with tiny, concealed eyes and no teeth on lower jaw |
| tortoise | *Testudinidae* | 10–140 | S Europe, Africa, Asia, C and S America | mainly herbivorous | includes smallest species of turtle, the Speckled Cape tortoise (10cm) and one of the longest-lived turtles, the spur-thighed tortoise with a possible life span of over a century |
| tuatara | *Sphenodontidae* | 45–61 | islands off New Zealand | ground insects, geckos, skinks, birds' eggs | lizard-like reptile with a third eye in the top of its head |
| turtle, Afro-American side-necked | *Pelomedusidae* | 12–90 | S America, Africa, Madagascar, Seychelles and Mauritius | herbivorous and omnivorous species | seabed-dweller that rarely requires to come to the surface |
| turtle, American mud and musk | *Kinosternidae* | 11–27 | N and S America | molluscs, insects, crustaceans, fish, plants | lives permanently or semi-permanently in freshwater; glands produce distinctive and evil smelling secretion |
| turtle, Austro-American side-necked | *Chelidae* | 14–48 | S America, Australia and New Guinea | omnivorous and carnivorous species | family includes the peculiar looking matamata, the most adept of the ambush-feeders at the gape and suck technique of capturing prey |
| turtle, big-headed | *Platyssternidae* | 20 | SE Asia | small invertebrates | distinctive large head which cannot be retracted; active at night; exceptionally good climber |
| turtle, Central American river | *Dermatemydidae* | to 65 | Vera Cruz, Mexico, Honduras | fish, insects, fruit, leaves, plants | freshwater creature with well-developed shell |
| turtle, Mexican musk | *Staurotypidae* | to 38 | Mexico to Honduras | worms, fish, newts | freshwater creature dwelling in marshes and swamps |
| turtle, pig-nosed softshell | *Carettochelyidae* | 55 or over | New Guinea and N Australia | crustaceans, insects, molluscs, fish, aquatic plants, fruit | specialized swimmer named for its plateless skin and fleshy, pig-like snout |
| turtle, pond and river | *Emydidae* | 11.4–80 | N and C America, S Europe, N Africa, Asia and Argentina | insects, molluscs, vertebrates, plants | family ranges from tiny bog turtle (11.4cm) to the largest of the river turtles, the Malaysian giant turtle; includes box turtle with possible life span of over a century, also species of terrapin |

| Name | Family | Size (cm)[1] | Distribution | Food | Special features |
|---|---|---|---|---|---|
| turtle, sea | *Cheloniidae* | 75–213 | pantropical, and some subtropical and temperate regions | sponges, jellyfish, mussels, crabs, sea urchins, fish | rapid movement through water contrasts with characteristically slow movements of turtles on land |
| turtle, snapping | *Chelydridae* | 47–66 | N and C America | carrion, insects, fish, turtles, molluscs, plant food | large-headed, aggressive sea-bed dweller; includes other turtles in its diet; ambush feeder with rapid snapping movements; alligator snapping turtle has unique worm-like projection on the tongue which fills with blood, turns red, and acts as lure to catch fish |
| turtle, softshell | *Trionychidae* | 30–115 | N America, Africa, Asia and Indo-Australian archipelago | insects, crustaceans, fish | named after its leathered, plateless skin; noted for its prominent, pointed snout |
| viper | *Viperidae* | 25–365 | N and S America, Africa, Europe and Asia | vertebrates | famous, venomous family of snakes, including the rattlesnake which vibrates its tail when disturbed, and the sidewinder with its distinctive sideways movements |
| whiptail and racerunner | *Teiidae* | 37–45 | N and S Asia | small mammals, birds, fish, frogs, tadpoles, lizards, insects, snails, plants | captured and eaten by South American Indians, the fat and flesh also being used in traditional medicines |
| xenosaur | *Xenosauridae* | 10–15 | Mexico, Guatemala and S China | insects, tadpoles, fish | terrestrial, sedentary and secretive |

[1]To convert cm to inches, multiply by 0.3937.

## Fish

| Name | Family | Size (cm)[1] | Habitat | Distribution | Special features |
|---|---|---|---|---|---|
| albacore | *Scombridae* | to 130 | open waters | tropical, warm temperate | tuna fish with large pectoral fins; prized food and sport fish |
| anchovy | *Engraulidae* | 9–12 | surface ocean | temperate | important food fish in S Europe, Black Sea, Peru |
| angler fish | *Chaunacidae* | 5–8 | deep ocean | tropical, temperate | large jaws; fishing lure at tip of modified dorsal ray |
| barracuda | *Sphyraenidae* | 30–240 | surface ocean | tropical, warm temperate | carnivorous; voracious; large teeth |
| blenny | *Blennidae* | 20–49 | sea bed | temperate, tropical | devoid of scales |
| bonito | *Scombridae* | to 90 | open sea surface water | temperate, warm | commercially important; member of tuna family; food fish; sport fish |
| bream | *Cyprinidae* | 41–80 | freshwater lakes, rivers | temperate (N Europe) | deep-bodied; food fish |
| brill | *Scophthalmidae* | to 70 | sea bed | temperate | flat fish; eyes on left side; food fish |
| butterfly fish | *Chaetodontidae* | to 15 | reefs | tropical | deep, compressed body; brightly coloured |
| carp | *Cyprinidae* | 51–61 | beds of freshwater lakes, rivers | temperate | important food fish; used in aquaculture |
| catfish | *Ictaluridae* | 90–135 | sea bed | temperate (N America) | females lay eggs in nest scooped out in mud; important food fish |
| chub | *Cyprinidae* | 30–60 | lakes, rivers | temperate (Europe) | popular sport fish |
| cod | *Gadidae* | to 120 | ocean shelf | temperate, N hemisphere | common cod very important food fish |

| Name | Family | Size (cm)[1] | Habitat | Distribution | Special features |
|---|---|---|---|---|---|
| conger eel | *Congridae* | 274 | sea bed, deep inshore pools | temperate | rounded cylindrical body; upper jaw longer than lower |
| dab | *Pleuronectidae* | 20–40 | shallow sea bed | temperate (Europe) | flat fish; eyes on right side; food fish |
| dace | *Cyprinidae* | 15–30 | freshwater lakes, rivers | temperate (Europe, former USSR) | sport fish |
| damsel fish | *Pomacentridae* | 5–15 | reefs, rocky shores | tropical, temperate | brightly coloured |
| dogfish | *Scyliorhinidae* | 60–100 | sea bed | temperate (Europe) | skin very rough; food fish (sold as rock salmon) |
| dolphin fish (dorado) | *Corypaenidae* | to 200 | surface | tropical, warm temperate | predatory; prized sport fish; food fish |
| dory | *Zeidae* | 30–60 | mainly shallow ocean | temperate | deep-bodied; food fish |
| eagle ray | *Myliobatidae* | to 200 | mainly inshore sea bed | tropical, temperate | pectoral fins form 'wings'; young born live |
| eel | *Anguillidae* | to 50 (male), to 100 (female) | rivers, mid-ocean | temperate | elongate cylindrical body form; adults live in rivers but spawn in sea; important food fish |
| electric eel | *Electrophoridae* | to 240 | shallow streams | Orinoco, Amazon basins (S America) | produces powerful electric shocks to stun prey and as defence |
| electric ray (or torpedo ray) | *Torpenidae* | to 180 | sea bed | tropical, temperate | produces strong electric shocks to stun prey |
| file fish | *Monacanthidae* | 5–13 | reefs, shallow water | tropical, warm temperate | rough skin; food fish |
| flounder | *Pleuronectidae* | to 51 | shallow sea bed, saline estuaries, lakes | temperate (Europe) | flat fish (eyes may be on right or left side); locally important food fish |
| flying fish | *Exocoetidae* | 25–50 | surface ocean | tropical, warm temperate | enlarged pelvic and pectoral fins give ability to jump and glide above water surface |
| goat fish ► red mullet | | | | | |
| goby | *Gobiidae* | 1–27 | shallow sea bed, rocky pools | tropical, temperate | pelvic fins joined to form single sucker-like fin |
| goldfish | *Cyprinidae* | to 30 | freshwater ponds, rivers | temperate | popular ornamental fish |
| grenadier ► rat-tail | | | | | |
| grey mullet | *Mugilidae* | to 75 | coastal sea bed; occasionally tropical freshwaters | tropical, temperate | food fish |
| grouper | *Serranidae* | 5–370 | deep sea | tropical, warm temperate | common around reefs, wrecks; prized sport and food fish |
| gurnard (or sea robin) | *Triglidae* | to 75 | sea bed | tropical, warm temperate | bony plates on head; many produce audible sounds |
| hake | *Merlucciidae* | to 180 | continental shelf waters | temperate | large head and jaws; food fish |
| halibut | *Pleuronectidae* | to 250 | sea bed | temperate (Atlantic) | flat fish; eyes on right side; prized food fish |
| herring | *Clupeidae* | to 40 | surface ocean | temperate (N Atlantic, Arctic) | important food fish |
| lamprey | *Petromyzonidae* | to 91 | streams, rivers; parasitic in open sea | temperate (N Atlantic) | primitive jawless fish; mouth sucker-like; food fish |
| lantern fish | *Myctophidae* | 2–15 | deep sea, but many migrate to surface at night | tropical, temperate | body has numerous light organs |

| Name | Family | Size (cm)[1] | Habitat | Distribution | Special features |
|---|---|---|---|---|---|
| lemon sole | *Pleuronectidae* | to 66 | sea bed | temperate | flat fish; specialized feeder on polychaete worms; food fish |
| loach | *Cobitidae* | to 15 | freshwater lakes, rivers | temperate (Europe, Asia) | popular aquarium fish |
| mackerel | *Scombridae* | to 66 | surface ocean | temperate (N Atlantic) | seasonal migrations; important food fish |
| manta ray (or devil ray) | *Mobulidae* | 120–900 (width) | surface ocean | tropical | fleshy 'horns' at side of head; young born, not hatched |
| minnow | *Cyprinidae* | to 12 | fast flowing freshwater lakes, rivers | temperate (N Europe, Asia) | locally abundant |
| monkfish | *Squatinidae* | to 180 | sea bed | temperate (N Atlantic, Mediterranean) | pectoral fins very broad, tail slender, intermediate in shape between shark and ray; food fish |
| moorish idol | *Zanclidae* | to 22 | reefs | tropical (Indo-Pacific) | body deep, tall dorsal and anal fins; bold black/white stripes with some yellow |
| moray eel | *Muraenidae* | to 130 | rocky shores | temperate, tropical | pointed snout; long, sharp teeth; aggressive |
| parrot fish | *Scaridae* | 25–190 | reefs | tropical | jaw teeth fused to form parrot-like beak for scraping algal growth from reefs, and for breaking coral |
| perch | *Percidae* | 30–50 | freshwater lakes, rivers, Baltic Sea | temperate | food fish; sport fish |
| pike | *Escocidae* | to 130 | freshwater lakes, rivers | temperate | snout pointed; jaws large; predatory; prized by anglers |
| pilchard (or sardine) | *Clupeidae* | to 25 | surface | temperate (N Atlantic, Mediterranean) | important food fish, often canned |
| pipefish | *Syngnathidae* | 15–160 | shallow seas | tropical, warm temperate | slender segmented body; males of some species carry eggs in brood pouch |
| plaice | *Pleuronectidae* | 50–90 | shallow sea bed | temperate (Europe) | flatfish; eyes on right side; important food fish |
| puffer | *Tetraodontidae* | 3–25 | inshore shallow seas, reefs | tropical, warm temperate | body often spiny; some organs and tissues very poisonous, but a food delicacy in Japan |
| rat-tail (or grenadier) | *Macrouridae* | 40–110 | close to deep-sea bed | temperate, tropical | large head, tapering body; some species make sounds by resonating swim bladder |
| ray | *Rajidae* | 39–113 | sea bed | temperate | skate and ray family; front part of body flattened with large pectoral fins |
| red mullet (or goat fish) | *Mullidae* | to 40 | sea bed | tropical, temperate | food fish |
| remora | *Echeneidae* | 12–46 | open sea | tropical, warm temperate | large sucking disc on head, with which it attaches itself to other fish, especially sharks |
| roach | *Cyprinidae* | 35–53 | freshwater lakes, rivers | temperate (Europe, former USSR) | popular sport fish |
| sailfish | *Istiophoridae* | to 360 | open ocean surface | tropical, warm temperate | long tall dorsal fin; prized sport fish |
| salmon | *Salmonidae* | to 150 | surface ocean; rivers | temperate | swims upriver to breed; prized sport and food fish |
| sandeel | *Ammodytidae* | to 20 | inshore sea bed | temperate (N hemisphere) | very important food for seabirds |
| sardine ► pilchard | | | | | |

| Name | Family | Size (cm)[1] | Habitat | Distribution | Special features |
|---|---|---|---|---|---|
| scorpion-fish | *Scorpaenidae* | to 50 | shallow sea bed, reefs | tropical, temperate | distinctive fin and body spines; venom glands |
| sea bass | *Percichthyidae* | 60–100 | inshore waters; reefs | tropical, temperate | food fish; popular sport fish |
| sea robin ► gurnard | | | | | |
| sea-bream | *Sparidae* | 35–51 | close to sea bed | tropical, temperate | food fish; sport fish |
| seahorse | *Syngnathidae* | to 15 | surface ocean | tropical, warm temperate | snout extended to form horse-like head; swims upright |
| shark, basking | *Cetorhinidae* | 870–1350 | surface ocean | tropical, temperate | feeds on plankton; second largest living fish |
| shark, great white | *Isuridae* | to 630 | surface ocean | tropical | fierce; voracious; young born, not hatched |
| shark, hammerhead | *Sphyrnidae* | 360–600 | mainly surface ocean | tropical, warm temperate | head flattened into hammer shape; voracious; young born, not hatched |
| shark, tiger | *Galeorhinidae* | 360–600 | surface ocean | tropical, warm temperate | vertical stripes on body; fierce |
| shark, whale | *Rhincodontidae* | 1 020–1 800 | surface ocean | tropical | largest living fish; feeds on plankton |
| skate | *Rajidae* | 200–285 | mid-ocean, sea bed | temperate | food fish |
| smelt | *Osmeridae* | 20–30 | freshwater lakes, rivers; inshore seas | temperate | related to salmon and trout; food fish |
| sole | *Soleidae* | 30–60 | sea bed | tropical, temperate | flat fish; eyes on right side; food fish |
| sprat | *Clupeidae* | 13–16 | surface–mid-ocean | temperate | food fish; called whitebait when small |
| squirrel fish | *Holocentridae* | 12–30 | reefs | tropical | brightly coloured; nocturnal stickleback |
| | *Gasterosteidae* | 5–10 | freshwater lakes, rivers; inshore seas | temperate (N hemisphere) | male builds nest, guards eggs |
| sting ray | *Dasyatidae* | 106–140 | sea bed; tropical freshwaters | tropical, temperate | tail whip-like, armed with poison spine(s) |
| sturgeon | *Acipenseridae* | 100–500 | shallow sea bed; rivers | temperate (N hemisphere) | primitive fish; eggs prized as caviar |
| sunfish | *Molidae* | to 400 | surface–mid open ocean | tropical, warm temperate | tail fin absent; body almost circular |
| surgeon fish (or tang) | *Acanthuridae* | 20–45 | reefs | tropical, subtropical | brightly coloured; sharp spine on sides of tail can be erected for defence |
| swordfish | *Xiphiidae* | 200–500 | surface–mid open ocean | tropical, temperate | upper jaw extended to form flathead 'sword'; food and sport fish |
| tang ► surgeon fish | | | | | |
| trigger fish | *Balistidae* | 10–60 | sea bed outside reefs | tropical | colourful; dorsal spine can be erected to wedge fish in crevice as defence; food fish, but can be poisonous |
| trout | *Salmonidae* | 23–140 | surface ocean; freshwater lakes, rivers | temperate | brown trout confined to fresh water; sea trout migratory; prized food fish |
| tuna, skipjack | *Scombridae* | to 100 | mid-ocean | tropical, temperate | fast swimmer; important food fish |
| tuna, yellow fin | *Scombridae* | to 200 | surface ocean | tropical, warm temperate | elongated body, long dorsal and anal fins; important food fish |
| turbot | *Scophthalamidae* | 50–100 | shallow sea bed | temperate (N Atlantic) | flat fish; eyes on left side of body; prized food fish |
| wrasse | *Labridae* | 7–210 | reefs, rocky coasts | tropical, warm temperate | brightly coloured |

[1] To convert cm to inches multiply by 0.3937

## Invertebrates

For molluscs, lengths given are normally maximum shell lengths, but (b) indicates body length; for spiders, lengths are body lengths, although legs may be much longer; for insects, sizes given are normally body lengths, but (w) indicates wingspan.

| Name | Species | Length | Range and habitat | Notable features |
|---|---|---|---|---|
| **MOLLUSCS: Phylum Mollusca** | | | | |
| ❑ **Slugs and snails/Gastropoda (c.50 000 species)** | | | | |
| abalone | *Haliotis* (several species) | <30cm | warm seas worldwide | feed on seaweeds; mainly in coastal waters; collected for food and for the pearly shells |
| conch | *Strombus* (several species) | <33cm | tropical seas | feed on seaweeds; shells with a broad 'wing', often used as trumpets |
| cone shell | *Conus* (c.600 species) | <23cm | warm seas worldwide | feed on fish and molluscs, killed by poison darts; some species dangerous to humans; beautiful shells much sought by collectors |
| cowrie | (c.150 species in several genera) | <10cm | warm seas worldwide | feed on sea anemones and other small creatures; shiny, china-like shells were once used as money |
| limpet, common | *Patella vulgata* | <5.5cm | worldwide | feeds on seaweeds in intertidal zone; conical shell pulled tightly down on rocks when tide is out |
| limpet, slipper | *Crepidula fornicata* | <6cm | originally N America, now common on coasts of Europe | strains food particles from the water; slipper-like shells cling together in chains; a serious pest in oyster and mussel farms, settling on the shells and cutting off their food supplies |
| periwinkle, common | *Littorina littorea* | <2.5cm | N Atlantic and adjacent seas; rocky shores | feeds on seaweeds; thick, dull brown shell; the fishmonger's winkle |
| sea butterfly | (c.100 species in several genera) | <5cm | oceans worldwide; most common in warm waters | carnivorous, eating a variety of small marine creatures; with or without shells, they swim by flapping wing-like extensions of the foot |
| slug, great grey | *Limax maximus* | <20cm (b) | Europe | mainly feeds on fungi and rotting matter; mottled grey and brown; common in gardens; mates in mid-air, hanging from a rope of slime |
| snail, giant African | *Achatina fulica* | <15cm | originally Africa, now tropical Asia and Pacific | vegetarian; a serious agricultural pest; lays hard-shelled eggs as big as those of a thrush |
| snail, great ramshorn | *Planorbarius corneus* | <3cm | Europe; still and slow-moving freshwater | vegetarian, often browsing on algae; shell forms a flat spiral; body has bright red blood |
| snail, roman | *Helix pomatia* | <5cm | C and S Europe; lime soils | vegetarian; often a pest, but cultivated for food in some areas |
| whelk | *Buccinum undatum* | <12cm | N Atlantic and neighbouring seas | carnivorous, feeding on living and dead animals; large numbers are collected for human consumption |

| Name | Species | Length | Range and habitat | Notable features |
|---|---|---|---|---|
| **❑ Bivalves/Lamellibranchia (c.8 000 species)** | | | | |
| cockle, common | *Cardium edule* | <5cm | European coasts | burrows in sand and mud near low-tide level; important food for fish and wading birds |
| mussel, common | *Mytilus edulis* | <11cm | coasts of Europe and eastern North America | bluish shell clings to rocks with tough threads; farmed on a large scale for human consumption, especially in S Europe |
| oyster | *Ostrea edulis* | <15cm | coasts of Europe and Africa | cements trough-shaped lower valve to stones, with flat upper valve sitting on it like a lid; large numbers farmed for human consumption |
| piddock | *Pholas dactylus* | <12cm | coasts of Europe and eastern North America | uses rasp-like shell to bore into soft rocks and wood, making an inescapable tomb; sucks in water and food through long siphons |
| razor-shell, pod | *Ensis siliqua* | <20cm | European coasts | long, straight shell, shaped like a cut-throat razor, is open at both ends; burrows in sand |
| scallop, great | *Pecten maximus* | <15cm | European coasts; usually below tide level | strongly ribbed, eared shells with one valve flatter than the other; lives freely on seabed and swims by opening and closing its valves |
| **❑ Squids and octopuses/Cephalopoda (c.750 species)** | | | | |
| cuttlefish, common | *Sepia officinalis* | <30cm | coastal waters of Atlantic and neighbouring seas | eats shrimps and other crustaceans, caught with tentacles; lives on seabed; flat, oval body can change colour; cuttle-bone is the internal shell |
| octopus, blue-ringed | *Hapalochlaena maculosa* | 10cm (span) | Australian coasts | the most dangerous species, despite its size; the only octopus whose venom is known to have killed people |
| octopus, common | *Octopus vulgaris* | <3m (span) | Atlantic and Mediterranean coastal waters | eats small fish and crustaceans, killed by a poisonous bite; not dangerous to people |
| squid, common | *Loligo vulgaris* | <50cm | Atlantic and Mediterranean coastal waters | eats fish, crustaceans and smaller squids; cylindrical body with a triangular fin at the rear; deep pink in life, fading to grey after death |
| squid, giant | *Architeuthis princeps* | <15m | oceans worldwide | largest invertebrate, although tentacles account for over half its length; eats fish, seals and small whales; main food of the sperm whale |
| **CRUSTACEANS: Phylum Arthropoda** | | | | |
| **❑ Crustacea (c.30 000 species)** | | | | |
| barnacle, acorn | *Semibalanus balanoides* | <1.5cm (diam.) | worldwide | cemented to intertidal rocks; the shell opens when the tide is in and the animal combs food particles from the water with its legs |
| crab, edible | *Cancer pagurus* | <20cm | eastern N Atlantic and neighbouring seas | scavenger; inhabits rocky coasts to depths of about 50m; widely caught for human consumption |

| Name | Species | Length | Range and habitat | Notable features |
|---|---|---|---|---|
| crab, fiddler | *Uca* (many species) | <3cm | tropical seashores and mangrove swamps | scavengers; male has one big, colourful claw, often much bigger than the rest of his body, which he waves to attract females |
| crab, hermit | (several species and genera) | <15cm | worldwide; mainly in coastal waters | scavengers; elongated, soft-bodied crabs use empty seashells as portable homes |
| crab, robber | *Birgus latro* | <45cm | islands and coasts of Indian and Pacific oceans | related to hermit crab, but does not live in discarded shells; terrestrial scavenger, feeds mainly on carrion; often climbs trees |
| crayfish, noble | *Astacus astacus* | <15cm | Europe | inhabits shallow, well aerated streams, feeding on other animals, living or dead; reared in large numbers for human consumption, especially in France |
| krill | *Euphausia superba* | <5cm | mainly the southern oceans | planktonic shrimp-like animal; the main food of the whalebone whales and many other animals in the southern oceans |
| lobster, common | *Homarus vulgaris* | <70cm | European coasts | scavenger; lives on rocky coasts down to depths of about 30m; bluish black in life; now rare in many places through overfishing |
| lobster, Norway | *Nephrops norvegicus* | <25cm | European seas | a spiny scavenger; lives on sandy and muddy seabeds at depths of 30–200m; marketed as scampi |
| lobster, spiny | *Palinurus vulgaris* | <45cm | Mediterranean and Atlantic; rocky coasts | very spiny, with stout antennae much longer than the body; no pincers; feeds on molluscs; a popular food in S Europe; also known as crayfish |
| prawn, common | *Palaemon serratus* | <10cm | European coasts; usually stony or rocky shores | scavenger; almost transparent in life; differs from shrimps in its serrated rostrum |
| shrimp, common | *Crangon crangon* | <7cm | coasts of Europe and eastern North America | eats other small animals, living or dead; common on sand and mud, and much used for human consumption; front legs stout and clawed |
| water flea | *Daphnia* (many species) | <0.5cm | worldwide; freshwater | reddish brown or greenish, abundant in muddy ponds and other freshwater; swims by waving long antennae; a major food of small fish and much used, living or dried, to feed aquarium fish |
| woodlouse | (many genera and species) | <2.5cm | worldwide | scavengers; feed mainly on decaying plant material; the only major group of terrestrial crustaceans, but still confined to damp places; also called sow-bugs and slaters |
| **SPIDERS: Phylum Arthropoda** | | | | |
| ❑ **Arachnida (c.40 000 species)** | | | | |
| bird-eating spider | (c.800 species in several genera) | <10cm | warmer parts of the Americas and southern Africa | stout-bodied, hairy hunting spiders, often in trees, where they sometimes capture nestling birds; venom not dangerous to people, although the hairs may cause a painful rash; often called tarantulas |

| Name | Species | Length | Range and habitat | Notable features |
|---|---|---|---|---|
| black widow | *Latrodectus mactans* | <1.6cm | most warm parts of the world, including S Europe | black with red markings beneath; a dangerous spider that has caused many human deaths, but bites are now quickly cured with antivenin; female sometimes eats the smaller male after mating |
| bolas spider | (several species and genera) | <1.5cm | North and South America, Africa and Australasia | catch moths by whirling a single thread of silk with a blob of sticky gum on the end |
| crab spider | (c.3 000 species in numerous genera) | <2cm | worldwide | mostly squat, crab-like spiders that lie in wait for prey — often in flowers — and grab it with their long front legs |
| funnel-web spider | *Atrax* (3 species) | <5cm | Australia | among the deadliest spiders, although antivenins are now available for treating bites; inhabit tubular webs in the ground or among rocks |
| garden spider | *Araneus diadematus* | <1.2cm | N hemisphere | black to ginger, with a white cross on the back; makes orb-webs up to 50cm across on fences and vegetation; not only in gardens |
| gladiator spider | *Dinopis* (several species) | <2.5cm | warm regions and some cooler parts of North America and Australia | slender spiders with enormous eyes; make sticky webs which they throw at passing prey, usually at night |
| house spider | *Tegenaria* (c.90 species) | <2cm | mostly N hemisphere | long-legged, fast-running spiders often seen running over floors at night; make scruffy triangular webs in neglected corners; harmless |
| jumping spider | (c.4 000 species in many genera) | <1.5cm | worldwide | large-eyed, day-active spiders that leap onto their prey; often brilliantly coloured |
| money spider | (many species and genera) | <0.6cm | worldwide, but most common in cooler areas of N hemisphere | believed to bring wealth or good fortune, perhaps because of the silvery appearance of their little hammock-like webs which cover grassland and glisten with dew on autumn mornings |
| orb-web spider | (c.2 500 species in many genera) | <3cm | worldwide | the makers of the familiar wheel-shaped webs, up to a metre or more in diameter; mostly brown, but some are very colourful; not dangerous |
| raft spider | *Dolomedes* (c.100 species) | <2.5cm | worldwide | hunting spiders that lurk at the edge of pools or on floating objects, picking up vibrations of prey (insects and small fish) and streaking after them |
| spitting spider | *Scytodes thoracica* | <0.6cm | worldwide; normally only in buildings | catches small insects by spitting strands of sticky, venom-coated gum at them |
| tarantula | *Lycosa narbonensis* | <3cm | S Europe | a wolf spider whose bite was believed to be curable only by performing a frantic dance — the tarantella; although painful, the bite is not really dangerous; the name is now often applied to the hairy bird-eating spiders |
| trapdoor spider | (c.700 species in several genera) | <3cm | most warm parts of the world, including S Europe | live in burrows closed by hinged lids of silk and debris; spiders lie in wait under the lid and grab passing prey |

| Name | Species | Length | Range and habitat | Notable features |
|---|---|---|---|---|
| water spider | *Argyroneta aquatica* | <1.5cm | Eurasia; in ponds and slow-moving streams | the world's only truly aquatic spider, living in an air-filled, thimble-shaped web fixed to water plants; darts out to catch passing prey |
| wolf spider | (c.2 500 species in many genera) | <3cm | worldwide, but most common in cooler parts of N hemisphere | large-eyed hunting spiders, mostly ground-living; some chase their prey at speed; generally harmless but some of the larger species have dangerous bites |
| zebra spider | *Salticus scenicus* | <0.6cm | N hemisphere; often in and around houses | black and white jumping spider, commonly hunting on rocks and walls, especially those covered with lichen |
| **INSECTS: Phylum Arthropoda** | | | | |
| ❑ **Bristletails/Thysanura (c.600 species)** | | | | |
| silverfish | *Lespisma saccharina* | 10mm | worldwide | wingless scavenger of starchy foods in houses |
| ❑ **Mayflies/Ephemeroptera (c.2 500 species)** | | | | |
| Mayfly | *Hexagenia bilineata* | 16mm | worldwide | flimsy insects with 2 or 3 long 'tails'; they grow up in water and have a very short adult life, often only a few hours |
| ❑ **Dragonflies/Odonata (c.5 000 species)** | | | | |
| Dragonfly | (many species) | <20–130mm | worldwide | long-bodied insects, with gauzy wings spanning up to 150mm; most fly rapidly and catch insects in mid-air; they grow up in water |
| ❑ **Crickets and grasshoppers/Orthoptera (c.17 000 species)** | | | | |
| cricket, bush | (thousands of species) | <150mm | worldwide, apart from coldest areas | omnivorous or insect-eating; like grasshoppers but with very long antennae; several N American species are called katydids |
| cricket, house | *Acheta domesticus* | <20mm | worldwide | scavenger in houses and rubbish dumps |
| locust, desert | *Schistocerca gregaria* | 85mm | Africa and S Asia | herbivorous; swarms periodically destroy crops in Africa |
| locust, migratory | *Locusta migratoria* | <50mm | Africa and S Europe | herbivorous; swarm in Africa, but solitary in Europe |
| ❑ **Stick insects and leaf insects/Phasmida (c.2 500 species, mostly tropical)** | | | | |
| insect, leaf | (c.50 species) | <90mm | SE Asia | very flat, leaf-like, green or brown herbivores |
| stick, insect | (over 2 400 species) | <350mm | warm areas, including S Europe | herbivorous; stick-like green or brown bodies with or without wings; often kept as pets |
| ❑ **Earwigs/Dermaptera (c.1 300 species)** | | | | |
| earwig | (many species) | <30mm | originally Africa, now worldwide | slender, brownish insects, with or without wings and always with prominent pincers at the rear; most are omnivorous scavengers |
| ❑ **Cockroaches and mantids/Dictyoptera (c.5 500 species)** | | | | |
| American cockroach | *Periplaneta americana* | 40mm | worldwide | scavenger, living outside (if warm) or in buildings; chestnut brown |
| praying mantis | (c.2 000 species) | <75mm | all warm areas | catch other insects with spiky front legs |

| Name | Species | Length | Range and habitat | Notable features |
|---|---|---|---|---|
| **□ Termites/Isoptera (over 2 000 species)** | | | | |
| termites | (many species) | <22mm | mostly tropical | small and ant-like, with or without wings; colonies in mounds of earth, in dead wood or underground; many are timber pests |
| **□ Bugs/Hemiptera (c.70 000 species)** | | | | |
| aphid | (numerous species) | <5mm | worldwide | sap-sucking insects, with or without wings; many, including trackfly and greenfly, are serious pests |
| bedbug | *Cimex lectularius* | 5mm | worldwide | bloodsucking; hides by day and feeds at night, often attacking people in their beds |
| cicada | (numerous species) | <40mm (w) | worldwide, mainly in warm climates | sap-sucking; males make loud, shrill sounds; young stages live underground on roots; one American species takes 17 years to mature |
| froghopper | *Philaenus spumarius* | 6mm | N hemisphere | sap-sucker; young stages live in froth, often called cuckoo-spit |
| pondskater | *Gerris lacustris* | 10mm | N hemisphere | skims across the surface of still water and catches other insects |
| **□ Thrips/Thysanoptera (over 3 000 species)** | | | | |
| thrips | (many species) | 2.5mm | worldwide | tiny winged or wingless herbivorous insects, many of which grow up in crops and cause much damage; they fly in huge numbers in sultry weather in summer and are often called thunder-bugs |
| **□ Lacewings/Neuroptera (over 6 000 species)** | | | | |
| antlion | *Myrmeleon formicarius* | 90mm (w) | Eurasia | larvae make small pits in sandy soil and feed on ants and other insects that fall into them |
| green lacewing | (several genera and many species) | <50mm | worldwide | predators of aphids and other small insects in a wide range of habitats; delicate green wings |
| **□ Scorpion flies/Mecoptera (c.400 species)** | | | | |
| scorpion fly | *Panorpa* | 20mm | worldwide | scavenging insects in which the male abdomen is usually turned up like a scorpion's tail, although they are quite harmless |
| **□ Butterflies and moths/Lepidoptera (c.150 000 species)** | | | | |
| **Butterflies (c. 18 000 species)** | | | | |
| birdwing butterfly | (several genera and species) | <300mm (w) | SE Asia and N Australia | tropical forests; they include the world's largest butterflies; many are becoming rare through collecting and loss of habitat |
| cabbage white butterfly | *Pieris brassicae* | <70mm (w) | Eurasia, N Africa | flowery places; caterpillar is a serious pest of cabbages and other brassicas |
| fritillary butterfly | (many genera and species) | <80mm (w) | mostly N hemisphere | mostly orange with black spots above and silvery spots below; live in woods and open spaces including arctic tundra |
| monarch butterfly | *Danaus plexippus* | <100mm (w) | mostly Pacific area and North America | orange with black markings; a great migrant; it hibernates in huge swarms in Mexico and southern USA; a rare visitor to Europe |

| Name | Species | Length | Range and habitat | Notable features |
|---|---|---|---|---|
| skipper butterfly | (many genera and species) | <80mm (w) | worldwide | mostly small brown or orange grassland insects with darting flight |
| **Moths (c. 132 000 species)** | | | | |
| swallowtail butterfly | (many genera and species) | <120mm (w) | worldwide, but mostly tropical | large, usually colourful and with prominent 'tails' on hindwings; many becoming rare through collecting and loss of habitat |
| burnet moth | *Zygaena* (many species) | <40mm (w) | Eurasia and N Africa | slow, night- and day-flying moths, protected by foul-tasting body fluids and gaudy black and red colours |
| clothes moth | (several species) | <15mm (w) | worldwide | small, often rather shiny moths whose caterpillars damage woollen fabrics; live mainly in buildings |
| death's head hawkmoth | *Acherontia atropos* | <135mm (w) | Africa and Eurasia | sturdy moth with a skull-like pattern on its thorax; larvae on potato and related plants |
| hummingbird hawkmoth | *Macroglossum stellatarum* | <60mm (w) | Eurasia | day-flying, producing loud hum as it hovers in front of flowers to feed; larvae on bedstraws |
| pine processionary moth | *Thaumetopoea pityocampa* | <40mm (w) | S and C Europe | greyish moth whose larvae live in silken tents on pine trees and go out to feed in long processions at night; a serious forest pest |
| silk moth | *Bombyx mori* | <60mm (w) | native of China; now unknown in the wild | cream-coloured moth bred for the fine silk obtained from its cocoon — over 1km from a single cocoon; larvae eat mulberry leaves; all cultured moths flightless |
| tiger moth | (many genera and species) | <100mm (w) | worldwide | mostly brightly coloured and hairy, with evil-tasting body fluids |
| ❑ **True flies/Diptera (c.90 000 species, a few without wings)** | | | | |
| crane fly (or leather-jacket) | (many genera and species) | <35mm (w) | worldwide | slender, long-legged flies, often resting with wings outstretched; larvae of many are leather-jackets that damage crop roots |
| house fly | *Musca domestica* | 7mm | worldwide | abundant on farms and rubbish dumps; becoming less common in houses; breeds in dung and other decaying matter and carries germs |
| hover fly | (many genera and species) | <40mm | worldwide | many have amazing hovering ability; adults feed on pollen and nectar; many are black and yellow mimics of bees and wasps |
| mosquito | (many genera and species) | <15mm | worldwide | females are bloodsuckers; spread malaria and other diseases |
| tsetse fly | *Glossina* (c.20 species) | 10mm | tropical Africa | bloodsuckers; spread human sleeping sickness, cattle diseases |
| ❑ **Fleas/Siphonaptera (c.1 800 species)** | | | | |
| European flea | (many species) | 3mm | worldwide | wingless, bloodsucking parasites feeding on birds and mammals; long hind legs enable them to jump many times their own lengths; the maggot-like larvae are not parasitic |

| Name | Species | Length | Range and habitat | Notable features |
|---|---|---|---|---|
| ❑ **Bees, wasps and ants/Hymenoptera (over 120 000 species)** | | | | |
| ant, army | (several genera and species) | <40mm | tropics | live in mobile colonies, some of over a million ants; kill any animal unable to get out of their way; workers much smaller than the 40mm-long queen; African species often called driver ants |
| ant, honeypot | (several genera and species) | 20mm | deserts across the world | some workers gorge themselves with sugar-rich food and become living honeypots from which other ants can feed |
| bee, bumble | *Bombus* (many species) | <35mm | worldwide, except Australia | plump, hairy bees living in annual colonies; only mated queen survives winter to start new colonies in spring |
| bee, honey | *Apis mellifera* | <20mm | worldwide (probably native of SE Asia) | less hairy than bumble bee; lives in permanent colonies, sometimes in hollow trees but mostly in artificial hives; stores honey for winter |
| hornet, European | *Vespa crabro* | <35mm | Eurasia and now America | large brown and yellow wasp; nests in hollow trees and feeds young on other insects |
| ichneumon | (thousands of genera and species) | <50mm | worldwide | parasites, mostly laying their eggs in young stages of other insects; the young grow inside their hosts and gradually kill them |
| sawfly | (numerous families) | <50mm | worldwide | named after the saw-like ovipositor of most females, used to cut slits in plants before laying eggs there; larvae all vegetarians |
| weaver, ant | *Oecophylla* (several species) | 10mm | Old World tropics | nest made from leaves, joined by sticky silk produced by the grubs |
| ❑ **Beetles/Coleopteria (over 350 000 species; front wings usually form casing over body)** | | | | |
| sexton beetle | *Nicrophorus* (several species) | <25mm | worldwide | often orange and black; beetles work in pairs to bury small dead animals, near which they then lay their eggs |
| click beetle (or wireworm) | (many genera and species) | <40mm | worldwide | bullet-shaped beetles which flick into the air to turn over, making a loud click; larvae, called wireworms, damage crop roots |
| colorado beetle | *Leptinotarsa decemlineata* | 10mm | N America and now Europe | black and yellow adults and pink grubs both seriously damage potato crops |
| deathwatch beetle | *Xestobium rufovillosum* | 7mm | N hemisphere | tunnelling larvae do immense damage to old building timbers; adults tap wood as mating call; also found in dead trees |
| devil's coach-horse | *Staphylinus olens* | 25mm | Eurasia | slender black beetle with short front wings; lives in gardens and often enters houses; also called cocktail because it raises its rear end |
| glow-worm | *Lampyris noctiluca* | 15mm | Europe | wingless female glows with greenish light to attract males flying overhead; feeds on snails |
| furniture beetle (or woodworm) | *Anobium punctatum* | 5mm | worldwide | larvae, known as woodworm, tunnel in dead wood and cause much damage to furniture and building timbers |
| goliath beetle | *Goliathus* (several species) | <150mm | Africa | world's heaviest beetles, up to 100g; fly well and feed on fruit |

| Name | Species | Length | Range and habitat | Notable features |
|---|---|---|---|---|
| grain weevil | *Sitophilus granarius* | 3mm | worldwide | a serious pest, breeding in and destroying all kinds of stored grain |
| ladybird | (c.3 500 species in many genera) | 10mm | worldwide | aphid-eating habits make them friends of gardeners; most are red or yellow, with various spot patterns |
| scarab beetle | *Scarabaeus* (many species) | <30mm | most warm parts of the world | dung-feeding — some form the dung into balls and roll it around before burying it; known as tumblebugs in N America; introduced into Australia to deal with sheep and cattle dung |
| stag beetle | *Lucanus cervus* | 50mm | Eurasia | males have huge antler-like jaws, with which they wrestle rivals |
| woodworm ► furniture beetle | | | | |

## Endangered species (Mammals, birds, reptiles)

Species are classified as endangered when they are in danger of extinction through drastic depletion of their numbers or habitats. Although the majority of endangered species are included in this list, there is space for only a few of the endangered subspecies. Many more species may actually be endangered, but there is not enough information known about them to determine whether they are endangered, vulnerable or just rare. (A few examples of these are included below, coded [2].) Also included in this list are taxa that may be extinct now, but have definitely been seen in the wild in the past 50 years.

| Name | Species | Location | Cause of endangerment |
|---|---|---|---|
| ❑ **Mammals** | | | |
| addax | *Addax nasomaculatus* | Chad; Mali; Mauritania; Niger | |
| anoa, lowland | *Bubalus depressicornis* (*Anoa depressicornis*) | Sulawesi, Indonesia | hunting; destruction of habitat |
| anoa, mountain | *Bubalus quarlesi* (*Anoa quarlesi*) | Sulawesi and Buton, Indonesia | hunting; destruction of habitat |
| antelope, giant sable | *Hippotragus niger variani* | Angola | human settlement; destruction of habitat |
| armadillo, Brazilian three-banded | *Tolypeutes tricinctus* | Brazil | |
| ass, African wild | *Equus africanus* (*Equus asinus*) | Ethiopia; Somalia | hunting for the medical properties of its meat and fat; poaching; human disturbance in the form of tourism; droughts; competition for pasture and water from domestic livestock |
| aye-aye | *Daubentonia madagascariensis* | Madagascar | primate threatened by loss of forest habitat |
| bandicoot, giant | *Peroryctes broadbenti* | Papua New Guinea | |
| bandicoot, golden | *Isoodon auratus* | Australia | |
| bandicoot, western barred | *Perameles bougainville* | Australia | |
| bat, Bulmer's fruit | *Aproteles bulmerae* | Papua New Guinea | |
| bat, cusp-toothed fruit | *Pteralopex atrata* | Solomon Is | |
| bat, golden-capped fruit | *Acerodon jubatus* | Philippines | |
| bat, gray | *Myotis grisescens* | SE USA | disturbance of habitat by caving, vandalism |
| bat, Philippines tube-nosed fruit | *Nyctimene rabori* | Philippines | |

| Name | Species | Location | Cause of endangerment |
|---|---|---|---|
| bat, Seychelles sheath-tailed | *Coleura seychellensis* | Seychelles | |
| bat (a species of) | *Pteralopex acrodonta* | Fiji | |
| bat (a species of) | *Pteralopex anceps* | Papua New Guinea | |
| bat (a species of) | *Pteralopex pulchra* | Solomon Is | |
| bear, Baluchistan | *Selenarctos thibetanus gedrosianus* (*Ursus thibetanus gedrosianus*) | Iran; Pakistan | human persecution; hunting because of its damage to crops and the threat posed by it to domestic stock |
| bettong, northern | *Bettongia tropica* | Australia | |
| boodie | *Bettongia lesueur* | Australia | |
| buffalo, wild water | *Bubalus arnee* | Bhutan; India; Nepal; Thailand | |
| cat, Iriomote | *Prionailurus bengalensis iriomotensis* (*Prionailurus iriomotensis*) | Iriomote I, Japan | loss of natural habitat to agriculture |
| cat, Pakistan sand | *Felis margarita scheffeli* | Pakistan | animal trade |
| cheetah, Asiatic | *Acinonyx jubatus venaticus* | Iran | fur trade; decline in population of its natural prey, the gazelle |
| chuditch | *Dasyurus geoffroii* | Australia | |
| civet, Malabar large spotted | *Viverra megaspila civettina* | S India | possibly already extinct due to persecution, loss of habitat to agriculture |
| cougar, Florida | *Puma concolor coryi* (*Felis concolor coryi*) | SE USA | loss of habitat; hunting; decreased prey on which to feed |
| deer, Argentinian pampas | *Ozotoceros bezoarticus celer* | Argentina | hunting; disease; loss of habitat to agriculture, domestic livestock |
| deer, Calamian hog | *Axis calamianensis* | Calamian Is, Philippines | |
| deer, Key | *Odocoileus virginianus clavium* | Washington and Oregon, USA | loss of habitat to agriculture |
| deer, Kuhl's hog or Bawean | *Axis kuhlii* | Bawean I, Indonesia | |
| deer, Manipur brow-antlered | *Cervus eldii eldii* | India | hunting; loss of habitat to domestic stock grazing, cultivation, logging, burning |
| deer, Père David's | *Elaphurus davidianus* | China | |
| deer, Persian fallow | *Dama mesopotamica* | Iran | hunting; loss of forest habitat to irrigation, agriculture, grazing of domestic livestock |
| deer, Siberian musk | *Moschus moschiferus* (*Moschus sibiricus*) | China; Korea; Mongolia; Russia | |
| deer, swamp | *Cervus duvauceli* | India; Nepal | poaching, human disturbance; competition for grazing from domestic livestock |
| deer, Thailand brow-antlered | *Cervus eldi siamensis* | Thailand; Laos; Cambodia; Vietnam | hunting; loss or destruction of habitat by the effects of war, agriculture, land development, shifting cultivation, forest clearance |
| deer, Visayan spotted | *Cervus alfredi* | Visayan Is, Philippines | |

| Name | Species | Location | Cause of endangerment |
|---|---|---|---|
| deer, Yarkand | *Cervus elaphus yarkandensis* | China | poaching; human disturbance; deterioration of habitat caused by domestic livestock, particularly grazing sheep |
| dibbler | *Parantechinus apicalis* (*Antechinus apicalis*) | Australia | |
| dog, wild | *Lycaon pictus* | Africa, South of the Sahara | human hunting, persecution |
| dog, Mexican prairie | *Cynomys mexicanus* | Mexico | |
| dolphin, Indus River | *Platanista minor* (*Platanista indi*) | Indus River, Pakistan | withdrawal of water for irrigation; illegal exploitation by fishermen |
| dolphin, Yangtse River (or baiji) | *Lipotes vexillifer* | Chiang Jiang River, China | |
| drill | *Mandrillus leucophaeus* (*Papio leucophaeus*) | Cameroon; Equatorial Guinea; Nigeria | hunting; loss of habitat due to clearance of forest, cultivation of land |
| duiker, Jentink's | *Cephalophus jentinki* | Liberia; Sierra Leone; Côte d'Ivoire | destruction of natural habitat; almost extinct |
| dunnart, Julia creek | *Sminthopsis douglasi* | Australia | |
| echidna, long-beaked | *Zaglossus bruijni* | Indonesia; Papua New Guinea | |
| elephant, Indian | *Elephas maximus* | Asia | severe loss of natural habitat |
| ferret, black-footed | *Mustela nigripes* | USA | poisoning; loss of grassland habitat |
| flying fox, Chuuk | *Pteropus insularis* | Federated States of Micronesia | |
| flying fox, Comoro black | *Pteropus livingstonei* | Comoros | |
| flying fox, Guam[1] | *Pteropus tokudae* | Guam, Mariana Is, USA | hunting; loss of forest areas |
| flying fox, Mortlock Island | *Pteropus phaecephalus* | Federated States of Micronesia | |
| flying fox, Pemba | *Pteropus voeltzkowi* | Tanzania | |
| flying fox, Pohnpei | *Pteropus molossinus* | Federated States of Micronesia | |
| flying fox, Rodrigues | *Pteropus rodricensis* | Rodrigues I, Mauritius | almost total loss of natural habitat |
| flying fox, Ryuku | *Pteropus dasymallus* | Japan; Taiwan | |
| fox, Simien (or Ethiopian wolf) | *Canis simensis* | Ethiopia | hunting; loss of habitat; decreasing availability of rodents as food |
| gazelle, Arabian sand | *Gazella subgutturosa marica* | Jordan and Arabian peninsula | hunting; deterioration of habitat due to overgrazing |
| gazelle, Cuvier's | *Gazella cuvieri* | Algeria; Morocco; Tunisia | hunting; loss of habitat to overgrazing by livestock, forest plantation |
| gazelle, dama | *Gazella dama* | Burkina Faso; Chad; Mali; Niger; The Sudan | |
| gazelle, slender-horned | *Gazella leptoceros* | Algeria; Chad; Egypt; Libya; Mali; Niger; The Sudan; Tunisia | hunting; deterioration of habitat |
| genet, crested | *Genetta cristata* | Cameroon; Nigeria | |
| gibbon, black | *Hylobates concolor* | Cambodia; China; Laos; Vietnam | |
| gibbon, hoolock | *Hylobates hoolock* | Bangladesh; China; India; Myanmar (Burma) | |

| Name | Species | Location | Cause of endangerment |
|---|---|---|---|
| gibbon, Mentawai | *Hylobates klossi* | Indonesia | |
| gibbon, pileated | *Hylobates pileatus* | Cambodia; Laos; Thailand | loss of forest habitat |
| gibbon, silvery | *Hylobates moloch* | Indonesia | destruction of forest habitat for timber, human settlement |
| glider, Mahogany | *Petaurus gracilis* | Australia | |
| guenon, Preuss's | *Cercopithecus preussi* | Cameroon; Equatorial Guinea | |
| guenon, red-bellied | *Cercopithecus erythrogaster* | Nigeria; Togo | |
| guenon, sun-tailed | *Cercopithecus solatus* | Gabon | |
| guenon, white-throated | *Cercopithecus sclateri* | Nigeria | |
| hare, hispid | *Caprolagus hispidus* | Bangladesh; India; Nepal | loss of habitat due to human settlement; cultivation; forestry; burning of thatchlands; also illegally hunted for food |
| hartebeest, Swayne's | *Alcelaphus buselaphus swaynei* | Ethiopia | hunting; destruction of habitat |
| hartebeest, Tora | *Alcelaphus buselaphus tora* | Ethiopia; The Sudan; Egypt | hunting; loss of habitat; disease |
| hirola | *Damaliscus hunteri* | Kenya; Somalia | |
| hog, pygmy | *Sus salvanius* | N India | destruction of thatchland habitat by settlement, forestry, fires; also hunted for its meat |
| horse, Przewalski's[1] | *Equus ferus przewalskii* | China; Mongolia | severe competition for natural pasture and water from domestic livestock; possibly already extinct in the wild |
| huemul, South Andean | *Hippocamelus bisulcus* | Argentina; Chile | |
| hutia, Cabrera's | *Capromys angelcabrerai (Mesocapromys angelcabrerai)* | Cuba | |
| hutia, dwarf | *Capromys nanus (Mesocapromys nanus)* | Cuba | |
| hutia, Garrido's | *Capromys garridoi (Mysateles garridoi)* | Cuba | |
| hutia, large-eared | *Capromys auritus (Mesocapromys auritus)* | Cuba | |
| hutia, little earth | *Capromys sanfelipensis (Mesocapromys sanfelipensis)* | Cuba | |
| hyena, Barbary | *Hyaena hyaena barbara* | N Africa | loss of habitat due to human settlement, agriculture |
| ibex, Pyrenean | *Capra pyrenaica pyrenaica* | Spain | hunting; now virtually extinct |
| ibex, Walia | *Capra walia* | Ethiopia | destruction of habitat by agriculture, livestock |
| impala, black-faced | *Aepyceros melampus petersi* | Angola; Namibia | hunting; low reproductive rate |
| indri | *Indri indri* | Madagascar | primate threatened by widespread destruction of forests |
| kangaroo rat, Morro Bay | *Dipodomys heermanni morroensis* | California, USA | loss or change of natural habitat; urban development; predation by domestic cats |
| kangaroo rat, Stephens' | *Dipodomys stephensi* | USA | |
| kangaroo rat, San Quintin | *Dipodomys elator* | Mexico | |

| Name | Species | Location | Cause of endangerment |
|---|---|---|---|
| kangaroo, Goodfellow's tree | *Dendrolagus goodfellowi* | Papua New Guinea | |
| kangaroo, Scott's tree | *Dendrolagus scottae* | Papua New Guinea | |
| kouprey | *Bos sauveli* (*Novibos sauveli*) | Cambodia; Laos; Thailand; Vietnam | hunting for meat, horns; effects of warfare; low reproductive rate |
| kowari | *Dasycercus byrnei* | Australia | |
| lemur, broad-nosed gentle | *Hapalemur sinus* | Madagascar | |
| lemur, crowned | *Eulemur coronatus* | Madagascar | |
| lemur, golden bamboo | *Hapalemur aureus* | Madagascar | |
| lemur, mongoose | *Eulemur mongoz* (*Lemur mongoz*) | Comoros; Madagascar | |
| lemur, ruffed | *Varecia variegata* | Madagascar | |
| lemur, hairy-eared dwarf | *Allocebus trichotis* (*Cheirogaleus trichotis*) | Madagascar | |
| leopard, Amur | *Panthera pardus orientalis* | China; DPR Korea; Russia | human persecution; depletion of natural prey |
| leopard, S Arabian | *Panthera pardus nimr* | Oman; Saudi Arabia; Yemen | persecution by shepherds protecting their flocks |
| leopard, snow | *Uncia uncia* (*Panthera uncia*) | Afghanistan; Bhutan; China; India; Nepal; Russia | hunting for fur and because of the threat it poses to domestic livestock; loss of natural prey |
| leopard, Sri Lankan | *Panthera pardus kotiya* | Sri Lanka | human persecution; depletion of natural prey |
| lion, Asiatic | *Panthera leo persica* | India | loss of natural habitat and prey |
| lynx, Spanish | *Lynx pardinus* (*Felis pardinus*) | Portugal; Spain | loss of habitat due to reforestation; the effects of myxomatosis on its main prey, the rabbit; incidental killing, trapping |
| macaque, lion-tailed | *Macaca silenus* | S India | loss of habitat; hunting for meat; animal trade |
| mala | *Lagorchestes hirsutus* | Australia | |
| mangabey, Tana River | *Cercocebus galeritus galeritus* | Kenya; Tanzania | primate threatened by loss of habitat due to agriculture |
| markhor | *Capra falconeri* | Afghanistan; Pakistan; India | hunting; loss of habitat to stock grazing |
| marmoset, buffy-headed | *Callithrix flaviceps* | SE Brazil | destruction of natural habitat |
| marmoset, buffy-tufted ear | *Callithrix aurita* | Brazil | |
| marmot, Vancouver Island | *Marmota vancouverensis* | Vancouver I, Canada | collection; exploitation; loss of habitat due to logging |
| mink, European | *Mustela lutreola* | Belarus; Estonia; France; Georgia; Russia; Spain | |
| mongoose, Liberian | *Liberiictis kuhni* | Liberia; Côte d'Ivoire; Guinea | |
| monkey, C American (or red-backed squirrel monkey) | *Saimiri oerstedii* | Panama; Costa Rica | animal exportation; loss of forest habitat |
| monkey, Douc | *Pygaturix nemaeus* | Cambodia; China; Laos | |
| monkey, François's leaf | *Trachypithecus francoisi* | China; Laos; Vietnam | |
| monkey, grizzled leaf | *Presbytis comata* (*Presbytis aygula*) | Indonesia | |
| monkey, Ka'apor capuchin | *Cebus kaapori* | Brazil | |

| Name | Species | Location | Cause of endangerment |
|---|---|---|---|
| monkey, mentawai leaf | *Presbytis potenziani* | Indonesia | |
| monkey, pig-tailed snub-nosed | *Nasalis concolor* (*Simias concolor*) | Indonesia | |
| monkey, tonkin snub-nosed | *Pygathrix avunculus* (*Rhinopithecus avunculus*) | Vietnam | |
| monkey, woolly spider (or muriqui monkey) | *Brachyteles arachnoides* | São Paulo state, Brazil | hunting; clearance of forest habitat for fuel, agriculture, human settlement |
| monkey, yellow-tailed woolly | *Lagothrix flavicauda* | Peru | hunting for its skin, meat; destruction of its habitat for human settlement |
| mouse, saltmarsh harvest | *Reithrodontomys raviventris* | California, USA | water pollution; loss of habitat due to urban, industrial development |
| muntjac, Fea's | *Muntiacus feae* | China; Myanmar (Burma) | hunting for the meat of this small deer which is highly valued |
| numbat | *Myrmecobius fasciatus* | Australia | |
| nyala, mountain | *Tragelaphus buxtoni* | Ethiopia | |
| orang-utan | *Pongo pygmaeus* | Indonesia; Malaysia | animal trade; felling of forests by timber industry |
| oryx, Arabian | *Oryx leucoryx* | Oman | hunting for its meat, skin, medical uses |
| oryx, scimitar-horned | *Oryx dammah* (*Oryx tao*) | Chad | |
| otter-civet | *Cynogale bennettii* | Brunei; Indonesia; Malaysia; Thailand | |
| ox, Vu Quang | *Pseudoryx nghetinhensis* | Vietnam | |
| pacarana | *Dinomys branickii* | Bolivia; Brazil; Colombia; Ecuador; Peru; Venezuela | |
| peccary, Chacoan | *Catagonus wagneri* | Argentina; Bolivia; Paraguay | |
| phascogale, red-tailed | *Phascogale calura* | Australia | |
| pig, Visayan warty | *Sus cebifrons* | Philippines | |
| possum, Fergusson Island striped | *Dactilopsila tatei* | Papua New Guinea | |
| possum, Leadbetter's | *Gymnbelideus leadbeateri* | Victoria, Australia | felling of forest areas has led to loss of habitat |
| possum, Mountain pygmy | *Burramys parvus* | Australia | |
| potoroo, long-footed | *Potorus longipes* | Australia | |
| pronghorn, Baja Californian | *Antilocapra americana peninsularis* | Mexico | hunting; competition for fodder from domestic livestock |
| pronghorn, Sonoran | *Antilocapra americana sonoriensis* | Mexico; Arizona, USA | destruction of habitat; competition for food and water from livestock; hunting |
| rabbit, Amami | *Pentalagus furnessi* | Ryukyu I, Japan | loss of habitat; predation by wild dogs |
| rabbit, Omilteme | *Sylvilagus insonus* | Mexico | |
| rabbit, riverine | *Bunologus monticularis* | South Africa | |
| rabbit, Sumatran | *Nesolagus netscheri* | Indonesia | |
| rabbit, Tehuantepec jack- | *Lepus flavigularis* | Mexico | |
| rabbit, Tres Marias | *Sylvilagus graysoni* | Tres Marias Is, Mexico | |

| Name | Species | Location | Cause of endangerment |
|---|---|---|---|
| rabbit, volcano | *Romerolagus diazi* | Mexico | loss of habitat; wanton destruction by shooting |
| rat, Anthony's wood | *Neotoma anthonyi* | Todos Santos I, Mexico | |
| rat, Bunker's wood | *Neotoma bunkeri* | Mexico | |
| rat, central rock | *Zyzomys pedunculatus* | Australia | |
| rat, Poncelet's giant | *Solomys ponceleti* | Papua New Guinea | |
| rat, San Martin Island wood | *Neotoma martinensis* | San Martin I, Mexico | |
| rat (a species of) | *Phaenomys ferrugineus* | Brazil | |
| rat (a species of) | *Rhagomys rufescens* | Brazil | |
| rat (a species of) | *Juscelinomys candango* | Brazil | |
| rhinoceros, black | *Diceros bicornis* | Africa | |
| rhinoceros, great Indian | *Rhinoceros unicornis* | Bhutan; India; Nepal | hunting; poaching for rhino horn; loss of habitat to agriculture, stock grazing |
| rhinoceros, Javan | *Rhinoceros sondaicus* | Cambodia; Java; Laos; Vietnam | hunting for rhino horn, medical properties of rhino blood; loss of habitat to human settlement |
| rhinoceros, northern white | *Ceratotherium simum cottoni* | DR Congo | hunting for the supposed aphrodisiac qualities of the rhino horn; disturbance by military operations |
| rhinoceros, Sumatran | *Dicerorhincus sumatrensis* (*Didermocerus sumatrensis*) | SE Asia | hunting for the aphrodisiac and medical qualities of the horn and other parts of the carcass which fetches high prices; loss of forest habitat to timber exploitation, human settlement |
| seal, Hawaiian monk | *Monachus schauinslandi* | Hawaiian Is, USA | initial decline in population due to 19th-c seal fishermen; present population threatened by attacks by sharks; human disturbance of breeding grounds leading to low rates of reproduction, high rates of juvenile mortality |
| seal, Mediterranean monk | *Monachus monachus* | N Africa; Lebanon; Cyprus; Turkey; Albania | persecution by fishermen; human disturbance; marine pollution |
| serow, Sumatran | *Capricornis sumatraensis sumatraensis* | Sumatra; Malaysia | hunting; destruction of habitat |
| sheep, dwarf blue | *Pseudois schaeferi* | China | |
| shrew, nimba otter | *Micropotamogale lamottei* | Côte d'Ivoire; Guinea; Liberia | |
| sifaka, diademed | *Propithecus diadema* | Madagascar | |
| sifaka, golden-crowned | *Propithecus tattersalli* | Madagascar | |
| sika, Formosan[1] | *Cervus nippon taiouanus* | Taiwan | hunting for meat, antlers; the medical properties of the carcass; loss of habitat to agriculture; probably already extinct in the wild |
| sika, N China | *Cervus nippon mandarinus* | China | hunting; loss of habitat; possibly already extinct in the wild |
| sika, Ryukyu | *Cervus nippon keramae* | Ryukyu Is, Japan | drought; low qualities of feeding vegetation; competition with goats for grazing fodder |

| Name | Species | Location | Cause of endangerment |
|---|---|---|---|
| sika, Shansi[1] | *Cervus nippon grassianus* | China | hunting for the antler trade; clearance of forest habitat for agriculture |
| sika, S China | *Cervus nippon pseudaxis* (*Cervus nippon kopschi*) | China; Vietnam | hunting for the antler trade; trapping; loss of habitat |
| sloth, maned | *Bradypus torquatus* | Brazil | loss of forest habitat |
| solenodon, Cuban | *Solenodon cubanus* | Cuba | |
| solenodon, Haitian | *Solenodon paradoxus* | Dominican Republic; Haiti | land development; deforestation |
| squirrel, Delmarva fox | *Sciurus niger cinereus* | Maryland, USA | loss of habitat due to logging |
| tamaraw | *Bubalus mindorensis* | Philippines | hunting; loss of forest habitat |
| tamarin, cotton-top | *Saguinus oedipus oedipus* | NW Colombia | animal trade; loss of habitat to agriculture |
| tamarin, black-faced lion | *Leontopithecus caissara* | Brazil | |
| tamarin, golden-headed lion | *Leontopithecus rosalia chrysomelas* | E Brazil | loss of Atlantic rainforest |
| tamarin, golden lion | *Leontopithecus rosalia* | Brazil | loss of forest habitat to agriculture, urban development |
| tamarin, golden-rumped lion | *Leontopithecus rosalia chrysopygus* | São Paulo area of Brazil | loss of forest habitat; possibly careless use of defoliants by farmers |
| tamarin, white-footed | *Saguinus leucopus* | Colombia | |
| tapir, Malayan | *Tapirus indicus* | Indonesia; Myanmar (Burma); Thailand; Vietnam; Malaysia | human disturbance; loss of forest habitat to logging, oil exploration, human settlement, mining, agriculture |
| tapir, mountain | *Tapirus pinchaque* (*Tapirus roulini*) | S America | human disturbance; competition for natural habitat with livestock |
| tiger | *Panthera tigris* | Eurasia | loss of habitat and prey; hunting for sport; because of the threat posed by it to both humans and domestic livestock |
| uakari, bald | *Cacajao calvus* | Brazil; Peru | primate threatened by hunting; animal trade |
| uakari, black | *Cacajao melanocephalus* | Brazil; Colombia; Venezuela | |
| vaquita | *Phocoena sinus* | Mexico | |
| wallaby, Alpine | *Thylogale calabyi* | Papua New Guinea | |
| wallaby, banded hare | *Logostrophus fasciatus* | Australia | |
| wallaby, bridle nailtail | *Onychogalea fraenata* | Queensland, Australia | loss of natural habitat to settlement; introduction of livestock; predation from foxes |
| wallaby, prosperine rock | *Petrogale persephone* | Australia | |
| weasel, Colombian | *Mustela felipei* | Colombia; Ecuador | |
| whale, blue | *Balaenoptera musculus* | Atlantic, Pacific and Indian Oceans | whaling |
| whale, northern right | *Eubalaena glacialis* (*Baleana glacialus*) | Northern temperate and sub-polar waters (North Atlantic and North Pacific) | whaling |
| wolf, Ethiopian ► fox, Simien | | | |
| wolf, red | *Canis rufus* (*Canis niger*) | Texas and Louisiana, USA | loss of habitat; hunting; trapping; hybridization with coyotes |
| wombat, northern hairy-nosed | *Lasiorhinus krefftii* | Australia | |

| Name | Species | Location | Cause of endangerment |
|---|---|---|---|
| woylie | *Bettongia penicillata* | Australia | |
| yak, wild | *Bos mutus* (*Bos grunniens*) | Tibet; Kashmir; W China | hunting |
| zebra, Grevy's | *Equus grevyi* | Ethiopia; Kenya | hunted because of its attractive, highly-prized skin |
| ❑ **Birds** | | | |
| adjutant, greater | *Leptoptilos dubius* | India | |
| 'akialoa, Kauai | *Hemignathus obscurus* | Kauai, Hawaiian Is, USA | disease; overgrazing of forest habitat by livestock; competition with imported birds; predation by rats |
| 'akiapola'au | *Hemignathus wilsoni* | Hawaiian Is, USA | deterioration of forest habitat; disease; competition with imported birds; predation by rats |
| albatross, Amsterdam Island | *Diomedea amsterdamensis* | Amsterdam I, French Southern and Antarctic Territories | |
| albatross, short-tailed | *Diomedea albatrus* | Japan | loss of habitat; exploitation for feathers; low rate of reproduction |
| alethe, Cholo | *Alethe choloensis* | Malawi; Mozambique | |
| antbird, grey-headed | *Myrmeciza griseiceps* | Ecuador; Peru | |
| antpitta, brown-banded[1] | *Grallaria milleri* | Colombia | |
| antpitta, moustached[1] | *Grallaria alleni* | Colombia | |
| antpitta, Tachira | *Grallaria chthonia* | Venezuela | |
| antwren, Alagoas | *Myrmotherula snowi* (*Terenura sicki*) | Brazil | destruction of tropical forest habitat |
| antwren, ash-throated | *Herpsilochmus parkeri* | Peru | |
| antwren, black-hooded | *Formicivora erythronotos* | Brazil | |
| antwren, Restinga | *Formicivora littoralis* | Brazil | |
| attila, ochraceous | *Attila torridus* | Colombia; Ecuador; Peru | |
| becard, slaty | *Pachyramphus spodiurus* | Ecuador; Peru | |
| blackbird, Forbes's | *Curaeus forbesi* | Brazil | |
| blackbird, yellow-shouldered | *Agelaius xanthomus* | Puerto Rico | |
| booby, Abbott's | *Papasula abbotti* (*Sula abbotti*) | Christmas I and Cocos Is, Australia; Indonesia | |
| bushbird, recurve-billed | *Clytoctantes alixii* | Colombia; Venezuela | |
| calyptura, kinglet[1] | *Calyptura cristata* | Brazil | |
| cockatoo, Philippine | *Cacatua haematuropygia* | Philippines | |
| cockatoo, salmon-crested | *Cacatua moluccensis* | Indonesia | |
| cockatoo, Tanimbar | *Cacatua goffini* | Tanimbar Is, Indonesia | |
| cockatoo, white | *Cacatua alba* | Indonesia | |
| condor, California | *Gymnogyps californianus* | California | low reproductive potential; shooting, trapping, poisoning, egg-collecting; extinction appears inevitable |

| Name | Species | Location | Cause of endangerment |
|---|---|---|---|
| coquette, short-crested | *Lophornis brachylopha* | Mexico | |
| coucal, green-billed | *Centropus chlororhynchus* | Sri Lanka | |
| crane, whooping | *Grus americana* | Canada | pollution; destruction, disturbance of wetland habitat |
| creeper, oahu | *Paroreomyza maculata* | Hawaiian Is, USA | disease to which Hawaiian honeycreepers have limited immunity; destruction of rainforest habitat by grazing livestock; competition from imported birds; predation by mammals |
| crow, Hawaiian | *Corvus hawaiiensis* | Hawaiian Is, USA | disease; loss of habitat to wild pigs, cattle, goats; predation by black rats |
| crow, Mariana | *Corvus kubaryi* | Guam, Mariana Is, USA | |
| curassow, Alagoas | *Mitu mitu* | Brazil | seriously threatened with extinction by hunting; loss of rainforest habitat |
| curassow, blue-knobbed | *Crax alberti* | Colombia | |
| curassow, helmeted | *Pauxi pauxi* | Colombia; Venezuela | |
| curlew, Eskimo[1] | *Numenius borealis* | Arctic tundra: Canada, Alaska; S America | shooting; loss of prairie habitat to agriculture; climatic changes possibly altering migratory and reproductive processes |
| dove, blue-eyed ground | *Columbina cyanopis* | Brazil | |
| dove, Grenada | *Leptotila wellsi* | Grenada | |
| dove, ochre-bellied | *Leptotila ochraceiventris* | Ecuador; Peru | |
| dove, purple-winged ground[1] | *Claravis godefrida* | Argentina; Brazil; Paraguay | |
| dove, Socorro | *Zenaida graysoni* | Revillagigedo Is, Mexico | |
| eagle, Adalbert's | *Aquila adalberti* | Portugal; Spain | poisoning and contamination by pesticides; shooting; loss of habitat to forest clearance, overgrazing |
| eagle, Great Philippine | *Pithecophaga jefferyi* | Philippines | shooting; animal trade; destruction of forest habitat |
| eagle, Madagascar fish | *Haliaeetus vociferoides* | Madagascar | hunting; human persecution |
| eagle, Madagascar serpent | *Eutriorchis astur* | Madagascar | clearing of forest habitat |
| emerald, Honduran | *Amazilia luciae* | Honduras | |
| finch, Cochabamba mountain- | *Poospiza garleppi* | Bolivia | |
| finch, Laysan | *Telespiza cantans* | Hawaiian Is, USA | |
| finch, Nihoa | *Telespiza ultima* | Hawaiian Is, USA | |
| finch, pale-headed brush-[1] | *Atlapetes pallidiceps* | Ecuador | |
| finch, rufous-breasted warbling- | *Poospiza rubecula* | Peru | |
| fire-eye, fringe-backed | *Pyriglena atra* | Brazil | loss of tropical forest habitat to human settlement; industrial, agricultural development |
| florican, Bengal | *Eupodotis bengalensis* (*Houbaropsis bengalensis*) | India; Nepal; Vietnam | |
| florican, lesser | *Eupodotis indica* (*Sypheotides indica*) | India; Nepal | |

| Name | Species | Location | Cause of endangerment |
|---|---|---|---|
| flycatcher, Guam | *Myiagra freycineti* | Guam | |
| flycatcher, Tahiti monarch | *Pomarea nigra* | Tahiti | causes of decline are unknown |
| fody, Mauritius | *Foudia rubra* | Mauritius | destruction of montane evergreen forest habitat; competition from other species of fody; predation of nests by macaque monkeys, black rats |
| fody, Yellow | *Foudia flavicans* | Rodrigues I, Mauritius | destruction of forest habitat; competition from other species of fody |
| foliage-gleaner, Alagoas | *Philydor novaesi* | Brazil | |
| foliage-gleaner, rufous-necked | *Automolus ruficollis* | Ecuador; Peru | |
| francolin, ochre-breasted | *Francolinus ochropectus* | Djibouti | |
| grebe, Alaotra | *Tachybaptus rufolavatus* | Madagascar | |
| grebe, Colombian[1] | *Podiceps andinus* | Colombia | competition for food from trout; possible contamination by pesticides |
| grebe, Puna | *Podiceps taczanowskii* | Peru | pollution of lake habitat by copper mining |
| guan, Trinidad piping | *Pipile pipile* | Trinidad | hunting; loss of forest habitat; may already be extinct |
| guan, white-winged | *Penelope albipennis* | Peru | hunting; loss of forest habitat to charcoal burning |
| guineafowl, white-breasted | *Agelastes meleagrides* | Côte d'Ivoire; Liberia; Sierra Leone | |
| hawk, grey-backed | *Leucopternis occidentalis* | Ecuador; Peru | |
| heron, white-bellied | *Ardea insignis* (*Ardea imperialis*) | Bangladesh; Bhutan; India; Myanmar (Burma) | |
| heron, white-eared night | *Gorsachius magnificus* | China | |
| honeyeater, Tagula[2] | *Meliphaga vicina* | Tagula I, Papua New Guinea | alteration of habitat; destruction of habitat by fire; competition with other species |
| ibis, crested | *Nipponia nippon* | Sado I, Japan | hunting; loss of forest habitat |
| ibis, Waldrapp | *Geronticus eremita* | Morocco | hunting; nest disturbance; poaching for eggs; animal, zoo trade; reproductive failure due to pesticide contamination |
| jacamar, three-toed | *Jacamaralcyon tridactyla* | Brazil | |
| jay, dwarf | *Cyanolyca nana* | Mexico | |
| junco, Guadalupe | *Junco insularis* | Guadalupe I, Mexico | |
| kagu | *Rhynochetos jubatus* | New Caledonia | trapping; animal trade; destruction of forest habitat by nickel mining; predation by dogs, cats, pigs, rats |
| kakapo | *Strigops habroptilus* | New Zealand | human disturbance; loss of forest habitat; competition for food; predation by rats, stoats |
| kamao | *Myadestes myadestinus* | Hawaiian Is, USA | |
| kestrel, Mauritius | *Falco punctatus* | Mauritius | destruction of forest habitat; hunting; predation of nests by macaque monkeys |
| kokako | *Callaeas cinerea* | New Zealand | |
| lark, Raso | *Alauda razae* | Raso I, Cape Verde | |

| Name | Species | Location | Cause of endangerment |
|---|---|---|---|
| macaw, blue-throated | *Ara glaucogularis* | Bolivia | |
| macaw, glaucous[1] | *Anodorhynchus glaucus* | S America | possibly already extinct |
| macaw, Lear's or indigo | *Anodorhynchus leari* | S America | rare bird in great demand among aviculturists who threaten its continued existence in the wild |
| macaw, little blue | *Cyanopsitta spixii* | Brazil | |
| malimbe, Ibadan | *Malimbus ibadanensis* | Nigeria | |
| merganser, Brazilian | *Mergus octosetaceus* | Argentina; Brazil; Paraguay | |
| mockingbird, Charles | *Nesomimus trifasciatus* | Galapagos Is, Ecuador | |
| mockingbird, Socorro | *Mimodes graysoni* | Socorro I, Mexico | |
| monal, Chinese | *Lophophorus lhuysii* | W China | hunting |
| myna, Bali (or Rothschild's starling) | *Leucopsar rothschildi* | Bali, Indonesia | loss of forest habitat to human settlement; competition from other starlings; trapping for the cagebird trade |
| nightjar, white-winged | *Caprimulgus candicans* | Brazil | |
| nukupu'u | *Hemignathus lucidus* | Hawaiian Is, USA | disease; predation by rats; competition from other birds |
| olomao | *Myadestes lanaiensis* | Hawaiian Is, USA | |
| oo, bishop's | *Moho bishopi* | Hawaiian Is, USA | |
| oo, kauai | *Moho braccatus* | Hawaiian Is, USA | |
| oriole, Martinique | *Icterus bonana* | Martinique | |
| 'o'u | *Psittirostra psittacea* | Hawaiian Is, USA | loss of forest habitat due to overgrazing by livestock; competition with imported birds; disease; predation |
| owl, Madagascar red[2] | *Tyto soumagnei* | Madagascar | loss of humid forest habitat |
| owl, Sokeke scops- | *Otus ireneae* | Kenya | over-collecting; destruction of evergreen forest habitat by felling, banana cultivation |
| oystercatcher, Chatham Islands | *Haematopus unicolor chathamensis* | Chatham Is, New Zealand | destruction of vegetation by grazing sheep |
| palila | *Loxioides bailleui* | Hawaiian Is, USA | |
| parakeet, Mauritius | *Psittacula echo* | Mauritius | loss of evergreen forest habitat; competition for nest sites; nest predation by macaque monkeys, rats |
| parrot, ground | *Pezoporus wallicus* | SW Australia | clearing, burning, draining of grassland and wetland habitat |
| parrot, Imperial | *Amazona imperialis* | Dominica | hunting for meat, sport |
| parrot, indigo-winged | *Hapalopsittaca fuertesi* | Colombia | |
| parrot, Paradise[1] | *Psephotus pulcherrimus* | Australia | drought; expansion of livestock grazing; last confirmed sighting was in 1927, but there have been more recent unconfirmed sightings |
| parrot, Puerto Rican | *Amazona vittata* | Puerto Rico | clearance of lowland forest habitat; predation of nests by rats |
| parrot, red-faced | *Hapalopsittaca pyrrhops* | Ecuador; Peru | |
| parrot, red-tailed | *Amazona brasiliensis* | SE Brazil | animal trade; loss of forest habitat |

| Name | Species | Location | Cause of endangerment |
|---|---|---|---|
| parrot, St Lucia | *Amazona versicolor* | St Lucia, W Indies | hunting; loss of forest habitat to agriculture |
| parrot, yellow-eared | *Ognorhynchus icterotis* | Colombia; Ecuador | |
| partridge, bearded wood- | *Dendrortyx barbatus* | Mexico | |
| partridge, Hainan | *Arborophila ardens* | China | |
| partridge, Sichuan | *Arborophila rufipectus* | China | |
| petrel, Bermuda | *Pterodroma cahow* | Bermuda | human persecution; disturbance, predation by rats, wild pigs; competition for nesting sights with tropical birds |
| petrel, black | *Procellaria parkinsoni* | New Zealand | predation on breeding adults and fledglings by cats |
| petrel, Chatham Islands | *Pterodroma axillaris* | Chatham Is, New Zealand | competition from other subspecies |
| petrel, Galapagos | *Pterodroma phaeopygia* | Galapagos Is, Ecuador | destruction of habitat due to agriculture; predation by dogs, pigs, black rats |
| petrel, Guadalupe storm- | *Oceanodroma macrodactyla* | Guadalupe I, Mexico | |
| petrel, Hawaiian dark-rumped | *Pterodroma phaeopygia sandwichensis* | Hawaiian Is, USA | predation by black rats, cats, mongooses |
| petrel, Madeira | *Pterodroma madeira* | Madeira | |
| petrel, magenta | *Pterodroma magentae* | New Zealand | predation by cats, rats; deterioration of forest habitat due to overgrazing of livestock, presence of other herbivores |
| petrel, Mascarene | *Pterodroma aterrima* (*Pseudobulweria aterrima*) | Réunion | |
| pheasant, brown-eared | *Crossoptilon mantchuricum* | N China | human persecution; loss of forest habitat |
| pheasant, cheer | *Catreus wallichii* | India; Nepal; Pakistan | hunting; destruction of forest habitat |
| pheasant, Elliot's | *Syrmaticus ellioti* | E China | hunting; destruction of forest habitat |
| pigeon, Marquesan imperial- | *Ducula galeata* | Nukuhiva, French Polynesia | hunting for its meat; loss of habitat to human disturbance, grazing of cattle, pigs, goats |
| pigeon, pink | *Columba mayeri* (*Nesoenas mayeri*) | Mauritius | predation of nests by macaque monkeys, black rats; hunting; loss of forest habitat |
| pigeon, plain[2] | *Columba inornata wetmorei* | Puerto Rico | human persecution; plundering of nests; loss of forest habitat to housing development |
| pitta, Gurney's | *Pitta gurneyi* | Thailand | |
| pitta, Schneider's | *Pitta schneideri* | Indonesia | |
| plantcutter, Peruvian | *Phytotoma raimondii* | Peru | |
| plover, shore | *Charadrius novaseelandiae* (*Thinornis novaseelandiae*) | Chatham Is, New Zealand | animal trade; destruction of vegetation by grazing sheep |
| pochard, Madagascar | *Aytha innotata* | Madagascar | |
| poorwill, Jamaican[1] | *Siphonorhis americanus* | Jamaica | |
| puaiohi | *Myadestes palmeri* | Hawaiian Is, USA | |
| puffleg, black-breasted | *Eriocnemis nigrivestis* | Ecuador | |
| puffleg, turquoise-throated[1] | *Eriocnemis godini* | Colombia; Ecuador | |

| Name | Species | Location | Cause of endangerment |
|---|---|---|---|
| rail, Austral[1] | *Rallus antarcticus* | Argentina; Chile | |
| rail, bar-winged | *Nesoclopeus poecilopterus* | Fiji | predation by mongooses, cats, rats |
| rail, junin | *Laterallus tuerosi* | Peru | |
| rail, Lord Howe | *Gallirallus sylvestris* (*Tricholimnas sylvestris*) | Lord Howe I, Australia | damage to vegetation by wild goats, pigs; predation of eggs by rats |
| rail, plain-flanked | *Rallus wetmorei* | Venezuela | |
| recurvebill, Bolivian | *Simoxenops striatus* | Bolivia | |
| redstart, yellow-faced | *Myiobarus pariae* | Venezuela | |
| robin, Chatham | *Petroica traversi* | Chatham Is, New Zealand | destruction and deterioration of scrub forest habitat by human disturbance, climatic conditions; nesting of petrels |
| robin, Seychelles magpie | *Copsychus sechellarum* | Seychelles | predation by cats; competition for nest sites; decreased availability of food |
| scrub-bird, noisy | *Atrichornis clamosus* | SW Australia | clearance of eucalyptus forest habitat; drought; predation by cats |
| seedeater, hooded[1] | *Sporophila melanops* | Brazil | |
| seedeater, Narosky's | *Sporophila zelichi* | Argentina | |
| seedeater, Tumaco[1] | *Sporophila insulata* | Tumaco I, Colombia | |
| shama, black | *Copsychus cebuensis* | Philippines | |
| shelduck, crested | *Tadorna cristata* | China; DPR Korea; Russia | |
| siskin, red | *Carduelis cucullata* | Colombia; Venezuela | trapping for the cagebird trade |
| spinetail, blackish-headed | *Synallaxis tithys* | Ecuador; Peru | |
| spoonbill, black-faced | *Platalea minor* | China; DPR Korea | |
| starling, Rarotonga | *Aplonis cinerascens* | Cook Is | |
| starling, Rothschild's ► myna, Bali | | | |
| stilt, black | *Himantopus novasealandiae* | New Zealand | loss of breeding and feeding habitat |
| stork, Oriental | *Ciconia boyciana* | China, Russia | shooting; contamination by mercury causing mortality or reproductive failure; loss of wetland habitat to agriculture; extinct in Europe |
| sunbird, Prigogine's double-collared | *Nectarinia prigoginei* | DR Congo | |
| takahe | *Porphyrio mantelli* (*Notornis mantelli*) | South I, New Zealand | |
| tanager, cherry-throated[1] | *Nemosia rourei* | SE Brazil | unrecorded for over a century, probably already extinct |
| tanager, cone-billed[1] | *Conothraupis mesoleuca* | Brazil | |
| tapaculo, chestnut-sided | *Scytalopus psychopompus* | Brazil | |
| thicketbird, long-legged | *Trichocichla rufa* | Fiji | predation by cats, rats, mongooses |
| thrasher, white-breasted | *Ramphocinclus brachyurus* | Martinique | hunting; predation by rats, mongooses |
| tinamou, Kalinowski's[1] | *Nothoprocta kalinowskii* | Peru | hunting; loss of forest habitat |
| tit-spinetail, white-browed | *Leptasthenura xenothorax* | Peru | |

| Name | Species | Location | Cause of endangerment |
|---|---|---|---|
| tit-tyrant, ash-breasted | *Anairetes alpinus* | Bolivia; Peru | |
| tragopan, Cabot's | *Tragopan caboti* | SE China | loss of forest habitat to agricultural cultivation |
| tragopan, western | *Tragopan melanocephalus* | India; Pakistan | hunting; trapping; disturbance by humans, goats; destruction of forest habitat |
| turaco, Bannerman's | *Tauraco bannermani* | Cameroon | |
| tyrannulet, Alagoas | *Phylloscartes ceciliae* | Brazil | |
| vireo, black-capped | *Vireo atricapillus* | Mexico; USA | |
| warbler, Aldabra bush- | *Nesillas aldabrana* | Seychelles | |
| warbler, Bachman's[1] | *Vermivora bachmanii* | USA | destruction of deciduous swampland forest habitat for timber, agriculture, sugar cane plantation; now N America's rarest songbird |
| warbler, Kirtland's | *Dendroica kirtlandii* | USA | loss of forest habitat; reduced breeding due to invasion by cowbirds who have parasitized nests |
| warbler, Nauru reed- | *Acrocephalus rehsei* | Nauru | |
| warbler, Rodrigues brush- | *Bebrornis rodericanus* (*Acrocephalus rodericamus*) | Rodrigues I, Mauritius | human disturbance; clearance of thicket habitat |
| warbler, Semper's[1] | *Leucopeza semperi* | St Lucia, West Indies | predation by mongooses |
| wattle-eye, banded | *Platysteira laticincta* | Cameroon | |
| weaver, Clarke's | *Ploceus golandi* | Kenya | |
| white-eye, Seychelles grey | *Zosterops modestus* | Seychelles | |
| white-eye, Truk | *Rukia ruki* | Caroline Is, Federated States of Micronesia | occupies limited and unprotected range of mountain forest habitat |
| white-eye, white-chested | *Zosterops albogularis* | Norfolk I | almost complete destruction of rainforest habitat |
| woodpecker, American ivory-billed[1] | *Campephilus principalis* | Cuba; SE USA | bird collection; clearance of swampland habitat; human disturbance |
| woodpecker, Imperial[1] | *Campephilus imperialis* | Mexico | shooting; loss of forest habitat due to logging |
| woodpecker, ivory-billed[1] | *Campephilus principalis* | Cuba; USA | shooting; loss of pine forest habitat to timber trade, sugar cane plantation |
| woodpecker, Okinawa | *Sapheopipo noguchii* | Okinawa, Japan | loss of woodland habitat to woodcutting, fires |
| woodpecker, red-cockaded | *Picoides borealis* | USA | |
| woodstar, Chilean[2] | *Eulidua yarrellii* | Chile | reasons for decline in population are unknown |
| woodstar, Esmeraldas | *Acestrura berlepschi* | Ecuador | |
| woodstar, little | *Acestrura bombus* | Ecuador; Peru | |
| wren, New Zealand bush | *Xenicus longipes* | New Zealand | predation by black rats |
| ❑ **Reptiles** | | | |
| alligator, Chinese | *Alligator sinensis* | E China | exploitation for meat, leather; extermination as vermin |

| Name | Species | Location | Cause of endangerment |
|---|---|---|---|
| anole, giant or Culebra Island giant[1] | *Anolis roosevelti* | Puerto Rico | loss of habitat, probably already extinct |
| blue tongue, pygmy | *Tiliqua adelaidensis* | Australia | |
| boa, Round Island[1] | *Bolyeria multocarinata* | Round I, near Mauritius | deterioration of palm forest habitat, possibly already extinct |
| boa, Round Island keel-scaled | *Casarea dussumieri* | Round I, near Mauritius | deterioration of palm forest habitat |
| chamaeleon, Smith's dwarf | *Bradypodion taeniabronchum* | South Africa | |
| cobra, C Asian or Oxus[2] | *Naja oxiana* | C Asia (Afghanistan) | loss of natural habitat |
| crocodile, Cuban | *Crocodylus rhombifer* | Cuba | exploitation for skins; loss of habitat; hybridization |
| crocodile, Mindoro or Philippines | *Crocodylus mindorensis* | Philippines | |
| crocodile, Orinoco | *Crocodylus intermedius* | Colombia; Venezuela | hunting; exploitation for skins |
| crocodile, Siamese | *Crocodylus siamensis* | Cambodia; Indonesia; Malaysia; Thailand | hunting; exploitation for skins |
| gecko, Monito | *Sphaerodactylus micropithecus* | Puerto Rico | |
| gecko, Round Island day | *Phelsuma guentheri* | Mauritius | |
| gharial | *Gavialis gangeticus* | Bangladesh; India; Pakistan; Nepal | hunting for its skin; human disturbance; loss of habitat to cultivation |
| gharial, false | *Tomistoma schlegelii* | Malay Peninsula; Sumatra; Borneo | trapping, hunting for its hide |
| iguana, Acklin's ground[2] | *Cyclura rileyi* | The Bahamas | hunting; poaching; zoo trade |
| iguana, Anegada ground | *Cyclura pinguis* | Virgin Is, USA | loss of habitat; human disturbance; predation by pets, wild animals |
| iguana, Jamaica ground | *Cyclura collei* (*Cychera lophoma*) | Jamaica | |
| lerista, Allan's | *Lerista allanae* | Australia | |
| lizard, black or Californian legless[2] | *Anniella pulchra niger* | California, USA | loss of habitat |
| lizard, blunt-nosed (or San Joaquin leopard lizard) | *Gambelia silus* (*Crotaphytus wislizenii silus*) | USA; Mexico | destruction of habitat by agriculture |
| lizard, Hierro giant | *Gallotia simonyi* | Hierro, Canary Is | human disturbance; loss of habitat |
| lizard, St Croix ground | *Ameiva polops* | Virgin Is, USA | loss of habitat; predation by the mongoose |
| lizard (a species of) | *Liolaemus gravenhorstii* | Chile | |
| racer, Antiguan | *Alsophis antiguae* | Antigua and Barbuda | |
| racer, black | *Alsophis ater* | Jamaica | |
| skink, Blue Mountain water | *Eulamprus leuraensis* | Australia | |
| skink, Chevron | *Leiolopisma bomalonotum* | New Zealand | |
| skink, Lancelin Island | *Ctenotus lancelini* | Australia | |
| snake, black strziped | *Simoselaps calonotus* | Australia | |
| snake, Kikuzato's brook | *Opisthotropis kikuzatoi* (*Liopeltis kikuzatoi*) | Japan | |
| snake, San Francisco garter | *Thamnophis sirtalis tetrataenia* | California, USA | collecting as specimens; loss of habitat to drainage, housing developments |
| snake (a species of) | *Liophis cursor* | Martinique | |

| Name | Species | Location | Cause of endangerment |
|---|---|---|---|
| snake (a species of) | *Liophis ornatus* | St Lucia, West Indies | |
| terrapin, Batagur | *Batagur baska* | Bangladesh; India; Indonesia; Malaysia | water pollution; damage to nesting areas by commercial sand removal, tin mining, flooding, silt deposits |
| terrapin, painted | *Callagur borneoensis* | Indonesia; Malaysia; Thailand | |
| tortoise, Bolson | *Gopherus flavomarginatus* | Mexico | |
| tortoise, Madagascar | *Geochelone yniphora* | Madagascar | |
| tuatara, Brother's Island | *Sphendon guntheri* | New Zealand | |
| turtle, green | *Chelonia mydas* | warm waters, especially Indian Ocean; Australia; Indonesia | exploitation of turtle meat, hides, eggs, shells; killing of turtles in the trawling nets of fishermen; human disturbance; loss of natural habitat; international trade in turtles |
| turtle, hawksbill | *Eretmochelys imbricata* | tropical and subtropical seas: Atlantic, Indian and Pacific Oceans, Gulf of Mexico and Caribbean | exploitation for tortoiseshell, skin, stuffed turtles as souvenirs |
| turtle, Kemp's Ridley | *Lepidochelys kempii* | Gulf of Mexico; USA | exploitation of turtles for eggs; leather; killing of turtles by trawlers fishing for shrimps |
| turtle, leatherback | *Dermochelys coriacea* | tropical and subtropical seas: Atlantic, Indian and Pacific Oceans; some temperate regions | exploitation for eggs which are considered a delicacy |
| turtle, Olive Ridley | *Lepidochelys olivacea* | tropical and subtropical seas: Atlantic, Indian and Pacific Oceans; India; Costa Rica; Mexico | exploitation for eggs, skin, oil |
| turtle, S American river | *Podocnemis expansa* | northern S America (Bolivia, Brazil) | exploitation for meat, eggs, oil; animal trade |
| turtle, western swamp | *Pseudemydura umbrina* | near Perth, W Australia | drainage and clearance of habitat for agriculture; disruption by wildfires; predation by foxes, wild dogs |
| viper, Cyclades blunt-nosed | *Vipera schweizeri* (*Macrovipera schweizeri*) | Greece | |
| viper, Latifi's | *Vipera latifii* | Lar Valley, Iran | loss of habitat to hydroelectric plant |
| woma | *Aspidites ramsayi* | Australia | |
| *common name not known* | *Aprasia aurita* | Australia | |
| *common name not known* | *Abronia montecristoi* | El Salvador | |
| *common name not known* | *Diploglossus anelpistus* | Dominican Republic | |

[1]Denotes species is certainly endangered and probably extinct.

[2] Denotes there is not enough information available to enable placing of species in rare, vulnerable or endangered category.

Some supplementary information for this edition of *Book of Facts* supplied by the 1994 IUCN (International Union for the Conservation of Nature and Natural Resources) *Red List of Threatened Animals*, compiled by the World Conservation Monitoring Centre.

# HUMAN LIFE

## Main types of vitamin

| Vitamin | Chemical name | Deficiency symptoms | Source |
|---|---|---|---|
| **❑ Fat soluble vitamins** | | | |
| A | retinol (carotene) | night blindness; rough skin; impaired bone growth | milk, butter, cheese, egg yolk, liver, fatty fish, dark green vegetables, yellow/red fruits and vegetables, especially carrots |
| D | cholecalciferol | rickets; osteomalacia | egg yolk, liver, fatty fish; made on skin in sunlight |
| E | tocopherols | multiple diseases produced in laboratory animals; in humans, multiple symptoms follow impaired fat absorption | vegetable oils |
| K | phytomenadione | haemorrhagic problems | green leafy vegetables, beef, liver |
| **❑ Water soluble vitamins** | | | |
| $B_1$ | thiamin | beri-beri, Korsakov's syndrome | germ and bran of seeds, grains, yeast |
| $B_2$ | riboflavin | skin disorders; failure to thrive | liver, milk, cheese, eggs, green leafy vegetables, pulses, yeast |
| $B_6$ | pyridoxine | dermatitis; neurological disorders | liver, meats, fruits, cereals, leafy vegetables |
| | pantothenic acid | dermatitis; neurological disorders | widespread in plants and animals; destroyed in heavily-processed food |
| | biotin | dermatitis | liver, kidney, yeast extract; made by micro-organisms in large intestine |
| $B_{12}$ | cyanocobalamin | anaemia; neurological disturbance | liver, kidney, milk; none found in plants |
| | folic acid | anaemia | liver, green leafy vegetables, peanuts; cooking and processing can cause serious losses in food |
| C | ascorbic acid | scurvy | blackcurrants, citrus fruits, other fruits, green leafy vegetables, potatoes; losses occur during storage and cooking |

## Main trace minerals

| Mineral | Deficiency symptoms | Source |
|---|---|---|
| calcium | rickets in children; osteoporosis in adults | milk, butter, cheese, sardines, green leafy vegetables, citrus fruits |
| chromium | adult-onset diabetes | brewer's yeast, black pepper, liver, wholemeal bread, beer |
| copper | anaemia; Menkes' syndrome | green vegetables, fish, oysters, liver |
| fluorine | tooth decay; possibly osteoporosis | fluoridated drinking water, seafood, tea |
| iodine | goitre; cretinism in new-born children | seafood, salt water fish, seaweed, iodized salt, table salt |
| iron | anaemia | liver, kidney, green leafy vegetables, egg yolk, dried fruit, potatoes, molasses |
| magnesium | irregular heart beat; muscular weakness; insomnia | green leafy vegetables (eaten raw), nuts, whole grains |

| Mineral | Deficiency symptoms | Source |
|---|---|---|
| manganese | not known in humans | legumes, cereal grains, green leafy vegetables, tea |
| molybdenum | not known in humans | legumes, cereal grains, liver, kidney, some dark green vegetables |
| phosphorus | muscular weakness; bone pain; loss of appetite | meat, poultry, fish, eggs, dried beans and peas, milk products |
| potassium | irregular heart beat; muscular weakness; fatigue; kidney and lung failure | fresh vegetables, meat, orange juice, bananas, bran |
| selenium | not known in humans | seafood, cereals, meat, egg yolk, garlic |
| sodium | impaired acid-base balance in body fluids (very rare) | table salt, other naturally occurring salts |
| zinc | impaired wound healing; loss of appetite; impaired sexual development | meat, whole grains, legumes, oysters, milk |

## Composition of selected foods

Approximate values given are for 100g of the food named.

| Food | Calories[1] | Protein (g) | Carbohy-drates (g) | Fat (g) | Fibre (g) |
|---|---|---|---|---|---|
| almonds | 564 | 19 | 20 | 54 | 15 |
| apples | 38 | trace | 15 | trace | 2 |
| apricots, dried | 182 | 5 | 67 | 1 | 24 |
| apricots, raw | 25 | 1 | 13 | trace | 2 |
| asparagus, cooked | 18 | 2 | 4 | trace | 1 |
| aubergine (or eggplant), cooked | 14 | 1 | 4 | trace | 2 |
| avocados | 221 | 2 | 6 | 16 | 2 |
| bacon, back, grilled | 271 | 15 | 2 | 24 | 0 |
| bacon, streaky, grilled | 308 | 16 | 2 | 27 | 0 |
| bananas | 85 | 1 | 22 | trace | 2 |
| beans, broad, cooked | 46 | 4 | 66 | 1 | 4 |
| beans, dried white, cooked | 118 | 8 | 21 | 7 | 25 |
| beans, green, cooked | 25 | 2 | 5 | trace | 4 |
| beef, rump steak, grilled | 218 | 30 | 0 | 12 | 0 |
| beetroot, cooked | 43 | 1 | 7 | trace | 2 |
| biscuits, chocolate digestive | 506 | 6 | 64 | 25 | 4 |
| biscuits, digestive | 486 | 7 | 62 | 23 | 5 |
| blackberries, raw | 29 | 1 | 13 | 1 | 7 |
| blackcurrants | 29 | 2 | 14 | trace | 9 |
| brazil nuts, raw | 618 | 14 | 11 | 67 | 9 |
| bread, white | 232 | 10 | 58 | 2 | 3 |
| bread, wholemeal | 216 | 10 | 55 | 3 | 9 |
| broccoli, cooked | 26 | 3 | 5 | trace | 4 |
| brussel sprouts, cooked | 18 | 4 | 6 | trace | 3 |
| butter, salted | 740 | 1 | trace | 82 | 0 |
| cabbage, cooked | 11 | 2 | trace | trace | 2 |
| cabbage, raw | 25 | 2 | 5 | trace | 3 |
| carrots, cooked | 20 | 1 | 5 | trace | 3 |
| carrots, raw | 25 | 1 | 6 | trace | 3 |
| cauliflower, cooked | 22 | 2 | 4 | trace | 2 |
| celery, raw | 36 | 1 | 2 | trace | 2 |
| cheese, Brie | 314 | 19 | 2 | 23 | 0 |
| cheese, Cheddar | 414 | 25 | 2 | 32 | 0 |
| cheese, cottage | 96 | 17 | 2 | 4 | 0 |
| cheese, Edam | 314 | 30 | trace | 23 | 0 |
| cherries, raw | 70 | 1 | 17 | trace | 1 |
| chick peas, dry | 320 | 20 | 50 | 6 | 15 |
| chicken, meat only, roast | 142 | 19 | 0 | 4 | 0 |
| chocolate bar, plain | 510 | 4 | 63 | 29 | 0 |
| cod, cooked | 94 | 19 | 0 | 1 | 0 |

| Food | Calories[1] | Protein (g) | Carbohy-drates (g) | Fat (g) | Fibre (g) |
|---|---|---|---|---|---|
| corn (on the cob) | 91 | 3 | 21 | 1 | 5 |
| courgettes, cooked | 14 | 1 | 3 | trace | 1 |
| crab, cooked | 129 | 18 | 1 | 5 | 0 |
| cream, double | 446 | 2 | 3 | 48 | 0 |
| crisps | 517 | 6 | 40 | 37 | 11 |
| cucumber, raw | 15 | 1 | 3 | trace | trace |
| dates | 214 | 2 | 73 | 1 | 7 |
| egg, boiled | 163 | 13 | 1 | 12 | 0 |
| eggplant ► aubergine | | | | | |
| figs, dried | 214 | 4 | 69 | 1 | 19 |
| flour, white | 350 | 9 | 80 | 1 | 4 |
| flour, wholemeal | 318 | 13 | 56 | 2 | 10 |
| grapefruit | 41 | 1 | 11 | trace | trace |
| grapes, raw | 69 | 1 | 16 | 1 | 1 |
| haddock, cooked | 96 | 19 | 0 | 1 | 0 |
| ham, lean | 168 | 22 | 0 | 5 | 0 |
| honey | 289 | trace | 82 | 0 | 0 |
| jam | 261 | 1 | 79 | trace | 1 |
| lamb chop, boned, grilled | 353 | 24 | 0 | 29 | 0 |
| leeks, cooked | 25 | 1 | 7 | 0 | 4 |
| lentils, cooked | 106 | 8 | 19 | trace | 4 |
| lettuce, raw | 12 | 1 | 3 | trace | 1 |
| liver, cooked | 254 | 20 | 6 | 13 | 0 |
| lobster, cooked | 119 | 20 | trace | 3 | 0 |
| mackerel, cooked | 188 | 25 | 0 | 11 | 0 |
| margarine | 730 | trace | 1 | 80 | 0 |
| melon, honeydew | 21 | 1 | 5 | trace | 1 |
| melon, water | 21 | trace | 5 | trace | 1 |
| milk, cow's, skimmed | 36 | 4 | 5 | trace | 0 |
| milk, cow's, whole | 65 | 4 | 5 | 4 | 0 |
| mushrooms, raw | 14 | 3 | 4 | trace | 2 |
| mussels, cooked | 86 | 17 | 0 | 1 | 0 |
| nectarines | 64 | 1 | 17 | trace | 2 |
| oatmeal, cooked | 399 | 2 | 10 | 1 | 7 |
| oats, porridge | 377 | 10 | 70 | 7 | 7 |
| oil, vegetable | 900 | 0 | 0 | 100 | 0 |
| onions, raw | 38 | 2 | 9 | trace | 1 |
| orange juice | 45 | 1 | 10 | trace | 0 |
| oranges, peeled, raw | 49 | 1 | 12 | trace | 2 |
| parsnip, cooked | 50 | 1 | 17 | trace | 4 |
| pasta, dry | 353 | 12 | 71 | 2 | 4 |
| peaches, raw | 38 | 1 | 8 | trace | 1 |
| peanuts, fresh | 571 | 26 | 19 | 48 | 8 |
| pears, raw | 61 | 1 | 15 | trace | 2 |
| peas, fresh, cooked | 54 | 5 | 4 | trace | 5 |
| pepper, green, raw | 14 | 1 | 5 | trace | 1 |
| pepper, red, raw | 20 | 1 | 7 | trace | 1 |
| pineapple, raw | 46 | trace | 14 | trace | 1 |
| pork chop, boned, grilled | 328 | 28 | 0 | 24 | 0 |
| potatoes, baked in skin | 86 | 3 | 21 | trace | 2 |
| potatoes, boiled in skin | 75 | 2 | 17 | trace | 2 |
| prawns, cooked | 107 | 18 | 0 | 1 | 0 |
| prunes | 136 | 1 | 77 | trace | 14 |
| raisins | 246 | 3 | 77 | trace | 7 |
| raspberries, raw | 25 | 1 | 14 | 1 | 7 |
| rice, brown, cooked | 129 | 3 | 26 | 1 | 1 |
| rice, white, cooked | 121 | 3 | 33 | trace | 1 |
| salmon, cooked | 196 | 20 | 0 | 13 | 0 |
| spinach, cooked | 23 | 3 | 4 | trace | 6 |
| strawberries, raw | 37 | 1 | 8 | 1 | 2 |

| Food | Calories[1] | Protein (g) | Carbohy-drates (g) | Fat (g) | Fibre (g) |
|---|---|---|---|---|---|
| sugar | 394 | 0 | 100 | 0 | 0 |
| swede, cooked | 18 | 1 | 4 | trace | 3 |
| tomatoes, raw | 14 | 1 | 5 | trace | 1 |
| tuna, canned in brine | 118 | 28 | 0 | 1 | 0 |
| turkey, meat only, roast | 140 | 36 | 0 | 3 | 0 |
| turnip, cooked | 14 | 1 | 5 | trace | 2 |
| walnuts | 525 | 15 | 16 | 64 | 5 |
| yogurt, skimmed milk | 50 | 3 | 5 | 2 | 0 |
| yogurt, whole milk | 62 | 3 | 5 | 3 | 0 |

[1] To convert calories into kilojoules multiply by 4.187.

## E-Numbers

### Glossary

| | |
|---|---|
| acidifiers | impart a sharp flavour; control acidity, eg for setting jams |
| anti-caking agents | prevent particles sticking together to enable the product to flow freely, eg in salt and icing sugar |
| anti-foaming agents | prevent excessive froth and scum formation during boiling |
| antioxidants | prevent or inhibit the harmful effects of oxidation in fat and oils, thus preventing fatty foods from turning rancid; also used to prevent discolouration due to oxidation eg in cut fruits |
| azo dyes | have a particular chemical structure and may be responsible for allergic reactions eg attacks of asthma and eczema, nettle rash, watering eyes and nose, blurred vision and hyperactivity in children; include E102, E107, E110, E122, E123, E124, E128, E151, 154, 155, E181 |
| bases | added to reduce acidity or increase alkalinity; also react with acids to make carbon dioxide for aeration |
| bleaching agents | artificially bleach and whiten flour |
| buffers | maintain the acid–alkali balance at a constant level |
| bulking agents | add to the bulk of foods without increasing their energy value, eg in slimming products |
| chelating agents | combine chemically with toxic substances such as trace metals, rendering them harmless |
| coal tar dyes | dyes formerly made from coal, now made industrially; may have same configuration as **azo dyes**; include those additives listed under azo dyes above plus E104, E127, E131, E132, 133 |
| colours | make food, particularly processed food, look more attractive and 'realistic' |
| emulsifiers | plant gums, chemicals or plant derivatives which allow the mixing of fats and oils with water and enhance smooth creamy textures; also slow down process of baked foods going stale (► **stabilizers**) |
| emulsifying salts | mixture of citrates, phosphates and tartrates added during processing of cheese to prevent it turning stringy |
| firming agents | calcium and magnesium salts that ensure fruits and vegetables retain their crispness and firmness and do not go soft during processing |
| flavour modifiers or enhancers | reduce or enhance taste or smell of a food without imparting their own smell or flavour |
| glazing agents | provide a protective coating or shiny appearance |
| humectants | prevent food from drying out by absorbing water from the atmosphere |
| plasticizers | make a substance more flexible |
| preservatives, antibacterial, antimicrobial etc | inhibit growth of bacteria, fungi and viruses which cause food poisoning or food decay, thus increasing storage time |
| release agents | used to coat machinery or food to prevent sticking during manufacture, and also to enable food to slip easily out of packaging |
| sequestrants | attach themselves to trace metals eg iron or copper to prevent them speeding up oxidation and thus causing the deterioration of food |
| stabilizers | like **emulsifiers**, they prevent mixtures from separating out and enhance smooth creamy textures; they also delay the process of baked foods going stale |
| thickeners | increase the viscosity of a food; usually of plant origin (except 551, silicon dioxide) |

| Number | Name | Function |
|---|---|---|
| **❑ Colours** | | |
| E100 | Curcumin | orange-yellow |
| E101 | Riboflavin | yellow/orange-yellow |
| 101 (a) | Riboflavin-5′ - phosphate | yellow/orange-yellow; vitamin $B_2$ |
| E102 | Tartrazine | yellow |
| E104 | Quinoline yellow | dull yellow/greenish yellow |
| 107 | Yellow 2G | yellow |
| E110 | Sunset Yellow FCF | yellow |
| E120 | Cochineal | red |
| E122 | Carmoisine | red |
| E123 | Amaranth | purplish red |
| E124 | Poncean 4R | red |
| E127 | Erythrosine | pink/red |
| 128 | Red 2G | red |
| 129 | Allura red AC | red (prohibited throughout EC) |
| E131 | Patent blue V | dark bluish-violet; diagnostic agent |
| E132 | Indigo carmine | blue; diagnostic agent |
| 133 | Brilliant blue FCF | blue/green |
| E140 | Chlorophyll | olive/dark green |
| E141 | copper complexes of Chlorophyll and Chlorophyllins | olive green/green |
| E142 | Green S | green |
| E150 | Caramel colour | brown/black |
| E151 | Black PN | black |
| E153 | Carbon black | black |
| 154 | Brown FK | brown |
| 155 | Brown HT | brown |
| E160 (a) | Alpha-carotene, beta-carotene, gamma-carotene | orange-yellow; becomes vitamin A in the body |
| E160 (b) | Annatto, Bixin, Norbixin | yellow/peach/red |
| E160 (c) | Capsanthin | red/orange |
| E160 (d) | Lycopene | red |
| E160 (e) | beta-apo-8′-carotenal | orange/yellowish-red |
| E160 (f) | Ethyl ester of beta-apo-8′-carotenoic acid | orange/yellow |
| E161 (a) | Xanthophylls Flavoxanthin | yellow |
| E161 (b) | Xanthophylls Lutein | yellow/reddish |
| E161 (c) | Xanthophylls Cryptoxanthin | yellow |
| E161 (d) | Xanthophylls Rubixanthin | yellow |
| E161 (e) | Xanthophylls Violoxanthin | yellow |
| E161 (f) | Xanthophylls Rhodoxanthin | yellow |
| E161 (g) | Xanthophylls Canthaxanthin | orange |
| E162 | Beetroot red | purplish-red |
| E163 | Anthocyanins | red/blue/violet |
| E170 | Calcium carbonate | white surface food colour; also alkali for deacidification of wine; firming agent; releasing agent; calcium supplement |
| E171 | Titanium dioxide | white; increases opacity |
| E172 | Iron oxides, iron hydroxides | yellow/red/orange/brown/black |
| E173 | Aluminium | metallic surface colour |
| E174 | Silver | metallic surface colour |
| E175 | Gold | metallic surface colour |
| E180 | Pigment Rubine | reddish |
| **❑ Preservatives** | | |
| E200 | Sorbic acid | active against yeast and moulds (in a slightly acid medium) |
| E201 | Sodium sorbate | |
| E202 | Potassium sorbate | antifungal and antibacterial |
| E203 | Calcium sorbate | antifungal and antibacterial |
| E210 | Benzoic acid | antifungal and antibacterial (in an acid medium) |

| Number | Name | Function |
|---|---|---|
| E211 | Sodium benzoate | antifungal and antibacterial (in a slightly acid medium) |
| E212 | Potassium benzoate | antifungal and antibacterial |
| E213 | Calcium benzoate | antifungal and antibacterial |
| E214 | Ethyl 4-hydroxybenzoate | antifungal and antibacterial |
| E215 | Ethyl 4-hydroxybenzoate, sodium salt | antifungal and antibacterial |
| E216 | Propyl 4-hydroxybenzoate | antimicrobial |
| E217 | Propyl 4-hydroxybenzoate, sodium salt | antimicrobial |
| E218 | Methyl 4-hydroxybenzoate | antimicrobial |
| E219 | Methyl 4-hydroxybenzoate, sodium salt | active against fungi and yeasts, less active against bacteria |
| E220 | Sulphur dioxide | also bleaching agent; improving agent; stabilizer; antioxidant; used in beer and wine making |
| E221 | Sodium sulphite | antimicrobial; also sterilizer; prevents discolouration |
| E222 | Sodium hydrogen sulphite | preservative for alcoholic beverages |
| E223 | Sodium metabisulphite | antimicrobial; also antioxidant; bleaching agent |
| E224 | Potassium metabisulphite | antimicrobial; also antibrowning agent |
| E226 | Calcium sulphite | also firming agent; disinfectant |
| E227 | Calcium hydrogen sulphite | also firming agent; used in washing beer casks and to prevent secondary fermentation |
| E230 | Biphenyl | fungistatic agent; acts against *Penicillium* |
| E231 | 2-Hydroxybiphenyl | antibacterial and antifungal |
| E232 | Sodium biphenyl-2-yl oxide | antifungal (alternative to E231) |
| E233 | 2 (Thiazol-4-yl) benzimidazole | fungicide; treatment of nematode worms in man |
| 234 | Nisin | |
| E236 | Formic acid | antibacterial; also flavour adjunct (prohibited in UK) |
| E237 | Sodium formate | (prohibited in UK) |
| E238 | Calcium formate | (prohibited in UK) |
| E239 | Hexamine | antimicrobial |
| E249 | Potassium nitrate | also curing agent; prevents growth of *Clostridium botulinum* (the bacterium responsible for botulism) |
| E250 | Sodium nitrite | prevents growth of *Clostridium botulinum*; also used in curing salt; red meat colour |
| E251 | Sodium nitrate | also used in curing salt; colour fixative |
| E252 | Potassium nitrate | also used in curing salt; colour fixative |
| E260 | Acetic acid | antibacterial; also food acidity stabilizer; colour diluent; flavouring agent |
| E261 | Potassium acetate | preservative of natural colour; also neutralizing agent; acidity regulator |
| E262 | Sodium hydrogen diacetate | antimicrobial; also acidity regulator; sequestrant |
| 262 | Sodium acetate | buffer |
| E263 | Calcium acetate | antimould agent; anti-rope (development of sticky yellow patches in bread) agent; sequestrant; firming agent; stabilizer; buffer |
| E270 | Lactic acid | also increases antioxidant effect of other substances; acid and flavouring |
| E280 | Propionic acid | antifungal |
| E281 | Sodium propionate | antimicrobial |
| E282 | Calcium propionate | antimicrobial |
| E283 | Potassium propionate | antimould (especially against 'rope' micro-organisms in bread) |
| E290 | Carbon dioxide | also coolant; freezant (liquid form); packaging gas; aerator |
| 296 | Malic acid | also acid; flavouring |
| 297 | Fumaric acid | also acidifier, raising agent; antioxidant |

| Number | Name | Function |
|---|---|---|
| **❑ Antioxidants** | | |
| E300 | L-Ascorbic acid | also Vitamin C; antibrowning agent; flour improving agent; meat colour preservative |
| E301 | Sodium L-ascorbate | also Vitamin C; colour preservative |
| E302 | Calcium L-ascorbate | also Vitamin C; meat colour preservative |
| E304 | 6-0-Palmitoyl-L-ascorbic acid | same function as Vitamin C; also colour preservative; antibrowning agent |
| E306 | Extracts of natural origin rich in tocopherols | also Vitamin E |
| E307 | Synthetic alpha-tocopherol | also Vitamin E |
| E308 | Synthetic gamma-tocopherol | also Vitamin E |
| E309 | Synthetic delta-tocopherol | also Vitamin E |
| E310 | Propyl gallate | antioxidant in oils and fats |
| E311 | Octyl gallate | |
| E312 | Dodecyl gallate | |
| E320 | Butylated hydroxyanisole | |
| E321 | Butylated hydroxytoluene | |
| **❑ Emulsifiers, stabilizers and others** | | |
| E322 | Lecithins | emulsifier |
| E325 | Sodium lactate | humectant; glycerol substitute; increases antioxidant effect of other substances; bodying agent |
| E326 | Potassium lactate | increases antioxidant effect of other substances; buffer |
| E327 | Calcium lactate | antioxidant; buffer; firming agent; fruit and vegetable colour preservative; powdered and condensed milk improver; yeast food; dough conditioner |
| E330 | Citric acid | enhances effects of antioxidants; fruit colour preservative; retains Vitamin C; acidity stabilizer; sequestrant; flavouring; setting agent |
| E331 (a) | Sodium dihydrogen citrate | enhances effects of antioxidants; acidity-controlling and carbonation-retaining buffer; emulsifying salt; sequestrant; prevents curds forming and cream clotting in aerosols |
| E331 (b) | *di* Sodium citrate | antioxidant; enhances effects of antioxidants; buffer; emulsifying salt |
| E331 (c) | *tri* Sodium citrate | antioxidant; buffer; emulsifying salt; sequestrant; stabilizer; used with polyphosphates and flavours to inject into chickens before freezing |
| E332 | Potassium dihydrogen citrate | buffer; emulsifying salt; yeast food |
| E332 | *tri* Potassium citrate | antioxidant; buffer in confectionery and artifically sweetened jellies and preserves; emulsifying salt; sequestrant |
| E333 | *mono, di* and *tri* Calcium citrate | buffers to neutralize acids in jams, jellies and confectionery; firming agents; emulsifying salts; sequestrants; flour improvers |
| E334 | L-(+)-Tartaric acid | antioxidant; enhances effects of antioxidants; acidity adjuster; sequestrant; food colour diluent; flavouring; acid |
| E335 | *mono* Sodium L-(+)-tartrate and *di* Sodium L-(+)-tartrate | antioxidant; enhances effects of antioxidants; buffer; emulsifying salt; sequestrant |
| E336 | *mono* Potassium L-(+)-tartrate (cream of tartar) | acid; buffer; emulsifying salt; raising agent for flour, used with sodium bicarbonate; inverting agent for sugar |
| E336 | *di* Potassium L-(+)-tartrate | antioxidant; enhances effects of antioxidants; buffer; emulsifying salt |
| E337 | Potassium sodium L-(+)-tartrate | buffer for confectionery and preserves; emulsifying salt; stabilizer; enhances effects of antioxidants |

| Number | Name | Function |
|---|---|---|
| E338 | Orthophosphoric acid | enhances effects of antioxidants; acidulant; flavouring agent; acidifier in cheese and beer production; sequestrant |
| E339 | Sodium dihydrogen orthophosphate | texture improver; speeds brine penetration; enhances effects of antioxidants; buffer; nutrient; gelling agent; stabilizer; sugar clarifying agent |
| E340 (a) | Potassium dihydrogen orthophosphate | buffer; sequestrant; emulsifying salt; enhances effects of antioxidants |
| E340 (b) | *di* Potassium hydrogen orthophosphate | buffer; emulsifying salt; enhances effects of antioxidants; yeast food; sequestrant |
| E340 (c) | *tri* Potassium orthophosphate | emulsifying salt; enhances effects of antioxidants; buffer; sequestrant |
| E341 (a) | Calcium tetrahydrogen diorthophosphate | bakery improving agent; firming agent; sequestrant; yeast food; aerator-acidulant; enhances effects of antioxidants; texturizer |
| E341 (b) | Calcium hydrogen orthophosphate | firming agent; yeast food; nutrient mineral supplement; enhances effects of antioxidants; animal feed supplement; abrasive in toothpaste; dough conditioner |
| E341 (c) | *tri* Calcium *di* orthophosphate | anti-caking agent; nutrient yeast food; vegetable extract diluent; clarifying agent |
| 350 | Sodium malate | buffer; seasoning agent |
| 350 | Sodium hydrogen malate | buffer |
| 351 | Potassium malate | buffer |
| 352 | Calcium malate | buffer; firming agent; seasoning agent |
| 352 | Calcium hydrogen malate | firming agent |
| 353 | Metatartaric acid | sequestrant (wine) |
| 355 | Adipic acid | acid buffer; neutralizing agent; flavouring agent; raising agent in baking powders |
| 363 | Succinic acid | acid; buffer; neutralizing agent |
| 370 | 1,4-Heptonolactone | acid; sequestrant |
| 375 | Nicotinic acid | B vitamin; colour protector |
| 380 | *tri* Ammonium citrate | buffer; emulsifying salt; softening agent |
| 381 | Ammonium ferric citrate | dietary iron supplement; raises red blood cell level |
| 381 | Ammonium ferric citrate, green | dietary iron supplement |
| 385 | Calcium disodium ethylenediamine-NNN'N' tetra-acetate (EDTA) | chelating agent; antioxidant |
| E400 | Alginic acid | alginate production |
| E401 | Sodium alginate | stabilizer; suspending agent; thickening agent; gelling agent (with a source of calcium); copper fining agent in brewing |
| E402 | Potassium alginate | emulsifier; stabilizer; boiled water additive; gelling agent |
| E403 | Ammonium alginate | emulsifier; stabilizer; colour diluent; thickener |
| E404 | Calcium alginate | emulsifier; stabilizer; thickener; gelling agent |
| E405 | Propane-1,2-diol alginate | emulsifier; stabilizer; thickener; solvent; foam stabilizing agent |
| E406 | Agar | thickener; stabilizer; gelling agent; humectant; copper fining agent in brewing |
| E407 | Carrageenan | stabilizer; thickener; suspending and gelling agent; texture modifier |
| E410 | Locust gum or Carob bean gum | gelling agent; stabilizer; emulsifier; thickening agent; texture modifier |
| E412 | Guar gum | thickening agent; emulsion stabilizer; suspending agent; dietary bulking agent; helps diabetics control blood sugar levels |
| E413 | Tragacanth | emulsifier; stabilizer; thickener; prevents crystallization of sugar; converts royal icing to a paste |

| Number | Name | Function |
|---|---|---|
| E414 | Gum arabic | retards sugar crystallization; thickener; converts royal icing to a paste; emulsifier; stabilizer; glazing agent; copper fining agent in brewing |
| E415 | Xanthan gum | stabilizer; thickener; emulsifier; 'pseudo-plasticizer' to improve pouring; gelling agent (with guar gum) |
| 416 | Karaya gum | stabilizer; emulsifier; thickener; binding agent in meat products; prevents formation of ice crystals; filling agent; citrus and spice flavouring agent |
| E420 | Sorbitol syrup | sweetening agent; glycerol substitute; retards crystallization; masks taste of saccharin; texturizing agent; humectant; stabilizer |
| E421 | Mannitol | texturizing agent; dietary supplement; humectant; sweetener; anti-caking agent; anti-sticking agent |
| E422 | Glycerol | solvent; humectant; sweetener; bodying agent (with gelatins and gums); plasticizer |
| 430 | Polyoxyethylene (8) stearate | emulsifier; stabilizer |
| 431 | Polyoxyethylene (40) stearate | emulsifier; makes bread 'feel fresh' |
| 432 | Polyoxyethylene (20) sorbitan monolaurate | emulsifier; stabilizer; dispersing agent |
| 433 | Polyoxyethylene (20) sorbitan mono-oleate | emulsifier; de-foamer; preserves moistness; prevents oil leaking from artificial whipped cream; solubility improver |
| 434 | Polyoxyethylene (20) sorbitan monopalmitate | emulsifier; stabilizer; dispersing agent (flavours); defoaming agent; wetting agent |
| 435 | Polyoxyethylene (20) sorbitan monostearate | emulsifier; stabilizer; prevents leakage of oils; preserves moistness; wetting and dispersing agent; prevents greasy taste; foaming agent |
| 436 | Polyoxyethylene (20) sorbitan tristearate | emulsifier; prevents leakage of oils and water; preserves moistness; wetting and solution agent; defoaming agent; flavour dispersing agent |
| E440 (a) | Pectin | emulsifying and gelling agent in acid media; bodying agent; syrups; stabilizer |
| E440 (b) | Amidated pectin | emulsifier; stabilizer; gelling agent; thickener |
| 442 | Ammonium phosphatides | stabilizer; emulsifier |
| E450 (a) | *di* Sodium dihydrogen diphosphate | buffer; sequestrant; emulsifier; raising agent (with sodium bicarbonate); colour improver; chelating agent |
| E450 (a) | *tri* Sodium diphosphate | buffer; sequestrant; emulsifier; colour improver; chelating agent |
| E450 (a) | *tetra* Sodium diphosphate | buffer; emulsifying salt; sequestrant; gelling agent; stabilizer; hydration aid |
| E450 (a) | *tetra* Potassium diphosphate | emulsifying salt; buffer; sequestrant; stabilizer |
| E450 (b) | *penta* Sodium triphosphate | emulsifying salt; texturizer; buffer; sequestrant; stabilizer; water-binding agent; protein solubilization agent |
| E450 (b) | *penta* Potassium triphosphate | emulsifying salt; texturizer; buffer; sequestrant; stabilizer |
| E450 (c) | Sodium polyphosphates | emulsifying salts; sequestrants; stabilizers; texturizers |
| E450 (c) | Potassium polyphosphates | emulsifying salts; stabilizers; sequestrants |
| E460 | Microcrystalline cellulose | bulking agent; binder; anti-caking agent; dietary fibre; hydration aid; emulsion stabilizer; heat stabilizer; alternative ingredient; tablet binder and disintegrant; quickdrying carrier and dispersant; cellulose component; texture modifier |
| E460 | Alpha-cellulose | bulking aid; anti-caking agent; binder; dispersant; thickening agent; filter aid; assists isinglass finings in brewing |

| Number | Name | Function |
|---|---|---|
| E461 | Methylcellulose | emulsifier; stabilizer; thickener; bulking agent; binding agent; film former; water-soluble gum substitute; useful in sugar- and gluten-free diets; fat barrier |
| E463 | Hydroxypropylcellulose | stabilizer; emulsifier; thickener; suspending agent |
| E464 | Hydroxypropylmethylcellulose | gelling or suspending agent; emulsifier; stabilizer and thickening agent; fat barrier |
| E465 | Ethylmethylcellulose | emulsifier; foam stabilizer; thickener; suspending agent |
| E466 | Carboxymethylcellulose, sodium salt | thickening agent; texture modifier; stabilizer; moisture migration controller; gelling agent; bulking agent; prevents crystal growth and syneresis (drawing together of particles in a gel); decreases fat absorption; foam stabilizer |
| E470 | Sodium, potassium and calcium salts of fatty acids | emulsifiers; stabilizers; anti-caking agents |
| E471 | Mono- and di-glycerides of fatty acids | retains foaming power of egg protein in presence of fat (in cakes); emulsifier; stabilizer; thickening agent |
| E472 (a) | Acetic acid esters of mono- and di-glycerides of fatty acids | emulsifiers; stabilizers; coating agents; texture modifiers; solvents; lubricants |
| E472 (b) | Lactic acid esters of mono- and di-glycerides of fatty acids | emulsifiers; stabilizers |
| E472 (c) | Citric acid esters of mono- and di-glycerides of fatty acids | emulsifiers; stabilizers |
| E472 (d) | Tartaric acid esters of mono- and di-glycerides of fatty acids | emulsifiers; stabilizers |
| E472 (e) | Mono- and di-acetyltartaric acid esters of mono- and di-glycerides of fatty acids | emulsifiers; stabilizers |
| E473 | Sucrose esters of fatty acids | emulsifiers; stabilizers |
| E474 | Sucroglycerides | emulsifiers; stabilizers |
| E475 | Polyglycerol esters of fatty acids | emulsifiers; stabilizers |
| 476 | Polyglycerol esters of polycondensed fatty acids of castor oil | emulsifiers; stabilizers; improves chocolate fluidity (with lecithin) for coating |
| E477 | Propane-1,2-diol esters of fatty acids | emulsifiers; stabilizers |
| 478 | Lactylated fatty acid esters of glycerol and propane-1,2-diol | emulsifiers; stabilizers; whipping agents; plasticizers; surface-active agents |
| E481 | Sodium stearoyl-2-lactylate | emulsifier; stabilizer |
| E482 | Calcium stearoyl-2-lactylate | emulsifier; stabilizer; whipping aid |
| E483 | Stearyl tartrate | emulsifier; stabilizer; flour improver |
| 491 | Sorbitan monostearate | emulsifier; stabilizer; glazing agent |
| 492 | Sorbitan tristearate | emulsifier; stabilizer |
| 493 | Sorbitan monolaurate | emulsifier; stabilizer; anti-foaming agent |
| 494 | Sorbitan mono-oleate | emulsifier; stabilizer |
| 495 | Sorbitan monopalmitate | oil-soluble emulsifier; stabilizer |
| 500 | Sodium carbonate | base; removal of testinic acid in brewing |
| 500 | Sodium hydrogen carbonate | base; aerating agent; diluent |
| 500 | Sodium sesquicarbonate | base |
| 501 | Potassium carbonate and potassium hydrogen carbonate | base; alkali |
| 503 | Ammonium carbonate | buffer; neutralizing agent; raising agent |
| 503 | Ammonium hydrogen carbonate | alkali; buffer; aerating agent; raising agent |
| 504 | Magnesium carbonate | alkali; anti-caking agent; acidity regulator; anti-bleaching agent |
| 507 | Hydrochloric acid | acid; for consistent quality in beer |
| 508 | Potassium chloride | gelling agent; salt substitute; dietary supplement |
| 509 | Calcium chloride | sequestrant; firming agent; for consistent quality in beer |
| 510 | Ammonium chloride | yeast food; flavour |

| Number | Name | Function |
|---|---|---|
| 513 | Sulphuric acid | acid; for consistent quality in beer |
| 514 | Sodium sulphate | diluent; for consistent quality in beer |
| 515 | Potassium sulphate | salt substitute |
| 516 | Calcium sulphate | firming agent; sequestrant; nutrient; yeast food; inert excipient; for consistent quality in beer |
| 518 | Magnesium sulphate | dietary supplement; firming agent; used in beer-making |
| 524 | Sodium hydroxide | alkali; soap making |
| 525 | Potassium hydroxide | base; oxidizing agent (black olives) |
| 526 | Calcium hydroxide | firming agent; neutralizing agent; removes testinic acid and ensures consistent quality in beer making |
| 527 | Ammonium hydroxide | food colouring diluent and solvent; alkali |
| 528 | Magnesium hydroxide | alkali |
| 529 | Calcium oxide | alkali; nutrient |
| 530 | Magnesium oxide | anti-caking agent; alkali |
| 535 | Sodium ferrocyanide | anti-caking agent; crystal modifier |
| 536 | Potassium ferrocyanide | anti-caking agent; metals removal in wine making ('blue finings') |
| 540 | *di* Calcium diphosphate | neutralizing agent; dietary supplement; buffering agent; yeast food; mineral supplement (little used in UK) |
| 541 | Sodium aluminium phosphate | aerator acidulant (raising agent) |
| 541 | Sodium aluminium phosphate, basic | emulsifying salt |
| 542 | Edible bone phosphate | anti-caking agent; mineral supplement; tablet filler |
| 544 | Calcium polyphosphates | emulsifying salts; mineral supplements; calcium source; firming agents (not used in UK) |
| 545 | Ammonium polyphosphates | emulsifiers; emulsifying salts; sequestrants; yeast foods; stabilizers |
| **❑ Anti-caking agents** | | |
| 551 | Silicon dioxide | also suspending agent; thickener; stabilizer; assists isinglass finings in clearing beer |
| 552 | Calcium silicate | also antacid (pharmacology); glazing, polishing and release agent (sweets); dusting agent (chewing gum); coating agent (rice); suspending agent |
| 553 (a) | Magnesium silicate, synthetic and magnesium trisilicate | also tablet excipient; antacid (pharmacology); glazing, polishing and release agent (sweets); dusting agent (chewing gum); coating agent (rice) |
| 553 (b) | Talc | also release agent; chewing gum component; filtering aid; dusting powder |
| 554 | Aluminium sodium silicate | |
| 556 | Aluminium calcium silicate | |
| 558 | Bentonite | also clarifying agent; filtration aid; emulsifier; suspending agent |
| 559 | Kaolin, heavy, and Kaolin, light | also clarifying agent |
| 570 | Stearic acid | |
| 572 | Magnesium stearate | also emulsifier; release agent |
| 575 | D-Glucono-1,5-lactone | also acid; sequestrant; prevents formation of milkstone (magnesium, calcium phosphate deposits) and beerstone |
| 576 | Sodium gluconate | also sequestrant; dietary supplement |
| 577 | Potassium gluconate | also sequestrant |
| 578 | Calcium gluconate | also buffer; firming agent; sequestrant |

| Number | Name | Function |
|---|---|---|
| ❑ **Flavour enhancers** | | |
| 620 | L-Glutamic acid | also salt substitute |
| 621 | *mono* Sodium glutamate | |
| 622 | Potassium hydrogen L-glutamate | also salt substitute |
| 623 | Calcium dihydrogen di-L-glutamate | also salt substitute |
| 627 | Guanosine 5′-(*di* Sodium phosphate) | |
| 631 | Inosine 5′-(*di* Sodium phosphate) | |
| 635 | Sodium 5′-ribonucleotide | |
| 636 | Maltol | 'freshly baked' flavour |
| 637 | Ethyl maltol | sweet flavour |
| 900 | Dimethylpolysiloxane | also water repellent; anti-foaming agent; chewing gum base; anti-caking agent; used in beer making |
| ❑ **Glazing agents** | | |
| 901 | Beeswax, white, and beeswax, yellow | also release agent; fruit and honey flavourings |
| 903 | Carnauba wax | also enhances hardness and lustre of other waxes; used in cosmetics |
| 904 | Shellac | |
| 905 | Mineral hydrocarbons | also sealing agent; chewing gum ingredient; defoaming agent; coating for fresh fruit and vegetables; lubricant and binder for capsules and tablets; lubricant in food-processing equipment and meat-packing plants |
| 907 | Refined microcrystalline wax | also chewing gum ingredient; polishing and release agent; stiffening agent; tablet coating |
| ❑ **Improving agents** | | |
| 920 | L-cysteine hydrochloride and L-cysteine hydrochloride monohydrate | also flavouring (chicken); used in shampoo |
| 924 | Potassium bromate | also flour-maturing agent; used in beer making |
| 925 | Chlorine | also flour bleaching; drinking water |
| 926 | Chlorine dioxide | also bleaching agent; oxidizing agent; water purifying agent; taste and odour control of water; bactericide and antiseptic |
| 927 | Azo dicarbonamide | also flour maturing agent |

## Infectious diseases and infections

| Name | Cause | Transmission | Incubation | Symptoms |
|---|---|---|---|---|
| AIDS (Acquired Immune Deficiency Syndrome) | human immunodeficiency virus (HIV) | sexual intercourse, sharing of syringes, blood transfusion | several years | fever, lethargy, weight loss, diarrhoea, lymph node enlargement, viral and fungal infections |
| amoebiasis | *Entamoeba histolytica* | organism in contaminated food | up to several years | fever, diarrhoea, exhaustion, rectal bleeding |
| anthrax | *Bacillus antracis* bacterium | animal hair | 1–3 days | small red pimple on hand or face enlarges and discharges pus |
| appendicitis | usually *E. coli* organism | not transmitted | sudden onset | abdominal pain which moves from left to right after a few hours, nausea |
| bilharziasis (schistosomiasis) | *Schistosoma haematobium*, (also called Bilharzia) *S. mansoni* or *S. japonicum* | certain snails living in calm water | varies with lifespan of parasite | fever, muscle aches, abdominal pain, headaches |
| bronchiolitis (babies only) | respiratory syncytical virus (RSV) | droplet infection | 1–3 days | blocked or runny nose, irritability |
| brucellosis | *Brucella abortus* or *B. meliteusis* bacteria | cattle or goats | 3–6 days | fever, drenching sweats, weight loss, muscle and joint pains, confusion and poor memory |
| bubonic plague | *Yersinia pestis* bacterium | fleas | 3–6 days | fever, muscle aches, headaches, exhaustion, enlarged lymph glands ('buboes') |
| chicken pox (varicella) | varicella-zoster virus | droplet infection | 14–21 days | blister-like eruptions, lethargy, headaches, sore throat |
| cholera | *Vibrio cholerae* | contaminated water | a few hours to 5 days | severe diarrhoea, vomiting |
| common cold (coryza) | Rhinoviruses | droplet infection | 1–3 days | blocked or runny nose, sneezing, sore throat, runny eyes |
| conjunctivitis | virus, bacterium or allergy | variable | variable | if viral, water discharge from eyes; if bacterial, sticky yellow discharge from eyes |
| dengue fever (break-bone fever) | B group of arboviruses | mosquito | 5–6 days | fever, severe muscle cramps, enlarged lymph nodes |
| diphtheria | *Corynebacterium diphtheriae* | droplet infection | 4–6 days | grey exudate across throat; swelling of throat tissues may lead to asphyxiation; toxin secreted by bacteria may seriously damage heart |
| dysentery | *Shigella* genus of bacteria | contaminated food or water | variable; can cause death within 48 hours | diarrhoea, with or without bleeding |
| gastro-enteritis | bacteria, viruses and food poisoning | droplet infection of food | variable | varies from nausea to severe fever, vomiting and diarrhoea |
| German measles (rubella) | togavirus | droplet infection | 18 days | 1–2 days catarrh and sore throat, then red rash, enlargement of lymph nodes |

| Name | Cause | Transmission | Incubation | Symptoms |
|---|---|---|---|---|
| glandular fever (infectious mononucleosis) | Epstein–Barr virus | saliva of infected person | 1–6 weeks | sore throat, fever, enlargement of tonsils and lymph nodes, lethargy, depression |
| gonorrhoea | *Neisseria gonorrhoeae* bacterium | usually sexually transmitted | 2–10 days | in men, burning sensation on urination and discharge from urethra; in women (if any), vaginal discharge |
| hepatitis | hepatitis A, B or C virus | contaminated food or water (type A); sexual relations, sharing syringes, transfusion (type B) | 3–6 weeks (type A); up to a few weeks (type B) | often no symptoms, otherwise similar to 'flu; loss of appetite, tenderness below right ribs, jaundice |
| influenza ('flu) | influenza A, B or C virus | droplet infection | 1–3 days | fever, sweating, muscle aches |
| kala-azar (leishmaniasis) | parasites, Genus leishmania | sandfly | usually 1–2 months, can be up to 10 years | lymph gland, spleen and liver enlargement |
| laryngitis | same viruses that cause colds and 'flu, ie adeno and rhinoviruses | droplet infection | 1–3 days | sore throat, coughing, hoarseness |
| lassa fever | arenavirus | urine | 3 weeks | fever, sore throat, muscle aches and pains, haemorrhage into the skin |
| Legionnaire's disease | *Legionella pneumophila* bacterium | water droplets in infected humidifiers, cooling towers; stagnant water in cisterns and shower heads | 1–3 days | 'flu and pneumonia-like symptoms, fever, diarrhoea, mental confusion |
| leprosy | *Mycobacterium leprae* bacterium | droplet infection; minimally contagious | variable | insensitive white patches on skin, nodules, thickening of and damage to nerves |
| malaria | *Plasmodium falciparium, P. vivax, P. ovale, P. malariae* | anopheles mosquito | several weeks for *P. falciparium*, to several months for *P. vivax* | severe swinging fever, cold sweats, shivers |
| Marburg (or green monkey) disease | unclassified virus | monkeys, body fluids | 5–9 days | fever, diarrhoea; affects brain, kidneys and lungs |
| measles | paramyxovirus | droplet infection | 14 days | fever, severe cold symptoms, bloody red rash |
| meningitis | various bacteria, viruses or fungi eg *Cryptococcus* | droplet infection | variable | severe headache, stiffness in neck muscles, dislike of the light, nausea, vomiting, confusion |
| mumps | paramyxovirus | droplet infection | 18 days | lethargy, fever, pain at the angle of the jaw, swelling of parotid gland(s) |
| orchitis | bacterium or virus; if bacterial, urinary infection due to eg gonorrhoea; if viral, due to eg mumps | see cause | variable | painful red and swollen testes, fever, nausea |

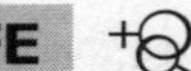



| Name | Cause | Transmission | Incubation | Symptoms |
|---|---|---|---|---|
| osteomyelitis | usually staphylococci organisms | infection spreads from eg boil or impetigo | 1–10 days | abrupt onset of fever, and pain at site of infected bone (usually tibia or femur) |
| parotitis | bacterium or virus | common in mumps (viral), may follow severe febrile illness or abdominal operation | 1–10 days | inflammation of one or both parotid glands |
| pericarditis | bacterium or virus eg *Coxsackie B* | infection follows a chest disease or heart attack | variable | inflamed pericardium (fibrous bag which encloses the heart); tight chest pain |
| peritonitis | usually *E. coli* organism; sometimes chemical irritation | usually appendicitis; perforation of the gut allows escape of barrel contents into peritoneal cavity | 1–10 days | severe abdominal pain, vomiting, rigidity, shock |
| pharyngitis | bacteria or virus | droplet infection | 3–5 days | sore throat, fever, pain on swallowing, enlarged neck glands |
| pneumonia | *Streptococcus pneumoniae* bacterium, *Legionella pneumophila* etc | droplet infection | 1–3 weeks | cough, fever, chest pain |
| poliomyelitis | three types of polio virus | droplet infection and hand to mouth infection from faeces | 7–14 days | affects spinal cord and brain; headache, fever, neck and muscle stiffness; may result in meningitis or paralysis |
| proctitis | fungal infection possible | contact | variable | inflammation of the rectum and anus resulting from thrush, piles or fissures; pain on defecation |
| psittacosis | *Chlamydis psittaci* | infected birds (eg parrots) | 1–2 weeks | headache, chest pain, fever, nausea |
| puerperal fever | infection within uterine cavity or vagina | follows childbirth | 1–10 days | fever; often fatal in past, now rare |
| pylitis | bacteria | kidney infection | 1–10 days | fever, rigor, loin pain, burning on passing urine |
| rabies | virus | bite or lick by infected animal | 2–6 weeks | headache, sickness, excitability, fear of drinking water, convulsions, coma and death |
| river blindness (or onchocerciasis) | *Onchocerca volvulus* worm | bites of infected flies of genus *Simulium* | worms mature in 2–4 months, may live 12 years | worms inhabit skin, causing nodules and sometimes blindness |
| salpingitis | infection of the Fallopian tubes | usually gonorrhoea | variable | abdominal pain, fever, irregular periods, vaginal discharge |
| scarlet fever | *haemolytic streptococcus* | droplet infection or streptococci-infected milk or ice cream | 2–4 days | sudden onset; headache, sore throat, fever, vomiting, red skin rash |
| shingles | *Herpes zoster* virus (also causes chicken pox) | dormant virus in body becomes active following a minor infection | variable | pain, numbness, blisters |
| sinusitis | virus or bacteria | droplet infection; common with a cold | 1–3 days | fever, sinus pain, nasal discharge |

| Name | Cause | Transmission | Incubation | Symptoms |
|---|---|---|---|---|
| sleeping sickness (or African trypanosomiasis) | 1. *Trypanosoma brucei gambieuse* or 2. *Tb. rhodesieuse* | bites by infected tsetse fly | 1. weeks–months; 2. 7–14 days | fever, lymph node enlargement, headache, behavioural change, drowsiness, coma, sometimes death |
| smallpox | variole major or minor virus | now eradicated worldwide | 12 days | fever, rash followed by pustules on face and extremities |
| syphilis | *Treponema pallidum* | sexually transmitted: organism enters bloodstream through a mucous membrane, usually genital skin | ulcer after 2–6 weeks, skin rash after weeks or months | late syphilis damages brain, heart and main blood vessels, and unborn babies |
| tetanus | *Clostridium tetani* | bacteria from soil infect wounds | 2 days–4 weeks | muscular spasms cause lockjaw and affect breathing; potentially fatal |
| thrush | *Candida albicans* yeast | the yeast is present on skin of most people and multiplies when resistance to infection is low; during pregnancy or when taking contraceptive pill | variable | white spots on tongue and cheeks; irritant vaginal discharge; rash in genital area or between folds of skin |
| tonsillitis | usually same viruses responsible for colds; sometimes bacterial (streptococci) | droplet infection | 1–3 days | red inflamed tonsils, sore throat |
| trachoma | *Chlamydia trachomatis* organism | poor hygiene: organism infects eye | 5 days | conjunctivitis, swelling and scarring in cornea, often leading to blindness |
| tuberculosis | *Myobacterium tuberculosis* bacterium | inhalation of bacterium from person with active tuberculosis pneumonia or from infected milk | up to several years | cough with bloodstained sputum, weight loss, chest pain |
| typhoid | *Salmonella typhi* bacillus | contaminated water or food | 10–14 days | slow onset of fever, abdominal discomfort, cough, rash, constipation then diarrhoea, delirium, coma; potentially fatal |
| typhus | *Rickettsiae* parasites | bite by infected flea, tick, mite or louse | 7–14 days | fever, rigor, headache, muscular pain, rash |
| urethritis | virus or bacteria | may occur with cystitis or venereal infection | variable | bloody stools, abdominal pain, burning on urination |
| whooping cough | *Bordetella pertussis* | droplet infection | 7–14 days | severe coughing followed by 'whoop' of respiration |
| yellow fever | zoonosis virus | mosquitoes infected by monkeys | 3–6 days | rigor, high fever, bone pain, headache, nausea, jaundice, kidney failure, coma; potentially fatal |

## Major causes of death

Death from respiratory ailments, infectious diseases and injuries (other than traffic accidents) tends to be lower in the developed world due to preventative medicine, safer living conditions and powerful modern drugs; however, people in the developed world are the most likely to die from cancer or heart disease.

The table below shows the standardized death rate per 100 000 of the population in various countries from the selected causes listed. AIDS is not included in these statistics.

| Country | Infectious and parasitic diseases | Malignant neoplasms (Cancer) | Diseases of the circulatory system | Diseases of the respiratory system (Heart disease) | Motor vehicle accidents | Homicide |
|---|---|---|---|---|---|---|
| Argentina | 24.1 | 119.0 | 267.8 | 44.2 | 10.1 | 4.0 |
| Australia | 3.8 | 126.2 | 168.3 | 32.0 | 10.0 | 1.7 |
| The Bahamas | 14.7 | 112.9 | 211.0 | 56.7 | 5.8 | 13.3 |
| Canada | 3.7 | 126.1 | 142.1 | 32.6 | 9.8 | 1.5 |
| Chile | 14.9 | 120.3 | 154.8 | 62.8 | 12.1 | 2.8 |
| Cuba | 11.9 | 108.4 | 221.6 | 47.0 | 16.7 | 6.8 |
| Estonia | 11.6 | 140.5 | 416.6 | 29.8 | 22.7 | 19.8 |
| Finland | 4.3 | 107.2 | 211.3 | 32.2 | 6.9 | 2.7 |
| France | 5.7 | 130.8 | 107.9 | 23.2 | 12.9 | 1.1 |
| Germany | 3.7 | 130.8 | 202.6 | 26.5 | 10.7 | 1.1 |
| Israel | 7.3 | 114.6 | 183.7 | 18.3 | 10.2 | 1.4 |
| Italy | 2.0 | 133.7 | 166.0 | 22.1 | 12.4 | 1.5 |
| Latvia | 18.0 | 137.0 | 471.7 | 36.1 | 27.7 | 16.0 |
| Mauritius | 16.4 | 68.8 | 346.2 | 75.1 | 17.6 | 1.2 |
| Mexico | 27.6 | 81.2 | 174.7 | 67.6 | 16.2 | 17.7 |
| The Netherlands | 4.3 | 136.7 | 160.9 | 35.8 | 6.9 | 1.1 |
| Poland | 5.9 | 149.0 | 323.6 | 23.3 | 16.7 | 2.5 |
| Russia | 19.6 | 142.5 | 501.2 | 56.5 | 20.4 | 26.6 |
| Singapore | 12.3 | 130.8 | 186.6 | 94.7 | 7.6 | 1.5 |
| Spain | 5.8 | 120.8 | 143.8 | 33.8 | 12.4 | 0.8 |
| Sweden | 3.5 | 106.6 | 172.8 | 25.5 | 4.9 | 1.0 |
| Trinidad and Tobago | 12.4 | 102.5 | 308.9 | 51.6 | 10.4 | 11.4 |
| UK | 3.9 | 137.1 | 192.6 | 63.7 | 5.6 | 1.0 |
| USA | 7.9 | 130.8 | 187.5 | 41.6 | 14.9 | 9.4 |
| Venezuela | 41.0 | 95.8 | 248.7 | 48.1 | 24.0 | 15.1 |

Source: *World Health Statistics Annual 1996* (WHO, 1998)

## An A to Z of phobias

| Technical term | Everyday term |
|---|---|
| acero- | sourness |
| achluo- | darkness |
| acro- | heights |
| aero- | air |
| agora- | open spaces |
| aichuro- | points |
| ailuro- | cats |
| akoustico- | sound |
| algo- | pain |
| amaka- | carriages |
| amatho- | dust |
| andro- | men |
| anemo- | wind |
| angino- | narrowness |
| anthropo- | man |
| antlo- | flood |
| apeiro- | infinity |
| arachno- | spiders |
| astheno- | weakness |
| astra- | lightning |
| ate- | ruin |
| aulo- | flute |
| aurora- | Northern Lights |
| bacilli- | microbes |
| baro- | gravity |
| baso- | walking |
| batracho- | reptiles |
| belone- | needles |
| bronto- (tonitro-, kerauno-) | thunder |
| cheima- | cold |
| chiono- | snow |
| chrometo- | money |
| chrono- | duration |
| chrystallo- | crystals |
| claustro- | closed spaces |
| cnido- | stings |
| cometo- | comets |
| cromo- | colour |
| cyno- | dogs |
| demo- | crowds |
| demono- | demons |
| dermato- | skin |
| dike- | injustice |
| dora- | fur |
| eisoptro- | mirrors |
| electro- | electricity |
| entomo- | insects |
| eoso- | dawn |
| eremo- | solitude |
| erete- | pins |
| ereuthro- | blushing |
| ergasio- | work |
| geno- | sex |
| geuma- | taste |
| grapho- | writing |

| Technical term | Everyday term |
|---|---|
| gymno- | nudity |
| gyno- | women |
| hamartio- | sin |
| haphe- | touch |
| harpaxo- | robbers |
| hedono- | pleasure |
| haemato- | blood |
| helmintho- | worms |
| hodo- | travel |
| homichlo- | fog |
| horme- | shock |
| hydro- | water |
| hypegia- | responsibility |
| hypno- | sleep |
| ideo- | ideas |
| kakorraphia- | failure |
| katagelo- | ridicule |
| keno- | void |
| kineso- | motion |
| klepto- | stealing |
| kopo- | fatigue |
| kristallo- | ice |
| lalio- | stuttering |
| linono- | string |
| logo- | words |
| lysso- (mania-) | insanity |
| mastigo- | flogging |
| mechano- | machinery |
| metallo- | metals |
| meteoro- | meteors |
| miso- | contamination |
| mono- | one thing |
| musico- | music |
| muso- | mice |
| necro- | corpses |
| nelo- | glass |
| neo- | newness |
| nepho- | clouds |
| noso- (patho-) | disease |
| ocho- | vehicles |
| odonto- | teeth |
| oiko- | home |
| olfacto- | smell |
| ommato- | eyes |
| oneiro- | dreams |
| ophidio- | snakes |
| ornitho- | birds |
| ourano- | heaven |
| pan- (panto-) | everything |
| partheno- | girls |
| patroio- | heredity |
| penia- | poverty |
| phasmo- | ghosts |
| phobo- | fears |
| photo- | light |
| pnigero- | smothering |
| poine- | punishment |

| Technical term | Everyday term |
|---|---|
| poly- | many things |
| poto- | drink |
| pterono- | feathers |
| pyro- | fire |
| rypo- | soiling |
| Satano- | Satan |
| sela- | flashes |
| sidero- | stars |
| sito- | food |
| sperma- (spermato-) | germs |
| stasi- | standing |
| stygio- (hade-) | hell |
| syphilo- | syphilis |
| thaaso- | sitting |
| thalasso- | sea |
| thanato- | death |
| theo- | God |
| thermo- | heat |
| toxi- | poison |
| tremo- | trembling |
| triskaideka- | thirteen |
| xeno- | strangers |
| zelo- | jealousy |
| zoo- | animals |

| Everyday term | Technical term |
|---|---|
| air | aero- |
| animals | zoo- |
| birds | ornitho- |
| blood | haemato- |
| blushing | ereutho- |
| carriages | amaka- |
| cats | ailuro- |
| closed spaces | claustro- |
| clouds | nepho- |
| cold | cheima- |
| colour | cromo- |
| comets | cometo- |
| contamination | miso- |
| corpses | necro- |
| crowds | demo- |
| crystals | chrystallo- |
| darkness | achluo- |
| dawn | eoso- |
| death | thanato- |
| demons | demono- |
| disease | noso- (patho-) |
| dogs | cyno- |
| dreams | oneiro- |
| drink | poto- |
| duration | chrono- |
| dust | amatho- |
| electricity | electro- |
| everything | pan- (panto-) |
| eyes | ommato- |
| failure | kakorraphia- |

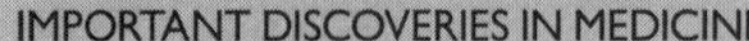




| Everyday term | Technical term | Everyday term | Technical term | Everyday term | Technical term |
|---|---|---|---|---|---|
| fatigue | kopo- | metals | metallo- | snakes | ophidio- |
| fears | phobo- | meteors | meteoro- | snow | chiono- |
| feathers | pterono- | mice | muso- | soiling | rypo- |
| fire | pyro- | microbes | bacilli- | solitude | eremo- |
| flashes | sela- | mirrors | eisoptro- | sound | akoustico- |
| flogging | mastigo- | money | chrometo- | sourness | acero- |
| flood | antlo- | motion | kineso- | spiders | arachno- |
| flute | aulo- | music | musico- | standing | stasi- |
| fog | homichlo- | narrowness | angino- | stars | sidero- |
| food | sito- | needles | belone- | stealing | klepto- |
| fur | dora- | newness | neo- | stings | cnido- |
| germs | sperma- (spermato-) | Northern Lights | aurora- | strangers | xeno- |
| ghosts | phasmo- | nudity | gymno- | string | linono- |
| girls | partheno- | one thing | mono- | stuttering | lalio- |
| glass | nelo- | open spaces | agora- | syphilis | syphilo- |
| God | theo- | pain | algo- | taste | geuma- |
| gravity | baro- | pins | erete- | teeth | odonto- |
| heat | thermo- | pleasure | hedono- | thirteen | triskaideka- |
| heaven | ourano- | points | aichuro- | thunder | bronto- (tonitro-, kerauno-) |
| heights | acro- | poison | toxi- | touch | haphe- |
| hell | stygio- (hade-) | poverty | penia- | travel | hodo- |
| heredity | patroio- | punishment | poine- | trembling | tremo- |
| home | oiko- | reptiles | batracho- | vehicles | ocho- |
| ice | kristallo- | responsibility | hypegia- | void | keno- |
| ideas | ideo- | ridicule | katagelo- | walking | baso- |
| infinity | apeiro- | robbers | harpaxo- | water | hydro- |
| injustice | dike- | ruin | ate- | weakness | astheno- |
| insanity | lysso- (mania-) | Satan | Satano- | wind | anemo- |
| insects | entomo- | sea | thalasso- | women | gyno- |
| jealousy | zelo- | sex | geno- | words | logo- |
| light | photo- | shock | horme- | work | ergasio- |
| lightning | astra- | sin | hamartio- | worms | helmintho- |
| machinery | mechano- | sitting | thaaso- | writing | grapho- |
| man | anthropo- | skin | dermato- | | |
| many things | poly- | sleep | hypno- | | |
| men | andro- | smell | olfacto- | | |
| | | smothering | pnigero- | | |

## Important discoveries in medicine

| Discovery | Date | Discoverer(s) | Nationality |
|---|---|---|---|
| adrenal gland, function of | 1856 | Vulpian (b.1826)[1] | French |
| adrenaline | 1901 | Jokichi Takamine (1854–1922) based on work by Edward Sharpey-Schafer (1850–1935) and Oliver | Japanese UK |
| AIDS (Aquired Immune Deficiency Syndrome) | 1981 | scientists in Los Angeles | — |
| allergenic nature of hay fever | 1906 | Clemens Peter von Pirquet (b.1874) | Austrian |
| allergy recognized in skin's reaction to tuberculin | 1906 | Clemens Peter von Pirquet (b.1874) | Austrian |
| anaesthetic, epidural | 1885 | James Leonard Corning (1855–1923) | US |
| anaesthetic, general | c.1840 | priority claimed by Crawford Long (1815–78) Gardner Cotton (1814–98) Horace Wells (1815–48) Charles Jackson (1805–80) | all US |
| anaesthetic, local (mandrake leaves and polenta) | described in *Natural History* | Pliny the Elder (23–79AD) | Roman |

| Discovery | Date | Discoverer(s) | Nationality |
|---|---|---|---|
| anaphylaxis | 1902 | Charles Robert Richet (1850–1935) | French |
| | | Pierre Portier | French |
| androsterone | 1931 | Adolf Friedrich Johann Butenandt (1903–95) | German |
| anthrax bacillus | 1850 | Casimir Joseph Davaine (1812–82) | French |
| anthrax bacillus | 1876 | Louis Pasteur (1822–95) | French |
| | | Robert Koch (1843–1910) | German |
| anthrax, serum against | 1895 | Achille Sclavo (b.1861) | Italian |
| | | E Marchoux | French |
| antihistamine | 1937 | Bonet | |
| | | Hans Staub (b.1890) | Swiss |
| antipyretic agent (lowers temperature) | 4th–5th century BC | Hippocrates (c.460–c.377 or 359BC) | Greek |
| antisepsis | 1865 | Joseph Lister (1827–1912) | UK |
| asepsis by boiling and by dry heat autoclave | 1883 | Octave Terrillon | French |
| | | Louis-Félix Terrier (b.1837) | French |
| atropine (isolated) | 1819 | Rudolph Brondes | — |
| bacillus ► diphtheria, gangrene, tuberculosis, typhus bacteria | 1673 | Anton van Leeuwenhoek (1632–1723) | Dutch |
| benzoadiazepines (tranquillizers) ('the time pill') | 1986 | Fred W Turck | US |
| | | Susan Losee Olsen | US |
| blood circulation | 1628 | William Harvey (1578–1677) | UK |
| blood groups A, O, B, AB | 1901 | Karl Landsteiner (1868–1943) | Austrian–US |
| blood groups M, N and P | 1927 | Karl Landsteiner (1868–1943) | Austrian–US |
| | | Philip Levine | US |
| blood pressure greater than atmospheric pressure | 1733 | Stephen Hales (1677–1761) | UK |
| brain, electric activity in the (► EEG) | 1875 | Richard Caton | UK |
| cellular division | 1855 | Rudolph Virchow (1821–1902) | German |
| chloroform, anaesthetic properties of | 1847 | James Young Simpson (1811–70) | UK |
| cholera vibrion | 1883 | Robert Koch (1843–1910) | German |
| chromosome X, heredity linked to sex | 1909 | Thomas Hunt Morgan (1866–1945) | US |
| chromosomes | 1888 | Thomas Hunt Morgan (1866–1945) | US |
| chromosomes (48) in man | — | Herbert McLean Evans (1882–1971) | US |
| circadian rhythm of 25 hours | 1972 | Michel Siffre | — |
| coagulation, role of fibrin in | 1771 | William Henson | UK |
| coagulation (formation of fibrin following dissolution of fibrinogen under influence of thrombin) | 1876 | Olaf Hammarsten (b.1841) | Swedish |
| cochlea or inner ear, stimulation mechanism of | 1961 | Georg von Békésy (1899–1972) | Hungarian–US |
| corpuscles, red | 1675 or 1684 | Anton van Leeuwenhoek (1632–1723) | Dutch |
| cortisone (adrenal cortex hormone) (isolated) | 1934 | Edward Calvin Kendall (1886–1972) | US |
| cyclosporin-A, immunosuppressive properties of | 1972 | J-F Borel | Swiss |
| digestion system | — | Claude Bernard (1813–78) | French |
| diphtheria bacillus | 1882 | Theodor Albrecht Edwin Klebs (b.1834) | Swiss–US |
| diphtheria, serum against | 1892 | Emil Adolf von Behring (1854–1917) | German |
| | | Shibasaburo Kitasato (1852–1931) | Japanese |
| | | Pierre Émile Roux (1853–1933) | French |
| disinfection of wounds, chemical | 1825 | Antoine Labarraque | French |
| DNA, structure of | 1953, 1961 | Francis Harry Crompton Crick (1916– ) | UK |
| | | James D Watson (1928– ) | US |
| Down's Syndrome, cause of ('the extra chromosome') | 1958 | Turpin | French |
| | | Gautier | French |
| | | Lejeune | French |

| Discovery | Date | Discoverer(s) | Nationality |
|---|---|---|---|
| electro-encephalogram (EEG) (spontaneous activity of the brain) | 1929 | Hans Berger (1873–1941) | German |
| endorphins | 1975 | John Hughes | US |
| | | Roger Guillemin (1924– ) | French–US |
| enzymes | 1833 | Anselme Payen | French |
| | | Jean-François Persoz | French |
| enzymes, restriction | 1970 | Hamilton Smith | US |
| estrogen produced by ovarian follicle | 1924 | Courrier | French |
| estrone | 1929 | Edward Adelbert Doisy (1893–1986) | US |
| | | Adolf Friedrich Johann Butenandt (1903–95) | German |
| ether first used as anaesthetic | 1846 | William Thomas Morton (1819–68) | US |
| fertilization | 1875 | Oskar Hertwig | German |
| gangrene, gas bacillus of | 1878 | Louis Pasteur (1822–95) | French |
| genes, chemical regulation by | 1952 | Jacques Monod (1910–76) | French |
| | | Edwin Joseph Cohn (1892–1953) | US |
| gonococcus | 1879 | Albert Ludwig Siegmund Neisser (1855–1916) | German |
| heparin (anticoagulant secreted by liver cells) | 1916 | Jay McLean | US |
| hepatitis-C virus | 1989 | Dr Qui-Lim-Choo's research team of the Chiron Corporation | US |
| heredity | 1865 | Gregor Johann Mendel (1822–84) | Austrian |
| HIV virus (isolated) | 1983 | Luc Montaigner and others | French |
| HLA (human leucocyte locus A) system (responsible for transplant rejection) | 1950–77 | Jean Dausset (1916– ) | French |
| hormone ► adrenaline, cortisone, estradiol, inhibin, insulin, progesterone, testosterone | | | |
| inhibin | 1985 | Roger Guillemin (1924– ) | French–US |
| insulin (isolated) | 1921 | Frederick Grant Banting (1891–1941) | Canadian |
| | | Charles Herbert Best (1899–1978) | Canadian |
| | | John James McLeod (1876–1935) | Canadian |
| insulin | 1921 | Nicolas Paulesco | Romanian |
| interferon | 1957 | Alick Isaacs (1921–67) | UK |
| | | J Lindemann | Swiss |
| interleukin 2 | 1985 | Steven Rosenberg | US |
| interleukin 3 | 1986 | Steven Clark | US |
| | | Yu Chang Yang | US |
| leprosy bacillus | 1869 | Gerhard Henrik Armauer Hansen (1841–1912) | Norwegian |
| malaria, plasmodium protozoan as agent of | 1880 | Charles-Louis-Alphonse Laveran (1845–1922) | French |
| microbes | 1762 | M A Plenciz (1705–86) | Austrian |
| morphine | 1805 | Friedrich Serturner | German |
| mosquitoes in infectious diseases, role of | 1895 | Ronald Ross (1857–1932) | UK |
| mosquitoes, transmission of filariae by | 1883 | Patrick Manson (1844–1922) | UK |
| nervous reaction, chemical transmission of | 1936 | Otto Loewi (1873–1961) | German–US |
| | | Henry Hallet Dale (1875–1968) | UK |
| nitrous oxide (laughing gas) | 1776 | Joseph Priestley (1733–1804) | UK |
| nitrous oxide, analgesic and laughter-provoking effect of | 1799 | Humphry Davy (1778–1829) | UK |
| nucleic acid | 1869 | Johann Friedrich Miescher (1844–95) | Swiss |
| oncogenes | 1981 | Robert Weinberg | US |
| | | Geoffrey Cooper | US |
| | | Michael Wigler | US |

| Discovery | Date | Discoverer(s) | Nationality |
|---|---|---|---|
| ovulation, substances acting against | 1921 | Haberlandt | German |
| penicillin | 1928 | Alexander Fleming (1881–1955) | UK |
| phagocytes (cells which devour infective organisms) | 1882–6 | Ilya Ilich Mechnikov (1845–1916) | Russian |
| phenol, disinfectant properties of | 1865 | Joseph Lister (1827–1912) | UK |
| Phenytoin (for treatment of epilepsy) | 1939 | — | — |
| pituitary, secretion of growth hormone | 1921 | Herbert McLean Evans (1882–1971) | US |
| prion (proteinaceous infectious particles) | 1982 | Stanley Prusiner | US |
| progesterone | 1929 | George Washington Corner (b.1889) | US |
| | | Edgar Allen (1892–1943) | US |
| protozoa (unicellular organisms) | 1675 | Anton van Leeuwenhoek (1632–1723) | Dutch |
| quinoline (later discovered to be antimicrobial agent) | 1834 | Friedlieb Ferdinand Runge (1795–1867) | German |
| rabies vaccination | 1885 | Louis Pasteur (1822–95) | French |
| relapsing fever, spirochaete of | 1873 | Obermeier | German |
| respiration, use of oxygen in | 1770–80 | Antoine Lavoisier (1743–94) | French |
| rhesus factor | 1939–40 | Karl Landsteiner (1868–1943) | Austrian–US |
| | | Philip Levine | US |
| scurvy, lemon juice treatment of | c.1740 | James Lind (1716–94) | UK |
| skin culture | 1950 | Howard Green | US |
| sleeping sickness, transmission by tsetse flies | 1895 | David Bruce (1855–1931) | UK |
| smallpox vaccination | 1796 | Edward Jenner (1749–1823) | UK |
| smallpox inoculation, introduction of | 1718 | Lady Mary Wortley Montagu (1689–1762) | UK |
| spermatozoa | 1677 | Anton van Leeuwenhoek (1632–1723) | Dutch |
| Staphylococcus and Streptococcus | 1880 | Louis Pasteur (1822–95) | French |
| streptomycin (antibiotic against tuberculosis) | 1943 | Selman Abraham Walksman (1888–1973) | US |
| sulphonamides (first antibiotics) | 1935 | Gerhard (Johannes Paul) Domagk (1895–1964) | German |
| T-lymphocytes | 1966 | J David | US |
| | | V Blum | US |
| testosterone (isolated) | 1929 | — | — |
| testosterone (synthesized) | 1935 | Leopold Stephen Ružička (1887–1976) | Swiss |
| tetanus, serum against | 1890 | Emil von Behring (1854–1917) | German |
| | | Shibasaburo Kitasato (1852–1931) | Japanese |
| | | Pierre-Paul-Émile Roux (1853–1933) | French |
| thyroxine (thyroid hormone) (isolated) | 1914 | Edward Calvin Kendall (1886–1972) | US |
| tomography | 1915 | André Bocage | French |
| tuberculosis bacillus | 1882 | Robert Koch (1843–1910) | German |
| tubocarine (muscle relaxant) | 1935 | Harold King | — |
| Tumor Necrosis Factor (TNF) | 1975 | Carswell | US |
| typhus bacillus | 1880 | Karl Joseph Eberth (1835–1926) | German |
| vaccination | c.10th century | — | Turkey and China |
| vaccination ► rabies, smallpox virus | 1892 | Dmitry Ivanovsky | Russian |
| viruses, cultivation of (on chicken embryos) | 1986 | Goodpasture | US |
| vitamin A | 1913 | Elmer Verner McCollum (b.1870) | US |
| | | M Davis | US |
| | | Thomas Burr Osborne (b.1859) | US |
| | | L B Mendel | US |
| vitamin B (niacin) (isolated) | 1913 | Casimir Funk (1884–1967) | Polish–US |
| vitamin $B_1$ (thiamin) | 1897 | Christiaan Eijkman (1858–1930) | Dutch |
| vitamin $B_2$ (riboflavin) | 1933 | R Kühn | German |
| | | P György | German |
| | | T Wagner-Jauregg | German |

| Discovery | Date | Discoverer(s) | Nationality |
|---|---|---|---|
| vitamin $B_3$ | 1937 | Madden | UK |
| | | Strong | UK |
| | | Woolley | UK |
| | | Elvehjem | UK |
| vitamin $B_5$ | 1933 | Williams | US |
| vitamin $B_6$ | 1936 | T W Birch | US |
| | | P György | German |
| vitamin $B_9$ | 1938 | Day | UK |
| vitamin $B_{12}$ | 1927 | Minot | UK |
| | | Murphy | UK |
| vitamin $B_{12}$ (isolated) | 1948 | E L Smith | UK |
| | | L F J Parke | UK |
| | same date | E L Rickes | US |
| | in US | N G Brink | US |
| | | F R Koniuszy | US |
| | | T R Wood | US |
| | | K Folkers | US |
| vitamin C (isolated but not recognized as a vitamin) | 1928 | Albert von Nagyrapolt Szent Györgyi (1893–1986) | Hungarian–US |
| vitamin C (isolated) | 1932 | Glen King | US |
| vitamin D (role in prevention of rickets)[2] | 1918 | E Mellenby | UK |
| vitamin D (isolated) | 1924 | Steenbock | German |
| | | Hass | German |
| | | Weinstock | German |
| vitamin E | 1923 | Herbert McLean Evans (1882–1971) | US |
| | | K S Bishop | US |
| vitamin $K_1$ | 1934 | K Dam | Danish |
| | | Schönheyder | Danish |
| vitamins, necessity of | 1906 | Sir Frederick Gowland Hopkins (1861–1947) | UK |
| X-rays | 1892 | Heinrich Hertz (1857–94) | German |
| X-rays, properties of | 1895 | Wilhelm Konrad von Röntgen (1845–1923) | German |
| yellow fever, transmission by *stegmyia* mosquito | 1881 | Ronald Ross (1857–1932) | UK |
| | | Carlos Juan Finlay (1833–1915) | Cuban |

[1] Vulpian = Edmé Félix Alfred Vulpian. [2] Not known as Vitamin D at this time.

## Alternative medicine

Alternative medicine is the treatment of diseases and disorders using procedures other than those traditionally practised in orthodox medicine. The term 'complementary medicine' is also used. The main types are explained below.

**acupressure** Ancient Chinese and Japanese healing massage using fingertip pressure on pain-relieving points around the body. These pressure points (acupoints) lie along the meridians (invisible body channels) used in **acupuncture**. Acupressure balances the flow of Qi (or Chi), the energy flowing through the meridians.

**acupuncture** A traditional Chinese method of healing in which symptoms are relieved by the insertion of special needles into one or more of 2 000 specific points (acupoints) that lie along invisible channels called meridians. This ancient therapy is believed to control the flow of Qi (or Chi), the energy flowing along the meridians. Used in the treatment of arthritis, allergy, back pain and many other disorders.

**Alexander technique** A system of body awareness which involves retraining the body's movements, positions and posture during all activities, including sitting or reading. The method, which must be learned from qualified teachers, is believed to encourage good mental and physical health, and resistance to stress, by promoting harmony between mind and body. Named after Australian-born physiotherapist F M Alexander (d.1955).

**aromatherapy** Use of concentrated plant oils — such as bergamot, eucalyptus or rosemary — to treat conditions including stress, headache and arthritis. Extracts, or essential oils, are generally massaged into the skin by aromatherapists, but can also be inhaled or added to baths.

**art therapy** Use of drawing and painting to encourage patients to explore and resolve deep-seated fears and emotions that they find difficult to

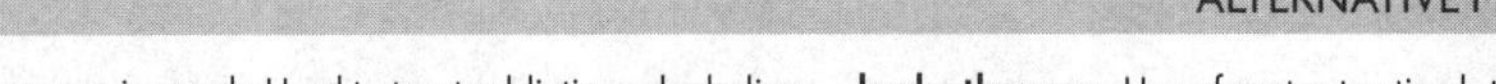



express in words. Used to treat addiction, alcoholism, anorexia and other conditions.

**aura therapy** An aura is said to be a magnetic field surrounding the body, visible to aura practitioners as lines of light. Aura therapy involves analysis of the aura, which is said to be indicative of a person's health, and balancing or recharging it to treat health problems.

**autogenics** Relaxation therapy used to reduce and control stress and fatigue by facilitating voluntary control of bodily tension. It is based on six taught mental exercises, which are repeated, sitting or lying down, twice or three times a day.

**autosuggestion** Form of self-**hypnotherapy** which empties the mind by the repetition of positive phrases or ideas to oneself in order to enhance wellbeing, relieve pain, and change attitudes or habits like addictions and phobias.

**Bach remedies** or **Bach flower healing** Use of wild flower preparations — chosen according to an individual's particular personality and emotional state — to treat physical and psychological disorders. Named after British physician Edward Bach (1880–1936).

**biochemic tissue salts** Use of 12 mineral salts to cure disorders by restoring the natural salt balance within the body.

**chiropractic** Manipulation of the spine and other joints to relieve musculo-skeletal complaints, especially back and neck pain.

**cranial osteopathy** Gentle manipulation of the bones of the skull and face to correct pressure changes to the brain and nerves in order to treat conditions such as migraine and neuralgia.

**craniosacral therapy (CST)** Gentle manipulation of the skull and face in order to release tensions and imbalances which are said to arise in the bones and membranes of the skull. Used to treat a wide range of physical and psychological symptoms.

**crystal healing** Selection and use of crystals that are said to promote healing and wellbeing in humans.

**dance movement therapy** Use of body movement to express deep feelings too difficult to explain in words. Used to treat depression and anxiety as well as more serious mental illnesses.

**Feldenkrais method** Technique of teaching people how to improve the way they move by learning how they are moving. The aim is to move with maximum efficiency and minimum movement. Believed to reduce risk of injury in eg dancers or athletes.

**herbal medicine** or **herbalism** Use of herbs to treat ailments, a practice that dates back thousands of years.

**homeopathy** Treatment of an illness using dilute doses of substances that produce symptoms similar to those of the illness itself (treating like with like). The aim is to restore the body's natural balance by boosting its healing powers.

**hydrotherapy** Use of water to stimulate the body's ability to heal itself, based on the fact that water is essential for life. Treatment includes hot and cold baths, and the steam baths found at spas and health farms. Used also to treat disability by developing movement in water.

**hypnotherapy** Use of suggestion under hypnosis to treat conditions including stress, phobias, and addiction to tobacco and alcohol.

**iridology** Diagnosis of disorders achieved by studying the patterns on the irises of the eyes. Iridologists believe that each section of the iris indicates the condition of a specific part of the body.

**kinesiology** Monitoring of muscle strength and tone, using gentle finger pressure, to indicate how the whole body is working. Based on the belief that muscle groups are linked to particular body organs. If imbalances are found, gentle massage is applied to pressure points to restore normal energy flow to muscles and their organs.

**macrobiotics** Dietary regime based on Chinese philosophy of yin (flexible and cool) and yang (strong and hot), balancing the two elements to complement an individual's nature and lifestyle. Believed to improve health and resistance to disease. In common usage, the term macrobiotics often refers to the devising and following of diets using whole grains and organically-grown fruit and vegetables, which are thought to prolong life.

**massage** Ancient therapy whereby one person uses hands and fingers to stroke, press and knead the body of another person who is lying horizontally. It is used to relax mind and body, and reduce tension, as well as treating disorders such as back pain.

**meditation** Achieving a tranquil mental state, without the use of drugs, to reduce tension, decrease blood pressure and regain confidence when stressed. This technique enables individuals to calm their bodies by controlling their thoughts. The meditative state is reached by focusing on a neutral thought or silently repeating a mantra while breathing in a controlled way.

**moxibustion** A form of **acupuncture**. A piece of burning moxa (a pithy material, eg sunflower pith or cotton wool) is placed on the head of an inserted acupuncture needle to heat it. Alternatively, the burning moxa is held above the acupuncture point to warm the skin. Both methods are used to relieve pain after operations, and for arthritis.

**naturopathy** Using natural cures to seek the underlying cause of illnesses rather than merely alleviating the symptoms. Naturopaths treat patients as whole individuals, taking into account their emotions and lifestyles. Evidently effective against stress and anxiety, as well as degenerative diseases such as emphysema and arthritis.

**negative ion therapy** Treatment whereby the body is exposed to harmless ions; claimed to effect various cures.

**osteopathy** Diagnosis and treatment of disorders of the bones, joints, muscles, tendons and nerves. Commonly used to treat back and neck problems, tension headaches and sports injuries. Based on the concept that the musculo-skeletal system plays a key role in the body's health. Osteopaths assess the damage, then manipulate the affected area.

**reflexology** Treatment of disorders by massaging the feet. Reflexologists relate different zones of the feet to different organs or parts of the body by way of meridians or energy channels. By massaging a particular foot region, they treat a particular organ or part of the body by releasing blocks in the meridians.

**Rolfing** Massaging of muscles and connective tissues in order to improve body posture and thereby improve the health and physical wellbeing of the whole body. Named after US physiotherapist Dr Ida Rolf (1897–1979).

**shiatsu** or **shiatzu** Ancient Japanese massage using the fingers or palms of the hand which, like **acupressure**, involves the application of pressure to points lying along the body's meridians in order to control the energy flow (Qi). Used in the treatment of many conditions including migraine, back pain, stress and digestive problems.

**t'ai chi ch'uan** Technique whereby people focus on their body and emotions by performing slow, circular, dance-like movements. T'ai chi is believed to remedy imbalances in the movement of the body's natural energy, Qi, so improving a person's wellbeing. It is also used as a system of exercise and self-defence.

**thalassotherapy** Treatment to detoxify and relax the body, involving the application of mud and seaweed compresses, seawater baths and massage.

**yoga** System of physical, mental and spiritual training designed to make the body more relaxed and more flexible. It involves adopting a series of postures while maintaining an inner calm of concentrated awareness. Yoga is used to help pain, especially back pain, stress and many other conditions.

## Commonly prescribed drugs

This list includes drugs that are commonly prescribed in the UK, the USA and other countries of the developed world. They are grouped according to their usage, and listed by their generic names, not by brand names.

**Anabolic steroids** Used to help muscle repair following injury. Abused by body builders and athletes to improve their physique.
◇ Nandrolene; Stanozolol.

**Analgesic drugs** Pain-relieving drugs. Non-opioid analgesics are used for mild pain; opioid analgesics for severe pain.
◇ **Non-opioid analgesics** Aspirin; Paracetamol; Benorylate; Nefopam; Sodium salicylate.
◇ **Opioid analgesics** Buprenorphine; Dihydrocodeine; Codeine; Morphine; Dextropropoxyphene; Pentazocine; Diamorphine; Pethidine.

**Antacid drugs** Neutralize stomach acids, relieving heartburn, peptic ulcers and other gastric complaints.
◇ Aluminium hydroxide; Magnesium carbonate; Magnesium trisilicate; Sodium bicarbonate.

**Anthelminthic drugs** Kill parasitic worms such as tapeworms, threadworms and roundworms.
◇ Bephenium; Piperazine; Mebendazole; Pyrantel; Niclosamide; Thiabendazole.

**Antibacterial drugs (antibiotics)** Used to treat bacterial infections.
◇ Amocycillin; Gentamicin; Ampicillin; Minocycline; Cefaclor; Cephradine; Oxytetracycline; Cephalexin; Phenoxymethyl penicillin; Doxycycline; Benzylpenicillin; Erythromycin; Streptomycin; Flucloxacillin; Tetracycline.

**Anticancer drugs** Used to treat certain cancers. Some are cytotoxic, which means they kill cancer cells; others (marked *) are similar to sex hormones or hormone antagonists, and, although not curative, may provide palliation of symptoms.
◇ Aminoglutethimide*; Lomustine; Chlorambucil; Medroxy-Cyclophosphamide; Progesterone*; Doxorubicin; Megestrol*; Ethinyloestradiol*; Metho-trexate; Etoposide; Procarbazine; Fluorouracil; Stilboestrol*; Tamoxifen*.

**Antidepressant drugs** ► Psychotherapeutic drugs on p169

**Antimuscarinic drugs** Block the transmission of impulses along parts of the nervous system. Used to treat asthma, irritable bowel syndrome, Parkinson's disease and other conditions.
◇ Atropine; Hyoscine; Ipratropium; Benzhexol; Orphenadrine; Dicyclomine.

**Anticoagulant drugs** Used both to prevent and to treat strokes or heart attacks by stopping the abnormal formation of blood clots.
◇ Heparin; Warfarin; Phenindione.

**Antidiarrhoeal drugs** Used to make faeces more bulky, or to slow down gut mobility.
◇ Codeine; Kaolin; Co-phenotrope; Loperamide.

**Antiemetic drugs** Used to treat vomiting and nausea.
◇ Chlorpromazine; Metoclopramide; Cinnarizine; Prochlorperazine; Dimenhydrinate; Promethazine; Hyoscine; Thiethylperazine.

**Antifungal drugs** Used to treat fungal infections including thrush, ringworm and athlete's foot.
◇ Amphotericin B; Ketoconazole; Clotrimazole; Miconazole; Econazole; Nystatin; Flucytosine; Tolnaftate; Griseofulvin.

**Antihistamine drugs** Used to treat allergic reactions such as hayfever and urticaria.
◊ Astemizole; Promethazine; Azatadine; Terfenadine; Chlorpheniramine; Trimeprazine; Triprolidine.

**Antihypertensive drugs** Used to treat high blood pressure to reduce the risk of heart failure or stroke.
◊ Atenolol; Hydrochlorothiazide; Captopril; Methyldopa; Clonidine; Minoxidil; Chlorthalidone; Nifedipine; Cyclopenthiazide; Oxprenolol; Diltiazem; Prazosin; Enalapril; Propanolol; Hydralazine; Verapamil.

**Antirheumatic drugs** Used to treat rheumatoid arthritis.
◊ Azathioprine; Gold; Chlorambucil; Penicillamine; Chloroquine; Prednisolone; Dexamethasone.

**Antispasmodic drugs** Used to control spasms in the wall of the bladder (causing irritable bladder) or intestine (causing irritable bowel syndrome).
◊ Dicyclomine; Peppermint oil; Hyoscine.

**Antiviral drugs** Used to treat infections caused by viruses.
◊ Acyclovir; Inosine pranobex; Amantadine; Zidovudine; Idoxuridine.

**Beta-blocker drugs** Used to reduce heart rate in treating anxiety, high blood pressure and angina.
◊ Acebutolol; Oxprenolol; Atenolol; Pindolol; Metoprolol; Propanolol; Nadolol.

**Bronchodilator drugs** Widen the airways to the lungs. Used to treat asthma and bronchitis.
◊ Aminophylline; Rimiterol; Fenoterol; Salbutamol; Terbutaline; Pirbuterol; Theophylline; Reproterol.

**Calcium channel blocker drugs** Used to treat irregular heartbeat, high blood pressure and angina by reducing the workload of the heart.
◊ Diltiazem; Verapamil; Nifedipine.

**Corticosteroid drugs** Wide-ranging uses include the treatment of rheumatoid arthritis, eczema and asthma, and Crohn's disease.
◊ Beclomethasone; Fludrocortisone; Betamethasone; Hydrocortisone; Cortisone; Prednisolone; Dexamethasone; Prednisone.

**Diuretic drugs** Used to treat high blood pressure and oedema (fluid retention) by increasing the amount of water lost from the body in urine.
◊ Amiloride; Cyclopenthiazide; Bendrofluazide; Frusemide; Bumetanide; Spironolactone; Chlorothiazide; Triamterene; Chlorthalidone.

**Hypoglycaemic drugs (oral)** Used to lower levels of glucose in the blood to normal levels in patients with one form of diabetes (type 2).
◊ Chlorpropamide; Glipizide; Glibenclamide; Tolazamide; Gliclazide; Tolbutamide.

**Immunosuppressant drugs** Used to suppress activity of the immune system so that it does not cause the rejection of a recently transplanted organ.
◊ Antilymphocyte Immunoglobulin; Cyclosporin; Methotrexate; Azathioprine; Prednisolone; Chlorambucil; Cyclophosphamide.

**NSAID (non-steroidal anti-inflammatory drugs)** Used to relieve pain and inflammation of joints in patients suffering from arthritis.
◊ Diclofenac; Indomethacin; Diflunisal; Ketoprofen; Fenbufen; Mefenamic acid; Fenoprofen; Naproxen; Flurbiprofen; Prioxicam; Ibuprofen.

**Oral contraceptive drugs** Used by women to prevent conception by stopping the release of eggs from the ovaries or thickening the mucus to block entry of sperm into the uterus.
◊ Ethinyloestradiol; Mestranol; Gestodene; Norethisterone; Levonorgestrel.

**Thrombolytic drugs** Used to dissolve blood clots in cases of heart attack or stroke.
◊ Anistreplase; Streptokinase.

## Common illegal drugs

| Type | Name | How taken | Major effects | Hazards associated with abuse |
|---|---|---|---|---|
| **Depressants** | Barbiturates — 'downers': amytal, nembutal, seconal | Taken orally or injected | Euphoria, tiredness, reduction in anxiety, slurred speech, slowed breathing and heart rate, confusion. | Dependence, tolerance; combination with alcohol may cause death. |
| **Narcotic analgesics** | Heroin | Sniffed, smoked or injected | Euphoria, reduction in pain, slurred speech, tiredness, loss of self-control, mood swings. | Dependence, tolerance; risk of overdose, or poisoning if heroin is impure; risk of HIV or hepatitis from needle sharing. |
| **Psychedelics/ hallucinogens** | Cannabis | Smoked or taken in food or tea | Euphoria, altered perception of time and sensory phenomena, hunger. | Long-term use may cause paranoia and anxiety in vulnerable users. |
| | Lysergic acid diethylamide (LSD) | Taken orally | Distortion of auditory and visual imagery, hallucinations, increased/ distorted feelings of sensory awareness, unpredictable behaviour. | Paranoia, flashbacks — recurrence of hallucinatory events without taking drug; possible long-term psychological damage. |
| **Solvents** | Various adhesives, cleaning fluid | Sniffed | Confusion, feeling of well-being, giddiness. | Brain, liver and kidney damage; may cause heart failure and sometimes death. |
| **Stimulants** | Amphetamines — 'uppers': benzedrine, dexedrine, methedrine | Taken orally, sniffed, injected or smoked | Feeling of self-confidence, hyperactivity, excitement, restlessness, racing pulse; often followed by depression. | Dependence, tolerance, paranoia, violent behaviour, weight loss, hallucinations; death from overdose. |
| | Cocaine | Sniffed, smoked or injected | Temporary feeling of euphoria and self-confidence, appetite loss, increased heart rate; often followed by anxiety, agitation, depression. | Long-term use may cause mental impairment, hallucinations, damage to nasal passages; risk of seizures or death from overdose. |
| | Crack cocaine | Smoked | Intense feelings of power and euphoria last for five minutes, followed by a 'crash' and a deep craving for another crack 'hit'. | Paranoia, violent behaviour, suicidal feelings, loss of sex drive, possible death from heart attack. |
| | MDMA — 'Ecstasy' | Taken orally | Mood elevation, increased energy, euphoria. | Severe dehydration, slight possibility of sudden death. |

## Psychotherapeutic drugs

These are used in the treatment of mental disorders, and can be very effective in the alleviation of both long- and short-term symptoms, though some carry risk of dependence.

| Drug class | Reasons for use | Drug names | How they work | Possible risks |
|---|---|---|---|---|
| Antianxiety drugs | To reduce feelings of tension, nervousness and anxiety if they interfere with a person's ability to cope with everyday life. | **Benzodiazepines**: Alprazolam, Chlordiazepoxide, Diazepam, Oxazepam | Depress action of the central nervous system, promoting drowsiness and relaxation. | Drug dependence and severe withdrawal symptoms; dizziness; drowsiness; impaired concentration. |
| | | **Beta-blockers**: Nadolol, Oxprenolol, Pindolol, Propranolol | Block nerve endings, stopping release of neurotransmitters, so reducing tremor, palpitations and sweating. | Breathing difficulties, cold hands and feet, tiredness, reduced capacity for strenuous exercise. |
| Antidepressant drugs | To treat serious depression by stimulating the nervous system to elevate the mood of the depressed individual. | **Selective serotonin re-uptake inhibitors (SSRIs)**: Fluroxetine (Prozac), Paroxetine (Seroxat), Fluroamine (Faverin) | Elevate level of the neurotransmitter serotonin, so stimulating brain cell activity; also used in the treatment of the eating disorder bulimia nervosa. | Nausea, nervousness, weight loss (rarely), insomnia, headache; known as the 'cleanest' of the anti-depressants, SSRIs are favoured for having relatively few side effects. |
| | | **Tricyclics**: Amitriptyline, Clomipramine, Dothiepin, Imipramine, Mianserin, Trazodone | Both tricyclics and MAOIs elevate the levels of two neurotransmitters — serotonin and noradrenalin — in the brain, so stimulating brain cell activity. | Weight gain, blurred vision, dry mouth, dizziness, drowsiness, constipation; overdose may cause coma or even death. |
| | | **Monoamine oxidase inhibitors (MAOIs)**: Isocarboxazid, Phenelzine, Tranylcypromine | | MAOIs can cause dangerously high blood pressure if taken with food containing tyramine: red wine, beer, cheese, pickles. |
| Antipsychotic drugs (major tranquillizers) | To treat abnormal behaviour shown by patients with psychotic disorders involving loss of contact with reality, particularly schizophrenia. | **Phenothiazines**: Chlorpromazine, Fluophenazine, Perphenazine, Thioridazine, Trifluoperazine<br>**Butyrophenones**: Haloperidol | Antipsychotic drugs block the action of the neurotransmitter dopamine, so inhibiting nerve activity in the brain. | Blurred vision, dry mouth, urine retention, drowsiness, lethargy, jerky movements of the mouth and face, involuntary movements of the limbs. |
| Other drugs | | **Lithium** | Used to treat manic depression; acts on brain neurotransmitters to reduce extreme mood swings. | Dry mouth; overdose may cause blurred vision, twitching, vomiting. |

## Immunization schedule for children up to age 18

| Age | Vaccine | How given |
|---|---|---|
| 2 months | Diphtheria, whooping cough (pertussis), tetanus | Combined DPT injection |
| | Polio | By mouth |
| 4 months | Diphtheria, whooping cough (pertussis), tetanus | Combined DPT injection |
| | Polio | By mouth |
| 6 months | Diphtheria, whooping cough (pertussis), tetanus | Combined DPT injection |
| | Polio | By mouth |
| 1–2 years | Measles, mumps, rubella (German measles) | Combined MMR injection |
| 4–5 years | Diphtheria and tetanus boosters | Combined injection |
| | Polio booster | By mouth |
| 10–13 years | BCG (tuberculosis) | Injection |
| 13–14 years | German measles (for girls who did not have the MMR injection at 12–24 months) | Injection |
| 16–18 years | Tetanus booster | Injection |
| | Polio booster | By mouth |

## Immunization for foreign travel

Immunization is recommended for travellers of all ages who are visiting countries where there is a chance of contracting serious or potentially fatal diseases. Travellers should check which immunizations are required for their destinations, and whether they require immunization certificates.

| Disease | Area where immunization needed | Effective for | Level of protection[1] |
|---|---|---|---|
| Cholera | Immunization no longer required by WHO but some countries still require evidence of vaccination. Check with embassy prior to travel. | 6 months | M |
| Hepatitis A | Countries with poor hygiene and sanitation. | 1 or 10 years | M |
| Meningococcal meningitis | For areas recommended by your doctor. | 3–5 years | H |
| Polio | For all areas, if no recent booster received. | 10 years | H |
| Rabies | Vaccine not recommended as routine. | 1–3 years | H |
| Tetanus | For all areas, if no recent booster received. | 10 years | H |
| Tuberculosis | For areas recommended by your doctor. | over 15 years | H |
| Typhoid fever | Countries with poor hygiene and sanitation. | 10 years | M |
| Yellow fever | Some African and South American countries. | 10 years | H |

[1] M = provides moderate level of protection; H = provides high level of protection.

## Measuring your Body Mass Index

Body Mass Index (BMI) gives an accurate measure of obesity. In order to determine your BMI, find out your height in metres and weight in kilograms. To convert height in inches to metres, multiply the number of inches by 0.0254; to convert weight in pounds to kilos, multiply the number of pounds by 0.4536.

$$\textbf{BMI} = \frac{\textbf{weight (kg)}}{\textbf{height (m)} \times \textbf{height (m)}}$$

BMI values:

Less than 18 – underweight

18 to 25 – in the ideal weight range

25 to 30 – overweight

Over 30 – obese; endangering health

## Optimum weight according to height

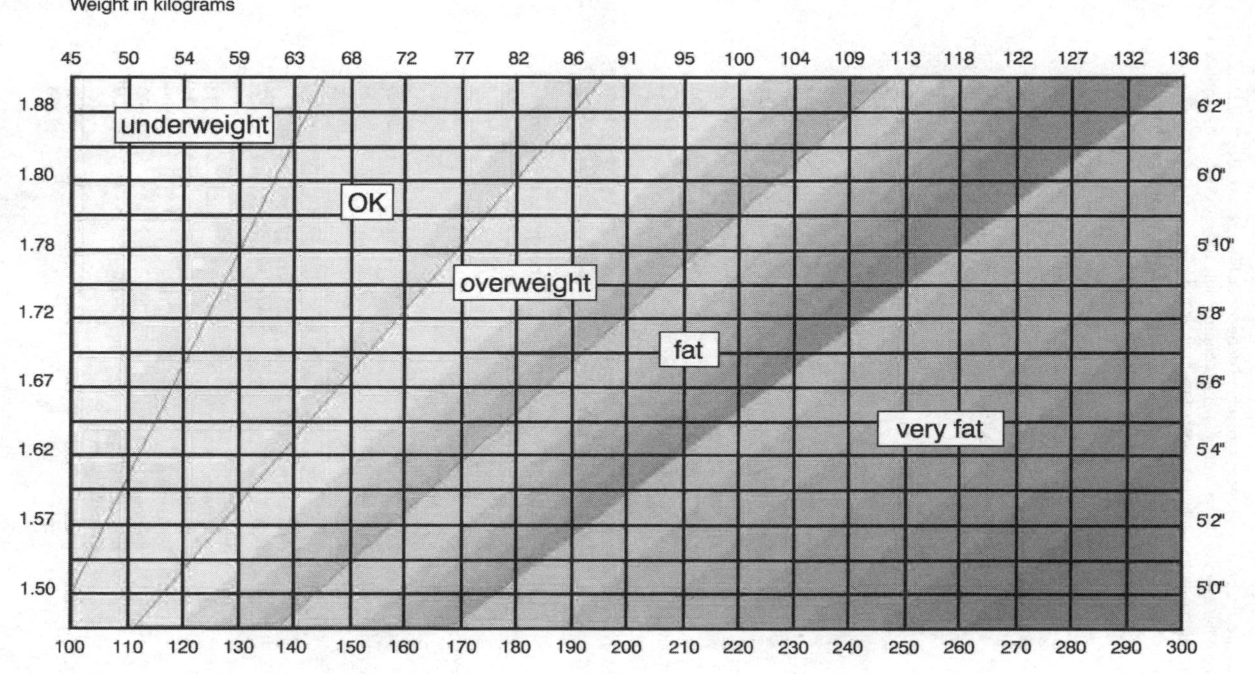

## Energy expenditure

During exercise, the amount of energy consumed depends on the age, sex, size and fitness of the individual, and how vigorous the exercise is. This table shows the approximate energy used up by a person of average size and fitness carrying out certain activities over a one-hour period.

| Activity | Energy used per hour kcals[1] | kJ[1] |
|---|---|---|
| Badminton | 340 | 1428 |
| Climbing stairs | 620 | 2604 |
| Cycling | 660 | 2772 |
| Football | 540 | 2268 |
| Gardening, heavy | 420 | 1764 |
| Gardening, light | 270 | 1134 |
| Golf | 270 | 1134 |
| Gymnastics | 420 | 1764 |
| Hockey | 540 | 2268 |
| Housework | 270 | 1134 |
| Jogging | 630 | 2646 |
| Rugby | 540 | 2268 |
| Squash | 600 | 2520 |
| Standing | 120 | 504 |
| Staying in bed | 60 | 252 |
| Swimming | 720 | 3024 |
| Tennis | 480 | 2016 |
| Walking, brisk | 300 | 1260 |
| Walking, easy | 180 | 756 |

[1] kcals = kilocalories; kJ =kilojoules.

## Average daily energy requirements

| CHILDREN Age | Energy used per day kcals[1] | kJ[1] |
|---|---|---|
| 0–3 months | 550 | 2300 |
| 3–6 months | 760 | 3200 |
| 6–9 months | 905 | 3800 |
| 9–12 months | 1000 | 4200 |
| 8 years | 2095 | 8800 |
| 15 years (female) | 2285 | 9600 |
| 15 years (male) | 3000 | 12600 |

| ADULT FEMALES Age | Energy used per day kcals[1] | kJ[1] |
|---|---|---|
| **18–55 years** | | |
| Inactive | 1900 | 7980 |
| Active | 2150 | 9030 |
| Very active | 2500 | 10500 |
| Pregnant | 2380 | 10000 |
| Breastfeeding | 2690 | 11300 |
| **Over 56 years** | | |
| Inactive | 1700 | 7140 |
| Active | 2000 | 8400 |

| ADULT MALES Age | Energy used per day kcals[1] | kJ[1] |
|---|---|---|
| **18–35 years** | | |
| Inactive | 2 500 | 10 500 |
| Active | 3 000 | 12 600 |
| Very active | 3 500 | 14 700 |
| **36–55 years** | | |
| Inactive | 2 400 | 10 080 |
| Active | 2 800 | 11 760 |
| Very active | 3 400 | 14 280 |
| **Over 56 years** | | |
| Inactive | 2 200 | 9 240 |
| Active | 2 500 | 10 500 |

[1] kcals = kilocalories; kJ = kilojoules.

## Dietary recommendations

### ❑ Dietary recommendations to protect the heart

Eat less fat, especially saturated fats.
Avoid sugary and processed foods.
Avoid obesity.
Eat plenty of fibre-rich foods.
Cut down on salt — too much salt can increase your blood pressure.

### ❑ Dietary recommendations to reduce cancer risks

Eat foods rich in fibre daily: these help to prevent bowel and colon cancers.
Eat fresh fruit and vegetables daily: these are rich in fibre and vitamins.
Eat less fat. There seems to be a close correlation between fat consumption and breast cancer.
Consume alcohol only in moderation. Excessive alcohol intake has been linked to cancers of the bowel, liver, mouth, oesophagus, stomach and throat, especially in smokers.
Eat fewer smoked and salted foods. High consumption of salt-cured meat and fish and nitrate-cured meat has been linked to throat and stomach cancers. There is also a link between eating pickled foods and stomach cancer.
Keep body weight at recommended level.

### ❑ Dietary recommendations to lose weight

To be healthy, a diet designed to reduce body weight needs to be in tune with the body's physiology. An effective diet should promote the loss of fatty, or adipose, tissue from the body so that its overall fat content is reduced. To do this successfully, the dieter should eat a well-balanced, high-carbohydrate, high-fibre, low-fat diet with an energy content of between 1 200 and 1 500 calories per day, combining this with regular exercise. Foods that can be consumed in this kind of low-calorie diet are shown (*below*) as Type A and Type B foods; Type C foods should be avoided, and fat-containing Type B foods, such as meat, should be eaten in moderation.

### ❑ Dieting tips

Reduce alcohol intake to a minimum.
Avoid convenience foods because many contain 'hidden' fats and sugar.
Exercise at least three times a week.
Remove fat from meat, and fatty skin from poultry.
Avoid frying food — bake, grill, microwave or steam instead.
Avoid mayonnaise and rich sauces.
If you overeat, work out why you do it (eg through boredom or depression) and find other ways of relieving these feelings.
Plan meals for the next day the night before, or early in the morning, to avoid impulse eating of high-calorie foods.
Use a smaller plate to make smaller helpings look larger than they really are.
Eat regularly. Do not miss meals but try to eat 3–5 small meals each day.
Avoid second helpings.
Avoid between-meal snacks, except for raw fruit and vegetables if very hungry.
Eat at a table rather than eg in front of the television, which may encourage you to eat more and faster.
Take more time when eating — chew well.

**Type A foods**

**Vegetarian foods**
Cereals (unsweetened)
Fruits — all except avocados
Vegetables — all, including potatoes
Vegetable protein, eg tofu
Wholemeal bread

**Meat, fish and dairy foods**
Chicken and other poultry (not duck) with skin removed
Cod, haddock and other non-oily fish
Mussels and other shellfish
Salmon (if tinned, in brine or water)
Tuna (if tinned, in brine or water)
Yoghurt (plain, low fat)

**Type B foods**

**Vegetarian foods**
Dried fruit
Margarine, polyunsaturated
Nuts, except peanuts
Pasta, especially wholewheat
Pulses, such as beans and lentils
Rice, especially wholegrain
Vegetable oils

**Meat, fish and dairy foods**
Beef, lean cuts
Eggs
Lamb, lean cuts
Oily fish such as herring or mackerel
Pork, lean cuts
Sardines (if tinned, in brine)

**Type C foods**

**Meat, fish and dairy foods**
Bacon
Beef, fatty cuts
Butter
Cheeses, apart from low-fat
Duck
Fish, fried
Ice cream
Lamb, fatty cuts
Mayonnaise
Milk, full cream
Pâté
Pork, fatty cuts
Salami
Sausages

**Convenience foods**
Biscuits
Burgers
Cakes
Chips
Chocolate
Crisps

## Culinary terms of foreign origin

**aïoli** a garlic-flavoured mayonnaise. [French; from Provençal *ai*, garlic]

**à la carte** said of a meal in a restaurant, with each dish priced and ordered separately. [French, = from the menu]

**à la mode** said of beef, larded and stewed with vegetables; said of desserts, served with ice cream (North American). [French, = in fashion]

**al dente** said of pasta and vegetables, cooked so as to remain firm when bitten. [Italian, = to the tooth]

**antipasto** (*plural* **antipasti**, **antipastos**) food served at the beginning of a meal to sharpen the appetite. [Italian]

**aperitif** an alcoholic drink taken before a meal to stimulate the appetite. [from French *apéritif*; from Latin *aperire*, to open]

**aqua vitae** a strong alcoholic drink, especially brandy. [Latin, = water of life]

**au gratin** covered with breadcrumbs and/or grated cheese, cooked in the oven and/or browned under the grill, so that a crisp, golden topping is formed. [French, = literally 'with the burnt scrapings'; from *gratter*, to scrape]

**au naturel** cooked plainly, or uncooked; served without dressing. [French, = in the natural state]

**bain-marie** a vessel of hot or boiling water into which a container of food can be cooked gently or kept warm. [French, = bath of Mary; from Latin *balneum Mariae*; origin uncertain, perhaps from Mary, or Miriam, sister of Moses, who reputedly wrote a book on alchemy]

**baklava** or **baclava** a rich cake of Middle Eastern origin made of layers of flaky pastry with a filling of honey, nuts and spices. [Turkish]

**balti** 1 a style of Indian cooking originating in Britain, in which food is both cooked and served in a pan resembling a wok. **2** the pan in which this is cooked. [Hindi, = bucket]

**béarnaise (sauce)** a rich sauce made from egg yolks, butter, shallots, tarragon, chervil and wine vinegar. [French; after *Bearn*, a region in SW France]

**béchamel (sauce)** a white sauce flavoured with onion and herbs and sometimes enriched with cream. [French; named after the Marquis de Béchamel (d.1703), a French courtier who attended Louis XIV]

**bhaji** an Indian appetizer of vegetables, chickpea flour, and spices, formed into a ball and deep-fried. [Hindi]

**biriani** or **biryani** (*plural* **birianis** or **biryanis**) a type of spicy Indian dish consisting mainly of rice, with meat or fish and vegetables, etc. [Urdu]

**bisque** a thick rich soup, usually made from shellfish, cream, and wine. [French]

**blanch** 1 to prepare (vegetables or meat) for cooking or freezing by boiling in water for a short time. 2 to remove the skins (from almonds, etc) by soaking them in boiling water. [from Old French *blanchir*]

**blancmange** a cold sweet jelly-like pudding made with milk. [from Old French *blanc*, white + *manger*, food]

**blanquette** a dish made with white meat such as chicken or veal, cooked in a white sauce. [from French *blanquette* (related to English blanket); from Old French *blankete*; from *blanc*, white]

**Bolognese** said especially of pasta, served with a tomato and meat sauce, usually also containing mushrooms, garlic, etc. [named after Bologna in N Italy]

**bombe** a dessert, usually ice cream, frozen in a round or melon-shaped mould. [French, = bomb]

**bonne femme** said of a dish, eg sole bonne femme, cooked simply and garnished with fresh vegetables and herbs. [from French *à la bonne femme*, in the manner of a good wife]

**bouillabaisse** a thick spicy fish soup from Provence. [French]

**bouillon** a thin clear soup made by boiling meat and vegetables in water, often used as a basis for thicker soups. [French; from *bouillir*, to boil]

**bouquet garni** a bunch or small packet of mixed herbs used to add flavour to food, usually removed before serving. [from French *bouquet* + *garnir*, to garnish]

**bourguignon** said of meat dishes, stewed with onion, mushrooms and Burgundy wine. [French, = Burgundian]

**braise** to cook (meat, etc) slowly with a small amount of liquid in a closed dish. [from French *braiser*, from *braise*, live coals]

**brochette** a small metal or wooden skewer for holding food together or steady while it is being cooked. [French; a diminutive of *broche*, brooch or needle]

**brioche** a type of bread-like cake made with a yeast dough, eggs, and butter. [French]

**brûlé** usually said of a dessert, having brown sugar on top and cooked so that the sugar melts. [French, = burnt]

**cacciatore** or **cacciatora** said of meat, especially chicken or veal, cooked with tomatoes, mushrooms, onions and herbs. [Italian, = hunter]

**calamari** *plural noun* squid. [Italian, plural of *calamaro*, squid]

**calzone** a folded round of pizza dough stuffed with a savoury filling. [Italian, = trouser leg]

**canapé** a type of food served at parties, etc consisting of a small piece of bread or toast spread or topped with something savoury. [French, = sofa]

**cannelloni** a kind of pasta in the form of large tubes, served with a filling of meat, cheese, etc. [Italian; from *cannello*, tube]

**cappuccino** (*plural* **cappuccinos**) coffee with frothy hot milk and usually chocolate powder on top. [Italian]

**ceviche** (Mexican cookery) raw fish marinated in lime juice and served as an hors d'oeuvre. [American Spanish]

**chapati** or **chapatti** in Indian cooking, a thin flat portion of unleavened bread. [from Hindi *capati*]

**chasseur** said of a sauce or food cooked in a sauce containing mushrooms, shallots, white wine and herbs. [French, = hunter]

**Chateaubriand** or **chateaubriand** a thick steak cut from grilled fillet of beef, usually served with fried potatoes and mushrooms. [named after François René, Vicomte de Chateaubriand (1768–1848), French author and statesman]

**chiffon** a light frothy mixture, made with beaten whites of eggs. [French, = rag]

**choux pastry** a very light pastry made with eggs. [from French *pâte choux*, cabbage pastry]

**ciabatta** Italian bread with a sponge-like texture, made with olive oil. [Italian, = slipper]

**consommé** thin clear soup made from meat stock. [French; from *consommer*, to eat, consume]

**cordon bleu** *noun* (*plural* **cordons bleus**) a cook of the highest standard; *adjective* said of a cook or cookery, being of the highest standard. [French, = blue ribbon]

**coupe** a dessert made with fruit and ice cream. [French, = glass, cup]

**couscous** a N African dish of crushed wheat steamed and served eg with meat. [French; from Arabic *kuskus*]

**crème fraîche** cream thickened with a culture of bacteria, used in cooking. [French, = fresh cream]

**crème** 1 cream, or a creamy food. 2 a liqueur. [French, = cream]

**crêpe** or **crepe** a thin pancake. [French; from Latin *crispus*, crisp]

**croissant** a crescent-shaped bread roll, made with a high proportion of fat, and flaky in consistency. [French, = crescent]

**croquante** a crisp pie or tart; a crisp cake containing almonds. [French]

**croquette** a ball or roll of eg minced meat, fish, or potato, coated in breadcrumbs and fried. [French; from *croquer*, to crunch]

**croûte** a thick slice of fried bread for serving entrées (► **en croûte**). [French, = crust]

**croûton** a small cube of fried or toasted bread, served in soup, salads etc. [French; a diminutive of *croûte*, crust]

**dal** or **dahl** or **dhal** 1 any of various edible dried split pea-like seeds. **2** a cooked dish made of any of these seeds. [from Hindi *dal*, to split]

**doner kebab** thin slices cut from a block of minced and seasoned lamb grilled on a spit and eaten on unleavened bread. [from Turkish *döner*, rotating]

**enchilada** (*plural* **enchiladas**) a Mexican dish consisting of a flour tortilla with a meat filling, served with a chilli-flavoured sauce. [from Spanish *enchilar*, to season with chilli]

**en croûte** wrapped in pastry and baked. [from French *croûte*, crust]

**entrecôte** a boneless steak cut from between two ribs. [French; from *entre*, between + *côte*, rib]

**entrée** 1 a small dish served after the fish course and before the main course at a formal dinner. **2** (chiefly US) a main course. [French, = entrance]

**escalope** a thin slice of boneless meat, especially veal. [French]

**espresso** (*plural* **espressos**) **1** coffee made by forcing steam or boiling water through ground coffee beans. **2** the machine for making it. [Italian, = pressed out]

**farce** stuffing or force-meat. [French]

**farci** stuffed. [from French *farce*, stuffing; from Latin *farcire*, to stuff]

**fettuccine** pasta in the form of flat wide ribbons. [Italian, a diminutive (plural) of *fettuccia*, tape]

**fines herbes** *plural noun* a mixture of herbs for use in cooking. [French, = fine herbs]

**flambé** *adjective* said of food, soaked in brandy and set alight before serving; *verb* (**flambéed, flambéing**) to serve (food) in this way. [from French *flamber*, to expose to flame]

**florentine** *adjective* containing or served with spinach, eg eggs florentine; *noun* a biscuit on a chocolate base covered on one side with preserved fruit and nuts. [from Latin *Florentinus*, from *Florentia* (Florence)]

**focaccia** a flat round of Italian bread topped with olive oil and herbs or spices. [Italian, = cake]

**fondue** 1 a Swiss dish of hot cheese sauce into which bits of bread are dipped. **2** a steak dish (also called **fondue bourguignonne**), the pieces of meat being cooked at the table by dipping them briefly into hot oil or stock. [French; from *fondre*, to melt]

**frankfurter** a type of spicy smoked sausage. [from German *Frankfurter Wurst*, Frankfurt sausage]

**fricassee** a cooked dish usually of pieces of meat or chicken served in a sauce. [from Old French *fricasser*, to cook chopped food in its own juice]

**fromage frais** a creamy low-fat cheese with the consistency of whipped cream. [French, = fresh cheese]

**fusilli** pasta shaped into short thick spirals. [Italian]

**galantine** a dish of boneless cooked white meat or fish served cold in jelly. [Old French]

**garam masala** a mixture of ground spices used to make curry. [Hindi, = hot mixture]

**garni** trimmed, garnished. [French; from *garnir*, to garnish]

**gateau** or **gâteau** (*plural* **gateaux, gateaus, gâteaux**) a large rich cake, especially filled with cream and decorated with fruit, nuts, etc. [French]

**ghee** butter made from cow's or buffalo's milk, purified by heating, used in Indian cooking. [from Hindi *ghi*]

**glacé** *adjective* **1** coated with a sugary glaze; candied: eg glacé cherries. **2** said of icing on cakes etc, made with icing sugar and liquid. **3** said of drinks etc, frozen or served with ice, eg mousse glacée; *verb* (**glacéed, glacéing**) **1** to crystallize fruit etc. **2** to ice cakes etc with glacé icing. [French]

**gnocchi** an Italian dish of small dumplings made with flour, cooked potato, or semolina, poached and served with various sauces. [Italian, = lumps]

**gougère** a kind of choux pastry that has grated cheese added to it before baking. [French]

**goujons** small strips of fish or chicken coated in seasoned flour, egg and breadcrumbs, and deep-fried. [from French *goujon*, gudgeon (the fish)]

**gratin** the golden brown crust covering a gratinated food or dish; ► **au gratin.**

**gratinate** to cook with a topping of buttered breadcrumbs and/or cheese browned until crisp; to cook au gratin; ► **au gratin**. [from French *gratiner*, to cook au gratin]

**gratiné** cooked or served au gratin; ► **au gratin**. [from French *gratiner*, to cook au gratin]

**gremolata** a colourful, flavoursome garnish, made of chopped parsley, lemon or orange peel, garlic, etc. [Italian]

**haute cuisine** cookery (especially French) of a very high standard. [French, = high cooking]

**hors d'oeuvre** a savoury appetiser served at the beginning of a meal. [French, = out of the work]

**hummus** or **hoummos** or **houmus** a Middle Eastern hors d'oeuvre or dip consisting of pureed cooked chickpeas and tahini paste, flavoured with lemon juice and garlic. [from Turkish *humus*]

**jardinière** an accompaniment of mixed vegetables for a meat dish. [from French *jardinière*, feminine of *jardinier*, gardener]

**jus** juice; gravy. [French]

**kofta** (*plural* **koftas**) (Indian cookery) minced and seasoned meat or vegetables, shaped into balls and fried. [Hindi, = pounded meat]

**lasagne** pasta in the form of thin flat sheets, often cooked in layers with a mixture of meat and tomatoes, and a cheese sauce. [Italian]

**lyonnaise** made with sautéed sliced potatoes and onions or potatoes in an onion sauce. [named after Lyon, France]

**macaroni** (*plural* **macaronis, macaronies**) pasta in the form of short tubes. [from Italian *maccaroni*]

**mascarpone** a soft Italian cream cheese. [Italian]

**mayonnaise** a cold creamy sauce made of egg yolk, oil, vinegar or lemon juice, and seasoning. [French]

**meringue** a crisp cooked mixture of sugar and egg whites, or a cake made from this. [French]

**mesclun** a mixed green salad of young leaves and shoots of rocket, chicory, fennel, etc. [French; from Niçois *mesclumo*, mixture]

**minestrone** thick soup containing vegetables and pasta. [Italian; from *minestrare*, to serve]

**moussaka** a dish made with minced meat, aubergines, onions, tomatoes, etc, covered with a cheese sauce and baked, traditionally eaten in Greece, Turkey and the Balkans. [Greek]

**mousse** **1** a dessert made from a whipped mixture of cream, eggs and flavouring, eaten cold. **2** a similar meat or fish dish. [French, = froth]

**mozzarella** a soft white Italian cheese, especially used as a topping for pizza. [Italian]

**muesli** a mixture of crushed grain, nuts and dried fruit, eaten with milk, especially for breakfast. [Swiss German]

**mulligatawny** a thick curry-flavoured meat soup, originally made in E India. [from Tamil *milagu-tannir*, pepper-water]

**nan** a slightly leavened Indian bread, similar to pitta bread. [Hindi]

**navarin** a stew of lamb or mutton with root vegetables such as turnip. [French]

**nougat** a chewy sweet containing nuts, etc. [French; from Latin *nux*, nut]

**nouvelle cuisine** a simple style of cookery characterized by much use of fresh produce and elegant presentation. [French, = new cookery]

**omelette** (*especially US* **omelet**) a dish of beaten eggs fried in a pan, often folded round a savoury or sweet filling such as cheese or jam. [from Old French *alemette*; from *lemelle*, knife-blade]

**paella** a Spanish dish of rice, fish, or chicken, vegetables and saffron. [Catalan; from Latin *patella*, pan]

**pakora** an Indian dish of chopped spiced vegetables formed into balls, coated in batter, and deep-fried. [Hindi]

**papillote** **1** frilled paper used to decorate the bones of chops, etc. **2** oiled or greased paper in which meat is cooked and served. [French, apparently from *papillon*, butterfly; from Latin *papilio, -onis*]

**Parmesan** a hard dry Italian cheese, especially served grated with pasta dishes. [from Italian *Parmegiano*, from Parma]

**passata** an Italian sauce of puréed and sieved tomatoes. [Italian, = passed (ie through a sieve)]

**pasta** **1** a dough made with flour, water, and eggs shaped in a variety of forms such as spaghetti, macaroni, lasagne, etc. **2** a cooked dish of this, usually with a sauce. [Italian; from Latin *pasta*, paste, dough; from Greek *pasta*, barley porridge]

**pâté** a spread made from ground or chopped meat, fish or vegetables blended with herbs, spices, etc. [French; formerly meaning pie or pasty]

**patisserie** a shop selling fancy cakes, sweet pastries, etc. [from French *pâtisserie*; from Latin *pasta*, dough]

**pesto** an Italian sauce originating in Liguria and made from fresh basil leaves, pine kernels, olive oil, garlic and Parmesan cheese. [Italian; from *pestare*, to crush, pound]

**petit four** (*plural* **petits fours**) a small sweet biscuit, usually decorated with icing. [French, = little oven]

**pilaf** or **pilaff** or **pilau** an oriental dish of spiced rice with chicken, fish, etc. [from Turkish *pilaw*]

**pizza** a circle of dough spread with cheese, tomatoes, etc and baked, made originally in Italy. [Italian]

**polenta** an Italian dish of cooked ground maize. [Italian; from Latin *polenta*, hulled and crushed grain]

**poppadum** or **poppadom** a paper-thin pancake grilled till crisp for serving with Indian dishes. [Tamil]

**praline** a sweet consisting of nuts in caramelized sugar. [named after Marshal Duplessis-Praslin (1598–1675), a French soldier whose cook invented it]

**pretzel** a salted and glazed biscuit in the shape of a knot. [German]

**profiterole** a small sweet or savoury confection of choux pastry. [French; said to be a diminutive from *profiter*, to profit]

**prosciutto** finely cured uncooked ham, often smoked. [Italian = pre-dried]

**provençale** a style of cookery that traditionally uses olive oil, tomatoes, onion, garlic and white wine, eg eggs à la provençale, and, in meat dishes, requires slow-cooking the beef, etc. [named after the area of Provence, SE France]

**pumpernickel** a dark heavy coarse rye bread, eaten especially in Germany. [German, = lout, perhaps literally 'stink-devil' or 'fart-devil']

**purée** *noun* a quantity of fruit or vegetables reduced to a pulp by liquidising or rubbing through a sieve; *verb* (**purées, puréed**) to reduce to a purée. [from French *purer*, to strain]

**puri** a small cake of unleavened Indian bread, deep-fried and served hot. [Hindi]

**quenelle** a dumpling of fish, chicken, veal, etc. [French]

**quesadilla** (Mexican cookery) a tortilla filled with cheese, chillis, etc, folded and fried or grilled. [Mexican Spanish; diminutive of *queseda*; from *quese*, cheese]

**quiche** a tart with a savoury filling usually made with eggs. [French; from German *Kuchen*, cake]

**ragout** a highly seasoned stew of meat and vegetables. [from French *ragoût*]

**ramekin** **1** a small baking dish for a single serving of food. **2** an individual serving of food, especially of a savoury dish containing cheese and eggs, served in a ramekin. [from French *ramequin*]

**ratafia** **1** a flavouring essence made with the essential oil of almonds. **2** a cordial or liqueur flavoured with fruit kernels and almonds. **3** an almond-flavoured biscuit or small cake. [French; probably from Creole or *tafia*, a type of rum]

**ratatouille** a southern French stew made with tomatoes, peppers, courgettes, aubergines, onions, and garlic. [French]

**ravioli** *plural noun* small, square pasta cases with a savoury filling of meat, cheese, etc. [Italian]

**risotto** (*plural* **risottos**) an Italian dish of rice cooked in a meat or seafood stock with onions, tomatoes, cheese, etc. [from Italian *riso*, rice]

**roti** (*plural* **rotis**) **1** a cake of unleavened bread, traditionally made in parts of India and the Caribbean. **2** a kind of sandwich made of this wrapped around curried vegetables, seafood, or chicken. [Hindi, = bread]

**roulade** meat, cake or soufflé mixture served rolled up, usually with a filling. [French]

**roux** (*plural* **roux**) a cooked mixture of flour and fat, used to thicken sauces. [from French *beurre roux*, brown butter]

**rugelach** or **ruggelach** *plural noun* (Jewish cookery) small, crescent-shaped pastries filled with fruit, nuts, cheese, etc. [from Yiddish *rugelekh*, plural of *rugele*]

**salami** (*plural* **salamis**) a highly seasoned type of sausage, usually served sliced. [Italian]

**salsa** (Mexican cookery) a spicy sauce made with tomatoes, onions, chillies and oil. [Spanish and Italian *salsa*, sauce]

**salsa verde** Italian green sauce, made with anchovies, garlic, capers, oil and herbs. [Spanish and Italian *salsa*, sauce]

**samosa** a small deep-fried triangular spicy meat or vegetable pasty of Indian origin. [Hindi]

**sauerkraut** shredded cabbage pickled in salt water, a popular German dish. [from German *sauerkraut*, sour cabbage]

**sauté** *verb* (**sautés, sautéd** *or* **sautéed**, **sautéing** *or* **sautéeing**) to fry gently for a short time; *adjective* fried in this way: eg sauté potatoes. [French, = tossed; from *sauter*, to jump]

**schnapps** in N Europe, any strong dry alcoholic spirit, especially Dutch gin distilled from potatoes. [German, = dram of liquor]

**schnitzel** a veal cutlet. [German]

**sorbet** a dish of sweetened fruit juice, frozen and served as a kind of ice cream; a water ice. [French; from Arabic *sharbah*, drink]

**soufflé** a light sweet or savoury baked dish, a frothy mass of whipped egg whites with other ingredients mixed in. [French; from *souffler*, to puff up]

**spaghetti** pasta in the form of long thin string-like strands. [Italian; from *spago*, cord]

**stroganoff** a dish, also called **beef stroganoff**, that is traditionally made with strips of sautéed fillet steak, onions and mushrooms, cooked in a lightly spiced, creamy white wine sauce and served with pilaf rice; there are many variations on this, including one that uses only vegetables. [named after Count Paul Stroganov, a 19th-century Russian diplomat]

**strudel** a baked roll of thin pastry with a filling of fruit, especially apple. [German, = whirlpool, ie from the rolling]

**table d'hôte** (*plural* **tables d'hôte**) a meal with a set number of choices and a set number of courses offered for a fixed price, especially to residents in a hotel. [French, = host's table]

**tagliatelle** pasta made in the form of long narrow ribbons. [Italian]

**tandoori** food cooked on a spit over charcoal in a clay oven. [from Hindi *tandoor*, clay oven]

**tapas** light savoury snacks or appetizers, especially those based on Spanish foods and cooking techniques and served with drinks. [from Spanish *tapa*, cover or lid]

**thermidor** *postpositive adjective* (eg lobster thermidor) denoting a method of preparation, the flesh being mixed with a cream sauce seasoned with mustard, and served in the shell. [from Greek *therme*, heat, and *doron* gift; Thermidor was the eleventh month of the French Revolutionary calendar, 19 July–17 August]

**tikka** in Indian cookery, meat that is marinated in yoghurt and spices and cooked in a clay oven. [Hindi]

**timbale** a dish of meat or fish, etc cooked in a cup-shaped mould or shell. [from French *timable*; from Spanish *atabal*; from Arabic *at-tabl*, the drum]

**tortilla** (*plural* **tortillas**) a thin round Mexican maize cake cooked on griddle and usually eaten hot, with a filling or topping of meat or cheese. [Spanish; a diminutive of *torta*, cake]

**tournedos** (*plural* **tournedos**) a small round thick fillet of beef. [French]

**vacherin** a dessert made with meringue and whipped cream, usually with ice cream, fruit, nuts, etc. [French]

**velouté** a smooth white sauce made with stock [French, = velvety]

**vermicelli** **1** pasta in very thin strands, thinner than spaghetti. **2** tiny splinters of chocolate used for desserts and cake decoration. [Italian, = little worms]

**vinaigrette** a salad dressing made by mixing oil, vinegar and seasonings, especially mustard. [French; from *vinaigre*, vinegar]

**vol-au-vent** a small round puff-pastry case with a savoury filling. [French, = flight in the wind]

**wurst** any of various types of large German sausage. [German, = something rolled; related to Latin *vertere*, to turn]

**yakitori** a Japanese dish of boneless pieces of chicken grilled on skewers and basted with a thick sweet sauce of sake, mirin and soy sauce. [Japanese; from *yaki*, grill + *tori*, bird]

**zabaglione** a dessert made from egg yolks, sugar and wine whipped together.

## Chefs, restaurateurs and cookery writers

**Allen, Betty** (1936– ) Scottish chef and restaurateur, born Bathgate, West Lothian. Since 1978 she and her husband have run the Airds Hotel in Port Appin, Argyll, where she and her son are chefs. It received a Michelin star in 1990.

**Beard, James** (1903–85) US chef and cookery writer, born Portland, Oregon. An influential teacher, he wrote many books including *The James Beard Cookbook* (1959) and *James Beard's American Cookery* (1972).

**Beeton, Mrs Isabella Mary**, née **Mayson** (1836–65) English cookery writer. Her *Book of Household Management* first appeared in a magazine owned by her husband, Samuel Beeton, in 1859–60. It made her a household name.

**Blanc, Raymond René** (1949– ) French chef and restaurateur, born near Besançon. He began to cook in 1975 in England and opened Les Quat' Saisons in Oxford in 1977, and Le Manoir aux Quat' Saisons in 1984. Books include *Blanc Mange* (1994) and *A Blanc Christmas* (1996).

**Bocuse, Paul** (1926– ) French restaurateur and cookery writer, born Collonges-au-Mont-d'Or. He took over the family business, now Restaurant Paul Bocuse, and runs the French Pavilion at Disneyworld, Orlando. Books include *La Bonne chére* (1995).

**Brown, David** (1951– ) and **Hilary** (1952– ) Scottish husband and wife team of restaurateurs, both born Glasgow. In 1975 they opened La Potiniére in Gullane, East Lothian, where she is the chef. It received a Michelin star in 1990.

**Carluccio, Antonio Mario Gaetano** (1937– ) Italian restaurateur, cookery writer and broadcaster, born Vietri sul Mare. He became restaurateur at Neal Street Restaurant in 1981 (proprietor since 1989). His books include *An Invitation to Italian Cooking* (1986), *A Passion for Pasta* (1993), *Antonio Carluccio's Italian Feasts* (1996, also television series) and *Complete Italian Food* (1997).

**Child, Julia**, née **McWilliams** (1912– ) US cookery writer and broadcaster, born Pasadena, California. She co-founded a cooking school in Paris in 1951, co-wrote *Mastering the Art of French Cooking* in 1961, among other books, and hosted the television series *The French Chef* (1963–76).

**Claiborne, Craig** (1920– ) US food critic and cookery writer, born Sunflower, Missouri. He was food editor of the *New York Times* (1957–88). Books include the *New York Times Cook Book* (1961) and *Craig Claiborne's Memorable Meals* (1985).

**David, Elizabeth** (1913–92) English cookery writer, born Sussex. She drew from her time spent abroad to write such influential books as *French Provincial Cooking* (1960).

**Delmonico, Lorenzo** (1813–81) US restaurateur, born Marengo, Switzerland. After arriving in New York with his uncles in 1832, he opened Delmonico's c.1834. He started a new restaurant culture by introducing European standards and foods (eg fresh salads, vegetables) and longer opening hours.

**Diat, Louis Felix** (1885–1957) US restaurateur, born Montmarault, France. Known as 'Monsieur Louis', he was chef at the New York Ritz-Carlton hotel's famous restaurant (1910–51) and championed French cooking there and through his books, eg *Cooking á la Ritz* (1941). He created vichysoisse.

**Dimbleby, Josceline Rose** (1943– ) English cookery writer; writer for Sainsbury's (1978– ) and cookery editor for the *Sunday Telegraph* (1982– ). Books include *A Taste of Dreams* (1976), *Salads for all Seasons* (1981) and *Josceline Dimbleby's Complete Cookbook* (1997).

**Eriksen, Gunn** (1956– ) Scottish chef and restaurateur, born Grimstad, Norway. An artist by training, in 1980 she joined Fred Brown, owner of the Altnaharrie Inn across Loch Broom from Ullapool, and began to develop her now renowned characteristic cooking style.

**Escoffier, Auguste** (c.1847–1935) French chef, born Villeneuve-Loubet. He used his culinary skills in the Franco-Prussian War and at the Grand Hotel in Monte Carlo before going to the London Savoy and then to the Carlton. He invented the *bombe Nero* and *pèche melba*.

**Farmer, Fannie Merritt** (1857–1915) US cookery expert, born Boston. She was a director of the Boston Cooking School and edited its bestselling cook book (now called 'Fannie Farmer's') in 1896 before founding Miss Farmer's School of Cookery — the first to cater for housewives and nurses rather than servants and teachers.

**Fisher, F(rances) K(ennedy)**, née **Kennedy** (1908–92) US cookery writer, born Albion, Michigan. Her books, which are like collections of culinary essays celebrating US regional food, include *How to Cook a Wolf* (1942) and *The Art of Eating* (1976).

**Floyd, Keith** (1943– ) English cookery writer and broadcaster, born Somerset. He is known for his flamboyant style on television and for his many *Floyd on ...* books, eg *Floyd on France, Floyd on Fish*.

**Franey, Pierre** (1921–96) US chef and restaurateur, born Tonnerre, France. He was chef at Le Pavillon in New York, collaborated on books and articles with **Craig Claiborne**, and published his own articles written for the *New York Times*.

**Gray, Rose** (1939– ) British chef and restaurateur. In 1987 she and Ruth Rogers opened the successful Italian-cooking based River Café in Hammersmith, London. *The River Café Cook Book* followed.

**Grigson, (Heather) Jane**, née **McIntyre** (1928–90) English cookery writer. She was correspondent for the *Observer* and wrote the cookery classics *English Food* (1974), *Jane Grigson's Vegetable Book* (1978) and *Jane Grigson's Fruit Book* (1982), all influenced by her country lifestyle.

**Grigson, Sophie (Hester Sophia Frances)** (1959– ) English cookery writer and broadcaster, and cookery correspondent for newspapers including the *Evening Standard* (1986–93) and the *Independent* (1991–4). Television series and related books include *Eat your Greens* (1993), *Travels á la Carte* (1994), *Sophie's Meat Course* (1995) and *Taste of the Times* (1997); she also contributed to *Fair World Cookbook* (1997).

**Grossman, Loyd Daniel Gilman** (1950– ) US chef, broadcaster and cookery writer. Books include *The World on a Plate* (1997).

**Guérard, Michel Etienne** (1933– ) French chef, restaurateur and cookery writer, born Vetheuil. His restaurant le Pot au Feu in Asniéres has two Michelin stars. Books include *Minceur Exquise* (1989).

**Harvey, Frederick Henry** (1835–1901) US restaurateur, born London, England. Starting in 1876 at the railroad depot in Kansas, he created a chain of restaurants along the Atchison, Topeka and Santa Fe railroad; these became known for their good food, fresh linens, and their trained waitresses or 'Harvey Girls'.

**Heathcote, Paul** (1960– ) English chef and restaurateur, born Bolton. His first restaurant, Paul Heathcote's in Longridge, has two Michelin stars. Others include Heathcote's Brasserie in Preston and Simply Heathcote's in Manchester (1996).

**Hom, Ken(neth)** (1949– ) US chef, cookery writer and broadcaster. He has earned renown as a food consultant and for popularizing Chinese cooking. His books and television series include *Hot Wok* (1996).

**Jaffrey, Madhur** (1933– ) US cookery writer, broadcaster and actress, born Delhi, India. She began publishing the recipes sent to her by her mother in India. Books include *Flavours of India* (1995).

**Johnstone, (Christian) Isobel**, pseudonym **Margaret Dods** (1781–1857) Scottish cookery writer and novelist, born Fife. She had a huge success in 1826 with 'Meg Dod's Cookery', properly *The Cook and Housewife's Manual* by Mistress Margaret Dods.

**Kerr, Graham Victor** (1934– ) New Zealand cookery writer and broadcaster, born in London, England. He became known for his widely-screened television show *The Galloping Gourmet*, and for such books as the *Graham Kerr Cookbook* (1966) and *Galloping Gourmets* (1969).

**Ladenis, Nico (Nicholas Peter)** (1934– ) Kenyan chef and restaurateur. He and his wife opened the Chez Nico restaurant, specializing in French cuisine, in 1971, followed by two more, and then Chez Nico at Ninety

Park Lane in 1992. Books include *My Gastronomy* (1987) and *Nico* (1996).

**Leith, Prue (Prudence Margaret)** (1940– ) English chef, restaurateur and cookery writer. She started Leith's restaurant in 1969 (one Michelin star) and Leith's School of Food and Wine in 1975. Books include *Leith's Cookery Bible* (1991).

**Little, (Robert) Alastair** (1950– ) English chef and restaurateur, born Colne, Lancashire. He opened the London restaurant Alastair Little in 1985, and became food columnist for the *Daily Mail* in 1993. Books include *Keep it Simple* (1993) and *Alastair Little's Italian Kitchen* (1996).

**Mosimann, Anton** (1947– ) Swiss chef, restaurateur, cookery writer and broadcaster. His first position as chef in the UK was at the Dorchester Hotel, London. He opened the restaurant Mosimann's in 1988. His television series and related books include *Anton Mosimann Naturally* (1991–2); other books include *Mosimann's World* (1996).

**Nairn, Nick** (1959– ) Scottish chef and broadcaster. He and his wife opened the Braeval restaurant in 1986 (one Michelin star) and also run a cooking school in Aberfoyle, Scotland. Television appearances include *Ready Steady Cook* and *Nick Nairn's Wild Harvest.*

**Oliver, Jamie** (1975– ) English chef, cookery writer and broadcaster. He wrote the bestseller, *The Naked Chef* (1999) after his successful TV series of the same name, following it up with the sequels *The Return of the Naked Chef* (2000) and *Happy Days with the Naked Chef* (2001).

**Prudhomme, Paul** (1940– ) US chef, restaurateur, cookery writer and broadcaster, born Opelousa, Louisiana. In 1979 he and his wife opened K-Paul's Louisiana Kitchen in New Orleans which is known for its cajun and creole cooking. He often appears on television and has published *Paul Prudhomme's Louisiana Kitchen* (1984).

**Ramsay, Gordon** (1967– ) Scottish chef and restaurateur, born Renfrewshire. He trained under Marco Pierre White, the Roux brothers, Guy Savoy and Joël Robuchon, and now runs the Aubergine restaurant in London, which has two Michelin stars. Books include *Passion for Flavour: Recipes from the Aubergine*.

**Rhodes, Gary** (1960– ) English chef, restaurateur and broadcaster. He worked at the Castle Hotel, Taunton, and the Greenhouse in Mayfair, London, before launching his own restaurants, eg City Rhodes. Books include *Fabulous Foods* (1997).

**Robuchon, Joël** (1945– ) French chef and restaurateur, born Poitiers. He ran the Restaurant Jamin in Paris (1981–94) and Restaurant Joël Robuchon (1994–6) before retiring in 1996. Books include *Simply French* (1991).

**Rombauer, Irma**, née **Louisa von Starkloff** (1877–1962) US cookery writer, born St Louis, Missouri. She wrote the perpetual bestseller, *The Joy of Cooking* (illustrated and revised in later editions by her daughter Marion Rombauer Becker, 1903–76). An encyclopedic collection of classic American and European recipes, culinary techniques and food preparation instructions, it has sold around 8 million copies, and has had an immeasurable influence on American cuisine.

**Roux, Albert Henri** (1935– ) and **Michel André** (1941– ) French chefs and restaurateurs, born Semur-en-Brionnais. They opened Le Gavroche in London in 1967, which is now run by Albert; Michel runs the Waterside Inn in Bray, Berkshire. The Waterside Inn has three Michelin stars. Their television appearances include *At Home with the Roux Brothers* (1988), and books include *Desserts: A Lifelong Passion* (1994).

**Sardi, (Melchior Pio Vi) Vincent** (1885–1969) US restaurateur, born in San Marzano Oliveto, Italy. From c.1907 he lived in New York City, where Sardi's, his restaurant in the theatre district, became a favourite haunt of many theatre-goers.

**Savoy, Guy** (1953– ) French chef and restaurateur, born Nevers. His restaurants in Paris include the Guy Savoy (opened 1980) and Le Bistrot de l'Etoile (opened 1988), and his books *La Gourmandise apprivoisée* (1987, 'Tamed Greed').

**Smith, Delia** (1941– ) English cookery writer and broadcaster, born Woking, Surrey. She followed her first of many books, *How to Cheat at Cooking* (1973), with several television series and bestsellers, eg *Delia Smith's Summer Collection* (1993) and *Delia Smith's Winter Collection* (1995).

**Soyer, Alexis** (1809–58) French chef, born Meaux. The most famous of his time, he was chef in the Reform Club in London (1837–50). He wrote *Culinary Campaign in the Crimea* (1857) after trying to reform the food supply system in the Crimea by introducing the 'Soyer stove'.

**Spry, Constance** (1886–1960) English flower arranger and cookery writer, born Derby. She ran flower shops and cookery schools, held advisory positions and wrote *The Constance Spry Cookbook* (1956).

**Stein, Rick** (c.1948– ) English chef and restaurateur, born Churchill, near Chipping Norton. Specializing in seafood, he runs the Seafood Restaurant in Padstow, Cornwall, which he and his wife opened in 1975. He became known through the television series *Taste of the Sea* (1995) and *Fruits of the Sea* (1997) and related publications. He also wrote *English Seafood Cookery* (1989).

**Tovey, John** (1933– ) English chef, restaurateur, broadcaster and cookery writer, born Lancashire. He opened Miller Howe in 1971. He now concentrates on television broadcasting and writing.

**Two Fat Ladies** Clarissa Dickson Wright (1946– ) and Jennifer Paterson (1928–99). Both professional cooks (Paterson also wrote for *The Spectator* and *The Oldie*), they came to fame with the television series *Two Fat Ladies* and related publications, eg *Two Fat Ladies Ride Again* (1997).

**White, Marco Pierre** (1961– ) English chef and

restaurateur, born Leeds. He learned from Albert Roux, Nico Ladenis and Raymond Blanc, and opened his first (of several) restaurants, Harveys, in 1987. Publications include *Canteen Cuisine* (1995), and *The Mirabelle Cookbook* (1999).

**Wilson, David** (1938– ) Scottish chef and restaurateur, born Bishopbriggs, near Glasgow. In 1972 he and his wife took over the Peat Inn in Fife, which has gained international renown and a Michelin rosette (1987).

**Worrall Thompson, Antony** (1952– ) English chef, restaurateur and cookery writer. His London restaurants include Ménage à Trois, 190 Queensgate, Dell'ugo and Woz. He has also appeared on television in *Ready Steady Cook* and *The Food and Drink Programme*.

## Varieties of wines and grapes

Wines are often named after the grape from which they are made, or the region or château in which they are produced.

**Alsace** mainly dry, white wine produced in the Alsace region of NE France; the wines are named after the grapes, eg Riesling, Gewürztraminer, Sylvaner, Pinot Blanc and Pinot Gris.

**Anjou Blanc** a dry white wine produced in the western Loire region of France and made from blends of such grape varieties as Chenin Blanc, Chardonnay and Sauvignon.

**Asti Spumante** a sweet, aromatic sparkling wine made from the Muscat grape and named after the town of Asti in Piedmont, Italy.

**Auslese** an expensive full-flavoured, sweet wine made in Germany from exceptionally high-quality mature grapes, particularly the Riesling grape.

**Beaujolais** a large area in southern Burgundy, France, famous for light, fruity red wines made from the Gamay grape.

**Beaujolais Nouveau** a young red wine from the Beaujolais area, available in late November.

**Beaune** French town in the centre of Burgundy with its own vineyard sites which are known for their soft, fragrant red wines.

**Bordeaux** French city and seaport in the centre of the famous wine-producing region of Bordeaux in SW France where red wines (known as claret) and white wines are produced. The finest wines come from the areas Médoc, Graves, St-Émilion and Pomerol.

**Burgundy 1** famous wine-producing region in France, divided into five districts: Chablis, Côte d'Or, Chalonnais, Mâconnais and Beaujolais. **2** a French wine made in the Burgundy region; most are red, some are white, all are dry. Burgundy's vineyards are divided into the Grands crus, Premier crus, and the remainder which are named after communes. **3** any similar red wine.

**Cabernet Sauvignon 1** a red-wine grape which is the basis of most Bordeaux wine; an adaptable variety originally from Bordeaux, it is now grown throughout the world. **2** the wine produced from this grape.

**Carignan** a red-wine grape used to make table wine and dessert wine; grown in the Midi, N and C America, N Africa and Australia.

**Chablis** a dry white wine made from the Chardonnay grape in the Burgundy region of central France, named after the small French town near to where it is made.

**Chardonnay 1** a white grape variety used in Burgundy and Champagne; originally from Burgundy, it is now also grown in California, Australia, New Zealand, etc. **2** a dry white wine made from this grape.

**Chateauneuf-du-Pape** a district of the Rhône region of France known especially for its expensive red wine; the wine is blended, using mainly Grenache, Syrah and Cinsault grapes.

**Chenin Blanc** a white-wine grape widely grown in the Loire Valley in France, and in South Africa (called Steen) and California; it is used to make Vouvray and Saumur wines.

**Chianti** a dry, usually red, blended Italian wine made in Tuscany.

**Cinsault** a red-wine grape grown especially in the Rhône valley and, being low in tannin, is used in blended wines eg Chateauneuf-du-Pape.

**Colombard** a white-wine grape, used especially in South Africa.

**Corbières** a district of the Languedoc-Roussillon area where red, white and rosé wines are made.

**Côtes du Rhône** the appellation for the lesser red, white and rosé wines produced in the Rhône valley.

**Dão** a mountain district in northern Portugal where mainly red wine is produced.

**Fitou** a red wine produced from the Carignan grape in the Languedoc-Roussillon area of France.

**Frascati** a full-bodied, fragrant white wine made in the town of Frascati, S Italy.

**Gamay** a red-wine grape used widely in France and elsewhere; used in Beaujolais, and in Anjou as a base for rosé wines.

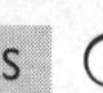



**Gewürztraminer** a spicy variety of white grape grown especially in the Alsace region which is used to make a medium-dry aromatic wine.

**Grenache** a fruity grape used for making strong, sweet wines; grown in Europe (especially Spain), N Africa, Australia, C and N America; used in rosé wines and in blended wines eg Chateauneuf-du-Pape.

**Graves** a large area within the Bordeaux region in France which produces red and white wines.

**Lambrusco** a red or white-wine grape; used to make a light, sweet sparkling red wine of the same name in northern Italy.

**Liebfraumilch** a white blended wine from the Rhine region of Germany; by law it is made with Riesling, Sylvaner or Müller-Thurgau grapes from the regions of Rheinhessen, Nahe, Rheinpfalz or Rheingau.

**Mâcon** a town in southern Burgundy where white and red wine is produced.

**Madeira** a fortified wine made on the N Atlantic island of Madeira.

**Malaga** a dark dessert wine from Andalucia, Spain, made from grapes that are partially sun-dried before use.

**Marsala** a brown, fortified wine made in the town of Marsala, Sicily.

**Médoc** the premier area of Bordeaux in France known for its fine red wines; many famous châteaux are situated here, eg Château Mouton-Rothschild.

**Merlot** **1** an important variety of black grape often used often in blends with Cabernet Sauvignon and in many soft fruity wines for drinking young. **2** a red wine that is produced in France, Italy and the USA from, or mainly from, this variety of grape.

**Minervois** a well-rated district in the Languedoc-Roussillon area which produces well-balanced, robust red wines made from Carignan, Cinsault and Grenache grapes.

**Moselle** or **Mosel** the region around the Moselle river which runs through NE France, Luxembourg and Germany; it is known for its light, crisp, perfumed dry white wine made mainly from the Riesling grape.

**Müller-Thurgau** a white-wine grape widely used in Germany, as well as in California, England and New Zealand; similar to the Muscat grape in flavour.

**Muscadet** **1** a white-wine grape successfully grown in the Loire valley in France. **2** a dry white wine, the best-known of those made in the Loire eg Muscadet de Sèvre-et-Maine.

**Muscat** or **Muscadelle** or **Moscatello** names of a large family of white and red grapes; they have a musky smell, and are dried for raisins as well as used to make scented, grapey wines; most wines from the Muscat grape are sweet, except that made in Alsace.

**Niersteiner** a well-known German wine made from the Riesling grape in the Nierstein district of the Rheinhessen region in Germany.

**Pinot** an important variety of black and white grape grown throughout the world. Pinot Noir is the traditional grape of Burgundy and is used in making champagne; as it is difficult to grow elsewhere, it is an irresistible challenge to wine-makers.

**Pinotage** a red-wine grape used especially in South Africa.

**Pomerol** a district of Bordeaux which produces red and white vines, including the high-quality red wine Château Petrus.

**Riesling** a white-wine grape grown most successfully in Germany, but also in Alsace, Austria and elsewhere; it is used to make wine ranging from dry to very sweet.

**Rioja** a small wine-making area in NE Spain, which produces mainly dry red wine.

**St-Émilion** a fine, fruity red wine made particularly from the Merlot grape in the St-Émilion area of Bordeaux.

**Sancerre** a district in the Loire Valley known especially for its pale, dry white wines, and for its rosés, which are made from the Pinot Noir grape.

**Saumur** a district of Anjou in NW France where both still and sparkling wines are made.

**Sauternes** an appellation used by five communes (Sauternes, Barsac, Bommes, Fargues and Preignac) in the Graves district of Bordeaux which produce sweet white wine, mainly from the Sémillon grape.

**Sauvignon Blanc** a white-wine grape used in Bordeaux and Sancerre; makes excellent wine in New Zealand and California.

**Sémillon** a white grape used in Bordeaux whites, especially the Sauternes district where is it harvested half rotten and therefore with a high concentration of sugar; it is also successful in Australia's Hunter Valley region.

**Soave** a light, dry, flowery white wine made near the village of Soave, NE Italy.

**Spätlese** a German term for wine made from grapes that have been harvested late, resulting in a wine with more body and sweetness than other German white wines.

**Sylvaner** a German white-wine grape used to make fruity wines and grown in Europe, N and S America and Australia.

**Syrah** a red-wine grape, the foremost grape of the hot Rhône valley; particularly at home in Australia, where it is known as Shiraz.

**Tarragona** a wine region in Spain, where much red and white table wine, and the sweet, red fortified wine Tarragona are produced.

**Valpolicella** a light, fragrant red wine made near the village of Valpolicella in the Veneto region of NE Italy.

**Vouvray** a usually sweet, but always fresh and fruity, white wine produced from the Chenin Blanc grape in Touraine, in the Loire Valley.

**Zinfandel** a red-wine grape used widely in California for making dry red wine.

## Terms relating to wine-making and wine-tasting

**acetic** tasting or smelling of vinegar, due to the presence of acetic acid; caused by oxidization or by faulty fermentation or bottling.

**acidity** the taste caused by the natural organic acids in wine, which in the correct proportions make a wine well-balanced.

**aftertaste** the taste that remains in the mouth or comes into it after tasting wine.

**appellation contrôlée** and **appellation d'origine contrôlée** (French; abbreviation AC or AOC) **1** the system which within France designates and controls the names especially of wine, but also of cognac, armagnac, calvados and some foods, guaranteeing the authenticity of the producing region and the methods of production, and which outside France protects the generic names from misappropriation. **2** the highest designation of French wine awarded under this system.

**argol** the harmless crystalline potassium deposit that is left on the sides of wine vats during fermentation. Also called tartrate.

**balance** a noun describing a wine's combination of alcoholic strength, acidity, residual sugar and tannins.

**big** amply flavoured, often with a high alcohol content.

**body** the 'weight' of a wine on the palate, or the sensation of fullness it imparts due to its density or viscosity. Wines range from being light-bodied to full-bodied.

**bouquet** the delicate smell of wine. [French; a diminutive of *bois*, a wood]

**breathe** to develop flavour when exposed to the air.

**brut** said especially of champagne: very dry.

**Buck's fizz** or **buck's fizz** a drink consisting of champagne, or sparkling white wine, and orange juice. [named after Buck's Club, London]

**chambré** said of wine: at room temperature.

**character** having positive, distinctive characteristics.

**château** used in names of wines, especially from the Bordeaux area: a vineyard estate around a castle or house.

**claret** a French red wine, especially from the Bordeaux area.

**clarity** the quality of being clear and pure; the clarity of a wine is an indication of both its condition (faulty wine often appears cloudy), and of how much clarification (the removal of suspended material, the lees) has been carried out.

**clean** pure-tasting and pure-smelling; a term usually applied to white wine.

**coarse** rough or crude; lacking refinement.

**common** plain and of no distinctive character, though not necessarily low quality.

**corked** said of wine: spoiled as a result of having a faulty cork, which has affected the taste of the wine.

**crisp** with a dry, refreshing taste; usually said of white wines with a pleasantly high level of acidity.

**cru** specialist term for a high-quality vineyard; often translated in English as 'growth'; eg grand cru, premier cru.

**decant** to pour (wine, etc) from one bottle or container to another, leaving any sediment behind.

**decanter** an ornamental bottle with a stopper, used for decanted wine, sherry, whisky, etc.

**demijohn** a large bottle with a short narrow neck and one or two small handles, used for storing eg wine.

**DOC** *abbreviation* said of wine: *Denominazione di Origine Controllata* (Italian), the Italian equivalent of appellation contrôlée. Compare DOCG.

**DOCG** *abbreviation* said of wine: *Denominazione di Origine Controllata Garantita* (Italian), a designation of wines, guaranteeing quality, strength, etc. Compare DOC.

**dry** said of wine, etc: not sweet.

**earthy** with a flavour and bouquet enhanced by characteristics of the soil in which the vine was grown (usually applicable only to grapes grown in a hot climate).

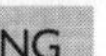



**en primeur** said of tasting, buying or investing in wine: when the wine is new.
**fat** full-bodied and viscous, but unbalanced due to insufficient acidity.
**fine** an ill-defined term, usually referring to the superior wines of the classic regions of Europe, eg Bordeaux and Burgundy.
**finesse** refinement; having the best possible characteristics a wine can have.
**finish** aftertaste.
**flabby** lacking in acidity; like a fat wine, well flavoured but with little 'bite'.
**flinty** usually said of highly rated white wines: having a dry, clean, hard taste reminiscent of gun flint, eg Pouilly Blanc Fumé.
**flowery** containing the scent of flowers in the bouquet.
**fortify** to add extra alcohol to (wine) in the course of production, in order to produce sherry, port, etc.
**fresh** refreshing.
**frizzante** an Italian term for semi-sparkling.
**fruity** smelling strongly of fruit, eg blackberries, blackcurrants, gooseberries or raspberries as well as grapes.
**full** or **full-bodied** having a rich flavour or quality.
**generous** rich, invigorating.
**glühwein** or **Glühwein** mulled wine, especially as prepared in Germany, Austria, etc.
**grand cru** produced by a famous vineyard or group of vineyards.
**grapey** having a strong flavour of grapes, eg wine made from the Muscat grape.
**grappa** a brandy (originally from Italy) distilled from what is left after the grapes have been pressed for wine-making.
**green** too acid, usually due to having been made from unripe grapes.
**hanepoot** a kind of grape for eating and wine-making.
**hard** with an unpleasant excess of tannin and lack of fruit; hard wines usually improve with time.
**hearty** usually said of red wines, eg from the Rhône valley: with a generous, warm flavour.
**heavy** too alcoholic; or full-bodied but lacking in finesse.
**hock** a white wine, originally only the one made in Hochheim, on the River Main, in Germany, but now applied to all white wines from the Rhine valley.
**honest** ordinary and undistinguished; unremarkable, eg an honest wine.
**hot** too alcoholic.
**lay down** to store (wine) in a cellar.
**lees** the sediment that settles at the bottom of liquids and alcoholic drinks, especially wine.
**legs** ► **tears**
**length** persistence of flavour on the palate; length is an indicator of quality.
**light** pleasantly slender in body and low in alcohol.
**lively** said of white wine: young and fresh, often with a slight natural sparkle.
**long** with an impressively enduring aftertaste, usually indicating high quality.
**maceration** in the making of red wine, the process in which the tannins etc are dissolved from the skins, seeds and stem fragments of the grapes to be added to the juice or new wine.
**madeirized** said of white wines: tinged with brown because of old age.
**magnum** a champagne or wine bottle that holds approximately 1.5 litres, ie twice the normal amount.
**malic acid** (formula $H_6C_4O_5$) an acid found in unripe fruits, and occurring in wines.
**malmsey** a strong sweet wine originally from Greece but now usually from Spain, Madeira, etc.
**marc** **1** the leftover skins and stems of grapes used in winemaking. **2** a kind of brandy made from these.
**mature** having a fully developed flavour.
**medium** neither dry nor sweet.
**mellow** fully flavoured with age; well matured.
**mirin** a sweet rice wine used in Japanese cookery.
**mull** to spice, sweeten and warm, eg mulled wine.
**muscatel** a rich sweet white wine made from Muscat grapes.
**must** the juice of grapes or other fruit before it is completely fermented to become wine.
**noble rot** on white grapes: a rot caused by the fungus *Botrytis cinerea*, which aids the production of sweet white wine.

**nose** a scent or aroma, especially a wine's bouquet.

**nutty** usually said of sherries or red wines: having a flavour reminiscent of nuts, eg walnuts or hazlenuts, which usually indicates good quality.

**oenology** the study or knowledge of wine (*adjective* **oenological**, *noun* **oenologist**).

**oenophile** a lover or connoisseur of wine; an oenologist.

**oxidation** a fault caused by exposure to oxygen, making any wine smell bad and making white wine darker.

**palate** an ability to discriminate between wines, different qualities of wine, etc.

**pétillant** lightly sparkling; a French term for a wine sparkling more than when *perlant* but not as much as when *mousseux*.

**pipe** 1 a cask or butt of varying capacity, but usually about 105 gallons in Britain (equal to 126 US gallons or 477 litres), used for wine or oil. **2** a measure of this amount.

**piquant** usually said of white wine: with an agreeably sharp flavour caused by high levels of acidity, eg wine from some areas of the Rhine, Loire and Mosel.

**plonk** *colloq* cheap, undistinguished wine.

**port** a sweet dark-red or tawny fortified wine. [from Oporto, the city in Portugal from where it was originally exported]

**prädikat** 1 in Germany: a distinction awarded to a wine, based on the ripeness of the grapes used to produce it. **2** a wine that qualifies for this award.

**race** said of wine: the special flavour by which its origin may be recognized.

**rack** to draw off (wine or beer) from its sediment.

**racy** said of wine: with a distinctive flavour imparted by the soil.

**rape** the refuse of grapes left after wine-making and used in making vinegar.

**red biddy** *colloq* a cheap alcoholic drink made from red wine and methylated spirits.

**remuage** in wine-making, the process of turning the bottles so that the sediment collects at the cork end for removal.

**retsina** a Greek white or rosé wine flavoured with pine resin.

**Rhenish** Rhine wine.

**Rhine wine** an imprecise term for any wine made from grapes grown in the valley of the River Rhine.

**ripe** said of the flavour or taste of wine: rich or strong.

**robust** said of wine: with a full, rich quality.

**rosé** a light-pink wine properly made by removing the skins of red grapes after fermentation has begun; it is sometimes also made by mixing red and white wines.

**rouge** *in full* vin rouge, French red wine.

**sack** a dry white wine from Spain, Portugal and the Canary Islands.

**sangria** a Spanish drink of red wine, fruit juice, sugar and spices.

**sec** 1 said of wine: dry. **2** said of champagne: medium sweet.

**Sekt** a German term for sparkling wines.

**severe** very sharp, almost astringent; this sourness is usually due to the wine being too acid and/or immature.

**sharp** sour-tasting, but not as sour as a severe wine; sharpness may be intentional, or a fault caused by immaturity or by the use of unripe grapes.

**sherry** 1 a fortified wine ranging in colour from pale gold to dark brown. **2** *loosely* a similar type of wine produced elsewhere. [from Jerez de la Frontera, the S Spanish town where it is produced].

**short** opposite of long; with little or no aftertaste.

**smooth** pleasantly textured with a mellow flavour.

**soft** a term describing the impact of the wine on the palate.

**spicy** with a flavour of spices and herbs, eg wines made from the Gewürztraminer grape.

**spritzer** a drink of white wine and soda water.

**spritzig** 1 a slightly sparkling, usually German, wine. **2** in wine-tasting: the slight prickle on the tongue that is affected by this kind of wine.

**spumante** an Italian term for fully sparkling, usually sweet wine, eg Asti Spumante.

**stalky** with an unpleasant taste of damp twigs; a fault caused by leaving the grape stalks in contact with the grapes for too long.

**stum** *noun* partly fermented grape juice that is added to a wine which has lost its strength, flavour, sharpness, etc in order to perk it up; *verb* to add stum to (a wine) and so restart the fermentation process.

**sulphurous acid** or (*US*) **sulfurous acid** (formula $H_2SO_3$) a colourless weakly acidic solution of sulphur dioxide in water that acts as a preservative in wine-making. A sulphury wine contains too much sulphur, but

usually improves an hour or two after opening.
**supple** usually said of red wine: a term evoking pliability in describing the impact on the palate.
**sweet** said of wine: having some taste of sugar or fruit; not dry.
**tannin** any of several substances in the pips, skins and stalks of the grapes which give a distinctive flavour to red wine. The tannin should mellow as the wine matures; if not, the wine tastes hard and disagreeable and is described as tannic.
**tart** very sharp.
**tartar** a deposit that forms a hard brownish-red crust on the insides of wine casks during fermentation.
**tears** (rhymes with 'ears') a noun used to describe the droplets that cling to the glass just above the surface of a glass of wine; a wine high in alcohol.
**temperature** an ideal tasting temperature for both red and white wines is 15–20°C/59–68°F.
**thin** insipid and watery.
**tierce** a former measure of wine, equal to one-third of a pipe, ie approx. 35 British or 42 US gallons (159 litres).
**tun** *noun* a large cask or liquid measure equivalent to 252 British or 303 US gallons (1 146 litres) of wine; *verb* to put or store (liquid, eg ale, beer or wine) in a tun.
**ullage** 1 the amount of wine, etc by which a container falls short of being full. **2** the quantity of liquid lost from a container through leakage, evaporation, etc. **3** *slang* the dregs remaining in a glass, etc.
**vault** a wine cellar.
**VDQS** *abbreviation: vins délimités de qualité supérieure* (French); wines of superior quality from approved vineyards, the interim wine quality designation between vin de pays and appellation contrôlée.
**velvety** said of the feel of the wine, not the flavour: very soft and smooth.
**vermouth** an alcoholic drink consisting of wine flavoured with aromatic herbs, originally wormwood.
**vin de pays** country or local wine.
**vin ordinaire** inexpensive table wine for everyday use.
**vine** any of various woody climbing plants that produce grapes.
**vineyard** a plantation of grape-bearing vines, especially for wine-making.
**vinho verde** a light, sharp young Portuguese wine.
**viniculture** the cultivation of grapes for wine-making.
**vino** *slang* wine, especially of poor quality.
**vinosity** a wine-like character; the characteristic qualities of a particular wine; an acceptable standard, with good, balanced characteristics.
**vinous** 1 belonging or relating to, or resembling, wine. **2** caused by or indicative of an excess of wine, eg a vinous complexion.
**vintage** said of wine: good quality and from a specified year.
**vintner** *formal* a wine-merchant.
**viticulture** the cultivation of grapes for making wine; viniculture.
**weighty** usually said of full-bodied red wine: with great depth and character.
**well-balanced** having good balance.
**white** said of wine: made from white grapes or from skinned black grapes.
**wine cellar** 1 a cellar in which to store wines. **2** the stock of wine stored there.
**wine cooler** a receptacle for cooling wine in bottles, ready for serving.
**wine glass** 1 a drinking-glass typically consisting of a small bowl on a stem, with a wide base flaring out from the stem. **2** the capacity of this; a wineglassful.
**wine list** a list of the wines available, eg in a restaurant.
**wine tasting** 1 the sampling of a variety of wines. **2** a gathering specifically for this.
**wine vault** 1 a vaulted wine cellar. **2** a place where wine is tasted or drunk.
**winepress** in the manufacture of wine: a machine in which grapes are pressed to extract the juice.
**winery** *chiefly US* a place where wine is prepared and stored.
**wineskin** *historical* the skin of a goat or sheep sewn up and used for holding wine.
**wino** *slang* someone, especially a down-and-out, addicted to cheap wine; an alcoholic.
**winy** or **winey** having a wine-like flavour.
**woody** with a flavour of wood; if overpowering, this may be a fault caused by the wine being left too long in the cask, or a problem with the cask.
**yeasty** with a smell of yeast, suggesting a second fermentation has or is about to happen.

## Wine bottle sizes

| Name | Capacity | | Name | Capacity | |
|---|---|---|---|---|---|
| wine bottle | 75cl | ($26\frac{2}{3}$ fl oz) (standard size) | jeroboam | 3 l | (4 standard bottles) |
| magnum | 1.5 l | (2 standard bottles) | salmanazar | 9 l | (12 standard bottles) |
| flagon | 1.13 l or 2 pints | | balthazar | 12 l | (16 standard bottles) |
| methuselah | 6 l | (8 standard bottles) | nebuchadnezzar | 15 l | (20 standard bottles) |
| rehoboam | 4.5 l | (6 standard bottles) | | | |

# HISTORY

## Journeys of exploration

| Date | Name | Exploration |
|---|---|---|
| 490BC | Hanno | Makes voyage round part of the coast of Africa |
| 325BC | Alexander the Great | Leads fleet along the N Indian coast and up the Persian Gulf |
| 84AD | Agricola | His fleet circumnavigates Britain |
| 1003 | Leif Ericsson | Voyages to N America and discovers 'Vinland' (possibly Nova Scotia) |
| 1418 | João Gonçalves Zarco | Discovers Madeira (dispatched by Henry the Navigator) |
| 1434 | Gil Eanes | Sails round Cape Bojadar (dispatched by Henry the Navigator) |
| 1446 | Dinís Dias | Discovers Cape Verde and the Senegal River (dispatched by Henry the Navigator) |
| 1488 | Bartolomeu Dias | Sails round the Cape of Storms (Cape of Good Hope) |
| 1492 | Christopher Columbus | Discovers the New World |
| 1493 | Christopher Columbus | Discovers Puerto Rico, Antigua and Jamaica |
| 1497 | John Cabot | Explores the coast of Newfoundland |
| 1497 | Vasco da Gama | Voyages round the Cape of Good Hope |
| 1498 | Vasco da Gama | Explores coast of Mozambique and discovers sea route to India |
| 1498 | Christopher Columbus | Discovers Trinidad and Venezuela |
| 1499 | Amerigo Vespucci | Discovers mouth of the River Amazon |
| 1500 | Pedro Alvares Cabral | Discovers Brazil |
| 1500 | Diogo Dias | Discovers Madagascar |
| 1500 | Gaspar Corte Real | Explores east coast of Greenland and Labrador |
| 1501 | Amerigo Vespucci | Explores S American coast |
| 1502 | Christopher Columbus | Explores Honduras and Panama |
| 1513 | Vasco Núñez de Balboa | Crosses the Panama Isthmus to discover the Pacific Ocean |
| 1520 | Ferdinand Magellan | Discovers the Straits of Magellan |
| 1521 | Ferdinand Magellan | Discovers the Philippines |
| 1524 | Giovanni da Verrazano | Discovers New York Bay and the Hudson River |
| 1526 | Sebastian Cabot | Explores the Rio de la Plata |
| 1534 | Jacques Cartier | Explores the Gulf of St Lawrence |
| 1535 | Jacques Cartier | Navigates the St Lawrence River |
| 1536 | Pedro de Mendoza | Founds Buenos Aires and explores Parana and Paraguay rivers |
| 1539 | Hernando de Soto | Explores Florida |
| 1540 | García López de Cárdenas | Discovers the Grand Canyon |
| 1580 | Francis Drake | Completes circumnavigation of the globe |
| 1585 | John Davis | Discovers Davis Strait on expedition to Greenland |
| 1595 | Walter Raleigh | Explores the Orinoco River |
| 1610 | Henry Hudson | Discovers Hudson's Bay |
| 1616 | William Baffin | Discovers Baffin Bay during search for the NW Passage |
| 1617 | Walter Raleigh | Begins expedition to Guiana |
| 1642 | Abel Janszoon Tasman | Discovers Tasmania and New Zealand |
| 1678 | Robert Cavelier de la Salle | Explores the Great Lakes of Canada |
| 1692 | Ijsbrand Iders | Explores the Gobi Desert |
| 1736 | Anders Celsius | Undertakes expedition to Lapland |
| 1761 | Carsten Niebuhr | Undertakes expedition to Arabia |
| 1766 | Louis de Bougainville | Voyage of discovery in Pacific, names Navigator Is |
| 1769 | James Cook | Names Society Is; charts coasts of New Zealand and E Australia |
| 1770 | James Cook | Lands at Botany Bay, Australia |
| 1772 | James Bruce | Explores Abyssinia and the confluence of the Blue Nile and White Nile |

| Date | Name | Exploration |
|---|---|---|
| 1774 | James Cook | Discoveries and rediscoveries in the Pacific; discovers and names S Georgia and the S Sandwich Is |
| 1778 | James Cook | Discovers Hawaiian group; surveys coast of Bering Straits |
| 1787 | Horace Saussure | Makes first ascent of Mont Blanc |
| 1790 | George Vancouver | Explores the coast of NW America |
| 1795 | Mungo Park | Explores the course of the Niger |
| 1818 | John Ross | Attempts to discover NW Passage |
| 1819 | John Barrow | Enters Barrow Straits in the N Arctic |
| 1823 | Walter Oudney | Discovers Lake Chad in C Africa |
| 1841 | David Livingstone | Discovers Lake Ngami |
| 1845 | John Franklin | Attempts to discover NW Passage |
| 1854 | Richard Burton and John Speke | Explore interior of Somaliland |
| 1855 | David Livingstone | Discovers the Victoria Falls on the Zambesi River |
| 1858 | Richard Burton and John Speke | Discover Lake Tanganyika |
| 1875 | Henry Morton Stanley | Traces the Congo to the Atlantic |
| 1888 | Fridtjof Nansen | Crosses Greenland |
| 1893 | Fridtjof Nansen | Attempts to reach N Pole |
| 1905 | Roald Amundsen | Sails through NW Passage |
| 1909 | Robert Edwin Peary | Reaches N Pole |
| 1911 | Roald Amundsen | Reaches S Pole |
| 1912 | Robert Falcon Scott | Reaches S Pole |
| 1914 | Ernest Shackleton | Leads expedition to the Antarctic |
| 1953 | Edmund Hillary and Tenzing Norgay | Make first ascent of Mt Everest |
| 1961 | Yuri Gagarin | Becomes first man in space |
| 1969 | Neil Armstrong and Buzz Aldrin | Make first landing on the moon |

This table comprises mainly European explorers; 'discovers' is used to indicate the first recorded visit by a European.

## Major battles and wars

| Date | Event | Explanation |
|---|---|---|
| c.1200BC | Trojan Wars | Greeks v. Trojans |
| 490–479BC | Persian Wars | Persia v. Greek city states |
| 490BC | Battle of Marathon | Athens defeat of Persia |
| 460–445BC | First Peloponnesian War | Sparta v. Athens |
| 431–404BC | Second Peloponnesian War | Sparta, Corinth, Persia v. Athens |
| 334–323BC | Conquests of Alexander the Great<br>Battle of Granicus (334BC)<br>Battle of Issus (333BC)<br>Battle of Guagmela (331BC) | v. Persia, Indian states |
| 306BC | Battle of Ipsus | 'Battle of the Kings', warring 'successors' of Alexander the Great |
| 264–241BC | First Punic War | Rome v. Carthage |
| 218–202BC | Second Punic War | Rome v. Carthage |
| 149–146BC | Third Punic War | Destruction of Carthage |
| 112–106BC | Numidian War | Rome v. Juguertia, King of Numidia |
| 73–71BC | Revolt of Spartacus | Slaves v. Rome |
| 58–51BC | Gallic Wars of Caesar | Rome v. Celtic tribes of Gaul (ancient France) |
| 55BC | Caesar's expedition to Britain | Rome v. British tribes |
| 48BC | Battle of Pharsalus | Julius Caesar's defeat of Pompey |
| 31BC | Battle of Actium | Octavian's defeat of Anthony and Cleopatra |
| 70AD | Siege of Jerusalem | Rome v. Israel (destruction of the Temple) |
| 84AD | Battle of Mons Graupius | Rome (Agricola) v. Scottish tribes |
| 375–454 | Hun raids on the Roman Empire | Attila v. tribes of Gaul and Italy |
| 665 | Battle of Basra | Arabs conquered by Muslims |
| 771–814 | Conquests of Charlemagne (Charles the Great) | v. Saxons, Lombards, Arabs (in Spain) |

| Date | Event | Explanation |
|---|---|---|
| 800–1016 | Viking Raids | v. Britain, Normandy, Russia, Spain, Morocco, Italy |
| 1066 | Battle of Hastings and Norman Conquest of England | William (the Conqueror) v. Harold II (King of Anglo Saxons) |
| 1089–94 | El Cid's conquest of Valencia | v. the Moors |
| 1095–1272 | The Crusades | Christians v. Muslims |
| 1190–1227 | Conquests of Genghis Khan | v. Naimans, Uigurs, N China, Kara-Chitai empire, Kharezm empire |
| 1211–1227 | Genghis Khan's conquest of N China and development of the Mongol empire | |
| 1206–1405 | Mongol Conquests | v. China |
| 1208–29 | Albigensian Crusade | Inquisition v. Cathars |
| 1220 | Fall of Samarkand to Genghis Khan | |
| 1282–1302 | War of the Sicilian Vespers | Sicilian rebels v. French rulers |
| 1297–1305 | Revolt of William Wallace | Scots v. English |
| 1314 | Battle of Bannockburn | Scots (under Robert Bruce) v. English |
| 1337–1453 | Hundred Years' War | England v. France |
| | Battle of Sluys (1340) | English defeat of French |
| | Battle of Crécy (1346) | English defeat of French |
| | Battle of Poitiers (1356) | English defeat of French |
| | Battle of Agincourt (1415) | English defeat of French |
| 1360–1405 | Conquests of Tamerlane (Timur) | v. Mongols, Persia, Prussia, India |
| 1388 | Battle of Otterburn (Chevy Chase) | Scots' defeat of English (under Sir Henry Percy, 'Hotspur') |
| 1403 | Battle of Shrewsbury | Glendower and Percies defeated by Henry V |
| 1411 | Battle of Harlaw | Highland v. Lowland Scots |
| 1429 | Siege of Orleans | Joan of Arc's defeat of English |
| 1453 | The Fall of Constantinople | Turkish conquest of Byzantine Empire |
| 1455–85 | Wars of the Roses | Series of civil wars in England (House of York v. House of Lancaster) |
| | Battle of St Albans (1455) | First battle of war: Yorkist victory |
| | Battle of Bosworth Field (1485) | Lancastrian victory: death of Richard III, accession of Henry VII |
| 1491–2 | The Siege of Granada | Spanish defeat of Moors |
| 1494–1559 | Habsburg–Valois Wars | |
| 1513 | Battle of Flodden | English defeat of Scots |
| 1542 | Battle of Solway Moss | English defeat of Scots |
| 1546–7 | War of the Schmalkaldic League | France v. German Protestant Estates |
| 1562 | Massacre at Vassy | Huguenots killed by de Guize |
| 1562–98 | French Wars of Religion | Catholics v. Huguenots |
| 1568–1648 | Dutch Wars of Independence | Successful revolt of Netherlands v. Philip II of Spain |
| 1571 | Battle of Lepanto | Spanish and Italian defeat of Turkish navy |
| 1572 | St Bartholomew's Day Massacre | Slaughter of French Huguenots by Charles IX |
| 1585–9 | War of the Three Henries | Henry IV secures succession to French throne |
| 1587 | Sack of Cadiz by Drake | Defeat of Philip II's Spanish ships |
| 1588 | Defeat of the Spanish Armada | English defeat of Spanish navy |
| 1592–9 | Japanese invasion of Korea | |
| 1596–1603 | Tyrone's Rebellion in Ireland | Irish v. English |
| 1605 | Gunpowder Plot | Catholic conspiracy against James I and the English Parliament |
| 1609–14 | War of the Julich Succession | Protestant v. Catholic powers of Europe |
| 1618–48 | Thirty Years' War | French king v. Habsburg rulers |
| 1620 | Battle of the White Mountain (Prague) | Defeat of Bohemian Protestants |
| 1628–31 | War of the Mantuan Succession | France v. Spain |
| 1639 | First Bishops' War | Scotland v. England |
| 1640 | Second Bishops' War | Scots' defeat of English |
| 1641–9 | Great Irish Rebellion | Ireland v. England |
| 1642–6 | English Civil War | Royalist forces of Charles I v. Parliamentarians under Cromwell |

## MAJOR BATTLES AND WARS

| Date | Event | Explanation |
|---|---|---|
| | Battle of Marston Moor (1644) | Parliamentary defeat of Royalists |
| 1688 | The Glorious Revolution | William III and Mary II ascend English throne after flight of James II |
| 1688–97 | War of the League of Augsburg | European alliance's defeat of Louis XIV |
| 1689 | Battle of Killiecrankie | Highland Scots' defeat of government |
| 1690 | Battle of the Boyne | Defeat of James II's Catholic forces by Protestant William III |
| 1692 | The Glencoe Massacre | Slaughter of McDonalds by Campbells (anti-Jacobite forces) |
| 1701–14 | War of the Spanish Succession | Grand Alliance v. Louis XIV of France |
| 1702–13 | Queen Anne's War | Britain v. France |
| 1704 | Battle of Blenheim | Allied troops' defeat of Louis XIV |
| 1715–16 | Jacobite Rebellion | Led by Earl of Mar v. Hanoverians |
| | Battle of Sherrifmuir (1715) | Hanoverians v. Jacobites, indecisive battle |
| 1739–43 | War of Jenkin's Ear | Britain v. Spain |
| 1740–48 | War of the Austrian Succession | Prussia v. Austria |
| 1745–6 | Jacobite Rebellion | Led by Charles Edward Stuart (Bonnie Prince Charlie) |
| | Battle of Prestonpans (1745) | Jacobite defeat of Hanoverians |
| | Battle of Culloden (1746) | Jacobite Highlanders crushed by Hanoverian forces |
| 1756–63 | Seven Years' War | Austria, France, Russia, Sweden and Saxony v. Prussia, Britain and Portugal |
| 1759 | Battle of Quebec | British defeat of French |
| 1763–6 | Pontiac's War | Unsuccessful uprising of Native Americans v. British colonists |
| 1775–83 | US War of Independence | American settlers v. British government forces |
| | Battle of Bunker Hill (1775) | First battle of war; heavy British losses |
| | Battle of Stillwater or Saratoga (1777) | American defeat of British |
| | Battle of Yorktown (1781) | American defeat of British, decisive campaign of war |
| 1789–92 | French Revolution | Popular movement overthrowing *ancien régime* to establish new constitution |
| 1792–1802 | French Revolutionary Wars | French campaigns v. various neighbouring states |
| 1792 | Battle of Valmy | French defeat of Prussians |
| 1798 | Battle of Aboukir Bay or the Nile | Napoleon's French fleet destroyed by Nelson |
| 1800–15 | Napoleonic Wars | Fought to preserve new French constitution and influence under Napoleon Bonaparte |
| | Battle of Austerlitz (1805) | French defeat of Austro-Russian army |
| | Battle of Trafalgar (1805) | English defeat of Napoleonic fleet |
| 1808–14 | Peninsular War | France v. Britain |
| | Battle of Corunna (1809) | British commander Sir John Moore killed by French |
| 1812 | Napoleon's retreat from Moscow | |
| 1814–16 | Gurkha War | Gurkhas v. British in India |
| 1815 | Battle of Waterloo | Napoleon defeated by Allied forces under Duke of Wellington |
| 1821–32 | Greek War of Independence | Greek rebellion v. Turkish rule |
| 1836 | Texan War of Independence, Battle of the Alamo | Americans v. Mexican rule |
| 1838–9 | Boer–Zulu War | |
| 1839–42 | First Opium War in China | British defeat of China |
| 1843–51 | Siege of Montevideo | Combined Argentine–Uruguayan army v. Montevideo with French and English support |
| 1844–7 | First Maori War | Maoris v. British settlers in New Zealand |
| 1846–7 | Mexican War | USA v. Mexico |
| 1853–6 | Crimean War | Britain v. Russia |
| | Battle of Balaclava (1856) | Unsuccessful Russian attack on British base; heavy British losses |

| Date | Event | Explanation |
|---|---|---|
| 1856–60 | Second Opium War in China | British defeat of China |
| 1857–8 | Mormon Utah War | Mormons v. Federal Government of USA |
| 1859 | John Brown's raid on Harper Ferry | Abolitionist attack on Federal arsenal |
| 1859–61 | Italian War of Unification | Austria v. Italy and France |
| | Battle of Solferino (1859) | French defeat of Austria |
| 1860–72 | Second Maori War | Maoris v. British settlers in New Zealand |
| 1861–5 | American Civil War | North (Union states) v. South (Confederate) |
| | Battle of Shiloh (1862) | Heavy losses to both sides |
| | Battle of Gettysburg (1863) | Unionist defeat of Confederates |
| | Battles of Petersburg (1864) | Successful Unionist campaign v. Confederates |
| 1866 | Seven Weeks' War | Prussia and Italy's defeat of Austria and allies |
| 1876 | Battle of Little Bighorn (Custer's Last Stand) | Defeat of US cavalry under General Custer by Sioux and Cheyenne |
| 1879 | Zulu War | British defeat of Zulu |
| 1879–84 | War of the Pacific | Chile v. Peru and Bolivia |
| 1880–1 | First Boer War | Boers' defeat of British |
| 1885 | Fall of Khartoum | Mahdi defeat of Egyptians; death of British General Gordon |
| 1890 | Massacre of Wounded Knee | US defeat of Sioux |
| 1899–1901 | Boxer Uprising in China | Unsuccessful anti-foreign uprising |
| 1899–1902 | Great Boer War | Boers v. British |
| | Battle of Ladysmith (1900) | Sieges of the British by the Boers |
| | Battle of Mafeking (1900) | |
| 1911–12 | Chinese Revolution | Overthrow of Manchu dynasty |
| 1914–18 | World War I | Triple Alliance (Britain, France and Russia) v. Triple Entente (Germany, Austria–Hungary and Turkey) |
| | Battles of Liège, Marne, Ypres and Tannenberg (1914) | Allied v. German forces |
| | Dardanelles and Gallipoli Campaigns (1915) | Unsuccessful Allied operations |
| | Battles of Loos and Ypres (1915) | Britain v. Germany |
| | Battle of Jutland (1916) | British fleet v. German fleet |
| | Battle of Verdun (1916) | France v. Germany |
| | Battle of Passchendaele (1917) | Third battle of Ypres, Britain v. Germany |
| | Battles of Amiens, Antwerp and the Second Battle of the Somme (1918) | Allied v. German forces |
| 1916 | Easter Rebellion in Dublin | Unsuccessful revolt by Irish nationalists v. British rule |
| 1917 | Russian Revolution | Overthrow of monarchy and beginning of Communism |
| 1918 | Hungarian Revolution | Communist revolt |
| 1932–7 | Communist rebellion in China | |
| 1935–6 | Italian invasion of Ethiopia | Mussolini's troops v. Ethiopia under Haile Selassie |
| 1936–9 | Spanish Civil War | Republicans v. Nationalists |
| | Battle of Ebro River (1938) | Nationalist defeat of Republicans |
| 1939–45 | World War II | Allied forces (Britain, France, USA, USSR) v. Germany, Japan, Italy |
| | Battle of Britain, Battle of Flanders, Evacuation of Dunkirk, Fall of France (1940) | Allied forces v. Germany |
| | Babi Yar Massacre (1941) | German slaughter of Jews |
| | Bombing of Pearl Harbor (1941) | Japanese attack on US naval base |
| | Battle of Stalingrad and Moscow (1941–2) | Soviet defeat of Germany |
| | Battle of Tobruk (1941–2) | Allied v. German forces |
| | Battle of Midway Island (1942) | US defeat of Japanese air force |
| | Battle of El Alamein (1942) | British defeat of Rommel's Afrika Corps |
| | Battle of Singapore (1942) | Japanese siege and occupation |
| | Battle of Salerno, Invasion of Sicily (1943) | Allied defeat of Germany and Italy |

| Date | Event | Explanation |
|---|---|---|
| | Burma Campaigns (1943–5) | British–Indian forces v. Japan |
| | D-Day allied invasion of Normandy (1944) | Allied defeat of Germany |
| | Battles of Anzio, Arnhem and Monte Cassino (1944) | Allied forces v. Germany |
| | Battle of the Bulge in the Ardennes (1944–5) | Eventual Allied defeat of Germany |
| | Battle of Iwo Jima (1945) | Allied capture of Japanese air-base |
| | Battle of the Rhine (1945) | Allied defeat of Germany |
| 1945–9 | Chinese Civil War | Communist v. non-communist forces |
| 1946–54 | French War of Indochina | Nationalist revolt v. France |
| 1947–8 | Indian Civil War | Pakistan v. India |
| 1950–3 | Korean War | Communist v. non-communist forces |
| 1952–6 | Mau-Mau uprisings in Kenya | Kikuyu revolt v. white settlers |
| 1956 | Suez War | Israel, Britain and France v. Egypt |
| 1956–1975 | Vietnam War | North Vietnam (communist) v. South Vietnam (non-communist) and US forces |
| 1960–8 | Civil War in the Congo | Military coup created first Marxist state in Africa, 1968 |
| 1961 | Bay of Pigs Invasion | Cuban defeat of exiles supported by USA |
| 1962–74 | Mozambique War of Independence | Nationalist revolt against Portuguese rule |
| 1967 | Six-Day War | Israel v. Arab states |
| 1967–70 | Nigerian–Biafran War | Nigerian defeat of Biafra |
| 1968 | Soviet invasion of Czechoslovakia | Defeat of attempt at liberalization from communism |
| 1968 | Tet offensive in Vietnam | Viet Cong v. South Vietnam and USA |
| 1970–1 | Jordanian Civil War | Jordan v. Palestinian guerillas |
| 1970–5 | Cambodian War | Cambodia, South Vietnam and USA v. North Vietnam, Viet Cong and Khmer Rouge |
| 1971 | Civil War in Pakistan | East v. West Pakistan |
| 1971 | My Lai massacre | Slaughter of Vietnamese villagers by US troops |
| 1973 | Chilean Revolution | Marxist government overthrown in military coup |
| 1974 | Turkish invasion of Cyprus | Turkey v. Greek Cypriots |
| 1975–88 | Angolan Civil War | Internal fighting after independence |
| 1978–9 | Ugandan Civil War | Ugandan exiles and Tanzanian defeat of Idi Amin Dada's regime |
| 1978 | Lebanese Civil War | Israeli invasion of S Lebanon |
| 1979– | Afghan Civil War and Soviet Invasion | Afghan resistance to Soviet invasion and to the Soviet-backed government remaining after their withdrawal in 1988, and subsequent internal disputes between Islamic factions |
| 1979 | Iranian Islamic Revolution | Republic established under Ayatollah Khomeini |
| 1980–8 | Iran–Iraq Gulf War | |
| 1982 | Falklands War | British defeat of Argentina |
| 1982–90 | Nicaraguan Civil War | Contras (supported by USA) v. Sandinista (socialist junta) |
| 1983 | Invasion of Grenada | US troops on peace-restoring mission |
| 1983– | Civil War in Sri Lanka | Buddhist v. Hindu groups |
| 1986 | Civil War in Haiti | Military coup and new constitution |
| 1991 | Gulf War | Iraqi invasion of Kuwait in 1990 resulted in the defeat of Iraq by US-led allies (29 countries, including UK) |
| 1991–5 | Civil War in Yugoslavia | Declaration of independence from Yugoslavia by Slovenia, Macedonia and Croatia, joined by Bosnia-Herzegovina in 1992, developed into civil war between Croats, Bosnians (mainly Slavic Muslims) and Serbs |
| 1990–6 | Civil War in Rwanda | Tutsi v. Hutu groups |
| 1996–7 | Civil War in Zaïre | Rebellion by forces of the Alliance of Democratic Forces for the Liberation of Congo-Zaïre (ADFL), led by Laurent Kabila |
| 1997– | Civil War in Sierra Leone | Military coup led by Major Johnny Paul Koroma |

# Monarchs

## Belgium

Belgium became an independent kingdom in 1831. A national congress elected Prince Leopold of Saxe-Coburg as king.

| Regnal dates | Name |
|---|---|
| 1831–65 | Leopold I |
| 1865–1909 | Leopold II |
| 1909–34 | Albert I |
| 1934–51 | Leopold III |
| 1951–93 | Baudouin |
| 1993– | Albert II |

## Denmark

| Regnal dates | Name |
|---|---|
| 1448–81 | Kristian I |
| 1481–1513 | Johan |
| 1513–23 | Kristian II |
| 1523–34 | Frederik I |
| 1534–59 | Kristian III |
| 1559–88 | Frederik II |
| 1588–1648 | Kristian IV |
| 1648–70 | Frederik III |
| 1670–99 | Kristian V |
| 1699–1730 | Frederik IV |
| 1730–46 | Kristian VI |
| 1746–66 | Frederik V |
| 1766–1808 | Kristian VII |
| 1808–39 | Frederik VI |
| 1839–48 | Kristian VIII |
| 1848–63 | Frederik VII |
| 1863–1906 | Kristian IX |
| 1906–12 | Frederik VIII |
| 1912–47 | Kristian X |
| 1947–72 | Frederik IX |
| 1972– | Margrethe II |

## England

| Regnal dates | Name |
|---|---|
| *West Saxon Kings* | |
| 802–39 | Egbert |
| 839–58 | Æthelwulf |
| 858–60 | Æthelbald |
| 860–5 | Æthelbert |
| 866–71 | Æthelred |
| 871–99 | Alfred |
| 899–924 | Edward (the Elder) |
| 924–39 | Athelstan |
| 939–46 | Edmund |
| 946–55 | Edred |
| 955–9 | Edwy |
| 959–75 | Edgar |
| 975–8 | Edward (the Martyr) |
| 978–1016 | Æthelred (the Unready) |
| 1016 | Edmund (Ironside) |
| *Danish Kings* | |
| 1016–35 | Knut (Canute) |
| 1035–7 | Harold *Regent* |
| 1037–40 | Harold I (Harefoot) |
| 1040–2 | Hardaknut |
| 1042–66 | Edward (the Confessor) |
| 1066 | Harold II |
| *House of Normandy* | |
| 1066–87 | William I (the Conqueror) |
| 1087–1100 | William II (Rufus) |
| 1100–35 | Henry I |
| *House of Blois* | |
| 1135–54 | Stephen |
| *House of Plantagenet* | |
| 1154–89 | Henry II |
| 1189–99 | Richard I (Cœur de Lion) |
| 1199–1216 | John |
| 1216–72 | Henry III |
| 1272–1307 | Edward I |
| 1307–27 | Edward II |
| 1327–77 | Edward III |
| 1377–99 | Richard II |
| *House of Lancaster* | |
| 1399–1413 | Henry IV |
| 1413–22 | Henry V |
| 1422–61 | Henry VI |
| *House of York* | |
| 1461–70 | Edward IV |
| *House of Lancaster* | |
| 1470–1 | Henry VI |
| *House of York* | |
| 1471–83 | Edward IV |
| 1483 | Edward V |
| 1483–5 | Richard III |
| *House of Tudor* | |
| 1485–1509 | Henry VII |
| 1509–47 | Henry VIII |
| 1547–53 | Edward VI |
| 1553–8 | Mary I |
| 1558–1603 | Elizabeth I |

## France

France became a republic in 1793, and an empire in 1804 under Napoleon Bonaparte. The monarchy was restored in 1814 and then once more dissolved in 1848.

| Regnal dates | Name |
|---|---|
| 987–996 | Hugh Capet |
| 996–1031 | Robert II |
| 1031–60 | Henry I |
| 1060–1108 | Philip I |
| 1108–37 | Louis VI |
| 1137–80 | Louis VII |
| 1180–1223 | Philip II Augustus |
| 1223–6 | Louis VIII |
| 1226–70 | Louis IX |
| 1270–85 | Philip III |
| 1285–1314 | Philip IV |
| 1314–16 | Louis X |
| 1316 | John I |
| 1316–22 | Philip V |
| 1322–8 | Charles IV |
| 1328–50 | Philip VI |
| 1350–64 | John II |
| 1364–80 | Charles V |
| 1380–1422 | Charles VI |
| 1422–61 | Charles VII |
| 1461–83 | Louis XI |
| 1483–98 | Charles VIII |
| 1498–1515 | Louis XII |
| 1515–47 | Francis I |
| 1547–59 | Henry II |
| 1559–60 | Francis II |
| 1560–74 | Charles IX |
| 1574–89 | Henry III |
| 1589–1610 | Henry IV (of Navarre) |
| 1610–43 | Louis XIII |
| 1643–1715 | Louis XIV |
| 1715–74 | Louis XV |
| 1774–92 | Louis XVI |
| 1814–24 | Louis XVIII |
| 1824–30 | Charles X |
| 1830–48 | Louis-Philippe |

## Germany

Modern Germany was united under Prussia in 1871; it became a republic (1919) after World War I and the abdication of William II in 1918.

| Regnal dates | Name |
|---|---|
| 1871–88 | William I |
| 1888 | Frederick |
| 1888–1918 | William II |

## Greece

In 1832 the Greek National Assembly elected Otto of Bavaria as King of modern Greece. In 1917 Constantine I abdicated the throne in favour of his son Alexander. In 1920 a plebiscite voted for his return. In 1922 he again abdicated. In 1923 the monarchy was deposed and a republic was proclaimed in 1924. In 1935 a plebiscite restored the monarchy until in 1967 a military junta staged a coup. The monarchy was formally abolished in 1973; Greece became a republic again in 1975.

| Regnal dates | Name |
|---|---|
| 1832–62 | Otto of Bavaria |
| 1863–1913 | George I (of Denmark) |
| 1913–17 | Constantine I |
| 1917–20 | Alexander |
| 1920–2 | Constantine I |
| 1922–3 | George II |
| 1935–47 | George II |
| 1947–64 | Paul |
| 1964–7 | Constantine II |

## Italy

Modern Italy became a united kingdom in 1861; it voted by referendum to become a republic in 1946.

| Regnal dates | Name |
|---|---|
| 1861–78 | Victor-Emanuel II |
| 1878–1900 | Humbert I |
| 1900–46 | Victor-Emanuel III |
| 1946 | Humbert II |

## Luxembourg

The Duchy of Luxembourg formally separated from the Netherlands in 1890.

| Regnal dates | Name |
|---|---|
| 1890–1905 | Adolf of Nassau |
| 1905–12 | William |
| 1912–19 | Marie Adélaïde |
| 1919–64 | Charlotte |
| 1964– | Jean |

## Netherlands

| Regnal dates | Name |
|---|---|
| 1572–84 | William the Silent |
| 1584–1625 | Maurice |
| 1625–47 | Frederick Henry |
| 1647–50 | William II |
| 1672–1702 | William III |
| 1747–51 | William IV |
| 1751–95 | William V |
| 1806–10 | Louis Bonaparte |
| 1813–40 | William I |
| 1840–9 | William II |
| 1849–90 | William III |
| 1890–1948 | Wilhelmina |
| 1948–80 | Juliana |
| 1980– | Beatrix |

## Portugal

From 1383 to 1385 the Portuguese throne was the subject of a dispute between John of Castile and John of Aviz. In 1826 Peter IV (I of Brazil) renounced his right to the Portuguese throne in order to remain in Brazil. His abdication was contingent upon his successor and daughter, Maria II marrying her uncle, Miguel. In 1828 Miguel usurped the throne on his own behalf. In 1834 Miguel was deposed and Maria II was restored to the throne. In 1910 Manuel II was deposed and Portugal became a republic.

| Regnal dates | Name |
|---|---|
| 1095–1112 | Henry of Burgundy |
| 1112–85 | Alfonso I |
| 1185–1211 | Sancho I |
| 1211–23 | Alfonso II |
| 1223–45 | Sancho II |
| 1245–79 | Alfonso III |
| 1279–1325 | Diniz |
| 1325–57 | Alfonso IV |
| 1357–67 | Peter I |
| 1367–83 | Ferdinand |
| 1385–1433 | John I of Aviz |
| 1433–8 | Edward |
| 1438–81 | Alfonso V |
| 1481–95 | John II |
| 1495–1521 | Manuel I |
| 1521–57 | John III |
| 1557–78 | Sebastian |
| 1578–80 | Henry |
| 1580–98 | Philip I (II of Spain) |
| 1598–1621 | Philip II (III of Spain) |
| 1621–40 | Philip III (IV of Spain) |
| 1640–56 | John IV of Braganza |
| 1656–83 | Alfonso VI |
| 1683–1706 | Peter II |
| 1706–50 | John V |
| 1750–77 | Joseph |
| 1777–1816 | Maria I |
| 1777–86 | Peter III (King Consort) |
| 1816–26 | John VI |
| 1826 | Peter IV (I of Brazil) |
| 1826–8 | Maria II |
| 1828–34 | Miguel |
| 1834–53 | Maria II |
| 1853–61 | Peter V |
| 1861–89 | Luis |
| 1889–1908 | Charles |
| 1908–10 | Manuel II |

## Russia

In 1610 Vasili Shuisky was deposed as Tsar and the throne remained vacant until the election of Michael Romanov in 1613. In 1682 a condition of the succession was that the two step-brothers, Ivan V and Peter I (the Great) should jointly be proclaimed as Tsars. In 1917 the empire was overthrown and Tsar Nicholas II was forced to abdicate.

| Regnal dates | Name |
|---|---|
| 1283–1303 | Daniel |
| 1303–25 | Yuri |
| 1325–41 | Ivan I |
| 1341–53 | Semeon |
| 1353–9 | Ivan II |
| 1359–89 | Dimitri Donskoy |
| 1389–1425 | Vasili I |
| 1425–62 | Vasili II |
| 1462–1505 | Ivan III (the Great) |
| 1505–33 | Vasili III |
| 1533–84 | Ivan IV (the Terrible) |

| Regnal dates | Name |
|---|---|
| 1584–98 | Feodor I |
| 1598–1605 | Boris Godunov |
| 1605 | Feodor II |
| 1605–6 | Dimitri II |
| 1606–10 | Vasili IV Shuisky |
| 1613–45 | Michael Romanov |
| 1645–76 | Alexei |
| 1676–82 | Feodor III |
| 1682–96 | Ivan V |
| 1682–1725 | Peter I (the Great) |
| 1725–7 | Catherine I |
| 1727–30 | Peter II |
| 1730–40 | Anne |
| 1740–1 | Ivan VI |
| 1741–62 | Elizabeth |
| 1762 | Peter III |
| 1762–96 | Catherine II (the Great) |
| 1796–1801 | Paul |
| 1801–25 | Alexander I |
| 1825–55 | Nicholas I |
| 1855–81 | Alexander II |
| 1881–94 | Alexander III |
| 1894–1917 | Nicholas II |

## Scotland

| Regnal dates | Name |
|---|---|
| 1005–34 | Malcolm II |
| 1034–40 | Duncan I |
| 1040–57 | Macbeth |
| 1057–8 | Lulach |
| 1058–93 | Malcolm III |
| 1093–4 | Donald Bane Deposed 1094 Restored 1094–7 |
| 1094 | Duncan II |
| 1097–1107 | Edgar |
| 1107–24 | Alexander I |
| 1124–53 | David I |
| 1153–65 | Malcolm IV |
| 1165–1214 | William I |
| 1214–49 | Alexander II |
| 1249–86 | Alexander III |
| 1286–90 | Margaret |
| 1290–2 | (Interregnum) |
| 1292–96 | John Balliol |
| 1296–1306 | (Interregnum) |
| 1306–29 | Robert I (the Bruce) |
| 1329–71 | David II |
| 1371–90 | Robert II |
| 1390–1406 | Robert III |
| 1406–37 | James I |
| 1437–60 | James II |
| 1460–88 | James III |
| 1488–1513 | James IV |
| 1513–42 | James V |
| 1542–67 | Mary Queen of Scots |
| 1567–1625 | James VI [1] |

[1] In 1603, James VI succeeded Elizabeth I to the English throne (Union of the Crowns) and united the thrones of Scotland and England.

## Spain

Philip V abdicated in favour of Luis in 1724, but returned to the throne in the same year following Luis' death. After the French invasion of Spain in 1808, Napoleon set up Joseph Bonaparte as king. In 1814 Ferdinand was restored to the crown. In 1868 a revolution deposed Isabella II. In 1870 Amadeus of Savoy was elected as king. In 1873 he resigned the throne and a temporary republic was formed. In 1874 Alfonso XII restored the Bourbon dynasty to the throne. In 1931 Alfonso XIII was deposed and a republican constitution was proclaimed. From 1939 Franco ruled Spain under a dictatorship until his death in 1975 and the restoration of King Juan Carlos.

| Regnal dates | Name |
|---|---|
| 1516–56 | Charles I (Emperor Charles V) |
| 1556–98 | Philip II |
| 1598–1621 | Philip III |
| 1621–65 | Philip IV |
| 1665–1700 | Charles II |
| 1700–24 | Philip V |
| 1724 | Luis |
| 1724–46 | Philip V |
| 1746–59 | Ferdinand VI |
| 1759–88 | Charles III |
| 1788–1808 | Charles IV |
| 1808 | Ferdinand VII |
| 1808–14 | Joseph Bonaparte |
| 1814–33 | Ferdinand VII |
| 1833–68 | Isabella II |
| 1870–3 | Amadeus of Savoy |
| 1874–85 | Alfonso XII |
| 1886–1931 | Alfonso XIII |
| 1975– | Juan Carlos |

## United Kingdom

| Regnal dates | Name |
|---|---|
| *House of Stuart* | |
| 1603–25 | James I (VI of Scotland) |
| 1625–49 | Charles I |
| *Commonwealth and Protectorate* | |
| 1649–53 | *Council of State* |
| 1653–8 | Oliver Cromwell *Lord Protector* |
| 1658–9 | Richard Cromwell *Lord Protector* |
| *House of Stuart (restored)* | |
| 1660–85 | Charles II |
| 1685–8 | James II |
| 1689–94 | William III (*jointly with* Mary II) |
| 1694–1702 | William III (*alone*) |
| 1702–14 | Anne |
| *House of Hanover* | |
| 1714–27 | George I |
| 1727–60 | George II |
| 1760–1820 | George III |
| 1820–30 | George IV |
| 1830–7 | William IV |
| 1837–1901 | Victoria |
| *House of Saxe-Coburg* | |
| 1901–10 | Edward VII |
| *House of Windsor* | |
| 1910–36 | George V |
| 1936 | Edward VIII |
| 1936–52 | George VI |
| 1952– | Elizabeth II |

## Roman kings

The founding of Rome by Romulus is a Roman literary tradition.

| Regnal dates | Name |
|---|---|
| 753–715BC | Romulus |
| 715–673BC | Numa Pompilius |
| 673–642BC | Tullus Hostilius |
| 642–616BC | Ancus Marcius |
| 616–578BC | Tarquinius Priscus |
| 578–534BC | Servius Tullius |
| 534–509BC | Tarquinius Superbus |

## Roman emperors

Dates overlap where there are periods of joint rule (eg Marcus Aurelius and Lucius Verus) and where the government of the empire divides between east and west.

| Regnal dates | Name |
|---|---|
| 27BC–14AD | Augustus (Caesar Augustus) |
| 14–37 | Tiberius |
| 37–41 | Caligula (Gaius Caesar) |
| 41–54 | Claudius |
| 54–68 | Nero |
| 68–69 | Galba |
| 69 | Otho |
| 69 | Vitellius |
| 69–79 | Vespasian |
| 79–81 | Titus |
| 81–96 | Domitian |
| 96–98 | Nerva |
| 98–117 | Trajan |
| 117–138 | Hadrian |
| 138–161 | Antoninus Pius |
| 161–180 | Marcus Aurelius |
| 161–169 | Lucius Verus |
| 176–192 | Commodus |
| 193 | Pertinax |
| 193 | Didius Julianus |
| 193–211 | Septemius Severus |
| 198–217 | Caracalla |
| 209–212 | Geta |
| 217–218 | Macrinus |
| 218–222 | Elagabalus |
| 222–235 | Alexander Severus |
| 235–238 | Maximin |
| 238 | Gordian I |
| 238 | Gordian II |
| 238 | Maximus |
| 238 | Balbinus |
| 238–244 | Gordian III |
| 244–249 | Philip |
| 249–251 | Decius |
| 251 | Hostilian |
| 251–253 | Gallus |
| 253 | Aemilian |
| 253–260 | Valerian |
| 253–268 | Gallienus |
| 268–269 | Claudius II (the Goth) |
| 269–270 | Quintillus |
| 270–275 | Aurelian |
| 275–276 | Tacitus |
| 276 | Florian |
| 276–282 | Probus |
| 282–283 | Carus |
| 283–285 | Carinus |
| 283–284 | Numerian |
| 284–305 | Diocletian–(East) |
| 286–305 | Maximian–(West) |
| 305–311 | Galerius–(East) |
| 305–306 | Constantius I |
| 306–307 | Severus–(West) |
| 306–312 | Maxentius–(West) |
| 306–337 | Constantine I |
| 308–324 | Licinius–(East) |
| 337–340 | Constantine II |
| 337–350 | Constans I |
| 337–361 | Constantius II |
| 350–351 | Magnentius |
| 360–363 | Julian |
| 364–375 | Valentinian I–(West) |
| 364–378 | Valens–(East) |
| 365–366 | Procopius–(East) |
| 375–383 | Gratian–(West) |
| 375–392 | Valentinian II–(West) |
| 379–395 | Theodosius I |
| 395–408 | Arcadius–(East) |
| 395–423 | Honorius–(West) |
| 408–450 | Theodosius II–(East) |
| 421–423 | Constantius III–(West) |
| 423–455 | Valentinian III–(West) |
| 450–457 | Marcian–(East) |
| 455 | Petronius Maximus –(West) |
| 455–456 | Avitus–(West) |
| 457–474 | Leo I–(East) |
| 457–461 | Majorian–(West) |
| 461–467 | Libius Severus–(West) |
| 467–472 | Anthemius–(West) |
| 472–473 | Olybrius–(West) |
| 474–480 | Julius Nepos–(West) |
| 474 | Leo II–(East) |
| 474–491 | Zeno–(East) |
| 475–476 | Romulus Augustus –(West) |

## Emperors of the Holy Roman Empire

| Regnal dates | Name |
|---|---|
| 800–814 | Charlemagne (Charles I) |
| 814–840 | Louis I (the Pious) |
| 840–843 | *Civil War* |
| 843–855 | Lothair |
| 855–875 | Louis II |
| 875–877 | Charles II (the Bald) |
| 877–881 | *Interregnum* |
| 881–887 | Charles III (the Fat) |
| 887–891 | *Interregnum* |
| 891–894 | Guido of Spoleto |
| 892–898 | Lambert of Spoleto[1] |
| 896–899 | Arnulf[2] |
| 901–905 | Louis III |
| 911–918 | Conrad I[2] |
| 905–924 | Berengar |
| 919–936 | Henry I |
| 936–973 | Otto I (the Great) |
| 973–983 | Otto II |
| 983–1002 | Otto III |
| 1002–24 | Henry II (the Saint) |
| 1024–39 | Conrad II |
| 1039–56 | Henry III (the Black) |
| 1056–1106 | Henry IV |
| 1077–80 | Rudolf[2] |
| 1081–93 | Hermann[2] |
| 1093–1101 | Conrad[2] |
| 1106–25 | Henry V |
| 1125–37 | Lothair II |
| 1138–52 | Conrad III |
| 1152–90 | Frederick I (Barbarossa) |
| 1190–7 | Henry VI |
| 1198–1208 | Philip[2] |
| 1198–1214 | Otto IV |
| 1215–50 | Frederick II |
| 1246–7 | Henry Raspe[2] |
| 1247–56 | William of Holland[2] |
| 1250–4 | Conrad IV |

| Regnal dates | Name | Regnal dates | Name | Regnal dates | Name |
|---|---|---|---|---|---|
| 1254–73 | *Great Interregnum* | 1410–37 | Sigismund | 1711–40 | Charles VI |
| 1257–72 | Richard[2] | 1438–9 | Albert II | 1740–42 | *Interregnum* |
| 1257–75 | Alfonso (Alfonso X of Castile)[2] | 1440–93 | Frederick III | 1742–5 | Charles VII |
| | | 1493–1519 | Maximilian I | 1745–65 | Francis I |
| 1273–91 | Rudolf I | 1519–56 | Charles V | 1765–90 | Joseph II |
| 1292–8 | Adolf | 1556–64 | Ferdinand I | 1790–2 | Leopold II |
| 1298–1308 | Albert I | 1564–76 | Maximilian II | 1792–1806 | Francis II |
| 1308–13 | Henry VII | 1576–1612 | Rudolf II | | |
| 1314–26 | Frederick (III)[3] | 1612–19 | Matthias | | |
| 1314–46 | Louis IV | 1619–37 | Ferdinand II | | |
| 1346–78 | Charles IV | 1637–57 | Ferdinand III | | |
| 1378–1400 | Wenceslas | 1658–1705 | Leopold I | | |
| 1400–10 | Rupert | 1705–11 | Joseph I | | |

[1] Co-emperor [2] Rival [3] Co-regent

## Popes

Antipopes (who claimed to be pope in opposition to those canonically chosen) are given in square brackets.

| | | | | | |
|---|---|---|---|---|---|
| until c.64 | Peter | 402–17 | Innocent I | 678–81 | Agatho |
| c.64–c.76 | Linus | 417–18 | Zosimus | 682–3 | Leo II |
| c.76–c.90 | Anacletus | 418–22 | Boniface I | 684–5 | Benedict II |
| c.90–c.99 | Clement I | [418–19 | Eulalius] | 685–6 | John V |
| c.99–c.105 | Evaristus | 422–32 | Celestine I | 686–7 | Cono |
| c.105–c.117 | Alexander I | 432–40 | Sixtus III | [687 | Theodore] |
| c.117–c.127 | Sixtus I | 440–61 | Leo I | [687–92 | Paschal] |
| c.127–c.137 | Telesphorus | 461–8 | Hilarus | 687–701 | Sergius I |
| c.137–c.140 | Hyginus | 468–83 | Simplicius | 701–5 | John VI |
| c.140–c.154 | Pius I | 483–92 | Felix III (II) | 705–7 | John VII |
| c.154–c.166 | Anicetus | 492–6 | Gelasius I | 708 | Sisinnius |
| c.166–c.175 | Soter | 496–8 | Anastasius II | 708–15 | Constantine |
| 175–89 | Eleutherius | 498–514 | Symmachus | 715–31 | Gregory II |
| 189–98 | Victor I | [498, 501–5 | Laurentius] | 731–41 | Gregory III |
| 198–217 | Zephyrinus | 514–23 | Hormisdas | 741–52 | Zacharias |
| 217–22 | Callistus I | 523–6 | John I | 752 | Stephen II (*not consecrated)* |
| [217–c.235 | Hippolytus] | 526–30 | Felix IV (III) | | |
| 222–30 | Urban I | 530–2 | Boniface II | 752–7 | Stephen II (III) |
| 230–5 | Pontian | [530 | Dioscorus] | 757–67 | Paul I |
| 235–6 | Anterus | 533–5 | John II | [767–9 | Constantine II] |
| 236–50 | Fabian | 535–6 | Agapetus I | [768 | Philip] |
| 251–3 | Cornelius | 536–7 | Silverius | 768–72 | Stephen III (IV) |
| [251–c.258 | Novatian] | 537–55 | Vigilius | 772–95 | Hadrian I |
| 253–4 | Lucius I | 556–61 | Pelagius I | 795–816 | Leo III |
| 254–7 | Stephen I | 561–74 | John III | 816–17 | Stephen IV (V) |
| 257–8 | Sixtus II | 575–9 | Benedict I | 817–24 | Paschal I |
| 259–68 | Dionysius | 579–90 | Pelagius II | 824–7 | Eugenius II |
| 269–74 | Felix I | 590–604 | Gregory I | 827 | Valentine |
| 275–83 | Eutychianus | 604–6 | Sabinianus | 827–44 | Gregory IV |
| 283–96 | Caius | 607 | Boniface III | [844 | John] |
| 296–304 | Marcellinus | 608–15 | Boniface IV | 844–7 | Sergius II |
| 308–9 | Marcellus I | 615–18 | Deusdedit *or* Adeodatus I | 847–55 | Leo IV |
| 310 | Eusebius | | | 855–8 | Benedict III |
| 311–14 | Miltiades | 619–25 | Boniface V | [855 | Anastasius Bibliothecarius] |
| 314–35 | Sylvester I | 625–38 | Honorius I | | |
| 336 | Mark | 640 | Severinus | 858–67 | Nicholas I |
| 337–52 | Julius I | 640–2 | John IV | 867–72 | Hadrian II |
| 352–66 | Liberius | 642–9 | Theodore I | 872–82 | John VIII |
| [355–65 | Felix II] | 649–55 | Martin I | 882–4 | Marinus I |
| 366–84 | Damasus I | 654–7 | Eugenius I[1] | 884–5 | Hadrian III |
| [366–7 | Ursinus] | 657–72 | Vitalian | 885–91 | Stephen V (VI) |
| 384–99 | Siricius | 672–6 | Adeodatus II | 891–6 | Formosus |
| 399–401 | Anastasius I | 676–8 | Donus | 896 | Boniface VI |

| | |
|---|---|
| 896–7 | Stephen VI (VII) |
| 897 | Romanus |
| 897 | Theodore II |
| 898–900 | John IX |
| 900–3 | Benedict IV |
| 903 | Leo V |
| [903–4 | Christopher] |
| 904–11 | Sergius III |
| 911–13 | Anastasius III |
| 913–14 | Lando |
| 914–28 | John X |
| 928 | Leo VI |
| 928–31 | Stephen VII (VIII) |
| 931–5 | John XI |
| 936–9 | Leo VII |
| 939–42 | Stephen IX |
| 942–6 | Marinus II |
| 946–55 | Agapetus II |
| 955–64 | John XII |
| 963–5 | Leo VIII |
| 964–6 | Benedict V |
| 965–72 | John XIII |
| 973–4 | Benedict VI |
| [974, 984–5 | Boniface VII] |
| 974–83 | Benedict VII |
| 983–4 | John XIV |
| 985–96 | John XV |
| 996–9 | Gregory V |
| [997–8 | John XVI] |
| 999–1003 | Sylvester II |
| 1003 | John XVII |
| 1004–9 | John XVIII |
| 1009–12 | Sergius IV |
| 1012–24 | Benedict VIII |
| [1012 | Gregory] |
| 1024–32 | John XIX |
| 1032–44 | Benedict IX |
| 1045 | Sylvester III |
| 1045 | Benedict IX *(second reign)* |
| 1045–6 | Gregory VI |
| 1046–7 | Clement II |
| 1047–8 | Benedict IX *(third reign)* |
| 1048 | Damasus II |
| 1048–54 | Leo IX |
| 1055–7 | Victor II |
| 1057–8 | Stephen IX (X) |
| [1058–9 | Benedict X] |
| 1059–61 | Nicholas II |
| 1061–73 | Alexander II |
| [1061–72 | Honorius II] |
| 1073–85 | Gregory VII |
| [1080, 1084–1100 | Clement VII] |
| 1086–7 | Victor III |
| 1088–99 | Urban II |
| 1099–1118 | Paschal II |
| [1100–2 | Theodoric] |
| [1102 | Albert] |
| [1105–11 | Sylvester IV] |
| 1118–19 | Gelasius II |
| [1118–21 | Gregory VIII] |
| 1119–24 | Callistus II |
| 1124–30 | Honorius II |
| [1124 | Celestine II] |
| 1130–43 | Innocent II |
| [1130–8 | Anacletus II] |
| [1138 | Victor IV][2] |
| 1143–4 | Celestine II |
| 1144–5 | Lucius II |
| 1145–53 | Eugenius III |
| 1153–4 | Anastasius IV |
| 1154–9 | Hadrian IV |
| 1159–81 | Alexander III |
| [1159–64 | Victor IV][2] |
| [1164–8 | Paschal III] |
| [1168–78 | Callistus III] |
| [1179–80 | Innocent III] |
| 1181–5 | Lucius III |
| 1185–7 | Urban III |
| 1187 | Gregory VIII |
| 1187–91 | Clement III |
| 1191–8 | Celestine III |
| 1198–1216 | Innocent III |
| 1216–27 | Honorius III |
| 1227–41 | Gregory IX |
| 1241 | Celestine IV |
| 1243–54 | Innocent IV |
| 1254–61 | Alexander IV |
| 1261–4 | Urban IV |
| 1265–8 | Clement IV |
| 1271–6 | Gregory X |
| 1276 | Innocent V |
| 1276 | Hadrian V |
| 1276–7 | John XXI[3] |
| 1277–80 | Nicholas III |
| 1281–5 | Martin IV |
| 1285–7 | Honorius IV |
| 1288–92 | Nicholas IV |
| 1294 | Celestine V |
| 1294–1303 | Boniface VIII |
| 1303–4 | Benedict XI |
| 1305–14 | Clement V |
| 1316–34 | John XXII |
| [1328–30 | Nicholas V] |
| 1334–42 | Benedict XII |
| 1342–52 | Clement VI |
| 1352–62 | Innocent VI |
| 1362–70 | Urban V |
| 1370–8 | Gregory XI |
| 1378–89 | Urban VI |
| [1378–94 | Clement VII] |
| 1389–1404 | Boniface IX |
| [1394–1423 | Benedict XIII] |
| 1404–6 | Innocent VII |
| 1406–15 | Gregory XII |
| [1409–10 | Alexander V] |
| [1410–15 | John XXIII] |
| 1417–31 | Martin V |
| [1423–9 | Clement VIII] |
| [1425–30 | Benedict XIV] |
| 1431–47 | Eugenius IV |
| [1439–49 | Felix V] |
| 1447–55 | Nicholas V |
| 1455–8 | Callistus III |
| 1458–64 | Pius II |
| 1464–71 | Paul II |
| 1471–84 | Sixtus IV |
| 1484–92 | Innocent VIII |
| 1492–1503 | Alexander VI |
| 1503 | Pius III |
| 1503–13 | Julius II |
| 1513–21 | Leo X |
| 1522–3 | Hadrian VI |
| 1523–34 | Clement VII |
| 1534–49 | Paul III |
| 1550–5 | Julius III |
| 1555 | Marcellus II |
| 1555–9 | Paul IV |
| 1559–65 | Pius IV |
| 1566–72 | Pius V |
| 1572–85 | Gregory XIII |
| 1585–90 | Sixtus V |
| 1590 | Urban VII |
| 1590–1 | Gregory XIV |
| 1591 | Innocent IX |
| 1592–1605 | Clement VIII |
| 1605 | Leo XI |
| 1605–21 | Paul V |
| 1621–3 | Gregory XV |
| 1623–44 | Urban VIII |
| 1644–55 | Innocent X |
| 1655–67 | Alexander VII |
| 1667–9 | Clement IX |
| 1670–6 | Clement X |
| 1676–89 | Innocent XI |
| 1689–91 | Alexander VIII |
| 1691–1700 | Innocent XII |
| 1700–21 | Clement XI |
| 1721–4 | Innocent XIII |
| 1724–30 | Benedict XIII |
| 1730–40 | Clement XII |
| 1740–58 | Benedict XIV |
| 1758–69 | Clement XIII |
| 1769–74 | Clement XIV |
| 1775–99 | Pius VI |
| 1800–23 | Pius VII |
| 1823–9 | Leo XII |
| 1829–30 | Pius VIII |
| 1831–46 | Gregory XVI |
| 1846–78 | Pius IX |
| 1878–1903 | Leo XIII |
| 1903–14 | Pius X |
| 1914–22 | Benedict XV |
| 1922–39 | Pius XI |
| 1939–58 | Pius XII |
| 1958–63 | John XXIII |
| 1963–78 | Paul VI |
| 1978 | John Paul I |
| 1978– | John Paul II |

[1] Elected during the banishment of Martin I. [2] Different individuals. [3] There was no John XX.

## Japanese emperors

The first 14 emperors (to Chuai) are regarded as legendary, and the regnal dates for the 15th to the 28th emperor (Senka), taken from the early Japanese chronicle, 'Nihon shoki', are not considered to be authentic.

| Regnal dates | Name |
|---|---|
| 660–585BC | Jimmu |
| 581–549BC | Suizei |
| 549–511BC | Annei |
| 510–477BC | Itoku |
| 475–393BC | Kosho |
| 392–291BC | Koan |
| 290–215BC | Korei |
| 214–158BC | Kogen |
| 158–98BC | Kaika |
| 97–30BC | Sujin |
| 29BC–70AD | Suinin |
| 71–130 | Keiko |
| 131–190 | Seimu |
| 192–200 | Chuai |
| 270–310 | Ojin |
| 313–399 | Nintoku |
| 400–405 | Richu |
| 406–410 | Hanzei |
| 412–453 | Ingyo |
| 453–456 | Anko |
| 456–479 | Yuryaku |
| 480–484 | Seinei |
| 485–487 | Kenzo |
| 488–498 | Ninken |
| 498–506 | Buretsu |
| 507–531 | Keitai |
| 531–535 | Ankan |
| 535–539 | Senka |
| 539–571 | Kimmei |
| 572–585 | Bidatsu |
| 585–587 | Yomei |
| 587–592 | Sushun |
| 592–628 | Suiko (Empress) |
| 629–641 | Jomei |
| 642–645 | Kogyoku (Empress) |
| 645–654 | Kotuko |
| 655–661 | Saimei (Empress) |
| 662–671 | Tenji |
| 671–672 | Kobun |
| 673–686 | Temmu |
| 686–697 | Jito (Empress) |
| 697–707 | Mommu |
| 707–715 | Gemmei (Empress) |
| 715–724 | Gensho (Empress) |
| 724–749 | Shomu |
| 749–758 | Koken (Empress) |
| 758–764 | Junnin |
| 764–770 | Shotoku (Empress) |
| 770–781 | Konin |
| 781–806 | Kammu |
| 806–809 | Heizei |
| 809–823 | Saga |
| 823–833 | Junna |
| 833–850 | Nimmyo |
| 850–858 | Montoku |
| 858–876 | Seiwa |
| 876–884 | Yozei |
| 884–887 | Koko |
| 887–897 | Uda |
| 897–930 | Daigo |
| 930–946 | Suzaku |
| 946–967 | Murakami |
| 967–969 | Reizei |
| 969–984 | En-yu |
| 984–986 | Kazan |
| 986–1011 | Ichijo |
| 1011–16 | Sanjo |
| 1016–36 | Go-Ichijo |
| 1036–45 | Go-Suzaku |
| 1045–68 | Go-Reizei |
| 1068–72 | Go-Sanyo |
| 1072–86 | Shirakawa |
| 1086–1107 | Horikawa |
| 1107–23 | Toba |
| 1123–41 | Sutoku |
| 1141–55 | Konoe |
| 1155–8 | Go-Shirakawa |
| 1158–65 | Nijo |
| 1165–8 | Rokujo |
| 1168–80 | Takakura |
| 1180–3 | Antoku |
| 1183–98 | Go-Toba |
| 1198–1210 | Tsuchimikado |
| 1210–21 | Juntoku |
| 1221 | Chukyo |
| 1221–32 | Go-Horikawa |
| 1232–42 | Shijo |
| 1242–6 | Go-Saga |
| 1246–59 | Go-Fukakusa |
| 1259–74 | Kameyama |
| 1274–87 | Go-Uda |
| 1287–98 | Fushimi |
| 1298–1301 | Go-Fushimi |
| 1301–8 | Go-Nijo |
| 1308–18 | Hanazono |
| 1318–39 | Go-Daigo |
| 1339–68 | Go-Murakami |
| 1368–83 | Chokei |
| 1383–92 | Go-Kameyama |
| *Northern Court* | |
| 1331–3 | Kogon |
| 1336–48 | Komyo |
| 1348–51 | Suko |
| 1352–71 | Go-Kogon |
| 1371–82 | Go-Enyu |
| 1382–1412 | Go-Komatsu |
| 1412–28 | Shoko |
| 1428–64 | Go-Hanazono |
| 1464–1500 | Go-Tsuchimikado |
| 1500–26 | Go-Kashiwabara |
| 1526–57 | Go-Nara |
| 1557–86 | Ogimachi |
| 1586–1611 | Go-Yozei |
| 1611–29 | Go-Mizuno-o |
| 1629–43 | Meisho (Empress) |
| 1643–54 | Go-Komyo |
| 1654–63 | Go-Sai |
| 1663–87 | Reigen |
| 1687–1709 | Higashiyama |
| 1709–35 | Nakamikado |
| 1735–47 | Sakuramachi |
| 1747–62 | Momozono |
| 1762–70 | Go-Sakuramachi |
| 1770–9 | Go-Momozono |
| 1779–1817 | Kokaku |
| 1817–46 | Ninko |
| 1846–66 | Komei |
| 1867–1912 | Meiji |
| 1912–26 | Taisho |
| 1926–89 | Hirohito |
| 1989– | Akihito |

## Ancient Egyptian dynasties

| Date BC | Dynasty | Period |
|---|---|---|
| c.3100–2890 | I | **Early Dynastic Period** |
| c.2890–2686 | II | (First use of stone in building.) |
| c.2686–2613 | III | **Old Kingdom** |
| c.2613–2494 | IV | (The age of the great pyramid |
| c.2494–2345 | V | builders. Longest reign in |
| c.2345–2181 | VI | history: Pepi II, 90 years.) |
| c.2181–2173 | VII | **First Intermediate Period** |
| c.2173–2160 | VIII | (Social order upset; few |
| c.2160–2130 | IX | monuments built.) |
| c.2130–2040 | X | |
| c.2133–1991 | XI | |
| 1991–1786 | XII | **Middle Kingdom** |
| 1786–1633 | XIII | (Golden age of art and |
| | | craftsmanship.) |
| 1786–c.1603 | XIV | **Second Intermediate Period** |
| 1674–1567 | XV | (Country divided into |
| | | principalities.) |
| c.1684–1567 | XVI | |
| c.1660–1567 | XVII | |
| 1567–1320 | XVIII | **New Kingdom** |
| 1320–1200 | XIX | (Began with colonial expansion, |
| 1200–1085 | XX | ended in divided rule.) |
| 1085–945 | XXI | **Third Intermediate Period** |
| 945–745 | XXII | (Revival of prosperity and |
| 745–718 | XXIII | restoration of cults.) |
| 718–715 | XXIV | |
| 715–668 | XXV | |
| 664–525 | XXVI | **Late Period** |
| 525–404 | XXVII | (Completion of Nile–Red Sea |
| 404–399 | XXVIII | canal. Alexander the Great |
| 399–380 | XXIX | reached Alexandria in 332BC.) |
| 380–343 | XXX | |
| 343–332 | XXXI | |

## Chinese dynasties

| Regnal dates | Name |
|---|---|
| c.22nd–18th-cBC | Hsia |
| c.18th–12th-cBC | Shang or Yin |
| c.1111–256BC | Chou |
| c.1111–770BC | Western Chou |
| 770–256BC | Eastern Chou |
| 770–476BC | Ch'un Ch'iu Period |
| 475–221BC | Warring States Period |
| 221–206BC | Ch'in |
| 206BC–220AD | Han |
| 206BC–9AD | Western Han |
| 9–23 | Hsin Interregnum |
| 25–220 | Eastern Han |
| 220–265 | Three Kingdoms Period |
| 265–420 | Chin |
| 265–317 | Western Chin |
| 317–420 | Eastern Chin |
| 420–589 | Northern and Southern Dynasties |
| 581–618 | Sui |
| 618–907 | Tang |
| 907–960 | Five Dynasties and Ten Kingdoms Period |
| 960–1279 | Sung |
| 960–1127 | Northern Sung |
| 1127–1279 | Southern Sung |
| 1115–1234 | Chin (Jurchen Tartars) |
| 1279–1368 | Yuan (Mongol) |
| 1368–1644 | Ming |
| 1644–1912 | Ch'ing or Qing (Manchu) |

## Mughal emperors

The 2nd Mughal emperor, Humayun, lost his throne in 1540, became a fugitive, and did not regain his title until 1555.

| Regnal dates | Name |
|---|---|
| 1526–30 | Babur |
| 1530–56 | Humayun |
| 1556–1605 | Akbar |
| 1605–27 | Jahangir |
| 1627–58 | Shah Jahan |
| 1658–1707 | Aurangzeb (Alamgir) |
| 1707–12 | Bahadur Shah I (or Shah Alam I) |
| 1712–13 | Jahandar Shah |
| 1713–19 | Farruksiyar |
| 1719 | Rafid-ud-Darajat |
| 1719 | Rafi-ud-Daulat |
| 1719 | Nekusiyar |
| 1719 | Ibrahim |
| 1719–48 | Muhammad Shah |
| 1748–54 | Ahmad Shah |
| 1754–9 | Alamgir II |
| 1759–1806 | Shah Alam II |
| 1806–37 | Akbar II |
| 1837–57 | Bahadur Shah II |

# Political leaders 1900–2001

Countries and organizations are listed alphabetically, with former or alternative names given in parentheses. Rulers are named chronologically since 1900 or (for new nations) since independence. For some major English-speaking nations, relevant details are also given of pre-20th-century rulers, along with a note of any political affiliation.

The list does not distinguish successive terms of office by a single ruler.

There is no universally agreed way of transliterating proper names in non-Roman alphabets; variations from the spellings given are therefore to be expected, especially in the case of Arabic rulers.

Minor variations in the titles adopted by Chiefs of State, or in the name of an administration, are not given; these occur most notably in countries under military rule.

Listings complete to December 2001.

## Afghanistan

### ❑ Afghan Empire

*Monarch*

1881–1901 Abdur Rahman Khan
1901–19 Habibullah Khan
1919–29 Amanullah Khan
1929 Habibullah Ghazi
1929–33 Nadir Shah
1933–73 Zahir Shah

### ❑ Republic of Afghanistan

*Prime Minister*

1973–8 Mohammad Daoud Khan

### ❑ Democratic Republic of Afghanistan

*Revolutionary Council - President*

1978–9 Nour Mohammad Taraki
1979 Hafizullah Amin

**Soviet Invasion**

1979–86 Babrak Karmal
1986–7 Haji Mohammad Chamkani *Acting President*
1987–92 Mohammad Najibullah
1992 Sebghatullah Mojaddedi *Acting President*

*General Secretary*

1978–86 *As President*
1986–92 Mohammad Najibullah

*Prime Minister*

1929–46 Sardar Mohammad Hashim Khan
1946–53 Shah Mahmoud Khan Ghazi
1953–63 Mohammad Daoud
1963–5 Mohammad Yousef
1965–7 Mohammad Hashim Maiwandwal
1967–71 Nour Ahmad Etemadi
1972–3 Mohammad Mousa Shafiq
1973–9 *As President*
1979–81 Babrak Karmal
1981–8 Sultan Ali Keshtmand

### ❑ Republic of Afghanistan (from 1987)

1988–9 Mohammad Hasan Sharq
1989–90 Sultan Ali Keshtmand
1990–2 Fazal Haq Khaliqyar
1992–3 Abdul Sabour Fareed
1993–6 Gulbuddin Hekmatyar

### ❑ Islamic State of Afghanistan

*President*

1992–2001 Burhanuddin Rabbani

*Chairman Interim Government*

2001– Hamid Karzai

## Albania

*Monarch*

1928–39 Zog I (Ahmed Zogu)
1939–44 *Italian rule*

### ❑ People's Socialist Republic (from 1946)

*President*

1944–85 Enver Hoxha
1985–92 Ramiz Alia

### ❑ Republic of Albania (from 1991)

1992–7 Sali Berisha
1997– Rexhep Mejdani

*Prime Minister*

1914 Turhan Pashë Permëti
1914 Esad Toptani
1914–18 Abdullah Rushdi
1918–20 Turhan Pashë Permëti
1920 Sulejman Deluina
1920–1 Iljaz Bej Vrioni
1921 Pandeli Evangeli
1921 Xhafer Ypi
1921–2 Omer Vrioni
1922–4 Ahmed Zogu
1924 Iljaz Bej Vrioni
1924–5 Fan Noli
1925–8 Ahmed Zogu
1928–30 Koço Kota
1930–5 Pandeli Evangeli
1935–6 Mehdi Frashëri
1936–9 Koço Kota
1939–41 Shefqet Verlaci

1941–3 Mustafa Merlika-Kruja
1943 Eqrem Libohova
1943 Maliq Bushati
1943 Eqrem Libohova
1943 *Provisional Executive Committee* (Ibrahim Biçakçlu)
1943 *Council of Regents* (Mehdi Frashëri)
1943–4 Rexhep Mitrovica
1944 Fiori Dine
1944–54 Enver Hoxha
1954–81 Mehmed Shehu
1981–91 Adil Carcani
1991 Ylli Buffi
1991 Fatos Nano
1991–2 Vilson Ahmeti
1992–7 Aleksander Meksi
1997 Bashkim Fino
1997–8 Fatos Nano
1998–9 Pandeli Majko
1999– Ilir Meta

## Algeria

*President*

1962–5 Ahmed Ben Bella
1965–78 Houari Boumédienne
1979–92 Chandli Benjedid
1992 *High Commission of State: Chair* Mohamed Boudiaf
1992–4 Ali Kafi
1994–9 Liamine Zeroual
1999– Abdelaziz Bouteflika

## Andorra

There are two heads of state, called Co-Princes: the President of France (see pp217–8) and the Bishop of Urgell, Spain (Joan Martí Alanis since 1971).

*President of the Executive Council*

1982–4 Óscar Ribas Reig
1984–90 Josep Pintat Solens
1990–4 Óscar Ribas Reig
1994– Marc Forné Molné

## Angola

*President*

1975–9 Antonio Agostinho Neto
1979– José Eduardo dos Santos

## Antigua and Barbuda

*Prime Minister*

1981–94 Vere Cornwall Bird
1994– Lester Bird

## Argentina

*President*

1898–1904 Julio Argentino Roca
1904–6 Manuel Quintana
1906–10 José Figueroa Alcorta
1910–14 Roque Sáenz Peña
1914–16 Victorino de la Plaza
1916–22 Hipólito Yrigoyen
1922–8 Marcelo T de Alvear
1928–30 Hipólito Yrigoyen
1930–2 José Félix Uriburu
1932–8 Augustin Pedro Justo
1938–40 Roberto M Ortiz
1940–3 Ramón S Castillo
1943–4 Pedro P Ramírez
1944–6 Edelmiro J Farrell
1946–55 Juan Perón
1955–8 Eduardo Lonardi
1958–62 Arturo Frondizi
1962–3 José María Guido
1963–6 Arturo Illia
1966–70 Juan Carlos Onganía
1970–1 Roberto Marcelo Levingston
1971–3 Alejandro Agustin Lanusse
1973 Héctor J Cámpora
1973–4 Juan Perón
1974–6 Martínez de Perón
1976–81 *Military Junta* (Jorge Rafaél Videla)
1981 *Military Junta* (Roberto Eduardo Viola)
1981–2 *Military Junta* (Leopoldo Galtieri)
1982–3 Reynaldo Bignone
1983–8 Raúl Alfonsín
1988–99 Carlos Saúl Menem
1999–2001 Fernando de la Rúa
2001 *Three Interim Presidents*
2002– Eduardo Duhalde

## Armenia

*President*

1991–8 Levon Ter-Petrossian
1998– Robert Kocharyan

## Australia

Chief of State: British monarch, represented by Governor General

*Prime Minister*

1901–3 Edmund Barton *Prot*
1903–4 Alfred Deakin *Prot*
1904 John Christian Watson *Lab*
1904–5 George Houston Reid *Free*
1905–8 Alfred Deakin *Prot*
1908–9 Andrew Fisher *Lab*
1909–10 Alfred Deakin *Fusion*
1910–13 Andrew Fisher *Lab*
1913–14 Joseph Cook *Lib*
1914–15 Andrew Fisher *Lab*
1915–17 William Morris Hughes *Nat Lab*
1917–23 William Morris Hughes *Nat*
1923–9 Stanley Melbourne Bruce *Nat*
1929–32 James Henry Scullin *Lab*
1932–9 Joseph Aloysius Lyons *Un*
1939 Earle Christmas Page Co
1939–41 Robert Gordon Menzies *Un*
1941 Arthur William Fadden Co
1941–5 John Joseph Curtin *Lab*
1945 Francis Michael Forde *Lab*

| | |
|---|---|
| 1945–9 | Joseph Benedict Chifley *Lab* |
| 1949–66 | Robert Gordon Menzies *Lib* |
| 1966–7 | Harold Edward Holt *Lib* |
| 1967–8 | John McEwen Co |
| 1968–71 | John Grey Gorton *Lib* |
| 1971–2 | William McMahon *Lib* |
| 1972–5 | Edward Gough Whitlam *Lab* |
| 1975–83 | John Malcolm Fraser *Lib* |
| 1983–91 | Robert James Lee Hawke *Lab* |
| 1991–6 | Paul Keating *Lab* |
| 1996– | John Howard *Lib* |

| | |
|---|---|
| *Co* = Country | *Nat* = Nationalist |
| *Con* = Conservative | *Nat Lab* = National Labor |
| *Free* = Free Trade | *Prot* = Protectionist |
| *Lab* = Labor | *Un* = United |
| *Lib* = Liberal | |

## Austria

*President*

| | |
|---|---|
| 1918–20 | Karl Sätz |
| 1920–8 | Michael Hainisch |
| 1928–38 | Wilhelm Miklas |
| 1938–45 | *German rule* |
| 1945–50 | Karl Renner |
| 1950–7 | Theodor Körner |
| 1957–65 | Adolf Schärf |
| 1965–74 | Franz Jonas |
| 1974–86 | Rudolf Kirchsläger |
| 1986–92 | Kurt Waldheim |
| 1992– | Thomas Klestil |

*Chancellor*

| | |
|---|---|
| 1918–20 | Karl Renner |
| 1920–1 | Michael Mayr |
| 1921–2 | Johann Schober |
| 1922 | Walter Breisky |
| 1922 | Johann Schober |
| 1922–4 | Ignaz Seipel |
| 1924–6 | Rudolph Ramek |
| 1926–9 | Ignaz Seipel |
| 1929–30 | Ernst Streeruwitz |
| 1930 | Johann Schober |
| 1930 | Carl Vaugoin |
| 1930–1 | Otto Ender |
| 1931–2 | Karl Buresch |
| 1932–4 | Engelbert Dollfus |
| 1934–8 | Kurt von Schuschnigg |
| 1938–45 | *German rule* |
| 1945 | Karl Renner |
| 1945–53 | Leopold Figl |
| 1953–61 | Julius Raab |
| 1961–4 | Alfons Gorbach |
| 1964–70 | Josef Klaus |
| 1970–83 | Bruno Kreisky |
| 1983–6 | Fred Sinowatz |
| 1986–97 | Franz Vranitzky |
| 1997–2000 | Viktor Klima |
| 2000– | Wolfgang Schüssel |

## Azerbaijan

*President*

| | |
|---|---|
| 1991–2 | Ayaz Mutalibov |
| 1992 | Yakub Mamedov *Acting President* |
| 1992–3 | Abul Faz Elchibey |
| 1993– | Heidar Aliyev |

## The Bahamas

Chief of State: British monarch, represented by Governor General

*Prime Minister*

| | |
|---|---|
| 1973–92 | Lynden O Pindling |
| 1992– | Hubert A Ingraham |

## Bahrain

*Emir*

| | |
|---|---|
| 1971–99 | Isa Bin Salman Al-Khalifa |
| 1999– | Hamad Bin Isa Al-Khalifa |

*Prime Minister*

| | |
|---|---|
| 1971– | Khalifa Bin Salman Al-Khalifa |

## Bangladesh

*President*

| | |
|---|---|
| 1971–2 | Sayed Nazrul Islam *Acting President* |
| 1972 | Mujibur Rahman |
| 1972–3 | Abu Saeed Chowdhury |
| 1974–5 | Mohammadullah |
| 1975 | Mujibur Rahman |
| 1975 | Khondaker Mushtaq Ahmad |
| 1975–7 | Abu Saadat Mohammad Sayem |
| 1977–81 | Zia Ur-Rahman |
| 1981–2 | Abdus Sattar |
| 1982–3 | Abdul Fazal Mohammad Ahsanuddin Chowdhury |
| 1983–90 | Hossain Mohammad Ershad |
| 1990–1 | Shehabuddin Ahmed *Acting President* |
| 1991–6 | Abdur Rahman Biswas |
| 1996–2001 | Shehabuddin Ahmed |
| 2001– | A Q M Badruddoza Chowdhury |

*Prime Minister*

| | |
|---|---|
| 1971–2 | Tajuddin Ahmed |
| 1972–5 | Mujibur Rahman |
| 1975 | Mohammad Monsur Ali |
| 1975–9 | *Martial Law* |
| 1979–82 | Mohammad Azizur Rahman |
| 1982–4 | *Martial Law* |
| 1984–5 | Ataur Rahman Khan |
| 1986–8 | Mizanur Rahman Chowdhury |
| 1988–90 | Kazi Zafar Ahmed |
| 1991–6 | Khaleda Zia |
| 1996 | Mohammad Habibur Rahman |
| 1996–2001 | Sheikh Hasina Wajed |
| 2001– | Khaleda Zia |

## Barbados

*Prime Minister*

1966–76 Errol Walton Barrow
1976–85 JMG (Tom) Adams
1985–6 H Bernard St John
1986–7 Errol Walton Barrow
1987–94 L Erskine Sandiford
1994– Owen Arthur

## Belarus (Byelorussia)

*Chair of Supreme Soviet*

1991–4 Stanislav Shushkevich
1994–6 Mecheslav Grib

*President*

1994– Alexander Lukashenko

## Belgium

*Monarch*

1865–1909 Leopold II
1909–34 Albert I
1934–50 Leopold III
1950–93 Baudoin I
1993– Albert II

*Prime Minister*

1899–1907 Paul de Smet de Nayer
1907–8 Jules de Trooz
1908–11 Frans Schollaert
1911–18 Charles de Broqueville
1918 Gerhard Cooreman
1918–20 Léon Delacroix
1920–1 Henri Carton de Wiart
1921–5 Georges Theunis
1925 Alois van de Vyvere
1925–6 Prosper Poullet
1926–31 Henri Jaspar
1931–2 Jules Renkin
1932–4 Charles de Broqueville
1934–5 Georges Theunis
1935–7 Paul van Zeeland
1937–8 Paul Émile Janson
1938–9 Paul Spaak
1939–45 Hubert Pierlot
1945–6 Achille van Acker
1946 Paul Spaak
1946 Achille van Acker
1946–7 Camille Huysmans
1947–9 Paul Spaak
1949–50 Gaston Eyskens
1950 Jean Pierre Duvieusart
1950–2 Joseph Pholien
1952–4 Jean van Houtte
1954–8 Achille van Acker
1958–61 Gaston Eyskens
1961–5 Théodore Lefèvre
1965–6 Pierre Harmel
1966–8 Paul Vanden Boeynants
1968–72 Gaston Eyskens
1973–4 Edmond Leburton
1974–8 Léo Tindemans
1978 Paul Vanden Boeynants
1979–81 Wilfried Martens
1981 Marc Eyskens
1981–91 Wilfried Martens
1992–9 Jean-Luc Dehaene
1999– Guy Verhofstadt

## Belize

Chief of State: British Monarch, represented by Governor General

*Prime Minister*

1981–4 George Cadle Price
1985–9 Manuel Esquivel
1989–93 George Cadle Price
1993–8 Manuel Esquivel
1998– Said Musa

## Benin

*President*

### ❑ Dahomey

1960–3 Hubert Coutoucou Maga
1963–4 Christophe Soglo
1964–5 Sourou Migan Apithy
1965 Justin Tométin Ahomadegbé
1965 Tairou Congacou
1965–7 Christophe Soglo
1967–8 Alphonse Amadou Alley
1968–9 Émile Derlin Zinsou
1969–70 *Presidential Committee* (Maurice Kouandete)
1970–2 *Presidential Committee* (Hubert Coutoucou Maga)
1972–5 Mathieu Kérékou

### ❑ People's Republic of Benin

1975–90 Mathieu (*from 1980* Ahmed) Kérékou

### ❑ Republic of Benin

1990–1 Ahmed Kérékou
1991–6 Nicéphore Soglo
1996– Ahmed Kérékou

*Prime Minister*

1958–9 Sourou Migan Apithy
1959–60 Hubert Coutoucou Maga
1960–4 *As President*
1964–5 Justin Tométin Ahomadegbé
1965–7 *As President*
1967–8 Maurice Kouandete
1968–96 *As President*
1996–8 Adrien Houngbedji

## Bhutan

*Monarch (Druk Gyalpo)*

1907–26 Uggyen Wangchuk
1926–52 Jigme Wangchuk
1952–72 Jigme Dorji Wangchuk
1972– Jigme Singye Wangchuk

## Bolivia

*President*

1899–1904 José Manuel Pando
1904–9 Ismael Montes
1909–13 Heliodoro Villazón
1913–17 Ismael Montes
1917–20 José N Gutiérrez Guerra
1920–5 Bautista Saavedra
1925–6 José Cabina Villanueva
1926–30 Hernando Siles
1930 Roberto Hinojusa *President of Revolutionaries*
1930–1 Carlos Blanco Galindo
1931–4 Daniel Salamanca
1934–6 José Luis Tejado Sorzano
1936–7 David Toro
1937–9 Germán Busch
1939 Carlos Quintanilla
1940–3 Enrique Peñaranda y del Castillo
1943–6 Gualberto Villaroel
1946 Nestor Guillen
1946–7 Tomas Monje Gutiérrez
1947–9 Enrique Hertzog
1949 Mamerto Urriolagoitía
1951–2 Hugo Ballivián
1952 Hernán Siles Suazo
1952–6 Víctor Paz Estenssoro
1956–60 Hernán Siles Suazo
1960–4 Víctor Paz Estenssoro
1964–5 René Barrientos Ortuño
1965–6 René Barrientos Ortuño *and* Alfredo Ovando Candía
1966 Alfredo Ovando Candía
1966–9 René Barrientos Ortuño
1969 Luis Adolfo Siles Salinas
1969–70 Alfredo Ovando Candía
1970 Rogelio Mirando
1970–1 Juan José Torres Gonzales
1971–8 Hugo Banzer Suárez
1978 Juan Pereda Asbún
1978–9 *Military Junta* (David Padilla Arericiba)
1979 Walter Guevara Arze
1979–80 Lydia Gueiler Tejada
1980–1 *Military Junta* (Luis García Meza)
1981–2 *Military Junta* (Celso Torrelio Villa)
1982 Guido Vildoso Calderón
1982–5 Hernán Siles Suazo
1985–9 Víctor Paz Estenssoro
1989–93 Jaime Paz Zamora
1993–97 Gonzalo Sánchez de Lozada
1997–2001 Hugo Bánzer Suárez
2001– Jorge Quiroga Ramírez

## Bosnia-Herzegovina

*President*

**❑ Republic**

1990–8 Alija Izetbegovic
1998–9 Zivko Radišic
1999–2000 Ante Jelavic
2000 Alija Izetbegovic
2000–1 Zivko Radišic
2001– Jozo Krizanovic

**❑ Federation**

1994–7 Kresimir Zubak
1997 Vladimir Soljic
1997–8 Ejup Ganic
1999–2000 Ivo Andric Luzanic
2000 Ejup Ganic
2001– Karlo Filipovic

**❑ Republika Srpska**

1992–6 Radovan Karadzic
1996–8 Biljana Plavsic
1998–9 Nikola Poplasen
2000– Mirko Šarovic

## Botswana

*President*

1966–80 Seretse Khama
1980–98 Ketumile Masire
1998– Festus Mogae

## Brazil

*President*

1898–1902 Manuel Ferraz de Campos Sales
1902–6 Francisco de Paula Rodrigues Alves
1906–9 Alfonso Pena
1909–10 Nilo Peçanha
1910–14 Hermes Rodrigues da Fonseca
1914–18 Venceslau Brás Pereira Gomes
1918–19 Francisco de Paula Rodrigues Alves
1919–22 Epitácio Pessoa
1922–6 Artur da Silva Bernardes
1926–30 Washington Luís Pereira de Sousa
1930–45 Getúlio Dorneles Vargas
1945–51 Eurico Gaspar Dutra
1951–54 Getúlio Dorneles Vargas
1954–5 João Café Filho
1955 Carlos Coimbra da Luz
1955–6 Nereu de Oliveira Ramos
1956–61 Juscelino Kubitschek de Oliveira
1961 Jânio da Silva Quadros
1961–3 João Belchior Marques Goulart
1963 Pascoal Ranieri Mazilli
1963–4 João Belchior Marques Goulart
1964 Pascoal Ranieri Mazilli
1964–7 Humberto de Alencar Castelo Branco
1967–9 Artur da Costa e Silva
1969–74 Emílio Garrastazu Médici
1974–9 Ernesto Geisel
1979–85 João Baptista de Oliveira Figueiredo
1985–90 José Sarney

1990–2 Fernando Collor de Mello
1992–4 Itamar Franco
1994– Fernando Henrique Cardoso

## Brunei

*Monarch (Sultan)*

1967– Muda Hassanal Bolkiah Mu'izzadin Waddaulah

## Bulgaria

*Monarch*

1887–1908 Ferdinand *Prince*
1908–18 Ferdinand I
1918–43 Boris III
1943–6 Simeon II

### ❑ Republic of Bulgaria

*President*

1946–7 Vasil Kolarov
1947–50 Mincho Naichev
1950–8 Georgi Damianov
1958–64 Dimitro Ganev
1964–71 Georgi Traikov
1971–89 Todor Zhivkov
1989–90 Petar Mladenov

### ❑ New Republic

1990–7 Zhelyu Zhelev
1997– Petar Stoyanov

*Premier*

1946–9 Georgi Dimitrov
1949–50 Vasil Kolarov
1950–6 Vulko Chervenkov
1956–62 Anton Yugov
1962–71 Todor Zhivkov
1971–81 Stanko Todorov
1981–6 Grisha Filipov
1986–90 Georgy Atanasov
1990 Andrei Lukanov
1990–1 Dimitur Popov

*First Secretary*

1946–53 Vulko Chervenkov
1953–89 Todor Zhivkov
1989–90 Petar Mladenov
1990 Alexander Lilov

*Prime Minister*

1991–2 Filip Dimitrov
1992–4 Lyuben Berov
1994–5 Renate Indzhova *Acting Prime Minister*
1995–7 Zhan Videnov
1997 Stefan Sofiyanski *Acting Prime Minister*
1997–2001 Ivan Kostov
2001– Simeon Sakskoburggotski (Simeon II)

## Burkina Faso

*President*

### ❑ Upper Volta

1960–6 Maurice Yaméogo
1966–80 Sangoulé Lamizana
1980 Saye Zerbo

**People's Salvation Council**

1982–3 Jean-Baptiste Ouedraugo *Chairman*

**National Revolutionary Council**

1983–4 Thomas Sankara *Chairman*

### ❑ Burkina Faso

1984–7 Thomas Sankara *Chairman*
1987– Blaise Compaoré

## Burma ► Myanmar, Union of

## Burundi

*Monarch*

1962–6 Mwambutsa IV
1966 Ntare V

### ❑ Republic of Burundi

*President*

1966–77 Michel Micombero
1977–87 Jean-Baptiste Bagaza
1987–93 *Military Junta* (Pierre Buyoya)
1993 Melchior Ndadaye
1994 Cyprien Ntaryamira
1994–6 Sylvestre Ntibantunganya
1996– *Military Junta* (Pierre Buyoya)

## Cambodia (Kampuchea)

*Monarch*

1941–55 Norodom Sihanouk II
1955–60 Norodom Suramarit

*Chief of State*

1960–70 Prince Norodom Sihanouk

### ❑ Khmer Republic (from 1970)

1970–2 Cheng Heng *Acting Chief of State*
1972–5 Lon Nol
1975–6 Prince Norodom Sihanouk
1976–81 Khieu Samphan
1981–91 Heng Samrin

### ❑ Government in exile (until 1991)

*President*

1970–5 Prince Norodom Sihanouk
1982–93 Prince Norodom Sihanouk

*Monarch*

1993– King Norodom Sihanouk

*Prime Minister*

1945–6 Son Ngoc Thanh
1946–8 Prince Monireth
1948–9 Son Ngoc Thanh
1949–51 Prince Monipong
1951 Son Ngoc Thanh
1951–2 Huy Kanthoul
1952–3 Norodom Sihanouk II

1953 Samdech Penn Nouth
1953–4 Chan Nak
1954–5 Leng Ngeth
1955–6 Prince Norodom Sihanouk
1956 Oum Chheang Sun
1956 Prince Norodom Sihanouk
1956 Khim Tit
1956 Prince Norodom Sihanouk
1956 Sam Yun
1956–7 Prince Norodom Sihanouk
1957–8 Sim Var
1958 Ek Yi Oun
1958 Samdech Penn Nouth *Acting Prime Minister*
1958 Sim Var
1958–60 Prince Norodom Sihanouk
1960–1 Pho Proung
1961 Samdech Penn Nouth
1961–3 Prince Norodom Sihanouk
1963–6 Prince Norodom Kantol
1966–7 Lon Nol
1967–8 Prince Norodom Sihanouk
1968–9 Samdech Penn Nouth
1969–72 Lon Nol

❑ **Khmer Republic (from 1970)**

1972 Sisovath Sivik Matak
1972 Son Ngoc Thanh
1972–3 Hang Thun Hak
1973 In Tam
1973–5 Long Boret
1975–6 Samdech Penn Nouth
1976–9 Pol Pot
1979–81 Khieu Samphan
1981–5 Chan Si
1985–93 Hun Sen

**Government in exile (until 1991)**

1970–3 Samdech Penn Nouth
1982–91 Son Sann
1993–7 Norodom Ranariddh *First Prime Minister*
Hun Sen *Second Prime Minister*
1997 Ung Huot *First Prime Minister*
Hun Sen *Second Prime Minister*
1998– Hun Sen

## Cameroon

*President*

1960–82 Ahmadun Ahidjo
1982– Paul Biya

## Canada

Chief of State: British monarch, represented by Governor General

*Prime Minister*

1867–73 John A MacDonald *Con*
1873–8 Alexander Mackenzie *Lib*
1878–91 John A MacDonald *Con*
1891–2 John J C Abbot *Con*
1892–4 John S D Thompson *Con*
1894–6 Mackenzie Bowell *Con*
1896 Charles Tupper *Con*
1896–1911 Wilfrid Laurier *Lib*
1911–20 Robert Borden *Con/Un*
1920–1 Arthur Meighen *Un/Con*
1921–6 William Lyon Mackenzie King *Lib*
1926 Arthur Meighen *Con*
1926–30 William Lyon Mackenzie King *Lib*
1930–5 Richard Bedford Bennett *Con*
1935–48 William Lyon Mackenzie King *Lib*
1948–57 Louis St Laurent *Lib*
1957–63 John George Diefenbaker *Con*
1963–8 Lester Bowles Pearson *Lib*
1968–79 Pierre Elliott Trudeau *Lib*
1979–80 Joseph Clark *Con*
1980–4 Pierre Elliott Trudeau *Lib*
1984 John Turner *Lib*
1984–93 Brian Mulroney *Con*
1993 Kim Campbell *Con*
1993– Jean Chrétien *Lib*

*Con* = Conservative *Lib* = Liberal *Un* = Unionist

## Cape Verde

*President*

1975–91 Arístides Pereira
1991– Antonio Mascarenhas Monteiro

*Prime Minister*

1975–91 Pedro Pires
1991–2001 Carlos Wahnon Veiga
2001– Pedro Pires

## Central African Republic

*President*

1960–6 David Dacko
1966–79 Jean-Bédel Bokassa (*from 1977*, Emperor Bokassa I)
1979–81 David Dacko
1981–93 André Kolingba
1993– Ange-Félix Patasse

## Chad

*President*

1960–75 François Tombalbaye
1975–9 *Supreme Military Council* (Félix Malloum)
1979 Goukouni Oueddi
1979 Mohammed Shawwa
1979–82 Goukouni Oueddi
1982–90 Hissène Habré
1990– Idriss Déby

## Chile

*President*

1900–1 Federico Errázuriz Echaurren
1901 Aníbal Zañartu *Vice President*
1901–3 Germán Riesco
1903 Ramón Barros Luco *Vice President*

1903–6 Germán Riesco
1906–10 Pedro Montt
1910 Ismael Tocornal *Vice President*
1910 Elías Fernández Albano *Vice President*
1910 Emiliano Figueroa Larraín *Vice President*
1910–15 Ramón Barros Luco
1915–20 Juan Luis Sanfuentes
1920–4 Arturo Alessandri
1924–5 *Military Juntas*
1925 Arturo Alessandri
1925 Luis Barros Borgoño *Vice President*
1925–7 Emiliano Figueroa
1927–31 Carlos Ibáñez
1931 Pedro Opaso Letelier *Vice President*
1931 Juan Esteban Montero *Vice President*
1931 Manuel Trucco Franzani *Vice President*
1931–2 Juan Estaban Montero
1932 *Military Juntas*
1932 Carlos G Dávila *Provisional President*
1932 Bartolomé Blanche *Provisional President*
1932 Abraham Oyanedel *Vice President*
1932–8 Arturo Alessandri Palma
1938–41 Pedro Aguirre Cerda
1941–2 Jerónimo Méndez Arancibia *Vice President*
1942–6 Juan Antonio Ríos Morales
1946–52 Gabriel González Videla
1952–8 Carlos Ibáñez del Campo
1958–64 Jorge Alessandri Rodríguez
1964–70 Eduardo Frei Montalva
1970–3 Salvador Allende Gossens
1973–90 Augusto Pinochet Ugarte
1990–3 Patricio Aylwin Azócar
1993–9 Eduardo Frei Ruíz-Tagle
2000– Ricardo Lagos Escobar

## China

### ❑ Qing (Ch'ing) dynasty

*Emperor*

1875–1908 Guangxu (Kuang-hsü)
1908–12 Xuantong (Hsüan-t'ung)

*Prime Minister*

1901–3 Ronglu (Jung-lu)
1903–11 Prince Qing (Ch'ing)
1912 Lu Zhengxiang (Lu Cheng-hsiang)
1912 Yuan Shikai (Yüan Shih-k'ai)

### ❑ Republic of China

*President*

1912 Sun Yat-sen (Sun Yixian) *Provisional*
1912–16 Yuan Shikai (Yüan Shih-k'ai)
1916–17 Li Yuanhong (Li Yüan-hung)
1917–18 Feng Guozhang (Feng Kuo-chang)
1918–22 Xu Shichang (Hsü Shih-ch'ang)
1921–5 Sun Yat-sen *Canton Administration*
1922–3 Li Yuanhong
1923–4 Cao Kun (Ts'ao K'un)
1924–6 Duan Qirui (Tuan Ch'i-jui)
1926–7 *Civil Disorder*
1927–8 Zhang Zuolin (Chang Tso-lin)
1928–31 Chiang K'ai-shek (Jiang Jieshi)
1931–2 Cheng Minxu (Ch'eng Ming-hsü) *Acting President*
1932–43 Lin Sen (Lin Sen)
1940–4 Wang Jingwei (Wang Ching-wei) *In Japanese-occupied territory*
1943–9 Chiang K'ai-shek
1945–9 *Civil War*
1949 Li Zongren (Li Tsung-jen)

*Premier*

1912 Tang Shaoyi (T'ang Shao-i)
1912–13 Zhao Bingjun (Chao Ping-chün)
1912–13 Xiong Xiling (Hsiung Hsi-ling)
1914 Sun Baoyi (Sun Pao-chi)
1915–16 *no Premier*
1916–17 Duan Qirui (Tuan Ch'i-jui)
1917–18 Wang Shizhen (Wang Shih-chen)
1918 Duan Qirui
1918–19 Qian Nengxun (Ch'ien Neng-hsün)
1919 Gong Xinzhan (Kung Hsin-chan)
1919–20 Jin Yunpeng (Chin Yün-p'eng)
1920 Sa Zhenbing (Sa Chen-ping)
1920–1 Jun Yunpeng
1921–2 Liang Shiyi (Liang Shih-i)
1922 Zhou Ziqi (Chow Tzu-ch'i) *Acting Premier*
1922 Yan Huiqing (Yen Hui-ch'ing)
1922 Wang Chonghui (Wang Ch'ung-hui)
1922–3 Wang Daxie (Wang Ta-hsieh)
1923 Zhang Shaozeng (Chang Shao-ts'eng)
1923–4 Gao Lingwei (Kao Ling-wei)
1924 Sun Baoyi (Sun Pao-ch'i)
1924 Gu Weijun (Ku Wei-chün) *Acting Premier*
1924 Yan Huiqing
1924–5 Huang Fu (Huang Fu) *Acting Premier*
1925 Duan Qirui
1925–6 Xu Shiying (Hsü Shih-ying)
1926 Jia Deyao (Chia Te-yao)
1926 Hu Weide (Hu Wei-te)
1926 Yan Huiqing
1926 Du Xigui (Tu Hsi-kuei)
1926–7 Gu Weijun
1927 *Civil Disorder*

*President of the Executive Council*

1928–30 Tan Yankai (T'an Yen-k'ai)
1930 T V Soong (Sung Tzu-wen) *Acting Premier*
1930 Wang Jingwei (Wang Ching-wei)
1930–1 Chiang K'ai-shek
1931–2 Sun Fo (Sun Fo)
1932–5 Wang Jingwei
1935–7 Chiang K'ai-shek
1937–8 Wang Chonghui (Wang Ch'ung-hui) *Acting Premier*
1938–9 Kong Xiangxi (K'ung Hsiang-hsi)
1939–44 Chiang K'ai-shek
1944–7 T V Soong
1945–9 *Civil War*
1948 Wang Wenhao (Wong Wen-hao)

1948–9 Sun Fo
1949 He Yingqin (Ho Ying-ch'in)
1949 Yan Xishan (Yen Hsi-shan)

**❑ People's Republic of China**

*President*

1949–59 Mao Zedong (Mao Tse-tung)
1959–68 Liu Shaoqi (Liu Shao-ch'i)
1968–75 Dong Biwu (Tung Pi-wu)
1975–6 Zhu De (Chu Te)
1976–8 Sung Qingling (Sung Ch'ing-ling)
1978–83 Ye Jianying (Yeh Chien-ying)
1983–8 Li Xiannian (Li Hsien-nien)
1988–93 Yang Shangkun (Yang Shang-k'un)
1993– Jiang Zemin (Chiang Tse-min)

*Prime Minister*

1949–76 Zhou Enlai (Chou En-lai)
1976–80 Hua Guofeng (Huo Kuo-feng)
1980–7 Zhao Ziyang (Chao Tzu-yang)
1987–98 Li Peng (Li P'eng)
1998– Zhu Rongji

**Communist Party**

*Chairman*

1935–76 Mao Zedong
1976–81 Hua Guofeng
1981–2 Hu Yaobang (Hu Yao-pang)

*General Secretary*

1982–7 Hu Yaobang
1987–9 Zhao Ziyang
1989– Jiang Zemin

## CIS (Commonwealth of Independent States) ▸ Armenia, Azerbaijan, Belarus, Georgia, Kazakhstan, Kyrgyzstan, Moldova, Russia, Tajikistan, Turkmenistan, Ukraine, Uzbekistan

## Colombia

*President*

1900–4 José Manuel Marroquín *Vice President*
1904–9 Rafael Reyes
1909–10 Ramón González Valencia
1910–14 Carlos E Restrepo
1914–18 José Vicente Concha
1918–21 Marco Fidel Suárez
1921–2 Jorge Holguín *President Designate*
1922–6 Pedro Nel Ospina
1926–30 Miguel Abadía Méndez
1930–4 Enrique Olaya Herrera
1934–8 Alfonso López
1938–42 Eduardo Santos
1942–5 Alfonso López
1945–6 Alberto Lleras Camargo *President Designate*
1946–50 Mariano Ospina Pérez
1950–3 Laureano Gómez
1953–7 Gustavo Rojas Pinilla
1957 *Military Junta*
1958–62 Alberto Lleras Camargo
1962–6 Guillermo León Valencia
1966–70 Carlos Lleras Restrepo
1970–4 Misael Pastrana Borrero
1974–8 Alfonso López Michelsen
1978–82 Julio César Turbay Ayala
1982–6 Belisario Betancur
1986–90 Virgilio Barco Vargas
1990–4 César Gaviria Trujillo
1994–8 Ernesto Samper Pizano
1998– Andrés Pastrana Arango

## Commonwealth

*Secretary-General*

1965–75 Arnold Smith
1975–90 Shridath S Ramphal
1990–2000 Emeka Anyaoku
2000– Donald C McKinnon

## Comoros

*President*

1976–78 Ali Soilih
1978–89 Ahmed Abdallah Abderemane
1989–96 Said Mohammed Djohar
1996–8 Mohammad Taki Abdoulkarim
1998–9 Majiddine Ben Said Massonde *Interim President*
1999– *Military Junta* (Azali Assoumani)

## Congo

*President*

1960–3 Abbé Fulbert Youlou
1963–8 Alphonse Massemba-Debat
1968 Marien Ngouabi
1968 Alphonse Massemba-Debat
1968–9 Alfred Raoul
1969–77 Marien Ngouabi
1977–9 Joachim Yhomby Opango
1979–92 Denis Sassou-Nguesso
1992–7 Pascal Lissouba
1997– Denis Sassou-Nguesso

## Congo, Democratic Republic of (Zaïre)

*President*

1960–5 Joseph Kasavubu
1965–97 Mobutu Sese Seko (*formerly* Joseph Mobutu)

**❑ Democratic Republic of Congo**

1997–2001 Laurent Kabila
2001– Joseph Kabila

*Prime Minister*

1960 Patrice Lumumba
1960 Joseph Ileo
1960–1 *College of Commissioners*
1961 Joseph Ileo
1961–4 Cyrille Adoula
1964–5 Moïse Tshombe
1965 Evariste Kimba

| | |
|---|---|
| 1965–6 | Mulamba Nyungu wa Kadima |
| 1966–77 | *As President* |
| 1977–80 | Mpinga Kasenga |
| 1980 | Bo-Boliko Lokonga Monse Mihambu |
| 1980–1 | Nguza Karl I Bond |
| 1981–3 | Nsinga Udjuu |
| 1983–6 | Léon Kengo Wa Dondo |
| 1986–8 | *No Prime Minister* |
| 1988 | Sambura Pida Nbagui |
| 1988–90 | Léon Kengo Wa Dondo |
| 1990–1 | Lunda Bululu |
| 1991 | Mulumba Lukeji |
| 1991 | Etienne Tshisekedi |
| 1991 | Bernardin Mungul Diaka |
| 1991–2 | Karl I Bond |
| 1992–3 | Etienne Tshisekedi |
| 1993–4 | Faustin Birindwa |
| 1994–7 | Léon Kengo Wa Dondo |
| 1997 | Etienne Tshisekedi |
| 1997 | Likulia Bolongo |

## Costa Rica

*President*

| | |
|---|---|
| 1894–1902 | Rafael Yglesias y Castro |
| 1902–6 | Ascención Esquivel Ibarra |
| 1906–10 | Cleto González Viquez |
| 1910–12 | Ricardo Jiménez Oreamuno |
| 1912–14 | Cleto González Víquez |
| 1914–17 | Alfredo González Flores |
| 1917–19 | Federico Tinoco Granados |
| 1919 | Julio Acosta García |
| 1919–20 | Juan Bautista Quiros |
| 1920–4 | Julio Acosta García |
| 1924–8 | Ricardo Jiménez Oreamuno |
| 1928–32 | Cleto González Víquez |
| 1932–6 | Ricardo Jiménez Oreamuno |
| 1936–40 | León Cortés Castro |
| 1940–4 | Rafael Ángel Calderón Guardia |
| 1944–8 | Teodoro Picado Michalski |
| 1948 | Santos Léon Herrera |
| 1948–9 | *Civil Junta* (José Figueres Ferrer) |
| 1949–52 | Otilio Ulate Blanco |
| 1952–3 | Alberto Oreamuno Flores |
| 1953–8 | José Figueres Ferrer |
| 1958–62 | Mario Echandi Jiménez |
| 1962–6 | Francisco José Orlich Bolmarcich |
| 1966–70 | José Joaquín Trejos Fernández |
| 1970–4 | José Figueres Ferrer |
| 1974–8 | Daniel Oduber Quirós |
| 1978–82 | Rodrigo Carazo Odio |
| 1982–6 | Luis Alberto Monge Álvarez |
| 1986–90 | Oscar Arias Sánchez |
| 1990–4 | Rafael Angel Calderón Fournier |
| 1994–8 | José Maria Figueres Olsen |
| 1998– | Miguel Angel Rodríguez Echevarría |

## Côte d'Ivoire

*President*

| | |
|---|---|
| 1960–93 | Félix Houphouët-Boigny |
| 1993–9 | Henri Konan-Bédié |
| 1999–2000 | Robert Guëi |
| 2000– | Laurent Gbagbo |

## Croatia

*President*

| | |
|---|---|
| 1992–9 | Franjo Tudjman |
| 1999–2000 | Vlatko Pavletic *Acting President* |
| 2000 | Zlatko Tomcic *Acting President* |
| 2000 | Stjepan Mesic |

## Cuba

*President*

| | |
|---|---|
| 1902–6 | Tomas Estrada Palma |
| 1906–9 | *US rule* |
| 1909–13 | José Miguel Gómez |
| 1913–21 | Mario García Menocal |
| 1921–5 | Alfredo Zayas y Alfonso |
| 1925–33 | Gerardo Machado y Morales |
| 1933 | Carlos Manuel de Céspedes |
| 1933–4 | Ramón Grau San Martín |
| 1934–5 | Carlos Mendieta |
| 1935–6 | José A Barnet y Vinagres |
| 1936 | Miguel Mariano Gómez y Arias |
| 1936–40 | Federico Laredo Bru |
| 1940–4 | Fulgencio Batista |
| 1944–8 | Ramón Grau San Martín |
| 1948–52 | Carlos Prío Socarrás |
| 1952–9 | Fulgencio Batista |
| 1959 | Manuel Urrutia |
| 1959–76 | Osvaldo Dorticós Torrado |
| 1959–76 | Fidel Castro Ruz *Prime Minister and First Secretary* |
| 1976– | Fidel Castro Ruz *President* |

## Cyprus

*President*

| | |
|---|---|
| 1960–77 | Archbishop Makarios III |
| 1977–88 | Spyros Kyprianou |
| 1988–93 | Georgios Vassiliou |
| 1993– | Glafcos Clerides |

## Czechoslovakia

In 1993 Czechoslovakia divided into two separate states, the Czech Republic (see below) and Slovakia, or the Slovak Republic (see p238).

*President*

| | |
|---|---|
| 1918–35 | Tomáš Garrigue Masaryk |
| 1935–8 | Edvard Beneš |
| 1938–9 | Emil Hácha |

**German Occupation**

| | |
|---|---|
| 1938–45 | Edvard Beneš *President in Exile* |
| 1939–45 | Emil Hácha *State President* |
| 1939–45 | Jozef Tiso *Slovak Republic President* |

**Post-war**

| | |
|---|---|
| 1945–8 | Edvard Beneš |
| 1948–53 | Klement Gottwald |
| 1953–7 | Antonín Zápotocký |
| 1957–68 | Antonín Novotný |
| 1968–75 | Ludvík Svoboda |
| 1975–89 | Gustáv Husák |
| 1989–93 | Václav Havel |

*Prime Minister*

1918–19 Karel Kramář
1919–20 Vlastimil Tusar
1920–1 Jan Černý
1921–2 Edvard Beneš
1922–6 Antonín Švehla
1926 Jan Černý
1926–9 Antonín Švehla
1929–32 František Udržal
1932–5 Jan Malypetr
1935–8 Milan Hodža
1938 Jan Syrový
1938–9 Rudolf Beran
1940–5 Jan Šrámek *in exile*
1945–6 Zdeněk Fierlinger
1946–8 Klement Gottwald
1948–53 Antonín Zápotocký
1953–63 Viliám Široký
1963–8 Josef Lenárt
1968–70 Oldřich Černík
1970–88 Lubomír Štrougal
1988–9 Ladislav Adamec
1989–92 Marian Calfa
1992 Jan Strasky

*First Secretary*

1948–52 Rudolf Slánsky
1953–68 Antonín Novotný
1968–9 Alexander Dubček
1969–87 Gustáv Husák
1987–9 Miloš Jakeš
1989 Karel Urbánek
1989–93 Ladislav Adamec

### ❑ Czech Republic

*President*

1993– Václav Havel

*Prime Minister*

1993–7 Václav Klaus
1997–8 Josef Tosovsky
1998– Miloš Zeman

## Denmark

*Monarch*

1863–1906 Kristian IX
1906–12 Frederik VIII
1912–47 Kristian X
1947–72 Frederik IX
1972– Margrethe II

*Prime Minister*

1900–1 H Sehested
1901–5 J H Deuntzer
1905–8 J C Christensen
1908–9 N Neergaard
1909 L Holstein-Ledreborg
1909–10 C Th Zahle
1910–13 Klaus Berntsen
1913–20 C Th Zahle
1920 Otto Liebe
1920 M P Frlls
1920–4 N Neergaard
1924–6 Thorvald Stauning
1926–9 Th Madsen-Mygdal
1929–42 Thorvald Stauning
1942 Wilhelm Buhl
1942–3 Erik Scavenius
1943–5 *No government*
1945 Wilhelm Buhl
1945–7 Knud Kristensen
1947–50 Hans Hedtoft
1950–3 Erik Eriksen
1953–5 Hans Hedtoft
1955–60 Hans Christian Hansen
1960–2 Viggo Kampmann
1962–8 Jens Otto Krag
1968–71 Hilmar Baunsgaard
1971–2 Jens Otto Krag
1972–3 Anker Jorgensen
1973–5 Poul Hartling
1975–82 Anker Jorgensen
1982–93 Poul Schlüter
1993–2001 Poul Nyrup Rasmussen
2001– Anders Fogh Rasmussen

## Djibouti

*President*

1977–99 Hassan Gouled Aptidon
1999– Ismael Omar Guelleh

*Prime Minister*

1977–8 Abdallah Mohammed Kamil
1978–2001 Barkat Gourad Hamadou
2001– Dileita Mohamed Dileita

## Dominica

*President*

1977 Louis Cods-Lartigue *Interim President*
1978–9 Frederick E Degazon
1979–80 Lenner Armour *Acting President*
1980–4 Aurelius Marie
1984–93 Clarence Augustus Seignoret
1993–8 Crispin Anselm Sorhaindo
1998– Vernon Shaw

*Prime Minister*

1978–9 Patrick Roland John
1979–80 Oliver Seraphine
1980–95 Mary Eugenia Charles
1995–2000 Edison James
2000 Rosie Douglas
2000 Pierre Charles

## Dominican Republic

*President*

1899–1902 Juan Isidro Jiménez
1902–3 Horacio Vásquez
1903 Alejandro Wos y Gil
1903–4 Juan Isidro Jiménez
1904–6 Carlos Morales

| | |
|---|---|
| 1906–11 | Ramon Cáceres |
| 1911–12 | Eladio Victoria |
| 1912–13 | Adolfo Nouel y Bobadilla |
| 1913–14 | José Bordas y Valdés |
| 1914 | Ramon Báez |
| 1914–16 | Juan Isidro Jiménez |
| 1916–22 | *US occupation* (Francisco Henríquez y Carrajal) |
| 1922–4 | *US occupation* (Juan Batista Vicini Burgos) |
| 1924–30 | Horacio Vásquez |
| 1930 | Rafael Estrella Urena |
| 1930–8 | Rafael Leónidas Trujillo y Molina |
| 1938–40 | Jacinto Bienvenudo Peynado |
| 1940–2 | Manuel de Jesus Troncoso de la Concha |
| 1942–52 | Rafael Leónidas Trujillo y Molina |
| 1952–60 | Hector Bienvenido Trujillo |
| 1960–2 | Joaquín Videla Balaguer |
| 1962 | Rafael Bonnelly |
| 1962 | *Military Junta* (Huberto Bogaert) |
| 1962–3 | Rafael Bonnelly |
| 1963 | Juan Bosch Gavino |
| 1963 | *Military Junta* (Emilio de los Santos) |
| 1963–5 | Donald Reid Cabral |
| 1965 | *Civil War* |
| 1965 | Elias Wessin y Wessin |
| 1965 | Antonio Imbert Barreras |
| 1965 | Francisco Caamaño Deñó |
| 1965–6 | Héctor Garcia Godoy Cáceres |
| 1966–78 | Joaquín Videla Balaguer |
| 1978–82 | Antonio Guzmán Fernández |
| 1982–6 | Salvador Jorge Blanco |
| 1986–96 | Joaquín Videla Balaguer |
| 1996–2000 | Leonel Fernández |
| 2000– | Hipólito Mejía |

## Ecuador

*President*

| | |
|---|---|
| 1895–1901 | Eloy Alfaro |
| 1901–5 | Leónides Plaza Gutiérrez |
| 1905–6 | Lizardo García |
| 1906–11 | Eloy Alfaro |
| 1911 | Emilio Estrada |
| 1911–12 | Carlos Freile Zaldumbide |
| 1912–16 | Leónides Plaza Gutiérrez |
| 1916–20 | Alfredo Baquerizo Moreno |
| 1920–4 | José Luis Tamayo |
| 1924–5 | Gonzálo S de Córdova |
| 1925–6 | *Military Juntas* |
| 1926–31 | Isidro Ayora |
| 1931 | Luis A Larrea Alba |
| 1932–3 | Juan de Dios Martínez Mera |
| 1933–4 | Abelardo Montalvo |
| 1934–5 | José María Velasco Ibarra |
| 1935 | Antonio Pons |
| 1935–7 | Federico Páez |
| 1937–8 | Alberto Enriquez Gallo |
| 1938 | Manuel María Borrero |
| 1938–9 | Aurelio Mosquera Narváez |
| 1939–40 | Julio Enrique Moreno |
| 1940–4 | Carlos Alberto Arroya del Río |
| 1944–7 | José María Velasco Ibarra |
| 1947 | Carlos Mancheno |
| 1947–8 | Carlos Julio Arosemena Tola |
| 1948–52 | Galo Plaza Lasso |
| 1952–6 | José María Velasco Ibarra |
| 1956–60 | Camilo Ponce Enríquez |
| 1960–1 | José María Velasco Ibarra |
| 1961–3 | Carlos Julio Arosemena Monroy |
| 1963–6 | *Military Junta* |
| 1966 | Clemente Yerovi Indaburu |
| 1966–8 | Otto Arosemena Gómez |
| 1968–72 | José María Velasco Ibarra |
| 1972–6 | Guillermo Rodríguez Lara |
| 1976–9 | *Military Junta* |
| 1979–81 | Jaime Roldós Aguilera |
| 1981–4 | Oswaldo Hurtado Larrea |
| 1984–8 | León Febres Cordero |
| 1988–92 | Rodrigo Borja Cevallos |
| 1992–6 | Sixto Durán Ballén |
| 1996–7 | Abdalá Bucaram Ortiz |
| 1997 | Rosalia Arteaga *(Acting President)* |
| 1997–8 | Fabián Alarcón Rivero |
| 1998–2000 | Jamil Mahuad Witt |
| 2000– | Gustavo Noboa |

## Egypt

*Khedive*

| | |
|---|---|
| 1895–1914 | Abbas Helmi II |

*Sultan*

| | |
|---|---|
| 1914–17 | Hussein Kamel |
| 1917–22 | Ahmed Fouad |

### ❑ Kingdom of Egypt

*Monarch*

| | |
|---|---|
| 1922–36 | Fouad I |
| 1936–7 | Farouk *Trusteeship* |
| 1937–52 | Farouk I |

### ❑ Republic of Egypt

*President*

| | |
|---|---|
| 1953–4 | Mohammed Najib |
| 1954–70 | Gamal Abdel Nasser |
| 1970–81 | Mohammed Anwar El-Sadat |
| 1981– | Mohammed Hosni Mubarak |

*Prime Minister*

| | |
|---|---|
| 1895–1908 | Mustafa Fahmy |
| 1908–10 | Butros Ghali |
| 1910–14 | Mohammed Said |
| 1914–19 | Hussein Rushdi |
| 1919 | Mohammed Said |
| 1919–20 | Yousuf Wahba |
| 1920–1 | Mohammed Tewfiq Nazim |
| 1921 | Adli Yegen |
| 1922 | Abdel Khaliq Tharwat |
| 1922–3 | Mohammed Tewfiq Nazim |
| 1923–4 | Yehia Ibrahim |
| 1924 | Saad Zaghloul |
| 1924–6 | Ahmed Zaywan |

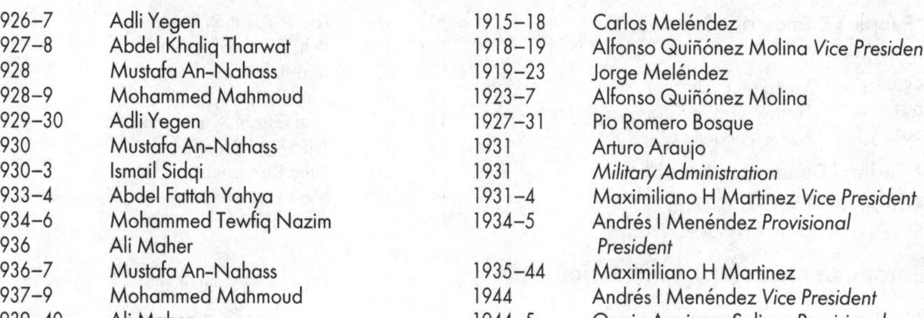

| | |
|---|---|
| 1926–7 | Adli Yegen |
| 1927–8 | Abdel Khaliq Tharwat |
| 1928 | Mustafa An-Nahass |
| 1928–9 | Mohammed Mahmoud |
| 1929–30 | Adli Yegen |
| 1930 | Mustafa An-Nahass |
| 1930–3 | Ismail Sidqi |
| 1933–4 | Abdel Fattah Yahya |
| 1934–6 | Mohammed Tewfiq Nazim |
| 1936 | Ali Maher |
| 1936–7 | Mustafa An-Nahass |
| 1937–9 | Mohammed Mahmoud |
| 1939–40 | Ali Maher |
| 1940 | Hassan Sabri |
| 1940–2 | Hussein Sirry |
| 1942–4 | Mustafa An-Nahass |
| 1944–5 | Ahmed Maher |
| 1945–6 | Mahmoud Fahmy El-Nuqrashi |
| 1946 | Ismail Sidqi |
| 1946–8 | Mahmoud Fahmy El-Nuqrashi |
| 1948–9 | Ibrahim Abdel Hadi |
| 1949–50 | Hussein Sirry |
| 1950–2 | Mustafa An-Nahass |
| 1952 | Ali Maher |
| 1952 | Najib El-Hilali |
| 1952 | Hussein Sirry |
| 1952 | Najib El-Hilali |
| 1952 | Ali Maher |
| 1952–4 | Mohammed Najib |
| 1954 | Gamal Abdel Nasser |
| 1954 | Mohammed Najib |
| 1954–62 | Gamal Abdel Nasser |
| 1958–61 | *United Arab Republic* |
| 1962–5 | Ali Sabri |
| 1965–6 | Zakariya Mohyi Ed-Din |
| 1966–7 | Mohammed Sidqi Soliman |
| 1967–70 | Gamal Abdel Nasser |
| 1970–2 | Mahmoud Fawzi |
| 1972–3 | Aziz Sidki |
| 1973–4 | Mohammed Anwar El-Sadat |
| 1974–5 | Abdel Aziz Hijazy |
| 1975–8 | Mamdouh Salem |
| 1978–80 | Mustafa Khalil |
| 1980–1 | Mohammed Anwar El-Sadat |
| 1981–2 | Mohammed Hosni Mubarak |
| 1982–4 | Fouad Monyi Ed-Din |
| 1984 | Kamal Hassan Ali |
| 1985–6 | Ali Lotfi |
| 1986–96 | Atif Sidqi |
| 1996–9 | Ahmed Kamal Al-Ganzouri |
| 1999– | Atef Muhammed Ebeid |

## El Salvador

*President*

| | |
|---|---|
| 1899–1903 | Tomás Regalado |
| 1903–7 | Pedro José Escalon |
| 1907–11 | Fernando Figueroa |
| 1911–13 | Manuel Enrique Araujo |
| 1913–14 | Carlos Meléndez *President Designate* |
| 1914–15 | Alfonso Quiñónez Molina *President Designate* |
| 1915–18 | Carlos Meléndez |
| 1918–19 | Alfonso Quiñónez Molina *Vice President* |
| 1919–23 | Jorge Meléndez |
| 1923–7 | Alfonso Quiñónez Molina |
| 1927–31 | Pio Romero Bosque |
| 1931 | Arturo Araujo |
| 1931 | *Military Administration* |
| 1931–4 | Maximiliano H Martinez *Vice President* |
| 1934–5 | Andrés I Menéndez *Provisional President* |
| 1935–44 | Maximiliano H Martinez |
| 1944 | Andrés I Menéndez *Vice President* |
| 1944–5 | Osmin Aguirre y Salinas *Provisional President* |
| 1945–8 | Salvador Castaneda Castro |
| 1948–50 | *Revolutionary Council* |
| 1950–6 | Oscar Osorio |
| 1956–60 | José María Lemus |
| 1960–1 | *Military Junta* |
| 1961–2 | *Civil-Military Administration* |
| 1962 | Rodolfo Eusebio Cordón *Provisional President* |
| 1962–7 | Julio Adalberto Rivera |
| 1967–72 | Fidel Sánchez Hernández |
| 1972–7 | Arturo Armando Molina |
| 1977–9 | Carlos Humberto Romero |
| 1979–82 | *Military Juntas* |
| 1982–4 | *Government of National Unanimity* (Alvaro Magaña) |
| 1984–9 | José Napoleón Duarte |
| 1989–94 | Alfredo Cristiani |
| 1994–9 | Armando Calderón Sol |
| 1999– | Francisco Flores |

## Equatorial Guinea

*President*

| | |
|---|---|
| 1968–79 | Francisco Macias Nguema |
| 1979– | Teodoro Obiang Nguema Mbasogo |

## Eritrea

*President*

| | |
|---|---|
| 1993– | Issaias Afewerki |

## Estonia

*President*

| | |
|---|---|
| 1990–2 | Arnold Rüütel |
| 1992–2001 | Lennart Meri |
| 2001– | Arnold Rüütel |

## Ethiopia

*Monarch*

| | |
|---|---|
| 1889–1911 | Menelik II |
| 1911–16 | Lij Iyasu (Joshua) |
| 1916–28 | Zawditu |
| 1928–74 | Haile Selassie *Emperor from 1930* |

**Provisional Military Administrative Council**

*Chairman*

| | |
|---|---|
| 1974–7 | Teferi Benti |
| 1977–87 | Mengistu Haile Mariam |

❑ **People's Democratic Republic**

*President*

1987–91 Mengistu Haile Mariam
1991 Tesfaye Gebre Kidan *Acting President*
1991–5 Meles Zenawi

❑ **Federal Democratic Republic**

1995–2001 Negasso Gidada
2001– Girma Wolde-Giorgis

## European Union (EU) Commission

*President*

1967–70 Jean Rey
1970–2 Franco M Malfatti
1972–3 Sicco L Mansholt
1973–7 Francois-Xavier Ortoli
1977–81 Roy Jenkins
1981–5 Gaston Thorn
1985–95 Jacques Delors
1995–9 Jacques Santer
1999– Romano Prodi

## Fiji

Chief of State until 1987: British monarch, represented by Governor General

*Prime Minister*

1970–87 Kamisese Mara
1987 Timoci Bavadra

**Interim Administration**

*Governor General*

1987 Penaia Ganilau
1987 *Military Administration* (Sitiveni Rabuka)

❑ **Republic**

*Chairman*

1987 Sitiveni Rabuka

*President*

1987–94 Penaia Ganilau
1994–2000 Kamisese Mara
2000 *Interim Military Government* (Frank Bainimarama)
2000 Ratu Josefa Iloilovatu Uluivuda *Interim President*

*Prime Minister*

1987–92 Kamisese Mara
1992–9 Sitiveni Rabuka
1999–2000 Mahendra Chaudhry
2000 Ratu Tevita Momoedonu *Acting Prime Minister*
2000 Ratu Epeli Nailatika *Interim Prime Minister*
2000–1 Laisenia Qarase
2001 Ratu Tevita Momoedonu
2001 Laisenia Qarase

## Finland

*President*

1919–25 Kaarlo Juho Ståhlberg
1925–31 Lauri Kristian Relander
1931–7 Pehr Evind Svinhufvud
1937–40 Kyösti Kallio
1940–4 Risto Ryti
1944–6 Carl Gustaf Mannerheim
1946–56 Juho Kusti Paasikivi
1956–81 Urho Kekkonen
1982–94 Mauno Koivisto
1994– Martti Ahtisaari

*Prime Minister*

1917–18 Pehr Evind Svinhufvud
1918 Juho Kusti Paasikivi
1918–19 Lauri Johannes Ingman
1919 Kaarlo Castrén
1919–20 Juho Vennola
1920–1 Rafael Erich
1921–2 Juho Vennola
1922 Aino Kaarlo Cajander
1922–4 Kyösti Kallio
1924 Aino Kaarlo Cajander
1924–5 Lauri Johannes Ingman
1925 Antti Agaton Tulenheimo
1925–6 Kyösti Kallio
1926–7 Väinö Tanner
1927–8 Juho Emil Sunila
1928–9 Oskari Mantere
1929–30 Kyösti Kallio
1930–1 Pehr Evind Svinhufvud
1931–2 Juhu Emil Sunila
1932–6 Toivo Kivimäki
1936–7 Kyösti Kallio
1937–9 Aino Kaarlo Cajander
1939–41 Risto Ryti
1941–3 Johann Rangell
1943–4 Edwin Linkomies
1944 Andreas Hackzell
1944 Urho Jonas Castrén
1944–5 Juho Kusti Paasikivi
1946–8 Mauno Pekkala
1948–50 Karl August Fagerholm
1950–3 Urho Kekkonen
1953–4 Sakari Tuomioja
1954 Ralf Törngren
1954–6 Urho Kekkonen
1956–7 Karl August Fagerholm
1957 Väinö Johannes Sukselainen
1957–8 Rainer von Fieandt
1958 Reino Ilsakki Kuuskoski
1958–9 Karl August Fagerholm
1959–61 Väinö Johannes Sukselainen
1961–2 Martti Miettunen
1962–3 Ahti Karjalainen
1963–4 Reino Ragnar Lehto
1964–6 Johannes Virolainen
1966–8 Rafael Paasio
1968–70 Mauno Koivisto
1970 Teuvo Ensio Aura
1970–1 Ahti Karjalainen
1971–2 Teuvo Ensio Aura
1972 Rafael Paasio
1972–5 Kalevi Sorsa

1975 Keijo Antero Liinamaa
1975–7 Martti Miettunen
1977–9 Kalevi Sorsa
1979–82 Mauno Koivisto
1982–7 Kalevi Sorsa
1987–91 Harri Holkeri
1991–5 Esko Aho
1995–2000 Paavo Lipponen
2000 Tarja Halonen

## France

*President*

### ❑ Third Republic

1899–1906 Emile Loubet
1906–13 Armand Fallières
1913–20 Raymond Poincaré
1920 Paul Deschanel
1920–4 Alexandre Millerand
1924–31 Gaston Doumergue
1931–2 Paul Doumer
1932–40 Albert Lebrun

### ❑ Fourth Republic

1947–54 Vincent Auriol
1954–8 René Coty

### ❑ Fifth Republic

1958–69 Charles de Gaulle
1969–74 Georges Pompidou
1974–81 Valéry Giscard d'Estaing
1981–95 François Mitterrand
1995– Jacques Chirac

*Prime Minister*

### ❑ Third Republic

1899–1902 Pierre Waldeck-Rousseau
1902–5 Emile Combes
1905–6 Maurice Rouvier
1906 Jean Sarrien
1906–9 Georges Clemenceau
1909–11 Aristide Briand
1911 Ernest Monis
1911–12 Joseph Caillaux
1912–13 Raymond Poincaré
1913 Aristide Briand
1913 Jean Louis Barthou
1913–14 Gaston Doumergue
1914 Alexandre Ribot
1914–15 René Viviani
1915–17 Aristide Briand
1917 Alexandre Ribot
1917 Paul Painlevé
1917–20 Georges Clemenceau
1920 Alexandre Millerand
1920–1 Georges Leygues
1921–2 Aristide Briand
1922–4 Raymond Poincaré
1924 Frédéric François-Marsal
1924–5 Édouard Herriot
1925 Paul Painlevé
1925–6 Aristide Briand
1926 Édouard Herriot
1926–9 Raymond Poincaré
1929 Aristide Briand
1929–30 André Tardieu
1930 Camille Chautemps
1930 André Tardieu
1930–1 Théodore Steeg
1931–2 Pierre Laval
1932 André Tardieu
1932 Édouard Herriot
1932–3 Joseph Paul-Boncour
1933 Édouard Daladier
1933 Albert Sarrault
1933–4 Camille Chautemps
1934 Édouard Daladier
1934 Gaston Doumergue
1934–5 Pierre-Étienne Flandin
1935 Fernand Bouisson
1935–6 Pierre Laval
1936 Albert Sarrault
1936–7 Léon Blum
1937–8 Camille Chautemps
1938 Léon Blum
1938–40 Édouard Daladier
1940 Paul Reynaud
1940 Philippe Pétain

### ❑ Vichy Government

1940–4 Philippe Pétain

### ❑ Provisional Government of the French Republic

1944–6 Charles de Gaulle
1946 Félix Gouin
1946 Georges Bidault

### ❑ Fourth Republic

1946–7 Léon Blum
1947 Paul Ramadier
1947–8 Robert Schuman
1948 André Marie
1948 Robert Schuman
1948–9 Henri Queuille
1949–50 Georges Bidault
1950 Henri Queuille
1950–1 René Pleven
1951 Henri Queuille
1951–2 René Pleven
1952 Edgar Faure
1952–3 Antoine Pinay
1953 René Mayer
1953–4 Joseph Laniel
1954–5 Pierre Mendès-France
1955–6 Edgar Faure
1956–7 Guy Mollet
1957 Maurice Bourgès-Maunoury
1957–8 Félix Gaillard
1958 Pierre Pfimlin
1958–9 Charles de Gaulle

❑ **Fifth Republic**

1959–62 Michel Debré
1962–8 Georges Pompidou
1968–9 Maurice Couve de Murville
1969–72 Jacques Chaban Delmas
1972–4 Pierre Mesmer
1974–6 Jacques Chirac
1976–81 Raymond Barre
1981–4 Pierre Mauroy
1984–6 Laurent Fabius
1986–8 Jacques Chirac
1988–91 Michel Rocard
1991–2 Édith Cresson
1992–3 Pierre Bérégovoy
1993–5 Édouard Balladur
1995–7 Alain Juppé
1997– Lionel Jospin

## Gabon

*President*

1960–7 Léon M'ba
1967– Omar (Bernard-Albert, *to 1973*) Bongo

*Prime Minister*

1960–75 *As President*
1975–90 Léon Mébiame (Mébiane)
1991–3 Casimir Oyé M'ba
1993–8 Paulin Obame-Nguema
1999– Jean-François Ntoutoume-Emane

## The Gambia

*President*

1965–94 Dawda Kairaba Jawara
1994– Yahya Jammeh

## Georgia

*President*

1991–2 Zviad Gamsakhurdia
1992 *Military Council*
1992– Eduard Shevardnaze

## Germany

❑ **German Empire**

*Emperor*

1888–1918 Wilhelm II

*Chancellor*

1909–17 Theobald von Bethmann Hollweg
1917 Georg Michaelis
1917–18 Georg Graf von Hertling
1918 Prince Max von Baden
1918 Friedrich Ebert

❑ **German Republic**

*President*

1919–25 Friedrich Ebert
1925–34 Paul von Hindenburg

*Reich Chancellor*

1919 Philipp Scheidemann
1919–20 Gustav Bauer
1920 Hermann Müller
1920–1 Konstantin Fehrenbach
1921–2 Karl Joseph Wirth
1922–3 Wilhelm Cuno
1923 Gustav Stresemann
1923–4 Wilhelm Marx
1925–6 Hans Luther
1926–8 Wilhelm Marx
1928–30 Hermann Müller
1930–2 Heinrich Brüning
1932 Franz von Papen
1932–3 Kurt von Sleicher
1933 Adolf Hitler

*Chancellor and Führer*

1933–45 Adolf Hitler (*Führer from 1934*)
1945 Karl Dönitz

❑ **German Democratic Republic (East Germany)**

*President*

1949–60 Wilhelm Pieck

*Chairman of the Council of State*

1960–73 Walter Ernst Karl Ulbricht
1973–6 Willi Stoph
1976–89 Erich Honecker
1989 Egon Krenz
1989–90 Gregor Gysi *General Secretary as Chairman*

*Premier*

1949–64 Otto Grotewohl
1964–73 Willi Stoph
1973–6 Horst Sindermann
1976–89 Willi Stoph
1989–90 Hans Modrow
1990 Lothar de Maizière

❑ **German Federal Republic (West Germany)**

*President*

1949–59 Theodor Heuss
1959–69 Heinrich Lübke
1969–74 Gustav Heinemann
1974–9 Walter Scheel
1979–84 Karl Carstens
1984–90 Richard von Weizsäcker

*Chancellor*

1949–63 Konrad Adenauer
1963–6 Ludwig Erhard
1966–9 Kurt Georg Kiesinger
1969–74 Willy Brandt
1974–82 Helmut Schmidt
1982–90 Helmut Kohl

❑ **Germany**

*President*

1990–4 Richard von Weizsäcker

| | |
|---|---|
| 1994–9 | Roman Herzog |
| 1999– | Johannes Rau |

*Chancellor*

| | |
|---|---|
| 1990–8 | Helmut Kohl |
| 1998– | Gerhard Schröder |

## Ghana

*President*

| | |
|---|---|
| 1960–6 | Kwame Nkrumah |

**National Liberation Council**

*Chairman*

| | |
|---|---|
| 1966–9 | Joseph Arthur Ankrah |
| 1969 | Akwasi Amankwa Afrifa |
| 1969–70 | *Presidential Committee* |

*President*

| | |
|---|---|
| 1970–2 | Edward Akufo-Addo |

*Chairman*

| | |
|---|---|
| 1972–8 | *National Redemption Council* (Ignatius Kuti Acheampong) |
| 1978–9 | *Supreme Military Council* (Fred W Akuffo) |
| 1979 | *Armed Forces Revolutionary Council* (Jerry John Rawlings) |

*President*

| | |
|---|---|
| 1979–81 | Hilla Limann |

**Provisional National Defence Council**

*Chairman*

| | |
|---|---|
| 1981–2001 | Jerry John Rawlings (*President from 1992*) |

*President*

| | |
|---|---|
| 2001– | John Agyekum Kufuor |

*Prime Minister*

| | |
|---|---|
| 1960–9 | *As President* |
| 1969–72 | Kufi Abrefa Busia |
| 1972–8 | *As President* |
| 1978– | *No Prime Minister* |

## Greece

*Monarch*

| | |
|---|---|
| 1863–1913 | George I |
| 1913–17 | Constantine I |
| 1917–20 | Alexander |
| 1920–2 | Constantine I |
| 1922–3 | George II |
| 1923–4 | Paul Koundouriotis *Regent* |

❑ **Republic**

*President*

| | |
|---|---|
| 1924–6 | Paul Koundouriotis |
| 1926 | Theodore Pangalos |
| 1926–9 | Paul Koundouriotis |
| 1929–35 | Alexander T Zaïmis |

*Monarch*

| | |
|---|---|
| 1935 | George Kondylis *Regent* |
| 1935–47 | George II |
| 1947–64 | Paul |
| 1964–7 | Constantine II |
| 1967–73 | *Military Junta* |
| 1973 | George Papadopoulos *Regent* |

❑ **New Republic**

*President*

| | |
|---|---|
| 1973 | George Papadopoulos |
| 1973–4 | Phaedon Gizikis |
| 1974–5 | Michael Stasinopoulos |
| 1975–80 | Constantine Tsatsos |
| 1980–5 | Constantine Karamanlis |
| 1985–90 | Christos Sartzetakis |
| 1990–5 | Constantine Karamanlis |
| 1995– | Constantine Stephanopoulos |

*Prime Minister*

| | |
|---|---|
| 1899–1901 | George Theotokis |
| 1901–2 | Alexander T Zaïmis |
| 1902–3 | Theodore Deligiannis |
| 1903 | George Theotokis |
| 1903 | Demetrius G Rallis |
| 1903–4 | George Theotokis |
| 1904–5 | Theodore Deligiannis |
| 1905 | Demetrius G Rallis |
| 1905–9 | George Theotokis |
| 1909 | Demetrius G Rallis |
| 1909–10 | Kyriakoulis P Mavromichalis |
| 1910 | Stephen N Dragoumis |
| 1910–15 | Eleftherios K Venizelos |
| 1915 | Demetrius P Gounaris |
| 1915 | Eleftherios K Venizelos |
| 1915 | Alexander T Zaïmis |
| 1915–16 | Stephen Skouloudis |
| 1916 | Alexander T Zaïmis |
| 1916 | Nicholas P Kalogeropoulos |
| 1916–17 | Spyridon Lambros |
| 1917 | Alexander T Zaïmis |
| 1917–20 | Eleftherios K Venizelos |
| 1920–1 | Demetrius G Rallis |
| 1921 | Nicholas P Kalogeropoulos |
| 1921–2 | Demetrius P Gounaris |
| 1922 | Nicholas Stratos |
| 1922 | Peter E Protopapadakis |
| 1922 | Nicholas Triandaphyllakos |
| 1922 | Sortirios Krokidas |
| 1922 | Alexander T Zaïmis |
| 1922–3 | Stylianos Gonatas |
| 1924 | Eleftherios Venizelos |
| 1924 | George Kaphandaris |
| 1924 | Alexander Papanastasiou |
| 1924 | Themistocles Sophoulis |
| 1924–5 | Andreas Michalakopoulos |
| 1925–6 | Alexander N Chatzikyriakos |
| 1926 | Theodore Pangalos |
| 1926 | Athanasius Eftaxias |
| 1926 | George Kondylis |
| 1926–8 | Alexander T Zaïmis |
| 1928–32 | Eleftherios K Venizelos |
| 1932 | Alexander Papanastasiou |

1932 Eleftherios K Venizelos
1932–3 Panagiotis Tsaldaris
1933 Eleftherios K Venizelos
1933 Nicholas Plastiras
1933 Alexander Othonaos
1933–5 Panagiotis Tsaldaris
1935 George Kondylis
1935–6 Constantine Demertzis
1936–41 John Metaxas
1941 Alexander Koryzis
1941 *Chairman of Ministers* George II
1941 *German Occupation* (Emmanuel Tsouderos)
1941–2 George Tsolakoglou
1942–3 Constantine Logothetopoulos
1943–4 John Rallis

**Government in exile**

1941–4 Emmanuel Tsouderos
1944 Sophocles Venizelos
1944–5 George Papandreou

**Post-war**

1945 Nicholas Plastiras
1945 Peter Voulgaris
1945 Damaskinos, Archbishop of Athens
1945 Panagiotis Kanellopoulos
1945–6 Themistocles Sophoulis
1946 Panagiotis Politzas
1946–7 Constantine Tsaldaris
1947 Demetrius Maximos
1947 Constantine Tsaldaris
1947–9 Themistocles Sophoulis
1949–50 Alexander Diomedes
1950 John Theotokis
1950 Sophocles Venizelos
1950 Nicholas Plastiras
1950–1 Sophocles Venizelos
1951 Nicholas Plastiras
1952 Demetrius Kiusopoulos
1952–5 Alexander Papagos
1955 Stephen C Stefanopoulos
1955–8 Constantine Karamanlis
1958 Constantine Georgakopoulos
1958–61 Constantine Karamanlis
1961 Constantine Dovas
1961–3 Constantine Karamanlis
1963 Panagiotis Pipinellis
1963 Stylianos Mavromichalis
1963 George Papandreou
1963–4 John Parskevopoulos
1964–5 George Papandreou
1965 George Athanasiadis-Novas
1965 Elias Tsirimokos
1965–6 Stephen C Stefanopoulos
1966–7 John Paraskevopoulos
1967 Panagiotis Kanellopoulos
1967–74 *Military Junta*
1967 Constantine Kollias
1967–73 George Papadopoulos
1973 Spyridon Markezinis
1973–4 Adamantios Androutsopoulos
1974–80 Constantine Karamanlis
1980–1 George Rallis
1981–9 Andreas Papandreou
1989 Tzannis Tzannetakis
1989–90 Xenofon Zolotas
1990–3 Constantine Mitsotakis
1993–6 Andreous Papandreou
1996– Kostas Simitis

## Grenada

Chief of State: British monarch, represented by Governor General

*Prime Minister*

1974–9 Eric M Gairy
1979–83 Maurice Bishop
1983–4 Nicholas Brathwaite *Chairman of Interim Council*
1984–9 Herbert A Blaize
1989–90 Ben Jones
1990–5 Nicholas Brathwaite
1995– Keith Mitchell

## Guatemala

*President*

1898–1920 Manuel Estrada Cabrera
1920–2 Carlos Herrera y Luna
1922–6 José María Orellana
1926–30 Lázaro Chacón
1930 Baudillo Palma
1930–1 Manuel María Orellana
1931 José María Reyna Andrade
1931–44 Jorge Ubico Castañeda
1944 Federico Ponce Vaidez
1944–5 Jacobo Arbenz Guzmán
1945–51 Juan José Arévalo
1951–4 Jacobo Arbenz Guzmán
1954 *Military Junta* (Carlos Díaz)
1954 Elfego J Monzón
1954–7 Carlos Castillo Armas
1957 *Military Junta* (Oscar Mendoza Azurdia)
1957 Luis Arturo González López
1957–8 *Military Junta* (Guillermo Flores Avendaño)
1958–63 Miguel Ydígoras Fuentes
1963–6 *Military Junta* (Enrique Peralta Azurdia)
1966–70 Julio César Méndez Montenegro
1970–4 Carlos Araña Osorio
1974–8 Kyell Eugenio Laugerua García
1978–82 Romeo Lucas García
1982 Angel Aníbal Guevara
1982–3 Efraín Rios Montt
1983–6 Oscar Humberto Mejía Victores
1986–91 Marco Vinicio Cerezo Arévalo
1991–3 Jonge Serrano Elias
1993–6 Ramiro de León Carpio
1996–2000 Álvaro Arzú Irigoyen
2000– Alfonso Portillo Cabrera

## Guinea

*President*

1961–84 Ahmed Sékou Touré
1984– Lansana Conté

*Prime Minister*

1958–72 Ahmed Sékou Touré
1972–84 Louis Lansana Beavogui
1984–5 Diarra Traore
1985–96 *None*
1996–9 Sidia Toure
1999– Lamine Sidime

## Guinea-Bissau

*President*

1974–80 Luis de Almeida Cabral
1980–4 *Revolutionary Council* (João Bernardo Vieira)
1984–99 João Bernardo Vieira
1999–2000 Malai Bacai Sanhá *Interim President*
2000– Kumba Yalla

## Guyana

*President*

1970 Edward A Luckhoo
1970–80 Arthur Chung
1980–5 Linden Forbes Sampson Burnham
1985–92 Hugh Desmond Hoyte
1992–7 Cheddi Bharrat Jagan
1997 Samuel Hinds
1997–9 Janet Jagan
1999– Bharrat Jagdeo

*Prime Minister*

1966–85 Linden Forbes Sampson Burnham
1985–92 Hamilton Green
1992–7 Samuel Hinds
1997 Janet Jagan
1997– Samuel Hinds

## Haiti

*President*

1896–1902 P A Tirésias Simon Lam
1902 Boisrond Canal
1902–8 Alexis Nord
1908–11 Antoine Simon
1911–12 Michel Cincinnatus Leconte
1912–13 Tancrède Auguste
1913–14 Michael Oreste
1914 Oreste Zamor
1914–15 Joseph Davilmare Théodore
1915 Jean Velbrun-Guillaume
1915–22 Philippe Sudre Dartiguenave
1922–30 Joseph Louis Bornó
1930 Étienne Roy
1930–41 Sténio Joseph Vincent
1941–6 Élie Lescot
1946 *Military Junta* (Frank Lavaud)
1946–50 Dumarsais Estimé
1950 *Military Junta* (Frank Lavaud)
1950–6 Paul E Magloire
1956–7 François Sylvain
1957 *Military Junta*
1957 Léon Cantave
1957 Daniel Fignolé
1957 Antoine Kebreau
1957–71 François Duvalier ('Papa Doc')
1971–86 Jean-Claude Duvalier ('Baby Doc')
1986–8 Henri Namphy
1988 Leslie Manigat
1988 Henri Namphy
1988–90 Prosper Avril
1990 Ertha Pascal-Trouillot *President*
1990–6 Jean-Bertrand Aristide (*Government in exile 1991–4*)
1996–2000 René Préval
2000– Jean-Bertrand Aristide

## Honduras

*President*

1900–3 Terencio Sierra
1903 Juan Angel Arias
1903–7 Manuel Bonilla Chirinos
1907–11 Miguel R Dávila
1912–15 Manuel Bonilla Chirinos
1915–20 Francisco Bertrand
1920–4 Rafael López Gutiérrez
1924–5 Vicente Tosta Carrasco
1925–8 Miguel Paz Barahona
1929–32 Vicente Mejía Clindres
1932–49 Tiburcio Carías Andino
1949–54 Juan Manuel Gálvez

*Head of State*

1954–6 Julio Lozano Diaz
1956–7 *Military Junta*

*President*

1958–63 José Ramón Villeda Morales

*Head of State*

1963–5 Oswaldo López Arellano

*President*

1965–71 Oswaldo López Arellano
1971–2 Ramón Ernesto Cruz

*Head of State*

1972–5 Oswaldo López Arellano
1975–8 Juan Alberto Melgar Castro
1978–82 Policarpo Paz García

*President*

1982–6 Roberto Suazo Córdova
1986–9 José Azcona Hoyo
1989–93 Rafael Leonardo Callejas
1993–7 Carlos Roberto Reina
1997– Carlos Roberto Flores Facussé

## Hungary

*Monarch*

1900–16 Franz Josef I
1916–18 Charles IV

*President*

1919 Mihály Károlyi
1919 *Revolutionary Governing Council* (Sándor Garbai)
1920–44 Miklós Horthy *Regent*
1944–5 *Provisional National Assembly*
1946–8 Zoltán Tildy
1948–50 Árpád Szakasits
1950–2 Sándor Rónai
1952–67 István Dobi
1967–87 Pál Losonczi
1987–8 Károly Németh
1988–9 Brunó Ferenc Straub
1989–90 Mátyás Szúrös
1990–2000 Árpád Göncz
2000– Ferenc Madl

*Premier*

1899–1903 Kálmán Széll
1903 Károly Khuen-Héderváry
1903–5 István Tisza
1905–6 Géza Fejérváry
1906–10 Sándor Wekerle
1910–12 Károly Khuen-Héderváry
1912–13 Lázló Lukács
1913–17 István Tisza
1917 Móric Esterházy
1917–18 Sándor Wekerle
1918–19 Mihály Károlyi
1919 Dénes Berinkey
1919 *Revolutionary Governing Council*
1919 Gyula Peidl
1919 István Friedrich
1919–20 Károly Huszár
1920 Sándor Simonyi-Semadam
1920–1 Pál Teleki
1921–31 István Bethlen
1931–2 Gyula Károlyi
1932–6 Gyula Gömbös
1936–8 Kálman Darányi
1938–9 Béla Imrédy
1939–41 Pál Teleki
1941–2 Lázló Bárdossy
1942–4 Miklós Kállay
1944 Döme Sztójay
1944 Géza Lakatos
1944 Ferenc Szálasi
1944–5 *Provisional National Assembly* (Béla Dálnoki Miklós)
1945–6 Zoltán Tildy
1946–7 Ferenc Nagy
1947–8 Lajos Dinnyés
1948–52 István Dobi
1952–3 Mátyás Rákosi
1953–5 Imre Nagy
1955–6 András Hegedüs
1956 Imre Nagy
1956–8 János Kádár
1958–61 Ferenc Münnich
1961–5 János Kádár
1965–7 Gyula Kállai
1967–75 Jenö Fock
1975–87 György Lázár
1987–8 Károly Grosz
1988–90 Miklás Németh
1990–3 József Antall
1993–4 Péter Boross
1994–8 Gyula Horn
1998– Viktor Orban

*First Secretary*

1949–56 Mátyás Rákosi
1956 Ernö Gerö
1956–88 János Kádár
1988–90 Károly Grosz

## Iceland

*President*

1944–52 Sveinn Björnsson
1952–68 Ásgeir Ásgeirsson
1968–80 Kristján Eldjárn
1980–96 Vigdís Finnbogadóttir
1996– Ólafur Ragnar Grimsson

*Prime Minister*

1900–1 C Goos
1901–4 P A Alberti
1904–9 Hannes Hafstein
1909–11 Björn Jónsson
1911–12 Kristján Jónsson
1912–14 Hannes Hafstein
1914–15 Sigurđur Eggerz
1915–17 Einar Arnórsson
1917–22 Jón Magnússon
1922–4 Sigurđur Eggerz
1924–6 Jón Magnússon
1926–7 John þorláksson
1927–32 Tryggvi þórhallsson
1932–4 Ásgeir Ásgeirsson
1934–42 Hermann Jónasson
1942 Ólafur Thors
1942–4 Björn þórđarsson
1944–7 Ólafur Thors
1947–9 Stefán Jóhann Stefánsson
1949–50 Ólafur Thors
1950–3 Steingrímur Steinþórsson
1953–6 Ólafur Thors
1956–8 Hermann Jónasson
1958–9 Emil Jónsson
1959–61 Ólafur Thors
1961 Bjarni Benediktsson
1961–3 Ólafur Thors
1963–70 Bjarni Benediktsson
1970–1 Jóhann Hafstein
1971–4 Ólafur Jóhannesson
1974–8 Geir Hallgrímsson
1978–9 Ólafur Jóhannesson
1979 Benedikt Gröndal

| | |
|---|---|
| 1980–3 | Gunnar Thoroddsen |
| 1983–7 | Steingrímur Hermannsson |
| 1987–8 | Thorsteinn Pálsson |
| 1988–91 | Steingrímur Hermannsson |
| 1991– | Davíd Oddsson |

## India

*President*

| | |
|---|---|
| 1950–62 | Rajendra Prasad |
| 1962–7 | Sarvepalli Radhakrishnan |
| 1967–9 | Zakir Husain |
| 1969 | Varahagiri Venkatagiri *Acting President* |
| 1969 | Mohammed Hidayatullah *Acting President* |
| 1969–74 | Varahagiri Venkatagiri |
| 1974–7 | Fakhruddin Ali Ahmed |
| 1977 | B D Jatti *Acting President* |
| 1977–82 | Neelam Sanjiva Reddy |
| 1982–7 | Giani Zail Singh |
| 1987–92 | Ramaswami Venkataraman |
| 1992–7 | Shankar Dayal Sharma |
| 1997– | Kocheril Raman Narayanan |

*Prime Minister*

| | |
|---|---|
| 1947–64 | Jawaharlal Nehru |
| 1964 | Gulzari Lal Nanda *Acting Prime Minister* |
| 1964–6 | Lal Bahadur Shastri |
| 1966 | Gulzari Lal Nanda *Acting Prime Minister* |
| 1966–77 | Indira Gandhi |
| 1977–9 | Morarji Desai |
| 1979–80 | Charan Singh |
| 1980–4 | Indira Gandhi |
| 1984–9 | Rajiv Gandhi |
| 1989–90 | Vishwanath Pratap Singh |
| 1990–1 | Chandra Shekhar |
| 1991–6 | P V Narasimha Rao |
| 1996 | Atal Behari Vajpayee |
| 1996–7 | H D Deve Gowda |
| 1997 | Inder Kumar Gujral |
| 1998– | Atal Behari Vajpayee |

## Indonesia

*President*

| | |
|---|---|
| 1945–9 | Ahmed Sukarno |

### ❑ Republic

| | |
|---|---|
| 1949–66 | Ahmed Sukarno |
| 1966–98 | T N J Suharto |
| 1998–9 | B J Habibie |
| 1999–2001 | Abdurrahman Wahid |
| 2001– | Megawati Sukarnoputri |

*Prime Minister*

| | |
|---|---|
| 1945 | R A A Wiranatakusumah |
| 1945–7 | Sutan Sjahrir |
| 1947–8 | Amir Sjarifuddin |
| 1948 | Mohammed Hatta |
| 1948–9 | Sjarifuddin Prawiraranegara |
| 1949 | Susanto Tirtoprodjo |
| 1949 | Mohammed Hatta |
| 1950 | Dr Halim |
| 1950–1 | Mohammed Natsir |
| 1951–2 | Sukiman Wirjosandjojo |
| 1952–3 | Dr Wilopo |
| 1953–5 | Ali Sastroamidjojo |
| 1955–6 | Burhanuddin Harahap |
| 1956–7 | Ali Sastroamidjojo |
| 1957–9 | Raden Haji Djuanda Kurtawidjaja |
| 1959–63 | Ahmed Sukarno |
| 1963–6 | S E Subandrio |
| 1966– | *No Prime Minister* |

## Iran

*Shah*

| | |
|---|---|
| 1896–1907 | Muzaffar Ad-Din |
| 1907–9 | Mohammed Ali |
| 1909–25 | Ahmad Mirza |
| 1925–41 | Mohammed Reza Khan |
| 1941–79 | Mohammed Reza Pahlavi |

### ❑ Islamic Republic

*Leader of the Islamic Revolution*

| | |
|---|---|
| 1979–89 | Ruhollah Khomeini |
| 1989– | Sayed Ali Khamenei |

*President*

| | |
|---|---|
| 1980–1 | Abolhassan Bani-Sadr |
| 1981 | Mohammed Ali Rajai |
| 1981–9 | Sayed Ali Khamenei |
| 1989–97 | Ali Akbar Hashemi Rafsanjani |
| 1997– | Sayed Ayatollah Mohammad Khatami |

*Prime Minister*

| | |
|---|---|
| 1979 | Shahpur Bakhtiar |
| 1979–80 | Mehdi Bazargan |
| 1980–1 | Mohammed Ali Rajai |
| 1981 | Mohammed Javad Bahonar |
| 1981 | Mohammed Reza Mahdavi-Kani |
| 1981–9 | Mir Hossein Moussavi |

## Iraq

*Monarch*

| | |
|---|---|
| 1921–33 | Faisal I |
| 1933–9 | Ghazi I |
| 1939–58 | Faisal II (*Regent 1939–53*, Abdul Illah) |

### ❑ Republic

*Commander of the National Forces*

| | |
|---|---|
| 1958–63 | Abdul Karim Qassem |

*Head of Council of State*

| | |
|---|---|
| 1958–63 | Mohammed Najib Ar-Rubai |

*President*

| | |
|---|---|
| 1963–6 | Abdus Salaam Mohammed Arif |
| 1966–8 | Abdur Rahman Mohammed Arif |
| 1968–79 | Said Ahmad Hassan Al-Bakr |
| 1979– | Saddam Hussein At-Takriti |

## Ireland

*Governor General*

1922–7 Timothy Michael Healy
1927–32 James McNeill
1932–6 Donald Buckley

*President*

1938–45 Douglas Hyde
1945–59 Sean Thomas O'Kelly
1959–73 Éamon de Valera
1973–4 Erskine H Childers
1974–6 Carroll Daly
1976–90 Patrick J Hillery
1990–7 Mary Robinson
1997– Mary McAleese

*Prime Minister*

1919–21 Éamon de Valera
1922 Arthur Griffiths
1922–32 William Cosgrave
1932–48 Éamon de Valera
1948–51 John Aloysius Costello
1951–4 Éamon de Valera
1954–7 John Aloysius Costello
1957–9 Éamon de Valera
1959–66 Sean Lemass
1966–73 John Lynch
1973–7 Liam Cosgrave
1977–9 John Lynch
1979–82 Charles Haughey
1982–7 Garrett Fitzgerald
1987–92 Charles Haughey
1992–4 Albert Reynolds
1994–7 John Bruton
1997– Bertie Ahern

## Israel

*President*

1948–52 Chaim Weizmann
1952–63 Itzhak Ben-Zvi
1963–73 Zalman Shazar
1973–8 Ephraim Katzair
1978–83 Yitzhak Navon
1983–93 Chaim Herzog
1993–2000 Ezer Weizman
2000– Moshe Katsav

*Prime Minister*

1948–53 David Ben-Gurion
1954–5 Moshe Sharett
1955–63 David Ben-Gurion
1963–9 Levi Eshkol
1969–74 Golda Meir
1974–7 Yitzhak Rabin
1977–83 Menachem Begin
1983–4 Yitzhak Shamir
1984–8 Shimon Peres
1988–92 Yitzhak Shamir
1992–5 Yitzhak Rabin
1995–6 Shimon Peres *Acting Prime Minister*
1996–9 Binyamin Netanyahu
1999–2001 Ehud Barak
2001– Ariel Sharon

## Italy

❑ **Kingdom of Italy**

*Monarch*

1900–46 Victor Emmanuel III

❑ **Italian Republic**

*President*

1946–8 Enrico de Nicola
1948–55 Luigi Einaudi
1955–62 Giovanni Gronchi
1962–4 Antonio Segni
1964–71 Giuseppe Saragat
1971–8 Giovanni Leone
1978–85 Alessandro Pertini
1985–92 Francesco Cossiga
1992–9 Oscar Luigi Scalfaro
1999– Carlo Azeglio Ciampi

❑ **Kingdom of Italy**

*Prime Minister*

1900–1 Giuseppe Saracco
1901–3 Giuseppe Zanardelli
1903–5 Giovanni Giolitti
1905–6 Alessandro Fortis
1906 Sydney Sonnino
1906–9 Giovanni Giolitti
1909–10 Sydney Sonnino
1910–11 Luigi Luzzatti
1911–14 Giovanni Giolitti
1914–16 Antonio Salandra
1916–17 Paolo Boselli
1917–19 Vittorio Emmanuele Orlando
1919–20 Francesco Saverio Nitti
1920–1 Giovanni Giolitti
1921–2 Ivanoe Bonomi
1922 Luigi Facta
1922–43 Benito Mussolini
1943–4 Pietro Badoglio
1944–5 Ivanoe Bonomi
1945 Ferrucio Parri
1945 Alcide de Gasperi

❑ **Italian Republic**

1946–53 Alcide de Gasperi
1953–4 Giuseppe Pella
1954 Amintore Fanfani
1954–5 Mario Scelba
1955–7 Antonio Segni
1957–8 Adone Zoli
1958–9 Amintore Fanfani
1959–60 Antonio Segni
1960 Fernando Tambroni
1960–3 Amintore Fanfani
1963 Giovanni Leone
1963–8 Aldo Moro
1968 Giovanni Leone
1968–70 Mariano Rumor
1970–2 Emilio Colombo
1972–4 Giulio Andreotti
1974–6 Aldo Moro
1976–8 Giulio Andreotti

1979–80 Francisco Cossiga
1980–1 Arnaldo Forlani
1981–2 Giovanni Spadolini
1982–3 Amintore Fanfani
1983–7 Bettino Craxi
1987 Amintore Fanfani
1987–8 Giovanni Goria
1988–9 Ciriaco de Mita
1989–92 Giulio Andreotti
1992–3 Giuliano Amato
1993–4 Carlo Azeglio Ciampi
1994 Silvio Berlusconi
1995–6 Lamberto Dini
1996–8 Romano Prodi
1998–2000 Massimo D'Alema
2000–1 Giuliano Amato
2001– Silvio Berlusconi

## Jamaica

Chief of State: British monarch, represented by Governor General

*Prime Minister*

1962–7 William Alexander Bustamante
1967 Donald Burns Sangster
1967–72 Hugh Lawson Shearer
1972–80 Michael Norman Manley
1980–9 Edward Phillip George Seaga
1989–92 Michael Norman Manley
1992– Percival James Patterson

## Japan

*Chief of State (Emperor)*

1867–1912 Mutsuhito (Meiji Era)
1912–26 Yoshihito (Taisho Era)
1926–89 Hirohito (Showa Era)
1989– Akihito (Heisei Era)

*Prime Minister*

1900–1 Hirobumi Ito
1901–6 Taro Katsura
1906–8 Kimmochi Saionji
1908–11 Taro Katsura
1911–12 Kimmochi Saionji
1912–13 Taro Katsura
1913–14 Gonnohyoe Yamamoto
1914–16 Shigenobu Okuma
1916–18 Masatake Terauchi
1918–21 Takashi Hara
1921–2 Korekiyo Takahashi
1922–3 Tomosaburo Kato
1923–4 Gonnohyoe Yamamoto
1924 Keigo Kiyoura
1924–6 Takaaki Kato
1926–7 Reijiro Wakatsuki
1927–9 Giichi Tanaka
1929–31 Osachi Hamaguchi
1931 Reijiro Wakatsuki
1931–2 Tsuyoshi Inukai
1932–4 Makoto Saito
1934–6 Keisuke Okada
1936–7 Koki Hirota
1937 Senjuro Hayashi
1937–9 Fumimaro Konoe
1939 Kiichiro Hiranuma
1939–40 Nobuyuki Abe
1940 Mitsumasa Yonai
1940–1 Fumimaro Konoe
1941–4 Hideki Tojo
1944–5 Kuniaki Koiso
1945 Kantaro Suzuki
1945 Naruhiko Higashikuni
1945–6 Kijuro Shidehara
1946–7 Shigeru Yoshida
1947–8 Tetsu Katayama
1948 Hitoshi Ashida
1948–54 Shigeru Yoshida
1954–6 Ichiro Hatoyama
1956–7 Tanzan Ishibashi
1957–60 Nobusuke Kishi
1960–4 Hayato Ikeda
1964–72 Eisaku Sato
1972–4 Kakuei Tanaka
1974–6 Takeo Miki
1976–8 Takeo Fukuda
1978–80 Masayoshi Ohira
1980–2 Zenko Suzuki
1982–7 Yasuhiro Nakasone
1987–9 Noburu Takeshita
1989 Sasuke Uno
1989–91 Toshiki Kaifu
1991–93 Kiichi Miyazawa
1993 Morihiro Hosokawa
1994 Tsutoma Hata
1994–6 Tomiichi Murayama
1996–8 Ryutaro Hashimoto
1998–2000 Kenzo Obuchi
2000 Mikio Aoki *Acting Prime Minister*
2000–1 Yoshiro Mori
2001– Junichiro Koizumi

## Jordan

*Monarch*

1921–51 Abdullah ibn Hussein I
1951–2 Talal I
1952–99 Hussein ibn Talal
1999– Abdullah ibn Hussein II

*Prime Minister*

1921 Rashid Tali
1921 Muzhir Ar-Raslan
1921–3 Rida Ar-Riqabi
1923 Muzhir Ar-Raslan
1923–4 Hassan Khalid
1924–33 Rida Ar-Riqabi
1933–8 Ibrahim Hashim
1939–45 Taufiq Abul-Huda
1945–8 Ibrahim Hashim
1948–50 Taufiq Abul-Huda
1950 Said Al-Mufti
1950–1 Samir Ar-Rifai
1951–3 Taufiq Abul-Huda
1953–4 Fauzi Al-Mulqi
1954–5 Taufiq Abul-Huda

1955 Said Al-Mufti
1955 Hazza Al-Majali
1955–6 Ibrahim Hashim
1956 Samir Ar-Rifai
1956 Said Al-Mufti
1956 Ibrahim Hashim
1956–7 Suleiman Nabulsi
1957 Hussein Fakhri Al-Khalidi
1957–8 Ibrahim Hashim
1958 Nuri Pasha Al-Said
1958–9 Samir Ar-Rifai
1959–60 Hazza Al-Majali
1960–2 Bahjat Talhuni
1962–3 Wasfi At-Tall
1963 Samir Ar-Rifai
1963–4 Sharif Hussein Bin Nasir
1964 Bahjat Talhuni
1965–7 Wasfi At-Tall
1967 Sharif Hussein Bin Nasir
1967 Saad Jumaa
1967–9 Bahjat Talhuni
1969 Abdul Munem Rifai
1969–70 Bahjat Talhuni
1970 Abdul Munem Rifai
1970 *Military Junta* (Mohammed Daud)
1970 Mohamed Ahmed Tugan
1970–1 Wasfi At-Tall
1971–3 Ahmad Lozi
1973–6 Zeid Rifai
1976–9 Mudar Badran
1979–80 Sharif Abdul Hamid Sharaf
1980 Kassem Rimawi
1980–4 Mudar Badran
1984–5 Ahmad Ubayat
1985–9 Zeid Ar-Rifai
1989 Sharif Zaid ibn Shaker
1989–91 Mudar Badran
1991 Taher Al-Masri
1991–3 Sharif Zaid ibn Shaker
1993–5 Abdel Salam Al-Majali
1995–7 Abdul Karim Kabariti
1997–8 Abdel Salam Al-Majali
1998–9 Fayez Tarawneh
1999–2000 Abdul Raouf Rawabdeh
2000– Ali Abu al-Ragheb

## Kazakhstan

*President*

1991– Nursultan Nazarbayev

## Kenya

*President*

1963–78 Mzee Jomo Kenyatta
1978– Daniel arap Moi

## Kiribati

*President*

1979–91 Ieremia T Tabai
1991–4 Teatao Teannaki
1994– Teburoro Tito

## Korea, Democratic People's Republic of (North Korea)

*President*

1948–57 Kim Doo-bong
1957–72 Choi Yong-kun
1972–94 Kim Il-sung
1994–7 *position vacant*
1998– Kim Jong Il

*Prime Minister*

1948–76 Kim Il-sung
1976–7 Park Sung-chul
1977–84 Li Jong-ok
1984–6 Kang Song-san
1986–8 Yi Kun-mo
1988–92 Yon Hyong-muk
1992–7 Kang Song-san
1997– Hong Song-nam

## Korea, Republic of (South Korea)

*President*

1948–60 Syngman Rhee
1960 Ho Chong *Acting President*
1960 Kwak Sang-hun *Acting President*
1960 Ho Chong *Acting President*
1960–3 Yun Po-sun
1963–79 Park Chung-hee
1979–80 Choi Kyu-hah
1980 Park Choong-hoon *Acting President*
1980–8 Chun Doo-hwan
1988–92 Roh Tae-woo
1993–7 Kim Young-sam
1997– Kim Dae-jung

*Prime Minister*

1948–50 Lee Pom-sok
1950 Shin Song-mo *Acting Prime Minister*
1950–1 John M Chang
1951–2 Ho Chong *Acting Prime Minister*
1952 Lee Yun-yong *Acting Prime Minister*
1952 Chang Taek-sang
1952–4 Paik Too-chin
1954–6 Pyon Yong-tae
1956–60 Syngman Rhee
1960 Ho Chong
1960–1 John M Chang
1961 Chang To-yong
1961–2 Song Yo-chan
1962–3 Kim Hyun-chul
1963–4 Choe Tu-son
1964–70 Chung Il-kwon
1970–1 Paik Too-chin
1971–5 Kim Jong-pil
1975–9 Choi Kyu-hah
1979–80 Shin Hyun-hwak
1980 Park Choong-hoon *Acting Prime Minister*
1980–2 Nam Duck-woo
1982 Yoo Chang-soon

1982–3 Kim Sang-hyup
1983–5 Chin Lee-chong
1985–8 Lho Shin-yong
1988 Lee Hyun-jae
1988–90 Kang Young-hoon
1990–1 Ro Jai-bong
1991–2 Chung Won-shik
1992–3 Hyun Soong-jong
1993 Hwang In-sung
1993–4 Lee Hoi-chang
1994 Lee Yung-duck
1994–5 Yi Hong-ku
1995–7 Lee Soo-sung
1997–8 Koh Kun
1998–2000 Kim Jong-pil
2000 Park Tae-joon
2000 Lee Hun jai *Acting Prime Minister*
2000– Lee Han-dong

## Kuwait

*Emir*

*Family name*: al-Sabah

1896–1915 Mubarak
1915–17 Jaber II
1917–21 Salem Al-Mubarak
1921–50 Ahmed Al-Jaber
1950–65 Abdallah Al-Salem
1965–77 Sabah Al-Salem
1978– Jaber Al-Ahmed Al-Jaber

*Prime Minister*

1962–3 Abdallah Al-Salem
1963–5 Sabah Al-Salem
1965–78 Jaber Al-Ahmed Al-Jaber
1978– Saad Al-Abdallah Al-Salem

## Kyrgyzstan (Kirghizia)

*President*

1991– Askar Akayev

## Laos

*Monarch*

1904–59 Sisavang Vong
1959–75 Savang Vatthana

### ❑ Lao People's Democratic Republic

*President*

1975–87 Souphanouvong
1987–91 Phoumi Vongvichit
1991–2 Kaysone Phomvihane
1992–8 Nouhak Phoumsavan
1998– Khamtai Siphandone

*Prime Minister*

1951–4 Souvanna Phouma
1954–5 Katay Don Sasorith
1956–8 Souvanna Phouma
1958–9 Phoui Sahanikone
1959–60 Sunthone Patthamavong
1960 Kou Abhay
1960 Somsanith
1960 Souvana Phouma
1960 Sunthone Patthamavong
1960 Quinim Pholsena
1960–2 Boun Oum Na Champassac
1962–75 Souvanna Phouma
1975–91 Kaysone Phomvihane
1991–8 Khamtai Siphandone
1998–2001 Sisavat Keobouriphan
2001– Boungnang Vorachith

## Latvia

*President*

1990–3 Anatolijs Gorbunovs
1993–9 Guntis Ulmanis
1999– Vaira Vike-Freiberga

## Lebanon

*President*

1943–52 Bishara Al-Khoury
1952–8 Camille Shamoun
1958–64 Fouad Shehab
1964–70 Charle Hilo
1970–6 Suleiman Frenjieh
1976–82 Elias Sarkis
1982 Bashir Gemayel
1982–8 Amin Gemayel
1988–9 *No President*
1989 Rene Muawad
1989–98 Elias Hrawi
1998– Emile Lahoud

*Prime Minister*

1943 Riad Solh
1943–4 Henry Pharaon
1944–5 Riad Solh
1945 Abdul Hamid Karame
1945–6 Sami Solh
1946 Saadi Munla
1946–51 Riad Solh
1951 Hussein Oweini
1951–2 Abdullah Yafi
1952 Sami Solh
1952 Nazem Accari
1952 Saeb Salam
1952 Fouad Chehab
1952–3 Khaled Chehab
1953 Saeb Salam
1953–5 Abdullah Yafi
1955 Sami Solh
1955–6 Rashid Karami
1956 Abdullah Yafi
1956–8 Sami Solh
1958–60 Rashid Karami
1960 Ahmad Daouq
1960–1 Saeb Salam
1961–4 Rashid Karami
1964–5 Hussein Oweini
1965–6 Rashid Karami
1966 Abdullah Yafi
1966–8 Rashid Karami

| | |
|---|---|
| 1968–9 | Abdullah Yafi |
| 1969–70 | Rashid Karami |
| 1970–3 | Saeb Salam |
| 1973 | Amin al-Hafez |
| 1973–4 | Takieddine Solh |
| 1974–5 | Rashid Solh |
| 1975 | Noureddin Rifai |
| 1975–6 | Rashid Karami |
| 1976–80 | Selim al-Hoss |
| 1980 | Takieddine Solh |
| 1980–4 | Chafiq al-Wazan |
| 1984–8 | Rashid Karami |
| 1988–90 | Michel Aoun/Selim al-Hoss |
| 1990–2 | Umar Karami |
| 1992–8 | Rafiq al-Hariri |
| 1998–2000 | Selim al-Hoss |
| 2000– | Rafiq al-Hariri |

## Lesotho

*Monarch*

| | |
|---|---|
| 1966–90 | Moshoeshoe II |
| 1991–4 | Letsie III |
| 1995–6 | Moshoeshoe II |
| 1996– | Letsie III |

*Prime Minister*

| | |
|---|---|
| 1966–86 | Leabua Jonathan |

*Chairman of Military Council*

| | |
|---|---|
| 1986–91 | Justin Metsing Lekhanya |
| 1991–3 | Elias Tutsoane Ramaema |

*Prime Minister*

| | |
|---|---|
| 1993–8 | Ntsu Mokhehle |
| 1998– | Bethuel Pakalitha Mosisili |

## Liberia

*President*

| | |
|---|---|
| 1900–4 | Garretson Wilmot Gibson |
| 1904–12 | Arthur Barclay |
| 1912–20 | Daniel Edward Howard |
| 1920–30 | Charles Dunbar Burgess King |
| 1930–43 | Edwin J Barclay |
| 1943–71 | William V S Tubman |
| 1971–80 | William Richard Tolbert |

**People's Redemption Council**

*Chairman*

| | |
|---|---|
| 1980–6 | Samuel K Doe |

*President*

| | |
|---|---|
| 1986–90 | Samuel K Doe |
| 1991–4 | Amos Sawyer *Interim President* |

**Council of State**

*Chairman*

| | |
|---|---|
| 1994–5 | David Kpormakor |
| 1995–6 | Wilton Sankawulo |
| 1996–7 | Ruth Perry |

*President*

| | |
|---|---|
| 1997– | Charles Taylor |

## Libya

*Monarch*

| | |
|---|---|
| 1951–69 | Mohammed Idris Al-Mahdi Al-Senussi |

**Revolutionary Command Council**

*Chairman*

| | |
|---|---|
| 1969–77 | Muammar Al-Gaddafi (Qaddafi) |

**General Secretariat**

*Secretary General*

| | |
|---|---|
| 1977–9 | Muammar Al-Gaddafi |
| 1979–84 | Abdul Ati Al-Ubaidi |
| 1984–6 | Mohammed Az-Zaruq Rajab |
| 1986–90 | Omar Al-Muntasir |
| 1990–4 | Abu Zayd 'Umar Durda |
| 1994– | Zanati Mohammed Al-Zanati |

*Leader of the Revolution*

| | |
|---|---|
| 1969– | Muammar Al-Gaddafi |

## Liechtenstein

*Prince*

| | |
|---|---|
| 1858–1929 | Johann II |
| 1929–38 | Franz von Paula |
| 1938–89 | Franz Josef II |
| 1989– | Hans Adam II |

*Prime Minister*

| | |
|---|---|
| 1928–45 | Franz Josef Hoop |
| 1945–62 | Alexander Friek |
| 1962–70 | Gérard Batliner |
| 1970–4 | Alfred J Hilbe |
| 1974–8 | Walter Kieber |
| 1978–93 | Hans Brunhart |
| 1993 | Markus Büchel |
| 1994–2001 | Mario Frick |
| 2001– | Otmar Hasler |

## Lithuania

*President*

| | |
|---|---|
| 1990–3 | Vytautas Landsbergis |
| 1993–8 | Algirdas Brazauskas |
| 1998– | Valdas Adamkus |

## Luxembourg

*Grand Dukes and Duchesses*

| | |
|---|---|
| 1890–1905 | Adolf |
| 1905–12 | William IV |
| 1912–19 | Marie Adelaide |
| 1919–64 | Charlotte (*in exile 1940–4*) |
| 1964–2000 | Jean |
| 2000– | Henri |

*Prime Minister*

| | |
|---|---|
| 1889–1915 | Paul Eyschen |
| 1915 | Mathias Mongenast |
| 1915–16 | Hubert Loutsch |
| 1916–17 | Victor Thorn |
| 1917–18 | Léon Kaufmann |
| 1918–25 | Emil Reuter |

1925–6 Pierre Prum
1926–37 Joseph Bech
1937–53 Pierre Dupong (*in exile 1940-4*)
1953–8 Joseph Bech
1958 Pierre Frieden
1959–69 Pierre Werner
1969–79 Gaston Thorn
1979–84 Pierre Werner
1984–95 Jacques Santer
1995– Jean-Claude Juncker

## Macedonia, Former Yugoslav Republic of

*President*

1991–5 Kiro Gligorov
1995–8 Stojan Andov *Acting President*
1998–9 Kiro Gligorov
1999– Boris Trajkovski

*Prime Minister*

1991–2 Branko Crvenkovski
1992–6 Petar Gosev
1996–8 Branko Crvenkovski
1998– Ljubco Georgievski

## Madagascar

*President*

1960–72 Philibert Tsiranana
1972–5 Gabriel Ramanantsoa
1975 Richard Ratsimandrava
1975 Gilles Andriamahazo
1975–93 Didier Ratsiraka
1993–7 Albert Zafy
1997– Didier Ratsiraka

*Prime Minister*

1960–75 *As President*
1975–6 Joël Rakotomala
1976–7 Justin Rakotoriaina
1977–88 Désiré Rakotoarijaona
1988–91 Victor Ramahatra
1991–3 Guy Willy Razanamasy
1993–5 Francisque Ravony
1995–6 Emmanuel Rakotovahiny
1996–7 Norbert Ratsirahonana
1997–8 Paskal Rakotmavo
1998– Tantely Adrianarivo

## Malawi

*President*

1966–94 Hastings Kamuzu Banda
1994– Bakili Muluzi

## Malaysia

*Chief of State (Yang di-Pertuan Agong)*

1957–63 Abdul Rahman
1963–5 Syed Putra Jamalullah
1965–70 Ismail Nasiruddin Shah
1970–5 Abdul Halim Muadzam Shah
1975–9 Yahya Petra Ibrahim
1979–84 Haji Ahmad Shah Al-Mustain Billah
1984–9 Mahmood Iskandar Shah
1989–94 Azlan Muhibuddin Shah
1994–9 Jaafar Ibni Abdul Rahman
1999–2001 Salehuddin Abdul Aziz Shah
2001– Tuanku Syed Sirajuddin

*Prime Minister*

### ❑ Malaya

1957–63 Abdul Rahman Putra Al-Haj

### ❑ Malaysia

1963–70 Abdul Rahman Putra Al-Haj
1970–6 Abdul Razak bin Hussein
1976–9 Haji Hussein bin Onn
1979–97 Mahathir bin Mohamad
1997 Anwar Ibrahim *Acting Prime Minister*
1997– Mahathir bin Mohamad

## Maldives

*Monarch (Sultan)*

1954–68 Mohammed Farid Didi

### ❑ Republic

*President*

1968–78 Ibrahim Nasir
1978– Maumoon Abdul Gayoom

## Mali

*President*

1960–8 Modibo Keita
1969–91 Moussa Traoré
1991–2 Amadou Toumani Touré
1992– Alpha Oumar Konaré

*Prime Minister*

1986–88 Mamadou Dembelé
1988–91 *No Prime Minister*
1991–2 Soumana Sacko
1992-3 Younoussi Touré
1993–4 Abdoulaye Sekou Sow
1994–2000 Ibrahim Boubacar Keita
2000– Mande Sidibe

## Malta

*President*

1974–6 Anthony Mamo
1976–81 Anton Buttigieg
1982–7 Agatha Barbara
1987–9 Paul Xuereb *Acting President*
1989–94 Vincent Tabone
1994–9 Ugo Mifsud Bonnici
1999– Guido de Marco

*Prime Minister*

1962–71 G Borg Olivier
1971–84 Dom Mintoff
1984–7 Carmelo Mifsud Bonnici
1987–96 Edward Fenech Adami
1996–8 Alfred Sant
1998– Edward Fenech Adami

## Marshall Islands

*President*

1990–6 Amata Kabua
1996–7 Kunio Lemari *Acting President*
1997–2000 Imata Kabua
2000– Kessai Note

## Mauritania

*President*

1961–78 Mokhtar Ould Daddah
1979 Mustapha Ould Mohammed Salek
1979–80 Mohammed Mahmoud Ould Ahmed Louly
1980–4 Mohammed Khouna Ould Haydallah
1984– Maaouya Ould Sidi Ahmed Taya

## Mauritius

Chief of State until 1992: British monarch, represented by Governor General

*Prime Minister*

1968–82 Seewoosagur Ramgoolam
1982–95 Anerood Jugnauth
1995–2000 Navin Ramgoolam
2000– Anerood Jugnauth

### ❑ Republic

*President*

1992 Veerasamy Ringadoo
1992– Cassam Uteem

## Mexico

*President*

1876–1911 Porfirio Diaz
1911 Francisco León de la Barra
1911–13 Francisco I Madero
1913–14 Victoriano Huerta
1914 Francisco Carvajal
1914 Venustiano Carranza
1914–15 Eulalio Gutiérrez *Provisional President*
1915 Roque González Garza *Provisional President*
1915 Francisco Lagos Chazaro *Provisional President*
1917–20 Venustiano Carranza
1920 Adolfo de la Huerta
1920–4 Alvaro Obregón
1924–8 Plutarco Elías Calles
1928–30 Emilio Portes Gil
1930–2 Pascual Ortíz Rubio
1932–4 Abelardo L Rodríguez
1934–40 Lazaro Cardenas
1940–6 Manuel Avila Camacho
1946–52 Miguel Alemán
1952–8 Adolfo Ruiz Cortines
1958–64 Adolfo López Mateos
1964–70 Gustavo Díaz Ordaz
1970–6 Luis Echeverría
1976–82 José López Portillo
1982–8 Miguel de la Madrid Hurtado
1988–94 Carlos Salinas de Gortari
1994–2000 Ernesto Zedillo Ponce de León
2000– Vincente Fox Quesada

## Micronesia, Federated States of

*President*

1991–7 Bailey Olter (Pohnpei)
1997–9 Jacob Nena (Kosrae)
1999– Leo Falcam (Pohnpei)

## Moldova (Moldavia)

*President*

1991–6 Mircea Snegur
1996–2001 Petru Lucinschi
2001– Vladimir Voronin

## Monaco

*Head of State*

1889–1922 Albert
1922–49 Louis II
1949– Rainier III

## Mongolia

*Prime Minister*

1924–8 Tserendorji
1928–32 Amor
1932–6 Gendun
1936–8 Amor
1939–52 Korloghiin Choibalsan
1952–74 Yumsjhagiin Tsedenbal

*Chairman of the Praesidium*

1948–53 Gonchighlin Bumatsende
1954–72 Jamsarangiin Sambu
1972–4 Sonomyn Luvsan
1974–84 Yumsjhagiin Tsedenbal
1984–90 Jambyn Batmunkh

*President*

1990–7 Punsalmaagiyn Ochirbat
1997– Natsagiyn Bagabandi

*Premier*

1974–84 Jambyn Batmunkh
1984–90 Dumaagiyn Sodnom
1990–2 Dashiyn Byambasuren
1992–6 Puntsagiyn Jasray
1996–8 Mendsaihany Enkhsahan
1998 Tsahiagiyin Elbegdorj
1998–9 Janlaviyn Narantsatsralt
1999–2000 Rinchinnyamiyn Amarjagal
2000– Nambaryn Enkhbayar

## Montenegro ▸ Yugoslavia

## Morocco

*Monarch*

1927–61 Mohammed V
1961–99 Hassan II
1999– Mohammed VI

*Prime Minister*

| | |
|---|---|
| 1955–8 | Si Mohammed Bekkai |
| 1958 | Ahmad Balfrej |
| 1958–60 | Abdullah Ibrahim |
| 1960–3 | *As Monarch* |
| 1963–5 | Ahmad Bahnini |
| 1965–7 | *As Monarch* |
| 1967–9 | Moulay Ahmed Laraki |
| 1969–71 | Mohammed Ben Hima |
| 1971–2 | Mohammed Karim Lamrani |
| 1972–9 | Ahmed Othman |
| 1979–83 | Maati Bouabid |
| 1983–6 | Mohammed Karim Lamrani |
| 1986–92 | Izz Id-Dien Laraki |
| 1992–4 | Mohammed Karim Lamrani |
| 1994–8 | Abdellatif Filali |
| 1998– | Abderrahmane el-Yousifi |

## Mozambique

*President*

| | |
|---|---|
| 1975–86 | Samora Moïses Machel |
| 1986– | Joaquim Alberto Chissano |

## Myanmar, Union of (Burma)

The Socialist Republic of the Union of Burma offically became the Union of Myanmar in 1989, following the military coup of 1988, but it is still often referred to as Burma.

*President*

| | |
|---|---|
| 1948–52 | Sao Shwe Thaik |
| 1952–7 | Agga Maha Thiri Thudhamma Ba U |
| 1957–62 | U Wing Maung |
| 1962 | Sama Duwa Sinwa Nawng |

**Revolutionary Council**

| | |
|---|---|
| 1962–74 | Ne Win |

**State Council**

| | |
|---|---|
| 1974–81 | Ne Win |
| 1981–8 | U San Yu |
| 1988 | U Sein Lwin |
| 1988 | Maung Maung |
| 1988–92 | Saw Maung |
| 1992 | Than Shwe |

*Prime Minister*

| | |
|---|---|
| 1947–56 | Thakin Nu |
| 1956–7 | U Ba Swe |
| 1957–8 | U Nu |
| 1958–60 | Ne Win |
| 1960–2 | U Nu |
| 1962–74 | Ne Win |
| 1974–7 | U Sein Win |
| 1977–8 | U Maung Maung Ka |
| 1988 | U Tun Tin |
| 1988–92 | Saw Maung |
| 1992– | Than Shwe |

## Namibia

*President*

| | |
|---|---|
| 1990– | Sam Daniel Nujoma |

## Nauru

*President*

| | |
|---|---|
| 1968–86 | Hammer de Roburt |
| 1986 | Kennan Adeang |
| 1986–9 | Hammer de Roburt |
| 1989 | Kenas Aroi |
| 1989–95 | Bernard Dowiyogo |
| 1995–6 | Lagumot Harris |
| 1996 | Bernard Dowiyogo |
| 1996–7 | Kennan Adeang |
| 1997–8 | Kinza Clodumar |
| 1998–9 | Bernard Dowiyogo |
| 1999–2000 | Rene Harris |
| 2000–1 | Bernard Dowiyogo |
| 2001– | Rene Harris |

## Nepal

*Monarch*

| | |
|---|---|
| 1881–1911 | Prithvi Bir Bikram Shah |
| 1911–50 | Tribhuvan Bir Bikram Shah |
| 1950–2 | Bir Bikram |
| 1952–5 | Tribhuvan Bir Bikram Shah |
| 1956–72 | Mahendra Bir Bikram Shah |
| 1972–2001 | Birendra Bir Bikram Shah Dev |
| 2001 | Dipendra Bir Bikram Shah Dev |
| 2001– | Gyanendra Bir Bikram Shah Dev |

*Prime Minister*

| | |
|---|---|
| 1901–29 | Chandra Sham Sher Jang Bahadur Rana |
| 1929–31 | Bhim Cham Sham Sher Jang Bahadur Rana |
| 1931–45 | Juddha Sham Sher Rana |
| 1945–8 | Padma Sham Sher Jang Bahadur Rana |
| 1948–51 | Mohan Sham Sher Jang Bahadur Rana |
| 1951–2 | Matrika Prasad Koirala |
| 1952–3 | Tribhuvan Bir Bikram Shah |
| 1953–5 | Matrika Prasad Koirala |
| 1955–6 | Mahendra Bir Bikram Shah |
| 1956–7 | Tanka Prasad Acharya |
| 1957–9 | *King also Prime Minister* |
| 1959–60 | Sri Bishawa Prasad Koirala |
| 1960–3 | *No Prime Minister* |
| 1963–5 | Tulsi Giri |
| 1965–9 | Surya Bahadur Thapa |
| 1969–70 | Kirti Nidhi Bista |
| 1970–1 | *King also Prime Minister* |
| 1971–3 | Kirti Nidhi Bista |
| 1973–5 | Nagendra Prasad Rijal |
| 1975–7 | Tulsi Giri |
| 1977–9 | Kirti Nidhi Bista |
| 1979–83 | Surya Bahadur Thapa |
| 1983–6 | Lokendra Bahadur Chand |
| 1986–91 | Marich Man Singh Shrestha |
| 1991–4 | Girija Prasad Koirala |
| 1994–5 | Man Mohan Adhikari |
| 1995–7 | Sher Bahadur Deuba |
| 1997 | Lokendra Bahadur Chand |
| 1997 | Surya Bahadur Thapa |
| 1998–9 | Girija Prasad Koirala |
| 1999–2000 | Krishna Prasad Bhattari |

2000–1 Girija Prasad Koirala
2001– Sher Bahadur Deuba

## The Netherlands

*Monarch*

1890–1948 Wilhelmina
1948–80 Juliana
1980– Beatrix

*Prime Minister*

1897–1901 Nicholas G Pierson
1901–5 Abraham Kuyper
1905–8 Theodoor H de Meester
1908–13 Theodorus Heemskerk
1913–18 Pieter W A Cort van der Linden
1918–25 Charles J M Ruys de Beerenbrouck
1925–6 Hendrikus Colijn
1926 Dirk J de Geer
1926–33 Charles J M Ruys de Beerenbrouck
1933–9 Hendrikus Colijn
1939–40 Dirk J de Geer
1940–5 Pieter S Gerbrandy *(in exile)*
1945–6 Willem Schemerhorn/Willem Drees
1946–8 Louis J M Beel
1948–51 Willem Drees/Josephus R H van Schaik
1951–8 Willem Drees
1958–9 Louis J M Beel
1959–63 Jan E de Quay
1963–5 Victor G M Marijnen
1965–6 Joseph M L T Cals
1966–7 Jelle Zijlstra
1967–71 Petrus J S de Jong
1971–3 Barend W Biesheuvel
1973–7 Joop M Den Uyl
1977–82 Andreas A M van Agt
1982–94 Ruud F M Lubbers
1994– Wim Kok

## New Zealand

Chief of State: British monarch, represented by Governor General

*Prime Minister*

1893–1906 Richard John Seddon *Lib*
1906 William Hall-Jones *Lib*
1906–12 Joseph George Ward *Lib/Nat*
1912 Thomas Mackenzie *Nat*
1912–25 William Ferguson Massey *Ref*
1925 Francis Henry Dillon Bell *Ref*
1925–8 Joseph Gordon Coates *Ref*
1928–30 Joseph George Ward *Lib/Nat*
1930–5 George William Forbes *Un*
1935–40 Michael Joseph Savage *Lab*
1940–9 Peter Fraser *Lab*
1949–57 Sidney George Holland *Nat*
1957 Keith Jacka Holyoake *Nat*
1957–60 Walter Nash *Lab*
1960–72 Keith Jacka Holyoake *Nat*
1972 John Ross Marshall *Nat*
1972–4 Norman Eric Kirk *Lab*
1974–5 Wallace Edward Rowling *Lab*
1975–84 Robert David Muldoon *Nat*
1984–89 David Russell Lange *Lab*
1989–90 Geoffrey Palmer *Lab*
1990 Mike Moore *Lab*
1990–7 James Bolger *Nat*
1997–9 Jenny Shipley *Nat*
1999– Helen Clark *Lab*

*Lab* = Labor *Nat* = National *Un* = United
*Lib* = Liberal *Ref* = Reform

## Nicaragua

*President*

1893–1909 José Santos Zelaya
1909–10 José Madriz
1910–11 José Dolores Estrada
1911 Juan José Estrada
1911–17 Adolfo Díaz
1912 Luis Mena *rival President*
1917–21 Emiliano Chamorro Vargas
1921–3 Riego Manuel Chamorro
1923–4 Martínez Bartolo
1925–6 Carlos Solórzano
1926 Emiliano Chamorro Vargas
1926–8 Adolfo Díaz
1926 Juan Bautista Sacasa *rival President*
1928–32 José Marcia Moncada
1933–6 Juan Bautista Sacasa
1936 Carlos Brenes Jarquin
1937–47 Anastasio Somoza García
1947 Leonardo Argüello
1947 Benjamin Lascayo Sacasa
1947–50 Victor Manuel Román y Reyes
1950–6 Anastasio Somoza García
1956–63 Luis Somoza Debayle
1963–6 René Schick Gutiérrez
1966–7 Lorenzo Guerrero Gutiérrez
1967–72 Anastasio Somoza Debayle
1972–4 *Triumvirate*
1974–9 Anastasio Somoza Debayle
1979–84 *Government Junta of National Reconstruction*
1984–90 Daniel Ortega Saavedra
1990–7 Violeta Barrios de Chamorro
1997– Arnoldo Alemán Lacayo

## Niger

*President*

1960–74 Hamani Diori
1974–87 Seyni Kountché
1987–91 Ali Saibou
1993–6 Mahamane Ousmane
1996–9 Ibrahim Baré Maïnassara
1999 Daouda Malam Wanke
1999– Tandja Mamadou

## Nigeria

*President*

1960–6 Nnamdi Azikiwe

*Prime Minister*

1960–6 Abubakar Tafawa Balewa

*Military Government*

1966 J T U Aguiyi-Ironsi
1966–75 Yakubu Gowon
1975–6 Murtala R Mohamed
1976–9 Olusegun Obasanjo

*President*

1979–83 Alhaji Shehu Shagari

*Military Government*

1983–4 Mohammadu Buhari
1985–93 Ibrahim B Babangida
1993 Ernest Shonekan *Interim President*
1993–8 Sani Abacha
1998–9 Abdulsalami Abubakar
1999– Olusegun Obasanjo

## North Korea ► Korea, Democratic People's Republic of

## Norway

*Monarch*

1872–1905 Oscar II *union with Sweden*
1905–57 Haakon VII
1957–91 Olav V
1991– Harald V

*Prime Minister*

1898–1902 Johannes Steen
1902–3 Otto Albert Blehr
1903–5 George Francis Hagerup
1905–7 Christian Michelsen
1907–8 Jørgen Løvland
1908–10 Gunnar Knudsen
1910–12 Wollert Konow
1912–13 Jens Bratlie
1913–20 Gunnar Knudsen
1920–1 Otto Bahr Halvorsen
1921–3 Otto Albert Blehr
1923 Otto Bahr Halvorsen
1923–4 Abraham Berge
1924–6 Johan Ludwig Mowinckel
1926–8 Ivar Lykke
1928 Christopher Hornsrud
1928–31 Johan Ludwig Mowinckel
1931–2 Peder L Kolstad
1932–3 Jens Hundseid
1933–5 Johan Ludwig Mowinckel
1935–45 Johan Nygaardsvold
1945–51 Einar Gerhardsen
1951–5 Oscar Torp
1955–63 Einar Gerhardsen
1963 John Lyng
1963–5 Einar Gerhardsen
1965–71 Per Borten
1971–2 Trygve Bratteli
1972–3 Lars Korvald
1973–6 Trygve Bratteli
1976–81 Odvar Nordli
1981 Gro Harlem Brundtland
1981–6 Kåre Willoch
1986–9 Gro Harlem Brundtland
1989–90 Jan P Syse
1990–6 Gro Harlem Brundtland
1996–7 Thorbjørn Jagland
1997–2000 Kjell Magne Bondevik
2000–1 Jens Stoltenberg
2001– Kjell Magne Bondevik

## Oman

*Sultan*

1888–1913 Faisal Bin Turki
1913–32 Taimur Bin Faisal
1932–70 Said Bin Taimur
1970– Qaboos Bin Said

## Pakistan

*President*

1956–8 Iskander Mirza
1958–69 Mohammad Ayoub Khan
1969–71 Agha Mohammad Yahya Khan
1971–3 Zulfikar Ali Bhutto
1973–8 Fazal Elahi Chawdry
1978–88 Mohammad Zia Ul-Haq
1988–93 Ghulam Ishaq Khan
1993–7 Farooq Ahmad Khan Leghari
1997 Wasim Sajjad *Acting President*
1998–2001 Muhammed Rafiq Tarar
2001– Pervez Musharraf

*Prime Minister*

1947–51 Liaqat Ali Khan
1951–3 Khawaja Nazimuddin
1953–5 Mohammad Ali
1955–6 Chawdry Mohammad Ali
1956–7 Hussein Shahid Suhrawardi
1957 Ismail Chundrigar
1957–8 Malik Feroz Khan Noon
1958 Mohammad Ayoub Khan
1958–73 *No Prime Minister*
1973–7 Zulfikar Ali Bhutto
1977–85 *No Prime Minister*
1985–8 Mohammad Khan Junejo
1988 Mohammad Aslam Khan Khattak
1988–90 Benazir Bhutto
1990 Ghulam Mustafa Jatoi
1990–3 Mian Mohammad Nawaz Sharif
1993–6 Benazir Bhutto
1996–7 Meraj Khalid *Acting Prime Minister*
1997–9 Mian Mohammad Nawaz Sharif
1999– *No Prime Minister*

## Panama

*President*

1904–8 Manuel Amador Guerrero
1908–10 José Domingo de Obaldia
1910 Federico Boyd
1910 Carlos Antonio Mendoza
1910–12 Pablo Arosemena
1912 Rodolfo Chiari
1912–16 Belisario Porras
1916–18 Ramón Maximiliano Valdés

1918 Pedro Antonio Diaz
1918 Cirilo Luis Urriola
1918–20 Belisario Porras
1920 Ernesto T Lefevre
1920–4 Belisario Porras
1924–8 Rodolfo Chiari
1928 Tomás Gabriel Duque
1928–31 Florencio Harmodio Arosemena
1931 Harmodio Arias
1931–2 Ricardo Joaquín Alfaro
1932–6 Harmodio Arias
1936–9 Juan Demóstenes Arosemena
1939 Ezequiel Fernández Jaén
1939–40 Augusto Samuel Boyd
1940–1 Arnulfo Arias Madrid
1941 Ernesto Jaén Guardia
1941 José Pezet
1941–5 Ricardo Adolfo de la Guardia
1945–8 Enrique Adolfo Jiménez Brin
1948–9 Domingo Diaz Arosemena
1949 Daniel Chanis
1949 Roberto Francisco Chiari
1949–51 Arnulfo Arias Madrid
1951–2 Alcibiades Arosemena
1952–5 José Antonio Remón
1955 José Ramón Guizado
1955–6 Ricardo Manuel Arias Espinosa
1956–60 Ernesto de la Guardia
1960–4 Roberto Francisco Chiari
1964–8 Marco A Robles
1968 Arnulfo Arias Madrid
1968 *Military Junta*
1968–9 Omar Torrijos Herrera
1969–78 Demetrio Basilio Lakas
1978–82 Aristides Royo
1982–4 Ricardo de la Esoriella
1984 Jorge Enrique Illueca Sibauste
1984–5 Nicolás Ardito Barletta
1985–8 Eric Arturo Delvalle
1988–9 Manuel Solís Palma
1989–94 Guillermo Endara Galimany
1994–9 Ernesto Pérez Balladares
1999– Mireya Moscoso Rodriguez

## Papua New Guinea

*Prime Minister*

1975–80 Michael T Somare
1980–2 Julius Chan
1982–5 Michael T Somare
1985–8 Paias Wingti
1988–92 Rabbie Namaliu
1992–4 Paias Wingti
1994–7 Julius Chan
1997 John Giheno *Acting Prime Minister*
1997 Julius Chan
1997–9 Bill Skate
1999– Sir Mekere Morauta

## Paraguay

*President*

1898–1902 Emilio Azeval
1902 Hector Carvallo
1902–4 Juan Antonio Escurra
1904–5 Juan Gaona
1905–6 Cecilio Baez
1906–8 Benigno Ferreira
1908–10 Emiliano González Navero
1910–11 Manuel Gondra
1911 Albino Jara
1911 Liberato Marcial Rojas
1912 Pedro Peña
1912 Emiliano González Navero
1912–16 Eduardo Schaerer
1916–19 Manuel Franco
1919–20 José P Montero
1920–1 Manuel Gondra
1921 Félix Paiva
1921–3 Eusebio Ayala
1923–4 Eligio Ayala
1924 Luis Alberto Riart
1924–8 Eligio Ayala
1928–31 José Particio Guggiari
1931–2 Emiliano González Navero
1932 José Particio Guggiari
1932–6 Eusebio Ayala
1936–7 Rafael Franco
1937–9 Félix Paiva
1939–40 José Félix Estigarribia
1940–8 Higino Moríñigo
1948 Juan Manuel Frutos
1948–9 Juan Natalicio González
1949 Raimundo Rolón
1949 Felipe Molas López
1949–54 Federico Chaves
1954 Tomás Romero Pareira
1954–89 Alfredo Stroessner
1989–93 Andrés Rodríguez
1993–8 Juan Carlos Wasmosy
1998–9 Raúl Cubas Grau
1999– Luis González Macchi

## Peru

*President*

1899–1903 Eduardo López de Romaña
1903–4 Manuel Candamo
1904 Serapio Calderón
1904–8 José Pardo y Barreda
1908–12 Augusto B Leguía
1912–14 Guillermo Billinghurst
1914–15 Oscar R Benavides
1915–19 José Pardo y Barreda
1919–30 Augusto B Leguía
1930 Manuel Ponce
1930–1 Luis M Sánchez Cerro
1931 Leoncio Elías
1931 Gustavo A Jiménez
1931 David Samanez Ocampo
1931–3 Luis M Sánchez Cerro
1933–9 Oscar R Benavides
1939–45 Manuel Prado
1945–8 José Luis Bustamante y Rivero
1948–56 Manuel A Odría

| | |
|---|---|
| 1956–62 | Manuel Prado |
| 1962–3 | *Military Junta* |
| 1963–8 | Fernando Belaúnde Terry |
| 1968–75 | *Military Junta* (Juan Velasco Alvarado) |
| 1975–80 | *Military Junta* (Francisco Morales Bermúdez) |
| 1980–5 | Fernando Belaúnde Terry |
| 1985–90 | Alan García Pérez |
| 1990–2000 | Alberto Keinya Fujimori |
| 2000–1 | Valentín Paniagua *Interim President* |
| 2001– | Alejandro Toledo Manrique |

## Philippines

*President*

### ❑ Commonwealth

| | |
|---|---|
| 1935–44 | Manuel L Quezon |

### Japanese Occupation

| | |
|---|---|
| 1943–4 | José P Laurel |

### ❑ Commonwealth

| | |
|---|---|
| 1944–6 | Sergio Osmeña |

### ❑ First Republic

| | |
|---|---|
| 1946–8 | Manuel A Roxas |
| 1948–53 | Elpidio Quirino |
| 1953–7 | Ramon Magsaysay |
| 1957–61 | Carlos P Garcia |
| 1961–5 | Diosdado Macapagal |
| 1965–72 | Ferdinand E Marcos |

### Martial Law

| | |
|---|---|
| 1972–81 | Ferdinand E Marcos |

### ❑ New Republic

| | |
|---|---|
| 1981–6 | Ferdinand E Marcos |
| 1986–92 | Corazon C Aquino |
| 1992–8 | Fidel V Ramos |
| 1998–2001 | Joseph Estrada |
| 2001– | Gloria Macapagel-Arroyo |

## Poland

### ❑ Republic of Poland

*President*

| | |
|---|---|
| 1945–7 | Bolesław Bierut *Acting President* |
| 1947–52 | Bolesław Bierut |
| 1952–64 | Aleksander Zawadzki |
| 1964–8 | Edward Ochab |
| 1968–70 | Marian Spychalski |
| 1970–2 | Józef Cyrankiewicz |
| 1972–85 | Henryk Jabłonski |
| 1985–90 | Wojciech Jaruzelski *President 1989* |
| 1990–5 | Lech Wałesa |
| 1995– | Aleksander Kwaśniewski |

*Prime Minister*

| | |
|---|---|
| 1947–52 | Józef Cyrankiewicz |
| 1952–4 | Bolesław Bierut |
| 1954–70 | Józef Cyrankiewicz |
| 1970–80 | Piotr Jecoszewicz |
| 1980 | Edward Babiuch |
| 1980–1 | Józef Pinkowski |
| 1981–5 | Wojciech Jaruzelski |
| 1985–8 | Zbigniew Messner |
| 1988–9 | Mieczyslaw Rakowski |
| 1989 | Czeslaw Kiszczak |
| 1989–90 | Tadeusz Mazowiecki |
| 1991 | Jan Krzysztof Bielecki |
| 1991–2 | Jan Olszewski |
| 1992 | Waldemar Pawlak |
| 1992–3 | Hanna Suchocka |
| 1993–5 | Waldemar Pawlak |
| 1995–6 | Józef Oleksy |
| 1996–7 | Wlodzimierz Cimoszewicz |
| 1997–2001 | Jerzy Buzek |
| 2001– | Leszek Miller |

*First Secretary*

| | |
|---|---|
| 1945–8 | Władysław Gomułka |
| 1948–56 | Bolesław Bierut |
| 1956 | Edward Ochab |
| 1956–70 | Władysław Gomułka |
| 1970–80 | Edward Gierek |
| 1980–1 | Stanisław Kania |
| 1981–9 | Wojciech Jaruzelski |
| 1989 | Mieczyslaw Rakowski |

## Portugal

*President*

### ❑ First Republic

| | |
|---|---|
| 1910–11 | Teófilo Braga |
| 1911–15 | Manuel José de Arriaga |
| 1915 | Teófilo Braga |
| 1915–17 | Bernardino Machado |
| 1917–18 | Sidónio Pais |
| 1918–19 | Joâo do Canto e Castro |
| 1919–23 | António José de Almeida |
| 1923–5 | Manuel Teixeira Gomes |
| 1925–6 | Bernardino Machado |

### ❑ New State

| | |
|---|---|
| 1926 | *Military Junta* (José Mendes Cabeçadas) |
| 1926 | *Military Junta* (Manuel de Oliveira Gomes da Costa) |
| 1926–51 | António Oscar Fragoso Carmona |
| 1951–8 | Francisco Craveiro Lopes |
| 1958–74 | Américo de Deus Tomás |

### ❑ Second Republic

| | |
|---|---|
| 1974 | *Military Junta* (António Spínola) |
| 1974–6 | *Military Junta* (Francisco da Costa Gomes) |

### ❑ Third Republic

| | |
|---|---|
| 1976–86 | António dos Santos Ramalho Eanes |
| 1986–96 | Mário Soares |
| 1996– | Jorge Sampaio |

*Prime Minister*

| | |
|---|---|
| 1932–68 | António de Oliveira Salazar |
| 1968–74 | Marcelo Caetano |
| 1974 | Adelino da Palma Carlos |

1974–5 Vasco Gonçalves
1975–6 José Pinheiro de Azevedo
1976–8 Mário Soares
1978 Alfredo Nobre da Costa
1978–9 Carlos Alberto de Mota Pinto
1979 Maria de Lurdes Pintasilgo
1980–1 Francisco de Sá Carneiro
1981–3 Francisco Pinto Balsemão
1983–5 Mário Soares
1985–95 Aníbal Cavaço Silva
1995–2001 António Guterres

## Qatar

*Emir*
*Family name*: al-Thani

1971–2 Ahmad Bin Ali
1972–95 Khalifah Bin Hamad
1995– Ahmad Bin Khalifa

## Romania

*Monarch*

1881–1914 Carol I
1914–27 Ferdinand I
1927–30 Michael *Prince*
1930–40 Carol II
1940–7 Michael I

### ❑ Republic

*President*

1947–8 Mihai Sadoveanu *Interim*
1948–52 Constantin I Parhon
1952–8 Petru Groza
1958–61 Ion Georghe Maurer
1961–5 Georghe Gheorghiu-Dej
1965–7 Chivu Stoica
1967–89 Nicolae Ceauşescu
1989–96 Ion Iliescu
1996– Emil Constantinescu

*General Secretary*

1955–65 Georghe Gheorghiu-Dej
1965–89 Nicolae Ceauşescu

*Prime Minister*

1900–1 Petre P Carp
1901–6 Dimitrie A Sturdza
1906–7 Gheorge Grigore Cantacuzino
1907–9 Dimitrie A Sturdza
1909 Ionel Brătianu
1909–10 Mihai Pherekyde
1910–11 Ionel Brătianu
1911–12 Petre P Carp
1912–14 Titu Maiorescu
1914–18 Ionel Brătianu
1918 Alexandru Averescu
1918 Alexandru Marghiloman
1918 Constantin Coandă
1918 Ionel Brătianu
1919 Artur Văitoianu
1919–20 Alexandru Vaida-Voevod
1920–1 Alexandru Averescu
1921–2 Take Ionescu
1922–6 Ionel Brătianu
1926–7 Alexandru Averescu
1927 Ionel Brătianu
1927–8 Vintila I C Brătianu
1928–30 Juliu Maniu
1930 Gheorghe C Mironescu
1930 Juliu Maniu
1930–1 Gheorghe C Mironescu
1931–2 Nicolae Iorga
1932 Alexandru Vaida-Voevod
1932–3 Juliu Maniu
1933 Alexandru Vaida-Voevod
1933 Ion G Duca
1933–4 Constantin Angelescu
1934–7 Gheorghe Tătărescu
1937 Octavian Goga
1937–9 Miron Cristea
1939 Armand Călinescu
1939 Gheorghe Argeşanu
1939 Constantine Argetoianu
1939–40 Gheorghe Tătărescu
1940 Ion Gigurtu
1940–4 Ion Antonescu
1944 Constantin Savbnătescu
1944–5 Nicolae Rădescu
1945–52 Petru Groza
1952–5 Gheorghe Gheorghiu-Dej
1955–61 Chivu Stoica
1961–74 Ion Gheorghe Maurer
1974–80 Manea Mănescu
1980–3 Ilie Verdet
1983–9 Constantin Dăscălescu
1989–91 Petre Roman
1991–2 Theodor Stolojan
1992–6 Nicolae Vacaroiu
1996–8 Victor Ciorbea
1998 Gavril Dejeu *Interim Prime Minister*
1998–9 Radu Vasile
1999 Alexandru Athanesiu *Interim Prime Minister*
1999– Mugur Isarescu

## Russia

*President*

1991–9 Boris Yeltsin
2000– Vladimir Putin

*Prime Minister*

1991–2 Boris Yeltsin
1992 Yegor Gaidar *Acting Prime Minister*
1992–8 Viktor Chernomyrdin
1998 Sergei Kiriyenko
1998 Viktor Chernomyrdin *Acting Prime Minister*
1998–9 Yevgeny Primakov
1999 Sergei Stepashin
1999–2000 Vladimir Putin
2000– Mikhail Kasyanov

## Rwanda

*President*

1962–73 Grégoire Kayibanda

1973–94 Juvénal Habyarimana
1994–2000 Pasteur Bizimungu
2000– Paul Kagame

## St Kitts and Nevis

Chief of State: British monarch, represented by Governor General

*Prime Minister*

1983–95 Kennedy A Simmonds
1995– Denzil Douglas

## St Lucia

Chief of State: British monarch, represented by Governor General

*Prime Minister*

1979 John Compton
1979–81 Allan Louisy
1981–3 Winston Francis Cenac
1983–96 John Compton
1996–7 Vaughan Lewis
1997– Kenny Anthony

## St Vincent and the Grenadines

Chief of State: British monarch, represented by Governor General

*Prime Minister*

1979–84 Milton Cato
1984–2000 James Fitz-Allen Mitchell
2000–1 Arnhim Eustace
2001– Ralph Gonsalves

## Samoa (Western Samoa)

*President*

1962–3 Tupua Tamesehe Mea'ole *and* Malietoa Tanumalfi II *Joint Presidents*
1963– Malietoa Tanumafili II

*Prime Minister*

1962–1970 Fiame Mata'afa Faumuina Mulinu'u II
1970–6 Tupua Tamasese Leolofi IV
1976–82 Tupuola Taisi Efi
1982 Va'ai Kolone
1982 Tupuola Taisi Efi
1982–6 Tofilau Eti Alesana
1986–8 Va'ai Kolone
1988–98 Tofilau Eti Alesana
1998– Tuilaepa Sailele Malielegaoi

## San Marino

*Regent*

2 regents appointed every 6 months

## São Tomé and Príncipe

*President*

1975–91 Manuel Pinto da Costa
1991–2001 Miguel Trovoada
2001– Fradrique de Menezes

## Saudi Arabia

*Monarch*

*Family name*: al-Saud

1932–53 Abdulaziz Bin Abdur-Rahman
1953–64 Saud Bin Abdulaziz
1964–75 Faisal Bin Abdulaziz
1975–82 Khalid Bin Abdulaziz
1982–96 Fahd Bin Abdulaziz
1996 Abdullah Bin Abdulaziz *Acting Monarch*
1996– Fahd Bin Abdulaziz

## Senegal

*President*

1960–80 Léopold Sédar Senghor
1981–2000 Abdou Diouf
2000– Abdoulaye Wade

## Serbia ▸ Yugoslavia

## Seychelles

*President*

1976–7 James R Mancham
1977– France-Albert René

## Sierra Leone

*President*

1971 Christopher Okero Cole
1971–85 Siaka Stevens
1985–92 Joseph Saidu Momoh
1992–6 Valentine Strasser
1996–7 Ahmad Tejan Kabbah
1997 *Military coup*
1997 Johnny Paul Koroma
1997– Ahmad Tejan Kabbah

*Prime Minister*

❑ **Commonwealth**

1961–4 Milton Margai
1964–7 Albert Michael Margai
1967 Siaka Stevens
1967 David Lansana
1967 Ambrose Genda
1967–8 *National Reformation Council* (Andrew Saxon-Smith)
1968 John Bangura
1968–71 Siaka Stevens

❑ **Republic**

1971–5 Sorie Ibrahim Koroma
1975–8 Christian Alusine Kamara Taylor
1978– *No Prime Minister*

## Singapore

*President (Yang di-Pertuan Negara)*

1959–70 Yusof bin Ishak
1970–81 Benjamin Henry Sheares
1981–5 Chengara Veetil Devan Nair
1985–93 Wee Kim Wee
1993–9 Ong Teng Cheong
1999– Sellapan Ramanathan Nathan

*Prime Minister*

1959–90 Lee Kuan Yew
1990– Goh Chok Tong

## Slovakia

*President*

1993–8 Michal Kovác
1998– Rudolf Schuster

*Prime Minister*

1993–4 Vladimír Mečiar
1994 Jozef Moravčik
1994–8 Vladimír Mečiar
1998– Mikuláš Dzurinda

## Slovenia

*President*

1991– Milan Kučan

## Solomon Islands

Chief of State: British monarch, represented by Governor General

*Prime Minister*

1978–82 Peter Kenilorea
1982–4 Solomon Mamaloni
1984–6 Peter Kenilorea
1986–9 Ezekiel Alebua
1989–93 Solomon Mamaloni
1993–4 Francis Billy Hilly
1994–7 Solomon Mamaloni
1997–2000 Bartholomew Ulufa'alu
2000–1 Manasseh Sogavare
2001– Allan Kemakeza

## Somalia

*President*

1961–7 Aden Abdallah Osman
1967–9 Abdirashid Ali Shermarke

**Supreme Revolutionary Council**

1969–80 Mohammed Siad Barre

### ❑ Republic

1980–91 Mohammed Siad Barre
1991–7 Ali Mahdi Mohammed
2000 Abdullahi Derow Isaq *Acting President*
2000– Abd-al-Qassim Salad Hasan

### ❑ Somaliland Republic (from 1989)

*Prime Minister*

1961–4 Abdirashid Ali Shermarke
1964–7 Abdirizak Haji Hussein
1967–9 Mohammed Haji Ibrahim Egal
1987–90 Mohammed Ali Samater
1990–1 Mohammed Hawadie Madar
1991–7 Umar Arteh Ghalib
2000–1 Ali Khalif Galaid
2001– Hassan Abshir Farah

## South Africa

*Governor General*

1910–14 Herbert, Viscount Gladstone
1914–20 Sydney, Earl Buxton
1920–4 Arthur, Duke of Connaught
1924–31 Alexander, Earl of Athlone
1931–7 George Herbert Hyde Villiers
1937–43 Patrick Duncan
1943–5 Nicolaas Jacobus de Wet
1945–51 Gideon Brand Van Zyl
1951–9 Ernest George Jansen
1959 Lucas Cornelius Steyn
1959–61 Charles Robberts Swart

### ❑ Republic

*President*

1961–7 Charles Robberts Swart
1967 Theophilus Ebenhaezer Dönges
1967–8 Jozua François Nandé
1968–75 Jacobus Johannes Fouché
1975–8 Nicolaas Diederichs
1978–9 Balthazar Johannes Vorster
1979–84 Marais Viljoen
1984–89 Pieter Willem Botha
1989–94 Frederick Willem de Klerk
1994–9 Nelson Rolihlahla Mandela
1999– Thabo Mbeki

*Prime Minister*

1910–19 Louis Botha *SAf*
1919–24 Jan Christiaan Smuts *SAf*
1924–39 James Barry Munnick Hertzog *Nat*
1939–48 Jan Christiaan Smuts *Un*
1948–54 Daniel François Malan *Nat*
1954–8 Johannes Gerardus Strijdom *Nat*
1958–66 Hendrik Frensch Verwoerd *Nat*
1966–78 Balthazar Johannes Vorster *Nat*
1978–84 Pieter Willem Botha *Nat*
1984– *No Prime Minister*

*Nat* = National *Un* = United
*SAf* = South African Party

## South Korea ► Korea, Republic of

## Spain

*Monarch*

1886–1931 Alfonso XIII

### ❑ Second Republic

*President*

1931–6 Niceto Alcalá Zamora y Torres
1936 Diego Martínez Barrio *Acting President*

*Civil War*

1936–9 Manuel Azaña y Díez
1936–9 Miguel Cabanellas Ferrer

### ❑ Nationalist Government

*Chief of State*

1936–75 Francisco Franco Bahamonde

*Monarch*

1975– Juan Carlos I

*Prime Minister*

1900–1 Marcelo de Azcárraga y Palmero
1901–2 Práxedes Mateo Sagasta
1902–3 Francisco Silvela y Le-Vielleuze
1903 Raimundo Fernández Villaverde
1903–4 Antonio Maura y Montaner
1904–5 Marcelo de Azcárraga y Palmero
1905 Raimundo Fernández Villaverde
1905 Eugenio Montero Ríos
1905–6 Segismundo Moret y Prendergast
1906 José López Domínguez
1906 Segismundo Moret y Prendergast
1906–7 Antonio Aguilar y Correa
1907–9 Antonio Maura y Montaner
1909–10 Segismundo Moret y Prendergast
1910–12 José Canalejas y Méndez
1912 Álvaro Figueroa y Torres
1912–13 Manuel García Prieto
1913–15 Eduardo Dato y Iradier
1915–17 Álvaro Figueroa y Torres
1917 Manuel García Prieto
1917 Eduardo Dato y Iradier
1917–18 Manuel García Prieto
1918 Antonio Maura y Montaner
1918 Manuel García Prieto
1918–19 Álvaro Figueroa y Torres
1919 Antonio Maura y Montaner
1919 Joaquín Sánchez de Toca
1919–20 Manuel Allendesalazar
1920–1 Eduardo Dato y Iradier
1921 Gabino Bugallal Araujo *Acting Prime Minister*
1921 Manuel Allendesalazar
1921–2 Antonio Maura y Montaner
1922 José Sánchez Guerra y Martínez
1922–3 Manuel García Prieto
1923–30 Miguel Primo de Rivera y Oraneja
1930–1 Dámaso Berenguer y Fusté
1931 Juan Bautista Aznar-Cabañas
1931 Niceto Alcalá Zamora y Torres
1931–3 Manuel Azaña y Díez
1933 Alejandro Lerroux y García
1933 Diego Martínez Barrio
1933–4 Alejandro Lerroux y García
1934 Ricardo Samper Ibáñez
1934–5 Alejandro Lerroux y García
1935 Joaquín Chapaprieta y Terragosa
1935–6 Manuel Portela Valladares
1936 Manuel Azaña y Díez
1936 Santiago Casares Quiroga
1936 Diego Martínez Barrio
1936 José Giral y Pereyra
1936–7 Francisco Largo Caballero
1937–9 Juan Negrín

*Chairman of the Council of Ministers*

1939–73 Francisco Franco Bahamonde

*Prime Minister*

1973 Torcuato Fernández Miranda y Hevía *Acting Prime Minister*
1973–6 Carlos Arias Navarro
1976–81 Adolfo Suárez
1981–2 Calvo Sotelo
1982–96 Felipe González
1996– José María Aznar

## Sri Lanka

*President*

1972–8 William Gopallawa
1978–89 Junius Richard Jayawardene
1989–93 Ranasinghe Premadasa
1994– Chandrika Bandaranaike Kumaratunga

*Prime Minister*

### ❑ Ceylon

1947–52 Don Stephen Senanayake
1952–3 Dudley Shelton Senanayake
1953–6 John Lionel Kotelawala
1956–9 Solomon West Ridgeway Dias Bandaranaike
1960 Dudley Shelton Senanayake
1960–5 Sirimavo Ratwatte Dias Bandaranaike
1965–70 Dudley Shelton Senanayake

### ❑ Sri Lanka

1970–7 Sirimavo Ratwatte Dias Bandaranaike
1977–89 Ranasinghe Premadasa
1989–93 Dingiri Banda Wijetunge
1993–4 Ranil Wickremasinghe
1994 Chandrika Bandaranaike Kumaratunga
1994–2000 Sirimavo Ratwatte Dias Bandaranaike
2000–1 Ratnasiri Wickremanayake
2001– Ranil Wickremasinghe

## The Sudan

*Chief of State*

1956–8 *Council of State*
1958–64 Ibrahim Abboud
1964–5 *Council of Sovereignty*
1965–9 Ismail Al-Azhari
1969–85 Jaafar Mohammed Nimeiri *President from 1971*
1993– Omar Hassan Ahmed Al-Bashir *President from 1996*

**Transitional Military Council**

*Chairman*

1985–6 Abd Al-Rahman Siwar Al-Dahab

**Supreme Council**

*Chairman*

1986–9 Ahmad Al-Mirghani
1989– *As Prime Minister*

*Prime Minister*

1955–6 Ismail Al-Azhari
1956–8 Abdullah Khalil
1958–64 *As President*
1964–5 Serr Al-Khatim Al-Khalifa
1965–6 Mohammed Ahmed Mahjoub
1966–7 Sadiq Al-Mahdi
1967–9 Mohammed Ahmed Mahjoub
1969 Babiker Awadalla
1969–76 *As President*
1976–7 Rashid Al-Tahir Bakr
1977–85 *As President*
1985–6 *Transitional Military Council* (Al-Jazuli Dafallah)
1986–9 Sadiq Al-Mahdi *Military Council, Prime Minister*
1989– Omar Hassan Ahmed Al-Bashir

## Suriname

*President*

1975–80 J H E Ferrier
1980–2 Henk Chin-a-Sen
1982–8 L F Ramdat-Musier *Acting President*
1988–90 Ramsewak Shankar
1990–1 Johan Kraag
1991–6 Ronald Venetiaan
1996–2000 Jules Wijdenbosch
2000– Ronald Venetiaan

**National Military Council**

*Chairman*

1980–7 Desi Bouterse
1987 Iwan Granoogst *Acting Premier*

*Prime Minister*

1975–80 Henk Arron
1980 Henk Chin-a-Sen
1980–2 *No Prime Minister*
1982–3 Henry Weyhorst
1983–4 Errol Alibux
1984–6 Wim Udenhout
1986–7 Pretaapnarain Radhakishun
1987–8 Jules Wijdenbosch
1988–90 Henk Arron
1990–1 Jules Wijdenbosch
1991–6 Jules Ajodhia

## Swaziland

*Monarch*

1967–82 Sobhuza II *Chief since 1921*
1983 Dzeliwe *Queen Regent*
1983–6 Ntombi *Queen Regent*
1986– Mswati III

*Prime Minister*

1967–78 Prince Makhosini
1978–9 Prince Maphevu Dlamini
1979–83 Prince Mbandla Dlamini
1983–6 Prince Bhekimpi Dlamini
1986–9 Sotsha Dlamini
1989-93 Obed Dlamini *Acting Prime Minister*
1993–6 Jameson Mbilini Dlamini
1996– Barnabus S Dlamini

## Sweden

*Monarch*

1872–1907 Oskar II
1907–50 Gustav V
1950–73 Gustav VI Adolf
1973– Carl XVI Gustaf

*Prime Minister*

1900–2 Fredrik von Otter
1902–5 Erik Gustaf Boström
1905 Johan Ramstedt
1905 Christian Lundeberg
1905–6 Karl Staaf
1906–11 Arvid Lindman
1911–14 Karl Staaf
1914–17 Hjalmar Hammarskjöld
1917 Carl Swartz
1917–20 Nils Edén
1920 Hjalmar Branting
1920–1 Louis de Geer
1921 Oscar von Sydow
1921–3 Hjalmar Branting
1923–4 Ernst Trygger
1924–5 Hjalmar Branting
1925–6 Rickard Sandler
1926–8 Carl Gustaf Ekman
1928–30 Arvid Lindman
1930–2 Carl Gustaf Ekman
1932 Felix Hamrin
1932–6 Per Albin Hansson
1936 Axel Pehrsson-Branstorp
1936–46 Per Albin Hansson
1946–69 Tage Erlander
1969–76 Olof Palme
1976–8 Thorbjörn Fälldin
1978–9 Ola Ullsten
1979–82 Thorbjörn Fälldin

| | |
|---|---|
| 1982–6 | Olof Palme |
| 1986–91 | Ingvar Carlsson |
| 1991–4 | Carl Bildt |
| 1994–6 | Ingvar Carlsson |
| 1996– | Göran Persson |

## Switzerland

*President*

| | |
|---|---|
| 1900 | Walter Hauser |
| 1901 | Ernst Brenner |
| 1902 | Joseph Zemp |
| 1903 | Adolf Deucher |
| 1904 | Robert Comtesse |
| 1905 | Marc-Emile Ruchet |
| 1906 | Ludwig Forrer |
| 1907 | Eduard Müller |
| 1908 | Ernst Brenner |
| 1909 | Adolf Deucher |
| 1910 | Robert Comtesse |
| 1911 | Marc-Emile Ruchet |
| 1912 | Ludwig Forrer |
| 1913 | Eduard Müller |
| 1914 | Arthur Hoffmann |
| 1915 | Giuseppe Motta |
| 1916 | Camille Decoppet |
| 1917 | Edmund Schulthess |
| 1918 | Felix Calonder |
| 1919 | Gustave Ador |
| 1920 | Giuseppe Motta |
| 1921 | Edmund Schulthess |
| 1922 | Robert Haab |
| 1923 | Karl Scheurer |
| 1924 | Ernest Chuard |
| 1925 | Jean-Marie Musy |
| 1926 | Heinrich Häberlin |
| 1927 | Giuseppe Motta |
| 1928 | Edmund Schulthess |
| 1929 | Robert Haab |
| 1930 | Jean-Marie Musy |
| 1931 | Heinrich Häberlin |
| 1932 | Giuseppe Motta |
| 1933 | Edmund Schulthess |
| 1934 | Marcel Pilet-Golaz |
| 1935 | Rudolf Minger |
| 1936 | Albert Meyer |
| 1937 | Giuseppe Motta |
| 1938 | Johannes Baumann |
| 1939 | Philipp Etter |
| 1940 | Marcel Pilet-Golaz |
| 1941 | Ernst Wetter |
| 1942 | Philipp Etter |
| 1943 | Enrico Celio |
| 1944 | Walter Stampfli |
| 1945 | Eduard von Steiger |
| 1946 | Karl Kobelt |
| 1947 | Philipp Etter |
| 1948 | Enrico Celio |
| 1949 | Ernst Nobs |
| 1950 | Max Petitpierre |
| 1951 | Eduard von Steiger |
| 1952 | Karl Kobelt |
| 1953 | Philipp Etter |
| 1954 | Rodolphe Rubattel |
| 1955 | Max Petitpierre |
| 1956 | Markus Feldmann |
| 1957 | Hans Streuli |
| 1958 | Thomas Holenstein |
| 1959 | Paul Chaudet |
| 1960 | Max Petitpierre |
| 1961 | Friedrich Wahlen |
| 1962 | Paul Chaudet |
| 1963 | Willy Spühler |
| 1964 | Ludwig von Moos |
| 1965 | Hans Peter Tschudi |
| 1966 | Hans Schaffner |
| 1967 | Roger Bonvin |
| 1968 | Willy Spühler |
| 1969 | Ludwig von Moos |
| 1970 | Hans Peter Tschudi |
| 1971 | Rudolf Gnägi |
| 1972 | Nello Celio |
| 1973 | Roger Bonvin |
| 1974 | Ernst Brugger |
| 1975 | Pierre Graber |
| 1976 | Rudolf Gnägi |
| 1977 | Kurt Furgler |
| 1978 | Willi Ritschard |
| 1979 | Hans Hürlimann |
| 1980 | Georges-André Chevallaz |
| 1981 | Kurt Furgler |
| 1982 | Fritz Honegger |
| 1983 | Pierre Aubert |
| 1984 | Leon Schlumpf |
| 1985 | Kurt Furgler |
| 1986 | Alphons Egli |
| 1987 | Pierre Aubert |
| 1988 | Otto Stich |
| 1989 | Jean-Pascal Delamuraz |
| 1990 | Arnold Koller |
| 1991 | Flavio Cotti |
| 1992 | René Felber |
| 1993 | Adolf Ogi |
| 1994 | Otto Stich |
| 1995 | Kaspar Villiger |
| 1996 | Jean-Pascal Delamuraz |
| 1997 | Arnold Koller |
| 1998 | Flavio Cotti |
| 1999 | Ruth Dreifuss |
| 2000 | Adolf Ogi |
| 2001 | Moritz Leuenberger |

## Syria

*President*

| | |
|---|---|
| 1943–9 | Shukri Al-Quwwatli |
| 1949 | Husni Az-Zaim |
| 1949–51 | Hashim Al-Atassi |
| 1951–4 | Adib Shishaqli |
| 1954–5 | Hashim Al-Atassi |
| 1955–8 | Shukri Al-Quwwatli |
| 1958–61 | *Part of United Arab Republic* |
| 1961–3 | Nazim Al-Qudsi |
| 1963 | Luai Al-Atassi |

1963–6 Amin Al-Hafiz
1966–70 Nureddin Al-Atassi
1970–1 Ahmad Al-Khatib
1971–2000 Hafez Al-Assad
2000– Bashar Al-Assad

*Prime Minister*

1946–8 Jamil Mardam Bey
1948–9 Khalid Al-Azm
1949 Husni Az-Zaim
1949 Muhsi Al-Barazi
1949 Hashim Al-Atassi
1949 Nazim Al-Qudsi
1949–50 Khalid Al-Azm
1950–1 Nazim Al-Qudsi
1951 Khalid Al-Azm
1951 Hassan Al-Hakim
1951 Maruf Ad-Dawalibi
1951–3 Fauzi As-Salu
1953–4 Adib Shishaqli
1954 Shewqet Shuqair
1954 Sabri Al-Asali
1954 Said Al-Ghazzi
1954–5 Faris Al-Khuri
1955 Sabri Al-Asali
1955–6 Said Al-Ghazzi
1956–8 Sabri Al-Asali
1958–61 *Part of United Arab Republic*
1961 Abd Al-Hamid As-Sarraj
1961 Mamun Kuzbari
1961 Izzat An-Nuss
1961–2 Maruf Ad-Dawalibi
1962 Bashir Azmah
1962–3 Khalid Al-Azm
1963 Salah Ad-Din Al-Bitaar
1963 Sami Al-Jundi
1963 Salah Ad-Din Al-Bitaar
1963–4 Amin Al-Hafez
1964 Salah Ad-Din Al-Bitaar
1964–5 Amin Al-Hafez
1965 Yousif Zeayen
1966 Salah Ad-Din Al-Bitaar
1966–8 Yousif Zeayen
1968–70 Nureddin Al-Atassi *Acting Prime Minister*
1970–1 Hafez Al-Assad
1971–2 Abdel Rahman Khleifawi
1972–6 Mahmoud Bin Saleh Al-Ayoubi
1976–8 Abdul Rahman Khleifawi
1978–80 Mohammed Ali Al-Halabi
1980–7 Abdel Rauof Al-Kasm
1987–2000 Mahmoud Al-Zubi
2000– Mustafa Mero

## Taiwan (Republic of China)

*President*

1950–75 Chiang Kai-shek
1975–8 Yen Chia-kan
1978–87 Chiang Ching-kuo
1987–2000 Lee Teng-hui
2000– Chen Shui-bian

*President of Executive Council*

1950–4 Ch'eng Ch'eng
1954–8 O K Yui
1958–63 Ch'eng Ch'eng
1963–72 Yen Chia-ken
1972–8 Chiang Ching-kuo
1978–84 Sun Yun-suan
1984–9 Yu Kuo-hwa
1989–90 Lee Huan
1990–3 Hau Pei-tsun
1993–6 Lien Chan

*Prime Minister*

1996–7 Lien Chan
1997–2000 Vincent Siew
2000– Chang Chun-hsiung

## Tajikistan (Tadzhikistan)

*President*

1991–2 Rakhman Nabiev
1992 Akbarsho Iskandrov *Acting*
1992– Imamoli Rakhmanov

## Tanzania

*President*

1964–85 Julius Kambarage Nyerere
1985–95 Ali Hassan Mwinyi
1995– Benjamin William Mkapa

*Prime Minister*

1964–72 Rashid M Kawawa *Vice President*
1972–7 Rashid M Kawawa
1977–80 Edward M Sokoine
1980–3 Cleopa D Msuya
1983–4 Edward M Sokoine
1984–5 Salim A Salim
1985–90 Joseph S Warioba
1990–4 John Malecela
1994–5 Cleopa Msuya
1995– Frederick Tulway Sumaye

## Thailand

*Monarch*

1868–1910 Chulalongkorn, Rama V
1910–25 Rama VI
1925–35 Rama VII
1935–9 Rama VIII (Ananda Mahidol)
1939–46 Nai Pridi Phanomyong *Regent*
1946 Rama IX
1946–50 Rangsit of Chainat *Regent*
1950– Bhumibol Adulyadej

*Prime Minister*

1932–3 Phraya Manopakom
1933–8 Phraya Phahon Phonphahuyasena
1938–44 Luang Phibun Songgram
1945 Thawi Bunyaket
1945–6 Mom Rachawongse Seni Pramoj
1946 Nai Khuang Aphaiwong

| | |
|---|---|
| 1946 | Nai Pridi Phanomyong |
| 1946–7 | Luang Thamrong Nawasawat |
| 1947–8 | Nai Khuang Aphaiwong |
| 1948–57 | Luang Phibun Songgram |
| 1957 | Sarit Thanarat |
| 1957 | Nai Pote Sarasin |
| 1957–8 | Thanom Kittikatchom |
| 1958–63 | Sarit Thanarat |
| 1963–73 | Thanom Kittikatchom |
| 1973–5 | Sanya Dharmasaki |
| 1975–6 | Mom Rachawongse Kukrit Pramoj |
| 1976 | Seni Pramoj |
| 1976–7 | Thanin Kraivichien |
| 1977–80 | Kriangsak Chammanard |
| 1980–7 | Prem Tinsulanonda |
| 1987–91 | Chatichai Choonhaven |
| 1991–2 | Anand Panyarachun |
| 1992 | Suchinda Kraprayoon |
| 1992 | Anand Panyarachun |
| 1992–5 | Chuan Leekpai |
| 1995–6 | Banharn Silpa-Archa |
| 1996–7 | Chavalit Yongchaiyudh |
| 1997–2001 | Chuan Leekpai |
| 2001– | Thaksin Shinawatra |

## Togo

*President*

| | |
|---|---|
| 1960–3 | Sylvanus Olympio |
| 1963–7 | Nicolas Grunitzky |
| 1967– | Gnassingbé Eyadéma |

## Tonga

*Monarch*

| | |
|---|---|
| 1893–1918 | George Tupou II |
| 1918–65 | Salote Tupou III |
| 1965– | Taufa'ahau Tupou IV |

*Prime Minister*

| | |
|---|---|
| 1970–91 | Fatafehi Tu'ipelehake |
| 1991–2000 | Baron Vaea |
| 2000– | Prince 'Ulukalala Lavaka Ata |

## Trinidad and Tobago

*President*

| | |
|---|---|
| 1976–87 | Ellis Emmanuel Clarke |
| 1987–97 | Noor Mohammed Hassanali |
| 1997– | Raymond Robinson |

*Premier*

| | |
|---|---|
| 1956–62 | Eric Williams |

*Prime Minister*

| | |
|---|---|
| 1962–81 | Eric Williams |
| 1981–6 | George Chambers |
| 1986–91 | Raymond Robinson |
| 1991–5 | Patrick Manning |
| 1995– | Basdeo Panday |

## Tunisia

*Bey*

| | |
|---|---|
| 1943–57 | Muhammad VIII |

*President*

| | |
|---|---|
| 1957–87 | Habib Bourguiba |
| 1987– | Zine Al-Abidine Bin Ali |

*Prime Minister*

| | |
|---|---|
| 1956–7 | Habib Bourguiba |
| 1957–69 | *No Prime Minister* |
| 1969–70 | Bahi Ladgham |
| 1970–80 | Hadi Nouira |
| 1980–6 | Mohammed Mezali |
| 1986–7 | Rashid Sfar |
| 1987 | Zine Al-Abidine Bin Ali |
| 1987–9 | Hadi Baccouche |
| 1989–99 | Hamed Karoui |
| 1999– | Mohammed Ghannouchi |

## Turkey

*Sultan of the Ottoman Empire*

| | |
|---|---|
| 1876–1909 | Abdülhamit |
| 1909–18 | Mehmet Reşat |
| 1918–22 | Mehmet Vahideddin |

### ❑ Turkish Republic

*President*

| | |
|---|---|
| 1923–38 | Mustafa Kemal Atatürk |
| 1938–50 | İsmet İnönü |
| 1950–60 | Celal Bayar |
| 1961–6 | Cemal Gürsel |
| 1966–73 | Cevdet Sunay |
| 1973–80 | Fahri S Korutürk |
| 1980 | Ihsan Çaglayangil *Acting President* |
| 1982–9 | Kenan Evren |
| 1989–93 | Turgut Özal |
| 1993–2000 | Süleyman Demirel |
| 2000– | Ahmet Necdet Sezer |

*Prime Minister*

| | |
|---|---|
| 1923–4 | İsmet İnönü |
| 1924–5 | Ali Fethi Okyar |
| 1925–37 | İsmet İnönü |
| 1937–9 | Celal Bayar |
| 1939–42 | Dr Refik Saydam |
| 1942–6 | Şükrü Saracoğlu |
| 1946–7 | Recep Peker |
| 1947–9 | Hasan Saka |
| 1949–50 | Şemşettin Günaltay |
| 1950–60 | Adnan Menderes |
| 1960–1 | Cemal Gürsel |
| 1961–5 | İsmet İnönü |
| 1965 | S Hayri Ürgüplü |
| 1965–71 | Süleyman Demirel |
| 1971–2 | Nihat Erim |
| 1972–3 | Ferit Melen |
| 1973–4 | Naim Talu |
| 1974 | Bülent Ecevit |
| 1974–5 | Sadi Irmak |

1975–7 Süleyman Demirel
1977 Bülent Ecevit
1977–8 Süleyman Demirel
1978–9 Bülent Ecevit
1979–80 Süleyman Demirel
1980–3 Bülent Ülüsü
1983–9 Turgut Özal
1989–91 Yildrim Akbulut
1991 Mesut Yilmaz
1991–3 Süleyman Demirel
1993–6 Tansu Çiller
1996 Mesut Yilmaz
1996–7 Necmettin Erbakan
1997–8 Mesut Yilmaz
1999– Bülent Ecevit

## Turkmenistan

*President*

1991– Saparmurad Niyazov

## Tuvalu

Chief of State: British monarch, represented by Governor General

*Prime Minister*

1978–81 Toalipi Lauti
1981–9 Tomasi Puapua
1989–93 Bikenibeu Paeniu
1993–6 Kamuta Lataasi
1996–9 Bikenibeu Paeniu
1999–2000 Ionatana Ionatana
2000–1 Lagitupu Tuilimu *Acting Prime Minister*
2001 Faimalaga Luka
2001– Koloa Talake

## Uganda

*President*

1962–6 Edward Muteesa II
1967–71 Apollo Milton Obote
1971–9 Idi Amin
1979 Yusuf Kironde Lule
1979–80 Godfrey Lukongwa Binaisa
1981–5 Apollo Milton Obote
1985–6 *Military Council (Tito Okello Lutwa)*
1986– Yoweri Kaguta Museveni

*Prime Minister*

1962–71 Apollo Milton Obote
1971–81 *No Prime Minister*
1981–5 Eric Otema Alimadi
1985 Paulo Muwanga
1985–6 Abraham N Waliggo
1986–91 Samson B Kisekka
1991–4 George Cosmas Adyebo
1994–9 Kintu Musoke
1999– Apollo Nsimbabi

## Ukraine

*President*

1991–4 Leonid Kravchuk
1994– Leonid Kuchma

## United Arab Emirates

*President*

1971– Zayed Bin Sultan al-Nahayan

*Prime Minister*

1971–9 Maktoum Bin Rashid al-Maktoum
1979–91 Rashid Bin Said al-Maktoum
1991– Maktoum Bin Rashid al-Maktoum

### ❑ Abu Dhabi

*Tribe*: al Bu Falah *or* al Nahyan (Bani Yas)

*Family name*: al-Nahyan

*Shaikh*

1855–1909 Zayed
1909–12 Tahnoun
1912–22 Hamdan
1922–6 Sultan
1926–8 Saqr
1928–66 Shakhbout
1966– Zayed

### ❑ Ajman

*Tribe*: al Bu Kharayban (Naim)

*Family name*: al-Nuaimi

*Shaikh*

1900–10 Abdel-Aziz
1910–28 Humaid
1928–81 Rashid
1981– Humaid

### ❑ Dubai

*Tribe*: al Bu Flasah (Bani Yas)

*Family name*: al-Maktoum

*Shaikh*

1894–1906 Maktoum
1906–12 Butti
1912–58 Said
1958–90 Rashid
1990– Maktoum

### ❑ Fujairah

*Tribe*: Sharqiyyin

*Family name*: al-Sharqi

*Shaikh*

1952–75 Mohammed
1975– Hamad

### ❑ Ras al-Khaimah

*Tribe*: Huwalah

*Family name*: al-Qasimi

*Shaikh*

1921–48 Sultan
1948– Saqr

### ❑ Sharjah

*Tribe*: Huwalah

*Family name*: al-Qasimi

*Shaikh*

| | |
|---|---|
| 1883–1914 | Saqr |
| 1914–24 | Khaled |
| 1924–51 | Sultan |
| 1951–65 | Saqr |
| 1965–72 | Khaled |
| 1972–87 | Sultan |
| 1987 | Abdel-Aziz |
| 1987– | Sultan |

### ❑ Umm al-Qaiwain

*Tribe*: al-Ali

*Family name*: al-Mualla

*Shaikh*

| | |
|---|---|
| 1873–1904 | Ahmad |
| 1904–22 | Rashid |
| 1922–3 | Abdullah |
| 1923–9 | Hamad |
| 1929–81 | Ahmad |
| 1981– | Rashid |

## United Kingdom

For list of previous monarchs see p195

*Monarch*

*House of Hanover*

| | |
|---|---|
| 1714–27 | George I |
| 1727–60 | George II |
| 1760–1820 | George III |
| 1820–30 | George IV |
| 1830–7 | William IV |
| 1837–1901 | Victoria |

*House of Saxe-Coburg*

| | |
|---|---|
| 1901–10 | Edward VII |

*House of Windsor*

| | |
|---|---|
| 1910–36 | George V |
| 1936 | Edward VIII |
| 1936–52 | George VI |
| 1952– | Elizabeth II |

*Prime Minister*

| | |
|---|---|
| 1721–42 | Robert Walpole *Whig* |
| 1742–3 | Earl of Wilmington (Spencer Compton) *Whig* |
| 1743–54 | Henry Pelham *Whig* |
| 1754–6 | Duke of Newcastle (Thomas Pelham-Holles) *Whig* |
| 1756–7 | Duke of Devonshire (William Cavendish) *Whig* |
| 1757–62 | Duke of Newcastle *Whig* |
| 1762–3 | Earl of Bute (John Stuart) *Tory* |
| 1763–5 | George Grenville *Whig* |
| 1765–6 | Marquess of Rockingham (Charles Watson Wentworth) *Whig* |
| 1766–70 | Duke of Grafton (Augustus Henry Fitzroy) *Whig* |
| 1770–82 | Lord North (Frederick North) *Tory* |
| 1782 | Marquess of Rockingham *Whig* |
| 1782–3 | Earl of Shelburne (William Petty-Fitzmaurice) *Whig* |
| 1783 | Duke of Portland (William Henry Cavendish) *Coal* |
| 1783–1801 | William Pitt *Tory* |
| 1801–4 | Henry Addington *Tory* |
| 1804–6 | William Pitt *Tory* |
| 1806–7 | Lord Grenville (William Wyndham) *Whig* |
| 1807–9 | Duke of Portland *Tory* |
| 1809–12 | Spencer Perceval *Tory* |
| 1812–27 | Earl of Liverpool (Robert Banks Jenkinson) *Tory* |
| 1827 | George Canning *Tory* |
| 1827–8 | Viscount Goderich (Frederick John Robinson) *Tory* |
| 1828–30 | Duke of Wellington (Arthur Wellesley) *Tory* |
| 1830–4 | Earl Grey (Charles Grey) *Whig* |
| 1834 | Viscount Melbourne (William Lamb) *Whig* |
| 1834–5 | Robert Peel *Con* |
| 1835–41 | Viscount Melbourne *Whig* |
| 1841–6 | Robert Peel *Con* |
| 1846–52 | Lord John Russell *Lib* |
| 1852 | Earl of Derby (Edward George Smith Stanley) *Con* |
| 1852–5 | Lord Aberdeen (George Hamilton-Gordon) *Peelite* |
| 1855–8 | Viscount Palmerston (Henry John Temple) *Lib* |
| 1858–9 | Earl of Derby *Con* |
| 1859–65 | Viscount Palmerston *Lib* |
| 1865–6 | Lord John Russell *Lib* |
| 1866–8 | Earl of Derby *Con* |
| 1868 | Benjamin Disraeli *Con* |
| 1868–74 | William Ewart Gladstone *Lib* |
| 1874–80 | Benjamin Disraeli *Con* |
| 1880–5 | William Ewart Gladstone *Lib* |
| 1885–6 | Marquess of Salisbury (Robert Gascoyne-Cecil) *Con* |
| 1886 | William Ewart Gladstone *Lib* |
| 1886–92 | Marquess of Salisbury *Con* |
| 1892–4 | William Ewart Gladstone *Lib* |
| 1894–5 | Earl of Rosebery (Archibald Philip Primrose) *Lib* |
| 1895–1902 | Marquess of Salisbury *Con* |
| 1902–5 | Arthur James Balfour *Con* |
| 1905–8 | Henry Campbell-Bannerman *Lib* |
| 1908–15 | Herbert Henry Asquith *Lib* |
| 1915–16 | Herbert Henry Asquith *Coal* |
| 1916–22 | David Lloyd George *Coal* |
| 1922–3 | Andrew Bonar Law *Con* |
| 1923–4 | Stanley Baldwin *Con* |
| 1924 | James Ramsay MacDonald *Lab* |
| 1924–9 | Stanley Baldwin *Con* |
| 1929–31 | James Ramsay MacDonald *Lab* |
| 1931–5 | James Ramsay MacDonald *Nat* |

| | |
|---|---|
| 1935–7 | Stanley Baldwin *Nat* |
| 1937–40 | Arthur Neville Chamberlain *Nat* |
| 1940–5 | Winston Churchill *Coal* |
| 1945–51 | Clement Attlee *Lab* |
| 1951–5 | Winston Churchill *Con* |
| 1955–7 | Anthony Eden *Con* |
| 1957–63 | Harold Macmillan *Con* |
| 1963–4 | Alec Douglas-Home *Con* |
| 1964–70 | Harold Wilson *Lab* |
| 1970–4 | Edward Heath *Con* |
| 1974–6 | Harold Wilson *Lab* |
| 1976–9 | James Callaghan *Lab* |
| 1979–90 | Margaret Thatcher *Con* |
| 1990–7 | John Major *Con* |
| 1997– | Tony Blair *Lab* |

*Coal* = Coalition *Lab* = Labour *Nat* = Nationalist
*Con* = Conservative *Lib* = Liberal

## United Nations

*Secretary-General*

| | |
|---|---|
| 1946–53 | Trygve Lie *Norway* |
| 1953–61 | Dag Hammarskjöld *Sweden* |
| 1962–71 | U Thant *Burma* |
| 1972–81 | Kurt Waldheim *Austria* |
| 1982–91 | Javier Pérez de Cuéllar *Peru* |
| 1992–6 | Boutros Boutros-Ghali *Egypt* |
| 1997– | Kofi Annan *Ghana* |

## United States of America

*President*

*Vice President in parentheses*

| | |
|---|---|
| 1789–97 | George Washington (1st)<br>(John Adams) |
| 1797–1801 | John Adams (2nd) *Fed*<br>(Thomas Jefferson) |
| 1801–9 | Thomas Jefferson (3rd) *Dem-Rep*<br>(Aaron Burr, 1801–5)<br>(George Clinton, 1805–9) |
| 1809–17 | James Madison (4th) *Dem-Rep*<br>(George Clinton, 1809–12)<br>*no Vice President 1812–13*<br>(Elbridge Gerry, 1813–14)<br>*no Vice President 1814–17* |
| 1817–25 | James Monroe (5th) *Dem-Rep*<br>(Daniel D Tompkins) |
| 1825–9 | John Quincy Adams (6th) *Dem-Rep*<br>(John C Calhoun) |
| 1829–37 | Andrew Jackson (7th) *Dem*<br>(John C Calhoun, 1829–32)<br>*no Vice President 1832–3*<br>(Martin van Buren, 1833–7) |
| 1837–41 | Martin van Buren (8th) *Dem*<br>(Richard M Johnson) |
| 1841 | William Henry Harrison (9th) *Whig*<br>(John Tyler) |
| 1841–5 | John Tyler (10th) *Whig*<br>*no Vice President* |
| 1845–9 | James Knox Polk (11th) *Dem*<br>(George M Dallas) |
| 1849–50 | Zachary Taylor (12th) *Whig*<br>(Millard Fillmore) |
| 1850–3 | Millard Fillmore (13th) *Whig*<br>*no Vice President* |
| 1853–7 | Franklin Pierce (14th) *Dem*<br>(William R King, 1853)<br>*no Vice President 1853–7* |
| 1857–61 | James Buchanan (15th) *Dem*<br>(John C Breckinridge) |
| 1861–5 | Abraham Lincoln (16th) *Rep*<br>(Hannibal Hamlin, 1861–5)<br>(Andrew Johnson, 1865) |
| 1865–9 | Andrew Johnson (17th) *Dem-Nat*<br>*no Vice President* |
| 1869–77 | Ulysses Simpson Grant (18th) *Rep*<br>(Schuyler Colfax, 1869–73)<br>(Henry Wilson, 1873–5)<br>*no Vice President 1875–7* |
| 1877–81 | Rutherford Birchard Hayes (19th) *Rep*<br>(William A Wheeler) |
| 1881 | James Abram Garfield (20th) *Rep*<br>(Chester A Arthur) |
| 1881–5 | Chester Alan Arthur (21st) *Rep*<br>*no Vice President* |
| 1885–9 | Grover Cleveland (22nd) *Dem*<br>(Thomas A Hendricks, 1885)<br>*no Vice President 1885–9* |
| 1889–93 | Benjamin Harrison (23rd) *Rep*<br>(Levi P Morton) |
| 1893–7 | Grover Cleveland (24th) *Dem*<br>(Adlai E Stevenson) |
| 1897–1901 | William McKinley (25th) *Rep*<br>(Garrat A Hobart, 1897–9)<br>*no Vice President 1899–1901*<br>(Theodore Roosevelt, 1901) |
| 1901–9 | Theodore Roosevelt (26th) *Rep*<br>*no Vice President 1901–5*<br>(Charles W Fairbanks, 1905–9) |
| 1909–13 | William Howard Taft (27th) *Rep*<br>(James S Sherman, 1909–12)<br>*no Vice President 1912–13* |
| 1913–21 | Woodrow Wilson (28th) *Dem*<br>(Thomas R Marshall) |
| 1921–3 | Warren Gamaliel Harding (29th) *Rep*<br>(Calvin Coolidge) |
| 1923–9 | Calvin Coolidge (30th) *Rep*<br>*no Vice President 1923–5*<br>(Charles G Dawes, 1925–9) |
| 1929–33 | Herbert Clark Hoover (31st) *Rep*<br>(Charles Curtis) |
| 1933–45 | Franklin Delano Roosevelt (32nd) *Dem*<br>(John N Garner, 1933–41)<br>(Henry A Wallace, 1941–5)<br>(Harry S Truman, 1945) |
| 1945–53 | Harry S Truman (33rd) *Dem*<br>*no Vice President 1945–9*<br>(Alben W Barkley, 1949–53) |
| 1953–61 | Dwight David Eisenhower (34th) *Rep*<br>(Richard M Nixon) |
| 1961–3 | John Fitzgerald Kennedy (35th) *Dem*<br>(Lyndon B Johnson) |

| | |
|---|---|
| 1963–9 | Lyndon Baines Johnson (36th) *Dem*<br>*no Vice President 1963–5*<br>(Hubert H Humphrey, 1965–9) |
| 1969–74 | Richard Milhous Nixon (37th) *Rep*<br>(Spiro T Agnew, 1969–73)<br>*no Vice President 1973, Oct–Dec*<br>(Gerald R Ford, 1973–4) |
| 1974–7 | Gerald Rudolph Ford (38th) *Rep*<br>*no Vice President 1974, Aug–Dec*<br>(Nelson A Rockefeller, 1974–7) |
| 1977–81 | Jimmy Carter (39th) *Dem*<br>(Walter F Mondale) |
| 1981–9 | Ronald Wilson Reagan (40th) *Rep*<br>(George H W Bush) |
| 1989–93 | George Herbert Walker Bush (41st) *Rep*<br>(J Danforth Quayle) |
| 1993–2001 | William Jefferson Blythe IV Clinton (42nd) *Dem*<br>(Albert Gore) |
| 2001– | George W Bush (43rd) *Rep*<br>(Dick Cheney) |

*Dem* = Democrat *Nat* = National Union
*Fed* = Federalist *Rep* = Republican

## Uruguay

*President*

| | |
|---|---|
| 1899–1903 | Juan Lindolfo Cuestas |
| 1903–7 | José Batlle y Ordóñez |
| 1907–11 | Claudio Williman |
| 1911–15 | José Batlle y Ordóñez |
| 1915–19 | Feliciano Viera |
| 1919–23 | Baltasar Brum |
| 1923–7 | José Serrato |
| 1927–31 | Juan Capisteguy |
| 1931–8 | Gabriel Terra |
| 1938–43 | Alfredo Baldomir |
| 1943–7 | Juan José de Amézaga |
| 1947 | Tomás Berreta |
| 1947–51 | Luis Batlle Berres |
| 1951–5 | Andrés Martínez Trueba |

**National Government Council (1955–67)**

| | |
|---|---|
| 1955–6 | Luis Batlle Berres |
| 1956–7 | Alberto F Zubiría |
| 1957–8 | Alberto Lezama |
| 1958–9 | Carlos L Fischer |
| 1959–60 | Martín R Etchegoyen |
| 1960–1 | Benito Nardone |
| 1961–2 | Eduardo Victor Haedo |
| 1962–3 | Faustino Harrison |
| 1963–4 | Daniel Fernández Crespo |
| 1964–5 | Luis Giannattasio |
| 1965–6 | Washington Beltrán |
| 1966–7 | Alberto Heber Usher |
| 1967 | Oscar Daniel Gestido |
| 1967–72 | Jorge Pacheco Areco |
| 1972–6 | Juan María Bordaberry Arocena |
| 1976–81 | Aparicio Méndez |
| 1981–4 | Gregorio Conrado Álvarez Armelino |
| 1984–90 | Julio María Sanguinetti Cairolo |
| 1990–4 | Luis Alberto Lacalle Herrera |
| 1994–9 | Julio María Sanguinetti |
| 1999– | Jorge Batlle Ibáñez |

## USSR (Union of Soviet Socialist Republics)

No longer in existence, but included for reference.

*President*

| | |
|---|---|
| 1917 | Leo Borisovich Kamenev |
| 1917–19 | Yakov Mikhailovich Sverlov |
| 1919–46 | Mikhail Ivanovich Kalinin |
| 1946–53 | Nikolai Shvernik |
| 1953–60 | Klimentiy Voroshilov |
| 1960–4 | Leonid Brezhnev |
| 1964–5 | Anastas Mikoyan |
| 1965–77 | Nikolai Podgorny |
| 1977–82 | Leonid Brezhnev |
| 1982–3 | Vasily Kuznetsov *Acting President* |
| 1983–4 | Yuri Andropov |
| 1984 | Vasily Kuznetsov *Acting President* |
| 1984–5 | Konstantin Chernenko |
| 1985 | Vasily Kuznetsov *Acting President* |
| 1985–8 | Andrei Gromyko |
| 1988–90 | Mikhail Gorbachev |

*Executive President*

| | |
|---|---|
| 1990–91 | Mikhail Gorbachev |
| 1991 | Gennady Yanayev *Acting President* |
| 1991 | Mikhail Gorbachev |

*Chairman (Prime Minister)*

**Council of Ministers**

| | |
|---|---|
| 1917 | Georgy Evgenyevich Lvov |
| 1917 | Aleksandr Fyodorovich Kerensky |

**Council of People's Commissars**

| | |
|---|---|
| 1917–24 | Vladimir Ilyich Lenin |
| 1924–30 | Aleksei Ivanovich Rykov |
| 1930–41 | Vyacheslav Mikhailovich Molotov |
| 1941–53 | Josef Stalin |

**Council of Ministers**

| | |
|---|---|
| 1953–5 | Georgiy Malenkov |
| 1955–8 | Nikolai Bulganin |
| 1958–64 | Nikita Khrushchev |
| 1964–80 | Alexei Kosygin |
| 1980–5 | Nikolai Tikhonov |
| 1985–90 | Nikolai Ryzhkov |
| 1990–1 | Yuri Maslyukov *Acting Chairman* |
| 1991 | Valentin Pavlov |
| 1991 | Ivan Silayev *Acting* |

*General Secretary*

| | |
|---|---|
| 1922–53 | Josef Stalin |
| 1953 | Georgiy Malenkov |
| 1953–64 | Nikita Khrushchev |
| 1964–82 | Leonid Brezhnev |
| 1982–4 | Yuri Andropov |
| 1984–5 | Konstantin Chernenko |
| 1985–91 | Mikhail Gorbachev |

See separate entries for former constituent states of USSR from 1990/91.

## Uzbekistan

*President*

1991– Islam Karimov

## Vanuatu

*President*

1980–9 George Sokomanu (*formerly* Kalkoa)
1989–94 Fred Timakata
1994–9 Jean-Marie Leye
1999– John Bani

*Prime Minister*

1980–91 Walter Lini
1991 Donald Kalpokas
1991–5 Maxime Carlot Korman
1995–6 Serge Vohor
1996 Maxime Carlot Korman
1996–8 Serge Vohor
1998–9 Donald Kalpokas
1999–2001 Barak Sope
2001– Edward Natapei

## Venezuela

*President*

1899–1908 Cipriano Castro
1908–36 Juan Vicente Gomez
1936–41 Eleazar Lopez Contreras
1941–5 Isaias Medina Angarita
1945–7 *Military Junta* (Rómulo Betancourt)
1947–8 Romulo Gallegos
1948–50 *Military Junta* (Carlos Delgado Chalbaud)
1950–9 *Military Junta* (Marcos Pérez Jiménez)
1959–64 Rómulo Betancourt
1964–9 Raul Leoni
1969–74 Rafael Caldera Rodriguez
1974–9 Carlos Andres Pérez
1979–84 Luis Herrera Campins
1984–9 Jaime Lusinchi
1989–93 Carlos Andres Pérez
1994–8 Rafael Caldera Rodríguez
1998– Hugo Chávez Frías

## Vietnam

*President*

❑ **Democratic Republic of Vietnam**

1945–69 Ho Chi Minh
1969–76 Ton Duc Thang

❑ **State of Vietnam**

1949–55 Bao Dai

❑ **Republic of Vietnam**

1955–63 Ngo Dinh Diem
1963–4 Duong Van Minh
1964 Nguyen Khanh
1964–5 Phan Khac Suu
1965–75 Nguyen Van Thieu
1975 Tran Van Huong
1975 Duong Van Minh
1975–6 *Provisional Revolutionary Government* (Huynh Tan Phat)

❑ **Socialist Republic of Vietnam**

1976–80 Ton Duc Thang
1980–1 Nguyen Hun Tho *Acting President*
1981–7 Truongh Chinh
1987–92 Vo Chi Cong
1992–7 Le Duc Anh
1997– Tran Duc Luong

*Prime Minister*

❑ **Democratic Republic of Vietnam**

1955–76 Pham Van Dong

❑ **State of Vietnam**

1949–50 Nguyen Van Xuan
1950 Nguyen Phan Long
1950–2 Tran Van Huu
1952 Tran Van Huong
1952–3 Nguyen Van Tam
1953–4 Buu Loc
1954–5 Ngo Dinh Diem

❑ **Republic of Vietnam**

1955–63 Ngo Dinh Diem
1963–4 Nguyen Ngoc Tho
1964 Nguyen Khan
1964–5 Tran Van Huong
1965 Phan Huy Quat
1965–7 Nguyen Cao Ky
1967–8 Nguyen Van Loc
1968–9 Tran Van Huong
1969–75 Tran Thien Khiem
1975 Nguyen Ba Can
1975–6 Vu Van Mau

❑ **Socialist Republic of Vietnam**

*Premier*

1976–87 Pham Van Dong
1987–8 Pham Hung
1988 Vo Van Kiet *Acting Premier*
1988–91 Do Muoi
1991–7 Vo Van Kiet
1997– Phan Van Khai

*General Secretary*

1960–80 Le Duan
1986 Truong Chinh
1986–92 Nguyen Van Linh

## Western Samoa ► Samoa

## Yemen

### ❑ Yemen Arab Republic (North Yemen)

*Monarch (Imam)*

| | |
|---|---|
| 1918–48 | Yahya Mohammed Bin Mohammed |
| 1948–62 | Ahmed Bin Yahya |
| 1962–70 | Mohammed Bin Ahmed |
| 1962 | *Civil War* |

*President*

| | |
|---|---|
| 1962–7 | Abdullah Al-Sallal |
| 1967–74 | Abdur Rahman Al-Iriani |
| 1974–7 | *Military Command Council* (Ibrahim Al-Hamadi) |
| 1977–8 | Ahmed Bin Hussein Al-Ghashmi |
| 1978–90 | Ali Abdullah Saleh |

*Prime Minister*

| | |
|---|---|
| 1964 | Hamud Al-Jaifi |
| 1965 | Hassan Al-Amri |
| 1965 | Ahmed Mohammed Numan |
| 1965 | *As President* |
| 1965–6 | Hassan Al-Amri |
| 1966–7 | *As President* |
| 1967 | Muhsin Al-Aini |
| 1967–9 | Hassan Al-Amri |
| 1969–70 | Abd Allah Kurshumi |
| 1970–1 | Muhsin Al-Aini |
| 1971 | Abdel Salam Sabra *Acting Prime Minister* |
| 1971 | Ahmed Mohammed Numan |
| 1971 | Hassan Al-Amri |
| 1971–2 | Muhsin Al-Aini |
| 1972–4 | Qadi Abdullah Al-Hijri |
| 1974 | Hassan Makki |
| 1974–5 | Muhsin Al-Aini |
| 1975 | Abdel Latif Deifallah *Acting Prime Minister* |
| 1975–90 | Abdel-Aziz Abdel-Ghani |

### ❑ People's Democratic Republic of Yemen (South Yemen)

*President*

| | |
|---|---|
| 1967–9 | Qahtan Mohammed Al-Shaabi |
| 1969–78 | Salim Ali Rubai |
| 1978 | Ali Nasir Mohammed Husani |
| 1978–80 | Abdel Fattah Ismail |
| 1980–6 | Ali Nasir Mohammed Husani |
| 1986–90 | Haidar Abu Bakr Al-Attas |

*Prime Minister*

| | |
|---|---|
| 1969 | Faisal Abd Al-Latif Al-Shaabi |
| 1969–71 | Mohammed Ali Haithem |
| 1971–85 | Ali Nasir Mohammed Husani |
| 1985–6 | Haidar Abu Bakr Al-Attas |
| 1986–90 | Yasin Said Numan |

### ❑ Republic of Yemen

*President*

| | |
|---|---|
| 1990– | Ali Abdullah Saleh |

*Prime Minister*

| | |
|---|---|
| 1990–3 | Haidar Abu Bakr Al-Attas |
| 1993–7 | Abdel Aziz Abdel-Ghani |
| 1997 | Farag Said Ben Ghanem |
| 1998–2001 | Abdul Ali Al-Karim Al-Iryani |
| 2001– | Abd al-Qadir Abd al-Rahman Bajammal |

## Yugoslavia

*Monarch*

| | |
|---|---|
| 1921–34 | Aleksandar II |
| 1934–45 | Petar II (*in exile from 1941*) |

### ❑ Republic

**National Assembly**

*Chairman*

| | |
|---|---|
| 1945–53 | Ivan Ribar |

*President*

| | |
|---|---|
| 1953–80 | Josip Broz Tito |

**Collective Presidency**

| | |
|---|---|
| 1980 | Lazar Koliševski |
| 1980–1 | Cvijetin Mijatović |
| 1981–2 | Serghei Kraigher |
| 1982–3 | Petar Stambolić |
| 1983–4 | Mika Spiljak |
| 1984–5 | Veselin Đuranović |
| 1985–6 | Radovan Vlajković |
| 1986–7 | Sinan Hasani |
| 1987–8 | Lazar Mojsov |
| 1988–9 | Raif Dizdarević |
| 1989–90 | Janez Drnovsek |
| 1990–1 | Borisav Jovic |
| 1991 | Stipe Mesic |

*Prime Minister*

| | |
|---|---|
| 1929–32 | Pear Živkovic |
| 1932 | Vojislav Marinković |
| 1932–4 | Milan Srškić |
| 1934 | Nikola Uzunović |
| 1934–5 | Bogoljub Jevtić |
| 1935–9 | Milan Stojadinović |
| 1939–41 | Dragiša Cvetković |
| 1941 | Dušan Simović |

**Government in exile**

| | |
|---|---|
| 1942 | Slobodan Jovanović |
| 1943 | Miloš Trifunović |
| 1943–4 | Božidar Purić |
| 1944–5 | Ivan Šubašić |
| 1945 | Drago Marušić |

**Home government**

1941–4 Milan Nedić
1943–63 Josip Broz Tito
1963–7 Petar Stambolić
1967–9 Mika Špiljak
1969–71 Mitja Ribičič
1971–7 Džemal Bijedić
1977–82 Veselin Đuranović
1982–6 Milka Planinc
1986–9 Branko Mikulić
1989–91 Ante Marković

**Communist Party**

*First Secretary*

1937–52 Josip Broz Tito

**League of Communists**

1952–80 Josip Broz Tito

**League of Communists Central Committee**

*President*

1979–80 Stevan Doronjski *Acting President*
1980–1 Lazar Mojsov
1981–2 Dušan Dragosavac
1982–3 Mitja Ribičič
1983–4 Dragoslav Marković
1984–5 Ali Sukrija
1985–6 Vidoje Žarkovic
1986–7 Milanko Renovica
1987–8 Boško Krunić
1988–9 Stipe Suvar
1989–90 Milan Pancevski
1990 Miomir Grbovic

❑ **Federal Republic of Yugoslavia**

*President*

1992–3 Dobrica Cosic
1993–7 Zoran Lilic
1997–2000 Slobodan Milosevic
2000– Vojislav Kostunica

*Prime Minister*

1992–3 Milan Panic
1993–8 Radoje Kontic
1998–2000 Momir Bulatovic
2000–1 Zoran Zizic
2001– Dragisa Pesic

❑ **Serbia**

*President*

1992–7 Slobodan Milosevic
1997 Vojislav Šešelj
1997– Milan Milutinovic

❑ **Montenegro**

*President*

1993–7 Momir Bulatovic
1997– Milo Djukanović

Civil War broke out in 1991. Four of Yugoslavia's six republics declared their independence. Serbia and Montenegro remain part of the Federal Republic of Yugoslavia (declared 1992).

► **Bosnia-Herzegovina, Croatia, Macedonia, Slovenia**.

## Zaïre ► Congo, Democratic Republic of

## Zambia

*President*

1964–91 Kenneth Kaunda
1991– Frederick Chiluba

*Prime Minister*

1964–73 Kenneth Kaunda
1973–5 Mainza Chona
1975–7 Elijah Mudenda
1977–8 Mainza Chona
1978–81 Daniel Lisulu
1981–5 Nalumino Mundia
1985–9 Kebby Musokotwane
1989–91 Malimba Masheke
1991– *No Prime Minister*

## Zimbabwe

*President*

1980–7 Canaan Sodindo Banana
1987– Robert Gabriel Mugabe

*Prime Minister*

1980–7 Robert Gabriel Mugabe

# SOCIAL STRUCTURE

## Major cities of the world

Cities are listed alphabetically followed by population figures, with year of estimate in brackets; those without 'e' indicate the year of census.

|  |  |  |
|---|---|---|
| **Abidjan** | Côte d'Ivoire | 2 797 000 (1995e) |
| **Abu Dhabi** | United Arab Emirates | 928 360 (1995) |
| **Acapulco** | Mexico | 597 000 (1996e) |
| **Accra** | Ghana | 1 781 100 (1995e) |
| **Adana** | Turkey | 1 047 300 (1994e) |
| **Addis Ababa** | Ethiopia | 2 316 400 (1994e) |
| **Adelaide** | Australia | 1 081 000 (1995e) |
| **Aden** | Yemen | 303 000 (1996e) |
| **Agadir** | Morocco | 1 370 000 (1994e) |
| **Agra** | India | 1 025 000 (1996e) |
| **Ahmadabad** | India | 3 372 000 (1996e) |
| **Ahvaz** | Iran | 731 500 (1996e) |
| **Ajme** | India | 497 000 (1996e) |
| **Albuquerque** | USA | 411 994 (1994e) |
| **Algiers** | Algeria | 3 208 000 (1995e) |
| **Aligarh** | India | 595 000 (1996e) |
| **Aleppo** | Syria | 1 591 400 (1994e) |
| **Alexandria** | Egypt | 3 382 000 (1994e) |
| **Allahabad** | India | 993 000 (1996e) |
| **Alma-Ata** | Kazakhstan | 1 150 500 (1995e) |
| **Amagasaki** | Japan | 488 574 (1995) |
| **Amman** | Jordan | 963 440 (1994) |
| **Amritsar** | India | 885 000 (1996e) |
| **Amsterdam** | Netherlands | 722 245 (1995e) |
| **Ankara** | Turkey | 2 782 000 (1994e) |
| **Anshan** | China | 1 546 000 (1996e) |
| **Antananarivo** | Madagascar | 1 052 835 (1994) |
| **Antwerp** | Belgium | 459 072 (1995e) |
| **Anyang** | China | 484 000 (1996e) |
| **Aracaju** | Brazil | 451 000 (1996e) |
| **Archangel** | Russia | 374 000 (1995e) |
| **Arequipa** | Peru | 619 156 (1994e) |
| **Asahikawa** | Japan | 360 569 (1995) |
| **Ashkhabad** | Turkmenistan | 518 000 (1994e) |
| **Astrakhan** | Russia | 486 000 (1995e) |
| **Asunción** | Paraguay | 502 426 (1993) |
| **Athens** | Greece | 824 000 (1996e) |
| **Atlanta** | USA | 396 052 (1994e) |
| **Auckland** | New Zealand | 353 670 (1996) |
| **Austin** | USA | 514 013 (1994e) |
| **Baghdad** | Iraq | 4 478 000 (1995e) |
| **Bakhtaran** | Iran | 698 000 (1996e) |
| **Baku** | Azerbaijan | 1 087 000 (1994e) |
| **Baltimore** | USA | 702 979 (1994e) |
| **Bamako** | Mali | 800 000 (1995e) |
| **Bandung** | Indonesia | 1 921 000 (1995e) |
| **Bangalore** | India | 2 869 000 (1991) |
| **Bangkok** | Thailand | 5 584 228 (1994e) |
| **Bangui** | Central African Republic | 524 000 (1994e) |
| **Banjarmasin** | Indonesia | 514 500 (1996e) |
| **Banjul** | The Gambia | 42 407 (1994) |
| **Baoding** | China | 577 800 (1996e) |
| **Baoji** | China | 378 000 (1996e) |
| **Baotou** | China | 1 110 000 (1996e) |
| **Barcelona** | Spain | 1 630 867 (1994e) |
| **Barcelona** | Venezuela | 237 000 (1996e) |
| **Bareilly** | India | 726 000 (1996e) |
| **Bari** | Italy | 338 949 (1994e) |
| **Barnaul** | Russia | 596 000 (1995e) |
| **Barquisimeto** | Venezuela | 648 000 (1996e) |
| **Barranquilla** | Colombia | 1 064 255 (1995e) |
| **Basra** | Iraq | 663 000 (1996e) |
| **Beijing (Peking)** | China | 8 200 000 (1996e) |
| **Beirut** | Lebanon | 1 564 000 (1995e) |
| **Belém** | Brazil | 1 309 000 (1995e) |
| **Belfast** | UK | 297 100 (1994e) |
| **Belgorod** | Russia | 322 000 (1995e) |
| **Belgrade** | Yugoslavia | 1 301 000 (1996e) |
| **Belo Horizonte** | Brazil | 2 628 000 (1995e) |
| **Bengpu** | China | 523 000 (1996e) |
| **Benxi** | China | 891 000 (1996e) |
| **Berlin** | Germany | 3 472 009 (1995e) |
| **Berne** | Switzerland | 128 422 (1995e) |
| **Bhavnagar** | India | 499 000 (1996e) |
| **Bhilai Nagar** | India | 485 000 (1996e) |
| **Bhopal** | India | 1 297 000 (1996e) |
| **Bilbao** | Spain | 371 787 (1994e) |
| **Birmingham** | UK | 1 008 400 (1994e) |

**Bissau** Guinea-Bissau 236 000 (1996e)
**Bochum** Germany 401 129 (1995e)
**Bogota** Colombia 5 237 635 (1995e)
**Bologna** Italy 394 969 (1994e)
**Bombay (Greater)** India 9 925 891 (1996e)
**Bonn** Germany 239 072 (1995e)
**Boston** USA 547 725 (1994e)
**Brasilia** Brazil 1 962 000 (1995e)
**Brasov** Romania 324 104 (1994e)
**Bratislava** Slovakia 450 776 (1995e)
**Brazzaville** Congo 998 000 (1996e)
**Bremen** Germany 549 182 (1995e)
**Brisbane** Australia 1 489 100 (1995e)
**Bristol** UK 399 200 (1994e)
**Brno** Czech Republic 389 576 (1995e)
**Brussels** Belgium 951 580 (1995e)
**Bryansk** Russia 462 000 (1995e)
**Bucaramanga** Colombia 351 737 (1995e)
**Bucharest** Romania 2 343 824 (1994e)
**Budapest** Hungary 1 909 000 (1996)
**Buenos Aires** Argentina 2 988 006 (1995e)
**Buffalo** USA 312 965 (1994e)
**Bulawayo** Zimbabwe 699 000 (1996e)
**Bursa** Turkey 996 600 (1994e)
**Bydgoszcz** Poland 385 700 (1995e)
**Cairo** Egypt 6 849 000 (1994e)
**Calcutta** India 5 490 000 (1996e)
**Calgary** Canada 767 059 (1996)
**Cali** Colombia 1 718 871 (1995e)
**Calicut** India 487 000 (1996e)
**Callao** Peru 615 046 (1994)
**Caloocan City** Philippines 642 670 (1994e)
**Campinas** Brazil 765 000 (1996e)
**Campo Grande** Brazil 401 000 (1996e)
**Campos** Brazil 379 900 (1996e)
**Canberra** Australia 303 700 (1995e)
**Canton (Guangzhou)** China 4 218 000 (1995e)
**Cape Town** South Africa 1 013 000 (1996e)
**Caracas** Venezuela 4 039 000 (1996e)
**Cardiff** UK 290 000 (1997e)
**Cartagena** Colombia 745 689 (1995e)
**Casablanca** Morocco 2 943 000 (1994e)
**Catania** Italy 327 163 (1994e)
**Cebu City** Philippines 688 196 (1994e)
**Chandigarh** India 663 000 (1996e)
**Changchun** China 2 021 000 (1996e)
**Changsha** China 1 477 000 (1996e)
**Changzhou** China 557 000 (1996e)
**Charlotte** USA 437 797 (1994e)
**Cheboksary** Russia 450 000 (1995e)
**Chelyabinsk** Russia 1 086 000 (1995e)
**Chemnitz** Germany 274 162 (1995e)
**Chengdu** China 2 033 000 (1966e)
**Cherepovets** Russia 320 000 (1995e)
**Chiba** Japan 856 882 (1995)
**Chicago** USA 2 731 743 (1995e)
**Chiclayo** Peru 430 000 (1996e)
**Chifeng** China 393 000 (1996e)
**Chihuahua** Mexico 411 000 (1996e)
**Chimkent** Kazakhstan 397 600 (1995e)
**Chita** Russia 322 000 (1995e)
**Chittagong** Bangladesh 1 995 000 (1996e)
**Chongjin** Korea, Democratic People's Republic of (North Korea) 601 000 (1996e)
**Chongju** Korea, Republic of (South Korea) 531 195 (1995)
**Chongqing** China 3 325 000 (1996e)
**Chonju** Korea, Republic of (South Korea) 563 406 (1995)
**Christchurch** New Zealand 313 969 (1996)
**Chungho** Taiwan 387 123 (1995e)
**Cincinnati** USA 358 170 (1994e)
**Ciudad Guayana** Venezuela 577 000 (1996e)
**Ciudad Juárez** Mexico 673 000 (1996e)
**Cleveland** USA 492 901 (1994e)
**Cluj-Napoca** Romania 321 850 (1993e)
**Cochabamba** Bolivia 448 756 (1994e)
**Cochin** India 708 000 (1996e)
**Coimbatore** India 998 000 (1996e)
**Cologne** Germany 963 817 (1995e)
**Colombo** Sri Lanka 754 000 (1996e)
**Columbus** USA 635 913 (1994e)
**Conakry** Guinea 1 508 000 (1995e)
**Constanta** Romania 348 985 (1994e)
**Constantine** Algeria 537 000 (1996e)
**Contagem** Brazil 480 000 (1996e)
**Copenhagen** Denmark 1 353 333 (1995)
**Córdoba** Argentina 1 130 000 (1996e)
**Coventry** UK 302 500 (1994e)
**Cracow** Poland 746 000 (1995e)
**Cucuta** Colombia 479 309 (1995e)
**Culiacan** Mexico 383 000 (1996e)
**Curitiba** Brazil 1 513 000 (1995e)
**Dakar** Senegal 785 071 (1994e)
**Dalian** China 2 014 000 (1996e)
**Dallas** USA 1 022 830 (1994e)
**Damascus** Syria 1 549 932 (1994e)
**Da Nang** Vietnam 415 000 (1996e)
**Dandong** China 586 000 (1996e)
**Daqing** China 726 000 (1996e)
**Dar es Salaam** Tanzania 1 630 000 (1995e)
**Datong** China 901 000 (1996e)
**Davao City** Philippines 960 910 (1994e)
**Delhi** India 8 865 000 (1996e)
**Denver** USA 493 559 (1994e)
**Detroit** USA 992 038 (1994e)

|  |  |
|---|---|
| **Dhaka** Bangladesh | 4 241 000 (1996e) |
| **Diyarbakir** Turkey | 448 300 (1994e) |
| **Dnepropetrovsk** Ukraine | 1 147 000 (1996e) |
| **Doha** Qatar | 356 000 (1996e) |
| **Donetsk** Russia | 1 088 000 (1996e) |
| **Dortmund** Germany | 600 918 (1995e) |
| **Douala** Cameroon | 1 491 000 (1996e) |
| **Dresden** Germany | 474 443 (1995e) |
| **Dubai** United Arab Emirates | 679 000 (1996e) |
| **Dublin** Ireland | 952 700 (1996) |
| **Duisburg** Germany | 536 106 (1995e) |
| **Dukou** China | 470 000 (1996e) |
| **Duque de Caxias** Brazil | 723 000 (1996e) |
| **Durban** South Africa | 833 000 (1996e) |
| **Durgapur** India | 505 000 (1996e) |
| **Dushanbe** Tajikistan | 524 000 (1994e) |
| **Düsseldorf** Germany | 572 638 (1995e) |
| **Dzhambul** Kazakhstan | 310 600 (1995e) |
| **Edinburgh** UK | 447 600 (1995e) |
| **Edmonton** Canada | 637 442 (1995) |
| **El Giza** Egypt | 2 270 000 (1996e) |
| **El Mahalla el-Koubra** Egypt | 423 000 (1996e) |
| **El Mansoura** Egypt | 398 000 (1996e) |
| **El Paso** USA | 579 307 (1994e) |
| **Eskisehir** Turkey | 451 000 (1994e) |
| **Essen** Germany | 617 955 (1995e) |
| **Faisalabad** Pakistan | 1 875 000 (1995e) |
| **Faridabad** India | 666 000 (1996e) |
| **Feira de Santana** Brazil | 403 000 (1996e) |
| **Fez** Morocco | 564 000 (1994e) |
| **Florence** Italy | 392 800 (1994e) |
| **Fortaleza** Brazil | 1 952 000 (1995) |
| **Fort Worth** USA | 451 814 (1994e) |
| **Frankfurt am Main** Germany | 652 412 (1995e) |
| **Freetown** Sierra Leone | 581 000 (1996e) |
| **Fujisawa** Japan | 368 636 (1995) |
| **Fukuoka** Japan | 1 284 741 (1995) |
| **Fukuyama** Japan | 374 510 (1995) |
| **Funabashi** Japan | 540 814 (1995) |
| **Fushun** China | 1 413 000 (1996e) |
| **Fuxin** China | 755 000 (1996e) |
| **Fuzhou** China | 1 005 000 (1996e) |
| **Ganzhou** China | 434 000 (1996e) |
| **Gaziantep** Turkey | 716 000 (1994e) |
| **Gdańsk** Poland | 463 100 (1995e) |
| **Genoa** Italy | 659 754 (1994) |
| **Georgetown** Guyana | 298 000 (1996e) |
| **Gifu** Japan | 407 145 (1995) |
| **Glasgow** UK | 674 800 (1995e) |
| **Goiania** Brazil | 993 000 (1996e) |
| **Gomel** Belarus | 512 000 (1996e) |
| **Gorakhpur** India | 607 000 (1996e) |
| **Gorky** Russia | 1 383 000 (1995e) |

|  |  |
|---|---|
| **Gorlovka** Ukraine | 322 000 (1996e) |
| **Gothenburg** Sweden | 449 189 (1996e) |
| **Grozny** Russia | 364 000 (1994e) |
| **Guadalajara** Mexico | 1 807 000 (1995e) |
| **Guarulhos** Brazil | 805 000 (1996e) |
| **Guatemala City** Guatemala | 823 301 (1994e) |
| **Guayaquil** Ecuador | 1 925 479 (1996e) |
| **Guilin** China | 427 000 (1996e) |
| **Guiyang** China | 1 116 000 (1996e) |
| **Gujranwala** Pakistan | 1 663 000 (1995e) |
| **Guntur** India | 579 000 (1996e) |
| **Gwalior** India | 853 000 (1996e) |
| **Gwangju** Korea, Republic of (South Korea) | 1 257 504 (1995) |
| **Hachioji** Japan | 503 320 (1995) |
| **The Hague** Netherlands | 442 105 (1995e) |
| **Haiphong** Vietnam | 811 000 (1996e) |
| **Hakodate** Japan | 298 868 (1995) |
| **Hamamatsu** Japan | 561 568 (1995) |
| **Hamburg** Germany | 1 705 872 (1995e) |
| **Hamhumg** Korea, Democratic People's Republic of (North Korea) | 771 000 (1996e) |
| **Hamilton** Canada | 318 947 (1994) |
| **Handan** China | 925 000 (1996e) |
| **Hangzhou** China | 1 237 000 (1996e) |
| **Hanoi** Vietnam | 2 692 000 (1996e) |
| **Hanover** Germany | 525 763 (1995e) |
| **Harare** Zimbabwe | 1 339 000 (1996e) |
| **Harbin** China | 2 917 000 (1996e) |
| **Havana** Cuba | 2 241 000 (1995e) |
| **Hefei** China | 863 000 (1996e) |
| **Hegang** China | 581 000 (1996e) |
| **Helsinki** Finland | 525 031 (1996) |
| **Hengyang** China | 550 000 (1996e) |
| **Hermosillo** Mexico | 336 000 (1996e) |
| **Higashiosaka** Japan | 517 228 (1995) |
| **Himeji** Japan | 470 986 (1995) |
| **Hirakata** Japan | 400 130 (1995) |
| **Hiroshima** Japan | 1 108 868 (1995) |
| **Ho Chi Minh City** Vietnam | 4 675 000 (1996e) |
| **Hohot** China | 739 000 (1996e) |
| **Homs** Syria | 644 204 (1994e) |
| **Hong Kong** Hong Kong | 6 218 000 (1996) |
| **Honolulu** USA | 385 881 (1994e) |
| **Houston** USA | 1 702 086 (1994e) |
| **Howrah** India | 1 075 000 (1996e) |
| **Huaibei** China | 412 000 (1996e) |
| **Huainan** China | 761 000 (1996e) |
| **Huangshi** China | 537 000 (1996e) |
| **Hubli-Dharwar** India | 803 000 (1996e) |
| **Hunjiang** China | 617 000 (1996e) |
| **Hyderabad** India | 3 253 000 (1996e) |
| **Hyderabad** Pakistan | 1 107 000 (1995e) |

|  |  |
|---|---|
| **Iasi** Romania | 337 643 (1994e) |
| **Ibadan** Nigeria | 1 365 000 (1995e) |
| **Icel** Turkey | 493 000 (1996e) |
| **Ichikawa** Japan | 440 527 (1995) |
| **Inchon** Korea, Republic of (South Korea) | 2 307 618 (1995) |
| **Indianapolis** USA | 752 279 (1994e) |
| **Indore** India | 1 307 000 (1996e) |
| **Irkutsk** Russia | 585 000 (1995e) |
| **Isfahan** Iran | 1 433 000 (1996e) |
| **Istanbul** Turkey | 7 615 500 (1994e) |
| **Ivanovo** Russia | 474 000 (1995e) |
| **Iwaki** Japan | 360 497 (1995) |
| **Izhevsk** Russia | 654 000 (1995e) |
| **Jabalpur** India | 901 000 (1996e) |
| **Jaboatoa** Brazil | 508 000 (1996e) |
| **Jacksonville** USA | 665 070 (1994e) |
| **Jaipur** India | 1 575 000 (1995e) |
| **Jakarta** Indonesia | 9 367 000 (1995e) |
| **Jalandhar** India | 644 000 (1996e) |
| **Jamshedpur** India | 571 000 (1996e) |
| **Jedda** Saudi Arabia | 1 947 000 (1995e) |
| **Jerusalem** Israel | 591 400 (1996e) |
| **Jiamusi** China | 561 000 (1996e) |
| **Jiaozuo** China | 449 000 (1996e) |
| **Jilin** China | 1 385 000 (1996e) |
| **Jinan** China | 1 494 000 (1996e) |
| **Jingdezhen** China | 390 000 (1996e) |
| **Jinzhou** China | 797 000 (1996e) |
| **Jixi** China | 801 000 (1996e) |
| **Joao Pessoa** Brazil | 433 000 (1996e) |
| **Jodhpur** India | 799 000 (1996e) |
| **Johannesburg** South Africa | 1 725 000 (1995e) |
| **Juiz de Fora** Brazil | 423 000 (1996e) |
| **Kabul** Afghanistan | 700 000 (1994e) |
| **Kaesong** Korea, Democratic People's Republic of (North Korea) | 391 000 (1996e) |
| **Kagoshima** Japan | 546 294 (1995) |
| **Kaifeng** China | 584 000 (1996e) |
| **Kalinin** Russia | 455 000 (1995e) |
| **Kaliningrad** Russia | 419 000 (1995e) |
| **Kaluga** Russia | 347 000 (1995e) |
| **Kampala** Uganda | 952 000 (1996e) |
| **Kanazawa** Japan | 453 977 (1995) |
| **Kano** Nigeria | 657 300 (1995e) |
| **Kanpur** India | 2 120 000 (1996e) |
| **Kansas City** USA | 443 878 (1994e) |
| **Kaohsiung** Taiwan | 1 426 518 (1996e) |
| **Karachi** Pakistan | 9 863 000 (1995e) |
| **Karaganda** Kazakhstan | 573 700 (1995e) |
| **Karaj** Iran | 462 000 (1996e) |
| **Kathmandu** Nepal | 535 000 (1994e) |
| **Katowice** Poland | 355 100 (1995e) |
| **Kaunas** Lithuania | 429 000 (1994e) |
| **Kawaguchi** Japan | 448 801 (1995) |
| **Kawasaki** Japan | 1 202 811 (1995) |
| **Kayseri** Turkey | 454 000 (1994e) |
| **Kazan** Russia | 1 085 000 (1995e) |
| **Keelung** Taiwan | 370 049 (1996e) |
| **Kemerovo** Russia | 503 000 (1995e) |
| **Kenitra** Morocco | 234 000 (1994e) |
| **Khabarovsk** Russia | 618 000 (1995e) |
| **Kharkov** Ukraine | 1 555 000 (1996e) |
| **Khartoum** The Sudan | 924 505 (1994) |
| **Khartoum North** The Sudan | 879 105 (1994) |
| **Kherson** Ukraine | 363 000 (1996e) |
| **Khulna** Bangladesh | 812 000 (1996e) |
| **Kiev** Ukraine | 2 630 000 (1996e) |
| **Kigali** Rwanda | 419 000 (1996e) |
| **Kingston** Jamaica | 538 100 (1995) |
| **Kingston upon Hull** UK | 269 100 (1994e) |
| **Kinshasa** Congo, Democratic Republic of | 4 655 313 (1994e) |
| **Kirkuk** Iraq | 667 000 (1996e) |
| **Kirov** Russia | 464 000 (1995e) |
| **Kishinyov** Moldova | 662 000 (1994e) |
| **Kitakyushu** Japan | 1 019 562 (1995) |
| **Kitchener** Canada | 184 600 (1996) |
| **Kitwe** Zambia | 398 000 (1996e) |
| **Kobe** Japan | 1 423 830 (1995) |
| **Kochi** Japan | 322 077 (1995) |
| **Kolhapur** India | 526 000 (1996e) |
| **Komsomolosk** Russia | 309 000 (1995e) |
| **Konya** Turkey | 576 000 (1994e) |
| **Koriyama** Japan | 326 831 (1995) |
| **Kota** India | 624 000 (1996e) |
| **Krasnodar** Russia | 646 000 (1995e) |
| **Krasnoyarsk** Russia | 869 000 (1995e) |
| **Krivoy Rog** Ukraine | 720 000 (1996e) |
| **Kuala Lumpur** Malaysia | 1 388 000 (1995e) |
| **Kumamoto** Japan | 650 322 (1995) |
| **Kumasi** Ghana | 441 000 (1996e) |
| **Kunming** China | 1 728 000 (1996e) |
| **Kurashiki** Japan | 422 824 (1995) |
| **Kurgan** Russia | 363 000 (1995e) |
| **Kursk** Russia | 442 000 (1995e) |
| **Kuwait City** Kuwait | 31 241 (1994e) |
| **Kuybyshev** Russia | 1 184 000 (1995e) |
| **Kyoto** Japan | 1 463 601 (1995) |
| **Lagos** Nigeria | 1 484 000 (1995e) |
| **Lahore** Pakistan | 5 085 000 (1995e) |
| **Lanzhou** China | 1 434 000 (1996e) |
| **La Paz** Bolivia | 829 000 (1996e) |
| **La Plata** Argentina | 688 000 (1996e) |
| **Las Palmas** Grand Canary | 371 787 (1994e) |
| **Leeds** UK | 724 400 (1994e) |

**Leicester** UK 293 400 (1994e)
**Leipzig** Germany 481 121 (1995e)
**Leon** Mexico 681 000 (1996e)
**Leshan** China 405 000 (1996e)
**Lianyungang** China 396 000 (1996e)
**Liaoyang** China 573 000 (1996e)
**Liaoyuan** China 399 000 (1996e)
**Libreville** Gabon 362 386 (1994e)
**Lima** Peru 5 706 127 (1994e)
**Lipetsk** Russia 474 000 (1995e)
**Lisbon** Portugal 913 000 (1996e)
**Liupanshui** China 399 000 (1996e)
**Liuzhou** China 691 000 (1996e)
**Liverpool** UK 474 000 (1994e)
**Ljubljana** Slovenia 276 119 (1995e)
**Lodz** Poland 828 500 (1995e)
**Lomé** Togo 431 000 (1996e)
**London** Canada 331 600 (1995)
**London** UK 6 967 500 (1994e)
**Londrina** Brazil 391 000 (1996e)
**Long Beach** USA 433 852 (1994e)
**Los Angeles** USA 3 448 613 (1994e)
**Luanda** Angola 2 001 000 (1994e)
**Lublin** Poland 352 500 (1995e)
**Lucknow** India 1 723 000 (1996e)
**Ludhiana** India 1 233 000 (1996e)
**Luoyang** China 858 000 (1996e)
**Lusaka** Zambia 971 000 (1996e)
**Luxembourg** Luxembourg 76 446 (1995e)
**Lyons** France 436 000 (1996e)
**Maceio** Brazil 558 000 (1996e)
**Machida** Japan 360 408 (1995)
**Madras** India 4601 000 (1996e)
**Madrid** Spain 3 041 101 (1994e)
**Madurai** India 1 146 000 (1996e)
**Magnitogorsk** Russia 427 000 (1995e)
**Makassar** Indonesia 929 000 (1996e)
**Makeyevka** Ukraine 409 000 (1996e)
**Makhachkala** Russia 339 000 (1995e)
**Malaga** Spain 531 443 (1994e)
**Malang** Indonesia 611 000 (1996e)
**Managua** Nicaragua 1 195 000 (1995e)
**Manaus** Brazil 933 000 (1996e)
**Manchester** UK 431 000 (1994e)
**Mandelay** Myanmar (Burma) 698 000 (1996e)
**Manila** Philippines 1 894 667 (1994e)
**Maputo** Mozambique 1 231 000 (1996e)
**Maracaibo** Venezuela 1 346 000 (1995e)
**Maracay** Venezuela 991 000 (1996e)
**Mar del Plata** Argentina 540 000 (1996e)
**Mariupal** Ukraine 510 000 (1996)
**Marrakesh** Morocco 602 000 (1994e)
**Marseilles** France 846 000 (1996e)
**Masan** Korea, Republic of (South Korea) 441 358 (1995)
**Matsudo** Japan 461 489 (1995)
**Matsuyama** Japan 460 870 (1995)
**Mecca** Saudi Arabia 701 000 (1996e)
**Medan** Indonesia 2 200 000 (1996e)
**Medellin** Colombia 1 621 356 (1995e)
**Meerut** India 933 000 (1996e)
**Meknes** Morocco 401 000 (1994e)
**Melbourne** Australia 3 218 100 (1995e)
**Memphis** USA 614 289 (1994e)
**Mendoza** Argentina 727 000 (1996e)
**Meshed** Iran 1 916 000 (1995e)
**Mexicali** Mexico 395 000 (1996e)
**Mexico City** Mexico 8 650 000 (1996e)
**Miami** USA 373 024 (1994e)
**Milan** Italy 1 334 171 (1994e)
**Milwaukee** USA 617 044 (1994e)
**Minneapolis** USA 354 590 (1994e)
**Minsk** Belarus 1 700 000 (1996e)
**Mogadishu** Somalia 742 000 (1996e)
**Mogilyov** Belarus 367 000 (1996e)
**Mombasa** Kenya 488 000 (1996e)
**Monrovia** Liberia 536 000 (1996e)
**Monterrey** Mexico 1 215 000 (1996e)
**Montevideo** Uruguay 1 378 707 (1996)
**Montreal** Canada 1 017 666 (1994)
**Moradabad** India 551 000 (1996e)
**Moscow** Russia 8 717 000 (1995e)
**Mosul** Iraq 640 000 (1996e)
**Mudanjiang** China 662 000 (1996e)
**Multan** Pakistan 1 257 000 (1995e)
**Munich** Germany 1 244 676 (1995e)
**Murcia** Spain 341 531 (1994e)
**Murmansk** Russia 407 000 (1995e)
**Mysore** India 597 000 (1996e)
**Naberezhnye Chelny** Russia 526 000 (1995e)
**Nagano** Japan 358 512 (1995)
**Nagasaki** Japan 438 724 (1995)
**Nagoya** Japan 2 152 258 (1995)
**Nagpur** India 1 756 000 (1995e)
**Naha** Japan 301 928 (1995)
**Nairobi** Kenya 1 697 000 (1995e)
**Namangan** Uzbekistan 341 000 (1994e)
**Nanchang** China 1 256 000 (1996e)
**Nanjing** China 2 394 000 (1996e)
**Nanning** China 771 000 (1996e)
**Nantong** China 380 000 (1996e)
**Naples** Italy 1 061 000 (1994e)
**Nara** Japan 359 234 (1995)
**Nashville** USA 504 505 (1994e)
**Nassau** The Bahamas 191 000 (1996e)
**Natal** Brazil 574 000 (1996e)

| | |
|---|---|
| **N'Djamena** Chad | 530 965 (1994e) |
| **Ndola** Zambia | 479 000 (1996e) |
| **Netzahualcóyotl** Mexico | 1 455 000 (1996e) |
| **Newark** USA | 258 751 (1994e) |
| **Newcastle** Australia | 466 000 (1995e) |
| **New Delhi** India | 345 000 (1996e) |
| **New Orleans** USA | 484 149 (1994e) |
| **New York** USA | 7 333 253 (1994e) |
| **Niamey** Niger | 439 000 (1996e) |
| **Nice** France | 465 000 (1996e) |
| **Nicosia** Cyprus | 186 400 (1994e) |
| **Niigata** Japan | 494 785 (1995) |
| **Nikolayev** Ukraine | 508 700 (1996e) |
| **Ningbo** China | 634 000 (1996e) |
| **Niš** Yugoslavia | 689 000 (1996e) |
| **Nishinomiya** Japan | 390 388 (1995) |
| **Niteroi** Brazil | 485 000 (1996e) |
| **Nizhny Tagil** Russia | 409 000 (1995e) |
| **Nova Iguacu** Brazil | 1 426 000 (1996e) |
| **Nouakchott** Mauritania | 755 000 (1995e) |
| **Novokuznetsk** Russia | 572 000 (1995e) |
| **Novosibirsk** Russia | 1 369 000 (1995e) |
| **Nuremberg** Germany | 495 845 (1995e) |
| **Oakland** USA | 366 926 (1994e) |
| **Odessa** Ukraine | 1 046 000 (1996e) |
| **Ogbomosho** Nigeria | 711 900 (1995e) |
| **Oita** Japan | 426 981 (1995) |
| **Okayama** Japan | 616 056 (1995) |
| **Oklahoma City** USA | 463 201 (1994e) |
| **Olinda** Brazil | 369 500 (1996e) |
| **Omaha** USA | 345 033 (1994e) |
| **Omdurman** The Sudan | 1 267 077 (1994) |
| **Omiya** Japan | 433 768 (1995) |
| **Omsk** Russia | 1 163 000 (1995e) |
| **Oporto** Portugal | 394 000 (1996e) |
| **Oran** Algeria | 696 000 (1996e) |
| **Ordzhonikidze** Russia | 312 000 (1995e) |
| **Orenburg** Russia | 532 000 (1995e) |
| **Oryol** Russia | 348 000 (1995e) |
| **Osaka** Japan | 2 602 352 (1995) |
| **Osasco** Brazil | 677 000 (1996e) |
| **Osijek** Croatia | 240 000 (1996e) |
| **Oslo** Norway | 487 908 (1996e) |
| **Ostrava** Czech Republic | 325 827 (1995e) |
| **Ottawa** Canada | 313 971 (1994) |
| **Oujda** Morocco | 331 000 (1994e) |
| **Padang** Indonesia | 790 000 (1996e) |
| **Palembang** Indonesia | 1 561 000 (1996e) |
| **Palermo** Italy | 694 749 (1994e) |
| **Palma** Majorca | 322 008 (1994e) |
| **Panama City** Panama | 445 902 (1994e) |
| **Panchiao** Taiwan | 539 115 (1995e) |
| **Panshan** China | 339 000 (1996e) |
| **Paris** France | 2 336 000 (1996e) |
| **Patna** India | 1 141 000 (1996e) |
| **Pavlodar** Kazakhstan | 340 700 (1995e) |
| **Penza** Russia | 534 000 (1995e) |
| **Perm** Russia | 1 032 000 (1995e) |
| **Perth** Australia | 1 262 600 (1995e) |
| **Peshawar** Pakistan | 1 676 000 (1995e) |
| **Philadelphia** USA | 1 524 249 (1994e) |
| **Phoenix** USA | 1 048 949 (1994e) |
| **Pingdingshan** China | 502 000 (1996e) |
| **Pingxiang** China | 506 000 (1996e) |
| **Pittsburgh** USA | 358 883 (1994e) |
| **Plovdiv** Bulgaria | 344 326 (1996e) |
| **Poltava** Ukraine | 321 000 (1996e) |
| **Pontianak** Indonesia | 419 000 (1996e) |
| **Poona** India | 1 688 000 (1995e) |
| **Port-au-Prince** Haiti | 846 247 (1995e) |
| **Port Elizabeth** South Africa | 797 000 (1996e) |
| **Portland** USA | 450 777 (1994e) |
| **Port Louis** Mauritius | 144 776 (1994e) |
| **Port Moresby** Papua New Guinea | 176 000 (1996e) |
| **Porto Alegre** Brazil | 1 569 000 (1996e) |
| **Port of Spain** Trinidad | 70 000 (1996e) |
| **Port Said** Egypt | 460 000 (1994e) |
| **Poznań** Poland | 582 300 (1995e) |
| **Prague** Czech Republic | 1 213 299 (1995e) |
| **Pretoria** South Africa | 925 000 (1996e) |
| **Puebla** Mexico | 991 000 (1996e) |
| **Pusan** Korea, Republic of (South Korea) | 3 813 814 (1995) |
| **Pyongyang** Korea, Democratic People's Republic of (North Korea) | 2 716 000 (1995e) |
| **Qinhuangdao** China | 405 000 (1996e) |
| **Qiqihar** China | 1 261 000 (1996e) |
| **Qom** Iran | 624 000 (1996e) |
| **Quebec** Canada | 175 039 (1994) |
| **Quezon City** Philippines | 1 676 644 (1994e) |
| **Quito** Ecuador | 1 444 363 (1996e) |
| **Rabat** Morocco | 1 220 000 (1994e) |
| **Raipur** India | 540 000 (1996e) |
| **Rajkot** India | 666 000 (1996e) |
| **Ranchi** India | 739 000 (1996e) |
| **Rangoon** Myanmar (Burma) | 3 851 000 (1995e) |
| **Rawalpindi** Pakistan | 1 290 000 (1995e) |
| **Recife** Brazil | 1 496 000 (1995e) |
| **Reykjavik** Iceland | 104 276 (1995e) |
| **Ribeirao Preto** Brazil | 444 000 (1996e) |
| **Riga** Latvia | 839 670 (1995e) |
| **Rio de Janeiro** Brazil | 6 574 000 (1995e) |
| **Riyadh** Saudi Arabia | 1 800 000 (1995e) |
| **Rome** Italy | 2 687 881 (1994e) |

**Rosario** Argentina 1 136 000 (1996e)
**Rostov-na-Donu** Russia 1 026 000 (1995e)
**Rotterdam** Netherlands 599 414 (1995e)
**Sacramento** USA 373 964 (1994e)
**Safi** Morocco 278 000 (1994)
**Sagamihara** Japan 570 594 (1995)
**St Catharines-Niagara** Canada 125 887 (1994)
**St Louis** USA 368 215 (1994e)
**St Petersburg** Russia 4 838 000 (1995e)
**Sakai** Japan 802 965 (1995)
**Salem** India 445 000 (1996e)
**Salonika** Greece 453 000 (1996e)
**Salvador** Brazil 2 203 000 (1995e)
**Samarkand** Uzbekistan 368 000 (1994e)
**San'a** Yemen 503 600 (1995e)
**San Antonio** USA 998 905 (1994e)
**San Cristobal** Venezuela 413 000 (1996e)
**San Diego** USA 1 151 977 (1994e)
**San Francisco** USA 734 676 (1994e)
**San José** USA 816 884 (1994e)
**San Juan** Puerto Rico 438 076 (1995e)
**San Luis Potosí** Mexico 412 000 (1996e)
**San Miguel de Tucumán** Argentina 551 000 (1996e)
**San Pedro Sula** Honduras 368 500 (1994e)
**San Salvador** El Salvador 439 000 (1996e)
**Santa Cruz de la Sierra** Bolivia 767 260 (1994e)
**Santiago** Chile 5 076 808 (1995e)
**Santiago de Cuba** Cuba 440 084 (1994e)
**Santo André** Brazil 734 000 (1996e)
**Santo Domingo** Dominican Republic 2 138 262 (1994e)
**Santos** Brazil 505 000 (1996e)
**São Bernardo do Campo** Brazil 613 000 (1996e)
**São Gonçalo** Brazil 777 000 (1996e)
**São João de Meriti** Brazil 513 000 (1996e)
**São José dos Campos** Brazil 389 000 (1996e)
**São Luis** Brazil 623 000 (1996e)
**São Paulo** Brazil 9 393 753 (1996)
**Sapporo** Japan 1 756 968 (1995)
**Saragossa** Spain 606 620 (1994e)
**Sarajevo** Bosnia-Herzegovina 250 000 (1995e)
**Saransk** Russia 320 000 (1995e)
**Saratov** Russia 895 000 (1995e)
**Scarborough** Canada 510 000 (1994)
**Seattle** USA 520 947 (1994e)
**Semarang** Indonesia 1 477 000 (1995e)
**Semipalatinsk** Kazakhstan 320 200 (1995e)
**Sendai** Japan 971 263 (1995)
**Seoul** Korea, Republic of (South Korea) 10 229 262 (1995)
**Shanchung** Taiwan 382 880 (1995e)
**Shanghai** China 7 830 000 (1996e)
**Shantou** China 602 000 (1996e)
**Shaoguan** China 404 000 (1996e)
**Sheffield** UK 530 100 (1994e)
**Shenyang** China 4 449 000 (1996e)
**Shihezi** China 376 000 (1996e)
**Shijiazhuang** China 1 333 000 (1996e)
**Shiraz** Iran 1 009 000 (1996e)
**Shizuoka** Japan 474 089 (1995)
**Sholapur** India 744 000 (1996e)
**Shoubra el-Kheima** Egypt 956 000 (1996e)
**Shuangyashan** China 467 000 (1996e)
**Sialkot** Pakistan 366 000 (1996e)
**Sian (Xian)** China 2 410 000 (1996e)
**Simferopol** Ukraine 348 000 (1996e)
**Singapore** Singapore 3 045 000 (1996e)
**Sinuiju** Korea, Democratic People's Republic of (North Korea) 361 000 (1996e)
**Skopje** Macedonia 541 280 (1994e)
**Smolensk** Russia 355 000 (1995e)
**Smyrna** Turkey 1 959 000 (1995e)
**Sochi** Russia 355 000 (1995e)
**Sofia** Bulgaria 1 116 823 (1996e)
**Songnam** Korea, Republic of (South Korea) 869 243 (1995)
**Sorocaba** Brazil 327 468 (1987e)
**Srinagar** India 742 000 (1996e)
**Stavropol** Russia 342 000 (1995e)
**Stockholm** Sweden 711 119 (1996e)
**Stuttgart** Germany 588 482 (1995e)
**Suita** Japan 342 794 (1995)
**Surabaya** Indonesia 2 726 000 (1995e)
**Surakarta** Indonesia 588 000 (1996e)
**Surat** India 1 620 000 (1995e)
**Suva** Fiji 73 1000 (1996e)
**Suwon** Korea, Republic of (South Korea) 755 502 (1995)
**Suzhou** China 778 000 (1996e)
**Sverdlovsk** Russia 1 280 000 (1995e)
**Sydney** Australia 3 772 700 (1995e)
**Szczecin** Poland 419 600 (1995e)
**Tabriz** Iran 1 301 000 (1995e)
**Taegu** Korea, Republic of (South Korea) 2 449 139 (1995)
**Taejon** Korea, Republic of (South Korea) 1 272 143 (1995)
**Taichung** Taiwan 857 590 (1996e)
**Tainan** Taiwan 707 658 (1996e)
**Taipei** Taiwan 2 626 138 (1996e)
**Taiyuan** China 1 861 000 (1996e)
**Takamatsu** Japan 330 997 (1995)
**Takatsuki** Japan 362 259 (1995)
**Tallinn** Estonia 434 763 (1995e)
**Tambov** Russia 316 000 (1995e)

|  |  |
|---|---|
| **Tangier** Morocco | 307 700 (1994e) |
| **Tangshan** China | 1 213 000 (1996e) |
| **Tanta** Egypt | 396 000 (1996e) |
| **Tashkent** Uzbekistan | 2 106 000 (1994e) |
| **Tbilisi** Georgia | 1 295 000 (1995e) |
| **Tegucigalpa** Honduras | 775 300 (1994e) |
| **Tehran** Iran | 6 632 000 (1996e) |
| **Tel Aviv** Israel | 355 900 (1996e) |
| **Teresina** Brazil | 588 000 (1996e) |
| **Tetouan** Morocco | 272 000 (1994e) |
| **Thane** India | 956 000 (1996e) |
| **Tianjin (Tientsin)** China | 5 479 000 (1996e) |
| **Tijuana** Mexico | 479 000 (1996e) |
| **Timisoura** Romania | 325 359 (1994e) |
| **Tirana** Albania | 257 000 (1996e) |
| **Tiruchchirapalli** India | 475 000 (1996e) |
| **Tokyo** Japan | 7 966 195 (1995) |
| **Toledo** USA | 322 550 (1994e) |
| **Tolyatti** Russia | 702 000 (1995e) |
| **Tomsk** Russia | 470 000 (1995e) |
| **Tonghua** China | 378 000 (1996e) |
| **Toronto** Canada | 590 838 (1994) |
| **Toulouse** France | 385 500 (1996e) |
| **Toyama** Japan | 341 038 (1995) |
| **Toyohasi** Japan | 352 913 (1995) |
| **Toyonaka** Japan | 325 303 (1995) |
| **Toyota** Japan | 398 912 (1995) |
| **Tripoli** Libya | 626 000 (1996e) |
| **Trivandrum** India | 707 000 (1996e) |
| **Trujillo** Peru | 509 312 (1994e) |
| **Tucson** USA | 434 726 (1994e) |
| **Tula** Russia | 532 000 (1995e) |
| **Tulsa** USA | 374 851 (1994e) |
| **Tunis** Tunisia | 674 100 (1994e) |
| **Turin** Italy | 945 551 (1994e) |
| **Tyumen** Russia | 494 000 (1995e) |
| **Ufa** Russia | 1 094 000 (1995e) |
| **Ulan Bator** Mongolia | 619 000 (1994e) |
| **Ulan-Ude** Russia | 366 000 (1995e) |
| **Ulsan** Korea, Republic of (South Korea) | 967 394 (1995) |
| **Ulyanovsk** Russia | 678 000 (1995e) |
| **Urawa** Japan | 453 000 (1995) |
| **Urumqi** China | 1 203 000 (1996e) |
| **Ust-Kamenogorsk** Kazakhstan | 326 300 (1995e) |
| **Utsunomiya** Japan | 435 446 (1995) |
| **Vadodara** India | 1 357 000 (1996e) |
| **Valencia** Spain | 764 293 (1994e) |
| **Valencia** Venezuela | 1 466 000 (1996e) |
| **Valladolid** Spain | 336 917 (1994e) |
| **Vancouver** Canada | 508 814 (1994) |
| **Varanasi** India | 1 217 000 (1996e) |
| **Vargas** Venezuela | 395 000 (1996e) |
| **Varna** Bulgaria | 301 421 (1996e) |
| **Venice** Italy | 306 439 (1994e) |
| **Veracruz** Mexico | 315 000 (1996e) |
| **Victoria** Seychelles | 25 000 (1994e) |
| **Vienna** Austria | 1 690 000 (1996e) |
| **Vientiane** Laos | 457 000 (1996e) |
| **Vijayawada** India | 881 000 (1996e) |
| **Vilnius** Lithuania | 590 100 (1993e) |
| **Vina del Mar** Chile | 322 220 (1995e) |
| **Vinnitsa** Ukraine | 388 000 (1996e) |
| **Virginia Beach** USA | 430 295 (1994e) |
| **Visakhapatnam** India | 928 000 (1996e) |
| **Vitebsk** Belarus | 365 000 (1996e) |
| **Vladimir** Russia | 339 000 (1995e) |
| **Vladivostok** Russia | 632 000 (1995e) |
| **Volgograd** Russia | 1 003 000 (1995e) |
| **Voronezh** Russia | 908 000 (1995e) |
| **Voroshilovgrad** Ukraine | 487 000 (1996e) |
| **Wakayama** Japan | 339 951 (1995) |
| **Warangal** India | 549 000 (1996e) |
| **Warsaw** Poland | 1 640 700 (1995e) |
| **Washington** USA | 567 094 (1994e) |
| **Weifang** China | 412 000 (1996e) |
| **Wellington** New Zealand | 158 275 (1996) |
| **Wenzhou** China | 475 900 (1996e) |
| **Windhoek** Namibia | 184 000 (1996e) |
| **Winnipeg** Canada | 641 700 (1994) |
| **Wroclaw** Poland | 642 900 (1995e) |
| **Wuhan** China | 4 015 000 (1996e) |
| **Wuhu** China | 506 000 (1996e) |
| **Wuppertal** Germany | 383 776 (1995e) |
| **Wuxi** China | 927 000 (1996e) |
| **Xiamen** China | 448 000 (1996e) |
| **Xiangfan** China | 447 000 (1996e) |
| **Xiangtan** China | 515 000 (1996e) |
| **Xiangyang** China | 468 000 (1996e) |
| **Xining** China | 639 000 (1996e) |
| **Xinxiang** China | 549 000 (1996e) |
| **Xuzhou** China | 932 000 (1996e) |
| **Yakeshi** China | 464 000 (1996e) |
| **Yangquan** China | 421 000 (1996e) |
| **Yantai** China | 461 000 (1996e) |
| **Yaounde** Cameroon | 824 000 (1996e) |
| **Yaroslavl** Russia | 629 000 (1995e) |
| **Yerevan** Armenia | 1 226 000 (1994e) |
| **Yichang (Ichang)** China | 417 000 (1996e) |
| **Yichun (Ichun)** China | 951 000 (1996e) |
| **Yinchuan** China | 392 000 (1996e) |
| **Yingkou** China | 482 000 (1996e) |
| **Yogyakarta** Indonesia | 583 000 (1996e) |
| **Yokohama** Japan | 3 307 408 (1995) |
| **Yukosuko** Japan | 432 202 (1995) |
| **Zagreb** Croatia | 845 000 (1996e) |

**Zamboanga City** Philippines 464 466 (1994e)
**Zaporozhye** Ukraine 882 000 (1996e)
**Zarqa** Jordan 344 524 (1994)
**Zhangjiakou** China 615 000 (1996e)
**Zhengzhou** China 1 333 000 (1996e)
**Zhenjiang** China 424 000 (1996e)
**Zhuzhou** China 465 000 (1996e)
**Zibo** China 992 000 (1996e)
**Zigong** China 469 000 (1996e)
**Zürich** Switzerland 342 872 (1995e)

## Largest cities by population

### ❑ World

**Seoul** Korea, Republic of (South Korea) 10 229 262
**Bombay** India 9 925 891
**Karachi** Pakistan 9 863 000
**Mexico City** Mexico 9 815 795
**São Paulo** Brazil 9 393 753
**Delhi** India 8 865 000
**Moscow** Russia 8 717 000
**Jakarta** Indonesia 8 259 266
**Beijing (Peking)** China 8 200 000
**Tokyo** Japan 7 966 195

### ❑ Europe

**Moscow** Russia 8 717 000
**Istanbul** Turkey 7 615 500
**London** UK 6 967 500
**St Petersburg** Russia 4 838 000
**Berlin** Germany 3 472 009
**Madrid** Spain 3 041 101
**Rome** Italy 2 687 227
**Bucharest** Romania 2 343 824
**Paris** France 2 175 200
**Budapest** Hungary 1 909 000

### ❑ USA

**New York** New York 7 333 253
**Los Angeles** California 3 448 613
**Chicago** Illinois 2 731 743
**Houston** Texas 1 702 086
**Philadelphia** Pennsylvania 1 524 249
**San Diego** California 1 170 200
**Phoenix** Arizona 1 048 949
**Dallas** Texas 1 022 830
**San Antonio** Texas 998 905
**Detroit** Michigan 992 038

## Nations of the world

In the case of countries that do not use the Roman alphabet (such as the Arabic countries), there is variation in the spelling of names and currencies, depending on the system of transliteration used.
Where more than one language is shown within a country, the status of the languages may not be equal. Some languages have a 'semi-official' status, or are used for a restricted set of purposes, such as trade or tourism.
Population census estimates are for 1999.
* The euro is now the currency, with euro notes and coins introduced from 1 January 2002. 1 euro (€) = 100cents

| English name | Local name | Official name (in English) | Capital (English name in parentheses) | Official language(s) | Currency | Population |
|---|---|---|---|---|---|---|
| Afghanistan | Afghānestān | Islamic State of Afghanistan | Kābul | Dari, Pushtu | 1 Afghani (Af) = 100 puls | 25 825 000 inc. nomads |
| Albania | Shqīpëri | Republic of Albania | Tiranë (Tirana) | Albanian | 1 Lek (Lk) = 100 qindarka | 3 365 000 |
| Algeria | Al-Jazā'ir (Arabic) Algérie (French) | Democratic and Popular Republic of Algeria | El Djazair (Algiers) | Arabic | 1 Algerian Dinar (AD, DA) = 100 centimes | 31 133 000 |
| Andorra | Andorra | Principality of Andorra; the Valleys of Andorra | Andorra la Vella | Catalan, French, Spanish | 1 French Franc (Fr) = 100 centimes; 1 Peseta (Pta, Pa) =100 céntimos | 65 900 |
| Angola | Angola | Republic of Angola | Luanda | Portuguese | 1 New Kwanza (Kzrl) = 100 lwei | 11 178 000 |
| Antigua and Barbuda | Antigua and Barbuda | State of Antigua and Barbuda | St John's | English | 1 East Caribbean Dollar (EC$) = 100 cents | 64 200 |
| Argentina | Argentina | Argentine Republic | Buenos Aires | Spanish | 1 Peso = 10 000 australes | 36 738 000 |
| Armenia | Hayastani Hanrapetoutiun | Republic of Armenia | Yerevan | Armenian | 1 Dram (Drm) =100 louma | 3 409 000 |
| Australia | Australia | Commonwealth of Australia | Canberra | English | 1 Australian Dollar ($A) = 100 cents | 18 784 000 |
| Austria | Österreich | Republic of Austria | Vienna | German | *1 Schilling (S, Sch) = 100 groschen | 8 139 000 |
| Azerbaijan | Azarbaijan | Republic of Azerbaijan | Baku | Azeri | 1 Manat =100 gopik | 7 980 000 |
| The Bahamas | Bahamas | Commonwealth of the Bahamas | Nassau | English | 1 Bahamian Dollar (BA$, B$) = 100 cents | 283 700 |
| Bahrain | Dawlat Al-Bahrayn | State of Bahrain | Al-Manāmah (Manama) | Arabic | 1 Bahraini Dinar (BD) = 1 000 fils | 629 100 |
| Bangladesh | Gana Prajatantri Bangladesh | People's Republic of Bangladesh | Dhaka (Dacca) | Bengali | 1 Taka (TK) = 100 poisha | 127 118 000 |

| English name | Local name | Official name (in English) | Capital (English name in parentheses) | Official language(s) | Currency | Population |
|---|---|---|---|---|---|---|
| Barbados | Barbados | Barbados | Bridgetown | English | 1 Barbados Dollar (BD$) = 100 cents | 259 200 |
| Belarus | Belarus | Republic of Belarus | Minsk | Belarusian, Russian | 1 Rouble =100 kopeks | 10 402 000 |
| Belgium | Belgique (French) België (Flemish) | Kingdom of Belgium | Bruxelles (Brussels) | Flemish, French, German | *1 Belgian Franc (BFr) = 100 centimes | 10 182 000 |
| Belize | Belize | Belize | Belmopan | English | 1 Belize Dollar (BZ$) = 100 cents | 235 800 |
| Benin | Bénin | Republic of Benin | Porto-Novo | French | 1 CFA Franc (CFAFr) = 100 centimes | 6 306 000 |
| Bhutan | Druk-Yul | Kingdom of Bhutan | Thimbu/Thimphu | Dzongkha | 1 Ngultrum (Nu) = 100 chetrum | 1 952 000 |
| Bolivia | Bolivia | Republic of Bolivia | La Paz/Sucre | Spanish | 1 Boliviano ($b) = 100 centavos | 7 983 000 |
| Bosnia-Herzegovina | Bosnia-Herzegovina | Republic of Bosnia-Herzegovina | Sarajevo | Bosnian, Serbian, Croatian | 1 Dinar (D, din) = 100 paras | 3 482 000 |
| Botswana | Botswana | Republic of Botswana | Gaborone | English, Setswana | 1 Pula (P, Pu) = 100 thebe | 1 464 000 |
| Brazil | Brasil | Federative Republic of Brazil | Brasilia | Portuguese | 1 Real = 100 centavos | 171 853 000 |
| Brunei | Brunei | State of Brunei, Abode of Peace | Bandar Seri Begawan | Malay, English | 1 Brunei Dollar (B$) = 100 sen | 323 000 |
| Bulgaria | Bălgarija | Republic of Bulgaria | Sofija (Sofia) | Bulgarian | 1 Lev (Lv) = 100 stotinki | 8 195 000 |
| Burkina Faso | Burkina Faso | Burkina Faso | Ouagadougou | French | 1 CFA Franc (CFAFr) = 100 centimes | 11 576 000 |
| Burma ► Myanmar | | | | | | |
| Burundi | Burundi | Republic of Burundi | Bujumbura | French, Kirundi | 1 Burundi Franc (BuFr, FBu) = 100 centimes | 5 736 000 |
| Cambodia | Preah Reach Ana Pak Kampuchea | State of Cambodia | Phnum Pénh (Phnom Penh) | Khmer | 1 Riel (CRI) = 100 sen | 11 627 000 |
| Cameroon | Cameroon | Republic of Cameroon | Yaoundé | English, French | 1 CFA (Franc) (CFAFr) = 100 centimes | 15 456 000 |
| Canada | Canada | Canada | Ottawa | English, French | 1 Canadian Dollar (C$, Can$) = 100 cents | 31 006 000 |
| Cape Verde | Cabo Verde | Republic of Cape Verde | Praia | Portuguese | 1 Escudo Caboverdiano (CVEsc) = 100 centavos | 405 700 |

| English name | Local name | Official name (in English) | Capital (English name in parentheses) | Official language(s) | Currency | Population |
|---|---|---|---|---|---|---|
| Central African Republic | République Centrafricaine | Central African Republic | Bangui | French, Sango | 1 CFA Franc (CFAFr) = 100 centimes | 3 445 000 |
| Chad | Tchad | Republic of Chad | N'Djamena | French, Arabic | 1 CFA Franc (CFAFr) = 100 centimes | 7 557 000 |
| Chile | Chile | Republic of Chile | Santiago | Spanish | 1 Chilean Peso (Ch$) = 100 centavos | 14 974 000 |
| China | Zhonghua | People's Republic of China | Beijing (Peking) | Mandarin Chinese | 1 Renminbi Yuan (RMBY, $, Y) = 10 jiao = 100 fen | 1 246 872 000 |
| Colombia | Colombia | Republic of Colombia | Bogotá | Spanish | 1 Colombian Peso (Col$) = 100 centavos | 39 309 000 |
| Comoros | Comores | Federal Islamic Republic of the Comoros | Moroni | French, Arabic | 1 Comorian Franc (KMF) = 100 centimes | 562 700 |
| Congo | Congo | Republic of Congo | Brazzaville | French, Kikongo, Lingala | 1 CFA Franc (CFAFr) = 100 centimes | 2 717 000 |
| Congo, Democratic Republic of | Congo | Democratic Republic of Congo | Kinshasa | French, Kikongo, Lingala | 1 New Zaïre = 100 makuta (*sing.* likuta) | 50 481 000 |
| Costa Rica | Costa Rica | Republic of Costa Rica | San José | Spanish | 1 Costa Rican Colón (CR₡) = 100 céntimos | 3 647 000 |
| Côte d'Ivoire (Ivory Coast) | Côte d'Ivoire | Republic of Côte d'Ivoire | Abidjan/ Yamoussoukro | French | 1 CFA Franc (CFAFr) = 100 centimes | 15 818 000 |
| Croatia | Hrvatska | Republic of Croatia | Zagreb | Croatian | 1 Kuna = 100 lipa | 4 677 000 |
| Cuba | Cuba | Republic of Cuba | La Habana (Havana) | Spanish | 1 Cuban Peso (Cub$) = 100 centavos | 11 096 000 |
| Cyprus | Kipros (Greek) Kibris (Turkish) | Republic of Cyprus | Levkosia (Nicosia) | Greek, Turkish | 1 Cyprus Pound (C£) = 100 cents | 754 100 |
| Czech Republic | Česká Republika | Czech Republic | Praha (Prague) | Czech | 1 Koruna (Kčs) = 100 haléřu | 10 281 000 |
| Denmark | Danmark | Kingdom of Denmark | København (Copenhagen) | Danish | 1 Danish Krone (Dkr) = 100 øre | 5 357 000 |
| Djibouti | Djibouti | Republic of Djibouti | Djibouti | Arabic, French | 1 Djibouti Franc (DF, DjFr) = 100 centimes | 447 400 |
| Dominica | Dominica | Commonwealth of Dominica | Roseau | English, French Creole | 1 East Caribbean Dollar (EC$) = 100 cents | 64 900 |
| Dominican Republic | República Dominicana | Dominican Republic | Santo Domingo | Spanish | 1 Dominican Republic Peso (RD$, DR$) = 100 centavos | 8 130 000 |

| English name | Local name | Official name (in English) | Capital (English name in parentheses) | Official language(s) | Currency | Population |
|---|---|---|---|---|---|---|
| Ecuador | Ecuador | Republic of Ecuador | Quito | Spanish, Quechua | 1 Sucre (Su, S/.) = 100 centavos | 12 562 000 |
| Egypt | Jumhuriyat Misr Al-Arabiya | Arab Republic of Egypt | Al-Qāhirah (Cairo) | Arabic | 1 Egyptian Pound (£E, LE) = 100 piastres | 62 274 000 |
| El Salvador | El Salvador | Republic of El Salvador | San Salvador | Spanish | 1 Colón (₡ES) = 100 centavos | 5 839 000 |
| Equatorial Guinea | Guinea Ecuatorial | Republic of Equatorial Guinea | Malabo | Spanish, French | 1 CFA Franc (CFAFr) = 100 centimes | 465 700 |
| Eritrea | Ertra | Eritrea | Asmara | Arabic, Tigrinya | 1 Nakfa = 100 cents | 3 985 000 |
| Estonia | Eesti Vabariik | Republic of Estonia | Tallinn | Estonian, Russian | 1 Kroon = 100 sents | 1 409 000 |
| Ethiopia | Ityopiya | Federal Democratic Republic of Ethiopia | Adis Abeba (Addis Ababa) | Amharic | 1 Ethiopian Birr (EB) = 100 cents | 59 680 000 |
| Faroe Islands | Faroyar/ Faeroerne | Faroe Islands | Torshavn | Faroese, Danish | 1 Danish Krone (DKr) = 100 øre | 41 100 |
| Federated States of Micronesia ► Micronesia | | | | | | |
| Fiji | Matanitu Ko Viti | Republic of Fiji | Suva | Fijian, Hindi | 1 Fiji Dollar (F$) = 100 cents | 812 900 |
| Finland | Suomen Tasavalta | Republic of Finland | Helsinki | Finnish, Swedish | *1 Markka (FMk) = 100 penniä | 5 158 000 |
| France | République Française | French Republic | Paris | French | *1 French Franc (Fr) = 100 centimes | 58 978 000 |
| French Guiana | Guyane Française | French Guiana | Cayenne | French Creole | 1 French Franc (Fr) = 100 centimes | 168 000 |
| French Polynesia | Territoire de la Polynesie Française | French Polynesia | Papeete | Polynesian, French | 1 CPA Franc (CPAFr) = 100 centimes | 197 400 |
| Gabon | République Gabonaise | Gabonese Republic | Libreville | French | 1 CFA Franc (CFAFr) = 100 centimes | 1 226 000 |
| The Gambia | Gambia | Republic of the Gambia | Banjul | English | 1 Dalasi (D) = 100 butut | 1 336 000 |
| Georgia | Sakartvelos Respublica | Republic of Georgia | Tbilisi | Georgian, Russian | 1 Lari (GEL) = 100 tetri | 5 066 000 |
| Germany | Bundesrepublik Deutschland | Federal Republic of Germany | Berlin | German | *1 Deutsche Mark (DM) = 100 pfennig | 82 087 000 |
| Ghana | Ghana | Republic of Ghana | Accra | English | 1 Cedi (₵) = 100 pesewas | 18 888 000 |
| Greece | Elliniki Dimokratia | Hellenic Republic | Athínai (Athens) | Greek | *1 Drachma (Dr) = 100 leptae | 10 707 000 |
| Greenland | Grønland (Danish) Kalaallit Nunaat | Greenland | Godthåb/Nuuk | Danish, Greenlandic | 1 Danish Krone (DKr) = 100 øre | 59 800 |

| English name | Local name | Official name (in English) | Capital (English name in parentheses) | Official language(s) | Currency | Population |
|---|---|---|---|---|---|---|
| Grenada | Grenada | Grenada | St George's | English | 1 East Caribbean Dollar (EC$) = 100 cents | 97 000 |
| Guatemala | Guatemala | Republic of Guatemala | Guatemala City | Spanish | 1 Quetzal (Q) = 100 centavos | 12 336 000 |
| Guinea | République de Guinée | Republic of Guinea | Conakry | French | 1 Guinea Franc (GFr) = 100 centimes | 7 539 000 |
| Guinea-Bissau | Republica da Guiné-Bissau | Republic of Guinea-Bissau | Bissau | Portuguese, Guinean Creole | 1 CFA Franc (CFAFr) = 100 centimes | 1 235 000 |
| Guyana | Guyana | Co-operative Republic of Guyana | Georgetown | English | 1 Guyana Dollar (G$) = 100 cents | 705 200 |
| Haiti | République d'Haïti | Republic of Haiti | Port-au-Prince | French, Creole | 1 Gourde (G, Gde) = 100 centimes | 6 884 000 |
| Holland ► Netherlands, The | | | | | | |
| Honduras | Honduras | Republic of Honduras | Tegucigalpa | Spanish | 1 Lempira (L, La) = 100 centavos | 5 997 000 |
| Hungary | Magyar Koztarsasag | Republic of Hungary | Budapest | Hungarian | 1 Forint (Ft) = 100 fillér | 10 186 000 |
| Iceland | Ísland | Republic of Iceland | Reykjavik | Icelandic | 1 Króna (IKr, ISK) = 100 aurar | 272 500 |
| India | Bhārat (Hindi) | Republic of India | New Delhi | Hindi, English | 1 Indian Rupee (Re, Rs) = 100 paisa | 1 000 849 000 |
| Indonesia | Republik Indonesia | Republic of Indonesia | Jakarta | Bahasa Indonesia | 1 Rupiah (Rp) = 100 sen | 216 108 000 |
| Iran | Jomhoori-e-Islami-e-Iran | Islamic Republic of Iran | Tehrān (Tehran) | Farsi | 1 Iranian Rial (Rls, Rl) = 100 dinars | 65 180 000 |
| Iraq | Jumhouriya al Iraquia | Republic of Iraq | Baghdād (Baghdad) | Arabic | 1 Iraqi Dinar (ID) = 1 000 fils | 22 427 000 |
| Ireland | Poblacht na hEireann | Republic of Ireland | Baile Átha Cliath (Dublin) | Irish, English | *1 Irish Pound/Punt (£, IR£) = 100 pence | 3 633 000 |
| Israel | Medinat Israel | State of Israel | Yerushalayim (Jerusalem) | Hebrew, Arabic | 1 Shekel (IS) = 100 agora | 5 750 000 |
| Italy | Repubblica Italiana | Italian Republic | Roma (Rome) | Italian | *1 Italian Lira (L, Lit) = 100 centesimi | 56 735 000 |
| Ivory Coast ► Côte d'Ivoire | | | | | | |
| Jamaica | Jamaica | Jamaica | Kingston | English | 1 Jamaican Dollar (J$) = 100 cents | 2 652 000 |

| English name | Local name | Official name (in English) | Capital (English name in parentheses) | Official language(s) | Currency | Population |
|---|---|---|---|---|---|---|
| Japan | Nihon | Japan | Tōkyō (Tokyo) | Japanese | 1 Yen (Y, ¥) = 100 sen | 126 182 000 |
| Jordan | Al'Urdunn | Hashemite Kingdom of Jordan | 'Ammān (Amman) | Arabic | 1 Jordanian Dinar (JD) = 1 000 fils | 4 561 000 |
| Jugoslavia ► Yugoslavia | | | | | | |
| Kampuchea ► Cambodia | | | | | | |
| Kazakhstan | Kazak Respublikasy | Republic of Kazakhstan | Astanta | Kazakh | 1 Tenge = 100 tiyn | 16 825 000 |
| Kenya | Jamhuri ya Kenya | Republic of Kenya | Nairobi | Swahili, English | 1 Kenyan shilling (Ksh) = 100 cents | 28 809 000 |
| Kiribati | Kiribati | Republic of Kiribati | Bairiki, on Tarawa | English, I-Kiribati | 1 Australian Dollar ($A) = 100 cents | 85 500 |
| Korea, North | Chosōn Minjujuüi In'min Konghwaguk | Democratic People's Republic of Korea | P'yŏngyang (Pyongyang) | Korean | 1 Won (NKW) = 100 chon | 21 386 000 |
| Korea, South | Taehan-Min'guk | Republic of Korea | Sŏul (Seoul) | Korean | 1 Won (W) = 100 jeon | 46 885 000 |
| Kuwait | Dowlat al-Kuwayt | State of Kuwait | Al-Kuwayt (Kuwait City) | Arabic | 1 Kuwaiti Dinar (KD) = 1 000 fils | 1 991 000 |
| Kyrgyzstan | Kyrgyz Respublikasy | Republic of Kyrgyzstan | Bishkek | Kyrgyz, Russian | 1 Som (Kgs) = 100 tyiyn | 4 546 000 |
| Laos | Lao | Lao People's Democratic Republic | Viangchan (Vientiane) | Lao | 1 Kip (Kp) = 100 at | 5 407 000 |
| Latvia | Latvijas Republika | Republic of Latvia | Riga | Latvian | 1 Lat = 100 santims | 2 354 000 |
| Lebanon | Al-Lubnān | Republic of Lebanon | Bayrūt (Beirut) | Arabic | 1 Lebanese Pound/Livre (LL, L£) = 100 piastres | 3 563 000 |
| Lesotho | Lesotho | Kingdom of Lesotho | Maseru | English, Sesotho | 1 Loti (*plural* Maloti) (M, LSM) = 100 lisente | 2 129 000 |
| Liberia | Liberia | Republic of Liberia | Monrovia | English | 1 Liberian Dollar (L$) = 100 cents | 2 924 000 |
| Libya | Lībyā | Socialist People's Libyan Arab Jamahiriya | Tarābulus (Tripoli) | Arabic | 1 Libyan Dinar (LD) = 1 000 dirhams | 4 993 000 |
| Liechtenstein | Furstentum Liechtenstein | Principality of Liechtenstein | Vaduz | German | 1 Swiss Franc (SFr, SwF) = 100 centimes = 100 rappen | 32 100 |
| Lithuania | Lietuva | Republic of Lithuania | Vilnius | Lithuanian | 1 Litas (Lt) = 100 centas | 3 585 000 |
| Luxembourg | Lëtzebuerg (Letz) Luxembourg (Fr) Luxemburg (Ger) | Grand Duchy of Luxembourg | Luxembourg | French, German, Lëtzebuergesch | *1 Luxembourg Franc (LF) = 100 centimes | 429 100 |

| English name | Local name | Official name (in English) | Capital (English name in parentheses) | Official language(s) | Currency | Population |
|---|---|---|---|---|---|---|
| Macedonia | Republika Makedonija | Former Yugoslav Republic of Macedonia | Skopje | Macedonian | 1 Denar (D, den) = 100 paras | 2 023 000 |
| Madagascar | Republikan'i Madagasikara | Democratic Republic of Madagascar | Antananarivo | Malagasy, French | 1 Malagasy Franc (FMG, MgFr) = 100 centimes | 14 873 000 |
| Malawi | Dziko la Malaŵi | Republic of Malawi | Lilongwe | Chichewa, English | 1 Kwacha (MK) = 100 tambala | 10 000 000 |
| Malaysia | Federation of Malaysia | Malaysia | Kuala Lumpur | Bahasa Malaysia | 1 Malaysian Dollar/Ringgit (M$) = 100 cents | 21 376 000 |
| Maldives | Maldives Divehi Jumhuriya | Republic of Maldives | Malé | Dhivehi | 1 Rufiyaa (MRf, Rf) = 100 laaris | 300 200 |
| Mali | Mali | Republic of Mali | Bamako | French | 1 CFA Franc (CFAFr) = 100 centimes | 10 429 000 |
| Malta | Malta | Republic of Malta | Valletta | English, Maltese | 1 Maltese Lira (LM) = 100 cents = 1 000 mils | 381 600 |
| Marshall Islands | Marshall Islands | Republic of the Marshall Islands | Majuro | Marshallese, English | 1 US Dollar ($, US$) = 100 cents | 66 000 |
| Martinique | Martinique | Martinique | Fort-de-France | French Creole | 1 French Franc (Fr) = 100 centimes | 411 500 |
| Mauritania | Mauritanie (French) Mūrītāniyā (Arabic) | Islamic Republic of Mauritania | Nouakchott | Arabic | 1 Ouguiya (U, UM) = 5 khoums | 2 582 000 |
| Mauritius | Mauritius | Republic of Mauritius | Port Louis | English | 1 Mauritian Rupee (MR, MauRe) = 100 cents | 1 182 000 |
| Mexico | México | United Mexican States | Ciudad de México (Mexico City) | Spanish | 1 Mexican Peso (Mex$) = 100 centavos | 100 294 000 |
| Micronesia | Micronesia | Federated States of Micronesia | Palikir, on Ponape | English | 1 US Dollar (US$) = 100 cents | 131 500 |
| Moldova | Republica Moldovenească | Republic of Moldova | Kishinev (Chisinau) | Moldovan | 1 Leu (Mld) = 100 bani | 4 461 000 |
| Monaco | Monaco | Principality of Monaco | Monaco | French | 1 French Franc (Fr) = 100 centimes | 32 100 |
| Mongolia | Mongol Ard Uls | State of Mongolia | Ulaanbaatar (Ulan Bator) | Khalka Mongolian | 1 Tugrik (Tug) = 100 möngö | 2 617 000 |
| Morocco | Mamlaka Al-Maghrebia | Kingdom of Morocco | Rabat | Arabic | 1 Dirham (DH) = 100 centimes | 29 662 000 |

| English name | Local name | Official name (in English) | Capital (English name in parentheses) | Official language(s) | Currency | Population |
|---|---|---|---|---|---|---|
| Mozambique | Republica de Moçambique | Republic of Mozambique | Maputo | Portuguese | 1 Metical (Mt, MZM) = 100 centavos | 19 124 000 |
| Myanmar (Burma) | Myanmar | Union of Myanmar | Yangon (Rangoon) | Burmese | 1 Kyat = 100 pyas | 48 081 000 |
| Namibia | Namibia | Republic of Namibia | Windhoek | English | 1 Namibian Dollar = 100 cents | 1 648 000 |
| Nauru | Naeoro (Nauruan) Nauru (English) | Republic of Nauru | Yaren District | Nauruan, English | 1 Australian Dollar ($A) = 100 cents | 10 600 |
| Nepal | Nepal Adhirajya | Kingdom of Nepal | Kathmandu | Nepali | 1 Nepalese Rupee (NRp, NRs) = 100 paise/pice | 24 303 000 |
| The Netherlands | Koninkrijk der Nederlanden | Kingdom of the Netherlands | Amsterdam 's-Gravenhage (The Hague) | Dutch | *1 Dutch Guilder (Gld)/Florin (f) = 100 cents | 15 808 000 |
| Netherlands Antilles | De Nederlandse Antillen | Netherlands Antilles | Willemstad | Papiamento, Dutch | 1 Netherlands Antilles Guilder (ANG) = 100 cents | 207 800 |
| New Zealand | New Zealand | New Zealand | Wellington | English, Maori | 1 New Zealand Dollar (NZ$) = 100 cents | 3 662 000 |
| Nicaragua | Nicaragua | Republic of Nicaragua | Managua | Spanish | 1 Córdoba Oro (C$) = 100 centavos | 4 717 000 |
| Niger | Niger | Republic of Niger | Niamey | French | 1 CFA Franc (CFAFr) = 100 centimes | 9 962 000 |
| Nigeria | Nigeria | Federal Republic of Nigeria | Abuja | English, Hausa | 1 Naira (N, ₦) = 100 kobo | 113 829 000 |
| Norway | Kongeriket Norge | Kingdom of Norway | Oslo | Norwegian | 1 Norwegian Krone (NKr) = 100 øre | 4 439 000 |
| Oman | Saltanat 'Uman | Sultanate of Oman | Masqat (Muscat) | Arabic | 1 Rial Omani (RO) = 1 000 baizas | 2 447 000 |
| Pakistan | Pākistān | Islamic Republic of Pakistan | Islāmābād (Islamabad) | Urdu | 1 Pakistan Rupee (PRs, Rp) = 100 paisa | 138 123 000 |
| Palau | Palau | Republic of Palau | Koror | Palauan, English | 1 US Dollar ($, US$) = 100 cents | 18 500 |
| Panama | Panamá | Republic of Panama | Panamá (Panama City) | Spanish | 1 Balboa (B, Ba) = 100 centésimos | 2 779 000 |
| Papua New Guinea | Papua New Guinea | Papua New Guinea | Port Moresby | English, Tok Pisin, Hiri Motu | 1 Kina (K) = 100 toea | 4 705 00 |
| Paraguay | Paraguay | Republic of Paraguay | Asunción | Spanish | 1 Guaraní (Gs) = 100 céntimos | 5 434 000 |
| Peru | Perú | Republic of Peru | Lima | Spanish, Quechua | 1 New Sol (Pes) = 100 cénts | 26 625 000 |

| English name | Local name | Official name (in English) | Capital (English name in parentheses) | Official language(s) | Currency | Population |
|---|---|---|---|---|---|---|
| Philippines | Pilipinas | Republic of the Philippines | Manila | Filipino, English | 1 Philippine Peso (PHP) = 100 centavos | 79 346 000 |
| Poland | Rzeczpospolita Polska | Republic of Poland | Warszawa (Warsaw) | Polish | 1 Złoty (Zl) = 100 groszy | 38 609 000 |
| Portugal | Portugal | Republic of Portugal | Lisboa (Lisbon) | Portuguese | *1 Escudo (Esc) = 100 centavos | 9 918 000 |
| Puerto Rico | Puerto Rico | Commonwealth of Puerto Rico | San Juan | Spanish, English | 1 US Dollar ($, US$) = 100 cents | 3 888 000 |
| Qatar | Dowlat Qatar | State of Qatar | Ad-Dawhah (Doha) | Arabic | 1 Qatar Riyal (QR) = 100 dirhams | 723 500 |
| Romania | România | Romania | București (Bucharest) | Romanian | 1 Leu (*plural* Lei) = 100 bani | 22 334 000 |
| Russia | Rossiya | The Russian Federation | Moskva (Moscow) | Russian | 1 Rouble (R) = 100 kopeks | 146 394 000 |
| Rwanda | Rwanda | Republic of Rwanda | Kigali | Kinyarwanda, French, English | 1 Rwanda Franc (RF, RWFr) = 100 centimes | 8 155 000 |
| St Kitts and Nevis | St Kitts and Nevis | Federation of St Kitts and Nevis | Basseterre | English | 1 East Caribbean Dollar (EC$) = 100 cents | 42 800 |
| St Lucia | St Lucia | St Lucia | Castries | English | 1 East Caribbean Dollar (EC$) = 100 cents | 154 000 |
| St Vincent and the Grenadines | St Vincent and the Grenadines | St Vincent and the Grenadines | Kingstown | English | 1 East Caribbean Dollar (EC$) = 100 cents | 120 500 |
| Samoa | Samoa | Independent State of Samoa | Apia | Samoan, English | 1 Tala (S$) = 100 sene | 230 000 |
| San Marino | San Marino | Republic of San Marino | San Marino | Italian | 1 San Marino Lira (SML) = 100 centesimi | 25 100 |
| São Tomé and Príncipe | São Tomé e Príncipe | Democratic Republic of São Tomé and Príncipe | São Tomé | Portuguese | 1 Dobra (Db) = 100 centavos | 154 900 |
| Saudi Arabia | Al-'Arabīyah as Sa'ūdīyah | Kingdom of Saudi Arabia | Ar-Riyād (Riyadh) | Arabic | 1 Saudi Arabian Riyal (SR, SRls) = 20 qursh = 100 halala | 21 505 000 |
| Senegal | Sénégal | Republic of Senegal | Dakar | French, Wolof | 1 CFA Franc (CFAFr) = 100 centimes | 10 052 000 |
| Seychelles | Seychelles | Republic of Seychelles | Victoria | French Creole, English, French | 1 Seychelles Rupee (SR) = 100 cents | 79 200 |
| Sierra Leone | Sierra Leone | Republic of Sierra Leone | Freetown | English, Mende, Temnel | 1 Leone (Le) = 100 cents | 5 297 000 |
| Singapore | Singapore | Republic of Singapore | Singapore City | Chinese, English, Malay, Tamil | 1 Singapore Dollar (S$) = 1 Ringgit = 100 cents | 3 532 000 |
| Slovakia | Slovenska Republika | Republic of Slovakia | Bratislava | Slovak | 1 Koruna (Kčs) = 100 halierov | 5 396 000 |
| Slovenia | Republika Slovenija | Slovenian Republic | Ljubljana | Slovene | 1 Tolar (SIT) =100 stotin | 1 971 000 |

| English name | Local name | Official name (in English) | Capital (English name in parentheses) | Official language(s) | Currency | Population |
|---|---|---|---|---|---|---|
| Solomon Islands | Solomon Islands | Solomon Islands | Honiara | English | 1 Solomon Islands Dollar (SI$) = 100 cents | 455 400 |
| Somalia | Somaliya | Somali Democratic Republic | Muqdisho (Mogadishu) | Arabic, Somali | 1 Somali Shilling (SoSh) = 100 cents | 7 141 000 |
| South Africa | South Africa | Republic of South Africa | Pretoria/Cape Town | Afrikaans, English | 1 Rand (R) = 100 cents | 43 426 000 |
| Spain | España | Kingdom of Spain | Madrid | Spanish | *1 Peseta (Pta, Pa) = 100 céntimos | 39 168 000 |
| Sri Lanka | Sri Lanka | Democratic Socialist Republic of Sri Lanka | Colombo | Sinhala, Tamil | 1 Sri Lankan Rupee (SLR, SLRs) = 100 cents | 19 145 000 |
| The Sudan | As-Sūdān | Democratic Republic of the Sudan | Al-Khartūm (Khartoum) | Arabic | 1 Sudanese Dinar (SD) = 10 pounds | 34 476 000 |
| Suriname | Suriname | Republic of Suriname | Paramaribo | Dutch | 1 Suriname Guilder (SGld)/ Florin (f) = 100 cents | 431 200 |
| Swaziland | Umbouso we Swatini | Kingdom of Swaziland | Mbabane | Swazi, English | 1 Lilangeni (*plural* Emalangeni) (Li, E) = 100 cents | 985 300 |
| Sweden | Konungariket Sverige | Kingdom of Sweden | Stockholm | Swedish | 1 Swedish Krona (Skr) = 100 øre | 8 911 000 |
| Switzerland | Schweiz (German) Suisse (French) Svizzera (Italian) | Swiss Confederation | Bern (Berne) | French, German, Italian, Romansch | 1 Swiss Franc (SFr, SwF) = 100 centimes = 100 rappen | 7 275 000 |
| Syria | As-Sūrīyah | Syrian Arab Republic | Dimashq (Damascus) | Arabic | 1 Syrian pound (LS, S$) = 100 piastres | 17 214 000 |
| Taiwan | T'aiwan | Republic of China | T'aipei (Taipei) | Mandarin Chinese | 1 New Taiwan Dollar (NT$) = 100 cents | 22 113 000 |
| Tajikistan | Jumkhurii Tojikistan | Republic of Tajikistan | Dushanbe | Tajik, Uzbek, Russian | 1 Tajik Rouble (TJR) = 100 tanga | 6 103 000 |
| Tanzania | Tanzania | United Republic of Tanzania | Dodoma | (Ki)Swahili, English | 1 Tanzanian Shilling (TSh) = 100 cents | 31 271 000 |
| Thailand | Prathet Thai | Kingdom of Thailand | Bangkok | Thai | 1 Baht (B) = 100 satang | 60 609 000 |
| Togo | Togo | Republic of Togo | Lomé | French | 1 CFA Franc (CFAFr) = 100 centimes | 5 081 000 |
| Tonga | Tonga | Kingdom of Tonga | Nuku'alofa | English, Tongan | 1 Pa'anga/Tongan Dollar (T$) = 100 seniti | 109 100 |

| English name | Local name | Official name (in English) | Capital (English name in parentheses) | Official language(s) | Currency | Population |
|---|---|---|---|---|---|---|
| Trinidad and Tobago | Trinidad and Tobago | Republic of Trinidad and Tobago | Port of Spain | English | 1 Trinidad and Tobago Dollar (TT$) = 100 cents | 1 102 000 |
| Tunisia | Tunisiya | Republic of Tunisia | Tunis | Arabic, French | 1 Tunisian Dinar (TD, D) = 1 000 millimes | 9 514 000 |
| Turkey | Tūrkiye | Republic of Turkey | Ankara | Turkish | 1 Turkish Lira (TL) = 100 kurus | 65 599 000 |
| Turkmenistan | Turkmenostan | Republic of Turkmenistan | Ashkhabad | Turkmen, Russian, Uzbek | 1 Manat (TMM) = 100 tenesi | 4 366 000 |
| Tuvalu | Tuvalu | Tuvalu | Fongafale (on Funafuti) | Tuvaluan, English | 1 Australian Dollar (A$) = 100 cents | 10 600 |
| Uganda | Uganda | Republic of Uganda | Kampala | English, Swahili | 1 Uganda Shilling = 100 cents | 22 805 000 |
| Ukraine | Ukraina | Ukraine | Kiev | Ukrainian | 1 Hryvna = 100 kopiykas | 49 811 000 |
| United Arab Emirates | Ittihād al-Imārāt al-'Arabīyah | United Arab Emirates | Abū Zaby (Abu Dhabi) | Arabic, English | 1 Dirham (DH) = 100 fils | 2 344 000 |
| United Kingdom | United Kingdom | United Kingdom of Great Britain and Northern Ireland | London | English | 1 Pound Sterling (£) = 100 pence | 59 500 900 |
| United States of America | United States of America | United States of America | Washington, DC | English | 1 US Dollar ($, US$) = 100 cents | 272 640 000 |
| Uruguay | Uruguay | Oriental Republic of Uruguay | Montevideo | Spanish | 1 New Uruguayan Peso (NUr$, UrugN$) = 100 centésimos | 3 309 000 |
| Uzbekistan | Uzbekistan | Republic of Uzbekistan | Tashkent | Uzbek | 1 Sum = 100 tiyin | 24 102 000 |
| Vanuatu | Vanuatu | Republic of Vanuatu | Port Vila | Bislama, English, French | 1 Vatu (V, VT) = 100 centimes | 189 000 |
| Vatican City | Citta' del Vaticano | Vatican City State | Vatican City | Italian | 1 Italian Lira (L,Lit) = 100 centesimi | 870 |
| Venezuela | Venezuela | Republic of Venezuela | Caracas | Spanish | 1 Bolívar (Bs) = 100 centesimi | 23 203 000 |
| Vietnam | Viêt-nam | Socialist Republic of Vietnam | Ha-noi (Hanoi) | Vietnamese | 1 Dông (D) = 10 hào = 100 xu | 77 311 000 |
| Western Samoa ► Samoa | | | | | | |
| Yemen | Al-Yamaniya | Republic of Yemen | Sana'a | Arabic | 1 Yemeni Riyal (YR, YRI) = 100 fils | 16 942 000 |
| Yugoslavia | Jugoslavija | Federal Republic of Yugoslavia | Beograd (Belgrade) | Serbo-Croat (Serbian) | 1 New Dinar (D, Din) = 100 paras | 11 206 900 |
| Zaire ► Congo, Democratic Republic of | | | | | | |
| Zambia | Zambia | Republic of Zambia | Lusaka | English | 1 Kwacha (K) = 100 ngwee | 9 664 000 |
| Zimbabwe | Zimbabwe | Republic of Zimbabwe | Harare | English | 1 Zimbabwe Dollar (Z$) = 100 cents | 11 163 000 |

## World population estimates

| Date (AD) | Millions | Date (AD) | Millions | Date (AD) | Millions |
|---|---|---|---|---|---|
| 1 | 300 | 1900 | 1 650 | 1995 | 5 716 |
| 1000 | 310 | 1950 | 1 520 | 2000 | 6 160 |
| 1250 | 400 | 1960 | 3 050 | 2015 | 7 470 |
| 1500 | 500 | 1970 | 3 700 | 2025 | 8 290 |
| 1750 | 790 | 1980 | 4 450 | 2050 | 9 830 |
| 1800 | 980 | 1985 | 4 845 | | |
| 1850 | 1 260 | 1990 | 5 246 | | |

The above are based on United Nations estimates and predictions published in 1995. In contrast to the predictions in the first edition of this book (e.g. 11 000 000 000 world population by 2050), the totals are down, mainly due to government-sponsored birth-control schemes in China. By that year, China is expected to be overtaken by India as the world's most-populous nation (see below).

## Population of the six most populous nations [1]

| | 1950 | | 2050 | |
|---|---|---|---|---|
| China | 1st | 555m | 2nd | 1 606m |
| India | 2nd | 358m | 1st | 1 640m |
| USA | 3rd | 152m | 4th | 349m |
| USSR | 4th | 103m | — | — |
| Japan | 5th | 84m | 17th | 110m |
| Indonesia | 6th | 80m | 6th | 319m |
| Pakistan | 13th | 40m | 3rd | 381m |

[1] compared for 2050 against 1950 in medium-variant predictions.

## Counties of England

| | Abbreviation[1] | Area sq km | Area sq mi | Population[2] | Persons per sq km |
|---|---|---|---|---|---|
| *Metropolitan counties* | | | | | |
| Greater Manchester | none | 1 286 | 497 | 2 577 000 | 2 003 |
| Merseyside | none | 655 | 253 | 1 403 600 | 2 143 |
| South Yorkshire | S Yorks | 1 559 | 602 | 1 302 400 | 835 |
| Tyne and Wear | none | 540 | 208 | 1 108 500 | 2 053 |
| West Midlands | W Midlands | 899 | 347 | 2 626 500 | 2 922 |
| West Yorkshire | W Yorks | 2 034 | 785 | 2 115 400 | 1 040 |
| *Non-metropolitan counties* | | | | | |
| Bedfordshire | Beds | 1 192 | 460 | 378 900 | 318 |
| Buckinghamshire | Bucks | 1 568 | 605 | 482 600 | 308 |
| Cambridgeshire | Cambs | 3 056 | 1 180 | 568 400 | 186 |
| Cheshire | Ches | 2 081 | 803 | 670 700 | 322 |
| Cornwall and Isles of Scilly | none | 3 559 | 1 374 | 494 700 | 139 |
| Cumbria | [Cumb] | 6 824 | 2 635 | 491 800 | 72 |
| Derbyshire | Derby | 2 551 | 985 | 737 700 | 289 |
| Devon | [Dev] | 6 562 | 2 534 | 697 700 | 106 |
| Dorset | [Dors] | 2 542 | 981 | 389 200 | 153 |
| Durham | Dur | 2 232 | 862 | 506 200 | 227 |
| East Sussex | [E Suss] | 1 713 | 661 | 496 200 | 290 |
| Essex | [Ess] | 3 469 | 1 339 | 1 306 200 | 377 |
| Gloucestershire | Glos | 2 653 | 1 024 | 561 900 | 212 |
| Hampshire | Hants | 3 689 | 1 424 | 1 248 800 | 339 |
| Hertfordshire | Herts | 1 639 | 633 | 1 043 000 | 636 |
| Kent | none | 3 543 | 1 368 | 1 344 000 | 379 |
| Lancashire | Lancs | 2 897 | 1 119 | 1 137 100 | 393 |

| | Abbreviation[1] | Area sq km | sq mi | Population[2] | Persons per sq km |
|---|---|---|---|---|---|
| Leicestershire | Leics | 2 084 | 805 | 606 800 | 291 |
| Lincolnshire | Lincs | 5 921 | 2 286 | 628 600 | 106 |
| London[3] | none | 1 579 | 610 | 7 285 000 | 4 614 |
| Norfolk | [Norf] | 5 372 | 2 074 | 796 500 | 148 |
| Northamptonshire | Northants | 2 367 | 914 | 621 200 | 262 |
| Northumberland | Northumb | 5 026 | 1 941 | 310 200 | 61 |
| North Yorkshire | N Yorks | 8 038 | 3 103 | 569 800 | 71 |
| Nottinghamshire | Notts | 2 085 | 805 | 748 400 | 359 |
| Oxfordshire | Oxon | 2 606 | 1 006 | 626 200 | 240 |
| Shropshire | [Shrops] | 3 197 | 1 234 | 282 500 | 88 |
| Somerset | Som | 3 452 | 1 333 | 493 100 | 143 |
| Staffordshire | Staffs | 2 623 | 1 013 | 809 800 | 309 |
| Suffolk | [Suff] | 3 798 | 1 466 | 674 600 | 178 |
| Surrey | [Sur] | 1 677 | 647 | 1 078 100 | 643 |
| Warwickshire | War | 1 979 | 764 | 507 900 | 257 |
| West Sussex | [W Suss] | 1 988 | 768 | 760 700 | 383 |
| Wiltshire | Wilts | 3 246 | 1 253 | 429 100 | 132 |
| Worcestershire | Worcs | 1 761 | 680 | 539 900 | 307 |
| *Unitary authorities* | | | | | |
| Bath and North East Somerset | none | 351 | 136 | 168 600 | 480 |
| Blackburn with Darwen | none | 137 | 53 | 138 400 | 1 010 |
| Blackpool | none | 35 | 14 | 150 000 | 4 286 |
| Bournemouth | none | 46 | 18 | 162 500 | 3 532 |
| Bracknell Forest | none | 109 | 42 | 111 500 | 1 023 |
| Brighton and Hove | none | 82 | 32 | 258 100 | 3148 |
| Bristol, City of | none | 110 | 42 | 405 200 | 3 684 |
| Darlington | none | 197 | 76 | 100 500 | 510 |
| Derby | none | 78 | 30 | 236 400 | 3 031 |
| East Riding of Yorkshire | none | 2 415 | 932 | 315 700 | 131 |
| Halton | none | 74 | 29 | 121 100 | 1 636 |
| Hartlepool | none | 94 | 36 | 92 100 | 980 |
| Herefordshire, County of | [Herefs] | 2 162 | 835 | 168 300 | 78 |
| Isle of Wight | IOW | 380 | 147 | 128 200 | 337 |
| Kingston upon Hull, City of | none | 71 | 27 | 257 900 | 3 632 |
| Leicester | none | 73 | 28 | 290 900 | 3 985 |
| Luton | none | 43 | 17 | 183 300 | 4 263 |
| Medway | none | 192 | 74 | 243 200 | 1 267 |
| Middlesbrough | none | 54 | 21 | 144 300 | 2 672 |
| Milton Keynes | none | 309 | 119 | 206 900 | 670 |
| North East Lincolnshire | none | 192 | 74 | 156 000 | 813 |
| North Lincolnshire | none | 833 | 322 | 152 000 | 182 |
| North Somerset | N Som | 373 | 144 | 189 800 | 509 |
| Nottingham | none | 75 | 29 | 284 300 | 3 791 |
| Peterborough | none | 344 | 133 | 156 500 | 455 |
| Plymouth | none | 80 | 31 | 253 200 | 3 165 |
| Poole | none | 65 | 25 | 140 800 | 2 166 |
| Portsmouth | none | 40 | 15 | 188 800 | 4 720 |
| Reading | none | 40 | 15 | 147 300 | 3 683 |
| Redcar and Cleveland | none | 245 | 95 | 137 100 | 560 |
| Rutland | none | 394 | 152 | 37 000 | 94 |
| Slough | none | 27 | 10 | 111 100 | 4 115 |
| Southampton | none | 50 | 19 | 215 300 | 4 306 |
| South Gloucestershire | S Glos | 497 | 192 | 244 500 | 492 |
| Southend-on-Sea | none | 42 | 16 | 176 600 | 4 205 |
| Stockton-on-Tees | none | 204 | 79 | 182 500 | 895 |
| Stoke-on-Trent | none | 93 | 36 | 250 800 | 2 697 |
| Swindon | none | 230 | 89 | 181 200 | 788 |
| Telford and Wrekin | none | 290 | 112 | 149 900 | 517 |
| Thurrock | none | 164 | 63 | 134 800 | 822 |

| | Abbreviation[1] | Area sq km | sq mi | Population[2] | Persons per sq km |
|---|---|---|---|---|---|
| Torbay | none | 63 | 24 | 124 100 | 1 970 |
| Warrington | none | 176 | 68 | 190 700 | 1 084 |
| West Berkshire | W Berks | 704 | 272 | 144 600 | 205 |
| Windsor and Maidenhead | none | 198 | 76 | 141 200 | 713 |
| Wokingham | none | 179 | 69 | 144 800 | 809 |
| York | none | 271 | 105 | 177 800 | 656 |
| TOTAL | | 130 423 | 50 354 | 49 752 900 | 381 |

[1] Square brackets denote that the abbreviation is not generally regarded as established. Those without square brackets are generally accepted abbreviations.

[2] Mid-1999 estimated figures.

[3] London is divided into Inner London and Outer London, and comprises 32 boroughs and the City of London.

Note: Figures do not add exactly because of rounding. Total area includes inland, but not tidal, water.



## Council areas of Scotland

| Unitary authority[1] | Admin centre | Area sq km | sq mi | Population[2] | Persons per sq km |
|---|---|---|---|---|---|
| Aberdeen City | Aberdeen | 186 | 72 | 212 650 | 1 143 |
| Aberdeenshire | Aberdeen | 6 318 | 2 439 | 227 440 | 36 |
| Angus | Forfar | 2 181 | 842 | 109 840 | 50 |
| Argyll and Bute | Lochgilphead | 6 930 | 2 675 | 87 780 | 13 |
| Clackmannanshire | Alloa | 157 | 61 | 48 530 | 309 |
| Dumfries and Galloway | Dumfries | 6 439 | 2 485 | 146 800 | 23 |
| Dundee City | Dundee | 67 | 26 | 144 430 | 2 222 |
| East Ayrshire | Kilmarnock | 1 252 | 483 | 120 940 | 97 |
| East Dunbartonshire | Kirkintilloch | 172 | 66 | 110 690 | 644 |
| East Lothian | Haddington | 678 | 262 | 90 430 | 133 |
| East Renfrewshire | Giffnock | 173 | 67 | 89 280 | 516 |
| Edinburgh, City of | Edinburgh | 262 | 101 | 451 710 | 1 724 |
| Falkirk | Falkirk | 299 | 115 | 144 370 | 483 |
| Fife | Glenrothes | 1 323 | 511 | 349 200 | 264 |
| Glasgow City | Glasgow | 175 | 68 | 611 440 | 3 494 |
| Highland | Inverness | 25 784 | 9 953 | 208 600 | 8 |
| Inverclyde | Greenock | 182 | 70 | 85 190 | 526 |
| Midlothian | Dalkeith | 356 | 137 | 81 680 | 229 |
| Moray | Elgin | 2 238 | 864 | 85 210 | 38 |
| North Ayrshire | Irvine | 884 | 341 | 139 410 | 158 |
| North Lanarkshire | Motherwell | 474 | 183 | 327 940 | 692 |
| Orkney Islands | Kirkwall | 992 | 383 | 19 600 | 20 |
| Perth and Kinross | Perth | 5 311 | 2 050 | 134 030 | 25 |
| Renfrewshire | Paisley | 261 | 101 | 177 230 | 679 |
| Scottish Borders | Newton St Boswells | 4 734 | 1 827 | 106 400 | 22 |
| Shetland Islands | Lerwick | 1 438 | 555 | 22 740 | 16 |
| South Ayrshire | Ayr | 1 202 | 464 | 114 250 | 95 |
| South Lanarkshire | Hamilton | 1 771 | 684 | 307 520 | 174 |
| Stirling | Stirling | 2 196 | 848 | 84 700 | 39 |
| West Dunbartonshire | Dumbarton | 162 | 63 | 94 980 | 586 |
| Western Isles (Eilean Siar, Comhairle nan) | Stornoway | 3 134 | 1 210 | 27 560 | 9 |
| West Lothian | Livingston | 425 | 164 | 154 680 | 364 |
| TOTAL[3] | | 78 789 | 30 420 | 5 119 200 | 66 |

[1] The counties of Scotland were replaced by 9 regional and 53 district councils in 1975; these in turn became 29 Unitary Authorities or Council Areas on 1 April 1996, the 3 island councils remaining as before.

[2] 30 June 1999 estimated figures.

[3] Figures may not add exactly because of rounding. Total area includes inland, but not tidal, water.

SOCIAL STRUCTURE

## Council areas of Wales

| Unitary authority[1] | Admin centre | Area sq km | sq mi | Population[2] | Persons per sq km |
|---|---|---|---|---|---|
| Anglesey, Isle of | Llangefni | 719 | 277 | 65 400 | 91 |
| Blaenau Gwent | Ebbw Vale | 109 | 42 | 71 700 | 658 |
| Bridgend | Bridgend | 246 | 95 | 131 600 | 535 |
| Caerphilly | Hengoed | 279 | 108 | 170 100 | 610 |
| Cardiff | Cardiff | 139 | 54 | 324 400 | 2 334 |
| Carmarthenshire | Carmarthen | 2 398 | 926 | 168 900 | 70 |
| Ceredigion | Aberaeron | 1797 | 694 | 71 700 | 40 |
| Conwy | Conwy | 1 130 | 436 | 112 100 | 99 |
| Denbighshire | Ruthin | 844 | 326 | 91 000 | 108 |
| Flintshire | Mold | 437 | 169 | 147 400 | 337 |
| Gwynedd | Caernarfon | 2 548 | 984 | 116 400 | 46 |
| Merthyr Tydfil | Merthyr Tydfil | 111 | 43 | 56 200 | 506 |
| Monmouthshire | Cwmbran | 851 | 328 | 86 600 | 102 |
| Neath Port Talbot | Port Talbot | 442 | 171 | 138 200 | 313 |
| Newport | Newport | 191 | 74 | 138 300 | 724 |
| Pembrokeshire | Haverfordwest | 1 590 | 614 | 113 700 | 72 |
| Powys | Llandrindod Wells | 5 204 | 2 009 | 126 300 | 24 |
| Rhondda, Cynon, Taff | Clydach Vale | 424 | 164 | 240 500 | 567 |
| Swansea | Swansea | 378 | 146 | 229 800 | 608 |
| Torfaen | Pontypool | 126 | 49 | 89 800 | 713 |
| Vale of Glamorgan | Barry | 337 | 130 | 121 300 | 360 |
| Wrexham | Wrexham | 499 | 193 | 125 500 | 252 |
| TOTAL | | 20 799 | 8 032 | 2 936 900 | 141 |

[1] The eight counties of Wales established in 1974 were replaced by 22 Unitary Authorities or Council Areas on 1 April 1996.

[2] Mid-1999 estimated figures.

Population data source: ONS, © Crown copyright 2000.

## UK islands

| Name | Admin centre | Area sq km | sq mi | Population (1999 est) |
|---|---|---|---|---|
| Isle of Man | Douglas | 572 | 221 | 73 110 |
| Jersey | St Helier | 116 | 45 | 88 910 |
| Guernsey | St Peter Port | 63 | 24 | 64 020 |
| Alderney (dependency of Guernsey) | St Anne | 8 | 3 | 2 147 |
| Sark (dependency of Guernsey) | — | 4 | 2 | 570 |

## Districts of Northern Ireland

| District | Area sq km | Area sq mi | Population (1999) | Admin centre | Formerly part of |
|---|---|---|---|---|---|
| Antrim | 563 | 217 | 50 700 | Antrim | Antrim |
| Ards | 369 | 142 | 71 400 | Newtownards | Down |
| Armagh | 672 | 259 | 54 000 | Armagh | Armagh |
| Ballymena | 638 | 246 | 59 200 | Ballymena | Antrim |
| Ballymoney | 419 | 162 | 25 900 | Ballymoney | Antrim |
| Banbridge | 444 | 171 | 39 900 | Banbridge | Down |
| Belfast | 140 | 54 | 284 400 | — | Antrim |
| Carrickfergus | 87 | 34 | 37 900 | Carrickfergus | Antrim |
| Castlereagh | 85 | 33 | 66 800 | Belfast | Down, Antrim |
| Coleraine | 485 | 187 | 55 700 | Coleraine | Antrim |
| Cookstown | 623 | 240 | 31 700 | Cookstown | Tyrone |
| Craigavon | 382 | 147 | 79 700 | Craigavon | Armagh, Down, Antrim |
| Derry | 382 | 147 | 106 600 | — | Londonderry |
| Down | 646 | 249 | 63 800 | Downpatrick | Down |
| Dungannon | 779 | 301 | 48 200 | Dungannon | Tyrone, Armagh |
| Fermanagh | 1 876 | 715 | 57 500 | Enniskillen | Fermanagh |
| Larne | 338 | 131 | 30 900 | Larne | Antrim |
| Limavady | 587 | 227 | 31 900 | Limavady | Londonderry |
| Lisburn | 444 | 171 | 111 200 | Lisburn | Antrim, Down |
| Magherafelt | 573 | 221 | 39 000 | Magherafelt | Londonderry |
| Moyle | 495 | 191 | 15 400 | Ballycastle | Antrim |
| Newry and Mourne | 895 | 346 | 87 700 | Newry | Down, Armagh |
| Newtownabbey | 152 | 59 | 81 300 | Newtownabbey | Antrim |
| North Down | 73 | 28 | 75 700 | Bangor | Down |
| Omagh | 1 129 | 436 | 47 800 | Omagh | Tyrone |
| Strabane | 870 | 336 | 37 600 | Strabane | Tyrone |

## Europe — administrative divisions

### ❑ Albania

| Province | Area sq km | Area sq mi | Population (1993 est) |
|---|---|---|---|
| Berat | 939 | 363 | 136 939 |
| Bulqizë | 469 | 181 | 43 363 |
| Delvinë | 348 | 134 | 29 926 |
| Devoll | 429 | 166 | 37 744 |
| Dibrë | 1 088 | 420 | 91 916 |
| Durrës | 433 | 167 | 162 846 |
| Elbasan | 1 372 | 530 | 215 240 |
| Fier | 785 | 303 | 208 646 |
| Gjirokastër | 1 752 | 439 | 60 547 |
| Gramsh | 695 | 268 | 42 087 |
| Has | 393 | 152 | 21 271 |
| Kavajë | 414 | 160 | 85 120 |
| Kolonjë | 805 | 311 | 25 089 |
| Korçë | 1 752 | 676 | 171 205 |
| Krujë | 333 | 129 | 59 997 |
| Kucovë | 84 | 32 | 40 035 |
| Kukës | 938 | 362 | 78 061 |
| Kurbin | 273 | 105 | 50 712 |
| Lezhë | 479 | 185 | 65 075 |
| Librazhd | 1 023 | 395 | 75 300 |
| Lushnjë | 712 | 275 | 136 865 |

| Province | Area sq km | Area sq mi | Population (1993 est) |
|---|---|---|---|
| Malesia e Madhe | 555 | 214 | 43924 |
| Mallakastër | 393 | 152 | 36287 |
| Mat | 1029 | 397 | 75436 |
| Mirditë | 867 | 335 | 49900 |
| Peqin | 109 | 42 | 29831 |
| Permet | 930 | 359 | 36979 |
| Pogradec | 725 | 280 | 72203 |
| Pukë | 1034 | 399 | 47621 |
| Sarandë | 749 | 289 | 53730 |
| Shkodër | 1973 | 762 | 195424 |
| Skrapar | 775 | 299 | 44339 |
| Tepelenë | 817 | 315 | 42365 |
| Tiranë | 1238 | 478 | 384010 |
| Tropojë | 1043 | 403 | 44761 |
| Vlorë | 1609 | 621 | 171131 |

❑ **Austria**

| State | Area sq km | Area sq mi | Population (1998 est) | Capital |
|---|---|---|---|---|
| Burgenland | 3966 | 1531 | 277600 | Eisenstadt |
| Carinthia (Kärnten) | 9533 | 3681 | 564100 | Klagenfurt |
| Lower Austria (Niederösterreich) | 19172 | 7402 | 1536400 | Sankt Pölten |
| Salzburg | 7154 | 2762 | 514000 | Salzburg |
| Styria (Steiermark) | 16387 | 6327 | 1203600 | Graz |
| Tyrol (Tirol) | 12647 | 4883 | 655400 | Innsbruck |
| Upper Austria (Oberösterreich) | 11980 | 4626 | 1375300 | Linz |
| Vienna (Wien) | 415 | 160 | 1599500 | — |
| Vorarlberg | 2601 | 1004 | 346900 | Bregenz |

❑ **Belgium**

| Province | Area sq km | Area sq mi | Population (1999 est) | Capital |
|---|---|---|---|---|
| Antwerp | 2867 | 1107 | 1637857 | Antwerp |
| E Flanders | 2982 | 1151 | 1357576 | Ghent |
| Flemish Brabant | 2106 | 813 | 1007882 | Leuven |
| Hainaut | 3787 | 1462 | 1282783 | Mons |
| Liège | 3862 | 1491 | 1016762 | Liège |
| Limburg | 2422 | 935 | 783927 | Hasselt |
| Luxembourg | 4441 | 1715 | 243790 | Arlon |
| Namur | 3665 | 1415 | 438864 | Namur |
| Walloon Brabant | 1091 | 421 | 344508 | Wavre |
| W Flanders | 3314 | 1210 | 1125140 | Bruges |

❑ **Bulgaria**

| Province | Area sq km | Area sq mi | Population (1999 est) | Capital |
|---|---|---|---|---|
| Burgas | 14724 | 5683 | 847000 | Burgas |
| Khaskovo | 13824 | 5336 | 889000 | Khashkovo |
| Lovech | 15150 | 5848 | 990000 | Lovech |
| Montana | 10606 | 4098 | 616000 | Montana (formerly Mikhailovgrad) |
| Plovdiv | 13585 | 5244 | 1214000 | Plovdiv |
| Ruse | 10842 | 4185 | 760000 | Ruse |
| Sofiya | 19021 | 7342 | 967000 | Sofia (Sofiya) |
| Varna | 11928 | 4604 | 901000 | Varna |

### ❑ Cyprus

| District | Area sq km | sq mi | Population (1998 est) | Capital |
|---|---|---|---|---|
| Famagusta | 1979 | 764 | 34300 | Famagusta |
| Larnaca | 1126 | 435 | 110900 | Larnaca |
| Limassol | 1393 | 538 | 191500 | Limassol |
| Nicosia | 2717 | 1049 | 269200 | Nicosia |
| Paphos | 1395 | 539 | 57400 | Paphos |

### ❑ Czech Republic

| Region | Area sq km | sq mi | Population (1996 est) | Capital |
|---|---|---|---|---|
| C Bohemia (Středocesky) | 11013 | 4251 | 1106738 | Prague |
| E Bohemia (Východočeský) | 11240 | 4339 | 1235641 | Hradec Králové |
| N Bohemia (Severočeský) | 7799 | 3010 | 1178208 | Ústí nad Labem |
| N Moravia (Severomoravský) | 11067 | 4273 | 1972336 | Ostrava |
| Prague (city) | 496 | 192 | 1209855 | — |
| S Bohemia (Jihočeský) | 11345 | 4380 | 700831 | České Budějovice |
| S Moravia (Jihomoravský) | 15028 | 5802 | 2057239 | Brno |
| W Bohemia (Západočeský) | 10875 | 4199 | 860469 | Plzeň |

### ❑ Denmark

| County | Area sq km | sq mi | Population (1998 est) | Capital |
|---|---|---|---|---|
| Aarhus (Aerhus) | 4561 | 1761 | 631586 | Acerhus |
| Bornholm | 588 | 227 | 44786 | Rønne |
| Copenhagen (København) | 526 | 203 | 610261 | — |
| Frederiksborg | 1347 | 520 | 359839 | Hillerød |
| Fyn | 3486 | 1346 | 471837 | Odense |
| N Jutland (Nordjylland) | 6173 | 2383 | 493114 | Aalborg (Aelborg) |
| Ribe | 3131 | 1209 | 223818 | Ribe |
| Ringkøbing | 4853 | 1874 | 271978 | Ringkøbing |
| Roskilde | 891 | 344 | 228202 | Roskilde |
| S Jutland (Sønderjylland) | 3938 | 1520 | 253836 | Aebeurace |
| Storstrøm | 3398 | 1312 | 258295 | Nykøbing Falster |
| Vejle | 2997 | 1157 | 344507 | Vejle |
| Viborg | 4122 | 1592 | 233143 | Viborg |
| W Zealand (Vestsjaelland) | 2984 | 1152 | 258295 | Sorø |

### ❑ Finland

| Province | Area sq km | sq mi | Population (1997 est) | Capital |
|---|---|---|---|---|
| Åland | 1527 | 590 | 25392 | Mariehamn |
| Eastern Finland | 48727 | 18813 | 603724 | Mikkeli |
| Lapland | 93057 | 35929 | 199051 | Rovaniemi |
| Oulu | 56868 | 21957 | 452942 | Oulu |
| Southern Finland | 30229 | 11671 | 2037147 | Hämeenlinna |
| Western Finland | 74186 | 28643 | 1829093 | Turku |

### France

| Region | Area sq km | Area sq mi | Population (1999 est) | Admin centre |
|---|---|---|---|---|
| Alsace | 8 280 | 3 197 | 1 734 100 | Strasbourg |
| Aquitaine | 41 309 | 15 950 | 2 908 400 | Bordeaux |
| Auvergne | 26 013 | 10 044 | 1 308 900 | Clermont-Ferrand |
| Brittany (Bretagne) | 27 209 | 10 505 | 2 906 200 | Rennes |
| Burgundy (Bourgogne) | 31 582 | 12 194 | 1 610 100 | Dijon |
| Centre | 39 151 | 15 116 | 2 440 300 | Orléans |
| Champagne-Ardenne | 25 606 | 9 887 | 1 342 400 | Reims |
| Corsica (Corse) | 8 680 | 3 351 | 260 200 | Ajaccio |
| Franche-Comté | 16 202 | 6 256 | 1 117 100 | Besançon |
| Île de France | 12 011 | 4 637 | 10 952 000 | Paris |
| Languedoc-Roussillon | 27 376 | 10 570 | 2 295 600 | Montpellier |
| Limousin | 16 942 | 6 541 | 710 900 | Limoges |
| Lorraine | 23 547 | 9 092 | 2 310 400 | Nancy |
| Midi-Pyrénées | 45 349 | 17 509 | 2 551 700 | Toulouse |
| Nord-Pas-de-Calais | 12 413 | 479 | 3 996 900 | Lille |
| Normandy, Lower (Basse-Normandie) | 17 589 | 6 791 | 1 422 200 | Caen |
| Normandy, Upper (Haute-Normandie) | 12 318 | 4 756 | 1 780 200 | Rouen |
| Pays de la Loire | 32 082 | 1 237 | 3 222 100 | Nantes |
| Picardy (Picardie) | 19 399 | 7 490 | 1 857 800 | Amiens |
| Poitou-Charentes | 25 809 | 9 965 | 1 640 100 | Poitiers |
| Provence Alpes-Côte d'Azur | 31 400 | 12 124 | 4 506 200 | Marseilles |
| Rhône-Alpes | 43 698 | 16 872 | 5 645 400 | Lyons |

### Germany

| District | Area sq km | Area sq mi | Population (1995 est) | Capital |
|---|---|---|---|---|
| Baden-Württemberg | 35 751 | 13 804 | 10 272 000 | Stuttgart |
| Bayern | 70 546 | 27 239 | 11 922 000 | Munich |
| Berlin | 889 | 340 | 3 472 000 | Berlin |
| Brandenburg | 29 481 | 11 379 | 2 537 000 | Potsdam |
| Bremen | 404 | 156 | 680 000 | Bremen |
| Hamburg | 755 | 292 | 1 706 000 | Hamburg |
| Hessen | 21 114 | 8 152 | 5 981 000 | Wiesbaden |
| Mecklenburg-Vorpommern | 23 170 | 8 944 | 1 832 000 | Schwerin |
| Niedersachsen | 47 609 | 18 271 | 7 715 000 | Hannover |
| Nordrhein-Westfalen | 34 070 | 13 155 | 17 816 000 | Düsseldorf |
| Rheinland-Pfalz | 19 849 | 7 664 | 3 952 000 | Mainz |
| Saarland | 2 570 | 992 | 1 084 000 | Saarbrücken |
| Sachsen | 18 412 | 7 080 | 4 584 000 | Dresden |
| Sachsen-Anhalt | 20 445 | 7 894 | 2 759 000 | Magdeburg |
| Schleswig-Holstein | 15 739 | 6 077 | 2 708 000 | Kiel |
| Thüringen | 16 171 | 6 242 | 2 518 000 | Erfurt |

### Greece

| Region | Area sq km | Area sq mi | Population (1991) | Admin centre |
|---|---|---|---|---|
| Attica (Attikí) | 3 808 | 1 470 | 3 523 407 | Athens |
| C Greece (Stereá Ellás) | 15 549 | 6 004 | 582 280 | Lamia |
| C Macedonia (Kedrikí Makedhonía) | 19 147 | 7 393 | 1 710 513 | Thessaloniki |
| Crete (Kríti) | 8 336 | 3 218 | 540 054 | Heraklion |

| County | Area sq km | Area sq mi | Population (1991) | Admin centre |
|---|---|---|---|---|
| E Macedonia and Thrace (Anatolikí Makedhonía kaí Thráki) | 14 157 | 5 466 | 570 496 | Comotini |
| Epirus (Ípiros) | 9 203 | 3 553 | 339 728 | Ioannina |
| Ionian Is (Iónioi Nísoi) | 2 307 | 891 | 193 734 | Corfu |
| N Aegean (Vóreion Aiyaíon) | 3 836 | 1 481 | 199 231 | Mytilene |
| Peleponnese (Pelopónnisos) | 15 490 | 5 981 | 607 428 | Tripolis |
| S Aegean (Nótion Aiyaíon) | 5 286 | 2 041 | 257 481 | Hermoupolis |
| Thessaly (Thessalía) | 14 037 | 5 420 | 734 846 | Larissa |
| W Greece (Dhytikí Ellás) | 11 350 | 4 382 | 707 687 | Patras |
| W Macedonia (Dhytikí Makedhonía) | 9 451 | 3 649 | 293 015 | Kozani |

## ❑ Greenland

| County/commune | Area sq km | Area sq mi | Population (2000 est) |
|---|---|---|---|
| Avanersuaq (Nordgrønland) (county) | 106 700 | 41 200 | — |
| Qaanaaq (Thule) | | | 864 |
| Kitaa (Vestgrønland) (county) | 119 100 | 46 000 | — |
| Aasiaat (Egedesminde) | | | 3 446 |
| Ilulissat (Jakobshavn) | | | 4 663 |
| Ivittuut (Ivigtut) | | | 164 |
| Kangaatsiaq (Kangaetsiaq) | | | 1 495 |
| Maniitsoq (Sukkertoppen) | | | 3 725 |
| Nanortalik | | | 2 555 |
| Narsaq (Narssaq) | | | 2 082 |
| Nuuk (Godthaeb) | | | 13 838 |
| Paamiut (Frederikshaeb) | | | 2 085 |
| Qaqortoq (Julianehaeb) | | | 3 416 |
| Qasigiannguit (Christianshaeb) | | | 1 516 |
| Qeqertarsuaq (Godhavn) | | | 1 050 |
| Sisimiut (Holsteinsborg) | | | 5 371 |
| Upernavik | | | 2 902 |
| Uummannaq (Umanaq) | | | 2 761 |
| Tunu (Owstgrønland) (county) | 115 900 | 44 700 | — |
| Ittoqqortoormiit (Scoresbysund) | | | 551 |
| Tasiilaq (Angmagssalik) | | | 2 991 |

## ❑ Hungary

| County | Area sq km | Area sq mi | Population (1995 est) | Capital |
|---|---|---|---|---|
| Baranya | 4 487 | 1 732 | 415 000 | Pécs |
| Bács-Kiskun | 8 362 | 3 229 | 541 000 | Kecskemét |
| Békés | 5 632 | 2 175 | 405 000 | Bekéscsaba |
| Borsod-Abaúj-Zemplén | 7 247 | 2 798 | 750 000 | Miskolc |
| Budapest (capital) [1] | 525 | 203 | 4 487 000 | — |
| Csongrád | 4 263 | 1 646 | 429 000 | Szeged |
| Fejér | 4 373 | 1 688 | 426 000 | Székesfehérvár |
| Györ-Moson-Sopron | 4 062 | 1 568 | 426 000 | Györ |
| Hajdú-Bihar | 6 211 | 2 398 | 550 000 | Debrecen |
| Heves | 3 637 | 1 404 | 330 000 | Eger |

| County | Area sq km | Area sq mi | Population (1995) | Capital |
|---|---|---|---|---|
| Jász-Nagykun-Szolnok | 5 607 | 2 165 | 423 000 | Szolnok |
| Komárom-Esztergom | 2 251 | 869 | 313 000 | Tatabánya |
| Nógrád | 2 544 | 982 | 224 000 | Salgótarján |
| Pest | 6 394 | 2 469 | 973 000 | Budapest |
| Somogy | 6 036 | 2 331 | 338 000 | Kapsovár |
| Szabolcs-Szatmár-Bereg | 5 938 | 2 293 | 573 000 | Nyíregyháza |
| Tolna | 3 704 | 1 430 | 250 000 | Szekszárd |
| Vas | 3 337 | 1 288 | 273 000 | Szombathely |
| Vezprém | 4 639 | 1 791 | 379 000 | Veszprém |
| Zala | 3 784 | 1 461 | 302 000 | Zalaegerszeg |

[1] Budapest has county status.

## ❑ Iceland

| Region | Area sq km | Area sq mi | Population (1991 est) | Admin centre |
|---|---|---|---|---|
| Austurland | 21 991 | 8 491 | 11 189 | Egilsstadhir |
| Höfudhborgarsvaedhi | 1 982[1] | 765 | 172 257 | Reykjavik |
| Nordhurland eystra | 22 368 | 8 636 | 27 293 | Akureyri |
| Nordhurland vestra | 13 093 | 5 055 | 10 331 | Saudhárkrókur |
| Sudhurland | 25 214 | 9 735 | 16 247 | Selfoss |
| Sudhurnes | —[1] | —[1] | 15 318 | Keflavik |
| Vestfirdhir | 9 470 | 3 657 | 7 123 | Ísafjördhur |
| Vesturland | 8 701 | 3 360 | 14 359 | Borgarnes |

[1] Höfudhborgarsvaedhi includes Sudhurnes.

## ❑ Ireland

| County | Area sq km | Area sq mi | Population (1996 est) | Admin centre |
|---|---|---|---|---|
| Carlow | 896 | 346 | 41 616 | Carlow |
| Cavan | 1 891 | 730 | 52 944 | Cavan |
| Clare | 3 188 | 1 231 | 94 006 | Ennis |
| Cork | 7 459 | 2 880 | 420 510 | Cork |
| Donegal | 4 830 | 1 865 | 129 994 | Lifford |
| Dublin | 922 | 356 | 1 058 264 | Dublin |
| Galway | 5 939 | 2 293 | 188 854 | Galway |
| Kerry | 4 701 | 1 815 | 126 130 | Tralee |
| Kildare | 1 694 | 654 | 134 992 | Naas |
| Kilkenny | 2 062 | 796 | 75 336 | Kilkenny |
| Laoighis (Leix) | 1 720 | 664 | 52 945 | Portlaoise |
| Leitrim | 1 526 | 589 | 25 057 | Carrick |
| Limerick | 2 686 | 1 037 | 165 042 | Limerick |
| Longford | 1 044 | 403 | 30 166 | Longford |
| Louth | 821 | 317 | 92 166 | Dundalk |
| Mayo | 5 398 | 2 084 | 111 524 | Castlebar |
| Meath | 2 339 | 903 | 109 732 | Trim |
| Monaghan | 1 290 | 498 | 51 313 | Monaghan |
| Offaly | 1 997 | 771 | 59 117 | Tullamore |
| Roscommon | 2 463 | 951 | 51 975 | Roscommon |
| Sligo | 1 795 | 693 | 55 821 | Sligo |
| Tipperary | 4 254 | 1 642 | 133 535 | Clonmel |
| Waterford | 1 839 | 710 | 94 680 | Waterford |
| Westmeath | 1 764 | 681 | 63 314 | Mullingar |
| Wexford | 2 352 | 908 | 104 371 | Wexford |
| Wicklow | 2 025 | 782 | 102 683 | Wicklow |

### Italy

| Region | Area sq km | Area sq mi | Population (1997 est) | Capital |
|---|---|---|---|---|
| Abruzzi | 10794 | 4168 | 1276040 | L'Aquila |
| Basilicata | 9992 | 3858 | 610330 | Potenza |
| Calabria | 15080 | 5823 | 2070992 | Catanzaro |
| Campania | 13595 | 5249 | 5796899 | Naples (Napoli) |
| Emilia-Romagna | 22124 | 8542 | 3947102 | Bologna |
| Friuli-Venezia Giulia | 7844 | 3029 | 1184654 | Trieste |
| Lazio | 17227 | 6649 | 5242709 | Rome (Roma) |
| Liguria | 5418 | 2092 | 1641835 | Genoa (Genova) |
| Lombardy (Lombardia) | 23859 | 9214 | 8988951 | Milan (Milano) |
| Marche | 9693 | 3743 | 1450879 | Ancona |
| Molise | 4438 | 1713 | 329894 | Campobasso |
| Piedmont (Piemonte) | 25399 | 9807 | 4291441 | Turin (Torino) |
| Puglia | 19357 | 7473 | 4090068 | Bari |
| Sardinia (Sardegna) | 24090 | 9301 | 1661429 | Cagliari |
| Sicily (Sicilia) | 25707 | 9926 | 5108067 | Palermo |
| Tuscany (Toscana) | 22992 | 8877 | 3527303 | Florence (Firenze) |
| Trentino-Alto Adige | 13607 | 5252 | 924281 | Bozen (Bolzano) [1], Trent, Trient (Trento) [1] |
| Umbria | 8456 | 3265 | 831714 | Perugia |
| Valle d'Aosta | 3262 | 1259 | 119610 | Aosta |
| Veneto | 18365 | 7090 | 4469156 | Venice (Venezia) |

[1] Joint regional capitals.

### Liechtenstein

| Commune | Area sq km | Area sq mi | Population (1998 est) |
|---|---|---|---|
| Balzers | 19.6 | 7.6 | 4118 |
| Eschen | 10.3 | 4.0 | 3571 |
| Gamprin | 6.1 | 2.4 | 1173 |
| Mauren | 7.5 | 2.9 | 3114 |
| Planken | 5.3 | 2.0 | 347 |
| Ruggell | 7.4 | 2.9 | 1693 |
| Schaan | 26.8 | 10.3 | 5262 |
| Schellenberg | 3.5 | 1.4 | 955 |
| Triesen | 26.4 | 10.2 | 4168 |
| Triesenberg | 29.8 | 11.5 | 2508 |
| Vaduz | 17.3 | 6.7 | 5106 |

### Luxembourg

| District/canton | Area sq km | Area sq mi | Population (1995 est) |
|---|---|---|---|
| Diekirch (district) | 1157 | 447 | 55910 |
| Clervaux | 332 | 128 | 10050 |
| Diekirch | 239 | 92 | 22930 |
| Redange | 267 | 103 | 10880 |
| Vianden | 54 | 21 | 2710 |
| Wiltz | 265 | 102 | 9340 |
| Grevenmacher (district) | 525 | 203 | 41370 |
| Echternach | 186 | 72 | 11300 |
| Grevenmacher | 211 | 82 | 17610 |
| Remich | 128 | 49 | 12460 |
| Luxembourg (district) | 904 | 349 | 277620 |
| Capellen | 199 | 77 | 30290 |
| Esch | 243 | 94 | 113960 |
| Luxembourg (city) | 238 | 92 | 114830 |
| Mersch | 224 | 86 | 18540 |

SOCIAL STRUCTURE

### ❑ Malta

| Census region | Area sq km | sq mi | Population (1995 est) |
|---|---|---|---|
| Gozo and Comino | 70 | 27 | 29 026 |
| Inner Harbour | 15 | 6 | 88 761 |
| N Malta | 78 | 30 | 44 852 |
| Outer Harbour | 32 | 12 | 112 882 |
| SE Malta | 53 | 20 | 50 650 |
| W Malta | 69 | 27 | 51 961 |

### ❑ The Netherlands

| Province | Area sq km | sq mi | Population (1998 est) | Capital |
|---|---|---|---|---|
| Drenthe | 2 680 | 1 025 | 464 700 | Assen |
| Flevoland | 2 412 | 549 | 293 300 | Lelijstad |
| Friesland | 5 741 | 1 295 | 618 100 | Leeuwarden |
| Gelderland | 5 143 | 1 935 | 1 895 700 | Arnhem |
| Groningen | 2 967 | 906 | 558 000 | Groningen |
| Limburg | 2 196 | 838 | 1 137 900 | Maastricht |
| N Brabant (Noord-Brabant) | 5 016 | 1 910 | 2 319 300 | 's-Hertogenbosch |
| N Holland (Noord-Holland) | 4 059 | 1 029 | 2 486 100 | Haarlem |
| Overijssel | 3 420 | 1 289 | 1 063 500 | Zwolle |
| S Holland (Zuid-Holland) | 3 446 | 1 123 | 3 359 000 | The Hague |
| Utrecht | 1 434 | 514 | 1 088 600 | Utrecht |
| Zeeland | 2 932 | 692 | 369 900 | Middelburg |

### ❑ Norway

| County | Area sq km | sq mi[1] | Population (1998 est) | Capital |
|---|---|---|---|---|
| Akershus | 4 917 | 1 898 | 453 490 | — |
| Aust-Agder | 9 212 | 3 557 | 101 152 | Arendal |
| Buskerud | 14 927 | 5 763 | 232 967 | Drammen |
| Finnmark | 48 637 | 18 779 | 74 879 | Vadsø |
| Hedmark | 27 388 | 10 575 | 186 118 | Hamar |
| Hordaland | 15 634 | 6 036 | 428 823 | Bergen |
| Møre og Romsdal | 15 104 | 5 832 | 241 972 | Molde |
| Nordland | 38 327 | 14 798 | 239 280 | Bodø |
| Nord-Trøndelag | 22 463 | 8 673 | 126 785 | Steinkjer |
| Oppland | 25 260 | 9 753 | 182 162 | Lillehammer |
| Oslo | 454 | 175 | 499 693 | Oslo |
| Østfold | 4 183 | 1 615 | 243 585 | Moss |
| Rogaland | 9 141 | 3 529 | 364 341 | Stavanger |
| Sogn og Fjordane | 18 634 | 7 195 | 107 790 | Leikanger |
| Sør-Trøndelag | 18 831 | 7 271 | 259 177 | Trondheim |
| Telemark | 15 315 | 5 913 | 163 857 | Skien |
| Troms | 25 954 | 10 021 | 150 288 | Tromsø |
| Vest-Agder | 7 281 | 2 811 | 152 553 | Kristiansand |
| Vestfold | 2 216 | 856 | 208 687 | Tønsberg |

[1] Excludes Svalbard and Jay Mayen (63 080 sq km/24 360 sq mi).

❑ **Poland**

| Voivodships (Provinces) | Area sq km | sq mi | Population (1999 est) |
|---|---|---|---|
| Dolnoslaskie | 19948 | 7700 | 2985000 |
| Kujawsko-Pomorskie | 17940 | 6936 | 2098000 |
| Lódzkie | 18219 | 7033 | 2673000 |
| Lubelski | 25115 | 9694 | 2242000 |
| Malopolskie | 15144 | 5846 | 3207000 |
| Mazowieckie | 35597 | 13740 | 5065000 |
| Opolskie | 9412 | 3633 | 1091000 |
| Podkarpackie | 17926 | 6919 | 2117000 |
| Pomorskie | 18293 | 7061 | 2179000 |
| Slaskie | 12294 | 4475 | 4894000 |
| Swietokrzyskie | 11672 | 5505 | 1328000 |
| Warminsko-Mazurskie | 24203 | 9342 | 1460000 |
| Wielkopolskie | 29826 | 11513 | 3346000 |
| Zachodniopomorskie | 22902 | 8840 | 1730300 |

❑ **Portugal**

| Region | Area sq km | sq mi | Population (1999 est) | Admin centre |
|---|---|---|---|---|
| Aveiro | 2808 | 1084 | 689100 | Aveiro |
| Beja | 10225 | 3948 | 153150 | Beja |
| Braga | 2695 | 1041 | 796160 | Braga |
| Bragança | 6597 | 2546 | 147720 | Bragança |
| Castelo Branco | 6616 | 2553 | 199890 | Castelo Branco |
| Coimbra | 3971 | 1532 | 420410 | Coimbra |
| Évora | 7393 | 2854 | 166330 | Évora |
| Faro | 4986 | 1924 | 349740 | Faro |
| Guarda | 5540 | 2138 | 176220 | Guarda |
| Leiria | 3508 | 1354 | 435340 | Leiria |
| Lisboa | 2758 | 1064 | 2056100 | Lisboa (Lisbon) |
| Portalegre | 6065 | 2342 | 123070 | Portalegre |
| Porto | 2341 | 904 | 1714690 | Porto |
| Santarém | 6707 | 2588 | 437850 | Santarém |
| Setúbal | 5064 | 1955 | 744700 | Setúbal |
| Viana do Castelo | 2210 | 853 | 250690 | Viano do Costelo |
| Vila Real | 4305 | 1661 | 229550 | Vila Real |
| Viseu | 5007 | 1933 | 399320 | Viseu |
| **Autonomous regions** | | | | |
| The Azores | 2247 | 868 | 246030 | Ponta Delgada |
| Madeira | 794 | 306 | 261530 | Funchal |

❑ **Romania**

| County | Area sq km | Area sq mi | Population (1997 est) | Capital |
|---|---|---|---|---|
| Alba | 6 242 | 2 409 | 402 097 | Alba Iulia |
| Arad | 7 754 | 2 993 | 476 988 | Arad |
| Argeş | 6 826 | 2 634 | 676 005 | Piteşti |
| Bacău | 6 621 | 2 555 | 746 131 | Bacău |
| Bihor | 7 544 | 2 911 | 625 596 | Oradea |
| Bistriţa-Năsăud | 5 355 | 2 067 | 326 539 | Bistriţa |
| Botoşani | 4 986 | 1 924 | 460 115 | Botoşani |
| Brăila | 4 766 | 1 840 | 388 891 | Brăila |
| Braşov | 5 363 | 2 070 | 636 434 | Braşov |
| Buzău | 6 103 | 2 355 | 508 492 | Buzău |
| Caraş-Severin | 8 520 | 3 288 | 332 884 | Reşiţa |
| Călăraşi | 5 088 | 1 964 | 360 773 | Călăraşi |
| Cluj | 6 674 | 2 576 | 724 355 | Cluj-Napoka |
| Constanţa | 7 071 | 2 729 | 746 686 | Constanţa |
| Covasna | 3 705 | 1 431 | 231 491 | Sfîntu Gheorghe |
| Dîmboviţa | 4 054 | 1 565 | 553 986 | Tîrgovişte |
| Dolj | 7 413 | 2 862 | 749 311 | Craiova |
| Galaţi | 4 466 | 1 721 | 641 647 | Galaţi |
| Giurgiu | 3 526 | 1 361 | 298 795 | Giurgiu |
| Gorj | 5 602 | 2 163 | 397 714 | Tîrgu Jiu |
| Harghita | 6 639 | 2 562 | 343 330 | Miercurea-Ciuc |
| Hunedoara | 7 063 | 2 726 | 543 109 | Deva |
| Ialomiţa | 4 453 | 1 720 | 304 740 | Slobozia |
| Iaşi | 5 476 | 2 113 | 823 735 | Iaşi |
| Maramureş | 6 304 | 2 433 | 533 672 | Baia Mare |
| Mehedinţi | 4 933 | 1 904 | 325 344 | Drobeta-Turnu-Severin |
| Mureş | 6 714 | 2 592 | 602 626 | Tîrgu Mureş |
| Neamţ | 5 896 | 2 276 | 583 141 | Piatra Neamţ |
| Olt | 5 498 | 2 129 | 513 961 | Slatina |
| Prahova | 4 716 | 1 819 | 864 159 | Ploieşti |
| Sălaj | 3 864 | 1 492 | 295 305 | Zalău |
| Satu Mare | 4 418 | 1 705 | 392 054 | Satu Mare |
| Sibiu | 5 432 | 2 097 | 444 701 | Sibiu |
| Suceava | 8 555 | 3 303 | 711 568 | Suceava |
| Teleorman | 5 790 | 2 235 | 466 010 | Alexandria |
| Timiş | 8 697 | 3 358 | 692 870 | Timişoara |
| Tulcea | 8 499 | 3 280 | 265 778 | Tulcea |
| Vaslui | 5 318 | 2 053 | 433 356 | Vaslui |
| Vâlcea | 5 765 | 2 225 | 460 854 | Râmnicu Vâlcea |
| Vrancea | 4 857 | 1 874 | 391 762 | Focşani |
| **Municipality** | | | | |
| Bucharest | 1 821 | 703 | 2 072 512 | Bucharest |

### ❑ Slovakia

| Region | Area sq km | Area sq mi | Population (1996 est) | Capital |
|---|---|---|---|---|
| Bratislava (city) | 367 | 142 | 450 775 | — |
| C Slovakia (Strĕdoslovenský) | 17 986 | 6 944 | 1 636 003 | Banská Bystrica |
| E Slovakia (Východoslovenský) | 16 191 | 6 251 | 1 544 077 | Košice |
| W Slovakia (Západoslovenský) | 14 492 | 5 595 | 1 725 352 | Bratislava |

### ❑ Slovenia

Has 148 municipalities, 11 of which are urban.

### ❑ Spain

| Province | Area sq km | Area sq mi | Population (1998 est) | Capital |
|---|---|---|---|---|
| Álava | 3 047 | 1 176 | 284 595 | Vitoria Gasteiz |
| Albacete | 14 862 | 5 737 | 358 597 | Albacete |
| Alicante | 5 863 | 2 263 | 1 388 933 | Alicante |
| Almería | 8 774 | 3 387 | 505 448 | Almería |
| Asturias | 10 565 | 4 078 | 1 081 834 | Oviedo |
| Ávila | 8 048 | 3 106 | 167 132 | Ávila |
| Badajoz | 21 657 | 8 360 | 663 803 | Badajoz |
| Beleares (Balearic Is) | 5 014 | 1 935 | 796 483 | Palma |
| Barcelona | 7 733 | 2 985 | 4 666 271 | Barcelona |
| Burgos | 14 309 | 5 523 | 346 355 | Burgos |
| Cáceres | 19 945 | 7 699 | 405 616 | Cáceres |
| Cádiz | 7 385 | 2 850 | 1 107 484 | Cádiz |
| Cantabria (Santander) | 5 289 | 2 041 | 527 137 | Santander |
| Castellón | 6 679 | 2 579 | 461 712 | Castellón |
| Ciudad Real | 19 749 | 7 519 | 479 474 | Ciudad Real |
| Córdoba | 13 718 | 5 295 | 767 175 | Córdoba |
| La Coruña | 7 876 | 3 040 | 1 106 325 | La Coruña |
| Cuenca | 17 061 | 6 585 | 199 086 | Cuenca |
| Girona (Gerona) | 5 886 | 2 272 | 543 191 | Girona |
| Granada | 12 531 | 4 387 | 801 177 | Granada |
| Guadalajara | 12 190 | 4 705 | 159 331 | Guadalajara |
| Guipúzcoa | 1 997 | 771 | 676 439 | San Sebastián |
| Huelva | 10 885 | 4 202 | 453 958 | Huelva |
| Huesca | 15 613 | 6 027 | 204 956 | Huesca |
| Jaén | 13 498 | 5 210 | 645 792 | Jáen |
| León | 15 468 | 5 971 | 506 365 | León |

| Province | Area sq km | Area sq mi | Population (1998 est) | Capital |
|---|---|---|---|---|
| Lérida | 12 028 | 4 642 | 357 903 | Lérida |
| Lugo | 9 803 | 3 784 | 367 751 | Lugo |
| Madrid | 7 995 | 3 086 | 5 091 336 | Madrid |
| Málaga | 7 276 | 2 808 | 1 240 580 | Malaga |
| Murcia | 11 317 | 4 368 | 1 115 068 | Murcia |
| Navarra | 10 421 | 4 022 | 530 819 | Pamplona |
| Orense | 7 278 | 2 809 | 344 170 | Orense |
| Palencia | 8 035 | 3 101 | 179 623 | Palencia |
| Las Palmas | 4 072 | 1 572 | 849 863 | Las Palmas |
| Pontevedra | 4 477 | 1 728 | 906 298 | Vigo |
| La Rioja | 5 034 | 1 943 | 263 644 | Logrono |
| Salamanca | 12 336 | 4 761 | 349 550 | Salamanca |
| Santa Cruz de Tenerife | 3 170 | 1 224 | 780 152 | Santa Cruz de Tenerife |
| Segovia | 6 949 | 2 682 | 146 755 | Segovia |
| Sevilla | 14 001 | 5 404 | 1 714 845 | Sevilla |
| Soria | 10 287 | 3 971 | 91 593 | Soria |
| Tarragona | 6 283 | 2 425 | 580 245 | Tarragona |
| Teruel | 14 785 | 5 707 | 136 840 | Teruel |
| Toledo | 15 368 | 5 932 | 519 664 | Toledo |
| Valencia | 10 763 | 4 154 | 2 172 796 | Valencia |
| Valladolid | 8 202 | 3 166 | 492 029 | Valladolid |
| Vizcaya | 2 217 | 856 | 1 137 594 | Bilbao |
| Zamora | 10 559 | 4 076 | 205 021 | Zamora |
| Zaragoza | 17 252 | 6 659 | 841 438 | Zaragoza |

❑ **Sweden**

| County | Area sq km | Area sq mi | Population (1998 est) | Capital |
|---|---|---|---|---|
| Blekinge | 2 941 | 1 136 | 151 414 | Karlskrona |
| Dalarna | 28 194 | 10 886 | 282 898 | Falun |
| Gävleborg | 18 191 | 7 024 | 282 226 | Gävle |
| Gotland | 3 140 | 1 212 | 57 643 | Visby |
| Halland | 5 454 | 2 106 | 272 539 | Halmstad |
| Jämtland | 49 443 | 19 090 | 131 766 | Östersund |
| Jönköping | 9 944 | 3 839 | 328 059 | Jönköping |
| Kalmar | 11 170 | 4 313 | 238 104 | Kalmar |
| Kronoberg | 8 458 | 3 266 | 178 078 | Växjö |
| Norrbotten | 98 913 | 39 191 | 260 473 | Lulece |
| Örebro | 8 519 | 3 289 | 274 584 | Örebro |
| Östergötland | 10 562 | 4 078 | 412 411 | Linköping |
| Skåne | 10 025 | 3 870 | 1 120 426 | Malmö |
| Södermanland | 6 060 | 2 340 | 256 269 | Nyköping |
| Stockholm | 6 488 | 2 505 | 1 783 440 | Stockholm |
| Uppsala | 6 989 | 2 698 | 291 413 | Uppsala |
| Värmland | 17 584 | 6 789 | 278 313 | Karlstad |
| Västerbotten | 55 401 | 21 390 | 257 803 | Umeå |
| Västernorrland | 21 678 | 8 370 | 251 884 | Härnösand |
| Västmanland | 6 302 | 2 433 | 257 661 | Västeraces |
| Västra Götalands | 23 942 | 9 244 | 1 486 918 | Gothenburg |

## ❑ Switzerland

| Canton | Area sq km | sq mi | Population (1998 est) | Capital |
|---|---|---|---|---|
| Aargau | 1 395 | 540 | 536 462 | Aarau |
| Appenzell Ausser-Rhoden[1] | 243 | 94 | 53 816 | Herisau |
| Appenzell Inner-Rhoden[1] | 172 | 66 | 14 873 | Appenzell |
| Basle (Basel-Landschaft)[1] | 428 | 165 | 256 761 | Liestal |
| Basle (Basel-Stadt)[1] | 37 | 14 | 190 505 | Basel |
| Berne | 5 932 | 2 290 | 941 144 | Berne |
| Fribourg | 1 591 | 614 | 232 086 | Fribourg |
| Geneva (Genève) | 245 | 94 | 398 910 | Geneva |
| Glarus | 684 | 264 | 38 698 | Glarus |
| Graubünden (Fr: Grisons) | 7 106 | 2 744 | 186 118 | Chur (Coire) |
| Jura | 837 | 323 | 68 995 | Delémont |
| Lucerne (Luzern) | 1 429 | 552 | 343 254 | Lucerne |
| Neuenberg (Neuchâtel) | 716 | 276 | 165 594 | Neuchâtel |
| Nidwalden[1] | 241 | 93 | 37 320 | Stans |
| Obwalden[1] | 480 | 186 | 31 989 | Sarnen |
| St Gall (Sankt Gallen) | 1 950 | 752 | 444 891 | St Gall |
| Schaffhausen | 298 | 115 | 73 725 | Schaffhausen |
| Schwyz | 851 | 328 | 126 479 | Schwyz |
| Solothurn | 791 | 305 | 243 450 | Solothurn |
| Thurgau | 863 | 333 | 226 479 | Frauenfeld |
| Ticino | 2 738 | 1 056 | 306 179 | Bellinzona |
| Uri | 1 057 | 408 | 35 612 | Altdorf |
| Valais | 5 213 | 2 015 | 274 458 | Sion |
| Vaud | 2 822 | 1 090 | 611 613 | Lausanne |
| Zug | 207 | 80 | 96 517 | Zug |
| Zürich | 1 661 | 641 | 1 187 609 | Zürich |

[1] Demicanton — functions as a full canton.

## ❑ Turkey

| Geographic region | Area sq km | sq mi | Population (1990 est) |
|---|---|---|---|
| Black Sea Coast (Karadeniz Kiyisi) | 81 295 | 31 388 | 6 900 805 |
| C Anatolia (Iç Anadolu) | 236 347 | 91 254 | 13 154 473 |
| E Anatolia (Doğu Anadolu) | 176 311 | 68 074 | 6 909 594 |
| Marmara and Aegean coasts (Marmara ve Ege kiyilari) | 85 560 | 33 035 | 11 784 535 |
| Mediterranean Coast (Akdeniz kiyisi) | 59 395 | 22 933 | 5 497 536 |
| SE Anatolia (Güneydoğu) | 39 749 | 15 347 | 2 793 894 |
| Thrace (Trakya) | 23 764 | 9 175 | 6 021 591 |
| W Anatolia (Bati Anadolu) | 77 031 | 29 742 | 3 906 681 |

## States of the USA

Population (Pop): figures from the 2000 population census.
Abbreviations are given after each state name: the first is the common abbreviation, the second the ZIP (postal) code.

**Alabama** (Ala; AL)
*Entry to Union* 1819 (22nd)
*Pop* 4 447 100
*Nickname* Camellia State, Heart of Dixie
*Inhabitant* Alabamian
*Area* 131 443 sq km/50 750 sq mi
*Capital* Montgomery
*Bird* Yellowhammer
*Fish* Tarpon
*Flower* Camellia
*Tree* Southern Pine

**Alaska** (Alaska; AK)
*Entry to Union* 1959 (49th)
*Pop* 626 932
*Nickname* Mainland State, The Last Frontier
*Inhabitant* Alaskan
*Area* 1 477 268 sq km/570 373 sq mi
*Capital* Juneau
*Bird* Willow Ptarmigan
*Fish* King Salmon
*Flower* Forget-me-not
*Gemstone* Jade
*Tree* Sitka Spruce

**Arizona** (Ariz; AZ)
*Entry to Union* 1912 (48th)
*Pop* 5 130 632
*Nickname* Apache State, Grand Canyon State
*Inhabitant* Arizonan
*Area* 295 276 sq km/114 006 sq mi
*Capital* Phoenix
*Bird* Cactus Wren
*Flower* Saguaro Cactus
*Gemstone* Turquoise
*Tree* Paloverde

**Arkansas** (Ark; AR)
*Entry to Union* 1836 (25th)
*Pop* 2 673 400
*Nickname* Bear State, Land of Opportunity
*Inhabitant* Arkansan
*Area* 137 754 sq km/53 187 sq mi
*Capital* Little Rock
*Bird* Mockingbird
*Flower* Apple Blossom
*Gemstone* Diamond
*Tree* Pine

**California** (Calif; CA)
*Entry to Union* 1850 (31st)
*Pop* 33 871 648
*Nickname* Golden State
*Inhabitant* Californian
*Area* 403 971 sq km/155 973 sq mi
*Capital* Sacramento
*Animal* California Grizzly Bear
*Bird* California Valley Quail
*Fish* South Fork Golden Trout
*Flower* Golden Poppy
*Tree* California Redwood

**Colorado** (Colo; CO)
*Entry to Union* 1876 (38th)
*Pop* 4 301 261
*Nickname* Centennial State
*Inhabitant* Coloradan
*Area* 268 658 sq km/103 729 sq mi
*Capital* Denver
*Animal* Rocky Mountain Bighorn Sheep
*Bird* Lark Bunting
*Flower* Columbine
*Gemstone* Aquamarine
*Tree* Blue Spruce

**Connecticut** (Conn; CT)
*Entry to Union* 1788 (5th)
*Pop* 3 405 565
*Nickname* Nutmeg State, Constitution State
*Inhabitant* Nutmegger
*Area* 12 547 sq km/4 844 sq mi
*Capital* Hartford
*Bird* American Robin
*Flower* Mountain Laurel
*Gemstone* Garnet
*Tree* White Oak

**Delaware** (Del; DE)
*Entry to Union* 1787 (1st)
*Pop* 783 600
*Nickname* Diamond State, First State
*Inhabitant* Delawarean
*Area* 5 133 sq km/1 982 sq mi
*Capital* Dover
*Bird* Blue Hen Chicken
*Flower* Peach Blossom
*Tree* American Holly

**District of Columbia** (DC; DC)
*Pop* 572 059
*Inhabitant* Washingtonian
*Area* 159 sq km/61 sq mi
*Capital* Washington
*Bird* Woodthrush
*Flower* American Beauty Rose
*Tree* Scarlet Oak

**Florida** (Fla; FL)
*Entry to Union* 1845 (27th)
*Pop* 15 982 378
*Nickname* Everglade State, Sunshine State
*Inhabitant* Floridian
*Area* 139 697 sq km/53 937 sq mi
*Capital* Tallahassee
*Bird* Mockingbird
*Flower* Orange Blossom
*Gemstone* Agatized Coral
*Tree* Sabal Palm

**Georgia** (Ga; GA)
*Entry to Union* 1788 (4th)
*Pop* 8 186 453
*Nickname* Empire State of the South, Peach State
*Inhabitant* Georgian
*Area* 152 571 sq km/58 908 sq mi
*Capital* Atlanta
*Bird* Brown Thrasher
*Flower* Cherokee Rose
*Tree* Live Oak

**Hawaii** (Hawaii; HI)
*Entry to Union* 1959 (50th)
*Pop* 1 211 537
*Nickname* Aloha State
*Inhabitant* Hawaiian
*Area* 16 636 sq km/6 423 sq mi
*Capital* Honolulu
*Bird* Nene (Hawaiian Goose)
*Flower* Yellow Hibiscus
*Tree* Kukui

**Idaho** (Idaho; ID)
*Entry to Union* 1890 (43rd)
*Pop* 1 293 953
*Nickname* Gem State
*Inhabitant* Idahoan
*Area* 214 325 sq km/82 751 sq mi
*Capital* Boise
*Bird* Mountain Bluebird
*Flower* Syringa
*Gemstone* Idaho Star Garnet
*Tree* Western White Pine

**Illinois** (Ill; IL)
*Entry to Union* 1818 (21st)
*Pop* 12 419 293
*Nickname* Prairie State, Land of Lincoln
*Inhabitant* Illinoisan
*Area* 144 123 sq km/55 646 sq mi
*Capital* Springfield
*Bird* Cardinal
*Flower* Butterfly Violet
*Tree* White Oak

**Indiana** (Ind; IN)
*Entry to Union* 1816 (19th)
*Pop* 6 080 485
*Nickname* Hoosier State
*Inhabitant* Hoosier
*Area* 92 903 sq km/35 870 sq mi
*Capital* Indianapolis
*Bird* Cardinal
*Flower* Peony
*Tree* Tulip Poplar

**Iowa** (Iowa; IA)
*Entry to Union* 1846 (29th)
*Pop* 2 926 324
*Nickname* Hawkeye State, Corn State
*Inhabitant* Iowan
*Area* 144 716 sq km/55 875 sq mi
*Capital* Des Moines
*Bird* Eastern Goldfinch
*Flower* Wild Rose
*Tree* Oak

**Kansas** (Kans; KS)
*Entry to Union* 1861 (34th)
*Pop* 2 688 418
*Nickname* Sunflower State, Jayhawker State
*Inhabitant* Kansan
*Area* 211 922 sq km/81 823 sq mi
*Capital* Topeka
*Animal* Bison
*Bird* Western Meadowlark
*Flower* Native Sunflower
*Tree* Cottonwood

**Kentucky** (Ky; KY)
*Entry to Union* 1792 (15th)
*Pop* 4 041 769
*Nickname* Bluegrass State
*Inhabitant* Kentuckian
*Area* 102 907 sq km/39 732 sq mi
*Capital* Frankfort
*Bird* Cardinal
*Flower* Goldenrod
*Tree* Kentucky Coffee Tree

**Louisiana** (La; LA)
*Entry to Union* 1812 (18th)
*Pop* 4 468 976
*Nickname* Pelican State, Sugar State, Creole State
*Inhabitant* Louisianian
*Area* 112 836 sq km/43 566 sq mi
*Capital* Baton Rouge
*Bird* Eastern Brown Pelican
*Flower* Magnolia
*Tree* Bald Cypress

**Maine** (Maine; ME)
*Entry to Union* 1820 (23rd)
*Pop* 1 274 923
*Nickname* Pine Tree State
*Inhabitant* Downeaster
*Area* 79 931 sq km/30 861 sq mi
*Capital* Augusta
*Bird* Chickadee
*Flower* White Pine Cone and Tassel
*Gemstone* Tourmaline
*Tree* Eastern White Pine

**Maryland** (Md; MD)
*Entry to Union* 1788 (7th)
*Pop* 5 296 486
*Nickname* Old Line State, Free State
*Inhabitant* Marylander
*Area* 25 316 sq km/9 775 sq mi
*Capital* Annapolis
*Bird* Baltimore Oriole
*Fish* Striped Bass
*Flower* Black-eyed Susan
*Tree* White Oak

**Massachusetts** (Mass; MA)
*Entry to Union* 1788 (6th)
*Pop* 6 349 097
*Nickname* Bay State, Old Colony
*Inhabitant* Bay Stater
*Area* 20 300 sq km/7 838 sq mi
*Capital* Boston
*Bird* Chickadee

*Flower* Mayflower
*Tree* American Elm

**Michigan** (Mich; MI)
*Entry to Union* 1837 (26th)
*Pop* 9 938 444
*Nickname* Wolverine State, Great Lake State
*Inhabitant* Michigander
*Area* 150 544 sq km/58 125 sq mi
*Capital* Lansing
*Bird* Robin
*Fish* Trout
*Flower* Apple Blossom
*Gemstone* Chlorastrolik
*Tree* White Pine

**Minnesota** (Minn; MN)
*Entry to Union* 1858 (32nd)
*Pop* 4 919 479
*Nickname* Gopher State, North Star State
*Inhabitant* Minnesotan
*Area* 206 207 sq km/79 617 sq mi
*Capital* St Paul
*Bird* Common Loon
*Fish* Walleye
*Flower* Moccasin Flower
*Gemstone* Lake Superior Agate
*Tree* Red Pine

**Mississippi** (Miss; MS)
*Entry to Union* 1817 (20th)
*Pop* 2 844 658
*Nickname* Magnolia State
*Inhabitant* Mississippian
*Area* 123 510 sq km/47 687 sq mi
*Capital* Jackson
*Bird* Mockingbird
*Flower* Magnolia
*Tree* Magnolia

**Missouri** (Mo; MO)
*Entry to Union* 1821 (24th)
*Pop* 5 595 211
*Nickname* Bullion State, Show Me State
*Inhabitant* Missourian
*Area* 178 446 sq km/68 898 sq mi
*Capital* Jefferson City
*Bird* Bluebird
*Flower* Hawthorn
*Tree* Dogwood

**Montana** (Mont; MT)
*Entry to Union* 1889 (41st)
*Pop* 902 195
*Nickname* Treasure State, Big Sky Country
*Inhabitant* Montanan
*Area* 376 991 sq km/145 556 sq mi
*Capital* Helena
*Bird* Western Meadowlark
*Flower* Bitterroot
*Gemstone* Sapphire, Agate
*Tree* Ponderosa Pine

**Nebraska** (Nebr; NE)
*Entry to Union* 1867 (37th)
*Pop* 1 711 263
*Nickname* Cornhusker State, Beef State
*Inhabitant* Nebraskan
*Area* 199 113 sq km/76 878 sq mi
*Capital* Lincoln
*Bird* Western Meadowlark
*Flower* Goldenrod
*Gemstone* Blue Agate
*Tree* Cottonwood

**Nevada** (Nev; NV)
*Entry to Union* 1864 (36th)
*Pop* 1 998 257
*Nickname* Silver State, Sagebrush State, Battle Born State
*Inhabitant* Nevadan
*Area* 273 349 sq km/105 540 sq mi
*Capital* Carson City
*Bird* Mountain Bluebird
*Flower* Sagebrush
*Tree* Single-leaf Piñon

**New Hampshire** (NH; NH)
*Entry to Union* 1788 (9th)
*Pop* 1 235 786
*Nickname* Granite State
*Inhabitant* New Hampshirite
*Area* 23 292 sq km/8 993 sq mi
*Capital* Concord
*Bird* Purple Finch
*Flower* Purple Lilac
*Tree* White Birch

**New Jersey** (NJ; NJ)
*Entry to Union* 1787 (3rd)
*Pop* 8 414 350
*Nickname* Garden State
*Inhabitant* New Jerseyite
*Area* 19 210 sq km/7 417 sq mi
*Capital* Trenton
*Bird* Eastern Goldfinch
*Flower* Purple Violet
*Tree* Red Oak

**New Mexico** (N Mex; NM)
*Entry to Union* 1912 (47th)
*Pop* 1 819 046
*Nickname* Sunshine State, Land of Enchantment
*Inhabitant* New Mexican
*Area* 314 334 sq km/121 364 sq mi
*Capital* Santa Fe
*Animal* Black Bear
*Bird* Roadrunner
*Fish* Cutthroat Trout
*Flower* Yucca
*Gemstone* Turquoise
*Tree* Piñon

**New York** (NY; NY)
*Entry to Union* 1788 (11th)
*Pop* 18 976 457
*Nickname* Empire State
*Inhabitant* New Yorker
*Area* 122 310 sq km/47 224 sq mi
*Capital* Albany
*Bird* Bluebird

*Flower* Rose
*Gemstone* Garnet
*Tree* Sugar Maple

**North Carolina** (NC; NC)
*Entry to Union* 1789 (12th)
*Pop* 8 049 313
*Nickname* Old North State, Tar Heel State
*Inhabitant* North Carolinian
*Area* 126 180 sq km/48 718 sq mi
*Capital* Raleigh
*Animal* Grey Squirrel
*Bird* Cardinal
*Fish* Channel Bass
*Flower* Dogwood
*Gemstone* Emerald
*Tree* Longleaf Pine

**North Dakota** (N Dak; ND)
*Entry to Union* 1889 (39th)
*Pop* 642 200
*Nickname* Flickertail State, Sioux State, Peace Garden State
*Inhabitant* North Dakotan
*Area* 178 695 sq km/68 994 sq mi
*Capital* Bismarck
*Bird* Western Meadowlark
*Fish* Northern Pike
*Flower* Wild Prairie Rose
*Gemstone* Teredo petrified wood
*Tree* American Elm

**Ohio** (Ohio; OH)
*Entry to Union* 1803 (17th)
*Pop* 11 353 140
*Nickname* Buckeye State
*Inhabitant* Ohioan
*Area* 106 067 sq km/40 952 sq mi
*Capital* Columbus
*Bird* Cardinal
*Flower* Scarlet Carnation
*Tree* Buckeye

**Oklahoma** (Okla; OK)
*Entry to Union* 1907 (46th)
*Pop* 3 450 654
*Nickname* Sooner State
*Inhabitant* Oklahoman
*Area* 177 877 sq km/68 678 sq mi
*Capital* Oklahoma City
*Bird* Scissor-tailed Flycatcher
*Flower* Mistletoe
*Tree* Redbud

**Oregon** (Oreg; OR)
*Entry to Union* 1859 (33rd)
*Pop* 3 421 399
*Nickname* Sunset State, Beaver State
*Inhabitant* Oregonian
*Area* 251 385 sq km/97 060 sq mi
*Capital* Salem
*Animal* Beaver
*Bird* Western Meadowlark
*Fish* Chinook Salmon
*Flower* Oregon Grape
*Gemstone* Thunder Egg
*Tree* Douglas Fir

**Pennsylvania** (Pa; PA)
*Entry to Union* 1787 (2nd)
*Pop* 12 281 054
*Nickname* Keystone State
*Inhabitant* Pennsylvanian
*Area* 116 083 sq km/44 820 sq mi
*Capital* Harrisburg
*Animal* Whitetail Deer
*Bird* Ruffed Grouse
*Flower* Mountain Laurel
*Tree* Hemlock

**Rhode Island** (RI; RI)
*Entry to Union* 1790 (13th)
*Pop* 1 048 319
*Nickname* Little Rhody, Plantation State
*Inhabitant* Rhode Islander
*Area* 2 707 sq km/1 045 sq mi
*Capital* Providence
*Bird* Rhode Island Red
*Flower* Violet
*Tree* Red Maple

**South Carolina** (SC; SC)
*Entry to Union* 1788 (8th)
*Pop* 4 012 012
*Nickname* Palmetto State
*Inhabitant* South Carolinian
*Area* 77 988 sq km/30 111 sq mi
*Capital* Columbia
*Animal* Whitetail Deer
*Bird* Carolina Wren
*Fish* Striped Bass
*Flower* Yellow Jessamine
*Tree* Cabbage Palmetto

**South Dakota** (S Dak; SD)
*Entry to Union* 1889 (40th)
*Pop* 754 844
*Nickname* Sunshine State, Coyote State
*Inhabitant* South Dakotan
*Area* 196 576 sq km/75 898 sq mi
*Capital* Pierre
*Animal* Coyote
*Bird* Ring-necked Pheasant
*Flower* Pasque
*Gemstone* Fairburn Agate
*Tree* Black Hills Spruce

**Tennessee** (Tenn; TN)
*Entry to Union* 1796 (16th)
*Pop* 5 689 283
*Nickname* Volunteer State
*Inhabitant* Tennessean
*Area* 106 759 sq km/41 220 sq mi
*Capital* Nashville
*Animal* Raccoon
*Bird* Mockingbird
*Flower* Iris
*Gemstone* Pearl
*Tree* Tulip Poplar

**Texas** (Tex; TX)
*Entry to Union* 1845 (28th)
*Pop* 20 851 820
*Nickname* Lone Star State
*Inhabitant* Texan
*Area* 678 358 sq km/261 914 sq mi
*Capital* Austin
*Bird* Mockingbird
*Flower* Bluebonnet
*Gemstone* Topaz
*Tree* Pecan

**Utah** (Utah; UT)
*Entry to Union* 1896 (45th)
*Pop* 2 233 169
*Nickname* Mormon State, Beehive State
*Inhabitant* Utahn
*Area* 212 816 sq km/82 168 sq mi
*Capital* Salt Lake City
*Bird* Sea Gull
*Flower* Sego Lily
*Gemstone* Topaz
*Tree* Blue Spruce

**Vermont** (Vt; VT)
*Entry to Union* 1791 (14th)
*Pop* 608 827
*Nickname* Green Mountain State
*Inhabitant* Vermonter
*Area* 23 955 sq km/9 249 sq mi
*Capital* Montpelier
*Animal* Morgan Horse
*Bird* Hermit Thrush
*Flower* Red Clover
*Tree* Sugar Maple

**Virginia** (Va; VA)
*Entry to Union* 1788 (10th)
*Pop* 7 078 515
*Nickname* Old Dominion State, Mother of Presidents
*Inhabitant* Virginian
*Area* 102 558 sq km/39 598 sq mi
*Capital* Richmond
*Bird* Cardinal
*Flower* Dogwood
*Tree* Flowering Dogwood

**Washington** (Wash; WA)
*Entry to Union* 1889 (42nd)
*Pop* 5 894 121
*Nickname* Evergreen State, Chinook State
*Inhabitant* Washingtonian
*Area* 172 447 sq km/66 582 sq mi
*Capital* Olympia
*Bird* Willow Goldfinch
*Fish* Steelhead Trout
*Flower* Western Rhododendron
*Gemstone* Petrified Wood
*Tree* Western Hemlock

**West Virginia** (W Va; WV)
*Entry to Union* 1863 (35th)
*Pop* 1 808 344
*Nickname* Panhandle State, Mountain State
*Inhabitant* West Virginian
*Area* 62 758 sq km/24 231 sq mi
*Capital* Charleston
*Animal* Black Bear
*Bird* Cardinal
*Flower* Big Rhododendron
*Tree* Sugar Maple

**Wisconsin** (Wis; WI)
*Entry to Union* 1848 (30th)
*Pop* 5 363 675
*Nickname* Badger State, America's Dairyland
*Inhabitant* Wisconsinite
*Area* 145 431 sq km/56 151 sq mi
*Capital* Madison
*Animal* Badger, Whitetail Deer
*Bird* Robin
*Fish* Muskellunge
*Flower* Wood Violet
*Tree* Sugar Maple

**Wyoming** (Wyo; WY)
*Entry to Union* 1890 (44th)
*Pop* 493 782
*Nickname* Equality State
*Inhabitant* Wyomingite
*Area* 251 501 sq km/97 105 sq mi
*Capital* Cheyenne
*Bird* Meadowlark
*Flower* Indian Paintbrush
*Gemstone* Jade
*Tree* Cottonwood

## Australian states and territories

| Name | Area sq km | Area sq mi | State Capital |
|---|---|---|---|
| Australian Capital Territory | 2432 | 939 | Canberra |
| New South Wales | 801 427 | 309 431 | Sydney |
| Northern Territory | 1 346 200 | 519 768 | Darwin |
| Queensland | 1 732 700 | 668 995 | Brisbane |
| South Australia | 984 376 | 380 070 | Adelaide |
| Tasmania | 68 331 | 26 383 | Hobart |
| Victoria | 227 600 | 87 876 | Melbourne |
| Western Australia | 2 525 500 | 975 096 | Perth |

## Canadian provinces

| Name | Area sq km | Area sq mi | Provincial Capital |
|---|---|---|---|
| Alberta | 661 185 | 255 284 | Edmonton |
| British Columbia | 944 735 | 364 667 | Victoria |
| Manitoba | 647 797 | 250 050 | Winnipeg |
| New Brunswick | 72 908 | 28 142 | Fredericton |
| Newfoundland and Labrador | 405 212 | 156 412 | St John's |
| Northwest Territories | 1 346 106 | 519 597 | Yellowknife |
| Nova Scotia | 55 284 | 21 340 | Halifax |
| Nunavut | 2 093 190 | 807 971 | Iqaluit |
| Ontario | 1 076 395 | 415 488 | Toronto |
| Prince Edward Island | 5660 | 2185 | Charlottetown |
| Quebec | 1 542 056 | 595 234 | Quebec City |
| Saskatchewan | 651 036 | 251 300 | Regina |
| Yukon Territory | 482 443 | 186 223 | Whitehorse |

## United Nations membership

Grouped according to year of entry.

1945 Argentina, Australia, Belgium, Byelorussian SSR (Belarus, 1991), Bolivia, Brazil, Canada, Chile, China (Taiwan to 1971), Colombia, Costa Rica, Cuba, Czechoslavakia (to 1993), Denmark, Dominican Republic, Ecuador, Egypt, El Salvador, Ethiopia, France, Greece, Guatemala, Haiti, Honduras, India, Iran, Iraq, Lebanon, Liberia, Luxembourg, Mexico, Netherlands, New Zealand, Nicaragua, Norway, Panama, Paraguay, Peru, Philippines, Poland, Saudi Arabia, South Africa, Syria, Turkey, Ukrainian SSR (Ukraine, 1991), USSR (Russia, 1991), UK, USA, Uruguay, Venezuela, Yugoslavia (to 1992)

1946 Afghanistan, Iceland, Sweden, Thailand

1947 Pakistan, Yemen (N, to 1990)

1948 Burma (Myanmar, 1989)

1949 Israel

1950 Indonesia

1955 Albania, Austria, Bulgaria, Kampuchea (Cambodia, 1989), Ceylon (Sri Lanka, 1970), Finland, Hungary, Ireland, Italy, Jordan, Laos, Libya, Nepal, Portugal, Romania, Spain

1956 Japan, Morocco, The Sudan, Tunisia

1957 Ghana, Malaya (Malaysia, 1963)

1958 Guinea

1960 Cameroon, Central African Republic, Chad, Congo, Côte d'Ivoire (Ivory Coast), Cyprus, Dahomey (Benin, 1975), Gabon, Madagascar, Mali, Niger, Nigeria, Senegal, Somalia, Togo, Upper Volta (Burkina Faso, 1984), Zaïre (Democratic Republic of Congo, 1997)

1961 Mauritania, Mongolia, Sierra Leone, Tanganyika (within Tanzania, 1964)

1962 Algeria, Burundi, Jamaica, Rwanda, Trinidad and Tobago, Uganda

1963 Kenya, Kuwait, Zanzibar (within Tanzania, 1964)

1964 Malawi, Malta, Zambia, Tanzania

1965 The Gambia, Maldives, Singapore

1966 Barbados, Botswana, Guyana, Lesotho, Yemen (S, to 1990)

1968 Equatorial Guinea, Mauritius, Swaziland

1970 Fiji

1971 Bahrain, Bhutan, China (People's Republic), Oman, Qatar, United Arab Emirates

| | |
|---|---|
| 1973 | The Bahamas, German Democratic Republic (within GFR 1990), German Federal Republic |
| 1974 | Bangladesh, Grenada, Guinea-Bissau |
| 1975 | Cape Verde, Comoros, Mozambique, Papua New Guinea, São Tomé and Príncipe, Suriname |
| 1976 | Angola, Seychelles, Western Samoa (Samoa, 1997) |
| 1977 | Djibouti, Vietnam |
| 1978 | Dominica, Solomon Islands |
| 1979 | St Lucia |
| 1980 | St Vincent and the Grenadines, Zimbabwe |
| 1981 | Antigua and Barbuda, Belize, Vanuatu |
| 1983 | St Kitts and Nevis |
| 1984 | Brunei |
| 1990 | Liechtenstein, Namibia, Yemen (formerly N Yemen and S Yemen) |
| 1991 | Estonia, Federated States of Micronesia, Latvia, Lithuania, Marshall Islands, N Korea, S Korea |
| 1992 | Armenia, Azerbaijan, Bosnia-Herzegovina, Croatia, Georgia, Kazakhstan, Kyrgyzstan, Moldova, San Marino, Slovenia, Tajikistan, Turkmenistan, Uzbekistan |
| 1993 | Andorra, Czech Republic, Eritrea, Former Yugoslav Republic of Macedonia, Monaco, Slovakia |
| 1994 | Palau |
| 1999 | Kiribati, Nauru, Tonga |
| 2000 | Tuvalu, Yugoslavia |

## United Nations — specialized agencies

| Abbreviated form | Full title | Area of concern |
|---|---|---|
| ILO | International Labour Organization | Social justice |
| FAO | Food and Agriculture Organization | Improvement of the production and distribution of agricultural products |
| UNESCO | United Nations Educational, Scientific and Cultural Organization | Stimulation of popular education and the spread of culture |
| ICAO | International Civil Aviation Organization | Encouragement of safety measures in international flight |
| IBRD | International Bank for Reconstruction and Development | Aid of development through investment |
| IMF | International Monetary Fund | Promotion of international monetary co-operation |
| UPU | Universal Postal Union | Uniting members within a single postal territory |
| WHO | World Health Organization | Promotion of the highest standards of health for all people |
| ITU | International Telecommunication Union | Allocation of frequencies and regulation of procedures |
| WMO | World Meteorological Organization | Standardization and utilization of meteorological observations |
| IFC | International Finance Corporation | Promotion of the international flow of private capital |
| IMCO | Inter-governmental Maritime Consultative Organization | Co-ordination of safety at sea |
| IDA | International Development Association | Credit on special terms to provide assistance for less developed countries |
| WIPO | World Intellectual Property Organization | Protection of copyright, designs, inventions, etc |
| IFAD | International Fund for Agricultural Development | Increase of food production in developing countries by the generation of grants or loans |

## Commonwealth membership

The Commonwealth is an informal association of sovereign states.
Member countries are grouped by year of entry.

| | |
|---|---|
| 1931 | Australia, Canada, New Zealand, United Kingdom, South Africa (left 1961, rejoined 1994) |
| 1947 | India, Pakistan (left 1972, rejoined 1989, suspended 1999) |
| 1948 | Sri Lanka |
| 1957 | Ghana, Malaysia |
| 1960 | Nigeria (suspended 1995, readmitted 1999) |
| 1961 | Cyprus, Sierra Leone, Tanzania |
| 1962 | Jamaica, Trinidad and Tobago, Uganda |
| 1963 | Kenya, Malawi |
| 1964 | Malawi, Malta, Zambia |
| 1965 | The Gambia, Singapore |
| 1966 | Barbados, Botswana, Guyana, Lesotho |
| 1968 | Mauritius, Nauru, Swaziland |
| 1970 | Tonga, Western Samoa, Fiji (left 1987, rejoined 1997) |
| 1972 | Bangladesh |
| 1973 | The Bahamas |
| 1974 | Grenada |
| 1975 | Papua New Guinea |
| 1976 | Seychelles |
| 1978 | Dominica, Solomon Islands, Tuvalu |
| 1979 | Kiribati, St Lucia, St Vincent and the Grenadines |
| 1980 | Vanuatu, Zimbabwe |
| 1981 | Antigua and Barbuda, Belize |
| 1982 | Maldives |
| 1983 | St Kitts and Nevis |
| 1984 | Brunei |
| 1990 | Namibia |
| 1995 | Cameroon, Mozambique |
| 1999 | Nauru |

The Republic of Ireland resigned from the Commonwealth in 1949.

## European Union Membership

Member countries are listed by year of entry.

| | |
|---|---|
| 1958 | Belgium |
| 1958 | France |
| 1958 | Germany |
| 1958 | Italy |
| 1958 | Luxembourg |
| 1958 | The Netherlands |
| 1973 | Denmark |
| 1973 | Republic of Ireland |
| 1973 | United Kingdom |
| 1981 | Greece |
| 1986 | Portugal |
| 1986 | Spain |
| 1995 | Austria |
| 1995 | Finland |
| 1995 | Sweden |

Applications from Cyprus, Estonia, Hungary, Poland, Switzerland and the Czech Republic are under consideration. Slovenia gained associate membership in 1996.

## European Community organizations

| Abbreviation | Full title | Area of concern |
|---|---|---|
| — | European Court of Justice | Adjudication of disputes arising from application of the Treaties |
| CAP | Common Agricultural Policy | Aiming to ensure reasonable standards of living for farmers; its policies have led to surpluses in the past |
| EMS | European Monetary System | Assistance of trading relations between member countries; all members of the community are in the EMS except Denmark, Sweden and the UK |
| EIB | European Investment Bank | Financing of capital investment projects to assist development of the Community |
| ECSC | European Coal and Steel Community | Regulation of prices and trade in these commodities |
| EURATOM | European Atomic Energy Community | Creation of technical and industrial conditions to produce nuclear energy on a large scale |

## Political definitions

Politics is the science of government: it studies and regulates the creation of legislation, as well as defining the role of the individual within society. Below are 50 concise definitions of the most widely used political terms.

**Act of Parliament** Bill passed through both houses of the UK Parliament.

**Anarchism** Rejection of the state and other forms of authority.

**Authoritarianism** Government not dependent on the consent of society.

**Bill, parliamentary** Draft of proposed new law for consideration by legislature.

**Cabinet** Group of senior ministers usually heading government departments.

**Civil disobedience** Strategy to achieve political goals by refusing to co-operate with a government or its agents.

**Civil rights** Rights guaranteed by a state to its citizens.

**Coalition** Arrangement between countries or political parties to pursue a common goal.

**Communism** Political ideology featuring common ownership of property, associated with the theories of Karl Marx (1818–83), published in his *Communist Manifesto* (1848).

**Conservatism** Political beliefs stressing adherence to established authority.

**Constitution** Principles that determine the way a country may be governed, usually in the form of a written document.

**Democracy** Rule by the people, usually with decision-making in the hands of popularly elected representatives.

**Devolution** Delegation of authority from central government to a subordinate elected institution.

**Dictatorship** Rule by a single person, or several people (eg military dictatorship), unelected and authoritarian in character.

**Dissidents** People who oppose a regime and may suffer discrimination.

**Fascism** Nationalistic and authoritarian movement associated with the 1930s.

**Federalism** Territorial political organization aiming to maintain national unity while permitting regional diversity.

**Green** Movement opposing ecological and environmental effects caused by technological and economic policies.

**House of Commons** Lower (and effectively ruling) chamber of UK Parliament.

**House of Lords** Non-elected house of UK Parliament, containing hereditary and life peers.

**House of Representatives** One of the two chambers of the US legislature.

**Human rights** Fundamental rights beyond those prescribed by law.

**Ideology** Set of beliefs and attitudes that support particular interests.

**Imperialism** Extension of state power through acquisition of other territories.

**Left wing** Political position occupied by those with radical and reforming tendencies towards social and political order.

**Legislature** Institution with power to pass laws.

**Liberalism** Doctrine that urges freedom of the individual, religion, trade and economics (*laissez faire*).

**Nationalism** Doctrine that views the nation as the principal unit of political organization.

**Nationalization** Taking an industry into state ownership.

**Ombudsman** Official who investigates complaints regarding government actions.

**Pluralism** Existence within a society of a variety of groups, limiting the power of any one group.

**Pressure group** Organization formed to support a particular political interest.

**Privatization** Transfer to private ownership of organizations owned by the state.

**Privy Council** Body advising the British monarch, appointed by the Crown.

**Proletariat** In socialist philosophy, term denoting working class.

**Proportional representation** Voting system ensuring that the representation of voters is in proportion to their numbers.

**Racism** Ideology alleging inferiority of racial or ethnic groups in terms of their biological or physical characteristics.

**Radicalism** Ideology arguing for substantial political and social change.

**Referendum** Device whereby the electorate can vote on a measure put before it by a government.

**Right wing** Political position of support for established institutions and opposition to socialist developments.

**Sanction** Penalty imposed by one state against another, such as denial of trade.

**Sectarianism** Excessive loyalty or attachment to a particular sect or party.

**Senate** One of the two chambers of a national or state legislature.

**Separatism** Demand for separation from territorial and political sovereignty of the state to which the separatists belong.

**Socialism** Doctrine favouring state intervention to create an egalitarian society.

**Terrorism** Violent behaviour to promote a particular political cause, often aimed at overthrow of the established order.

**Totalitarianism** System in which political opposition is suppressed and decision-making is highly centralized.

**Trade union** Association of people, usually in the same trade, joining together to improve pay and working conditions.

**Tribunal** Official body appointed to inquire into and give judgement on some matter of dispute.

**Welfare state** System whereby state is responsible for protecting and promoting citizens' welfare in areas such as health, employment, pensions and education.

## Legislative systems of government

A bicameral political system is one in which there are two chambers in the legislature, whereas a unicameral system has only one chamber.

❑ **Bicameral**

**Africa**
Burkina Faso, Central African Republic, Liberia, Madagascar, Mauritania, Swaziland

**Asia**
India, Japan, Philippines, Thailand

**Australasia**
Australia, Fiji

**Europe**
Austria, Belgium, Czech Republic, France, Germany, Ireland, Italy, Netherlands, Poland, Romania, Russian Federation, Spain, Switzerland, UK, Yugoslavia (Serbia and Montenegro)

**Middle East**
Afghanistan, Jordan

**North America**
Antigua and Barbuda, The Bahamas, Barbados, Belize, Canada, Dominican Republic, Grenada, Haiti, Jamaica, Puerto Rico, St Lucia, Trinidad and Tobago, USA

**South America**
Argentina, Bolivia, Chile, Columbia, Paraguay, Peru, Uruguay, Venezuela

❑ **Unicameral**

**Africa**
Algeria, Angola, Benin, Botswana, Burundi, Cameroon, Cape Verde, Chad, Comoros, Congo, Côte d'Ivoire, Democratic Republic of Congo, Djibouti, Equatorial Guinea, Gabon, The Gambia, Ghana, Guinea-Bissau, Kenya, Lesotho, Malawi, Mali, Mauritius, Mozambique, Namibia, Nigeria, São Tomé and Príncipe, Senegal, Seychelles, Sierra Leone, The Sudan, Tanzania, Togo, Tunisia, Zambia

**Asia**
Bangladesh, Bhutan, Brunei, Cambodia, China, Indonesia, Kazakhstan, Laos, Nepal, North Korea, Singapore, South Korea, Sri Lanka, Turkmenistan, Uzbekistan, Vietnam

**Australasia**
Kiribati, New Zealand, Papua New Guinea, Solomon Islands, Tonga, Tuvalu, Vanuatu, Samoa

**Europe**
Albania, Andorra, Belarus, Bulgaria, Croatia, Cyprus, Denmark, Estonia, Finland, Gibraltar, Greece, Greenland, Hungary, Iceland, Liechtenstein, Lithuania, Luxembourg, Macedonia, Malta, Moldova, Norway, Portugal, San Marino, Slovakia, Slovenia, Sweden, Ukraine

**Middle East**
Armenia, Azerbaijan, Egypt, Iran, Iraq, Israel, Kuwait, Lebanon, Syria, Turkey, United Arab Emirates, Yemen

**North America**
Costa Rica, Cuba, El Salvador, Guatemala, Honduras, Nicaragua, Panama, St Kitts and Nevis, St Vincent and the Grenadines

**South America**
Ecuador, Guyana, Suriname

## Passage of a public bill to law in the UK

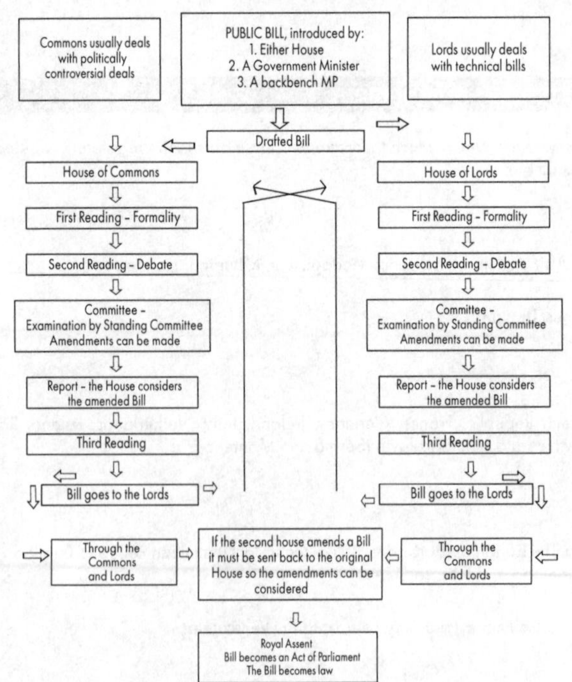

## Passage of a public bill to law in the USA

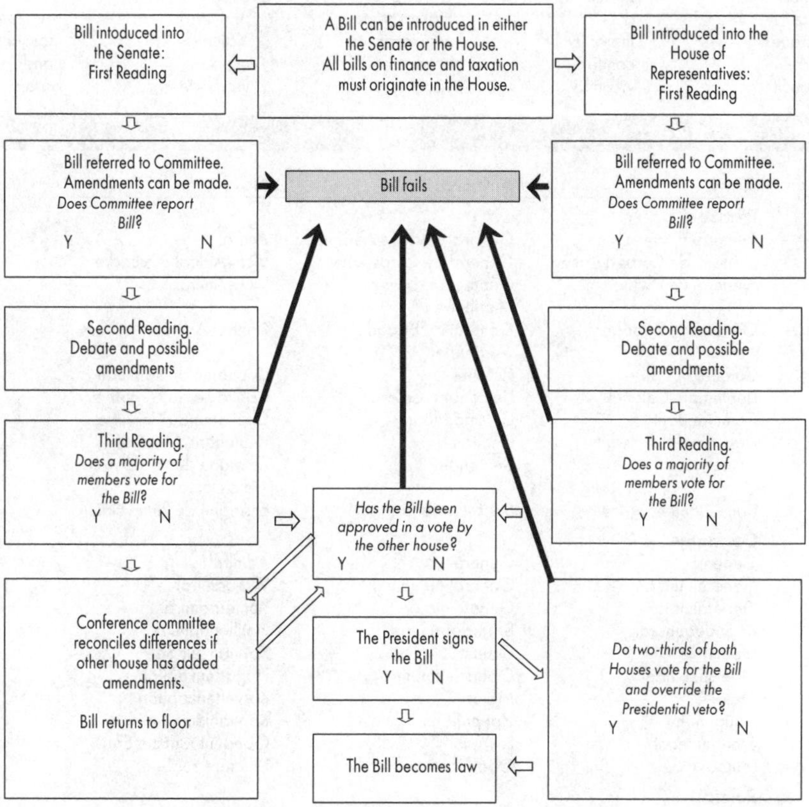

## Ranks of the aristocracy

| England | France | Holy Roman Empire (Germany) | Italy | Spain |
|---|---|---|---|---|
| king | roi | Kaiser | re | rey |
| prince | prince | Herzog | duca | duque |
| duke | duc | Pfalzgraf | principe | principe |
| marquess | marquis | Markgraf | marchese | marques |
| earl | comte | Landgraf | conde | conde |
| viscount | vicomte | visconte | vizconde | baron |

## Military ranks

| Army | Air Force | Navy |
|---|---|---|
| **France** | | |
| Général d'Armée | Général d'Armée Aérienne | Amiral |
| Général de Corps d'Armée | Général de Corps Aérien | Vice-Amiral d'Escadre |
| Général de Division | Général de Division Aérienne | Vice-Amiral |
| Général de Brigade | Général de Brigade Aérienne | Contre-Amiral |
| Colonel | Colonel | Capitaine de Vaisseau |
| Lieutenant-Colonel | Lieutenant-Colonel | Capitaine de Frégate |
| Commandant | Commandant | Capitaine de Corvette |
| Capitaine | Capitaine | Lieutenant de Vaisseau |
| Lieutenant | Lieutenant | Enseigne de Vaisseau de 1ère classe |
| Sous-Lieutenant | Sous-Lieutenant | Enseigne de 2ème classe |
| **Germany** | | |
| General | General | Admiral |
| Generalleutnant | Generalleutnant | Vizeadmiral |
| Generalmajor | Generalmajor | Konteradmiral |
| Brigadegeneral | Brigadegeneral | Flotillenadmiral |
| Oberst | Oberst | Kapitan zur See |
| Oberstleutnant | Oberstleutnant | Fregattenkapitän |
| Major | Major | Korvettenkapitän |
| Hauptmann | Hauptmann | Kapitänleutnant |
| Oberleutnant | Leutnant | Oberleutnant zur See |
| Leutnant | Oberfahnrich | Leutnant zur See |
| **Russia** | | |
| Marshal of the Army of the Russian Federation | Marshal of the Air Force of the Russian Federation | Admiral of the Fleet of the Russian Federation |
| Army General | General of the Air Force | Admiral of the Fleet |
| Colonel-General | Colonel-General | Admiral |
| Lieutenant-General | Lieutenant-General | Vice-Admiral |
| Major-General | Major-General | Rear-Admiral |
| Colonel | Colonel | Captain 1st class |
| Lieutenant-Colonel | Lieutenant-Colonel | Captain 2nd class |
| Major | Major | Captain 3rd class |
| Captain | Captain | Captain-Lieutenant |
| Senior Lieutenant | Senior Lieutenant | Senior Lieutenant |
| Lieutenant | Lieutenant | Lieutenant |
| Junior Lieutenant | Junior Lieutenant | Junior Lieutenant |

| Army | Air Force | Navy |
|---|---|---|
| **UK** | | |
| Field Marshal | Marshal of the Royal Air Force | Admiral of the Fleet |
| General | Air Chief Marshal | Admiral |
| Lieutenant-General | Air Marshal | Vice-Admiral |
| Major-General | Air Vice-Marshal | Rear-Admiral |
| Brigadier | Air Commodore | Commodore Admiral |
| Colonel | Group Captain | Captain RN |
| Lieutenant-Colonel | Wing Commander | Commander |
| Major | Squadron Leader | Lieutenant Commander |
| Captain | Flight Lieutenant | Lieutenant |
| Lieutenant | Flying Officer | Sub-Lieutenant |
| Second-Lieutenant | Pilot Officer | Midshipman |
| **USA** | | |
| General of the Army | General of the Air Force | Fleet Admiral |
| General | General | Admiral |
| Lieutenant-General | Lieutenant-General | Vice-Admiral |
| Major-General | Major-General | Rear-Admiral |
| Brigadier-General | Brigadier-General | Commodore Admiral |
| Colonel | Colonel | Captain |
| Lieutenant-Colonel | Lieutenant-Colonel | Commander |
| Major | Major | Lieutenant-Commander |
| Captain | Captain | Lieutenant |
| First-Lieutenant | First-Lieutenant | Lieutenant Junior Grade |
| Second-Lieutenant | Second-Lieutenant | Ensign |

## Honours: Europe

### ❑ Denmark

**Order of Dannebrog** Believed to have been founded in 1219 and one of the oldest orders in existence, revived in 1671, with six main classes: Grand Commanders, Knights Grand Cross, Commanders of the First Degree, Commanders, Knights of the First Degree and Knights, and an auxiliary class known as the Badge of Honour.

**Order of the Elephant** Founded in 1462 and revived by King Christian V in 1693; the premier order of Denmark.

### ❑ France

**Croix de Guerre** Military award established in 1915 to commemorate individuals mentioned in despatches.

**Légion d'Honneur** Instituted by Napoleon in 1802 to reward distinguished military or civil service, and divided into five classes: Grands Croix, Grands Officiers, Commandeurs, Officiers and Chevaliers.

### ❑ Germany

**The Iron Cross** Established by Frederick William in 1813 as an award for gallantry in action; various grades of award.

**Order of Merit** Instituted by the Federal German Republic in 1951, and divided into eight classes: Grand Cross (three grades), Large Merit Cross (three grades) and Merit Cross (two grades).

### ❑ Italy

**Al Merita della Republica Italiana** Established in 1952, with five classes of award: Grand Cross, Grand Officer, Commander, Officer and Member.

### ❑ Netherlands

**Huisorde van Oranje** Established in 1905, awarded for outstanding services to the Royal House; corresponds to the Royal Victorian Order in the United Kingdom.

**Militaire Willemsorde** Founded by King William I in 1815; the highest military decoration open to members of the forces of all ranks and to civilians for acts of bravery and devotion to duty.

**Nederlandsche Leeuw** Founded by King William I in 1815, awarded to those of proven patriotism, outstanding zeal and devotion to civil duty, and to those with extraordinary ability in the arts and sciences; open to civilians, members of the military and foreigners; divided into three classes: Grand Cross, Commander and Knight, with an attached brotherhood whose members are nominated for acts of distinction, self-sacrifice and philanthropy.

**Orde van Oranje Nassau** Established in 1892; awarded to Netherlanders and foreigners for distinguished performance to the state or society; open to civilians or members of the forces; divided into five classes: Grand Cross, Grand Officer, Knight Commander, Officer and Knight.

## Honours: UK

**CBE ► The Most Excellent Order of the British Empire**

**The Distinguished Service Order (DSO)** Established in 1886; bestowed as a reward for the distinguished service in action of commissioned officers in the Navy, Army and Royal Air Force; extended in 1942 to cover officers of the Merchant Navy.

**The George Cross (GC)** Instituted in 1940 as a reward for gallantry, and conferred upon those responsible for 'acts of the greatest heroism or of the most conspicuous courage in circumstances of extreme danger'.

**The Imperial Service Order (ISO)** Instituted in 1902 to reward members of the Civil Service; one class of membership; numbers limited to 1 700 in total, 1 100 belonging to the Home Civil Service, and 600 coming from the Overseas Civil Service.

**MBE ► The Most Excellent Order of the British Empire**

**The Most Ancient and Most Noble Order of the Thistle (KT)** An ancient order revived by King James II in 1687, and re-established by Queen Anne in 1703; limited to 16 knights.

**The Most Distinguished Order of St Michael and St George** Founded in 1818 by King George III; conferred upon British subjects for services abroad or in the British Commonwealth, with the motto 'Auspicium melioris aevi' (Token of a better age), and divided into three classes: Knight Grand Cross (GCMG), Knight Commander (KCMG) and Companion (CMG).

**The Most Excellent Order of the British Empire** An order of knighthood, the first to be granted to both sexes equally; instituted 1917; divided into military and civil divisions in 1918, with five divisions: Knight or Dame Grand Cross (GBE), Knight or Dame Commander (KBE/DBE), Commander (CBE), Officer (OBE) and Member (MBE).

**The Most Honourable Order of the Bath** Founded in 1399, revived by King George in 1725; originally a military order, the civil branch was established in 1847; women became eligible in 1971; the order has three divisions: Knight or Dame Grand Cross (GCB), Knight or Dame Commander (KCB/DCB), and Companion (CB).

**The Most Noble Order of the Garter (KG)** Instituted in 1348 by Edward III; limited to 24 knights companion only, and with the motto 'Honi soit qui mal y pense' (Shame on him who thinks evil of it).

**OBE ► The Most Excellent Order of the British Empire**

**The Order of Merit (OM)** Instituted in 1902, with civil and military divisions, and limited to 24 in number.

**The Order of the Companions of Honour** Instituted in 1917 at the same time as the Most Excellent Order of the British Empire; it carries no title or precedence and consists of one class ranking immediately after the first class of the Order of the British Empire; membership is limited to 65 in number, excluding honorary members.

**The Royal Red Cross** Instituted by Queen Victoria in 1883; the first military order designed solely for women, and conferred upon members of the nursing services for their efforts in the field, and for others undertaking voluntary work on behalf of the sick or wounded or on behalf of the Red Cross.

**The Royal Victorian Chain** Founded in 1902 by King Edward VII, it confers no precedence on the holder, and is largely, although not exclusively, awarded to foreign monarchs.

**The Royal Victorian Order** Established by Queen Victoria in 1896, with no limit to the number of members; conferred for services to the sovereign or Royal Family; bestowed upon foreigners as well as British subjects; women became eligible in 1936.

**The Victoria Cross (VC)** Instituted by Queen Victoria in 1856 to reward conspicuous bravery, and the most highly coveted of British military decorations.

## Honours: USA

**The Bronze Star** Established in 1944; awarded to members of the forces for acts of heroism or merit and for services beyond the call of duty, but not sufficiently outstanding to merit the Silver Star or Legion of Merit.

**The Congressional Medal of Honor** Instituted in 1861/1862, and first awarded during the American Civil War; conferred upon members of the forces showing exceptional gallantry and bravery in action.

**The Distinguished Service Cross** Instituted in 1918; confined to the army, and awarded to those showing extraordinary heroism in circumstances which do not justify the Congressional Medal of Honor.

**The Legion of Merit** Instituted in 1942; awarded to members of both the United States and foreign forces for distinguished service and meritorious conduct over a period of time.

**The Purple Heart** First instituted by George Washington in 1782 and reinstituted by Congress in 1932; awarded to those wounded in military action, and bears the inscription 'For Military Merit'.

**The Medal for Merit** Established by President Roosevelt in 1942 to award civilians of the United States or her allies for distinguished and meritorious service.

**The Silver Star** First authorised during World War I, it takes precedence over the Legion of Merit.

## Charities (UK)

This chart gives information on the top 25 UK charities by voluntary income in 1997 (excluding legacies).

| Abbreviated name | Full name | Date founded | Voluntary income in £million |
|---|---|---|---|
| — | Church Commissioners for England | 1948 | 107.1 |
| CAF | Charities Aid Foundation | 1974 | 107 |
| — | Oxfam | 1942 | 76.6 |
| — | National Trust | 1895 | 53.5 |
| ICRF | Imperial Cancer Research Fund | 1902 | 39.7 |
| — | British Heart Foundation | 1962 | 36.9 |
| — | United Bible Societies' Trust Association | 1946 | 36.1 |
| — | Help the Aged | 1961 | 35.5 |
| — | British Red Cross Society | 1870 | 35.1 |
| — | Barnardo's | 1866 | 30.3 |
| — | Cancer Relief Macmillan Fund | 1911 | 28.9 |
| — | Save the Children Fund | 1919 | 28.8 |
| — | ACTIONAID | 1972 | 28.3 |
| NSPCC | National Society for the Prevention of Cruelty to Children | 1884 | 26 |
| — | Marie Curie Memorial Foundation | 1948 | 23.9 |
| RNLI | Royal National Lifeboat Institution | 1824 | 20.8 |
| — | Tear Fund | 1968 | 19.7 |
| — | Christian Aid | 1949 | 19 |
| — | Royal British Legion | 1921 | 18.7 |
| RSPB | Royal Society for the Protection of Birds | 1889 | 17.1 |
| — | Salvation Army International Trust | 1865 | 16 |
| — | Institute of Cancer Research | 1909 | 15.6 |
| — | Royal Opera House Covent Garden | 1946 | 15.2 |
| — | Institute of Physics | 1874 | 15 |
| — | The National Gallery | 1824 | 14.7 |

Data from *Baring Asset Management Top 3000 Charities 1997*, published by Caritas Data Ltd.

SOCIAL STRUCTURE

## Charities (USA)

| Abbreviated name | Full name | Date founded | Income in US$000 [1] |
|---|---|---|---|
| ALSAC-SJCRH | ALSAC-St Jude Children's Research Hospital | 1957 | 126782 |
| ACS | American Cancer Society | 1913 | 335758 |
| AHA | American Heart Association | 1924 | 248776 |
| — | American National Red Cross | 1881 | 985175 |
| AF | AmeriCares Foundation | 1979 | 69373 |
| — | Arthritis Foundation | 1948 | 55534 |
| BGEA | Billy Graham Evangelistic Association | 1950 | 89178 |
| — | Boys Town/Father Flanagan's Boys' Home | 1917 | 64779 |
| — | Campus Crusade for Christ | 1951 | 129734 |
| — | CARE USA | 1945 | 329126 |
| CRS | Catholic Relief Services | 1943 | 288296 |
| CTW | Children's Television Workshop | 1969 | 71333 |
| CCF | Christian Children's Fund | 1938 | 101744 [2] |
| — | City of Hope | 1913 | 133013 |
| CH | Covenant House | 1969 | 88167 |
| LSA | Leukemia Society of America | 1949 | 54439 |
| — | March of Dimes Birth Defects Foundation | 1938 | 119655 |
| MDA | Muscular Dystrophy Association | 1950 | 111498 |
| NBA | National Benevolant Association of the Christian Church | 1887 | 81421 |
| NJCIRM | National Jewish Center for Immunology and Respiratory Medicine | 1899 | 62439 |
| NMSS | National Multiple Sclerosis Society | 1946 | 65590 |
| NWF | National Wildlife Federation | 1936 | 78753 |
| — | The Nature Conservancy | 1951 | 168554 |
| PPHF | People-to-People Health Foundation | 1958 | 53200 |
| — | Rotary Foundation of Rotary International | 1917 | 106276 |
| SCF | Save the Children Federation | 1932 | 84301 |
| — | Shriner's Hospital for Crippled Children | 1922 | 339266 |
| UJA | United Jewish Appeal | 1939 | 367863 |
| WV | World Vision | 1950 | 188735 |

[1] Data from 1988 or 1989.

[2] Includes income from related organizations in Germany and Australia.

# COMMUNICATION

## Languages: number of speakers

### Language families

Estimates of the numbers of speakers in the main language families of the world in the early 1980s. The list includes Japanese and Korean, which are not clearly related to any other languages.

| Main language families | |
|---|---|
| Indo-European | 2 000 000 000 |
| Sino-Tibetan | 1 040 000 000 |
| Niger-Congo | 260 000 000 |
| Afro-Asiatic | 230 000 000 |
| Austronesian | 200 000 000 |
| Dravidian | 140 000 000 |
| Japanese | 120 000 000 |
| Altaic | 90 000 000 |
| Austro-Asiatic | 60 000 000 |
| Korean | 60 000 000 |
| Tai | 50 000 000 |

| Main language families | |
|---|---|
| Nilo-Saharan | 30 000 000 |
| Amerindian (North, Central, South America) | 25 000 000 |
| Uralic | 23 000 000 |
| Miao-Yao | 7 000 000 |
| Caucasian | 6 000 000 |
| Indo-Pacific | 3 000 000 |
| Khoisan | 50 000 |
| Australian aborigine | 50 000 |
| Palaeosiberian | 25 000 |

### Specific languages

The first column gives estimates (in millions) for mother-tongue speakers of the 20 most widely used languages. The second column gives estimates of the total population of all countries where the language has official or semi-official status; these totals are often over-estimates, as only a minority of people in countries where a second language is recognized may actually be fluent in it.

| Mother-tongue speakers | |
|---|---|
| 1 Chinese | 1 000 |
| 2 English | 350 |
| 3 Spanish | 250 |
| 4 Hindi | 200 |
| 5 Arabic | 150 |
| 6 Bengali | 150 |
| 7 Russian | 150 |
| 8 Portuguese | 135 |
| 9 Japanese | 120 |
| 10 German | 100 |
| 11 French | 70 |
| 12 Panjabi | 70 |
| 13 Javanese | 65 |
| 14 Bihari | 65 |
| 15 Italian | 60 |
| 16 Korean | 60 |
| 17 Telugu | 55 |
| 18 Tamil | 55 |
| 19 Marathi | 50 |
| 20 Vietnamese | 50 |

| Official language populations | |
|---|---|
| 1 English | 1 400 |
| 2 Chinese | 1 000 |
| 3 Hindi | 700 |
| 4 Spanish | 280 |
| 5 Russian | 270 |
| 6 French | 220 |
| 7 Arabic | 170 |
| 8 Portuguese | 160 |
| 9 Malay | 160 |
| 10 Bengali | 150 |
| 11 Japanese | 120 |
| 12 German | 100 |
| 13 Urdu | 85 |
| 14 Italian | 60 |
| 15 Korean | 60 |
| 16 Vietnamese | 60 |
| 17 Persian | 55 |
| 18 Tagalog | 50 |
| 19 Thai | 50 |
| 20 Turkish | 50 |

## Speakers of English

The first column gives figures for countries where English is used as a mother-tongue or first language; for countries where no figure is given, English is not the first language of a significant number of people. (A question-mark indicates that no agreed estimates are available.) The second column gives total population figures (mainly 1996 estimates) for countries where English has official or semi-official status as a medium of communication. These totals are likely to bear little correlation with the real use of English in the area.

| Country | First language speakers of English | Country population |
|---|---|---|
| Anguilla | | 1 650 |
| Antigua and Barbuda | 61 400 | 64 400 |
| Australia | 17 700 000 | 18 287 000 |
| The Bahamas | 230 000 | 280 000 |
| Bangladesh | 3 200 000 | 123 100 000 |
| Barbados | 265 000 | 265 000 |
| Belize | 111 000 | 219 000 |
| Bermuda | 61 000 | 61 400 |
| Bhutan | ? | 1 622 000 |
| Botswana | 590 000 | 1 478 000 |
| Brunei | 10 000 | 290 000 |
| Cameroon | 2 720 000 | 13 609 000 |
| Canada | 18 112 000 | 29 784 000 |
| Dominica | ? | 73 800 |
| Fiji | 160 000 | 802 000 |
| Ghana | ? | 16 904 000 |
| Gibraltar | 24 000 | 27 100 |
| Grenada | 97 900 | 97 900 |
| Guyana | 700 000 + | 825 000 |
| India | 330 000 | 952 969 000 |
| Ireland | 3 599 000 | 3 599 000 |
| Jamaica | 2 505 000 | 2 505 000 |
| Kenya | | 29 137 000 |
| Kiribati | | 81 800 |
| Lesotho | | 2 017 000 |
| Liberia | 570 000 | 2 110 000 |
| Malawi | 540 000 | 9 453 000 |
| Malaysia | 100 000 | 20 359 000 |
| Malta | 8 000 | 373 000 |
| Mauritius | 2 000 | 1 141 000 |
| Montserrat | 12 000 | 12 000 |
| Namibia | 13 000 | 1 709 000 |
| Nauru | 800 | 10 600 |
| Nepal | ? | 20 892 000 |
| New Zealand | 3 290 000 | 3 619 000 |
| Nigeria | ? | 103 912 000 |
| Pakistan | ? | 133 500 000 |
| Papua New Guinea | 70 000 | 4 400 000 |
| Philippines | | 71 750 000 |
| St Kitts and Nevis | 39 400 | 39 400 |
| St Lucia | 29 000 | 144 000 |
| St Vincent and the Grenadines | 100 000 + | 113 000 |
| Seychelles | 2 000 | 76 100 |
| Sierra Leone | 700 000 | 4 617 000 |
| Singapore | 1 139 000 | 3 045 000 |
| Solomon Islands | | 396 000 |
| South Africa | 3 800 000 | 41 734 000 |
| Sri Lanka | 10 000 | 18 318 000 |
| Suriname | | 436 000 |
| Swaziland | | 934 000 |
| Tanzania | 900 000 | 29 165 000 |
| Tonga | | 101 000 |
| Trinidad and Tobago | 1 262 000 | 1 262 000 |
| Tuvalu | | 9 500 |
| Uganda | 190 000 | 20 158 000 |
| UK | 57 190 000 | 58 784 000 |
| USA | 228 700 000 | 265 455 000 |
| US territories in Pacific | ? | 196 300 |
| Vanuatu | 60 000 | 172 000 |
| Samoa | 1 000 | 214 000 |
| Zambia | 300 000 | 9 715 000 |
| Zimbabwe | 260 000 | 11 515 000 |
| Other British territories | ? | 106 167 |
| TOTALS | 349 764 500 | 2 038 046 117 |

## Foreign words and phrases

**ab initio** (Lat) 'from the beginning'.

**à bon marché** (Fr) 'good market'; at a good bargain, cheap.

**ab ovo** (Lat) 'from the egg'; from the beginning.

**absit omen** (Lat) a superstitious formula; may there be no ill omen (as in a reference just made).

**a cappella** (Ital) 'in the style of the chapel'; sung without instrumental accompaniment.

**Achtung** (Ger) 'Look out! Take care!'.

**acushla** (Ir) term of endearment; darling.

**addendum** *plural* **addenda** (Lat) 'that which is to be added'; supplementary material for a book.

**à deux** (Fr) 'for two'; often denotes a dinner or conversation of a romantic nature.

**ad hoc** (Lat) 'towards this'; for this special purpose.

**ad hominem** (Lat) 'to the man'; appealing not to logic or reason but to personal preferences or feelings.

**ad infinitum** (Lat) 'to infinity'; denotes endless repetition.

**ad litem** (Lat) 'for the lawsuit'; used of a guardian appointed to act in court (eg because of insanity or insufficient years of the litigant).

**ad nauseam** (Lat) 'to the point of sickness'; disgustingly endless or repetitive.

**ad referendum** (Lat) 'for reference'; to be further considered.

**ad valorem** (Lat) 'to value'; 'according to what it is worth'; often used of taxes etc.

**advocatus diaboli** (Lat) 'devil's advocate'; person opposing an argument in order to expose any flaws in it.

**affaire** (Fr) liaison, intrigue; an incident arousing speculation and scandal.

**afflatus** (Lat) 'blowing or breathing'; inspiration (often divine).

**aficionado** (Span) 'amateur'; an ardent follower; a 'fan'.

**a fortiori** (Lat) 'from the stronger' (argument); denotes the validity and stronger reason of a proposition.

**agent provocateur** (Fr) 'provocative agent'; someone who incites others, by pretended sympathy, to commit crimes.

**aggiornamento** (Ital) 'modernization'; reform (often political).

**aide-de-camp** (Fr) 'assistant on the field'; an officer who acts as a confidential personal assistant for an officer of higher rank.

**aide-mémoire** (Fr) 'help-memory'; a reminder; memorandum-book; a written summary of a diplomatic agreement.

**à la carte** (Fr) 'from the menu'; each dish individually priced.

**à la mode** (Fr) 'in fashion, fashionable'; also in cooking, of meat braised and stewed with vegetables; with ice-cream (American English).

**al dente** (Ital) 'to the tooth'; culinary term denoting (usually) pasta fully cooked but still firm.

**al fresco** (Ital) 'fresh'; painting on fresh or moist plaster; in the fresh, cool or open air.

**alma mater** (Lat) 'bountiful mother'; one's former school, college, or university; official college or university song (American English).

**aloha** (Hawaiian) 'love'; a salutation, 'hello' or 'goodbye'.

**alumnus** *plural* **alumni** (Lat) 'pupil' or 'foster son'; a former pupil or student.

**ambiance** (Fr) surroundings, atmosphere.

**amende honorable** (Fr) a public apology satisfying the honour of the injured party.

**amour-propre** (Fr) 'own love, self-love'; legitimate self-esteem, sometimes exaggerated; vanity, conceit.

**ancien régime** (Fr) 'old regime'; a superseded and outdated political system or ruling elite.

**angst** (Ger) 'anxiety'; an unsettling feeling produced by awareness of the uncertainties and paradoxes inherent in the state of being human.

**anno Domini** (Lat) 'in the year of the Lord'; used in giving dates of the Christian era, counting forward from the year of Christ's birth.

**annus mirabilis** (Lat) 'year of wonders'; a remarkably successful or auspicious year.

**Anschluss** (Ger) 'joining together'; union, especially the political union of Germany and Austria in 1938.

**ante-bellum** (Lat) 'before the war'; denotes a period before a specific war, especially the American Civil War.

**ante meridiem** (Lat) 'before midday'; between midnight and noon, abbreviated to am.

**à point** (Fr) 'into the right condition'; to a nicety, a culinary term.

**a posteriori** (Lat) 'from the later'; applied to reasoning from experience, from effect to cause; inductive reasoning.

**apparatchik** (Russ) a Communist spy or agent; (humorous) any bureaucratic hack.
**appellation contrôlée** (Fr) 'certified name'; used in the labelling of French wines, a guarantee of specified conditions of origin, strength, etc.
**après-ski** (Fr) 'after-ski'; pertaining to the evening's amusements after skiing.
**a priori** (Lat) 'from the previous'; denotes argument from the cause to the effect; deductive reasoning.
**atelier** (Fr) a workshop; an artist's studio.
**au contraire** (Fr) 'on the contrary'.
**au fait** (Fr) 'to the point'; highly skilled; knowledgeable or familiar with something.
**au fond** (Fr) 'at the bottom'; fundamentally.
**au naturel** (Fr) 'in the natural state'; naked; also as a culinary term: cooked plainly, raw, or without dressing.
**au pair** (Fr) 'on an equal basis'; originally an arrangement of mutual service without payment; now used of a girl (usually foreign) who performes domestic duties for board, lodging and pocket money.
**auto-da-fé** (Port) 'act of the faith'; the public declaration or carrying out of a sentence imposed on heretics in Spain and Portugal by the Inquisition, eg burning at the stake.
**avant-garde** (Fr) 'front guard'; applied to those in the forefront of an artistic movement.
**ave atque vale** (Lat) hail and farewell.
**babushka** (Russ) 'grandmother'; granny; a triangular headscarf worn under the chin.
**bain-marie** (Fr) 'bath of Mary'; a water-bath; a vessel of boiling water in which another is placed for slow and gentle cooking, or for keeping food warm.
**baksheesh** (Persian) a gift or present of money, particularly in the East (India, Turkey, Egypt, etc).
**bal costumé** (Fr) a fancy-dress ball.
**banzai** (Jap) a Japanese battle cry, salute to the emperor, or exclamation of joy.
**barrio** (Span) 'district, suburb'; a community (usually poor) of Spanish-speaking immigrants (esp American English).
**batik** (Javanese) 'painted'; method of producing patterns on fabric by drawing with wax before dyeing.
**beau geste** (Fr) 'beautiful gesture'; a magnanimous action.
**belle époque** (Fr) 'fine period'; the time of gracious living for the well-to-do immediately preceding World War I.
**bête noire** (Fr) 'black beast'; a bugbear; something one especially dislikes.
**Bildungsroman** (Ger) 'educational novel'; a novel concerning its hero's early spiritual and emotional development and education.
**blasé** (Fr) 'cloyed'; dulled to enjoyment.
**blitzkrieg** (Ger) 'lightning war'; a sudden overwhelming attack by ground and air forces; a burst of intense activity.
**bodega** (Span) a wine shop that usually sells food as well; a building for wine storage.
**bona fides** (Lat) 'good faith'; genuineness.
**bonne-bouche** (Fr) 'good mouth'; a delicious morsel eaten at the end of a meal.
**bonsai** (Jap) art of growing miniature trees in pots; a dwarf tree grown by this method.
**bon vivant** (Fr) 'good living (person)'; one who lives well, particularly enjoying good food and wine; a jovial companion.
**bon voyage** (Fr) have a safe and pleasant journey.
**bourgeois** (Fr) 'citizen'; a member of the middle class; a merchant; conventional, conservative.
**camera obscura** (Lat) 'dark room'; a light-free chamber in which an image of outside objects is thrown upon a screen.
**canard** (Fr) 'duck'; a false rumour; a second wing fitted as a horizontal stabilizer near the nose of an aircraft.
**carpe diem** (Lat) 'seize the day'; enjoy the pleasures of the present moment while they last.
**carte blanche** (Fr) 'blank sheet of paper'; freedom of action.
**casus belli** (Lat) 'occasion of war'; whatever sparks off or justifies a war or quarrel.
**cause célèbre** (Fr) a very notable or famous trial; a notorious controversy.
**caveat emptor** (Lat) 'let the buyer beware'; warns the buyer to examine carefully the article about to be purchased.
**c'est la vie** (Fr) 'that's life'; denotes fatalistic resignation.
**chacun à son goût** (Fr) 'each to his own taste'; implies surprise at another's choice.
**chambré** (Fr) 'put into a room'; (of red wine) at room temperature.

**chargé-d'affaires** (Fr) a diplomatic agent of lesser rank; an ambassador's deputy.

**chef d'oeuvre** (Fr) a masterpiece; the best piece of work by a particular artist, writer, etc.

**chicano** (Span) *mejicano* 'Mexican'; or an American of Mexican descent.

**chutzpah** (Yiddish) 'effrontery'; nerve to do or say outrageous things.

**cinéma vérité** (Fr) 'cinema truth'; realism in films usually sought by photographic scenes of real life.

**cinquecento** (Ital) 'five hundred'; of the Italian art and literature of the 16th-c Renaissance period.

**circa** (Lat) 'surrounding'; of dates and numbers: approximately.

**cliché** (Fr) 'stereotype printing block'; the impression made by a die in any soft metal; a hackneyed phrase or concept.

**cognoscente** *plural* **cognoscenti** (Ital) 'one who knows'; one who professes critical knowledge of art, music, etc; a connoisseur.

**coitus interruptus** (Lat) 'interrupted intercourse'; coitus intentionally interrupted by withdrawal before semen is ejaculated; anticlimax when something ends prematurely.

**comme il faut** (Fr) 'as it is necessary'; correct; genteel.

**compos mentis** (Lat) 'having control of one's mind'; sane.

**contra mundum** (Lat) 'against the world'; denotes defiant perseverance despite universal criticism.

**cordon bleu** (Fr) 'blue ribbon'; denotes food cooked to a very high standard; a dish made with ham and cheese and a white sauce.

**coup de foudre** (Fr) 'flash of lightning'; a sudden and astonishing happening; love at first sight.

**coup de grâce** (Fr) 'blow of mercy'; a finishing blow to end pain; a decisive action which ends a troubled enterprise.

**coup d'état** (Fr) 'blow of state'; a violent overthrow of a government or subversive stroke of state policy.

**coupé** (Fr) 'cut'; (usually) two-door motor-car with sloping roof.

**crème de la crème** (Fr) 'cream of the cream'; the very best.

**cuisine minceur** (Fr) 'slenderness cooking'; a style of cooking characterized by imaginative use of light, simple, low-fat ingredients.

**cul-de-sac** (Fr) 'bottom of the bag'; a road closed at one end.

**cum grano salis** (Lat) with a grain (pinch) of salt.

**curriculum vitae** (Lat) 'course of life'; denotes a summary of someone's educational qualifications and work experience for presenting to a prospective employer.

**décolleté** (Fr) 'with bared neck and shoulders'; with neck uncovered; (of dress) low cut.

**de facto** (Lat) 'from the fact'; in fact; actually; irrespective of what is legally recognized.

**de gustibus non est disputandum** (Lat) (often in English shortened for convenience to *de gustibus*) 'there is no disputing about tastes'; there is no sense in challenging people's preferences.

**déjà vu** (Fr) 'already seen'; in any of the arts: original material; an illusion of having experienced something before; something seen so often it has become tedious.

**de jure** (Lat) 'according to law'; denotes the legal or theoretical position, which may not correspond with reality.

**delirium tremens** (Lat) 'trembling delirium'; psychotic condition caused by alcoholism, involving anxiety, shaking, hallucinations, etc.

**Deo volente** (Lat) 'God willing'; a sort of good-luck talisman.

**de rigueur** (Fr) 'of strictness'; compulsory; required by strict etiquette.

**derrière** (Fr) 'behind'; the buttocks.

**déshabillé** (Fr) 'undressed'; state of being only partially dressed, or of being casually dressed.

**de trop** (Fr) 'of too much'; superfluous; in the way.

**deus ex machina** (Lat) 'a god from a machine'; a contrived solution to a difficulty in a plot.

**distingué** (Fr) 'distinguished'; having an aristocratic or refined demeanour; striking.

**dolce far niente** (Ital) 'sweet doing nothing'; denotes the pleasure of idleness.

**doppelgänger** (Ger) 'double goer'; a ghostly duplicate of a living person; a wraith; someone who looks exactly like someone else.

**double entendre** (Fr) 'double meaning'; ambiguity (normally with indecent connotations).

**doyen** (Fr) 'dean'; most distinguished member or representative by virtue of seniority, experience, and often also excellence.

**droit du seigneur** (Fr) 'the lord's right'; originally the alleged right of a feudal superior to take the virginity of a vassal's bride; any excessive claim imposed on a subordinate.

**Dummkopf** (Ger) 'dumb-head'; blockhead; idiot.

**echt** (Ger) 'real, genuine'; denotes authenticity, typicality.

**Eheu fugaces** (Lat); opening of a quotation (Horace *Odes* II, XIV, 1–2) 'Alas! the fleeting years slip away'; bemoans the brevity of human existence.

**élan** (Fr) 'dash, rush, bound'; flair; flamboyance.

**El Dorado** (Span) 'the gilded man'; the golden land (or city) imagined by the Spanish conquerors of America; any place which offers the opportunity of acquiring fabulous wealth.

**embarras de richesse** (Fr) 'embarrassment of wealth'; a perplexing amount of wealth or an abundance of any kind.

**embonpoint** (Fr) *en bon point* 'in fine form'; well-fed; stout; plump.

**emeritus** (Lat) 'having served one's time'; eg of a retired professor, honourably discharged from a public duty; holding a position on an honorary basis only.

**éminence grise** (Fr) 'grey eminence'; someone exerting power through their influence over a superior.

**enfant terrible** (Fr) 'terrible child'; a precocious child whose sayings embarrass its parents; a person whose behaviour is indiscreet, embarrassing to his associates.

**ennui** (Fr) 'boredom'; world-weary listlessness.

**en passant** (Fr) 'in passing'; by the way; incidentally; applied in chess to the taking of a pawn that has just moved two squares as if it had moved only one.

**en route** (Fr) 'on the way, on the road'; let us go.

**entente** (Fr) 'understanding'; a friendly agreement between nations.

**épater le bourgeois** (Fr) 'shock the middle class'; to disconcert the prim and proper; commonly used of artistic productions which defy convention.

**erratum** *plural* **errata** (Lat) an error in writing or printing.

**ersatz** (Ger) 'replacement, substitute'; connotes a second-rate substitute; a supplementary reserve from which waste can be made good.

**et al** (Lat) *et alii* 'and other things'; used to avoid giving a complete and possibly over-lengthy list of all items eg of authors.

**Et tu, Brute?** (Lat) 'You too, Brutus?' (Caesar's alleged exclamation when he saw Brutus among his assassins); denotes surprise and dismay that a supposed friend has joined in a conspiracy against one.

**eureka** (Gr) *heureka* 'I have found!'; cry of triumph at a discovery.

**ex cathedra** (Lat) 'from the seat'; from the chair of office; authoritatively; judicially.

**ex gratia** (Lat) 'from favour'; of a payment; one that is made as a favour, without any legal obligation and without admitting legal liability.

**ex officio** (Lat) 'from office, by virtue of office'; used as a reason for membership of a body.

**ex parte** (Lat) 'from (one) part, from (one) side'; on behalf of one side only in legal proceedings; partial; prejudiced.

**fait accompli** (Fr) 'accomplished fact'; already done or settled, and therefore irreversible.

**fata Morgana** (Ital) a striking kind of mirage, attributed to witchcraft.

**fatwa** (Arabic) 'the statement of a formal legal opinion'; a formal legal opinion delivered by an Islamic religious leader.

**faute de mieux** (Fr) 'for lack of anything better'.

**faux ami** (Fr) 'false friend'; a word in a foreign language that does not mean what it appears to.

**faux-naïf** (Fr) 'falsely naive'; seeming or pretending to be unsophisticated, innocent, etc.

**faux pas** (Fr) 'false step'; a social blunder.

**femme fatale** (Fr) 'fatal woman'; an irresistibly attractive woman who brings difficulties or disasters on men; a siren.

**fidus Achates** (Lat) 'the faithful Achates' (Aeneas' friend); a loyal follower.

**film noir** (Fr) 'black film'; a bleak and pessimistic film.

**fin de siècle** (Fr) 'end of the century'; of the end of the 19th-c in Western culture or of an era; decadent.

**floruit** (Lat) 'he or she flourished'; denotes a period during which a person lived.

**fons et origo** (Lat) 'the source and origin'.

**force de frappe** (Fr) 'strike force'; equivalent of the 'independent nuclear deterrent'.

**force majeure** (Fr) 'superior force'; an unforseeable or uncontrollable course of events, excusing one from fulfilling a contract; a legal term.

**Führer** (Ger) 'leader, guide'; an insulting term for anyone bossily asserting authority.

**Gastarbeiter** (Ger) 'guest-worker'; an immigrant worker, especially one who does menial work.

**Gauleiter** (Ger) 'district leader'; a chief official of a district under the Nazi régime; an overbearing wielder of petty authority.
**gemütlich** (Ger) amiable; comfortable; cosy.
**gestalt** (Ger) 'form, shape'; original whole or unit, more than the sum of its parts.
**Gesundheit** (Ger) 'health', 'your health'; said to someone who has just sneezed.
**glasnost** (Russ) 'publicity'; the policy of openness and forthrightness followed by the Soviet government, initiated by Mikhail Gorbachev.
**Gnothi seauton** (Gr) 'Know thyself'.
**Götterdämmerung** (Ger) 'twilight of the gods'; the downfall of any once powerful system.
**goy** plural **goys** or **goyim** (Hebrew) non-Jewish, a gentile.
**grand mal** (Fr) 'large illness'; a violently convulsive form of epilepsy.
**grand prix** (Fr) 'great prize'; any of several international motor races; any competition of similar importance in other sports.
**gran turismo** (Ital) 'great touring, touring on a grand scale'; a motor car designed for high speed touring in luxury (abbreviation GT).
**gratis** (Lat) *gratiis* 'kindness, favour'; free of charge.
**gravitas** (Lat) 'weight'; seriousness; weight of demeanour; avoidance of unseemly frivolity.
**gringo** (Mexican-Spanish) 'foreigner'.
**guru** (Hindi) a spiritual leader; a revered instructor or mentor.
**habeas corpus** (Lat) 'you should have the body'; a writ to a jailer to produce a prisoner in person, and to state the reasons for detention; maintains the right of the subject to protection from unlawful imprisonment.
**haiku** (Jap) 'amusement poem'; a Japanese poem consisting of only three lines, containing respectively five, seven, and five syllables.
**hajj** (Arabic) 'pilgrimage'; the Muslim pilgrimage to Mecca.
**haka** (Maori) a Maori ceremonial war dance; a similar dance performed by New Zealanders eg before a rugby game.
**halal** (Arabic) 'lawful'; meat from an animal killed in strict accordance with Islamic law.
**haute couture** (Fr) 'higher tailoring'; fashionable, expensive dress designing and tailoring.
**haut monde** (Fr) 'high world'; high society; fashionable society; composed of the aristocracy and the wealthy.
**hic jacet** (Lat) 'here lies'; the first words of an epitaph; memorial inscription.
**hoi polloi** (Gr) 'the many'; the rabble; the vulgar.
**hombre** (Span) 'man'.
**honoris causa** (Lat) 'for the sake of honour'; a token of respect; used to designate honorary university degrees.
**hors concours** (Fr) 'out of the competition'; not entered for a contest; unequalled.
**ibidem** (Lat) 'in the same place'; used in footnotes to indicate that the same book (or chapter) has been cited previously.
**id** (Lat) 'it'; the sum total of the primitive instinctive forces in an individual.
**idée fixe** (Fr) 'a fixed idea'; an obsession.
**idem** (Lat) 'the same'.
**ikebana** (Jap) 'living flowers'; the Japanese art of flower arrangement.
**in absentia** (Lat) 'in absence'; used for occasions, such as the receiving of a degree award, when the recipient would normally be present.
**in camera** (Lat) 'in the room'; in a private room; in secret.
**incommunicado** (Span) 'unable to communicate'; deprived of the right to communicate with others.
**in extremis** (Lat) 'in the last'; at the point of death; in desperate circumstances.
**in flagrante delecto** (Lat) 'with the crime blazing'; in the very act of committing the crime.
**infra dig** (Lat) 'below dignity'; below one's dignity.
**in loco parentis** (Lat) 'in place of a parent'.
**in Shallah** (Arabic) 'if God wills'; ► **Deo volente**
**inter alia** (Lat) 'among other things'; used to show that a few examples have been chosen from many possibilities.
**in vitro** (Lat) 'in glass'; in the test tube.
**ipso facto** (Lat) 'by the fact itself'; thereby.
**je ne sais quoi** (Fr) 'I do not know what'; an indefinable something.

**jihad** (Arabic) 'struggle'; a holy war undertaken by Muslims against unbelievers.

**Jugendstil** (Ger) 'youth style'; the German term for art nouveau.

**kamikaze** (Jap) 'divine wind'; Japanese pilots making a suicide attack; any reckless, potentially self-destructive act.

**kanaka** (Hawaiian) 'man'; used by Europeans (and Australians) to mean South Sea islander.

**karaoke** (Jap) 'empty orchestra'; in bars, clubs, etc members of the public sing a solo to a recorded backing.

**karma** (Sanskrit) 'act'; the concept that the actions in a life determine the future condition of an individual.

**kibbutz** (Hebrew) a Jewish communal agricultural settlement in Israel.

**kitsch** (Ger) 'rubbish'; work in any of the arts that is pretentious and inferior or in bad taste.

**kvetch** (Yiddish) 'complain, whine (incessantly)'.

**la dolce vita** (Ital) 'the sweet life'; the name of a film made by Federico Fellini in 1960 showing a life of wealth, pleasure and self-indulgence.

**laissez-faire** (Fr) 'let do'; a general principle of non-interference.

**Lebensraum** (Ger) 'life space'; room to live; used by Hitler to justify his acquisition of land for Germany.

**leitmotiv** (Ger) 'leading motive'; a recurrent theme.

**lèse-majesté** (Fr) 'injured majesty'; offence against the sovereign power; treason.

**lingua franca** (Ital) 'Frankish language'; originally a mixed Italian trading language used in the Levant, subsequently any language chosen as a means of communication among speakers of different languages.

**locum tenens** (Lat) 'place holder'; a deputy or substitute, especially for a doctor or a clergyman.

**macho** (Mexican-Spanish) 'male'; originally a positive term denoting masculinity or virility, it has come in English to describe an ostentatious virility.

**magnum opus** (Lat) 'great work'; a person's greatest achievement, especially a literary work.

**maharishi** (Sanskrit) a Hindu sage or spiritual leader; a guru.

**mañana** (Span) 'tomorrow'; an unspecified time in the future.

**mea culpa** (Lat) 'through my fault'; originally part of the Latin mass; an admission of fault and an expression of repentance.

**memento mori** (Lat) 'remember that you must die'; an object, such as a skull, or anything to remind one of mortality.

**ménage à trois** (Fr) 'household of three'; a household comprising a husband and wife and the lover of one of them.

**mens sana in corpore sano** (Lat) 'a sound mind in a sound body' (Juvenal *Satires* X, 356); the guiding rule of the 19th-c English educational system.

**mirabile dictu** (Lat) 'wonderful to tell'; an expression of (sometimes ironic) amazement.

**modus operandi** (Lat) 'mode of working'; the characteristic methods employed by a particular criminal.

**modus vivendi** (Lat) 'mode of living'; an arrangement or compromise by means of which those who differ may get on together for a time.

**mot juste** (Fr) 'exact word'; the word which fits the context exactly.

**multum in parvo** (Lat) 'much in little'; a large amount in a small space.

**mutatis mutandis** (Lat) 'with the necessary changes made'.

**négociant** (Fr) 'merchant, trader'; often used for *négociant en vins* 'wine merchant'.

**ne plus ultra** (Lat) 'not more beyond'; extreme perfection.

**netsuke** (Jap) a small Japanese carved ornament used to fasten small objects, eg a purse, tobacco pouch, or medicine box, to the sash of a kimono. They are now collectors' pieces.

**noblesse oblige** (Fr) 'nobility obliges'; rank imposes obligations.

**non sequitur** (Lat) 'it does not follow'; a conclusion that does not follow logically from the premise; a remark that has no relation to what has gone before.

**nostalgie de la boue** (Fr) 'hankering for mud'; a craving for a debased physical life without civilized refinements.

**nota bene** (Lat) 'observe well, note well'; often abbreviated NB.

**nouveau riche** (Fr) 'new rich'; one who has only lately acquired wealth (without acquiring good taste).

**nouvelle cuisine** (Fr) 'new cooking'; a style of simple French cookery that aims to produce dishes that are light and healthy, utilizing fresh fruit and vegetables, and avoiding butter and cream.

**nouvelle vague** (Fr) 'new wave'; a movement in the French cinema aiming at imaginative quality films.

**obiter dictum** (Lat) 'something said in passing'; originally a legal term for something said by a trial judge that was incidental to the case in question.

**origami** (Jap) 'paper-folding'; Japanese art of folding paper to make shapes suggesting birds, boats, etc.

**O tempora! O mores!** (Lat) 'O the times! O the manners' (Cicero *In Catilinam*); a condemnation of present times, as contrasted with a past which is seen as golden.

**outré** (Fr) 'gone to excess'; beyond what is customary or proper; eccentric.

**pace** (Lat) 'peace'; by your leave (indicating polite disagreement).

**panem et circenses** (Lat) 'bread and circuses', or 'food and the big match' (Juvenal *Satires* X, 80); amusements which divert the populace from unpleasant realities.

**passim** (Lat) 'everywhere, throughout'; dispersed through a book.

**per capita** (Lat) 'by heads'; per head of the population in statistical contexts.

**perestroika** (Russ) 'reconstruction'; restructuring of an organization.

**persona non grata** (Lat) one who is not welcome or favoured (originally a term in diplomacy).

**pied à terre** (Fr) 'foot to the ground'; a flat, small house etc kept for temporary or occasional accommodation.

**plus ça change** (Fr) abbreviated form of **plus ça change, plus c'est la même chose** 'the more things change, the more they stay the same'; a comment on the unchanging nature of the world.

**post meridiem** (Lat) 'after midday, after noon'; abbreviated to pm.

**post mortem** (Lat) 'after death'; an examination of a body in order to determine the cause of death; an after-the-event discussion.

**poule de luxe** (Fr) 'luxurious hen'; a sexually attractive promiscuous young woman; a prostitute.

**pour encourager les autres** (Fr) 'to encourage the others' (Voltaire *Candide*, on the execution of Admiral Byng); exemplary punishment.

**premier cru** (Fr) 'first growth'; wine of the highest quality in a system of classification.

**prêt-à-porter** (Fr) 'ready to wear'; refers to 'designer' clothes that are made in standard sizes as opposed to made-to-measure clothes.

**prima donna** (Ital) 'first lady'; leading female singer in an opera; a person who is temperamental and hard to please.

**prima facie** (Lat) 'at first sight'; a legal term for evidence that is assumed to be true unless disproved by other evidence.

**primus inter pares** (Lat) 'first among equals'.

**prix fixe** (Fr) 'fixed price'; used of a meal in a restaurant offered at a set price for a restricted choice. Compare **table d'hôte**.

**pro bono publico** (Lat) 'for the public good'; something done for no fee.

**quid pro quo** (Lat) 'something for something'; something given or taken as equivalent to another, often as retaliation.

**quod erat demonstrandum** (Lat) 'which was to be shown'; often used in its abbreviated form **qed**.

**raison d'être** (Fr) 'reason for existence'.

**rara avis** (Lat) 'rare bird' (Juvenal *Satires* VI, 165); something or someone remarkable and unusual.

**realpolitik** (Ger) 'politics of realism'; practical politics based on the realities and necessities of life, rather than moral or ethical ideas.

**recherché** (Fr) 'sought out'; carefully chosen; particularly choice; rare or exotic.

**reculer pour mieux sauter** (Fr) 'move backwards in order to jump better'; a strategic withdrawal to wait for a better opportunity.

**reductio ad absurdum** (Lat) 'reduction to absurdity'; originally used in logic to mean the proof of a proposition by proving the falsity of its contradictory; the application of a principle so strictly that it is carried to absurd lengths.

**répondez, s'il vous plaît** (Fr) 'reply, please'; in English mainly in its abbreviated form, **RSVP**, on invitations.

**revenons à nos moutons** (Fr) 'let us return to our sheep'; let us get back to our subject.

**rijsttafel** (Dutch) 'rice table'; an Indonesian rice dish served with a variety of foods.

**risqué** (Fr) 'risky, hazardous'; audaciously bordering on the unseemly.

**Rus in urbe** (Lat) 'The country in the town' (Martial *Epigrams* XII, 57); the idea of country charm in the centre of a city.

**Salus populi suprema est lex** (Lat) 'Let the welfare of the people be the chief law' (Cicero *De Legibus* III, 3).

**samizdat** (Russ) 'self-publisher'; the secret printing and distribution of banned literature in the former USSR and other Eastern European countries previously under Communist rule.

**sanctum sanctorum** (Lat) 'holy of holies'; the innermost chamber of the temple, where the Ark of the Covenant was kept; any private room reserved for personal use.

**sang froid** (Fr) 'cold blood'; self possession; coolness under stress.
**savoir faire** (Fr) 'knowing what to do'; knowing what to do and how to do it in any situation.
**schadenfreude** (Ger) 'hurt joy'; pleasure in others' misfortunes.
**shlimazel** (Yiddish) 'bad luck'; a persistently unlucky person.
**shlock** (Yiddish) 'broken or damaged goods'; inferior; shoddy.
**shmaltz** (Yiddish) 'melted fat, grease'; showy sentimentality, particularly in writing, music, art, etc
**shmuck** (Yiddish) 'penis'; a (male) stupid person.
**shogun** (Jap) 'leader of the army'; ruler of feudal Japan.
**sic** (Lat) 'so, thus'; used in brackets within printed matter to show that the original is faithfully reproduced even if incorrect.
**sic transit gloria mundi** (Lat) 'so passes away earthly glory'.
**sine die** (Lat) 'without a day'; the adjournment of a meeting (often in court), indicating that no day has been fixed for its resumption; an indefinite adjournment.
**sine qua non** (Lat) 'without which not'; an indispensable condition.
**sotto voce** (Ital) 'below the voice'; in an undertone; aside.
**status quo** (Lat) 'the state in which'; the existing condition.
**sub judice** (Lat) 'under a judge'; under consideration by a judge or a court of law.
**subpoena** (Lat) 'under penalty'; a writ commanding attendance in court.
**sub rosa** (Lat) 'under the rose'; in secret; privately.
**succès de scandale** (Fr) 'success of scandal'; the success of a book, film, etc due not to merit but to its connection with, or reference to, a scandal.
**summa cum laude** (Lat) 'with the highest praise'; with great distinction; the highest class of degree award that can be gained by a US college student.
**summum bonum** (Lat) 'the chief good'.
**table d'hôte** (Fr) 'host's table'; a set meal at a fixed price. Compare **prix fixe**.
**tabula rasa** (Lat) 'scraped table'; a cleaned tablet; a mind not yet influenced by outside impressions and experience.
**t'ai chi** (Chin) 'great art of boxing'; a system of exercise and self-defence in which good use of balance and co-ordination allows effort to be minimized.
**tempus fugit** (Lat) 'time flies'; delay cannot be tolerated.
**terra incognita** (Lat) 'unknown land'; an unknown land (so marked on early maps); an area of study about which very little is known.
**touché** (Fr) 'touched'; claiming or acknowledging a hit made in fencing; claiming or acknowledging a point scored in an argument.
**tour de force** (Fr) 'turning movement'; feat of strength or skill.
**trompe l'oeil** (Fr) 'deceives the eye'; an appearance of reality achieved by the use of perspective and detail in painting, architecture, etc.
**tsunami** (Jap) 'wave in harbour'; a wave generated by movement of the earth's surface underwater; commonly (and erroneously) called a 'tidal wave'.
**Übermensch** (Ger) 'over-person'; superman.
**ultra vires** (Lat) 'beyond strength, beyond powers'; beyond one's power or authority.
**urbi et orbi** (Lat) 'to the city and the world'; used of the Pope's pronouncements; to everyone.
**vade-mecum** (Lat) 'go with me'; a handbook; pocket companion.
**vin du pays** (Fr) 'wine of the country'; a locally produced wine for everyday consumption.
**vis-à-vis** (Fr) 'face to face'; one who faces or is opposite another; in relation to.
**viva voce** (Lat) 'with the living voice'; in speech, orally; an oral examination, particularly at a university (commonly 'viva' alone).
**volte-face** (Fr) 'turn-face'; a sudden and complete change in opinion or in views expressed.
**vox populi** (Lat); 'voice of the people'; public or popular opinion.
**Weltschmerz** (Ger) 'world pain'; sympathy with universal misery; thoroughgoing pessimism.
**wunderkind** (Ger) 'wonder-child'; a 'child prodigy'; one who shows great talent and/or achieves great success at an early (or comparatively early) age.
**zeitgeist** (Ger) 'time-spirit'; the spirit of the age.

## Common abbreviations

See also **Computer Languages** p330

**AA** Alcoholics Anonymous
**AA** Automobile Association
**AAA** Amateur Athletics Association
**AAA** American Automobile Association
**ABA** Amateur Boxing Association
**ABA** American Booksellers Association
**ABC** American Broadcasting Corporation
**ABC** Australian Broadcasting Corporation
**ABM** antiballistic missile
**ABTA** Association of British Travel Agents
**AC/ac** alternating current
**ACAS** Advisory, Conciliation, and Arbitration Service
**ACLU** American Civil Liberties Union
**ACT** Australian Capital Territory
**ACTH** adrenocorticotrophic hormone
**ACTU** Australian Council of Trade Unions
**AD** anno Domini (in the year of Our Lord)
**A-D** analog-to-digital (in computing)
**ADH** antidiuretic hormone
**ADP** adenosine diphosphate
**AEA** Atomic Energy Authority (UK)
**AEC** Atomic Energy Commission (USA)
**AFC** American Football Conference
**AFL/CIO** American Federation of Labor/ Congress of Industrial Organizations
**AFV** armoured fighting vehicle
**AGM** annual general meeting
**AGR** advanced gas-cooled reactor
**AH** anno Hegirae (in the year of Hegira)
**AHF** anti-haemophilic factor
**AI** artificial intelligence
**AID** artificial insemination by donor
**AIDS** Acquired Immune Deficiency Syndrome
**AIF** Australian Imperial Force
**AIH** artificial insemination by husband
**ALCM** air-launched cruise missile
**ALP** Australian Labor Party
**ALU** arithmetic and logic unit
**AM** amplitude modulation
**am** ante meridiem (before noon)
**AMA** American Medical Association
**amu** atomic mass unit
**ANC** African National Congress
**ANS** autonomic nervous system
**ANSI** American National Standards Institute
**ANZAC** Australian and New Zealand Army Corps
**ANZUS** Australia, New Zealand and the United States
**AOB** any other business
**AONB** Area of Outstanding Natural Beauty
**APEX** Association of Professional, Executive, Clerical, and Computer Staff
**APR** annual percentage rate
**APRA** Alianza Popular Revolutionaria Americana (American Popular Revolutionary Alliance)
**AR** aspect ratio
**ARCIC** Anglican Roman Catholic International Commission
**A/S** Advanced/Supplementary
**ASA** American Standards Association
**ASCII** American Standards Code for Information Interchange
**ASDIC** Admiralty Submarine Detection Investigation Committee
**ASEAN** Association of South-East Asian Nations
**ASL** American Sign Language
**ASLEF** Associated Society of Locomotive Engineers and Firemen
**ASLIB** Association of Special Libraries and Information Bureaux
**ASM** air-to-surface missile
**ASPCA** American Society for the Prevention of Cruelty to Animals
**ASSR** Autonomous Soviet Socialist Republic
**ASTMS** Association of Scientific, Technical, and Managerial Staffs
**ATP** adenosine triphosphate
**ATS** Auxiliary Territorial Service
**ATV** Associated Television
**AU** astronomical unit
**AV** audio-visual
**AVC** Additional Voluntary Contribution
**AWACS** Airborne Warning and Control System
**AWU** Australian Workers' Union
**BAFTA** British Academy of Film and Television Arts
**BALPA** British Airline Pilots' Association
**B&W** black and white
**BASIC** (English) British American Scientific International Commercial
**BBC** British Broadcasting Corporation
**BC** before Christ
**BCD** binary coded decimal
**BCE** Before the Common Era
**BCG** bacille (bacillus) Calmette Guérin
**BCS** Bardeen, Cooper & Schrieffer (theory)
**BEF** British Expeditionary Force
**BEV** Black English Vernacular
**BIA** Bureau of Indian Affairs
**BIS** Bank for International Settlements
**BLAISE** British Library Automated Information Service
**BMA** British Medical Association
**BOSS** Bureau of State Security (South Africa)
**BP** blood pressure
**BSE** bovine spongiform encephalopathy
**BSI** British Standards Institution
**BST** British Summer Time
**btu** British thermal unit
**BUF** British Union of Fascists
**BUPA** British United Provident Association
**CAA** Civil Aviation Authority
**CAB** Citizen's Advice Bureau
**CACM** Central American Common Market

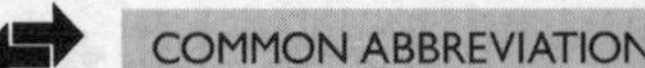


**CAD** computer aided design
**CAI** computer aided instruction
**CAL** computer aided learning
**CAM** computer aided manufacture
**CAP** Common Agricultural Policy
**CARICOM** Caribbean Community
**CARIFTA** Caribbean Free Trade Area
**CATV** cable television
**CB** citizen's band (radio)
**CBE** Commander of the (Order of the) British Empire
**CBI** Confederation of British Industry
**CCD** charge-coupled device
**CCK** cholecystokinin-pancreozymin
**CCR** camera cassette recorder
**CCTV** closed circuit television
**CD** Civil Defence
**CD-ROM** compact disc read-only memory
**CDU** Christian Democratic Union
**CE** Common Era
**CENTO** Central Treaty Organization
**CERN** Organisation Européene pour la Recherche Nucléaire (formerly, Conseil Européen pour la Recherche Nucléaire)
**CFC** chlorofluorocarbon
**CGS** centimetre-gram-second
**CGT** capital gains tax
**CGT** Confédération Générale du Travail
**CH** Companion of Honour
**CHAPS** Clearing House Automated Clearance System
**CHIPS** Clearing House Interbank Payments System
**CIA** Central Intelligence Agency
**CID** Criminal Investigation Department
**CIO** Congress of Industrial Organizations
**CIS** Commonwealth of Independent States
**CJD** Creutzfeldt-Jakob disease
**CM** Congregation of the Mission
**CMG** Companion of (the Order of) St Michael and St George
**CNAA** Council for National Academic Awards
**CND** Campaign for Nuclear Disarmament
**CNES** Centre National d'Espace
**CNN** Cable News Network
**CNS** central nervous system
**COMECON** Council for Mutual Economic Assistance
**CORE** Congress of Racial Equality
**CP** Congregation of the Passion
**CPI** Consumer Price Index
**CP/M** control program monitor
**CPR** cardio-pulmonary resuscitation
**CPU** central processing unit
**CRO** cathode-ray oscilloscope
**CRT** cathode-ray tube
**CSE** Certificate of Secondary Education
**CSF** cerebrospinal fluid
**CSIRO** Commonwealth Scientific and Industrial Research Organization
**CSO** colour separation overlay
**CTT** capital transfer tax
**CV** cultivar (*culti*vated *v*ariety)
**CV** curriculum vitae
**CVO** Commander of the Royal Victorian Order
**CVS** chorionic villus sampling
**CWA** County Women's Association
**CWS** Co-operative Wholesale Society
**D-A** digital-to-analog (in computing)
**DALR** dry adiabatic lapse rate
**D&C** dilation and curettage
**DBE** Dame Commander of the (Order of the) British Empire
**DBMS** database management system
**DBS** direct broadcasting from satellite
**DC/dc** direct current
**DCF** discounted cash flow
**DCMG** Dame Commander of (the Order of) St Michael and St George
**DCVO** Dame Commander of the Royal Victorian Order
**DDT** dichloro-diphenyl-trichloroethane
**DES** Department of Education and Science
**DES** diethylstilboestrol
**DFC** Distinguished Flying Cross
**DHA** District Health Authority
**DIA** Defense Intelligence Agency
**DLP** Democratic Labor Party (Australia)
**DMSO** dimethyl sulphoxide
**DNA** deoxyribonucleic acid
**DOS** Disk Operating System
**DPP** Director of Public Prosecutions
**DSN** Deep Space Network
**DSO** Distinguished Service Order
**DST** daylight saving time
**DTP** desk top publishing
**EAC** European Atomic Commission
**EA-ROM** electrically alterable read-only memory
**EBCDIC** Extended Binary-Coded Decimal Interchange Code
**EBU** European Boxing Union
**EBU** European Broadcasting Union
**EC** European Community
**ECA** European Commission on Agriculture
**ECF** extracellular fluid
**ECG** electrocardiograph
**ECM** European Common Market
**ECO** European Coal Organization
**ECOSOC** Economic and Social Council (of the United Nations)
**ECOWAS** Economic Community of West African States
**ECSC** European Coal and Steel Community
**ECT** electroconvulsive therapy
**ECTG** European Channel Tunnel Group
**ECU** European Currency Unit
**EDC** European Defence Community
**EDF** European Development Fund
**EDVAC** Electronic Discrete Variable Automatic Computer
**EEC** European Economic Community
**EEG** electroencephalography
**EEOC** Equal Employment Opportunity Commission
**EE-ROM** electrically erasable read-only memory
**EFA** European Fighter Aircraft

| | |
|---|---|
| **EFC** | European Forestry Commission |
| **EFTA** | European Free Trade Association |
| **EGF** | epidermal growth factor |
| **EI** | Exposure Index |
| **ELDO** | European Launcher Development Organization |
| **ELF** | Eritrea Liberation Front |
| **emf** | electromotive force |
| **EMS** | European Monetary System |
| **EMS** | Emergency Medical Service |
| **emu** | electromagnetic units |
| **EMU** | Economic Monetary Union |
| **EMU** | European and Monetary Union |
| **ENIAC** | Electronic Numeral Indicator and Calculator |
| **EOKA** | Ethniki Organosis Kipriakou Agonos (National Organization of Cypriot Struggle) |
| **EP** | European Parliament |
| **EPA** | Environmental Protection Agency |
| **EPR** | Einstein-Podolsky-Rosen (paradox) |
| **EPR** | electron paramagnetic resonance |
| **EP-ROM** | electronically programmable read-only memory |
| **ERNIE** | Electronic Random Number Indicator Equipment |
| **ERW** | enhanced radiation weapon |
| **ESA** | Environmentally Sensitive Area |
| **ESA** | European Space Agency |
| **ESC** | electronic stills camera |
| **ESCU** | European Space Operations Centre |
| **ESO** | European Southern Observatory |
| **ESP** | extra-sensory perception |
| **ESRO** | European Space Research Organization |
| **ESTEC** | European Space Research and Technology Centre |
| **ETU** | Electricians Trade Union |
| **EUFA** | European Union Football Associations |
| **EURATOM** | European Atomic Energy Community |
| **FA** | Football Association |
| **FAA** | Federal Aviation Administration |
| **FAO** | Food and Agriculture Organization |
| **FBI** | Federal Bureau of Investigation |
| **FCA** | Farm Credit Administration |
| **FCC** | Federal Communications Commission |
| **FDIC** | Federal Deposit Insurance Corporation |
| **FIFA** | Fédération Internationale de Football Association (International Association Football Federation) |
| **FIMBRA** | Financial Intermediaries, Managers and Brokers Regulatory Association |
| **FLN** | Front de Liberation Nationale |
| **FM/fm** | frequency modulation |
| **FORTRAN** | Formula Translation |
| **FPS** | foot-pound-second |
| **FRELIMO** | Frente de Libertação de Moçambique |
| **FSH** | follicle-stimulating hormone |
| **FTC** | Federal Trade Commission |
| **GAR** | Grand Army of the Republic |
| **GATT** | General Agreement on Tariffs and Trade |
| **GBE** | Knight/Dame Grand Cross of the (Order of the) British Empire |
| **GBH** | grievous bodily harm |
| **GC** | George Cross |
| **GCC** | Gulf Co-operation Council |
| **GCE** | General Certificate of Education |
| **GCHQ** | Government Communications Headquarters |
| **GCMG** | Knight/Dame Grand Cross of (the Order of) St Michael and St George |
| **GCSE** | General Certificate of Secondary Education |
| **GCVO** | Knight/Dame Grand Cross of the Royal Victorian Order |
| **GDI** | gross domestic income |
| **GDP** | gross domestic product |
| **GEO** | geosynchronous Earth orbit |
| **GESP** | generalized extra-sensory perception |
| **GH** | growth hormone |
| **GLC** | gas-liquid chromatography |
| **GLCM** | ground-launched cruise missile |
| **GM** | George Medal |
| **GMC** | General Medical Council |
| **GMT** | Greenwich Mean Time |
| **GNP** | gross national product |
| **GnRH** | gonadotrophin-releasing hormone |
| **GP** | General Practitioner |
| **GPSS** | General Purpose System Simulator |
| **GUTS** | grand unified theories |
| **HCG** | human chorionic gonadotrophin |
| **HE** | His/Her Excellency |
| **HEP** | hydro-electric power |
| **HF** | high frequency |
| **HGV** | heavy goods vehicle |
| **HIH** | His/Her Imperial Highness |
| **HIM** | His/Her Imperial Majesty |
| **HLA** | human leucocyte antigen |
| **HM** | His/Her Majesty |
| **HMG** | His/Her Majesty's Government |
| **HMI** | His/Her Majesty's Inspectorate |
| **HMO** | Health Maintenance Organization |
| **HMS** | His/Her Majesty's Ship/Service |
| **HMSO** | His/Her Majesty's Stationery Office |
| **HNC** | Higher National Certificate |
| **HND** | Higher National Diploma |
| **hp** | horsepower |
| **HQ** | headquarters |
| **HR** | House of Representatives |
| **HRH** | His/Her Royal Highness |
| **IAEA** | International Atomic Energy Agency |
| **IBRD** | International Bank for Reconstruction and Development |
| **IC** | integrated circuit |
| **ICAO** | International Civil Aviation Organization |
| **ICFTU** | International Confederation of Free Trade Unions |
| **ICI** | Imperial Chemical Industries |
| **IDA** | International Development Agency |
| **IFAD** | International Fund for Agricultural Development |

**IFC** International Finance Corporation
**ILO** International Labour Organization
**IMCO** Intergovernmental Maritime Consultative Organization
**IMF** International Monetary Fund
**INLA** Irish National Liberation Army
**INRI** Iesus Nazarenus Rex Iudeorum (Jesus of Nazareth, King of the Jews)
**IPA** International Phonetic Alphabet
**IQ** intelligence quotient
**IR** infrared
**IRA** Irish Republican Army
**IRB** Irish Republican Brotherhood
**IRBM** intermediate-range ballistic missile
**ISBN** International Standard Book Number
**ISO** International Organization for Standardization
**ISSN** International Standard Serial Number
**ITA** Initial Teaching Alphabet
**ITC** Independent Television Commission
**ITCZ** intertropical convergence zone
**ITN** Independent Television News
**ITO** International Trade Organization
**ITT** International Telephone and Telegraph Corporation
**ITU** International Telecommunication Union
**ITV** Independent Television
**IUCN** International Union for the Conservation of Nature and Natural Resources
**IUD** intra-uterine device
**IUPAC** International Union of Pure and Applied Chemistry
**IUPAP** International Union of Pure and Applied Physics
**IVF** in vitro fertilization
**IVR** International Vehicle Registration
**IWW** Industrial Workers of the World
**JP** Justice of the Peace
**JET** Joint European Torus
**KADU** Kenya African Democratic Union
**KANU** Kenya African National Union
**KB** Knight Bachelor; Knight of the Bath
**KBE** Knight Commander of the (Order of the) British Empire
**KC** King's Counsel
**KCB** Knight Commander of the Bath
**KCMG** Knight Commander of (the Order of) St Michael and St George
**KCVO** Knight Commander of the Royal Victorian Order
**KG** Knight of the (Order of the) Garter
**KGB** Komitet Gosudarstvennoye Bezhopaznosti (Committee of State Security)
**KKK** Ku Klux Klan
**KMT** Kuomintang
**kpc** kiloparsec
**KT** Knight of the Thistle
**LAFTA** Latin-American Free Trade Association
**LAN** local area network
**LAUTRO** Life Assurance and Unit Trust Regulatory Organization
**LCD** liquid crystal display
**LDC** less developed country
**LEA** Local Education Authority
**LED** light-emitting diode
**LEO** low Earth orbit
**LFA** Less Favoured Area
**LH** luteinizing hormone
**LHRH** luteinizing-hormone-releasing hormone
**LIFFE** London International Financial Futures Exchange
**LISP** List Processing
**LMS** London Missionary Society
**LPG** liquefied petroleum gas
**LSD** lysergic acid diethylamide
**LSI** large-scale integration
**LVO** Lieutenant of the Royal Victorian Order
**MAC** Multiplexed Analog Component
**MAO** monoamine oxidase
**MATV** Master Antenna Television
**MBE** Member of the (Order of the) British Empire
**MC** Master of Ceremonies
**MCA** Monetary Compensation Amount
**MCC** Marylebone Cricket Club
**MDMA** methylenedioxymethamphetamine
**ME** myalgic encephalomyelitis
**MH** Medal of Honor
**MHD** magnetohydrodynamics
**MICR** magnetic ink character recognition
**Mired** micro reciprocal degrees
**MIRV** multiple independently targetted re-entry vehicle
**MKSA** metre-kilogram-second-ampere
**MLR** minimum lending rate
**mmf** magnetomotive force
**MMI** man-machine interaction
**MOH** Medal of Honor
**mpc** megaparsec
**MPS** marginal propensity to save
**MPTP** methylphenyltetrahydropyridine
**MRA** Moral Rearmament
**MS** multiple sclerosis; manuscript
**MSC** Manpower Services Commission
**MSG** monosodium glutamate
**MSH** melanocyte-stimulating hormone
**MVD** Ministerstvo Vnutrennikh Del (Ministry for Internal Affairs)
**MVO** Member of the Royal Victorian Order
**NAACP** National Association for the Advancement of Colored People
**NANC** non-adrenergic, non-cholinergic
**NASA** National Aeronautics and Space Administration
**NASDA** National Space Development Agency
**NATO** North Atlantic Treaty Organization
**NDE** near-death experience
**NEDO** National Economic Development Office
**NEP** New Economic Policy
**NF** National Front
**NFC** National Football Conference
**NGC** New General Catalogue

**NGF** nerve growth factor
**NHL** National Hockey League
**NHS** National Health Service
**NIH** National Institutes of Health
**NKVD** Narodnyi Komissariat Vnutrennikh Del (People's Commissariat of Internal Affairs)
**NLRB** National Labor Relations Board
**NMR** nuclear magnetic resonance
**NOW** National Organization for Women
**NPT** Non-Proliferation Treaty
**NRA** National Recovery Administration
**NRAO** National Radio Astronomy Observatory
**NSF** National Science Foundation
**NSPCC** National Society for the Prevention of Cruelty to Children
**NTSC** National Television System Commission
**NUM** National Union of Mineworkers
**NUT** National Union of Teachers
**NVC** non-verbal communication
**OAPEC** Organization of Arab Petroleum Exporting Countries
**OAS** Organisation de l'Armée Secrète (Secret Army Organization)
**OAS** Organization of American States
**OAU** Organization of African Unity
**OB** Order of the Bath
**OB** outside broadcast
**OBE** Officer of the (Order of the) British Empire
**OCarm** Order of the Brothers of the Blessed Virgin Mary of Mount Carmel
**OCart** Order of Carthusians
**OCR** optical character recognition/reader
**OCSO** Order of the Reformed Cistercians of the Strict Observance
**OD** ordnance datum
**ODC** Order of Discalced Carmelites
**ODECA** Organización de Estados Centro-americanos (Organization of Central American States)
**OECD** Organization for Economic Co-operation and Development
**OEEC** Organization for European Economic Co-operation
**OEM** Original Equipment Manufacturer
**OFM** Order of Friars Minor
**OFMCap** Order of Friars Minor Capuchin
**OFMConv** Order of Friars Minor Conventual
**OGPU** Otdelenie Gosurdarstvenni Politcheskoi Upravi (Special Government Political Administration)
**OM** Order of Merit
**OMCap** Order of Friars Minor of St Francis Capuccinorum
**OOBE** out-of-the-body experience
**OP** Order of Preachers
**OPEC** Organization of Petroleum Exporting Countries
**OSA** Order of the Hermit Friars of St Augustine
**OSB** Order of St Benedict
**OSFC** Order of Friars Minor of St Francis Capuccinorum
**OTC** over-the-counter (stocks and shares, drugs)
**OTEC** ocean thermal energy conversion
**OU** Open University
**OXFAM** Oxford Committee for Famine Relief
**PA** personal assistant
**PAC** Pan-African Congress
**PAC** political action committee
**PAL** phase alternation line
**PAYE** pay as you earn
**pc** parsec
**PC** personal computer
**PC** Poor Clares
**PCP** phenylcyclohexylpiperidine
**PDGF** platelet-derived growth factor
**PDR** precision depth recorder
**PEN** International Association of Poets, Playwrights, Editors, Essayists, and Novelists
**PEP** personal equity plan
**PEP** Political and Economic Planning
**PF** Patriotic Front
**PGA** Professional Golfers' Association
**PH** Purple Heart
**PIN** personal identification number
**PK** psychokinesis
**PKU** phenylketonuria
**PLA** People's Liberation Army
**plc** public limited company
**PLO** Palestine Liberation Organization
**pm** post meridiem (after noon)
**PM of F** Presidential Medal of Freedom
**PNLM** Palestine National Liberation Movement
**POW** prisoner of war
**PPI** plan position indicator
**PR** proportional representation
**PRO** Public Record Office
**PRO** public relations officer
**PSBR** public sector borrowing requirement
**PTA** parent-teacher association
**PTO** please turn over
**PTFE** polytetrafluorethylene
**PVA** polyvinyl acetate
**PVC** polyvinyl chloride
**PWA** Public Works Administration
**PWR** pressurized-water reactor
**PYO** pick-your-own
**QC** Queen's Counsel
**QCD** quantum chromodynamics
**QED** quantum electrodynamics
**RA** Royal Academy
**R&A** Royal & Ancient Golf Club of St Andrews
**RAAF** Royal Australian Air Force
**RADA** Royal Academy of Dramatic Art
**RAF** Royal Air Force
**RAM** random access memory
**RAM** Royal Academy of Music
**RAN** Royal Australian Navy
**RDA** recommended daily allowance
**REM** rapid eye movement

**RHA** Regional Health Authority
**RISC** reduced interaction set computer
**RKKA** Rabochekrest'yanshi Krasny (Red Army of Workers and Peasants)
**RM** Royal Marines
**rms** root-mean-square
**RN** Royal Navy
**RNA** ribonucleic acid
**RNLI** Royal National Lifeboat Institution
**ROM** read-only memory
**RP** received pronunciation
**RPI** retail price index
**RPM** resale price maintenance
**rpm** revolutions per minute
**RRP** recommended retail price
**RS** Royal Society
**RSPB** Royal Society for the Protection of Birds
**RSPCA** Royal Society for the Prevention of Cruelty to Animals
**RSVP** répondez s'il vous plaît (please reply)
**RTG** radio-isotope thermo-electric generator
**RVO** Royal Victorian Order
**SA** Sturm Abteilung (Storm Troopers)
**sae** stamped addressed envelope
**SALR** saturated adiabatic lapse rate
**SALT** Strategic Arms Limitation Talks
**SAS** Special Air Service
**SAT** scholastic aptitude test
**SBR** styrene butadiene rubber
**SCID** severe combined immuno-deficiency
**SCLC** Southern Christian Leadership Conference
**SDI** selective dissemination of information
**SDI** strategic defense initiative
**SDP** Social Democratic Party
**SDR** special drawing rights
**SDS** Students for a Democratic Society
**SDU** Social Democratic Union
**SEAQ** Stock Exchange Automated Quotations
**SEATO** South East Asia Treaty Organization
**SEC** Securities and Exchange Commission
**SECAM** Séquence Electronique Couleur avec Mémoire (Electronic Colour Sequence with Memory)
**SERPS** State Earnings Related Pension Scheme
**SHAEF** Supreme Headquarters Allied Expeditionary Force
**SHAPE** Supreme Headquarters Allied Powers, Europe
**SHF** super high frequency
**SI** Système International (International System)
**SIB** Securities and Investments Board
**SIOP** Single Integrated Operation Plan
**SJ** Society of Jesus
**SLBN** submarine-launched ballistic missile
**SLCM** sea-launched cruise missile
**SLDP** Social and Liberal Democratic Party
**SLE** systemic lupus erythematosus
**SLR** single lens reflex
**SNCC** Student Non-Violent Co-ordinating Committee
**SNP** Scottish National Party
**SOCist** Cistercians of Common Observance
**SOE** Special Operations Executive
**SONAR** sound navigation and ranging
**SP** starting price
**SQUID** superconducting quantum interference device
**SR** Socialist Revolutionaries
**SRO** self-regulatory organization
**SS** Schutzstaffel (Protective Squad)
**SSR** Soviet Socialist Republic
**SSSI** Site of Special Scientific Interest
**START** Strategic Arms Reduction Talks
**STD** subscriber trunk dialling
**STD** sexually transmitted disease
**STOL** short take-off and landing
**SWAPO** South West Africa People's Organization
**SWS** slow wave sleep
**TAB** Totalisator Agency Board
**TARDIS** Time and Relative Dimensions in Space
**TASS** Telegrafnoye Agentsvo Sovietskovo Soyuza (Telegraph Agency of the Soviet Union)
**TB** tuberculosis
**TCDD** tetrachlorodibenzo-p-dioxin
**TEFL** Teaching English as a Foreign Language
**TESL** Teaching English as a Second Language
**TESOL** Teaching English to Speakers of Other Languages
**TGWU** Transport and General Workers Union
**TNT** trinitrotoluene
**TSB** Trustee Savings Bank
**TT** Tourist Trophy
**TTL** through the lens
**TUC** Trades Union Congress
**TV** television
**TVA** Tennessee Valley Authority
**UAE** United Arab Emirates
**UAP** United Australia Party
**UCAR** Union of Central African Republics
**UCCA** Universities' Central Council on Admissions
**UDA** Ulster Defence Association
**UDI** Unilateral Declaration of Independence
**UEFA** Union of European Football Associations
**UFO** unidentified flying object
**UHF** ultra high frequency
**UHT** ultra high temperature
**UK** United Kingdom
**UN** United Nations
**UNCTAD** United Nations Conference on Trade and Development
**UNDC** United Nations Disarmament Commission
**UNDP** United Nations Development Programme

**UNEP** United Nations Environment Programme
**UNESCO** United Nations Educational, Scientific, and Cultural Organization
**UNFAO** United Nations Food and Agriculture Organization
**UNGA** United Nations General Assembly
**UNHCR** United Nations High Commission for Refugees
**UNHRC** United Nations Human Rights Commission
**UNICEF** United Nations Children's Fund (formerly United Nations International Children's Emergency Fund)
**UNIDO** United Nations Industrial Development Organization
**UNO** United Nations Organization
**UNRWA** United Nations Relief and Works Agency for Palestine Refugees in the Near East
**UNSC** United Nations Security Council
**UNSG** United Nations Secretary General
**UNTT** United Nations Trust Territory
**UPU** Universal Postal Union
**USA** United States of America
**USAF** United States Air Force
**USCG** United States Coast Guard
**USIS** United States Information Service
**USSR** Union of Soviet Socialist Republics
**UV** ultraviolet
**VA** Veterans Administration
**VAT** value-added tax
**VC** Victoria Cross
**VCR** video cassette recorder
**VD** venereal disease
**VDU** visual display unit
**VHF** very high frequency
**VHS** Video Home Service
**VIP** vasoactive intestinal polypeptide
**VIP** very important person
**VLF** very low frequency
**VLSI** very large scale interpretation
**VOA** Voice of America
**VSEPR** valence shell electron pair repulsion
**VSO** Voluntary Service Overseas
**VTOL** vertical take-off and landing
**VTR** video tape recorder
**WAAC** Women's Auxiliary Army Corps
**WAAF** Women's Auxiliary Air Force
**WAC** Women's Army Corps
**WASP** White Anglo-Saxon Protestant
**WBA** World Boxing Association
**WBC** World Boxing Council
**WCC** World Council of Churches
**WEA** Workers' Educational Association
**WFTU** World Federation of Trade Unions
**WHO** World Health Organization
**WI** (National Federation of) Women's Institutes
**WIPO** World Intellectual Property Organization
**WMO** World Meteorological Organization
**WPA** Work Projects Administration
**WRAC** Women's Royal Army Corps
**WRAF** Women's Royal Air Force
**WRNS** Women's Royal Naval Service
**WRVS** Women's Royal Voluntary Service
**WVS** Women's Voluntary Service
**WWF** World Wide Fund for Nature (formerly World Wildlife Fund)
**YHA** Youth Hostels Association
**YMCA** Young Men's Christian Association
**YMHA** Young Men's Hebrew Association
**YWCA** Young Women's Christian Association
**YWHA** Young Women's Hebrew Association

# Alphabets

There is no agreement over the use of a single transliteration system in the case of Hebrew. The equivalents given below are widely used, but several other possibilities can be found.

## Hebrew

| Letter | Name | Transliteration |
|---|---|---|
| א | 'aleph | ’ |
| ב | beth | b |
| ג | gimel | g |
| ד | daleth | d |
| ה | he | h |
| ו | waw | w |
| ז | zayin | z |
| ח | heth | h |
| ט | teth | t |
| י | yodh | y, j |
| כ ך | kaph | k |
| ל | lamedh | l |
| מ ם | mem | m |
| נ ן | nun | n |
| ס | samekh | s |
| ע | ayin | ‘ |
| פ ף | pe | p, f |
| צ ץ | saddhe | s |
| ק | qoph | q |
| ר | resh | r |
| ש | shin | sh, ś |
| ש | sin | ś |
| ת | taw | t |

## Greek

| Letter | Name | Transliteration |
|---|---|---|
| Α α | alpha | a |
| Β β | beta | b |
| Γ γ | gamma | g |
| Δ δ | delta | d |
| Ε ε | epsilon | e |
| Ζ ζ | zeta | z |
| Η η | eta | e, ė |
| Θ θ | theta | th |
| Ι ι | iota | i |
| Κ κ | kappa | k |
| Λ λ | lambda | l |
| Μ μ | mu | m |
| Ν ν | nu | n |
| Ξ ξ | xi | x |
| Ο ο | omicron | o |
| Π π | pi | p |
| Ρ ρ | rho | r |
| Σ σ, ς | sigma | s |
| Τ τ | tau | t |
| Υ υ | upsilon | y |
| Φ φ | phi | ph |
| Χ χ | chi | ch, kh |
| Ψ ψ | psi | ps |
| Ω ω | omega | o, ȯ |

## Nato Alphabet

| Letter | Code name | Pronunciation |
|---|---|---|
| A | Alpha | AL-FAH |
| B | Bravo | BRAH-VOH |
| C | Charlie | CHAR-LEE |
| D | Delta | DELL-TAH |
| E | Echo | ECK-OH |
| F | Foxtrot | FOKS-TROT |
| G | Golf | GOLF |
| H | Hotel | HOH-TELL |
| I | India | IN-DEE-AH |
| J | Juliet | JEW-LEE-ETT |
| K | Kilo | KEY-LOH |
| L | Lima | LEE-MAH |
| M | Mike | MIKE |
| N | November | NO-VEM-BER |
| O | Oscar | OSS-CAH |
| P | Papa | PAH-PAH |
| Q | Quebec | KEY-BECK |
| R | Romeo | ROW-ME-OH |
| S | Sierra | SEE-AIR-RAH |
| T | Tango | TAN-GO |
| U | Uniform | YOU-NEE-FORM |
| V | Victor | VIK-TAH |
| W | Whiskey | WISS-KEY |
| X | Xray | ECKS-RAY |
| Y | Yankee | YANG-KEY |
| Z | Zulu | ZOO-LOO |

## Morse & Braille

| Letters | Morse | Braille |
|---|---|---|
| A | ·– | ⠁ |
| B | –··· | ⠃ |
| C | –·–· | ⠉ |
| D | –·· | ⠙ |
| E | · | ⠑ |
| F | ··–· | ⠋ |
| G | ––· | ⠛ |
| H | ···· | ⠓ |
| I | ·· | ⠊ |
| J | ·––– | ⠚ |
| K | –·– | ⠅ |
| L | ·–·· | ⠇ |
| M | –– | ⠍ |
| N | –· | ⠝ |
| O | ––– | ⠕ |
| P | ·––· | ⠏ |
| Q | ––·– | ⠟ |
| R | ·–· | ⠗ |
| S | ··· | ⠎ |
| T | – | ⠞ |
| U | ··– | ⠥ |
| V | ···– | ⠧ |
| W | ·–– | ⠺ |
| X | –··– | ⠭ |
| Y | –·–– | ⠽ |
| Z | ––·· | ⠵ |

## Typefaces

The typefaces shown are modern versions of the main groups under which most typefaces may be classified. The dates indicating the introduction of each group are approximate.

### Gothic
ABCDEFGHIJKLMNOPQRSTUVWXYZ
abcdefghijklmnopqrstuvwxyz
15 & 7pt Old English Text (c. 1450)

### Venetian
ABCDEFGHIJKLMNOPQRSTUVWXYZ
abcdefghijklmnopqrstuvwxyz
15 & 7pt Centaur (c. 1470)

### Old Face
ABCDEFGHIJKLMNOPQRSTUVWXYZ
abcdefghijklmnopqrstuvwxyz
15 & 7pt Caslon Old Face (c. 1495)

### Transitional
ABCDEFGHIJKLMNOPQRSTUVWXYZ
abcdefghijklmnopqrstuvwxyz
15 & 7pt Baskerville (c. 1761)

### Modern
ABCDEFGHIJKLMNOPQRSTUVWXYZ
abcdefghijklmnopqrstuvwxyz
15 & 7pt Bodoni (c. 1765)

### Sans Serif
ABCDEFGHIJKLMNOPQRSTUVWXYZ
abcdefghijklmnopqrstuvwxyz
15 & 7pt Univers (c. 1816)

### Egyptian
ABCDEFGHIJKLMNOPQRSTUVWXYZ
abcdefghijklmnopqrstuvwxyz
12 & 7pt Rockwell (c. 1830)

### Old Style
ABCDEFGHIJKLMNOPQRSTUVWXYZ
abcdefghijklmnopqrstuvwxyz
15 & 7pt Goudy Old Style (c. 1850)

### Newspaper
ABCDEFGHIJKLMNOPQRSTUVWXYZ
abcdefghijklmnopqrstuvwxyz
12pt Century Bold & 7pt Century Roman (c. 1890)

### Contemporary
ABCDEFGHIJKLMNOPQRSTUVWXYZ
abcdefghijklmnopqrstuvwxyz
12 & 7pt Times New Roman (c. 1932)

## First name meanings in the UK and USA

The meanings of the most popular first names in the UK and USA are given below, along with a few other well-known names.

| Name | Original meaning |
|---|---|
| **Aaron** | high mountain (*Hebrew*) |
| **Adam** | redness (*Hebrew*) |
| **Alan** | harmony (*Celtic*) |
| **Albert** | nobly bright (*Germanic*) |
| **Alexander** | defender of men (*Greek*) |
| **Alexis** | helper (*Greek*) |
| **Alison** | *French diminutive of* Alice; of noble kind |
| **Amanda** | fit to be loved (*Latin*) |
| **Amy** | loved (*French*) |
| **Andrea** | *female form of* Andrew |
| **Andrew** | manly (*Greek*) |
| **Angela** | messenger, angel (*Greek*) |
| **Ann(e)** | *English forms of* Hannah |
| **Anthony** | *Roman family name* |
| **April** | name of the month |
| **Arthur** | ?bear, stone (*Celtic*) |
| **Ashley** | *Germanic place name*; ashwood |
| **Austin** | *English form of* Augustus; venerated |
| **Barbara** | strange, foreign (*Greek*) |
| **Barry** | spear, javelin (*Celtic*) |
| **Beatrice** | bringer of joy (*Latin*) |
| **Benjamin** | son of my right hand (*Hebrew*) |
| **Bernard** | bear + brave (*Germanic*) |
| **Beth** | *pet form of* Elizabeth |
| **Betty** | *pet form of* Elizabeth |
| **Bill/Billy** | *pet form of* William |
| **Bob** | *pet form of* Robert |
| **Brandi** | *variant of* Brandy, *from the common noun* |
| **Brandon** | *place name*; broom-covered hill (*Germanic*) |
| **Brian** | ?hill (?*Celtic*) |
| **Candice** | *meaning unknown* |
| **Carl** | man, husbandman (*Germanic*) |
| **Carol(e)** | *forms of* Caroline, *Italian female form of* Charles |
| **Catherine** | pure (*Greek*) |
| **Charles** | man, husbandman (*Germanic*) |
| **Christine** | *French form of* Christina, *ultimately from* Christian; anointed |
| **Christopher** | carrier of Christ (*Greek*) |
| **Claire** | bright, shining (*Latin*) |
| **Colin** | *form of* Nicholas |
| **Craig** | rock (*Celtic*) |
| **Crystal** | *female use of the common noun* |
| **Daniel** | God is my judge (*Hebrew*) |
| **Danielle** | *female form of* Daniel |
| **Darren** | *Irish surname* |
| **Darryl** | *surname; uncertain origin* |
| **David** | beloved, friend (*Hebrew*) |
| **Dawn** | *female use of the common noun* |
| **Dean** | *surname*; valley or leader |
| **Deborah** | bee (*Hebrew*) |
| **Dennis** | of Dionysus (*Greek*), *the god of wine* |
| **Derek** | *form of* Theodoric; ruler of the people (*Germanic*) |
| **Diane** | *French form of* Diana; divine (*Latin*) |
| **Donald** | world mighty (*Gaelic*) |
| **Donna** | lady (*Latin*) |
| **Doreen** | *from* Dora, *a short form of* Dorothy; gift of God |
| **Doris** | woman from Doris (*Greek*) |
| **Dorothy** | gift of God (*Greek*) |
| **Ebony** | *female use of the common noun* |
| **Edward** | property guardian (*Germanic*) |
| **Eileen** | *Irish form of* ?Helen |
| **Elizabeth** | oath/perfection of God (*Hebrew*) |
| **Emily** | *Roman family name* |
| **Emma** | all-embracing (*Germanic*) |
| **Eric** | ruler of all (*Norse*) |
| **Erica** | *female form of* Eric |
| **Eugenie** | *French form of* Eugene; well-born (*Greek*) |
| **Frank** | *pet form of* Francis; Frenchman |
| **Frederick** | peaceful ruler (*Germanic*) |
| **Gail** | *pet form of* Abigail; father rejoices (*Hebrew*) |
| **Gareth** | gentle (*Welsh*) |
| **Gary** | *US place name* |
| **Gavin** | *Scottish form of* Gawain; hawk + white (*Welsh*) |
| **Gemma** | gem (*Italian*) |
| **Geoffrey** | ?peace (*Germanic*) |
| **George** | husbandman, farmer (*Greek*) |
| **Graham** | *Germanic place name* |
| **Hannah** | grace, favour (*Hebrew*) |
| **Harold** | army power/ruler (*Germanic*) |
| **Harry** | *pet form of* Henry; home ruler (*Germanic*) |
| **Hayley** | *English place name*; hay-meadow |
| **Heather** | *plant name* |
| **Helen** | bright/shining one (*Greek*) |
| **Ian** | *modern Scottish form of* John |
| **Irene** | peace (*Greek*) |
| **Jacob** | he seized the heel (*Hebrew*) |
| **Jacqueline** | *French female form of* Jacques (James) |
| **James** | *Latin form of* Jacob |
| **Jane** | *from Latin* Johanna, *female form of* John |
| **Janet** | *diminutive form of* Jane |
| **Jasmine** | flower name (*Persian*) |
| **Jason** | *form of* Joshua; Jehovah is salvation (*Hebrew*) |
| **Jeffrey** | *US spelling of* Geoffrey |
| **Jean** | *French form of* Johanna, *from* John |
| **Jennifer** | fair/white + yielding/smooth (*Celtic*) |
| **Jeremy** | *English form of* Jeremiah; Jehova exalts (*Hebrew*) |
| **Jessica** | he beholds (*Hebrew*) |
| **Joan** | *contracted form of* Johanna, *from* John |
| **Joanne** | *French form of* Johanna, *from* John |
| **John** | Jehovah has been gracious (*Hebrew*) |

| Name | Original meaning |
|---|---|
| **Jonathan** | Jehovah's gift (*Hebrew*) |
| **Jordan** | flowing down (*Hebrew*) |
| **Joseph** | Jehovah adds (*Hebrew*) |
| **Joshua** | Jehovah is gracious (*Hebrew*) |
| **Joyce** | ?joyful (?*Latin*) |
| **Julie** | *French female form of Latin* Julius; descended from Jove |
| **Karen** | *Danish form of* Katarina (Catherine) |
| **Katherine** | *US spelling of* Catherine |
| **Kathleen** | *English form of Irish* Caitlin (*from* Catherine) |
| **Kelly** | *Irish surname*; warlike one |
| **Kenneth** | *English form of Gaelic*; fair one or fire-sprung |
| **Kerry** | *Irish place name* |
| **Kevin** | handsome at birth (*Irish*) |
| **Kimberly** | *South African place name* |
| **Lakisha** | La + ?Aisha; woman (*Arabic*) |
| **Latoya** | La + *form of* Tonya (Antonia) |
| **Laura** | bay, laurel (*Latin*) |
| **Lauren** | *diminutive of* Laura |
| **Lee** | *Germanic place name*; wood, clearing |
| **Leslie** | *Scottish place name* |
| **Lilian** | lily (*Italian*) |
| **Linda** | serpent (symbol of wisdom) (*Germanic*) |
| **Lindsay** | *Scottish place name* |
| **Lisa** | *pet form of* Elizabeth |
| **Margaret** | pearl (*Greek*) |
| **Marjorie** | *from* Marguerite, *French form of* Margaret |
| **Mark** | *English form of* Marcus, *from Mars, god of war* |
| **Martin** | *from Mars, god of war* (*Latin*) |
| **Mary** | *Greek form of* Miriam (*Hebrew*); *unknown meaning* |
| **Matthew** | gift of the Lord (*Hebrew*) |
| **Megan** | *pet form of* Margaret |
| **Melissa** | bee (*Greek*) |
| **Michael** | like the Lord (*Hebrew*) |
| **Michelle** | *English spelling of French* Michèle, *from* Michael |
| **Morgan** | ?sea + ?circle (*Welsh*) |
| **Nancy** | *pet form of* Ann |
| **Natalie** | birthday of the Lord (*Latin*) |
| **Neil** | champion (*Irish*) |
| **Nicholas** | victory people (*Greek*) |
| **Nicola** | *Italian female form of* Nicholas |
| **Nicole** | *French female form of* Nicholas |
| **Pamela** | ?all honey (*Greek*) |
| **Patricia** | noble (*Latin*) |
| **Paul** | small (*Latin*) |
| **Pauline** | *French female form of* Paul |
| **Peter** | stone, rock (*Greek*) |
| **Philip** | fond of horses (*Greek*) |
| **Rachel** | ewe (*Hebrew*) |
| **Rebecca** | ?noose (*Hebrew*) |
| **Richard** | strong ruler (*Germanic*) |
| **Robert** | fame bright (*Germanic*) |
| **Ronald** | counsel + power (*Germanic*) |
| **Ruth** | ?vision of beauty (*Hebrew*) |
| **Ryan** | *Irish surname* |
| **Sally** | *pet form of* Sarah |
| **Samantha** | *female form of* Samuel; heard/name of God (*Hebrew*) |
| **Sandra** | *pet form of* Alexandra |
| **Sarah** | princess (*Hebrew*) |
| **Scott** | *surname*; from Scotland |
| **Sharon** | the plain (*Hebrew*) |
| **Shaun** | *English spelling of Irish* Sean, *from* John |
| **Shirley** | bright clearing (*Germanic*) |
| **Simon** | *form of* Simeon; listening attentively (*Hebrew*) |
| **Stephanie** | *French female form of* Stephen |
| **Stephen** | crown (*Greek*) |
| **Stuart** | steward (*Germanic*) |
| **Susan** | *short form of* Susannah; lily (*Hebrew*) |
| **Teresa** | woman of Theresia (*Greek*) |
| **Thomas** | twin (*Hebrew*) |
| **Tiffany** | manifestation of God (*Greek*) |
| **Timothy** | honouring God (*Greek*) |
| **Trac(e)y** | ?*pet form of* Teresa |
| **Vera** | faith (*Slavic*) |
| **Victoria** | victory (*Latin*) |
| **Vincent** | conquer (*Latin*) |
| **Virginia** | maiden (*Latin*) |
| **Walter** | ruling people (*Germanic*) |
| **Wayne** | *surname*; wagon-maker |
| **William** | will + helmet (*Germanic*) |
| **Zachary** | Jehovah has remembered (*Hebrew*) |
| **Zoë** | life (*Greek*) |

## Forms of address

In the fomulae given below, *F* stands for forename and *S* for surname.

- Very formal ceremonial styles for closing letters are now seldom used: 'Yours faithfully' is assumed below, unless otherwise indicated.
- Forms of spoken address are given only where a special style is followed.
- Holders of courtesy titles are addressed according to their rank, but without 'The', 'The Right Hon.', or 'The Most Hon.'.
- Ranks in the armed forces, and ecclesiastical and ambassadorial ranks, precede titles in the peerage, eg 'Colonel the Earl of ——' or 'The Rev the Marquess of ——'.
- Although the correct forms of address are given below for members of the Royal Family, it is more normal practice for letters to be addressed to their private secretary, equerry, or lady-in-waiting.
- More detailed information about forms of address is to be found in Debrett's *Correct Form* and Black's *Titles and Forms of Address*.

**Ambassadors** (foreign)
*Address on envelope*: 'His/Her Excellency the Ambassador of ——' or 'His/Her Excellency the —— Ambassador'. (The wife of an ambassador is not entitled to the style 'Her Excellency'.) *Begin*: 'Your Excellency'. (Within the letter, refer to 'Your Excellency' once, thereafter as 'you'.) *Close*: 'I have the honour to be, Sir/Madam (or according to rank), Your Excellency's obedient servant'. *Spoken address*: 'Your Excellency' at least once, and then 'Sir' or 'Madam' by name.

**Archbishop** (Anglican communion)
*Address on envelope*: 'The Most Reverend the Lord Archbishop of ——'. (The Archbishops of Canterbury and York are Privy Counsellors, and should be addressed as 'The Most Reverend and Right Hon. the Lord Archbishop of ——'.) *Begin*: 'Dear Archbishop' or 'My Lord Archbishop'. *Spoken address*: 'Your Grace'. *Begin an official speech*: 'My Lord Archbishop'.

**Archbishop** (Roman Catholic)
*Address on envelope*: 'His Grace the Archbishop of ——'. *Begin*: 'My Lord Archbishop'. *Close*: 'I remain, Your Grace, Yours faithfully' or 'Yours faithfully'. *Spoken address*: 'Your Grace'.

**Archdeacon**
*Address on envelope*: 'The Venerable the Archdeacon of ——'. *Begin*: 'Dear Archdeacon' or 'Venerable Sir'. *Spoken address*: 'Archdeacon'. *Begin an official speech*: 'Venerable Sir'.

**Baron**
*Address on envelope*: 'The Right Hon. the Lord ——'. *Begin*: 'My Lord'. *Spoken address*: 'My Lord'.

**Baron's wife** (Baroness)
*Address on envelope*: 'The Right Hon. the Lady [S——]'. *Begin*: 'Dear Lady'. *Spoken address*: 'Madam'.

**Baroness** (in her own right)
*Address on envelope*: either as for Baron's wife, or 'The Right Hon. the Baroness [S——]'. Otherwise, as for Baron's wife.

**Baronet**
*Address on envelope*: 'Sir [F——S——], Bt'. *Begin*: 'Dear Sir'. *Spoken address*: 'Sir [F——]'.

**Baronet's wife**
*Address on envelope*: 'Lady [S——]'. If she has the title 'Lady' by courtesy, 'Lady [F——S——]'. If she has the courtesy style 'The Hon.', this precedes 'Lady'. *Begin*: 'Dear Madam'. *Spoken address*: 'Madam'.

**Bishop** (Anglican communion)
*Address on envelope*: 'The Right Reverend the Lord Bishop of ——'. (The Bishop of London is a Privy Counsellor, so is addressed as 'The Right Rev and Right Hon. the Lord Bishop of London'. The Bishop of Meath is styled 'The Most Reverend'.) *Begin*: 'Dear Bishop' or 'My Lord'. *Spoken address*: 'Bishop'. *Begin an official speech*: 'My Lord'.

**Bishop** (Episcopal Church in Scotland)
*Address on envelope*: 'The Right Reverend [F——S——], Bishop of ——'. Otherwise as for a bishop of the Anglican communion. The bishop who holds the position of Primus is addressed as 'The Most Reverend the Primus'. *Begin*: 'Dear Primus'. *Spoken address*: 'Primus'.

**Bishop** (Roman Catholic)
*Address on envelope*: 'His Lordship the Bishop of ——' or 'The Right Reverend [F——S——], Bishop of ——'. In Ireland, 'The Most Reverend' is used instead of 'The Right Reverend'. If an auxiliary bishop, address as 'The Right Reverend [F——S——], Auxiliary Bishop of ——'. *Begin*: 'My Lord' or (more rarely) 'My Lord Bishop'. *Close*: 'I remain, My Lord' or (more rarely), 'My Lord Bishop, Yours faithfully', or simply 'Yours faithfully'. *Spoken address*: 'My Lord' or (more rarely) 'My Lord Bishop'.

**Cabinet Minister ► Secretary of State**

**Canon** (Anglican communion)
*Address on envelope*: 'The Reverend Canon [F——S——]'. *Begin*: 'Dear Canon' or 'Dear Canon [S——]'. *Spoken address*: 'Canon' or 'Canon [S——]'.

**Canon** (Roman Catholic)
*Address on envelope*: 'The Very Reverend Canon [F——S——]'. *Begin*: 'Very Reverend Sir'. *Spoken address*: 'Canon [S——]'.

**Cardinal**
*Address on envelope*: 'His eminence Cardinal [S——]'. If an archbishop, 'His Eminence the Cardinal Archbishop of ——'. *Begin*: 'Your Eminence' or (more rarely) 'My Lord Cardinal'. *Close*: 'I remain, Your Eminence (or 'My Lord Cardinal'), Yours faithfully'. *Spoken*: 'Your Eminence'.

**Clergy** (Anglican communion)
*Address on envelope*: 'The Reverend [F——S——]'. *Begin*: 'Dear Sir/Madam' or 'Dear Mr/Mrs [S——]'.

**Clergy** (Roman Catholic)
*Address on envelope*: 'The Reverend [F——S——]'. If a member of a religious order, the initials of the order should be added after the name. *Begin*: 'Dear Reverend Father'.

**Clergy** (Other churches)
*Address on envelope*: 'The Reverend [F——S——]'. *Begin*: 'Dear Sir/Madam' or 'Dear Mr/Mrs [S——]'.

**Countess**
*Address on envelope*: 'The Right Hon. the Countess of ——'. *Begin*: 'Dear Madam'. *Spoken address*: 'Madam'.

**Dean** (Anglican)
*Address on envelope*: 'The Very Reverend the Dean of ——'. *Begin* 'Dear Dean' or 'Very Reverend Sir/Madam'. *Spoken address*: 'Dean'. *Begin an official speech*: 'Very Reverend Sir/Madam'.

**Doctor**
Physicians, anaesthetists, pathologists and radiologists are addressed as 'Doctor'. Surgeons, whether they hold the degree of Doctor of Medicine or not, are known as 'Mr/Mrs'. In England and Wales, obstetricians and gynaecologists are addressed as 'Mr/Mrs', but in Scotland, Ireland and elsewhere as 'Doctor'. In addressing a letter to the holder of a doctorate, the initials DD, MD, etc are placed after the ordinary form of address, eg 'The Rev John Smith DD', the 'Rev Dr Smith' and 'Dr John Brown' are also used.

**Dowager**
*Address on envelope*: On the marriage of a peer or baronet, the widow of the previous holder of the title becomes 'Dowager' and is addressed 'The Right Hon. the Dowager Countess of ——', 'The Right Hon. the Dowager Lady ——', etc. If there is already a Dowager still living, she retains this title, the later widow being addressed 'The Most Hon. [F——], Marchioness of ——', 'The Right Hon. [F——], Lady ——', etc. However, many Dowagers prefer the style which includes their Christian names to that including the title Dowager. *Begin*, etc as for a peer's wife.

**Duchess**
*Address on envelope*: 'Her Grace the Duchess of ——'. *Begin*: 'Dear Madam'. *Spoken address*: 'Your Grace'. (For Royal Duchess ► **Princess**.)

**Duke**
*Address on envelope*: 'His Grace the Duke of ——'. *Begin*: 'My Lord Duke'. *Spoken address*: 'Your Grace'. (For Royal Duke ► **Prince**.)

**Earl**
*Address on envelope*: 'The Right Hon. the Earl of ——'. *Begin*: 'My Lord'. *Spoken address*: 'My Lord'. (For Earl's wife ► **Countess**.)

**Governor of a colony** or **Governor-General**
*Address on envelope*: 'His Excellency [ordinary designation], Governor(-General) of ——'. (The Governor-General of Canada has the rank of 'Right Honourable', which he retains for life.) The wife of a Governor-General is styled 'Her Excellency' within the country her husband administers. *Begin*: according to rank. *Close*: 'I have the honour to be, Sir (or 'My Lord', if a peer), Your Excellency's obedient servant'. *Spoken address*: 'Your Excellency'.

**Judge, High Court**
*Address on envelope*: if a man, 'The Hon. Mr Justice [S——]'; if a woman, 'The Hon. Mrs Justice [S——]'. *Begin*: 'Dear Sir/Madam'; if on judicial matters, 'My Lord/Lady'. *Spoken address*: 'Sir/Madam'; only on the bench or when dealing with judicial matters should a High Court Judge be addressed as 'My Lord/Lady' or referred to as 'Your Lordship/Ladyship'.

**Judge, Circuit**
*Address on envelope*: 'His/Her Honour Judge [S——]'. If a Knight, 'His Honour Judge Sir [F——S——]'. *Begin*: 'Dear Sir/Madam'. *Spoken address*: 'Sir/Madam'; address as 'Your Honour' only when on the bench or dealing with judicial matters.

**Justice of the Peace** (England and Wales)
When on the bench, refer to and address as 'Your Worship'; otherwise according to rank. The letters 'JP' may be added after the person's name in addressing a letter, if desired.

**Knight Bachelor**
As Baronet, except that 'Bt' is omitted. Knight of the Bath, of St Michael and St George, etc. *Address on envelope*: 'Sir [F——S——]', with the initials 'GCB', 'KCB', etc added. *Begin*: 'Dear Sir'.

**Knight's wife**
As Baronet's wife, or according to rank.

**Lady Mayoress**
*Address on envelope*: 'The Lady Mayoress of ——'. *Begin*: 'My Lady Mayoress'. *Spoken address*: '(My) Lady Mayoress'.

**Lord Mayor**
*Address on envelope*: The Lord Mayors of London, York, Belfast, Cardiff, Dublin and also Melbourne, Sydney, Adelaide, Perth, Brisbane and Hobart are styled 'The Right Hon. the Lord Mayor of ——'. Other Lord Mayors are styled 'The Right Worshipful the Lord Mayor of ——'. *Begin*: 'My Lord Mayor', even if the holder of the office is a woman. *Spoken address*: '(My) Lord Mayor'.

**Marchioness**
*Address on envelope*: 'The Most Hon. the Marchioness of ——'. *Begin*: 'Dear Madam'. *Spoken address*: 'Madam'.

**Marquess**
*Address on envelope*: 'The Most Hon. the Marquess of ——'. *Begin*: 'My Lord'. *Spoken address*: 'My Lord'.

**Mayor**
*Address on envelope*: 'The Worshipful the Mayor of ——'; in the case of cities and certain towns, 'The Right Worshipful'. *Begin*: 'Mr Mayor'. *Spoken address*: 'Mr Mayor'.

**Mayoress**
*Address on envelope*: 'The Mayoress of ——'. *Begin*: 'Madam Mayoress' is traditional, but some now prefer 'Madam Mayor'. *Spoken address*: 'Mayoress' (or 'Madam Mayor').

**Member of Parliament**
*Address on envelope*: Add 'MP' to the usual form of address. *Begin*: according to rank.

**Monsignor**
*Address on envelope*: 'The Reverend Monsignor [F——S——]'. If a canon, 'The Very Reverend Monsignor (Canon) [F——S——]'. *Begin*: 'Reverend Sir'. *Spoken address*: 'Monsignor [S——]'.

**Officers in the Armed Forces**
*Address on envelope*: The professional rank is prefixed to any other rank, eg 'Admiral the Right Hon. the Earl of ——', 'Lieut.-Col. Sir [F——S——], KCB'. Officers below the rank of Rear-Admiral, and Marshal of the Royal Air Force, are entitled to 'RN' (or 'Royal Navy') and 'RAF' respecively after their name. Army officers of the rank of Colonel or below may follow their name with the name of their regiment or corps (which may be abbreviated). Officers in the women's services add 'WRNS', 'WRAF', 'WRAC'. *Begin*: according to social rank.

**Officers** (retired and former)
*Address on envelope*: Officers above the rank of Lieutenant (in the Royal Navy), Captain (in the Army) and Flight Lieutenant (in the Royal Air Force) may continue to use and be addressed by their armed forces rank after being placed on the retired list. The word 'retired' (or in an abbreviated form) should not normally be placed after the person's name. Former officers in the women's services do not normally continue to use their ranks.

**Pope**
*Address on envelope*: 'His Holiness, the Pope'. *Begin*: 'Your Holiness' or 'Most Holy Father'. *Close*: if a Roman Catholic, 'I have the honour to be your Holiness's most devoted and obedient child' (or 'most humble child'); if not Roman Catholic, 'I have the honour to be (or 'remain') Your Holiness's obedient servant'. *Spoken address*: 'Your Holiness'.

**Prime Minister**
*Address on envelope*: according to rank. The Prime Minister is a Privy Counsellor (see separate entry) and the letter should be addressed accordingly. *Begin*, etc according to rank.

**Prince**
*Address on envelope*: If a Duke, 'His Royal Highness the Duke of ——'; if not a Duke, 'His Royal Highness the Prince

[F——]', if a child of the sovereign; otherwise 'His Royal Highness Prince [F——] of [Kent or Gloucester]'. *Begin*: 'Sir'. Refer to as 'Your Royal Highness'. *Close*: 'I have the honour to remain (or 'be'), Sir, Your Royal Highness's most humble and obedient servant'. *Spoken address*: 'Your Royal Highness' once, thereafter 'Sir'.

**Princess**
*Address on envelope*: If a Duchess, 'Her Royal Highness the Duchess of ——'; if not a Duchess, the daughter of a sovereign is addressed as 'Her Royal Highness the Princess [F——]', followed by any title she holds by marriage. 'The' is omitted in addressing a princess who is not the daughter of a sovereign. A Princess by marriage is addressed 'HRH Princess [husband's F——] of ——'. *Begin*: 'Madam'. Refer to as 'Your Royal Highness'. *Close*: as for Prince, substituting 'Madam' for 'Sir'. *Spoken address*: 'Your Royal Highness' once, thereafter 'Ma'am'.

**Privy Counsellor**
*Address on envelope*: If a peer, 'The Right Hon. the Earl of ——, PC'; if not a peer, 'The Right Hon. [F——S——]', without the 'PC'. *Begin*, etc according to rank.

**Professor**
*Address on envelope*: 'Professor [F——S——]'; the styles 'Professor Lord [S——]' and 'Professor Sir [F——S——]' are often used, but are deprecated by some people. If the professor is in holy orders, 'The Reverend Professor'. *Begin*: 'Dear Sir/Madam', or according to rank. *Spoken address*: according to rank.

**Queen**
*Address on envelope*: 'Her Majesty the Queen'. *Begin*: 'Madam, with my humble duty'. Refer to as 'Your Majesty'. *Close*: 'I have the honour to remain (or 'be'), Madam, Your Majesty's most humble and obedient servant'. *Spoken address*: 'Your Majesty' once, thereafter 'Ma'am'. *Begin an official speech*: 'May it please Your Majesty'.

**Rabbi**
*Address on envelope*: 'Rabbi [initial and S——]' or, if a doctor, 'Rabbi Doctor [initial and S——]'. *Begin*: 'Dear Sir'. *Spoken address*: 'Rabbi [S——]' or '[Doctor S——]'.

**Secretary of State**
*Address on envelope*: 'The Right Hon. [F——S——], MP, Secretary of State for ——', or 'The Secretary of State for ——'. Otherwise according to rank.

**Viscount**
*Address on envelope*: 'The Right Hon. the Viscount ——'. *Begin*: 'My Lord'. *Spoken address*: 'My Lord'.

**Viscountess**
*Address on envelope*: 'The Right Hon. the Viscountess ——'. *Begin*: 'Dear Madam'. *Spoken address*: 'Madam'.

## Computer languages

| Name | Full name | Main use |
|---|---|---|
| Ada | — | Complex on-line real-time monitoring and control (eg military applications) |
| AED | Algol Extended for Design | Computer-aided design |
| ALGOL | Algorithmic Language | Concise expression of mathematical and logical processes and the control of these processes |
| APL | A Programming Language | Educational; mathematical problems particularly those concerned with multidimensional arrays |
| APT | Automatically Programmed Tools | Operate machine tools using numeric codes |
| BASIC | Beginners All-purpose Symbolic Instruction Code | Education, games |
| BCPL | B Combined Programming Language | Mathematical, scientific, systems programming |
| C | — | Operating systems (eg UNIX), business, scientific, games |
| C++ | — | Operating systems, business, scientific, games |
| CHILL | — | Real-time language used for programming computer-based telecommunication systems and computer-controlled telephone exchanges |
| COBOL | Common Business Oriented Language | Business data processing |
| COGO | Co-ordinate Geometry | Solving coordinate geometry problems in civil engineering |
| COMAL | Common Algorithmic Language | Education |
| CORAL | Computer On-line Real-time Application Language | Military applications |
| FORTH | — | Astronomy, robotics, control applications |
| FORTRAN | Formula Translation | Mathematical, engineering, scientific |
| GPSS | General Purpose Systems Simulation | Simulation programs |
| HTML | Hypertext Markup Language | Web page construction |
| JAVA | — | Internet applications |
| LISP | List Processing | Linguistics, Artificial Intelligence, manipulation of mathematical and arithmetic logic |
| LOGO | — | Education, turtle graphics |
| ML | Meta Language | Dynamic programming |
| MO2 | — | Parallel computations (derivative of Pascal) |
| OCCAM | — | Artificial Intelligence applications |
| Pascal | — | Education |
| PL1 | Programming Language 1 | Educational; commercial and scientific work |
| PL/M | Programming Language for Microcomputers | Educational; commercial and scientific work |
| PROLOG | Programming in Logic | Artificial Intelligence, expert systems |
| SGML | Standard Generalized Mark-up Language | Print applications |
| SIMULA | Simulation Language | Simulation programs |
| Smalltalk | | Object-orientated language |
| SNOBOL | String Oriented Symbolic Language | Manipulation of textual data |
| SQL | Structured Query Language | Database querying |
| XML | Extensible Mark-up Language | Web pages with multimedia content |

## News agencies

| Press name | Full name | Date founded | Location |
|---|---|---|---|
| **AAP** | Australian Associated Press | 1935 | Sydney |
| **AASA** | Agence Arabe Syrienne d'Information | 1966 | Damascus |
| **ADN** | Allgemeiner Deutscher Nachrichtendienst | 1946 | Berlin |
| **AE** | Agence Europe | 1952 | Brussels |
| **AFP** | Agence France-Presse | 1944 | Paris |
| **AIO** | Agencia Informativa Orbe de Chile | 1952 | Santiago |
| **AIP** | Agence Ivoirienne de Presse | 1961 | Abidjan |
| **ALD** | Agencia Los Diarios | 1910 | Buenos Aires |
| **ALI** | Agencia Lusa de Informacao | 1987 | Lisbon |
| **AM** | Agencia Meridional | 1931 | Rio de Janeiro |
| **ANA** | Athenagence | 1896 | Athens |
| **ANP** | Algemeen Nederlands Persbureau | 1934 | The Hague |
| **ANSA** | Agenzia Nazionale Stampa Associate | 1945 | Rome |
| **ANTARA** | Indonesian National News Agency | 1937 | Jakarta |
| **AN** | Agencia Nacional | 1946 | Brasilia |
| **APA** | Austria Presse-Agentur | 1946 | Vienna |
| **APP** | Agence Parisienne de Presse | 1949 | Paris |
| **APP** | Associated Press of Pakistan | 1948 | Islamabad |
| **APS** | Agence de Presse Senegalaise | 1959 | Dakar |
| **APS** | Algeria Presse Service | 1962 | Algiers |
| **AP** | Associated Press | 1848 | New York |
| **ATA** | Albanian Telegraphic Agency | 1945 | Tirana |
| **AUP** | Australian United Press | 1928 | Melbourne |
| **BELGA** | Agence Belga | 1920 | Brussels |
| **BERNAMA** | Malaysia National News Agency | 1967 | Kuala Lumpur |
| **BOPA** | Botswana Press Agency | 1981 | Gaborone |
| **BTA** | Bulgarska Telegrafitscheka Agentzia | 1898 | Sofia |
| **CANA** | Caribbean News Agency | 1976 | Bridgetown |
| **CIP** | Centre d'Information de Presse | 1946 | Brussels |
| **CNA** | Central News Agency | 1924 | Taipei |
| **CNA** | Cyprus News Agency | 1976 | Nicosia |
| **CNS** | China News Service | 1952 | Beijing |
| **COLPRENSA** | Colprensa | 1980 | Bogota |
| **CP** | Canadian Press | 1917 | Toronto |
| **CTK** | Ceskoslovenska Tiskova Kancelar | 1918 | Prague |
| **DPA** | Deutsche Presse-Agentur | 1949 | Hamburg |
| **EFE** | Agencia EFE | 1939 | Madrid |
| **ENA** | Eastern News Agency | 1970 | Dhaka |
| **EXTEL** | Exchange and Telegraph Company | 1872 | London |
| **FIDES** | Agenzia Internazionale Fides | 1926 | Vatican City |
| **GNA** | Agence Guinéenne de Presse | 1981 | Conakry |
| **GNA** | Ghana News Agency | 1957 | Accra |
| **GNA** | Guyana News Agency | 1981 | Georgetown |
| **HHA** | Hurriyet Haber Ajasi | 1963 | Istanbul |
| **IC** | Inforpress Centroamericana | 1972 | Guatemala |
| **INA** | Iraqi News Agency | 1959 | Baghdad |
| **IPS** | Inter Press Service | 1964 | Rome |
| **IRNA** | Islamic Republic News Agency | 1936 | Tehran |
| **ITAR-TASS** | Information and Telegraphic Agency of Russia-Telegraphic Agency of the Sovereign States | 1992/1904 | Moscow |
| **JAMPRESS** | Jampress | 1984 | Kingston |
| **JANA** | Jamahiriya News Agency | — | Tripoli |
| **JIJI** | Jiji Tsushin-Sha | 1945 | Tokyo |
| **JTA** | Jewish Telegraphic Agency | 1919 | Jerusalem |
| **KCNA** | Korean Central News Agency | 1946 | Pyongyang |
| **KNA** | Kenya News Agency | 1963 | Nairobi |

| Press name | Full name | Date founded | Location |
|---|---|---|---|
| **KPL** | Khao San Pathet Lao | 1968 | Vientiane |
| **KUNA** | Kuwait News Agency | 1976 | Kuwait City |
| **KYODO** | Kyodo Tsushin | 1945 | Tokyo |
| **LAI** | Logos Agencia de Informacion | 1929 | Madrid |
| **MENA** | Middle East News Agency | 1955 | Cairo |
| **MTI** | Magyar Tavariti Iroda | 1880 | Budapest |
| **NAB** | News Agency of Burma | 1963 | Rangoon |
| **NAEWOE** | Naewoe Press | 1974 | Seoul |
| **NAN** | News Agency of Nigeria | 1978 | Lagos |
| **NA** | Noticias Argentinas | 1973 | Buenos Aires |
| **NOTIMEX** | Noticias Mexicanas | 1968 | Mexico City |
| **NOVOSTI** | Agentstvo Pechati Novosti | 1961 | Moscow |
| **NPS** | Norsk Presse Service | 1960 | Oslo |
| **NTB** | Norsk Telegrambyra | 1867 | Oslo |
| **NZPA** | New Zealand Press Agency | 1879 | Wellington |
| **OPA** | Orbis Press Agency | 1977 | Prague |
| **OTTFNB** | Oy Suomen Tietoimisto Notisbyran Ab | 1887 | Helsinki |
| **PANA** | Pan-African News Agency | 1979 | Dakar |
| **PAP** | Polska Agencija Prasowa | 1944 | Warsaw |
| **PA** | Press Association | 1868 | London |
| **PETRA** | Jordan News Agency | 1965 | Amman |
| **PNA** | Philippines News Agency | 1973 | Manila |
| **PPI** | Pakistan Press International | 1959 | Karachi |
| **PRELA** | Prensa Latina | 1959 | Havana |
| **PS** | Presse Services | 1929 | Paris |
| **PTI** | Press Trust of India | 1949 | Bombay |
| **RB** | Ritzaus Bureau | 1866 | Copenhagen |
| **REUTERS** | Reuters | 1851 | London |
| **ROMPRESS** | Romanian News Agency | 1949 | Bucharest |
| **SAPA** | South African Press Association | 1938 | Johannesburg |
| **SDA** | Schweizerische Depeschenagentur | 1894 | Berne |
| **SIP** | Svensk-Internationella Pressbyran | 1927 | Stockholm |
| **SLENA** | Sierre Leone News Agency | 1980 | Freetown |
| **SOFIAPRES** | Sofia Press Agency | 1967 | Sofia |
| **SOPAC-NEWS** | South Pacific News Service | 1948 | Wellington |
| **SPA** | Saudi Press Agency | 1970 | Riyadh |
| **TANJUG** | Novinska Agencija Tanjug | 1943 | Belgrade |
| **TAP** | Tunis Afrique Presse | 1961 | Tunis |
| **TT** | Tidningarnes Telegrambyra | 1921 | Stockholm |
| **UNI** | United News of India | 1961 | New Delhi |
| **UPI** | United Press International | 1958 | New York |
| **UPP** | United Press of Pakistan | 1949 | Karachi |
| **XINHUA** | Xinhua | 1937 | Beijing |
| **YONHAP** | Yonhap (United) Press Agency | 1980 | Seoul |
| **ZIANA** | Zimbabwe Inter-Africa News Agency | 1981 | Harare |

## National newspapers — Europe

| Name | Location | Circulation[1] | Date founded |
|---|---|---|---|
| ABC | Madrid | 350 000 | 1905 |
| Algemeen Dagblad | Rotterdam | 415 800 | 1946 |
| Apogevmatini | Athens | 67 300 | 1956 |
| Avriani | Athens | 115 000 | 1980 |
| B.T. | Copenhagen | 175 600 | 1916 |
| Berliner Zeitung | Berlin | 230 600 | 1877 |
| Berlingske Tidende | Copenhagen | 155 400 | 1749 |
| Bild am Sonntag (s) | Hamburg | 2 639 000 | 1956 |
| Bild Zeitung | Hamburg | 4 643 900 | 1952 |
| Blick | Zürich | 335 100 | 1959 |
| Correio do Manha | Lisbon | 90 000 | 1979 |
| Corriere della Sera | Milan | 720 200 | 1876 |
| Dagbladet | Oslo | 228 000 | 1869 |
| De Standaard/Het Nieuwsblad/De Gentenaar | Brussels | 331 000 | n/a |
| De Telegraaf | Amsterdam | 743 000 | 1893 |
| De Volkskrant | Amsterdam | 361 200 | 1919 |
| Diario de Noticias | Lisbon | 41 900 | 1864 |
| Diario Popular | Lisbon | 29 200 | 1942 |
| Die Welt | Bonn | 214 700 | 1946 |
| Die Zeit (weekly) | Hamburg | 494 100 | 1946 |
| Ekstra Bladet | Copenhagen | 190 600 | 1904 |
| El Pais | Madrid | 412 300 | 1976 |
| El Periodico | Barcelona | 215 600 | 1978 |
| Ethnos | Athens | 58 800 | 1981 |
| Evening Herald | Dublin | 99 200 | 1891 |
| Evening Press | Dublin | 52 600 | 1954 |
| Expressen | Stockholm | 566 600 | 1944 |
| France-Dimanche (s) | Paris | 721 000 | n/a |
| France-Soir | Paris | 424 000 | 1944 |
| Frankfurter Allgemeine Zeitung | Frankfurt | 360 000 | 1949 |
| Gazeta Wyborcza | Warsaw | 500 000 | n/a |
| Gazet Van Antwerpen | Antwerp | 170 000 | 1891 |
| Helsingin Sanomat | Helsinki | 463 500 | 1889 |
| Het Laatste Nieuws | Brussels | 306 800 | 1888 |
| Il Giornale | Milan | 238 800 | 1974 |
| Il Giorno | Milan | 255 400 | 1965 |
| Il Messaggero | Rome | 426 100 | 1878 |
| Il Sole 24 Ore | Milan | 340 000 | 1865 |
| International Herald Tribune | Paris | 190 700 | 1887 |
| Irish Independent | Dublin | 147 100 | 1905 |
| Irish Times | Dublin | 95 300 | 1859 |
| La Libre Belgique | Brussels | 82 800 | 1884 |
| La Dernière Heure | Brussels | 93 400 | 1906 |
| La Lanterne | Brussels | 132 800 | 1944 |
| La Repubblica | Rome | 620 000 | 1976 |
| La Stampa | Turin | 420 600 | 1867 |
| La Vanguardia | Barcelona | 208 000 | 1881 |
| La Voix du Nord | Lille | 400 000 | 1944 |
| Le Figaro | Paris | 424 000 | 1828 |
| Le Monde | Paris | 379 100 | 1944 |
| Le Parisien Libère | Paris | 339 300 | 1944 |
| Les Echos | Paris | 121 000 | 1908 |
| Le Soir | Brussels | 148 900 | 1887 |
| L'Humanité | Paris | 117 000 | 1904 |
| L'Humanité Dimanche (s) | Paris | 360 000 | 1946 |
| Libération | Paris | 171 100 | 1973 |

| Name | Location | Circulation[1] | Date founded |
|---|---|---|---|
| Luxemburger Wort/La Voix du Luxembourg | Luxembourg | 82 800 | 1848 |
| Népszabadság | Budapest | 320 000 | 1942 |
| Neue Kronenzeitung | Vienna | 1 047 800 | n/a |
| Ouest France | Rennes | 790 000 | 1944 |
| Politiken | Copenhagen | 150 300 | 1884 |
| Rude Pravo | Prague | 400 000 | 1920 |
| Süddeutsche Zeitung | Munich | 405 400 | 1945 |
| Sunday Independent (s) | Dublin | 276 200 | 1905 |
| Sunday Press (s) | Dublin | 154 100 | 1949 |
| Sunday World (s) | Dublin | 232 100 | 1973 |
| Täglich Alles | Vienna | 542 000 | 1992 |
| Ta Nea | Athens | 135 000 | 1944 |
| Vers L'Avenir | Namur | 119 600 | 1918 |
| Welt am Sonntag (s) | Hamburg | 394 400 | n/a |
| Ya | Madrid | 380 000 | 1935 |

(s) published on Sundays only

[1] 1997 figures (rounded to nearest 100).

## National newspapers — UK

| Name | Location | Circulation[1] | Date founded |
|---|---|---|---|
| Daily Express | London | 1 076 000 | 1900 |
| Daily Mail | London | 2 394 000 | 1896 |
| Daily Mirror | London | 2 230 000 | 1903 |
| Daily Star | London | 617 000 | 1978 |
| Daily Telegraph | London | 1 029 000 | 1855 |
| Financial Times | London | 462 000 | 1880 |
| The Guardian | London | 393 000 | 1821 |
| The Independent on Sunday (s) | London | 243 000 | 1990 |
| The Independent | London | 226 000 | 1986 |
| The Mail on Sunday (s) | London | 2 303 000 | 1982 |
| News of the World (s) | London | 3 981 000 | 1843 |
| Observer (s) | London | 429 000 | 1791 |
| The Sunday People (s) | London | 1 506 000 | 1881 |
| Scotland on Sunday (s) | Edinburgh | 114 000 | 1988 |
| The Scotsman | Edinburgh | 105 000 | 1817 |
| The Sun | London | 3 570 000 | 1964 |
| The Sunday Express (s) | London | 975 000 | 1918 |
| The Sunday Mirror (s) | London | 1 891 000 | 1963 |
| The Sunday Telegraph (s) | London | 802 000 | 1961 |
| The Sunday Times (s) | London | 1 341 000 | 1822 |
| The Times | London | 724 000 | 1785 |

(s) published on Sundays only

[1] June 2000 (rounded to nearest 1000).

## Major newspapers — USA

Includes national newspapers and local newspapers having an all-day, morning, or evening circulation of 250 000 or more.

| Name | Location | Circulation[1] | Date founded |
|---|---|---|---|
| Arizona Republic | Phoenix, Ariz | 482 300 | 1890 |
| Atlanta Constitution | Atlanta, Ga | 433 100 | 1868 |
| Baltimore Sun | Baltimore, Md | 328 300 | 1837 |
| Boston Globe | Boston, Mass | 477 100 | 1872 |
| Boston Herald | Boston, Mass | 265 700 | 1892 |
| Buffalo News | Buffalo, NY | 316 300 | 1880 |
| Chicago Sun-Times | Chicago, Ill | 482 200 | 1948 |
| Chicago Tribune | Chicago, Ill | 674 600 | 1847 |
| Cleveland Plain Dealer | Cleveland, Ohio | 379 000 | 1842 |
| Columbus Dispatch | Columbus, Ohio | 252 700 | 1871 |
| Dallas Morning News | Dallas, Texas | 496 200 | 1885 |
| Denver Post | Denver, Colo | 413 700 | 1892 |
| Denver Rocky Mountain News | Denver, Colo | 446 500 | 1859 |
| Detroit Free Press | Detroit, Mich | 603 400 | 1831 |
| Detroit News | Detroit, Mich | 361 200 | 1873 |
| Forth Worth Star-Telegram | Fort Worth, Texas | 267 700 | 1906 |
| Houston Chronicle | Houston, Texas | 553 500 | 1901 |
| Indianapolis Star | Indianapolis, Ind | 267 600 | 1903 |
| Kansas City Star | Kansas City, Mo | 275 700 | 1880 |
| Los Angeles Times | Los Angeles, Cal | 1 153 700 | 1881 |
| Miami Herald | Miami, Fla | 443 600 | 1910 |
| Milwaukee Sentinel | Milwaukee, Wisc | 279 200 | 1837 |
| Minneapolis Star Tribune | Minneapolis, Minn | 406 400 | 1867 |
| New Orleans Times-Picayune | New Orleans, La | 276 800 | 1837 |
| New York Daily News | New York, NY | 730 500 | 1919 |
| New York Post | New York, NY | 436 500 | 1801 |
| New York Times[2] | New York, NY | 1 149 600 | 1851 |
| Newark Star-Ledger | Newark, NJ | 406 600 | 1832 |
| Newsday | Melville, NY | 575 600 | 1940 |
| Orange County Register | Santa Ana, Cal | 368 500 | 1905 |
| Orlando Sentinel | Orlando, Fla | 269 500 | 1876 |
| Philadelphia Inquirer | Philadelphia, Pa | 404 900 | 1829 |
| Portland Oregonian | Portland, Ore | 358 800 | 1850 |
| Sacramento Bee | Sacramento, Cal | 296 600 | 1857 |
| San Diego Union | San Diego, Cal | 381 300 | 1868 |
| San Francisco Chronicle | San Francisco, Cal | 566 600 | 1865 |
| San Jose Mercury News | San Jose, Cal | 289 500 | 1851 |
| Seattle Times | Seattle, Wash | 403 900 | 1886 |
| St Louis Post-Dispatch | St Louis, Mo | 309 000 | 1878 |
| St Petersburg Times | St Petersburg, Fla | 343 700 | 1884 |
| Sun-Sentinel | Fort Lauderdale, Fla | 275 000 | 1910 |
| Tampa Tribune | Tampa, Fla | 261 500 | 1893 |
| USA Today[2] | Arlington, Va | 1 757 700 | 1982 |
| Wall Street Journal[2] | New York, NY | 1 812 600 | 1889 |
| Washington Post | Washington, DC | 812 600 | 1877 |

[1] 1997 figures (rounded to nearest 100).

[2] National newspapers.

## Symbols in general use

| | |
|---|---|
| &, | ampersand (*and*) |
| &c. | et cetera |
| @ | at; per (in costs) |
| × | by (measuring dimensions, eg 3 x 4) |
| £ | pound |
| $ | dollar (also peso, escudo, etc in certain countries) |
| ¢ | cent (also centavo, etc in certain countries) |
| © | copyright |
| ® | registered |
| ¶ | new paragraph |
| § | new section |
| ″ | ditto |
| * | born (in genealogy) |
| † | died |
| * | hypothetical or unacceptable form (in linguistics) |
| ☠ | poison; danger |
| ♂, □ | male |
| ♀, ○ | female |
| ✠ | bishop's name follows |
| ☏ | telephone number follows |
| ☞ | this way |
| ✂ ✂··· | cut here |

**In astronomy**

| | |
|---|---|
| ● | new moon |
| ☽ | moon first quarter |
| ○ | full moon |
| ☾ | moon last quarter |

**In meteorology**

| | |
|---|---|
| ▲▲▲ | cold front |
| ◗◗◗ | warm front |
| ▲◗▲ | stationary front |
| ▲◗▲◗ | occluded front |

**In cards**

| | |
|---|---|
| ♥ | hearts |
| ♦ | diamonds |
| ♠ | spades |
| ♣ | clubs |

## Clothes care symbols

Do not iron

Can be ironed with *cool* iron (up to 110°C)

Can be ironed with *warm* iron (up to 150°C)

Can be ironed with *hot* iron (up to 200°C)

Hand wash only

Can be washed in a washing machine
The number shows the most effective washing temperature (in °C)

Reduced (medium) washing conditions

Much reduced (minimum) washing conditions (for wool products)

Do not wash

Can be tumble dried (one dot within the circle means a low temperature setting; two dots for higher temperatures)

Do not tumble dry

Do not dry clean

Ⓐ Dry cleanable (letter indicates which solvents can be used)
A: all solvents

Ⓕ Dry cleanable
F: white spirit and solvent 11 can be used

Ⓟ Dry cleanable
P: perchloroethylene (tetrachloroethylene), white spirit, solvent 113 and solvent 11 can be used

Dry cleanable, if special care taken

Chlorine bleach may be used with care

Do not use chlorine bleach

## Car index marks — UK[1]

|  |  |
|---|---|
| AA | Bournemouth |
| AB | Worcester |
| AC | Coventry |
| AD | Gloucester |
| AE | Bristol |
| AF | Truro |
| AG | Beverley |
| AH | Norwich |
| AJ | Middlesbrough |
| AK | Sheffield |
| AL | Nottingham |
| AM | Swindon |
| AN | Reading |
| AO | Carlisle |
| AP | Brighton |
| AR | Chelmsford |
| AS | Inverness |
| AT | Beverley |
| AU | Nottingham |
| AV | Peterborough |
| AW | Shrewsbury |
| AX | Cardiff |
| AY | Leicester |
| AZ | Belfast |
| BA | Manchester |
| BB | Newcastle upon Tyne |
| BC | Leicester |
| BD | Northampton |
| BE | Lincoln |
| BF | Stoke-on-Trent |
| BG | Liverpool |
| BH | Luton |
| BJ | Ipswich |
| BK | Portsmouth |
| BL | Reading |
| BM | Luton |
| BN | Manchester |
| BO | Cardiff |
| BP | Portsmouth |
| BR | Newcastle upon Tyne |
| BS | Inverness |
| BT | Leeds |
| BU | Manchester |
| BV | Preston |
| BW | Oxford |
| BX | Swansea |
| BY | Stanmore |
| BZ | Downpatrick |
| CA | Chester |
| CB | Manchester |
| CC | Bangor |
| CD | Brighton |
| CE | Peterborough |
| CF | Reading |
| CG | Bournemouth |
| CH | Nottingham |
| CJ | Gloucester |
| CK | Preston |
| CL | Norwich |
| CM | Liverpool |
| CN | Newcastle upon Tyne |
| CO | Exeter |
| CP | Leeds |
| CR | Portsmouth |
| CS | Glasgow |
| CT | Lincoln |
| CU | Newcastle upon Tyne |
| CV | Truro |
| CW | Preston |
| CX | Leeds |
| CY | Swansea |
| CZ | Belfast |
| DA | Birmingham |
| DB | Manchester |
| DC | Middlesbrough |
| DD | Gloucester |
| DE | Swansea |
| DF to DG | Gloucester |
| DH | Dudley |
| DJ | Liverpool |
| DK | Manchester |
| DL | Portsmouth |
| DM | Chester |
| DN | Leeds |
| DO | Lincoln |
| DP | Reading |
| DR | Exeter |
| DS | Glasgow |
| DT | Sheffield |
| DU | Coventry |
| DV | Exeter |
| DW | Cardiff |
| DX | Ipswich |
| DY | Brighton |
| DZ | Ballymena |
| EA | Dudley |
| EB | Peterborough |
| EC | Preston |
| ED | Liverpool |
| EE | Lincoln |
| EF | Middlesbrough |
| EG | Peterborough |
| EH | Stoke-on-Trent |
| EJ | Swansea |
| EK | Liverpool |
| EL | Bournemouth |
| EM | Liverpool |
| EN | Manchester |
| EO | Preston |
| EP | Swansea |
| ER | Peterborough |
| ES | Dundee |
| ET | Sheffield |
| EU | Bristol |
| EV | Chelmsford |
| EW | Peterborough |
| EX | Norwich |
| EY | Bangor |
| EZ | Belfast |
| FA | Stoke-on-Trent |
| FB | Bristol |
| FC | Oxford |
| FD | Dudley |
| FE | Lincoln |
| FF | Bangor |
| FG | Brighton |
| FH | Gloucester |
| FJ | Exeter |
| FK | Dudley |
| FL | Peterborough |
| FM | Chester |
| FN | Maidstone |
| FO | Gloucester |
| FP | Leicester |
| FR | Preston |
| FS | Edinburgh |
| FT | Newcastle upon Tyne |
| FU | Lincoln |
| FV | Preston |
| FW | Lincoln |
| FX | Bournemouth |
| FY | Liverpool |
| FZ | Belfast |
| GA to GB | Glasgow |
| GC | Wimbledon |
| GD to GE | Glasgow |
| GF | Wimbledon |
| GG | Glasgow |
| GH | Wimbledon |
| GJ to GK | Wimbledon |
| GL | Truro |
| GM | Reading |
| GN to GP | Wimbledon |
| GR | Newcastle upon Tyne |
| GS | Luton |
| GT | Wimbledon |
| GU | Sidcup |
| GV | Ipswich |
| GW to GX | Sidcup |
| GZ | Belfast |
| HA | Dudley |
| HB | Cardiff |
| HC | Brighton |
| HD | Leeds |
| HE | Sheffield |
| HF | Liverpool |
| HG | Preston |
| HH | Carlisle |
| HJ to HK | Chelmsford |
| HL | Sheffield |
| HM | Wimbledon |
| HN | Middlesbrough |
| HO | Bournemouth |

| | |
|---|---|
| **HP** | Coventry |
| **HR** | Swindon |
| **HS** | Glasgow |
| **HT** to **HU** | Bristol |
| **HV** | Wimbledon |
| **HW** | Bristol |
| **HX** | Wimbledon |
| **HY** | Bristol |
| **HZ** | Omagh |
| **IA** | Ballymena |
| **IB** | Armagh |
| **IJ** | Downpatrick |
| **IL** | Enniskillen |
| **IW** | Coleraine |
| **JA** | Manchester |
| **JB** | Reading |
| **JC** | Bangor |
| **JD** | Wimbledon |
| **JE** | Peterborough |
| **JF** | Leicester |
| **JG** | Maidstone |
| **JH** | Reading |
| **JI** | Omagh |
| **JJ** | Maidstone |
| **JK** | Brighton |
| **JL** | Lincoln |
| **JM** | Reading |
| **JN** | Chelmsford |
| **JO** | Oxford |
| **JP** | Liverpool |
| **JR** | Newcastle upon Tyne |
| **JS** | Inverness |
| **JT** | Bournemouth |
| **JU** | Leicester |
| **JV** | Lincoln |
| **JW** | Birmingham |
| **JX** | Leeds |
| **JY** | Exeter |
| **JZ** | Downpatrick |
| **KA** to **KD** | Liverpool |
| **KE** | Maidstone |
| **KF** | Liverpool |
| **KG** | Cardiff |
| **KH** | Beverley |
| **KJ** to **KP** | Maidstone |
| **KR** | Maidstone |
| **KS** | Edinburgh |
| **KT** | Maidstone |
| **KU** | Sheffield |
| **KV** | Coventry |
| **KW** | Sheffield |
| **KX** | Luton |
| **KY** | Sheffield |
| **KZ** | Ballymena |
| **LA** to **LF** | Stanmore |
| **LG** | Chester |
| **LH** | Stanmore |
| **LJ** | Bournemouth |
| **LK** to **LP** | Stanmore |
| **LR** | Stanmore |
| **LS** | Edinburgh |
| **LT** to **LU** | Stanmore |
| **LV** | Liverpool |
| **LW** to **LY** | Stanmore |
| **LZ** | Armagh |
| **MA** to **MB** | Chester |
| **MC** to **MH** | Chelmsford |
| **MJ** | Luton |
| **MK** to **MM** | Chelmsford |
| **MN** | *(not used)* |
| **MO** | Reading |
| **MP** | Chelmsford |
| **MR** | Swindon |
| **MS** | Edinburgh |
| **MT** to **MU** | Chelmsford |
| **MV** | Sidcup |
| **MW** | Swindon |
| **MX** to **MY** | Sidcup |
| **NA** to **NF** | Manchester |
| **NG** | Norwich |
| **NH** | Northampton |
| **NJ** | Brighton |
| **NK** | Luton |
| **NL** | Newcastle upon Tyne |
| **NM** | Luton |
| **NN** | Nottingham |
| **NO** | Chelmsford |
| **NP** | Worcester |
| **NR** | Leicester |
| **NS** | Glasgow |
| **NT** | Shrewsbury |
| **NU** | Nottingham |
| **NV** | Northampton |
| **NW** | Leeds |
| **NX** | Dudley |
| **NY** | Cardiff |
| **NZ** | Coleraine |
| **OA** to **OC** | Birmingham |
| **OD** | Exeter |
| **OE** to **OH** | Birmingham |
| **OI** | Belfast |
| **OJ** to **ON** | Birmingham |
| **OO** | Chelmsford |
| **OP** | Birmingham |
| **OR** | Portsmouth |
| **OS** | Glasgow |
| **OT** | Portsmouth |
| **OU** | Bristol |
| **OV** | Birmingham |
| **OW** | Portsmouth |
| **OX** | Birmingham |
| **OY** | Stanmore |
| **OZ** | Belfast |
| **PA** to **PF** | Wimbledon |
| **PG** to **PH** | Guildford |
| **PJ** to **PM** | Guildford |
| **PN** | Brighton |
| **PO** | Portsmouth |
| **PP** | Luton |
| **PR** | Bournemouth |
| **PS** | Aberdeen |
| **PT** | Newcastle upon Tyne |
| **PU** | Chelmsford |
| **PV** | Ipswich |
| **PW** | Norwich |
| **PX** | Portsmouth |
| **PY** | Middlesbrough |
| **PZ** | Belfast |
| **QA** to **QH** | Wimbledon |
| **QJ** to **QN** | Wimbledon |
| **QP** to **QY** | Wimbledon |
| **RA** to **RC** | Nottingham |
| **RD** | Reading |
| **RE** to **RF** | Stoke-on-Trent |
| **RG** | Newcastle upon Tyne |
| **RH** | Beverley |
| **RJ** | Manchester |
| **RK** | Stanmore |
| **RL** | Truro |
| **RM** | Carlisle |
| **RN** | Preston |
| **RO** | Luton |
| **RP** | Northampton |
| **RR** | Nottingham |
| **RS** | Aberdeen |
| **RT** | Ipswich |
| **RU** | Bournemouth |
| **RV** | Portsmouth |
| **RW** | Coventry |
| **RX** | Reading |
| **RY** | Leicester |
| **RZ** | Ballymena |
| **SA** | Aberdeen |
| **SB** | Glasgow |
| **SC** | Edinburgh |
| **SCY** | Truro (Isles of Scilly) |
| **SD** | Glasgow |
| **SE** | Aberdeen |
| **SF** to **SH** | Edinburgh |
| **SJ** | Glasgow |
| **SK** | Inverness |

| | |
|---|---|
| **SL** | Dundee |
| **SM** | Carlisle |
| **SN** | Dundee |
| **SO** | Aberdeen |
| **SP** | Dundee |
| **SR** | Dundee |
| **SS** | Aberdeen |
| **ST** | Inverness |
| **SU** | Glasgow |
| **SV** | *spare* |
| **SW** | Carlisle |
| **SX** | Edinburgh |
| **SY** | *spare* |
| **SZ** | Downpatrick |
| **TA** | Exeter |
| **TB** | Liverpool |
| **TC** | Bristol |
| **TD** to **TE** | Manchester |
| **TF** | Reading |
| **TG** | Cardiff |
| **TH** | Swansea |
| **TJ** | Liverpool |
| **TK** | Exeter |
| **TL** | Lincoln |
| **TM** | Luton |
| **TN** | Newcastle upon Tyne |
| **TO** | Nottingham |
| **TP** | Portsmouth |
| **TR** | Portsmouth |
| **TS** | Dundee |
| **TT** | Exeter |
| **TU** | Chester |
| **TV** | Nottingham |
| **TW** | Chelmsford |
| **TX** | Cardiff |
| **TY** | Newcastle upon Tyne |
| **TZ** | Belfast |
| **UA** | Leeds |
| **UB** | Leeds |
| **UC** | Wimbledon |
| **UD** | Oxford |
| **UE** | Dudley |
| **UF** | Brighton |
| **UG** | Leeds |
| **UH** | Cardiff |
| **UI** | Londonderry |
| **UJ** | Shrewsbury |
| **UK** | Birmingham |
| **UL** | Wimbledon |
| **UM** | Leeds |
| **UN** to **UO** | Exeter |
| **UP** | Newcastle upon Tyne |
| **UR** | Luton |
| **US** | Glasgow |
| **UT** | Leicester |
| **UU** to **UW** | Wimbledon |
| **UX** | Shrewsbury |
| **UY** | Worcester |
| **UZ** | Belfast |
| **VA** | Peterborough |
| **VB** | Maidstone |
| **VC** | Coventry |
| **VD** | *series withdrawn* |
| **VE** | Peterborough |
| **VF** to **VG** | Norwich |
| **VH** | Leeds |
| **VJ** | Gloucester |
| **VK** | Newcastle upon Tyne |
| **VL** | Lincoln |
| **VM** | Manchester |
| **VN** | Middlesbrough |
| **VO** | Nottingham |
| **VP** | Birmingham |
| **VR** | Manchester |
| **VS** | Luton |
| **VT** | Stoke-on-Trent |
| **VU** | Manchester |
| **VV** | Northampton |
| **VW** to **VX** | Chelmsford |
| **VY** | Leeds |
| **VZ** | Omagh |
| **WA** to **WB** | Sheffield |
| **WC** | Chelmsford |
| **WD** | Dudley |
| **WE** to **WG** | Sheffield |
| **WH** | Manchester |
| **WJ** | Sheffield |
| **WK** | Coventry |
| **WL** | Oxford |
| **WM** | Liverpool |
| **WN** | Swansea |
| **WO** | Cardiff |
| **WP** | Worcester |
| **WR** | Leeds |
| **WS** | Bristol |
| **WT** to **WU** | Leeds |
| **WV** | Brighton |
| **WW** to **WY** | Leeds |
| **WZ** | Belfast |
| **XI** | Belfast |
| **XZ** | Belfast |
| **YA** to **YD** | Taunton |
| **YE** to **YF** | Wimbledon |
| **YG** | Leeds |
| **YH** | Wimbledon |
| **YJ** | Brighton |
| **YK** to **YP** | Wimbledon |
| **YR** | Wimbledon |
| **YS** | Glasgow |
| **YT** to **YY** | Wimbledon |
| **YZ** | Coleraine |

[1] Prior to September 2001.

## Car index marks — UK[2]

| | |
|---|---|
| **AA – AN** | Peterborough |
| **AO – AU** | Norwich |
| **AV – AY** | Ipswich |
| **BA – BY** | Birmingham |
| **CA – CO** | Cardiff |
| **CP – CV** | Swansea |
| **CW – CY** | Bangor |
| **DA – DK** | Chester |
| **DL – DY** | Shrewsbury |
| **EA – EY** | Essex |
| **FA – FN** | Nottingham |
| **FP** | Nottingham |
| **FR – FY** | Lincoln |
| **GA – GO** | Maidstone |
| **GP – GY** | Brighton |
| **HA – HJ** | Bournemouth |
| **HK – HV** | Portsmouth |
| **HW** | Isle of Wight |
| **HX – HY** | Portsmouth |
| **KA – KL** | Luton |
| **KM – KY** | Northampton |
| **LA – LJ** | Wimbledon |
| **LK – LT** | Stanmore |
| **LU – LY** | Sidcup |
| **MA – MY** | Manchester |
| **NA – NE** | Newcastle |
| **NG – NO** | Newcastle |
| **NP – NY** | Stockton |
| **OA – OY** | Oxford |
| **PA – PT** | Preston |
| **PU – PY** | Carlisle |
| **RA – RY** | Reading |
| **SA – SJ** | Glasgow |
| **SK – SO** | Edinburgh |
| **SP – ST** | Dundee |
| **SU – SW** | Aberdeen |
| **SX – SY** | Inverness |
| **VA – VY** | Worcester |
| **WA – WJ** | Exeter |
| **WK – WL** | Truro |
| **WM – WY** | Bristol |
| **YA – YK** | Leeds |
| **YL – YU** | Sheffield |
| **YV – YY** | Beverley |

[2] Introduced September 2001. Note that I and Q are not used in the new format.

## Car index marks — International

| | |
|---|---|
| **A** | Austria |
| **ADN** | Yemen |
| **AFG** | Afghanistan |
| **AL** | Albania |
| **AND** | Andorra |
| **AUS** | Australia* |
| **B** | Belgium |
| **BD** | Bangladesh* |
| **BDS** | Barbados* |
| **BG** | Bulgaria |
| **BH** | Belize |
| **BIH** | Bosnia-Herzegovina |
| **BR** | Brazil |
| **BRN** | Bahrain |
| **BRU** | Brunei* |
| **BS** | The Bahamas* |
| **BUR** | Myanmar (Burma) |
| **C** | Cuba |
| **CDN** | Canada |
| **CH** | Switzerland |
| **CI** | Côte d'Ivoire |
| **CL** | Sri Lanka* |
| **CO** | Colombia |
| **CR** | Costa Rica |
| **CY** | Cyprus* |
| **CZ** | Czech Republic |
| **D** | Germany |
| **DK** | Denmark |
| **DOM** | Dominican Republic |
| **DY** | Benin |
| **DZ** | Algeria |
| **E** | Spain[1] |
| **EAK** | Kenya* |
| **EAT** | Tanzania* |
| **EAU** | Uganda* |
| **EC** | Ecuador |
| **ES** | El Salvador |
| **EST** | Estonia |
| **ET** | Egypt |
| **ETH** | Ethiopia |
| **F** | France[2] |
| **FIN** | Finland |
| **FJI** | Fiji* |
| **FL** | Liechtenstein |
| **FO** | Faroe Is |
| **GB** | UK* |
| **GBA** | Alderney* |
| **GBG** | Guernsey* |
| **GBJ** | Jersey* |
| **GBM** | Isle of Man* |
| **GBZ** | Gibraltar |
| **GCA** | Guatemala |
| **GE** | Georgia |
| **GH** | Ghana |
| **GR** | Greece |
| **GUY** | Guyana* |
| **H** | Hungary |
| **HK** | Hong Kong* |
| **HKJ** | Jordan |
| **HR** | Croatia |
| **I** | Italy |
| **IL** | Israel |
| **IND** | India* |
| **IR** | Iran |
| **IRL** | Ireland* |
| **IRQ** | Iraq |
| **IS** | Iceland |
| **J** | Japan* |
| **JA** | Jamaica* |
| **K** | Cambodia |
| **KS** | Kyrgyzstan |
| **KWT** | Kuwait |
| **KZ** | Kazakhstan |
| **L** | Luxembourg |
| **LAO** | Laos |
| **LAR** | Libya |
| **LB** | Liberia |
| **LS** | Lesotho* |
| **LT** | Lithuania |
| **LV** | Latvia |
| **M** | Malta* |
| **MA** | Morocco |
| **MAL** | Malaysia* |
| **MC** | Monaco |
| **MEX** | Mexico |
| **MGL** | Mongolia |
| **MK** | Macedonia |
| **MS** | Mauritius* |
| **MW** | Malawi* |
| **N** | Norway |
| **NA** | Netherlands Antilles |
| **NAM** | Namibia* |
| **NIC** | Nicaragua |
| **NL** | Netherlands |
| **NZ** | New Zealand* |
| **P** | Portugal |
| **PA** | Panama |
| **PE** | Peru |
| **PK** | Pakistan* |
| **PL** | Poland |
| **PNG** | Papua New Guinea* |
| **PY** | Paraguay |
| **RA** | Argentina |
| **RB** | Botswana* |
| **RC** | China |
| **RCA** | Central African Republic |
| **RCB** | Congo |
| **RCH** | Chile |
| **RH** | Haiti |
| **RI** | Indonesia* |
| **RIM** | Mauritania |
| **RL** | Lebanon |
| **RM** | Madagascar |
| **RMM** | Mali |
| **RN** | Niger |
| **RO** | Romania |
| **ROK** | Korea, Republic of (South Korea) |
| **ROU** | Uruguay |
| **RP** | Philippines |
| **RSM** | San Marino |
| **RU** | Burundi |
| **RUS** | Russia |
| **RWA** | Rwanda |
| **S** | Sweden |
| **SD** | Swaziland* |
| **SGP** | Singapore* |
| **SK** | Slovakia |
| **SLO** | Slovenia |
| **SME** | Suriname* |
| **SN** | Senegal |
| **SU** | Belarus |
| **SY** | Seychelles* |
| **SYR** | Syria |
| **T** | Thailand* |
| **TG** | Togo |
| **TJ** | Tajikistan |
| **TM** | Turkmenistan |
| **TN** | Tunisia |
| **TR** | Turkey |
| **TT** | Trinidad and Tobago* |
| **UA** | Ukraine |
| **USA** | USA |
| **UZ** | Uzbekistan |
| **V** | Vatican City |
| **VN** | Vietnam |
| **WAG** | The Gambia |
| **WAL** | Sierra Leone |
| **WAN** | Nigeria |
| **WD** | Dominica* |
| **WG** | Grenada* |
| **WL** | St Lucia* |
| **WS** | Samoa |
| **WV** | St Vincent and the Grenadines* |
| **YU** | Yugoslavia, Federal Republic of |
| **YV** | Venezuela |
| **Z** | Zambia* |
| **ZA** | South Africa* |
| **ZRE** | Congo, Democratic Republic of |
| **ZW** | Zimbabwe* |

*In countries so marked, the rule of the road is to drive on the left; in other countries, vehicles drive on the right.

[1]Including Balearic Islands, Canary Islands and Spanish enclaves.

[2]Including French Overseas Possessions.

## UK airports

| | |
|---|---|
| **Alderney** | Channel Is |
| **Baltasound** | Unst, Shetlands |
| **Belfast City** | |
| **Belfast International** | |
| **Benbecula** | Hebrides |
| **Biggin Hill** | Kent |
| **Blackpool** | Lancashire |
| **Bournemouth** | Dorset |
| **Bristol** | Avon |
| **Cambridge** | |
| **Cardiff** | |
| **Coventry** | West Midlands |
| **Dundee** | |
| **Dyce** | Aberdeen |
| **East Midlands** | Derbyshire |
| **Exeter** | Devon |
| **Fair Isle** | Shetlands |
| **Gatwick** | London |
| **Glenegedale** | Islay |
| **Glasgow** | |
| **Grimsetter** | Orkney |
| **Guernsey** | Channel Is |
| **Heathrow** | London |
| **Humberside** | |
| **Inverness** | |
| **Jersey** | Channel Is |
| **Kirkwall** | Orkney |
| **Leeds-Bradford** | |
| **Liverpool** | |
| **London City** | |
| **Luton** | Bedfordshire |
| **Lydd** | Kent |
| **Manchester** | |
| **Newcastle** | |
| **North Bay** | Barra, Hebrides |
| **Norwich** | Norfolk |
| **Penzance** | Cornwall |
| **Plymouth (Roborough)** | Devon |
| **Prestwick** | Ayrshire |
| **Ronaldsway** | Isle of Man |
| **Saint Mary's** | Scilly Isles |
| **Sandown** | Isle of Wight |
| **Scatsa** | Shetlands |
| **Southampton** | Hampshire |
| **Southend** | Essex |
| **Stansted** | London |
| **Stornoway** | Hebrides |
| **Sumburgh** | Shetlands |
| **Swansea** | |
| **Teeside** | Cleveland |
| **Tingwall** | Lerwick, Shetlands |
| **Tiree** | Hebrides |
| **Tresco** | Scilly Isles |
| **Turnhouse** | Edinburgh |
| **West Midlands** | Birmingham |
| **Westray** | Orkney |
| **Wick** | Caithness |

## International airports

| | |
|---|---|
| **Abadan International** | Iran |
| **Abu Dhabi** | United Arab Emirates |
| **Adana** | Turkey |
| **Adelaide** | Australia |
| **Agno** | Lugano, Switzerland |
| **Ain el Bay** | Constantine, Algeria |
| **Albany County** | New York, USA |
| **Alborg Roedslet** | Norresundbyr, Denmark |
| **Albuquerque** | New Mexico, USA |
| **Alexandria** | Egypt |
| **Alfonso Bonilla Aragon** | Cali, Colombia |
| **Alicante** | Spain |
| **Alma Ata** | Kazakhstan |
| **Almeria** | Spain |
| **Amarillo** | Texas, USA |
| **Amborovy** | Majunga, Madagascar |
| **Amilcar Cabral International** | Sal I, Cape Verde |
| **Aminu International** | Kano, Nigeria |
| **Anchorage** | Alaska, USA |
| **Archangel** | Russia |
| **Arlanda** | Stockholm, Sweden |
| **Arnos Vale** | St Vincent |
| **Arrecife** | Lanzarote, Canary Is |
| **Arturo Marino Benitez** | Santiago, Chile |
| **Ashkabad** | Turkmenistan |
| **Asmara International** | Eritrea |
| **Asturias** | Spain |
| **Atatürk** | Istanbul, Turkey |
| **Auckland** | New Zealand |
| **Augusto C Sandino** | Managua, Nicaragua |
| **Baghdad International** | Iraq |
| **Bahrain International** | Bahrain |
| **Bali International/ Ngurah Rai** | Denpasar, Indonesia |
| **Balice** | Kracow, Poland |
| **Bandar Seri Begawan** | Brunei |
| **Baneasa** | Bucharest, Romania |
| **Bangkok International** | Thailand |
| **Barajas** | Madrid, Spain |
| **Barcelona** | Spain |
| **Basle-Mulhouse** | Basle, Switzerland |
| **Beijing (Peking)** | China |
| **Beira** | Mozambique |
| **Beirut International** | Khaldeh, Lebanon |
| **Belfast International** | UK |
| **Belgrade** | Yugoslavia |
| **Belize City International** | Belize |
| **Ben Gurion** | Tel Aviv, Israel |
| **Benina** | Benghazi, Libya |
| **Benito Juarez** | Mexico City, Mexico |
| **Berlin-Schonefeld** | Berlin, Germany |

| | |
|---|---|
| **Berline-Tegel** | Berlin, Germany |
| **Berne** | Switzerland |
| **Billund** | Denmark |
| **Birmingham** | Alabama, USA |
| **Bishkek-Manas** | Manas, Kyrgyzstan |
| **Blackburne/Plymouth** | Montserrat |
| **Blagnac** | Toulouse, France |
| **Bole** | Addis Ababa, Ethiopia |
| **Bombay** | India |
| **Borispol** | Kiev, Ukraine |
| **Boukhalef** | Tangier, Morocco |
| **Boulogne** | France |
| **Bourgas** | Bulgaria |
| **Bradley International** | Hartford, Connecticut, USA |
| **Brasilia International** | Brazil |
| **Bremen** | Germany |
| **Brisbane** | Australia |
| **Brnik** | Ljubljana, Slovenia |
| **Bromma** | Stockholm, Sweden |
| **Brussels National** | Belgium |
| **Buffalo** | New York, USA |
| **Bujumbura** | Burundi |
| **Bulawayo** | Zimbabwe |
| **Butmir** | Sarajevo, Bosnia-Herzegovina |
| **Cairns** | Queensland, Australia |
| **Cairo International** | Egypt |
| **Calabar** | Nigeria |
| **Calcutta** | India |
| **Calgary International** | Canada |
| **Cancun** | Mexico |
| **Cannon International** | Reno, Nevada, USA |
| **Canton** | Akron, Ohio, USA |
| **Capodichino** | Naples, Italy |
| **Carrasco** | Montevideo, Uruguay |
| **Carthage** | Tunis, Tunisia |
| **Cebu** | Philippines |
| **Chiang Kai Shek** | Taipei, Taiwan |
| **Changi** | Singapore |
| **Charleroi (Gossilies)** | Belgium |
| **Charles de Gaulle** | Paris, France |
| **Charleston** | South Carolina, USA |
| **Charleston** | West Virginia, USA |
| **Charlotte** | North Carolina, USA |
| **Château Bougon** | Nantes, France |
| **Christchurch** | New Zealand |
| **Ciampino** | Rome, Italy |
| **Cologne-Bonn** | Cologne, Germany |
| **Columbus** | Ohio, USA |
| **Congonhas** | São Paulo, Brazil |
| **Copenhagen International** | Kastrup, Denmark |
| **Cork** | Ireland |
| **Costa Smerelda** | Olbia, Sardinia |
| **Côte d'Azure** | Nice, France |
| **Cotonou** | Benin |
| **Cristoforo Colombo** | Genoa, Italy |
| **Crown Point** | Scarborough, Tobago |
| **Cuscatlan** | Comalapa, El Salvador |
| **D F Malan** | Cape Town, South Africa |
| **Dalaman** | Turkey |

| | |
|---|---|
| **Dallas/Fort Worth** | Dallas, Texas, USA |
| **Damascus** | Syria |
| **Dar es Salaam** | Tanzania |
| **Darwin** | Australia |
| **Des Moines** | Iowa, USA |
| **Detroit-Wayne County** | Detroit, Michigan, USA |
| **Deurne** | Antwerp, Belgium |
| **Dhahran International** | Al Khobar, Saudi Arabia |
| **Djibouti** | Djibouti |
| **Doha** | Qatar |
| **Dois de Julho International** | Salvador, Brazil |
| **Domodedovo** | Moscow, Russia |
| **Don Miguel Hidalgo y Castilla** | Guadalajara, Mexico |
| **Dorval International** | Montreal, Canada |
| **Douala** | Cameroon |
| **Dresden** | Germany |
| **Dubai** | United Arab Emirates |
| **Dublin** | Ireland |
| **Dubrovnik** | Croatia |
| **Dulles International** | Washington DC, USA |
| **Dusseldorf** | Germany |
| **Ecterdingen** | Stuttgart, Germany |
| **Edmonton International** | Canada |
| **Eduardo Gomes** | Manaus, Brazil |
| **Eindhoven** | Netherlands |
| **El Alto** | La Paz, Bolivia |
| **El Dorado** | Bogata, Colombia |
| **El Paso** | Texas, USA |
| **Elat** | Israel |
| **Elmas** | Cagliari, Italy |
| **Entebbe** | Uganda |
| **Entzheim** | Strasbourg, France |
| **Eppley Airfield** | Omaha, Nebraska, USA |
| **Erie** | Pennsylvania, USA |
| **Ernesto Cortissoz** | Barranquilla, Colombia |
| **Esbjerg** | Denmark |
| **Esenboga** | Ankara, Turkey |
| **Faleolo** | Apia, Samoa |
| **Faro** | Portugal |
| **Ferihegy** | Budapest, Hungary |
| **Findel** | Luxembourg |
| **Fiumicino (Leonardo da Vinci)** | Rome, Italy |
| **Flesland** | Bergen, Norway |
| **Fontanarossa** | Catonia, Sicily |
| **Fornebu** | Oslo, Norway |
| **Fort de France** | Lamentin, Martinique |
| **Fort Lauderdale** | Florida, USA |
| **Fort Myers** | Florida, USA |
| **Frankfurt am Main** | Germany |
| **Freeport International** | The Bahamas |
| **Frejorgues** | Montpellier, France |
| **Fuenterrabia** | San Sebastian, Spain |
| **Fuerteventura** | Canary Is |
| **Fuhlsbuttel** | Hamburg, Germany |
| **G Marconi** | Bologna, Italy |
| **Galileo Galilei** | Pisa, Italy |
| **Gatwick** | London, UK |

| Airport | Location |
|---|---|
| **G'Bessia** | Conakry, Guinea |
| **General Abelard L Rodriguez** | Tijuana, Mexico |
| **General Juan N Alvarez** | Acapulco, Mexico |
| **General Manuel Marquez de Leon** | La Paz, Mexico |
| **General Mariano Escobedo** | Monterrey, Mexico |
| **General Mitchell** | Milwaukee, Wisconsin, USA |
| **General Rafael Buelna** | Mazatlan, Mexico |
| **Geneva** | Switzerland |
| **Gerona/Costa Brava** | Gerona, Spain |
| **Gillot** | St Denis, Réunion |
| **Golden Rock** | St Kitts |
| **Goleniow** | Szczecin, Poland |
| **Glasgow** | UK |
| **Granada** | Spain |
| **Grantley Adams International** | Bridgetown, Barbados |
| **Greater Cincinnati** | Ohio, USA |
| **Greater Pittsburgh** | Pennsylvania, USA |
| **Guam** | Guam |
| **Guararapes International** | Recife, Brazil |
| **Guarulhos International** | São Paulo, Brazil |
| **Halifax** | Canada |
| **Halim Perdanakusama** | Jakarta, Indonesia |
| **Hamilton Kindley Field** | Hamilton, Bermuda |
| **Hancock Field** | Syracuse, New York State, USA |
| **Hannover-Langenhagen** | Hannover, Germany |
| **Hanoi** | Vietnam |
| **Harare** | Zimbabwe |
| **Harrisburg** | Pennsylvania, USA |
| **Hartsfield** | Atlanta, Georgia, USA |
| **Hassan** | Laayoune, Morocco |
| **Hato** | Curaçao, Netherlands Antilles |
| **Hahaya International** | Moroni, Comoros |
| **Hanedi** | Tokyo, Japan |
| **Heathrow** | London, UK |
| **Hellenikon** | Athens, Greece |
| **Henderson Field** | Honiari, Solomon Is |
| **Heraklion** | Crete, Greece |
| **Hewanorra International** | St Lucia |
| **Ho Chi Minh City** | Vietnam |
| **Hong Kong International** | Hong Kong |
| **Hongqiao** | Shanghai, China |
| **Honolulu** | Hawaii, USA |
| **Hopkins** | Cleveland, Ohio, USA |
| **Houari Boumedienne International** | Dar-el-Beida, Algeria |
| **Houston** | Texas, USA |
| **Ibiza** | Balearic Is, Spain |
| **Indianapolis** | Indiana, USA |
| **Indira Ghandi International** | Delhi, India |
| **Inezgane** | Agadir, Morocco |
| **Islamabad** | Pakistan |
| **Isle Verde** | San Juan, Puerto Rico |
| **Izmir** | Turkey |
| **Itazuke** | Fukuoka, Japan |

| Airport | Location |
|---|---|
| **Ivanka** | Bratislava, Slovakia |
| **Ivato** | Antananarivo, Madagascar |
| **J F Kennedy** | New York, USA |
| **Jackson Field** | Port Moresby, Papua New Guinea |
| **Jacksonville** | Florida, USA |
| **James M Cox** | Dayton, Ohio, USA |
| **Johannesburg International** | South Africa |
| **Jomo Kenyatta** | Nairobi, Kenya |
| **Jorge Chavez International** | Lima, Peru |
| **Jose Marti International** | Havana, Cuba |
| **Juan Santa Maria International** | Alajuela, Costa Rica |
| **Kagoshima** | Japan |
| **Kalmar** | Sweden |
| **Kamazu** | Lilongwe, Malawi |
| **Kansas City** | Missouri, USA |
| **Kaohsiung** | Taiwan |
| **Karachi** | Pakistan |
| **Karpathos** | Karpathos, Greece |
| **Katunayake** | Colombo, Sri Lanka |
| **Keflavik** | Reykjavik, Iceland |
| **Kent County** | Grand Rapids, Michigan, USA |
| **Kerkyra** | Corfu, Greece |
| **Key West** | Florida, USA |
| **Khartoum** | The Sudan |
| **Khoramaksar** | Aden, Yemen |
| **Khwaja Rawash** | Kabul, Afghanistan |
| **Kigali** | Rwanda |
| **Kimpo International** | Seoul, Korea, Republic of (South Korea) |
| **King Abdul Aziz** | Jeddah, Saudi Arabia |
| **King Khaled** | Riyadh, Saudi Arabia |
| **Kingsford Smith** | Sydney, Australia |
| **Kjevik** | Kristiansand, Norway |
| **Klagenfurt** | Austria |
| **Komaki** | Nagoya, Japan |
| **Kos** | Greece |
| **Košice** | Slovakia |
| **Kota Kinabulu** | Sabah, Malaysia |
| **Kotoka** | Accra, Ghana |
| **Kranebitten** | Innsbruck, Austria |
| **Kuching** | Sarawak, Malaysia |
| **Kungsangen** | Norrköping, Sweden |
| **Kuwait International** | Kuwait |
| **La Aurora** | Guatemala City, Guatemala |
| **La Coruña** | Spain |
| **La Guardia** | New York, USA |
| **La Mesa** | San Pedro Sula, Honduras |
| **La Parra** | Jerez de la Frontera, Spain |
| **Lahore** | Pakistan |
| **Landvetter** | Gothenburg, Sweden |
| **Larnaca International** | Cyprus |
| **Las Americas International** | Santo Domingo, Dominican Republic |

| | |
|---|---|
| **Las Palmas** | Gran Canaria, Canary Is |
| **Le Raizet** | Point-à-Pitre, Guadeloupe |
| **Leipzig** | Germany |
| **Les Angades** | Oujda, Morocco |
| **Lesquin** | Lille, France |
| **Lester B Pearson International** | Toronto, Canada |
| **Libreville** | Gabon |
| **Lic Gustavo Diaz Ordaz** | Puerto Vallarta, Mexico |
| **Lic Manuel Crecencio Rejon** | Merida, Mexico |
| **Liège (Bierset)** | Belgium |
| **Liepaja International** | Latvia |
| **Linate** | Milan, Italy |
| **Lincoln** | Nebraska, USA |
| **Lindbergh International** | San Diego, USA |
| **Linz** | Austria |
| **Lisbon** | Portugal |
| **Little Rock** | Arkansas, USA |
| **Llabanère** | Perpignan, France |
| **Logan International** | Boston, Massachusetts, USA |
| **Lomé** | Togo |
| **London City** | UK |
| **Long Beach** | California, USA |
| **Los Angeles** | California, USA |
| **Loshitsa** | Minsk, Belarus |
| **Louis Botha** | Durban, South Africa |
| **Louisville** | Kentucky, USA |
| **Luanda** | Angola |
| **Luano** | Lubumashi, Congo, Democratic Republic of |
| **Lubbock** | Texas, USA |
| **Luis Munoz Marin International** | San Juan, Puerto Rico |
| **Lungi** | Freetown, Sierra Leone |
| **Luqa** | Malta |
| **Lusaka** | Zambia |
| **Luxor** | Egypt |
| **Maastricht** | Netherlands |
| **McCarran International** | Las Vegas, Nevada, USA |
| **McCoy International** | Orlando, Florida, USA |
| **Mactan International** | Cebu, Philippines |
| **Mahon** | Menorca |
| **Mais Gate** | Port-au-Prince, Haiti |
| **Malaga** | Spain |
| **Male** | Maldives |
| **Malpensa** | Milan, Italy |
| **Managua** | Nicaragua |
| **Manchester** | New Hampshire, USA |
| **Manchester** | UK |
| **Maputo** | Mozambique |
| **Marco Polo** | Venice, Italy |
| **Mariscal Sucre** | Quito, Ecuador |
| **Maseru** | Lesotho |
| **Matsapha** | Manzini, Swaziland |
| **Maupertus** | Cherbourg, France |
| **Maxglan** | Salzburg, Austria |
| **Maya Maya** | Brazaville, Congo |
| **Medina** | Saudi Arabia |
| **Meenambakkam International** | Madras, India |
| **Mehrabad International** | Tehran, Iran |
| **Melita** | Djerba, Tunisia |
| **Memphis** | Tennessee, USA |
| **Menara** | Marrakesh, Morocco |
| **Merignac** | Bordeaux, France |
| **Miami** | Florida, USA |
| **Midway** | Chicago, Illinois, USA |
| **Ministro Pistarini** | Buenos Aires, Argentina |
| **Minneapolis/St Paul** | Minneapolis, USA |
| **Mirabel** | Montreal, Canada |
| **Mogadishu** | Somalia |
| **Mohamed V** | Casablanca, Morocco |
| **Moi International** | Mombasa, Kenya |
| **Monroe County** | Rochester, New York State, USA |
| **Morelos** | Mexico City, Mexico |
| **Münster/Osnabrück** | Germany |
| **Murmansk** | Russia |
| **Murtala Muhammed** | Lagos, Nigeria |
| **Nadi International** | Fiji |
| **Nagasaki** | Japan |
| **Narita** | Tokyo, Japan |
| **Narssarsuaq** | Greenland |
| **Nashville** | Tennessee, USA |
| **Nassau International** | The Bahamas |
| **Nauru** | Nauru |
| **N'Djamena** | Chad |
| **N'Djili** | Kinshasa, Congo, Democratic Republic of |
| **Nejrab** | Aleppo, Syria |
| **Newcastle** | UK |
| **New Orleans** | Louisiana, USA |
| **Newark** | New York, USA |
| **Niamey** | Niger |
| **Ninoy Aquino International** | Manila, Philippines |
| **Niš** | Yugoslavia |
| **Norfolk International** | Virginia, USA |
| **Norman Manley International** | Kingston, Jamaica |
| **North Front** | Gibraltar |
| **Nouadhibou** | Mauritania |
| **Nouakchott** | Mauritania |
| **Novo-Alexeyevka** | Tblisi, Georgia |
| **Nuremberg** | Germany |
| **Oakland International** | California, USA |
| **Octeville** | Le Havre, France |
| **Odense** | Denmark |
| **O'Hare** | Chicago, Illinois, USA |
| **Okecie** | Warsaw, Poland |
| **Okinawa** | Naha, Japan |
| **Oran** | Algeria |
| **Orebro** | Sweden |
| **Orlando** | Florida, USA |
| **Orly** | Paris, France |
| **Osaka** | Japan |
| **Osvaldo Veira** | Bissau, Guinea-Bissau |
| **Otopeni** | Bucharest, Romania |
| **Ouagadougou** | Burkina Faso |

| | |
|---|---|
| **Owen Roberts** | Grand Cayman, West Indies |
| **Pago Pago** | Samoa |
| **Palese** | Bari, Italy |
| **Palma** | Majorca |
| **Pamplona** | Spain |
| **Panama City** | Panama |
| **Paphos** | Cyprus |
| **Papola Casale** | Brindisi, Italy |
| **Paradisi** | Rhodes, Greece |
| **Patenga** | Chittagong, Bangladesh |
| **Penang** | Malaysia |
| **Peninsula** | Monterey, California, USA |
| **Peretola** | Florence, Italy |
| **Perth** | Australia |
| **Peshawar** | Pakistan |
| **Peterson Field** | Colorado Springs, Colorado, USA |
| **Philadelphia** | Pennsylvania, USA |
| **Piarco** | Port of Spain, Trinidad |
| **Pleso** | Zagreb, Croatia |
| **Pochentong** | Phnom Penh, Cambodia |
| **Point Salines** | Grenada |
| **Pointe Noire** | Congo |
| **Polonia** | Medan, Indonesia |
| **Ponta Delgado** | São Miguel, Azores |
| **Poprad Tatry** | Poprad, Slovakia |
| **Port Bouet** | Abidjan, Côte d'Ivoire |
| **Port Harcourt** | Nigeria |
| **Portland** | Maine, USA |
| **Portland** | Oregon, USA |
| **Port Sudan** | The Sudan |
| **Porto Pedra Rubras** | Oporto, Portugal |
| **Praia** | Cape Verde |
| **Prestwick** | UK |
| **Provence** | Marseille, France |
| **Pula** | Croatia |
| **Pulkovo** | St Petersburg, Russia |
| **Punta Arenas International** | Chile |
| **Punta Raisi** | Palermo, Sicily |
| **Queen Alia** | Amman, Jordan |
| **Queen Beatrix** | Aruba, Netherlands Antilles |
| **Raleigh/Durham** | North Carolina, USA |
| **Ras al Khaimah** | United Arab Emirates |
| **Rabiechowo** | Gdańsk, Poland |
| **Regina** | Canada |
| **Reina Sofia** | Tenerife, Canary Is |
| **Rejon** | Merida, Mexico |
| **Richmond** | Virginia, USA |
| **Riem** | Munich, Germany |
| **Rio de Janeiro International** | Brazil |
| **Riyadh International** | Saudi Arabia |
| **Roberts International** | Monrovia, Liberia |
| **Rochambeau** | Cayenne, French Guiana |
| **Robert Mueller Municipal Airport** | Austin, Texas, USA |
| **Ronchi dei Legionari** | Trieste, Italy |
| **Rotterdam** | Netherlands |
| **Ruzyne** | Prague, Czech Republic |
| **Saab** | Linköping, Sweden |
| **Saint Eufemia** | Lamezia Terma, Italy |
| **Saint Louis** | Missouri, USA |
| **Saint Thomas** | Virgin Is |
| **Sainte Foy** | Quebec, Canada |
| **Sale** | Rabat, Morocco |
| **Salgado Filho International** | Pôrto Alegre, Brazil |
| **Salt Lake City** | Utah, USA |
| **San Antonio** | Texas, USA |
| **San Diego** | California, USA |
| **San Francisco** | California, USA |
| **San Giusto** | Pisa, Italy |
| **San Javier** | Murcia, Spain |
| **San José** | California, USA |
| **San Pablo** | Seville, Spain |
| **San Salvador** | El Salvador |
| **Sanaa International** | Yemen |
| **Sangster International** | Montego Bay, Jamaica |
| **Santa Caterina** | Funchal, Madeira |
| **Santa Cruz** | La Palma, Canary Is |
| **Santa Isabel** | Malabo, Guinea |
| **Santander** | Spain |
| **Santiago** | Spain |
| **Santos Dumont** | Rio de Janeiro, Brazil |
| **São Tomé** | São Tomé |
| **Satolas** | Lyon, France |
| **Schipol** | Amsterdam, Netherlands |
| **Schwechat** | Vienna, Austria |
| **Seeb** | Muscat, Oman |
| **Senou** | Bamako, Mali |
| **Seychelles International** | Mahe, Seychelles |
| **Sfax** | Tunisia |
| **Shannon** | Ireland |
| **Sharjah** | United Arab Emirates |
| **Sheremetyevo** | Moscow, Russia |
| **Silvio Pettirossi** | Asunción, Paraguay |
| **Simon Bolivar** | Caracas, Venezuela |
| **Simon Bolivar** | Guayaquil, Ecuador |
| **Sir Seewoosagur Ramgoolam** | Plaisance, Mauritius |
| **Sir Seretse Khama** | Gaborone, Botswana |
| **Skanes** | Monastir, Morocco |
| **Skopje** | Macedonia |
| **Sky Harbour** | Phoenix, Arizona, USA |
| **Sliac** | Slovakia |
| **Snilow** | Lwow, Ukraine |
| **Sofia International** | Bulgaria |
| **Sola** | Stavanger, Norway |
| **Sondica** | Bilbao, Spain |
| **Søndre Strømfjord** | Greenland |
| **Spilve** | Riga, Latvia |
| **Split** | Croatia |
| **Spokane** | Washington, USA |
| **Stansted** | UK |
| **Stapleton International** | Denver, Colorado, USA |
| **Sturup** | Malmö, Sweden |
| **Subang International** | Kuala Lumpur, Malaysia |

**Sunan** Pyongyang, Korea, Democratic People's Republic of (North Korea
**Tacoma** Seattle, USA
**Tallahassee** Florida, USA
**Tamatve** Madagascar
**Tampa** Florida, USA
**Tarbes-Ossun-Lourdes** Jullian, France
**Tegucigalpa** Toncontin, Honduras
**Thalerhof** Graz, Austria
**Theodore Francis** Providence, Rhode I, USA
**Thessalonika** Greece
**Timehri International** Georgetown, Guyana
**Timişoara** Romania
**Tirana** Albania
**Tito Menniti** Reggio Calabria, Italy
**Tontouta** Noumea, New Caledonia
**Townsville** Australia
**Tribhuyan** Kathmandu, Nepal
**Tripoli** Libya
**Trivandrum** India
**Truax Field** Madison, Wisconsin, USA
**Tucson** Arizona, USA
**Tullamarine** Melbourne, Australia
**Turin** Italy
**Turku** Finland
**Turnhouse** Edinburgh, UK
**Ulemiste** Tallinn, Estonia
**Unokovo** Moscow, Russia
**Uplands** Ottawa, Canada
**V C Bird International** Antigua
**Vaasa** Finland
**Vagar** Faroe Is
**Valencia** Spain
**Vancouver International** Canada
**Vantaa** Helsinki, Finland
**Varna International** Bulgaria
**Verona** Italy
**Victoria** British Columbia, Canada
**Vigie** St Lucia
**Vigo** Spain
**Vilnius** Lithuania
**Vilo de Porto** Santa Maria, Azores
**Viracopos** São Paulo, Brazil
**Vitoria** Spain
**Washington International** Baltimore, Maryland, USA
**Wattay** Vientiane, Laos
**Wellington** New Zealand
**Wichita** Kansas, USA
**Will Rogers** Oklahoma City, Oklahoma, USA
**Winnipeg International** Manitoba, Canada
**Yangon** Myanmar (Burma)
**Yoff** Dakar, Senegal
**Yundum** Banjul, The Gambia
**Zakynthos** Greece
**Zia International** Dhaka, Bangladesh
**Zürich** Switzerland

## Airline designators

| Code | Airline | Country |
|---|---|---|
| AA | American Airlines | USA |
| AC | Air Canada | Canada |
| AF | Air France | France |
| AH | Air Algerie | Algeria |
| AI | Air India | India |
| AJ | Air Belgium | Belgium |
| AM | Aeromexico | Mexico |
| AN | Ansett Australia | Australia |
| AQ | Aloha Airlines | Hawaii |
| AR | Aerolineas Argentinas | Argentina |
| AS | Alaska Airlines | USA |
| AT | Royal Air Maroc | Morocco |
| AV | Avianca | Colombia |
| AY | Finnair | Finland |
| AZ | Alitalia | Italy |
| BA | British Airways | UK |
| BD | British Midland | UK |
| BG | Biman Bangladesh Airlines | Bangladesh |
| BH | Transtate Airlines | Australia |
| BI | Royal Brunei Airlines | Brunei |
| BL | Pacific Airlines | Vietnam |
| BO | Bouraq Indonesia Airlines | Indonesia |
| BP | Air Botswana | Botswana |
| BT | Air Baltic | Latvia |
| BU | Braathens SAFE | Norway |
| BW | BWIA International Trinidad and Tobago Airways | Trinidad |
| BY | Britannia Airways | UK |
| CA | Air China | China |
| CB | Suckling Airways | UK |
| CI | China Airlines | Taiwan |
| CJ | China North Airlines | Taiwan |
| CK | China Airlines Cargo | China |
| CM | COPA (Compania Panamena de Aviación) | Panama |
| CO | Continental Airlines | USA |
| CP | Canadian Airlines International | Canada |
| CS | Micronesia Continental | Mariana Is |
| CT | Air Sofia | Bulgaria |
| CU | Cubana | Cuba |
| CW | Air Marshall Islands | Marshall Is |
| CX | Cathay Pacific Airways | Hong Kong |
| CY | Cyprus Airways | Cyprus |
| CZ | China Southern Airlines | China |
| DA | Air Georgia | Georgia |

| Code | Airline | Country |
|---|---|---|
| DI | Deutsche BA | Germany |
| DL | Delta Air Lines | USA |
| DT | TAAG-Angola Airlines | Angola |
| DX | Danish Air Transport | Denmark |
| EI | Aer Lingus | Ireland |
| EK | Emirates | United Arab Emirates |
| ET | Ethiopian Airlines | Ethiopia |
| EU | Ecuatoriana | Ecuador |
| EW | Eastwest Airlines | Australia |
| FE | Royal Khmer Airlines | Cambodia |
| FF | Tower Air | USA |
| FG | Ariana Afghan Airlines | Afghanistan |
| FI | Icelandair | Iceland |
| FJ | Air Pacific | Fiji |
| FM | Shanghai Airlines | China |
| FQ | Air Aruba | Netherlands Antilles |
| FR | Ryanair | Ireland |
| FU | Air Littoral | France |
| GA | Garuda Indonesia | Indonesia |
| GF | Gulf Air | Bahrain |
| GH | Ghana Airways | Ghana |
| GL | Gronlandsfly | Greenland |
| GM | Air Slovakia | Slovakia |
| GN | Air Gabon | Gabon |
| GR | Aurigny Air Services | Channel Is |
| GT | GB Airways | Gibraltar |
| GV | Riga Airlines | Latvia |
| GY | Guyana Airways | Guyana |
| HA | Hawaiian Airlines | USA |
| HM | Air Seychelles | Seychelles |
| HP | America West Airlines | USA |
| HV | Transavia Airlines | Netherlands |
| HY | Uzbekistan Airlines | Uzbekistan |
| IB | Iberia | Spain |
| IC | Indian Airlines | India |
| IE | Solomon Airlines | Solomon Is |
| IF | Great China Airlines | China |
| IL | Istanbul Airways | Turkey |
| IN | Macedonian Airlines | Macedonia |
| IP | Airlines of Tasmania | Australia |
| IR | Iran Air | Iran |
| IV | Fujian Airlines | China |
| IY | Yemenia Airways | Yemen |
| JA | Air Bosnia | Bosnia-Herzegovina |
| JE | Manx Airlines | Isle of Man |
| JG | Air Greece | Greece |
| JL | Japan Airlines | Japan |
| JM | Air Jamaica | Jamaica |
| JP | Adria Airways | Macedonia |
| JQ | Air Jamaica Express | Jamaica |
| JS | Air Koryo | Korea, Democratic People's Republic of (North Korea) |
| JU | JAT (Jugoslovenski Aerotransport) | Yugoslavia |
| JY | Jersey European Airways | Channel Is |
| KA | Dragonair | Hong Kong |
| KE | Korean Air Lines | Korea, Republic of (South Korea) |
| KL | KLM | Netherlands |
| KM | Air Malta | Malta |
| KP | Kiwi International Airlines | USA |
| KQ | Kenya Airways | Kenya |
| KT | Kampuchea Airlines | Cambodia |
| KU | Kuwait Airways | Kuwait |
| KV | Kavminvodyaria | Russia |
| KX | Cayman Airways | Cayman Is |
| KZ | Nippon Cargo Airlines | Japan |
| LA | LAN-Chile | Chile |
| LG | Luxair | Luxembourg |
| LH | Lufthansa | Germany |
| LJ | Sierra National Airlines | Sierra Leone |
| LM | ALM (Antillean Airlines) | Netherlands Antilles |
| LN | Jamahiriya Libyan Arab Airlines | Libya |
| LO | LOT-Polish Airlines | Poland |
| LR | LACSA | Costa Rica |
| LT | LTU International Airways | Germany |
| LU | Theron Airways | South Africa |
| LV | Albanian Airlines | Albania |
| LX | Crossair | Switzerland |
| LY | El Al Israel Airlines | Israel |
| LZ | Balkan-Bulgarian Airlines | Bulgaria |
| MA | Malev | Hungary |
| MD | Air Madagascar | Madagascar |
| MH | Malaysian Airlines | Malaysia |
| MK | Air Mauritius | Mauritius |
| MN | Commercial Airways | South Africa |
| MR | Air Mauritanie | Mauritania |
| MS | Egyptair | Egypt |
| MX | Mexicana | Mexico |
| NF | Air Vanuatu | Vanuatu |
| NG | Lauda Air | Austria |
| NH | All Nippon Airways | Japan |
| NM | Mount Cook Airlines | New Zealand |
| NU | Japan Transocean Air | Japan |
| NV | Northwest Territorial Airways | Canada |
| NW | Northwest Airlines | USA |
| NY | Air Iceland | Iceland |
| NZ | Air New Zealand | New Zealand |
| OA | Olympic Airways | Greece |
| OG | Go | UK |
| OK | Czech Airlines | Czech Republic |
| OM | MAIT-Mongolian Airlines | Mongolia |
| ON | Air Nauru | Australia |
| OO | Skywest Airlines | Australia |
| OS | Austrian Airlines | Austria |
| OU | Croatia Airlines | Croatia |
| OV | Estonian Air | Estonia |
| PC | Fiji Air | Fiji |
| PE | Air Europe | Italy |
| PG | Bangkok Airways | Thailand |
| PH | Polynesian Airlines | Samoa |

| Code | Airline | Country |
|---|---|---|
| PK | Pakistan International Airlines | Pakistan |
| PL | Aeroperu | Peru |
| PR | Philippine Airlines | Philippines |
| PS | Ukraine International Airlines | Ukraine |
| PU | Pluna (Primerias Lineas Uruguayas de Navegación Aerea) | Uruguay |
| PX | Air Niugini | Papua New Guinea |
| PY | Surinam Airways | Suriname |
| PZ | TAM (Transportes Aereos del Mercosur) | Paraguay |
| QF | Qantas Airways | Australia |
| QL | Air Lesotho | Lesotho |
| QM | Air Malawi | Malawi |
| QR | Qatar Airways | Qatar |
| QS | Tatra Air | Slovakia |
| QU | Uganda Airlines | Uganda |
| QV | Lao Aviation | Laos |
| QW | Turks and Caicos Airways | Turks and Caicos |
| QX | Horizon Air | USA |
| QZ | Zambia Airways | Zambia |
| RA | Royal Nepal Airlines | Nepal |
| RB | Syrian Arab Airlines | Syria |
| RG | Varig | Brazil |
| RJ | Royal Jordanian | Jordan |
| RK | Air Afrique | Côte d'Ivoire |
| RM | Air Moldova | Moldova |
| RO | Tarom | Romania |
| RR | Royal Air Force | UK |
| SA | South African Airways | South Africa |
| SB | Air Caledonie International | New Caledonia |
| SD | Sudan Airways | The Sudan |
| SK | SAS (Scandinavian Airlines) | Sweden |
| SN | Sabena Belgian World Airlines | Belgium |
| SQ | Singapore Airlines | Singapore |
| SR | Swissair | Switzerland |
| SU | Aeroflot | Russia |
| SV | Saudia | Saudi Arabia |
| SW | Air Namibia | Namibia |
| TC | Air Tanzania | Tanzania |
| TE | Lithuanian Airlines | Lithuania |
| TG | Thai Airways International | Thailand |
| TI | Angkor Airlines | Cambodia |
| TK | Turkish Airlines | Turkey |
| TM | LAM (Linhas Aereas de Moçambique) | Mozambique |
| TN | Air Tahiti Nui | Tahiti |
| TP | TAP Air Portugal | Portugal |
| TR | Transbrasil SA Linhas Aereas | Brazil |
| TU | Tunis Air | Tunisia |

| Code | Airline | Country |
|---|---|---|
| TT | Air Lithuania | Lithuania |
| TV | Virgin Express | Belgium |
| TW | TWA (Trans World Airlines) | USA |
| UA | United Airlines | USA |
| UB | Myanmar Airlines | Myanmar (Burma) |
| UC | Ladeco | Chile |
| UF | Turkestan Airlines | Kazakhstan |
| UK | KLM UK | UK |
| UL | Sri Lanka Airlines | Sri Lanka |
| UM | Air Zimbabwe | Zimbabwe |
| UN | Transaero Airlines | Russia |
| UP | Bahamasair | The Bahamas |
| US | USAir | USA |
| UY | Cameroon Airlines | Cameroon |
| VE | Avensa | Venezuela |
| VN | Vietnam Airlines | Vietnam |
| VO | Tyrolean Airways | Austria |
| VP | VASP (Viacäo Aèrea São Paulo) | Brazil |
| VR | Transportes Aereos de Cabo Verde | Cape Verde |
| VS | Virgin Atlantic Airways | UK |
| VT | Air Tahiti | Tahiti |
| VV | Aerorosvit Airlines | Ukraine |
| VX | Aces (Aerolineas Centrales de Colombia) | Colombia |
| WH | China Northwest Airlines | China |
| WJ | Labrador Airways | Canada |
| WM | Windward Islands Airways | Canada |
| WN | Southwest Airlines | USA |
| WR | Royal Tongan Airlines | Tonga |
| WT | Nigeria Airways | Nigeria |
| WX | Cityjet | Ireland |
| WY | Oman Aviation Services | Oman |
| YJ | National Airlines | South Africa |
| YK | Cyprus Turkish Airlines | Cyprus |
| YN | Air Creebec | Canada |
| YP | Aero Lloyd | Germany |
| YU | Dominair | Dominican Republic |
| YZ | Transportes Aereos Da Guiné-Bissau | Guinea-Bissau |
| ZB | Monarch Airlines | UK |
| ZC | Royal Swazi National Airways | Swaziland |
| ZP | Air St Thomas | Virgin Is |
| ZQ | Ansett New Zealand | New Zealand |
| ZX | Air BC | Canada |
| 2J | Air Burkino | Burkino Faso |
| 3D | Denim Air | Netherlands |

## Air distances

Air distances between some major cities, given in statute miles. To convert to kilometres, multiply number given by 1.6093.

* Shortest route.

| | Amsterdam | Anchorage | Beijing | Buenos Aires | Cairo | Chicago | Delhi | Hong Kong | Honolulu | Istanbul | Johannesburg | Lagos | London | Los Angeles | Mexico City | Montreal | Moscow | Nairobi | Paris | Perth | Rome | Santiago | Sydney | Tokyo |
|---|---|---|---|---|---|---|---|---|---|---|---|---|---|---|---|---|---|---|---|---|---|---|---|---|
| Anchorage | 4475 | | | | | | | | | | | | | | | | | | | | | | | |
| Beijing | 6566 | 4756 | | | | | | | | | | | | | | | | | | | | | | |
| Buenos Aires | 7153 | 8329 | 12000 | | | | | | | | | | | | | | | | | | | | | |
| Cairo | 2042 | 6059 | 6685 | 7468 | | | | | | | | | | | | | | | | | | | | |
| Chicago | 4109 | 28 | 7599 | 5587 | 6135 | | | | | | | | | | | | | | | | | | | |
| Delhi | 3985 | 8925 | 2368 | 8340 | 2753 | 8119 | | | | | | | | | | | | | | | | | | |
| Hong Kong | 5926 | 5063 | 1235 | 3124 | 5098 | 7827 | 2345 | | | | | | | | | | | | | | | | | |
| Honolulu | 8368 | 2780 | 6778 | 8693 | 9439 | 4246 | 7888 | 5543 | | | | | | | | | | | | | | | | |
| Istanbul | 1373 | 6024 | 4763 | 7783 | 764 | 5502 | 2833 | 5998 | 9547 | | | | | | | | | | | | | | | |
| Johannesburg | 5606 | 1042 | 10108 | 5725 | 4012 | 8705 | 6765 | 6728 | 12892 | 4776 | | | | | | | | | | | | | | |
| Lagos | 3161 | 7587 | 8030 | 4832 | 2443 | 7065 | 5196 | 7541 | 10367 | 3207 | 2854 | | | | | | | | | | | | | |
| London | 217 | 4472 | 5054 | 6985 | 2187 | 3956 | 4169 | 5979 | 7252 | 1552 | 5640 | 3115 | | | | | | | | | | | | |
| Los Angeles | 5559 | 2333 | 6349 | 6140 | 7589 | 1746 | 8717 | 7231 | 2553 | 6994 | 10443 | 7716 | 5442 | | | | | | | | | | | |
| Mexico City | 5724 | 3751 | 7912 | 4592 | 7730 | 1687 | 9806 | 8794 | 4116 | 7255 | 10070 | 7343 | 5703 | 1563 | | | | | | | | | | |
| Montreal | 3422 | 3100 | 7557 | 5640 | 5431 | 737 | 7421 | 8564 | 4923 | 4795 | 8322 | 5595 | 3252 | 2482 | 2307 | | | | | | | | | |
| Moscow | 1338 | 4291 | 3604 | 8382 | 1790 | 5500 | 2698 | 4839 | 8802 | 1089 | 6280 | 4462 | 1550 | 6992 | 6700 | 4393 | | | | | | | | |
| Nairobi | 4148 | 8714 | 8888 | 7427 | 2203 | 8177 | 4956 | 7301 | 11498 | 2967 | 1809 | 2377 | 4246 | 9688 | 9949 | 7498 | 3951 | | | | | | | |
| Paris | 261 | 4683 | 5108 | 6892 | 1995 | 4140 | 4089 | 5987 | 7463 | 1394 | 5422 | 2922 | 220 | 5633 | 5714 | 3434 | 1540 | 4031 | | | | | | |
| Perth | 9118 | 8368 | 4987 | 9734 | 7766 | 11281 | 5013 | 3752 | 7115 | 7846 | 5564 | 10209 | 9246 | 9535 | 11098 | 12402 | 8355 | 7373 | 12587 | | | | | |
| Rome | 809 | 5258 | 5306 | 6931 | 1329 | 4828 | 3679 | 5773 | 8150 | 852 | 4802 | 2497 | 898 | 6340 | 6601 | 5431 | 1478 | 3349 | 688 | 8309 | | | | |
| Santiago | 7714 | 7919 | 13622 | 710 | 8029 | 5328 | 12715 | 3733 | 8147 | 10109 | 5738 | 6042 | 8568 | 5594 | 4168 | 5551 | 10118 | 7547 | 461 | 15129 | 7548 | | | |
| Sydney | 1039 | 8522 | 5689 | 7760 | 9196 | 9324 | 6495 | 4586 | 5078 | 9883 | 7601 | 11700 | 10565 | 7498 | 9061 | 9980 | 9425 | 9410 | 10150 | 2037 | 10149 | 13092 | | |
| Tokyo | 6006* | 3443 | 1313 | 13100 | 6362 | 6286 | 3656 | 1807 | 3831 | 5757 | 8535 | 9130* | 6218 | 5451 | 7014 | 6913 | 4668 | 8565 | 6208* | 4925 | 6146 | 11049 | 4640 | |
| Washington | 3854 | 3430 | 7930 | 6097 | 5859 | 590 | 7841 | 8385 | 4822 | 5347 | 8199 | 5472 | 3672 | 2294 | 1871 | 493 | 4884 | 7918 | 3843 | 11829 | 4495 | 5061 | 9792 | 6763 |

## Flying times

Approximate flying times between some major cities. Timings quoted (in hours and minutes) are for 'flying time' only. In many cases in order to travel between two points chosen, it is necessary to change aircraft one or more times. Time between flights has not been included.

| | Amsterdam | Anchorage | Beijing | Buenos Aires | Cairo | Chicago | Delhi | Hong Kong | Honolulu | Istanbul | Johannesburg | Lagos | London | Los Angeles | Mexico City | Montreal | Moscow | Nairobi | Paris | Perth | Rome | Santiago | Sydney | Tokyo |
|---|---|---|---|---|---|---|---|---|---|---|---|---|---|---|---|---|---|---|---|---|---|---|---|---|
| Anchorage | 9.00 | | | | | | | | | | | | | | | | | | | | | | | |
| Beijing | 16.50 | 11.45 | | | | | | | | | | | | | | | | | | | | | | |
| Buenos Aires | 17.45 | 10.48 | 28.31 | | | | | | | | | | | | | | | | | | | | | |
| Cairo | 4.20 | 13.20 | 13.15 | 20.40 | | | | | | | | | | | | | | | | | | | | |
| Chicago | 8.35 | 5.44 | 15.15 | 15.40 | 18.40 | | | | | | | | | | | | | | | | | | | |
| Delhi | 8.15 | 16.50 | 6 40 | 26.20 | 7.00 | 20.05 | | | | | | | | | | | | | | | | | | |
| Hong Kong | 15.15 | 11.40 | 3.00 | 29.35 | 10.55 | 17.05 | 6.05 | | | | | | | | | | | | | | | | | |
| Honolulu | 16.42 | 5.45 | 10.55 | 19.00 | 22.50 | 9.25 | 16.50 | 13.05 | | | | | | | | | | | | | | | | |
| Istanbul | 3.15 | 12.15 | 15.40 | 18.45 | 2.00 | 12.20 | 7.35 | 17.35 | 21.05 | | | | | | | | | | | | | | | |
| Johannesburg | 13.15 | 19.50 | 20.10 | 12.30 | 8.55 | 21.40 | 23.45 | 14.55 | 30.25 | 16.30 | | | | | | | | | | | | | | |
| Lagos | 6.40 | 14.55 | 22.35 | 9.55 | 8.20 | 14.55 | 14.55 | 22.30 | 23.40 | 8.05 | 6.55 | | | | | | | | | | | | | |
| London | 1.05 | 8.30 | 18.05 | 16.35 | 5.35 | 8.30 | 10.35 | 16.05 | 17.15 | 3.50 | 13.10 | 6.25 | | | | | | | | | | | | |
| Los Angeles | 11.15 | 6.13 | 15.25 | 13.45 | 21.00 | 5.00 | 19.30 | 15.50 | 5.15 | 14.50 | 24.10 | 17.25 | 11.00 | | | | | | | | | | | |
| Mexico City | 12.27 | 10.49 | 18.45 | 10.25 | 16.47 | 5.15 | 20.42 | 19.10 | 8.35 | 15.42 | 25.42 | 19.07 | 14.35 | 3.20 | | | | | | | | | | |
| Montreal | 7.40 | 7.91 | 27.30 | 16.00 | 12.35 | 2.20 | 17.35 | 23.05 | 12.50 | 10.15 | 20.10 | 13.25 | 7.00 | 6.40 | 4.45 | | | | | | | | | |
| Moscow | 3.15 | 12.15 | 8.40 | 22.05 | 5.25 | 12.15 | 7.35 | 18.00 | 21.00 | 4.40 | 13.30 | 10.10 | 3.45 | 14.45 | 18.10 | 10.45 | | | | | | | | |
| Nairobi | 8.15 | 17.00 | 16.00 | 24.55 | 4.55 | 17.00 | 10.45 | 12.45 | 25.45 | 7.15 | 3.45 | 6.20 | 8.30 | 19.30 | 20.42 | 15.30 | 12.50 | | | | | | | |
| Paris | 1.10 | 9.00 | 16.35 | 15.35 | 5.05 | 9.00 | 10.45 | 16.40 | 18.05 | 3.10 | 15.50 | 7.45 | 1.05 | 12.50 | 13.25 | 6.25 | 4.00 | 9.20 | | | | | | |
| Perth | 20.35 | 17.25 | 11.15 | 25.20 | 17.10 | 23.00 | 9.30 | 8.15 | 17.25 | 15.25 | 14.20 | 25.55 | 19.30 | 19.30 | 22.50 | 26.30 | 19.40 | 23.00 | 21.40 | | | | | |
| Rome | 2.20 | 12.00 | 16.10 | 14.40 | 3.25 | 11.35 | 8.50 | 15.10 | 19.13 | 2.35 | 12.25 | 6.55 | 2.25 | 14.35 | 5.35 | 8.10 | 4.10 | 7.20 | 1.55 | 20.00 | | | | |
| Santiago | 20.50 | 19.13 | 22.34 | 2.10 | 25.10 | 17.15 | 29.05 | 19.15 | 8.35 | 21.00 | 19.55 | 24.25 | 21.55 | 16.00 | 12.00 | 14.50 | 24.05 | 29.05 | 19.45 | 26.00 | 18.50 | | | |
| Sydney | 23.05 | 16.35 | 16.15 | 20.45 | 17.20 | 21 10 | 13.50 | 10.35 | 11.50 | 18.40 | 31.50 | 28.35 | 21.55 | 18.10 | 18.05 | 24.50 | 19.40 | 31.35 | 25.05 | 4.35 | 23.50 | 24.30 | | |
| Tokyo | 11.40 | 7.20 | 3.50 | 28.30 | 19.40 | 12.55 | 9.45 | 4.20 | 7.05 | 14.05 | 25.00 | 18.40 | 11.50 | 11.55 | 16.25 | 18.55 | 9.25 | 19.55 | 16.45 | 10.05 | 17.40 | 27.55 | 9.15 | |
| Washington | 8.55 | 7.25 | 25.50 | 11.00 | 14.20 | 1.45 | 20.10 | 24.15 | 10.55 | 11.25 | 21.20 | 14.45 | 8.10 | 5.25 | 7.50 | 2.50 | 12.30 | 17.10 | 9.25 | 22.45 | 12.40 | 17.40 | 23.35 | 12.40 |

## European road distances

Road distances between some cities, given in kilometres.
To convert to statute miles, multiply number given by 0.6214.

| | Athens | Barcelona | Brussels | Calais | Cherbourg | Cologne | Copenhagen | Geneva | Gibraltar | Hamburg | Hook of Holland | Lisbon | Lyons | Madrid | Marseilles | Milan | Munich | Paris | Rome | Stockholm |
|---|---|---|---|---|---|---|---|---|---|---|---|---|---|---|---|---|---|---|---|---|
| Barcelona | 3313 | | | | | | | | | | | | | | | | | | | |
| Brussels | 2963 | 1318 | | | | | | | | | | | | | | | | | | |
| Calais | 3175 | 1326 | 204 | | | | | | | | | | | | | | | | | |
| Cherbourg | 3339 | 1294 | 583 | 460 | | | | | | | | | | | | | | | | |
| Cologne | 2762 | 1498 | 206 | 409 | 785 | | | | | | | | | | | | | | | |
| Copenhagen | 3276 | 2218 | 966 | 1136 | 1545 | 760 | | | | | | | | | | | | | | |
| Geneva | 2610 | 803 | 677 | 747 | 853 | 1662 | 1418 | | | | | | | | | | | | | |
| Gibraltar | 4485 | 1172 | 2256 | 2224 | 2047 | 2436 | 3196 | 1975 | | | | | | | | | | | | |
| Hamburg | 2977 | 2018 | 597 | 714 | 1115 | 460 | 460 | 1118 | 2897 | | | | | | | | | | | |
| Hook of Holland | 3030 | 1490 | 172 | 330 | 731 | 269 | 269 | 895 | 2428 | 550 | | | | | | | | | | |
| Lisbon | 4532 | 1304 | 2084 | 2052 | 1827 | 2290 | 2971 | 1936 | 676 | 2671 | 2280 | | | | | | | | | |
| Lyons | 2753 | 645 | 690 | 739 | 789 | 714 | 1458 | 158 | 1817 | 1159 | 863 | 1778 | | | | | | | | |
| Madrid | 3949 | 636 | 1558 | 1550 | 1347 | 1764 | 2498 | 1439 | 698 | 2198 | 1730 | 668 | 1281 | | | | | | | |
| Marseilles | 2865 | 521 | 1011 | 1059 | 1101 | 1035 | 1778 | 425 | 1693 | 1479 | 1183 | 1762 | 320 | 1157 | | | | | | |
| Milan | 2282 | 1014 | 925 | 1077 | 1209 | 911 | 1537 | 328 | 2185 | 1238 | 1098 | 2250 | 328 | 1724 | 618 | | | | | |
| Munich | 2179 | 1365 | 747 | 977 | 1160 | 583 | 1104 | 591 | 2565 | 805 | 851 | 2507 | 724 | 2010 | 1109 | 331 | | | | |
| Paris | 3000 | 1033 | 285 | 280 | 340 | 465 | 1176 | 513 | 1971 | 877 | 457 | 1799 | 471 | 1273 | 792 | 856 | 821 | | | |
| Rome | 817 | 1460 | 1511 | 1662 | 1794 | 1497 | 2050 | 995 | 2631 | 1751 | 1683 | 2700 | 1048 | 2097 | 1011 | 586 | 946 | 1476 | | |
| Stockholm | 3927 | 2868 | 1616 | 1786 | 2196 | 1403 | 650 | 2068 | 3886 | 949 | 1500 | 3231 | 2108 | 3188 | 2428 | 2187 | 1754 | 1827 | 2707 | |
| Vienna | 1991 | 1802 | 1175 | 1381 | 1588 | 937 | 1455 | 1019 | 2974 | 1155 | 1205 | 2935 | 1157 | 2409 | 1363 | 898 | 428 | 1249 | 1209 | 2105 |

## UK road distances

Road distances between British centres are given in statute miles, using routes recommended by the Automobile Association based on the quickest travelling time. To convert to kilometres, multiply number given by 1.6093.

| | Aberdeen | Birmingham | Bristol | Cambridge | Cardiff | Dover | Edinburgh | Exeter | Glasgow | Holyhead | Hull | Leeds | Liverpool | Manchester | Newcastle | Norwich | Nottingham | Oxford | Penzance | Plymouth | Shrewsbury | Southampton | Stranraer | York |
|---|---|---|---|---|---|---|---|---|---|---|---|---|---|---|---|---|---|---|---|---|---|---|---|---|
| Birmingham | 430 | | | | | | | | | | | | | | | | | | | | | | | |
| Bristol | 511 | 85 | | | | | | | | | | | | | | | | | | | | | | |
| Cambridge | 468 | 101 | 156 | | | | | | | | | | | | | | | | | | | | | |
| Cardiff | 532 | 107 | 45 | 191 | | | | | | | | | | | | | | | | | | | | |
| Dover | 591 | 202 | 198 | 121 | 234 | | | | | | | | | | | | | | | | | | | |
| Edinburgh | 130 | 293 | 373 | 337 | 395 | 457 | | | | | | | | | | | | | | | | | | |
| Exeter | 584 | 157 | 81 | 233 | 119 | 248 | 446 | | | | | | | | | | | | | | | | | |
| Glasgow | 149 | 291 | 372 | 349 | 393 | 490 | 45 | 444 | | | | | | | | | | | | | | | | |
| Holyhead | 457 | 151 | 232 | 246 | 209 | 347 | 325 | 305 | 319 | | | | | | | | | | | | | | | |
| Hull | 361 | 136 | 227 | 157 | 246 | 278 | 229 | 297 | 245 | 215 | | | | | | | | | | | | | | |
| Leeds | 336 | 115 | 216 | 143 | 236 | 265 | 205 | 288 | 215 | 163 | 59 | | | | | | | | | | | | | |
| Liverpool | 361 | 98 | 178 | 195 | 200 | 295 | 222 | 250 | 220 | 104 | 126 | 72 | | | | | | | | | | | | |
| Manchester | 354 | 88 | 167 | 153 | 188 | 283 | 218 | 239 | 214 | 123 | 97 | 43 | 34 | | | | | | | | | | | |
| Newcastle | 239 | 198 | 291 | 224 | 311 | 348 | 107 | 361 | 150 | 260 | 121 | 91 | 170 | 141 | | | | | | | | | | |
| Norwich | 501 | 161 | 217 | 62 | 252 | 167 | 365 | 295 | 379 | 309 | 153 | 173 | 232 | 183 | 258 | | | | | | | | | |
| Nottingham | 402 | 59 | 151 | 82 | 170 | 202 | 268 | 222 | 281 | 174 | 92 | 73 | 107 | 71 | 156 | 123 | | | | | | | | |
| Oxford | 497 | 63 | 74 | 82 | 109 | 148 | 361 | 152 | 354 | 218 | 188 | 171 | 164 | 153 | 253 | 144 | 104 | | | | | | | |
| Penzance | 696 | 272 | 195 | 346 | 232 | 362 | 561 | 112 | 559 | 419 | 411 | 401 | 366 | 355 | 477 | 407 | 336 | 265 | | | | | | |
| Plymouth | 624 | 199 | 125 | 275 | 164 | 290 | 488 | 45 | 486 | 347 | 341 | 328 | 294 | 281 | 410 | 336 | 265 | 193 | 78 | | | | | |
| Shrewsbury | 412 | 48 | 128 | 142 | 110 | 243 | 276 | 201 | 272 | 104 | 164 | 116 | 64 | 69 | 216 | 205 | 85 | 113 | 315 | 242 | | | | |
| Southampton | 571 | 128 | 75 | 133 | 123 | 155 | 437 | 114 | 436 | 296 | 253 | 235 | 241 | 227 | 319 | 192 | 171 | 67 | 227 | 155 | 190 | | | |
| Stranraer | 241 | 307 | 386 | 361 | 406 | 503 | 130 | 457 | 88 | 332 | 259 | 232 | 234 | 226 | 164 | 393 | 295 | 371 | 572 | 502 | 287 | 447 | | |
| York | 325 | 128 | 221 | 153 | 241 | 274 | 191 | 291 | 208 | 190 | 38 | 24 | 100 | 71 | 83 | 185 | 86 | 185 | 406 | 340 | 144 | 252 | 228 | |
| London | 543 | 118 | 119 | 60 | 155 | 77 | 405 | 170 | 402 | 263 | 215 | 196 | 210 | 199 | 280 | 115 | 128 | 56 | 283 | 215 | 162 | 76 | 419 | 209 |

## International E-road network ('Euroroutes')

Reference and intermediate roads (class A roads) have two-digit numbers; branch, link, and connecting roads (class B roads, not listed here), have three-digit numbers.

North–South orientated reference roads have two-digit odd numbers ending in the figure 5, and increasing from west to east. East–West orientated roads have two-digit even numbers ending in the figure 0, and increasing from north to south.

Intermediate roads have two-digit odd numbers (for N–S roads) or two-digit even numbers (for E–W roads) falling within the numbers of the reference roads between which they are located.

Only a selection of the towns and cities linked by E-roads are given here.

[...] indicates a sea crossing.

### ❑ West–East orientation

#### Reference roads

E10 Narvik — Kiruna — Luleå
E20 Shannon — Dublin ... Liverpool — Hull ... Esbjerg — Nyborg ... Korsør-Køge — Copenhagen ... Malmö — Stockholm ... Tallinn — St Petersburg
E30 Cork — Rosslare ... Fishguard — London — Felixstowe ... Hook of Holland — Utrecht — Hannover — Berlin — Warsaw — Smolensk — Moscow
E40 Calais — Brussels — Aachen — Cologne — Dresden — Krakow — Kiev — Rostov na Donu
E50 Brest — Paris — Metz — Nuremberg — Prague — Mukačevo
E60 Brest — Tours — Besançon — Basle — Innsbruck — Vienna — Budapest — Bucharest — Constanța
E70 La Coruña — Bilbao — Bordeaux — Lyons — Torino — Verona — Trieste — Zagreb — Belgrade — Bucharest — Varna
E80 Lisbon — Coimbra — Salamanca — Pau — Toulouse — Nice — Genoa — Rome — Pescara ... Dubrovnik — Sofia — Istanbul — Erzincan — Iran
E90 Lisbon — Madrid — Barcelona ... Mazara del Vallo — Messina ... Reggio di Calabria — Brindisi ... Igoumenitsa — Thessaloniki — Gelibolu ... Lapseki — Ankara — Iraq

#### Intermediate roads

E06 Olderfjord — Kirkenes
E12 Mo i Rana — Umeå ... Vaasa — Helsinki
E14 Trondheim — Sundsvall
E16 Londonderry — Belfast ... Glasgow — Edinburgh
E18 Craigavon — Larne ... Stranraer — Newcastle ... Stavanger — Oslo — Stockholm — Kappelskär ... Mariehamn ... Turku — Helsinki — St Petersburg
E22 Holyhead — Manchester — Immingham ... Amsterdam — Hamburg — Sassnitz ... Trelleborg — Norrköping
E24 Birmingham — Ipswich
E26 Hamburg — Berlin
E28 Berlin — Gdańsk
E32 Colchester — Harwich
E34 Antwerp — Bad Oeynhausen
E36 Berlin — Legnica
E42 Dunkirk — Aschaffenburg
E44 Le Havre — Luxembourg — Giessen
E46 Cherbourg — Liège
E48 Schweinfurt — Prague
E52 Strasbourg — Salzburg
E54 Paris — Basle — Munich
E56 Nuremberg — Sattledt
E58 Vienna — Bratislava
E62 Nantes — Geneva — Tortona
E64 Turin — Brescia
E66 Fortezza — Székesfehérvár
E68 Szeged — Brașov
E72 Bordeaux — Toulouse
E74 Nice — Alessandria
E76 Migliarino — Florence
E78 Grosseto — Fano
E82 Porto — Tordesillas
E84 Keșan — Silivri
E86 Krystalopigi — Yefira
E88 Ankara — Refahiye
E92 Igoumenitsa — Volos
E94 Corinth — Athens
E96 Izmir — Sivrihisar
E98 Topbogazi — Syria

❑ **North–South orientation**

**Reference roads**

E05 Greenock — Birmingham — Southampton ... Le Havre — Paris — Bordeaux — Madrid — Algeciras
E15 Inverness — Edinburgh — London — Dover ... Calais — Paris — Lyons — Barcelona — Algeciras
E25 Hook of Holland — Luxembourg — Strasbourg — Basle — Geneva — Turin — Genoa
E35 Amsterdam — Cologne — Basle — Milan — Rome
E45 Gothenburg ... Frederikshavn — Hamburg — Munich — Innsbruck — Bologna — Rome — Naples — Villa S Giovanni ... Messina — Gela
E55 Kemi-Tornio — Stockholm — Helsingborg ... Heslingør — Copenhagen — Gedser ... Rostock — Berlin — Prague — Salzburg — Rimini — Brindisi ... Igoumenitsa — Kalamata
E65 Malmö — Ystad ... Świnoujście — Prague — Zagreb — Dubrovnik — Bitolj — Antirrion ... Rion — Kalamata ... Kissamos — Chania
E75 Karasjok — Helsinki ... Gdańsk — Budapest — Belgrade — Athens ... Chania — Sitia
E85 Černovcy — Bucharest — Alexandropouli
E95 St Petersburg — Moscow — Yalta

**Intermediate roads**

E01 Larne — Dublin — Rosslare ... La Coruña — Lisbon — Seville
E03 Cherbourg — La Rochelle
E07 Pau — Zaragoza
E09 Orléans — Barcelona
E11 Vierzon — Montpellier
E13 Doncaster — London
E17 Antwerp — Beaune
E19 Amsterdam — Brussels — Paris
E21 Metz — Geneva
E23 Metz — Lausanne
E27 Belfort — Aosta
E29 Cologne — Sarreguemines
E31 Rotterdam — Ludwigshafen
E33 Parma — La Spezie
E37 Bremen — Cologne
E39 Kristiansand — Aalborg
E41 Dortmund — Altdorf
E43 Würzburg — Bellinzona
E47 Nordkap — Oslo — Copenhagen — Rødby ... Puttgarden — Lübeck
E49 Magdeburg — Vienna
E51 Berlin — Nuremberg
E53 Plzeň — Munich
E57 Sattledt — Ljubljana
E59 Prague — Zagreb
E61 Klagenfurt — Rijeka
E63 Sodankylä — Naantali ... Stockholm — Gothenburg
E67 Warsaw — Prague
E69 Tromsø — Tornio
E71 Košice — Budapest — Split
E73 Budapest — Metković
E77 Gdańsk — Budapest
E79 Oradea — Calafat ... Vidín — Thessaloniki
E81 Halmeu — Piteśti
E83 Bjala — Sofia
E87 Tulcea — Eceabat ... Çanakkale — Antalya
E89 Gerede — Ankara
E91 Toprakkale — Syria
E93 Orel — Odessa
E97 Trabzon — Aşkale
E99 Doğubeyazit — Ş Urfa

## Deepwater ports of the world

**Aalborg** Denmark
**Aarhus** Denmark
**Abadan** Iran
**Aberdeen** UK
**Abidjan** Côte d'Ivoire
**Abu Dhabi** United Arab Emirates
**Acajutla** El Salvador
**Acapulco** Mexico
**Accra** Ghana
**Adelaide** Australia
**Aden** Yemen
**Agadir** Morocco
**Ajaccio** Corsica
**Alcudia** Majorca
**Alexandria** Egypt
**Algeciras** Spain
**Algiers** Algeria
**Alicante** Spain
**Almeria** Spain
**Amsterdam** Netherlands
**Anchorage** USA
**Ancona** Italy
**Annaba** Algeria
**Antofagasta** Chile
**Antwerp** Belgium
**Apia** Samoa
**Aqaba** Jordan
**Archangel** Russia
**Arica** Chile
**Ashdod** Israel
**Asunción** Paraguay
**Auckland** New Zealand
**Aveiro** Portugal
**Aviles** Spain
**Bahia Blanca** Argentina
**Baku** Azerbaijan
**Balboa** Panama
**Baltimore** USA
**Bandar Abbas** Iran
**Bangkok** Thailand
**Banjul** The Gambia
**Barcelona** Spain
**Bari** Italy
**Barranquilla** Colombia
**Basrah** Iraq
**Batumi** Georgia
**Beira** Mozambique
**Beirut** Lebanon
**Belem** Brazil
**Belfast** UK
**Belize City** Belize
**Benghazi** Libya
**Bergen** Norway
**Bilbao** Spain
**Bissau** Guinea-Bissau
**Bizerta** Tunisia
**Bombay** India
**Bordeaux** France
**Boston** USA
**Boulogne** France
**Bourgas** Bulgaria
**Brazzaville** Congo
**Bremen** Germany
**Brest** France
**Bridgetown** Barbados
**Brindisi** Italy
**Brisbane** Australia
**Bristol** UK
**Buena Ventura** Colombia
**Buenos Aires** Argentina
**Buffalo** USA
**Busan** Korea, Republic of (South Korea)
**Cabinda** Angola
**Cadiz** Spain
**Caen** France
**Cagliari** Sardinia
**Calabar** Nigeria
**Calais** France
**Calcutta** India
**Caldera** Costa Rica
**Calicut** India
**Callao** Peru
**Cannes** France
**Cape Town** South Africa
**Cap Haitian** Haiti
**Cardiff** UK
**Cartagena** Colombia
**Cartagena** Spain
**Casablanca** Morocco
**Catania** Sicily
**Cayenne** French Guiana
**Cebu** Philippines
**Charleston** USA
**Cherbourg** France
**Chiba** Japan
**Chicago** USA
**Chittagong** Bangladesh
**Cienfuegos** Cuba
**Cleveland** USA
**Coatzacoalcos** Mexico
**Cochin** India
**Cologne** Germany
**Colombo** Sri Lanka
**Conakry** Guinea
**Constanta** Romania
**Copenhagen** Denmark
**Corinth** Greece
**Corinto** Nicaragua
**Cork** Ireland
**Cotonou** Benin
**Dakar** Senegal
**Dalian** China
**Dammam** Saudi Arabia
**Dampier** Australia
**Dar es Salaam** Tanzania
**Darwin** Australia
**Davao** Philippines
**Detroit** USA
**Dieppe** France
**Djibouti** Djibouti
**Doha** Qatar
**Dordrecht** Netherlands
**Douala** Cameroon
**Douglas** Isle of Man
**Dover** UK
**Dubai** United Arab Emirates
**Dublin** Ireland
**Dubrovnik** Croatia
**Duisburg** Germany
**Duluth** USA
**Dundee** UK
**Dunedin** New Zealand
**Dunkirk** France
**Durban** South Africa
**Durres** Albania
**East London** South Africa
**Elat** Israel
**Emden** Germany
**Esbjerg** Denmark
**Europoort** Netherlands
**Famagusta** Cyprus
**Faro** Portugal
**Felixstowe** UK
**Flensburg** Germany
**Flushing** Netherlands
**Folkestone** UK
**Fortaleza** Brazil
**Fort de France** Martinique
**Frankfurt** Germany
**Fray Bentos** Uruguay
**Fredericia** Denmark
**Frederikshavn** Denmark
**Fredrikstad** Norway
**Freeport** The Bahamas
**Freeport** USA
**Freetown** Sierra Leone
**Fremantle** Australia
**Funchal** Madeira
**Galveston** USA
**Galway** Ireland
**Gateshead** UK
**Gavle** Sweden
**Gdańsk** Poland
**Gdynia** Poland
**Geelong** Australia
**Genoa** Italy
**Georgetown** Cayman Is
**Georgetown** Guyana
**Ghent** Belgium
**Gibraltar** Gibraltar
**Gijon** Spain

| Port | Country |
|---|---|
| **Glasgow** | UK |
| **Godthaab** | Greenland |
| **Goole** | UK |
| **Gothenburg** | Sweden |
| **Grangemouth** | UK |
| **Gravesend** | UK |
| **Great Yarmouth** | UK |
| **Greenock** | UK |
| **Grimsby** | UK |
| **Guayaquil** | Ecuador |
| **Haifa** | Israel |
| **Hakodate** | Japan |
| **Halifax** | Canada |
| **Halmstad** | Sweden |
| **Hamburg** | Germany |
| **Hamilton** | Bermuda |
| **Hamilton** | Canada |
| **Harstad** | Norway |
| **Hartlepool** | UK |
| **Harwich** | UK |
| **Havana** | Cuba |
| **Hay Point** | Australia |
| **Helsingborg** | Sweden |
| **Helsinki** | Finland |
| **Hiroshima** | Japan |
| **Hobart** | Australia |
| **Ho Chi Minh City** | Vietnam |
| **Hodeida** | Yemen |
| **Holyhead** | UK |
| **Hong Kong** | Hong Kong |
| **Honiari** | Solomon Is |
| **Honolulu** | Hawaii |
| **Houston** | USA |
| **Hull** | UK |
| **Ibiza** | Ibiza |
| **Inchon** | Korea, Republic of (South Korea) |
| **Iskenderun** | Turkey |
| **Istanbul** | Turkey |
| **Izmir** | Turkey |
| **Jacksonville** | USA |
| **Jakarta** | Indonesia |
| **Jarrow** | UK |
| **Jeddah** | Saudi Arabia |
| **Juneau** | USA |
| **Kagoshima** | Japan |
| **Kalmar** | Sweden |
| **Kandla** | India |
| **Kaohsiung** | Taiwan |
| **Karachi** | Pakistan |
| **Kawasaki** | Japan |
| **Khulna** | Bangladesh |
| **Kiel** | Germany |
| **Kingston** | Jamaica |
| **Kirkcaldy** | UK |
| **Kitakyushu** | Japan |
| **Klaipeda** | Lithuania |
| **Kobe** | Japan |
| **Kompong Som** | Cambodia |
| **Koper** | Slovenia |
| **Kota Kinabalu** | Malaysia |
| **Kowloon** | Hong Kong |
| **Kristiansand** | Norway |
| **Kuching** | Malaysia |
| **Kushiro** | Japan |
| **Kuwait** | Kuwait |
| **Lagos** | Nigeria |
| **La Guaira** | Venezuela |
| **Langesund** | Norway |
| **La Plata** | Argentina |
| **Larnaca** | Cyprus |
| **Larne** | UK |
| **Las Palmas** | Grand Canary |
| **La Spezia** | Italy |
| **Lattakia** | Syria |
| **La Coruña** | Spain |
| **Launceton** | Australia |
| **La Union** | El Salvador |
| **Le Havre** | France |
| **Leith** | UK |
| **Libreville** | Gabon |
| **Liège** | Belgium |
| **Limassol** | Cyprus |
| **Limerick** | Ireland |
| **Lisbon** | Portugal |
| **Liverpool** | UK |
| **Livingstone** | Guatemala |
| **Livorno** | Italy |
| **Lobito** | Angola |
| **Lomé** | Togo |
| **London** | UK |
| **Long Beach** | USA |
| **Los Angeles** | USA |
| **Lowestoft** | UK |
| **Luanda** | Angola |
| **Lübeck** | Germany |
| **Lüda** | China |
| **Macao** | China |
| **Madras** | India |
| **Malaga** | Spain |
| **Malmö** | Sweden |
| **Manama** | Bahrain |
| **Manaus** | Brazil |
| **Manchester** | UK |
| **Manila** | Philippines |
| **Mannheim** | Germany |
| **Manzanillo** | Mexico |
| **Maputo** | Mozambique |
| **Mar del Plata** | Argentina |
| **Maracaibo** | Venezuela |
| **Mariehamn** | Finland |
| **Marsala** | Sicily |
| **Marseilles** | France |
| **Masan** | Korea, Republic of (South Korea) |
| **Matanzas** | Cuba |
| **Melbourne** | Australia |
| **Mersin** | Turkey |
| **Messina** | Sicily |
| **Miami** | USA |
| **Middlesbrough** | UK |
| **Milwaukee** | USA |
| **Mina Qaboos** | Oman |
| **Mina Sulman** | Bahrain |
| **Mindelo** | Cape Verde |
| **Mizushima** | Japan |
| **Mobile** | USA |
| **Mogadishu** | Somalia |
| **Mombasa** | Kenya |
| **Monrovia** | Liberia |
| **Montego Bay** | Jamaica |
| **Montevideo** | Uruguay |
| **Montreal** | Canada |
| **Mormugao** | India |
| **Moulmein** | Myanmar (Burma) |
| **Murmansk** | Russia |
| **Muscat** | Oman |
| **Nacala** | Mozambique |
| **Nagasaki** | Japan |
| **Nagoya** | Japan |
| **Nampo** | Korea, Democratic People's Republic of (North Korea) |
| **Nantes** | France |
| **Napier** | New Zealand |
| **Naples** | Italy |
| **Narvik** | Norway |
| **Nassau** | The Bahamas |
| **Natal** | Brazil |
| **Nelson** | New Zealand |
| **New Amsterdam** | Guyana |
| **Newcastle** | Australia |
| **Newcastle** | UK |
| **New Haven** | USA |
| **New Mangalore** | India |
| **New Orleans** | USA |
| **New Plymouth** | New Zealand |
| **Newport** | UK |
| **New York** | USA |
| **Nice** | France |
| **Nouakchott** | Mauritania |
| **Noumea** | New Caledonia |
| **Novorossiysk** | Russia |
| **Nukualofa** | Tonga |
| **Nyborg** | Denmark |
| **Oakland** | USA |
| **Odense** | Denmark |
| **Odessa** | Ukraine |
| **Oporto** | Portugal |
| **Oran** | Algeria |
| **Osaka** | Japan |
| **Oslo** | Norway |
| **Ostend** | Belgium |
| **Oulu** | Finland |
| **Pago Pago** | Samoa |
| **Palermo** | Sicily |

| Port | Country |
|---|---|
| **Palma** | Majorca |
| **Palm Beach** | USA |
| **Panama Canal** | Panama |
| **Papeete** | Tahiti |
| **Paradip** | India |
| **Paramaribo** | Suriname |
| **Paranagua** | Brazil |
| **Paris** | France |
| **Pasajes** | Spain |
| **Pasir Gudang** | Malaysia |
| **Penang** | Malaysia |
| **Philadelphia** | USA |
| **Phnom Penh** | Cambodia |
| **Piraeus** | Greece |
| **Plymouth** | UK |
| **Point-a-Pitre** | Guadeloupe |
| **Pointe-Noire** | Congo |
| **Pondicherry** | India |
| **Ponta Delgada** | Azores |
| **Poole** | UK |
| **Port Adelaide** | Australia |
| **Port-au-Prince** | Haiti |
| **Port Cartier** | Canada |
| **Port Elizabeth** | South Africa |
| **Port Georgetown** | Guyana |
| **Port Gentil** | Gabon |
| **Port Harcourt** | Nigeria |
| **Port Hedland** | Australia |
| **Pork Kelang** | Malaysia |
| **Port Kembla** | Australia |
| **Portland** | USA |
| **Port Limon** | Costa Rica |
| **Port Louis** | Mauritius |
| **Port Moresby** | Papua New Guinea |
| **Port of Spain** | Trinidad |
| **Port Said** | Egypt |
| **Port Sudan** | The Sudan |
| **Port Talbot** | UK |
| **Port Victoria** | Seychelles |
| **Porto Alegre** | Brazil |
| **Portsmouth** | UK |
| **Prince Rupert** | Canada |
| **Providence** | USA |
| **Puerto Cortés** | Honduras |
| **Pula** | Croatia |
| **Punta Arenas** | Chile |
| **Pusan** | Korea, Republic of (South Korea) |
| **Quebec** | Canada |
| **Ramsgate** | UK |
| **Rangoon** | Myanmar (Burma) |
| **Ravenna** | Italy |
| **Recife** | Brazil |
| **Reykjavik** | Iceland |
| **Richards Bay** | South Africa |
| **Richmond** | USA |
| **Riga** | Latvia |
| **Rijeka** | Croatia |
| **Rimini** | Italy |
| **Rio de Janeiro** | Brazil |
| **Rio Grande** | Brazil |
| **Rosaria** | Argentina |
| **Rostock** | Germany |
| **Rotterdam** | Netherlands |
| **Rouen** | France |
| **Sacramento** | USA |
| **Safi** | Morocco |
| **St George's** | Grenada |
| **St Helier** | Jersey |
| **St John** | Canada |
| **St John's** | Antigua |
| **St John's** | Canada |
| **St Malo** | France |
| **St Nazaire** | France |
| **St Petersburg** | Russia |
| **Sakai** | Japan |
| **Salerno** | Italy |
| **Salina Cruz** | Mexico |
| **Salonica** | Greece |
| **Salvador** | Brazil |
| **Samsun** | Turkey |
| **San Diego** | USA |
| **San Francisco** | USA |
| **San José** | Guatemala |
| **San Juan** | Puerto Rico |
| **San Juan del Sur** | Nicaragua |
| **San Lorenzo** | Argentina |
| **San Pedro** | Côte d'Ivoire |
| **San Remo** | Italy |
| **San Sebastián** | Spain |
| **Santa Cruz de Tenerife** | Tenerife |
| **Santa Fé** | Argentina |
| **Santa Marta** | Colombia |
| **Santander** | Spain |
| **Santiago de Cuba** | Cuba |
| **Santo Domingo** | Dominican Republic |
| **Santos** | Brazil |
| **São Tomé** | São Tomé |
| **Sasebo** | Japan |
| **Sassandra** | Côte d'Ivoire |
| **Savannah** | USA |
| **Savona** | Italy |
| **Seattle** | USA |
| **Sevastopol** | Ukraine |
| **Seville** | Spain |
| **Sfax** | Tunisia |
| **Shanghai** | China |
| **Shimizu** | Japan |
| **Singapore** | Singapore |
| **Sitra** | Bahrain |
| **Sittwe** | Myanmar (Burma) |
| **Sousse** | Tunisia |
| **Southampton** | UK |
| **Split** | Croatia |
| **Stavanger** | Norway |
| **Stockholm** | Sweden |
| **Stockton** | USA |
| **Stralsund** | Germany |
| **Suez** | Egypt |
| **Sunderland** | UK |
| **Sundsvall** | Sweden |
| **Surabaya** | Indonesia |
| **Suva** | Fiji |
| **Swansea** | UK |
| **Sydney** | Australia |
| **Sydney** | Canada |
| **Syracuse** | Sicily |
| **Szczecin** | Poland |
| **Tacoma** | USA |
| **Takamatsu** | Japan |
| **Takoradi** | Ghana |
| **Tallinn** | Estonia |
| **Tampa** | USA |
| **Tampico** | Mexico |
| **Tanga** | Tanzania |
| **Tangier** | Morocco |
| **Taranto** | Italy |
| **Tarragona** | Spain |
| **Tauranga** | New Zealand |
| **Three Rivers (Trois Rivières)** | Canada |
| **Thunder Bay** | Canada |
| **Timaru** | New Zealand |
| **Tianjin** | China |
| **Toamasina** | Madagascar |
| **Tokyo** | Japan |
| **Toledo** | USA |
| **Toronto** | Canada |
| **Torshavn** | Faroes |
| **Toulon** | France |
| **Townsville** | Australia |
| **Toyama** | Japan |
| **Trebizond** | Turkey |
| **Trieste** | Italy |
| **Tripoli** | Lebanon |
| **Tripoli** | Libya |
| **Trondheim** | Norway |
| **Tunis** | Tunisia |
| **Turku** | Finland |
| **Tuticorin** | India |
| **Tyre** | Lebanon |
| **Ulsan** | Korea, Republic of (South Korea) |
| **Vaasa** | Finland |
| **Valencia** | Spain |
| **Valetta** | Malta |
| **Valparaíso** | Chile |
| **Vancouver** | Canada |
| **Varna** | Bulgaria |
| **Venice** | Italy |
| **Velsen** | Netherlands |
| **Veracruz** | Mexico |
| **Vigo** | Spain |
| **Visakhapatnam** | India |
| **Vitoria** | Brazil |

| | | | | | |
|---|---|---|---|---|---|
| **Vlaardingen** | Netherlands | **Willemstad** | Netherlands Antilles | **Yokohama** | Japan |
| **Vladivostok** | Russia | **Wilmington** | USA | **Zamboanga** | Philippines |
| **Volgograd** | Russia | **Xingang** | China | **Zanzibar** | Tanzania |
| **Walvis Bay** | Namibia | **Yangon** | Myanmar (Burma) | **Zeebrugge** | Belgium |
| **Wellington** | New Zealand | | | **Zhdanov** | Ukraine |

## Map of Europe

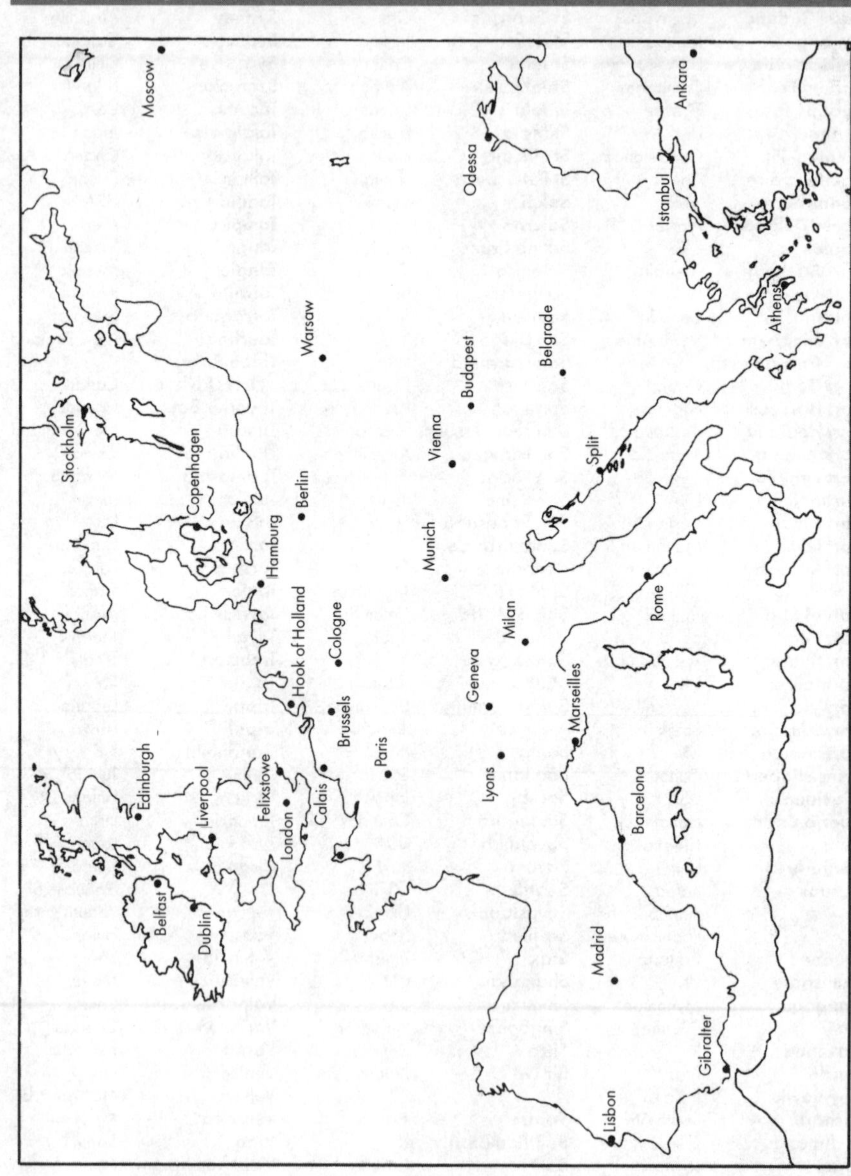

# SCIENCE, ENGINEERING AND MEASUREMENT

## Scientists

**Airy, Sir George Biddell** (1802–92) English astronomer and geophysicist, born Alnwick. Astronomer Royal (1835–81) who reorganized the Greenwich Observatory. Initiated measurement of Greenwich Mean Time, determined the mass of the Earth from gravity experiments in mines, and carried out extensive work in optics.

**Alzheimer, Alois** (1864–1915) German psychiatrist and neuropathologist, born Markbreit. Gave full clinical and pathological description of pre-senile dementia (Alzheimer's disease) (1907).

**Ampère, André Marie** (1775–1836) French mathematician and physicist, born Lyons. Laid the foundations of the science of electrodynamics. His name is given to the basic SI unit of electric current (ampere, amp).

**Appleton, Sir Edward Victor** (1892–1965) English physicist, born Bradford. Researched propagation of wireless waves, and discovered the existence of a layer of electrically charged particles in the upper atmosphere (the Appleton layer) which plays an essential role in radio communication. Received the Nobel prize for physics (1947) for studies of Earth's atmosphere.

**Archimedes** (c.287–212BC) Greek mathematician, born Syracuse. Discovered formulae for the areas and volumes of plane and solid geometrical figures using methods which anticipated theories of integration to be developed 1 800 years later. Also founded the science of hydrostatics; in popular tradition remembered for the cry of 'Eureka' when he discovered the principle of upthrust on a floating body.

**Aristotle** (384–322BC) Greek philosopher and scientist, born Stagira. One of the most influential figures in the history of Western thought and scientific tradition. Wrote enormous amounts on biology, zoology, physics and psychology.

**Avogadro, Amedeo** (1776–1856) Italian physicist, born Turin. Formulated the hypothesis (Avogadro's law) that equal volumes of gas contain equal numbers of molecules, when at the same temperature and pressure.

**Axelrod, Julius** (1912– ) American pharmacologist, born New York City. Discovered the substance which inhibits neural impulses, laying the basis for significant advances in the treatment of disorders such as schizophrenia. Joint winner of the 1970 Nobel prize for physiology or medicine.

**Babbage, Charles** (1791–1871) English mathematician, born Teignmouth. Attempted to build two calculating machines — the 'difference engine', to calculate logarithms and similar functions by repeated addition performed by trains of gear wheels, and the 'analytical engine', to perform much more varied calculations. Babbage is regarded as the pioneer of modern computers.

**Bacon, Francis, Baron Verulam of Verulam, Viscount St Albans** (1561–1626) English statesman and natural philosopher, born London. Creator of scientific induction; stressed the importance of experiment in interpreting nature, giving significant impetus to future scientific investigation.

**Baird, John Logie** (1888–1946) Scottish engineer, born Helensburgh. Gave first demonstration of a television image in 1926. Also researched radar and infrared television, and succeeded in producing 3-D and colour images (1944), as well as projection onto a screen and stereophonic sound.

**Barnard, Christiaan Neethling** (1922–2001) South African surgeon, born Beaufort West. Performed first successful heart transplant in December 1967 at Groote Schuur Hospital. Although the recipient died 18 days later from pneumonia, a second patient operated on in January 1968 survived for 594 days.

**Beaufort, Sir Francis** (1774–1857) Irish naval officer and hydrographer, born Navan, County Meath. Devised the Beaufort scale of wind force and a tabulated system of weather registration.

**Becquerel, Antoine Henri** (1852–1908) French physicist, born Paris. While researching fluorescence (the ability of substances to give off visible light), discovered radioactivity in the form of rays emitted by uranium salts, leading to the beginnings of modern nuclear physics. For this he shared the 1903 Nobel prize for physics with Marie and Pierre Curie.

**Bell, Alexander Graham** (1847–1922) Scottish–American inventor, born Edinburgh. After researching and teaching methods in speech therapy and experimenting with various acoustical devices, produced the first intelligible telephonic transmission on 5 June 1875, and patented the telephone in 1876. Founded the Bell Telephone Company in 1877.

**Bishop, (John) Michael** (1936– ) American molecular biologist and virologist, born York, Pennsylvania. Awarded 1989 Nobel prize for physiology or medicine (jointly with Harold Varmus 1939– ), for their discovery of oncogenes. This discovery is crucial to the understanding of cancer mechanisms.

**Bohr, Niels Henrik David** (1885–1962) Danish physicist, born Copenhagen. Greatly extended the theory of atomic structure by explaining the spectrum of hydrogen by means of an atomic model and quantum theory (1913). Awarded the Nobel prize for physics in 1922. Assisted in atom bomb research in America during World War II.

**Boltzmann, Ludwig Eduard** (1844–1906) Austrian physicist, born Vienna. Carried out important work on the kinetic theory of gases and established Boltzmann's law, or the principle of equipartition of energy.

**Boyle, The Hon Robert** (1627–91) Irish physicist and chemist, born Munster. One of the first members of the Royal Society. Carried out experiments on air, vacuum, combustion and respiration, and in 1662 arrived at Boyle's law, which states that the pressure and volume of a gas are inversely proportional at constant temperature.

**Brahe, Tycho** or **Tyge** (1546–1601) Danish astronomer, born Knudstrup, Sweden (then under Danish crown). After seeing the partial solar eclipse of 1569, became obsessed with astronomy. Accurately measured and compiled catalogues of the positions of stars, providing vital information for later astronomers and recorded unique observations of a new star in Cassiopeia in 1572 (a nova now known as Tycho's star).

**Brunel, Isambard Kingdom** (1806–59) English engineer and inventor, born Portsmouth. Helped to plan the Thames Tunnel and later planned the Clifton Suspension Bridge. Designed the first steamship to cross the Atlantic, the first ocean screw-steamer. In 1833 appointed engineer to the Great Western Railway and constructed all tunnels, bridges and viaducts on that line; also constructed and improved many docks.

**Celsius, Anders** (1701–44) Swedish astronomer, born Uppsala. Devised the centigrade, or 'Celsius', scale of temperature. Also advocated the introduction of the Gregorian calendar, and made observations of the aurora borealis, or northern lights.

**Chadwick, Sir James** (1891–1974) English physicist, born near Macclesfield. Studied radioactivity and as a result of the Curies' work, was able to confirm the existence of the neutron which Rutherford had postulated in 1920. Built Britain's first cyclotron in 1935 and assisted in atomic bomb research in America during World War II.

**Copernicus, Nicolaus** (1473–1543) Polish astronomer, born Torún. Studied mathematics, optics, perspective and canon law before a varied career involving law, medicine and astronomy. Published theory in 1543 that the Sun is at the centre of the Universe; this was not initially accepted due to opposition from the Church which held that the Universe was Earth-centred.

**Coulomb, Charles Augustin de** (1736–1806) French physicist, born Angoulême. Experimented on friction, and invented the torsion balance for measuring the force of magnetic and electrical attraction. The unit of electric charge (coulomb) is named after him.

**Crick, Francis Harry Compton** (1916– ) English biologist, born Northampton. Constructed a molecular model of the complex genetic material deoxyribonucleic acid (DNA). Later research on nucleic acids led to far-reaching discoveries concerning the genetic code. Joint winner of the Nobel prize for physiology or medicine in 1962 with James Watson (1928– ).

**Curie, Marie** (originally **Manya**) née **Sklodowska** (1867–1934) Polish–French physicist, born Warsaw. After graduating from the Sorbonne worked on magnetism and radioactivity, isolating radium and polonium. Shared the Nobel prize for physics in 1903 with her husband, Pierre Curie, and Antoine Henri Becquerel. Became professor of physics at the Sorbonne in 1906; awarded the Nobel prize for chemistry in 1911. Element 96 is named curium after the Curies.

**Curie, Pierre** (1859–1906) French chemist and physicist, born Paris. Carried out research on magnetism and radioactivity with his wife, Marie Curie, for which they were jointly awarded the Nobel prize for physics in 1903, with Antoine Henri Becquerel.

**Cuvier, Georges (Léopold Chrétien Frédéric Dagobert)** (1769–1832) French anatomist, born Montbéliard. Known as the father of comparative anatomy and palaeontology. Opponent of the Theory of Descent, and originated the natural system of animal classification. Linked comparative anatomy and palaeontology through studies of animal and fish fossils.

**Dalton, John** (1766–1844) English chemist, born Eaglesfield, near Cockermouth. Researched mixed gases, the force of steam, the elasticity of vapours and deduced the law of partial pressures, or Dalton's law. Also made important contributions in atomic theory.

**Darwin, Charles Robert** (1809–82) English naturalist, born Shrewsbury. Recommended as naturalist for a scientific survey of South American waters (1831–6) on HMS *Beagle*, during which he made many geological and zoological discoveries which led him to speculate on the origin of species. In 1859 published theory of evolution in *The Origin of Species by Means of Natural Selection*.

**Davy, Sir Humphry** (1778–1829) English chemist, born Penzance. Experimented with newly discovered gases, and discovered the anaesthetic effect of laughing gas. Discovered the new metals potassium, sodium, barium, strontium and magnesium and the metallic element calcium. Also investigated volcanic action, devised safety lamps for use in mining and was important in promoting science within industry.

**Delbrück, Max** (1906–81) German–American biophysicist, born Berlin. Made significant contributions in the creation of bacterial and bacteriophage genetics, and in 1946 showed that viruses can recombine genetic material. Joint winner of the 1969 Nobel prize for physiology or medicine for his work in viral genetics.

**Descartes, René** (1596–1650) French philosopher and mathematician, born near Tours. Creator of analytical or co-ordinate geometry, also named after him as Cartesian geometry. Also theorized extensively in physics and physiology, and is regarded as the father of modern philosophy.

**Dirac, Paul Adrien Maurice** (1902–84) English mathematical physicist, born Bristol. Published complete mathematical formulation of the relativity theory of Albert Einstein after work on quantum mechanics. Joint winner of the Nobel prize for physics in 1933.

**Doherty, Peter Charles** (1940– ) Australian immunologist, born Brisbane. Joint winner of 1996 Nobel prize for physiology or medicine (with Swiss immunologist Rolf M Zinkernagel, 1944– ), for his research into the human immune system. Also received the Paul Ehrlich prize in 1983 and became FRS in 1987.

**Doppler, Christian Johann** (1803–53) Austrian physicist, born Salzburg. The Doppler effect, described in a paper in 1842, explains the increase and decrease of wave frequency observed when a wave source and the observer respectively approach or recede from one another.

**Duchenne, Guillaume Benjamin Amand** (1806–75) French physician, born Boulogne. Pioneer in electrophysiology and founder of electrotherapeutics. First to describe locomotor ataxia, in 1858.

**Dulbecco, Renato** (1914– ) Italian–American biologist, born Catanzaro. Showed how certain viruses can transform some cells into a cancerous state, giving a valuable simple model system for which he shared the 1975 Nobel prize for physiology or medicine.

**Edison, Thomas Alva** (1847–1931) American inventor and physicist, born Milan, Ohio. Took out more than 1 000 patents, including the gramophone (1877), the incandescent light bulb (1879) and an improved microphone for Bell's telephone. Also discovered thermionic emission, formerly called the Edison effect.

**Ehrlich, Paul** (1854–1915) German bacteriologist, born Strehlen (now Strzelin), Silesia. Pioneer in haematology and chemotherapy, he synthesized salvarsan as a treatment for syphilis and propounded the side-chain theory in immunology. Joint winner of the 1908 Nobel prize for physiology or medicine.

**Einstein, Albert** (1879–1955) German–Swiss–American mathematical physicist, born Ulm, Bavaria. Achieved world fame through his special and general theories of relativity; also studied gases and discovered the photoelectric effect, for which he was awarded the Nobel prize for physics in 1921. Element 99 was named einsteinium after him.

**Ernst, Richard Robert** (1933– ) Swiss physical chemist, born Winterthur. Awarded 1991 Nobel prize for chemistry for innovations in nuclear magnetic resonance (NMR) spectroscopy. Also received the 1986 Benoist prize and the 1990 Ampère prize.

**Euler, Leonhard** (1707–83) Swiss mathematician, born Basel. Published over 800 different books and papers on mathematics, physics and astronomy, introducing many new functions and carrying out important work in calculus. Introduced the notations e and *gp*, still used today. Also studied motion and celestial mechanics.

**Eysenck, Hans Jurgen** (1916–97) German–British psychologist, born Berlin. Researched the variations in human personality and intelligence, and frequently championed the view that genetic factors are to a large extent responsible for psychological differences between people.

**Fahrenheit, Gabriel Daniel** (1686–1736) German physicist, born Danzig. Devised the alcohol thermometer (1709) and later invented the mercury thermometer (1714). Also devised the temperature scale named after him, and was the first to show that the boiling point of liquids varies at different atmospheric pressures.

**Faraday, Michael** (1791–1867) English chemist and physicist, born Grenoble. Discovered electro-magnetic induction (1831), the laws of electrolysis (1833) and the rotation of polarized light by magnetism (1845). First to isolate benzene and to synthesize chlorocarbons.

**Fermi, Enrico** (1901–54) Italian–American nuclear physicist, born Rome. Published method of calculating atomic particles, and in 1943 succeeded in splitting the nuclei of uranium atoms, producing artificial radioactive substances. Awarded the 1938 Nobel prize for physics, and constructed the first American nuclear reactor at Chicago (1942). Element 100 was named fermium after him.

**Feynman, Richard Phillips** (1918–88) American physicist, born New York City. Made considerable theoretical advances in quantum electrodynamics, for which he was joint winner of the Nobel prize for physics in 1965. Involved in building the first atomic bomb during World War II.

**Fleming, Sir Alexander** (1881–1955) Scottish bacteriologist, born Loudoun, Ayrshire. First to use anti-typhoid vaccines on humans and pioneered the use of salvarsan to treat syphilis. In 1928 discovered penicillin by chance, for which he was joint winner of the 1945 Nobel prize for physiology or medicine.

**Foucault, Jean Bernard Léon** (1819–68) French physicist, born Paris. Determined the velocity of light by the revolving mirror method and proved that light travels more slowly in water than in air (1850). In 1851 by means of a freely suspended pendulum, he proved that the Earth rotates. In 1852 constructed the gyroscope and in 1857 the Foucault prism.

**Frisch, Karl von** (1886–1982) Austrian ethologist and zoologist, born Vienna. Developed ethology using field observation of animals combined with ingenious experiments. Showed that forager bees communicate information (on the location of food sources) in part by use of coded dances. Joint winner of the Nobel prize for physiology or medicine in 1973.

**Gadolin, Johan** (1760–1852) Finnish chemist, born Turku. He is remembered for his investigations of the rare earth elements, analysing a new black mineral from Ytterby, Sweden, and isolating from it a rare earth mineral, yttria, in 1794. This was an important step towards identifying the remaining undiscovered elements. Element 64 was named gadolinium after him.

**Gajdusek, Daniel Carleton** (1923– ) American virologist, born Yonkers, New York. Studied the origin and dissemination of infectious diseases amongst the Fore people of Papua New Guinea. Joint winner of the 1976 Nobel prize for physiology or medicine.

**Galilei, Galileo**, known as **Galileo** (1564–1642) Italian astronomer, mathematician and natural philosopher, born Pisa. Inferred the value of a pendulum for exact measurement of time, proved that all falling bodies, great or small, descend due to gravity at the same rate. Perfected the refracting telescope and pursued astronomical observations which revealed mountains and valleys on the Moon, four satellites of Jupiter, and sunspots, convincing him of the correctness of the Copernican theory. His advocation of the Copernican theory led to his imprisonment by the Inquisition; he remained under house arrest until his death.

**Gauss, Carl Friedrich** (1777–1855) German mathematician, astronomer and physicist, born Brunswick. Made significant new advances in number theory, studied errors of observation and devised the method of least squares. Also carried out much work on pure mathematics, studied the Earth's magnetism and was involved in the development of the magnetometer, as well as giving a mathematical theory of optical systems of lenses.

**Geiger, Hans Wilhelm** (1882–1945) German physicist, born Neustadt-an-der-Haart. Investigated beta-ray radioactivity and, with Walther Müller, devised a counter to measure it.

**Halley, Edmond** (1656–1742) English astronomer and mathematician, born London. Studied the Solar System and correctly predicted the return (in 1758, 1835 and 1910) of a comet that had been observed in 1583, and is now named after him.

**Harvey, William** (1578–1657) English physician, born Folkestone. Discovered the circulation of the blood.

**Hawking, Stephen William** (1942– ) English theoretical physicist, born Oxford. Research on relativity led him to study gravitational singularities such as the 'big bang', out of which the Universe originated, and 'black holes', which result from the death of stars. His book *A Brief History of Time* is a popular account of modern cosmology. Since the 1960s he has suffered from a highly disabling progressive neuromotor disease.

**Heisenberg, Werner Karl** (1901–76) German theoretical physicist, born Würzburg. Developed quantum mechanics and formulated the principle of indeterminacy (uncertainty principle). Awarded the 1932 Nobel prize for physics. In 1958, with Wolfgang Pauli, announced the formulation of a unified field theory.

**Helmholtz, Hermann (Ludwig Ferdinand von)** (1821–94) German physiologist and physicist, born Potsdam. Researched physiology of vision, the ear and the nervous system as well as making important contributions in fluid dynamics, studies of vibrations and the spectrum, and studies of the development of electric current within a galvanic battery.

**Henle, Friedrich Gustav Jakob** (1809–85) German anatomist, born Fürth. Discovered the tubules in the kidney which are named after him and wrote treatises on systematic anatomy.

**Herschel, Sir John Frederick William** (1792–1871) English astronomer, born Slough. Son of Sir William Herschel; continued his father's research and discovered 525 nebulae and clusters. Pioneered celestial photography and researched photoactive chemicals and the wave theory of light.

**Herschel, Sir (Frederick) William** (1738–1822) German–British astronomer, born Hanover. Made a reflecting telescope (1773–4) with which he discovered the planet Uranus in 1781. Also discovered satellites of Uranus and Saturn, the rotation of Saturn's rings and Saturn's rotation period. Researched binary stars, nebulae and the Milky Way.

**Hertz, Heinrich Rudolph** (1857–94) German physicist, born Hamburg. Confirmed James Clerk Maxwell's predictions in 1887 by his discovery of invisible electromagnetic waves, of the same fundamental form as light waves.

**Hooke, Robert** (1635–1703) English chemist, physicist and architect, born Freshwater, Isle of Wight. Anticipated the invention of the steam engine, formulated Hooke's Law of the extension and compression of elastic bodies, and anticipated Isaac Newton's inverse square law of gravitation. Constructed first Gregorian telescope and inferred rotation of Jupiter. Materially invented the microscope, the quadrant and a marine barometer.

**Hubble, Edwin Powell** (1889–1953) American astronomer, born Marshfield, Missouri. Demonstrated that some nebulae are independent galaxies, and in 1929 discovered galaxy 'redshift': distant galaxies are receding from us and the apparent speed of recession of a galaxy is proportional to its distance from us.

**Hutton, James** (1726–97) Scottish geologist, born Edinburgh. Formed the basis of modern geology with the Huttonian theory, emphasizing the igneous origin of many rocks and deprecating the assumption of causes other than those still seen at work.

**Huxley, Thomas Henry** (1825–95) English biologist, born Ealing. Assistant surgeon on surveying expedition to the South Seas (1846–50), during which he collected marine animal specimens; became foremost scientific supporter of Charles Darwin's theory of evolution. Also studied fossils and later turned to philosophy.

**Huygens, Christiaan** (1629–93) Dutch physicist, born The Hague. Made pendulum clock (1657), and developed the doctrine of accelerated motion under gravity. Discovered the rings and fourth satellite of Saturn, and the laws of collision of elastic bodies.

**Jansky, Karl Guthe** (1905–50) American radio engineer, born Norman, Oklahoma. Discovered astronomical radio sources by chance while investigating interference on short-wave radio telephone transmissions, initiating the science of radio astronomy. The SI unit of radio emission strength, the jansky, is named after him.

**Jeans, Sir James Hopwood** (1877–1946) English physicist and astronomer, born Ormskirk, near Southport. Made important contributions to the dynamical theory of gases, radiation, quantum theory and stellar evolution; best known for his role in popularizing physics and astronomy.

**Joule, James Prescott** (1818–89) English physicist, born Salford. Showed experimentally that heat is a form of energy and established the mechanical equivalent of heat; this became the basis for the theory of conservation of energy. With Lord Kelvin he studied temperatures of gases and formulated the absolute scale of temperature. The joule, a unit of work or energy, is named after him.

**Kant, Immanuel** (1724–1804) German philosopher, born Königsberg, Prussia (now Kaliningrad, Russia). Researched astronomy and geophysics, and predicted the existence of the planet Uranus before its discovery. Philosophical works had enormous influence.

**Katz, Sir Bernard** (1911– ) German–British biophysicist, born Leipzig. Discovered how the neural transmitter acetylcholine is released by neural impulses. Joint winner of the 1970 Nobel prize for physiology or medicine.

**Kelvin, William Thomson, 1st Baron** (1824–1907) Irish–Scottish physicist and mathematician, born Belfast. Solved important problems in electrostatics, proposed the absolute, or Kelvin, temperature scale and established the second law of thermodynamics simultaneously with Rudolf Clausius. Also investigated geomagnetism and hydrodynamics, and invented innumerable instruments.

**Kepler, Johannes** (1571–1630) German astronomer, born Weil der Stadt, Württemberg. Formulated laws of planetary motion describing elliptical orbits and forming the starting point of modern astronomy. Also made discoveries in optics, general physics and geometry.

**Kirchhoff, Gustav Robert** (1824–87) German physicist, born Königsberg. Carried out important research in electricity, heat, optics and spectrum analysis, his work leading to the discovery of caesium and rubidium (1859).

**Krebs, Sir Edwin Gerhard** (1918– ) American biochemist, born Lansing, Iowa. Elected FRS in 1947. Researched the activation of glycogen enzymes together with Edmond Fischer (1920– ), for which they were awarded the 1992 Nobel prize for physiology or medicine. Krebs later studied the structure of the kinases and the properties of phosphatases.

**Krebs, Sir Hans Adolf** (1900–81) German–British biochemist, born Hildesheim. Discovered the series of chemical reactions known as the urea cycle (1932). Joint winner of the 1953 Nobel prize for physiology or medicine for research into metabolic processes, particularly the 'Krebs cycle'.

**Kroto, Sir Harold Walter** (1939– ) English chemist, born Wisbech, Cambridgeshire. Distinguished for his work in detecting unstable molecules, interstellar polyyne molecules and the third allotrope of carbon C. Joint winner of the 1996 Nobel prize for chemistry (with Robert Curl, 1933– , and Richard Smalley, 1943– ).

**Lamarck, Jean (Baptiste Pierre Antoine de Monet) Chevalier de** (1744–1829) French naturalist, born Bazentin. Made the basic distinction between vertebrates and invertebrates. On evolution he postulated that acquired characteristics can be inherited by later generations, preparing the way for the Darwinian theory of evolution.

**Langmuir, Irving** (1881–1959) American physical chemist, born New York City. He worked at the General Electric Company for 41 years, and his many inventions include the gas-filled tungsten lamp and an improved vacuum pump. He was awarded the 1932 Nobel prize for chemistry for his work on solid and liquid surfaces.

**Lawrence, Ernest Orlando** (1901–58) American physicist, born Canton, South Dakota. Constructed the first cyclotron for the production of artificial radioactivity (1929), fundamental to the development of the atomic bomb. Became the first director of the radiation laboratory at Berkeley, California, in 1936 and received the Nobel prize for physics in 1939. Element 103 was named lawrencium after him.

**Leibniz, Gottfried Wilhelm** (1646–1716) German mathematician and philosopher, born Leipzig. Discovered calculus around the same time as Isaac Newton; also made original contributions in the fields of optics, mechanics, statistics, logic and probability, and laid the foundations of 18th-century philosophy.

**Leishman, Sir William Boog** (1865–1926) Scottish bacteriologist, born Glasgow. Discovered an effective vaccine for inoculation against typhoid and was first to discover the parasite of the disease kala-azar.

**Linnaeus, Carolus (Carl von Linné)** (1707–78) Swedish naturalist and physician, born Raceshult. Founder of modern scientific nomenclature for plants and animals.

**Lorentz, Hendrik Antoon** (1853–1928) Dutch physicist, born Arnhem. Carried out important work in

electromagnetism; joint winner of the Nobel prize for physics in 1902 for explaining the effect whereby atomic spectral lines are split in the presence of magnetic fields.

**Lorenz, Konrad Zacharias** (1903–89) Austrian zoologist and ethologist, born Vienna. Regarded as the father of ethology, favouring the study of the instinctive behaviour of animals in the wild. In 1935 published observations on imprinting in young birds by which hatchlings 'learn' to recognize substitute parents, and argued that while aggressive behaviour in humans is inborn, it may be channelled into other forms of activity, whereas in other animals it is purely survival-motivated.

**Lyell, Sir Charles** (1797–1875) Scottish geologist, born Kinnordy, Fife. Established the principle of uniformitarianism in geology: geological changes have been gradual and produced by forces still at work, not catastrophic changes. His work significantly influenced Charles Darwin, although Lyell never accepted the theory of evolution by natural selection.

**Mach, Ernst** (1838–1916) Austrian physicist and philosopher, born Turas, Moravia. Carried out experimental work on projectiles and the flow of gases. His name has been given to the ratio of the speed of flow of a gas to the speed of sound (Mach number) and to the angle of a shock wave to the direction of motion (Mach angle).

**Malpighi, Marcello** (1628–94) Italian anatomist, born near Bologna. Discovered capillary blood vessels and made many pioneering discoveries in microscopic anatomy.

**Marconi, (Marquis) Guglielmo** (1874–1937) Italian physicist and inventor, born Bologna. Experimented with converting electromagnetic waves into electricity and achieved wireless telegraphy in 1895. In 1898 transmitted signals across the English Channel and in 1901 succeeded in sending Morse code signals across the Atlantic. Joint winner of the 1909 Nobel prize for physics. Later developed short-wave radio equipment and established a worldwide radio telegraph network for the British government.

**Maxwell, James Clerk** (1831–79) Scottish physicist, born Edinburgh. Produced mathematical theory of electromagnetism and identified light as electromagnetic radiation. Also suggested that invisible electromagnetic waves could be generated in a laboratory, as later carried out by Hertz. Other research included the kinetic theory of gases, the nature of Saturn's rings, colour perception and colour photography.

**Medawar, Sir Peter Brian** (1915–87) British zoologist and immunologist, born Rio de Janeiro. Pioneered experiments in skin grafting and the prevention of rejection in transplant operations. Joint winner of the Nobel prize for physiology or medicine in 1960.

**Mendel, Gregor Johann** (1822–84) Austrian biologist and botanist, born near Udrau, Silesia. Became abbot in 1868. Researched inheritance characteristics in plants leading to the formulation of Mendel's law of segregation and the law of independent assortment; his principles became the basis of modern genetics.

**Mendeleyev, Dmitri Ivanovich** (1834–1907) Russian chemist, born Tobolsk. Formulated the periodic law from which he predicted the existence of several elements which were subsequently discovered. Element 101 was named mendelevium after him.

**Michaelis, Leonor** (1875–1949) German–American biochemist, born Berlin. Made early deductions on enzyme action and is best known for the Michaelis–Menten equation on enzyme-catalyzed reactions.

**Michelson, Albert Abraham** (1852–1931) German–American physicist, born Strelno (now Strzelno, Poland). Carried out famous Michelson–Morley experiment which confirmed the non-existence of 'ether', a result which set Einstein on the road to the theory of relativity. First American scientist to win a Nobel prize (physics) in 1907.

**Millikan, Robert Andrews** (1868–1953) American physicist, born Illinois. Awarded the Nobel prize for physics in 1923 for determining the charge on the electron, and carried out important work on cosmic rays.

**Mullis, Kary Banks** (1944– ) American biochemist, born Lenoir, North Carolina. Discovered 'polymerase chain reaction' technique, which allows tiny amounts of DNA to be copied millions of times. This has many analytical uses, including HIV virus tests. Joint winner of the 1993 Nobel prize for chemistry (with Michael Smith 1932–2000).

**Napier, John** (1550–1619) Scottish mathematician, born Edinburgh. He is famous for the invention of logarithms to simplify computation, and for devising a calculating machine using a set of rods, known as 'Napier's Bones'.

**Newton, Sir Isaac** (1642–1727) English scientist and mathematician, born Woolsthorpe, Lincolnshire. Formulated complete theory of gravitation by 1684; also carried out important work in optics, concluding that the different colours of light making up white light have different refrangibility, developed the reflecting telescope, and invented calculus around the same time as Leibniz.

**Parkinson, James** (1755–1824) English physician, born London. Gave first description of paralysis agitans, or Parkinson's disease. Described appendicitis and perforation, and was first to recognize perforation as a cause of death.

**Pascal, Blaise** (1623–62) French mathematician and physicist, born Clermont-Ferrand. Carried out important work in geometry, invented a calculating machine, demonstrated that air pressure decreases with altitude as previously predicted and developed probability theory. The SI unit of pressure (pascal) and the modern computer programming language, Pascal, are named after him.

**Pasteur, Louis** (1822–95) French chemist, born Dôle. Father of modern bacteriology. Discovered possibility of attenuating the virulence of injurious micro-organisms by exposure to air, by variety of culture, or by transmission through various animals, and demonstrated that the attenuated organisms could be used for immunization. From this he developed vaccinations against anthrax and rabies. Also introduced pasteurization (moderate heating) to kill disease-producing organisms in wine, milk and other foods, and disymmetry in molecules.

**Pauli, Wolfgang** (1900–58) Austrian–American theoretical physicist, born Vienna. Formulated the exclusion principle (1924), that no two electrons can be in the same energy state, producing important advances in the application of quantum theory to the periodic table of elements; for this he was awarded the Nobel prize for physics in 1945.

**Pauling, Linus** (1901–94) American chemist, born Portland, Oregon. He made important discoveries concerning chemical bonding and complex molecular structures; this led him into work on the chemistry of biological molecules and the chemical basis of hereditary disease. He was awarded the 1954 Nobel prize for chemistry, and also the 1962 Nobel peace prize.

**Pavlov, Ivan Petrovich** (1849–1936) Russian physiologist, born near Ryazan. Studied physiology of circulation, digestion and 'conditioned' or acquired reflexes, believing the brain's only function to be to couple neurones to produce reflexes. Awarded the Nobel prize for physiology or medicine in 1904.

**Perutz, Max Ferdinand** (1914–2002) Austrian–British biochemist, born Vienna. Studied the structure of haemoglobin. Joint winner of the 1962 Nobel prize for chemistry.

**Planck, Max Karl Ernst** (1858–1947) German theoretical physicist, born Kiel. Researched thermodynamics and black-body radiation, leading him to formulate quantum theory (1900), which assumes energy changes take place in abrupt instalments or quanta. Awarded the Nobel prize for physics in 1918.

**Ptolemy** or **Claudius Ptolemaeus** (c.90–168) Egyptian astronomer and geographer, believed born Ptolemaeus Hermion. Corrected and improved the astronomical work of his predecessors to form the Ptolemaic System, described by Plato and Aristotle, with the Earth at the centre of the Universe and heavenly bodies revolving round it; beyond this lay the sphere of the fixed stars. Also compiled geographical catalogues and maps.

**Purkinje, Jan Evangelista** (1787–1869) Czech physiologist, born Libochowitz. Carried out research on the eye, brain, muscles, embryology, digestion and sweat glands, studying 'Purkinje's figure', an effect by which one can see in one's own eye the shadows of the retinal blood vessels, and 'Purkinje's cells', cells in the middle layer of the cerebellar cortex.

**Pythagoras** (6th century BC) Greek mathematician and philosopher, born Samos. Associated with mathematical discoveries involving the chief musical intervals, the relations of numbers and the relations between the lengths of sides of right-angled triangles (Pythagoras's theorem). Profoundly influenced Plato and later astronomers and mathematicians.

**Ramón y Cajal, Santiago** (1852–1934) Spanish physician and histologist, born Petilla de Aragon. Carried out important work on the brain and nerves, isolated the neuron and discovered how nerve impulses are transmitted to brain cells. Joint winner of the 1906 Nobel prize for physiology or medicine.

**Rathke, Martin Heinrich** (1793–1860) German biologist, born Danzig (now Gdańsk, Poland). Discovered gill-slits and gill-arches in embryo birds and mammals. 'Rathke's pocket' is the name given to the small pit on the dorsal side of the oral cavity of developing vertebrates.

**Rayleigh, John William Strutt, 3rd Baron** (1842–1919) English physicist, born near Maldon, Essex. Carried out valuable research on vibratory motion, the theory of sound and the wave theory of light. With Sir William Ramsay (1852–1916) discovered argon (1894). Awarded the Nobel prize for physics in 1904.

**Richter, Charles Francis** (1900–85) American seismologist, born near Hamilton, Ohio. Devised the scale of earthquake strength which bears his name (1927–35).

**Röntgen, Wilhelm Konrad von** (1845–1923) German physicist, born Lennep, Prussia. Discovered the electromagnetic rays which he called X-rays (also known as Röntgen rays) in 1895. For his work on X-rays he was joint winner of the Rumford medal in 1896 and winner of the 1901 Nobel prize for physics. Also carried out important work on the heat conductivity of crystals, the specific heat of gases, and the electromagnetic rotation of polarized light.

**Rutherford, Ernest Rutherford, 1st Baron Rutherford of Nelson** (1871–1937) New Zealand–British physicist, born Spring Grove, near Nelson. Made first successful wireless transmissions over two miles, discovered the three types of uranium radiations, formulated a theory of atomic disintegration and determined the nature of alpha particles; this led to a new atomic model in which the mass is concentrated in the nucleus. Also discovered that alpha-ray bombardment could produce atomic transformation and predicted the existence of the neutron. Awarded the Nobel prize for chemistry in 1908.

**Schrödinger, Erwin** (1887–1961) Austrian physicist, born Vienna. Originated the study of wave mechanics as part of the quantum theory with the celebrated Schrödinger wave equation, for which he was joint winner of the 1933 Nobel prize for physics. Also made contributions to field theory.

**Schwann, Theodor** (1810–82) German physiologist, born Neuss. Discovered the enzyme pepsin, investigated muscle contraction, demonstrated the role of micro-organisms in putrefaction and extended the cell theory, previously applied to plants, to animal tissues.

**Sharp, Phillip Allen** (1944– ) American molecular biologist, born Kentucky. Invented the mapping technique used in the analysis of RNA molecules, leading to the discovery that genes are split into several sections, separated by stretches of DNA ('introns') which appear to carry no genetic information. Received the 1993 Nobel prize for physiology or medicine, which he shared with Richard Roberts (1943– ).

**Sörensen, Sören Peter Lauritz** (1868–1939) Danish biochemist, born Havrabjerg, Slagelsi. Carried out pioneering research on hydrogen concentration and invented the pH scale for measuring acidity in 1909.

**Szent-Györgyi, Albert von Nagyrapolt** (1893–1986) Hungarian–American biochemist, born Budapest. Discovered actin, isolated vitamin C and was awarded the Nobel prize for physiology or medicine in 1937. Also made important studies of biological combustion, muscular contraction and cellular oxidation.

**Thomson, Sir Joseph John** (1856–1940) English physicist, born Cheetham Hill, near Manchester. Studied gaseous conductors of electricity and the nature of cathode rays; this led to his discovery of the electron. Also pioneered mass spectrometry and discovered the existence of isotopes of elements. Awarded the Nobel prize for physics in 1906.

**Thomson, Sir William ▸ Kelvin, 1st Baron**

**Tinbergen, Nikolaas** (1907–88) Dutch ethologist, born The Hague. Co-founder with Konrad Lorenz of the science of ethology (study of animal behaviour in natural surroundings). Analysed social behaviour of certain animals and insects as an evolutionary process with considerable relevance to human behaviour, especially courtship and aggression. Joint winner of the 1973 Nobel prize for physiology or medicine.

**Van de Graaff, Robert Jemison** (1901–67) American physicist, born Tuscaloosa, Alabama. Conceived of an improved type of electrostatic generator, in which electric charge could be built up on a hollow metal sphere; constructed first model, later to be known as the Van de Graaff generator, giving possibility of generating potentials of over a million volts. Developed the generator for use as a particle accelerator for atomic and nuclear physicists. Generator was also adapted to produce high-energy X-rays for cancer treatment and examination of the interior structure of heavy ordnance.

**Varmus, Harold** (1939– ) American molecular biologist, born New York. Awarded the 1989 Nobel prize for physiology or medicine (jointly with Michael Bishop, 1936– ) for the discovery of oncogenes.

**Volta, Alessandro Giuseppe Anastasio, Count** (1745–1827) Italian physicist, born Como. Developed the theory of current electricity, discovered the electric composition of water, invented an electric battery, the electrophorus, an electroscope, and made investigations into heat and gases. His name is given to the SI unit of electric potential difference, the volt.

**Waals, Johannes Diderik van der** (1837–1923) Dutch physicist, born Leiden. Formulated van der Waals equation, defining the physical state of a gas or liquid, and investigated the weak attractive forces (van der Waals forces) between molecules. Awarded the Nobel prize for physics in 1910.

**Warburg, Otto Heinrich** (1883–1970) German biochemist, born Freiburg, Baden. Carried out important cancer research. Awarded the 1931 Nobel prize for physiology or medicine, and in 1944 was offered a second Nobel Prize which, as a Jew, he was prevented from accepting by Hitler.

**Watt, James** (1736–1819) Scottish engineer and inventor, born Greenock. Developed and improved early models of the steam engine, and manufactured it from 1774. The watt, a unit of power, is named after him, and the term horsepower was first used by him.

**Wien, Wilhelm** (1864–1928) German physicist, born Gaffken, East Prussia. Awarded the Nobel prize for physics in 1911 for work on the radiation of energy from black bodies. Research also included investigation of X-rays and hydrodynamics.

**Young, Thomas** (1773–1829) English physicist and physician, born Milverton, Somerset. Expounded the phenomenon of interference, which established the undulatory theory of light. Also made valuable contributions in insurance, haemodynamics and deciphering the inscriptions on the Rosetta Stone.

## Scientific terms



**Bold** type indicates that a definition of a word or phrase in an entry is given elsewhere in the glossary.

In this glossary $10^{12}$ is used to mean 1 followed by 12 zeros and $10^{-27}$ is used to mean 1 occurring 27 places after a decimal point.

**aberration** In an image-forming system, such as a curved mirror or lens, the failure to produce a true image when different colours of light or light incident on different parts of the mirror or lens are focused to different positions.

**absolute alcohol** Water-free **ethanol**.

**absolute zero** The least possible temperature for all substances, when the **molecules** of any substance possess no heat energy. A figure of −273.15°C is generally accepted as the value of absolute zero.

**ac ► alternating current**

**acid** Normally, a substance which (a) dissolves in water with the formation of hydrogen **ions**, (b) dissolves metals with the liberation of hydrogen gas, or (c) more generally, a substance which tends to lose a **proton** or to accept an **electron** pair.

**acid rain** Rain that is unnaturally **acid** as a result of pollution of the atmosphere with oxides of nitrogen and sulphur from the burning of coal and oil.

**acoustic imaging** Determination of distance and direction of objects, such as submarines, by the reception of the reflection of a sound pulse. Also known as sonar.

**acquired character** In zoology, a modification of an organ during the lifetime of an individual due to use or disuse, and not inherited from a previous generation. **► natural selection**.

**adaptation** In zoology, any structural, physiological or behavioural characteristic which fits an organism to the conditions under which it lives; the genetic or developmental processes by which such characteristics arise. **► natural selection**.

**adiabatic process** In physics, a process which occurs without interchange of heat with surroundings.

**adsorption** In chemistry, the taking up of one substance at the surface of another.

**aerosol** (1) A system in the form of a **colloid**, such as a mist or a fog, in which the dispersion medium is a gas. (2) Pressurized container with built-in spray mechanism used for packaging insecticides, deodorants, paints, etc.

**aerospace** The Earth's atmosphere together with the space beyond; the branch of technology or of industry concerned with the flight of spacecraft through this.

**algae** A group of simple plants containing **chlorophyll** but without roots, stems or leaves, which live in aquatic conditions.

**alkali** A substance which, when dissolved in water, forms a solution containing hydroxyl **ions**, negatively charged ions containing oxygen and hydrogen, and with a **pH value** of more than 7.

**allotropy** The existence of two or more forms of an **element** in one phase of matter (ie solid, liquid or gas), called allotropes.

**alloy** A mixture of metals, or of a metal with a non-metal in which the metal is the major component.

**alpha particle** The **nucleus** of a helium **atom**, emitted from natural or radioactive **isotopes**. Often written α-particle. **► radioactivity**.

**alternating current** Generally abbreviated to ac. An electric **current** whose flow alternates in direction.

**AM (amplitude modulation) ► modulation**

**amino acid** A fatty acid in which an amino group ($NH_2$) and a carboxyl group (COOH) are attached to an **organic molecule**. They play an important part in the bodies of animals and plants, often combining in different forms to produce **protein**.

**amorphous** Non-crystalline.

**amu ► atomic mass unit**

**anaerobic** Living in the absence of oxygen. Anaerobic respiration is the liberation of energy which does not require the presence of oxygen.

**anion** A negative **ion**, ie **atom** or **molecule** which has gained one or more **electrons**.

**anisotropic** Said of crystalline material for which physical properties, such as its ability to conduct electrical **current**, depend on the direction relative to the crystal axes.

**annihilation** Spontaneous conversion of a particle and its **antiparticle** into **radiation**.

**annual** A plant that flowers and dies within a period of one year from germination.

**annulus** A plane surface bounded by two concentric circles, like a washer.

**anode** A positively charged **conductor** used in conjunction with a **cathode** to lead an electric current into or out of a solid, liquid or gas.

**antibody** A defensive substance produced in an organism in response to the action of a foreign body, such as the toxin of a **parasite**.

**anticyclone** A distribution of atmospheric pressure in which the pressure increases towards the centre. Winds in such a system circulate in a clockwise direction in the northern hemisphere and in a counterclockwise direction in the southern hemisphere.

**antigen** A substance which stimulates the production of an **antibody**.

**antiparticle** The antiparticle of a given particle has the same mass but opposite values for all its other properties, such as charge. A particle and its

antiparticle, eg the **electron** and **positron**, destroy each other on contact in the process of **annihilation**.

**aperture** (1) The opening, usually circular, through which light enters an optical system, such as a camera lens; its area may be varied by an iris diaphragm to control the amount of light passing. ► **f-number**. (2) The rectangular opening at which motion picture film is exposed in a camera or projector.

**Archimedes' principle** The principle that when a body is wholly or partly immersed in a fluid it experiences an upwards force equal to the weight of fluid it displaces.

**aromatic compounds** Organic compounds containing **benzene** or with similar chemical properties.

**asteroid** One of thousands of rocky objects found in the **solar system**, normally between the orbits of Mars and Jupiter, ranging in size from 1 to 1 000km.

**astigmatism** (1) In medicine, unequal curvature of the focusing surfaces of the eye, which prevents incident light rays from reaching a common focus point on the retina, resulting in blurred eyesight. (2) In physics, a defect in an optical system on account of which, instead of a point image being formed of a point object, two short line images (focal lines) are produced at slightly different positions and at right angles to each other.

**astronomical unit** The mean distance of the Earth from the Sun, about 149 600 000km or 93 000 000mi.

**atom** The smallest particle of an element which can take part in a chemical reaction. A central nucleus containing **protons** and **neutrons** is surrounded by shells of **electrons**.

**atomic mass unit** Exactly one twelfth the mass of a neutral **atom** of the most abundant **isotope** of carbon ($1.660 \times 10^{-27}$kg).

**aurora** Luminous curtains or streamers of light seen in the night sky at high latitudes, caused when electrically charged particles from the Sun are guided by the Earth's magnetic field to the polar regions, there colliding with atoms in the upper atmosphere. In the northern hemisphere known as aurora borealis and in the southern as aurora australis.

**background radiation Radiation** which causes **ionization** coming from natural sources such as the Earth's rocks, soil and atmosphere.

**bacteriophage** A **virus** which infects bacteria.

**benthos** Collectively, the immobile animal and plant life living on the sea bottom.

**benzene** A **molecule** consisting of a ring or closed chain of six carbon **atoms** each with a hydrogen atom attached.

**beta decay** The radioactive disintegration with the emission of an **electron** or **positron**. ► **radioactivity**.

**biennial** A plant that flowers and dies between its first and second years from germination and which does not flower in its first year.

**Big Bang** Hypothetical model of the universe which postulates that all matter and energy were once concentrated into an unimaginably dense state, from which it has been expanding from a creation event between 13 000 000 000 and 20 000 000 000 years ago.

**bioassay** The quantitative determination of a substance by measuring its biological effect on eg growth, ie the use of an organism to test the environment.

**biogenesis** The formation of living organisms from their ancestors and of minute **cell** structures from their predecessors.

**bioluminescence** The production of light by living organisms, such as glow-worms, some deep-sea fish, some bacteria and some fungi.

**biosphere** The part of the Earth (upwards at least to a height of 10 000m, and downwards to the depths of the ocean, and a few hundred metres below the land surface) and the atmosphere surrounding it, which is able to support life. The term may be expanded theoretically to other planets.

**bit** In computer science, a digit in binary notation, ie 0 or 1. It is the smallest unit of storage (from *B*inary dig*IT*).

**black hole** A region in space from which matter and energy cannot escape. A black hole could be a **star** or the central part of a **galaxy** which has collapsed in on itself to the point where the speed required for matter to escape exceeds the speed of light.

**buckyballs Molecules** consisting of 60 carbon **atoms** arranged symmetrically. Familiar name for buckminsterfullerene.

**byte** In computer science, a fixed number of **bits**, often corresponding to a single character and operated on as a unit.

**calculus** The branch of mathematics dealing with continuously varying quantities or functions.

**carat** or **karat** (1) A standard weight for precious stones equal to 200 milligrams. (2) The standard of fineness for gold, such that 24 carats represents pure gold, and 23 carat gold has $\frac{1}{24}$ part impurity.

**carbohydrates** Compounds of carbon, hydrogen and oxygen, the last two being in the same proportion as in water. Form the main source of energy in food as sugars and starches.

**carbon dating** or **radiocarbon dating** The estimation of the date of death of an **organic** material from the amount of a radioactive **isotope** of carbon in it. The quantity of the radioactive carbon naturally decreases with time. ► **radioactivity**.

**carcinogen** Substance which encourages the growth of cancer.

**carnivore** A flesh-eating mammal.

**catalysis** The acceleration or retardation of a chemical reaction by a substance, a catalyst, which itself undergoes no permanent chemical change, or which can be recovered when the chemical reaction is completed.

**cathode** A negatively charged **conductor** used in conjunction with an **anode** to lead an electric current into or out of a solid, liquid or gas.

**caustic** Said of a material which is destructive or corrosive to living tissue; an agent which burns or destroys living tissue.

**cell** In biology, the unit from which plants and animals are composed.

**cellulose** A **carbohydrate** forming the chief component of **cell** walls in plants and in wood.

**Celsius scale** The **SI** name for centigrade scale. Temperature scale in which the freezing point of water is 0°C and the boiling point is 100°C.

**centigrade scale ► Celsius scale**

**centrifuge** Machine which uses the force produced by rotation to separate molecules from solution, particles and solids from liquids, and liquids which do not mix from each other.

**CGS unit** Abbreviation for Centimetre-Gram-Second unit, based on the centimetre, the gram and the second as the fundamental units of length, mass and time. For most purposes superseded by **SI units**. (► pp389–90)

**chaos theory** The theory which describes how the behaviour of a system which obeys well-known physical laws can become unpredictable if a very large number of accurately known quantities or a very extensive description of its initial state is required to predict its development. This leads to unpredictability in eg weather forecasting.

**chip** The popular name for an **integrated circuit**.

**chlorophylls** Green pigments involved in the process of **photosynthesis**. *Chlorophyll a* is the primary photosynthetic pigment in all organisms that release oxygen, ie all plants and **algae**.

**cholesterol** A white crystalline solid found in nerve tissues, gall stones, and in other tissues of the body.

**chromosome** Rod-like structures found in the **nucleus** of a **cell**, which perform an important role in cell division and transmission of hereditary features.

**clone** Organisms, **cells** or micro-organisms all derived from a single progenitor. They have therefore an almost identical **genotype**.

**colloid** A solid dispersed through a liquid such that, though apparently dissolved, it cannot pass through a membrane.

**comet** A small member of the solar system, made of ice, dust and gas, becoming visible as it approaches the Sun. A bright nucleus is often seen, and sometimes a tail which points away from the Sun.

**conductor** A material used for the transference of heat or electrical energy.

**congenital** Said of diseases or deformities dating from birth, but not passed on from a previous generation.

**continental drift** A hypothesis to explain the distribution of the continents and oceans and the structural, geological and physical similarities which exist between them. The continents were believed to have been formed from one large land mass and to have drifted apart. ► **plate tectonics**.

**convection** The transfer of heat in a fluid by the circulation flow due to temperature differences. The regions of higher temperature, being less dense, rise, while the regions of lower temperature move down to take their place.

**Coriolis effect** The effect whereby an object falling freely towards the Earth is slightly deviated from a straight line and will fall to a point east of the point directly below its initial position, due to the rotation of the Earth underneath as it falls.

**cosmic rays** Highly penetrating rays from interstellar space, consisting of particles such as **protons**, **electrons** and **positrons**.

**cracking** The breaking down of heavier crude-oil **molecules** to form lighter molecules by heat, pressure and the use of **catalysis**.

**current** The flow of electric charge in a substance, solid, liquid or gas.

**cyclone** (1) A region of low pressure, or depression. (2) A tropical revolving storm in the Arabian Sea, Bay of Bengal and South Indian Ocean.

**Darwinian theory ► natural selection**

**desertification** Formation of deserts from zones previously supporting plant life by the action of drought and/or increased populations of humans and grass-eating animals.

**diffraction** The spreading of light or other waves passing through a narrow opening or by the edge of an opaque body.

**diffusion** General transport of matter whereby **molecules** or **ions** mix through normal movement of particles due to their heat energy.

**dimorphism** (1) In chemistry, the crystallization into two distinct forms of an **element** or compound, eg carbon as diamond and graphite. (2) In biology, the condition of having two different forms, as animals which show marked differences between male and female (sexual dimorphism), animals which have two different kinds of offspring, and colonial animals in which the members of the colony are of two different kinds.

**direct current** Generally abbreviated to dc. An electric current which flows in one direction only.

**dispersion** The separation of visible light into its various colours when passing between media of different density, such as air and glass. Occurs because light passing between the media is deviated from a straight path by an amount which depends on the wavelength, ie the colour.

**diurnal** During a day. The term is used in astronomy and meteorology to indicate the variations of an astronomical quantity or weather phenomenon during an average day.

**DNA** or **deoxyribonucleic acid** In its double-stranded form the genetic material of organisms. Usually, two strands of DNA form a double-helix, the strands running in opposite directions.

**dominant** Of a **gene** which shows its effect in those individuals who received it from only one parent. Also describes an inherited feature due to a dominant gene.

**Doppler effect** The apparent change of frequency of light or sound because of the relative motion of the source of radiation and the observer, eg the change in frequency of sound heard when a train or aircraft is moving towards or away from an observer.

**dry ice** Solid (frozen) carbon dioxide, used in refrigeration (storage) and engineering.

**dwarf star** The name given to a small low-luminosity star. ► **white dwarf**.

**ecosystem** Conceptual view of a plant and animal community, emphasizing the interactions between living and non-living parts, and the flow of materials and energy between these parts.

**El Niño** An occasional warm tropical ocean current that moves from the East Indies to the South American coast, sometimes causing devastating changes in weather patterns leading to torrential rain and flooding in some areas, and drought in others.

**electric field** The region in which forces are exerted on any electric charge present.

**electrode** A **conductor** whereby an electric current is led into or out of a solid, liquid or gas.

**electrolysis** Chemical change, generally decomposition of a compound, effected by a flow of current through a solution of the chemical, or its molten state, based on **ionization**.

**electromagnetic wave** A wave comprising two interdependent mutually perpendicular transverse waves of **electric** and **magnetic fields**. The spectrum of electromagnetic waves comprises **gamma-radiation**, **X-rays**, **ultraviolet radiation**, visible light, **infrared radiation**, **microwaves** and **radio waves**. The speed in free space for all such waves is around 300 000km (186 000 mi) per sec.

**electron** A subatomic particle with negative electric charge, which with the **proton** and **neutron**, is a basic constituent of the **atom**.

**element** A simple substance, composed of **atoms**, which cannot be resolved into simpler substances by normal chemical means.

**emulsion** (1) In chemistry, a suspension in the form of a **colloid** of one liquid in another. (2) In photography, a suspension of finely divided crystals in a medium such as gelatine which provides the light-sensitive coating on film, glass plates and paper.

**endothermic** Said of a chemical reaction which is accompanied by the absorption of heat.

**entropy** In thermal processes, a quantity which measures the extent to which the energy of a system is available for conversion to work.

**enzyme** A protein which provides **catalysis**, which is restricted to a limited set of reactions.

**epicentre** That point on the surface of the Earth lying immediately above the focus of an earthquake or nuclear explosion.

**equinox** Either of the two instants of time at which the Sun crosses the projected plane of the Earth's equator, around 21 March and 23 September.

**ethanol** or **ethyl alcohol** An alcohol with chemical formula CHOH, the active substance in alcoholic drinks.

**evolution** In biology, changes in the genetic composition of a population during successive generations. The gradual development of more complex organisms from simpler ones.

**exothermic** Said of a chemical reaction which is accompanied by the evolution of heat.

**f-number** A measure of the **aperture** of a lens, representing its light transmission; it expresses the diameter of the lens diaphragm as a fraction of its focal length, eg f/8, also written f:8 or f8.

**Fahrenheit scale** The temperature scale in which the freezing point of water is 32°F and the boiling point is 212°F.

**fault** A fracture in rocks along which some displacement has taken place. The displacement may vary from a few millimetres to thousands of metres. Movement along faults is the most common cause of earthquakes.

**feedback** Occurs when part of an output signal is fed back into the input of the system, which often occurs in electro-acoustic systems in which the microphone and loudspeaker are in the same room.

**fermentation** A slow decomposition process of **organic** substances induced by micro-organisms or **enzymes**. An important fermentation process is the alcoholic fermentation of sugar.

**fibre optics** ► **optical fibre**

**field theory** As yet an unverified attempt to link the properties of all force fields in physics into a unified system.

**fission** (1) In biology, the reproduction of some single-cell organisms from a single parent in which the **cell** divides into two more or less equal parts. (2) In physics, the spontaneous or induced disintegration of a heavy atomic **nucleus** into two or more lighter fragments. The energy released in the process is referred to as **nuclear energy**.

**fossil** The relic or trace of some plant or animal which has been preserved by natural processes in rocks of the past.

**fractal** A geometrical entity characterized by a basic pattern that is repeated at ever decreasing sizes.

**fraternal twins** ► **twins**

**fusion** (1) The process of forming a new atomic **nucleus** by combining lighter ones. The energy released in the process is referred to as **nuclear energy** or fusion energy. (2) The conversion of a solid into a liquid state. ► **atom**.

**Galaxy** (1) The name given to the belt of faint stars which encircles the heavens and which is known as

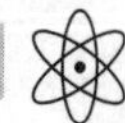



the Milky Way. (2) The name is also used for the entire system of dust, gases and stars within which the Sun moves. (3) More generally, galaxy is used to mean any extra-galactic nebula, each being a vast collection of stars, dust and gas.

**galvanized iron** Iron which has been subjected to galvanizing, eg zinc coating, to prevent corrosion due to moisture.

**gamma-radiation** **Electromagnetic waves** of high energy emitted after **nuclear reactions** or by radioactive atoms during the process of radioactive decay. ► **radioactivity**.

**gene** One of the units of **DNA**, arranged in linear fashion on the **chromosomes**, responsible for passing on specific features from parents to offspring.

**genetic code** The system by which **genes** pass on instructions that ensure transmission of features inherited from previous generations.

**genetic engineering** Biological science whose aims include the control of hereditary defects by the modification or elimination of certain **genes**, and the mass production of useful biological substances (eg insulin) by the transplanting of genes.

**genome** The full set of **chromosomes** of an individual; the total number of **genes** in such a set.

**genotype** The genetic constitution of an individual; a group of individuals all of which possess the same genetic constitution.

**genus** In biology, a taxonomic rank of closely related forms, which is lower than family and is further subdivided into species.

**geomorphology** The structure and development of land forms, including those under the sea; the study of this.

**geostationary** Said of an orbit lying above the equator, in which an artificial satellite moves at the same speed as the Earth rotates, thus maintaining position above a fixed point on the Earth's surface. Such a satellite would have an altitude of 35 800km (22 200mi) above the Earth's surface.

**geothermal power** Power generated by using the heat energy of rocks in the Earth's crust.

**gestation** In mammals, the act of retaining and nourishing the young in the uterus; pregnancy.

**giant star** A large and luminous star with low average density.

**gravitational waves** Waves which move through a gravitational field. Accelerating masses are expected to radiate gravitational waves, but so far this has not been observed directly.

**greenhouse effect** The phenomenon by which thermal radiation from the Sun is trapped by water vapour and carbon dioxide on a planet's surface. This leads to the temperature at the planet's surface being considerably higher than would otherwise be the case.

**gyroscope** or **gyro** An apparatus in which a heavy flywheel or top rotates at high speed, the turning movement resisting change of direction of axis.

**herbaceous** A soft and green plant organ or a plant without persistent woody tissues above ground.

**herbivore** A grass-eating animal.

**hermaphrodite** A person whose reproductive organs are anatomically ambiguous, so that they are not exclusively male or female.

**histamine** A substance present in all tissues of the body, being liberated into the blood, eg when the skin is cut or burnt or during allergic reactions, eg hay fever; large releases cause the contraction of nearly all smooth muscle, a fall of arterial blood pressure and shock.

**hologram** A photograph made without use of a lens by means of interference between two parts of a split **laser** beam, which when suitably illuminated shows as a three-dimensional image.

**hormone** A substance released by glands into the bloodstream which carries it to remote sites in the body where it has a specific physiological activating or repressing function.

**hybrid** In biology, the offspring of a cross between two different strains, varieties, races or species.

**identical twins** ► **twins**

**igneous rocks** Rock masses generally accepted as being formed by the solidification of the Earth's internal molten **magma**.

**immunity** The state of having a high resistance to a disease due to the formation of **antibodies** in response to the presence of **antigens**.

**imprinting** In biology, an aspect of learning in some species, through which attachment to the important parental figure develops and their social preferences become restricted to their own species.

**in vitro fertilization** The reproduction of the natural process of fertilization outside the living body, in laboratory apparatus.

**indigenous** Native; not imported.

**inertia** The property of a body, proportional to its mass, which opposes a change in the motion of the body.

**infinity** A number which is larger than any quantified concept. For many purposes it may be considered as one divided by zero.

**infrared radiation** **Electromagnetic waves** in the wavelength range from 0.000075 to 0.1cm, approximately, lying between the visible and **microwave** regions of the spectrum.

**infrasound** The sound of frequencies below the usual audible limit, ie of less than around 20 cycles per sec or hertz.

**inorganic** Said of chemical **elements** and their compounds, other than the compounds of carbon.

**integrated circuit** A very small circuit consisting of interconnected **semiconductor** devices in a single structure which cannot be subdivided without destroying its intended function.

**ion** Strictly, any **atom** or **molecule** which has resultant electric charge due to loss or gain of **electrons**. Free electrons are sometimes loosely classified as negative ions.

**ionization** The formation of **ions** by separating **molecules**, or adding or subtracting **electrons** from **atoms** by various methods.

**isobar** A line drawn on a map through places having the same atmospheric pressure at a given time.

**isomerism** The existence of more than one substance having a given molecular composition and molecular mass but differing in constitution or structure.

**isotope** One of a set of chemically identical species of **atom** which have the same number of **protons**, but different numbers of **neutrons**.

**jet stream** A fairly well-defined core of strong wind, around 200–300 mi (320–480 km) wide with wind speeds up to around 200mph (320kph) occurring more than 20 000ft (7 000m) above the Earth.

**Kelvin scale** Temperature scale in which **absolute zero** is assigned the value zero and the temperature interval is the same as that of the Celsius scale. The unit is abbreviated as K; the freezing point of water (0°C) on this scale is 273.15 K.

**La Niña** An occasional cold ocean current that moves westerly along the equator, sometimes causing devastating changes in weather patterns leading to torrential rain and flooding in some areas, and drought in others.

**laser** *L*ight *A*mplification by *S*timulated *E*mission of *R*adiation. A source of intense light of a very narrow wavelength range in the ultraviolet, visible or infrared region of **electromagnetic waves**.

**LED ► light-emitting diode**

**light-emitting diode** A **semiconductor** device which emits light when an electric current is passed through it, as used eg for displays in digital clocks and electronic calculators. Abbreviated as LED.

**light-year** An astronomical measure of distance, being the distance travelled by light in space during a year, which is approximately $9.46 \times 10^{12}$ km or $5.88 \times 10^{12}$ mi.

**lipids** or **lipoids** General terms for oils, fats, waxes and related products found in living tissues.

**litmus** A material of **organic** origin used as an indicator; its colour changes to red in the presence of **acids**, and to blue in the presence of **alkalis**.

**luminescence** The emission of light otherwise than due to heating, and so at a relatively cool temperature.

**Mach number** The ratio of the speed of a body, or of the flow of a fluid, to the speed of sound in the same medium. At Mach 1, the speed of the body is that of sound; below Mach 1, it is **subsonic**; above Mach 1, it is **supersonic**.

**magma** Molten rock, including dissolved water and other gases. It is formed by melting at depth in the Earth and rises either to the surface, as lava, or to whatever level it can reach before crystallizing again.

**magnetic field** A field of force which exists around a magnetized body. Also associated with electric **currents** and the motions of **electrons** in **atoms**.

**magnetic tape** Flexible plastic tape, typically 6 to 50mm wide, coated on one side with magnetic material, in which signals are registered for subsequent reproduction. Used for storing television images, sound or computer data.

**magnetism** The science which covers **magnetic fields** and their effects on materials.

**magnitude** A measure of the apparent or absolute brightness of an astronomical object. The brightest naked-eye stars are of around first magnitude and the dimmest around the sixth.

**matrix** A system of numbers arranged in a square or rectangular formation.

**metamorphic rocks** Rocks formed by alteration of existing rocks by heat, pressure or other processes in the Earth's crust.

**meteor** A 'shooting star'. A small body which enters the Earth's atmosphere from the space between the planets and burns up due to friction, flashing across the sky and generally ceasing to be visible before it falls to Earth.

**microwave background** A weak **radio wave** signal which is detectable in every direction in the sky with almost identical intensity. It is believed to be the relic of the early hot phase in the **Big Bang** universe.

**microwaves** Those electromagnetic waves with wavelengths between 1mm and 30cm, lying between **radio waves** and **infrared radiation** in the spectrum.

**Milky Way ► Galaxy**

**minor planet** A term used generally in professional astronomy for **asteroid**. Also known as planetoid.

**MKSA** Metre-Kilogram(me)-Sec-Ampere system of units, adopted by the International Electrotechnical Commission, in place of all other systems of units. **► SI units**.

**modulation** The process of impressing information (code, speech, video, data, etc) onto a higher frequency carrier wave. In frequency modulation (FM) the information is recorded as a variation in frequency, with constant amplitude, and in amplitude modulation (AM) as a variation in amplitude at constant frequency. Used in radio broadcasting.

**mole** The amount of substance that contains as many entities (**atom**, **molecules**, **ions**, **electrons**, **photons**, etc) as there are atoms in 12 of a certain **isotope** of carbon.

**molecule** An **atom** or a finite group of atoms which is capable of independent existence and has properties characteristic of the substance of which it is the basic unit. Molecular substances are those which have discrete molecules, such as water. Diamond and sodium chloride are examples of non-molecular substances.

**mutation** In biology, a genetic change that can be transmitted to offspring as an inheritable divergence from previous generations.

**natural selection** An evolutionary theory which postulates the survival of the best-adapted forms of a species, with the inheritance of those characteristics wherein their fitness lies, and which arise as random variations due to **mutation**; it was first propounded by Charles Darwin, and is often referred to as Darwinism or the Darwinian Theory.

**neap tides** High tides occurring when the Sun's tidal influence is working against that of the Moon.

**nebula** A term applied to any astronomical object which appears as a hazy smudge of light in an optical telescope, its usage predating photographic astronomy. It is now more properly restricted to true clouds of interstellar medium. **Galaxies** are sometimes referred to as extra-galactic nebulae.

**neuron** or **neurone** A nerve cell and its processes.

**neutrino** A fundamental particle with zero charge and zero mass which only interacts weakly with matter and is therefore difficult to detect.

**neutron star** A small body of very high density resulting from a **supernova** explosion in which a massive **star** collapses under its own gravitational forces, the **electrons** and **protons** combining to form **neutrons**.

**neutron** An uncharged subatomic particle, with mass approximately equal to that of the **proton**, which is found in the **nucleus** of the **atom**.

**noble gases** The elements helium, neon, argon, krypton, xenon and radon, which due to their stable structures do not take part in all the usual chemical reactions. Also known as inert gases, rare gases.

**node** The location of a minimum in the sound, pressure or particle motion when waves superimpose and result in standing waves.

**nova** Classically, any new star which suddenly becomes visible to the unaided eye. In modern astronomy, a star late in its evolutionary track which suddenly brightens by a factor of 10 000 or more.

**nuclear energy** In principle, the energy stored in an atomic **nucleus** which binds together the constituent particles. More usually, the energy released during nuclear reactions involving regrouping of such particles (eg **fission** or **fusion** processes).

**nuclear fission** The spontaneous or induced disintegration of the **nucleus** of a heavy **atom** into two lighter atoms. The process involves a loss of mass which is converted into **nuclear energy**.

**nuclear fusion** The process of forming **atoms** of new elements by the fusion of atoms of lighter ones. Usually the formation of helium by the fusion of hydrogen and its **isotopes**. The process involves a loss of mass which is converted into **nuclear energy**.

**nuclear reaction** A process in which an atomic **nucleus** interacts with another nucleus or particle, producing changes in energy and nuclear structure.

**nucleon** A general name for a **neutron** or **proton**.

**nucleus** (1) In biology, the compartment within a **cell** bounded by a double membrane and containing the genomic **DNA**. (2) In physics, the structure within an **atom** composed of **protons** and **neutrons** which constitutes almost all the mass of the atom.

**omnivore** An animal which eats both plants and animals.

**oncogene** A type of **gene** involved in the onset and development of cancer.

**optical fibre** Fibres of ultra-pure glass, having properties such that light can be transmitted through them by continuously reflecting round bends. Used eg in some communications systems.

**order of magnitude** The approximate size or number of something, usually measured in a scale from one value to ten times that value.

**organic** Said of the compounds of carbon. Owing to the ability of carbon atoms to combine together in long chains, these compounds are far more numerous than those of other elements and are the basis of living matter.

**orogenesis** The tectonic process whereby mountain chains are formed through movement of the Earth's crust.

**orthogenesis** The evolution of organisms systematically in definite directions and not accidentally in many directions; determinate variation.

**osmosis** Diffusion of a solvent through a semi-permeable membrane into a more concentrated solution, tending to equalize the concentrations on both sides of the membrane.

**oxidation** The addition of oxygen to a compound. More generally, any reaction involving the loss of **electrons** from an **atom**. It is always accompanied by reduction.

**ozone layer** The region of the Earth's atmosphere, between about 20 and 40km (12.5 and 25mi) above the surface, where ozone makes up a greater proportion of the air than at any other height. This layer exerts a vital influence by absorbing much of the **ultraviolet radiation** in sunlight and preventing it from reaching the Earth's surface where it has considerable biological effect.

**parasite** An organism which lives in or on another organism and derives subsistence from it without rendering it any service in return.

**parsec** The unit of length used for distances beyond the solar system, approximately equal to 3.26 **light-years**.

**parthenogenesis** The development of a new individual from a single, unfertilized reproductive cell, often an egg.

**pasteurization** Reduction of the number of micro-organisms in milk by maintaining it in a holder at a temperature of from 62.8° to 65.5°C for 30 minutes.

**pathogen** An organism, eg **parasite**, bacterium or **virus**, which causes disease.

**perennial** A plant that lives for more than two years.

**periodic table** A table displaying classification of chemical **elements** into periods (corresponding to the filling of successive shells of electrons in the atom) and groups (corresponding to the number of outer electrons present).

**pH value** A number used to express degrees of acidity or alkalinity in solutions, where a pH above 7 indicates alkalinity and below 7 indicates acidity. ► **acid** and **alkali**.

**phage** ► **bacteriophage**

**phosphorescence** (1) In biology, the production of light, usually (in animals) with little production of heat, as in glow-worms. (2) ► **luminescence.**

**photochemical reaction** The chemical reaction brought about by light or **ultraviolet radiation**.

**photoelectric effect** Any phenomenon resulting from the absorption of **photon** energy by **electrons**, leading to their release from a surface, when the photon energy exceeds that binding the electron to the surface, or otherwise allowing conduction when the photon energy exceeds the amount of energy binding an electron to the **atom**.

**photon** A unit of radiation in the **quantum theory** of light in which light is required to have particle character. May also be regarded as a unit of energy. Photons travel at the speed of light.

**photosensitive** Sensitive to the action of visible or invisible radiation.

**photosynthesis** The use of energy from light to drive chemical reactions, most notably the building-up of complex compounds by the **chlorophyll** apparatus of plants.

**plankton** Animals and plants floating in the waters of seas, rivers, ponds and lakes, as distinct from animals which are attached to, or crawl upon, the bottom; especially minute organisms and forms, possessing weak powers of motion.

**plasma** (1) In physics, a gaseous discharge containing **ions** in which there is no resultant charge, the number of positive and negative ions being equal, in addition to unionized **molecules** or **atoms**. (2) In biology, the bounding membrane of **cells** which controls the entry of molecules and the interaction of cells with their environment.

**plate tectonics** The interpretation of the Earth's structures and processes (including midocean ridges, mountain building, earthquake zones and volcanic belts) in terms of the movements of large plates of the Earth's crust acting as rigid slabs floating on the layer beneath.

**polarization** (1) In chemistry, the separation of the positive and negative charges of a molecule by an external agent. (2) In physics, non-random orientation of electric and magnetic fields of an **electromagnetic wave**, ie the restriction of the vibrations of light in certain planes.

**Polaroid®** The trademark for a range of photographic and optical products, including a transparent light-polarizing plastic sheet and methods of instant photography in black-and-white and colour. ► **polarization**.

**polymer** A plastic material built up from a series of smaller units. The molecular size of the polymer helps to determine the mechanical properties of the plastic material and ranges from a few hundred of the basic units to perhaps hundreds of thousands.

**polymorphism** (1) The presence in a population of two or more forms of a particular gene. (2) The occurrence of different structural forms at different stages of the life-cycle of the individual.

**positron** A particle of the same mass as and opposite charge to the (negative) **electron**. The **antiparticle** to the electron.

**precession of the equinoxes** The variation in the direction of the Earth's axis of rotation caused mainly by the attraction of the Sun and Moon on the equatorial bulge of the Earth, the change describing a full cone with a period of around 25 800 years.

**primary colours** Colours from which all other colours can be derived; red, yellow and blue.

**protein** Any member of a group of complex substances containing nitrogen that play an important part in the bodies of plants and animals.

**proton** The **nucleus** of the hydrogen **atom**, of positive charge. With **neutrons**, protons form the nuclei of all atoms.

**quantum mechanics** A branch of mechanics based on the **quantum theory**, used in predicting the behaviour of elementary particles.

**quantum theory** The theory of emission and absorption of energy not in continuous measures but in finite steps, applied to elementary particles.

**quark** A fundamental subatomic particle, currently seen as any of six types: bottom, top, up, down, charmed and strange. Although not yet observed directly, these are suggested to be the units out of which all other subatomic particles are formed.

**quasar** A distant, compact object far beyond our **Galaxy** which looks star-like on a photograph but appears to be much more distant than a star that we would be able to observe. The word is a contraction of quasi-stellar object. Thought to be the most luminous objects in the universe, their mechanisms are possibly related to **black holes**.

**radar** In general, a system using pulsed **radio waves** to measure the distance and direction of a target (from *RAdio Detection And Ranging*).

**radiation** The dissemination of energy from a source. The term is applied to **electromagnetic waves** and to emitted particles (**protons, neutrons**, etc).

**radio galaxy** A **galaxy** emitting a particularly high amount of **radio waves**.

**radio waves Electromagnetic waves** of frequency suitable for radio transmission, of wavelength greater than around 10cm, ie of longer wavelength than **microwaves**.

**radioactivity** Spontaneous disintegration of certain natural heavy **elements** (eg radium, actinium, uranium, thorium). The ultimate end-product of radioactive disintegration is an **isotope** of lead.

**rational number** A number which can be expressed as the ratio of two integers, eg $\frac{3}{4}$.

**recessive** Of a **gene**, showing its effect only in individuals that received it from both parents. Also describes an inheritable feature due to a recessive gene.

**recombination** Reassortment of genes or inheritable features in combinations different from what they were in the parents.

**red giant** A large, cool, luminous star with its hydrogen exhausted by **nuclear reaction** to helium.

**redshift** Generally, the decrease in frequency of light observed when a light source moves away from an observer due to the **Doppler effect**. Often referred to in the sense of redshifts observed in light from distant galaxies, indicating the expansion of the universe.

**reduction** Any process in which an electron is added to an **atom** or an **ion**. Always occurs accompanied by **oxidation**.

**refraction** Deflection of waves (light, sound, etc) which occurs when passing from one medium to another of different density.

**relative atomic mass** The mass of atoms of an element given on the scale where 1 unit is equal to $1.660 \times 10^{-27}$ kg. Devised by assigning the value 12 to a specific **isotope** of carbon.

**relativity** Einstein's Special Theory of Relativity (1905) postulates that all motion is relative and that the velocity of light is the same for all observers, and predicts the effects of these assumptions, including variations in the size and mass of objects and in the rate of passage of time, depending on the speed of the observer. His General Theory of Relativity (1916) predicts the variations involved due to acceleration and gravitation.

**remote sensing** A method in which remote detectors are used to collect data for transmission to a central computer; observation and collection of scientific data without direct contact, especially observation of the Earth's surface from the air or from space using **electromagnetic waves**.

**resonance** If a vibrating system is set into forced vibrations by a periodic driving force and the applied frequency is at or near the natural vibration frequency of the system, then resonance occurs, producing vibrations of maximum velocity amplitude.

**respiration** Breathing; the taking in of oxygen and giving out of carbon dioxide, with associated physiological processes.

**Richter scale** A scale of measurement from 1 to 10, used to indicate the magnitude of an earthquake.

**RNA** or **ribonucleic acid** Nucleic acid containing ribose, present in the living cells, where it plays an important part in the development of **proteins**. It can hold genetic information as in **viruses**, but is also the primary agent for transferring information from the **genome** to the protein synthetic machinery of the cell.

**saprophyte** A plant that feeds on dead organic matter.

**saturated compounds** Compounds to which no hydrogen atoms or their equivalent can be added, ie which contain neither a double nor a triple bond.

**sedimentary rocks** All those rocks which result from the wastage of pre-existing rocks. They include the fragments of rocks deposited as sheets of sediment on the floors of seas, lakes and rivers and on land, and also deposits formed of the hard parts of organisms. **Igneous** and **metamorphic** rocks are excluded.

**semiconductor** Said of a material (an **element** or a compound) having higher resistance to the flow of electricity than a **conductor**, but lower resistance than an insulator.

**sex determination** In many organisms (including vertebrates) sex is determined by the possession of a particular combination of **chromosomes**. In mammals, the female's chromosomes are designated XX and the male's are known as XY.

**SI** The system of coherent metric units (Système International d'Unités) proposed for international acceptance in 1960.

**sidereal time** Time measured by considering the rotation of the Earth relative to the distant stars (rather than the Sun, which is the basis of civil time).

**silicon chip ► chip**

**sine wave** A mathematical function which describes a waveform of a single frequency, indefinitely repeated in time. Its displacement can be expressed as the sine (or cosine) of a linear function of time or distance, or both.

**software package** A fully documented computer program, or set of programs, designed to perform a particular task.

**solar system** The term designating the Sun and the attendant bodies moving about it under gravitational attraction; comprises nine major planets, and a vast number of **asteroids**, **comets** and **meteors**.

**solstice** One of the two instants in the year when the Sun reaches its greatest excursion north or south of the equator, or the point reached then. The summer solstice occurs around 21 June, when the Sun reaches the tropic of Cancer, and the winter solstice occurs around 21 December, when the Sun reaches the tropic of Capricorn.

**sonar ► acoustic imaging**

**sonic boom** A noise phenomenon due to the shock waves projected from an aircraft travelling at **supersonic** speed. The waves create pressures which may be of sufficient intensity to cause damage to buildings, etc.

**species** A group of individuals that actually or potentially interbreed with each other but not with other such groups and show continuous **variation** within the group but which is distinct from other such groups.

**spore** A single-cell asexual reproductive body, sometimes extended to other reproductive bodies.

**spring tides** High tides occurring when the Sun and Moon are acting together to produce a maximum tide.

**stalactite** A deposit of calcium carbonate which hangs icicle-like from the roofs of limestone caverns.

**stalagmite** An upward-growing conical formation of calcium carbonate, precipitated from dripping solutions on the floors and walls of limestone caverns.

**star** A sphere of matter held together entirely by its own gravitational field and generating energy by means of **nuclear fusion** reactions in its deep interior.

**stellar evolution** The sequence of events and changes covering the entire life-cycle of a star.

**subsonic** Said of an object or flow which moves with a speed less than that of sound. ► **Mach number**, **supersonic.**

**superconductivity** The property of some pure metals and metallic alloys at very low temperature of having negligible resistance to the flow of an electric current. Each material has its own critical temperature above which it is a normal conductor. When a current is established, it persists almost indefinitely.

**supergiant star** A star of very high luminosity, enormous size and low density.

**supernova** A very bright **nova** resulting from an explosion which blows a star's material into space, leaving an expanding cloud of gas and sometimes a central compact object.

**supersonic** Faster than the speed of sound in that medium. Erroneously used for ultrasonic. ► **Mach number**, **subsonic**, **ultrasonic.**

**symbiosis** A mutually beneficial partnership between organisms of different kinds, especially such an association where one lives within the other.

**Système International d'Unités** ► **SI**

**thermonuclear energy** Energy released by a nuclear **fusion** reaction that occurs because of the high thermal energy of the interacting particles.

**tornado** An intensely destructive, advancing whirlwind formed from strongly ascending air current; also, in West Africa, the squall following thunderstorms between the wet and dry seasons.

**transition metal** One of the group which have an incomplete inner electron shell. Also known as transition element. ► **atom**

**transuranic elements** Elements of atomic number greater than that of uranium, ie with 93 or more protons in the atomic nuclei. These do not occur naturally but more than 12 have been artificially produced, including neptunium, plutonium, curium and lawrencium.

**tsunami** A series of waves produced in the ocean by violent movement of the sea floor, most commonly submarine faulting accompanied by an earthquake. Its amplitude in mid-ocean is very small; as it approaches land, the amplitude builds up and all the energy of the original disturbance is concentrated with devastating results. Erroneously called a tidal wave.

**turbulence** Particle motion which at any point varies rapidly in magnitude and direction.

**twins** (1) Identical twins arise from the same fertilized egg which has subsequently divided into two, each half developing into a separate individual. (2) In mammals, non-identical twins are produced from separate eggs fertilized at the same time.

**typhoon** A tropical revolving storm in the China Sea and western North Pacific.

**ultrasonic** Sound frequencies above the upper limit of the normal range of hearing, at or about 20 000 cycles per sec, or 20 kilohertz. Ultrasonics is the general term for the study and application of ultrasonic sound and vibrations.

**ultrasound** **Ultrasonic** sound used by some animals (eg bats, dolphins) for localization and communication, and in a variety of industrial applications.

**ultraviolet radiation** **Electromagnetic waves** in a wavelength range from 0.00004 to 0.000001cm approximately, ie between the visible and X-ray regions of the spectrum.

**uncertainty principle** The principle that there is a fundamental limit to the precision with which a position co-ordinate of a particle and its momentum in that direction can be simultaneously known. Also, there is a fundamental limit to the knowledge of the energy of a particle when it is measured for a finite time.

**unified field theory** ► **field theory**

**valency** A measure of the combining power of an **atom**, **molecule** or **ion**; the valency of an ion is equal to its charge.

**Van Allen radiation belts** Two belts encircling the Earth within which electrically charged particles from the Sun are trapped.

**variation** In biology, the differences between the offspring of a single mating; the differences between the individuals of a race, subspecies, or species; the differences between analogous groups of higher rank.

**vector** In mathematics, a vector or vector quantity is one which has magnitude and direction, eg force or velocity.

**very high frequencies** Those between 30 000 000 and 300 000 000 cycles per sec or between 30 and 300 megahertz. Abbreviated as VHF.

**virtual reality** Computer simulation which takes into account the motion of an observer to produce the illusion of reality in a computer-created situation, using complex graphics and sound reproduction.

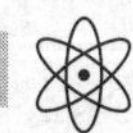



**virus** A **pathogen**, usually protein-coated particles of **DNA** or **RNA**, capable of increasing rapidly inside a living cell.

**vitamins** **Organic** substances required in relatively small amounts in the diet for the proper functioning of the organism, comprising vitamins A, C, D, E, K and the vitamins of the B complex.

**white dwarf** A small dim star in the final stages of its evolution. The masses of known white dwarfs do not exceed 1.4 times that of the Sun, with a typical diameter about the same as that of the Earth.

**X-chromosome ► sex determination**

**X-rays** **Electromagnetic waves** in a wavelength range from 0.0000000001 to 0.000001cm approximately, ie between the ultraviolet and gamma-ray regions of the spectrum.

**Y-chromosome ► sex determination**

**zenith** In astronomy, the point on the celestial sphere vertically above the observer's head.

**zodiac** A name, of Greek origin, given to the belt of stars, about 18° wide, through which the Sun appears to pass through the year. The zodiac lies approximately in the plane of the motions of the Sun, Moon and planets.

## Fields of scientific study

**acoustics** The science of mechanical waves including production and propagation properties.

**actinobiology** The study of the effects of radiation upon living organisms.

**aerodynamics** That part of the mechanics of fluids that deals with the dynamics of gases, particularly the study of forces acting upon bodies in motion in air.

**aerology** The study of the free atmosphere.

**aeronautics** All activities concerned with aerial locomotion.

**aerothermodynamics** The branch of thermodynamics relating to the heating effects associated with the dynamics of a gas; in particular the physical effects produced in the air flowing over a vehicle during launch and re-entry.

**aetiology** or **etiology** The medical study of the causation of disease.

**algology** The study of algae.

**angiology** The study or scientific account of the anatomy of blood and lymph vascular systems.

**astronautics** The science of space flight.

**astronomy** The study of all classes of celestial object and the universe as a whole.

**astrophysics** That branch of astronomy which applies the laws of physics to the study of interstellar matter and the stars, their constitution, evolution, luminosity, etc.

**autecology** The study of the ecology of any individual species. ► **synecology.**

**autonomics** Study of self-regulating systems for process control, optimizing performance.

**autoradiography** Originally used to show the distribution of radioactive molecules in cells and tissues after injecting the organism with, or growing the cells in a medium containing, a radioactive precursor. It is now widely used to show the distribution of radio-labelled molecules separated on the basis of size, charge, etc. Photographic film or emulsion is exposed after applying it to the section, fixed cell or separating medium and the distribution of developed grains viewed directly or under the microscope. Similar procedures exist for fluorescent and other labels.

**bacteriology** The scientific study of bacteria.

**ballistics** The study of the dynamics of the path taken by an object moving under the influence of a gravitational field.

**balneology** The scientific study of baths and bathing, and of their application to disease.

**bioclimatology** The study of the effects of climate on living organisms.

**biology** The study of living organisms and systems; the life sciences collectively, including botany, anatomy, physiology, zoology, etc.

**biometeorology** The study of the effects of atmospheric conditions on living things.

**biophysics** The physics of vital processes; the study of biological phenomena in terms of physical principles.

**biosystematics** The study of relationships with reference to the laws of classification of organisms; taxonomy.

**biotechnology** The use of organisms or their components in industrial or commercial processes, which can be aided by the techniques of genetic manipulation in developing eg novel plants for agriculture or industry.

**botany** The study of living organisms and systems.

**bronchography** The radiological examination of the trachea, bronchi, or the bronchial tree after the introduction of a contrast medium.

**cardiology** That part of medical science concerned with the function and diseases of the heart.

**chemistry** The study of the composition of substances and the changes that they undergo.

**chromatics** The science of colours as affected by phenomena determined by their differing wavelengths.

**cladistics** A method of classifying organisms into groups (taxa) based on 'recency of common descent' as judged by the possession of shared derived (ie not primitive) characteristics.

**climatology** The study of climate and its causes.

**cosmology** The study of the universe on the largest scales of length and time, particularly the propounding of theories concerning its origin, nature, structure and evolution. A cosmology is any model said to represent the observed universe. Western cosmology is entirely scientific in its approach, and has produced two famous models, the Big Bang and steady-state cosmology.

**cryogenics** The study of materials at very low temperatures.

**crystallography** The study of internal arrangements (ionic and molecular) and external forms of crystal species, and their classification into types.

**cybernetics** The study of control and communications in complex electronic systems and in animals, especially humans.

**cytogenetics** The study of the chromosomal complement of cells, and of chromosomal abnormalities and their inheritance.

**cytology** The study of the structure and functions of cells.

**dendrochronology** The science of reconstructing past climates from the information stored in tree trunks as annual radial increments of growth.

**dermatology** That branch of medical science which deals with the skin and its diseases.

**dynamics** That branch of applied mathematics which studies the way in which force produces motion.

**ecology** The scientific study of the interrelations between living organisms and their environment, emphasizing both relations between species and within species; the scientific study of the distribution and abundance of living organisms (ie exactly where they occur and precisely how many there are).

**econometrics** The application of statistical methods to economic phenomena.

**ecophysiology** The branch of physiology concerned with how organisms are adapted to their natural environment.

**electrocardiography** The study of electric currents produced in cardiac muscular activity.

**electrokinetics** The science of electric charges in motion, without reference to the accompanying magnetic field.

**electromagnetics** or **electromagnetism** The science of the properties of, and relationships between, magnetism and electric currents.

**electromyography** The study of electric currents set up in muscle fibres by bodily movement.

**electronics** The study and application of the movement of electrons.

**electrophysiology** The study of electrical phenomena associated with living organisms, particularly nervous conduction.

**electrostatics** That section of the science of electricity which deals with the phenomenon of electric charges substantially at rest.

**embryology** The study of the formation and development of embryos.

**endocrinology** The study of the internal secretory glands.

**energetics** The abstract study of the energy relations of physical and chemical changes. ► **thermodynamics**.

**entomology** The branch of zoology which deals with the study of insects.

**epidemiology** The study of disease in the population, defining its incidence and prevalence, examining the role of external influences such as infection, diet or toxic substances, and examining appropriate preventive or curative measures.

**epistemics** The scientific study of the perceptual, intellectual and linguistic processes by which knowledge and understanding are acquired and communicated.

**ergonomics** The application of various human studies to the area of work and leisure; includes anatomy, physiology and psychology.

**ethology** An approach to the study of animal behaviour in which attempts to explain behaviour combine questions about its immediate causation, development, function and evolution.

**etiology** ► **aetiology**

**eugenics** The study of the means whereby the characteristics of human populations might be improved by the application of genetics.

**exobiology** The study of (possible) living systems which probably must exist elsewhere in the universe.

**fluidics** The science of liquid flow in tubes etc which strongly simulates electron flow in conductors and conducting plasma. The interaction of streams of fluid can be used for the control of instruments or industrial processes without the use of moving parts.

**fractography** The microscopic study of fractures in metal surfaces.

**genecology** The branch of ecology which seeks genetic explanations of the patterns of distribution of plants and animals in time and space.

**genetics** The study of heredity; of how differences between individuals are passed on from one generation to the next; and of how the information in the genes is used in the development and functioning of the adult organism.

**geochronology** The study of time with respect to the history of the Earth, primarily through the use of absolute and relative age-dating methods.

**geology** The study of the planet Earth. It embraces mineralogy, petrology, geophysics, geochemistry, physical geology, palaeontology and stratigraphy. It increasingly involves the use of the chemical, physical, mathematical and biological sciences.

**geophysics** The study of physical properties of the Earth; it makes use of the data available in Earth measurement, seismology, meteorology and oceanography, as well as that relating to atmospheric electricity, terrestrial magnetism and tidal phenomena.

**gerontology** The scientific study of the processes of ageing.

**gynaecology** or **gynecology** That branch of medical science which deals with the functions and diseases peculiar to women's reproductive organs.

**histology** The study of the minute structure of tissues in organisms.

**horology** The science of time measurement, or of the construction of timepieces.

**hydraulics** The science relating to the flow of fluids.

**hydrodynamics** That branch of dynamics which studies the motion produced in fluids by applied forces.

**hydrogeology** The study of the geological aspects of the Earth's water.

**hydrography** The study, determination and publication of the conditions of seas, rivers and lakes, which involves surveying and charting of coasts, rivers, estuaries and harbours, and supplying particulars of depth, bottom, tides, currents, etc.

**hydrology** The study of water, including rain, snow and water on the Earth's surface, with reference to its properties, distribution, utilization, etc.

**hydroponics** The technique of growing plants without soil. The roots can be in either a nutrient solution or in an inert medium percolated by such a solution.

**hydrostatics** The branch of statics which studies the forces arising from the presence of fluids.

**immunology** The study of the biological responses of a living organism to its invasion by living bacteria, viruses or parasites, and its defence against these; also the study of the body's reaction to foreign substances.

**kinematics** That branch of applied mathematics which studies the way in which velocities and accelerations of various parts of a moving system are related.

**kinetics** The study of the rates at which chemical reactions and biological processes proceed.

**laryngology** That branch of medical science which treats diseases of the larynx and adjacent parts of the upper respiratory tract.

**limnology** The study of lakes.

**lithology** The systematic description of rocks, more especially sedimentary rocks. ► **petrology**.

**magnetohydrodynamics** The study of the motions of an electrically conducting fluid in the presence of a magnetic field. The motion of the fluid gives rise to induced electric currents which interact with the magnetic field which in turn modifies the motion. The phenomenon has applications both to magnetic fields in space and to the possibility of generating electricity.

**magnetostatics** The study of steady-state magnetic fields.

**malacology** The study of molluscs.

**mathematics** The study of the logical consequences of sets of axioms. Pure mathematics, roughly speaking, comprises those branches studied for their own sake or their relation to other branches. The most important of these are algebra, analysis and topology. The term applied mathematics is usually restricted to applications in physics. Applications in other fields, eg economics, mainly statistical, are sometimes referred to as applicable mathematics.

**mechanics** The study of forces on bodies and of the motions they produce. ► **dynamics**, **kinematics**, **statics**.

**metallography** The study of metals and their alloys with the aid of various procedures, eg microscopy, X-ray diffraction, etc.

**meteorology** The study of the Earth's atmosphere in its relation to weather and climate.

**metrology** The science of measuring.

**micropalaeontology** The study of microfossils.

**mineralogy** The study of the chemical composition, physical properties and occurrence of minerals.

**morphology** The study of the structure and forms of organisms, as opposed to the study of their functions.

**mycology** The study of fungi.

**myology** The study of muscles.

**neuroendocrinology** The study of interactions between the nervous system and endocrine organs, particularly pituitary gland and hypothalamic region of the brain.

**neurology** The study of the nervous system.

**neuropathology** The study of pathology of diseases of the nervous system.

**nosology** The systematic classification of diseases; the branch of medical science which deals with this.

**nucleonics** The science and technology of nuclear studies.

**obstetrics** That branch of medical science which deals with the problems and management of pregnancy and labour.

**oceanography** The study of the oceans, including geological, chemical, physical and biological processes.

**odontology** The study of the physiology, anatomy, pathology, etc of the teeth.

**oncology** That part of medical science dealing with new growths (tumours) of body tissue.

**oölogy** The study of ova.

**ophthalmology** The study of the eye and its diseases.

**optics** The study of light. Physical optics deals with the nature of light and its wave properties; geometrical optics ignores the wave nature of light and treats problems of reflection and refraction from the ray aspect.

**organography** A descriptive study of the external form of plants, with relation to function.

**ornithology** The study of birds.

**orthopaedics** or **orthopedics** That branch of surgery which deals with deformities arising from injury or disease of bones or of joints.

**osteology** The study of bones.

**otology** That part of surgical science dealing with the organ of hearing and its diseases.

**otorhinolaryngology** That part of surgical science which deals with diseases of the ear, nose and throat.

**palaeoclimatology** The study of climatic conditions in the geological record, using evidence from fossils, sediments and their structures, geophysics and geochemistry.

**palaeoecology** The study of fossil organisms in terms of their mode of life, their interrelationships, their environment, their manner of death and their eventual burial.

**palaeogeography** The study of the relative positions of land and water at particular periods in the geological past.

**palaeontology** The study of fossil animals and plants.

**palaeopathology** The study of disease of previous eras from examination of bodily remains or evidence from ancient writings.

**palaeozoology** The study of fossil animals. ► **palaeontology**.

**palynology** The study of fossil spores and pollen. They are very resistant to destruction and in many sedimentary rocks are the only fossils that can be used to determine the relationships of strata.

**parapsychology** The study of certain alleged phenomena, the paranormal, that are beyond the scope of ordinary psychology, eg ESP, psychokinesis, etc.

**parasitology** The study of parasites and their habits (usually confined to animal parasites).

**pathology** That part of medical science which deals with the causes and nature of disease, and with the bodily changes brought about by disease.

**pedology** The study of soil.

**petrology** That study of rocks which includes consideration of their mode of origin, present conditions, chemical and mineral composition, their alteration and decay.

**pharmacodynamics** The science of the action of drugs; pharmacology.

**pharmacology** The scientific study of the action of chemical substances on living systems.

**phenology** The study of plant development in relation to the seasons.

**phenomenology** In philosophy, the study of the psychic awareness that accompanies experience and that is the source of all meaning for the individual. In psychiatry, it refers to the description and classification of an individual's mental activity, including subjective experience and perceptions, mental performance (eg memory) and the somatic accompaniments of mental events (eg heart rate).

**phonetics** Study of speech and vocal acoustics. Used to describe the system of symbols which uniquely represent the spoken word of any language in writing, enabling the reader to pronounce words accurately in spite of spelling irregularities.

**photobiology** The study of light as it affects living organisms.

**phycology** The study of algae.

**physics** The study of electrical, luminescent, mechanical, magnetic, radioactive and thermal phenomena with respect to changes in energy states without change of chemical composition.

**physiography** The science of the surface of the Earth and the inter-relations of air, water and land.

**phytology** ► **botany**

**phytopathology** Plant pathology. The study of plant diseases, especially of plants in relation to their parasites.

**phytosociology** The study of the association of plant species.

**planetology** The study of the composition, origin and distribution of matter in the planets of the solar system.

**planigraphy** ► **tomography**

**prosthetics** That branch of surgical science involved in supplying artificial parts to the body.

**proxemics** The study of the spatial features of human social interaction, eg personal space.

**psychodynamics** A theory of the workings of the mind.

**psychometrics** The application of mathematical and statistical concepts to psychological data, particularly in the areas of mental testing and experimental data.

**psychopathology** The study of psychological disorders.

**psychopharmacology** The study and use of drugs that influence behaviour, emotions, perception and thought, by acting on the central nervous system.

**psychophysics** The branch of psychology that studies the relationship between characteristics of physical stimuli and the psychological experiences they produce.

**radiobiology** The branch of science involving study of the effect of radiation and radioactive materials on living matter.

**radiology** or **röntgenology** The science and application of X-rays, gamma-rays and other penetrating ionizing or non-ionizing radiations.

**rheology** The science of the flow of matter. The critical study of elasticity, viscosity and plasticity.

**robotics** The study of the design and use of robots, particularly for their use in manufacturing and related processes.

**röntgenology** ► **radiology**

**seismology** The study of earthquakes, particularly their shock waves. Studies of the speed and refraction of seismic waves enable the deeper structure of the Earth to be investigated.

**semeiology** The branch of medical science which is concerned with the symptoms of disease.

**semiotics** The study of communication.

**serology** The study of serums.

**sonics** A general term for the study of mechanical vibrations in matter.

**spelaeology** or **speleology** The study of the fauna and flora of caves.

**statics** That branch of applied mathematics which studies the way in which forces combine with each other usually so as to produce equilibrium. Until the early part of the 20th century the term also embraced the study of gravitational attractions, but this is now normally regarded as a separate subject.

**statistics** The branch of mathematics which deals with the collection and analysis of numerical data.

**stratigraphy** The definition and description of the stratified rocks of the Earth's crust, their relationships and structure, their arrangement into chronological groups, their mineral mass and the conditions of their formation, and their fossil contents.

**superaerodynamics** Aerodynamics at very low air densities occurring above 30 480m/100 000ft, ie for spacecraft on ascending and re-entry trajectories.

**symptomatology** The study of symptoms; a discourse or treatise on symptoms; the branch of medical science concerning symptoms of disease.

**synecology** The study of relationships between communities and their environment. ► **autecology.**

**systematics** The branch of biology which deals with classification and nomenclature.

**tectonics** The study of the major structural features of the Earth's crust.

**teleology** The interpretation of animal or plant structures in terms of purpose and utility.

**teratology** The study of monstrosities, as an aid to the understanding of normal development.

**thermionics** The study of the processes involved in the emission of electrons from hot bodies.

**thermodynamics** The study of heat and heat-related phenomena.

**topology** The study of those properties of shapes and space that are independent of distance.

**toxicology** The branch of medical science dealing with the nature and effects of poisons.

**urodynamics** The study of urine flow.

**urology** That part of medical science which deals with diseases and abnormalities of the urinary tract and their treatment.

**virology** The study of viruses.

**zoogeography** The study of animal distribution.

**zoology** The study of all aspects of animals.

**zootaxy** The science of the classification of animals.

## Periodic table

The elements, listed with their symbols and atomic numbers, lie horizontally in order of their atomic numbers. Those with chemically similar properties fall under one another in the columns. Elements with atomic numbers of 93 and over are man-made.

| | | | | | | | | | | | | | | | | | |
|---|---|---|---|---|---|---|---|---|---|---|---|---|---|---|---|---|---|
| 1<br>Hydrogen<br>H | | | | | | | | | | | | | | | | | 2<br>Helium<br>He |
| 3<br>Lithium<br>Li | 4<br>Beryllium<br>Be | | | | | | | | | | | 5<br>Boron<br>B | 6<br>Carbon<br>C | 7<br>Nitrogen<br>N | 8<br>Oxygen<br>O | 9<br>Fluorine<br>F | 10<br>Neon<br>Ne |
| 11<br>Sodium<br>Na | 12<br>Magnesium<br>Mg | | | | | | | | | | | 13<br>Aluminium<br>Al | 14<br>Silicon<br>Si | 15<br>Phosphorus<br>P | 16<br>Sulphur<br>S | 17<br>Chlorine<br>Cl | 18<br>Argon<br>Ar |
| 19<br>Potassium<br>K | 20<br>Calcium<br>Ca | 21<br>Scandium<br>Sc | 22<br>Titanium<br>Ti | 23<br>Vanadium<br>V | 24<br>Chromium<br>Cr | 25<br>Manganese<br>Mn | 26<br>Iron<br>Fe | 27<br>Cobalt<br>Co | 28<br>Nickel<br>Ni | 29<br>Copper<br>Cu | 30<br>Zinc<br>Zn | 31<br>Gallium<br>Ga | 32<br>Germanium<br>Ge | 33<br>Arsenic<br>As | 34<br>Selenium<br>Se | 35<br>Bromine<br>Br | 36<br>Krypton<br>Kr |
| 37<br>Rubidium<br>Rb | 38<br>Strontium<br>Sr | 39<br>Yttrium<br>Y | 40<br>Zirconium<br>Zr | 41<br>Niobium<br>Nb | 42<br>Molybdenum<br>Mo | 43<br>Technetium<br>Tc | 44<br>Ruthenium<br>Ru | 45<br>Rhodium<br>Rh | 46<br>Palladium<br>Pd | 47<br>Silver<br>Ag | 48<br>Cadmium<br>Cd | 49<br>Indium<br>In | 50<br>Tin<br>Sn | 51<br>Antimony<br>Sb | 52<br>Tellurium<br>Te | 53<br>Iodine<br>I | 54<br>Xenon<br>Xe |
| 55<br>Caesium<br>Cs | 56<br>Barium<br>Ba | 57-71<br>Lanthanide<br>Series | 72<br>Hafnium<br>Hf | 73<br>Tantalum<br>Ta | 74<br>Wolfram<br>W | 75<br>Rhenium<br>Re | 76<br>Osmium<br>Os | 77<br>Iridium<br>Ir | 78<br>Platinum<br>Pt | 79<br>Gold<br>Au | 80<br>Mercury<br>Hg | 81<br>Thallium<br>Tl | 82<br>Lead<br>Pb | 83<br>Bismuth<br>Bi | 84<br>Polonium<br>Po | 85<br>Astatine<br>At | 86<br>Radon<br>Rn |
| 87<br>Francium<br>Fr | 88<br>Radium<br>Ra | 89–103<br>Actinide<br>Series | 104<br>Rutherfordium | | | | | | | | | | | | | | |

| | | | | | | | | | | | | | |
|---|---|---|---|---|---|---|---|---|---|---|---|---|---|
| 57<br>Lanthanum<br>La | 58<br>Cerium<br>Ce | 59<br>Praseodymium<br>Pr | 60<br>Neodymium<br>Nd | 61<br>Prometheum<br>Pm | 62<br>Samarium<br>Sm | 63<br>Europium<br>Eu | 64<br>Gadolinium<br>Gd | 65<br>Terbium<br>Tb | 66<br>Dysprosium<br>Dy | 67<br>Holmium<br>Ho | 68<br>Erbium<br>Er | 69<br>Thulium<br>Tm | 70<br>Ytterbium<br>Yb | 71<br>Lutecium<br>Lu |
| 89<br>Actinium<br>Ac | 90<br>Thorium<br>Th | 91<br>Protactinium<br>Pa | 92<br>Uranium<br>U | 93<br>Neptunium<br>Np | 94<br>Plutonium<br>Pu | 95<br>Americium<br>Am | 96<br>Curium<br>Cm | 97<br>Berkelium<br>Bk | 98<br>Californium<br>Cf | 99<br>Einsteinium<br>Es | 100<br>Fermium<br>Fm | 101<br>Mendelevium<br>Md | 102<br>Nobelium<br>No | 103<br>Lawrencium<br>Lr |

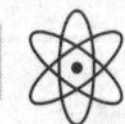



## Table of elements

Atomic weights are taken from the 1983 list of the International Union of Pure and Applied Chemistry. For radioactive elements, the mass number of the most stable isotope is given in square brackets.

| Symbol | Element | Derived from | Atomic No. | Atomic Weight | Discovered by | Date |
|---|---|---|---|---|---|---|
| Ac | actinium | Greek, *aktis* = ray | 89 | [227] | André-Louis Debierne (1874–1949) | 1899 |
| Ag | silver | Anglo-Saxon, *seolfor* | 47 | 107.8682 | Prehistoric | — |
| Al | aluminium | Latin, *alumen* = alum | 13 | 26.98154 | Friedrich Wöhler (1800–82) | 1828 |
| Am | americium | America | 95 | [243] | Glenn Theodore Seaborg (1912–99), Ralph James and others | 1944 |
| Ar | argon | Greek, *argos* = inactive | 18 | 39.948 | John Rayleigh (1842–1919) and William Ramsay (1852–1916) | 1894 |
| As | arsenic | Latin, *arsenicum* | 33 | 74.9216 | Prehistoric | — |
| At | astatine | Greek, *astatos* = unstable | 85 | [210] | Emilio Segrè (1905–89), Dale Corson and Mackenzie | 1940 |
| Au | gold | Anglo-Saxon, *gold* | 79 | 196.9665 | Prehistoric | — |
| B | boron | Persian, *brah* | 5 | 10.811 | Humphry Davy (1778–1829) | 1808 |
| Ba | barium | Greek, *barys* = heavy | 56 | 137.33 | Humphry Davy (1778–1829) | 1808 |
| Be | beryllium | Greek, *beryllion* = beryl | 4 | 9.01218 | Friedrich Wöhler (1800–82) | 1828 |
| Bi | bismuth | German (origin unknown) | 83 | 208.9804 | Basil Valentine | 1450 |
| Bk | berkelium | Berkeley, California | 97 | [247] | Glenn Theodore Seaborg (1912–99) and others | 1950 |
| Br | bromine | Greek, *bromos* = stench | 35 | 79.904 | Antoine Jérôme Balard (1802–76) | 1826 |
| C | carbon | Latin, *carbo* = charcoal | 6 | 12.011 | Prehistoric | — |
| Ca | calcium | Latin, *calx* = lime | 20 | 40.078 | Humphry Davy (1778–1829) | 1808 |
| Cd | cadmium | Greek, *kadmeia* = calamine | 48 | 112.41 | Friedrich Stromeyer (1776–1848) | 1817 |
| Ce | cerium | Planet Ceres | 58 | 140.12 | Jöns Jacob Berzelius (1779–1848) | 1803 |
| Cf | californium | California | 98 | [251] | Glenn Theodore Seaborg (1912–99) and others | 1950 |
| Cl | chlorine | Greek, *chloros* = green | 17 | 35.453 | Carl Wilhelm Scheele (1742–86) | 1774 |
| Cm | curium | Pierre and Marie Curie[1] | 96 | [249] | Glenn Theodore Seaborg (1912–99), Ralph James and others | 1944 |
| Co | cobalt | German, *Kobold* = goblin | 27 | 58.9332 | Georg Brandt (1694–1768) | 1739 |
| Cr | chromium | Greek, *chroma* = colour | 24 | 51.9961 | Nicolas-Louis Vauquelin (1763–1829) | 1797 |
| Cs | cesium/caesium | Latin, *caesium* = bluish-grey | 55 | 132.9054 | Robert Wilhelm Bunsen (1811–99) | 1860 |
| Cu | copper | Cyprus | 29 | 63.546 | Prehistoric | — |
| Dy | dysprosium | Greek, *dysprositos* | 66 | 162.50 | Paul Émile Lecoq de Boisbaudran (1838–1912) | 1886 |
| Er | erbium | Ytterby, a Swedish town | 68 | 167.26 | Carl Gustaf Mosander (1797–1858) | 1843 |
| Es | einsteinium | Albert Einstein[1] | 99 | [252] | Albert Ghiorso and others | 1952 |
| Eu | europium | Europe | 63 | 151.96 | Eugène Anatole Demarcay (1852–1903) | 1896 |
| F | fluorine | Latin, *fluo* = flow | 9 | 18.998403 | Carl Wilhelm Scheele (1742–86) | 1771 |
| Fe | iron | Anglo-Saxon, *iren* | 26 | 55.847 | Prehistoric | — |
| Fm | fermium | Enrico Fermi[1] | 100 | [257] | Albert Ghiorso and others | 1952 |
| Fr | francium | France | 87 | [223] | Marguerite Catherine Perey (1909–75) | 1939 |
| Ga | gallium | Latin, *Gallia* = France | 31 | 69.723 | Paul Émile Lecoq de Boisbaudran (1838–1912) | 1875 |
| Gd | gadolinium | Johan Gadolin[1] | 64 | 157.25 | Jean Charles Galissard de Marignac (1817–94) | 1880 |
| Ge | germanium | Latin, *Germania* | 32 | 72.59 | Clemens Alexander Winkler (1838–1904) | 1886 |
| H | hydrogen | Greek, *hydor* = water + *gen* | 1 | 1.00794 | Henry Cavendish (1766–1810) | 1766 |
| He | helium | Greek, *helios* = sun | 2 | 4.002602 | William Ramsay (1852–1916) | 1895 |
| Hf | hafnium | *Hafnia* = Copenhagen | 72 | 178.49 | Dirk Coster (1889–1950) and Georg Hevesey (1885–1966) | 1923 |
| Hg | mercury | Mercury (myth) | 80 | 200.59 | Prehistoric | — |
| Ho | holmium | *Holmia* = Stockholm | 67 | 164.9304 | Per Teodor Cleve (1840–1905) | 1879 |

| Symbol | Element | Derived from | Atomic No. | Atomic Weight | Discovered by | Date |
|---|---|---|---|---|---|---|
| I | iodine | Greek, *iodes* = violet | 53 | 126.9045 | Bernard Courtois (1777–1838) | 1811 |
| In | indium | Its indigo spectrum | 49 | 114.82 | Ferdinand Reich (1799–1882) and Hieronymous Theodor Richter (1824–98) | 1863 |
| Ir | iridium | Latin, *iris* = rainbow | 77 | 192.22 | Smithson Tennant (1761–1815) | 1803 |
| K | potassium | English, *potash* | 19 | 39.0983 | Humphry Davy (1778–1829) | 1807 |
| Kr | krypton | Greek, *kryptos* = hidden | 36 | 83.80 | William Ramsay (1852–1916) and Morris William Travers (1872–1961) | 1898 |
| La | lanthanum | Greek, *lanthanō* = conceal | 57 | 138.9055 | Carl Gustaf Mosander (1797–1858) | 1839 |
| Li | lithium | Greek, *lithos* = stone | 3 | 6.941 | Johan August Arfvedson | 1817 |
| Lu | lutetium | *Lutetia*, ancient name of Paris | 71 | 174.967 | Georges Urbain (1872–1938) and Karl Auer, Baron von Welsbach (1858–1929) | 1907 |
| Lw | lawrencium | Ernest Lawrence [1] | 103 | [260] | Albert Ghiorso and others | 1961 |
| Md | mendelevium | Dmitri Mendeleyev [1] | 101 | [258] | Glenn Theodore Seaborg (1912–99) and others | 1955 |
| Mg | magnesium | Magnesia, district in Thessaly | 12 | 24.305 | Antoine Alexandre Brutus Bussy (1794–1882) | 1829 |
| Mn | manganese | Latin, *magnes* = magnet | 25 | 54.9380 | Johan Gottlieb Gahn (1745–1818) | 1774 |
| Mo | molybdenum | Greek, *molybdos* = lead | 42 | 95.94 | Peter Jacob Hjelm (1746–1813) | 1782 |
| N | nitrogen | Greek, *nitron* = salpetre | 7 | 14.0067 | Daniel Rutherford (1749–1819) | 1772 |
| Na | sodium | English, *soda* | 11 | 22.98977 | Humphry Davy (1778–1829) | 1807 |
| Nb | niobium | Niobe (Greek myth) | 41 | 92.9064 | Charles Hatchett (1765–1847) | 1801 |
| Nd | neodymium | Greek, *neos* = new and *didymos* = twin | 60 | 144.24 | Karl Auer, Baron von Welsbach (1858–1929) | 1885 |
| Ne | neon | Greek, *neos* = new | 10 | 20.179 | William Ramsay (1852–1916) and Morris William Travers (1872–1961) | 1898 |
| Ni | nickel | Swedish, abbreviation of *kopparnickel* | 28 | 58.69 | Baron Axel Fredrik Cronstedt (1722–65) | 1751 |
| No | nobelium | Alfred Nobel [1] | 102 | [259] | Albert Ghiorso, Glenn Theodore Seaborg (1912–99) and others | 1957 |
| Np | neptunium | Planet Neptune | 93 | [237] | Edwin Mattison McMillan (1907–91) and Philip Hauge Abelson (1913– ) | 1940 |
| O | oxygen | Greek, *oxys* = acid + *gen* | 8 | 15.9994 | Joseph Priestley (1733–1804) | 1774 |
| Os | osmium | Greek, *osme* = odour | 76 | 190.2 | Smithson Tennant (1761–1815) | 1803 |
| P | phosphorus | Latin, from Greek 'light-bearing' | 15 | 30.97376 | Hennig Brand | 1669 |
| Pa | protactinium | Greek, *protos* = first + *actinium* | 91 | [231] | Otto Hahn (1879–1968) and Lise Meitner (1878–1968) | 1917 |
| Pb | lead | Anglo-Saxon, *lead* | 82 | 207.2 | Prehistoric | — |
| Pd | palladium | Planet Pallas | 46 | 106.42 | William Hyde Wollaston (1766–1828) | 1804 |
| Pm | promethium | Prometheus, stealer of fire from heaven (Greek myth) | 61 | [145] | Clinton Laboratories, Oak Ridge, Tennessee | 1940 |
| Po | polonium | Poland | 84 | [209] | Marie Curie (1867–1934) | 1898 |
| Pr | praseodymium | Greek, *prasios* = green and *didymos* = twin | 59 | 140.9077 | Karl Auer, Baron von Welsbach (1858–1929) | 1885 |
| Pt | platinum | Spanish, *platina* = silver | 78 | 195.08 | Antonio de Ulloa | 1735 |
| Pu | plutonium | Planet Pluto | 94 | [244] | Glenn Theodore Seaborg (1912–99), Edwin Mattison McMillan (1907–91), Wahl and Kennedy | 1940 |
| Ra | radium | Latin, *radius* = ray | 88 | [226] | Marie (1867–1934) and Pierre (1859–1906) Curie | 1898 |
| Rb | rubidium | Latin, *rubidus* = red | 37 | 85.4678 | Robert Wilhelm Bunsen (1811–99) | 1860 |
| Re | rhenium | German, *Rhein* | 75 | 186.207 | Walter Karl Friedrich Noddack (1893–1960) and Ida Eva Tacke (1896–1978) | 1925 |

| Symbol | Element | Derived from | Atomic No. | Atomic Weight | Discovered by | Date |
|---|---|---|---|---|---|---|
| Rh | rhodium | Greek, *rhodon* = rose | 45 | 102.9055 | William Hyde Wollaston (1766–1828) | 1804 |
| Rn | radon | Radium emanation | 86 | [222] | Friedrich Ernst Dorn (1848–1916) | 1901 |
| Ru | ruthenium | Latin, *Ruthenia* = Russia | 44 | 101.07 | Carl Ernst Claus (1796–1864) | 1845 |
| S | sulphur/sulfur | Latin, *sulfur* | 16 | 32.066 | Prehistoric | — |
| Sb | antimony | Latin, *antimonium* | 51 | 121.75 | Prehistoric | — |
| Sc | scandium | Scandinavia | 21 | 44.95591 | Lars Fredrik Nilson (1840–99) | 1879 |
| Se | selenium | Greek, *selene* = moon | 34 | 78.96 | Jöns Jacob Berzelius (1779–1848) | 1817 |
| Si | silicon | Latin, *silex* = flint | 14 | 28.0855 | Jöns Jacob Berzelius (1779–1848) | 1823 |
| Sm | samarium | Samarski, a Russian savant | 62 | 150.36 | Paul Émile Lecoq de Boisbaudran (1838–1912) | 1879 |
| Sn | tin | Anglo-Saxon, *tin* | 50 | 118.710 | Prehistoric | — |
| Sr | strontium | Strontian, a Scottish village | 38 | 87.62 | Humphry Davy (1778–1829) | 1808 |
| Ta | tantalum | Tantalus (Greek myth) | 73 | 180.9479 | Anders Gustaf Ekeberg (1767–1813) | 1802 |
| Tb | terbium | Ytterby, a Swedish town | 65 | 158.9254 | Carl Gustaf Mosander (1797–1858) | 1843 |
| Tc | technetium | Greek, *technetos* = artificial | 43 | [99] | Emilio Segrè (1905–89) and Carlo Perrier | 1937 |
| Te | tellurium | Latin, *tellus* = earth | 52 | 127.60 | Franz Joseph Müller, Baron von Reichenstein (1740–1825) | 1782 |
| Th | thorium | God Thor | 90 | 232.0381 | Jöns Jacob Berzelius (1779–1848) | 1828 |
| Ti | titanium | Latin, *Titanes* = sons of the earth | 22 | 47.88 | William Gregor (1761–1817) | 1789 |
| Tl | thallium | Greek, *thallos* = budding twig | 81 | 204.383 | William Crookes (1832–1919) | 1862 |
| Tm | thulium | Greek and Roman *Thule* = Northland | 69 | 168.9342 | Per Teodor Cleve (1840–1905) | 1879 |
| U | uranium | Planet Uranus | 92 | 238.0289 | Martin Heinrich Klaproth (1743–1817) | 1789 |
| Une | unnilennium | | 109 | [266] | | |
| Unh | unnilhexium | | 106 | [263] | | |
| Unp | unnilpentium | | 105 | [262] | | |
| Unq | unnilquadium | | 104 | [261] | | |
| Uns | unnilseptium | | 107 | [262] | | |
| V | vanadium | Goddess Vanadis (Freya) | 23 | 50.9415 | Nils Gabriel Sefström (1765–1829) | 1830 |
| W | tungsten | Swedish, heavy stone | 74 | 183.85 | Don Fausto d'Elhujar (1755–1833) | 1781 |
| Xe | xenon | Greek, *xenos* = stranger | 54 | 131.29 | William Ramsay (1852–1916) and Morris William Travers (1872–1961) | 1898 |
| Y | yttrium | Ytterby, a Swedish town | 39 | 88.9059 | Johan Gadolin (1760–1852) | 1794 |
| Yb | ytterbium | Ytterby, a Swedish town | 70 | 173.04 | Jean Charles Galissard de Marignac (1817–94) | 1878 |
| Zn | zinc | German, *zink* | 30 | 65.39 | — | c.1500 |
| Zr | zirconium | Persian, *zargun* = gold-coloured | 40 | 91.224 | Jöns Jacob Berzelius (1779–1848) | 1824 |

[1] For information on scientists who have given their names to certain elements, see pp359–66.

## Physical constants

1986 recommended values of the main fundamental physical constants of physics and chemistry.

| Quantity | Symbol | Value | Units |
|---|---|---|---|
| **❑ Universal constants** | | | |
| speed of light in vacuum | c | 299 792 458 | $m\,s^{-1}$ |
| permeability of vacuum | $\mu_0$ | $4\pi \times 10^{-7}$ | $N\,A^{-2}$ |
| | | = 12.566370614... | $10^{-7}\,N\,A^{-2}$ |
| permittivity of vacuum, $1/\mu_0\gamma^2$ | $\varepsilon_0$ | 8.854187817... | $10^{-12}\,F\,m^{-1}$ |
| Newtonian constant of gravitation | G | 6.67259 | $10^{-11}\,m^3 kg^{-1} s^{-2}$ |
| Planck constant | $h$ | 6.6260755 | $10^{-34}\,J\,s$ |
| $h/2\pi$ | $\hbar$ | 1.05457266 | $10^{-34}\,J\,s$ |
| **❑ Electromagnetic constants** | | | |
| elementary charge | e | 1.60217733 | $10^{-19}\,C$ |
| | e/h | 2.41798836 | $10^{14}\,A\,J^{-1}$ |
| magnetic flux quantum, $h/2e$ | $\Phi_0$ | 2.06783461 | $10^{-15}\,Wb$ |
| Josephson frequency-voltage quotient | 2e/h | 4.8359767 | $10^{14}\,Hz V^{-1}$ |
| Bohr magneton, $e\hbar/2m_e$ | $\mu_B$ | 9.2740154 | $10^{-24}\,J\,T^{-1}$ |
| nuclear magneton, $e\hbar/2m_p$ | $\mu_N$ | 5.0507866 | $10^{-27}\,J\,T^{-1}$ |
| **❑ Atomic constants** | | | |
| fine-structure constant, $\mu_0 c e^2/2h$ | $\alpha$ | 7.29735308 | $10^{-3}$ |
| | $\alpha^{-1}$ | 137.0359895 | |
| Rydberg constant, $m_e c\alpha^2/2h$ | $R_\infty$ | 10 973 731.534 | $m^{-1}$ |
| Bohr radius, $\alpha/4\pi R_\infty$ | $a_0$ | 0.529177249 | $10^{-10}\,m$ |
| quantum of circulation | $h/2m_e$ | 3.63694807 | $10^{-4}\,m^2 s^{-1}$ |
| | $h/m_e$ | 7.27389614 | $10^{-4}\,m^2 s^{-1}$ |
| **❑ Electron** | | | |
| electron mass | $m_e$ | 9.1093897 | $10^{-31}\,kg$ |
| | | 5.48579903 | $10^{-4}\,u$ |
| electron-muon mass ratio | $m_e/m_\mu$ | 4.83633218 | $10^{-3}$ |
| electron-proton mass ratio | $m_e/m_p$ | 5.44617013 | $10^{-4}$ |
| electron specific charge | $-e/m_e$ | -1.75881962 | $10^{11}\,C\,kg^{-1}$ |
| Compton wavelength, $h/m_e c$ | $\lambda_c$ | 2.42631058 | $10^{-12}\,m$ |
| $\lambda_C/2\pi = \alpha a_0 = \alpha^2/4\pi R_\infty$ | $\bar{\lambda}_c$ | 3.86159323 | $10^{-13}\,m$ |
| classical electron radius, $\alpha^2 a_0$ | $r_e$ | 2.81794092 | $10^{-15}\,m$ |
| electron magnetic moment | $\mu_e$ | 928.47701 | $10^{-26}\,J\,T^{-1}$ |
| electron $g$ factor, $2(1+a_e)$ | $g_e$ | 2.002319304386 | |
| electron-proton magnetic moment ratio | $\mu_e/\mu_p$ | 658.2106881 | |
| **❑ Muon** | | | |
| muon mass | $m_\mu$ | 1.8835327 | $10^{-28}\,kg$ |
| | | 0.113428913 | u |
| muon magnetic moment | $\mu_\mu$ | 4.4904514 | $10^{-26}\,J\,T^{-1}$ |
| muon $g$ factor, $2(1+a_\mu)$ | $g_\mu$ | 2.002331846 | |
| muon-proton magnetic moment ratio | $\mu_\mu/\mu_p$ | 3.18334547 | |
| **❑ Proton** | | | |
| proton mass | $m_p$ | 1.6726231 | $10^{-27}\,kg$ |
| | | 1.007276470 | u |
| proton Compton wavelength, $h/m_p c$ | $\lambda_{C,p}$ | 1.32141002 | $10^{-15}\,m$ |
| $\lambda_{C,p}/2\pi$ | $\bar{\lambda}_{C,p}$ | 2.10308937 | $10^{-6}\,m$ |
| proton magnetic moment | $\mu_p$ | 1.41060761 | $10^{-26}\,J\,T^{-1}$ |
| in Bohr magnetons | $\mu_p/\mu_B$ | 1.521032202 | $10^{-3}$ |
| in nuclear magnetons | $\mu_p/\mu_N$ | 2.792847386 | |
| proton gyromagnetic ratio | $\gamma_p$ | 26 752.2128 | $10^4 s^{-1} T^{-1}$ |
| | $\gamma_p/2\pi$ | 42.577469 | $MHz\,T^{-1}$ |
| uncorrected ($H_2O$, sph., 25°C) | $\gamma'_p$ | 26 751.5255 | $10^4 s^{-1} T^{-1}$ |
| | $\gamma'_p/2\pi$ | 42.576375 | $MHz\,T^{-1}$ |

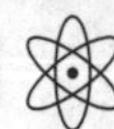



| Quantity | Symbol | Value | Units |
|---|---|---|---|
| **❑ Neutron** | | | |
| neutron mass | $m_n$ | 1.6749286 | $10^{-27}$ kg |
| | | 1.008664904 | u |
| neutron Compton wavelength, $h/m_n c$ | $\lambda_{C,n}$ | 1.31959110 | $10^{-15}$ m |
| $\lambda_{C,n}/2\pi$ | $\lambda_{C,n}$ | 2.10019445 | $10^{-16}$ m |
| **❑ Physico-chemical constants** | | | |
| Avogadro constant | $N_A, L$ | 6.0221367 | $10^{23}$ mol$^{-1}$ |
| atomic mass constant, $m_u = \frac{1}{12} m(^{12}C)$ | $m_u$ | 1.6605402 | $10^{-27}$ kg |
| Faraday constant, $N_A e$ | $F$ | 96 485.309 | C mol$^{-1}$ |
| molar gas constant | $R$ | 8.314510 | J mol$^{-1}$K$^{-1}$ |
| Boltzmann constant, $R/N_A$ | k | 1.380658 | $10^{-23}$ J K$^{-1}$ |
| molar volume (ideal gas), $RT/p$ | | | |
| $T = 273.15$ K, $p = 101\,325$ Pa | $V_m$ | 0.02241410 | m$^3$mol$^{-1}$ |
| Stefan-Boltzmann constant, $(\pi^2/60)\,k^4/\hbar^3c^2$ | $\sigma$ | 5.67051 | $10^{-8}$ W m$^{-2}$ K$^{-4}$ |
| first radiation constant, $2\pi hc^2$ | $c_1$ | 3.7417749 | $10^{-16}$ W m$^2$ |
| second radiation constant, $hc/k$ | $C_2$ | 0.01438769 | m K |

## Radiation

| Radiation | Approximate wavelengths | Discovered by | Date | Uses |
|---|---|---|---|---|
| Radio waves | >10 cm | Heinrich Hertz (German) | 1888 | communications; radio and TV broadcasting |
| Microwaves | 1mm – 10 cm | Heinrich Hertz (German) | 1886 | communications; radar; microwave ovens |
| Infrared | $10^{-3}$–$7.8 \times 10^{-7}$ m | William Herschel (German–British) | 1800 | night and smoke vision systems; intruder alarms; weather forecasting; missile guidance systems |
| Visible | $7.8 \times 10^{-7}$–$3 \times 10^{-7}$ m | — | — | human eyesight |
| Ultraviolet | $3 \times 10^{-7}$–$10^{-8}$ m | Johann Ritter (German) | 1801 | forensic science; medical treatment |
| X-rays | $10^{-8}$–$3 \times 10^{-11}$ m | Wilhelm Röntgen (German) | 1895 | medical X-ray photographs; material structure analysis |
| Gamma rays | $<3 \times 10^{-11}$ m | Ernest Rutherford (British) | 1902 | medical diagnosis |

## Properties of metals

| Name | Symbol | Valence no. | Atomic no. | Melting point (°C) |
|---|---|---|---|---|
| Aluminium | Al | 3 | 13 | 660.37 |
| Antimony (stibium) | Sb | 3 or 5 | 51 | 630.74 |
| Barium | Ba | 2 | 56 | 725 |
| Beryllium | Be | 2 | 4 | 1278 ± 5 |
| Bismuth | Bi | 3 or 5 | 83 | 271.3 |
| Cadmium | Cd | 1 or 2 | 48 | 320.9 |
| Caesium | Cs | 1 | 55 | 28.40 ± 0.01 |
| Calcium | Ca | 2 | 20 | 839 ± 2 |
| Cerium | Ce | 3 or 4 | 58 | 798 |
| Chromium | Cr | 2, 3 or 6 | 24 | 1857 ± 20 |
| Cobalt | Co | 2 or 3 | 27 | 1495 |
| Copper (cuprum) | Cu | 1 or 2 | 29 | 1083.4 ± 0.2 |
| Gallium | Ga | 3 | 31 | 29.78 |
| Gold (aurum) | Au | 1 or 3 | 79 | 1064.43 |
| Iridium | Ir | 2 or 4 | 77 | 2410 |
| Iron (ferrum) | Fe | 2 or 3 | 26 | 1535 |
| Lanthanum | La | 3 | 57 | 918 |
| Lead (plumbum) | Pb | 2 or 4 | 82 | 327.5 |

| Name | Symbol | Valence no. | Atomic no. | Melting point (°C) |
|---|---|---|---|---|
| Lithium | Li | 1 | 3 | 180.5 |
| Magnesium | Mg | 2 | 12 | 648.8 ± 0.5 |
| Manganese | Mn | 2, 3, 4, 6 or 7 | 25 | 1244 ± 3 |
| Mercury (hydrargyrum) | Hg | 1 or 2 | 80 | −38.87 |
| Molybdenum | Mo | 2 or 6 | 42 | 2617 |
| Nickel | Ni | 2 or 3 | 28 | 1453 |
| Osmium | Os | 2 or 8 | 76 | 3045 ± 30 |
| Palladium | Pd | 2 or 4 | 46 | 1554 |
| Platinum | Pt | 3 or 4 | 78 | 1772 |
| Plutonium | Pu | – | 94 | 641 |
| Potassium (kalium) | K | 1 | 19 | 63.25 |
| Rubidium | Rb | 1 | 37 | 38.89 |
| Silver (argentum) | Ag | 1 | 47 | 961.93 |
| Sodium (natrium) | Na | 1 | 11 | 97.81 ± 0.03 |
| Tin (stannum) | Sn | 2 or 4 | 50 | 231.97 |
| Titanium | Ti | 3 or 4 | 22 | 1660 ± 10 |
| Tungsten (wolfram) | W | 4 or 6 | 74 | 3410 ± 20 |
| Uranium | U | 2 or 6 | 92 | 1132 ± 0.8 |
| Vanadium | V | 5 | 23 | 1890 ± 10 |
| Zinc | Zn | 2 | 30 | 419.58 |

## Properties of polymers

| Polymer | Density ($kg\ m^{-3}$) | Tensile strength ($MN\ m^{-2}$) | Heat capacity ($J\ g^{-1} K^{-1}$) | Resistivity ($\Omega$ cm) |
|---|---|---|---|---|
| Acetals | 1420 | 65 | 1.46 | $10^{15}$ |
| Cellulose | 1480–1530 | 80–240 | 1.3–1.5 | $10^{7}$–$10^{14}$ |
| Cellulose acetate | | | | |
| Moulded | 1220–1340 | 12–58 | 1.26–1.8 | $10^{10}$–$10^{14}$ |
| Sheet | 1280–1320 | 30–52 | 1.26–2.1 | $10^{11}$–$10^{15}$ |
| Cellulose nitrate (celluloid) | 1350–1400 | 50 | 1.3–1.7 | $10^{10}$ |
| Epoxy cast resins | 1110–1400 | 26–85 | 1.0 | $10^{12}$–$10^{17}$ |
| Nylon-6 (Poly-E-caprolactam) | 1120–1170 | 45–90 | 1.6 | $10^{12}$–$10^{15}$ |
| Nylon-66 (Polyhexa-methylene-adipamide) | 1130–1150 | 60–80 | 1.7 | $10^{14}$–$10^{15}$ |
| Polyacrylonitrile | 1160–1180 | 200 | — | $10^{14}$ |
| Polycarbonates | 1200 | 52–62 | 1.17–1.25 | $10^{16}$ |
| Polyethylene | | | | |
| Low density | 910–925 | 4–15 | — | $10^{15}$–$10^{18}$ |
| Medium density | 926–940 | 8–22 | — | $10^{15}$–$10^{18}$ |
| High density | 940–965 | 20–36 | — | $10^{15}$–$10^{18}$ |
| Polyisoprene | | | | |
| Natural rubber | 906–913 | — | 1.88 | $10^{6}$ |
| Hard rubber | 1130–1180 | 39 | 1.38 | $10^{16}$ |
| Polypropylene | 902–906 | 28–36 | 1.92 | $>10^{16}$ |
| Polystyrene | 1040–1090 | 30–100 | 1.3–1.5 | $>10^{16}$ |
| Polyurethane | | | | |
| Cast liquid | 1100–1500 | 1–65 | 1.8 | $10^{11}$–$10^{15}$ |
| Elastomer | 1110–1250 | 29–55 | 1.8 | $10^{11}$–$10^{13}$ |
| Polyvinylchloride | 1300–1400 | 50 | 0.84–1.17 | $10^{16}$ |
| Silicone cast resin | 1300 | — | — | $10^{14}$–$10^{15}$ |

## SI units (International system of units)

| Concept | Symbol | Name of Unit | Abbreviation of Unit Name |
|---|---|---|---|
| Length | $l$ | metre | m |
| Mass | $m$ | kilogramme | kg |
| Time | $t$ | second | s |
| Electric current | $I$ | ampere | A |
| Thermodynamic temperature | $T$ | kelvin | K |
| Luminous intensity | $I$ | candela | cd |
| Amount of substance | | mole | mol |
| Plane angle | $\alpha, \beta, \theta$, etc | radian | rad |
| Solid angle | $\Omega, \omega$ | steradian | sr |
| Area | $A, a$ | square metre | $m^2$ |
| Volume | $V, v$ | cubic metre | $m^3$ |
| Velocity | $v, u$ | metre/second | $m\ s^{-1}$ |
| Acceleration | $a$ | metre/second$^2$ | $m\ s^{-2}$ |
| Density | $\rho$ | kilogramme/metre$^3$ | $kg\ m^{-3}$ |
| Mass rate of flow | $\dot{m}, \dot{M}$ | kilogramme/sec | $kg\ s^{-1}$ |
| Volume rate of flow | $\dot{V}$ | cubic metre/sec | $m^3\ s^{-1}$ |
| Moment of inertia | $I$ | kilogramme metre$^2$ | $kg\ m^2$ |
| Momentum | $p$ | kilogramme metre/sec | $kg\ m\ s^{-1}$ |
| Angular momentum | $I\omega$ | kilogramme metre$^2$/sec | $kg\ m^2\ s^{-1}$ |
| Force | $F$ | newton | N |
| Torque (moment of force) | $T\ (M)$ | newton metre | N m |
| Work (energy, heat) | $W\ (E)$ | joule | J |
| Potential energy | $V$ | joule | J |
| Kinetic energy | $T\ (W)$ | joule | J |
| Heat (enthalpy) | $Q\ (H)$ | joule | J |
| Power | $P$ | watt | W |
| Pressure (stress) | $p\ (\sigma, f)$ | newton/metre$^2$ | $N\ m^{-2}$ |
| Surface tension | $\gamma\ (\sigma)$ | newton/metre | $N\ m^{-1}$ |
| Viscosity, dynamic | $\eta, \mu$ | | $N\ s\ m^{-1}$ |
| Viscosity, kinematic | $\nu$ | | $m^2\ s^{-1}$ |
| Temperature | $\theta, T$ | degree Celsius, kelvin | °C, K |
| Velocity of light | $c$ | metre/sec | $m\ s^{-1}$ |
| Permeability of vacuum | $\mu_0$ | henry/metre | $H\ m^{-1}$ |
| Permittivity of vacuum | $\varepsilon_0$ | farad/metre | $F\ m^{-1}$ |
| Electric charge | $Q$ | coulomb | C |
| Electric potential (potential difference) | $V$ | volt | V |
| Electric field strength (electric force) | $E$ | volt/metre | $V\ m^{-1}$ |
| Electric resistance | $R$ | ohm | Ω |
| Conductance | $G$ | siemens | S |
| Electric flux | $\Psi$ | coulomb | $\Psi$=Q |
| Electric flux density (displacement) | $D$ | coulomb/metre$^2$ | $C\ m^{-2}$ |
| Frequency | $f$ | hertz | Hz |
| Permittivity | $\varepsilon$ | farad/metre | $F\ m^{-1}$ |
| Relative permittivity | $\varepsilon_r$ | | |
| Magnetic field strength | $H$ | amp. turn/metre | $At\ m^{-1}$ |
| Magnetic flux | $\Phi$ | weber | Wb |
| Magnetic flux density | $B$ | tesla | T |
| Permeability | $\mu$ | henry/metre | $H\ m^{-1}$ |
| Relative permeability | $\mu_r$ | | |
| Mutual inductance | $M$ | henry | H |
| Self inductance | $L$ | henry | H |
| Capacitance | $C$ | farad | F |
| Reactance | $X$ | ohm | Ω |
| Impedance | $Z$ | ohm | Ω |
| Susceptance | $B$ | siemens | S |
| Admittance | $Y$ | siemens | S |
| Total voltamperes | $S$ | volt amp | VA |

| Concept | Symbol | Name of Unit | Abbreviation of Unit Name |
|---|---|---|---|
| Reactive voltamperes | $Q$ | volt amp reactive | VAr |
| Power factor | p.f. | — | — |
| Luminous flux | $\Phi$ | lumen | lm |
| Illumination | $E$ | lux | lx |

## SI conversion factors

This table gives the conversion factors for many British and other units which are still in common use, showing their equivalents in terms of the international system of units (SI). The column labelled 'SI equivalent' gives the SI value of one unit of the type named in the first column, eg 1 calorie is 4.186 J.

| Unit name | Symbol | Quantity | SI equivalent | Unit |
|---|---|---|---|---|
| acre | | area | 0.405 | $hm^2$ |
| ångström[1] | Å | length | 0.1 | nm |
| astronomical unit | AU | length | 0.150 | Tm |
| atomic mass unit | amu | mass | $1.661 \times 10^{-27}$ | kg |
| bar[1] | bar | pressure | 0.1 | MPa |
| barn[1] | b | area | 100 | $fm^2$ |
| barrel (US) = 42 US gal | bbl | volume | 0.159 | $m^3$ |
| British thermal unit | Btu | energy | 1.055 | kJ |
| calorie | cal | energy | 4.186 | J |
| cubic foot | $ft^3$ | volume | 0.028 | $m^3$ |
| cubic inch | $in^3$ | volume | 16.387 | $cm^3$ |
| cubic yard | $yd^3$ | volume | 0.765 | $m^3$ |
| curie[1] | Ci | activity of radionuclide | 37 | GBq |
| degree = 1/90 rt angle | ° | plane angle | $\pi/180$ | rad |
| degree Celsius | °C | temperature | 1 | K |
| degree Centigrade | °C | temperature | 1 | K |
| degree Fahrenheit | °F | temperature | 5/9 | K |
| degree Rankine | °R | temperature | 5/9 | K |
| dyne | dyn | force | 10 | µN |
| electronvolt | eV | energy | 0.160 | aJ |
| erg | erg | energy | 0.1 | µJ |
| fathom (6ft) | | length | 1.829 | m |
| fermi | | length | 1 | fm |
| foot | ft | length | 30.48 | cm |
| foot per second | $ft\ s^{-1}$ | velocity | {0.305<br>{1.097 | $m\ s^{-1}$<br>$km\ h^{-1}$ |
| gallon (UK)[1] | gal | volume | 4.546 | $dm^3$ |
| gallon (US)[1] = 231 $in^3$ | gal | volume | 3.785 | $dm^3$ |
| gallon (UK) per mile | | consumption | 2.825 | $dm^3\ km^{-1}$ |
| gauss | Gs, G | magnetic flux density | 100 | µT |
| grade = 0.01 rt angle | | plane angle | $\pi/200$ | rad |
| grain | gr | mass | 0.065 | g |
| hectare[1] | ha | area | 1 | $hm^2$ |
| horsepower | hp | energy | 0.746 | kW |
| inch | in | length | 2.54 | cm |
| kilogram-force | kgf | force | 9.807 | N |
| knot[1] | | velocity | 1.852 | $km\ h^{-1}$ |
| light year | l.y. | length | $9.461 \times 10^{15}$ | m |
| litre | l | volume | 1 | $dm^3$ |
| maxwell | Mx | magnetic flux | 10 | nWb |
| metric carat | | mass | 0.2 | g |
| micron | µ | length | 1 | µm |
| mile (nautical)[1] | | length | 1.852 | km |
| mile (statute) | | length | 1.609 | km |
| mile per hour (mph) | $mile\ h^{-1}$ | velocity | 1.609 | $km\ h^{-1}$ |
| minute = (1/60)° | ′ | plane angle | $\pi/10\,800$ | rad |
| oersted | Oe | magnetic field strength | $1/(4\pi)$ | $kA\ m^{-1}$ |
| ounce (avoirdupois) | oz | mass | 28.349 | g |

| Unit name | Symbol | Quantity | SI equivalent | Unit |
|---|---|---|---|---|
| ounce (troy) = 480 gr | | mass | 31.103 | g |
| parsec | pc | length | 30 857 | Tm |
| phot | ph | illuminance | 10 | klx |
| pint (UK) | pt | volume | 0.568 | $dm^3$ |
| poise | p | viscosity | 0.1 | Pa s |
| pound | lb | mass | 0.454 | kg |
| pound-force | lbf | force | 4.448 | N |
| pound-force/$in^{-2}$ | | pressure | 6.895 | kPa |
| poundal | pdl | force | 0.138 | N |
| pounds per square inch | psi | pressure | $6.895 \times 10^3$ | K Pa |
| rad[1] | rad | absorbed dose | 0.01 | Gy |
| rem[1] | rem | dose equivalent | 0.01 | Sv |
| right angle = $\pi/2$ rad | | plane angle | 1.571 | rad |
| röntgen[1] | R | exposure | 0.258 | mC $kg^{-1}$ |
| second = (1/60)′ | ″ | plane angle | $\pi/648$ | mrad |
| slug | | mass | 14.594 | kg |
| solar mass | M | mass | $1.989 \times 10^{30}$ | kg |
| square foot | $ft^2$ | area | 9.290 | $dm^2$ |
| square inch | $in^2$ | area | 6.452 | $cm^2$ |
| square mile (statute) | | area | 2.590 | $km^2$ |
| square yard | $yd^2$ | area | 0.836 | $m^2$ |
| standard atmosphere | atm | pressure | 0.101 | MPa |
| stere | st | volume | 1 | $m^3$ |
| stilb | sb | luminance | 10 | kcd $m^{-2}$ |
| stokes | St | viscosity | 1 | $cm^2 s^{-1}$ |
| therm = $10^5$Btu | | energy | 0.105 | GJ |
| ton = 2 240 lb | | mass | 1.016 | Mg |
| ton-force | tonf | force | 9.964 | kN |
| ton-force/$in^{-2}$ | | pressure | 15.444 | MPa |
| tonne | t | mass | 1 | Mg |
| torr } mmHg } | torr | pressure | 0.133 | kPa |
| X unit | | length | 0.100 | pm |
| yard | yd | length | 0.915 | m |

[1] In temporary use with SI.

## SI prefixes

| Factor | Prefix | Symbol | Factor | Prefix | Symbol | Factor | Prefix | Symbol | Factor | Prefix | Symbol |
|---|---|---|---|---|---|---|---|---|---|---|---|
| $10^{18}$ | exa | E | $10^6$ | mega | M | $10^{-1}$ | deci | d | $10^{-9}$ | nano | n |
| $10^{15}$ | peta | P | $10^3$ | kilo | k | $10^{-2}$ | centi | c | $10^{-12}$ | pico | p |
| $10^{12}$ | tera | T | $10^2$ | hecto | h | $10^{-3}$ | milli | m | $10^{-15}$ | femto | f |
| $10^9$ | giga | G | $10^1$ | deca | da | $10^{-6}$ | micro | μ | $10^{-18}$ | atto | a |

## Temperature conversion

| To convert | To | Equation |
|---|---|---|
| °Fahrenheit | °Celsius | −32, × 5, ÷ 9 |
| °Fahrenheit | °Rankine | + 459.67 |
| °Fahrenheit | °Réaumur | −32, × 4, ÷ 9 |
| °Celsius | °Fahrenheit | × 9, ÷ 5, + 32 |
| °Celsius | Kelvin | + 273.15 |
| °Celsius | °Réaumur | × 4, ÷ 5 |
| Kelvin | °Celsius | −273.15 |
| °Rankine | °Fahrenheit | −459.67 |
| °Réaumur | °Fahrenheit | × 9, ÷ 4, + 32 |
| °Réaumur | °Celsius | × 5, ÷ 4 |

Carry out operations in sequence.

## Temperature conversion

**Degrees Fahrenheit (F) → Degrees Celsius (Centigrade) (C)**

| °F | → °C | °F | → °C | °F | → °C | °F | → °C |
|---|---|---|---|---|---|---|---|
| 1 | - 17.2 | 54 | 12.2 | 107 | 41.7 | 160 | 71.1 |
| 2 | - 16.7 | 55 | 12.8 | 108 | 42.2 | 161 | 71.7 |
| 3 | - 16.1 | 56 | 13.3 | 109 | 42.8 | 162 | 72.2 |
| 4 | - 15.5 | 57 | 13.9 | 110 | 43.3 | 163 | 72.8 |
| 5 | - 15.0 | 58 | 14.4 | 111 | 43.9 | 164 | 73.3 |
| 6 | - 14.4 | 59 | 15.0 | 112 | 44.4 | 165 | 73.9 |
| 7 | - 13.9 | 60 | 15.5 | 113 | 45.0 | 166 | 74.4 |
| 8 | - 13.3 | 61 | 16.1 | 114 | 45.5 | 167 | 75.0 |
| 9 | - 12.8 | 62 | 16.7 | 115 | 46.1 | 168 | 75.5 |
| 10 | - 12.2 | 63 | 17.2 | 116 | 46.7 | 169 | 76.1 |
| 11 | - 11.6 | 64 | 17.8 | 117 | 47.2 | 170 | 76.7 |
| 12 | - 11.1 | 65 | 18.3 | 118 | 47.8 | 171 | 77.2 |
| 13 | - 10.5 | 66 | 18.9 | 119 | 48.3 | 172 | 77.8 |
| 14 | - 10.0 | 67 | 19.4 | 120 | 48.9 | 173 | 78.3 |
| 15 | - 9.4 | 68 | 20.0 | 121 | 49.4 | 174 | 78.9 |
| 16 | - 8.9 | 69 | 20.5 | 122 | 50.0 | 175 | 79.4 |
| 17 | - 8.3 | 70 | 21.1 | 123 | 50.5 | 176 | 80.0 |
| 18 | - 7.8 | 71 | 21.7 | 124 | 51.1 | 177 | 80.5 |
| 19 | - 7.2 | 72 | 22.2 | 125 | 51.7 | 178 | 81.1 |
| 20 | - 6.7 | 73 | 22.8 | 126 | 52.2 | 179 | 81.7 |
| 21 | - 6.1 | 74 | 23.3 | 127 | 52.8 | 180 | 82.2 |
| 22 | - 5.5 | 75 | 23.9 | 128 | 53.3 | 181 | 82.8 |
| 23 | - 5.0 | 76 | 24.4 | 129 | 53.9 | 182 | 83.3 |
| 24 | - 4.4 | 77 | 25.0 | 130 | 54.4 | 183 | 83.9 |
| 25 | - 3.9 | 78 | 25.5 | 131 | 55.0 | 184 | 84.4 |
| 26 | - 3.3 | 79 | 26.1 | 132 | 55.5 | 185 | 85.0 |
| 27 | - 2.8 | 80 | 26.7 | 133 | 56.1 | 186 | 85.5 |
| 28 | - 2.2 | 81 | 27.2 | 134 | 56.7 | 187 | 86.1 |
| 29 | - 1.7 | 82 | 27.8 | 135 | 57.2 | 188 | 86.7 |
| 30 | - 1.1 | 83 | 28.3 | 136 | 57.8 | 189 | 87.2 |
| 31 | - 0.5 | 84 | 28.9 | 137 | 58.3 | 190 | 87.8 |
| 32 | 0 | 85 | 29.4 | 138 | 58.9 | 191 | 88.3 |
| 33 | 0.5 | 86 | 30.0 | 139 | 59.4 | 192 | 88.8 |
| 34 | 1.1 | 87 | 30.5 | 140 | 60.0 | 193 | 89.4 |
| 35 | 1.7 | 88 | 31.1 | 141 | 60.5 | 194 | 90.0 |
| 36 | 2.2 | 89 | 31.7 | 142 | 61.1 | 195 | 90.5 |
| 37 | 2.8 | 90 | 32.2 | 143 | 61.7 | 196 | 91.1 |
| 38 | 3.3 | 91 | 32.8 | 144 | 62.2 | 197 | 91.7 |
| 39 | 3.9 | 92 | 33.3 | 145 | 62.8 | 198 | 92.2 |
| 40 | 4.4 | 93 | 33.9 | 146 | 63.3 | 199 | 92.8 |
| 41 | 5.0 | 94 | 34.4 | 147 | 63.9 | 200 | 93.3 |
| 42 | 5.5 | 95 | 35.0 | 148 | 64.4 | 201 | 93.9 |
| 43 | 6.1 | 96 | 35.5 | 149 | 65.0 | 202 | 94.4 |
| 44 | 6.7 | 97 | 36.1 | 150 | 65.5 | 203 | 95.0 |
| 45 | 7.2 | 98 | 36.7 | 151 | 66.1 | 204 | 95.5 |
| 46 | 7.8 | 99 | 37.2 | 152 | 66.7 | 205 | 96.1 |
| 47 | 8.3 | 100 | 37.8 | 153 | 67.2 | 206 | 96.7 |
| 48 | 8.9 | 101 | 38.3 | 154 | 67.8 | 207 | 97.2 |
| 49 | 9.4 | 102 | 38.9 | 155 | 68.3 | 208 | 97.8 |
| 50 | 10.0 | 103 | 39.4 | 156 | 68.9 | 209 | 98.3 |
| 51 | 10.5 | 104 | 40.0 | 157 | 69.4 | 210 | 98.9 |
| 52 | 11.1 | 105 | 40.5 | 158 | 70.0 | 211 | 99.4 |
| 53 | 11.7 | 106 | 41.1 | 159 | 70.5 | 212 | 100.0 |

**Degrees Celsius (Centigrade) (C) → Degrees Fahrenheit (F)**

| °C | → °F | °C | → °F |
|---|---|---|---|
| 1 | 33.8 | 54 | 129.2 |
| 2 | 35.6 | 55 | 131.0 |
| 3 | 37.4 | 56 | 132.8 |
| 4 | 39.2 | 57 | 134.6 |
| 5 | 41.0 | 58 | 136.4 |
| 6 | 42.8 | 59 | 138.2 |
| 7 | 44.6 | 60 | 140.0 |
| 8 | 46.4 | 61 | 141.8 |
| 9 | 48.2 | 62 | 143.6 |
| 10 | 50.0 | 63 | 145.4 |
| 11 | 51.8 | 64 | 147.2 |
| 12 | 53.6 | 65 | 149.0 |
| 13 | 55.4 | 66 | 150.8 |
| 14 | 57.2 | 67 | 152.6 |
| 15 | 59.0 | 68 | 154.4 |
| 16 | 60.8 | 69 | 156.2 |
| 17 | 62.6 | 70 | 158.0 |
| 18 | 64.4 | 71 | 159.8 |
| 19 | 66.2 | 72 | 161.6 |
| 20 | 68.0 | 73 | 163.4 |
| 21 | 69.8 | 74 | 165.2 |
| 22 | 71.6 | 75 | 167.0 |
| 23 | 73.4 | 76 | 168.8 |
| 24 | 75.2 | 77 | 170.6 |
| 25 | 77.0 | 78 | 172.4 |
| 26 | 78.8 | 79 | 174.2 |
| 27 | 80.6 | 80 | 176.0 |
| 28 | 82.4 | 81 | 177.8 |
| 29 | 84.2 | 82 | 179.6 |
| 30 | 86.0 | 83 | 181.4 |
| 31 | 87.8 | 84 | 183.2 |
| 32 | 89.6 | 85 | 185.0 |
| 33 | 91.4 | 86 | 186.8 |
| 34 | 93.2 | 87 | 188.6 |
| 35 | 95.0 | 88 | 190.4 |
| 36 | 96.8 | 89 | 192.2 |
| 37 | 98.6 | 90 | 194.0 |
| 38 | 100.4 | 91 | 195.8 |
| 39 | 102.2 | 92 | 197.6 |
| 40 | 104.0 | 93 | 199.4 |
| 41 | 105.8 | 94 | 201.2 |
| 42 | 107.6 | 95 | 203.0 |
| 43 | 109.4 | 96 | 204.8 |
| 44 | 111.2 | 97 | 206.6 |
| 45 | 113.0 | 98 | 208.4 |
| 46 | 114.8 | 99 | 210.2 |
| 47 | 116.6 | 100 | 212.0 |
| 48 | 118.4 | | |
| 49 | 120.2 | | |
| 50 | 122.0 | | |
| 51 | 123.8 | | |
| 52 | 125.6 | | |
| 53 | 127.4 | | |

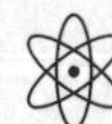



## Numerical equivalents

| Arabic | Roman | Greek | Binary numbers |
|---:|---|---|---:|
| 1 | I | α′ | 1 |
| 2 | II | β′ | 10 |
| 3 | III | γ′ | 11 |
| 4 | IV | δ′ | 100 |
| 5 | V | ε′ | 101 |
| 6 | VI | ς′ | 110 |
| 7 | VII | ζ′ | 111 |
| 8 | VIII | η′ | 1000 |
| 9 | IX | θ′ | 1001 |
| 10 | X | ι′ | 1010 |
| 11 | XI | ια′ | 1011 |
| 12 | XII | ιβ′ | 1100 |
| 13 | XIII | ιγ′ | 1101 |
| 14 | XIV | ιδ′ | 1110 |
| 15 | XV | ιε′ | 1111 |
| 16 | XVI | ις′ | 10000 |
| 17 | XVII | ιζ′ | 10001 |
| 18 | XVIII | ιη′ | 10010 |
| 19 | XIX | ιθ′ | 10011 |
| 20 | XX | κ′ | 10100 |
| 30 | XXX | λ′ | 11110 |
| 40 | XL | μ′ | 101000 |
| 50 | L | ν′ | 110010 |
| 60 | LX | ξ′ | 111100 |
| 70 | LXX | ο′ | 1000110 |
| 80 | LXXX | π′ | 1010000 |
| 90 | XC | ,ο′ | 1011010 |
| 100 | C | ρ′ | 1100100 |
| 200 | CC | σ′ | 11001000 |
| 300 | CCC | τ′ | 100101100 |
| 400 | CD | υ′ | 110010000 |
| 500 | D | ϕ′ | 111110100 |
| 1 000 | M | ,α | 1111101000 |
| 5 000 | V̄ | ,ε | 1001110001000 |
| 10 000 | X̄ | ,ι | 10011100010000 |
| 100 000 | C̄ | ,ρ | 11000011010100000 |

| % | D[1] | F[2] | % | D | F | % | D | F | % | D | F | % | D | F |
|---|---|---|---|---|---|---|---|---|---|---|---|---|---|---|
| 1 | 0.01 | $\frac{1}{100}$ | $12\frac{1}{2}$ | 0.125 | $\frac{1}{8}$ | 24 | 0.24 | $\frac{6}{25}$ | 36 | 0.36 | $\frac{9}{25}$ | 49 | 0.49 | $\frac{49}{100}$ |
| 2 | 0.02 | $\frac{1}{50}$ | 13 | 0.13 | $\frac{13}{100}$ | 25 | 0.25 | $\frac{1}{4}$ | 37 | 0.37 | $\frac{37}{100}$ | 50 | 0.50 | $\frac{1}{2}$ |
| 3 | 0.03 | $\frac{3}{100}$ | 14 | 0.14 | $\frac{7}{50}$ | 26 | 0.26 | $\frac{13}{50}$ | 38 | 0.38 | $\frac{19}{50}$ | 55 | 0.55 | $\frac{11}{20}$ |
| 4 | 0.04 | $\frac{1}{25}$ | 15 | 0.15 | $\frac{3}{20}$ | 27 | 0.27 | $\frac{27}{100}$ | 39 | 0.39 | $\frac{39}{100}$ | 60 | 0.60 | $\frac{3}{5}$ |
| 5 | 0.05 | $\frac{1}{20}$ | 16 | 0.16 | $\frac{4}{25}$ | 28 | 0.28 | $\frac{7}{25}$ | 40 | 0.40 | $\frac{2}{5}$ | 65 | 0.65 | $\frac{13}{20}$ |
| 6 | 0.06 | $\frac{3}{50}$ | $16\frac{2}{3}$ | 0.167 | $\frac{1}{6}$ | 29 | 0.29 | $\frac{29}{100}$ | 41 | 0.41 | $\frac{41}{100}$ | 70 | 0.70 | $\frac{7}{10}$ |
| 7 | 0.07 | $\frac{7}{100}$ | 17 | 0.17 | $\frac{17}{100}$ | 30 | 0.30 | $\frac{3}{10}$ | 42 | 0.42 | $\frac{21}{50}$ | 75 | 0.75 | $\frac{3}{4}$ |
| 8 | 0.08 | $\frac{2}{25}$ | 18 | 0.18 | $\frac{9}{50}$ | 31 | 0.31 | $\frac{31}{100}$ | 43 | 0.43 | $\frac{43}{100}$ | 80 | 0.80 | $\frac{4}{5}$ |
| $8\frac{1}{3}$ | 0.083 | $\frac{1}{12}$ | 19 | 0.19 | $\frac{19}{100}$ | 32 | 0.32 | $\frac{8}{25}$ | 44 | 0.44 | $\frac{11}{25}$ | 85 | 0.85 | $\frac{17}{20}$ |
| 9 | 0.09 | $\frac{9}{100}$ | 20 | 0.20 | $\frac{1}{5}$ | 33 | 0.33 | $\frac{33}{100}$ | 45 | 0.45 | $\frac{9}{20}$ | 90 | 0.90 | $\frac{9}{10}$ |
| 10 | 0.10 | $\frac{1}{10}$ | 21 | 0.21 | $\frac{21}{100}$ | $33\frac{1}{3}$ | 0.333 | $\frac{1}{3}$ | 46 | 0.46 | $\frac{23}{50}$ | 95 | 0.95 | $\frac{19}{20}$ |
| 11 | 0.11 | $\frac{11}{100}$ | 22 | 0.22 | $\frac{11}{50}$ | 34 | 0.34 | $\frac{17}{50}$ | 47 | 0.47 | $\frac{47}{100}$ | 100 | 1.00 | 1 |
| 12 | 0.12 | $\frac{3}{25}$ | 23 | 0.23 | $\frac{23}{100}$ | 35 | 0.35 | $\frac{7}{20}$ | 48 | 0.48 | $\frac{12}{25}$ | | | |

[1] Decimal [2] Fraction

| Fraction | Decimal | Fraction | Decimal |
|---|---|---|---|
| $\frac{1}{2}$ | 0.5000 | $\frac{9}{11}$ | 0.8181 |
| $\frac{1}{3}$ | 0.3333 | $\frac{10}{11}$ | 0.9090 |
| $\frac{2}{3}$ | 0.6667 | $\frac{1}{12}$ | 0.0833 |
| $\frac{1}{4}$ | 0.2500 | $\frac{5}{12}$ | 0.4167 |
| $\frac{3}{4}$ | 0.7500 | $\frac{7}{12}$ | 0.5833 |
| $\frac{1}{5}$ | 0.2000 | $\frac{11}{12}$ | 0.9167 |
| $\frac{2}{5}$ | 0.4000 | $\frac{1}{16}$ | 0.0625 |
| $\frac{3}{5}$ | 0.6000 | $\frac{3}{16}$ | 0.1875 |
| $\frac{4}{5}$ | 0.8000 | $\frac{5}{16}$ | 0.3125 |
| $\frac{1}{6}$ | 0.1667 | $\frac{7}{16}$ | 0.4375 |
| $\frac{5}{6}$ | 0.8333 | $\frac{9}{16}$ | 0.5625 |
| $\frac{1}{7}$ | 0.1429 | $\frac{11}{16}$ | 0.6875 |
| $\frac{2}{7}$ | 0.2857 | $\frac{13}{16}$ | 0.8125 |
| $\frac{3}{7}$ | 0.4286 | $\frac{15}{16}$ | 0.9375 |
| $\frac{4}{7}$ | 0.5714 | $\frac{1}{20}$ | 0.0500 |
| $\frac{5}{7}$ | 0.7143 | $\frac{3}{20}$ | 0.1500 |
| $\frac{6}{7}$ | 0.8571 | $\frac{7}{20}$ | 0.3500 |
| $\frac{1}{8}$ | 0.1250 | $\frac{9}{20}$ | 0.4500 |
| $\frac{3}{8}$ | 0.3750 | $\frac{11}{20}$ | 0.5500 |
| $\frac{5}{8}$ | 0.6250 | $\frac{13}{20}$ | 0.6500 |
| $\frac{7}{8}$ | 0.8750 | $\frac{17}{20}$ | 0.8500 |
| $\frac{1}{9}$ | 0.1111 | $\frac{19}{20}$ | 0.9500 |
| $\frac{2}{9}$ | 0.2222 | $\frac{1}{32}$ | 0.0312 |
| $\frac{4}{9}$ | 0.4444 | $\frac{3}{32}$ | 0.0937 |
| $\frac{5}{9}$ | 0.5556 | $\frac{5}{32}$ | 0.1562 |
| $\frac{7}{9}$ | 0.7778 | $\frac{7}{32}$ | 0.2187 |
| $\frac{8}{9}$ | 0.8889 | $\frac{9}{32}$ | 0.2812 |
| $\frac{1}{10}$ | 0.1000 | $\frac{11}{32}$ | 0.3437 |
| $\frac{3}{10}$ | 0.3000 | $\frac{13}{32}$ | 0.4062 |
| $\frac{7}{10}$ | 0.7000 | $\frac{15}{32}$ | 0.4687 |
| $\frac{9}{10}$ | 0.9000 | $\frac{17}{32}$ | 0.5312 |
| $\frac{1}{11}$ | 0.0909 | $\frac{19}{32}$ | 0.5937 |
| $\frac{2}{11}$ | 0.1818 | $\frac{21}{32}$ | 0.6562 |
| $\frac{3}{11}$ | 0.2727 | $\frac{23}{32}$ | 0.7187 |
| $\frac{4}{11}$ | 0.3636 | $\frac{25}{32}$ | 0.7812 |
| $\frac{5}{11}$ | 0.4545 | $\frac{27}{32}$ | 0.8437 |
| $\frac{6}{11}$ | 0.5454 | $\frac{29}{32}$ | 0.9062 |
| $\frac{7}{11}$ | 0.6363 | $\frac{31}{32}$ | 0.9687 |
| $\frac{8}{11}$ | 0.7272 | | |

## Multiplication table

| | 2 | 3 | 4 | 5 | 6 | 7 | 8 | 9 | 10 | 11 | 12 | 13 | 14 | 15 | 16 | 17 | 18 | 19 | 20 | 21 | 22 | 23 | 24 | 25 |
|---|---|---|---|---|---|---|---|---|---|---|---|---|---|---|---|---|---|---|---|---|---|---|---|---|
| **2** | 4 | 6 | 8 | 10 | 12 | 14 | 16 | 18 | 20 | 22 | 24 | 26 | 28 | 30 | 32 | 34 | 36 | 38 | 40 | 42 | 44 | 46 | 48 | 50 |
| **3** | 6 | 9 | 12 | 15 | 18 | 21 | 24 | 27 | 30 | 33 | 36 | 39 | 42 | 45 | 48 | 51 | 54 | 57 | 60 | 63 | 66 | 69 | 72 | 75 |
| **4** | 8 | 12 | 16 | 20 | 24 | 28 | 32 | 36 | 40 | 44 | 48 | 52 | 56 | 60 | 64 | 68 | 72 | 76 | 80 | 84 | 88 | 92 | 96 | 100 |
| **5** | 10 | 15 | 20 | 25 | 30 | 35 | 40 | 45 | 50 | 55 | 60 | 65 | 70 | 75 | 80 | 85 | 90 | 95 | 100 | 105 | 110 | 115 | 120 | 125 |
| **6** | 12 | 18 | 24 | 30 | 36 | 42 | 48 | 54 | 60 | 66 | 72 | 78 | 84 | 90 | 96 | 102 | 108 | 114 | 120 | 126 | 132 | 138 | 144 | 150 |
| **7** | 14 | 21 | 28 | 35 | 42 | 49 | 56 | 63 | 70 | 77 | 84 | 91 | 98 | 105 | 112 | 119 | 126 | 133 | 140 | 147 | 154 | 161 | 168 | 175 |
| **8** | 16 | 24 | 32 | 40 | 48 | 56 | 64 | 72 | 80 | 88 | 96 | 104 | 112 | 120 | 128 | 136 | 144 | 152 | 160 | 168 | 176 | 184 | 192 | 200 |
| **9** | 18 | 27 | 36 | 45 | 54 | 63 | 72 | 81 | 90 | 99 | 108 | 117 | 126 | 135 | 144 | 153 | 162 | 171 | 180 | 189 | 198 | 207 | 216 | 225 |
| **10** | 20 | 30 | 40 | 50 | 60 | 70 | 80 | 90 | 100 | 110 | 120 | 130 | 140 | 150 | 160 | 170 | 180 | 190 | 200 | 210 | 220 | 230 | 240 | 250 |
| **11** | 22 | 33 | 44 | 55 | 66 | 77 | 88 | 99 | 110 | 121 | 132 | 143 | 154 | 165 | 176 | 187 | 198 | 209 | 220 | 231 | 242 | 253 | 264 | 275 |
| **12** | 24 | 36 | 48 | 60 | 72 | 84 | 96 | 108 | 120 | 132 | 144 | 156 | 168 | 180 | 192 | 204 | 216 | 228 | 240 | 252 | 264 | 276 | 288 | 300 |
| **13** | 26 | 39 | 52 | 65 | 78 | 91 | 104 | 117 | 130 | 143 | 156 | 169 | 182 | 195 | 208 | 221 | 234 | 247 | 260 | 273 | 286 | 299 | 312 | 325 |
| **14** | 28 | 42 | 56 | 70 | 84 | 98 | 112 | 126 | 140 | 154 | 168 | 182 | 196 | 210 | 224 | 238 | 252 | 266 | 280 | 294 | 308 | 322 | 336 | 350 |
| **15** | 30 | 45 | 60 | 75 | 90 | 105 | 120 | 135 | 150 | 165 | 180 | 195 | 210 | 225 | 240 | 255 | 270 | 285 | 300 | 315 | 330 | 345 | 360 | 375 |
| **16** | 32 | 48 | 64 | 80 | 96 | 112 | 128 | 144 | 160 | 176 | 192 | 208 | 224 | 240 | 256 | 272 | 288 | 304 | 320 | 336 | 352 | 368 | 384 | 400 |
| **17** | 34 | 51 | 68 | 85 | 102 | 119 | 136 | 153 | 170 | 187 | 204 | 221 | 238 | 255 | 272 | 289 | 306 | 323 | 340 | 357 | 374 | 391 | 408 | 425 |
| **18** | 36 | 54 | 72 | 90 | 108 | 126 | 144 | 162 | 180 | 198 | 216 | 234 | 252 | 270 | 288 | 306 | 324 | 342 | 360 | 378 | 396 | 414 | 432 | 450 |
| **19** | 38 | 57 | 76 | 95 | 114 | 133 | 152 | 171 | 190 | 209 | 228 | 247 | 266 | 285 | 304 | 323 | 342 | 361 | 380 | 399 | 418 | 437 | 456 | 475 |
| **20** | 40 | 60 | 80 | 100 | 120 | 140 | 160 | 180 | 200 | 220 | 240 | 260 | 280 | 300 | 320 | 340 | 360 | 380 | 400 | 420 | 440 | 460 | 480 | 500 |
| **21** | 42 | 63 | 84 | 105 | 126 | 147 | 168 | 189 | 210 | 231 | 252 | 273 | 294 | 315 | 336 | 357 | 378 | 399 | 420 | 441 | 462 | 483 | 504 | 525 |
| **22** | 44 | 66 | 88 | 110 | 132 | 154 | 176 | 198 | 220 | 242 | 264 | 286 | 308 | 330 | 352 | 374 | 396 | 418 | 440 | 462 | 484 | 506 | 528 | 550 |
| **23** | 46 | 69 | 92 | 115 | 138 | 161 | 184 | 207 | 230 | 253 | 276 | 299 | 322 | 345 | 368 | 391 | 414 | 437 | 460 | 483 | 506 | 529 | 552 | 575 |
| **24** | 48 | 72 | 96 | 120 | 144 | 168 | 192 | 216 | 240 | 264 | 288 | 312 | 336 | 360 | 384 | 408 | 432 | 456 | 480 | 501 | 528 | 552 | 576 | 600 |
| **25** | 50 | 75 | 100 | 125 | 150 | 175 | 200 | 225 | 250 | 275 | 300 | 325 | 350 | 375 | 400 | 425 | 450 | 475 | 500 | 525 | 550 | 575 | 600 | 625 |

## Mathematical signs and symbols

|  |  |
|---|---|
| $+$ | plus; positive; underestimate |
| $-$ | minus; negative; overestimate |
| $\pm$ | plus or minus; positive or negative; degree of accuracy |
| $\mp$ | minus or plus; negative or positive |
| $\times$ | multiplies (colloq. 'times') (6x 4) |
| $\cdot$ | multiplies (colloq. 'times') (6.4); scalar product of two vectors (A • B) |
| $\div$ | divided by (6÷4) |
| $/$ | divided by; ratio of (6/4) |
| $-$ | divided by; ratio of ($\frac{6}{4}$) |
| $=$ | equals |
| $\neq$, $\neq$ | not equal to |
| $\equiv$ | identical with |
| $\not\equiv$, $\not\equiv$ | not identical with |
| $:$ | ratio of (6 : 4); scalar product of two tensors (X : Y) |
| $::$ | proportionately equals (1 : 2 :: 2 : 4) |
| $\approx$ | approximately equal to; equivalent to; similar to |
| $>$ | greater than |
| $\gg$ | much greater than |
| $\ngtr$ | not greater than |
| $<$ | less than |
| $\ll$ | much less than |
| $\nless$ | not less than |
| $\geqslant$, $\geqq$, $\gtreqless$ | equal to or greater than |
| $\leqslant$, $\leqq$, $\lesseqgtr$ | equal to or less than |
| $\propto$ | directly proportional to |
| ( ) | parentheses |
| [ ] | brackets |
| { } | braces |
| — | vinculum: division ($\overline{a-b}$); chord of circle or length of line ($\overline{AB}$); arithmetic mean ($\bar{X}$) |

|  |  |
|---|---|
| $\infty$ | infinity |
| $\rightarrow$ | approaches the limit |
| $\sqrt{}$ | square root |
| $\sqrt[3]{}$, $\sqrt[4]{}$ | cube root, fourth root, etc. |
| ! | factorial (4! = 4 x 3 x 2 x 1) |
| % | percent |
| ′ | prime; minute(s) of arc; foot/feet |
| ″ | double prime; second(s) of arc; inch(es) |
| $\frown$ | arc of circle |
| $^\circ$ | degree of arc |
| $\angle$, $\angle$s | angle(s) |
| $\veebar$ | equiangular |
| $\perp$ | perpendicular |
| $\parallel$ | parallel |
| ○, Ⓢ | circle(s) |
| $\triangle$, $\triangle$s | triangle(s) |
| □ | square(s) |
| ▭ | rectangle |
| ▱ | parallelogram |
| $\cong$ | congruent to |
| $\therefore$ | therefore |
| $\because$ | because |
| $\underline{\underline{m}}$ | measured by |
| $\triangle$ | increment |
| $\Sigma$ | summation |
| $\Pi$ | product |
| $\int$ | integral sign |
| $\nabla$ | del: differential operator |
| $\cap$ | union |
| $\cup$ | interaction |

## Squares and roots

| No. | Square | Cube | Square root | Cube root | No. | Square | Cube | Square root | Cube root |
|---|---|---|---|---|---|---|---|---|---|
| 1 | 1 | 1 | 1.000 | 1.000 | 13 | 169 | 2 197 | 3.606 | 2.351 |
| 2 | 4 | 8 | 1.414 | 1.260 | 14 | 196 | 2 744 | 3.742 | 2.410 |
| 3 | 9 | 27 | 1.732 | 1.442 | 15 | 225 | 3 375 | 3.873 | 2.466 |
| 4 | 16 | 64 | 2.000 | 1.587 | 16 | 256 | 4 096 | 4.000 | 2.520 |
| 5 | 25 | 125 | 2.236 | 1.710 | 17 | 289 | 4 913 | 4.123 | 2.571 |
| 6 | 36 | 216 | 2.449 | 1.817 | 18 | 324 | 5 832 | 4.243 | 2.621 |
| 7 | 49 | 343 | 2.646 | 1.913 | 19 | 361 | 6 859 | 4.359 | 2.668 |
| 8 | 64 | 512 | 2.828 | 2.000 | 20 | 400 | 8 000 | 4.472 | 2.714 |
| 9 | 81 | 729 | 3.000 | 2.080 | 25 | 625 | 15 625 | 5.000 | 2.924 |
| 10 | 100 | 1 000 | 3.162 | 2.154 | 30 | 900 | 27 000 | 5.477 | 3.107 |
| 11 | 121 | 1 331 | 3.317 | 2.224 | 40 | 1 600 | 64 000 | 6.325 | 3.420 |
| 12 | 144 | 1 728 | 3.464 | 2.289 | 50 | 2 500 | 125 000 | 7.071 | 3.684 |

## Common measures

### ❑ Metric units

| Length | | Imperial equivalent |
|---|---|---|
| | 1 millimetre | 0.03937 in |
| 10 mm | 1 centimetre | 0.39 in |
| 10 cm | 1 decimetre | 3.94 in |
| 100 cm | 1 metre | 39.37 in |
| 1 000 m | 1 kilometre | 0.62 mile |
| **Area** | | |
| | 1 square millimetre | 0.0016 sq in |
| | 1 square centimetre | 0.155 sq in |
| 100 sq cm | 1 square decimetre | 15.5 sq in |
| 10 000 sq cm | 1 square metre | 10.76 sq ft |
| 10 000 sq m | 1 hectare | 2.47 acres |
| **Volume** | | |
| | 1 cubic centimetre | 0.016 cu in |
| 1 000 cu cm | 1 cubic decimetre | 61.024 cu in |
| 1 000 cu dm | 1 cubic metre | 35.31 cu ft |
| | | 1.308 cu yds |
| *Liquid volume* | | |
| | 1 litre | 1.76 pints |
| 100 litres | 1 hectolitre | 22 gallons |
| **Weight** | | |
| | 1 gram | 0.035 oz |
| 1 000 g | 1 kilogram | 2.2046 lb |
| 1 000 kg | 1 tonne | 0.9842 ton |

### ❑ Imperial units

| Length | | Metric equivalent |
|---|---|---|
| | 1 inch | 2.54 cm |
| 12 in | 1 foot | 30.48 cm |
| 3 ft | 1 yard | 0.9144 m |
| 1 760 yd | 1 mile | 1.6093 km |
| **Area** | | |
| | 1 square inch | 6.45 sq cm |
| 144 sq in | 1 square foot | 0.0929 $m^2$ |
| 9 sq ft | 1 square yard | 0.836 $m^2$ |
| 4 840 sq yd | 1 acre | 0.405 ha |
| 640 acres | 1 square mile | 259 ha |

| Volume | | Metric equivalent |
|---|---|---|
| | 1 cubic inch | 16.3871 $cm^3$ |
| 1 728 cu in | 1 cubic foot | 0.028 $m^3$ |
| 27 cu ft | 1 cubic yard | 0.765 $m^3$ |
| *Liquid volume* | | |
| | 1 pint | 0.57 litre |
| 2 pints | 1 quart | 1.14 litres |
| 4 quarts | 1 gallon | 4.55 litres |
| **Weight** | | |
| | 1 ounce | 28.3495 g |
| 16 oz | 1 pound | 0.4536 kg |
| 14 lb | 1 stone | 6.35 kg |
| 8 stones | 1 hundredweight | 50.8 kg |
| 20 cwt | 1 ton | 1.016 tonnes |

## Conversion factors

### ❑ Imperial to metric

| Length | | | Multiply by |
|---|---|---|---|
| inches | → | millimetres | 25.4 |
| inches | → | centimetres | 2.54 |
| feet | → | metres | 0.3048 |
| yards | → | metres | 0.9144 |
| statute miles | → | kilometres | 1.6093 |
| nautical miles | → | kilometres | 1.852 |
| **Area** | | | |
| square inches | → | square centimetres | 6.4516 |
| square feet | → | square metres | 0.0929 |
| square yards | → | square metres | 0.8361 |
| acres | → | hectares | 0.4047 |
| square miles | → | square kilometres | 2.5899 |
| **Volume** | | | |
| cubic inches | → | cubic centimetres | 16.3871 |
| cubic feet | → | cubic metres | 0.0283 |
| cubic yards | → | cubic metres | 0.7646 |
| **Capacity** | | | |
| UK fluid ounces | → | litres | 0.0284 |
| US fluid ounces | → | litres | 0.0296 |
| UK pints | → | litres | 0.5682 |
| US pints | → | litres | 0.4732 |
| UK gallons | → | litres | 4.546 |
| US gallons | → | litres | 3.7854 |
| **Weight** | | | |
| ounces (avoirdupois) | → | grams | 28.3495 |
| ounces (troy) | → | grams | 31.1035 |
| pounds | → | kilograms | 0.4536 |
| tons (long) | → | tonnes | 1.016 |

| Length | | | Multiply by |
|---|---|---|---|
| millimetres | → | inches | 0.0394 |
| centimetres | → | inches | 0.3937 |
| metres | → | feet | 3.2808 |
| metres | → | yards | 1.0936 |
| kilometres | → | statute miles | 0.6214 |
| kilometres | → | nautical miles | 0.54 |
| **Area** | | | |
| square centimetres | → | square inches | 0.155 |
| square metres | → | square feet | 10.764 |
| square metres | → | square yards | 1.196 |
| hectares | → | acres | 2.471 |
| square kilometres | → | square miles | 0.386 |
| **Volume** | | | |
| cubic centimetres | → | cubic inches | 0.061 |
| cubic metres | → | cubic feet | 35.315 |
| cubic metres | → | cubic yards | 1.308 |
| **Capacity** | | | |
| litres | → | UK fluid ounces | 35.1961 |
| litres | → | US fluid ounces | 33.8150 |
| litres | → | UK pints | 1.7598 |
| litres | → | US pints | 2.1134 |
| litres | → | UK gallons | 0.2199 |
| litres | → | US gallons | 0.2642 |
| **Weight** | | | |
| grams | → | ounces (avoirdupois) | 0.0353 |
| grams | → | ounces (troy) | 0.0322 |
| kilograms | → | pounds | 2.2046 |
| tonnes | → | tons (long) | 0.9842 |

## Conversion tables: length

| in | cm | in | cm | cm | in |
|---|---|---|---|---|---|
| ⅛ | 0.3 | 16 | 40.6 | 1 | 0.39 |
| ¼ | 0.6 | 17 | 43.2 | 2 | 0.79 |
| ⅜ | 1 | 18 | 45.7 | 3 | 1.18 |
| ½ | 1.3 | 19 | 48.3 | 4 | 1.57 |
| ⅝ | 1.6 | 20 | 50.8 | 5 | 1.97 |
| ¾ | 1.9 | 21 | 53.3 | 6 | 2.36 |
| ⅞ | 2.2 | 22 | 55.9 | 7 | 2.76 |
| 1 | 2.5 | 23 | 58.4 | 8 | 3.15 |
| 2 | 5.1 | 24 | 61 | 9 | 3.54 |
| 3 | 7.6 | 25 | 63.5 | 10 | 3.94 |
| 4 | 10.2 | 26 | 66 | 11 | 4.33 |
| 5 | 12.7 | 27 | 68.6 | 12 | 4.72 |
| 6 | 15.2 | 28 | 71.1 | 13 | 5.12 |
| 7 | 17.8 | 29 | 73.7 | 14 | 5.51 |
| 8 | 20.3 | 30 | 76.2 | 15 | 5.91 |
| 9 | 22.9 | 40 | 101.6 | 16 | 6.30 |
| 10 | 25.4 | 50 | 127 | 17 | 6.69 |

| cm | in |
|---|---|
| 24 | 9.45 |
| 25 | 9.84 |
| 26 | 10.24 |
| 27 | 10.63 |
| 28 | 11.02 |
| 29 | 11.42 |
| 30 | 11.81 |
| 31 | 12.20 |
| 32 | 12.60 |
| 33 | 12.99 |
| 34 | 13.39 |
| 35 | 13.78 |
| 36 | 14.17 |
| 37 | 14.57 |
| 38 | 14.96 |
| 39 | 15.35 |
| 40 | 15.75 |

| in | mm |
|---|---|
| ⅛ | 3.2 |
| ¼ | 6.4 |
| ⅜ | 9.5 |
| ½ | 12.7 |
| ⅝ | 15.9 |
| ¾ | 19 |
| ⅞ | 22.2 |
| 1 | 25.4 |
| 2 | 50.8 |
| 3 | 76.2 |
| 4 | 101.6 |
| 5 | 127 |
| 6 | 152.4 |
| 7 | 177.8 |
| 8 | 203.2 |
| 9 | 228.6 |
| 10 | 254 |

| mm | in |
|---|---|
| 1 | 0.04 |
| 2 | 0.08 |
| 3 | 0.12 |
| 4 | 0.16 |
| 5 | 0.20 |
| 6 | 0.24 |
| 7 | 0.28 |
| 8 | 0.31 |
| 9 | 0.35 |
| 10 | 0.39 |
| 11 | 0.43 |
| 12 | 0.47 |
| 13 | 0.51 |
| 14 | 0.55 |
| 15 | 0.59 |
| 16 | 0.63 |
| 17 | 0.67 |

Exact conversions 1 in = 2.54 cm 1 cm = 0.3937 in 1 in = 25.40 mm 1 mm = 0.0394 in

| ft | m | m | ft | yd | m | m | yd | mi* | km | km | mi* |
|---|---|---|---|---|---|---|---|---|---|---|---|
| 1 | 0.3 | 1 | 3.3 | 1 | 0.9 | 1 | 1.1 | 1 | 1.6 | 1 | 0.6 |
| 2 | 0.6 | 2 | 6.6 | 2 | 1.8 | 2 | 2.2 | 2 | 3.2 | 2 | 1.2 |
| 3 | 0.9 | 3 | 9.8 | 3 | 2.7 | 3 | 3.3 | 3 | 4.8 | 3 | 1.9 |
| 4 | 1.2 | 4 | 13.1 | 4 | 3.7 | 4 | 4.4 | 4 | 6.4 | 4 | 2.5 |
| 5 | 1.5 | 5 | 16.4 | 5 | 4.6 | 5 | 5.5 | 5 | 8.0 | 5 | 3.1 |
| 6 | 1.8 | 6 | 19.7 | 6 | 5.5 | 6 | 6.6 | 6 | 9.7 | 6 | 3.7 |
| 7 | 2.1 | 7 | 23.0 | 7 | 6.4 | 7 | 7.7 | 7 | 11.3 | 7 | 4.3 |
| 8 | 2.4 | 8 | 26.2 | 8 | 7.3 | 8 | 8.7 | 8 | 12.9 | 8 | 5.0 |
| 9 | 2.7 | 9 | 29.5 | 9 | 8.2 | 9 | 9.8 | 9 | 14.5 | 9 | 5.6 |
| 10 | 3.0 | 10 | 32.8 | 10 | 9.1 | 10 | 10.9 | 10 | 16.1 | 10 | 6.2 |
| 15 | 4.6 | 15 | 49.2 | 15 | 13.7 | 15 | 16.4 | 15 | 24.1 | 15 | 9.3 |
| 20 | 6.1 | 20 | 65.5 | 20 | 18.3 | 20 | 21.9 | 20 | 32.2 | 20 | 12.4 |
| 25 | 7.6 | 25 | 82.0 | 25 | 22.9 | 25 | 27.3 | 25 | 40.2 | 25 | 15.5 |
| 30 | 9.1 | 30 | 98.4 | 30 | 27.4 | 30 | 32.8 | 30 | 48.3 | 30 | 18.6 |
| 35 | 10.7 | 35 | 114.8 | 35 | 32.0 | 35 | 38.3 | 35 | 56.3 | 35 | 21.7 |
| 40 | 12.2 | 40 | 131.2 | 40 | 36.6 | 40 | 43.7 | 40 | 64.4 | 40 | 24.9 |
| 45 | 13.7 | 45 | 147.6 | 45 | 41.1 | 45 | 49.2 | 45 | 72.4 | 45 | 28.0 |
| 50 | 15.2 | 50 | 164.0 | 50 | 45.7 | 50 | 54.7 | 50 | 80.5 | 50 | 31.1 |
| 75 | 22.9 | 75 | 246.1 | 75 | 68.6 | 75 | 82.0 | 55 | 88.5 | 55 | 34.2 |
| 100 | 30.5 | 100 | 328.1 | 100 | 91.4 | 100 | 109.4 | 60 | 96.6 | 60 | 37.3 |
| 200 | 61.0 | 200 | 656.2 | 200 | 182.9 | 200 | 218.7 | 65 | 104.6 | 65 | 40.4 |
| 300 | 91.4 | 300 | 984.3 | 220 | 201.2 | 220 | 240.6 | 70 | 112.7 | 70 | 43.5 |
| 400 | 121.9 | 400 | 1 312.3 | 300 | 274.3 | 300 | 328.1 | 75 | 120.7 | 75 | 46.6 |
| 500 | 152.4 | 500 | 1 640.4 | 400 | 365.8 | 400 | 437.4 | 80 | 128.7 | 80 | 49.7 |
| 600 | 182.9 | 600 | 1 968.5 | 440 | 402.3 | 440 | 481.2 | 85 | 136.8 | 85 | 52.8 |
| 700 | 213.4 | 700 | 2 296.6 | 500 | 457.2 | 500 | 546.8 | 90 | 144.8 | 90 | 55.9 |
| 800 | 243.8 | 800 | 2 624.7 | 600 | 548.6 | 600 | 656.2 | 95 | 152.9 | 95 | 59.0 |
| 900 | 274.3 | 900 | 2 952.8 | 700 | 640.1 | 700 | 765.5 | 100 | 160.9 | 100 | 62.1 |
| 1 000 | 304.8 | 1 000 | 3 280.8 | 800 | 731.5 | 800 | 874.9 | 200 | 321.9 | 200 | 124.3 |
| 1 500 | 457.2 | 1 500 | 4 921.3 | 880 | 804.7 | 880 | 962.4 | 300 | 482.8 | 300 | 186.4 |
| 2 000 | 609.6 | 2 000 | 6 561.7 | 900 | 823.0 | 900 | 984.2 | 400 | 643.7 | 400 | 248.5 |
| 2 500 | 762.0 | 2 500 | 8 202.1 | 1 000 | 914.4 | 1 000 | 1 093.6 | 500 | 804.7 | 500 | 310.7 |
| 3 000 | 914.4 | 3 000 | 9 842.5 | 1 500 | 1 371.6 | 1 500 | 1 640.4 | 750 | 1 207.0 | 750 | 466.0 |
| 3 500 | 1 066.8 | 3 500 | 11 482.9 | 2 000 | 1 828.8 | 2 000 | 2 187.2 | 1 000 | 1 609.3 | 1 000 | 621.4 |
| 4 000 | 1 219.2 | 4 000 | 13 123.4 | 2 500 | 2 286.0 | 2 500 | 2 734.0 | 2 500 | 4 023.4 | 2 500 | 1 553.4 |
| 5 000 | 1 524.0 | 5 000 | 16 404.2 | 5 000 | 4 572.0 | 5 000 | 5 468.1 | 5 000 | 8 046.7 | 5 000 | 3 106.9 |

* Statute miles

Exact conversions 1 ft = 0.3048 m 1 m = 3.2808 ft 1 yd = 0.9144 m 1 m = 1.0936 yd 1 mi = 1.6093 km 1 km = 0.6214 mi

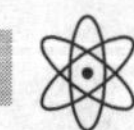



## Conversion tables: area

| sq in | sq cm | sq cm | sq in | sq ft | sq m | sq m | sq ft | acres | hectares | hectares | acres |
|---|---|---|---|---|---|---|---|---|---|---|---|
| 1 | 6.45 | 1 | 0.16 | 1 | 0.09 | 1 | 10.8 | 1 | 0.40 | 1 | 2.5 |
| 2 | 12.90 | 2 | 0.31 | 2 | 0.19 | 2 | 21.5 | 2 | 0.81 | 2 | 4.9 |
| 3 | 19.35 | 3 | 0.47 | 3 | 0.28 | 3 | 32.3 | 3 | 1.21 | 3 | 7.4 |
| 4 | 25.81 | 4 | 0.62 | 4 | 0.37 | 4 | 43.1 | 4 | 1.62 | 4 | 9.9 |
| 5 | 32.26 | 5 | 0.78 | 5 | 0.46 | 5 | 53.8 | 5 | 2.02 | 5 | 12.4 |
| 6 | 38.71 | 6 | 0.93 | 6 | 0.56 | 6 | 64.6 | 6 | 2.43 | 6 | 14.8 |
| 7 | 45.16 | 7 | 1.09 | 7 | 0.65 | 7 | 75.3 | 7 | 2.83 | 7 | 17.3 |
| 8 | 51.61 | 8 | 1.24 | 8 | 0.74 | 8 | 86.1 | 8 | 3.24 | 8 | 19.8 |
| 9 | 58.06 | 9 | 1.40 | 9 | 0.84 | 9 | 96.9 | 9 | 3.64 | 9 | 22.2 |
| 10 | 64.52 | 10 | 1.55 | 10 | 0.93 | 10 | 107.6 | 10 | 4.05 | 10 | 24.7 |
| 11 | 70.97 | 11 | 1.71 | 11 | 1.02 | 11 | 118.4 | 11 | 4.45 | 11 | 27.2 |
| 12 | 77.42 | 12 | 1.86 | 12 | 1.11 | 12 | 129.2 | 12 | 4.86 | 12 | 29.7 |
| 13 | 83.87 | 13 | 2.02 | 13 | 1.21 | 13 | 139.9 | 13 | 5.26 | 13 | 32.1 |
| 14 | 90.32 | 14 | 2.17 | 14 | 1.30 | 14 | 150.7 | 14 | 5.67 | 14 | 34.6 |
| 15 | 96.77 | 15 | 2.33 | 15 | 1.39 | 15 | 161.5 | 15 | 6.07 | 15 | 37.1 |
| 16 | 103.23 | 16 | 2.48 | 16 | 1.49 | 16 | 172.2 | 16 | 6.47 | 16 | 39.5 |
| 17 | 109.68 | 17 | 2.64 | 17 | 1.58 | 17 | 183 | 17 | 6.88 | 17 | 42 |
| 18 | 116.13 | 18 | 2.79 | 18 | 1.67 | 18 | 193.8 | 18 | 7.28 | 18 | 44.5 |
| 19 | 122.58 | 19 | 2.95 | 19 | 1.77 | 19 | 204.5 | 19 | 7.69 | 19 | 46.9 |
| 20 | 129.03 | 20 | 3.10 | 20 | 1.86 | 20 | 215.3 | 20 | 8.09 | 20 | 49.4 |
| 25 | 161.29 | 25 | 3.88 | 25 | 2.32 | 25 | 269.1 | 25 | 10.12 | 25 | 61.8 |
| 50 | 322.58 | 50 | 7.75 | 50 | 4.65 | 50 | 538.2 | 50 | 20.23 | 50 | 123.6 |
| 75 | 483.87 | 75 | 11.63 | 75 | 6.97 | 75 | 807.3 | 75 | 30.35 | 75 | 185.3 |
| 100 | 645.16 | 100 | 15.50 | 100 | 9.29 | 100 | 1 076.4 | 100 | 40.47 | 100 | 247.1 |
| 125 | 806.45 | 125 | 19.38 | 250 | 23.23 | 250 | 2 691 | 250 | 101.17 | 250 | 617.8 |
| 150 | 967.74 | 150 | 23.25 | 500 | 46.45 | 500 | 5 382 | 500 | 202.34 | 500 | 1 235.5 |
| | | | | 750 | 69.68 | 750 | 8 072.9 | 750 | 303.51 | 750 | 1 853.3 |
| | | | | 1 000 | 92.90 | 1 000 | 10 763.9 | 1 000 | 404.69 | 1 000 | 2 471.1 |
| | | | | | | | | 1 500 | 607.03 | 1 500 | 3 706.6 |

Exact conversions $1\ in^2 = 6.4516\ cm^2$ $1\ cm^2 = 0.155\ in^2$ $1\ ft^2 = 0.0929\ m^2$
$1\ m^2 = 10.7639\ ft^2$ 1 acre = 0.4047 hectares 1 hectare = 2.471 acres

| sq mi* → | sq km |
|---|---|
| 1 | 2.6 |
| 2 | 5.2 |
| 3 | 7.8 |
| 4 | 10.4 |
| 5 | 12.9 |
| 6 | 15.5 |
| 7 | 18.1 |
| 8 | 20.7 |
| 9 | 23.3 |
| 10 | 25.9 |
| 20 | 51.8 |
| 21 | 54.4 |
| 22 | 57.0 |
| 23 | 59.6 |
| 24 | 62.2 |
| 25 | 64.7 |
| 30 | 77.7 |
| 40 | 103.6 |
| 50 | 129.5 |
| 100 | 259.0 |
| 200 | 518.0 |
| 300 | 777.0 |
| 400 | 1 036.0 |
| 500 | 1 295.0 |

| sq km → | sq mi* |
|---|---|
| 1 | 0.39 |
| 2 | 0.77 |
| 3 | 1.16 |
| 4 | 1.54 |
| 5 | 1.93 |
| 6 | 2.32 |
| 7 | 2.70 |
| 8 | 3.09 |
| 9 | 3.47 |
| 10 | 3.86 |
| 20 | 7.72 |
| 21 | 8.11 |
| 22 | 8.49 |
| 23 | 8.88 |
| 24 | 9.27 |
| 25 | 9.65 |
| 30 | 11.58 |
| 40 | 15.44 |
| 50 | 19.31 |
| 100 | 38.61 |
| 200 | 77.22 |
| 300 | 115.83 |
| 400 | 154.44 |
| 500 | 193.05 |

| sq mi* | → sq km | sq km | → sq mi* |
|---|---|---|---|
| 600 | 1 554.0 | 600 | 231.66 |
| 700 | 1 813.0 | 700 | 270.27 |
| 800 | 2 072.0 | 800 | 308.88 |
| 900 | 2 331.0 | 900 | 347.49 |
| 1 000 | 2 590.0 | 1 000 | 386.1 |
| 1 500 | 3 885.0 | 1 500 | 579.2 |
| 2 000 | 5 180.0 | 2 000 | 772.2 |

* Statute miles

Exact conversions 1 sq mi = 2.589999 sq km 1 sq km = 0.3861 sq mi

## Conversion tables: volume

| cu in | cu cm | cu cm | cu in | cu ft | cu m | cu m | cu ft | cu yd | cu m | cu m | cu yd |
|---|---|---|---|---|---|---|---|---|---|---|---|
| 1 | 16.39 | 1 | 0.06 | 1 | 0.03 | 1 | 35.3 | 1 | 0.76 | 1 | 1.31 |
| 2 | 32.77 | 2 | 0.12 | 2 | 0.06 | 2 | 70.6 | 2 | 1.53 | 2 | 2.62 |
| 3 | 49.16 | 3 | 0.18 | 3 | 0.08 | 3 | 105.9 | 3 | 2.29 | 3 | 3.92 |
| 4 | 65.55 | 4 | 0.24 | 4 | 0.11 | 4 | 141.3 | 4 | 3.06 | 4 | 5.23 |
| 5 | 81.93 | 5 | 0.30 | 5 | 0.14 | 5 | 176.6 | 5 | 3.82 | 5 | 6.54 |
| 6 | 93.32 | 6 | 0.37 | 6 | 0.17 | 6 | 211.9 | 6 | 4.59 | 6 | 7.85 |
| 7 | 114.71 | 7 | 0.43 | 7 | 0.20 | 7 | 247.2 | 7 | 5.35 | 7 | 9.16 |
| 8 | 131.10 | 8 | 0.49 | 8 | 0.23 | 8 | 282.5 | 8 | 6.12 | 8 | 10.46 |
| 9 | 147.48 | 9 | 0.55 | 9 | 0.25 | 9 | 317.8 | 9 | 6.88 | 9 | 11.77 |
| 10 | 163.87 | 10 | 0.61 | 10 | 0.28 | 10 | 353.1 | 10 | 7.65 | 10 | 13.08 |
| 15 | 245.81 | 15 | 0.92 | 15 | 0.42 | 15 | 529.7 | 15 | 11.47 | 15 | 19.62 |
| 20 | 327.74 | 20 | 1.22 | 20 | 0.57 | 20 | 706.3 | 20 | 15.29 | 20 | 26.16 |
| 50 | 819.35 | 50 | 3.05 | 50 | 1.41 | 50 | 1 765.7 | 50 | 38.23 | 50 | 65.40 |
| 100 | 1 638.71 | 100 | 6.10 | 100 | 2.83 | 100 | 3 531.5 | 100 | 76.46 | 100 | 130.80 |

Exact conversions $1\ in^3 = 16.3871\ cm^3$ $1\ ft^3 = 0.0283\ m^3$ $1\ yd^3 = 0.7646\ m^3$
$1\ cm^3 = 0.0610\ in^3$ $1\ m^3 = 35.3147\ ft^3$ $1\ m^3 = 1.3080\ yd^3$

## Conversion tables: capacity

### ❑ Liquid measure

| UK fluid ounces | litres | US fluid ounces | litres | litres | UK fluid ounces | US fluid ounces |
|---|---|---|---|---|---|---|
| 1 | 0.0284 | 1 | 0.0296 | 1 | 35.2 | 33.8 |
| 2 | 0.0568 | 2 | 0.0592 | 2 | 70.4 | 67.6 |
| 3 | 0.0852 | 3 | 0.0888 | 3 | 105.6 | 101.4 |
| 4 | 0.114 | 4 | 0.118 | 4 | 140.8 | 135.3 |
| 5 | 0.142 | 5 | 0.148 | 5 | 176.0 | 169.1 |
| 6 | 0.170 | 6 | 0.178 | 6 | 211.2 | 202.9 |
| 7 | 0.199 | 7 | 0.207 | 7 | 246.4 | 236.7 |
| 8 | 0.227 | 8 | 0.237 | 8 | 281.6 | 270.5 |
| 9 | 0.256 | 9 | 0.266 | 9 | 316.8 | 304.3 |
| 10 | 0.284 | 10 | 0.296 | 10 | 352.0 | 338.1 |
| 11 | 0.312 | 11 | 0.326 | 11 | 387.2 | 372.0 |
| 12 | 0.341 | 12 | 0.355 | 12 | 422.4 | 405.8 |
| 13 | 0.369 | 13 | 0.385 | 13 | 457.5 | 439.6 |
| 14 | 0.397 | 14 | 0.414 | 14 | 492.7 | 473.4 |
| 15 | 0.426 | 15 | 0.444 | 15 | 527.9 | 507.2 |
| 20 | 0.568 | 20 | 0.592 | 20 | 703.9 | 676.3 |
| 50 | 1.42 | 50 | 1.48 | 50 | 1 759.8 | 1 690.7 |
| 100 | 2.84 | 100 | 2.96 | 100 | 3 519.6 | 3 381.5 |

Exact conversions 1 fl oz = 0.0284 l 1 l = 35.1961 UK fl oz
1 fl oz = 0.0296 l 1 l = 33.8140 US fl oz

| UK pints | litres |
|---|---|
| 1 | 0.57 |
| 2 | 1.14 |
| 3 | 1.70 |
| 4 | 2.27 |
| 5 | 2.84 |
| 6 | 3.41 |
| 7 | 3.98 |
| 8 | 4.55 |
| 9 | 5.11 |
| 10 | 5.68 |
| 11 | 6.25 |
| 12 | 6.82 |
| 13 | 7.38 |
| 14 | 7.95 |
| 15 | 8.52 |
| 20 | 11.36 |
| 50 | 28.41 |
| 100 | 56.82 |

| US pints | litres |
|---|---|
| 1 | 0.47 |
| 2 | 0.95 |
| 3 | 1.42 |
| 4 | 1.89 |
| 5 | 2.37 |
| 6 | 2.84 |
| 7 | 3.31 |
| 8 | 3.78 |
| 9 | 4.26 |
| 10 | 4.73 |
| 11 | 5.20 |
| 12 | 5.68 |
| 13 | 6.15 |
| 14 | 6.62 |
| 15 | 7.10 |
| 20 | 9.46 |
| 50 | 23.66 |
| 100 | 47.32 |

| litres | UK pints | US pints |
|---|---|---|
| 1 | 1.76 | 2.11 |
| 2 | 3.52 | 4.23 |
| 3 | 5.28 | 6.34 |
| 4 | 7.04 | 8.45 |
| 5 | 8.80 | 10.57 |
| 6 | 10.56 | 12.68 |
| 7 | 12.32 | 14.79 |
| 8 | 14.08 | 16.91 |
| 9 | 15.84 | 19.02 |
| 10 | 17.60 | 21.13 |
| 11 | 19.36 | 23.25 |
| 12 | 21.12 | 25.36 |
| 13 | 22.88 | 27.47 |
| 14 | 24.64 | 29.59 |
| 15 | 26.40 | 31.70 |
| 20 | 35.20 | 105.67 |
| 50 | 87.99 | 211.34 |
| 100 | 175.98 | 422.68 |

Exact conversions 1 UK pt = 0.5682 l 1 US pt = 0.4732 l 1 l = 1.7598 UK pt, 2.1134 US pt
1 UK pt = 1.20 US pt 1 US pt = 0.83 UK pt 1 US cup = 8 fl oz

| UK gallons | litres |
|---|---|
| 1 | 4.55 |
| 2 | 9.09 |
| 3 | 13.64 |
| 4 | 18.18 |
| 5 | 22.73 |
| 6 | 27.28 |
| 7 | 31.82 |
| 8 | 36.37 |
| 9 | 40.91 |
| 10 | 45.46 |
| 11 | 50.01 |
| 12 | 54.55 |
| 13 | 59.10 |
| 14 | 63.64 |
| 15 | 68.19 |
| 16 | 72.74 |
| 17 | 77.28 |
| 18 | 81.83 |
| 19 | 86.37 |
| 20 | 90.92 |
| 25 | 113.65 |
| 50 | 227.30 |
| 75 | 340.96 |
| 100 | 454.61 |

| US gallons | litres |
|---|---|
| 1 | 3.78 |
| 2 | 7.57 |
| 3 | 11.36 |
| 4 | 15.14 |
| 5 | 18.93 |
| 6 | 22.71 |
| 7 | 26.50 |
| 8 | 30.28 |
| 9 | 34.07 |
| 10 | 37.85 |
| 11 | 41.64 |
| 12 | 45.42 |
| 13 | 49.21 |
| 14 | 52.99 |
| 15 | 56.78 |
| 16 | 60.57 |
| 17 | 64.35 |
| 18 | 68.14 |
| 19 | 71.92 |
| 20 | 75.71 |
| 25 | 94.63 |
| 50 | 189.27 |
| 75 | 283.90 |
| 100 | 378.54 |

| litres | UK gallons | US gallons |
|---|---|---|
| 1 | 0.22 | 0.26 |
| 2 | 0.44 | 0.53 |
| 3 | 0.66 | 0.79 |
| 4 | 0.88 | 1.06 |
| 5 | 1.10 | 1.32 |
| 6 | 1.32 | 1.58 |
| 7 | 1.54 | 1.85 |
| 8 | 1.76 | 2.11 |
| 9 | 1.98 | 2.38 |
| 10 | 2.20 | 2.64 |
| 11 | 2.42 | 2.91 |
| 12 | 2.64 | 3.17 |
| 13 | 2.86 | 3.43 |
| 14 | 3.08 | 3.70 |
| 15 | 3.30 | 3.96 |
| 16 | 3.52 | 4.23 |
| 17 | 3.74 | 4.49 |
| 18 | 3.96 | 4.76 |
| 19 | 4.18 | 5.02 |
| 20 | 4.40 | 5.28 |
| 25 | 5.50 | 6.60 |
| 50 | 11.00 | 13.20 |
| 75 | 16.50 | 19.81 |
| 100 | 22.00 | 26.42 |

Exact conversions 1 UK gal = 4.546 l 1 US gal = 3.7854 l 1 l = 0.220 UK gal, 0.2642 US gal

SCIENCE, ENGINEERING AND MEASUREMENT

## Conversion tables: capacity

| UK gal | US gal |
|---|---|
| 1 | 1.2 |
| 2 | 2.4 |
| 3 | 3.6 |
| 4 | 4.8 |
| 5 | 6 |
| 6 | 7.2 |
| 7 | 8.4 |
| 8 | 9.6 |
| 9 | 10.8 |
| 10 | 12 |
| 11 | 13.2 |
| 12 | 14.4 |
| 13 | 15.6 |
| 14 | 16.8 |
| 15 | 18 |
| 20 | 24 |
| 25 | 30 |
| 50 | 60 |

| US gal | UK gal |
|---|---|
| 1 | 0.8 |
| 2 | 1.7 |
| 3 | 2.5 |
| 4 | 3.3 |
| 5 | 4.2 |
| 6 | 5 |
| 7 | 5.8 |
| 8 | 6.7 |
| 9 | 7.5 |
| 10 | 8.3 |
| 11 | 9.2 |
| 12 | 10 |
| 13 | 10.8 |
| 14 | 11.7 |
| 15 | 12.5 |
| 20 | 16.6 |
| 25 | 20.8 |
| 50 | 41.6 |

Exact conversions 1 UK gal = 1.200929 US gal 1 US gal = 0.832688 UK gal

### ❑ Dry capacity measures

| UK bushels | cu m | litres |
|---|---|---|
| 1 | 0.037 | 36.4 |
| 2 | 0.074 | 72.7 |
| 3 | 0.111 | 109.1 |
| 4 | 0.148 | 145.5 |
| 5 | 0.184 | 181.8 |
| 10 | 0.369 | 363.7 |

| US bushels | cu m | litres |
|---|---|---|
| 1 | 0.035 | 35.2 |
| 2 | 0.071 | 70.5 |
| 3 | 0.106 | 105.7 |
| 4 | 0.141 | 140.9 |
| 5 | 0.175 | 176.2 |
| 10 | 0.353 | 352.4 |

Exact conversions 1 UK bushel = 0.0369 $m^3$ 1 US bushel = 0.9353 $m^3$
1 UK bushel = 36.3677 l 1 US bushel = 35.2381 l

| cu m | UK bushels | US bushels |
|---|---|---|
| 1 | 27.5 | 28.4 |
| 2 | 55.0 | 56.7 |
| 3 | 82.5 | 85.1 |
| 4 | 110 | 113 |
| 5 | 137 | 142 |
| 10 | 275 | 284 |

| litres | UK bushels | US bushels |
|---|---|---|
| 1 | 0.027 | 0.028 |
| 2 | 0.055 | 0.057 |
| 3 | 0.082 | 0.085 |
| 4 | 0.110 | 0.114 |
| 5 | 0.137 | 0.142 |
| 10 | 0.275 | 0.284 |

Exact conversions 1 $m^3$ = 27.4962 UK bu 1 l = 0.0275 UK bu
1 $m^3$ = 28.3776 US bu 1 l = 0.0284 US bu

❑ **Dry capacity measures**

| UK pecks | litres | US pecks | litres |
|---|---|---|---|
| 1 | 9.1 | 1 | 8.8 |
| 2 | 18.2 | 2 | 17.6 |
| 3 | 27.3 | 3 | 26.4 |
| 4 | 36.4 | 4 | 35.2 |
| 5 | 45.5 | 5 | 44 |
| 10 | 90.9 | 10 | 88.1 |

| litres | UK pecks | US pecks |
|---|---|---|
| 1 | 0.110 | 0.113 |
| 2 | 0.220 | 0.226 |
| 3 | 0.330 | 0.339 |
| 4 | 0.440 | 0.454 |
| 5 | 0.550 | 0.567 |
| 10 | 1.100 | 1.135 |

Exact conversions 1 UK pk = 9.0919 l 1 US pk = 8.8095 l 1 l = 0.1100 UK pk = 0.1135 US pk

| US quarts | cu m | litres |
|---|---|---|
| 1 | 1 101 | 1.1 |
| 2 | 2 202 | 2.2 |
| 3 | 3 304 | 3.3 |
| 4 | 4 405 | 4.4 |
| 5 | 5 506 | 5.5 |
| 10 | 11 012 | 11 |

| US pints | cu m | litres |
|---|---|---|
| 1 | 551 | 0.55 |
| 2 | 1 101 | 1.10 |
| 3 | 1 652 | 1.65 |
| 4 | 2 202 | 2.20 |
| 5 | 2 753 | 2.75 |
| 10 | 5 506 | 5.51 |

Exact conversions 1 US qt = 1 101.2209 $cm^3$ 1 US pt = 550.6105 $cm^3$
1 US qt = 1.1012 l 1 US pt = 0.5506 l

## Conversion tables: tyre pressures

| lb per sq in | kg per sq cm | lb per sq in | kg per sq cm |
|---|---|---|---|
| 10 | 0.7 | 26 | 1.8 |
| 15 | 1.1 | 28 | 2 |
| 20 | 1.4 | 30 | 2.1 |
| 24 | 1.7 | 40 | 2.8 |

## Conversion tables: weight

| ounces* | grams | grams | ounces* | pounds | kilograms | pounds | kilograms | kilograms | pounds | kilograms | pounds |
|---|---|---|---|---|---|---|---|---|---|---|---|
| 1 | 28.3 | 1 | 0.04 | 1 | 0.45 | 19 | 8.62 | 1 | 2.2 | 19 | 41.9 |
| 2 | 56.7 | 2 | 0.07 | 2 | 0.91 | 20 | 9.07 | 2 | 4.4 | 20 | 44.1 |
| 3 | 85 | 3 | 0.11 | 3 | 1.36 | 25 | 11.34 | 3 | 6.6 | 25 | 55.1 |
| 4 | 113.4 | 4 | 0.14 | 4 | 1.81 | 30 | 13.61 | 4 | 8.8 | 30 | 66.1 |
| 5 | 141.7 | 5 | 0.18 | 5 | 2.27 | 35 | 15.88 | 5 | 11 | 35 | 77.2 |
| 6 | 170.1 | 6 | 0.21 | 6 | 2.72 | 40 | 18.14 | 6 | 13.2 | 40 | 88.2 |
| 7 | 198.4 | 7 | 0.25 | 7 | 3.18 | 45 | 20.41 | 7 | 15.4 | 45 | 99.2 |
| 8 | 226.8 | 8 | 0.28 | 8 | 3.63 | 50 | 22.68 | 8 | 17.6 | 50 | 110.2 |
| 9 | 255.1 | 9 | 0.32 | 9 | 4.08 | 60 | 27.24 | 9 | 19.8 | 60 | 132.3 |
| 10 | 283.5 | 10 | 0.35 | 10 | 4.54 | 70 | 31.78 | 10 | 22 | 70 | 154.4 |
| 11 | 311.7 | 20 | 0.71 | 11 | 4.99 | 80 | 36.32 | 11 | 24.3 | 80 | 176.4 |
| 12 | 340.2 | 30 | 1.06 | 12 | 5.44 | 90 | 40.86 | 12 | 26.5 | 90 | 198.5 |
| 13 | 368.5 | 40 | 1.41 | 13 | 5.90 | 100 | 45.36 | 13 | 28.7 | 100 | 220.5 |
| 14 | 396.9 | 50 | 1.76 | 14 | 6.35 | 200 | 90.72 | 14 | 30.9 | 200 | 440.9 |
| 15 | 425.2 | 60 | 2.12 | 15 | 6.80 | 250 | 113.40 | 15 | 33.1 | 250 | 551.2 |
| 16 | 453.6 | 70 | 2.47 | 16 | 7.26 | 500 | 226.80 | 16 | 35.3 | 500 | 1 102.3 |
| | | 80 | 2.82 | 17 | 7.71 | 750 | 340.19 | 17 | 37.5 | 750 | 1 653.5 |
| | | 90 | 3.18 | 18 | 8.16 | 1 000 | 453.59 | 18 | 39.7 | 1 000 | 2 204.6 |
| | | 100 | 3.53 | | | | | | | | |

* avoirdupois

Exact conversions 1 oz (avdp) = 28.3495 g 1 g = 0.0353 oz (avdp) 1 lb = 0.454 kg 1 kg = 2.205 lb

## CONVERSION TABLES: WEIGHT

Tons: long, UK 2 240 lb; short, US 2 000 lb

| UK tons | tonnes | US tons | tonnes | UK tons | US tons |
|---|---|---|---|---|---|
| 1 | 1.02 | 1 | 0.91 | 1 | 1.12 |
| 2 | 2.03 | 2 | 1.81 | 2 | 2.24 |
| 3 | 3.05 | 3 | 2.72 | 3 | 3.36 |
| 4 | 4.06 | 4 | 3.63 | 4 | 4.48 |
| 5 | 5.08 | 5 | 4.54 | 5 | 5.6 |
| 10 | 10.16 | 10 | 9.07 | 10 | 11.2 |
| 15 | 15.24 | 15 | 13.61 | 15 | 16.8 |
| 20 | 20.32 | 20 | 18.14 | 20 | 22.4 |
| 50 | 50.80 | 50 | 45.36 | 50 | 56 |
| 75 | 76.20 | 75 | 68.04 | 75 | 84 |
| 100 | 101.60 | 100 | 90.72 | 100 | 102 |

| tonnes | UK tons | US tons | US tons | UK tons |
|---|---|---|---|---|
| 1 | 0.98 | 1.10 | 1 | 0.89 |
| 2 | 1.97 | 2.20 | 2 | 1.79 |
| 3 | 2.95 | 3.30 | 3 | 2.68 |
| 4 | 3.94 | 4.40 | 4 | 3.57 |
| 5 | 4.92 | 5.50 | 5 | 4.46 |
| 10 | 9.84 | 11.02 | 10 | 8.93 |
| 15 | 14.76 | 16.53 | 15 | 13.39 |
| 20 | 19.68 | 22.05 | 20 | 17.86 |
| 50 | 49.21 | 55.11 | 50 | 44.64 |
| 75 | 73.82 | 82.67 | 75 | 66.96 |
| 100 | 98.42 | 110.23 | 100 | 89.29 |

Exact conversions 1 UK ton = 1.0160 tonnes 1 US ton = 0.9072 tonne 1 UK ton = 1.1199 US tons
1 tonne = 0.9842 UK ton = 1.1023 US tons 1 US ton = 0.8929 UK ton

Hundredweights: long, UK 112 lb; short, US 100 lb

| UK cwt | kilograms | US cwt | kilograms | UK cwt | US cwt |
|---|---|---|---|---|---|
| 1 | 50.8 | 1 | 45.4 | 1 | 1.12 |
| 2 | 102 | 2 | 90.7 | 2 | 2.24 |
| 3 | 152 | 3 | 136 | 3 | 3.36 |
| 4 | 203 | 4 | 181 | 4 | 4.48 |
| 5 | 254 | 5 | 227 | 5 | 5.6 |
| 10 | 508 | 10 | 454 | 10 | 11.2 |
| 15 | 762 | 15 | 680 | 15 | 16.8 |
| 20 | 1 016 | 20 | 907 | 20 | 22.4 |
| 50 | 2 540 | 50 | 2 268 | 50 | 56 |
| 75 | 3 810 | 75 | 3 402 | 75 | 84 |
| 100 | 5 080 | 100 | 4 536 | 100 | 102 |

| kilograms | UK cwt | US cwt | US cwt | UK cwt |
|---|---|---|---|---|
| 1 | 0.0197 | 0.022 | 1 | 0.89 |
| 2 | 0.039 | 0.044 | 2 | 1.79 |
| 3 | 0.059 | 0.066 | 3 | 2.68 |
| 4 | 0.079 | 0.088 | 4 | 3.57 |
| 5 | 0.098 | 0.11 | 5 | 4.46 |
| 10 | 0.197 | 0.22 | 10 | 8.93 |
| 15 | 0.295 | 0.33 | 15 | 13.39 |
| 20 | 0.394 | 0.44 | 20 | 17.86 |
| 50 | 0.985 | 1.10 | 50 | 44.64 |
| 75 | 1.477 | 1.65 | 75 | 66.96 |
| 100 | 1.970 | 2.20 | 100 | 89.29 |

Exact conversions 1 UK cwt = 50.8023 kg 1 US cwt = 45.3592 kg 1 UK cwt = 1.1199 US cwt
1 kg = 0.0197 UK cwt = 0.0220 US cwt 1 US cwt = 0.8929 UK cwt

| stones | pounds | stones | pounds |
|---|---|---|---|
| 1 | 14 | 11 | 154 |
| 2 | 28 | 12 | 168 |
| 3 | 42 | 13 | 182 |
| 4 | 56 | 14 | 196 |
| 5 | 70 | 15 | 210 |
| 6 | 84 | 16 | 224 |
| 7 | 98 | 17 | 238 |
| 8 | 112 | 18 | 252 |
| 9 | 126 | 19 | 266 |
| 10 | 140 | 20 | 280 |

| stones | kilograms |
|---|---|
| 1 | 6.35 |
| 2 | 12.70 |
| 3 | 19.05 |
| 4 | 25.40 |
| 5 | 31.75 |
| 6 | 38.10 |
| 7 | 44.45 |
| 8 | 50.80 |
| 9 | 57.15 |
| 10 | 63.50 |

1 st = 14 lb 1 lb = 0.07 st 1 st = 6.350 kg 1 kg = 0.1575 st

## International clothing sizes

Size equivalents are approximate, and may display some variation between manufacturers.

### ❑ Women's suits/dresses

| UK | USA | UK/ Continent |
|---|---|---|
| 8 | 6 | 36 |
| 10 | 8 | 38 |
| 12 | 10 | 40 |
| 14 | 12 | 42 |
| 16 | 14 | 44 |
| 18 | 16 | 46 |
| 20 | 18 | 48 |
| 22 | 20 | 50 |
| 24 | 22 | 52 |

### ❑ Adults' shoes

| UK | USA | UK/ Continent |
|---|---|---|
| 4 | 5½ | 37 |
| 4½ | 6 | 38 |
| 5 | 6½ | 38 |
| 5½ | 7 | 39 |
| 6 | 7½ | 39 |
| 6½ | 8 | 40 |
| 7 | 8½ | 41 |
| 7½ | 8½ | 42 |
| 8 | 9½ | 42 |
| 8½ | 9½ | 43 |
| 9 | 10½ | 43 |
| 9½ | 10½ | 44 |
| 10 | 11½ | 44 |
| 10½ | 11½ | 45 |
| 11 | 12 | 46 |

### ❑ Children's shoes

| UK/USA | UK/Continent |
|---|---|
| 0 | 15 |
| 1 | 17 |
| 2 | 18 |
| 3 | 19 |
| 4 | 20 |
| 5 | 22 |
| 6 | 23 |
| 7 | 24 |
| 8 | 25 |
| 8½ | 26 |
| 9 | 27 |
| 10 | 28 |
| 11 | 29 |
| 12 | 30 |
| 13 | 32 |

### ❑ Women's hosiery

| UK/USA | UK/Continent |
|---|---|
| 8 | 0 |
| 8½ | 1 |
| 9 | 2 |
| 9½ | 3 |
| 10 | 4 |
| 10½ | 5 |

### ❑ Men's suits and overcoats

| UK/USA | Continental |
|---|---|
| 36 | 46 |
| 38 | 48 |
| 40 | 50 |
| 42 | 52 |
| 44 | 54 |
| 46 | 56 |

### ❑ Men's socks

| UK/USA | UK/Continent |
|---|---|
| 9½ | 38–39 |
| 10 | 39–40 |
| 10½ | 40–41 |
| 11 | 41–42 |
| 11½ | 42–43 |

### ❑ Men's shirts

| UK/USA | UK/Continent |
|---|---|
| 12 | 30–31 |
| 12½ | 32 |
| 13 | 33 |
| 13½ | 34–35 |
| 14 | 36 |
| 14½ | 37 |
| 15 | 38 |
| 15½ | 39–40 |
| 16 | 41 |
| 16½ | 42 |
| 17 | 43 |
| 17½ | 44–45 |

SCIENCE, ENGINEERING AND MEASUREMENT

## International pattern sizes

**Young junior/teenage**

| | Bust | | Waist | | Hip | | Back waist length | |
|---|---|---|---|---|---|---|---|---|
| Size | cm | in | cm | in | cm | in | cm | in |
| 5/6 | 71 | 28 | 56 | 22 | 79 | 31 | 34.5 | 13½ |
| 7/8 | 74 | 29 | 58 | 23 | 81 | 32 | 35.5 | 14 |
| 9/10 | 78 | 30½ | 61 | 24 | 85 | 33½ | 37 | 14½ |
| 11/12 | 81 | 32 | 64 | 25 | 89 | 35 | 38 | 15 |
| 13/14 | 85 | 33½ | 66 | 26 | 93 | 36½ | 39 | 15⅜ |
| 15/16 | 89 | 35 | 69 | 27 | 97 | 38 | 40 | 15¾ |

**Misses**

| Size | cm | in | cm | in | cm | in | cm | in |
|---|---|---|---|---|---|---|---|---|
| 6 | 78 | 30½ | 58 | 23 | 83 | 32½ | 39.5 | 15½ |
| 8 | 80 | 31½ | 61 | 24 | 85 | 33½ | 40 | 15¾ |
| 10 | 83 | 32½ | 64 | 25 | 88 | 34½ | 40.5 | 16 |
| 12 | 87 | 34 | 67 | 26½ | 92 | 36 | 41.5 | 16¼ |
| 14 | 92 | 36 | 71 | 28 | 97 | 38 | 42 | 16½ |
| 16 | 97 | 38 | 76 | 30 | 102 | 40 | 42.5 | 16¾ |
| 18 | 102 | 40 | 81 | 32 | 107 | 42 | 43 | 17 |
| 20 | 107 | 42 | 87 | 34 | 112 | 44 | 44 | 17¼ |

**Half-sizes**

| Size | cm | in | cm | in | cm | in | cm | in |
|---|---|---|---|---|---|---|---|---|
| 10½ | 84 | 33 | 69 | 27 | 89 | 35 | 38 | 15 |
| 12½ | 89 | 35 | 74 | 29 | 94 | 37 | 39 | 15¼ |
| 14½ | 94 | 37 | 79 | 31 | 99 | 39 | 39.5 | 15½ |
| 16½ | 99 | 39 | 84 | 33 | 104 | 41 | 40 | 15¾ |
| 18½ | 104 | 41 | 89 | 35 | 109 | 43 | 40.5 | 15⅞ |
| 20½ | 109 | 43 | 96 | 37½ | 116 | 45½ | 40.5 | 16 |
| 22½ | 114 | 45 | 102 | 40 | 122 | 48 | 41 | 16⅛ |
| 24½ | 119 | 47 | 108 | 42½ | 128 | 50½ | 41.5 | 16¼ |

**Women's**

| Size | cm | in | cm | in | cm | in | cm | in |
|---|---|---|---|---|---|---|---|---|
| 38 | 107 | 42 | 89 | 35 | 112 | 44 | 44 | 17¼ |
| 40 | 112 | 44 | 94 | 37 | 117 | 46 | 44 | 17⅜ |
| 42 | 117 | 46 | 99 | 39 | 122 | 48 | 44.5 | 17½ |
| 44 | 122 | 48 | 105 | 41½ | 127 | 50 | 45 | 17⅝ |
| 46 | 127 | 50 | 112 | 44 | 132 | 52 | 45 | 17¾ |
| 48 | 132 | 52 | 118 | 46½ | 137 | 54 | 45.5 | 17⅞ |
| 50 | 137 | 54 | 124 | 49 | 142 | 56 | 46 | 18 |

## International paper sizes

### ❑ A series

| | mm | in |
|---|---|---|
| A0 | 841 × 1 189 | 33.11 × 46.81 |
| A1 | 594 × 841 | 23.39 × 33.1 |
| A2 | 420 × 594 | 16.54 × 23.39 |
| A3 | 297 × 420 | 11.69 × 16.54 |
| A4 | 210 × 297 | 8.27 × 11.69 |
| A5 | 148 × 210 | 5.83 × 8.27 |
| A6 | 105 × 148 | 4.13 × 5.83 |
| A7 | 74 × 105 | 2.91 × 4.13 |
| A8 | 52 × 74 | 2.05 × 2.91 |
| A9 | 37 × 52 | 1.46 × 2.05 |
| A10 | 26 × 37 | 1.02 × 1.46 |

### ❑ B series

| | mm | in |
|---|---|---|
| B0 | 1 000 × 1 414 | 39.37 × 55.67 |
| B1 | 707 × 1 000 | 27.83 × 39.37 |
| B2 | 500 × 707 | 19.68 × 27.83 |
| B3 | 353 × 500 | 13.90 × 19.68 |
| B4 | 250 × 353 | 9.84 × 13.90 |
| B5 | 176 × 250 | 6.93 × 9.84 |
| B6 | 125 × 176 | 4.92 × 6.93 |
| B7 | 88 × 125 | 3.46 × 4.92 |
| B8 | 62 × 88 | 2.44 × 3.46 |
| B9 | 44 × 62 | 1.73 × 2.44 |
| B10 | 31 × 44 | 1.22 × 1.73 |

### ❑ C series

| | mm | in |
|---|---|---|
| C0 | 917 × 1 297 | 36.00 × 51.20 |
| C1 | 648 × 917 | 25.60 × 36.00 |
| C2 | 458 × 648 | 18.00 × 25.60 |
| C3 | 324 × 458 | 12.80 × 18.00 |
| C4 | 229 × 324 | 9.00 × 12.80 |
| C5 | 162 × 229 | 6.40 × 9.00 |
| C6 | 114 × 162 | 4.50 × 6.40 |
| C7 | 81 × 114 | 3.20 × 4.50 |
| DL | 110 × 220 | 4.33 × 8.66 |
| C7/6 | 81 × 162 | 3.19 × 6.38 |

All sizes in these series have sides in the proportion of 1: $\sqrt{2}$.
A series is used for writing paper, books and magazines; B series for posters; C series for envelopes.

## Engineering: bridges

When a single date is given it is the date for completion of construction.

| Name | Location | Length (m)[1] | Type | Date |
|---|---|---|---|---|
| Akashi-Kaikyo | Honshu–Shikoku, Japan | 1 990 | (longest) suspension | 1978–98 |
| Alex Fraser (previously called Annacis) | Vancouver, Canada | 465 | cable-stayed | 1986 |
| Ambassador | Detroit, Michigan, USA | 564 | suspension | 1929 |
| Angostura | Cuidad Bolivar, Venezuela | 712 | suspension | 1967 |
| Astoria | Astoria, Oregon, USA | 376 | truss | 1966 |
| Bayonne (Kill van Kull) | New Jersey–Staten Island, USA | 504 | steel arch | 1932 |
| Bendorf | Rhine River, Coblenz, Germany | 1 030 | cement girder | 1965 |
| Benjamin Franklin | Philadelphia–Camden, USA | 534 | suspension | 1926 |
| Bosporus | Istanbul, Turkey | 1 074 | suspension | 1973 |
| Bosporus II | Istanbul, Turkey | 1 090 | suspension | 1986–8 |
| Bridge of Sighs | Doge's Palace–Pozzi Prison, Venice, Italy | c.5 | enclosed arch | 16th-c |
| Britannia tubular rail | Menai Strait, Wales | 420 | plate girder | 1845–50 |
| Brooklyn | Brooklyn–Manhattan Island, New York City, USA | 486 | suspension | 1869–83 |
| Chao Phraya | Bangkok, Thailand | 450 | (longest single-plane) cable-stayed | 1989 |
| Commodore Barry | Chester, Pennsylvania, USA | 501 | cantilever | 1974 |
| Cooper River | Charleston, S Carolina, USA | 488 | truss | 1989 |
| Delaware River | Chester, Pennsylvania, USA | 501 | cantilever | 1971 |
| Evergreen | Seattle, Washington, USA | longest span 2 293 | floating pontoon | 1963 |
| Forth (rail) | Firth of Forth, South Queensferry, Scotland | 1 658 (spans 521) | cantilever | 1882–90 |
| Forth Road Bridge (road) | Firth of Forth, South Queensferry, Scotland | 1 006 | suspension | 1958–64 |
| George Washington | Hudson River, New York City, USA | 1 067 | suspension | 1927–31 |
| Gladesville | Sydney, Australia | 305 | (longest) concrete arch | 1964 |
| Golden Gate | San Francisco, California, USA | 1 280 | suspension | 1937 |
| Grand Trunk rail-road | Niagara Falls, New York, USA | 250 | suspension | 1855 (survived until 1897) |
| Great Belt (Storebælt) East | Halsskov–Kudshoved, Denmark | 1 624 | suspension | 1998 |
| Greater New Orleans | Mississippi River, Louisiana, USA | 480 | cantilever | 1958 |
| High Coast | Västernorrland, Sweden | 1 210 | suspension | 1997 |
| Howrah (railroad) | Hooghly River, Calcutta, India | 457 | cantilever | 1936–43 |
| Humber Estuary | Hull–Grimsby, England | 1 410 | suspension | 1973–81 |
| Humen | Humen, China | 888 | suspension | 1996 |
| Jiangsu Yangtze | Jiangsu Province, China | 1 385 | suspension | 1999 |
| Kap Shui Mun | Lantau I–Ma Wan I, Hong Kong | 430 | cable-stayed (double-deck road/rail) | 1997 |
| Kincardine | Forth River, Scotland | 822 (swing span 111) | movable | 1936 |
| Lake Pontchartrain Causeway | Maudeville–Jefferson, Louisiana, USA | 38km | twin concrete trestle | 1963 |

| Name | Location | Length (m)[1] | Type | Date |
|---|---|---|---|---|
| Lion's Gate | Vancouver, Canada | 473 | suspension | 1938 |
| London | Southwark–City of London | centre span 46 | concrete arch | 1973 |
| Mackinac | Michigan, USA | 1 158 | suspension | 1957 |
| McCall's Ferry | Susquehanna River, Lancaster, Pennsylvania, USA | 110 | wooden covered | 1815 |
| Meiko Chuo | Tokyo Bay, Japan | 590 | cable-stayed | 1997 |
| Menai Strait | Menai Strait, N Wales | 177 | suspension | 1820–6 (reconstructed 1940) |
| Minami Bisan-Seto | Honshu–Shikoku, Japan | 1 118 | suspension | 1988 |
| New River Gorge | Fayetteville, West Virginia | 518 | (longest) steel arch | 1977 |
| Nord Sundet | Norway | 223 | lattice | 1989 |
| Normandie | Le Havre, France | 856 | cable-stayed | 1995 |
| Øresund | Flinterenden, Denmark–Malmö, Sweden | 1 092 (main span 490) | cable-stayed | 2000 |
| Plauen | Plauen, Germany | span 90 | (longest) masonry arch | 1903 |
| Pont d'Avignon | Rhône River, France | c.60 | arch | 1177–87 |
| Pontypridd | S Wales | 43 | single-span arch | 1750 |
| Quebec (railroad) | St Lawrence, Canada | 549 | (largest-span) cantilever | 1918 |
| Rainbow | Canada–USA, Niagara Falls | 300 | steel arch | 1941 |
| Ravenswood | West Virginia, USA | 525 | cantilever | 1981 |
| Rialto | Grand Canal, Venice, Italy | 25 | single-span arch | 1588–92 |
| Rio-Niteroi | Guanabara Bay, Brazil | centre span 300, length 14km | box and plate girder | 1972 |
| Salazar | Tagus River, Lisbon, Portugal | 1 014 | suspension | 1966 |
| Severn | Ironbridge, Shropshire, England | 31 | (first) cast-iron arch | 1779 |
| Severn | Beachley, England | 988 | suspension | 1961–6 |
| Severn II | Severn Estuary, England | 456 | cable-stayed | 1996 |
| Skarnsundet | Norway | 530 | cable-stayed | 1991 |
| Sky Train Bridge (rail) | Vancouver, Canada | 340 | cable-stayed | 1989 |
| Sydney Harbour | Sydney, Australia | 503 | steel arch | 1923–32 |
| Tacoma Narrows II | Puget Sound, Washington, USA | 854 | suspension | 1950 |
| Tagus II | Lisbon, Portugal | 420 | cable-stayed | 1997 |
| Tatara, Great | Japan | 890 | cable-stayed | 1999 |
| Tay (road) | Dundee, Scotland | 2 246 | box girder | 1966 |
| Thatcher Ferry | Panama Canal, C America | 344 | arch | 1962 |
| Tower | Thames River, London | 76 | movable | 1886–94 |
| Transbay | San Francisco, California, USA | 705 | suspension | 1933 |
| Trans-Tokyo Bay Highway | Kawasaki–Kisarazu, Japan | 590 | box girder | 1997 |
| Trois-Rivières | St Lawrence River, Quebec, Canada | 336 | steel arch | 1962 |
| Tsing Ma | Tsing Yi I–Ma Wan I, Hong Kong | 1 377 | suspension (double deck) | 1997 |
| Verrazano Narrows | Brooklyn–Staten Island, New York Harbour, USA | 1 298 | suspension | 1959–64 |
| Victoria Jubilee | St Lawrence River, Montreal, Canada | 2 742 | open steel | 1854–9 |
| Wheeling | Wheeling, Virginia, USA | 308 | suspension | 1849 |
| Xiling Yangtze | Three Gorges Dam, China | 900 | suspension | 1996 |
| Yokohama Bay (road) | Japan | 855 | suspension | 1989 |
| Zoo | Cologne, Germany | 259 | steel box girder | 1966 |

[1] To convert m to ft, multiply by 3.2808.

## Engineering: tunnels

When a single date is given it is the date for completion of construction.

| Name | Use | Location | Length[1] | Date |
|---|---|---|---|---|
| Aki | rail | Japan | 13km | 1975 |
| Box | rail | Wiltshire, England | 3km | 1841 |
| Cascade | rail | Washington, USA | 13km | 1929 |
| Channel | rail | Cheriton, England–Sargette, France | 50km | 1987–94 |
| Chesapeake Bay Bridge-Tunnel | road | USA | 28km | 1964 |
| Chesbrough | water supply | Chicago, USA | 3km | 1867 |
| Cumberland Mountain | underground parking | Cumberland Gap, USA | 1 402m | 1996 |
| Dai-shimizu | rail | Honshu, Japan | 22km | 1979 |
| Delaware Aqueduct | water supply | Catskill Mts, New York, USA | 169km | 1937–44 |
| Detroit River | rail | Detroit, Michigan, USA–Windsor, Ontario, Canada | 2km | 1910 |
| Eupalinus | water supply | Samos, Greece | 1 037m | c.525BC |
| FATIMA (Magerøy) | road | Norway | 6 820m (longest undersea road) | 1998 |
| Flathead | rail | Washington, USA | 13km | 1970 |
| Fréjus | rail | Modane, France–Bardonecchia, Italy | 13km | 1857–71 |
| Fucino | drainage | Lake Fucino, Italy | 6km | 41 |
| Great Apennine | rail | Vernio, Italy | 19km | 1934 |
| Hokuriku | rail | Japan | 15km | 1962 |
| Holland | road | Hudson River, New York City–Jersey City, New Jersey, USA | 3km | 1927 |
| Hoosac | rail | Massachusetts | 8km | 1876 |
| Hyperion | sewer | Los Angeles, California, USA | 8km | 1959 |
| Kanmon | rail | Kanmon Strait, Japan | 19km | 1975 |
| Keijo | rail | Japan | 11km | 1970 |
| Kilsby Ridge | rail | London–Birmingham line, England | 2km | 1838 |
| Languedoc (Canal du Midi) | canal | Malpas, France | 157m | 1666–92 |
| Lierasen | rail | Norway | 11km | 1973 |
| London and Southwark Subway | rail | London, England | 11km | 1890 |
| Lötschberg | rail | Switzerland | 15km | 1913 |
| Mersey | road | Mersey River, Birkenhead–Liverpool, England | 4km | 1934 |
| Moffat | rail | Colorado, USA | 10km | 1928 |
| Mont Blanc | road | France–Italy | 12km | 1965 |
| Mt MacDonald | rail | Canada | 15km | 1989 |
| NEAT (St Gotthard) | rail | Switzerland | 57km | under construction |
| NEAT (Bern–Lötschberg–Simplon) | rail | Switzerland | 38km | under construction |
| Orange-Fish River | irrigation | South Africa | (longest irrigation tunnel) 82km | 1975 |
| Øresund | road-rail | Copenhagen, Denmark–Malmö, Sweden | 3 750m (longest immersed tube) | 2000 |
| Owingsburg Landing | canal | Pennsylvania, USA | 137m | 1828 |
| Posilipo | road | Naples–Pozzuoli, Italy | 6km | c.36BC |
| Rogers Pass | rail | Calgary–Vancouver, Canada | 15km | 1982–8 |

| Name | Use | Location | Length[1] | Date |
|---|---|---|---|---|
| Rogers Pass | road | British Columbia, Canada | 35km | 1989 |
| Rokko | rail | Ōsaka–Kōbe, Japan | 16km | 1972 |
| Seikan | rail | Tsugaru Strait, Honshu–Hokkaido, Japan | (longest undersea rail) 54km | 1964–88 |
| Shin-shimizu | rail | Japan | 13km | 1961 |
| Simplon I and II | rail | Brigue, Switzerland–Iselle, Italy | 20km | 1906 and 1922 |
| St Gotthard | rail | Switzerland | 15km | 1882 |
| St Gotthard | road | Göschenen, Switzerland–Airolo, Italy | 16km | 1980 |
| (First) Thames | pedestrian, rail after 1865 | Wapping–Rotherhithe, London, England | 366m | 1825–43 |
| Tower Subway | rail | London, England | 411m | 1869–70 |
| Tronquoy | canal | France | 1 099m | 1810 |

[1] To convert m to ft, multiply by 3.2808; to convert km to mi, multiply by 0.6214.

## Engineering: dams

When a single date is given it is the date for completion of construction.

| Name | River, country | Height (m)[1] | Date |
|---|---|---|---|
| Afsluitdijk Sea | Zuider Zee, Netherlands | 20 (largest sea dam, length 31km) | 1927–32 |
| Aswan High | Nile, Egypt | 111 | 1970 |
| Atatürk | Euphrates, Turkey | 184 | 1990 |
| Bakun | Rajang, Malaysia | 204 | 2002 |
| Chicoasén | Grijalva, Mexico | 263 | 1980 |
| Chivor | Cundinamarca, Colombia | 237 | 1975 |
| Cipasang | Cimanuk, Indonesia | 200 | under construction |
| Daniel Johnson | Manicouagan, Canada | 214 | 1968 |
| Ertan | Yalong, China | 240 | 1998 |
| Grand Coulee | Columbia (Franklin D Roosevelt Lake), USA | 168 | 1933–42 |
| Grand Dixence | Dixence, Switzerland | 285 | 1961 |
| Guavio | Guaviare, Colombia | 245 | 1989 |
| Hoover | Colorado (Lake Mead), USA | 221 | 1931–6 |
| Inguri | Inguri, Georgia | 272 | 1980 |
| Itaipú | Paraná, Paraguay/Brazil border | 189; length 8km (world's largest hydroelectric complex) | opened 1982, completed 1991 |
| Kambarantinsk | Naryn, Kyrgyzstan | 255 | under construction |
| Katse | Malibamatso, Lesotho | 182 | 1996 |
| Kiev | Dneiper, Ukraine | 256 | 1964 |
| Kishau | Tons, India | 253 | under construction |
| La Grande 2A | La Grande, Canada | 168 | under construction |
| Longtan | Hongshui, China | 285 | under construction |
| Mauvoisin | Drance de Bagnes, Switzerland | 237 | 1957 |
| Mica | Columbia, Canada | 244 | 1973 |
| New China (Three Gorges) | Chang Jiang (Yangzte), China | 175 | 2009 |
| Nurek | Vakhsh, Tajikistan | 310 | 1980 |
| Oroville | Feather, California, USA | 235 | 1968 |
| Poti | Paraná, Argentina | 109 (most massive: volume 238 180 000 $m^3$) | under construction |
| Rogun | Vakhsh, Tajikistan | 335 (tallest) | 1973–96 |
| San Roque | Agno, Philippines | 210 | under construction |

| Name | River, country | Height (m) [1] | Date |
|---|---|---|---|
| Sardar Sarovar | Narmada, India | 163 | 1994 |
| Sayansk | Yenisey, Russia | 236 | 1980 |
| Tehri | Bhagirathi, India | 261 | 1997 |
| Thames Barrier | Thames, England | spans 520 (largest tidal barrier) | 1984 |
| Vaiont | Vaiont, Italy | 265 | 1961 (damaged by landslide 1963) |
| Xiaolangdi | Huang He, China | 154 | 2001 |

[1] To convert m to ft, multiply by 3.2808.

## Engineering: tallest buildings

| Name | Location | Height (m) [1] of construction | Date |
|---|---|---|---|
| Petronas I | Kuala Lumpur, Malaysia | 452 | 1996 |
| Petronas II | Kuala Lumpur, Malaysia | 452 | 1996 |
| Sears Tower | Chicago, USA | 443 | 1974 |
| Jin Mao Building | Shanghai, China | 420 | 1998 |
| World Trade Centre, One[2] | New York City, USA | 417 | 1972 |
| World Trade Centre, Two[2] | New York City, USA | 415 | 1973 |
| Empire State Building | New York City, USA | 381 | 1931 |
| Central Plaza | Hong Kong | 374 | 1992 |
| Bank of China | Hong Kong | 368 | 1989 |
| T&C Tower | Kaohsiung, Taiwan | 347 | 1989 |

[1] To convert m to ft, multiply by 3.2808.

[2] Destroyed by terrorists, September 2001.

## Inventions

| Name | Date | Inventor (nationality)* |
|---|---|---|
| adding machine | 1642 | Blaise Pascal (Fr) |
| adhesive (rubber-based glue) | 1850 | anon |
| adhesive (epoxy resin) | 1958 | Certas Co |
| aeroplane (steam powered) | 1886 | Clement Ader (Fr) |
| aeroplane | 1903 | Orville and Wilbur Wright (US) |
| aeroplane (swing-wing) | 1954 | Grumman Co (US) |
| aerosol | 1926 | Erik Rotheim (Nor) |
| airship (non-rigid) | 1851 | Henri Giffard (Fr) |
| airship (rigid) | 1900 | Graf Ferdinand von Zeppelin (Ger) |
| ambulance | 1792 | Jean Dominique Larrey (Fr) |
| aspirin (synthesization) | 1859 | Heinrich Kolbe (Ger) |
| aspirin (introduction into medicine) | 1899 | Felix Hoffmann (Ger) |
| atomic bomb | 1939–45 | Otto Frisch (Aus), Niels Bohr (D) and Rudolf Peierls (Ger) |
| balloon | 1783 | Jacques and Joseph Montgolfier (Fr) |
| barbed wire (first patent) | 1867 | Lucien B Smith (US) |
| barbed wire (manufacture) | 1874 | Joseph Glidden (US) |
| barbiturates (preparation of barbituric acid) | 1863 | Adolf von Baeyer (Pruss) |
| barometer | 1643 | Evangelista Torricelli (Ital) |
| battery (electric) | 1800 | Alessandro Volta (Ital) |
| bicycle | 1839–40 | Kirkpatrick MacMillan (UK) |

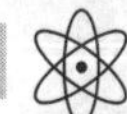



| Name | Date | Inventor (nationality)* |
|---|---|---|
| bifocal lens | 1780 | Benjamin Franklin (US) |
| blood (artificial) | 1966 | Clark and Gollan (US) |
| bronze (copper with tin) | c.3700BC | Pre-dynastic Egypt |
| bunsen burner | 1855 | Robert Wilhelm Bunsen (Pruss) |
| burglar alarm | 1858 | Edwin T Holmes (US) |
| cable-car | 1866 | W Ritter (Ger) or anon (US) |
| calendar (modern) | 525 | Dionysius Exiguus (Scythian) |
| camera (polaroid) | 1947 | Edwin Land (US) |
| canning | 1810 | Nicolas Appert (Fr) |
| cannon | 2nd-cBC | Archimedes (Gr) |
| car (three-wheeled steam tractor) | 1769 | Nicolas Cugnot (Fr) |
| car (internal combustion) | 1884 | Gottlieb Daimler (Ger) |
| car (petrol) | 1886 | Karl Benz (Ger) |
| car (air-conditioning) | 1902 | J Wilkinson (US) |
| car (disc brakes) | 1902 | Frederick W Lanchester (UK) |
| car (speedometer) | 1902 | Thorpe and Salter (UK) |
| carbon fibres | 1964 | Courtaulds Ltd (UK) |
| carburettor | 1876 | Gottlieb Daimler (Ger) |
| carpet sweeper | 1876 | Melville Bissell (US) |
| cash register | 1892 | William Burroughs (US) |
| celluloid | 1870 | John W Hyatt (US) |
| cement (Portland) | 1824 | Joseph Aspdin (UK) |
| chocolate (solid) | 1819 | François-Louis Cailler (Swiss) |
| chocolate (solid, milk) | 1875 | Daniel Peter (Swiss) |
| chronometer | 1735 | John Harrison (UK) |
| cinema | 1895 | Auguste and Louis Lumière (Fr) |
| cinema (wide screen) | 1900 | Raoul Grimoin-Sanson (Fr) |
| clock (mechanical) | 725 | I-Hsing (Chinese) |
| clock (pendulum) | 1657 | Christiaan Huygens (NL) |
| clock (quartz) | 1929 | Warren Alvin Marrison (US) |
| coffee (instant) | 1937 | Nestlé (Swiss) |
| compact disc | 1979 | Philips (NL) and Sony (Japanese) |
| compass (discovery of magnetite) | 1st-c | China |
| compass (first record of mariner's compass) | 1187 | Alexander Neckam (UK) |
| computer | 1835 | Charles Babbage (UK) |
| computer (electronic, digital) | 1946 | J Presper Eckert and John W Mauchly (US) |
| concrete | 1st-c | Rome |
| concrete (reinforced) | 1892 | François Hennebique (Fr) |
| contact lenses | 1887 | Adolph E Fick (Ger) |
| contraceptive pill | 1950 | Gregor Pincus (US) |
| corrugated iron | 1853 | Pierre Carpentier (Fr) |
| credit card | 1950 | Ralph Scheider (US) |
| crossword | 1913 | Arthur Wynne (US) in *New York World* |
| crystal | c.1450 | anon, Venice |
| decompression chamber | 1929 | Robert H Davis (UK) |
| dental plate | 1817 | Anthony A Plantson (US) |
| dental plate (rubber) | 1854 | Charles Goodyear (US) |
| detergents | 1916 | anon, Germany |
| diesel engine | 1892 | Rudolf Diesel (Ger) |
| dishwasher (automatic) | 1889 | Mrs W A Cockran (US) |
| drill (pneumatic) | 1861 | Germain Sommelier (Fr) |
| drill (electric, hand) | 1895 | Wilhelm Fein (Ger) |
| electric chair | 1888 | Harold P Brown and E A Kenneally (US) |
| electric flat iron | 1882 | Henry W Seeley (US) |
| electric generator | 1831 | Michael Faraday (UK) |
| electric guitar | 1931 | Adolph Rickenbacker, Barth and Beauchamp (US) |

| Name | Date | Inventor (nationality)* |
|---|---|---|
| electric heater | 1887 | W Leigh Burton (US) |
| electric light bulb | 1879 | Thomas Alva Edison (US) |
| electric motor (AC) | 1888 | Nikola Tesla (US) |
| electric motor (DC) | 1870 | Zenobe Gramme (Belg) |
| electric oven | 1889 | Bernina Hotel, Switzerland |
| electrocardiography | 1903 | Willem Einthoven (NL) |
| electromagnet | 1824 | William Sturgeon (UK) |
| encyclopedia | c.47BC | Marcus Terentius Varro (Roman) |
| endoscope | 1827 | Pierre Segalas (Fr) |
| escalator | 1892 | Jesse W Reno (US) |
| explosives (nitroglycerine) | 1847 | Ascanio Sobrero (Ital) |
| explosives (dynamite) | 1866 | Alfred Nobel (Swed) |
| extinguisher | 1866 | François Carlier (Fr) |
| facsimile machine (fax) | 1907 | Arthur Korn (Ger) |
| ferrofluids | 1968 | Ronald Rosensweig (US) |
| film (moving outlines) | 1874 | Jules Janssen (Fr) |
| | 1888 | Louis Le Prince (Fr) |
| | 1891 | Thomas Alva Edison (US) |
| film (with soundtrack) | 1896 | Lee De Forest (US) |
| forceps (obstetric) | c.1630 | Peter Chamberlen (UK) |
| freeze-drying | 1906 | Arsene D'Arsonval and Georges Bordas (Fr) |
| galvanometer | 1834 | André Marie Ampère (Fr) |
| gas lighting | 1792 | William Murdock (UK) |
| gearbox (automatic) | 1910 | Hermann Fottinger (Ger) |
| glass (heat-resistant) | 1884 | Carl Zeiss (Ger) |
| glass (stained) | pre-850 | Europe |
| glass (toughened) | 1893 | Leon Appert (Fr) |
| glass fibre | 1713 | René de Réaumur (Fr) |
| glass fibre (industrial) | 1931 | Owens Illinois Glass Co (US) |
| glassware | c.2600BC | Egypt |
| glider | 1853 | George Cayley (UK) |
| gramophone | 1877 | Thomas Alva Edison (US) |
| gun | 245BC | Ctesibius (Gr) |
| gyro-compass | 1911 | Elmer A Sperry (US) |
| heart (artificial) | 1937 | Vladimir P Demikhov (USSR) |
| | 1982 | Robert Jarvik (US) |
| heat pump | 1851 | William Thompson, Lord Kelvin (UK) |
| helicopter | 1907 | Louis and Jacques Breguet (Fr) |
| holography | 1948 | Denis Gabor (Hung/UK) |
| hovercraft | 1955 | Christopher Cockerell (UK) |
| integrated circuit (concept) | 1952 | Geoffrey Dummer (UK) |
| interferometry | 1802 | Thomas Young (UK) |
| interferometer | 1856 | J-C Jamin (Fr) |
| iron (working of) | c.1323BC | Hittites, Anatolia |
| jeans | 1872 | Levi-Strauss (US) |
| kidney (artificial) | 1945 | Willem Kolff (NL) |
| laser | 1960 | Theodore Maiman (US) |
| launderette | 1934 | J F Cantrell (US) |
| lawnmower | 1902 | James Edward Ransome (UK) |
| lift (mechanical) | 1851 | Elisha G Otis (US) |
| lightning conductor | 1752 | Benjamin Franklin (US) |
| linoleum | 1860 | Frederick Walton (UK) |
| lithography | 1796 | Aloys Senefelder (Bav) |
| locomotive (railed) | 1804 | Richard Trevithick (UK) |
| lock | c.4000BC | Mesopotamia |
| loom (power) | 1785 | Edmund Cartwright (UK) |
| loudspeaker | 1900 | Horace Short (UK) |
| machine gun | 1718 | James Puckle (UK) |
| maps | c.2250BC | Mesopotamia |

| Name | Date | Inventor (nationality)* |
|---|---|---|
| margarine | 1868 | Hippolyte Mergé-Mouriès (Fr) |
| match | 1680 | Robert Boyle (UK) |
| match (safety) | 1845 | Anton von Schrotter (Ger) |
| microchip | 1958 | Jack Saint Clair Kilby (US) |
| microphone | 1876 | Alexander Graham Bell and Thomas Alva Edison (US) |
| microprocessor | 1971 | Marcian E Hoff (US) |
| microscope | 1590 | Zacharias Janssen (NL) |
| microscope (electron) | 1933 | Max Knoll and Ernst Ruska (Ger) |
| microscope (scanning tunnelling) | 1982 | Gerd Binnig and Heinrich Rohrer (Swiss) |
| microscope (atomic force) | 1985 | Gerd Binnig and Heinrich Rohrer (Swiss) |
| microwave oven | 1945 | Percy Le Baron Spencer (US) |
| missile (air-to-air) | 1943 | Herbert Wagner (Ger) |
| motorcycle | 1885 | Gottlieb Daimler (Ger) |
| neon lamp | 1910 | Georges Claude (Fr) |
| newspaper | 59BC | Julius Caesar (Roman) |
| non-stick pan | 1954 | Marc Grégoir (Fr) |
| novel (serialized) | 1836 | Charles Dickens, Chapman and Hall Publishers (UK) |
| nylon | 1938 | Wallace H Carothers (US) |
| optical fibres | c.1955 | Navinder S Kapany (Ind) |
| optical sound recording | 1920 | Lee De Forest (US) |
| pacemaker (implantable) | 1956 | Wilson Greatbach (US) |
| paint (fluorescent) | 1933 | Joe and Bob Switzer (US) |
| paint (acrylic) | 1964 | Reeves Ltd (UK) |
| paper | AD105 | Ts'ai Lun (Chinese) |
| paper clip | 1900 | Johann Vaaler (Nor) |
| parachute | c.2nd-cBC | China |
| parachute (jump) | 1797 | André-Jacques Garnerin (Fr) |
| parachute (patent) | 1802 | André-Jacques Garnerin (Fr) |
| parchment | 2nd-cBC | Eumenes II of Pergamum (reigned 197–159BC) |
| parking meter | 1932 | Carlton C Magee (US) |
| pasteurization | 1863 | Louis Pasteur (Fr) |
| pen (fountain) | 1884 | Lewis Waterman (US) |
| pen (ball-point) | 1938 | Laszlo Biro (Hung) |
| pencil | 1795 | Nicholas Jacques Conté (Fr) |
| pentium processor | 1995 | Intel (US) |
| phonograph | 1877 | Thomas Alva Edison (US) |
| photoelectric cell | 1896 | Julius Elster and Hans F Geitel (Ger) |
| phototypesetting | 1894 | Eugene Porzott (Hung) |
| photographic lens (for camera obscura) | 1812 | William H Wollaston (UK) |
| photographic film | 1889 | George Eastman (US) |
| photography (on metal) | 1816 | Joseph Nicéphore Niepce (Fr) |
| photography (on paper) | 1838 | William Henry Fox Talbot (UK) |
| photography (colour) | 1861 | James Clerk Maxwell (UK) |
| pianoforte | 1720 | Bartolomeo Cristofori (Ital) |
| plastics | 1868 | John W Hyatt (US) |
| pocket calculator | 1972 | Jack Saint Clair Kilby, James Van Tassell and Jerry D Merryman (US) |
| porcelain | c.960 | China |
| pressure cooker | 1679 | Denis Papin (Fr) |
| printing press (wooden) | c.1450 | Johannes Gutenberg (Ger) |
| printing press (rotary) | 1845 | Richard Hoe (US) |
| propeller (boat, hand-operated) | 1775 | David Bushnell (US) |
| propeller (ship) | 1844 | Isambard Kingdom Brunel (UK) |
| radar (theory) | 1900 | Nikola Tesla (Croat) |
| radar (theory) | 1922 | Guglielmo Marconi (Ital) |

| Name | Date | Inventor (nationality)* |
|---|---|---|
| radar (application) | c.1930 | A Hoyt Taylor and Leo C Young (US) |
| radio telegraphy (discovery and production of sound waves) | 1888 | Heinrich Hertz (Ger) |
| radio (transatlantic) | 1901 | Guglielmo Marconi (Ital) |
| rails (iron) | 1738 | Abraham Barby (UK) |
| railway (underground) | 1843 | Charles Pearson (UK) |
| railway (electric) | 1878 | Ernst Werner von Siemens (Ger) |
| rayon | 1883 | Joseph Swan (UK) |
| razor (safety) | 1895 | King Camp Gillette (US) |
| razor (electric) | 1928 | Jacob Schick (US) |
| record (flat disc) | 1888 | Emil Berliner (Ger) |
| record (long-playing microgroove) | 1948 | Peter Goldmark (US) |
| refrigerator (compressed ether) | 1855 | James Harrison (UK) |
| refrigerator (absorption) | 1857 | Ferdinand Carré (Fr) |
| revolver | 1835 | Samuel Colt (US) |
| Richter seismographic scale | 1935 | Charles Francis Richter (US) |
| rocket (missile) | 1232 | Mongols, China |
| rubber (latex foam) | 1929 | E A Murphy, W H Chapman and John Dunlop (US) |
| rubber (butyl) | 1937 | Robert Thomas and William Sparks, Exxon (US) |
| rubber (vulcanized) | 1939 | Charles Goodyear (US) |
| Rubik cube | 1975 | Erno Rubik (Hung) |
| safety-pin | 1849 | Walter Hunt (US) |
| satellite (artificial) | 1957 | USSR |
| saw | c.4000BC | Egypt |
| scanner | 1973 | Godfrey N Hounsfield (UK) |
| scotch tape | 1930 | Richard Drew (US) |
| screw | 3rd-cBC | Archimedes (Gr) |
| serotherapy | 1890 | Emil von Behring (Ger) |
| sewing machine | 1830 | Barthelemy Thimonnier (Fr) |
| ship (steam) | 1775 | Jacques C Perier (Fr) |
| ship (turbine) | 1894 | Charles Parsons (UK) |
| ship (metal hull and propeller) | 1844 | Isambard Kingdom Brunel (UK) |
| silicon chip | 1961 | Texas Instruments (US) |
| silk (reeling) | c.2640BC | Hsi Ling Shi (Chinese) |
| skin (artificial) | c.1980 | John Tanner (US), Bell (US), Neveu (Fr), Ioannis Yannas (Gr), Howard Green (US) and Jacques Thivolet (Fr) |
| skyscraper | 1882 | William Le Baron Jenney (US) |
| slide rule | 1621 | William Oughtred (UK) |
| soap | c.2500BC | Sumer, Babylonia |
| soda (extraction of) | c.16th-cBC | Egypt |
| space shuttle | 1981 | NASA (US) |
| spectacles | c.1280 | Alessandro della Spina and Salvino degli Armati (Ital) |
| spinning frame | 1768 | Richard Arkwright (UK) |
| spinning jenny | c.1764 | James Hargreaves (UK) |
| spinning-mule | 1779 | Samuel Crompton (UK) |
| stapler | 1868 | Charles Henry Gould (UK) |
| starter motor | 1912 | Charles F Kettering (US) |
| steam engine | 1698 | Thomas Savery (UK) |
| steam engine (condenser) | 1769 | James Watt (UK) |
| steam engine (piston) | 1705 | Thomas Newcomen (UK) |
| steel (production) | 1854 | Henry Bessemer (UK) and William Kelly (US) |
| steel (stainless) | 1913 | Henry Brearley (UK) |
| stethoscope | 1816 | René Théophile Hyacinthe Laënnec (Fr) |
| stereotype | 1725 | William Ged (UK) |

| Name | Date | Inventor (nationality)* |
|---|---|---|
| submarine | c.1620 | Cornelis Brebbel or Van Drebbel (NL) |
| sun-tan cream | 1936 | Eugène Schueller (Fr) |
| suspension bridge | 25BC | China |
| syringe (scientific) | 1646 | Blaise Pascal (Fr) |
| syringe (hypodermic) | c.1835 | Charles Gabriel Pravaz (Fr) |
| table tennis | 1890 | James Gibb (UK) |
| tampon | 1930 | Earl Hass (US) |
| tank | 1916 | Ernest Swinton (UK) |
| telegraph (electric) | 1774 | Georges Louis Lesage (Swiss) |
| telegraph (transatlantic cable) | 1866 | William Thompson, Lord Kelvin (UK) |
| telegraph code | 1837 | Samuel F B Morse (US) |
| telephone (first practical) | 1876 | Alexander Graham Bell (US) |
| telephone (automatic exchange) | 1889 | Alman B Strowger (US) |
| telescope (refractor) | 1608 | Hans Lippershey (NL) |
| telescope (space) | 1990 | Edwin Hubble (US) |
| television (mechanical) | 1926 | John Logie Baird (UK) |
| television (colour) | 1940 | Peter Goldmark (US) |
| tennis | 1873 | Walter G Wingfield (UK) |
| thermometer | 3rd-cBC | Ctesibius (Gr) |
| thermometer (mercury) | 1714 | Gabriel Fahrenheit (Ger) |
| timeclock | 1894 | Daniel M Cooper (US) |
| toaster | 1927 | Charles Strite (US) |
| traffic lights | 1868 | J P Knight (UK) |
| traffic lights (automatic) | 1914 | Alfred Benesch (US) |
| transformer | 1831 | Michael Faraday (UK) |
| tranquillizers | 1952 | Henri Laborit (Fr) |
| transistor | 1948 | John Bardeen, Walter Brattain and William Shockley (US) |
| travel agency | 1841 | Thomas Cook (UK) |
| traveller's cheques | 1891 | American Express Travel Agency (US) |
| turbojet | 1928 | Frank Whittle (UK) |
| typewriter | 1829 | William Burt (US) |
| typewriter (electric) | 1872 | Thomas Alva Edison (US) |
| tyre (pneumatic, coach) | 1845 | Robert William Thomson (UK) |
| tyre (pneumatic, bicycle) | 1888 | John Boyd Dunlop (UK) |
| ultrasonography (obstetric) | 1958 | Ian Donald (UK) |
| universal joint | c.140BC | Fang Feng (Chinese) |
| vacuum cleaner (steam powered) | 1871 | Ives W McGaffrey (US) |
| vacuum cleaner (electric) | 1901 | Hubert Cecil Booth (UK) |
| vending machine | 1883 | Percival Everitt (UK) |
| ventilator | 1858 | Théophile Guibal (Fr) |
| videophone | 1927 | American Telegraph and Telephone Co |
| video recorder | 1956 | Ampex Co (US) |
| washing machine (electric) | 1907 | Hurley Machine Co (US) |
| watch | 1462 | Bartholomew Manfredi (Ital) |
| watch (waterproof) | 1927 | Rolex (Swiss) |
| wheel | c.3500BC | Mesopotamia |
| windmill | c.600 | Syria |
| word processor | 1965 | IBM (US) |
| writing (pictography) | c.3000BC | Egypt |
| xerography | 1938 | Chester Carlson (US) |
| zip-fastener | 1893 | Whitcomb L Judson (US) |

*Aus: Austrian
Bav: Bavarian
Belg: Belgian
Croat: Croatian
D: Danish
Fr: French
Ger: German
Gr: Greek
Hung: Hungarian
Ind: Indian
Ital: Italian
NL: Dutch
Nor: Norwegian
Pruss: Prussian
Swed: Swedish

## Industrialists and entrepreneurs

**Agnelli, Giovanni** (1866–1945) Italian, born Villa Perosa, Piedmont. Founder of Fiat (Fabbrica Italiana Automobili Torino) in 1899. Appointed as a senator in 1923 and mobilized Italian industry in World War II.

**Astor, John Jacob, 1st Baron Astor of Hever** (1886–1971) Anglo-American, born New York City. Elected MP for Dover (1922) and chairman of the Times Publishing Company.

**Astor, William Waldorf, 1st Viscount Astor** (1848–1919) Anglo-American, born New York City. After period as US minister to Italy, emigrated to Britain to become newspaper proprietor, acquiring the *Pall Mall Gazette*, *Pall Mall Magazine* and in 1911, the *Observer*.

**Austin, Herbert, 1st Baron Austin of Longbridge** (1866–1941) English, born Bucking-hamshire. After working in engineering shops in Australia, returned to England and produced his first three-wheel car with the Wolseley Co in 1895, forming his own company in 1905. Conservative MP from 1918 to 1924.

**Barclay, Robert** (1843–1913) English. Founder of Barclay and Co Ltd with the merger of 20 banks in 1896. In 1917 the name was changed to Barclay's Bank Limited.

**Beaverbrook, Max (William Maxwell Aitken), 1st Baron** (1879–1964) Anglo-Canadian, born Maple, Ontario. Originally stockbroker, before entering British parliament (1911–16); became minister of information (1918). Later acquired a number of major British newspapers, including the *Daily Express*.

**Benz, Karl Friedrich** (1844–1929) German, born Karlsruhe. Engineer and car manufacturer who developed two-stroke engine. Founded Benz & Co and produced one of the earliest petrol-driven vehicles; company later merged to become Daimler-Benz.

**Birdseye, Clarence** (1886–1956) American, born Brooklyn, New York City. Co-founder of the General Seafoods Co in 1924, after developing a process for freezing foods in small packages. Later president of Birdseye Frosted Foods (1930–4) and Birdseye Electric Company (1935–8). He is credited with around 300 patents.

**Boeing, William Edward** (1881–1956) American, born Detroit, Michigan. Formed Pacific Aero Products Co in 1916 to build seaplanes. Renamed as the Boeing Airplane Co in 1917; it became the largest aircraft manufacturer in the world. Also formed civilian airline Boeing Air Transport Co in 1927.

**Bond, Alan** (1938– ) Anglo-Australian, born London. At the age of 19 established his own company; the Bond Corporation developed extensive interests in Australian newspapers, television, brewing, oil and gas, and gold mining.

**Branson, Sir Richard Charles Nicholas** (1950– ) English entrepreneur and businessman, born London. Started Virgin mail-order business in 1969. Opened first branch of record chain in 1971 and founded record label 1973. Founded Virgin Atlantic Airlines 1984, and sold Virgin Music in 1992 for £560m to expand airline. Launched Virgin Radio in 1993 (sold to Chris Evans's Ginger Productions in 1997) and bought MGM UK high-street cinemas in 1995. Introduced personal banking services and Virgin Trains into the Virgin Group in the 1990s. By 1998 the Virgin Group consisted of 200 companies, with an annual turnover of £1.8 billion.

**Brierley, Sir Ron(ald Alfred)** (1937– ) New Zealand entrepreneur, born Wellington. Founded Brierley Investments in 1961. Sold Industrial Equities conglomerate just before 1987 crash and became chairman of Guinness Peat Group in 1990.

**Burrell, Sir William** (1861–1958) Scottish, born Glasgow. Ship-owner and art collector. Accumulated 8000 works of art from all over the world, which he donated to the city of Glasgow in 1944.

**Butlin, Sir William Edmund** (1899–1980) English, born South Africa. Holiday camp promoter; opened first camp at Skegness in 1936 and expanded business in the UK and abroad after World War II.

**Cadbury, George** (1839–1922) English, born Birmingham. Quaker businessman, son of John Cadbury. Took over father's business in 1861 and established for the workers the model village of Bournville, near Birmingham. Became proprietor of the *Daily News* in 1902.

**Cadbury, John** (1801–89) English, born Birmingham. Quaker businessman, founder of Cadbury's cocoa and chocolate business.

**Carnegie, Andrew** (1835–1918) Scottish, born Dunfermline. Invested in oil lands and a business which grew into the largest iron and steel works in America. Retired in 1901, a multimillionaire.

**Chandos, Oliver Lyttelton, 1st Viscount** (1893–1972) English, born London. Managing director of the British Metal Corporation from 1928. In 1940 entered the House of Commons and was made President of the Board of Trade. Resigned from politics to return to business in 1954.

**Christie, James** (1730–1803) English, born London. Founder of Christie's auctioneers in 1766.

**Citroën, André Gustave** (1878–1935) French, born Paris. Responsible for mass production of armaments during World War I. Later manufacturer of small low-priced cars but in 1934 lost control of the Citroën company.

**Conran, Sir Terence Orby** (1931– ) English, born Esher, Surrey. Businessman and designer who founded and ran the Habitat Company (1971). Has since been involved in management of Richard Shops, Conran Stores, Mothercare and several restaurants.

**Cunard, Sir Samuel** (1787–1865) Canadian, born Halifax. Merchant and ship-owner who emigrated to Britain in 1838 to found the British and North American Royal Mail Steam Packet Company, later known as the

Cunard Line, for the new steam mail service between Britain and America.

**du Pont Nemours, Eleuthère Irénée** (1771–1834) French–American, born Paris. Worked in father's printing plant until 1797. Emigrated to USA and in 1802 established a gunpowder factory which developed into one of the world's largest chemical concerns.

**du Pont, Pierre Samuel** (1870–1954) American, born Wilmington, Delaware. Joined family gunpowder company. As its president (1915–20) introduced and developed many new industrial management techniques. Became president of General Motors in 1920.

**Dunlop, John Boyd** (1840–1921) Scottish, born Dreghorn, Ayrshire. Credited with inventing the pneumatic tyre. In 1889 formed business which became the Dunlop Rubber Company Ltd; produced pneumatic tyres for bicycles, and later for cars.

**Firestone, Harvey Samuel** (1868–1938) American, born Columbiana, Ohio. Sold solid rubber carriage tyres in Chicago and in 1900 founded Firestone Tire and Rubber Company, which grew to be one of the biggest industrial corporations in the USA. Pioneered pneumatic tyres for Ford Model T, and non-skid treads. Started rubber plantations in Liberia in 1924.

**Ford, Henry II** (1917–87) American, born Dearborn, Michigan. Seized control of the Ford Motor Company from his grandfather Henry Ford in 1945. Stepped down as chief executive officer in 1979 and as chairman in 1980, but remained as member of the board of directors.

**Ford, Henry** (1863–1947) American, born Greenfield, Michigan. Apprentice to a machinist at the age of 15, produced his first petrol-driven car in 1893. In 1903 founded Ford Motor Company and pioneered mass-production techniques.

**Frick, Henry Clay** (1849–1919) American, born West Overton, Pennsylvania. Millionaire at 30 after forming company to supply the Pittsburgh steelworks with coke. Became chairman of the Carnegie steel company in 1889. A ruthless employer, he was shot and stabbed after forcefully breaking a strike in 1892, but subsequently recovered. Became a director of United States Steel in 1901.

**Gates, Bill (William Henry)** (1955– ) American computer scientist and businessman, born Seattle. Founded Microsoft Corporation in 1975 and licensed computer operating system (MS-DOS) to IBM in 1980. This system and their applications software have been phenomenally successful. Gates was a billionaire by 1986.

**Getty, Jean Paul** (1892–1976) American, born Minneapolis, Minnesota. Entered oil business in his early twenties and went on to acquire and control more than 100 companies. Also acquired an enormous and valuable art collection.

**Guinness, Sir Benjamin Lee** (1798–1868) Irish, born Dublin. Inherited Guinness's Brewery (1759) and made it the largest business of its kind in the world. First Lord Mayor of Dublin (1851) and MP (1865–8).

**Gulbenkian, Calouste Sarkis** (1869–1955) British–Ottoman–Turkish, born Scutari. Entered father's oil business in Baku in 1888. Later organized international oil company mergers and negotiated oil concessions between USA and Saudi Arabia.

**Hammer, Armand** (1899–1990) American, born New York City. Exported grain to the USSR in exchange for furs, dealing with Lenin and subsequent Soviet leaders. Founded the A Hammer Pencil Company in 1925 and maintained strong connections with the USSR, occasionally acting as intermediary between Soviet and American governments. Bought and expanded the small Occidental Petroleum Corporation in 1957, and founded Hammer Galleries Inc in New York in 1930.

**Harmsworth, Harold Sydney, 1st Viscount Rothermere** (1868–1940) Irish, born London. Newspaper magnate, founder of the *Glasgow Daily Record* and the *Sunday Pictorial*. Also controlled the *Daily Mail*, *Sunday Dispatch* and the *Daily Mirror*, for which he developed a circulation of three million in 1922.

**Heinz, Henry John** (1844–1919) American, born Pittsburgh, Pennsylvania. Co-founder of food manufacturing and packing company F & J Heinz, and president of the reorganized business H J Heinz Co from 1905 to 1919. Promoted pure food movement in the USA, and pioneered staff welfare work.

**Hilton, Conrad Nicholson** (1887–1979) American, born San Antonio, New Mexico. Took over family inn in 1918, then built up a chain of hotels in major cities in the USA. Formed Hilton Hotels Corporation in 1946 and Hilton International in 1948, and continued to expand until 1966 when his son became president.

**Honda, Soichiro** (1906–91) Japanese, born Iwata Gun. Became garage apprentice in 1922 and opened his own garage in 1928. By 1934 had opened a piston-ring production factory and later produced motor cycles. President of Honda Corporation (1948–73), remaining as a director, and appointed supreme advisor in 1983.

**Hoover, William Henry** (1849–1932) American, born Ohio. After running a tannery business, bought patent of an electric cleaning machine from a janitor and formed Electric Suction Sweeper Co in 1908 (later renamed Hoover) to manufacture and market it throughout the world.

**Hughes, Howard Robard** (1905–76) American, born Houston, Texas. Inherited father's oil-drilling equipment company and used profits to make Hollywood films. After working as a pilot, became involved in designing, building and flying aircraft, then abruptly returned to filmmaking. From 1966 lived in complete seclusion but continued to control his vast business interests.

**Iacocca, Lee (Lido Anthony)** (1924– ) American, born Allentown, Pennsylvania. Worked for Ford Motor Co, rising to become president in 1970. In 1978 joined

Chrysler Corporation as president and chief executive officer, restoring profitability during serious financial difficulties.

**Jobs, Steven** (1955– ) American computer inventor and entrepreneur, born San Fransisco. Together with Stephen Wozniak (1950– ) he set up Apple Computer Co in 1976, which became the fastest-growing company in USA. Jobs left Apple in 1985 and founded NeXT Inc.

**King (of Wartnaby), John Leonard King, Baron** (1917– ) English industrialist. Became chairman of Dennis Motor Holdings in 1970 and Babcock and Wilcox Ltd in 1972. He was appointed chairman of British Airways in 1981 and then life president in 1993.

**Krupp, Alfred** (1812–87) German, born Essen. Inherited father's iron forge and began manufacturing arms in 1837. Established a steel plant and became an international arms supplier. Also acquired large mines, collieries and docks.

**Lyons, Sir Joseph** (1848–1917) English, born London. Starting with a teashop in Piccadilly, made J Lyons and Co Ltd one of the largest catering businesses in Britain.

**Marks, Simon, 1st Baron Marks of Broughton** (1888–1964) English, born Leeds. Son of a Jewish immigrant from Poland from whom he inherited 60 Marks and Spencer 'penny bazaars'. With Israel (later Lord) Seif, established Marks and Spencer as a major high-quality retail chain.

**Maxwell (Ian) Robert** (1923–91) English, born Czechoslovakia. Founder of Pergamon Press and Labour MP (1964–70). As well as controlling Mirror Group Newspapers and the Maxwell Communication Corporation, he had extensive private business interests. After his death massive debts were revealed.

**Morita, Akio** (1921–99) Japanese businessman, born Nagoya. Founded Sony electronics firm together with Masaru Ibuka (1908–97) in 1958. Among Sony's most important products have been early tape recorders (c.1950) and the 'Walkman' (1980).

**Murdoch, (Keith) Rupert** (1931– ) Australian–American, born Melbourne. After becoming Australia's second largest publisher, expanded abroad acquiring newspapers in London and New York, including the *Sun*, the *Times* and the *New York Post*. Expanded communications empire in 1989 with the purchase of Collins the publishers and the inauguration of Sky Television. Later bought 20th Century-Fox film studios and New World Communications, and created the Fox Network, becoming the owner of television stations that reached up to 40 per cent of American viewership.

**Nobel, Alfred** (1833–96) Swedish, born Stockholm. Explosives expert who invented dynamite and gelignite. Created an industrial empire to manufacture his many inventions and left his fortune to endow annual Nobel prizes. Element 102 was named nobelium after him.

**Nuffield, William Richard Morris, 1st Viscount** (1877–1963) English, born Worcester. Started in bicycle repair business and by 1910 was manufacturing prototypes of Morris Oxford cars at Cowley in Oxford. First British manufacturer to develop mass production of cheap cars.

**Olivetti, Adriano** (1901–60) Italian, born Ivrea. Vastly increased and developed father's typewriter firm. Widely noted for his social concerns.

**Onassis, Aristotle Socrates** (1906–75) Greek, born Smyrna, Turkey. Made fortune in tobacco trade and built up one of the world's largest independent fleets of ships. Also pioneer in construction of supertankers. Married Jacqueline Kennedy, widow of American president John F Kennedy.

**Packer, Kerry Francis Bullmore** (1937– ) Australian, born Sydney. Inherited from his father the Australian Consolidated Press, newspaper publisher with television and radio interests. Involved in disputes and legal battles with national cricket bodies due to his creation and broadcasting of 'World Series Cricket'.

**Pilkington, Sir Lionel Alexander Bethune (Sir Alastair)** (1920–95) English, born Calcutta. Member of family firm of glass-makers, who researched and developed methods of producing defect-free plate glass.

**Pulitzer, Joseph** (1847–1911) Hungarian–American, born Makó, Hungary. Emigrated to USA in 1864 and joined the army. Later in St Louis he became a reporter, then began to acquire and revitalize old newspapers, including the *New York World* (1883). Established in his will annual Pulitzer prizes for literature, drama, music and journalism.

**Rockefeller, John Davison** (1839–1937) American, born Richford, New York. Founded the Standard Oil Co in 1870 and through it secured control of the oil trade of America. Gave over $500 million in aid of medical research, universities and Baptist churches; in 1913 established Rockefeller Foundation 'to promote the well-being of mankind'.

**Roddick, Anita Lucia** (1942– ) English, born Brighton. Founded the Body Shop International plc to sell natural cosmetics. Company has around 1 000 stores in 47 countries.

**Rolls, Charles Stewart** (1877–1910) English, born London. Motor car manufacturer, founded C S Rolls & Co in 1902, and later Rolls-Royce Ltd with Sir Henry Royce. In 1910 made first non-stop double crossing of the English Channel by aeroplane.

**Rowntree, Joseph** (1836–1925) English, born York. With his brother became a partner in a cocoa factory in York in 1869, and built up welfare organizations for employees.

**Royce, Sir (Frederick) Henry** (1863–1933) English, born near Peterborough. Founder of electrical and mechanical engineering firm Royce Ltd (1884) and co-founder of Rolls-Royce Ltd, manufacturer of car and aeroplane engines. Designed engines used in Spitfires and Hurricanes in World War II.

**Sainsbury, Alan John, Baron Sainsbury of Drury Lane** (1902–98) English, born Hornsey, Middlesex. Joined family grocery business in 1921 and from 1967

was joint president of major supermarket chain J Sainsbury plc.

**Selfridge, Harry Gordon** (1858–1947) English–American, born Ripon, Wisconsin. Chicago trader who in 1906 on a visit to London initiated the Selfridge business; the Oxford Street store opened in 1909.

**Sieff, Israel Moses, Baron Sieff of Brimpton** (1889–1972) English, born Manchester. With Simon Marks, developed Marks and Spencer. Joint managing director from 1926 to 1967 and succeeded Lord Marks as chairman (1964–7).

**Sinclair, Sir Clive (Marles)** (1940– ) English, born Surrey. Launched electronics company which has developed and successfully marketed calculators, miniature televisions and personal computers. Also manufactured Sinclair C5 'personal transport' vehicle powered by a washing-machine motor and rechargeable batteries.

**Tate, Sir Henry** (1819–99) English, born Chorley, Lancashire. Patented method for cutting sugar cubes (1872) and formed major sugar refinery. Gave nation Tate Gallery (1897) containing his own valuable private collection.

**Tiffany, Charles Lewis** (1812–1902) American, born Killingby, Connecticut. Goldsmith and jeweller who began dealing in 1837, and by 1883 was one of the largest silverware manufacturers in USA. Held appointments to 23 royal patrons, including the Tsar of Russia and Queen Victoria.

**Turner, Ted (Robert Edward)** (1938– ) American entrepreneur, born Cincinnati. Created the first 'superstation', WTBS, in the mid-1970s and created Cable News Network (CNN) in 1980. In 1985 he bought MGM and established a movie channel on television in 1988. Time Warner Inc merged with Turner Broadcasting System in 1996, creating the world's largest media company, with Turner as its vice-chairman.

**Wang, An** (1920–89) American–Chinese, born Shanghai. Graduated in science from Shanghai, then studied applied physics at Harvard. Invented the magnetic core memory and founded Wang Laboratories in Boston in 1951, now one of the world's largest automation systems firms. Also introduced desktop computers and calculators.

**Woolworth, Frank Winfield** (1852–1919) American, born Rodman, Jefferson County, New York. From inexpensive fixed-price goods stores built up a chain of over a thousand stores controlled from a New York headquarters. Most development outside USA was after the death of the founder.

# ARTS AND CULTURE

## Novelists

Selected works are listed.

**Abrahams, Peter (Henry)** (1919– ) South African novelist, born Vrededorp, near Johannesburg; *The View from Coyaba* (1985).

**Achebe, Chinua** (originally **Albert Chinualumogu**) (1930– ) Nigerian novelist, born Ogidi; *Things Fall Apart* (1959), *Anthills of the Savannah* (1987).

**Ackroyd, Peter** (1949– ) English novelist, biographer, poet, critic, born London; *Notes for a New Culture* (1976), *The Last Testament of Oscar Wilde* (1983), *T S Eliot* (1984), *Chatterton* (1988), *First Light* (1989), *English Music* (1992), *Milton in America* (1996).

**Adams, Douglas (Noël)** (1952–2001) English novelist, short-story writer, born Cambridge; *The Hitch Hiker's Guide to the Galaxy* (1979), *Dirk Gently's Holistic Detective Agency* (1987), *Mostly Harmless* (1992).

**Adams, Richard (George)** (1920– ) English novelist, short-story writer, born Newbury, Berkshire; *Watership Down* (1972), *Shardik* (1974), *The Girl in a Swing* (1980), *The Day Gone By* (autobiography) (1990).

**Aldiss, Brian (Wilson)** (1925– ) English novelist, poet, short-story writer, playwright, critic, born East Dereham, Norfolk; *The Helliconia Trilogy* (1985), *Forgotten Life* (1988), *Dracula Unbound* (1991), *Remembrance Day* (1993), *The Detached Retina* (1995).

**Aldridge, (Harold Edward) James** (1918– ) Australian novelist, short-story writer, playwright, born White Hills, Victoria; *The Diplomat* (1949), *The Hunter* (1950), *The Last Exile* (1961), *The True Story of Spit MacPhee* (1986), *The True Story of Lola MacKellar* (1993).

**Alvarez, Al(fred)** (1929– ) English novelist, poet, critic, born London; *The Savage God: A Study of Suicide* (non-fiction) (1971), *Hers* (1974), *Day of Atonement* (1991), *Night* (1995).

**Ambler, Eric** (1909–98) English novelist, playwright screenwriter, born London; *The Mask of Dimitrios* (1939), *The Intercom Conspiracy* (1970), *The Care of Time* (1981), *The Story So Far* (1993).

**Amis, Kingsley (William)** (1922–95) English novelist, poet, born London; *Lucky Jim* (1954), *That Uncertain Feeling* (1955), *Jake's Thing* (1978), *The Old Devils* (1986, Booker Prize).

**Amis, Martin (Louis)** (1949– ) English novelist, short-story writer, born Oxford; *The Rachel Papers* (1973), *Money* (1984), *London Fields* (1990), *Time's Arrow* (1991), *The Information* (1995).

**Anand, Mulk Raj** (1905– ) Indian novelist, short-story writer, born Peshawar; *Untouchable* (1935), *The Big Heart* (1945).

**Angelou, Maya** (pseudonym of **Marguerite Annie Johnson**) (1928– ) American novelist, poet, playwright, born St Louis, Missouri; *I Know Why The Caged Bird Sings* (1969), *All God's Children Need Travelling Shoes* (1986), *Wouldn't Take Nothing for My Journey Now* (1993), *Even the Stars Look Lonesome* (1998).

**Apuleius, Lucius** (c.123–after 161) Roman writer, born Madaura, Numidia, Africa; *Golden Ass* (the only Roman novel to survive complete), *Apologia*.

**Archer, Jeffrey (Howard) Archer, Baron** (1940– ) English novelist, short-story writer, born London; *Not a Penny More, Not a Penny Less* (1975), *Kane and Abel* (1979), *First Among Equals* (1984), *A Twist in the Tale* (short stories) (1989), *Honour Among Thieves* (1993), *The Eleventh Commandment* (1998).

**Asimov, Isaac** (1920–92) American novelist, short-story writer, born Petrovichi, Russia; *I Robot* (1950), *Foundation* (1951), *The Disappearing Man and other stories* (1985), *Nightfall* (1990).

**Atwood, Margaret (Eleanor)** (1939– ) Canadian novelist, poet, short-story writer, born Ottawa; *Bluebeard's Egg* (1983), *The Handmaid's Tale* (1986), *Cat's Eye* (1989), *The Robber Bride* (1993), *The Blind Assassin* (2000, Booker Prize).

**Auchincloss, Louis (Stanton)** (1917– ) American novelist, short-story writer, born Lawrence, New York; *The Great World and Timothy Colt* (1957), *A World of Profit* (1968), *Diary of a Yuppie* (1986), *Fellow Passengers* (1990), *Lady of Situations* (1991).

**Austen, Jane** (1775–1817) English novelist, born Steventon, Hampshire; *Sense and Sensibility* (1811), *Pride and Prejudice* (1813), *Mansfield Park* (1814), *Emma* (1816), *Persuasion* (1818).

**Bainbridge, Beryl (Margaret)** (1934– ) English novelist, born Liverpool; *The Dressmaker* (1973), *The Bottle Factory Outing* (1974), *Injury Time* (1977), *An Awfully Big Adventure* (1989), *Every Man for Himself* (1996), *Master Georgie* (1998).

**Ballantyne, R(obert) M(ichael)** (1825–94) Scottish novelist, born Edinburgh; *The Coral Island* (1857), *The Gorilla Hunters* (1862).

**Ballard, J(ames) G(raham)** (1930– ) English novelist, born Shanghai, China; *The Drowned World* (1962), *The Terminal Beach* (1964), *Empire of the Sun* (1984), *The Kindness of Women* (1991), *A User's Guide to the Millennium* (1996).

**Balzac, Honoré de** (1799–1850) French novelist, born Tours; *Comédie humaine* (1827–47), *Illusions perdues* (1837–43).

**Banks, Iain (Menzies)** (1954– ) Scottish novelist, born Dunfermline; *The Wasp Factory* (1984), *The Bridge* (1986), *Whit* (1995), *Excession* (1996), *A Song of Stone* (1997), *The Business* (1999).

**Banks, Lynne Reid** (1929– ) English novelist, playwright, born London; *The L-Shaped Room* (1961), *Defy the Wilderness* (1981), *The Warning Bell* (1987), *The Magic Hare* (1992), *Harry the Poisonous Centipede* (1996).

**Barker, Pat (Patricia Margaret)** (1943– ) English novelist, short-story writer, born Thornaby-on-Tees; *Union Street* (1982), *Blow Your House Down* (1984), *The Century's Daughter* (1986), *The Man Who Wasn't There* (1989), *Regeneration* (1991), *The Eye in the Door* (1993), *The Ghost Road* (1995, Booker Prize), *Another World* (1998).

**Barnes, Julian (Patrick)** (1946– ) English novelist, born Leicester; *Flaubert's Parrot* (1984), *Staring at the Sun* (1986), *A History of the World in $10\frac{1}{2}$ Chapters* (1989), *Love, Etc* (1992), *Cross Channel* (short stories) (1996).

**Barstow, Stan(ley)** (1928– ) English novelist, short-story writer, playwright, born Horbury, Yorkshire; *A Kind of Loving* (1960), *A Raging Calm* (1968), *Just You Wait and See* (1986), *Next of Kin* (1991), *In My Own Good Time* (1996).

**Barth, John (Simmons)** (1930– ) American novelist, short-story writer, born Cambridge, Maryland; *The Floating Opera* (1956), *Chimera* (1974), *The Tidewater Tales* (1987), *The Last Voyage of Somebody the Sailor* (1991), *Further Fridays* (1995).

**Bates, H(erbert) E(rnest)** (1905–74) English novelist, short-story writer, born Rushden, Northamptonshire; *Fair Stood the Wind for France* (1944), *The Jacaranda Tree* (1949), *Love for Lydia* (1952), *The Darling Buds of May* (1958).

**Bawden, Nina (Mary)** (née **Mabey**) (1925– ) English writer, born London; *The Birds on the Trees* (1970), *The Peppermint Pig* (children's) (1975), *The Ice House* (1983), *Circles of Deceit* (1987), *Family Money* (1991), *A Nice Change* (1997).

**Bedford, Sybille** (née **von Schoenebeck**) (1911– ) British novelist, born Charlottenburg, Germany; *A Legacy* (1956), *Jigsaw: An Unsentimental Education* (1989), *As It Was* (essays) (1990).

**Beerbohm, Sir (Henry) Max(imilian)** (1872–1956) English novelist, born London; *Zuleika Dobson* (1912).

**Behn, Aphra** (1640–89) English novelist, playwright, born Wye, Kent; *The Rover* (play) (1678), *Oroonoko* (1688).

**Bellow, Saul** (1915– ) Canadian novelist, born Lachine, Quebec; *Henderson the Rain King* (1959), *Herzog* (1964), *Humboldt's Gift* (1975, Pulitzer Prize 1976) *The Dean's December* (1982), *The Actual* (1997); Nobel Prize for Literature 1976.

**Bely, Andrei** (pseudonym of **Boris Nikolayvich Bugayev**) (1880–1934) Russian novelist, poet, born Moscow; *The Silver Dove* (1910), *Petersburg* (1913).

**Benedictus, David (Henry)** (1938– ) English novelist, playwright, born London; *The Fourth of June* (1962), *A World of Windows* (1971), *Local Hero* (novelization of screenplay) (1983), *The Stamp Collector* (1994).

**Bennett, (Enoch) Arnold** (1867–1931) English novelist, born Hanley, Staffordshire; *Anna of the Five Towns* (1902), The Old Wives' Tale (1908), *Clayhanger* series (1910–18).

**Berger, John (Peter)** (1926– ) English novelist, playwright, born Stoke Newington, London; *A Painter of Our Time* (1958), *A Fortunate Man* (non-fiction) (1967), *G* (1972, Booker Prize), *To The Wedding* (1995), *Photocopies* (1996).

**Berger, Thomas (Louis)** (1924– ) American novelist, born Cincinnati, Ohio; *Reinhart in Love* (1962), *Arthur Rex* (1978), *The Houseguest* (1988), *Suspects* (1996).

**Binchy, Maeve** (1940– ) Irish novelist, short-story writer, born Dublin; *Light a Penny Candle* (1982), *Echoes* (1985), *Firefly Summer* (1987), *Circle of Friends* (1990), *Copper Beech* (1992), *The Glass Lake* (1994), *Evening Class* (1996), *Tara Road* (1998).

**Blackmore, R(ichard) D(odderidge)** (1825–1900) English novelist, born Longworth, Berkshire; *Lorna Doone* (1869).

**Bleasdale, Alan** (1946– ) English novelist, playwright, born Liverpool; *Scully* (1975), *The Boys from the Blackstuff* (TV series) (1982), *Are You Lonesome Tonight?* (musical) (1985), *GBH* (TV series) (1991), *Jake's Progress* (TV series) (1995).

**Böll, Heinrich** (1917–85) German novelist, born Cologne; *And Never Said a Solitary Word* (1953), *The Unguarded House* (1954), *The Bread of Our Early Years* (1955); Nobel Prize for Literature 1972.

**Borges, Jorge Luis** (1899–1986) Argentinian poet, short-story writer, born Buenos Aires; *Ficciones* (1944), *El Aleph* (1949), *Labyrinths* (1962).

**Bowen, Elizabeth (Dorothea Cole)** (1899–1973) Anglo-Irish novelist, short-story writer, born Dublin; *The Death of the Heart* (1938), *The Heat of the Day* (1949).

**Bowles, Paul (Frederick)** (1910–99) American novelist, short-story writer, born New York City; *The Sheltering Sky* (1949), *Pages from Cold Point and other stories* (1968), *Midnight Mass* (stories) (1981).

**Boyd, William (Andrew Murray)** (1952– ) Scottish novelist, short-story writer, born Accra, Ghana; *A Good Man in Africa* (1982), *An Ice-Cream War*

(1983), *Brazzaville Beach* (1990), *The Blue Afternoon* (1993), *The Destiny of Nathalie X* (stories) (1995).

**Bradbury, Sir Malcolm (Stanley)** (1932–2000) English novelist, born Sheffield; *Eating People is Wrong* (1959), *The History Man* (1975).

**Bradbury, Ray(mond) (Douglas)** (1920– ) American novelist, short-story writer, born Waukegan, Illinois; *The Martian Chronicles* (short stories) (1950), *Fahrenheit 451* (1954), *Something Wicked this Way Comes* (1962), *A Graveyard for Lunatics* (1990).

**Bradford, Barbara Taylor** (1933– ) English novelist, born Leeds; *A Woman of Substance* (1979), *Hold the Dream* (1985), *Love in Another Town* (1995).

**Bragg, Melvin Bragg, Baron** (1939– ) English novelist, playwright, short-story writer, born Carlisle; *The Hired Man* (1969), *A Time to Dance* (1991).

**Braine, John (Gerard)** (1922–86) English novelist, born Bradford; *Room at the Top* (1957).

**Brink, André (Philippus)** (1935– ) South African novelist, short-story writer, playwright, born Vrede, Orange Free State; *Looking on Darkness* (1974), *Rumours of Rain* (1978), *A Dry White Season* (1979), *States of Emergency* (1988), *On the Contrary* (1993), *Imaginings of Sand* (1996).

**Brittain, Vera (Mary)** (1893–1970) English novelist, poet, born Newcastle-under-Lyme, Staffordshire; *Testament of Youth* (1933), *Testament of Friendship* (1940), *Testament of Experience* (1957) (all autobiographies).

**Bromfield, Louis** (1896–1956) American novelist, short-story writer, born Mansfield, Ohio; *Early Autumn* (1926), *Until the Day Break* (1942).

**Brontë, Anne** (1820–49) English novelist, poet, born Thornton, Yorkshire; *Agnes Grey* (1847), *The Tenant of Wildfell Hall* (1848).

**Brontë, Charlotte** (1816–55) English novelist, poet, born Thornton, Yorkshire; *Jane Eyre* (1847), *Shirley* (1849), *Villette* (1853).

**Brontë, Emily** (1818–48) English novelist, poet, born Thornton, Yorkshire; *Wuthering Heights* (1847).

**Brooke-Rose, Christine** (1926– ) English novelist, born Geneva, Switzerland; *The Languages of Love* (1957), *Thru* (1975), *Amalgamemnon* (1984), *Textermination* (1991), *Remake* (1996).

**Brookner, Anita** (1928– ) English novelist, born London; *Hotel du Lac* (1984, Booker Prize), *Family and Friends* (1985), *Brief Lives* (1991), *Altered States* (1996), *Visitors* (1997).

**Brophy, Brigid (Antonia)** (1929–95) English novelist, short-story writer, playwright, born London; *The Crown Princess and Other Stories* (1953), *The King of a Rainy Country* (1956), *In Transit* (1969).

**Brown, George Douglas** (1869–1902) Scottish novelist, born Ochiltree, Ayrshire; *House with the Green Shutters* (1901).

**Brown, George Mackay** (1921–96) Scottish novelist, poet, short-story writer, playwright, born Orkney; *Greenvoe* (1972), *Beside the Ocean of Time* (1994).

**Buchan, John** (1875–1940) Scottish novelist, poet, born Perth; *The Thirty-Nine Steps* (1915), *Greenmantle* (1916), *Sir Walter Scott* (biography) (1932).

**Buck, Pearl** (née **Sydenstricker**) (1892–1973) American novelist, born Hillsboro, West Virginia; *The Good Earth* (1913), *Pavilion of Women* (1946); Nobel Prize for Literature 1938.

**Bulgakov, Mikhail (Afanasievich)** (1891–1940) Russian novelist, short-story writer, born Kiev; *Diavoliada* (1925), *The Master and Margarita* (1967).

**Bunyan, John** (1628–88) English novelist, born Elstow, near Bedford; *Pilgrim's Progress* (1678).

**Burgess, Anthony** (pseudonym of **John Anthony Burgess Wilson**) (1917–93) English novelist, born Manchester; *A Clockwork Orange* (1962), *The Malayan Trilogy* (1972), *Earthly Powers* (1980), *Kingdom of the Wicked* (1985), *Any Old Iron* (1989).

**Burney, Fanny (Frances,** later **Mme d'Arblay)** (1752–1840) English novelist, born King's Lynn; *Evelina* (1778), *Cecilia* (1782).

**Burroughs, Edgar Rice** (1875–1950) American novelist, born Chicago; *Tarzan of the Apes* (1914), *The Land that Time Forgot* (1924).

**Burroughs, William S(eward)** (1914–97) American novelist, born St Louis, Missouri; *The Naked Lunch* (1959), *The Soft Machine* (1961), *The Wild Boys* (1971), *Exterminator!* (1974), *My Education: a Book of Dreams* (1995).

**Byatt, Dame A(ntonia) S(usan)** (1936– ) English novelist, born Sheffield; *The Shadow of a Sun* (1964), *The Virgin in the Garden* (1978), *Possession* (1989, Booker Prize 1990), *Babel Tower* (1996).

**Calvino, Italo** (1923–87) Italian novelist, short-story writer, born Santiago de Las Vegas, Cuba; *Invisible Cities* (1972), *The Castle of Crossed Destinies* (1969), *If on a Winter's Night a Traveller* (1979).

**Camus, Albert** (1913–60) French novelist, playwright, born Mondovi, Algeria; *The Outsider* (1942), *The Plague* (1948), *The Fall* (1957); Nobel Prize for Literature 1957.

**Canetti, Elias** (1905–94) Bulgarian novelist, born Russe, Bulgaria; *Auto da Fé* (1935, trans 1946), *Crowds and Power* (1960, trans 1962); Nobel Prize for Literature 1981.

**Capote, Truman** (1924–84) American playwright, novelist, short-story writer, born New Orleans; *Other Voices, Other Rooms* (1948), *Breakfast at Tiffany's* (1958).

**Carey, Peter (Philip)** (1943– ) Australian novelist, short-story writer, born Bacchus Marsh, Victoria; *Bliss* (1981), *Illywhacker* (1985), *Oscar and Lucinda* (1989, Booker Prize), *The Tax Inspector* (1991), *True Story of the Kelly Gang* (2001, Booker Prize).

**Carr, Philippa ► Holt, Victoria**

**Carter, Angela** (1940–92) English novelist, poet, playwright, born London; *The Magic Toyshop* (1967), *The Infernal Desire Machines of Dr Hoffman* (1972), *Nights at the Circus* (1984), *Wise Children* (1991).

**Cartland, Dame (Mary) Barbara (Hamilton)** (1901–2000) English novelist, born Birmingham; *The Husband Hunters* (1976), *The Castle Made for Love* (1985), *Love Solves the Problem* (1995).

**Cather, Willa (Silbert)** (1876–1947) American novelist, poet, born near Winchester, Virginia; *O Pioneers!* (1913), *My Antonia* (1918), *One of Ours* (1922), *The Professor's House* (1925), *My Mortal Enemy* (1926), *Death Comes for the Archbishop* (1927), *Sapphira and the Slave Girl* (1940).

**Cela, Camilo José** (1916–2002) Spanish novelist, born Iria Flavia; *La Familia de Pascual Duarte* (1942), *Mazurca para dos muertos* (1984, trans Mazurka for Two Dead People); Nobel Prize for Literature 1989.

**Cervantes (Saavedra), Miguel de** (1547–1616) Spanish novelist and poet, born Alcala de Henares; *La Galatea* (1585), *Don Quixote* (1605–15).

**Chandler, Raymond** (1888–1959) American novelist, born Chicago; *The Big Sleep* (1939), *Farewell, My Lovely* (1940), *The High Window* (1942), *The Lady in the Lake* (1943), *The Long Goodbye* (1953).

**Chesterton, G(ilbert) K(eith)** (1874–1936) English novelist, poet, born London; *The Napoleon of Notting Hill* (1904), *The Innocence of Father Brown* (1911).

**Christie, Dame Agatha (Mary Clarissa)** (née **Miller**) (1890–1976) English novelist, born Torquay, Devon; *Murder on the Orient Express* (1934), *Death on the Nile* (1937), *Ten Little Niggers* (1939), *Curtain* (1975).

**Clarke, Sir Arthur C(harles)** (1917– ) English novelist, short-story writer, born Minehead, Somerset; *Childhood's End* (1953), *The Fountains of Paradise* (1979), *The Garden of Rama* (1991), *The Hammer of God* (1993).

**Clavell, James (du Maresq)** (1922–94) American novelist, playwright, born England; *King Rat* (1962), *Tai-Pan* (1966), *Shogun* (1975).

**Cleary, Jon (Stephen)** (1917– ) Australian novelist, born Sydney; *You Can't See Around Corners* (1947), *The Safe House* (1975), *Pride's Harvest* (1991), *Dark Summer* (1992), *Autumn Maze* (1994), *Winter Chill* (1995), *Endpeace* (1996).

**Coetzee, J(ohn) M(ichael)** (1940– ) South African novelist, born Cape Town; *Life and Times of Michael K* (1983, Booker Prize), *Foe* (1986), *The Master of Petersburg* (1994), *Disgrace* (1999, Booker Prize).

**Colette, Sidonie Gabrielle** (1873–1954) French novelist, born Saint-Sauveur-en-Puisaye, Burgundy; *Claudine à l'école* (1900), *Chéri* (1920), *La Fin de Chéri* (1926), *Gigi* (1943).

**Collins, (William) Wilkie** (1824–89) English novelist, born London; *The Woman in White* (1860), *No Name* (1862), *Armadale* (1866), *The Moonstone* (1868).

**Compton-Burnett, Dame Ivy** (1884–1969) English novelist, born Pinner, Middlesex; *A House and its Head* (1935), *A Family and a Fortune* (1939), *Manservant and Maidservant* (1947).

**Condon, Richard (Thomas)** (1915–96) American novelist, born New York City; *The Manchurian Candidate* (1959), *Winter Kills* (1974), *Prizzi's Honor* (1982).

**Connell, Evan S(helby)** (1924– ) American novelist, born Kansas City, Missouri; *Mrs Bridge* (1958), *The Diary of a Rapist* (1966), *Mr Bridge* (1969).

**Conrad, Joseph** (originally **Jozef Teodor Konrad Nalecz Korzeniowski**) (1857–1924) Anglo-Polish novelist, short-story writer, born Berdichev, Poland, (now Ukraine); *Lord Jim* (1900), *Heart of Darkness* (1902), *Nostromo* (1904), *The Secret Agent* (1907), *Chance* (1914).

**Cookson, Dame Catherine (Ann)** (1906–98) English novelist, born Tyne Dock, County Durham; *Tilly Trotter* (1956), *The Glass Virgin* (1969), *The Black Candle* (1989).

**Cooper, Jilly** (1937– ) English novelist, born Hornchurch, Essex; *Men and Supermen* (1972), *Class* (1979), *Riders* (1985), *Rivals* (1988), *Polo* (1990), *The Man who made Husbands Jealous* (1993), *Appassionata* (1996), *Score* (1999).

**Cooper, William** (pseudonym of **Harry Summerfield Hoff**) (1910– ) English novelist, born Crewe, Cheshire; *Scenes from Provincial Life* (1950), *Disquiet and Peace* (1956), *Immortality At Any Price* (1991).

**Dahl, Roald** (1916–90) Welsh writer and playwright, born Llandaff; *Over to You* (1946), *Kiss, Kiss* (1960) (all short stories), *James and the Giant Peach* (1961), *Matilda* (1988).

**Davies, (William) Robertson** (1913–95) Canadian novelist, short-story writer, playwright, born Thamesville, Ontario; *The Rebel Angels* (1981), *'The Deptford Trilogy'* (1970–5), *What's Bred in the Bone* (1985).

**de Beauvoir, Simone** (1908–86) French novelist, born Paris; *The Second Sex* (1949, trans 1953), *Les Mandarins* (1954), *Memoirs of a Dutiful Daughter* (1959).

**Defoe, Daniel** (1660–1731) English novelist, born Stoke Newington, London; *Robinson Crusoe* (1719), *Moll Flanders* (1722), *A Journal of the Plague Year* (1722).

**Deighton, Len (Leonard Cyril)** (1929– ) English novelist, born London; *The Ipcress File* (1962), *Spy Hook* (1988), *Spy Line* (1989), *Spy Sinker* (1990).

**Delafield, E M** (pseudonym of **Edmée Elizabeth Monica Dashwood**) (née **de la Pasture**) (1890–1943) English novelist, born Llandogo, Monmouth, Wales; *The Diary of a Provincial Lady* (1931).

**DeLillo, Don** (1936– ) American novelist, born New York City; *End Zone* (1972), *Ratner's Star* (1976), *White Noise* (1985), *Mao II* (1991).

**de Quincey, Thomas** (1785–1859) English novelist, born Manchester; *Confessions of an English Opium Eater* (1822).

**Desai, Anita** (née **Mazumbar**) (1937– ) Indian novelist, short-story writer, born Mussoorie; *Cry, The Peacock* (1963), *Fire on the Mountain* (1977), *In*

*Custody* (1984), *Baumgartner's Bombay* (1988), *Journey to Ithaca* (1995).

**De Vries, Peter** (1910–93) American novelist, born Chicago; *The Tunnel of Love* (1954), *The Meckerel Plaza* (1958), *Slouching Towards Kalamazoo* (1983).

**Dickens, Charles** (1812–70) English novelist, born Landport, Portsmouth; *Oliver Twist* (1837–9), *David Copperfield* (1849–50), *Bleak House* (1852–3), *Great Expectations* (1860–1).

**Dickens, Monica** (1915–92) English novelist, born London; *One Pair of Hands* (1939), *Spring Comes to the World's End* (1973).

**Didion, Joan** (1934– ) American novelist, born Sacramento, California; *Run River* (1963), *A Book of Common Prayer* (1977), *Democracy* (1984), *The Last Thing He Wanted* (1996).

**Dinesen, Isak** (pseudonym of **Baroness Karen Blixen**) (1885–1962) Danish novelist, born Rungsted; *Seven Gothic Tales* (1934), *Out of Africa* (1937).

**Disraeli, Benjamin** (1804–81) English novelist, born London; *Coningsby* (1844), *Sybil* (1846), *Tancred* (1847).

**Donleavy, J(ames) P(atrick)** (1926– ) Irish–American novelist, playwright, born Brooklyn, New York City; *The Ginger Man* (1955), *Schultz* (1980), *Are You Listening, Rabbi Low?* (1987), *The Lady Who Liked Clean Rest Rooms* (1995).

**Dos Passos, John Roderigo** (1896–1970) American novelist, born Chicago; *Manhattan Transfer* (1925), *USA* (1930–6).

**Dostoevsky, Fyodor Mikhailovich** (1821–81) Russian novelist, born Moscow; *Notes from the Underground* (1864), *Crime and Punishment* (1866), *The Brothers Karamazov* (1880).

**Doyle, Sir Arthur Conan** (1859–1930) Scottish novelist, short-story writer, born Edinburgh; *The Memoirs of Sherlock Holmes* (1894), *The Hound of the Baskervilles* (1902), *The Lost World* (1912).

**Doyle, Roddy** (1958– ) Irish novelist, born Dublin; *The Commitments* (1987), *Paddy Clarke, Ha Ha Ha* (1993, Booker Prize), *The Woman Who Walked into Doors* (1996), *A Star Called Henry* (1999).

**Drabble, Margaret** (1939– ) English novelist, short-story writer, born Sheffield; *The Millstone* (1965), *The Ice Age* (1977), *The Gates of Ivory* (1991), *The Witch of Exmoor* (1996).

**Duffy, Maureen (Patricia)** (1933– ) English novelist, playwright, born Worthing, Sussex; *That's How It Was* (1962), *The Microcosm* (1966), *The Paradox Players* (1967), *Occam's Razor* (1993).

**Dumas, Alexandre** (in full **Alexandre Dumas Davy de la Pailleterie**), known as **Dumas père** (1802–70) French novelist and playwright, born Villers-Cotterêts, Aisne; *The Three Musketeers* (1844–5).

**Dumas, Alexandre**, known as **Dumas fils** (1824–95) French novelist, playwright, born Paris; *La Dame aux camélias* (1848).

**du Maurier, Dame Daphne** (1907–89) English novelist, born London; *Rebecca* (1938), *My Cousin Rachel* (1951).

**Dunn, Nell (Mary)** (1936– ) English novelist, playwright, born London; *Poor Cow* (1967), *Tears His Head Off His Shoulders* (1974), *The Only Child* (1978).

**Durrell, Gerald Malcolm** (1925–95) English writer, born Jamshedpur, India; *The Overloaded Ark* (1953), *My Family and Other Animals* (1956).

**Durrell, Lawrence George** (1912–90) English novelist, poet, born Julundur, India; *'Alexandria Quartet'* (1957–60).

**Eco, Umberto** (1932– ) Italian novelist, born Alessandria, Piedmont; *The Name of the Rose* (1980), *Foucault's Pendulum* (1989), *The Island of the Day Before* (1995).

**Edgeworth, Maria** (1767–1849) Irish novelist, born Blackbourton, Oxfordshire; *Castle Rackrent* (1800), *The Absentee* (1809).

**Eliot, George** (originally **Mary Ann**, later **Marian Evans**) (1819–80) English novelist, born Arbury, Warwickshire; *Adam Bede* (1858), *The Mill on the Floss* (1860), *Middlemarch* (1871–2), *Daniel Deronda* (1874–6).

**Elkin, Stanley (Lawrence)** (1930–95) American novelist, short-story writer, born Brooklyn, New York City; *Criers and Kibitzers, Kibitzers and Criers* (1966), *The Living End* (1979), *George Mills* (1982), *The Magic Kingdom* (1985).

**Ellis, Alice Thomas** (pseudonym of **Anna Margaret Haycraft**, née **Lindholm**) (1932– ) English novelist, born Liverpool; *The Sin Eater* (1977), *The 27th Kingdom* (1982), *The Inn at the Edge of the World* (1990), *Fairy Tale* (1996).

**Elton, Ben (Benjamin Charles)** (1959– ) English novelist, born London; *Stark* (1989), *Gridlock* (1991), *Popcorn* (1996), *Inconceivable* (1999).

**Fairbairns, Zoë (Ann)** (1948– ) English novelist, born Tunbridge Wells, Kent; *Stand We At Last* (1983), *Here Today* (1984), *Daddy's Girls* (1991).

**Farmer, Philip José** (1918– ) American novelist, short-story writer, born Indiana; *To Your Scattered Bodies Go* (1977), *The Magic Labyrinth* (1980), *Nothing Burns in Hell* (1998).

**Fast, Howard (Melvin)** (1914–92) American novelist, playwright, born New York City; *The Last Frontier* (1941), *Spartacus* (1951), *The Immigrants* (1977).

**Faulkner, William Harrison** (1897–1962) American novelist, born near Oxford, Mississippi; *Sartoris* (1929), *The Sound and the Fury* (1929), *Absalom, Absalom!* (1936); Nobel Prize for Literature 1949.

**Feinstein, Elaine** (1930– ) English novelist, poet, born Bootle, Lancashire; *The Circle* (1970), *The Border* (1989), *All You Need* (1991).

**Fielding, Henry** (1707–54) English novelist, born Sharpham Park, near Glastonbury, Somerset; *Joseph Andrews* (1742), *Tom Jones* (1749).

**Figes, Eva** (née **Unger**) (1932– ) British novelist, born Berlin, Germany; *Winter Journey* (1967), *Light* (1983), *The Tree of Knowledge* (1990).

**Fitzgerald, F(rancis) Scott (Key)** (1896–1940) American novelist, short-story writer, born St Paul, Minnesota; *The Great Gatsby* (1925), *Tender is the Night* (1934).

**Fitzgerald, Penelope (Mary)** (née **Knox**) (1916–2000) English novelist, born Lincoln; *The Bookshop* (1978), *Offshore* (1979, Booker Prize), *The Gate of Angels* (1990), *The Blue Flower* (1995).

**Flaubert, Gustave** (1821–80) French novelist, born Rouen; *Madame Bovary* (1857), *Salammbô* (1862).

**Fleming, Ian (Lancaster)** (1908–64) English novelist, born London; author of the 'James Bond' novels, eg *Casino Royale* (1953), *From Russia with Love* (1957), *Dr No* (1958), *Goldfinger* (1959), *The Man with the Golden Gun* (1965).

**Ford, Ford Madox** (originally **Ford Hermann Hueffer**) (1873–1939) English novelist, poet, born Merton, Surrey; *The Fifth Queen* (1906), *The Good Soldier* (1915), *Parade's End* (1924–8).

**Ford, Richard** (1944– ) American novelist, born Jackson, Mississippi; *A Piece of My Heart* (1976), *The Sportswriter* (1986), *Independence Day* (1995, Pulitzer Prize 1996).

**Forester, C(ecil) S(cott)** (1899–1966) British novelist, born Cairo, Egypt; *Payment Deferred* (1926), *The African Queen* (1935), *The Happy Return* (1937).

**Forster, E(dward) M(organ)** (1879–1970) English novelist, short-story writer, born London; *A Room with a View* (1908), *Howards End* (1910), *A Passage to India* (1922–4).

**Forsyth, Frederick** (1938– ) English novelist, short-story writer, born Ashford, Kent; *The Day of the Jackal* (1971), *The Odessa File* (1972), *The Fourth Protocol* (1984), *The Fist of God* (1993), *Icon* (1996).

**Fowles, John (Robert)** (1926– ) English novelist, born Leigh-on-Sea, Essex; *The Magus* (1965, revised 1977), *The French Lieutenant's Woman* (1969), *The Ebony Tower* (1974), *The Tree* (1991).

**Frame, Janet Paterson** (1924– ) New Zealand novelist, short-story writer, born Dunedin; *The Lagoon: Stories* (1952), *Scented Gardens for the Blind* (1963), *Living in the Maniototo* (1979); autobiography: *To the Island* (1982), *An Angel at My Table* (1984), *The Envoy from Mirror City* (1985).

**Francis, Dick (Richard Stanley)** (1920– ) English novelist, born Tenby, Pembrokeshire; *Dead Cert* (1962), *Slay-Ride* (1973), *The Edge* (1988), *Comeback* (1991) *To The Hilt* (1996), *10 lb Penalty* (1997).

**Fraser, Lady Antonia** (née **Pakenham**) (1932– ) English novelist, born London; *Mary, Queen of Scots* (1969), *Quiet as a Nun* (1977), *A Splash of Red* (1981), *Have a Nice Death* (1983), *Political Death* (1994).

**Frayn, Michael** (1933– ) English novelist, playwright, born Mill Hill, London; *The Tin Men* (1965), *A Very Private Life* (1968), *Sweet Dreams* (1973), *A Landing on the Sun* (1990), *Headlong* (1999).

**Freeling, Nicholas** (1927– ) English novelist, born London; *Love in Amsterdam* (1962), *Tsing-Boum* (1969), *Sand Castles* (1990), *A Dwarf Kingdom* (1996).

**French, Marilyn** (1929– ) American novelist, born New York City; *The Women's Room* (1977), *The Bleeding Heart* (1980), *Her Mother's Daughter* (1987), *The War Against Women* (1992).

**Fuller, Roy (Broadbent)** (1912–91) English novelist, poet, born Failsworth, Lancashire; *The Second Curtain* (1953), *The Ruined Boys* (1959), *My Child, My Sister* (1965).

**Gaddis, William** (1922–98) American novelist, born New York City; *The Recognitions* (1955), *JR* (1976), *Carpenter's Gothic* (1985), *A Frolic of His Own* (1994).

**Galsworthy, John** (1867–1933) English novelist, playwright, born Coombe, Surrey; *The Man of Property* (1906), *The Forsyte Saga* (1906–31); Nobel Prize for Literature 1932.

**García Márquez, Gabriel** (1928– ) Colombian novelist, born Aracataca; *One Hundred Years of Solitude* (1970), *Chronicle of a Death Foretold* (1982), *The General in His Labyrinth* (1991), *Of Love and Other Demons* (1995), *News of a Kidnapping* (non-fiction, 1997); Nobel Prize for Literature 1982.

**Garner, Helen** (1942– ) Australian novelist, born Geelong; *Monkey Gripp* (1977), *The Last Days of Chez Nous* (screenplay) (1993), *Cosmo Cosmolino* (1993).

**Gaskell, Mrs Elizabeth (Cleghorn)** (née **Stevenson**) (1810–65) English novelist, born Cheyne Row, Chelsea, London; *Mary Barton* (1848), *Cranford* (1853), *North and South* (1855), *Sylvia's Lovers* (1863).

**Gerhardie, William Alexander** (1895–1977) English novelist, born St Petersburg, Russia; *The Polyglots* (1925), *Resurrection* (1934).

**Gibbon, Lewis Grassic** (pseudonym of **James Leslie Mitchell**) (1901–35) Scottish novelist, born near Auchterless, Aberdeenshire; *Sunset Song* (1932), *Cloud Howe* (1933), *Grey Granite* (1934).

**Gibbons, Stella (Dorothea)** (1902–89) English novelist, born London; *Cold Comfort Farm* (1933).

**Gide, André (Paul Guillaume)** (1860–1951) French novelist, born Paris; *The Immoralist* (1902), *The Vatican Cellars* (1914).

**Gilliat, Penelope (Ann Douglas**, née **Conner)** (1932–93) English novelist, short-story writer, born London; *One by One* (1965), *The Cutting Edge* (1978), *Mortal Matters* (1983).

**Gissing, George Robert** (1857–1903) English novelist, short-story writer, born Wakefield, Yorkshire; *New Grub Street* (1891), *The Private Papers of Henry Ryecroft* (1902).

**Glasgow, Ellen** (1873–1945) American novelist, born Richmond, Virginia; *Barren Ground* (1925), *The Sheltered Life* (1932), *In This Our Life* (1941).

**Godden, (Margaret) Rumer** (1907–98) English novelist, poet, children's author, born Eastbourne, Sussex; *Black Narcissus* (1939), *Breakfast with the Nikolides*

(1942), *The Greengage Summer* (1958), *Coromandel Sea Change* (1991), *Pippa Passes* (1994).

**Godwin, William** (1756–1836) English novelist, born Wisbech, Cambridgeshire; *Caleb Williams* (1794), *Mandeville* (1817).

**Goethe, Johann Wolfgang von** (1749–1832) German novelist, poet, born Frankfurt am Main; *The Sorrows of Young Werther* (1774).

**Gogol, Nikolai Vasilievich** (1809–52) Russian novelist, short-story writer, playwright, born Sorochinstsi, Poltava; *The Overcoat* (1835), *Diary of a Madman* (1835), *Dead Souls* (1842), *The Odd Women* (1893).

**Gold, Herbert** (1924– ) American novelist, born Cleveland, Ohio; *Birth of a Hero* (1951), *The Man Who Was Not With It* (1956), *My Last Two Thousand Years* (autobiography) (1972).

**Golding, (Sir) William (Gerald)** (1911–93) English novelist, born St Columb Minor, Cornwall; *The Lord of the Flies* (1954), *The Inheritors* (1955), *Pincher Martin* (1956), *The Spire* (1964), *Darkness Visible* (1979), *Rites of Passage* (1980, Booker Prize), *The Paper Men* (1984), *Close Quarter* (1987), *Fire Down Below* (1989); Nobel Prize for Literature 1983.

**Goldman, William** (1931– ) American novelist, playwright, born Chicago; *Boys and Girls Together* (1964), *The Princess Bride* (1973), *The Silent Gondoliers* (1984), *Misery* (screenplay) (1990).

**Goldsmith, Oliver** (1728–74) Anglo-Irish playwright, novelist, poet, born Pallasmore, County Longford; *The Vicar of Wakefield* (1766).

**Gordimer, Nadine** (1923– ) South African novelist, short-story writer, born Springs, Transvaal; *Occasion for Loving* (1963), *A Guest of Honour* (1970), *The Conservationist* (1974, Booker Prize), *A Sport of Nature* (1987), *None to Accompany Me* (1994); Nobel Prize for Literature 1991.

**Gorky, Maxim** (pseudonym of **Aleksei Maksimovich Peshkov**) (1868–1936) Russian novelist, short-story writer, born Nizhni Novgorod (New Gorky); *The Mother* (1906–7), *Childhood* (1913), *The Life of Klim Samgin* (1925–36).

**Gosse, Sir Edmund William** (1849–1928) English novelist, poet, born London; *Father and Son* (1907).

**Graham, Winston (Mawdsley)** (1910– ) English novelist, born Victoria Park, Manchester; *Ross Poldark* (1945), *The Little Walls* (1955), *Marnie* (1961), *Poldark's Cornwall* (1983), *Tremor* (1995).

**Grass, Günter (Wilhelm)** (1927– ) German novelist, born Danzig; *The Tin Drum* (1959), *The Meeting at Telgte* (1979), *A Wide Field* (1995); Nobel Prize for Literature 1999.

**Graves, Robert (Ranke)** (1895–1985) English novelist, poet, born London; *I Claudius* (1934), *Claudius the God* (1934).

**Gray, Alasdair (James)** (1934– ) Scottish novelist, short-story writer, poet, born Glasgow; *Lanark* (1981), *Unlikely Stories, Mostly* (stories) (1983), *Janine* (1984), *Poor Things* (1992), *A History Maker* (1994).

**Greene, (Henry) Graham** (1904–91) English novelist, playwright, born Berkhamstead, Hertfordshire; *Brighton Rock* (1938), *The Power and the Glory* (1940), *The Third Man* (1950), *The Honorary Consul* (1973).

**Grossmith, George** (1847–1912) and **Weedon** (1852–1919) English writers, entertainers, both born London; *The Diary of a Nobody* (1892).

**Guterson, David** (1956– ) American novelist, short-story writer, born Seattle, Washington; *The Country Ahead of Us, The Country Behind* (stories) (1989), *Snow Falling on Cedars* (1995).

**Haggard, Sir (Henry) Rider** (1856–1925) English novelist, born Bradenham Hall, Norfolk; *King Solomon's Mines* (1885), *She* (1887), *Allan Quatermain* (1887).

**Hailey, Arthur** (1920– ) Anglo-Canadian novelist, playwright, born Luton, Bedfordshire; *Flight into Danger* (1958), *Airport* (1968), *The Evening News* (1990), *Detective* (1997).

**Hardy, Thomas** (1840–1928) English novelist, poet, born Higher Bockhampton, Dorset; *Far from the Madding Crowd* (1874), *The Mayor of Casterbridge* (1886), *Tess of the D'Urbervilles* (1891), *Jude the Obscure* (1895).

**Hartley, L(eslie) P(oles)** (1895–1972) English novelist, short-story writer, born near Peterborough; *The Shrimp and the Anemone* (1944), *The Go-Between* (1953), *The Hireling* (1957).

**Hawthorne, Nathaniel** (1804–64) American novelist, short-story writer, born Salem, Massachusetts; *The Scarlet Letter* (1850), *The House of the Seven Gables* (1851).

**Hazzard, Shirley** (1931– ) American novelist, short-story writer, born Sydney, Australia; *People in Glass Houses* (1967), *The Transit of Venus* (1980), *Countenance of Truth* (1990).

**Heinlein, Robert A(nson)** (1907–88) American novelist, born Missouri; *Stranger in a Strange Land* (1962), *The Moon is a Harsh Mistress* (1967).

**Heller, Joseph** (1923–99) American novelist, born Brooklyn, New York City; *Catch-22* (1961), *Something Happened* (1974), *Picture This* (1988), *Closing Time* (1994).

**Hemingway, Ernest (Millar)** (1899–1961) American novelist, short-story writer, born Oak Park (Chicago), Illinois; *A Farewell to Arms* (1929), *For Whom the Bell Tolls* (1940), *The Old Man and the Sea* (1952); Nobel Prize for Literature 1954.

**Hesse, Hermann** (1877–1962) German novelist, born Calw, Württemberg; *Rosshalde* (1914), *Steppenwolf* (1927), *The Glass Bead Game* (1943); Nobel Prize for Literature 1946.

**Heyer, Georgette** (1902–74) English novelist, born London; *The Black Moth* (1929), *Footsteps in the Dark* (1932), *Regency Buck* (1935), *The Corinthian* (1940), *Friday's Child* (1944), *The Grand Sophy* (1950), *Bath Tangle* (1955), *Venetia* (1958), *The Nonesuch* (1962), *Frederica* (1965).

**Highsmith, (Mary) Patricia** (née **Plangman**) (1921–95) American novelist, short-story writer, born Fort Worth, Texas; *This Sweet Sickness* (1960), *The Cry* of the *Owl* (1962), *The Boy Who Followed Ripley* (1980).

**Hill, Susan (Elizabeth)** (1942– ) English novelist, short-story writer, born Scarborough, Yorkshire; *I'm the King of the Castle* (1970), *Strange Meeting* (1972), *The Woman in Black* (1983), *Mrs de Winter* (1993).

**Hilton, James** (1900–54) English novelist, born Leigh, Lancashire; *Lost Horizon* (1933), *Goodbye Mr Chips* (1934).

**Hines, (Melvin) Barry** (1939– ) English novelist, playwright, born Barnsley, S Yorkshire; *A Kestrel for a Knave* (1968), *The Gamekeeper* (1975), *The Heart of It* (1994).

**Hoban, Russell (Conwell)** (1925– ) American novelist, playwright, children's writer, born Lansdale, Pennsylvania; *Turtle Diary* (1975), *Riddley Walker* (1980), *Pilgermann* (1983), *The Trokeville Way* (1996).

**Hogg, James, 'the Ettrick Shepherd'** (1770–1835) Scottish novelist, poet, born Ettrick, Selkirkshire; *Confessions of a Justified Sinner* (1824).

**Holt, Victoria** (pseudonym of **Eleanor Alice Burford Hibbert**) (1906–93) English novelist, also wrote as Philippa Carr, Jean Plaidy; *Catherine de' Medici* (1969, as JP), *Will You Love Me in September* (1981, as PC), *The Captive* (1989, as VH).

**Holtby, Winifred** (1898–1935) English novelist, born Rudston, Yorkshire; *The Crowded Street* (1924), *The Land of Green Ginger* (1927), *South Riding* (1936).

**Horgan, Paul** (1903–95) American novelist, poet, short-story writer, born Buffalo, New York; *The Fault of Angels* (1933), *Rome Eternal* (1957), *Mexico Bay* (1982).

**Howard, Elizabeth Jane** (1923– ) English novelist, born London; *The Sea Change* (1959), *After Julius* (1965), *The Light Years* (1990), *Marking Time* (1991), *Casting Off* (1995).

**Hughes, Thomas** (1822–96) English novelist, born Uffington, Berkshire; *Tom Brown's Schooldays* (1857).

**Hugo, Victor (Marie)** (1802–85) French novelist, dramatist, poet, born Besançon; *Notre Dame de Paris* (1831), *Les Misérables* (1862).

**Hulme, Keri (Ann Ruhi)** (1947– ) New Zealand novelist, born Christchurch; *The Bone People* (1983, Booker Prize 1985), *Lost Possessions* (1985).

**Hunter, Evan** (originally **Salvatore A Lambino**) (1926– ) American novelist, playwright, short-story writer, born New York City; *The Blackboard Jungle* (1954), *Strangers When We Meet* (1958), *The Paper Dragon* (1966), *Last Summer* (1968), *Privileged Conversation* (1996); also writes as Ed McBain.

**Hurston, Zora Neale** (1903–60) American novelist, born Eatonville, Florida; *Their Eyes Were Watching God* (1937), *Moses, Man of the Mountain* (1939).

**Huxley, Aldous (Leonard)** (1894–1963) English novelist, born Godalming, Surrey; *Brave New World* (1932), *Eyeless in Gaza* (1936), *Island* (1962).

**Innes, Michael** ► **Stewart, J I M**

**Innes, (Ralph) Hammond** (1913–98) English novelist, playwright, born Horsham, Sussex; *The Trojan Horse* (1940), *Atlantic Fury* (1962), *Isvik* (1991), *Delta Connection* (1996).

**Irving, John (Winslow)** (1942– ) American novelist, short-story writer, born Exeter, New Hampshire; *The World According to Garp* (1978), *The Hotel New Hampshire* (1981), *A Prayer for Owen Meany* (1989).

**Isherwood, Christopher (William Bradshaw)** (1904–86) Anglo-American novelist, born Disley, Cheshire; *Mr Norris Changes Trains* (1935), *Goodbye to Berlin* (1939), *Down There on a Visit* (1962).

**Ishiguro, Kazuo** (1954– ) British novelist, short-story writer, born Japan; *The Remains of the Day* (1989, Booker Prize), *The Unconsoled* (1995).

**James, Henry** (1843–1916) American novelist, born New York City; *Portrait of a Lady* (1881), *The Bostonians* (1886), *The Turn of the Screw* (1889), *The Awkward Age* (1899), *The Ambassadors* (1903), *The Golden Bowl* (1904).

**James, P(hyliss) D(orothy)** (1920– ) English novelist, born Oxford; *Cover Her Face* (1966), *Taste for Death* (1986), *Devices and Desires* (1989), *Original Sin* (1994).

**Jhabvala, Ruth Prawer** (1927– ) Anglo-Polish novelist, born Cologne, Germany; *Heat and Dust* (1975, Booker Prize), *In Search of Love and Beauty* (1983), *Poet and Dancer* (1993).

**Jong, Erica** (née **Mann**) (1942– ) American novelist, poet, born New York City; *Fear of Flying* (1973), *Fanny, Being the True History of the Adventures of Fanny Hackabout-Jones* (1980), *Serenissima* (1987).

**Joyce, James (Augustine Aloysius)** (1882–1941) Irish novelist, poet, born Dublin; *Dubliners* (1914), *A Portrait of the Artist as a Young Man* (1914–15), *Ulysses* (1922), *Finnegan's Wake* (1939).

**Kafka, Franz** (1883–1924) Austrian novelist, short-story writer, born Prague (now in Czech Republic); *Metamorphosis* (1916), *The Trial* (1925), *The Castle* (1926), *America* (1927).

**Kaplan, Johanna** (1942– ) American novelist, short-story writer, born New York City; *Other People's Lives* (1975), *O My America!* (1980).

**Kazantazakis, Nikos** (1883–1957) Greek novelist, poet, playwright, born Heraklion, Crete; *Zorba the Greek* (1946).

**Keane, Molly** (1904–96) Anglo-Irish novelist, born County Kildare, Ireland; *Devoted Ladies* (1934), *Good Behaviour* (1981), *Time After Time* (1983).

**Kelman, James (Alexander)** (1946– ) Scottish novelist, short-story writer, playwright, born Glasgow; *The Busconductor Hines* (1984), *A Chancer* (1985), *Greyhound for Breakfast* (1987), *A Disaffection* (1989), *How late it was, how late* (1994, Booker Prize).

**Keneally, Thomas (Michael)** (1935– ) Australian novelist, short-story writer, playwright, born Sydney; *Bring Larks and Heroes* (1967), *Three Cheers for a Paraclete* (1968), *The Survivor* (1969), *Schindler's Ark* (1982, Booker Prize), *Woman of the Inner Sea* (1992), *A River Town* (1995).

**Kennedy, Margaret (Moore)** (1896–1967) English novelist, playwright, born London; *The Ladies of Lyndon* (1923), *The Constant Nymph* (1924), *The Fool of the Family* (1930).

**Kerouac, Jack (Jean-Louis)** (1922–69) American novelist, born Lowell, Massachusetts; *On the Road* (1957), *The Dharma Bums* (1958).

**Kesey, Ken (Elton)** (1935–2001) American novelist, short-story writer, born La Junta, Colorado; *One Flew Over the Cuckoo's Nest* (1962), *Demon Box* (stories) (1987), *Sailor Song* (1990).

**King, Francis (Henry)** (1923– ) English novelist, short-story writer, born Adelboden, Switzerland; *To the Dark Tower* (1946), *The Widow* (1957), *The Custom House* (1961), *Visiting Cards* (1990), *Ash on an Old Man's Sleeve* (1996).

**King, Stephen (Edwin)** (1947– ) American novelist, short-story writer, born Portland, Maine; *Carrie* (1974), *The Shining* (1977), *Christine* (1983), *Pet Sematary* (1983), *Four Past Midnight* (1990).

**Kingsley, Charles** (1819–75) English novelist, born Holne vicarage, Dartmoor; *Westward Ho!* (1855), *The Water-Babies* (1863), *Hereward the Wake* (1866).

**Kipling, Rudyard** (1865–1936) English novelist, poet, short-story writer, born Bombay, India; *Barrack-room Ballads* (1892), *The Jungle Book* (1894), *Kim* (1901), *Just So Stories* (1902); Nobel Prize for Literature 1907.

**Kundera, Milan** (1929– ) French–Czech novelist, born Brno; *Life is Elsewhere* (1973), *The Farewell Party* (1976), *The Unbearable Lightness of Being* (1984), *Immortality* (1991), *Testaments Betrayed* (1995), *Slowness* (1996).

**Laclos, Pierre (Ambroise François) Choderlos de** (1741–1803) French novelist, born Amiens; *Les Liaisons Dangereuses* (Dangerous Liaisons) (1782).

**La Fayette, Marie Madeleine Pioche de Lavergne, Comtesse de** (1634–93) French novelist, born Paris; *Zaide* (1670), *La Princesse de Clèves* (1678).

**Lamming, George (Eric)** (1927– ) Barbadian novelist, born Carrington Village; *In the Castle of My Skin* (1953), *Season of Adventure* (1960), *Natives of My Person* (1972).

**Lampedusa, Giuseppe Tomasi di** (1896–1957) Italian novelist, born Palermo, Sicily; *Il Gattopardo* (The Leopard) (1958).

**Lawrence, D(avid) H(erbert)** (1885–1930) English novelist, poet, short-story writer, born Eastwood, Nottinghamshire; *Sons and Lovers* (1913), *The Rainbow* (1915), *Women in Love* (1920), *Lady Chatterley's Lover* (1928).

**Le Carré, John** (pseudonym of **David John Moore Cornwell**) (1931– ) English novelist, born Poole, Dorset; *Tinker, Tailor, Soldier, Spy* (1974), *Smiley's People* (1980), *The Little Drummer Girl* (1983), *A Perfect Spy* (1986), *The Russia House* (1989), *The Secret Pilgrim* (1991), *The Night Manager* (1993), *Our Game* (1995), *The Tailor of Panama* (1996).

**Lee, (Nelle) Harper** (1926– ) American novelist, born Monroeville, Alabama; *To Kill a Mockingbird* (1960, Pulitzer Prize 1961).

**Lee, Laurie** (1914–97) English novelist, poet, born Slad, Gloucestershire; *Cider with Rosie* (1959), *As I Walked Out One Midsummer Morning* (1969).

**Le Fanu, (Joseph) Sheridan** (1814–73) Irish novelist, short-story writer, born Dublin; *Uncle Silas* (1864), *In a Glass Darkly* (1872).

**Le Guin, Ursula K(roeber)** (1929– ) American novelist, poet, short-story writer, born Berkeley, California; *Rocannon's World* (1966), *The Left Hand of Darkness* (1969), *Searoad* (1991), *Fish Soup* (1992).

**Lehmann, Rosamond (Nina)** (1903–90) English novelist, born London; *Dusty Answer* (1927), *Invitation to the Waltz* (1932), *The Ballad and the Source* (1944).

**Lessing, Doris (May)** (née **Tayler**) (1919– ) Rhodesian novelist, short-story writer, born Kermanshah, Iran; *The Grass is Singing* (1950), *The Golden Notebook* (1962), *Canopus in Argus Archives* (1979–83), *The Good Terrorist* (1985), *Playing the Game* (1996).

**Levi, Primo** (1919–87) Italian novelist, born Turin; *If this is a Man* (1947), *The Periodic Table* (1984).

**Lewis, (Harry) Sinclair** (1885–1951) American novelist, born Sauk Center, Minnesota; *Main Street* (1920), *Babbitt* (1922), *Martin Arrowsmith* (1925), *Elmer Gantry* (1927); Nobel Prize for Literature 1930.

**Lively, Penelope (Margaret)** (née **Low**) (1933– ) English, born Cairo, Egypt; *The Road to Lichfield* (1977), *Moon Tiger* (1987, Booker Prize), *City of the Mind* (1991), *Heat Wave* (1996).

**Lodge, David (John)** (1935– ) English novelist, born London; *The British Museum is Falling Down* (1965), *Changing Places* (1975), *Small World* (1984), *Nice Work* (1988), *Paradise News* (1991), *Therapy* (1995).

**London, Jack (John) Griffith** (1876–1916) American novelist, born San Francisco; *Call of the Wild* (1903), *White Fang* (1907), *Martin Eden* (1909).

**Lowry, (Clarence) Malcolm** (1909–57) English novelist, born New Brighton, Merseyside; *Under The Volcano* (1947).

**Lurie, Alison** (1926– ) American novelist, born Chicago; *Love and Friendship* (1962), *The War Between the Tates* (1974), *Foreign Affairs* (1984, Pulitzer Prize 1985), *The Truth about Lorin Jones* (1988), *Women and Ghosts* (short stories) (1994).

**Macaulay, Dame (Emilie) Rose** (1881–1958) English novelist, born Rugby, Warwickshire; *Dangerous Ages* (1921), *The World, My Wilderness* (1950), *The Towers of Trebizond* (1956).

**MacDonald, George** (1824–1905) Scottish novelist, born Huntly, Aberdeenshire; *Robert Falconer* (1868), *The Princess and the Goblin* (1872), *Lilith* (1895).

**McEwan, Ian (Russell)** (1948– ) English novelist, short-story writer, playwright, born Aldershot, Hampshire; *First Love, Last Rites* (1975), *The Cement Garden* (1978), *The Innocent* (1990), *Enduring Love* (1997), *Amsterdam* (1998, Booker Prize).

**McIlvanney, William (Angus)** (1936– ) Scottish novelist, poet, born Kilmarnock, Ayrshire; *Remedy is None* (1966), *Docherty* (1975), *The Big Man* (1985), *Strange Loyalties* (1991).

**MacInnes, Colin** (1914–76) English novelist, born London; *City of Spades* (1959), *Absolute Beginners* (1959).

**MacKenzie, Sir (Edward Montague) Compton** (1883–1972) English novelist, born West Hartlepool, Cleveland; *Whisky Galore* (1942).

**MacKenzie, Henry** (1745–1831) Scottish novelist, born Edinburgh; *The Man of Feeling* (1771).

**MacLean, Alistair** (1922–87) Scottish novelist, born Glasgow; *The Guns of Navarone* (1957), *Ice Station Zebra* (1963), *Where Eagles Dare* (1967), *Force Ten from Navarone* (1968).

**Mahfouz, Naguib** (1911– ) Egyptian novelist, born Cairo; *The Thief and the Dogs* (1961), *Adrift on the Nile* (1966), *God's World* (1973), *The Cairo Trilogy* (1956–7); Nobel Prize for Literature 1988.

**Mailer, Norman (Kingsley)** (1923– ) American novelist, born Long Beach, New Jersey; *The Naked and the Dead* (1949), *Barbary Shore* (1951), *An American Dream* (1965), *The Executioner's Song* (1979, Pulitzer Prize 1980), *Harlot's Ghost* (1991), *Portrait of Picasso as a Young Man* (1995), *Oswald's Tale* (1995).

**Malamud, Bernard** (1914–86) American novelist, born Brooklyn, New York City; *The Fixer* (1966), *The Tenants* (1971).

**Malouf, David** (1934– ) Australian novelist, poet, born Brisbane; *An Imaginary Life* (1978), *Harland's Half Acre* (1984), *Remembering Babylon* (1993).

**Mankowitz, (Cyril) Wolf** (1924–98) English novelist, short-story writer, playwright, born London; *Make Me an Offer* (1952), *The Bespoke Overcoat* (play) (1954), *A Kid for Two Farthings* (1953), *My Old Man's a Dustman* (1956), *Exquisite Cadaver* (1990).

**Mann, Thomas** (1875–1955) German novelist, born Lübeck; *Death in Venice* (1912), *The Magic Mountain* (1924).

**Manning, Olivia** (1908–80) English novelist, short-story writer, born Portsmouth; *The Balkan Trilogy* (1960–5), *The Levant Trilogy* (1977–80).

**Mansfield, Katherine** (pseudonym of **Katherine Mansfield Beauchamp**) (1888–1923) New Zealand short-story writer, born Wellington; *Prelude* (1918), *Bliss, and other stories* (1920), *The Garden Party, and other stories* (1922).

**Markandaya, Kamala** (pseudonym of **Kamala Purnaiya Taylor**) (1924– ) Indian novelist; *Nectar in a Sieve* (1954), *A Silence of Desire* (1960), *The Coffer Dams* (1969).

**Mars-Jones, Adam** (1954– ) English short-story writer, critic, born London; *Lantern Lecture and Other Stories* (1981), *The Darker Proof; Stories From a Crisis* (with Edmund White) (1987), *The Waters of Thirst* (1993).

**Marsh, Ngaio** (1899–1982) New Zealand novelist, born Christchurch; *Death in a White Tie* (1958), *A Grave Mistake* (1978).

**Massie, Allan (Johnstone)** (1938– ) Scottish novelist, journalist, born Singapore; *Change and Decay in All Around I See* (1978), *The Last Peacock* (1980), *A Question of Loyalties* (1989), *The Sins of the Fathers* (1991), *King David* (1995).

**Maugham, (William) Somerset** (1874–1965) English novelist, born Paris; *Of Human Bondage* (1915), *The Moon and Sixpence* (1919), *The Razor's Edge* (1945).

**Maupassant, Guy de** (1850–93) French short-story writer, novelist, born Miromesnil; *Claire de Lune* (1884), *Bel Ami* (1885).

**Mauriac, François** (1885–1970) French novelist, born Bordeaux; *Le Baiser au Lépreux* (1922); Nobel Prize for Literature 1952.

**Melville, Herman** (1819–1909) American novelist, poet, born New York City; *Moby Dick* (1851).

**Meredith, George** (1828–1909) English novelist, poet, born Portsmouth; *The Egoist* (1879), *Diana of the Crossways* (1885).

**Michener, James A(lbert)** (1907–97) American novelist, short-story writer, born New York City; *Tales of the South Pacific* (1947, Pulitzer Prize 1948), *Hawaii* (1959), *Chesapeake* (1978), *Miracle in Seville* (1995).

**Miller, Henry Valentine** (1891–1980) American novelist, born New York City; *Tropic of Cancer* (1934), *Tropic of Capricorn* (1938), *The Rosy Crucifixion Trilogy* (1949–60).

**Mishima, Yukio** (pseudonym of **Hiraoka Kimitake**) (1925–70) Japanese novelist, born Tokyo; *Confessions of a Mask* (1960), *The Temple of the Golden Pavilion* (1959), *The Sea of Fertility* (1969–71).

**Mitchell, (Charles) Julian (Humphrey)** (1935– ) English novelist, playwright, born Epping, Essex; *The White Father* (1964), *The Undiscovered Country* (1968), *Another Country* (play) (1981).

**Mitchell, Margaret** (1900–49) American novelist, born Atlanta, Georgia; *Gone with the Wind* (1936).

**Mitchison, Naomi (Margaret)** (née **Haldane**) (1897–1999) Scottish novelist, poet, playwright, born Edinburgh; *The Corn King and the Spring Queen* (1931), *The Big House* (1950); memoirs: *Small Talk* (1973), *All Change Here* (1975), *You May Well Ask* (1979).

**Mitford, Nancy** (1904–73) English novelist, born London; *Love in a Cold Climate* (1949), *Don't Tell Alfred* (1960).

**Mo, Timothy (Peter)** (1950– ) British novelist, born Hong Kong; *The Monkey King* (1978), *Sour Sweet* (1982), *An Insular Possession* (1986), *The Redundancy of Courage* (1991).

**Monsarrat, Nicholas (John Turney)** (1910–79) English novelist, born Liverpool; *The Cruel Sea* (1951), *The Story of Esther Costello* (1953).

**Moorcock, Michael** (1939– ) English novelist, short-story writer, born London; *Gloriana* (1978), *Byzantium Endures* (1983), *The City in the Autumn Stars* (1986).

**Moore, Brian** (1921–99) Irish–Canadian novelist, born Belfast, Northern Ireland; *The Luck of Ginger Coffey* (1960), *The Temptation of Eileen Hughes* (1981), *The Colour of Blood* (1987), *Lies of Silence* (1990), *The Statement* (1995).

**Morrison, Toni (Chloe Anthony)** (née **Wofford**) (1931– ) American novelist, born Lorain, Ohio; *The Bluest Eye* (1970), *Song of Solomon* (1977), *Beloved* (1987, Pulitzer Prize 1988), *Paradise* (1998).

**Mortimer, Sir John (Clifford)** (1923– ) English novelist, short-story writer, playwright, born London; *A Cat Among the Pigeons* (1964), *Rumpole of the Bailey* (1978), *Paradise Postponed* (1985), *Under the Hammer* (1994).

**Mortimer, Penelope (Ruth)** (née **Fletcher**) (1918–99) Welsh novelist, playwright, born Rhyl; *A Villa in Summer* (1954), *The Pumpkin Eater* (1962), *My Friend Says It's Bullet-Proof* (1967), *The Home* (1971), *About Time* (autobiography) (1993).

**Mosley, Nicholas (3rd Baron Ravensdale)** (1923– ) English novelist, born London; *Spaces of the Dark* (1951), *Accident* (1965), *Hopeful Monsters* (1991), *Children of Darkness and Light* (1996).

**Murdoch, Dame (Jean) Iris** (1919–99) Irish novelist, philosopher, born Dublin; *The Bell* (1958), *The Sea, The Sea* (1978, Booker Prize), *The Philosopher's Pupil* (1983), *The Green Knight* (1993).

**Nabokov, Vladimir Vladimirovich** (1899–1977) Russian–American novelist, poet, born St Petersburg; *Lolita* (1955), *Look at the Harlequins!* (1974).

**Naipaul, Sir V(idiadhar) S(urajprasad)** (1932– ) Trinidadian novelist, born Chaguanas; *A House for Mr Biswas* (1961), *In a Free State* (1971, Booker Prize), *A Bend in the River* (1979), *A Way in the World* (1994).

**Newby, P(ercy) H(oward)** (1918–97) English novelist, born Crowborough, Sussex; *The Picnic at Sakkara* (1955), *Revolution and Roses* (1957), *The Barbary Light* (1962), *Something About Women* (1995).

**Ngugi wa Thiong'o** (formerly wrote as **James T Ngugi**) (1938– ) Kenyan novelist, short-story writer, playwright, born Kamiriithu, near Limura; *The River Between* (1963), *Weep Not, Child* (1964), *A Grain of Wheat* (1967), *Petals of Blood* (1977).

**Nye, Robert** (1939– ) English novelist, poet, short-story writer, playwright, born London; *Falstaff* (1976), *Merlin* (1978), *The Life and Death of My Lord Gilles de Rais* (1990), *Mrs Shakespeare: the complete works* (1993).

**Oates, Joyce Carol** (1938– ) American novelist, short-story writer, born Millersport, New York; *A Garden of Earthly Delights* (1967), *Them* (1969), *Wonderland* (1971), *What I Lived For* (1994).

**O'Brien, Edna** (1932– ) Irish novelist, short-story writer, born Tuamgraney, County Clare; *The Country Girls* (1960), *August is a Wicked Month* (1964), *A Pagan Place* (1971), *Lantern Slides* (stories) (1990), *Time and Tide* (1992), *Wild Decembers* (1999).

**Oë, Kenzaburo** (1935– ) Japanese novelist, born Shikoku; *Hiroshima Notes* (1981), *A Personal Matter* (1968), *The Silent Cry* (1974); Nobel Prize for Literature 1994.

**O'Flaherty, Liam** (1897–1984) Irish novelist, short-story writer, born Inishmore, Aran Islands; *The Informer* (1926), *Two Lovely Beasts* (1948).

**O'Hara, John (Henry)** (1905–70) American novelist, short-story writer, born Pottsville, Pennsylvania; *Spring Sowing* (1924), *Appointment in Samarra* (1934), *The Doctor's Son* (1935), *Butterfield 8* (1935), *Pal Joey* (1940).

**Okri, Ben** (1959– ) Nigerian novelist, born Minna; *The Famished Road* (1991, Booker Prize), *Dangerous Love* (1996), *Mental Fight* (1999).

**Oliphant, Margaret** (1828–97) Scottish novelist, born Wallyford, Midlothian; *The Athelings* (1857), *Salem Chapel* (1863).

**Ondaatje, (Philip) Michael** (1943– ) Canadian novelist, poet, born Ceylon (now Sri Lanka); *Coming Through Slaughter* (1976), *In the Skin of a Lion* (1987), *The English Patient* (1991, Booker Prize 1992).

**Orwell, George** (pseudonym of **Eric Arthur Blair**) (1903–50) English novelist, born Bengal, India; *Down and Out in Paris and London* (1933), *The Road to Wigan Pier* (1937), *Animal Farm* (1945), *Nineteen Eighty-Four* (1949).

**Ouida** (pseudonym of **Marie-Louise de la Ramée**) (1839–1908) English novelist, born Bury St Edmunds; *Held in Bondage* (1865), *Under Two Flags* (1867), *Folle-Farine* (1871).

**Ozick, Cynthia** (1928– ) American novelist, short-story writer, born New York City; *Trust* (1966), *The Pagan Rabbit and Other Stories* (1971), *The Cannibal Galaxy* (1983), *The Messiah of Stockholm* (1987), *Fame and Folly* (essays) (1996).

**Pasternak, Boris (Leonidovich)** (1890–1960) Russian novelist, born Moscow; *Doctor Zhivago* (1957); Nobel Prize for Literature 1958.

**Paton, Alan (Stewart)** (1903–88) South African novelist, short-story writer, born Pietermaritzburg, Natal; *Cry, the Beloved Country* (1948).

**Peacock, Thomas Love** (1785–1866) English novelist, poet, born Weymouth; *Melincourt* (1817), *Nightmare Abbey* (1818).

**Peake, Mervyn (Laurence)** (1911–68) English novelist, poet, born Kuling, China; *Titus Groan* (1946), *Gormenghast* (1950), *Titus Alone* (1959).

**Plaidy, Jean** ► **Holt, Victoria**

**Poe, Edgar Allan** (1809–49) American short-story writer, poet, born Boston, Massachusetts; *Tales of the Grotesque and Arabesque* (eg 'The Fall of the House of Usher') (1840), *The Pit and the Pendulum* (1843).

**Porter, Harold (Hal)** (1911–84) Australian novelist, playwright, poet, short-story writer, born Melbourne; *A Handful of Pennies* (1958), *The Right Thing* (1971).

**Porter, Katherine Anne (Maria Veronica Callista Russell)** (1890–1980) American novelist, short-story writer, born Indian Creek, Texas; *Pale Horse, Pale Rider* (1939), *Ship of Fools* (1962).

**Powell, Anthony (Dymoke)** (1905–2000) English nov-elist, born London; *A Dance to the Music of Time* (1951–75), *The Fisher King* (1986).

**Powys, John Cowper** (1872–1963) English novelist, born Shirley, Derbyshire; *Wolf Solent* (1929), *Owen Glendower* (1940).

**Priestley, J(ohn) B(oynton)** (1894–1984) English novelist, playwright, born Bradford, Yorkshire; *The Good Companions* (1929), *Angel Pavement* (1930).

**Pritchett, Sir V(ictor) S(awdon)** (1900–97) English novelist, short-story writer, playwright, born Ipswich, Suffolk; *Nothing like Leather* (1935), *Dead Man Leading* (1937), *Mr Beluncle* (1951), *The Key to My Heart* (1963), *Man of Letters* (essays) (1985).

**Proulx, E Annie** (1935– ) American novelist, short-story writer, born Connecticut; *Postcards* (1993), *The Shipping News* (1993, Pulitzer Prize 1994), *Heart Songs* (1996), *Accordion Crimes* (1996).

**Proust, Marcel** (1871–1922) French novelist, born Paris; *Remembrance of Things Past* (1913–27).

**Puzo, Mario** (1920–99) American novelist, born New York City; *The Godfather* (1969), *The Last Don* (1996), *Omerta* (2000).

**Pynchon, Thomas** (1937– ) American novelist, born Long Island, New York; *V* (1963), *Gravity's Rainbow* (1973), *Vineland* (1989), *Mason & Dixon* (1996).

**Queen, Ellery** (pseudonym of **Patrick Dannay** (1905–82) and his cousin **Manfred B Lee** (1905–71)) American novelists and short-story writers, both born Brooklyn, New York City; *The French Powder Mystery* (1930), *The Tragedy of X* (1940), *The Glass Village* (1954).

**Radcliffe, Ann** (1764–1823) English novelist, born London; *The Mysteries of Udolpho* (1794), *The Italian* (1797).

**Rao, Raja** (1909– ) Indian novelist, short-story writer, born Hassan, Mysore; *Kanthapura* (1938), *The Serpent and the Rope* (1960), *The Cat and Shakespeare* (1965).

**Raphael, Frederic (Michael)** (1931– ) American novelist, short-story writer, playwright, born Chicago; *The Earlsdon Way* (1958), *The Limits of Love* (1960), *Lindmann* (1963), *Heaven and Earth* (1985), *Old Scores* (1995).

**Read, Piers Paul** (1941– ) English novelist, born Beaconsfield, Buckinghamshire; *The Junkers* (1968), *Monk Dawson* (1969), *The Villa Golitsyn* (1981), *A Season in the West* (1988), *A Patriot in Berlin* (1995).

**Remarque, Erich Maria** (1898–1970) German nov-elist, born Osnabrück; *All Quiet on the Western Front* (1929), *The Road Back* (1931), *The Black Obelisk* (1957).

**Renault, Mary** (pseudonym of **Eileen Mary Challans**) (1905–83) English novelist, born London; *The King Must Die* (1958), *Fire from Heaven* (1969), *The Persian Boy* (1972).

**Rendell, Ruth (Barbara) Rendell, Baroness** (1930– ) English novelist, born London; *A Judgement in Stone* (1977), *The Killing Doll* (1980), *Heartstones*, (1987), *Blood Linen* (short stories) (1995); as Barbara Vine: *The House of Stairs* (1989).

**Rhys, Jean** (pseudonym of **Ella Gwendolyn Rees Williams**) (1894–1979) British novelist, short-story writer, born Dominica, West Indies; *After Leaving Mackenzie* (1930), *Wide Sargasso Sea* (1966), *Tigers are Better Looking* (1968).

**Richardson, Dorothy M(iller)** (1873–1957) English novelist, born Abingdon, Berkshire; *Pilgrimage* (12 vol, 1915–38).

**Richardson, Harry Handel** (pseudonym of **Ethel Florence Lindesay Richardson**) (1870–1946) Australian novelist, born Melbourne; *The Getting of Wisdom* (1910), *Ultima Thule* (1929).

**Richardson, Samuel** (1689–1761) English novelist, born near Derby; *Pamela* (1740), *Clarissa* (1747–8), *Sir Charles Grandison* (1753–4).

**Richler, Mordecai** (1931–2001) Canadian novelist, born Montreal, Quebec; *The Apprenticeship of Duddy Kravitz* (1959), *St Urbain's Horseman* (1971), *Solomon Gursky Was Here* (1990), *This Year in Jerusalem* (1994).

**Robbins, Harold** (pseudonym of **Francis Kane**) (1916–97) American novelist, born Hell's Kitchen, New York City; *Never Love a Stranger* (1948), *A Stone for Danny Fisher* (1951), *The Carpetbaggers* (1961), *The Betsy* (1971), *Tycoon* (1996).

**Rolfe, Frederick William** (styled **Baron Corvo**) (1860–1913) English novelist, born London; *Hadrian the Seventh* (1904), *The Desire and Pursuit of the Whole* (1934).

**Roth, Henry** (1906–95) American novelist, short-story writer, born Tysmenica, Austro-Hungary; *Call It Sleep* (1934).

**Roth, Philip Milton** (1933– ) American novelist, short-story writer, born Newark, New Jersey; *Goodbye Columbus* (1959), *Portnoy's Complaint* (1969), *The Great American Novel* (1973), *My Life as a Man* (1974), *Patrimony* (1991), *Sabbath's Theater* (1995), *American Pastoral* (1997, Pulitzer Prize 1998).

**Rushdie, (Ahmed) Salman** (1947– ) British nov-elist, short-story writer, born Bombay, India; *Midnight's Children* (1981, Booker Prize), *Shame* (1983), *The Satanic Verses* (1988), *The Moor's Last Sigh* (1995), *The Ground Beneath Her Feet* (1999).

**Sackville-West, Vita (Victoria May)** (1892–1962) English poet, novelist, short-story writer, born Knole, Kent; *The Edwardians* (1930), *All Passion Spent* (1931).

**Sade, Donatien Alphonse François, Comte de**, (known as **Marquis**) (1740–1814) French novelist, born Paris; *Les 120 Journées de Sodome* (1784), *Justine* (1791), *La Philosophie dans le boudoir* (1793), *Juliette* (1798), *Les Crimes de l'amour* (1800).

**Saki** (pseudonym of **Hector Hugh Munro**) (1870–1916) British novelist, short-story writer, born Akyab, Burma; *The Chronicles of Clovis* (1912), *The Unbearable Bassington* (1912).

**Salinger, J(erome) D(avid)** (1919– ) American novelist, born New York; *The Catcher in the Rye*

(1951), *Franny and Zooey* (1961), *Hapworth 16, 1924* (1997).

**Sand, George** (pseudonym of **Amandine Aurore Lucille Dupin, Baronne Dudevant**) (1804–76) French novelist, born Paris; *Lélia* (1833), *La Petite Fadette* (1849).

**Saroyan, William** (1908–81) American novelist, playwright, short-story writer, born Fresno, California; *The Daring Young Man on the Flying Trapeze* (1934), *My Name is Aram* (1940), *The Human Comedy* (1942).

**Sartre, Jean-Paul** (1905–80) French novelist, playwright, born Paris; *Nausea* (1949), *The Roads to Freedom* (1945–7); Nobel Prize for Literature 1964.

**Sayers, Dorothy Leigh** (1893–1957) English novelist, short-story writer, born Oxford; *Lord Peter Views the Body* (1928), *Gaudy Night* (1935).

**Schreiner, Olive** (1855–1920) South African novelist, born Wittebergen Mission Station, Cape of Good Hope; *The Story of an African Farm* (1883), *Trooper Peter Halkett of Mashonaland* (1897).

**Scott, Sir Walter** (1771–1832) Scottish novelist, poet, born Edinburgh; *Waverley* (1814), *Rob Roy* (1817), *The Heart of Midlothian* (1818), *The Bride of Lammermoor* (1819), *Ivanhoe* (1820).

**Selby, Hubert, Jr** (1928– ) American novelist, short-story writer, born Brooklyn, New York City; *Last Exit to Brooklyn* (1964), *The Room* (1971), *Requiem for a Dream* (1978), *Song of the Silent Snow* (1986).

**Sharpe, Tom (Thomas Ridley)** (1928– ) English novelist, born London; *Riotous Assembly* (1971), *Porterhouse Blue* (1974), *Blott on the Landscape* (1975), *Wilt* (1976), *Grantchester Grind* (1995), *The Midden* (1996).

**Shelley, Mary (Wollstonecraft)** (née **Godwin**) (1797–1851) English novelist, born London; *Frankenstein* (1818), *The Last Man* (1826), *Perkin Warbeck* (1830).

**Shields, Carol** (née **Warner**) (1935– ) Canadian–American novelist, born Oak Park, Illinois; *Small Ceremonies* (1976), *Happenstance* (1980), *Swann: A Mystery* (1987), *The Republic of Love* (1992), *The Stone Diaries* (1993, Pulitzer Prize 1995), *Larry's Party* (1997, Orange Prize 1998).

**Sholokhov, Mikhail Alexandrovich** (1905–84) Russian novelist, born near Veshenskayal; *And Quiet Flows the Don* (1928–40), *The Upturned Soil* (1940); Nobel Prize for Literature 1965.

**Shute, Nevil** (pseudonym of **Nevil Shute Norway**) (1899–1960) Anglo-Australian novelist, born Ealing, London; *The Pied Piper* (1942), *A Town Like Alice* (1950), *On the Beach* (1957).

**Sillitoe, Alan** (1928– ) English novelist, poet, short-story writer, born Nottingham; *Saturday Night and Sunday Morning* (1958), *The Loneliness of the Long Distance Runner* (1959), *The Broken Chariot* (1998).

**Simenon, Georges** (1903–89) French writer, born Liège, Belgium; almost 100 novels featuring Jules Maigret, and 400 other novels: *The Death of Monsieur Gallet* (1932), *The Crime of Inspector Maigret* (1933).

**Simon, Claude (Henri Eugène)** (1913– ) French novelist, born Tananarive, Madagascar; *The Wind* (1959), *The Flanders Road* (1962), *Triptych* (1977); Nobel Prize for Literature 1985.

**Singer, Isaac Bashevis** (1904–91) American novelist, playwright, born Radzymin, Poland; *The Family Moskat* (1950), *The Satan in Goray* (1955); Nobel Prize for Literature 1978.

**Smith, Iain Crichton** (Gaelic **Iain Mac A'Ghobhainn**) (1928–98) Scottish novelist, poet, short-story writer, playwright, born Glasgow; *Consider the Lilies* (1968), *Murdo and Other Stories* (1981), *The Dream* (1990).

**Smollett, Tobias George** (1721–71) Scottish novelist, born Dalquharn, Dunbartonshire; *Roderick Random* (1748), *The Adventures of Peregrine Pickle* (1751), *The Expedition of Humphrey Clinker* (1771).

**Snow, C(harles) P(ercy)** (1905–80) English novelist, born Leicester; *Strangers and Brothers* (1940–70).

**Solzhenitsyn, Aleksandr Isayevich** (1918– ) Russian novelist, born Kislovodsk, Caucasus; *One Day in the Life of Ivan Denisovich* (1962), *Cancer Ward* (1968), *The First Circle* (1969), *The Gulag Archipelago 1918–56* (3 vols 1973–6); Nobel Prize for Literature 1970.

**Spark, Dame Muriel (Sarah)** (née **Camberg**) (1918– ) Scottish novelist, short-story writer, poet, born Edinburgh; *The Ballad of Peckham Rye* (1960), *The Prime of Miss Jean Brodie* (1962), *The Girls of Slender Means* (1963), *A Far Cry from Kensington* (1988), *Aiding and Abetting* (2000).

**Spring, Howard** (1889–1965) Welsh novelist, born Cardiff; *Oh Absalom* (1938).

**Stead, C(hristian) K(arlson)** (1932– ) New Zealand novelist, poet, born Auckland; *Smith's Dream* (1971), *All Visitor's Ashore* (1984), *Sister Hollywood* (1990), *The Singing Whalcapapa* (1994).

**Stein, Gertrude** (1874–1946) American novelist, short-story writer, born Allegheny, Pennsylvania; *Three Lives* (1909), *Tender Buttons* (1914).

**Steinbeck, John Ernest** (1902–68) American novelist, born Salinas, California; *Of Mice and Men* (1937), *The Grapes of Wrath* (1939), *Cannery Row* (1945), *East of Eden* (1952); Nobel Prize for Literature 1962.

**Stendhal** (pseudonym of **Henri Marie Beyle**) (1788–1842) French novelist, born Grenoble; *Le Rouge et le noir* (1830), *La Chartreuse de Parme* (1839).

**Sterne, Lawrence** (1713–68) Irish novelist, born Clonmel, Tipperary; *Tristram Shandy* (1759–67), *A Sentimental Journey* (1768).

**Stevenson, Robert Louis (Balfour)** (1850–94) Scottish novelist, short-story writer, poet, born Edinburgh; *Travels with a Donkey* (1879), *Treasure Island* (1883), *Kidnapped* (1886), *The Strange Case of Dr Jekyll and Mr Hyde* (1886), *Weir of Hermiston* (1896).

**Stewart, J(ohn) I(nnes) M(ackintosh)** (1906–94) Scottish novelist, born Edinburgh; *A Use of Riches* (1957), *The Last Tresilians* (1963); as Michael Innes:

*Hamlet, Revenge!* (1937), *Appleby and the Ospreys* (1986).

**Stewart, Mary (Florence Elinor)** (1916– ) English novelist born Sunderland; *This Rough Magic* (1964), *The Last Enchantment* (1979), *The Prince and the Pilgrim* (1995).

**Stoker, Bram (Abraham)** (1847–1912) Irish novelist, short-story writer, born Dublin; *Dracula* (1897).

**Stone, Robert (Anthony)** (1937– ) American novelist, born Brooklyn, New York City; *Dog Soldiers* (1974), *A Flag for Sunrise* (1982).

**Storey, David (Malcolm)** (1933– ) English novelist, playwright, born Wakefield, Yorkshire; *This Sporting Life* (1960), *Radcliffe* (1963), *Saville* (1976, Booker Prize), *A Prodigal Child* (1982), *Phoenix* (1993).

**Stowe, Harriet (Elizabeth) Beecher** (1811–96) American novelist, born Litchfield, Connecticut; *Uncle Tom's Cabin* (1852).

**Styron, William (Clark)** (1925– ) American novelist, born Newport News, Virginia; *Lie Down in Darkness* (1951), *The Confessions of Nat Turner* (1967), *Sophie's Choice* (1979), *A Tidewater Morning* (1993).

**Suskind, Patrick** (1949– ) German novelist; *Perfume: the Story of a Murderer* (1985).

**Swift, Graham (Colin)** (1949– ) English novelist, born London; *The Sweet Shop Owner* (1980), *Waterland* (1983), *Out of This World* (1988), *Ever After* (1992), *Last Orders* (1996, Booker Prize).

**Swift, Jonathan** (1667–1754) Irish novelist, poet, born Dublin; *A Tale of a Tub* (1704), *Gulliver's Travels* (1726).

**Symons, Julian (Gustave)** (1912–94) English novelist, poet, short-story writer, playwright, born London; *The Thirty-First of February* (1950), *The Colour of Murder* (1957), *Sweet Adelaide* (1980).

**Tennant, Emma (Christina)** (1937– ) English novelist, born London; *Hotel de Dream* (1978), *Alice Fell* (1980), *Pemberley* (1993), *Elinor and Marianne* (1996).

**Thackeray, William Makepeace** (1811–63) English novelist, born Calcutta, India; *Vanity Fair* (1847–8), *Pendennis* (1848–50).

**Theroux, Paul (Edward)** (1941– ) American novelist, short-story writer, travel writer, born Medford, Massachusetts; *The Mosquito Coast* (1981), *The Kingdom by the Sea* (travel) (1983), *Doctor Slaughter* (1984), *Riding the Iron Rooster* (travel) (1988), *My Secret History* (1989), *My Other Life* (1996).

**Thomas, D(onald) M(ichael)** (1935– ) English novelist, poet, born Redruth, Cornwall; *The White Hotel* (1981); Russian Nights (quintet): *Ararat* (1983), *Swallow* (1984), *Sphinx* (1986), *Summit* (1987), *Lying Together* (1990); *Eating Pavlova* (1994).

**Tolkien, J(ohn) R(onald) R(euel)** (1892–1973) English novelist, born Bloemfontein, South Africa; *The Hobbit* (1937), *The Lord of the Rings* (1954–5).

**Tolstoy, Count Leo Nikolayevich** (1828–1910) Russian novelist, born Yasnaya Polyana, Central Russia; *War and Peace* (1863–9), *Anna Karenina* (1873–7), *Resurrection* (1899).

**Tranter, Nigel Godwin** (1909–99) Scottish novelist, born Glasgow; over 100 novels including *The Steps to the Empty Throne* (1969), *The Path of the Hero King* (1970), *The Price of the King's Peace* (1971), *Honours Even* (1995).

**Tremain, Rose** (née **Thomson**) (1943– ) English novelist, short-story writer, playwright, born London; *The Cupboard* (1981), *The Colonel's Daughter and Other Stories* (1984), *Restoration* (1989), *Sacred Country* (1992), *The Way I Found Her* (1997).

**Trevor, William** (properly **William Trevor Cox**) (1928– ) Irish novelist, short-story writer, born Mitchelstown, County Cork; *Fools of Fortune* (1983), *The Silence in the Garden* (1988), *Two Lives* (1991), *Felicia's Journey* (1994).

**Trollope, Anthony** (1815–82) English novelist, born London; *Barchester Towers* (1857), *Can You Forgive Her?* (1864), *The Way We Live Now* (1875).

**Trollope, Joanna** (1943– ) English novelist; *Eliza Stanhope* (1978), *The Choir* (1988), *A Village Affair* (1989), *The Rector's Wife* (1991), *Next of Kin* (1996).

**Tuohy, Frank (John Francis)** (1925–99) English novelist, short-story writer, born Uckfield, Sussex; *The Animal Game* (1957), *The Warm Nights of January* (1960), *The Ice Saints* (1964), *Fingers in the Door* (stories) (1970), *Collected Stories* (1984).

**Turgenev, Ivan Sergeevich** (1818–83) Russian novelist, born province of Oryel; *Sportsman's Sketches* (1952), *Fathers and Children* (1862).

**Tutuola, Amos** (1920–97) Nigerian novelist, short-story writer, born Abeokuta; *The Palm-Wine Drinkard and His Dead Palm-Wine Tapster in the Deads' Town* (1952), *The Wild Hunter in the Bush of the Ghosts* (1982), *Pauper, Brawler and Slanderer* (1987), *The Village Witchdoctor and Other Stories* (1990).

**Twain, Mark** (pseudonym of **Samuel Langhorne Clemens**) (1835–1910) American novelist, born Florida, Missouri; *The Celebrated Jumping Frog of Calaveras County* (1865), *The Adventures of Tom Sawyer* (1876), *The Prince and the Pauper* (1882), *The Adventures of Huckleberry Finn* (1884), *A Connecticut Yankee in King Arthur's Court* (1889).

**Tyler, Anne** (1941– ) American novelist, short-story writer, born Minneapolis, Minnesota; *If Morning Ever Comes* (1964), *Morgan's Passing* (1980), *The Accidental Tourist* (1985), *Breathing Lessons* (1988, Pulitzer Prize 1989), *Ladder of Years* (1995).

**Updike, John (Hoyer)** (1932– ) American novelist, short-story writer, born Shillington, Pennsylvania; *Rabbit, Run* (1960), *Pigeon Feathers and Other Stories* (1962), *Rabbit is Rich* (1982, Pulitzer Prize), *The Witches of Eastwick* (1984), *Rabbit at Rest* (1990, Pulitzer Prize 1991), *In the Beauty of the Lilies* (1996).

**Upward, Edward (Falaise)** (1903– ) English novelist, born Romford, Essex; *Journey to the Border* (1938), *In the Thirties* (1962), *The Rotten Elements* (1969).

**Uris, Leon (Marcus)** (1924– ) American novelist, born Baltimore, Maryland; *Battle Cry* (1953), *Exodus* (1958), *The Haj* (1984), *Redemption* (1995).

**Van der Post, Sir Laurens (Jan)** (1906–96) South African novelist, playwright, born Philippolis; *Flamingo Feather* (1955), *Journey into Russia* (1964), *A Far-Off Place* (1974).

**Vansittart, Peter** (1920– ) English novelist, born Bedford; *Quintet* (1976), *The Death of Robin Hood* (1981), *Parsifal* (1988), *In the Fifties* (1995).

**Vargas Llosa, Mario** (1936– ) Peruvian novelist, born Arequipa; *The Time of the Hero* (1963), *Aunt Julia and the Scriptwriter* (1977), *The War at the End of the World* (1982), *The Green House* (1986).

**Verne, Jules** (1828–1905) French novelist, born Nantes; *Voyage to the Centre of the Earth* (1864), *Twenty Thousand Leagues under the Sea* (1870).

**Vidal, Gore (Eugene Luther, Jr)** (1925– ) American novelist, short-story writer, playwright, born West Point, New York; *Williwaw* (1946), *The City and the Pillar* (1948), *The Judgement of Paris* (1952), *Myra Breckenridge* (1968), *Kalki* (1978), *Empire* (1987), *Hollywood* (1989), *The Season of Conflict* (1996).

**Vine, Barbara ► Rendell, Ruth**

**Voltaire, François-Marie Arouet de** (1694–1778) French novelist, poet, born Paris; *Zadig* (1747), *Candide* (1759).

**Vonnegut, Kurt, Jr** (1922– ) American novelist, short-story writer, born Indianapolis, Indiana; *Cat's Cradle* (1963), *Slaughterhouse-Five* (1969), *Hocus Pocus* (1990), *Timequake* (1997).

**Wain, John (Barrington)** (1925–94) English novelist, poet, short-story writer, playwright, born Stoke-on-Trent, Staffordshire; *Hurry on Down* (1953), *The Young Visitors* (1965), *Where the Rivers Meet* (1988).

**Walker, Alice (Malsenior)** (1944– ) American novelist, short-story writer, born Eatonville, Georgia; *The Third Life of Grange Copeland* (1970), *In Love and Trouble* (1973), *The Color Purple* (1983, Pulitzer Prize), *Everyday Use* (1994).

**Walpole, Horace** (1717–97) English novelist, poet, born London; *Letter from Xotto to his Friend Lien Chi at Pekin* (1757), *Anecdotes of Painting in England* (1761–71), *The Castle of Otranto* (1764), *The Mysterious Mother* (1768).

**Warner, Marina (Sarah)** (1946– ) English novelist, born London; *In a Dark Wood* (1977), *The Skating Party* (1982), *The Lost Father* (1988), *The Mermaids in the Basement* (1993), *No Go the Bogeyman* (1998).

**Warren, Robert Penn** (1905–89) American novelist, poet, born Guthrie, Kentucky; *Night Rider* (1939), *All the King's Men* (1943).

**Waterhouse, Keith (Spencer)** (1929– ) English novelist, playwright, born Leeds, Yorkshire; *Billy Liar* (1959), *Office Life* (1978), *Bimbo* (1990), *Unsweet Charity* (1992).

**Waugh, Evelyn (Arthur St John)** (1903–66) English novelist, born London; *Decline and Fall* (1928), *A Handful of Dust* (1934), *Brideshead Revisited* (1945).

**Weldon, Fay** (originally **Franklin Birkinshaw**) (1933– ) English novelist, born Alvechurch, Worcestershire; *Down Among the Women* (1971), *Female Friends* (1975), *Life and Loves of a She-Devil* (1983), *Worst Fears* (1996), *Big Women* (1998).

**Wells, H(erbert) G(eorge)** (1866–1946) English novelist, born Bromley, Kent; *The Time Machine* (1895), *The War of the Worlds* (1898).

**Welty, Eudora** (1909–2001) American novelist, shortstory writer, born Jackson, Mississippi; *A Curtain of Green* (1941), *The Robber Bridegroom* (1944), *The Golden Apples* (1949), *The Ponder Heart* (1954), *The Optimist's Daughter* (1972, Pulitzer Prize 1973), *A Writer's Eye: Collected Book Reviews* (1994).

**Wesley, Mary** (pseudonym of **Mary Aline Siepmann**) (née **Farmar**) (1912– ) English novelist, born Englefield Green, Berkshire; *The Camomile Lawn* (1984), *A Sensible Life* (1990), *Part of the Furniture* (1997).

**West, Morris (Langlo)** (1916–99) Australian novelist, playwright, born Melbourne, Victoria; *Children of the Sun* (non-fiction) (1957), *The Devil's Advocate* (1959), *Summer of the Red Wolf* (1971), *The Clowns of God* (1981), *The World is Made of Glass* (1983), *The Ringmaster* (1991), *Vanishing Point* (1996).

**West, Dame Rebecca** (pseudonym of **Cecily Isabel Andrews**) (née **Fairfield**) (1892–1983) Irish novelist, born County Kerry; *The Harsh Voice* (1935), *The Mountain Overflows* (1957).

**Wharton, Edith (Newbold)** (1862–1937) American novelist, short-story writer, born New York; *The House of Mirth* (1905), *Ethan Frome* (1911), *The Age of Innocence* (1920).

**White, Antonia** (pseudonym of **Eirene Adeline Botting**) (1899–1980) English novelist, born London; *Beyond the Glass* (1954), *Frost in May* (1983).

**White, Patrick Victor Martindale** (1912–90) Australian novelist, playwright, short-story writer, born London; *Voss* (1957), *The Vivisector* (1970), *A Fringe of Leaves* (1976); Nobel Prize for Literature 1973.

**White, T(erence) H(anbury)** (1906–64) English novelist, poet, born Bombay, India; *Darkness at Pemberley* (1932), *The Once and Future King* (1958).

**Wilde, Oscar (Fingal O'Flahertie Wills)** (1854–1900) Irish novelist, short-story writer, playwright, poet, born Dublin; *The Happy Prince and Other Tales* (1888), *The Picture of Dorian Gray* (1890), *The Importance of Being Earnest* (play) (1895).

**Wilder, Thornton Niven** (1897–1976) American novelist, playwright, born Madison, Wisconsin; *The Bridge of San Luis Rey* (1927), *The Woman of Andros* (1930), *Heaven's My Destination* (1935).

**Wilding, Michael** (1942– ) Australian novelist, short-story writer, born Worcester, England; *Living Together* (1974), *The West Midland Underground* (1975), *Pacific Highway* (1982).

**Wilson, A(ndrew) N(orman)** (1950– ) English novelist, born London; *Kindly Light* (1979), *Wise Virgin* (1982), *Daughters of Albion* (1991), *A Watch in the Night* (1996).

**Winterson, Jeanette** (1959– ) English novelist, born Manchester; *Oranges Are Not the Only Fruit* (1987), *The Passion* (1987), *Sexing the Cherry* (1989), *Gut Symmetries* (1997).

**Wodehouse, Sir P(elham) G(renville)** (1881–1975) English novelist, short-story writer, born Guildford, Surrey; *The Inimitable Jeeves* (1923), *Carry on, Jeeves* (1925).

**Wolfe, Thomas Clayton** (1900–38) American novelist, born Asheville, North Carolina; *Look Homeward, Angel* (1929), *Of Time and the River* (1935), *From Death to Morning* (1935).

**Wolfe, Tom (Thomas Kennerly)** (1931– ) American novelist, journalist, born Richmond, Virginia; *The Kandy-Kolored Tangerine-Flake Streamline Baby* (1965), *The Electric Kool-Aid Acid Test* (1968), *The Right Stuff* (1979), *The Bonfire of the Vanities* (1st novel) (1988), *A Man in Full* (1998).

**Wolff, Tobias** (1945– ) American novelist, short-story writer, born Birmingham, Alabama; *In the Garden of the North American Martyrs* (stories) (1981), *The Barracks Thief* (1984), *Back in the World* (stories) (1985).

**Woolf, (Adeline) Virginia** (1882–1941) English novelist, born London; *Mrs Dalloway* (1925), *To The Lighthouse* (1927), *Orlando* (1928), *A Room of One's Own* (1929), *The Waves* (1931).

**Wouk, Herman** (1915– ) American novelist, playwright, born New York City; *The Caine Mutiny* (1951), *The Winds of War* (1971), *War and Remembrance* (1978), *Inside, Outside* (1985), *The Hope* (1993), *The Glory* (1994).

**Wright, Richard Nathaniel** (1908–60) American novelist, short-story writer, born Mississippi; *Native Son* (1940), *Eight Men* (1961).

**Yerby, Frank (Garvin)** (1916–91) American novelist, born Augusta, Georgia; *The Golden Hawk* (1948), *The Dahomean* (1971), *A Darkness at Ingraham's Crest* (1979).

**Yourcenar, Marguerite** (pseudonym of **Marguerite de Crayencour**) (1903–87) French novelist, poet, born Brussels; *Memoirs of Hadrian* (1941).

**Zamyatin, Evgeny Ivanovich** (1884–1937) Russian novelist, short-story writer, born Lebedyan; *We* (1921), *The Dragon: Fifteen Stories* (1966).

**Zola, Émile** (1840–1902) French novelist, born Paris; *Thérèse Raquin* (1867), *Les Rougon-Macquart* (1871–93), *Germinal* (1885).

## Poets

Selected volumes of poetry are listed.

**Abse, Dannie (Daniel)** (1923– ) Welsh, born Cardiff; *After Every Green Thing* (1948), *Tenants of the House* (1957), *There Was a Young Man from Cardiff* (1991), *The Man Behind the Smile* (1996).

**Adcock, (Karen) Fleur** (1934– ) New Zealander, born Papakura; *The Eye of the Hurricane* (1964), *In Focus* (1977), *The Incident Book* (1986).

**Aiken, Conrad (Potter)** (1889–1973) American, born Georgia; *Earth Triumphant* (1914), *Preludes for Memnon* (1931).

**Akhamatova, Anna** (pseudonym of **Anna Andreevna Gorenko**) (1889–1966) Russian, born Odessa; *Evening* (1912), *Poem without a Hero* (1940–62), *Requiem* (1963).

**Angelou, Maya** (pseudonym of **Marguerite Annie Johnson**) (1928– ) American, born St Louis, Missouri; *And Still I Rise* (1978), *I Shall Not Be Moved* (1990).

**Apollinaire, Guillaume** (1880–1918) French, born Rome; *Alcools* (1913), *Calligrammes* (1918).

**Ariosto, Ludovico** (1474–1535) Italian, born Reggio; *Furioso* (1532).

**Auden, W(ystan) H(ugh)** (1907–73) British, naturalized American citizen, born York; *Another Time* (1940), *The Sea and the Mirror* (1944), *The Age of Anxiety* (1947).

**Baudelaire, Charles (Pierre)** (1821–67) French, born Paris; *Les Fleurs du mal* (1857).

**Beer, Patricia** (1919–99) English, born Exmouth, Devon; *The Loss of the Magyar* (1959), *The Lie of the Land* (1983), *Friend of Heraclitus* (1993).

**Belloc, (Joseph) Hillaire (Pierre)** (1870–1953) British, born St Cloud, France; *Cautionary Tales* (1907), *Sonnets and Verse* (1923).

**Berryman, John** (1914–72) American, born McAlester, Oklahoma; *Homage to Mistress Bradsheet* (1966), *Dream Songs* (1969).

**Betjeman, Sir John** (1906–84) English, born Highgate, London; *Mount Zion* (1931), *New Bats in Old Belfries* (1945), *A Nip in the Air* (1972).

**Bishop, Elizabeth** (1911–79) American, born Worcester, Massachusetts; *North and South* (1946), *Geography III* (1978).

**Blake, William** (1757–1827) English, born London; *The Marriage of Heaven and Hell* (1793), *The Vision of the Daughter of Albion* (1793), *Songs of Innocence and Experience* (1794), *Vala, or The Four Zoas* (1800), *Milton* (1810).

**Blunden, Edmund (Charles)** (1896–1974) English, born Yalding, Kent; *The Waggoner and Other Poems* (1920), *Undertones of War* (1928).

**Brodsky, Joseph** (originally **Iosif Aleksandrovich Brodsky**) (1940–96) Russian-American, born Leningrad (now St Petersburg); *Longer and Shorter Poems* (1965), *To Urania: Selected Poems 1965–1985* (1988); Nobel Prize for Literature 1987.

**Brooke, Rupert (Chawner)** (1887–1915) English, born Rugby; *Poems* (1911); *1914 and Other Poems* (1915), *New Numbers* (1915).

**Brooks, Gwendolyn (Elizabeth)** (1917–2000) American, born Topeka, Kansas; *A Street in Bronzeville* (1945), *Annie Allen* (1949, Pulitzer Prize 1950), *In The Mecca* (1968), *Blacks* (1987).

**Browning, Elizabeth Barrett** (née **Barrett**) (1806–61) English, born Coxhoe Hall, near Durham; *Sonnets from the Portuguese* (1850), *Aurora Leigh* (1855).

**Browning, Robert** (1812–89) English, born Camberwell, London; *Bells and Pomegranates* (1841–6), *Men and Women* (1855), *The Ring and the Book* (1868–9).

**Burns, Robert** (1759–96) Scottish, born Alloway, Ayr; *Poems, Chiefly in the Scottish Dialect* (1786), *Tam o'Shanter* (1790).

**Byron (of Rochdale), George Gordon, 6th Baron** (1788–1824) English, born London; *Hours of Idleness* (1807), *Childe Harolde* (1817), *Don Juan* (1819–24).

**Carver, Raymond** (1939–88) American poet, short-story writer, born Clatskanie, Oregon; story collections: *Will You Please Be Quiet, Please?* (1976), *What We Talk About When We Talk About Love* (1981), *Cathedral* (1983); poetry collections: *Where Water Comes Together with Other Water* (1985), *Ultramarine* (1985).

**Catullus, Gaius Valerius** (c.84–c.54BC) Roman, born Verona; lyric poet, over 100 poems survive.

**Causley, Charles** (1917– ) English, born Lanceton, Cornwall; *Union St* (1957), *Johnny Alleluia* (1961), *Underneath the Water* (1968), *All Day Saturday* (1994).

**Chaucer, Geoffrey** (c.1343–1400) English, born London; *Book of the Duchess* (1370), *Troilus and Cressida* (c.1385), *The Canterbury Tales* (1387–1400).

**Clampitt, Amy** (1920–94) American, born Iowa; *The Kingfisher* (1983), *Archaic Figure* (1987), *Westward* (1990).

**Clare, John** (1773–1864) English, born Helpstone, Northamptonshire; *Poems Descriptive of Rural Life* (1820), *The Shepherd's Calendar* (1827).

**Coleridge, Samuel Taylor** (1772–1834) English, born Otterly St Mary, Devon; *Poems on Various Subjects* (1796), *'Kubla Khan'* (1797), *'The Rime of the Ancient Mariner'* (1798), *Christabel and Other Poems* (1816), *Sybylline Leaves* (1817).

**Cowper, William** (1731–1800) English, born Great Berkhampstead, Hertfordshire; *The Task* (1785).

**Crabbe, George** (1754–1823) English, born Aldeburgh, Suffolk; *The Village* (1783).

**cummings, e(dward) e(stlin)** (1894–1962) American, born Cambridge, Massachusetts; *Tulips and Chimneys* (1923), *XLI Poems* (1925), *is 5* (1926).

**Dante, Alighieri** (1265–1321) Italian, born Florence; *Vita nuova* (1294), *Divine Comedy* (1321).

**Day Lewis, Cecil** (1904–72) Irish, born Ballintubbert, Laois; *Overtures to Death* (1938), *The Aeneid of Virgil* (1952).

**de la Mare, Walter** (1873–1956) English, born Charleston, Kent; *The Listeners* (1912), *The Burning Glass and Other Poems* (1945).

**Dickinson, Emily (Elizabeth)** (1830–86) American, born Amherst, Massachusetts; only 7 poems published in her lifetime; posthumous publications, eg *Poems* (1890).

**Donne, John** (c.1572–1631) English, born London; *Satires & Elegies* (1590s), *Holy Sonnets* (1610–11), *Songs and Sonnets*; most verse published posthumously.

**Doolittle, Hilda** (known as **H D**) (1886–1961) American, born Bethlehem, Pennsylvania; *Sea Garden* (1916), *The Walls Do Not Fall* (1944), *Helen in Egypt* (1961).

**Dryden, John** (1631–1700) English, born Adwinckle All Saints, Northamptonshire; *'Astrea Redux'* (1660), *'Absalom and Achitophel'* (1681), *'MacFlecknoe'* (1684).

**Duffy, Carol Ann** (1955– ) Scottish, born Glasgow; *Standing Female Nude* (1985), *Mean Time* (1993), *The World's Wife* (1999).

**Dunbar, William** (c.1460–c.1520) Scottish, birthplace probably E Lothian; *'The Thrissill and the Rois' (1503)*, *'Lament for the Makaris'* (c.1507).

**Dunn, Douglas (Eaglesham)** (1942– ) Scottish, born Inchinnan, Strathclyde; *Love or Nothing* (1974), *Elegies* (1985), *Dante's Drum-kit* (1993).

**Dutton, Geoffrey (Piers Henry)** (1922–98) Australian, born Kapunda; *Antipodes in Shoes* (1955), *Poems, Soft and Loud* (1968), *A Body of Words* (1977).

**Eliot, T(homas) S(tearns)** (1888–1965) American (British citizen 1927), born St Louis, Missouri; *Prufrock and Other Observations* (1917), *The Waste Land* (1922), *Ash Wednesday* (1930), *Four Quartets* (1944).

**Éluard, Paul** (pseudonym of **Eugène Grindel**) (1895–1952) French, born Saint-Denis; *La Vie immédiate* (1934), *Poésie et vérité* (1942).

**Emerson, Ralph Waldo** (1803–84) American, born Boston, Massachusetts; poems published posthumously in *Complete Works* (1903–4).

**Empson, Sir William** (1906–84) English, born Yokefleet, E Yorkshire; *Poems* (1935), *The Gathering Storm* (1940).

**Fitzgerald, Edward** (1809–83) English, born near Woodbridge, Suffolk; translator of *The Rubaiyat of Omar Khayyam* (1859).

**Fitzgerald, Robert (David)** (1902–87) Australian, born Hunters Hill, New South Wales; *To Meet the Sun* (1929), *The Wind at Your Door* (1959), *Product* (1974).

**Frost, Robert (Lee)** (1874–1963) American, born San Francisco; *North of Boston* (1914), *Mountain Interval* (1916), *New Hampshire* (1923), *In the Clearing* (1962).

**Ginsberg, Allen** (1926–97) American, born Newark, New Jersey; *Howl and Other Poems* (1956), *Empty Mirror* (1961), *The Fall of America* (1973).

**Graves, Robert (Ranke)** (1895–1985) English, born London; *Fairies and Fusiliers* (1917).

**Gunn, Thom(son William)** (1929– ) English, born Gravesend, Kent; *The Sense of Movement* (1957), *Touch* (1967), *Jack Straw's Castle* (1976), *The Passages of Joy* (1982), *The Man with Night Sweats* (1992).

**Heaney, Seamus (Justin)** (1939– ) Irish, born Castledawson, County Derry; *Death of a Naturalist* (1966), *Door into the Dark* (1969), *Field Work* (1979), *Seeing Things* (1991), *Spirit Level* (1995), *Beowulf* (2000, translation); Nobel Prize for Literature 1995.

**Henri, Adrian (Maurice)** (1932–2000) English, born Birkenhead; *Tonight at Noon* (1968), *City* (1969), *From the Loveless Motel* (1980), *Wish You Were Here* (1990), *Not Fade Away* (1994), *Robocat* (1998).

**Henryson, Robert** (c.1430–1506) Scottish, birthplace unknown; *Testament of Cresseid*, *Morall Fables of Esope the Phrygian*.

**Herbert, George** (1593–1633) English, born Montgomery, Wales; *The Temple* (1633).

**Herrick, Robert** (1591–1674) English, born London; *Hesperides* (1648).

**Hill, Geoffrey (William)** (1932– ) English, born Bromsgrove, Worcestershire; *King Log* (1968), *Mercian Hymns* (1971), *Tenebrae* (1978).

**Hodgson, Ralph (Edwin)** (1871–1962) English, born Yorkshire; *Poems* (1917), *The Skylark and Other Poems* (1958).

**Homer** (10th–8th-cBC) Greek, birthplace and existence disputed; he is credited with the writing or writing down of *The Iliad* and *The Odyssey*.

**Hopkins, Gerard Manley** (1844–89) English, born Stratford, London; *'The Wreck of the Deutschland'* (1876), posthumously published *Poems* (1918).

**Horace, Quintus Horatius Flaccus** (65–8BC) Roman, born Venusia, Apulia; *Epodes* (30BC), *Odes* (23–13BC).

**Housman, A(lfred) E(dward)** (1859–1936) English, born Flockbury, Worcestershire; *A Shropshire Lad* (1896), *Last Poems* (1922).

**Hughes, Ted** (1930–98) English, born Mytholmroyd, Yorkshire; *The Hawk in the Rain* (1957), *Lupereal* (1960), *Wodwo* (1967), *Crow* (1970), *Care Birds* (1975), *Season Songs* (1976), *Gaudete* (1977), *Moortown* (1979), *Wolfwatching* (1989), *Birthday Letters* (1998).

**Jennings, Elizabeth (Joan)** (1926–2001) English, born Boston, Lincolnshire; *Poems* (1953), *The Mind Has Mountains* (1966), *The Animals' Arrival* (1969), *Relationships* (1972), *Praises* (1998).

**Johnson, Samuel** (1709–84) English, born Lichfield, Staffordshire; *The Vanity of Human Wishes* (1749).

**Kavanagh, Patrick** (1905–67) Irish, born Inniskeen; *Ploughman and Other Poems* (1936), *The Great Hunger* (1942).

**Keats, John** (1795–1821) English, born London; *Endymion* (1818), *Lamia and Other Poems* (1820).

**Keyes, Sidney (Arthur Kilworth)** (1922–43) English, born Dartford, Kent; *The Iron Laurel* (1942), *The Cruel Solstice* (1943).

**La Fontaine, Jean de** (1621–95) French, born Château-Thierry, Champagne; *Contes et nouvelles en vers* (1665), *Fables choisies mises en vers* (1668).

**Langland** or **Langley, William** (c.1332–c.1400) English, birthplace uncertain, possibly Ledbury, Herefordshire; *Vision of William concerning Piers the Plowman* (1362–99).

**Larkin, Philip (Arthur)** (1922–85) English, born Coventry; *The North Ship* (1945), *The Whitsun Weddings* (1964), *High Windows* (1974).

**Longfellow, Henry (Wadsworth)** (1807–82) American, born Portland, Maine; *Voices of the Night* (1839), *Ballads and Other Poems* (1842), *Hiawatha* (1855), *'Divina Comedia'* (1872).

**Lowell, Amy (Laurence)** (1874–1925) American, born Brookline, Massachusetts; *A Dome of Many-Colored Glass* (1912), *Legends* (1921).

**Lowell, Robert (Traill Spence, Jr)** (1917–77) American, born Boston, Massachusetts; *Lord Weary's Castle* (1946), *Life Studies* (1959), *Prometheus Bound* (1967).

**Macaulay, Thomas (Babington)** (1800–59) English, born Rothey Temple, Leicestershire; *The Lays of Ancient Rome* (1842).

**MacCaig, Norman (Alexander)** (1910–96) Scottish, born Edinburgh; *Far Cry* (1943), *Riding Lights* (1955), *A Round of Applause* (1962), *A Man in My Position* (1969), *Voice-Over* (1988).

**MacDiarmid, Hugh** (pseudonym of **Christopher Murray Grieve**) (1892–1978) Scottish, born Langholm, Dumfriesshire; *A Drunk Man Looks at the Thistle* (1926).

**McGough, Roger** (1937– ) English, born Liverpool; *The Mersey Sound: Penguin Modern Poets 10* (with Adrian Henri and Brian Patten) (1967), *Gig* (1973), *Waving at Trains* (1982), *An Imaginary Menagerie* (1988), *The Spotted Unicorn* (1998).

**MacLean, Sorley** (Gaelic **Somhairle Macgill-Eain**) (1911–96) Scottish, born Isle of Raasay, off Skye; *Reothairt is Contraigh* (Spring Tide and Neap Tide) (1977).

**MacNeice, (Frederick) Louis** (1907–63) Irish, born Belfast; *Blind Fireworks* (1929), *Solstices* (1961).

**Mallarmé, Stéphane** (1842–98) French, born Paris; *L'Après-midi d'un faune* (1876), *Poésies* (1899).

**Marvell, Andrew** (1621–78) English, born Winestead, near Hull; *Miscellaneous Poems by Andrew Marvell, Esq.* (1681).

**Masefield, John (Edward)** (1878–1967) English, born Ledbury, Herefordshire; *Salt-Water Ballads* (1902).

**Millay, Edna St Vincent** (1892–1950) American, born Rockland, Maine; *A Few Figs from Thistles* (1920), *The Ballad of Harp-Weaver* (1922).

**Milton, John** (1608–74) English, born London; *Lycidas* (1637), *Paradise Lost* (1667), *Samson Agonistes* (1671).

**Moore, Marianne (Craig)** (1887–1972) American, born Kirkwood, Missouri; *The Pangolin and Other Verse* (1936).

**Muir, Edwin** (1887–1959) Scottish, born Deerness, Orkney; *First Poems* (1925), *Chorus of the Newly Dead* (1926), *Variations on a Time Theme* (1934), *The Labyrinth* (1949), *New Poems* (1949–51).

**Nash, (Frederick) Ogden** (1902–71) American, born Rye, New York; *Free Wheeling* (1931).

**O'Hara, Frank (Francis Russell)** (1926–66) American, born Baltimore, Maryland; *A City Winter and Other Poems* (1952), *Lunch Poems* (1964).

**Ovid** (in full **Publius Ovidius Naso**) (43BC–c.17AD) Roman, born Sulmo; *Amores* (c.16BC), *Metamorphoses, Ars Amatoria.*

**Owen, Wilfred (Edward Salter)** (1893–1918) English, born Oswestry, Shropshire; most poems published posthumously, 1920, by Siegfried Sassoon; 'Dulce et decorum est'.

**Patten, Brian** (1946– ) English, born Liverpool; *Penguin Modern Poets 10* (1967), *Notes to the Hurrying Man* (1969), *Grinning Jack* (1990), *Armada* (1996), *The Blue and Green Ark* (1999).

**Paz, Octavio** (1914–98) Mexican, born Mexico City; *Sun Stone* (1963), *The Bow and the Lyre* (1973), *Collected Poems 1957–87* (1987), *Glimpses of India* (1995); Nobel Prize for Literature 1990.

**Petrarch** (in full **Francesco Petrarca**) (1304–74) Italian, born Arezzo; *Canzoniere.*

**Plath, Sylvia** (1932–63) American, born Boston, Massachusetts; *The Colossus and Other Poems* (1960), *Ariel* (1965), *Crossing the Water* (1971), *Winter Trees* (1972).

**Porter, Peter (Neville Frederick)** (1929– ) Australian, born Brisbane; *Poems, Ancient and Modern* (1964), *English Subtitles* (1981), *The Automatic Oracle* (1987).

**Pound, Ezra (Weston Loomis)** (1885–1972) American, born Haile, Idaho; *The Cantos* (1917, 1948, 1959).

**Pushkin, Aleksandr (Sergeyevich)** (1799–1837) Russian, born Moscow; *Eugene Onegin* (1828), *Ruslam and Lyudmilla* (1820).

**Raine, Kathleen (Jessie)** (1908– ) English, born London; *Stone and Flower* (1943), *The Hollow Hill* (1965), *Living with Mystery* (1992).

**Rich, Adrienne (Cecile)** (1929– ) American, born Baltimore, Maryland; *The Diamond Cutters and Other Poems* (1955), *Snapshots of a Daughter-in-Law* (1963), *The Will to Change* (1971), *Dark Fields of the Republic* (1995).

**Riding, Laura** (née **Reichenfeld**) (1901–91) American, born New York; *The Close Chaplet* (1926).

**Rilke, Rainer Maria** (1875–1926) Austrian, born Prague; *Die Sonnettean Orpheus* (1923).

**Rimbaud, (Jean Nicholas) Arthur** (1854–91) French, born Charleville, Ardennes; *Les Illuminations* (1886).

**Rochester, John Wilmot, Earl of** (1647–80) English, born Ditchley, Oxfordshire; *A Satyre Against Mankind* (1675).

**Roethke, Theodore Huebner** (1908–63) American, born Saginaw, Michigan; *Open House* (1941), *The Lost Son and Other Poems* (1948).

**Rosenberg, Isaac** (1890–1918) English, born Bristol; *Night and Day* (1912), *Youth* (1915), *Poems* (1922).

**Saint-John Perse** (pseudonym of **Marie René Auguste Alexis Saint-Léger Léger**) (1887–1975) French, born St Léger des Feuilles; *Anabase* (1924), *Exil* (1942), *Chroniques* (1960); Nobel Prize for Literature 1960.

**Sassoon, Siegfried (Lorraine)** (1886–1967) English, born Brenchley, Kent; *Counter-Attack and Other Poems* (1917), *The Road to Ruin* (1933).

**Schwarz, Delmore** (1913–66) American, born New York City; *In Dreams Begin Responsibilities* (1938), *Vaudeville for a Princess and Other Poems* (1950).

**Seifert, Jaroslav** (1901–86) Czech, born Prague; *City of Tears* (1921), *All Love* (1923), *A Helmet of Earth* (1945); Nobel Prize for Literature 1984.

**Shelley, Percy Bysshe** (1792–1822) English, born Field Place, Horsham, Sussex; *Alastor* (1816), *The Revolt of Islam* (1818), *Julian and Maddalo* (1818), *The Triumph of Life* (1822).

**Sidney, Sir Philip** (1554–86) English, born Penshurst, Kent; *Arcadia* (1580), *Astrophel and Stella* (1591).

**Sitwell, Dame Edith (Louisa)** (1887–1964) English, born Scarborough; *Façade* (1922), *Colonel Fantock* (1926).

**Smart, Christopher** (1722–71) English, born Shipbourne, Kent; *Jubilate Agno* (first published 1939).

**Smith, Stevie** (pseudonym of **Florence Margaret Smith**) (1902–71) English, born Hull; *Not Waving but Drowning: Poems* (1957).

**Spender, Sir Stephen (Harold)** (1909–95) English, born London; *Poems* (1933).

**Spenser, Edmund** (1552–99) English, born London; *The Sheapheardes Calender* (1579), *The Faerie Queene* (1590, 1596).

**Stevens, Wallace** (1879–1955) American, born Reading, Pennsylvania; *Harmonium* (1923), *Transport to Summer* (1947).

**Szymborska, Wislawa** (1923– ) Polish, born Bnin; *A Great Number (1976), People on a Bridge* (1986), *View with a Grain of Sand* (1995); Nobel Prize for Literature 1996.

**Tennyson, Alfred, Lord** (1809–92) English, born Somersby Rectory, Lincolnshire; *Poems* (1832) (eg 'The Lotus-Eaters' and 'The Lady of Shalott'), *The Princess* (1847), *In Memoriam* (1850), *Idylls of the King* (1859), *Maud* (1885).

**Thomas, Dylan (Marlais)** (1914–53) Welsh, born Swansea; *Twenty-five Poems* (1936), *Deaths and Entrances* (1946), *In Country Sleep and Other Poems* (1952).

**Thomas, (Philip) Edward** (1878–1917) English, born London; *Six Poems* (1916), *Last Poems* (1918).

**Thomas, R(onald) S(tuart)** (1913–2000) Welsh, born Cardiff; *The Stones of the Field* (1946), *Song at the Year's Turning* (1955), *The Bread of Truth* (1963), *Between Here and Now* (1981), *Counterpoint* (1990), *No Truth with The Furies* (1995).

**Thomson, James** (1700–48) Scottish, born Ednam, Roxburghshire; *The Seasons* (1730), *The Castle of Indolence* (1748).

**Verlaine, Paul** (1844–96) French, born Metz; *Fêtes galantes* (1869), *Sagesse* (1881).

**Virgil, Publius Vergilius Maro** (70–19BC) Roman, born near Mantua; *Eclogues* (37BC), *Georgics* (29BC), *The Aeneid* (19BC).

**Walcott, Derek Alton** (1930– ) West Indian, born St Lucia; *Castaway* (1965), *Fortunate Traveller* (1981), *Selected Poetry* (1993), *The Bounty* (1997); Nobel Prize for Literature (1992).

**Webb, Francis Charles** (1925–73) Australian, born Adelaide; *A Drum for Ben Boyd* (1948), *The Ghost of the Cock* (1964).

**Whitman, Walt** (1819–92) American, born West Hills, Long Island, New York; *Leaves of Grass* (1855–89).

**Wordsworth, William** (1770–1850) English, born Cockermouth; *Lyrical Ballads* (with S T Coleridge, 1798), *The Prelude* (1799, 1805, 1850), *The Excursion* (1814).

**Wright, Judith (Arundell)** (1915–2000) Australian, born Armidale, New South Wales; *The Moving Image* (1946), *The Two Fires* (1955), *Birds* (1962), *Alive* (1973), *The Cry for the Dead* (1981).

**Wyatt, Sir Thomas** (1503–42) English, born Allington Castle, Kent; poems first published in *Tottel's Miscellany* (1557).

**Yeats, W(illiam) B(utler)** (1865–1939) Irish, born Sandymount, County Dublin; *The Wanderings of Oisin and Other Poems* (1889), *The Wind Among the Reeds* (1894), *The Wild Swans at Coole* (1917), *Michael Robartes and the Dancer* (1921), *The Winding Stair and Other Poems* (1933); Nobel Prize for Literature 1923.

## Poets laureate

| | |
|---|---|
| 1617 | Ben Jonson[1] |
| 1638 | Sir William Davenant[1] |
| 1668 | John Dryden |
| 1689 | Thomas Shadwell |
| 1692 | Nahum Tate |
| 1715 | Nicholas Rowe |
| 1718 | Laurence Eusden |
| 1730 | Colley Cibber |
| 1757 | William Whitehead |
| 1785 | Thomas Warton |
| 1790 | Henry Pye |
| 1813 | Robert Southey |
| 1843 | William Wordsworth |
| 1850 | Alfred, Lord Tennyson |
| 1896 | Alfred Austin |
| 1913 | Robert Bridges |
| 1930 | John Masefield |
| 1968 | Cecil Day Lewis |
| 1972 | Sir John Betjeman |
| 1984 | Ted Hughes |
| 1999 | Andrew Motion |

[1]The post was not officially established until 1668.

## Playwrights

Selected plays are listed.

**Aeschylus** (c.525–c.456BC) Athenian; *The Oresteia trilogy (Agamemnon, Choephoroe, Eumenides)* (458BC), *Prometheus Bound*, *Seven Against Thebes*.

**Albee, Edward Franklin, III** (1928– ) American, born Washington, DC; *The American Dream* (1961), *Who's Afraid of Virginia Woolf?* (1962), *A Delicate Balance* (1966, Pulitzer Prize), *Seascape* (1974), *Three Tall Women* (1991, Pulitzer Prize 1994), *Fragments* (1993).

**Amos, Robert** (1920– ) Australian, born Austria; *When the Gravediggers Come* (1961).

**Anouilh, Jean** (1910–87) French, born Bordeaux; *Antigone* (1944), *Médée* (1946), *L'Alouette* (1953), *Beckett; or, the Honour of God* (1960).

**Aristophanes** (c.448–c.385BC) Athenian; *The Acharnians* (425BC), *The Knights* (424BC), *The Clouds* (423BC), *The Wasps* (422BC), The Birds (414BC), *Lysistrata* (411BC), *The Frogs* (405BC).

**Ayckbourn, Sir Alan** (1939– ) English, born London; *Absurd Person Singular* (1973), *Absent Friends* (1975), *Joking Apart* (1979), *Way Upstream* (1982), *Woman in Mind* (1985), *Henceforward* (1987), *Man of the Moment* (1988), *Wildest Dreams* (1991), *Communicating Doors* (1994), *The Champion of Paribanou* (1996), *The Boy Who Fell Into a Book* (1998).

**Beaumont, Sir Francis** (1584–1616) English, born Grace-Dieu, Leicestershire, and **John Fletcher**; *Philaster* (1609), *The Maid's Tragedy* (1610).

**Beckett, Samuel (Barclay)** (1906–89) Irish, born Foxrock, near Dublin; *Waiting for Godot* (1955), *Endgame* (1958), *Krapp's Last Tape* (1958), *Happy Days* (1961), *Not I* (1973); Nobel Prize for Literature 1969.

**Beynon, Richard** (1925– ) Australian, born Carlton, Melbourne; *The Shifting Heart* (1956), *Time and Mr Strachan* (1958).

**Bond, (Thomas) Edward** (1934– ) English, born North London; *Early Morning* (1969), *Lear* (1971), *Summer* (1982), *The War Plays* (1985), *Olly's Prison* (1992), *Coffee: a tragedy* (1995), *Eleven Vests* (1997).

**Brecht, (Eugen) Bertolt (Friedrich)** (1898–1956) German, born Augsburg; *Galileo* (1938–9), *Mutter Courage and ihre Kinder* (Mother Courage and Her Children) (1941), *Der Gute Mensch von Setzuan* (The Good Woman of Setzuan) (1943), *Der Kaukasische Kreidekreis* (The Caucasian Chalk Circle) (1949).

**Brieux, Eugène** (1858–1932) French, born Paris; *Les Trois Filles de M Dupont* (1897), *The Red Robe* (1900).

**Chapman, George** (c.1559–1634) English, born near Hitchin, Hertfordshire; *Bussy D'Ambois* (1607).

**Chekhov, Anton Pavlovich** (1860–1904) Russian, born Taganrog; *The Seagull* (1895), *Uncle Vanya* (1900), *Three Sisters* (1901), *The Cherry Orchard* (1904).

**Congreve, William** (1670–1729) English, born Bardsey, near Leeds; *Love for Love* (1695), *The Way of the World* (1700).

**Corneille, Pierre** (1606–84) French, born Rouen; *Le Cid* (1636), *Horace* (1639), *Polyeucte* (1640).

**Coward, Sir Noël Peirce** (1899–1973) English, born Teddington, Middlesex; *Hay Fever* (1925), *Private Lives* (1933), *Blithe Spirit* (1941).

**Dekker, Thomas** (c.1570–1632) English, born London; *The Whore of Babylon* (1606).

**Dryden, John** (1631–1700) English, born Aldwinkle; *The Indian Queen* (1664), *Marriage à la Mode* (1672), *All for Love* (1678), *Amphitryon* (1690).

**Eliot, T(homas) S(tearns)** (1888–1965) American naturalized British, born St Louis, Missouri; *Murder in the Cathedral* (1935), *The Family Reunion* (1939), *The Cocktail Party* (1950).

**Esson, (Thomas) Louis (Buvelot)** (1879–1943) Australian, born Edinburgh; *The Drovers* (1920), *Andeganora* (1937).

**Euripides** (c.480–406BC) Athenian; *Medea* (431BC), *Electra* (413BC), *The Bacchae* (407BC).

**Fletcher, John** (1579–1625) English, born Rye, Sussex, *The Faithful Shepherdess* (1610), *A Wife for a Month* (1624).

**Fo, Dario** (1926– ) Italian, born Lombardy; *Accidental Death of an Anarchist* (1970), *Can't Pay! Won't Pay!* (1974), *The Pope and the Witch* (1989), *The Tricks of the Trade* (1991), *Il Diavolo con le Zinne* (1997).

**Ford, John** (1586–c.1640) English, born Devon; *'Tis Pity She's a Whore* (1633), *Perkin Warbeck* (1634).

**Galsworthy, John** (1867–1933) English, born Coombe, Surrey; *Strife* (1909), *Justice* (1910); Nobel Prize for Literature 1932.

**Genet, Jean** (1910–86) French, born Paris; *The Maids* (1948), *The Balcony* (1956).

**Giraudoux, (Hippolyte) Jean** (1882–1944) French, born Bellac; *Judith* (1931), *Ondine* (1939).

**Goethe, Johann Wolfgang von** (1749–1832) German, born Frankfurt am Main; *Faust* (1808, 1832).

**Gogol, Nikolai (Vasilievich)** (1809–52) Russian, born Ukraine; *The Inspector General* (1836).

**Goldsmith, Oliver** (1728–74) Irish, born Pallas, County Longford; *She Stoops to Conquer* (1773).

**Gray, Oriel** (1921– ) Australian, born Sydney; *The Torrents* (1955), *Burst of Summer* (1960).

**Greene, Robert** (1558–92) English, born Norwich; *Orlando Furioso* (1594), *James the Fourth* (1598).

**Hauptmann, Gerhart Johann Robert** (1862–1946) German, born Obersalzbrunn, Silesia; *Before Sunrise* (1889), *The Weavers* (1892); Nobel Prize for Literature 1912.

**Hayes, Alfred** (1911–85) American, born England; *The Girl on the Via Flaminia* (1954).

**Hebbel, (Christian) Friedrich** (1813–63) German, born Wesselburen, Dithmarschen; *Judith* (1841), *Maria Magdalena* (1844).

**Hewett, Dorothy (Coade)** (1923– ) Australian, born Wickepin, West Australia; *The Chapel Perilous* (1972), *This Old Man Comes Rolling Home* (1976), *Golden Valley* (1984).

**Heywood, Thomas** (c.1574–1641) English, born Lincolnshire; *A Woman Killed with Kindness* (1603), *The Fair Maid of the West* (1631), *The English Traveller* (1633).

**Hibberd, Jack** (1940– ) Australian, born Warracknabeal, Victoria; *Dimboola* (1969), *White with Wire Wheels* (1970), *A Stretch of the Imagination* (1973), *Squibs* (1984).

**Howard, Sidney (Coe)** (1891–1939) American, born Oakland, California; *They Knew What They Wanted* (1924), *The Silver Cord* (1926).

**Ibsen, Henrik** (1828–1906) Norwegian, born Skien; *Peer Gynt* (1867), *A Doll's House* (1879), *The Pillars of Society* (1880), *The Wild Duck* (1884), *Hedda Gabler* (1890), *The Master Builder* (1892).

**Inge, William Motter** (1913–73) American, born Kansas; *Picnic* (1953), *Where's Daddy?* (1966).

**Ionesco, Eugène** (1912–94) French, born Romania; *The Bald Prima Donna* (1948), *The Picture* (1958), *Le Rhinocéros* (1960).

**Jonson, Ben(jamin)** (c.1572–1637) English, born Westminster, London; *Every Man in His Humour* (1598), *Sejanus* (1603), *Volpone* (1606), *The Alchemist* (1610), *Bartholomew Fair* (1614).

**Kaiser, Georg** (1878–1945) German, born Magdeburg; *The Burghers of Calais* (1914), *Gas* (1920).

**Kushner, Tony** (1956– ) American, born New York City; *Yes, Yes, No, No* (1985), *Angels in America* (1992, Pulitzer Prize 1993), *Slavs!* (1995), *Henry Box Brown* (1997).

**Kyd, Thomas** (1558–94) English, born London; *The Spanish Tragedy* (1587).

**Lawler, Ray(mond Evenor)** (1922– ) Australian, born Melbourne; *The Summer of the Seventeenth Doll* (1955), *The Man Who Shot the Albatross* (1970), *Kid Stakes* (1975), *Other Times* (1976), *Godsend* (1982).

**Lorca, Federico García** (1899–1936) Spanish, born Fuente Vaqueros; *Blood Wedding* (1933), *The House of Bernarda Alba* (1945).

**Maeterlinck, Maurice, Count** (1862–1949) Belgian, born Ghent; *La Princesse Maleine* (1889), *Pélleas et Mélisande* (1892), *The Blue Bird* (1909).

**Mamet, David Alan** (1947– ) American, born Chicago; *Sexual Perversity in Chicago* (1974), *Duck Variations* (1974), *American Buffalo* (1975), *Edmond* (1982), *Glengarry Glen Ross* (1983, Pulitzer Prize), *Oleanna* (1992), *Death Defying Acts* (1996).

**Marlowe, Christopher** (1564–93) English, born Canterbury; *Tamburlaine the Great* (in two parts, 1587), *Dr Faustus* (1588), *The Jew of Malta* (c.1589), *Edward II* (1592).

**Marston, John** (1576–1634) English, born Wardington, Oxfordshire; *Antonio's Revenge* (1602), *The Malcontent* (1604).

**Miller, Arthur** (1915– ) American, born New York City; *All My Sons* (1947), *Death of a Salesman* (1949), *The Crucible* (1952), *A View from the Bridge* (1955), *The Misfits* (1961), *After the Fall* (1964), *The Creation of the World and Other Business* (1972), *Playing for Time* (1981), *Danger: Memory!* (1987), *The Ride Down Mount Morgan* (1991), *The Last Yankee* (1992), *Broken Glass* (1994), *Homely Girl* (1995).

**Molière** (pseudonym of **Jean-Baptiste Poquelin**) (1622–73) French, born Paris; *Le Bourgeois Gentilhomme* (The Bourgeois Gentleman) (1660), *Tartuffe* (1664), *Le Misanthrope* (The Misanthropist) (1666), *Le Malade Imaginaire* (The Hypochondriac) (1673).

**Oakley, Barry** (1931– ) Australian, born Melbourne; *The Feet of Daniel Mannix* (1975), *Bedfellows* (1975).

**O'Casey, Sean** (originally **John Casey**) (1880–1964) Irish, born Dublin; *Juno and the Paycock* (1924), *The Plough and the Stars* (1926).

**O'Neill, Eugene Gladstone** (1888–1953) American, born New York City; *Beyond the Horizon* (1920), *Desire under the Elms* (1924), *Mourning Becomes Electra* (1931), *Long Day's Journey into Night* (1941), *The Iceman Cometh* (1946); Nobel Prize for Literature 1936.

**Orton, Joe (John Kingsley)** (1933–67) English, born Leicester; *Entertaining Mr Sloane* (1964), *Loot* (1965), *What the Butler Saw* (1969).

**Osborne, John (James)** (1929–94) Welsh, born Fulham, London; *Look Back in Anger* (1956), *The Entertainer* (1957), *Inadmissible Evidence* (1965), *The Hotel in Amsterdam* (1968), *West of Suez* (1971), *Almost a Vision* (1976), *Déjà Vu* (1989).

**Otway, Thomas** (1652–85) English, born Milland, Sussex; *Don Carlos* (1676), *The Orphan* (1680), *Venice Preserv'd* (1682).

**Patrick, John** (1905–95) American, born Louisville, Kentucky; *The Teahouse of the August Moon* (1953).

**Pinter, Harold** (1930– ) English, born East London; *The Birthday Party* (1958), *The Caretaker* (1960), *The Homecoming* (1965), *Landscape* (1967), *Old Times* (1970), *No Man's Land* (1974), *Betrayal* (1978), *A Kind of Alaska* (1982), *One for the Road* (1984), *Party Time* (1991), *Ashes to Ashes* (1996).

**Pirandello, Luigi** (1867–1936) Italian, born near Agrigento, Sicily; *Six Characters in Search of an Author* (1921), *Henry IV* (1922); Nobel Prize for Literature 1934.

**Plautus, Titus Maccius** (c.250–184BC) Roman; *Menachmi, Miles Gloriosus*.

**Porter, Hal** (1911–84) Australian, born Melbourne; *The Tower* (1963), *The Professor* (1966), *Eden House* (1969).

**Racine, Jean** (1639–99) French, born near Soissons; *Andromaque* (1667), *Phèdre* (1677), *Bajazet* (1672), *Esther* (1689).

**Romeril, John** (1945– ) Australian, born Melbourne; *Chicago, Chicago* (1970), *I Don't Know Who to Feel Sorry For* (1973), *The Kelly Dance* (1986).

**Russell, Willy (William)** (1947– ) English, born Whiston, Merseyside; *Educating Rita* (1979), *Blood Brothers* (1983), *Shirley Valentine* (1986).

**Sackville, Thomas** (1553–1608) English, born Buckhurst, Sussex; *Gorboduc* (1592).

**Sartre, Jean-Paul** (1905–80) French, born Paris; *The Flies* (1943), *Huis Clos* (1945), *The Condemned of Altona* (1961).

**Schiller, Johann Christoph Friedrich von** (1759–1805) German, born Marbach; *The Robbers* (1781), *Wallenstein* (1799), *Maria Stuart* (1800).

**Seneca, Lucius Annaeus** (c.4BC–AD65) Roman, born Corduba; *Hercules, Medea, Thyestes*.

**Seymour, Alan** (1927– ) Australian, born Perth; *The One Day of the Year* (1962), *Swamp Creatures* (1958), *Danny Johnson* (1960).

**Shaffer, Peter (Levin)** (1926– ) English, born Liverpool; *The Royal Hunt of the Sun* (1964), *Equus* (1973), *Amadeus* (1979), *Yonadab* (1985), *The Gift of the Gorgon* (1992).

**Shakespeare, William** ► **Plays of Shakespeare** p446

**Shaw, George Bernard** (1856–1950) Irish, born Dublin; *Arms and the Man* (1894), *Man and Superman* (1903), *Pygmalion* (1913), *Saint Joan* (1924); Nobel Prize for Literature 1925.

**Shepard, Sam** (originally **Samuel Shepard Rogers**) (1943– ) American, born Fort Sheridan, Illinois; *La Turista* (1967), *Forensic and the Navigators* (1968), *The Tooth of Crime* (1972), *Buried Child* (1978), *The Curse of the Starving Class* (1976), *True West* (1979), *Fool for Love* (1983).

**Sheridan, Richard Brinsley** (1751–1816) Irish, born Dublin; *The Rivals* (1775), *The School for Scandal* (1777), *The Critic* (1779).

**Sherwood, Robert (Emmet)** (1896–1955) American, born New Rochelle, New York; *Idiot's Delight* (1936), *Abe Lincoln in Illinois* (1938), *There Shall Be No Night* (1940).

**Sophocles** (496–406BC) Athenian, born Colonus; *Antigone, Oedipus Rex, Oedipus at Colonus*.

**Soyinka, Wole** (in full **Akinwande Oluwole Soyinka**) (1934– ) Nigerian, born Abeokata, West Nigeria; *The Swamp Dwellers* (1958), *The Strong Breed* (1962), *The Road* (1964), *The Bacchae of Euripides* (1973), *Opera Wonyosi* (1978), *From Zia, with Love* (1991); Nobel Prize for Literature 1986.

**Stoppard, Sir Tom (Thomas Straussler)** (1937– ) English, born Czechoslovakia; *Rosencrantz and Guildenstern are Dead* (1966), *The Real Inspector Hound* (1968), *Travesties* (1974), *New-Found-Land* (1976), *Undiscovered Country* (1980), *Rough Crossing* (1984), *Arcadia* (1993), *Indian Ink* (1995), *Shakespeare in Love* (screenplay) (1998).

**Strindberg, (Johan) August** (1849–1912) Swedish, born Stockholm; *Master Olof* (1877), *Miss Julie* (1888), *The Dance of Death* (1901).

**Synge, (Edmund) J(ohn) M(illington)** (1871–1909) Irish, born near Dublin; *The Well of Saints* (1905), *The Playboy of the Western World* (1907).

**Webster, John** (c.1578–c.1632) English, born London; *The White Devil* (1612), *The Duchess of Malfi* (1614).

**Wilde, Oscar (Fingal O'Flahertie Wills)** (1854–1900) Irish, born Dublin; *Lady Windermere's Fan* (1892), *The Importance of Being Earnest* (1895), *Salomé* (1896).

**Wilder, Thornton (Niven)** (1897–1975) American, born Wisconsin; *Our Town* (1938), *The Merchant of Yonkers* (1938), *The Skin of Our Teeth* (1942), *The Matchmaker* (1954, later a musical *Hello, Dolly!*, 1964).

**Williams, Tennessee** (originally **Thomas Lanier Williams**) (1911–83) American, born Mississippi; *The Glass Menagerie* (1944), *A Streetcar Named Desire* (1947), *Cat on a Hot Tin Roof* (1955), *Sweet Bird of Youth* (1959).

**Williamson, David Keith** (1942– ) Australian, born Melbourne; *The Removalists* (1971), *Don's Party* (1971), *The Club* (1977), *The Perfectionist* (1981), *Sons of Cain* (1985).

**Wycherly, William** (1641–1715) English, born Clive, near Shrewsbury; *The Gentleman Dancing-Master* (1672), *The Country Wife* (1675), *The Plain-Dealer* (1676).

## Plays of Shakespeare

William Shakespeare (1564–1616), English playwright and poet, born Stratford-upon-Avon.

| Title | Date | Category | Title | Date | Category |
|---|---|---|---|---|---|
| The Two Gentlemen of Verona | 1590–1 | comedy | As You Like It | 1599–1600 | comedy |
| Henry VI Part One | 1592 | history | Hamlet, Prince of Denmark | 1600–1 | tragedy |
| Henry VI Part Two | 1592 | history | Twelfth Night, or What You Will | 1601 | comedy |
| Henry VI Part Three | 1592 | history | Troilus and Cressida | 1602 | tragedy |
| Titus Andronicus | 1592 | tragedy | Measure for Measure | 1603 | dark comedy |
| Richard III | 1592–3 | history | Othello | 1603–4 | tragedy |
| The Taming of the Shrew | 1593 | comedy | All's Well That Ends Well | 1604–5 | dark comedy |
| The Comedy of Errors | 1594 | comedy | Timon of Athens | 1605 | romantic drama |
| Love's Labours Lost | 1594–5 | comedy | The Tragedy of King Lear | 1605–6 | tragedy |
| Richard II | 1595 | history | Macbeth | 1606 | tragedy |
| Romeo and Juliet | 1595 | tragedy | Antony and Cleopatra | 1606 | tragedy |
| A Midsummer Night's Dream | 1595 | comedy | Pericles | 1607 | romance |
| King John | 1596 | history | Coriolanus | 1608 | tragedy |
| The Merchant of Venice | 1596–7 | comedy | The Winter's Tale | 1609 | romance |
| Henry IV Part One | 1596–7 | history | Cymbeline | 1610 | comedy |
| The Merry Wives of Windsor | 1597–8 | comedy | The Tempest | 1611 | comedy |
| Henry IV Part Two | 1597–8 | history | Henry VIII | 1613 | history |
| Much Ado About Nothing | 1598 | dark comedy | | | |
| Henry V | 1598–9 | history | | | |
| Julius Caesar | 1599 | tragedy | | | |

## Film and TV actors

Selected films and television productions are listed. Original and full names of actors are given in parentheses.

**Adams, Brooke** (1949– ) American, born New York City; *Invasion of the Body Snatchers* (1978), *A Man, a Woman, and a Bank* (1980), *Dead Zone* (1983), *Lace* (TV 1984), *Lace 2* (TV 1985), *Moonlighting* (TV 1987), *The Babysitter's Club* (1995).

**Adjani, Isabelle** (1955– ) French, born Paris; *The Story of Adele H* (1975), *Nosferatu* (1978), *Possession* (1980), *Quartet* (1981), *One Deadly Summer* (1983), *Subway* (1985), *Ishtar* (1987), *Camille Claudel* (1988), *La Reine Margot* (1992), *Diabolique* (1996).

**Agutter, Jenny** (1952– ) British, born Taunton; *The Railway Children* (1970), *Walkabout* (1971), *Logan's Run* (1976), *The Eagle Has Landed* (1977), *Equus* (1977), *The Man in the Iron Mask* (1977), *An American Werewolf in London* (1981), *Child's Play 2* (1990), *Blue Juice* (1995), *The Parole Officer* (2000).

**Aiello, Danny** (1935– ) American, born New York City; *Fort Apache The Bronx* (1981), *Once Upon a Time in America* (1984), *The Purple Rose of Cairo* (1984), *Moonstruck* (1987), *Do the Right Thing* (1988), *Harlem Nights* (1989), *Leon* (1994).

**Aimée, Anouk** (Françoise Sorya) (1934– ) French, born Paris; *Les Amants de Verone* (1949), *La Dolce Vita* (1960), *Lola* (1961), *Un Homme et une Femme* (1966), *Justine* (1969), *Flagrant Desire* (1985), *Scar* (1994), *Prêt-À-Porter* (1994), *Une pour toutes* (1999).

**Albert, Eddie** (Eddie Albert Heimberger) (1908– ) American, born Rock Island, Illinois; *Brother Rat* (1938), *Four Wives* (1939), *Smash Up* (1947), *Carrie* (1952), *Leave it to Larry* (TV 1952), *Roman Holiday* (1953), *Oklahoma!* (1955), *I'll Cry Tomorrow* (1955), *Attack!* (1956), *The Teahouse of the August Moon* (1956), *The Roots of Heaven* (1958), *Orders to Kill* (1958), *The Miracle of the White Stallions* (1962), *Green Acres* (TV 1965–70), *The Longest Yard* (1974), *Escape to Witch Mountain* (1975), *Switch* (TV 1975–6), *Yes, Giorgio* (1982), *Dreamscape* (1984), *Deadly Illusion* (1987), *The Big Picture* (1989), *The Barefoot Executive* (TV 1995).

**Alda, Alan** (1936– ) American, born New York City; *Paper Lion* (1968), *Catch-22* (1970), *M*A*S*H* (TV 1972–83), *California Suite* (1978), *Same Time Next Year* (1978), *The Four Seasons* (1981), *Sweet Liberty* (1986), *A New Life* (1988), *Crimes and Misdemeanors* (1989), *Betsy's Wedding* (1990), *Manhattan Murder Mystery* (1993), *Flirting With Disaster* (1996), *Mad City* (1997).

**Allen, Karen** (1951– ) American, born Carrollton, Illinois; *Animal House* (1978), *The Wanderers* (1979), *East of Eden* (TV 1980), *Raiders of the Lost Ark* (1981), *Shoot the Moon* (1981), *Starman* (1984), *The Glass Menagerie* (1987), *Scrooged* (1988), *Secret Weapon* (TV, 1990), *Sweet Talker* (1991), *Malcolm X* (1992), *The Turner* (1994), *Falling Sky* (1998).

**Allen, Nancy** (1950– ) American, born New York City; *Carrie* (1976), *I Wanna Hold Your Hand* (1978), *1941* (1979), *Dressed to Kill* (1980), *Blow Out* (1981), *The Philadelphia Experiment* (1984), *The Gladiator* (TV 1986), *Robocop* (1987), *Poltergeist III* (1988), *Robocop 2* (1990), *Robocop 3* (1994), *Les Patriotes* (1994), *The Man Who Wouldn't Die* (TV 1995).

**Allen, Woody** (Allen Stewart Konigsberg) (1935– ) American, born Brooklyn, New York City; *What's New, Pussycat?* (1965), *Casino Royale* (1967), *Bananas* (1971), *Play it Again Sam* (1972), *Sleeper* (1973), *Annie Hall* (1977), *Manhattan* (1979), *Stardust Memories* (1980), *Hannah and Her Sisters* (1986), *New York Stories* (1989), *Crimes and Misdemeanors* (1989), *Scenes from a Mall* (1991), *Husbands and Wives* (1992), *Manhattan Murder Mystery* (1993), *Mighty Aphrodite* (1995), *Deconstructing Harry* (1997), *Stanley Kubrick: A Life in Pictures* (2001).

**Alley, Kirstie** (1955– ) American, born Wichita, Kansas; *Star Trek II: The Wrath of Khan* (1982), *Blind Date* (1983), *Champions* (1983), *Runaway* (1984), *North and South* (TV 1986), *Summer School* (1987), *Cheers* (TV 1987–93), *Shoot to Kill* (1988), *Look Who's Talking* (1989), *Madhouse* (1990), *Loverboy* (1990), *Sibling Rivalry* (1990), *Look Who's Talking Too* (1991), *Look Who's Talking Now* (1993), *It Takes Two* (1995), *Drop Dead Gorgeous* (1999).

**Allyson, June** (Ella Geisman) (1917– ) American, born Westchester, New York; *Two Girls and a Sailor* (1944), *Music for Millions* (1944), *Little Women* (1949), *The Glen Miller Story* (1954), *The Shrike* (1955), *The June Allyson Show* (TV 1959–61), *That's Entertainment! III* (1994).

**Ameche, Don** (Dominic Felix Amici) (1908–93) American, born Kenosha, Wisconsin; *Ramona* (1936), *In Old Chicago* (1938), *The Three Musketeers* (1939), *Midnight* (1939), *The Story of Alexander Graham Bell* (1939), *Swanee River* (1939), *Four Sons* (1940), *Down Argentine Way* (1940), *That Night in Rio* (1941), *Heaven Can Wait* (1943), *Happy Land* (1943), *Trading Places* (1983), *Cocoon* (1985), *Bigfoot and the Hendersons* (1987), *Coming to America* (1988), *Things Change* (1988), *Cocoon: The Return* (1988), *Oscar* (1991), *Corrina, Corrina* (1994).

**Anderson, Dame Judith** (Frances Margaret Anderson) (1898–1992) Australian, born Adelaide; *Rebecca* (1940), *The Ten Commandments* (1956), *Cat on a Hot Tin Roof* (1958), *A Man Called Horse* (1970), *Star Trek III: The Search for Spock* (1984).

**Andress, Ursula** (1936– ) Swiss, born Berne; *Dr No* (1963), *She* (1965), *What's New, Pussycat?* (1965), *Casino Royale* (1967), *The Clash of the Titans* (1981), *Big Man* (1988).

**Andrews, Anthony** (1948– ) British, born London; *Danger UXB* (TV 1978), *Brideshead Revisited* (TV 1981), *The Scarlet Pimpernel* (TV 1982), *Under the Volcano* (1984), *The Lighthorsemen* (1987), *Lost in Siberia* (1991), *Haunted* (1995).

**Andrews, Dame Julie** (Julia Elizabeth Wells) (1935– ) British, born Walton-on-Thames, Surrey; *Mary Poppins* (1964), *The Americanization of Emily* (1964), *The Sound of Music* (1965), *Torn Curtain* (1966), *Thoroughly Modern Millie* (1967), *Star!* (1968), *SOB* (1981), *Victor/Victoria* (1982), *The Man Who Loved Women* (1983), *Tchin Tchin* (1990).

**Ann-Margret** (Ann-Margret Olsson) (1941– ) Swedish–American, born Valsobyn, Jamtland, Sweden; *State Fair* (1962), *Bye Bye Birdie* (1963), *The Cincinnati Kid* (1965), *Carnal Knowledge* (1971), *Tommy* (1975), *52 Pick-Up* (1986), *A New Life* (1988), *Newsies* (1991), *Grumpy Old Men* (1994), *Grumpier Old Men* (1996).

**Anthony, Lysette** (1963– ) British, born London; *Krull* (1983), *Three Up, Two Down* (TV 1987–8), *Jack the Ripper* (TV 1988), *Without a Clue* (1988), *The Lady and the Highway Man* (1989), *Campion* (TV 1989–90).

**Archer, Anne** (1947– ) American, born Los Angeles; *Bob and Carol and Ted and Alice* (TV 1973), *Paradise Alley* (1978), *Green Ice* (1980), *Fatal Attraction* (1987), *Love at Large* (1990), *Narrow Margin* (1990), *Body of Evidence* (1992), *Patriot Games* (1992), *Short Cuts* (1993), *Clear and Present Danger* (1994).

**Arquette, Rosanna** (1959– ) American, born New York City; *Shirley* (1979 TV), *SOB* (1981), *Johnny Belinda* (TV 1982), *The Executioner's Song* (TV 1982), *Desperately Seeking Susan* (1983), *Silverado* (1985), *After Hours* (1985), *Nobody's Fool* (1985), *Eight Million Ways to Die* (1987), *The Big Blue* (1988), *New York Stories* (1989), *The Black Rainbow* (1990), *The Player* (1992), *Nowhere to Run* (1993), *Pulp Fiction* (1994), *Crash* (1996), *Love is Murder* (1997).

**Ashcroft, Dame Peggy** (1907–91) British, born Croydon, Greater London; *The Thirty-Nine Steps* (1935), *Quiet Wedding* (1940), *Edward and Mrs Simpson* (TV 1978), *A Passage to India* (1984), *The Jewel in the Crown* (TV 1984), *Madame Sousatzka* (1988), *She's Been Away* (TV 1990).

**Asher, Jane** (1946– ) British, born London; *The Masque of the Red Death* (1964), *Deep End* (1971), *Dreamchild* (1985), *Paris by Night* (1988), *The Volunteer* (1993).

**Astaire, Fred** (Frederick Austerlitz) (1899–1987) American, born Omaha, Nebraska; *Flying Down to Rio* (1933), *The Gay Divorcee* (1934), *Top Hat* (1935), *Funny Face* (1957), *It Takes a Thief* (TV 1965–9), *Finian's Rainbow* (1968).

**Astor, Mary** (Lucille Langhanke) (1906–87) American, born Quincy, Illinois; *Beau Brummell* (1924), *Don Juan* (1926), *Dodsworth* (1936), *The Prisoner of Zenda* (1937), *The Great Lie* (1941), *The Maltese Falcon* (1941), *The Palm Beach Story* (1942), *Meet Me in St Louis* (1944), *Act of Violence* (1948), *Little Women* (1949), *Return to Peyton Place* (1961).

**Atkinson, Rowan** (1955– ) British, born Newcastle upon Tyne; *The Black Adder* (TV 1984), *Blackadder II* (TV 1985), *Blackadder III* (TV 1986), *Blackadder Goes Forth* (TV 1989), *The Tall Guy* (1989), *The Witches* (1990), *Mr Bean* (TV 1990–4), *Bean: The Ultimate Disaster Movie* (1997), *Maybe Baby* (2000).

**Attenborough, Richard Samuel Attenborough, Baron** (1923– ) British, born Cambridge; *In Which We Serve* (1942), *The Man Within* (1942), *Brighton Rock* (1947), *The Guinea Pig* (1949), *The Great Escape* (1963), *Brannigan* (1975), *Jurassic Park* (1993), *Miracle on 34th Street* (1994), *Elizabeth* (1998).

**Avalon, Frankie** (Francis Thomas Avallone) (1940–) American, born Philadelphia, Pennsylvania; *The Alamo* (1960), *Voyage to the Bottom of the Sea* (1962), *Beach Blanket Bingo* (1965), *Fireball 500* (1966), *Grease* (1978), *Blood Song* (1982), *Casino* (1995).

**Aykroyd, Dan** (1952– ) Canadian, born Ottawa, Ontario; *1949* (1979), *The Blues Brothers* (1980), *Neighbors* (1981), *Twilight Zone* (1983), *Ghostbusters* (1984), *Spies Like Us* (1986), *Dragnet* (1987), *The Couch Trip* (1988), *The Great Outdoors* (1988), *Caddyshack II* (1968), *Ghostbusters II* (1989), *My Stepmother is an Alien* (1989), *Driving Miss Daisy* (1989), *Loose Cannons* (1990), *My Girl* (1991), *Chaplin* (1992), *Sneakers* (1992), *Coneheads* (1993), *My Girl 2* (1994), *Getting Away With Murder* (1995), *Caspar* (1995), *Sgt Bilko* (1996), *Grosse Pointe Blank* (1996), *Blues Brothers 2000* (1998).

**Bacall, Lauren** (Betty Joan Perske) (1924– ) American, born New York City; *To Have and Have Not* (1944), *The Big Sleep* (1946), *How to Marry a Millionaire* (1953), *The Fan* (1981), *Mr North* (1988), *Misery* (1990), *Prêt-À-Porter* (1994), *The Mirror Has Two Faces* (1996).

**Bacon, Kevin** (1958– ) American, born Philadelphia, Pennsylvania; *Animal House* (1978), *Friday the 13th* (1980), *Diner* (1982), Footloose (1984), *She's Having a Baby* (1988), *Tremors* (1989), *Flatliners* (1990), *The Big Picture* (1990), *JFK* (1991), *A Few Good Men* (1992), *The River Wild* (1994), *Apollo 13* (1995), *Sleepers* (1996), *Stir of Echoes* (1999).

**Baker, Joe Don** (1936– ) American, born Groesbeck, Texas; *Cool Hand Luke* (1967), *Mongo's Back in Town* (TV 1971), *Charley Varrick* (1972), *Walking Tall* (1972), *Mitchell* (1974), *The Natural* (1984), *Fletch* (1984), *Getting Even* (1985), *The Living Daylights* (1987), *The Killing Time* (1987), *Cape Fear* (1991), *Golden Eye* (1995), *Mars Attacks!* (1996).

**Baker, Tom** (1935– ) British, born Liverpool; *Nicholas and Alexandra* (1971), *Doctor Who* (TV 1975–81), *The Life and Loves of a She-Devil* (TV 1987), *The Chronicles of Narnia* (TV 1990).

**Baldwin, Alec** (1958– ) American, born Massapequa, New York; *Sweet Revenge* (TV 1984), *She's Having a Baby* (1988), *Beetlejuice* (1988), *Working Girl* (1988), *Married to the Mob* (1988), *The Hunt for Red October* (1989), *Miami Blues* (1990), *Alice* (1991), *Glengarry Glen Ross* (1992), *Malice* (1993), *The Shadow* (1994), *Notting Hill* (1999), *Pearl Harbor* (2001).

**Ball, Lucille** (1910–89) American, born Celaron, New York; *Top Hat* (1935), *Stage Door* (1937), *The Affairs of Annabel* (1938), *Five Came Back* (1939), *The*

*Big Street* (1942), *Du Barry was a Lady* (1943), *Without Love* (1945), *Ziegfeld Follies* (1946), *Easy to Wed* (1946), *Her Husband's Affairs* (1947), *Fancy Pants* (1950), *I Love Lucy* (TV 1951–5), *The Long Long Trailer* (1954), *The Facts of Life* (1956), *The Lucy Show* (TV 1962–8), *Yours Mine and Ours* (1968), *Here's Lucy* (TV 1968–73), *Life with Lucy* (TV 1976).

**Bancroft, Anne** (Anna Maria Italiano) (1931– ) American, born The Bronx, New York City; *The Miracle Worker* (1962), *The Graduate* (1968), *Silent Movie* (1976), *The Elephant Man* (1980), *84 Charing Cross Road* (1986), *Torch Song Trilogy* (1988), *Bert Rigby, You're a Fool* (1989), *The Assassin* (1992), *Malice* (1993), *How To Make an American Quilt* (1995), *Dracula: Dead and Loving It* (1995), *GI Jane* (1997).

**Bankhead, Tallulah** (1902–68) American, born Huntsville, Texas; *Tarnished Lady* (1931), *A Royal Scandal* (1945).

**Bardot, Brigitte** (Camille Javal) (1934– ) French, born Paris; *And God Created Woman* (1956), *En Cas de Malheur* (1958), *Viva Maria!* (1965).

**Barkin, Ellen** (1959– ) American, born The Bronx, New York City; *Diner* (1982), *The Adventures of Buckeroo Banzai* (1984), *The Big Easy* (1987), *Johnny Handsome* (1990), *Switch* (1991), *Mac* (1993), *Trigger Happy* (1996), *Drop Dead Gorgeous* (1999).

**Barrymore, Drew** (1975– ) American, born Los Angeles; *ET* (1982), *Firestarter* (1984), *Cat's Eye* (1984), *Poison Ivy* (1992), *Wayne's World 2* (1993), *Batman Forever* (1995), *Charlie's Angels* (2000).

**Barrymore, Ethel** (Edith Blythe) (1879–1959) American, born Philadelphia, Pennsylvania; *Rasputin and the Empress* (1932), *None but the Lonely Heart* (1944), *The Farmer's Daughter* (1947), *Young at Heart* (1954).

**Barrymore, John** (John Blythe) (1882–1942) American, born Philadelphia, Pennsylvania; *Dr Jekyll and Mr Hyde* (1920), *Show of Shows* (1929), *Rasputin and the Empress* (1932), *Dinner at 8* (1933), *Midnight* (1939), *The Great Profile* (1940).

**Barrymore, Lionel** (Lionel Blythe) (1878–1954) American, born Philadelphia, Pennsylvania; *Peter Ibbetson* (1917), *The Copperhead* (1918), *The Bells* (1926), *Sadie Thompson* (1928), *A Free Soul* (1931), *The Man I Killed* (1932), *Arsène Lupin* (1932), *Rasputin and the Empress* (1932), Grand Hotel (1932), *Dinner at 8* (1933), *David Copperfield* (1934), *Captains Courageous* (1937), *A Family Affair* (1937), *Young Dr Kildare* (1938), *Calling Dr Gillespie* (1942), *On Borrowed Time* (1939), *Three Wise Fools* (1946), *It's a Wonderful Life* (1946), *Duel in the Sun* (1946), *Key Largo* (1948).

**Basinger, Kim** (1953– ) American, born Athens, Georgia; *From Here to Eternity* (TV 1980), *Hard Country* (1981), *Never Say Never Again* (1983), *The Natural* (1984), *9½ Weeks* (1985), *No Mercy* (1986), *Blind Date* (1987), *Nadine* (1987), *Batman* (1989), *My Stepmother is an Alien* (1989), *The Marrying Man* (1990), *Wayne's World 2* (1993), *Prêt-À-Porter* (1994), *Kansas City* (1996), *LA Confidential* (1997).

**Bates, Alan** (1934– ) British, born Allestree, Derbyshire; *A Kind of Loving* (1962), *Whistle Down the Wind* (1962), *Zorba the Greek* (1965), *Far from the Madding Crowd* (1967), *Women in Love* (1969), *The Rose* (1979), *A Prayer for the Dying* (1987), *We Think the World of You* (1988), *Hamlet* (1990), *Grotesque* (1995).

**Béart, Emmanuelle** (1965– ) French, born Gassin; *Manon des Sources* (1986), *Mission: Impossible* (1996).

**Beatty, Ned** (1937– ) American, born Louisville, Kentucky; *Deliverance* (1972), *Nashville* (1975), *Network* (1976), *All the President's Men* (1976), *Exorcist II: The Heretic* (1977), *Superman* (1978), *Friendly Fire* (TV 1979), *Incredible Shrinking Woman* (1981), *Superman II* (1981), *The Toy* (1983), *Hopscotch* (1983), *Stoker Ace* (1983), *Restless Natives* (1986), *The Big Easy* (1987), *The Fourth Protocol* (1987), *Switching Channels* (1988), *The Unholy* (1988), *Midnight Crossing* (1988), *After the Rain* (1988), *Purple People Eater* (1988), *Just Cause* (1995).

**Beatty, Warren** (Henry Warren Beaty) (1937– ) American, born Richmond, Virginia; *Splendor in the Grass* (1961), *The Roman Spring of Mrs Stone* (1961), *Bonnie and Clyde* (1967), *The Parallax View* (1974), *Shampoo* (1975), *Heaven Can Wait* (1978), *Reds* (1981), *Ishtar* (1987), *Dick Tracy* (1990), *Bugsy* (1991), *Love Affair* (1994), *Bulworth* (1998).

**Bedelia, Bonnie** (1952– ) American, born New York City; *They Shoot Horses Don't They?* (1969), *Love and Other Strangers* (1970), *Heart Like a Wheel* (1983), *The Prince of Pennsylvania* (1988), *Die Hard* (1988), *Die Hard II: Die Harder* (1990), *Presumed Innocent* (1990), *Ghost in the Machine* (1996).

**Belmondo, Jean-Paul** (1933– ) French, born Neuilly-sur-Seine, Paris; *À Bout de Souffle* (1959), *Moderato Cantabile* (1960), *Un Singe en Hiver* (1962), *That Man from Rio* (1964).

**Belushi, James** (1954– ) American, born Chicago; *Trading Places* (1983), *Salvador* (1986), *About Last Night* (1987), *Red Heat* (1988), *Only the Lonely* (1991), *Curly Sue* (1991), *Last Action Hero* (1993), *Separate Lives* (1995), *Jingle All The Way* (1996), *Rake's Progress* (1997).

**Belushi, John** (1949–82) American, born Chicago; *Animal House* (1978), *1941* (1979), *The Blues Brothers* (1981), *Neighbors* (1981).

**Berenger, Tom** (1950– ) American, born Chicago; *The Big Chill* (1983), *Platoon* (1987), *Shoot to Kill* (1988), *Betrayed* (1988), *Last Rites* (1988), *Born On The Fourth Of July* (1990), *Sliver* (1993), *The Substitute* (1996).

**Bergen, Candice** (1946– ) American, born Beverly Hills, California; *The Group* (1966), *The Magus* (1969), *Carnal Knowledge* (1971), *Rich and Famous* (1981), *Gandhi* (1982).

**Bergman, Ingrid** (1915–82) Swedish, born Stockholm; *Intermezzo* (1939), *Dr Jekyll and Mr Hyde* (1941), *Casablanca* (1943), *For Whom the Bell Tolls* (1943), *Gaslight* (1943), *Spellbound* (1945), *Anastasia* (1946), *Notorious* (1946), *Stromboli* (1950), *Indiscreet*

(1958), *Cactus Flower* (1969), *Murder on the Orient Express* (1974), *Autumn Sonata* (1978).

**Berkoff, Stephen** (1937– ) British, born London; *Octopussy* (1983), *Beverly Hills Cop* (1984), *Rambo* (1985), *War and Remembrance* (TV 1989).

**Bernhardt, Sarah** (Henriette Rosine Bernhardt) (1884–1923) French, born Paris; *Queen Elizabeth* (1912).

**Bisset, Jacqueline** (1944– ) British, born Weybridge, Surrey; *Cul-de-Sac* (1966), *Casino Royale* (1967), *Bullitt* (1968), *The Grasshopper* (1970), *Murder on the Orient Express* (1974), *The Deep* (1977), *Rich and Famous* (1981), *Class* (1983), *Under the Volcano* (1984), *High Season* (1987), *Scenes from the Class Struggle in Beverly Hills* (1989), *Wild Orchid* (1990).

**Blessed, Brian** (1936– ) British, born Mexborough, South Yorkshire; *Z Cars* (TV 1962–5), *I, Claudius* (TV 1976), *Flash Gordon* (1980), *Henry V* (1989), *Robin Hood: Prince of Thieves* (1991), *Much Ado About Nothing* (1993), *Macbeth* (1997).

**Bloom, Claire** (1931– ) British, born London; *Look Back in Anger* (1959), *The Haunting* (1963), *The Spy who Came in from the Cold* (1966), *Clash of the Titans* (1981), *Crimes and Misdemeanors* (1989), *Daylight* (1996).

**Bogarde, Sir Dirk** (Derek Niven Van Den Bogaerde) (1921–99) Anglo-Dutch, born Hampstead, London; *A Tale of Two Cities* (1958), *Victim* (1961), *The Servant* (1963), *Darling* (1965), *Death in Venice* (1971), *Providence* (1977), *These Foolish Things* (1990).

**Bogart, Humphrey** (De Forest) (1899–1957) American, born New York City; *Broadway's Like That* (1930), *The Petrified Forest* (1936), *High Sierra* (1941), *The Maltese Falcon* (1941), *Casablanca* (1942), *To Have and Have Not* (1944), *The Big Sleep* (1946), *The Treasure of the Sierra Madre* (1947), *The African Queen* (1952), *The Barefoot Contessa* (1954), *The Caine Mutiny* (1954).

**Bonham-Carter, Helena** (1966– ) British, born London; *Oxford Blues* (1984), *Lady Jane* (1985), *A Room with a View* (1985), *Hamlet* (1990), *Where Angels Fear to Tread* (1991), *Howards End* (1992), *Frankenstein* (1994), *Twelfth Night* (1996), *Wings of the Dove* (1997), *Fight Club* (1999).

**Borgnine, Ernest** (Ermes Borgnino) (1918– ) American, born Hamden, Connecticut; *From Here to Eternity* (1953), *Bad Day at Black Rock* (1954), *Marty* (1955), *The Catered Affair* (1956), *The Best Things in Life Are Free* (1956), *The Vikings* (1958), *Pay or Die* (1960), *McHale's Navy* (TV 1962–5), *The Dirty Dozen* (1967), *Ice Station Zebra* (1968), *The Wild Bunch* (1969), *The Poseidon Adventure* (1972), *Convoy* (1978), *The Black Hole* (1979), *Escape from New York* (1981), *Deadly Blessing* (1981), *Codename: Wildgeese* (1984), *Airwolf* (TV 1984–6), *Mel* (1999).

**Bow, Clara** (1905–65) American, born Brooklyn, New York City; *Mantrap* (1926), *It* (1927), *Wings* (1927).

**Bowie, David** (David Robert Jones) (1947– ) British, born Brixton, South London; *The Man Who Fell to Earth* (1976), *Cat People* (1982), *The Hunger* (1983), *Merry Christmas Mr Lawrence* (1983), *Into the Night* (1985), *Labyrinth* (1986), *The Last Temptation of Christ* (1988), *Twin Peaks: Fire Walk With Me* (1992).

**Branagh, Kenneth** (1960– ) British, born Belfast; *High Season* (1987), *A Month in the Country* (1988), *Henry V* (1989), *Dead Again* (1991), *Peter's Friends* (1992), *Much Ado About Nothing* (1993), *Frankenstein* (1994), *In the Bleak Mid Winter* (1995), *Othello* (1995), *Hamlet* (1996), *Love's Labour's Lost* (2000).

**Brandauer, Klaus Maria** (1944– ) Austrian, born Alt Aussee; *Mephisto* (1980), *Never Say Never Again* (1983), *Colonel Red* (1984), *Out of Africa* (1985), *Streets of Gold* (1986), *Hanussen* (1988), *The Russia House* (1990), *White Fang* (1991), *Becoming Colette* (1991), *The Poet* (1996).

**Brando, Marlon** (1924– ) American, born Omaha, Nebraska; *A Streetcar Named Desire* (1951), *Viva Zapata* (1952), *Julius Caesar* (1953), *The Wild One* (1953), *On the Waterfront* (1954), *Guys and Dolls* (1955), *The Teahouse of the August Moon* (1956), *The Young Lions* (1958), *One-Eyed Jacks* (1961), *Mutiny on the Bounty* (1962), *The Chase* (1966), *The Godfather* (1972), *Last Tango in Paris* (1972), *Superman* (1978), *Apocalypse Now* (1979), *A Dry White Season* (1988), *The Freshman* (1990), *Hearts of Darkness* (doc) (1991), *Christopher Columbus: The Discovery* (1992), *Don Juan de Marco* (1995).

**Bridges, Jeff** (1949– ) American, born Los Angeles; *The Last Picture Show* (1971), *Hearts of the West* (1975), *Stay Hungry* (1976), *King Kong* (1976), *Somebody Killed Her Husband* (1978), *Winter Kills* (1979), *Tron* (1982), *Against All Odds* (1983), *Starman* (1984), *The Jagged Edge* (1985), *8 Million Ways to Die* (1985), *The Morning After* (1986), *Nadine* (1987), *Tucker: The Man and His Dream* (1987), *The Fabulous Baker Boys* (1989), *Texasville* (1990), *The Fisher King* (1991), *The Vanishing* (1992), *Fearless* (1993), *The Mirror Has Two Faces* (1996), *The Big Lebowski* (1998).

**Bridges, Lloyd** (1913–98) American, born San Leandro, California; *Home of the Brave* (1949), *Try and Get Me* (1951), *The Rainmaker* (1956), *Sea Hunt* (TV 1957–60), *The Goddess* (1958), *The Love War* (TV 1970), *Roots* (TV 1977), *Airplane* (1980), *Hot Shots!* (1991), *Honey, I Blew Up the Kid* (1992), *Hot Shots! Part Deux* (1993).

**Broderick, Matthew** (1963– ) American, born New York City; *War Games* (1983), *Ladyhawke* (1984), *Ferris Bueller's Day Off* (1986), *Biloxi Blues* (1988), *Torch Song Trilogy* (1988), *Family Business* (1989), *Glory* (1989), *The Freshman* (1990), *The Cable Guy* (1996), *Inspector Gadget* (1999).

**Bronson, Charles** (Charles Buchinski) (1920– ) American, born Ehrenfield, Pennsylvania; *Drumbeat* (1954), *Vera Cruz* (1954), *The Magnificent Seven* (1960), *This Property is Condemned* (1966), *The Dirty Dozen* (1967), *Chato's Land* (1972), *The Mechanic* (1972), *The Valachi Papers* (1972), *Death Wish* (1974), *Hard Times* (1975), *Telefon* (1977), *Death Wish II* (1982), *Death Wish III* (1985), *Death Wish IV* (1987),

*Murphy's Law* (1987), *Messenger of Death* (1988), *Kinjite: Forbidden Subjects* (1989), *The Indian Runner* (1991), *Death Wish V* (1993).

**Brooks, Louise** (Leslie Gettman) (1906–85) American, born Cherryvale, Kansas; *Pandora's Box* (1929), *Diary of a Lost Girl* (1930).

**Brooks, Mel** (Melvin Kaminski) (1926– ) American, born New York City; *The Twelve Chairs* (1969), *Blazing Saddles* (1974), *Silent Movie* (1976), *High Anxiety* (1978), *History of the World Part One* (1981), *Spaceballs* (1987), *Robin Hood: Men in Tights* (1993), *Dracula: Dead and Loving It* (1995), *Svitati* (1999).

**Brown, Bryan** (1947– ) Australian, born Panania; *A Town Like Alice* (TV 1981), *The Thorn Birds* (TV 1983), *Eureka Stockade* (TV 1985), *F/X: Murder by Illusion* (1985), *Rebel* (1985), *Taipan* (1985), *The Shiralee* (TV 1987), *Cocktail* (1988), *Gorillas in the Mist* (1988), *Dead Heart* (1996).

**Brynner, Yul** (1915–85) Swiss–Russian, naturalized American, born Sakhalin, Siberia; *The King and I* (1956), *The Brothers Karamazov* (1958), *The Magnificent Seven* (1960), *Return of the Seven* (1966).

**Burton, Richard** (Richard Walter Jenkins) (1925–84) British, born Pontrhydfen, S Wales: *My Cousin Rachel* (1952), *Alexander the Great* (1956), *Look Back in Anger* (1959), *Cleopatra* (1962), *The Night of the Iguana* (1964), *The Spy Who Came in from the Cold* (1965), *Who's Afraid of Virginia Woolf?* (1966), *The Taming of the Shrew* (1967), *Where Eagles Dare* (1969), *Equus* (1977), *Exorcist II: The Heretic* (1977), *Absolution* (1979), *1984* (1984).

**Caan, James** (1939– ) American, born The Bronx, New York City; *Brian's Song* (TV 1971), *The Godfather* (1972), *The Godfather, Part II* (1974), *Rollerball* (1975), *A Bridge Too Far* (1977), *Dick Tracy* (1990), *Misery* (1990), *Eraser* (1996), *Mickey Blue Eyes* (1999).

**Cage, Nicolas** (Nicholas Coppola) (1964– ) American, born Long Beach, California; *Fast Times at Ridgemont High* (1982), *Rumblefish* (1983), *Racing with the Moon* (1984), *The Cotton Club* (1984), *Birdy* (1985), *Peggy Sue Got Married* (1986), *Raising Arizona* (1987), *Moonstruck* (1987), *Vampire's Kiss* (1988), *Wild at Heart* (1990), *Wings of the Apache* (1990), *Leaving Las Vegas* (1995), *The Rock* (1996), *Face Off* (1997), *Captain Corelli's Mandolin* (2001).

**Cagney, James** (Francis Jr) (1899–1986) American, born New York City; *Public Enemy* (1931), *Lady Killer* (1933), *A Midsummer Night's Dream* (1935), *The Roaring Twenties* (1939), *Yankee Doodle Dandy* (1942), *White Heat* (1949), *Love Me or Leave Me* (1955), *Mister Roberts* (1955), *One, Two, or Three* (1961), *Ragtime* (1981).

**Caine, Michael** (Maurice Micklewhite) (1933– ) British, born London; *Zulu* (1963), *The Ipcress File* (1965), *Alfie* (1966), *The Italian Job* (1969), *Sleuth* (1972), *The Man Who Would Be King* (1975), *The Eagle Has Landed* (1976), *California Suite* (1978), *Beyond the Poseidon Adventure* (1979), *Dressed to Kill* (1980), *Death Trap* (1983), *Educating Rita* (1983), *Hannah and Her Sisters* (1986), *The Whistle Blower* (1987), *Without a Clue* (1988), *Bullseye* (1990), *Shock to the System* (1990), *Mr Destiny* (1990), *Noises Off* (1992), *Blue Ice* (1992), *Little Voice* (1998).

**Callow, Simon** (1949– ) British, born London; also stage; *Amadeus* (1984), *A Room With a View* (1985), *Maurice* (1987), *Four Weddings and a Funeral* (1994), *Shakespeare in Love* (1998).

**Candy, John** (1950–94) Canadian, born Toronto, Ontario; *Stripes* (1981), *Splash!* (1984), *Summer Rental* (1984), *Brewster's Millions* (1985), *Little Shop of Horrors* (1986), *Spaceballs* (1987), *Planes, Trains, and Automobiles* (1988), *The Great Outdoors* (1988), *Who's Harry Crumb?* (1989), *Uncle Buck* (1989), *Only the Lonely* (1991), *JFK* (1991), *Cool Runnings* (1993).

**Cardinale, Claudia** (1939– ) Italian, born Tunis, Tunisia; *The Pink Panther* (1963), *Once Upon a Time in the West* (1969), *Escape to Athena* (1979), *Fitzcarraldo* (1982), *A Man in Love* (1987), *Torrents of Spring* (1988), *Son of the Pink Panther* (1993), *La Goulette* (1997).

**Carlyle, Robert** (1961– ) British, born Glasgow; *Riff Raff* (1990), *Priest* (1994), *Hamish Macbeth* (TV 1994–7), *Carla's Song* (1996), *Trainspotting* (1996), *The Full Monty* (1997), *Face* (1997), *Angela's Ashes* (1999).

**Caron, Leslie** (Claire Margaret) (1931– ) French, born Boulogne-Billancourt, near Paris; *An American in Paris* (1951), *Lili* (1953), *The Glass Slipper* (1954), *Daddy Long Legs* (1955), *Gigi* (1958), *Fanny* (1961), *The L-Shaped Room* (1962), *Father Goose* (1964), *QB VII* (TV 1974).

**Carradine, John** (Richmond Reed Carradine) (1906–88) American, born New York City; *Five Came Back* (1939), *Stagecoach* (1939), *The Grapes of Wrath* (1940), *Bluebeard* (1944), *House of Frankenstein* (1945), *The Man Who Shot Liberty Valance* (1962), *Peggy Sue Got Married* (1986).

**Carrey, Jim** (James Eugene) (1962– ) Canadian, born Ontario; *Earth Girls are Easy* (1989), *The Mask* (1994), *Batman Forever* (1995), *Liar Liar* (1997), *The Truman Show* (1998).

**Cassavetes, John** (1929–89) American, born New York City; *Johnny Staccato* (TV 1959), *The Dirty Dozen* (1967), *Rosemary's Baby* (1969), *The Fury* (1978), *Minnie and Moskovitz* (1979), *Whose Life is it Anyway?* (1981), *Tempest* (1982).

**Cates, Phoebe** (1963– ) American, born New York City; *Fast Times at Ridgemont High* (1982), *Paradise* (1982), *Private School* (1983), *Gremlins* (1984), *Lace* (TV 1984), *Lace 2* (TV 1985), *Bright Lights, Big City* (1988), *Shag* (1988), *Gremlins 2: The New Batch* (1990), *Heart of Dixie* (1990), *Drop Dead Fred* (1991), *Princess Caraboo* (1994).

**Chamberlain, Richard** (1935– ) American, born Beverly Hills, California; *Dr Kildare* (TV 1961–6), *The Music Lovers* (1970), *Lady Caroline Lamb* (1972), *The Slipper and the Rose* (1976), *The Man in the Iron Mask* (1977), *The Last Wave* (1978), *Shogun* (TV 1980), *The Thorn Birds* (TV 1983), *Island Son* (TV 1989).

**Chaplin, Charlie** (Sir Charles Spencer) (1889–1977) British, born London; *The Champion* (1915), *The*

*Tramp* (1915), *Easy Street* (1917), *A Dog's Life* (1918), *Shoulder Arms* (1918), *The Kid* (1920), *The Idle Class* (1921), *The Gold Rush* (1924), *City Lights* (1931), *Modern Times* (1936), *The Great Dictator* (1940), *Limelight* (1952), *A King in New York* (1957).

**Chaplin, Geraldine** (1944– ) American, born Santa Monica, California; *Doctor Zhivago* (1965), *The Three Musketeers* (1974), *Nashville* (1975), *Hidden Talent* (1984), *White Mischief* (1987), *The Moderns* (1988), *Mama Turns 100* (1988), *Chaplin* (1992), *Age of Innocence* (1993), *Jane Eyre* (1996).

**Charisse, Cyd** (Tula Ellice Funklea) (1922– ) American, born Amarillo, Texas; *Ziegfeld Follies* (1945), *The Unfinished Dance* (1947), *Singin' in the Rain* (1952), *The Band Wagon* (1953), *Brigadoon* (1954), *It's Always Fair Weather* (1955), *Invitation to the Dance* (1957), *Two Weeks in Another Town* (1962), *That's Entertainment! III* (1994).

**Chase, Chevy** (Cornelius Crane Chase) (1943– ) American, born New York City; *Foul Play* (1978), *Caddyshack* (1980), *Seems Like Old Times* (1980), *Vacation* (1983), *European Vacation* (1984), *Fletch* (1985), *Spies Like Us* (1985), *The Three Amigos* (1986), *The Couch Trip* (1988), *Caddy Shack II* (1988), *Funny Farm* (1988), *Fletch Lives* (1988), *Christmas Vacation* (1989), *LA Story* (1991), *Hero* (1992), *Last Action Hero* (1993), *Vegas Vacation* (1997).

**Cher** (Cherilyn Sarkisian La Pier) (1946– ) American, born El Centro, California; *Silkwood* (1983), *Mask* (1985), *Moonstruck* (1987), *Suspect* (1987), *The Witches of Eastwick* (1987), *Mermaids* (1990), *Faithful* (1995), *Tea with Mussolini* (1999).

**Chevalier, Maurice** (1888–1972) French, born Paris; *The Innocents of Paris* (1929), *One Hour with You* (1932), *Love Me Tonight* (1932), *The Love Parade* (1932), *Gigi* (1958).

**Christie, Julie** (1941– ) British, born Chukua, Assam, India; *The Fast Lady* (1963), *Billy Liar* (1963), *Doctor Zhivago* (1965), *Darling* (1965), *Farenheit 451* (1966), *Far from the Madding Crowd* (1967), *The Go-Between* (1971), *Don't Look Now* (1974), *Shampoo* (1975), *Heaven Can Wait* (1978), *Heat and Dust* (1982), *Power* (1985), *The Gold Diggers* (1988), *Dragon Heart* (1996), *Hamlet* (1996).

**Clark, Petula** (1932– ) British, born Epsom, Surrey; *Finian's Rainbow* (1968), *Goodbye Mr Chips* (1969).

**Cleese, John** (Marwood) (1939– ) British, born Weston-super-Mare; *The Frost Report* (TV 1966), *At Last the 1948 Show* (TV 1967), *Monty Python's Flying Circus* (TV 1969–74), *Monty Python and the Holy Grail* (1974), *Fawlty Towers* (TV 1975, 1979), *The Life of Brian* (1979), *Time Bandits* (1982), *The Meaning of Life* (1983), *Clockwise* (1985), *A Fish Called Wanda* (1988), *Erik the Viking* (1989), *Splitting Heirs* (1993), *Frankenstein* (1994), *Fierce Creatures* (1996).

**Clift, (Edward) Montgomery** (1920–66) American, born Omaha, Nebraska; *Red River* (1946), *The Search* (1948), *A Place in the Sun* (1951), *From Here to Eternity* (1953), *Suddenly Last Summer* (1959), *Freud* (1962).

**Close, Glenn** (1947– ) American, born Greenwich, Connecticut; *The World According to Garp* (1982), *The Big Chill* (1983), *The Natural* (1984), *Something About Amelia* (TV 1984), *Jagged Edge* (1985), *Maxie* (1985), *Fatal Attraction* (1987), *Dangerous Liaisons* (1988), *Immediate Family* (1989), *Reversal of Fortune* (1990), *Hamlet* (1990), *Meeting Venus* (1991), *Hook* (1991), *The Paper* (1994), *Mary Reilly* (1996), *101 Dalmatians* (1996), *Mars Attacks!* (1996), *102 Dalmations* (2000).

**Cobb, Lee J** (Lee Jacoby) (1911–76) American, born New York City; *Golden Boy* (1939), *The Moon is Down* (1943), *Anna and the King of Siam* (1946), *The Dark Past* (1948), *On the Waterfront* (1954), *The Man in the Grey Flannel Suit* (1956), *Twelve Angry Men* (1957), *The Brothers Karamazov* (1958), *The Virginian* (TV 1962–6), *Come Blow Your Horn* (1963), *Death of a Salesman* (TV 1966), *Coogan's Bluff* (1968), *They Came to Rob Las Vegas* (1968), *The Young Lawyers* (TV 1970–1), *The Exorcist* (1973).

**Coburn, James** (1928– ) American, born Laurel, Nebraska; *The Magnificent Seven* (1960), *The Great Escape* (1963), *Charade* (1963), *Our Man Flint* (1966), *In Like Flint* (1966), *A Fistful of Dynamite* (1971), *California Suite* (1978), *Loving Couples* (1980), *Young Guns II* (1990), *Sister Act 2: Back in the Habit* (1993), *Maverick* (1995), *Eraser* (1996), *The Nutty Professor* (1996).

**Collins, Joan** (Henrietta) (1933– ) British, born London; *Lady Godiva Rides Again* (1951), *The Virgin Queen* (1955), *The Bitch* (1979), *Dynasty* (TV 1981–9), *Decadence* (1993), *In the Bleak Midwinter* (1995).

**Coltrane, Robbie** (Robin McMillan) (1950– ) British, born Rutherglen, near Glasgow; *Mona Lisa* (1986), *The Fruit Machine* (1987), *Tutti Frutti* (TV 1987), *Henry V* (1989), *Nuns on the Run* (1990), *The Pope must Die* (1991), *Cracker* (TV 1993–6), *Golden Eye* (1995).

**Connery, Sir Sean** (Thomas Connery) (1930– ) British, born Edinburgh; *Dr No* (1963), *Marnie* (1964), *From Russia With Love* (1964), *Goldfinger* (1965), *The Hill* (1965), *Thunderball* (1965), *A Fine Madness* (1966), *You Only Live Twice* (1967), *The Molly Maguires* (1969), *The Anderson Tapes* (1970), *Diamonds are Forever* (1971), *The Offence* (1972), *Zardoz* (1973), *Murder on the Orient Express* (1974), *The Man Who Would Be King* (1975), *Robin and Marian* (1976), *Meteor* (1979), *Outland* (1981), *Time Bandits* (1981), *Never Say Never Again* (1983), *Highlander* (1985), *The Name of the Rose* (1986), *The Untouchables* (1987), *The Presidio* (1988), *Indiana Jones and the Last Crusade* (1989), *Family Business* (1989), *The Hunt for Red October* (1990), *The Russia House* (1990), *Highlander II: The Quickening* (1991), *Robin Hood: Prince of Thieves* (1991), *Medicine Man* (1991), *The Rising Sun* (1992), *Dreadnought* (1992), *Broken Dreams* (1992), *First Knight* (1995), *Dragon Heart* (1996), *Entrapment* (1999).

**Conti, Tom** (1941– ) British, born Paisley; *Merry Christmas Mr Lawrence* (1983), *Reuben Reuben* (1983), *Saving Grace* (1984), *Miracles* (1985), *Heavenly Pursuits* (1985), *Shirley Valentine* (1989).

**Cooper, Gary** (Frank J Cooper) (1901–61) American, born Helena, Montana; *The Winning of Barbara Worth* (1926), *Lilac Time* (1928), *The Virginian* (1929), *A Farewell to Arms* (1932), *City Streets* (1932), *The Lives of a Bengal Lancer* (1935), *Sergeant York* (1941), *For Whom the Bell Tolls* (1943), *The Fountainhead* (1949), *High Noon* (1952), *Friendly Persuasion* (1956).

**Costner, Kevin** (1955– ) American, born Los Angeles; *Night Shift* (1982), *American Flyers* (1984), *Silverado* (1985), *The Untouchables* (1987), *No Way Out* (1987), *Bull Durham* (1988), *Field of Dreams* (1989), *Revenge* (1990), *Dances with Wolves* (1990), *Robin Hood: Prince of Thieves* (1991), *JFK* (1991), *The Bodyguard* (1992), *A Perfect World* (1993), *The War* (1994), *Waterworld* (1995), *Tin Cup* (1996).

**Cotten, Joseph** (1905–94) American, born Petersburg, Virginia; *Citizen Kane* (1941), *The Magnificent Ambersons* (1942), *Journey into Fear* (1942), *Shadow of a Doubt* (1943), *I'll Be Seeing You* (1945), *Portrait of Jennie* (1948), *The Third Man* (1949), *Niagara* (1952), *Tora! Tora! Tora!* (1971).

**Courtenay, Tom** (1937– ) British, born Hull; also stage; *The Loneliness of the Long Distance Runner* (1962), *Billy Liar* (1963), *Doctor Zhivago* (1965), *The Dresser* (1983), *Let Him Have It* (1991).

**Cox, Ronny** (1938– ) American, born Cloudcroft, New Mexico; *Deliverance* (1972), *The Onion Field* (1978), *Taps* (1981), *Vision Quest* (1985), *Beverly Hills Cop* (1985), *Beverly Hills Cop II* (1987), *Robocop* (1987), *St Elsewhere* (TV 1989), *Total Recall* (1990).

**Crawford, Joan** (Lucille Le Sueur) (1906–77) American, born San Antonio, Texas; *Our Dancing Daughters* (1928), *Our Blushing Brides* (1933), *Dancing Lady* (1933), *The Women* (1939), *Mildred Pierce* (1945), *Possessed* (1947), *What Ever Happened to Baby Jane?* (1962), *Trog* (1970).

**Crenna, Richard** (1926– ) American, born Los Angeles; *Pride of St Louis* (1952), *Star!* (1968), *Body Heat* (1981), *Death Ship* (1981), *First Blood* (1982), *Breakheart Pass* (1983), *Table for Five* (1983), *The Flamingo Kid* (1984), *The Rape of Richard Beck* (TV 1985), *Summer Rental* (1985), *Rambo* (1986), *Rambo III* (1988), *Leviathan* (1989), *Hot Shots! Part Deux* (1993).

**Crosby, Bing** (Harry Lillis Crosby) (1904–77) American, born Tacoma, Washington; *King of Jazz* (1930), *Mississippi* (1935), *Anything Goes* (1936), *Road to Singapore* (1940), *Road to Zanzibar* (1941), *Holiday Inn* (1942), *Road to Morrocco* (1942), *Going My Way* (1944), *The Bells of St Mary's* (1945), *Blue Skies* (1946), *A Connecticut Yankee in King Arthur's Court* (1949), *White Christmas* (1954), *The Country Girl* (1954), *High Society* (1956), *Road to Hong Kong* (1962).

**Cruise, Tom** (Tom Cruise Mapother IV) (1962– ) American, born Syracuse, New York; *Taps* (1981), *Endless Love* (1981), *The Outsiders* (1983), *Legend* (1984), *Risky Business* (1984), *Top Gun* (1985), *The Color of Money* (1986), *Cocktail* (1988), *Rain Man* (1988), *Born on the Fourth of July* (1989), *Days of Thunder* (1990), *Far and Away* (1992), *A Few Good Men* (1992), *The Firm* (1993), *Interview with the Vampire* (1994), *Mission: Impossible* (1996), *Jerry Maguire* (1996), *Eyes Wide Shut* (1999).

**Crystal, Billy** (1947– ) American, born Long Beach, New York; *Throw Momma from the Train* (1987), *The Princess Bride* (1988), *When Harry met Sally ...* (1989), *City Slickers* (1991), *Mr Saturday Night* (1992), *Hamlet* (1996), *Analyze This* (1999).

**Culp, Robert** (1930– ) American, born Oakland, California; *I Spy* (TV 1965–7), *Bob and Carol and Ted and Alice* (1969), *The Greatest American Hero* (TV 1981–2), *The Gladiator* (TV 1986), *The Pelican Brief* (1994), *Spy Hard* (1996).

**Curtis, Jamie Lee** (1958– ) American, born Los Angeles; *Operation Petticoat* (TV 1978), *Halloween* (1979), *The Fog* (1980), *Halloween II* (1981), *Love Letters* (1983), *Trading Places* (1983), *Perfect* (1985), *A Fish Called Wanda* (1988), *Dominick and Eugene* (1988), *Blue Steel* (1990), *My Girl* (1991), *Forever Young* (1992), *My Girl 2* (1994), *Fierce Creatures* (1996), *Virus* (1999).

**Curtis, Tony** (Bernard Schwarz) (1925– ) American, born New York City; *Houdini* (1953), *Trapeze* (1956), *The Vikings* (1958), *Some Like it Hot* (1959), *Spartacus* (1960), *The Boston Strangler* (1968), The Persuaders (TV 1971–2).

**Cusack, Cyril** (James) (1910–93) Irish, born Durban, South Africa; *Odd Man Out* (1947), *The Blue Lagoon* (1949), *Jacqueline* (1965), *The Spy Who Came in From the Cold* (1965), *Fahrenheit 451* (1966), *Day of the Jackal* (1973), *1984* (1984), *Little Dorrit* (1987), *My Left Foot* (1989), *The Fool* (1990).

**Cushing, Peter** (1913–94) British, born Kenley, Surrey; *The Man in the Iron Mask* (1939), *Hamlet* (1947), *1984* (TV 1955), *The Curse of Frankenstein* (1957), *Dracula* (1958), *The Mummy* (1959), *The Hound of the Baskervilles* (1959), *Cash on Demand* (1963), *Dr Who and the Daleks* (1965), *Sherlock Holmes* (TV 1968), *Tales from the Crypt* (1972), *Horror Express* (1972), *Star Wars* (1977), *Biggles* (1988).

**Dafoe, Willem** (1955– ) American, born Appleton, Wisconsin; *Heaven's Gate* (1980), *Platoon* (1986), *The Last Temptation of Christ* (1988), *Mississippi Burning* (1988), *Triumph of the Spirit* (1989), *Born on the Fourth of July* (1989), *Wild At Heart* (1990), *Cry Baby* (1990), *Light Sleeper* (1992), *Body of Evidence* (1992), *Tom and Viv* (1994), *Clear and Present Danger* (1994), *The English Patient* (1996), *Shadow of the Vampire* (2000).

**Dalton, Timothy** (1946– ) British, born Wales; *The Lion in Winter* (1968), *Wuthering Heights* (1970), *Mary Queen of Scots* (1971), *Agatha* (1979), *Flash Gordon* (1980), *Centennial* (TV 1981–2), *The Living Daylights* (1987), *License to Kill* (1989), *The Rocketeer* (1991), *Last Action Hero* (1993), *Johnny Loves Suzy* (1996).

**Dance, Charles** (1946– ) British, born Rednal, Worcestershire; *For Your Eyes Only* (1981), *The Jewel in the Crown* (TV 1984), *The Golden Child* (1985), *Plenty* (1985), *Good Morning Babylon* (1987), *White*

*Mischief* (1987), *Pascali's Island* (1988), *Phantom of the Opera* (TV 1990), *Last Action Hero* (1993).

**D'Angelo, Beverly** (1953– ) American, born Columbus, Ohio; *First Love* (1977), *Every Which Way But Loose* (1978), *Hair* (1979), *Coal Miner's Daughter* (1980), *Paternity* (1981), *Honky Tonk Freeway* (1981), *Vacation* (1984), *European Vacation* (1985), *Aria* (1987), *High Spirits* (1988), *Christmas Vacation* (1989), *The Pope Must Die* (1991), *Judgement Day* (1993), *Vegas Vacation* (1997).

**Daniels, William** (1927– ) American, born Brooklyn, New York City; *Captain Nice* (TV 1966), *The Graduate* (1967), *1776* (1972), *The Parallax View* (1974), *The Blue Lagoon* (1981), *Reds* (1981), *St Elsewhere* (TV 1982–9), *Blind Date* (1987).

**Danson, Ted** (1947– ) American, born Flagstaff, Arizona; *The Onion Field* (1979), *Body Heat* (1981), *Cheers* (1982–93), *Creepshow* (1982), *Something About Amelia* (TV 1984), *Three Men and a Baby* (1988), *Cousins* (1989), *Dad* (1990), *Three Men and a Little Lady* (1990), *Made In America* (1993), *Loch Ness* (1995), *Saving Private Ryan* (1998).

**Darren, James** (James Ercolani) (1936– ) American, born Philadelphia, Pennsylvania; *Gidget* (1959), *The Guns of Navarone* (1961), *For Those Who Think Young* (1964), *Time Tunnel* (TV 1966), *T J Hooker* (TV 1983–6).

**Davenport, Nigel** (1928– ) British, born Shelford, Cambridge; *A Man for All Seasons* (1966), *The Virgin Soldiers* (1969), *Living Free* (1972), *The Island of Dr Moreau* (1977), *Longitude* (2000).

**Davis, Bette** (Ruth Elizabeth Davis) (1908–89) American, born Lowell, Massachusetts; *Bad Sister* (1931), *Dangerous* (1935), *Jezebel* (1938), *The Great Lie* (1941), *All About Eve* (1950), *What Ever Happened to Baby Jane?* (1962), *Strangers* (TV 1979), *The Whales of August* (1987).

**Davis, Geena** (1957– ) American, born Wareham, Massachusetts; *Tootsie* (1982), *Fletch* (1985), *The Fly* (1986), *Beetlejuice* (1988), *The Accidental Tourist* (1989), *Thelma and Louise* (1991), *A League of Their Own* (1993), *The Long Kiss Goodnight* (1996).

**Davis, Judy** (1956– ) Australian, born Perth; *My Brilliant Career* (1979), *Who Dares Wins* (1982), *A Passage to India* (1987), *High Tide* (1987), *Naked Lunch* (1991), *Barton Fink* (1991), *Husbands and Wives* (1992), *Deconstructing Harry* (1997).

**Day, Doris** (Doris von Kappelhoff) (1924– ) American, born Cincinnati, Ohio; *Romance on the High Seas* (1948), *Storm Warning* (1950), *Calamity Jane* (1953), *Young at Heart* (1954), *Love Me or Leave Me* (1955), *The Pajama Game* (1957), *Pillow Talk* (1959), *That Touch of Mink* (1962), *With Six You Get Egg Roll* (1968), *The Doris Day Show* (TV 1968–73).

**Day-Lewis, Daniel** (1958– ) Irish, born London; *Gandhi* (1983), *My Beautiful Laundrette* (1985), *Room with a View* (1985), *The Unbearable Lightness of Being* (1988), *Stars and Bars* (1988), *Nanou* (1988), *My Left Foot* (1989), *The Last of the Mohicans* (1992), *Age of Innocence* (1993), *In the Name of the Father* (1993), *The Crucible* (1996), *The Boxer* (1998).

**Dean, James** (Byron) (1931–55) American, born Fairmount, Indiana; *East of Eden* (1955), *Rebel without a Cause* (1955), *Giant* (1956).

**De Havilland, Olivia** (1916– ) British, born Tokyo, Japan; *Midsummer Night's Dream* (1935), *The Adventures of Robin Hood* (1938), *Gone with the Wind* (1939), *The Dark Mirror* (1946), *To Each His Own* (1946), *The Heiress* (1949).

**De Mornay, Rebecca** (1962– ) American, born Los Angeles; *Risky Business* (1984), *Runaway Train* (1985), *And God Created Woman* (1988), *Dealers* (1988), *Feds* (1988), *Backdraft* (1991), *The Hand that Rocks the Cradle* (1993), *The Winner* (1996).

**Dench, Dame Judi** (Judith Olivia Dench) (1934– ) British, born York; *The Third Secret* (1964), *Four in the Morning* (1966), *A Fine Romance* (TV 1981–4), *A Room With a View* (1985), *84 Charing Cross Road* (1987), *Henry V* (1989), *Jack and Sarah* (1995), *Hamlet* (1996), *Mrs Brown* (1997), *Shakespeare in Love* (1998), *Chocolat* (2000).

**Deneuve, Catherine** (Catherine Dorleac) (1943– ) French, born Paris; *Les Parapluies de Cherbourg* (1964), *Repulsion* (1965), *Belle de Jour* (1967), *Tristana* (1970), *The Hunger* (1983), *Indochine* (1991), *Les Voleurs* (1996).

**De Niro, Robert** (1943– ) American, born New York City; *Bang the Drum Slowly* (1973), *Mean Streets* (1973), *The Godfather, Part II* (1974), *1900* (1976), *Taxi Driver* (1976), *The Deer Hunter* (1978), *Raging Bull* (1980), *King of Comedy* (1982), *Brazil* (1985), *Angel Heart* (1987), *The Untouchables* (1987), *Midnight Run* (1988), *Jacknife* (1989), *Stanley & Iris* (1989), *We're No Angels* (1990), *Goodfellas* (1990), *Awakenings* (1990), *Backdraft* (1991), *Cape Fear* (1991), *The Mistress* (1992), *Mad Dog and Glory* (1992), *Night and The City* (1992), *This Boy's Life* (1992), *Frankenstein* (1994), *Casino* (1995), *Heat* (1995), *Sleepers* (1996), *Jackie Brown* (1998), *Ronin* (1998).

**Dennehy, Brian** (1940– ) American, born Bridgeport, Connecticut; *Foul Play* (1978), *Butch and Sundance* (1979), *Big Shamus Little Shamus* (TV 1979), *First Blood* (1982), *Gorky Park* (1983), *Cocoon* (1985), *Silverado* (1985), *Legal Eagles* (1986), *Belly of an Architect* (1987), *Best Seller* (1987), *Miles from Home* (1988), *Cocoon: The Return* (1988), *Return to Snowy River Part II* (1988), *Presumed Innocent* (1990).

**Depardieu, Gérard** (1948– ) French, born Châteauroux; *1900* (1976), *Get Out Your Handkerchiefs* (1977), *Loulou* (1980), *The Last Metro* (1980), *The Return of Martin Guerre* (1981), *Danton* (1982), *The Moon in the Gutter* (1983), *Police* (1985), *Jean de Florette* (1986), *Streets of Departure* (1986), *Under the Sun of Satan* (1987), *The Woman Next Door* (1987), *Cyrano de Bergerac* (1990), *Green Card* (1990), *Uranus* (1991), *Merci la Vie* (1991), *Mon Père, Ce Héros* (1991), *Tous les Matins du Monde* (1991), *Christopher Columbus* (1992), *Germinal* (1992), *Le Colonel Chabert* (1994), *Les Anges Gardiens* (1995),

*Unhook the Stars* (1996), *Hamlet* (1996), *Le Gaulois* (1997).

**Depp, Johnny** (1963– ) American, born Owensboro, Kentucky; *Nightmare on Elm Street* (1994), *Platoon* (1986), *Cry Baby* (1990), *Edward Scissorhands* (1990), *What's Eating Gilbert Grape?* (1993), *Ed Wood* (1994), *Don Juan de Marco* (1995), *Sleepy Hollow* (1999).

**Derek, Bo** (Mary Cathleen Collins) (1956– ) American, born Long Beach, California; *Orca* (1977), *'10'* (1979), *Tarzan, the Ape Man* (1981), *Bolero* (1984), *Ghosts Can't Do It* (1990), *Tommy Boy* (1995).

**Dern, Bruce** (MacLeish) (1936– ) American, born Chicago; *Marnie* (1964), *They Shoot Horses Don't They?* (1969), *Silent Running* (1972), *The Great Gatsby* (1974), *Family Plot* (1975), *Smile* (1975), *Coming Home* (1978), *The Driver* (1978), *Tattoo* (1981), *Middle Age Crazy* (1981), *That Championship Season* (1982), *Big Town* (1987), *1969* (1988), *World Gone Wild* (1988), *The 'Burbs* (1989), *After Dark My Sweet* (1990), *Last Man Standing* (1996), *The Haunting* (1999).

**Dern, Laura** (Elizabeth) (1966– ) American, born California; *Mask* (1985), *Smooth Talk* (1986), *Blue Velvet* (1986), *Wild at Heart* (1990), *Jurassic Park* (1993), *Citizen Ruth* (1996), *October Sky* (1999).

**De Vito, Danny** (1944– ) American, born Neptune, New Jersey; *One Flew Over the Cuckoo's Nest* (1975), *Taxi* (TV 1978–82), *Romancing the Stone* (1983), *Terms of Endearment* (1984), *The Jewel of the Nile* (1985), *Ruthless People* (1986), *Throw Momma from the Train* (1987), *Twins* (1988), *War of the Roses* (1989), *Batman Returns* (1992), *Renaissance Man* (1994), *Junior* (1994), *Get Shorty* (1995), *Matilda* (1996), *LA Confidential* (1997), *Man on the Moon* (1999).

**Dietrich, Marlene** (Maria Magdalena von Losch) (1901–92) German–American, born Berlin; *The Blue Angel* (1930), *Morocco* (1930), *Blond Venus* (1932), *Shanghai Express* (1932), *The Scarlett Empress* (1934), *The Devil is a Woman* (1935), *Desire* (1936), *Destry Rides Again* (1939), *A Foreign Affair* (1948), *Rancho Notorious* (1952), *Judgement at Nuremberg* (1961).

**Dillon, Matt** (1964– ) American, born Larchmont, New York; *Tex* (1982), *The Outsiders* (1983), *Rumble Fish* (1983), *The Flamingo Kid* (1984), *Target* (1985), *Big Town* (1987), *Kansas* (1988), *Drugstore Cowboy* (1989), *A Kiss Before Dying* (1991), *Singles* (1992), *Malcolm X* (1992), *Golden Gate* (1994), *Mr Wonderful* (1994), *Albino Alligator* (1996).

**Donat, Robert** (1905–58) British, born Manchester; *The Count of Monte Cristo* (1934), *The Thirty-Nine Steps* (1935), *The Ghost Goes West* (1936), *The Citadel* (1938), *Goodbye Mr Chips* (1939), *The Winslow Boy* (1948), *The Inn of the Sixth Happiness* (1958).

**Donohoe, Amanda** (c.1965– ) British; *Castaway* (1987), *The Lair of the White Worm* (1988), *The Rainbow* (1989), *LA Law* (TV 1990–2), *Paper Mask* (1990), *The Madness of King George* (1994), *The Last Day* (1996), *Liar Liar* (1997).

**Dors, Diana** (Diana Fluck) (1931–84) British, born Swindon, Wiltshire; *Oliver Twist* (1948), *Yield to the Night* (1956), *Deep End* (1970), *There's a Girl in My Soup* (1970), *The Amazing Mr Blunden* (1972), *Theatre of Blood* (1973), *Steaming* (1984).

**Douglas, Kirk** (Issur Danielovitch Demsky) (1916– ) American, born Amsterdam, New York; *The Strange Love of Martha Ivers* (1946), *Lust for Life* (1956), *Gunfight at the OK Corral* (1957), *Paths of Glory* (1957), *The Vikings* (1958), *Spartacus* (1960), *The Man from Snowy River* (1982), *Oscar* (1991), *Greedy* (1994).

**Douglas, Michael** (1944– ) American, born New Brunswick, New Jersey; *The Streets of San Francisco* (TV 1972–5), *Coma* (1978), *The China Syndrome* (1980), *The Star Chamber* (1983), *Romancing the Stone* (1984), *The Jewel of the Nile* (1985), *Fatal Attraction* (1987), *Wall Street* (1987), *Black Rain* (1989), *War of the Roses* (1989), *Shining Through* (1991), *Basic Instinct* (1992), *Falling Down* (1993), *Disclosure* (1994), *The Ghost in the Darkness* (1996), *The Game* (1997), *Traffic* (2000).

**Dreyfuss, Richard** (1947– ) American, born Brooklyn, New York City; *American Graffiti* (1973), *The Apprenticeship of Duddy Kravitz* (1974), *Jaws* (1975), *Close Encounters of the Third Kind* (1977), *The Goodbye Girl* (1977), *Whose Life is it Anyway?* (1981), *Down and Out in Beverly Hills* (1986), *Stakeout* (1987), *Tin Men* (1987), *Moon over Parador* (1988), *Always* (1989), *The Proud and the Free* (1991), *What About Bob?* (1991), *Prisoners of Honor* (1991), *Rosencrantz and Guilderstern are Dead* (1991), *Lost in Yonkers* (1993), *Another Stakeout* (1993), *The American President* (1995), *Trigger Happy* (1996).

**Dunaway, (Dorothy) Faye** (1941– ) American, born Bascom, Florida; *Bonnie and Clyde* (1967), *Little Big Man* (1970), *The Getaway* (1972), *Chinatown* (1974), *The Towering Inferno* (1974), *Network* (1976), *The Eyes of Laura Mars* (1978), *The Champ* (1979), *Mommie Dearest* (1981), *Barfly* (1987), *Midnight Crossing* (1988), *Burning Secret* (1988), *The Handmaid's Tale* (1990), *Scorchers* (1991), *Silhouette* (TV 1991), *Three Weeks in Jerusalem* (1991), *American Dreamers* (1992), *Don Juan de Marco* (1995), *Albino Alligator* (1996).

**Durbin, Deanna** (Edna Mae Durbin) (1921– ) Canadian, born Winnipeg, Manitoba; *Three Smart Girls* (1936), *One Hundred Men and a Girl* (1937), *Mad About Music* (1938), *That Certain Age* (1938), *Three Smart Girls Grow Up* (1939), *It Started With Eve* (1941), *Christmas Holiday* (1944), *Lady on a Train* (1945).

**Duvall, Robert** (1930– ) American, born San Diego, California; *To Kill a Mockingbird* (1963), *The Godfather* (1972), *The Godfather, Part II* (1974), *Ike* (TV 1979), *Apocalypse Now* (1979), *The Great Santini* (1980), *Tender Mercies* (1983), *The Natural* (1984), *Colors* (1988), *The Handmaid's Tale* (1990), *Days of Thunder* (1990), *Convicts* (1991), *Newsies* (1992), *An American Legend* (1993), *The Scarlet Letter* (1995), *Phenomenon* (1996), *A Civil Action* (1998).

**Duvall, Shelley** (1949– ) American, born Houston, Texas; *Thieves Like Us* (1974), *Annie Hall* (1977), *The*

*Shining* (1980), *Popeye* (1980), *Time Bandits* (1981), *Roxanne* (1987), *Suburban Commando* (1991), *The Portrait of a Lady* (1996), *Home Fries* (1998).

**Eastwood, Clint** (1930– ) American, born San Francisco, California; *Rawhide* (TV 1958–65), *A Fistful of Dollars* (1964), *For a Few Dollars More* (1965), *The Good, The Bad, and the Ugly* (1966), *Paint Your Wagon* (1969), *Coogan's Bluff* (1968), *Where Eagles Dare* (1969), *Play Misty for Me* (1971), *Dirty Harry* (1972), *High Plains Drifter* (1973), *Magnum Force* (1973), *The Enforcer* (1976), *The Outlaw Josey Wales* (1976), *Every Which Way But Loose* (1978), *Escape from Alcatraz* (1979), *Any Which Way You Can* (1980), *Firefox* (1982), *Honky Tonk Man* (1982), *Sudden Impact* (1983), *Tightrope* (1984), *Heartbreak Ridge* (1986), *Pink Cadillac* (1989), *The Dead Pool* (1989), *White Hunter Black Heart* (1990), *The Rookie* (1990), *Unforgiven* (1992), *In the Line of Fire* (1993), *A Perfect World* (1993), *The Bridges of Madison County* (1995), *Absolute Power* (1997), *True Crime* (1999).

**Eden, Barbara** (Barbara Huffman) (1934– ) American, born Tucson, Arizona; *Voyage to the Bottom of the Sea* (1961), *I Dream of Jeannie* (TV 1965–70), *Harper Valley PTA* (1978), *Harper Valley PTA* (TV 1981).

**Ekberg, Anita** (1931– ) Swedish, born Malmö; *La Dolce Vita* (1959), *The Summer is Short* (1962).

**Ekland, Britt** (Britt-Marie Ekland) (1942– ) Swedish, born Stockholm; *The Man with the Golden Gun* (1974), *Casanova* (1977), *Scandal* (1989), *Beverly Hills Vamp* (1989).

**Elliott, Denholm** (1922–92) British, born London; *Nothing but the Best* (1964), *Here We Go Round the Mulberry Bush* (1967), *A Bridge too Far* (1977), *Raiders of the Lost Ark* (1981), *Brimstone and Treacle* (1982), *Trading Places* (1983), *The Razor's Edge* (1984), *A Private Function* (1984), *A Room with a View* (1985), *Defence of the Realm* (1985), *Maurice* (1987), *Indiana Jones and the Last Crusade* (1989), *Toy Soldiers* (1991).

**Estevez, Emilio** (1962– ) American, born New York City; *The Outsiders* (1983), *Repo Man* (1984), *Breakfast Club* (1984), *St Elmo's Fire* (1985), *Stakeout* (1987), *Young Guns* (1988), *Young Guns 2* (1990), *Freejack* (1991), *The Mighty Ducks* (1992), *Another Stakeout* (1993), *Judgement Night* (1993), *Mission: Impossible* (1996).

**Evans, Dame Edith** (1888–1976) British, born London; *The Queen of Spades* (1948), *The Importance of Being Earnest* (1951).

**Everett, Rupert** (1960– ) British, born Norfolk; *Another Country* (1984), *Dance with a Stranger* (1985), *The Comfort of Strangers* (1990), *Prêt-À-Porter* (1994), *The Madness of King George* (1994), *My Best Friend's Wedding* (1997), *An Ideal Husband* (1999).

**Fairbanks, Douglas, Sr** (Douglas Elton Ullman) (1883–1939) American, born Denver, Colorado; *The Mark of Zorro* (1920), *The Three Musketeers* (1921), *Robin Hood* (1922), *The Thief of Baghdad* (1924), *The Black Pirate* (1926).

**Fairbanks, Douglas, Jr** (1909–2000) American, born New York City; *Catherine the Great* (1934), *The Prisoner of Zenda* (1937), *Sinbad the Sailor* (1947).

**Falk, Peter** (1927– ) American, born New York City; *It's a Mad, Mad, Mad, Mad, World* (1963), *The Great Race* (1965), *Columbo* (TV 1971–8), *The Princess Bride* (1987), *Cookie* (1988), *Vibes* (1988), *Wings of Desire* (1988), *Aunt Julia and the Scriptwriter* (1991), *The Player* (1992), *Pronto* (1996).

**Farrow, Mia** (Maria Farrow) (1945– ) American, born Los Angeles; *Peyton Place* (TV 1964–7), *Rosemary's Baby* (1968), *Blind Terror* (1971), *The Great Gatsby* (1973), *Death on the Nile* (1978), *A Wedding* (1978), *A Midsummer Night's Sex Comedy* (1982), *The Purple Rose of Cairo* (1985), *Hannah and Her Sisters* (1986), *Another Woman* (1988), *New York Stories* (1989), *Alice* (1991), *Shadows and Fogs* (1992), *Husbands and Wives* (1992), *Wolf* (1993), *Reckless* (1995), *Coming Soon* (1999).

**Fell, Norman** (1924–98) American, born Philadelphia, Pennsylvania; *The Graduate* (1967), *Bullitt* (1968), *The Man from UNCLE* (TV 1968), *Three's Company* (TV 1977–8), *The Ropers* (TV 1979–80), *Paternity* (1981).

**Field, Sally** (1946– ) American, born Pasadena, California; *Gidget* (TV 1965), *The Flying Nun* (TV 1967–9), *Sybil* (TV 1976), *Stay Hungry* (1976), *Heroes* (1977), *Smokey and the Bandit* (1977), *Hooper* (1978), *Norma Rae* (1979), *Beyond the Poseidon Adventure* (1979), *Smokey and the Bandit II* (1980), *Absence of Malice* (1981), *Places in the Heart* (1984), *Punchline* (1988), *Steel Magnolias* (1990), *Not Without my Daughter* (1991), *Mrs Doubtfire* (1993), *Forrest Gump* (1994), *A Cooler Climate* (1999).

**Fields, W C** (William Claude Dunkenfield) (1879–1946) American, born Philadelphia, Pennsylvania; *Pool Sharks* (1915), *International House* (1933), *It's a Gift* (1934), *The Old Fashioned Way* (1934), *David Copperfield* (1935), *My Little Chickadee* (1940), *The Bank Dick* (1940), *Never Give a Sucker an Even Break* (1941).

**Fiennes, Ralph** (Ralph Nathanial Fiennes) (1962– ) British; *Wuthering Heights* (1992), *Schindler's List* (1994), *Quiz Show* (1994), *The English Patient* (1996), *Oscar and Lucinda* (1998).

**Finch, Peter** (Frederick George Peter Ingle Finch) (1916–77) British, born London; *The Shiralee* (1957), *The Nun's Story* (1959), *No Love for Johnnie* (1961), *Far from the Madding Crowd* (1967), *Sunday, Bloody Sunday* (1971), *Network* (1976).

**Finney, Albert** (1936– ) British, born Salford, Lancashire; *The Entertainer* (1960), *Saturday Night and Sunday Morning* (1960), *Tom Jones* (1963), *Charlie Bubbles* (1968), *Murder on the Orient Express* (1974), *Shoot the Moon* (1981), *Annie* (1982), *The Dresser* (1983), *Miller's Crossing* (1990), *The Playboys* (1992), *Erin Brockovich* (2000).

**Firth, Peter** (1953– ) British, born Bradford, Yorkshire; *Equus* (1973), *Tess* (1980), *Life Force* (1985), *Letter to Brezhnev* (1985), *A State of Emergency* (1986), *Shadowlands* (1993), *Mighty Joe Young* (1999).

**Fisher, Carrie** (1956– ) American, born Beverly Hills, California; *Shampoo* (1975), *Star Wars* (1977), *The Blues Brothers* (1980), *The Empire Strikes Back* (1980), *Under the Rainbow* (1981), *Return of the Jedi* (1983), *The Man With One Red Shoe* (1985), *Hannah and Her Sisters* (1986), *The 'Burbs* (1989), *When Harry Met Sally ...* (1989), *Loverboy* (1990), *Sibling Rivalry* (1990), *Drop Dead Fred* (1991), *Soapdish* (1991), *This is My Life* (1991), *So I Married an Axe Murderer* (1992), *Scream 3* (2000).

**Fletcher, Louise** (1934– ) American, born Birmingham, Alabama; *One Flew Over the Cuckoo's Nest* (1975), *Exorcist II: The Heretic* (1977), *The Cheap Detective* (1978), *Brainstorm* (1983), *Firestarter* (1984), *The Boy Who Could Fly* (1985), *Two Moon Junction* (1988).

**Flynn, Errol** (1909–59) Australian–American, born Hobart, Tasmania; *In the Wake of the Bounty* (1933), *Captain Blood* (1935), *The Charge of the Light Brigade* (1936), *The Adventures of Robin Hood* (1938), *The Sea Hawk* (1940), *The Sun Also Rises* (1957).

**Fonda, Henry** (James) (1905–82) American, born Grand Island, Nebraska; *The Moon's Our Home* (1936), *A Farmer Takes A Wife* (1938), Young Mr Lincoln (1939), *The Grapes of Wrath* (1940), *The Lady Eve* (1941), *The Oxbow Incident* (1943), *My Darling Clementine* (1946), *Twelve Angry Men* (1957), *Stage Struck* (1957), *Fail Safe* (1964), *The Boston Strangler* (1968), *On Golden Pond* (1981).

**Fonda, Jane** (Seymour) (1937– ) American, born New York City; *Walk on the Wild Side* (1961), *Barbarella* (1968), *They Shoot Horses Don't They?* (1969), *Klute* (1971), *Julia* (1977), *Coming Home* (1978), *The Electric Horseman* (1979), *The China Syndrome* (1980), *Nine to Five* (1981), *On Golden Pond* (1981), *The Dollmaker* (TV 1983), *The Morning After* (1986), *Old Gringo* (1989), *Stanley and Iris* (1989).

**Fonda, Peter** (1939– ) American, born New York City; *Easy Rider* (1969), *Futureworld* (1976), *Cannonball Run* (1981), *Mercenary Fighters* (1988), *Escape From LA* (1996).

**Fontaine, Joan** (Joan de Havilland) (1917– ) British, born Tokyo, Japan; *Rebecca* (1940), *Suspicion* (1941), *Jane Eyre* (1943), *Frenchman's Creek* (1944), *From This Day Forward* (1946), *Letter from an Unknown Woman* (1948), *Born to Be Bad* (1950).

**Ford, Harrison** (1942– ) American, born Chicago; *Dead Heat on a Merry-Go-Round* (1966), *American Graffiti* (1974), *Star Wars* (1977), *Heroes* (1977), *Force 10 from Navarone* (1978), *The Frisco Kid* (1979), *Hanover Street* (1979), *Apocalypse Now* (1979), *The Empire Strikes Back* (1980), *Raiders of the Lost Ark* (1981), *Blade Runner* (1982), *Return of the Jedi* (1983), *Indiana Jones and the Temple of Doom* (1984), *Witness* (1985), *Mosquito Coast* (1986), *Frantic* (1988), *Working Girl* (1988), *Indiana Jones and the Last Crusade* (1989), *Presumed Innocent* (1990), *Regarding Henry* (1991), *Patriot Games* (1992), *The Fugitive* (1993), *Clear and Present Danger* (1994), *The Devil's Own* (1996), *What Lies Beneath* (2000).

**Foster, Jodie** (Ariane Munker) (1962– ) American, born The Bronx, New York City; *Bob and Carol and Ted and Alice* (TV 1973), *Paper Moon* (TV 1974), *Alice Doesn't Live Here Anymore* (1974), *Bugsy Malone* (1976), *Taxi Driver* (1976), *The Little Girl Who Lives Down the Lane* (1976), *Candleshoe* (1977), *Freaky Friday* (1977), *Siesta* (1987), *The Accused* (1988), *5 Corners* (1988), *Silence of the Lambs* (1991), *Little Man Tate* (1991), *Shadows and Fog* (1992), *Sommersby* (1993), *Maverick* (1994), *Nell* (1994), *Contact* (1997), *Anna and the King* (1999).

**Fox, James** (1939– ) British, born London; *The Magnet* (1950), *The Loneliness of the Long Distance Runner* (1963), *Those Magnificent Men in Their Flying Machines* (1965), *Thoroughly Modern Millie* (1967), *Performance* (1970), *A Passage to India* (1984), *Greystoke* (1984), *The Whistle Blower* (1987), *High Season* (1987), *She's Been Away* (TV 1990), *Hostage* (1992), *Never Ever* (1996).

**Fox, Michael J** (1961– ) Canadian, born Edmonton, Alberta; *Letters from Frank* (TV 1979), *Family Ties* (TV 1982–9), *Poison Ivy* (TV 1985), *Back to the Future* (1985), *Teenwolf* (1985), *The Secret of My Success* (1987), *Bright Lights Big City* (1988), *Casualties of War* (1989), *Back to the Future II* (1989), *Back to the Future III* (1990), *The Hard Way* (1991), *'Doc' Hollywood* (1991), *For Love or Money* (1993), *Life with Mikey* (1993), *Don't Drink the Water* (TV 1994), *The American President* (1995), *Blue in the Face* (1995), *Mars Attacks!* (1996).

**Freeman, Morgan** (1937– ) American, born Memphis, Tennessee; *The Electric Company* (TV 1971–6), *Street Smart* (1987), *Driving Miss Daisy* (1989), *Glory* (1989), *The Bonfire of the Vanities* (1990), *Robin Hood: Prince of Thieves* (1991), *Unforgiven* (1992), *The Shawshank Redemption* (1994), *Seven* (1995), *Deep Impact* (1998).

**Fry, Stephen** (John) (1957– ) English, born London; *A Fish Called Wanda* (1988), *A Bit of Fry and Laurie* (TV 1989–95), *Jeeves and Wooster* (TV 1990–3), *Peter's Friends* (1992), *Cold Comfort Farm* (TV 1995), *Wilde* (1997), *Longitude* (2000).

**Gabin, Jean** (Jean-Alexis Moncorgé) (1904–76) French, born Paris; *Chacun Sa Chance* (1930), *Pepé le Moko* (1936), *La Grande Illusion* (1937), *Quai des Brumes* (1938), *Le Jour se lève* (1939), *Touchez Pas Au Grisbi* (1953), *Archimède Le Clochard* (1958), *Un Singe en Hiver* (1962), *Le Chat* (1971), *L'Année Sainte* (1976).

**Gable, (William) Clark** (1901–60) American, born Cadiz, Ohio; *Red Dust* (1932), *It Happened One Night* (1934), *Mutiny on the Bounty* (1935), *San Francisco* (1936), *Gone with the Wind* (1939), *The Hucksters* (1947), *Mogambo* (1953), *Never Let Me Go* (1953), *Teacher's Pet* (1958), *The Misfits* (1961).

**Gabor, Zsa Zsa** (Sari Gabor) (1918– ) Hungarian, born Budapest; *Lovely to Look at* (1952), *Moulin Rouge* (1952), *Lili* (1953), *Public Enemy Number One* (1954), *Queen of Outer Space* (1959), *Up the Front* (1972).

**Gambon, Sir Michael** (1940– ) Irish, born Dublin; *Turtle Diary* (1985), *The Singing Detective* (TV 1986),

*The Cook, The Thief, His Wife and Her Lover* (1989), *Sleepy Hollow* (1999), *Longitude* (2000).

**Garbo, Greta** (Greta Lovisa Gustafsson) (1905–90) Swedish–American, born Stockholm; *Flesh and the Devil* (1927), *Anna Christie* (1930), *Grand Hotel* (1932), *Queen Christina* (1933), *Anna Karenina* (1935), *Camille* (1936), *Ninotchka* (1939).

**Gardner, Ava** (Lucy Johnson) (1922–90) American, born Smithfield, North Carolina; *The Killers* (1946), *The Hucksters* (1947), *Show Boat* (1951), *Pandora and the Flying Dutchman* (1951), *The Snows of Kilimanjaro* (1952), *Mogambo* (1953), *The Barefoot Contessa* (1954), *The Sun Also Rises* (1957), *The Night of the Iguana* (1964).

**Garland, Judy** (Frances Gumm) (1922–69) American, born Grand Rapids, Minnesota; *The Wizard of Oz* (1939), *Babes in Arms* (1939), *For Me and My Gal* (1942), *Meet Me in St Louis* (1944), *Ziegfeld Follies* (1945), *The Clock* (1945), *Easter Parade* (1948), *Summer Stock* (1950), *A Star is Born* (1954).

**Garner, James** (James Scott Baumgarner) (1928– ) American, born Norman, Oklahoma; *Maverick* (TV 1957–62), *The Great Escape* (1963), *The Americanization of Emily* (1964), *The Skin Game* (1971), *Rockford Files* (TV 1974–80), *The Fan* (1980), *Victor/Victoria* (1982), *Maverick* (1994), *My Fellow Americans* (1996).

**Garr, Teri** (1949– ) American, born Lakewood, Ohio; *Young Frankenstein* (1974), *Oh God* (1977), *Close Encounters of the Third Kind* (1977), *The Black Stallion* (1978), *Honky Tonk Freeway* (1981), *One from the Heart* (1982), *Tootsie* (1982), *The Sting II* (1982), *The Black Stallion Returns* (1983), *Mr Mom* (1983), *First Born* (1984), *After Hours* (1985), *Full Moon in Blue Water* (1988), *Perfect Alibi* (1994), *Prêt-À-Porter* (1994), *Dumb and Dumber* (1994).

**Gassman, Vittorio** (1922–2000) Italian, born Genoa; *Il Cavaliere Misterioso* (1948), *Riso Amaro* (1948), *La Vie est un Roman* (1983), *Sleepers* (1996).

**Gere, Richard** (1949– ) American, born Philadelphia, Pennsylvania; *Yanks* (1979), *American Gigolo* (1980), *An Officer and a Gentleman* (1982), *Breathless* (1983), *The Cotton Club* (1984), *No Mercy* (1986), *Miles from Home* (1988), *Internal Affairs* (1990), *Pretty Woman* (1990), *Rhapsody in August* (1991), *Final Analysis* (1992), *Mr North* (1992), *Sommersby* (1993), *First Knight* (1995), *Primal Fear* (1996), *The Jackal* (1997), *Runaway Bride* (1999).

**Gibson, Mel** (1956– ) American–Australian, born Peekshill, New York; *Tim* (1979), *Mad Max* (1979), *Gallipoli* (1981), *Mad Max 2: The Road Warrior* (1982), *The Year of Living Dangerously* (1982), *Mad Max Beyond Thunderdome* (1985), *Lethal Weapon* (1987), *Tequila Sunrise* (1988), *Lethal Weapon 2* (1989), *Bird on a Wire* (1990), *Air America* (1990), *Hamlet* (1990), *Lethal Weapon 3* (1992), *The Rest of Daniel* (1992), *Forever Young* (1992), *The Man Without A Face* (1993), *Maverick* (1994), *Braveheart* (1995), *Ransom* (1996), *Conspiracy Theory* (1997), *What Women Want* (2001).

**Gielgud, Sir John** (Arthur) (1904–2000) British, born London; also stage; *Julius Caesar* (1953), *The Charge of the Light Brigade* (1968), *Oh What a Lovely War* (1969), *Murder on the Orient Express* (1974), *Providence* (1977), *Brideshead Revisited* (TV 1981), *Arthur* (1981), *Gandhi* (1982), *The Whistle Blower* (1987), *Arthur 2: On the Rocks* (1988), *Loser Takes All* (1989), *Prospero's Books* (1991), *First Knight* (1995), *Haunted* (1995), *Hamlet* (1996), *Elizabeth* (1998).

**Gish, Lillian** (Diana) (Lillian de Guiche) (1896–1993) American, born Springfield, Ohio; *An Unseen Enemy* (1912), *Birth of a Nation* (1914), *Intolerance* (1916), *Broken Blossoms* (1919), *Way Down East* (1920), *Duel in the Sun* (1946), *Night of the Hunter* (1955), *The Whales of August* (1987).

**Glover, Danny** (1947– ) American, born San Francisco, California; *Silverado* (1985), *Witness* (1985), *Lethal Weapon* (1987), *Bat 21* (1988), *Lethal Weapon 2* (1989), *Predator 2* (1990), *Lethal Weapon 3* (1992), *The Saint of Fort Washington* (1993), *Bopha!* (1993), *Leathal Weapon 4* (1998), *The Patriot* (2000).

**Goldberg, Whoopi** (Caryn Johnson) (1949– ) American, born Manhattan, New York City; *The Color Purple* (1985), *Burglar* (1985), *Jumping Jack Flash* (1986), *Clara's Heart* (1988), *The Telephone* (1988), *Ghost* (1990), *Soapdish* (1991), *Sister Act* (1992), *Change of Heart* (1992), *The Player* (1992), *Made in America* (1993), *Sister Act 2: Back in the Habit* (1993), *Corrina Corrina* (1994), *Star Trek: Generations* (1994), *Girl Interrupted* (1999).

**Goldblum, Jeff** (1952– ) American, born Pittsburgh, Pennsylvania; *California Split* (1974), *Death Wish* (1974), *Nashville* (1975), *Invasion of the Body Snatchers* (1978), *Escape from Athena* (1979), *The Right Stuff* (1983), *The Big Chill* (1983), *Into the Night* (1985), *The Fly* (1985), *Vibes* (1988), *The Tall Guy* (1989), *Earth Girls Are Easy* (1989), *The Player* (1992), *Fathers and Sons* (1992), *Jurassic Park* (1993), *Nine Months* (1995), *Independence Day* (1996), *The Lost World: Jurassic Park* (1997).

**Goodman, John** (1953– ) American, born St Louis, Missouri; *True Stories* (1986), *The Big Easy* (1987), *Roseanne* (TV 1988–97), *Punchline* (1988), *Sea of Love* (1990), *Always* (1990), *Stella* (1990), *Arachnophobia* (1990), *King Ralph* (1991), *The Flintstones* (1994), *O Brother, Where Art Thou?* (2000).

**Gossett, Louis Jr** (1936– ) American, born Brooklyn, New York City; *Travels with My Aunt* (1972), *Roots* (TV 1977), *The Lazarus Syndrome* (TV 1979), *An Officer and a Gentleman* (1982), *The Powers of Matthew Starr* (TV 1982), *Jaws 3D* (1983), *Iron Eagle* (1985), *Iron Eagle II* (1988), *Cover Up* (1991), *Aces: Iron Eagle III* (1992), *The Highwayman* (1999).

**Granger, Stewart** (James Lablanche Stewart) (1913–93) British, born London; *The Man in Grey* (1943), *Waterloo Road* (1944), *Love Story* (1944), *Caesar and Cleopatra* (1945), *Captain Boycott* (1947), *King Solomon's Mines* (1950), *Scaramouch* (1952), *The Prisoner of Zenda* (1952), *Beau Brummell* (1954), *The Wild Geese* (1977).

**Grant, Cary** (Archibald Alexander Leach) (1904–86) Anglo-American, born Bristol, England; *This is the Night* (1932), *She Done Him Wrong* (1933), *The Awful Truth* (1937), *Bringing Up Baby* (1938), *His Girl Friday* (1940), *Arsenic and Old Lace* (1944), *Notorious* (1946), *To Catch a Thief* (1953), *North by Northwest* (1959).

**Grant, Hugh** (1960– ) British, born London; *Maurice* (1987), *The Lair of the White Worm* (1988), *Impromptu* (1991), *Bitter Moon* (1992), *Four Weddings and a Funeral* (1994), *An Awfully Big Adventure* (1995), *Sense and Sensibility* (1995), *Notting Hill* (1999), *Bridget Jones's Diary* (2001).

**Grant, Lee** (Lyova Rosenthal) (1930– ) American, born New York City; *Detective Story* (1951), *The Landlord* (1970), *Shampoo* (1975), *The Voyage of the Damned* (1976), *Damien: Omen II* (1978), *Big Town* (1987).

**Greenwood, Joan** (1921–87) British, born Chelsea, London; *Whisky Galore* (1949), *Kind Hearts and Coronets* (1949), *The Man in the White Suit* (1951), *The Importance of Being Earnest* (1952), *Tom Jones* (1963), *Little Dorrit* (1987).

**Griffith, Melanie** (1957– ) American, born New York City; *Something Wild* (1987), *Cherry 2000* (1988), *Working Girl* (1988), *Stormy Monday* (1988), *Pacific Heights* (1990), *Bonfire of the Vanities* (1990), *Paradise* (1991), *Shining Through* (1992), *Close to Eden* (1992), *Born Yesterday* (1993), *Nobody's Fool* (1994), *Lolita* (1996).

**Guinness, Sir Alec** (1914–2000) British, born London; *Oliver Twist* (1948), *Kind Hearts and Coronets* (1949), *The Mudlark* (1950), *The Lavender Hill Mob* (1951), *The Man in the White Suit* (1951), *The Card* (1952), *Father Brown* (1954), *The Ladykillers* (1955), *The Bridge on the River Kwai* (1957), *The Horse's Mouth* (1958), *Our Man in Havana* (1960), *Tunes of Glory* (1962), *Lawrence of Arabia* (1962), *Doctor Zhivago* (1966), *Star Wars* (1977), *Tinker, Tailor, Soldier, Spy* (TV 1979), *Smiley's People* (TV 1981), *Return of the Jedi* (1983), *A Passage to India* (1984), *Little Dorrit* (1987), *A Handful of Dust* (1988), *Kafka* (1991), *Foreign Field* (TV 1993).

**Guttenberg, Steve** (1958– ) American, born Massapequa, New York; *Diner* (1981), *Police Academy* (1984), *Police Academy II* (1985), *Cocoon* (1985), *Short Circuit* (1986), *The Bedroom Window* (1986), *Three Men and a Baby* (1988), *High Spirits* (1988), *Cocoon: The Return* (1988), *Three Men and a Little Lady* (1990), *Airborne* (1998).

**Gwynne, Fred** (1926–93) American, born New York City; *Car 54 Where are You?* (TV 1961–2), *The Munsters* (TV 1964–5), *On the Waterfront* (1954), *Munster Go Home* (1966), *The Cotton Club* (1984), *Fatal Attraction* (1987), *Kane and Abel* (TV 1988), *Pet Sematary* (1989), *Shadows and Fog* (1992), *My Cousin Vinny* (1992).

**Hackman, Gene** (1931– ) American, born San Bernardino, California; *Bonnie and Clyde* (1967), *I Never Sang for My Father* (1969), *French Connection* (1971), *The Poseidon Adventure* (1972), *Young Frankenstein* (1974), *French Connection II* (1975), *A Bridge Too Far* (1977), *Superman* (1978), *Superman II* (1981), *Target* (1985), *Superman IV* (1987), *Another Woman* (1988), *Bat 21* (1988), *Full Moon in Blue Water* (1988), *Mississippi Burning* (1989), *The Package* (1989), *Loose Cannons* (1990), *Postcards from the Edge* (1990), *Class Action* (1990), *Company Business* (1991), *Unforgiven* (1992), *The Firm* (1993), *Geronimo: An American Legend* (1993), *Get Shorty* (1995), *The Birdcage* (1996), *The Chamber* (1996), *Extreme Measures* (1996), *Absolute Power* (1997), *Behind Enemy Lines* (2001).

**Hagman, Larry** (Larry Hageman) (1931– ) American, born Weatherford, Texas; *Ensign Pulver* (1964), *I Dream of Jeannie* (TV 1965–70), *The Eagle Has Landed* (1976), *Superman* (1978), *Dallas* (TV 1978–90), *Nixon* (1995), *Primary Colors* (1998).

**Hamill, Mark** (1952– ) American, born Oakland, California; *Star Wars* (1977), *The Big Red One* (1979), *The Empire Strikes Back* (1980), *The Night the Lights Went out in Georgia* (1981), *Return of the Jedi* (1983), *Slipstream* (1988), *Flash II* (1991), *Village of the Damned* (1995).

**Hamlin, Harry** (1951– ) American, born Pasadena, California; *Clash of the Titans* (1981), *Dragonslayer* (1981), *Space* (TV 1985), *LA Law* (TV 1986–92).

**Hanks, Tom** (1957– ) American, born Oakland, California; *Bachelor Party* (1983), *Splash!* (1984), *The Man With One Red Shoe* (1985), *Dragnet* (1987), *Big* (1988), *Turner and Hooch* (1990), *Joe Versus the Volcano* (1990), *Bonfire of the Vanities* (1991), *A League of Their Own* (1992), *Benny and Joon* (1992), *Sleepless in Seattle* (1993), *Philadelphia* (1993), *Forrest Gump* (1994), *Apollo 13* (1995), *That Thing You Do* (1996), *Saving Private Ryan* (1998), *Cast Away* (2000).

**Hannah, Daryl** (1960– ) American, born Chicago; *Blade Runner* (1982), *Splash!* (1984), *Clan of the Cave Bear* (1986), *Legal Eagles* (1986), *Roxanne* (1987), *Wall Street* (1987), *High Spirits* (1988), *Steel Magnolias* (1989), *Crazy People* (1990), *At Play in the Fields of the Lord* (1991), *Memoirs of an Invisible Man* (1992), *Frankie the Fly* (1996).

**Hardy, Oliver** (Norvell Hardy Junior) (1892–1957) American, born near Atlanta, Georgia; many Laurel and Hardy films including *Putting Pants on Philip* (1927), *The Battle of the Century* (1927), *Two Tars* (1928), *The Perfect Day* (1929), *Laughing Gravy* (1931), *The Music Box* (1932), *Babes in Toyland* (1934), *Bonnie Scotland* (1935), *Way Out West* (1937), *The Flying Deuces* (1939), *Atoll K* (1950).

**Harlow, Jean** (Harlean Carpentier) (1911–37) American, born Kansas City, Missouri; *Red Dust* (1932), *Hell's Angels* (1930), *Platinum Blonde* (1931), *Red-Headed Woman* (1932), *Bombshell* (1933), *Dinner at 8* (1933), *Libelled Lady* (1936).

**Harrelson, Woody** (1961– ) American, born Midland, Texas; *Harper Valley PTA* (1978), *Wildcats* (1986), *LA Story* (1991), *'Doc' Hollywood* (1991), *Ted and Venus* (1991), *White Men Can't Jump* (1992),

*Indecent Proposal* (1993), *Natural Born Killers* (1994), *Kingpin* (1996), *The People vs Larry Flynt* (1996).

**Harris, Julie** (Julia Harris) (1925– ) American, born Grosspoint, Michigan; *The Member of the Wedding* (1953), *East of Eden* (1955), *The Haunting* (1963).

**Harris, Richard** (1930– ) Irish, born County Limerick; *The Guns of Navarone* (1961), *Mutiny on the Bounty* (1962), *This Sporting Life* (1963), *Camelot* (1967), *A Man Called Horse* (1969), *Cromwell* (1970), *The Cassandra Crossing* (1977), *Orca – Killer Whale* (1977), *The Wild Geese* (1978), *Tarzan the Ape Man* (1981), *The Field* (1990), *Gladiator* (2000).

**Harrison, Sir Rex** (Reginald Carey Harrison) (1908–90) British, born Huyton, Lancashire; *Major Barbara* (1940), *Blithe Spirit* (1945), *Anna and the King of Siam* (1946), *The Ghost and Mrs Muir* (1947), *The Reluctant Debutante* (1958), *The Constant Husband* (1955), *Cleopatra* (1962), *My Fair Lady* (1964), *Dr Doolittle* (1967).

**Hauer, Rutger** (1944– ) Dutch, born Amsterdam; *Nighthawks* (1981), *Blade Runner* (1982), *Eureka* (1983), *The Osterman Weekend* (1983), *The Hitcher* (1985), *Flesh and Blood* (1985), *Wanted Dead or Alive* (1986), *The Legend of the Holy Drinker* (1989), *Blind Fury* (1990), *Ocean Point* (1991), *On a Moonlit Night* (1991), *Split Second* (1992), *Buffy the Vampire Slayer* (1992), *Past Midnight* (1992), *Nostradamus* (1994), *Crossworlds* (1996).

**Hawn, Goldie** (Jeanne) (1945– ) American, born Washington DC; *Laugh In* (TV 1968–73), *Cactus Flower* (1969), *There's a Girl in My Soup* (1970), *Butterflies are Free* (1971), *Sugarland Express* (1974), *Shampoo* (1975), *Foul Play* (1978), *Seems Like Old Times* (1980), *Private Benjamin* (1980), *Best Friends* (1982), *Swing Shift* (1984), *Bird on a Wire* (1990), *CrissCross* (1991), *Deceived* (1991), *Housesitter* (1992), *Death Becomes Her* (1992), *The First Wives Club* (1996).

**Hawthorne, Sir Nigel** (Barnard) (1929–2001) British, born Coventry; *Yes Minister* (1980–92), *Yes, Prime Minister* (1986–8), *The Madness of King George* (1994), *Richard III* (1995), *Twelfth Night* (1996), *The Fragile Heart* (1996), *A Reasonable Man* (1999).

**Hay, Will** (1889–1949) British, born Stockton-on-Tees; *Good Morning Boys* (1937), *Old Bones of the River* (1938), *Oh Mr Porter* (1938), *Ask a Policeman* (1939), *The Ghost of St Michaels* (1941), *My Learned Friend* (1944).

**Hayward, Susan** (Edythe Marrenner) (1917–75) American, born Brooklyn, New York City; *Smash-Up: The Story of a Woman* (1947), *With a Song In My Heart* (1952), *I'll Cry Tomorrow* (1955), *I Want to Live!* (1958), *Where Love Has Gone* (1964), *Valley of the Dolls* (1967), *The Revengers* (1972).

**Hayworth, Rita** (Margarita Carmen Cansino) (1918–87) American, born New York City; *Only Angels Have Wings* (1939), *The Lady in Question* (1940), *The Strawberry Blonde* (1940), *Blood and Sand* (1941), *You'll Never Get Rich* (1941), *Cover Girl* (1944), *Gilda* (1946), *The Lady from Shanghai* (1948), *Separate Tables* (1958).

**Hepburn, Audrey** (Audrey Hepburn-Ruston) (1929–93) Anglo-Dutch, born Brussels, Belgium; *Roman Holiday* (1953), *War and Peace* (1956), *Funny Face* (1957), *The Nun's Story* (1959), *Breakfast at Tiffany's* (1961), *My Fair Lady* (1964), *How to Steal a Million* (1966), *Wait Until Dark* (1967), *Robin and Marian* (1976), *Always* (1989).

**Hepburn, Katharine** (1907– ) American, born Hartford, Connecticut; *A Bill of Divorcement* (1932), *Morning Glory* (1933), *Stage Door* (1937), *Bringing Up Baby* (1938), *Holiday* (1938), *The Philadelphia Story* (1940), *Woman of the Year* (1942), *Adam's Rib* (1949), *The African Queen* (1951), *Long Day's Journey into Night* (1962), *Guess Who's Coming to Dinner?* (1967), *Suddenly Last Summer* (1968), *The Lion in Winter* (1968), *The Glass Menagerie* (TV 1973), *Rooster Cogburn* (1975), *On Golden Pond* (1981), *Love Affair* (1994).

**Hershey, Barbara** (formerly Barbara Seagull, originally Herzstein) (1948– ) American, born Hollywood, California; *Last Summer* (1968), *Diamonds* (1975), *The Flood* (TV 1976), *The Stunt Man* (1978), *Angel on My Shoulder* (TV 1980), *The Entity* (1983), *The Right Stuff* (1983), *The Natural* (1984), *Passion Flower* (TV 1985), *Hannah and Her Sisters* (1986), *Tin Men* (1987), *A World Apart* (1988), *The Last Temptation of Christ* (1988), *Beaches* (1988), *Barton Fink* (1990), *Naked Lunch* (1991), *The Public Eye* (1991), *A Dangerous Woman* (1993), *Splitting Heirs* (1993), *The Portrait of a Lady* (1996).

**Heston, Charlton** (John Charlton Carter) (1922– ) American, born Evanston, Illinois; *Arrowhead* (1953), *The Ten Commandments* (1956), *Touch of Evil* (1958), *Ben Hur* (1959), *El Cid* (1961), *The Greatest Story Ever Told* (1965), *The War Lord* (1965), *Khartoum* (1966), *Planet of the Apes* (1968), *Earthquake* (1973), *Airport* (1975), *The Four Musketeers* (1975), *Almost an Angel* (1990), *Wayne's World 2* (1993), *Tombstone* (1993), *Hamlet* (1996), *Any Given Sunday* (1999).

**Hiller, Dame Wendy** (1912– ) British, born Bramhall, Cheshire; also stage; *Major Barbara* (1940), *I Know Where I'm Going* (1945), *Separate Tables* (1958), *Sons and Lovers* (1960), *A Man for All Seasons* (1966), *Murder on the Orient Express* (1974), *Voyage of the Damned* (1976), *The Elephant Man* (1980), *The Lonely Passion of Judith Hearne* (1987).

**Hoffman, Dustin** (1937– ) American, born Los Angeles; *The Graduate* (1967), *Midnight Cowboy* (1969), *Little Big Man* (1970), *Papillon* (1973), *Lenny* (1974), *All the President's Men* (1976), *Kramer vs Kramer* (1979), *Tootsie* (1982), *Death of a Salesman* (TV 1984), *Rain Man* (1988), *Dick Tracy* (1990), *Billy Bathgate* (1991), *Hook* (1991), *Hero* (1992), *Outbreak* (1995), *Sleepers* (1996), *Sphere* (1998).

**Hogan, Paul** (1939– ) Australian, born New South Wales; *Crocodile Dundee* (1986), *Crocodile Dundee II* (1988), *Almost an Angel* (1990), *Lightning Jack* (1994), *Flipper* (1996).

**Holbrook, Hal** (Harold Holbrook) (1925– ) American, born Cleveland, Ohio; *The Group* (1966),

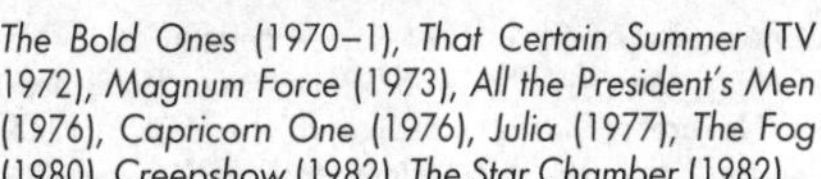



*The Bold Ones* (1970–1), *That Certain Summer* (TV 1972), *Magnum Force* (1973), *All the President's Men* (1976), *Capricorn One* (1976), *Julia* (1977), *The Fog* (1980), *Creepshow* (1982), *The Star Chamber* (1982).

**Holden, William** (William Franklin Beedle, Jr) (1918–82) American, born O'Fallon, Illinois; *Golden Boy* (1939), *Rachel and the Stranger* (1948), *Sunset Boulevard* (1950), *Born Yesterday* (1950), *Stalag 17* (1953), *Love is a Many-Splendored Thing* (1955), *Picnic* (1955), *The Bridge on the River Kwai* (1957), *Casino Royale* (1967), *The Wild Bunch* (1969), *The Towering Inferno* (1974), *Network* (1976), *Damien: Omen II* (1978), *Escape to Athena* (1979), *The Earthling* (1980), *SOB* (1981), *When Time Ran Out* (1981).

**Hope, Bob** (Leslie Townes Hope) (1903– ) Anglo-American, born Eltham, London; *Thanks for the Memory* (1938), *The Cat and the Canary* (1939), *Road to Singapore* (1940), *The Ghost Breakers* (1940), *Road to Zanzibar* (1941), *My Favorite Blonde* (1942), *Road to Morocco* (1942), *The Paleface* (1948), *Fancy Pants* (1950), *The Facts of Life* (1960), *Road to Hong Kong* (1961), *How to Commit Marriage* (1969).

**Hopkins, Anthony** (1941– ) Welsh-American, born Port Talbot, Wales; *The Lion in Winter* (1968), *When Eight Bells Toll* (1971), *War and Peace* (TV 1972), *The Lindbergh Kidnapping Case* (TV 1976), *Magic* (1978), *The Elephant Man* (1980), *The Bunker* (TV 1981), *The Bounty* (1983), *84 Charing Cross Road* (1986), *Desperate Hours* (1991), *Silence of the Lambs* (1991), *Spotswood* (1991), *Freejack* (1992), *Howards End* (1992), *Charlie* (1992), *The Innocent* (1992), *Dracula* (1992), *The Remains of the Day* (1993), *Shadowlands* (1993), *The Road to Wellville* (1994), *Legends of the Fall* (1994), *Nixon* (1995), *Surviving Picasso* (1996), *Meet Joe Black* (1998), *Hannibal* (2001).

**Hopper, Dennis** (1936– ) American, born Dodge City, Kansas; *Rebel Without a Cause* (1955), *Giant* (1956), *Cool Hand Luke* (1967), *Easy Rider* (1969), *Apocalypse Now* (1979), *Blue Velvet* (1986), *River's Edge* (1986), *Blood Red* (1990), *Catchfire* (1990), *Paris Trout* (1991), *The Indian Runner* (1991), *Money Men* (1992), *True Romance* (1993), *Speed* (1994), *Waterworld* (1995), *Bad City Blues* (1999).

**Hordern, Sir Michael** (1911–95) British, born Berkhampstead, Hertfordshire; *The Constant Husband* (1955), *The Spanish Gardener* (1956), *Dr Syn – Alias the Scarecrow* (1963), *A Funny Thing Happened on the Way to the Forum* (1966), *The Bed-Sitting Room* (1969), *The Slipper and the Rose* (1976), *The Missionary* (1982), *Paradise Postponed* (TV 1986), *The Fool* (1990).

**Hoskins, Bob** (Robert William) (1942– ) British, born Bury St Edmunds, Suffolk; *Pennies from Heaven* (TV 1978), *The Long Good Friday* (1980), *Pink Floyd: The Wall* (1982), *The Honorary Consul* (1983), *The Cotton Club* (1984), *Brazil* (1985), *Sweet Liberty* (1985), *Mona Lisa* (1986), *A Prayer for the Dying* (1987), *Who Framed Roger Rabbit?* (1988), *Heart Condition* (1990), *Mermaids* (1990), *Shattered* (1991), *Hook* (1991), *The Favour, the Watch and the very Big Fish* (1991), *The Inner Circle* (1992), *Rainbow* (1995), *Nixon* (1995), *Parting Shots* (1998).

**Howard, Leslie** (Leslie Howard Stainer) (1890–1943) British, born London; *Of Human Bondage* (1934), *The Scarlet Pimpernel* (1935), *Pygmalion* (1938), *Gone with the Wind* (1939).

**Howard, Trevor** (Wallace) (1916–88) British, born Cliftonville, Kent; *The Way Ahead* (1944), *Brief Encounter* (1946), *Green for Danger* (1946), *The Third Man* (1949), *The Heart of the Matter* (1953), *The Key* (1958), *Sons and Lovers* (1960), *Mutiny on the Bounty* (1962), *The Charge of the Light Brigade* (1968), *Ryan's Daughter* (1970), *The Night Visitor* (1971), *Catholics* (TV 1973), *Conduct Unbecoming* (1975), *Meteor* (1979), *Staying On* (TV 1980), *Gandhi* (1982), *White Mischief* (1987), *The Unholy* (1988).

**Hudson, Rock** (Roy Scherer, Jr) (1925–85) American, born Winnetka, Illinois; *Magnificent Obsession* (1954), *Giant* (1956), *Written on the Wind* (1956), *The Tarnished Angel* (1957), *Pillow Talk* (1959), *Send Me No Flowers* (1964), *Seconds* (1966), *Darling Lili* (1969), *McMillan and Wife* (TV 1971–5), *McMillan* (TV 1976), *Embryo* (1976), *The Martian Chronicles* (TV 1980), *Dynasty* (TV 1985).

**Hulce, Tom** (1953– ) American, born Plymouth, Michigan; *September 30, 1955* (1977), *Animal House* (1978), *Amadeus* (1984), *Dominick and Eugene* (1988), *Parenthood* (1989), *Shadow Man* (1990), *The Inner Circle* (1991), *Fearless* (1993), *Wings of Courage* (1995).

**Hunter, Holly** (1958– ) American, born Conyers, Georgia; *Raising Arizona* (1987), *Once Around* (1990), *The Piano* (1993), *The Positively True Adventures of the Alleged Texas Cheerleader-Murdering Mom* (TV 1993), *Copycat* (1995), *Crash* (1996), *O Brother, Where Art Thou?* (2000).

**Hunter, Kim** (Janet Cole) (1922– ) American, born Detroit, Michigan; *A Matter of Life and Death* (1945), *A Streetcar Named Desire* (1951), *Deadline USA* (1952), *Planet of the Apes* (1967), *The Swimmer* (1968), *Beneath the Planet of the Apes* (1970), *Escape from the Planet of the Apes* (1971).

**Huppert, Isabelle** (1955– ) French, born Paris; *César et Rosalie* (1972), *La Dentellière* (1977), *Violette Nozière* (1978), *Heaven's Gate* (1980), *The Possessed* (1987), *Une Affaire des Femmes* (1988), *Madame Bovary* (1991), *Pas de scandale* (1999).

**Hurt, John** (1940– ) British, born Chesterfield, Derbyshire; *A Man for All Seasons* (1966), *10 Rillington Place* (1971), *The Naked Civil Servant* (TV 1975), *Midnight Express* (1978), *Alien* (1979), *The Elephant Man* (1980), *History of the World Part One* (1981), *Champions* (1983), *1984* (1984), *Spaceballs* (1987), *Aria* (1987), *White Mischief* (1987), *Scandal* (1989), *Frankenstein Unbound* (1990), *King Ralph* (1991), *Resident Alien* (1991), *Dark at Noon* (1992), *Rob Roy* (1995), *Darkening* (1996), *New Blood* (1999).

**Hurt, William** (1950– ) American, born Washington, DC; *Altered States* (1981), *The Janitor* (1981), *Body*

*Heat* (1981), *The Big Chill* (1983), *Gorky Park* (1983), *Kiss of the Spider Woman* (1985), *Children of a Lesser God* (1986), *Broadcast News* (1987), *A Time of Destiny* (1988), *The Accidental Tourist* (1989), *Love You to Death* (1990), *Alice* (1990), *Until the End of the World* (1991), *The Doctor* (1991), *The Plague* (1992), *Second Best* (1994), *Smoke* (1995), *Jane Eyre* (1995).

**Hussey, Olivia** (1951– ) British, born Buenos Aires, Argentina; *Romeo and Juliet* (1968), *Lost Horizon* (1973), *Jesus of Nazareth* (TV 1977), *Death on the Nile* (1978), *The Man with Bogart's Face* (1980), *Ivanhoe* (TV 1982), *The Undiscovered* (1997).

**Huston, Anjelica** (1952– ) Irish–American, born Ireland; *The Last Tycoon* (1976), *Frances* (1982), *This is Spinal Tap* (1984), *Prizzi's Honor* (1985), *The Dead* (1987), *Gardens of Stone* (1987), *A Handful of Dust* (1988), *Mr North* (1988), *The Witches* (1990), *The Grifters* (1990), *The Addams Family* (1991), *Bitter Moon* (1992), *Addams Family Values* (1993), *Manhattan Murder Mystery* (1994), *The Crossing Guard* (1995), *Agnes Browne* (1999).

**Hyde-White, Wilfrid** (1903–91) British, born Gloucester; *The Third Man* (1949), *My Fair Lady* (1964), *The Associates* (TV 1979), *Buck Rogers* (TV 1980–2), *Oh God Book Two* (1980), *The Fog* (1982).

**Irons, Jeremy** (1948– ) British, born Cowes; *The French Lieutenant's Woman* (1981), *Brideshead Revisited* (TV 1981), *Swann in Love* (1984), *The Mission* (1985), *Dead Ringers* (1988), *Reversal of Fortune* (1990), *Kafka* (1991), *Waterland* (1992), *Damage* (1992), *M Butterfly* (1992), *Die Hard with a Vengeance* (1995), *Lolita* (1996), *Longitude* (2000).

**Jackson, Glenda** (1936– ) British, born Liverpool; *Women in Love* (1969), *Sunday, Bloody Sunday* (1971), *Mary Queen of Scots* (1971), *Elizabeth R* (TV 1971), *A Touch of Class* (1972), *Hedda* (1975), *Stevie* (1978), *The Patricia Neal Story* (TV 1981), *Turtle Diary* (1985), *Business as Usual* (1987), *Salome's Last Dance* (1988), *The Rainbow* (1989), *Doombeach* (1990), *A Murder of Quality* (TV 1991).

**Jackson, Gordon** (1923–89) British, born Glasgow; *Whisky Galore* (1948), *Tunes of Glory* (1960), *The Great Escape* (1963), *The Ipcress File* (1965), *The Prime of Miss Jean Brodie* (1969), *Upstairs Downstairs* (TV 1970–5), *Kidnapped* (1972), *The Medusa Touch* (1977), *The Professionals* (TV 1977–81), *A Town Like Alice* (TV 1980), *The Shooting Party* (1984), *The Whistle Blower* (1987), *Beyond Therapy* (1987).

**Jacobi, Sir Derek** (1938– ) British, born Leytonstone, London; *The Odessa File* (1964), *I Claudius* (TV 1976), *Burgess and MacLean* (TV 1977), *Little Dorrit* (1987), *The Fool* (1990), *Gladiator* (2000).

**Johnson, Don** (1950– ) American, born Flatt Creek, Missouri; *From Here to Eternity* (1979), *Miami Vice* (TV 1984–90), *The Long Hot Summer* (TV 1985), *Dead Bang* (1988), *The Hot Spot* (1990), *Harley Davidson and the Marlboro Man* (1991), *Paradise* (1991), *Born Yesterday* (1993), *Guilty as Sin* (1993), *Tin Cup* (1996).

**Jones, James Earl** (1931– ) American, born Tate County, Missouri; *The Great White Hope* (1970), *Jesus of Nazareth* (TV 1977), *Exorcist II: The Heretic* (1977), *Roots II* (TV 1979), *Beastmaster* (1982), *Coming to America* (1988), *Field of Dreams* (1988), *Three Fugitives* (1988), *The Hunt for Red October* (1989), *Best of the Best* (1990), *Clear and Present Danger* (1994).

**Jones, Jennifer** (Phyllis Isley) (1919– ) American, born Tulsa, Oklahoma; *The Song of Bernadette* (1943), *Duel in the Sun* (1946), *Portrait of Jennie* (1948), *Carrie* (1951), *Love is a Many-Splendored Thing* (1955), *A Farewell to Arms* (1958), *Tender is the Night* (1961), *The Towering Inferno* (1974).

**Julia, Raul** (1940–94) Puerto Rican, born San Juan; *The Eyes of Laura Mars* (1978), *One From the Heart* (1982), *Tempest* (1982), *Kiss of the Spider Woman* (1985), *The Morning After* (1986), *Moon over Parador* (1988), *The Penitent* (1988), *Tequila Sunrise* (1989), *Romero* (1990), *Presumed Innocent* (1990), *The Rookie* (1990), *Frankenstein Unbound* (1990).

**Karloff, Boris** (William Henry Pratt) (1887–1969) Anglo-American, born London; *Frankenstein* (1931), *The Mask of Fu Manchu* (1931), *The Lost Patrol* (1934), *The Raven* (1935), *The Bride of Frankenstein* (1935), *The Body Snatcher* (1945).

**Kaye, Danny** (David Daniel Kominski) (1913–87) American, born New York City; *Up in Arms* (1944), *The Secret Life of Walter Mitty* (1947), *Hans Christian Andersen* (1952), *White Christmas* (1954), *The Court Jester* (1956), *The Five Pennies* (1959), *Skokie* (TV 1981).

**Keaton, Buster** (Joseph Francis Keaton) (1895–1966) American, born Piqua, Kansas; *Our Hospitality* (1923), *The Navigator* (1924), *The General* (1927), *San Diego I Love You* (1944), *Sunset Boulevard* (1950), *Limelight* (1952), *It's a Mad, Mad, Mad, Mad World* (1963).

**Keaton, Diane** (Diane Hall) (1946– ) American, born Los Angeles, California; *The Godfather* (1972), *The Godfather, Part II* (1974), *Sleeper* (1973), *Annie Hall* (1977), *Manhattan* (1979), *Reds* (1981), *Shoot the Moon* (1982), *Mrs Soffel* (1984), *Baby Boom* (1987), *The Good Mother* (1988), *The Godfather, Part III* (1990), *Success* (1991), *Father of the Bride* (1991), *Manhattan Murder Mystery* (1993), *Father of the Bride II* (1995), *The First Wives Club* (1996).

**Keaton, Michael** (Michael Douglas) (1951– ) American, born Carapolis, Pennsylvania; *Night Shift* (1982), *Mr Mom* (1983), *Beetlejuice* (1988), *Batman* (1989), *The Dream Team* (1989), *Clean and Sober* (1989), *Pacific Heights* (1990), *Batman Returns* (1992), *Much Ado About Nothing* (1993), *My Life* (1993), *The Paper* (1994), *Desperate Measures* (1997).

**Keitel, Harvey** (1947– ) American, born Brooklyn, New York City; *Mean Streets* (1973), *Taxi Driver* (1976), *Bad Timing* (1980), *The Men's Club* (1986), *The Last Temptation of Christ* (1988), *The January Man* (1989), *Bugsy* (1991), *Thelma and Louise* (1991), *Reservoir Dogs* (1992), *The Bad Lieutenant* (1992), *Sister Act* (1992), *The Piano* (1993), *Pulp Fiction* (1994), *Smoke*

(1995), *Clockers* (1995), *Ulysses' Gaze* (1995), *Get Shorty* (1995), *Head Above Water* (1996), *Copland* (1997), *Holy Smoke* (1999).

**Kelly, Gene** (Eugene Curran Kelly) (1912–96) American, born Pittsburgh, Pennsylvania; *For Me and My Girl* (1942), *Cover Girl* (1944), *Anchors Aweigh* (1945), *Ziegfeld Follies* (1946), *The Pirate* (1948), *The Three Musketeers* (1948), *Take Me Out to the Ball Game* (1949), *On the Town* (1949), *Summer Stock* (1950), *An American in Paris* (1951), *Singin' in the Rain* (1952), *Brigadoon* (1954), *Invitation to Dance* (1956), *Les Girls* (1957), *Marjorie Morningstar* (1958), *Inherit the Word* (1960), *Sins* (TV 1987).

**Kelly, Grace** (Patricia) (1928–82) American, born Philadelphia, Pennsylvania; *High Noon* (1952), *Mogambo* (1953), *Dial M for Murder* (1954), *Rear Window* (1954), *The Country Girl* (1954), *To Catch a Thief* (1955), *High Society* (1956).

**Kennedy, George** (1925– ) American, born New York City; *Charade* (1963), *The Flight of the Phoenix* (1967), *The Dirty Dozen* (1967), *Cool Hand Luke* (1967), *Sarge* (TV 1971), *Thunderbolt and Lightfoot* (1974), *Earthquake* (1974), *The Blue Knight* (TV 1975–6), *The Eiger Sanction* (1977), *Death on the Nile* (1979), *Bolero* (1984), *Delta Force* (1985), *Creepshow 2* (1987), *Dallas* (TV 1988–91), *Naked Gun* (1989), *Naked Gun 2½: The Smell of Fear* (1991), *Naked Gun 33⅓: The Final Insult* (1994).

**Kerr, Deborah** (Deborah Jane Kerr-Trimmer) (1921– ) British, born Helensburgh, Scotland; *Major Barbara* (1940), *Love on the Dole* (1941), *The Life and Death of Colonel Blimp* (1943), *Perfect Strangers* (1945), *I See a Dark Stranger* (1945), *Black Narcissus* (1947), *From Here to Eternity* (1953), *The King and I* (1956), *Tea and Sympathy* (1956), *An Affair to Remember* (1957), *Separate Tables* (1958), *The Sundowners* (1960), *The Innocents* (1961), *The Night of the Iguana* (1964), *Casino Royale* (1967), *Prudence and the Pill* (1968), *The Assam Garden* (1985).

**Kingsley, Ben** (Krishna Banji) (1943– ) Anglo-Indian, born Snaiton, Yorkshire; *Gandhi* (1982), *Betrayal* (1982), *Turtle Diary* (1985), *Testimony* (1987), *Pascali's Island* (1988), *Without a Clue* (1988), *Slipstream* (1989), *Bugsy* (1991), *Sneakers* (1992), *Schindler's List* (1994), *Death and the Maiden* (1994), *Species* (1996), *Parting Shots* (1998).

**Kinski, Klaus** (Claus Gunther Nakszynski) (1926–94) Polish, born Sopot (Zoppot), Danzig; *For a Few Dollars More* (1965), *Dr Zhivago* (1965), *Aguirre: Wrath of God* (1972), *Nosferatu* (1978), *Fitzcarraldo* (1982), *Codename: Wildgeese* (1984).

**Kinski, Nastassja** (Nastassja Nakszynski) (1960– ) German, born Berlin; *Tess* (1979), *Cat People* (1982), *One from the Heart* (1982), *Paris, Texas* (1984), *Maria's Lovers* (1985), *Revolution* (1985), *Magdalane* (1988), *Torrents of Spring* (1989), *On a Moonlit Night* (1991), *The Secret* (1991), *Night Sun* (1992), *Terminal Velocity* (1994).

**Kline, Kevin** (1947– ) American, born St Louis, Missouri; *Sophie's Choice* (1983), *The Big Chill* (1983), *Silverado* (1985), *Cry Freedom* (1987), *A Fish Called Wanda* (1988), *January Man* (1989), *Love You to Death* (1990), *Soap Dish* (1991), *Dave* (1993), *Princess Caraboo* (1994), *Paris Match* (1995), *Fierce Creatures* (1996), *The Ice Storm* (1998).

**Ladd, Alan** (1913–64) American, born Hot Springs, Arkansas; *This Gun for Hire* (1942), *The Glass Key* (1942), *The Blue Dahlia* (1946), *The Great Gatsby* (1949), *Shane* (1953), *The Carpetbaggers* (1964).

**Lamarr, Hedy** (Hedwig Eva Maria Kiesler) (1913–2000) Austrian, born Vienna; *Algiers* (1938), *White Cargo* (1942), *Samson and Delilah* (1949).

**Lambert, Christopher** (1957– ) French, born New York City; *Greystoke* (1984), *Subway* (1985), *Highlander* (1985), *The Sicilian* (1987), *Why Me?* (1990), *Highlander 2: The Quickening* (1991), *Knight Moves* (1993), *Gunmen* (1994), *The Hunted* (1994), *Mortal Kombat* (1995), *Highlander III: The Sorcerer* (1995), *Alaska* (1996).

**Lamour, Dorothy** (Mary Leaton Dorothy Slaton) (1914–96) American, born New Orleans, Louisiana; *The Jungle Princess* (1936), *The Hurricane* (1937), *Road to Singapore* (1940), *Road to Zanzibar* (1941), *Manhandled* (1948), *Creepshow 2* (1987).

**Lancaster, Burt** (Stephen Burton) (1913–94) American, born New York City; *The Killers* (1946), *Brute Force* (1947), *The Flame and the Arrow* (1950), *Come Back Little Sheba* (1953), *From Here to Eternity* (1953), *Vera Cruz* (1954), *Gunfight at the OK Corral* (1957), *Elmer Gantry* (1960), *Birdman of Alcatraz* (1962), *The Professionals* (1966), *The Swimmer* (1967), *1900* (1976), *Atlantic City* (1980), *Local Hero* (1983), *Rocket Gibraltar* (1988), *Field of Dreams* (1988).

**Lange, Hope** (1933– ) American, born Redding Ridge, Connecticut; *Bus Stop* (1956), *Peyton Place* (1957), *Death Wish* (1974), *Nightmare on Elm Street II* (1985), *Blue Velvet* (1986), *Tune in Tomorrow* (1990), *Clear and Present Danger* (1994), *Just Cause* (1995).

**Lange, Jessica** (1949– ) American, born Cloquet, Minnesota; *King Kong* (1976), *All That Jazz* (1979), *The Postman Always Rings Twice* (1981), *Tootsie* (1982), *Frances* (1982), *Country* (1984), *Sweet Dreams* (1985), *Crimes of the Heart* (1986), *Far North* (1988), *Music Box* (1989), *Men Don't Leave* (1990), *Blue Sky* (1991), *Cape Fear* (1991), *Night and The City* (1992), *Losing Isaiah* (1995), *Rob Roy* (1995), *Titus* (1999).

**Lansbury, Angela** (Brigid) (1925– ) American, born London; *National Velvet* (1944), *Gaslight* (1944), *The Picture of Dorian Gray* (1945), *The Private Affairs of Bel Ami* (1947), *The Three Musketeers* (1948), *The Reluctant Debutante* (1958), *The Long Hot Summer* (1958), *The Dark at the Top of the Stairs* (1960), *The Manchurian Candidate* (1962), *The Greatest Story Ever Told* (1965), *Bedknobs and Broomsticks* (1971), *Death on the Nile* (1978), *The Lady Vanishes* (1979), *Lace* (TV 1984), *Company of Wolves* (1984), *Murder She Wrote* (TV 1984–96).

**Laughton, Charles** (1899–1962) British, born Scarborough; *The Sign of the Cross* (1932), *The Private Life of Henry VIII* (1932), *The Barretts of Wimpole Street*

(1934), *Ruggles of Red Gap* (1935), *Mutiny on the Bounty* (1935), *Les Misérables* (1935), *Rembrandt* (1936), *The Hunchback of Notre Dame* (1939), *Hobson's Choice* (1954), *Witness for the Prosecution* (1957), *Advise and Consent* (1962).

**Laurel, Stan** (Arthur Stanley Jefferson) (1890–1965) Anglo-American, born Ulverston, Lancashire; *Nuts in May* (1917), *Monsieur Don't Care* (1925); for films with Hardy ► **Hardy, Oliver**.

**Laurie, Piper** (Rosetta Jacobs) (1932– ) American, born Detroit, Michigan; *The Hustler* (1961), *Carrie* (1976), *Tim* (1979), *Mae West* (TV 1982), *The Thorn Birds* (TV 1983), *Tender is the Night* (TV 1985), *Return to Oz* (1985), *Children of a Lesser God* (1986), *Tiger Warsaw* (1988), *Twin Peaks* (TV 1991), *Other People's Money* (1991), *Storyville* (1992), *Wrestling Ernest Hemingway* (1993), *The Crossing Guard* (1995).

**Lee, Christopher** (1922– ) British, born London; *The Curse of Frankenstein* (1956), *Dracula* (1958), *The Man Who Could Cheat Death* (1959), *The Mummy* (1959), *The Face of Fu Manchu* (1965), *Horror Express* (1972), *The Three Musketeers* (1973), *The Man With the Golden Gun* (1974), *Return from Witch Mountain* (1976), *Howling II* (1985), *The Land of Faraway* (1988), *Gremlins 2: The New Batch* (1990), *The Knot* (1996), *Ivanhoe* (TV 1997), *The Lord of the Rings: The Fellowship of the Ring* (2001).

**Lee, Spike** (Shelton Jackson Lee) (1957– ) American, born Atlanta, Georgia; *She's Gotta Have It* (1986), *School Daze* (1988), *Do the Right Thing* (1989), *Mo' Better Blues* (1990), *Lonely in America* (1990), *Jungle Fever* (1991), *Malcolm X* (1992).

**Leigh, Janet** (Jeanette Helen Morrison) (1927– ) American, born Merced, California; *Little Women* (1949), *That Forsyte Woman* (1949), *Houdini* (1953), *My Sister Eileen* (1955), *The Vikings* (1958), *Psycho* (1960), *The Manchurian Candidate* (1962), *The Fog* (1980).

**Leigh, Vivien** (Vivien Hartley) (1913–67) British, born Darjeeling, India; *Dark Journey* (1937), *A Yank at Oxford* (1938), *Gone with the Wind* (1939), *Lady Hamilton* (1941), *Caesar and Cleopatra* (1945), *Anna Karenina* (1948), *A Streetcar Named Desire* (1951), *The Roman Spring of Mrs Stone* (1961), *Ship of Fools* (1965).

**Lemmon, Jack** (John Uhler Lemmon III) (1925–2001) American, born Boston, Massachusetts; *It Should Happen to You* (1953), *Mister Roberts* (1955), *Some Like It Hot* (1959), *The Apartment* (1960), *Irma La Douce* (1963), *The Great Race* (1965), *The Odd Couple* (1968), *The Prisoner of Second Avenue* (1975), *The China Syndrome* (1979), *Missing* (1982), *Dad* (1990), *JFK* (1991), *The Player* (1992), *Glengarry Glen Ross* (1992), *Short Cuts* (1993), *The Grass Harp* (1995), *Hamlet* (1996).

**Lewis, Jerry** (Joseph Levitch) (1926– ) American, born Newark, New Jersey; *My Friend Irma* (1949), *The Bellboy* (1960), *Cinderfella* (1960), *The Nutty Professor* (1963), *It's a Mad, Mad, Mad, Mad World* (1963), *The Family Jewels* (1965), *King of Comedy* (1983), *Smorgasbord* (1983), *Cookie* (1988), *Funny Bones* (1995).

**Lithgow, John** (1945– ) American, born Rochester, New York; *Blow Out* (1973), *High Anxiety* (1978), *The World According to Garp* (1982), *Twilight Zone* (1983), *Terms of Endearment* (1983), *The Day After* (TV 1983), *2010* (1984), *Footloose* (1984), *Distant Thunder* (1988), *Memphis Belle* (1990), *Ricochet* (1991), *Raising Cain* (1992), *Cliffhanger* (1993), *The Pelican Brief* (1993).

**Lloyd, Christopher** (1938– ) American, born Stanford, Connecticut; *Star Trek III: The Search for Spock* (1984), *Back to the Future* (1985), *Who Framed Roger Rabbit?* (1988), *Track 29* (1988), *Eight Men Out* (1988), *Back to the Future II* (1989), *Back to the Future III* (1990), *Why Me?* (1990), *The Addams Family* (1991), *Addams Family Values* (1993).

**Lloyd, Emily** (1970– ) British, born London; *Wish You Were Here* (1987), *Cookie* (1988), *In Country* (1989), *Chicago Joe and the Showgirl* (1989), *Scorchers* (1992), *The Poet* (1996), *Welcome to Sarajevo* (1997).

**Lloyd, Harold** (Clayton) (1893–1971) American, born Burchard, Nebraska; *High and Dizzy* (1920), *Grandma's Boy* (1922), *Safety Last* (1923), *Why Worry?* (1923), *The Freshman* (1925), *The Kid Brother* (1927), *Feet First* (1930), *Movie Crazy* (1932).

**Lockwood, Margaret** (Margaret Day) (1916–90) British, born Karachi, India; *Lorna Doone* (1934), *The Beloved Vagabond* (1936), *The Lady Vanishes* (1938), *Night Train to Munich* (1940), *The Man in Grey* (1943), *The Wicked Lady* (1945), *Cast a Dark Shadow* (1947), *The Slipper and the Rose* (1976).

**Loggia, Robert** (1930– ) American, born Staten Island, New York; *THE Cat* (TV 1966), *First Love* (1977), *SOB* (1981), *An Officer and a Gentleman* (1982), *Psycho 2* (1982), *Scarface* (1983), *Jagged Edge* (1985), *Over the Top* (1987), *Big* (1988), *Prizzi's Honor* (1988), *Mancuso FBI* (TV 1989–90), *The Marrying Man* (1991), *Innocent Blood* (1992).

**Lollobrigida, Gina** (1927– ) Italian, born Subiaco; *Belles de Nuit* (1952), *Bread, Love and Dreams* (1953), *Beautiful but Dangerous* (1955), *Trapeze* (1956), *Woman of Straw* (1964), *Falcon Crest* (TV 1984).

**Lom, Herbert** (Herbert Charles Angelo Kuchacevich ze Schluderpacheru) (1917– ) Czech, born Prague; *The Seventh Veil* (1946), *Duel Alibi* (1947), *State Secret* (1950), *The Ladykillers* (1950), *El Cid* (1961), *Phantom of the Opera* (1962), *A Shot in the Dark* (1964), *Murders in the Rue Morgue* (1972), *The Return of the Pink Panther* (1974), *The Pink Panther Strikes Again* (1977), *Revenge of the Pink Panther* (1978), *The Lady Vanishes* (1979), *Hopscotch* (1980), *The Dead Zone* (1983), *Whoops Apocalypse* (1986), *Going Bananas* (1988), *Ten Little Indians* (1989), *The Pope Must Die* (1991), *Son of the Pink Panther* (1993).

**Loren, Sophia** (Sofia Scicolone) (1934– ) Italian, born Rome; *Woman of the River* (1955), *Boy on a Dolphin* (1957), *The Key* (1958), *El Cid* (1961), *Two Women* (1961), *The Millionairess* (1961), *Marriage Italian Style* (1964), *Cinderella Italian Style* (1967), *A Special Day* (1977), *Prêt-À-Porter* (1994), *Grumpier Old Men* (1995).

**Lorre, Peter** (Laszlo Lowenstein) (1904–64) Hungarian, born Rosenberg; *M* (1931), *Mad Love*

(1935), *Crime and Punishment* (1935), *The Maltese Falcon* (1941), *Casablanca* (1942), *The Mask of Dimitrios* (1944), *Arsenic and Old Lace* (1944), *The Beast With Five Fingers* (1946), *My Favourite Brunette* (1947), *20 000 Leagues Under the Sea* (1954), *The Raven* (1963).

**Lowe, Rob** (1964– ) American, born Charlottesville, Virginia; *Class* (1983), *Oxford Blues* (1984), *St Elmo's Fire* (1985), *Youngblood* (1985), *About Last Night* (1987), *Illegally Yours* (1987), *Masquerade* (1988), *Bad Influence* (1990), *Wayne's World* (1991), *The Finest Hour* (1992), *Tommy Boy* (1995).

**Lugosi, Bela** (Bela Ferenc Denzso Blasko) (1882–1956) Hungarian–American, born Lugos (now Romania); *Dracula* (1930), *The Murders in the Rue Morgue* (1931), *White Zombie* (1932), *International House* (1933), *The Black Cat* (1934), *Son of Frankenstein* (1939), *Abbott and Costello Meet Frankenstein* (1948), *Plan 9 from Outer Space* (1956).

**Lumley, Joanna** (1946– ) British, born Kashmir, India; *On Her Majesty's Secret Service* (1969), *General Hospital* (TV 1974–5), *The New Avengers* (TV 1976–7), *Sapphire and Steel* (TV 1979), *Trail of the Pink Panther* (1982), *Curse of the Pink Panther* (1983), *Shirley Valentine* (1989), *Absolutely Fabulous* (TV 1992–7, 2001), *Maybe Baby* (2000).

**McCallum, David** (1933– ) British, born Glasgow; *Violent Playground* (1958), *The Great Escape* (1963), *The Man From UNCLE* (TV 1964–7), *The Greatest Story Ever Told* (1965), *Colditz* (TV 1972), *The Invisible Man* (TV 1975), *Sapphire and Steel* (TV 1979), *The Watcher in the Woods* (1980), *Return of the Man from UNCLE* (TV 1983), *Mother Love* (1989).

**McCarthy, Andrew** (1962– ) American, born New York City; *Class* (1983), *Pretty in Pink* (1986), *Mannequin* (1987), *Less Than Zero* (1987), *Fresh Horses* (1988), *Kansas* (1988), *Weekend at Bernie's* (1989), *Only You* (1992), *Dead Funny* (1994).

**McCarthy, Kevin** (1914– ) American, born Seattle, Washington; *Death of a Salesman* (1952); *Invasion of the Body Snatchers* (1956), *The Misfits* (1961), *The Prize* (1963), *Invasion of the Body Snatchers* (1978), *Piranha* (1978), *Flamingo Road* (1980–1), *The Howling* (1981), *SOB* (1981), *Private Benjamin* (1982), *My Tutor* (1983), *Twilight Zone* (1983), *Innerspace* (1987), *Love or Money* (1990), *The Distinguished Gentleman* (1992), *Just Cause* (1995).

**McCowen, Alec** (Alexander Duncan) (1925– ) British, born Tunbridge Wells; *The Cruel Sea* (1953), *The One That Got Away* (1957), *The Loneliness of the Long Distance Runner* (1962), *The Witches* (1966), *Frenzy* (1972), *Never Say Never Again* (1983), *Forever Young* (1984), *The Assam Garden* (1985), *Cry Freedom* (1987), *Henry V* (1989), *The Age of Innocence* (1993), *Longitude* (2000).

**MacDowell, Andie** (Rosalie Anderson MacDowell) (1958– ) American, born Gaffney, South Carolina; *St Elmo's Fire* (1985), *Sex, Lies and Videotape* (1990), *Green Card* (1990), *The Player* (1992), *Groundhog Day* (1993), *Short Cuts* (1993), *Four Weddings and a Funeral* (1993), *Michael* (1996).

**McGoohan, Patrick** (1928– ) Irish–American, born Long Island, New York; *The Dam Busters* (1954), *Hell Drivers* (1957), *Danger Man* (TV 1960–7), *The Prisoner* (TV 1968–9), *Ice Station Zebra* (1968), *Escape from Alcatraz* (1979).

**McGregor, Ewan** (1971– ) British, born Crieff; *Lipstick on Your Collar* (TV1993), *Scarlet and Black* (TV1993), *Shallow Grave* (1994), *Blue Juice* (1995), *Emma* (1995), *Trainspotting* (1996), *Brassed Off* (1996), *A Life Less Ordinary* (1997), *Star Wars Episode 1: The Phantom Menace* (1999), *Moulin Rouge* (2001).

**McKern, Leo** (Reginald) (1920– ) Australian, born Sydney; *Time without Pity* (1957), *The Mouse That Roared* (1959), *A Jolly Bad Fellow* (1964), *A Man for All Seasons* (1966), *Ryan's Daughter* (1970), *The Omen* (1976), *Candleshoe* (1977), *Rumpole of the Bailey* (TV 1978–80), *The Blue Lagoon* (1980), *The French Lieutenant's Woman* (1981), *Ladyhawke* (1984), *Monsignor Quixote* (TV 1986), *Travelling North* (1986).

**MacLaine, Shirley** (Shirley Beaty) (1934– ) American, born Richmond, Virginia; *The Trouble with Harry* (1955), *Ask any Girl* (1959), *The Apartment* (1959), *Irma La Douce* (1963), *Sweet Charity* (1968), *Terms of Endearment* (1983), *Madame Sousatzka* (1988), *Postcards from the Edge* (1990), *Defending Your Life* (1991), *Used People* (1992), *Guarding Tess* (1994), *The Evening Star* (1996).

**Macnee, (Daniel) Patrick** (1922– ) British, born London; *The Life and Death of Colonel Blimp* (1943), *Hamlet* (1948), *Scrooge* (1951), *Les Girls* (1957), *The Avengers* (TV 1960–8), *The New Avengers* (TV 1977–8), *The Sea Wolves* (1980), *This is Spinal Tap* (1984), *A View to a Kill* (1985), *Chill Factor* (1990).

**McQueen, Steve** (Terence Steven McQueen) (1930–80) American, born Slater, Missouri; *Wanted Dead or Alive* (TV 1958), *The Blob* (1958), *The Magnificent Seven* (1960), *The Great Escape* (1962), *Love with the Proper Stranger* (1963), *The Cincinnatti Kid* (1965), *Bullitt* (1968), *Le Mans* (1971), *Getaway* (1972), *Papillon* (1973), *The Towering Inferno* (1974), *An Enemy of the People* (1977).

**Madonna** (Madonna Louise Veronica Ciccone) (1958– ) American, born Bay City, Michigan; *Desperately Seeking Susan* (1985), *Shanghai Surprise* (1986), *Who's That Girl?* (1987), *Dick Tracy* (1990), *A League of Their Own* (1992), *Body of Evidence* (1993), *Shadows and Fog* (1991), *Blue in the Face* (1995), *Four Rooms* (1995), *Girl 6* (1996), *Evita* (1996).

**Malkovich, John** (1953– ) American, born Christopher, Illinois; *The Killing Fields* (1984), *Places in the Heart* (1984), *Empire of the Sun* (1987), *Dangerous Liaisons* (1988), *The Sheltering Sky* (1990), *Of Mice and Men* (1992), *In the Line of Fire* (1993), *Mary Reilly* (1996), *Being John Malovich* (1999), *Shadow of the Vampire* (2000).

**Mansfield, Jayne** (Vera Jayne Palmer) (1933–67) American, born Bryn Mawr, Pennsylvania; *The Girl Can't Help It* (1957), *The Sheriff of Fractured Jaw* (1959), *Too Hot to Handle* (1960), *The Challenge* (1960), *Promises! Promises!* (1965).

**Martin, Steve** (1945– ) American, born Waco, Texas; *Sgt Pepper's Lonely Hearts Club Band* (1978), *The Jerk* (1978), *Muppet Movie* (1979), *Pennies from Heaven* (1981), *Dead Men Don't Wear Plaid* (1982), *The Man With Two Brains* (1983), *The Lonely Guy* (1984), *All of Me* (1984), *The Three Amigos* (1986), *The Little Shop of Horrors* (1986), *Planes, Trains and Automobiles* (1987), *Roxanne* (1987), *Dirty, Rotten Scoundrels* (1989), *Parenthood* (1989), *My Blue Heaven* (1990), *LA Story* (1991), *Father of the Bride* (1991), *Grand Canyon* (1991), *Housesitter* (1992), *A Simple Twist of Faith* (1994), *Sgt Bilko* (1995).

**Marvin, Lee** (1924–87) American, born New York City; *The Wild One* (1954), *Attack* (1957), *The Killers* (1964), *Cat Ballou* (1965), *The Dirty Dozen* (1967), *Paint Your Wagon* (1969), *Gorky Park* (1983), *Dirty Dozen 2: The Next Mission* (TV 1985).

**Marx Brothers, The: Chico** (Leonard Marx) (1886–1961); **Harpo** (Adolph Marx) (1888–1964); **Groucho** (Julius Henry Marx) (1890–1977); **Zeppo** (Herbert Marx) (1901–79) all American, born New York City; (joint) *The Cocoanuts* (1929), *Monkey Business* (1931), *Horse Feathers* (1932), *Duck Soup* (1933), *A Night at the Opera* (1935), *A Day at the Races* (1937), *A Night in Casablanca* (1946).

**Mason, James** (1909–84) British, born Huddersfield; *I Met a Murderer* (1939), *The Night Has Eyes* (1942), *The Man in Grey* (1943), *Fanny by Gaslight* (1944), *The Seventh Veil* (1945), *The Wicked Lady* (1946), *Odd Man Out* (1946), *Pandora and the Flying Dutchman* (1951), *The Desert Fox* (1951), *Five Fingers* (1952), *The Prisoner of Zenda* (1952), *Julius Caesar* (1953), *20 000 Leagues Under the Sea* (1954), *A Star is Born* (1954), *Journey to the Center of the Earth* (1959), *Lolita* (1962), *The Pumpkin Eater* (1964), *Georgy Girl* (1966), *The Blue Max* (1966), *The Deadly Affair* (1967), *Voyage of the Damned* (1976), *Heaven Can Wait* (1978), *The Boys from Brazil* (1978), *Murder by Decree* (1979), *Evil Under the Sun* (1982), *The Verdict* (1982), *Yellowbeard* (1983), *The Shooting Party* (1984).

**Massey, Raymond** (1896–1983) American, born Toronto, Canada; *The Old Dark House* (1932), *The Scarlet Pimpernel* (1934), *Things to Come* (1936), *The Prisoner of Zenda* (1937), *Abe Lincoln in Illinois* (1940), *Arsenic and Old Lace* (1944), *The Fountainhead* (1949), *East of Eden* (1955), *I Spy* (TV 1955), *Dr Kildare* (TV 1961–6).

**Mastroianni, Marcello** (1924–96) Italian, born Fontana Liri, near Frosinone; *I Miserabili* (1947), *White Nights* (1957), *La Dolce Vita* (1959), *Divorce Italian Style* (1962), *Yesterday, Today and Tomorrow* (1963), *8½* (1963), *Casanova* (1970), *Diamonds for Breakfast* (1968), *Ginger and Fred* (1985), *Black Eyes* (1987), *The Two Lives of Mattia Pascal* (1988), *Traffic Jam* (1988), *Used People* (1992), *Prêt-À-Porter* (1994), *Beyond the Clouds* (1996).

**Matthau, Walter** (Matuschanskayasky) (1920–2000) American, born New York City; *A Face in the Crowd* (1957), *King Creole* (1958), *Charade* (1963), *Mirage* (1965), *The Fortune Cookie* (1966), *A Guide to the Married Man* (1967), *The Odd Couple* (1968), *Hello Dolly* (1969), *Cactus Flower* (1969), *Kotch* (1971), *Earthquake* (1974), *The Taking of Pelham One Two Three* (1974), *Hopscotch* (1980), *Pirates* (1986), *The Couch Trip* (1988), *JFK* (1991), *Grumpy Old Men* (1993), *Grumpier Old Men* (1995), *Out to Sea* (1997).

**Mature, Victor** (1913–99) American, born Louisville, Kentucky; *One Million BC* (1940), *My Darling Clementine* (1946), *Kiss of Death* (1947), *Samson and Delilah* (1949), *The Robe* (1953), *The Egyptian* (1954), *Safari* (1956), *The Long Haul* (1957), *After the Fox* (1966).

**Maura, Carmen** (1945– ) Spanish, born Madrid; *Dark Habits* (1983), *What Have I Done to Deserve This?* (1984), *Law of Desire* (1987), *Women on the Verge of a Nervous Breakdown* (1988), *Baton Rouge* (1988), *How to Be a Woman and Not Die Trying* (1991).

**Mercouri, Melina** (1923–94) Greek, born Athens; *Stella* (1954), *Never on Sunday* (1960), *Topkapi* (1964).

**Midler, Bette** (1945– ) American, born Honolulu, Hawaii; *The Rose* (1979), *Down and Out in Beverly Hills* (1986), *Ruthless People* (1986), *Outrageous Fortune* (1987), *Beaches* (1988), *Big Business* (1988), *Stella* (1989), *Scenes from a Mall* (1991), *For the Boys* (1991), *Hocus Pocus* (1993), *Gypsy* (1993), *Get Shorty* (1995), *The First Wives Club* (1996).

**Mills, Hayley** (1946– ) British, born London; *Tiger Bay* (1959), *Pollyanna* (1960), *The Parent Trip* (1961), *Whistle Down the Wind* (1961), *The Moonspinners* (1965), *Forbush and the Penguins* (1971), *Deadly Strangers* (1974), *After Midnight* (1989).

**Mills, Sir John** (Lewis Ernest Watts) (1908– ) British, born Felixstowe, Suffolk; *Those Were the Days* (1934), *Cottage to Let* (1941), *In Which We Serve* (1942), *Waterloo Road* (1944), *The Way to the Stars* (1945), *Great Expectations* (1946), *The October Man* (1947), *Scott of the Antarctic* (1948), *The History of Mr Polly* (1949), *The Rocking Horse Winner* (1950), *The Colditz Story* (1954), *Hobson's Choice* (1954), *Town on Trial* (1957), *Tiger Bay* (1959), *Swiss Family Robinson* (1959), *Tunes of Glory* (1960), *Ryan's Daughter* (1970), *Lady Caroline Lamb* (1972), *The Big Sleep* (1978), *The 39 Steps* (1978), *Quatermass* (TV 1979), *Young at Heart* (TV 1980–1), *Gandhi* (1982), *Sahara* (1983), *Who's That Girl?* (1987), *Hamlet* (1996).

**Minnelli, Liza** (1946– ) American, born Los Angeles; *Cabaret* (1972), *New York New York* (1977), *Arthur* (1981), *Arthur 2: On the Rocks* (1988), *Rent-a-Cop* (1988), *Stepping Out* (1991).

**Mirren, Helen** (1945– ) British, born London; *Miss Julie* (1973), *Excalibur* (1981), *Cal* (1984), *2010* (1985), *Heavenly Pursuits* (1985), *White Nights* (1986), *Mosquito Coast* (1986), *Pascali's Island* (1988), *The Cook, The Thief, His Wife and Her Lover* (1989), *The Comfort of Strangers* (1990), *Where Angels Fear to Tread* (1991), *Prime Suspect* (TV 1991–5), *The Hawk* (1993), *The Madness of King George* (1994), *Losing Chase* (1996).

**Mitchum, Robert** (1917–97) American, born Bridgeport, Connecticut; *The Story of GI Joe* (1945),

*Pursued* (1947), *Crossfire* (1947), *Out of the Past* (1947), *The Big Steal* (1949), *Night of the Hunter* (1955), *Home from the Hill* (1960), *The Sundowners* (1960), *Cape Fear* (1962), *The List of Adrian Messenger* (1963), *Ryan's Daughter* (1970), *Farewell My Lovely* (1975), *The Big Sleep* (1978), *The Winds of War* (TV 1983), *War and Remembrance* (TV 1987), *Mr North* (1988), *Scrooged* (1988), *Cape Fear* (1991), *Tombstone* (1993), *Backfire* (1994).

**Modine, Matthew** (1959– ) American, born Utah; *Private School* (1983), *Streamers* (1983), *Birdy* (1984), *Mrs Soffel* (1984), *Vision Quest* (1985), *Full Metal Jacket* (1988), *Married to the Mob* (1989), *Memphis Belle* (1990), *Pacific Heights* (1990), *Short Cuts* (1993).

**Monroe, Marilyn** (Norma Jean Mortenson or Baker) (1926–62) American, born Los Angeles; *How to Marry a Millionaire* (1953), *Gentlemen Prefer Blondes* (1953), *The Seven Year Itch* (1955), *Bus Stop* (1956), *Some Like It Hot* (1959), *The Misfits* (1960).

**Montand, Yves** (Ivo Levi) (1921–91) French, born Monsumagno, Italy; *The Wages of Fear* (1953), *Let's Make Love* (1962), *Jean de Florette* (1986), *Manon des Sources* (1986).

**Moore, Demi** (Demi Guines) (1962– ) American, born Roswell, New Mexico; *St Elmo's Fire* (1986), *About Last Night* (1987), *The Seventh Sign* (1988), *We're No Angels* (1990), *Ghost* (1990), *The Butcher's Wife* (1991), *A Few Good Men* (1992), *Indecent Proposal* (1993), *Disclosure* (1994), *The Scarlet Letter* (1995), *Striptease* (1996), *GI Jane* (1997).

**Moore, Dudley** (1935– ) British, born Dagenham, Essex; *Bedazzled* (1967), *Foul Play* (1978), *'10'* (1979), *Arthur* (1981), *Lovesick* (1983), *Unfaithfully Yours* (1983), *Micki and Maude* (1984), *Best Defense* (1985), *Santa Claus* (1985), *Arthur 2: On the Rocks* (1988), *Like Father, Like Son* (1989), *Crazy People* (1990), *Blame it on the Bellboy* (1992), *The Pickle* (1993).

**Moore, Roger** (George) (1927– ) British, born London; *Ivanhoe* (TV 1957), *The Saint* (TV 1963–8), *The Persuaders* (TV 1971–2), *Live and Let Die* (1973), *The Man with the Golden Gun* (1974), *Shout at the Devil* (1976), *The Spy Who Loved Me* (1977), *The Wild Geese* (1978), *Escape to Athena* (1979), *Moonraker* (1979), *For Your Eyes Only* (1981), *The Cannonball Run* (1981), *Octopussy* (1983), *A View to a Kill* (1985), *The Quest* (1996).

**Moorehead, Agnes** (1906–74) American, born Chinton, Massachusetts; *Citizen Kane* (1941), *The Magnificent Ambersons* (1942), *Jane Eyre* (1943), *The Lost Moment* (1947), *The Woman in White* (1948), *Johnny Belinda* (1948), *Summer Holiday* (1948), *The Bat* (1959), *How the West was Won* (1963), *Bewitched* (TV 1964–71).

**Moranis, Rick** (1953– ) Canadian, born Toronto, Ontario; *Strange Brew* (1982), *Ghostbusters* (1984), *Brewster's Millions* (1985), *Little Shop of Horrors* (1986), *Spaceballs* (1987), *Ghostbusters II* (1989), *Parenthood* (1989), *Honey, I Shrunk the Kids* (1990), *My Blue Heaven* (1990), *LA Story* (1991), *Honey, I Blew Up the Kid* (1992).

**Moreau, Jeanne** (1928– ) French, born Paris; *Les Amants* (1958), *Ascenseur Pour L'Échafaud* (1957), *Jules et Jim* (1961), *Eva* (1962), *The Trial* (1963), *Journal d'une Femme de Chambre* (1964), *Viva Maria* (1965), *Nikita* (1990), *La Vieille Qui Marchait Dans La Mer* (1991), *Ever After* (1998).

**Morgan, Frank** (Francis Phillip Wupperman) (1890–1949) American, born New York City; *Hallelujah I'm a Bum* (1933), *Bombshell* (1933), *The Affairs of Cellini* (1934), *The Great Ziegfeld* (1936), *Trouble for Two* (1936), *Piccadilly Jim* (1936), *Dimples* (1936), *The Last of Mr Cheyney* (1937), *The Wizard of Oz* (1939), *Boom Town* (1940), *The Vanishing Virginian* (1942), *Tortilla Flat* (1942), *The Human Comedy* (1943), *The Three Musketeers* (1948).

**Morgan, Harry** (Harry Bratsburg) (1915– ) American, born Detroit, Michigan; *High Noon* (1952), *December Bride* (TV 1954–8), *The Teahouse of the August Moon* (1956), *Dragnet* (TV 1969), *M*A*S*H* (TV 1976–83), *Aftermash* (TV 1983), *Dragnet* (TV 1987).

**Murphy, Eddie** (1961– ) American, born Brooklyn, New York City; *48 Hours* (1982), *Trading Places* (1983), *Beverly Hills Cop* (1985), *The Golden Child* (1986), *Beverly Hills Cop II* (1987), *Coming to America* (1988), *Harlem Nights* (1989), *Another 48 Hours* (1990), *Boomerang* (1992), *Distinguished Gentleman* (1992), *Beverly Hills Cop III* (1994), *The Nutty Professor* (1995), *The Metro* (1997).

**Murray, Bill** (1950– ) American, born Evanston, Illinois; *Meatballs* (1977), *Caddyshack* (1980), *Stripes* (1981), *Tootsie* (1982), *Ghostbusters* (1984), *Razor's Edge* (1984), *Little Shop of Horrors* (1986), *Scrooged* (1988), *Ghostbusters II* (1989), *What About Bob?* (1991), *Mad Dog and Glory* (1992), *Groundhog Day* (1993), *Ed Wood* (1994), *Kingpin* (1996).

**Neal, Patricia** (1926– ) American, born Packard, Kentucky; *The Fountainhead* (1949), *The Hasty Heart* (1950), *Diplomatic Courier* (1952), *Breakfast at Tiffany's* (1961), *Hud* (1963), *A Face in the Crowd* (1957), *All Quiet on the Western Front* (TV 1980).

**Neeson, Liam** (1952– ) British, born Ballymena, Northern Ireland; *Excalibur* (1981), *Suspect* (1987), *High Spirits* (1988), *The Good Mother* (1988), *The Dead Pool* (1988), *The Big Man* (1990), *Husbands and Wives* (1992), *Schindler's List* (1994), *Nell* (1994), *Rob Roy* (1995), *Michael Collins* (1996), *Star Wars Episode 1: The Phantom Menace* (1999).

**Neill, Sam** (1947– ) New Zealander, born Northern Ireland; *The Final Conflict* (1982), *Reilly: Ace of Spies* (TV 1983), *Robbery Under Arms* (TV 1985), *Plenty* (1985), *Kane and Abel* (TV 1988), *A Cry in the Dark* (1988), *Evil Angels* (1988), *The Hunt for Red October* (1990), *Jurassic Park* (1993).

**Newman, Paul** (1925– ) American, born Cleveland, Ohio; *Somebody Up There Likes Me* (1956), *The Long Hot Summer* (1958), *The Hustler* (1961), *Hud* (1963), *The Prize* (1963), *Torn Curtain* (1966), *Cool Hand Luke* (1967), *Butch Cassidy and the Sundance Kid* (1969), *Judge Roy Bean* (1972), *The Sting* (1973), *Absence of*

*Malice* (1981), *The Verdict* (1982), *The Color of Money* (1986), *Blaze* (1990), *Mr and Mrs Bridge* (1990), *The Hudsucker Proxy* (1994), *Nobody's Fool* (1994), *Magic Hour* (1997).

**Nicholson, Jack** (1937– ) American, born Neptune, New Jersey; *The Little Shop of Horrors* (1960), *Easy Rider* (1969), *Five Easy Pieces* (1970), *Carnal Knowledge* (1971), *The Last Detail* (1974), *Chinatown* (1974), *One Flew Over the Cuckoo's Nest* (1975), *Tommy* (1975), *The Shining* (1980), *The Postman Always Rings Twice* (1981), *Reds* (1981), *Terms of Endearment* (1983), *Prizzi's Honor* (1985), *Broadcast News* (1987), *Ironweed* (1987), *The Witches of Eastwick* (1987), *Batman* (1989), *Two Jakes* (1990), *The Death of Napoleon* (1991), *Man Trouble* (1992), *A Few Good Men* (1992), *Hoffa* (1992), *Wolf* (1994), *The Crossing Guard* (1995), *Blood and Wine* (1996), *Mars Attacks!* (1996), *As Good as it Gets* (1997).

**Nielsen, Leslie** (1926– ) Canadian, born Regina, Saskatchewan; *Forbidden Planet* (1956), *Incident in San Francisco* (TV 1970), *The Poseidon Adventure* (1972), *Airplane* (1980), *Prom Night* (1980), *Police Squad* (TV 1982), *Soul Man* (TV 1986), *The Patriot* (TV 1987), *Fatal Confession* (TV 1987), *Naked Gun* (1988), *Repossessed* (1990), *Naked Gun $2\frac{1}{2}$: The Smell of Fear* (1991), *Naked Gun $33\frac{1}{3}$: The Final Insult* (1994), *Dracula: Dead and Loving It* (1995), *Spy Hard* (1996).

**Nimoy, Leonard** (1931– ) American, born Boston, Massachusetts; *Star Trek* (TV 1966–8), *Mission Impossible* (TV 1970–2), *Invasion of the Body Snatchers* (1978), *Star Trek: The Motion Picture* (1979), *Star Trek II: The Wrath of Khan* (1982), *Star Trek III: The Search for Spock* (1984), *Star Trek IV: The Voyage Home* (1986), *Star Trek V: The Final Frontier* (1989), *Star Trek VI: The Undiscovered Country* (1991).

**Niven, David** (James David Graham Niven) (1910–83) British, born London; *Thank You Jeeves* (1936), *The Prisoner of Zenda* (1937), *Wuthering Heights* (1939), *Bachelor Mother* (1939), *Raffles* (1940), *The Way Ahead* (1944), *A Matter of Life and Death* (1946), *Carrington VC* (1955), *Around the World in Eighty Days* (1956), *Separate Tables* (1958), *The Guns of Navarone* (1961), *The Pink Panther* (1964), *Casino Royale* (1967), *Candleshoe* (1977), *Death on the Nile* (1978), *Escape to Athena* (1979), *Trail of the Pink Panther* (1982), *Curse of the Pink Panther* (1982).

**Nolte, Nick** (1940– ) American, born Omaha, Nebraska; *Rich Man Poor Man* (TV 1976), *Cannery Row* (1982), *48 Hours* (1982), *Down and Out in Beverly Hills* (1986), *Weeds* (1987), *Three Fugitives* (1989), *Another 48 Hours* (1990), *Cape Fear* (1991), *Prince of Tides* (1991), *The Player* (1992), *Lorenzo's Oil* (1992), *Blue Chips* (1993), *I'll Do Anything* (1994), *I Love Trouble* (1994), *Jefferson in Paris* (1995), *Nightwatch* (1996), *The Thin Red Line* (1998).

**Oberon, Merle** (Estelle Merle O'Brien Thompson) (1911–79) Anglo-Indian, born Bombay, India; *The Dark Angel* (1935), *The Scarlet Pimpernel* (1935), *The Divorce of Lady X* (1938), *Wuthering Heights* (1939), *That Uncertain Feeling* (1941), *Forever and a Day* (1943), *A Song to Remember* (1943), *The Oscar* (1966), *Hotel* (1967), *Interval* (1973).

**Oldman, Gary** (1959– ) British, born New Cross, South London; *Sid and Nancy* (1986), *Prick Up Your Ears* (1987), *We Think the World of You* (1988), *Track 29* (1988), *Rosencrantz and Guilderstern are Dead* (1990), *JFK* (1991), *Bram Stoker's Dracula* (1992), *True Romance* (1993), *Leon* (1994), *The Scarlet Letter* (1995), *The Fifth Element* (1996).

**Olivier, Sir Laurence** (Kerr) (1907–89) British, born Dorking; *The Divorce of Lady X* (1938), *Wuthering Heights* (1939), *Rebecca* (1940), *Pride and Prejudice* (1940), *Henry V* (1944), *Hamlet* (1948), *Richard III* (1956), *The Prince and the Showgirl* (1958), *The Devil's Disciple* (1959), *The Entertainer* (1960), *Sleuth* (1972), *Marathon Man* (1976), *A Bridge Too Far* (1977), *Brideshead Revisited* (TV 1981), *A Voyage Round My Father* (TV 1982), *The Last Days of Pompeii* (1984), *The Jigsaw Man* (1984), *The Bounty* (1984), *A Talent for Murder* (TV 1986), *War Requiem* (1988).

**O'Neal, Ryan** (Patrick Ryan O'Neal) (1941– ) American, born Los Angeles; *Peyton Place* (TV 1964–8), *Love Story* (1970), *What's Up, Doc?* (1972), *Paper Moon* (1973), *Nickelodeon* (1976), *A Bridge Too Far* (1977), *Green Ice* (1980), *Fever Pitch* (1985), *Tough Guys Don't Dance* (1987), *Chances Are* (1989).

**O'Neal, Tatum** (1963– ) American, born Los Angeles; *Paper Moon* (1973), *Nickelodeon* (1976), *International Velvet* (1978), *Little Darlings* (1980), *Little Noises* (1991), *Basquiat* (1996).

**O'Sullivan, Maureen** (1911–98) Irish, born Boyle; *Tarzan the Ape Man* (1932), *Tarzan and His Mate* (1934), *The Barretts of Wimpole Street* (1934), *Pride and Prejudice* (1940), *Never Too Late* (1965), *Hannah and Her Sisters* (1986), *Peggy Sue Got Married* (1986), *Stranded* (1987).

**O'Toole, Peter** (Seamus) (1932– ) Irish, born Kerry, Connemara; *Lawrence of Arabia* (1962), *How to Steal a Million* (1966), *The Lion in Winter* (1968), *Goodbye Mr Chips* (1969), *The Ruling Class* (1972), *The Stunt Man* (1980), *My Favourite Year* (1982), *The Last Emperor* (1987), *High Spirits* (1988), *Wings of Fame* (1989), *Isabelle Eberhardt* (1990), *King Ralph* (1991), *World's Apart* (1992).

**Pacino, Al** (Alfredo Pacino) (1940– ) American, born New York City; *The Godfather* (1972), *The Godfather, Part II* (1974), *Dog Day Afternoon* (1975), *Scarface* (1983), *Revolution* (1984), *Sea of Love* (1990), *Dick Tracy* (1990), *The Godfather, Part III* (1990), *Frankie and Johnny* (1991), *Glengarry Glen Ross* (1992), *Scent of a Woman* (1992), *Damon* (1992), *Carlito's Way* (1993), *Heat* (1995), *Donnie Brasco* (1997), *The Insider* (1999).

**Page, Geraldine** (1924–87) American, born Kirksville, Missouri; *Summer and Smoke* (1961), *Sweet Bird of Youth* (1962), *Dear Heart* (1965), *The Happiest Millionaire* (1966), *Interiors* (1978), *Harry's War* (1980), *Honky Tonk Freeway* (1981), *The Pope of Greenwich Village* (1984), *The Trip to Bountiful* (1985).

**Palance, Jack** (Walter Palanuik) (1919– ) American, born Lattimer, Pennsylvania; *Panic in the Streets* (1950), *Shane* (1953), *The Big Knife* (1953), *Arrowhead* (1953), *They Came to Rob Las Vegas* (1968), *Oklahoma Crude* (1973), *Ripley's Believe It or Not* (TV 1982–6), *Gor* (1988), *Batman* (1988), *Young Guns* (1988), *Tango and Cash* (1989), *City Slickers* (1991), *Tombstone* (1993), *Marco Polo* (1998).

**Palin, Michael** (1943– ) British, born Sheffield; *Monty Python's Flying Circus* (TV 1969–74), *And Now for Something Completely Different* (1970), *Monty Python and the Holy Grail* (1974), *Three Men in a Boat* (TV 1975), *Jabberwocky* (1976), *Ripping Yarns* (TV 1976–80), *The Life of Brian* (1978), *Time Bandits* (1980), *The Meaning of Life* (1982), *The Missionary* (1982), *A Private Function* (1984), *Brazil* (1985), *A Fish Called Wanda* (1988), *Around the World in 80 Days* (TV 1990), *American Friends* (1990), *GBH* (TV 1991), *Pole to Pole* (TV 1992), *Fierce Creatures* (1996), *Full Circle* (TV 1997).

**Peck, Gregory** (Eldred) (1916– ) American, born La Jolla, California; *The Keys to the Kingdom* (1944), *Spellbound* (1945), *Duel in the Sun* (1946), *Gentleman's Agreement* (1947), *The Macomber Affair* (1947), *The Paradine Case* (1947), *Twelve O'Clock High* (1949), *The Gunfighter* (1950), *Captain Horatio Hornblower* (1951), *The Million Pound Note* (1954), *The Purple Plain* (1955), *The Man in the Grey Flannel Suit* (1956), *The Big Country* (1958), *The Guns of Navarone* (1961), *Cape Fear* (1962), *To Kill a Mockingbird* (1963), *The Omen* (1976), *Old Gringo* (1989), *Other People's Money* (1991), *Cape Fear* (1991).

**Penn, Sean** (1960– ) American, born Burbank, California; *Taps* (1981), *Fast Times at Ridgemont High* (1982), *Racing with the Moon* (1984), *The Falcon and the Snowman* (1985), *At Close Range* (1986), *Shanghai Surprise* (1986), *Colors* (1988), *Judgement in Berlin* (1988), *Casualties of War* (1989), *State of Grace* (1990), *Carlito's Way* (1993), *Dead Man Walking* (1995), *The Thin Red Line* (1998).

**Perkins, Anthony** (1932–92) American, born New York City; *The Actress* (1953), *Desire Under the Elms* (1957), *Fear Strikes Out* (1957), *This Angry Age* (1958), *Psycho* (1960), *Five Miles to Midnight* (1962), *Murder on the Orient Express* (1974), *For the Term of His Natural Life* (TV 1982), *Psycho II* (1983), *Crimes of Passion* (1985), *Psycho III* (1986), *Destroyer* (1988), *Edge of Sanity* (1989), *Naked Target* (1991).

**Pesci, Joe** (1943– ) American, born Newark, New Jersey; *Raging Bull* (1980), *Lethal Weapon 2* (1989), *Goodfellas* (1990), *Home Alone* (1990), *JFK* (1991), *My Cousin Vinny* (1992), *Lethal Weapon 3* (1992), *Home Alone 2* (1992), *A Bronx Tale* (1993), *Jimmy Hollywood* (1994), *Lethal Weapon 4* (1998).

**Pfeiffer, Michelle** (1957– ) American, born Santa Ana, California; *Grease 2* (1982), *Scarface* (1983), *Sweet Liberty* (1982), *Into the Night* (1985), *The Witches of Eastwick* (1987), *Dangerous Liaisons* (1988), *Tequila Sunrise* (1988), *Married to the Mob* (1989), *The Fabulous Baker Boys* (1989), *The Russia House* (1990), *Frankie and Johnny* (1991), *Batman Returns* (1992), *Age of Innocence* (1993), *My Posse Don't Do Homework* (1994), *Wolf* (1994), *Up Close and Personal* (1995), *What Lies Beneath* (2000).

**Philipe, Gérard** (1922–59) French, born Cannes; *The Idiot* (1946), *Le Diable au Corps* (1947), *Une Si Jolie Petite Plage* (1949), *Fanfan la Tulipe* (1951), *Les Belles de Nuit* (1952), *Knave of Hearts* (1954), *Montparnasse* (1957), *Les Liaisons Dangereuses* (1959).

**Phoenix, River** (1970–93) American, born Madras, Oregon; *Explorers* (1985), *Mosquito Coast* (1986), *Running on Empty* (1988), *Jimmy Reardon* (1988), *Little Nikita* (1988), *Indiana Jones and the Last Crusade* (1989), *I Love You to Death* (1990), *Dogfight* (1991), *My Own Private Idaho* (1991), *Sneakers* (1992), *The Thing Called Love* (1993).

**Pickford, Mary** (Gladys Mary Smith) (1893–1979) Canadian, born Toronto, Ontario; *The Violin Maker of Cremona* (1909), *Rebecca of Sunnybrook Farm* (1917), *Poor Little Rich Girl* (1917), *Pollyanna* (1919), *Little Lord Fauntleroy* (1921), *Tess of the Storm Country* (1922), *The Taming of the Shrew* (1929), *Coquette* (1929), *Secrets* (1933).

**Pickup, Ronald** (Alfred) (1940– ) British, born Chester; *Day of the Jackal* (1973), *The 39 Steps* (1978), *Nijinski* (1980), *Never Say Never Again* (1983), *Fortunes of War* (TV 1987), *Testimony* (1987).

**Pitt, Brad** (William Bradley Pitt) (1963– ) American, born Shawnee, Oklahoma; *Thelma and Louise* (1991), *A River Runs Through It* (1992), *Kalifornia* (1993), *True Romance* (1993), *Interview with the Vampire* (1994), *Legends of the Fall* (1994), *Seven* (1995), *Twelve Monkeys* (1995), *Sleepers* (1996), *Seven Years in Tibet* (1997), *Fight Club* (1999).

**Pleasence, Donald** (1919–95) British, born Worksop; *Robin Hood* (TV 1955–7), *Battle of the Sexes* (1959), *Dr Crippen* (1962), *The Great Escape* (1963), *The Caretaker* (1964), *Cul-de-Sac* (1966), *Fantastic Voyage* (1966), *You Only Live Twice* (1967), *Escape to Witch Mountain* (1975), *The Eagle Has Landed* (1977), *Oh God* (1977), *Telefon* (1977), *Halloween* (1978), *Sgt Pepper's Lonely Hearts Club Band* (1979), *Escape from New York* (1981), *Halloween 4* (1988), *Hanna's War* (1988), *Ground Zero* (1988), *Halloween 5* (1989), *Ten Little Indians* (1989), *Shadows and Fog* (1992), *Halloween 6* (1995).

**Plowright, Joan** (1929– ) British, born Brigg, Lincolnshire; *The Entertainer* (1960), *Drowning by Numbers* (1988), *Tea with Mussolini* (1999).

**Plummer, Christopher** (1927– ) Canadian, born Toronto, Ontario; *The Fall of the Roman Empire* (1964), *The Sound of Music* (1965), *Waterloo* (1970), *The Man Who Would Be King* (1975), *The Return of the Pink Panther* (1975), *International Velvet* (1978), *Hanover Street* (1979), *Somewhere in Time* (1980), *The Janitor* (1981), *Dreamscape* (1984), *Where the Heart Is* (1990), *Liar's Edge* (1992), *Impolite* (1992), *Malcolm X* (1992), *Twelve Monkeys* (1995), *The Insider* (1999).

**Poitier, Sidney** (1927– ) American, born Miami, Florida; *No Way Out* (1950), *Cry, the Beloved Country* (1952), *The Blackboard Jungle* (1955), *The Defiant Ones* (1958), *Porgy and Bess* (1959), *Lilies of the Field* (1963), *To Sir with Love* (1967), *In the Heat of the Night* (1967), *Guess Who's Coming to Dinner* (1967), *Little Nikita* (1988), *Shoot to Kill* (1988), *Separate But Equal* (TV 1991), *Sneakers* (1992), *To Sir with Love II* (1996).

**Powell, Robert** (1944– ) British, born Salford, Lancashire; *The Italian Job* (1969), *Jesus of Nazareth* (TV 1977), *The 39 Steps* (1978), *Pygmalion* (TV 1981), *Frankenstein* (TV 1984), *Hannay* (TV 1988).

**Powers, Stefanie** (Stefania Federkiewicz) (1942– ) American, born Hollywood, California; *Experiment in Terror* (1962), *Fanatic* (1964), *Stagecoach* (1966), *The Girl from UNCLE* (1966), *Herbie Rides Again* (1973), *Escape to Athena* (1979), *Hart to Hart* (TV 1979–83), *Family Secrets* (TV 1984).

**Presley, Elvis** (Aaron) (1935–77) American, born Tupelo, Mississippi; *Love Me Tender* (1956), *Jailhouse Rock* (1957), *Loving You* (1957), *King Creole* (1958), *GI Blues* (1960), *Girl Happy* (1965), *That's the Way It Is* (1971).

**Price, Vincent** (1911–93) American, born St Louis, Missouri; *Tower of London* (1940), *Dragonwyck* (1946), *His Kind of Woman* (1941), *House of Wax* (1953), *The Story of Mankind* (1957), *The Fly* (1958), *The Fall of the House of Usher* (1961), *The Raven* (1963), *The Tomb of Ligeia* (1964), *City Under the Sea* (1965), *House of a Thousand Dolls* (1967), *The House of Long Shadows* (1983), *The Whales of August* (1987), *Dead Heat* (1988), *Edward Scissorhands* (1991).

**Pryor, Richard** (1940– ) American, born Peoria, Illinois; *Busy Body* (1967), *Lady Sings the Blues* (1972), *Silver Streak* (1976), *Blue Collar* (1978), *Stir Crazy* (1980), *Superman III* (1982), *Brewster's Millions* (1985), *Jo Jo Dancer Your Life is Calling* (1986), *Harlem Nights* (1989), *Lost Highway* (1997).

**Quaid, Dennis** (1954– ) American, born Houston, Texas; *Breaking Away* (1978), *Caveman* (1980), *The Night the Lights Went Out in Georgia* (1980), *Bill* (TV 1981), *All Night Long* (1981), *Johnny Belinda* (TV 1982), *The Right Stuff* (1983), *Jaws 3D* (1983), *Dreamscape* (1984), *The Big Easy* (1986), *Innerspace* (1987), *Suspect* (1987), *DOA* (1988), *Great Balls of Fire* (1989), *Come See the Paradise* (1990), *Postcards from the Edge* (1990), *Wilder Napalm* (1992), *Undercover Blues* (1993), *Wyatt Earp* (1995), *Dragon Heart* (1996), *Any Given Sunday* (1999).

**Quaid, Randy** (1950– ) American, born Houston, Texas; *The Last Picture Show* (1971), *What's Up, Doc?* (1972), *Paper Moon* (1973), *Midnight Express* (1978), *Vacation* (1983), *Parents* (1988), *Caddyshack II* (1988), *Christmas Vacation* (1989), *Days of Thunder* (1990), *Texasville* (1990).

**Quayle, Sir Anthony** (1913–89) British, born Ainsdale, Lancashire; *Ice Cold in Alex* (1958), *The Guns of Navarone* (1961), *Lawrence of Arabia* (1962).

**Quinn, Anthony** (Rudolph Oaxaca) (1915–2001) Irish–American, born Chihuahua, Mexico; *Viva Zapata* (1952), *La Strada* (1954), *Lust for Life* (1956), *The Guns of Navarone* (1961), *Zorba the Greek* (1964), *The Shoes of the Fisherman* (1968), *Revenge* (1989), *Ghosts Can't Do It* (1990), *Jungle Fever* (1991), *Mobsters* (1991), *Last Action Hero* (1993), *A Walk in the Clouds* (1995).

**Rampling, Charlotte** (1946– ) British, born Sturmer; *Georgy Girl* (1966), *The Dammed* (1969), *Zardoz* (1973), *Orca* (1977), *Stardust Memories* (1980), *The Verdict* (1982), *Max mon Amour* (1986), *Angel Heart* (1987), *Paris by Night* (1988), *DOA* (1988), *Head Games* (1996), *Wings of the Dove* (1997).

**Rathbone, Basil** (Philip St John) (1892–1967) British, born Johannesburg, South Africa; *David Copperfield* (1935), *Anna Karenina* (1935), *Captain Blood* (1935), *Romeo and Juliet* (1936), *The Adventures of Robin Hood* (1938), *The Hound of the Baskervilles* (1939), *The Adventures of Sherlock Holmes* (1939), *Spider Woman* (1944), *Heartbeat* (1946), *The Court Jester* (1956).

**Reagan, Ronald** (Wilson) (1911– ) American, born Tampico, Illinois; *King's Row* (1941), *Desperate Journey* (1942), *The Hasty Heart* (1949), *Bedtime for Bonzo* (1951), *The Killer* (1964).

**Redford, (Charles) Robert** (1937– ) American, born Santa Monica, California; *Barefoot in the Park* (1967), *Butch Cassidy and the Sundance Kid* (1969), *The Candidate* (1972), *The Great Gatsby* (1973), *The Sting* (1973), *All the President's Men* (1976), *The Electric Horseman* (1979), *The Natural* (1984), *Out of Africa* (1985), *Legal Eagles* (1986), *Havana* (1990), *Sneakers* (1992), *Indecent Proposal* (1993), *Up Close and Personal* (1995), *The Horse Whisperer* (1998).

**Redgrave, Sir Michael** (Scudamore) (1908–85) British, born Bristol; *The Lady Vanishes* (1938), *The Way to the Stars* (1945), *The Browning Version* (1951), *The Importance of Being Earnest* (1952), *The Dam Busters* (1955), *The Quiet American* (1958), *The Innocents* (1961), *Nicholas and Alexandra* (1971).

**Redgrave, Vanessa** (1937– ) British, born London; also stage; *Morgan!* (1965), *Blow-Up* (1966), *Camelot* (1967), *Mary, Queen of Scots* (1971), *Julia* (1977), *Playing for Time* (TV 1980), *The Bostonians* (1984), *Wetherby* (1985), *Three Sovereigns for Sarah* (TV 1985), *Prick Up Your Ears* (1987), *Consuming Passions* (1988), *The Ballad of The Sad Café* (1991), *What Ever Happened to Baby Jane?* (1991), *Howards End* (1992), *Little Odessa* (1994), *Mission: Impossible* (1996).

**Reed, Oliver** (Robert Oliver Reed) (1938–99) British, born Wimbledon, London; *The Damned* (1962), *The System* (1964), *The Jokers* (1966), *Women in Love* (1969), *The Brood* (1980), *Condorman* (1981), *Castaway* (1987), *Return of the Musketeers* (1989), *The Pit and the Pendulum* (1991), *Severed Ties* (1992), *Funny Bones* (1995), *Gladiator* (2000).

**Reeve, Christopher** (1952– ) American, born New York City; *Superman* (1978), *Superman II* (1980), *Somewhere in Time* (1980), *Monsignor* (1982), *Death Trap* (1982), *Superman III* (1983), *The Bostonians* (1984), *Superman IV* (1987), *Switching Channels*

(1988), *Noises Off* (1992), *The Remains of the Day* (1993), *The Sea Wolf* (TV 1993), *Morning Glory* (1993), *Speechless* (1994), *Village of the Damned* (1995).

**Reeves, Keanu** (1964– ) American, born Beirut, Lebanon; *River's Edge* (1986), *Prince of Pennsylvania* (1988), *The Night Before* (1988), *Dangerous Liaisons* (1988), *Permanent Record* (1988), *Bill and Ted's Excellent Adventure* (1989), *Parenthood* (1989), *Love You to Death* (1990), *Bill and Ted's Bogus Journey* (1991), *My Own Private Idaho* (1991), *Dracula* (1992), *Much Ado About Nothing* (1993), *Little Buddha* (1993), *Speed* (1994), *Even Cowgirls Get the Blues* (1994), *A Walk in the Clouds* (1995), *Feeling Minnesota* (1995), *Johnny Mnemonic* (1995), *The Matrix* (1999).

**Reynolds, Burt** (1935– ) American, born Waycross, Georgia; *Gunsmoke* (TV 1965–7), *Hunters Are for Killing* (TV 1970), *Deliverance* (1972), *Nickelodeon* (1976), *Smokey and the Bandit* (1977), *Hooper* (1978), *Starting Over* (1979), *Smokey and the Bandit II* (1980), *The Cannonball Run* (1981), *Sharkey's Machine* (1981), *The Best Little Whorehouse in Texas* (1982), *Stroker Ace* (1983), *The Man Who Loved Women* (1983), *City Heat* (1984), *Rent-a-Cop* (1988), *Switching Channels* (1988), *Breaking In* (1989), *Evening Shade* (TV 1990–4), *Modern Love* (1990), *Cop-and-a-Half* (1992), *The Player* (1992), *The Maddening* (1995), *Striptease* (1996), *Trigger Happy* (1996), *Boogie Nights* (1997).

**Richardson, Miranda** (1958– ) British, born Liverpool; *Dance with a Stranger* (1984), *The Innocent* (1985), *Blackadder II* (TV 1986), *Empire of the Sun* (1987), *A Month in the Country* (1988), *The Fool* (1990), *Enchanted April* (1991), *Damage* (1992), *The Crying Game* (1992), *Tom and Viv* (1994), *Kansas City* (1996), *Sleepy Hollow* (1999).

**Richardson, Sir Ralph** (1902–83) British, born Cheltenham; *Bulldog Jack* (1935), *Q Planes* (1939), *The Four Feathers* (1939), *Anna Karenina* (1948), *The Fallen Idol* (1948), *The Heiress* (1949), *Richard III* (1956), *Oscar Wilde* (1960), *Long Day's Journey into Night* (1962), *Dr Zhivago* (1966), *The Wrong Box* (1967), *A Doll's House* (1973), *The Man in the Iron Mask* (1977), *Time Bandits* (1980), *Dragonslayer* (1981), *Greystoke* (1984).

**Rickman, Alan** (1947– ) British, born London; *Die Hard* (1988), *Robin Hood: Prince of Thieves* (1991), *Truly, Madly, Deeply* (1991), *Sense and Sensibility* (1995), *Michael Collins* (1996), *Rasputin* (TV 1996), *Harry Potter and the Philosopher's Stone* (2001).

**Rigg, Dame Diana** (1938– ) British, born Doncaster, Yorkshire; *The Avengers* (TV 1965–7), *On Her Majesty's Secret Service* (1969), *Theatre of Blood* (1973), *Diana* (TV 1973–4), *Evil Under the Sun* (1981), *Mother Love* (TV 1989), *Snow White* (1989).

**Ringwald, Molly** (1968– ) American, born Rosewood, California; *The Facts of Life* (TV 1979–80), *Tempest* (1982), *Space Hunter 3D: Adventures in the Forbidden Zone* (1983), *Packin' It In* (TV 1983), *Sixteen Candles* (1984), *The Breakfast Club* (1985), *Pretty in Pink* (1986), *Maybe Baby* (1987), *The Pick-up Artist* (1987), *Fresh Horses* (1988), *For Keeps?* (1988), *Loser Takes All* (1989), *Betsy's Wedding* (1990), *Seven Sundays* (1994), *Malicious* (1995), *Office Killer* (1996).

**Robards, Jason** (Jr) (1922– ) American, born Chicago; *Tender is the Night* (1961), *Long Day's Journey into Night* (1962), *The Hour of the Gun* (1967), *Once Upon a Time in the West* (1969), *Tora! Tora! Tora!* (1970), *All the President's Men* (1976), *Julia* (1977), *Melvin and Howard* (1980), *The Legend of the Lone Ranger* (1981), *The Day After* (1983), *Sakharov* (TV 1984), *The Long Hot Summer* (TV 1985), *Bright Lights, Big City* (1988), *The Good Mother* (1988), *Parenthood* (1989), *Reunion* (1989), *Storyville* (1992), *Philadelphia* (1993), *The Trial* (1993), *The Paper* (1994), *My Antonia* (TV 1995).

**Robbins, Tim** (Timothy Francis) (1958– ) American, born New York City; *Bull Durham* (1988), *Cadillac Man* (1990), *Jacob's Ladder* (1990), *The Player* (1992), *Bob Roberts* (1992), *Short Cuts* (1993), *The Hudsucker Proxy* (1994), *The Shawshank Redemption* (1994), *Nothing to Lose* (1996), *Arlington Road* (1999).

**Roberts, Julia** (1967– ) American, born Smyrna, Georgia; *Mystic Pizza* (1988), *Steel Magnolias* (1989), *Flatliners* (1990), *Pretty Woman* (1990), *Sleeping with the Enemy* (1991), *Hook* (1991), *The Player* (1992), *The Pelican Brief* (1993), *I Love Trouble* (1994), *Prêt-À-Porter* (1994), *Michael Collins* (1996), *My Best Friend's Wedding* (1997), *Notting Hill* (1999), *Erin Brockovich* (2000).

**Robinson, Edward G** (Emanuel Goldenberg) (1893–1973) American, born Bucharest, Romania; *Little Caesar* (1930), *Five Star Final* (1931), *The Whole Town's Talking* (1935), *The Last Gangster* (1937), *A Slight Case of Murder* (1938), *The Amazing Dr Clitterhouse* (1938), *Dr Ehrlich's Magic Bullet* (1940), *Brother Orchid* (1940), *The Sea Wolf* (1941), *Double Indemnity* (1944), *The Woman in the Window* (1944), *Scarlet Street* (1945), *All My Sons* (1948), *Key Largo* (1948), *House of Strangers* (1949), *Two Weeks in Another Town* (1962), *The Cincinnati Kid* (1965), *Soylent Green* (1973).

**Rogers, Ginger** (Virginia Katherine McMath) (1911–95) American, born Independence, Missouri; *Young Man of Manhattan* (1930), *42nd Street* (1933), *Flying Down to Rio* (1933), *The Gay Divorcee* (1934), *Top Hat* (1935), *Follow the Fleet* (1936), *Stage Door* (1937), *Bachelor Mother* (1939), *Kitty Foyle* (1940), *Roxie Hart* (1942), *Lady in the Dark* (1944).

**Rogers, Will** (William Penn Adair) (1879–1935) American, born Colagah, Indian Territory (now Oklahoma); *Jubilo* (1919), *State Fair* (1933), *Judge Priest* (1934), *David Harum* (1934), *Handy Andy* (1934), *Life Begins at Forty* (1935), *Steamboat round the Bend* (1935).

**Rooney, Mickey** (Joe Yule, Jr) (1920– ) American, born Brooklyn, New York City; *A Midsummer Night's Dream* (1935), *Ah Wilderness* (1935), *A Family Affair* (1937), *Judge Hardy's Children* (1938), *Boys Town* (1938), *Babes in Arms* (1939), *The Human Comedy* (1943), *National Velvet* (1944), *Summer Holiday*

(1948), *The Bold and the Brave* (1956), *Breakfast at Tiffany's* (1961), *It's a Mad, Mad, Mad, Mad World* (1963), *Leave 'Em Laughing* (TV 1980), *Bill* (TV 1981), *Erik the Viking* (1989), *Home for Christmas* (TV 1990), *The Toy Maker* (1991), *The Legend of Wolf Mountain* (1992), *That's Entertainment! III* (1994), *Heidi* (1996).

**Rossellini, Isabella** (1952– ) Italian, born Rome; *White Nights* (1985), *Blue Velvet* (1986), *Siesta* (1987), *Zelly and Me* (1988), *Cousins* (1989), *Wild at Heart* (1990), *Death Becomes Her* (1992), *Fearless* (1993), *Wyatt Earp* (1994), *The Funeral* (1996).

**Roth, Tim** (1962– ) British, born London; *A World Apart* (1988), *The Cook, The Thief, His Wife and Her Lover* (1989), *Vincent and Theo* (1990), *Rosencrantz and Guildenstern are Dead* (1990), *Backsliding* (1991), *Jumpin' at the Boneyard* (1991), *Reservoir Dogs* (1992), *Bodies Rest and Motion* (1993), *Pulp Fiction* (1994), *Rob Roy* (1995), *Deceiver* (1997).

**Rourke, Mickey** (1956– ) American, born Schenectady, New York; *Body Heat* (1981), *Rumble Fish* (1983), *9½ Weeks* (1985), *The Year of the Dragon* (1985), *Angel Heart* (1987), *A Prayer for the Dying* (1987), *Johnny Handsome* (1990), *Wild Orchid* (1990), *Harley Davidson and the Marlboro Man* (1991), *Desperate Hours* (1991), *White Sands* (1992), *Bullet* (1995), *Exit in Red* (1996).

**Russell, Jane** (1921– ) American, born Bemidji, Minnesota; *The Outlaw* (1943), *The Paleface* (1948), *Gentlemen Prefer Blondes* (1953).

**Russell, Kurt** (1951– ) American, born Springfield, Massachusetts; *The Quest* (TV 1976), *Elvis* (TV 1979), *Escape from New York* (1981), *The Thing* (1982), *Silkwood* (1983), *Swing Shift* (1984), *Big Trouble in Little China* (1986), *Tequila Sunrise* (1988), *Tango and Cash* (1990), *Backdraft* (1991), *Unlawful Entry* (1992), *Tombstone* (1993), *Escape from LA* (1996), *Breakdown* (1997).

**Rutherford, Dame Margaret** (1892–1972) British, born London; *Blithe Spirit* (1945), *The Happiest Days of Your Life* (1950), *The Importance of Being Earnest* (1952), *The Smallest Show on Earth* (1957), *Murder She Said* (1961), *The VIPs* (1963), *Murder Most Foul* (1964), *Murder Ahoy* (1964).

**Ryan, Meg** (1962– ) American, born Fairfield, Connecticut; *Rich and Famous* (1981), *Top Gun* (1985), *Innerspace* (1987), *DOA* (1988), *Promised Land* (1988), *The Presidio* (1988), *When Harry Met Sally ...* (1989), *Joe Versus the Volcano* (1990), *The Doors* (1991), *Prelude to a Kiss* (1992), *Sleepless in Seattle* (1993), *Flesh and Bone* (1993), *French Kiss* (1995), *Courage Under Fire* (1996), *Easy Women* (1996), *You've Got Mail* (1998).

**Ryan, Robert** (1909–73) American, born Chicago; *Gangway for Tomorrow* (1943), *Crossfire* (1947), *The Set-Up* (1949), *Clash by Night* (1952), *God's Little Acre* (1958), *Odds Against Tomorrow* (1959), *Billy Budd* (1962), *The Dirty Dozen* (1967), *The Wild Bunch* (1969).

**Ryder, Winona** (1971– ) American, born Winona, Michigan; *Beetlejuice* (1988), *1969* (1988), *Heathers* (1989), *Great Balls of Fire* (1989), *Mermaids* (1990), *Night on Earth* (1992), *Dracula* (1992), *Age of Innocence* (1993), *Reality Bites* (1994), *Little Women* (1994), *How to Make an American Quilt* (1995), *The Crucible* (1996), *Girl Interrupted* (1999).

**Sabu** (Sabu Dastagir) (1924–63) Indian, born Karapur, Mysore; *Elephant Boy* (1937), *The Thief of Baghdad* (1940), *The Jungle Book* (1942), *The End of the River* (1947), *Black Narcissus* (1947).

**Sanders, George** (1906–73) British, born St Petersburg, Russia; *Lancer Spy* (1937), *Rebecca* (1940), *The Saint's Double Trouble* (1940), *The Moon and Sixpence* (1942), *The Picture of Dorian Gray* (1944), *Scandal in Paris* (1946), *The Ghost and Mrs Muir* (1947), *Forever Amber* (1947), *The Private Affairs of Bel Ami* (1947), *Lady Windermere's Fan* (1949), *All About Eve* (1950), *Village of the Damned* (1960), *A Shot in the Dark* (1964).

**Sands, Julian** (1958– ) British, born Yorkshire; *Oxford Blues* (1982), *The Killing Fields* (1984), *A Room with a View* (1985), *Gothic* (1987), *Siesta* (1987), *Vibes* (1988), *Warlock* (1989), *Arachnophobia* (1990), *Impromptu* (1990), *Grand Isle* (1991), *Naked Lunch* (1991), *Husbands and Lovers* (1992), *Boxing Helena* (1993), *Warlock, Part II* (1993), *Leaving Las Vegas* (1995), *One Night Stand* (1997).

**Sarandon, Susan** (Susan Abigail Tomalin) (1946– ) American, born New York City; *The Front Page* (1974), *Dragonfly* (1977), *Atlantic City* (1981), *Tempest* (1982), *The Hunger* (1983), *The Witches of Eastwick* (1987), *Bull Durham* (1988), *White Palace* (1991), *Thelma and Louise* (1991), *Light Sleeper* (1991), *Lorenzo's Oil* (1992), *The Client* (1994), *Little Women* (1995), *Dead Man Walking* (1995), *Stepmom* (1998).

**Savalas, Telly** (Aristotle Savalas) (1924–94) Greek–American, born Garden City, New York; *Birdman of Alcatraz* (1962), *The Battle of the Bulge* (1965), *The Dirty Dozen* (1967), *On Her Majesty's Secret Service* (1969), *Horror Express* (1972), *Visions of Death* (1972), *Kojak* (1973–7), *Escape to Athena* (1979), *Kojak* (TV 1989–90), *Backfire* (1994).

**Scheider, Roy** (1932– ) American, born Orange, New Jersey; *Paper Lion* (1968), *French Connection* (1971), *Jaws* (1975), *Jaws 2* (1978), *All That Jazz* (1979), *Blue Thunder* (1982), *Still of the Night* (1982), *2010* (1984), *52 Pick-Up* (1986), *Night Game* (1989), *The Russia House* (1990), *Naked Lunch* (1991), *Romeo Is Bleeding* (1994), *The Rainmaker* (1997).

**Schwarzenegger, Arnold** (1947– ) American, born Thal, near Graz, Austria; *Stay Hungry* (1976), *Pumping Iron* (1977), *Conan the Barbarian* (1982), *Conan the Destroyer* (1984), *The Terminator* (1984), *Red Sonja* (1985), *Commando* (1985), *Raw Deal* (1986), *Predator* (1987), *The Running Man* (1987), *Twins* (1988), *Red Heat* (1989), *Total Recall* (1990), *Kindergarten Cop* (1990), *Terminator 2: Judgement Day* (1991), *The Last Action Hero* (1993), *True Lies* (1994), *Junior* (1994), *Jingle All the Way* (1996), *Eraser* (1996), *Batman and Robin* (1997), *End of Days* (1999).

**Scofield, (David) Paul** (1922– ) British, born Hurstpierpoint, Sussex; *That Lady* (1955), *A Man for*

*All Seasons* (1966), *Henry V* (1989), *Hamlet* (1990), *Quiz Show* (1994), *The Crucible* (1996).

**Scott, George C** (1927–99) American, born Wise, Virginia; *Anatomy of a Murder* (1959), *The Hustler* (1962), *The List of Adrian Messenger* (1963), *Dr Strangelove* (1963), *Patton* (1970), *The Hospital* (1972), *Fear on Trial* (TV 1976), *The Changeling* (1980), *Taps* (1981), *Oliver Twist* (1982), *Firestarter* (1984), *A Christmas Carol* (TV 1984), *The Last Days of Patton* (TV 1986), *The Exorcist III* (1990), *Malice* (1993), *Family Rescue* (TV 1996).

**Selleck, Tom** (1945– ) American, born Detroit, Michigan; *Coma* (1977), *Magnum* (TV 1981–9), *High Road to China* (1983), *Lassiter* (1984), *Runaway* (1984), *Three Men and a Baby* (1988), *Three Men and a Little Lady* (1990), *Tokyo Diamond* (1991), *Christopher Columbus: The Discovery* (1992), *Mr Baseball* (1992), *Open Season* (1994).

**Sellers, Peter** (1925–80) British, born Southsea; *The Smallest Show on Earth* (1957), *The Ladykillers* (1959), *I'm Alright Jack* (1959), *Only Two Can Play* (1962), *Lolita* (1962), *Dr Strangelove* (1963), *The Pink Panther* (1963), *A Shot in the Dark* (1964), *Return of the Pink Panther* (1975), *The Pink Panther Strikes Again* (1976), *Revenge of the Pink Panther* (1978), *Being There* (1979).

**Seymour, Jane** (Joyce Frankenberg) (1951– ) British, born Hillingdon, Middlesex; *Live and Let Die* (1972), *Battle Star Galactica* (TV 1978), *East of Eden* (TV 1981), *Somewhere in Time* (1980), *The Scarlet Pimpernel* (TV 1982), *War and Remembrance* (TV 1987–9), *Matters of the Heart* (1991), *Angel of Death* (1991), *Dr Quinn, Medicine Woman* (TV 1992–3).

**Sharif, Omar** (Michael Shalhouz) (1932– ) Egyptian, born Alexandria; *Lawrence of Arabia* (1962), *Genghis Khan* (1965), *Doctor Zhivago* (1965), *Che!* (1969), *Green Ice* (1980), *The 13th Warrior* (1999).

**Shatner, William** (1931– ) Canadian, born Montreal, Quebec; *Star Trek* (TV 1966–8), *Horror at 37 000 Feet* (TV 1974), *Big Bad Mama* (1974), *Star Trek: The Motion Picture* (1979), *The Kidnapping of the President* (1980), *Star Trek II: The Wrath of Khan* (1982), *T J Hooker* (TV 1982–6), *Star Trek III: The Search for Spock* (1984), *Star Trek IV: The Voyage Home* (1987), *Star Trek V: The Final Frontier* (1989), *Star Trek VI: The Undiscovered Country* (1991), *Star Trek: Generations* (1994).

**Sheedy, Ally** (1962– ) American, born New York City; *Wargames* (1983), *The Breakfast Club* (1985), *St Elmo's Fire* (1986), *Short Circuit* (1986), *Heart of Dixie* (1990), *Betsy's Wedding* (1990), *Only the Lonely* (1991), *Man's Best Friend* (1993), *The Tin Soldier* (1995), *Myth America* (1997).

**Sheen, Charlie** (Carlos Irwin Estevez) (1965– ) American, born Santa Monica, California; *Ferris Bueller's Day Off* (1986), *Wall Street* (1987), *Platoon* (1987), *Eight Men Out* (1988), *Major League* (1989), *The Rookie* (1990), *Catchfire* (1990), *Navy Seals* (1990), *Back Track* (1991), *Hot Shots!* (1991), *Hot Shots! Part Deux* (1993), *The Three Musketeers* (1993), *Terminal Velocity* (1994), *The Shadow Conspiracy* (1996).

**Sheen, Martin** (Ramon Estevez) (1940– ) American, born Dayton, Ohio; *Catch-22* (1970), *Badlands* (1973), *The Execution of Private Slovik* (TV 1974), *The Little Girl Who Lives Down the Lane* (1976), *Apocalypse Now* (1979), *Gandhi* (1982), *That Championship Season* (1982), *The Dead Zone* (1983), *Firestarter* (1984), *Wall Street* (1987), *Siesta* (1987), *Da* (1988), *Judgement in Berlin* (1988), *Stockade* (1990), *JFK* (1991), *Gettysburg* (1993), *Finnegan's Wake* (1993), *Hot Shots! Part Deux* (1993), *A Hundred and One Nights* (1994), *The American President* (1995), *Lost and Found* (1999).

**Shepard, Sam** (Samuel Shepard Rogers) (1943– ) American, born Fort Sheridan, Illinois; *Frances* (1982), *The Right Stuff* (1983), *Country* (1984), *Crimes of the Heart* (1986), *Baby Boom* (1987), *Steel Magnolias* (1989), *Bright Angel* (1990), *Voyager* (1990), *Thunderheart* (1992), *The Pelican Brief* (1993), *Lily Dale* (TV 1996).

**Shepherd, Cybill** (1950– ) American, born Memphis, Tennessee; *The Last Picture Show* (1971), *Taxi Driver* (1976), *The Lady Vanishes* (1979), *The Long Hot Summer* (TV 1985), *Moonlighting* (TV 1985–9), *Texasville* (1990), *Alice* (1991), *Married to It* (1991), *Once Upon a Crime* (1992), *Cybill* (TV 1995–8).

**Signoret, Simone** (Simon-Henriette Charlotte Kaminker) (1921–85) French, born Wiesbaden, Germany; *La Ronde* (1950), *Casque d'Or* (1952), *Les Diaboliques* (1952), *Room at the Top* (1959), *Ship of Fools* (1965), *Le Chat* (1971), *Madame Rosa* (1973).

**Sim, Alastair** (1900–76) British, born Edinburgh; *Inspector Hornleigh* (1939), *Green for Danger* (1946), *The Happiest Days of Your Life* (1950), *Scrooge* (1951), *Laughter in Paradise* (1951), *The Bells of St Trinians* (1954).

**Simmons, Jean** (1929– ) British, born London; *Great Expectations* (1946), *Black Narcissus* (1946), *Hamlet* (1948), *The Blue Lagoon* (1948), *The Big Country* (1958), *Elmer Gantry* (1960), *Spartacus* (1960), *The Grass is Greener* (1961), *The Thorn Birds* (TV 1982), *Going Undercover* (1988), *Great Expectations* (TV 1991), *Sense and Sensibility* (TV 1990), *How to Make an American Quilt* (1995), *Paradise Road* (1996).

**Sinatra, Frank** (Francis Albert Sinatra) (1915–98) American, born Hoboken, New Jersey; *Anchors Aweigh* (1945), *On the Town* (1949), *From Here to Eternity* (1953), *The Man With the Golden Gun* (1955), *Pal Joey* (1957), *The Manchurian Candidate* (1962), *The Detective* (1963).

**Sinden, Sir Donald** (1923– ) British, born Plymouth; *Doctor in the House* (1954), *The National Health* (1973), *The Day of the Jackal* (1973), *The Island at the Top of the World* (1973), *Two's Company* (TV 1977–80), *Never the Twain* (TV 1981–91), *The Canterville Ghost* (TV 1996).

**Singer, Marc** (1948– ) Canadian, born Vancouver, British Columbia; *Beast Master* (1982), *If You Could See What I Hear* (1982), *V* (TV 1983), *V – The Final Battle* (TV 1984–5), *Dallas* (TV 1986), *Born to Race* (1988).

**Skerritt, Tom** (1933– ) American, born Detroit, Michigan; *M*A*S*H* (1970), *Big Bad Mama* (1974),

*Run, Run, Joe* (TV 1974), *The Devil's Rain* (1975), *Up in Smoke* (1978), *Alien* (1979), *Ice Castles* (1979), *The Dead Zone* (1983), *Top Gun* (1986), *Wisdom* (1986), *Cheers* (TV 1987–8), *Space Camp* (1988), *Poltergeist III* (1988), *Steel Magnolias* (1989), *Knight Moves* (1991), *A River Runs Through It* (1992), *Singles* (1992).

**Slater, Christian** (1969– ) American, born New York City; *The Name of the Rose* (1986), *Tucker: The Man and His Dream* (1988), *Heathers* (1989), *Young Guns II* (1990), *Pump Up the Volume* (1990), *Robin Hood: Prince of Thieves* (1991), *Kuffs* (1992), *Where the Day Takes You* (1992), *True Romance* (1993), *Jimmy Hollywood* (1994), *Interview with the Vampire* (1994), *Broken Arrow* (1996), *Hard Rain* (1998).

**Smith, Sir C Aubrey** (Charles Aubrey Smith) (1863–1948) British, born London; *Love Me Tonight* (1932), *Morning Glory* (1933), *Lives of a Bengal Lancer* (1935), *The Prisoner of Zenda* (1937), *The Four Feathers* (1939), *Rebecca* (1940), *And Then There Were None* (1945), *An Ideal Husband* (1947), *Little Women* (1949).

**Smith, Dame Maggie** (1934– ) British, born Ilford, Essex; *The VIPs* (1963), *The Pumpkin Eater* (1964), *The Prime of Miss Jean Brodie* (1969), *Travels with My Aunt* (1972), *California Suite* (1978), *A Room With a View* (1985), *Hook* (1991), *Sister Act* (1992), *The Secret Garden* (1993), *Sister Act 2: Back in the Habit* (1993), *Richard III* (1995), *The First Wives Club* (1996), *Washington Square* (1997), *Tea with Mussolini* (1999), *Harry Potter and the Philosopher's Stone* (2001).

**Spader, James** (1960– ) American, born Boston, Massachusetts; *Pretty in Pink* (1986), *Mannequin* (1987), *Less Than Zero* (1987), *Baby Boom* (1987), *Jack's Back* (1988), *Sex, Lies and Videotape* (1989), *The Rachel Papers* (1989), *Bad Influence* (1990), *White Palace* (1991), *True Colors* (1991), *Storyville* (1992), *Bob Roberts* (1992), *The Music of Chance* (1993), *Wolf* (1994), *Stargate* (1994), *Crash* (1996).

**Stallone, Sylvester** (1946– ) American, born New York City; *The Lords of Flatbush* (1973), *Rocky* (1976), *Paradise Alley* (1978), *Rocky II* (1979), *Victory* (1981), *Nighthawks* (1981), *First Blood* (1981), *Rocky III* (1981), *Rambo* (1985), *Rocky IV* (1985), *Rambo II* (1986), *Over the Top* (1987), *Rambo III* (1988), *Lock Up* (1989), *Tango and Cash* (1990), *Rocky V* (1990), *Oscar* (1991), *Stop, Or My Mom Will Shoot* (1992), *Bartholomew vs Neff* (1992), *Cliffhanger* (1992), *Demolition Man* (1993), *The Specialist* (1994), *Judge Dredd* (1995), *Daylight* (1996), *Copland* (1997).

**Stamp, Terence** (1939– ) British, born Stepney, London; *The Collector* (1965), *Far from the Madding Crowd* (1967), *Superman* (1978), *Superman II* (1981), *Company of Wolves* (1985), *Legal Eagles* (1986), *Wall Street* (1987), *The Sicilian* (1988), *Alien Nation* (1988), *Young Guns* (1988), *Genuine Risk* (1990), *Stranger in the House* (1991), *Priscilla Queen of the Desert* (1994), *Star Wars Episode 1: The Phantom Menace* (1999).

**Stanton, Harry Dean** (1926– ) American, born Kentucky; *How the West Was Won* (1962), *Cool Hand Luke* (1967), *The Godfather, Part II* (1974), *Alien* (1979), *The Rose* (1979), *Private Benjamin* (1980), *Young Doctors in Love* (1982), *Christine* (1983), *Repo Man* (1984), *Paris, Texas* (1984), *Pretty in Pink* (1986), *Mr North* (1988), *Stars and Bars* (1988), *The Last Temptation of Christ* (1988), *Twister* (1989), *Wild at Heart* (1990), *Twin Peaks: Fire Walk With Me* (1992).

**Stanwyck, Barbara** (Ruby Shaw) (1907–90) American, born Brooklyn, New York City; *Broadway Nights* (1927), *Miracle Woman* (1931), *Night Nurse* (1931), *The Bitter Tea of General Yen* (1933), *Baby Face* (1933), *Annie Oakley* (1935), *Stella Dallas* (1937), *Union Pacific* (1939), *The Lady Eve* (1941), *Meet John Doe* (1941), *Ball of Fire* (1941), *Double Indemnity* (1944), *The Strange Love of Martha Ivers* (1946), *The Furies* (1950), *Executive Suite* (1954), *Walk on the Wild Side* (1962), *The Big Valley* (TV 1965–9), *The Thorn Birds* (TV 1983).

**Steiger, Rod** (Rodney Stephen Steiger) (1925– ) American, born Westhampton, New York; *On the Waterfront* (1954), *Oklahoma!* (1955), *The Court Martial of Billy Mitchell* (1955), *The Harder They Fall* (1956), *Al Capone* (1958), *The Pawnbroker* (1964), *Doctor Zhivago* (1965), *In the Heat of the Night* (1967), *A Fistful of Dynamite* (1971), *The Amityville Horror* (1979), *Hollywood Wives* (TV 1984), *American Gothic* (1988), *The January Man* (1988), *Tennessee Nights* (1989), *Men of Respect* (1990), *Guilty as Charged* (1991), *The Player* (1992), *Genghis Khan* (1992), *Taking Liberties* (1993), *The Specialist* (1994), *Mars Attacks!* (1996), *End of Days* (1999).

**Stewart, James** (Maitland) (1908–97) American, born Indiana, Pennsylvania; *Seventh Heaven* (1937), *You Can't Take It With You* (1938), *Mr Smith Goes to Washington* (1939), *Destry Rides Again* (1939), *The Shop around the Corner* (1940), *The Philadelphia Story* (1940), *It's a Wonderful Life* (1946), *Harvey* (1950), *Broken Arrow* (1950), *The Glen Miller Story* (1953), *Rear Window* (1954), *The Man from Laramie* (1955), *Vertigo* (1958), *Anatomy of a Murder* (1959), *Mr Hobbs Takes a Vacation* (1962), *Shenandoah* (1965), *The Big Sleep* (1978), *North and South II* (TV 1986).

**Stockwell, Dean** (1936– ) American, born Hollywood, California; *The Green Years* (1946), *The Boy with Green Hair* (1948), *Kim* (1950), *Compulsion* (1959), *Sons and Lovers* (1959), *McCloud: Twas the Fight Before Christmas* (TV 1977), *Paris, Texas* (1984), *Dune* (1984), *The Legend of Billie Jean* (1985), *Blue Velvet* (1986), *Gardens of Stone* (1987), *Tucker: The Man and His Dream* (1988), *The Blue Iguana* (1988), *Married to the Mob* (1988), *Quantum Leap* (TV 1989–93), *Smokescreen* (1990), *Back Track* (1991), *The Player* (1992), *Chasers* (1994), *Midnight Blues* (1996).

**Stoltz, Eric** (1961– ) American, born California; *Fast Times at Ridgemont High* (1982), *Mask* (1985), *Some Kind of Wonderful* (1987), *Sister Sister* (1988), *Haunted Summer* (1988), *Fly II* (1989), *Memphis Belle* (1990), *The Waterdance* (1992), *Bodies Rest and Motion* (1993), *Killing Zoë* (1993), *Pulp Fiction* (1994), *Little Women* (1994), *Rob Roy* (1995), *Don't Look Back* (1996).

**Stone, Sharon** (1964– ) American, born Meadsville, Pennsylvania; *Deadly Blessing* (1981), *Action Jaction* (1987), *Total Recall* (1990), *He Said She Said* (1991), *Basic Instinct* (1992), *Diary of a Hitman* (1992), *Sliver* (1993), *Last Action Hero* (1993), *Intersection* (1994), *Casino* (1995), *Diabolique* (1996), *Gloria* (1999).

**Streep, Meryl** (Mary Louise Streep) (1949– ) American, born Summit, New Jersey: *Julia* (1977), *The Deer Hunter* (1978), *Kramer vs Kramer* (1979), *Manhattan* (1979), *The French Lieutenant's Woman* (1981), *Sophie's Choice* (1982), *Silkwood* (1983), *Plenty* (1985), *Out of Africa* (1986), *Ironweed* (1987), *A Cry in the Dark* (1988), *Evil Angels* (1988), *She-Devil* (1989), *Postcards from the Edge* (1990), *Defending Your Life* (1991), *Death Becomes Her* (1992), *The River Wild* (1994), *The Bridges of Madison County* (1995), *Music of the Heart* (1999).

**Streisand, Barbra** (Joan) (1942– ) American, born Brooklyn, New York City; *Funny Girl* (1968), *Hello Dolly* (1969), *On a Clear Day You Can See Forever* (1970), *What's Up, Doc?* (1972), *The Way We Were* (1973), *A Star is Born* (1976), *Yentl* (1983), *Nuts* (1987), *Prince of Tides* (1991), *The Mirror Has Two Faces* (1996).

**Sutherland, Donald** (1935– ) Canadian, born St John, New Brunswick; *The Dirty Dozen* (1967), *M*A*S*H* (1970), *Klute* (1971), *Casanova* (1976), *1900* (1976), *The Eagle Has Landed* (1977), *Animal House* (1978), *Invasion of the Body Snatchers* (1978), *Ordinary People* (1980), *Apprentice to Murder* (1988), *Lock Up* (1989), *A Dry White Season* (1989), *Backdraft* (1991), *Buffy the Vampire Slayer* (1992), *Benefit of the Doubt* (1993), *The Shadow Conspiracy* (1995), *The Poet* (1996), *Instinct* (1999).

**Sutherland, Kiefer** (1967– ) American, born Los Angeles; *Bright Lights, Big City* (1985), *Stand By Me* (1987), *The Lost Boys* (1987), *The Killing Time* (1987), *1969* (1988), *Promised Land* (1988), *Young Guns* (1988), *Renegades* (1989), *Chicago Joe and the Showgirl* (1989), *Flatliners* (1990), *Young Guns II* (1990), *Article 99* (1991), *A Few Good Men* (1992), *Twin Peaks: Fire Walk With Me* (1992), *The Vanishing* (1992), *The Three Musketeers* (1993), *Double Cross* (1995), *Truth or Consequences* (1996), *Ground Control* (1998).

**Swanson, Gloria** (Gloria May Josephine Svensson) (1897–1983) American, born Chicago; *Male and Female* (1919), *The Affairs of Anatol* (1921), *Manhandled* (1924), *Sadie Thompson* (1928), *Queen Kelly* (1928), *The Trespasser* (1929), *Sunset Boulevard* (1950).

**Swayze, Patrick** (1954– ) American, born Houston, Texas; *The Outsiders* (1983), *Red Dawn* (1984), *Young Blood* (1985), *North and South* (TV 1986), *North and South II* (TV 1986), *Dirty Dancing* (1987), *Tiger Warsaw* (1988), *Road House* (1989), *Next of Kin* (1989), *Ghost* (1990), *Point Break* (1991), *City of Joy* (1992), *Father Hood* (1993), *Tall Tale* (1995), *Three Wishes* (1995), *Without a Word* (1999).

**Tandy, Jessica** (1909–94) British, born London; *Dragonwyck* (1946), *The Birds* (1963), *Honky Tonk Freeway* (1981), *The World According to Garp* (1982), *Still of the Night* (1982), *The Bostonians* (1984), *Cocoon* (1985), *The House on Carroll Street* (1988), *Cocoon: The Return* (1988), *Driving Miss Daisy* (1989), *Fried Green Tomatoes* (1991), *Used People* (1992).

**Taylor, Dame Elizabeth** (Rosemond) (1932– ) British, born London; *National Velvet* (1944), *Little Women* (1949), *The Father of the Bride* (1950), *A Place in the Sun* (1951), *Giant* (1956), *Raintree Country* (1957), *Cat on a Hot Tin Roof* (1958), *Butterfield 8* (1960), *Cleopatra* (1962), *Who's Afraid of Virginia Woolf?* (1966), *Reflections in a Golden Eye* (1967), *The Taming of the Shrew* (1967), *Suddenly Last Summer* (1968), *A Little Night Music* (1977), *The Mirror Crack'd* (1981), *Malice in Wonderland* (TV 1985), *Poker Alice* (TV 1986), *Young Toscanini* (1988), *Sweet Bird of Youth* (TV 1989), *Faithful* (1992), *The Flintstones* (1994).

**Taylor, Robert** (Spangler Arlington Brugh) (1911–69) American, born Filley, Nebraska; *Magnificent Obsession* (1935), *Camille* (1936), *Three Comrades* (1938), *Yank at Oxford* (1938), *Waterloo Bridge* (1940), *Bataan* (1943), *Song of Russia* (1943), *Quo Vadis* (1951), *Ivanhoe* (1952), *Knights of the Round Table* (1953), *Party Girl* (1958), *The Detectives* (TV 1959–61), *The Miracle of the White Stallions* (1962).

**Taylor, Rod** (Robert Taylor) (1929– ) Australian, born Sydney; *The Time Machine* (1960), *The Birds* (1963), *The VIPs* (1963), *Thirty-Six Hours* (1964), *The Glass Bottom Boat* (1966), *A Rage in Harlem* (1991).

**Tearle, Sir Godfrey** (1884–1953) British, born New York City; also stage; *Romeo and Juliet* (1908), *The Thirty-nine Steps* (1935), *One of Our Aircraft is Missing* (1942), *The Titfield Thunderbolt* (1953).

**Temple, Shirley** (1928– ) American, born Santa Monica, California; *Little Miss Marker* (1934), *Curly Top* (1935), *Dimples* (1936), *Heidi* (1937), *The Little Princess* (1939).

**Terry-Thomas** (Thomas Terry Hoar-Stevens) (1911–90) British, born Finchley, London; *Private's Progress* (1956), *Carleton Browne of the FO* (1958), *The Naked Truth* (1958), *I'm All Right, Jack* (1959), *It's a Mad, Mad, Mad, Mad World* (1963), *How to Murder Your Wife* (1965), *Those Magnificent Men in Their Flying Machines* (1965), *Don't Look Now* (1968).

**Thompson, Emma** (1959– ) British, born Cambridge; *The Tall Guy* (1989), *Henry V* (1989), *Dead Again* (1989), *Impromptu* (1991), *Howards End* (1992), *Peter's Friends* (1992), *Much Ado About Nothing* (1993), *The Remains of the Day* (1993), *In the Name of the Father* (1993), *My Father the Hero* (1994), *Carrington* (1995), *Sense and Sensibility* (1995), *The Well of Loneliness* (1997), *Maybe Baby* (2000).

**Thompson, Lea** (1961– ) American, born Minneapolis, Minnesota; *Jaws 3D* (1983), *Red Dawn* (1984), *Back to the Future* (1985), *Howard: A New Breed of Hero* (1985), *Space Camp* (1986), *The Wizard of Loneliness* (1988), *Casual Sex?* (1988), *Going Undercover* (1988), *Back to the Future II* (1989), *Article 99* (1991), *Dennis the Menace* (1993).

**Tierney, Gene** (Eliza) (1920–91) American, born Brooklyn, New York City; *The Return of Frank James* (1940), *Tobacco Road* (1941), *Bell Star* (1941), *Heaven Can Wait* (1943), *Laura* (1944), *Leave Her to Heaven* (1945), *The Ghost and Mrs Muir* (1947), *Whirlpool* (1949), *Toys in the Attic* (1963), *The Pleasure Seekers* (1964).

**Tilly, Meg** (1960– ) Canadian, born Texada; *Fame* (1980), *The Big Chill* (1983), *Psycho II* (1983), *Agnes of God* (1985), *Masquerade* (1988), *Valmont* (1989), *The Two Jakes* (1991), *Leaving Normal* (1992), *Body Snatchers* (1994), *Double Cross* (1994), *Journey* (TV 1995).

**Tomlin, Lily** (1939– ) American, born Detroit, Michigan; *Nine to Five* (1980), *The Incredible Shrinking Woman* (1981), *All of Me* (1984), *Big Business* (1988), *Shadows and Fog* (1992), *The Beverly Hillbillies* (1993), *Short Cuts* (1993), *Even Cowgirls Get the Blues* (1993), *Blue in the Face* (1995), *Flirting with Disaster* (1996), *Tea with Mussolini* (1999).

**Tracy, Spencer** (1900–67) American, born Milwaukee, Wisconsin; *Twenty Thousand Years in Sing Sing* (1932), *The Power and the Glory* (1933), *A Man's Castle* (1933), *Fury* (1936), *San Francisco* (1936), *Libeled Lady* (1936), *Captains Courageous* (1937), *Boys Town* (1938), *Stanley and Livingstone* (1939), *Northwest Passage* (1939), *Edison the Man* (1940), *Dr Jekyll and Mr Hyde* (1941), *Woman of the Year* (1942), *The Seventh Cross* (1944), *State of the Union* (1948), *Adam's Rib* (1949), *Father of the Bride* (1950), *Bad Day at Black Rock* (1955), *The Last Hurrah* (1958), *Inherit the Wind* (1960), *Judgement at Nuremberg* (1961), *It's a Mad, Mad, Mad, Mad World* (1963), *Guess Who's Coming to Dinner* (1967).

**Travolta, John** (1954– ) American, born Englewood, New Jersey; *Welcome Back Kotter* (TV 1975–8), *Carrie* (1976), *Saturday Night Fever* (1977), *Grease* (1978), *Blow Out* (1981), *Staying Alive* (1983), *Two of a Kind* (1984), *Perfect* (1985), *Look Who's Talking* (1989), *Look Who's Talking Too* (1991), *Chains of Gold* (1991), *Pulp Fiction* (1994), *Get Shorty* (1995), *Broken Arrow* (1996), *Phenomenon* (1996), *Michael* (1996), *The Thin Red Line* (1998).

**Turner, Kathleen** (1954– ) American, born Springfield, Missouri; *The Doctors* (TV 1977–8), *Body Heat* (1981), *The Man With Two Brains* (1983), *Romancing the Stone* (1984), *Crimes of Passion* (1984), *The Jewel of the Nile* (1985), *Prizzi's Honor* (1985), *Peggy Sue Got Married* (1986), *Switching Channels* (1988), *Julia and Julia* (1988), *The Accidental Tourist* (1989), *War of the Roses* (1989), *V I Warshawski* (1991), *House of Cards* (1992), *Serial Mom* (1994), *Moonlight and Valentino* (1995).

**Turner, Lana** (Julia Jean Mildred Frances Turner) (1920–95) American, born Wallace, Indiana; *Dr Jekyll and Mr Hyde* (1940), *Somewhere I'll Find You* (1942), *The Three Musketeers* (1948), *Peyton Place* (1957).

**Turturro, John** (1957– ) American, born Brooklyn, New York City; *Raging Bull* (1980), *Hannah and Her Sisters* (1986), *Do the Right Thing* (1989), *Miller's Crossing* (1990), *Barton Fink* (1991), *Fearless* (1993), *O Brother, Where Art Thou?* (2000).

**Tushingham, Rita** (1942– ) British, born Liverpool; *A Taste of Honey* (1961), *Girl with Green Eyes* (1964), *The Knack* (1965), *Dr Zhivago* (1965), *Judgement in Stone* (1986), *Resurrected* (1988), *Paper Marriage* (1992), *An Awfully Big Adventure* (1995).

**Ullmann, Liv** (1938– ) Norwegian, born Tokyo, Japan; *Persona* (1966), *The Emigrants* (1972), *Face to Face* (1975), *Autumn Sonata* (1978), *Dangerous Moves* (1983), *Gaby – The True Story* (1987), *La Amiga* (1988), *The Rose Garden* (1989), *Mindwalk* (1990), *The Ox* (1991), *The Long Shadow* (1992).

**Ustinov, Sir Peter** (Alexander) (1921– ) British, born London; *Private Angelo* (1949), *Hotel Sahara* (1951), *Quo Vadis* (1951), *Beau Brummell* (1954), *The Sundowners* (1960), *Spartacus* (1960), *Romanoff and Juliet* (1961), *Topkapi* (1964), *Logan's Run* (1976), *Death on the Nile* (1978), *Evil Under the Sun* (1982), *Appointment with Death* (1988), *Lorenzo's Oil* (1992), *Stiff Upper Lips* (1997), *The Bachelor* (1999).

**Valentino, Rudolph** (Rodolpho Alphonso Guglielmi di Valentina d'Antonguolla) (1895–1926) Italian–American, born Castellaneta, Italy; *The Four Horsemen of the Apocalypse* (1921), *The Sheikh* (1921), *Blood and Sand* (1922), *The Young Rajah* (1922), *Monsieur Beaucaire* (1924), *The Eagle* (1925), *The Son of the Sheikh* (1926).

**Van Cleef, Lee** (1925–89) American, born Somerville, New Jersey; *High Noon* (1952), *For a Few Dollars More* (1967), *The Good, the Bad and the Ugly* (1967), *Return of Sabata* (1971), *The Magnificent Seven Ride* (1972), *Escape from New York* (1981), *Codename: Wildgeese II* (1986), *The Heist* (1988).

**Van Damme, Jean-Claude** (1961– ) Belgian, born Brussels; *No Retreat No Surrender* (1985), *Kickboxer* (1989), *Universal Soldier* (1992), *Nowhere to Run* (1993), *Last Action Hero* (1993), *Timecop* (1994), *Streetfighter* (1994), *The Quest* (1996).

**Van Dyke, Dick** (1925– ) American, born West Plains, Missouri; *The Dick Van Dyke Show* (TV 1961–6), *Mary Poppins* (1964), *Chitty Chitty Bang Bang* (1968), *The Cosmic* (1969), *Dropout Father* (TV 1982), *Dick Tracey* (1990), *The Brigade* (1996).

**Vaughn, Robert** (Francis Vaughn) (1932– ) American, born New York City; *The Magnificent Seven* (1960), *The Man from UNCLE* (TV 1964–7), The Towering Inferno (1974), *Washington Behind Closed Doors* (TV 1976), *Superman III* (1983), *Delta Force* (1985), *Black Moon Rising* (1986).

**Vincent, Jan-Michael** (1944– ) American, born Denver, Colorado; *The Mechanic* (1972), *The World's Greatest Athlete* (1973), *Bite the Bullet* (1974), *Hooper* (1978), *Hard Country* (1981), *Airwolf* (TV 1982–6), *The Winds of War* (TV 1983), *Alienator* (1989), *Beyond the Call of Duty* (1992), *Extreme* (1993), *Redline* (1995), *Russian Roulette* (1996).

**von Stroheim, Erich** (Hans Erich Maria Stroheim von Nordenwall) (1885–1957) Austrian, born Vienna;

*Foolish Wives* (1921), *La Grande Illusion* (1937), *Five Graves to Cairo* (1943), *Sunset Boulevard* (1950).

**von Sydow, Max** (Carl Adolf) (1929– ) Swedish, born Lund; *The Seventh Seal* (1956), *The Face* (1959), *The Greatest Story Ever Told* (1965), *Hawaii* (1966), *Through a Glass Darkly* (1966), *Hour of the Wolf* (1967), *The Shame* (1968), *The Emigrants* (1972), *The Exorcist* (1973), *Exorcist II: The Heretic* (1977), *Flash Gordon* (1980), *Never Say Never Again* (1983), *Hannah and Her Sisters* (1986), *Awakenings* (1990), *Dr Grassler* (1990), *The Father* (1990), *The Touch* (1992), *Needful Things* (1993), *Judge Dredd* (1995), *Snow Falling on Cedars* (1999).

**Wagner, Robert** (John Jr) (1930– ) American, born Detroit, Michigan; *The Silver Whip* (1953), *Prince Valiant* (1954), *A Kiss Before Dying* (1956), *The True Story of Jesse James* (1957), *All the Fine Young Cannibals* (1959), *The Condemned of Altona* (1963), *The Pink Panther* (1963), *It Takes a Thief* (TV 1965–9), *Colditz* (TV 1972–3), *The Towering Inferno* (1974), *Switch* (TV 1975–7), *Hart to Hart* (TV 1979–84), *Trail of the Pink Panther* (1982), *Curse of the Pink Panther* (1983), *Delirious* (1993), *The Bruce Lee Story* (1993).

**Walken, Christopher** (1943– ) American, born Astoria, New York; *The Anderson Tapes* (1970), *Annie Hall* (1977), *The Deer Hunter* (1978), *The Dogs of War* (1981), *Pennies from Heaven* (1981), *The Dead Zone* (1983), *Brainstorm* (1983), *A View to a Kill* (1984), *At Close Range* (1986), *The Milagro Beanfield War* (1987), *Biloxi Blues* (1988), *Puss in Boots* (1988), *The Comfort of Strangers* (1990), *Batman Returns* (1992), *True Romance* (1993), *Wayne's World 2* (1993), *Pulp Fiction* (1994), *Things to Do in Denver When You're Dead* (1995), *Darkening* (1996), *Sleepy Hollow* (1999).

**Walters, Julie** (1950– ) British, born Birmingham; *Educating Rita* (1983), *She'll Be Wearing Pink Pajamas* (1984), *Car Trouble* (1986), *Prick Up Your Ears* (1987), *Personal Services* (1987), *Buster* (1987), *Killing Dad* (1989), *Stepping Out* (1991), *Sister My Sister* (1995), *Intimate Relations* (1996), *Brazen Hussies* (1997).

**Wanamaker, Sam** (1919–93) American, born Chicago; *Those Magnificent Men in Their Flying Machines* (1965), *The Spy Who Came in from the Cold* (1965), *Voyage of the Damned* (1976), *Death on the Nile* (1978), *Private Benjamin* (1980), *Raw Deal* (1986), *Superman IV* (1986), *Baby Boom* (1987), *Judgement in Berlin* (1988), *Guilty by Suspicion* (1991).

**Warner, David** (1941– ) British, born Manchester; *Morgan* (1966), *The Bofors Gun* (1968), *The Engagement* (1970), *The Omen* (1976), *Holocaust* (TV 1978), *The 39 Steps* (1978), *Time Bandits* (1981), *The French Lieutenant's Woman* (1981), *Tron* (1982), *The Man with Two Brains* (1983), *Company of Wolves* (1984), *Mr North* (1988), *Hanna's War* (1988), *Star Trek V: The Final Frontier* (1989), *The Secret Life of Ian Fleming* (1990), *Star Trek VI: The Undiscovered Country* (1991), *The Unnameable Returns* (1992), *Tryst* (1994), *Darkening* (1996), *Titanic* (1997).

**Washington, Denzel** (1954– ) American, born Mt Vernon, New York; *St Elsewhere* (TV 1982–9), *Cry Freedom* (1987), *Queen and Country* (1988), *Glory* (1989), *Mo' Better Blues* (1990), *Mississippi Masala* (1991), *Ricochet* (1991), *Malcolm X* (1992), *Philadelphia* (1993), *The Pelican Brief* (1993), *Much Ado About Nothing* (1993), *Devil in a Blue Dress* (1995), *Crimson Tide* (1995), *The Preacher's Wife* (1996), *The Hurricane* (1999).

**Wayne, John** (Marion Michael Morrison) (1907–79) American, born Winterset, Iowa; *The Big Trail* (1930), *Stagecoach* (1939), *The Long Voyage Home* (1940), *Red River* (1948), *She Wore a Yellow Ribbon* (1949), *Sands of Iwo Jima* (1949), *The Quiet Man* (1952), *The High and the Mighty* (1954), *The Searchers* (1956), *Rio Bravo* (1959), *The Alamo* (1960), *True Grit* (1969), *The Shootist* (1976).

**Weaver, Sigourney** (Susan Weaver) (1949– ) American, born New York City; *Alien* (1979), *The Janitor* (1981), *The Year of Living Dangerously* (1982), *Ghostbusters* (1984), *Aliens* (1986), *Gorillas in the Mist* (1988), *Working Girl* (1988), *Ghostbusters II* (1989), *Alien 3* (1992), *1492* (1992), *Dave* (1993), *Death and The Maiden* (1994), *Copycat* (1995), *Ice Storm* (1996), *Alien: Resurrection* (1997), *Galaxy Quest* (1999).

**Welch, Raquel** (Raquel Tejada) (1940– ) American, born Chicago; *Fantastic Voyage* (1966), *One Million Years BC* (1967), *Myra Breckenridge* (1970), *The Three Musketeers* (1974), *The Four Musketeers* (1975), *Naked Gun* $33\frac{1}{3}$: The Final Insult (1994).

**Welles, Orson** (1915–85) American, born Kenosha, Wisconsin; *Citizen Kane* (1941), *Journey into Fear* (1942), *The Stranger* (1945), *The Lady from Shanghai* (1947), *The Third Man* (1949), *The Trial* (1962), *Touch of Evil* (1965), *A Man For All Seasons* (1966), *Casino Royale* (1967), *Voyage of the Damned* (1976), *History of the World Part One* (1981).

**West, Mae** (1892–1980) American, born Brooklyn, New York City; *She Done Him Wrong* (1933), *I'm No Angel* (1933), *My Little Chickadee* (1939), *Myra Breckenridge* (1970).

**Widmark, Richard** (1914– ) American, born Sunrise, Minnesota; *Kiss of Death* (1947), *Night and the City* (1950), *How the West Was Won* (1963), *The Bedford Incident* (1965), *Madigan* (1968), *Madigan* (TV 1972), *Murder on the Orient Express* (1974), *Who Dares Wins* (1982), *Hanky Panky* (1982), *Against all Odds* (1983), *True Colors* (1991).

**Wilder, Gene** (Jerome Silberman) (1935– ) American, born Milwaukee, Wisconsin; *Bonnie and Clyde* (1967), *The Producers* (1967), *Willy Wonka and the Chocolate Factory* (1971), *Blazing Saddles* (1974), *Young Frankenstein* (1974), *The Frisco Kid* (1979), *Stir Crazy* (1982), *Hanky Panky* (1982), *The Woman in Red* (1984), *Haunted Honeymoon* (1986), *See No Evil Hear No Evil* (1989), *Funny About Love* (1991).

**Williams, Kenneth** (1926–88) British, born London; *Carry on Sergeant* (1958), *Carry on Dick* (1974), *Follow that Camel* (1968).

**Williams, Robin** (1952– ) American, born Chicago; *Mork and Mindy* (TV 1978–82), *Popeye* (1980), *The World According to Garp* (1982), *Good Morning*

*Vietnam* (1987), *Dead Poets Society* (1989), *Cadillac Man* (1990), *Awakenings* (1990), *Dead Again* (1991), *The Fisher King* (1991), *Hook* (1991), *Toys* (1992), *Ferngully* (1992), *Being Human* (1992), *Mrs Doubtfire* (1993), *Jumanji* (1995), *Hamlet* (1996), *Father's Day* (1997), *Good Will Hunting* (1997), *Bicentennial Man* (1999).

**Williams, Treat** (Richard Williams) (1951– ) American, born Rowayton, Connecticut; *The Eagle Has Landed* (1977), *Hair* (1977), *1941* (1979), *Once Upon a Time in America* (1984), *Dempsey* (TV 1985), *Smooth Talk* (1985), *A Street Car Named Desire* (1986), *The Men's Club* (1986), *Dead Heat* (1988), *Heart of Dixie* (1990), *The Phantom* (1995), *Deep Rising* (1997).

**Williamson, Nicol** (1938– ) British, born Hamilton, near Glasgow; *Inadmissible Evidence* (1967), *The Bofors Gun* (1968), *The Reckoning* (1969), *Excalibur* (1981), *Sakharov* (TV 1985), *Return to Oz* (1985), *Black Widow* (1986), *The Exorcist III* (1990), *Apt Pupil* (1992).

**Willis, Bruce** (1955– ) American, born Penns Grove, New Jersey; *Moonlighting* (TV 1985–9), *Blind Date* (1987), *Die Hard* (1988), *Sunset* (1988), *In Country* (1989), *Die Hard 2: Die Harder* (1990), *Bonfire of the Vanities* (1991), *Hudson Hawk* (1991), *Billy Bathgate* (1991), *The Last Boy Scout* (1991), *Death Becomes Her* (1992), *Striking Distance* (1993), *Pulp Fiction* (1994), *Nobody's Fool* (1994), *Die Hard with a Vengeance* (1995), *Twelve Monkeys* (1995), *The Fifth Element* (1996), *The Jackal* (1997), *The Sixth Sense* (1999).

**Winger, Debra** (1955– ) American, born Columbus, Ohio; *Urban Cowboy* (1980), *Cannery Row* (1981), *An Officer and a Gentleman* (1982), *Terms of Endearment* (1983), *Legal Eagles* (1985), *Black Widow* (1987), *Made in Heaven* (1987), *Betrayed* (1988), *The Sheltering Sky* (1990), *Wilder Napalm* (1992), *A Dangerous Woman* (1993), *Shadowlands* (1993), *Forget Paris* (1995).

**Winters, Shelley** (Shirley Schrift) (1922– ) American, born St Louis, Missouri; *A Double Life* (1948), *The Big Knife* (1955), *The Night of the Hunter* (1955), *The Diary of Anne Frank* (1959), *Lolita* (1962), *A Patch of Blue* (1965), *Alfie* (1966), *The Poseidon Adventure* (1972), *SOB* (1981), *Purple People Eater* (1988), *Stepping Out* (1991), *Backfire* (1994), *The Portrait of a Lady* (1996), *Gideon* (1999).

**Wisdom, Norman** (1915– ) British, born London; *Trouble in Store* (1955), *Man of the Moment* (1955), *Just My Luck* (1958), *There was a Crooked Man* (1960), *On the Beat* (1962), *A Stitch in Time* (1963), *Sandwich Man* (1966), *The Night They Raided Minsky's* (1968), *What's Good for the Goose* (1969).

**Wood, Natalie** (Natasha Gurdin) (1938–81) American, born San Francisco, California; *Miracle on 34th Street* (1947), *The Ghost and Mrs Muir* (1947), *Rebel Without a Cause* (1955), *The Searchers* (1956), *Marjorie Morningstar* (1958), *All The Fine Young Cannibals* (1959), *Splendor in the Grass* (1961), *West Side Story* (1961), *Love with the Proper Stranger* (1964), *The Great Race* (1965), *This Property is Condemned* (1966), *Bob and Carol and Ted and Alice* (1969), *From Here to Eternity* (TV 1979), *Meteor* (1979), *Brainstorm* (1983).

**Woods, James** (1947– ) American, born Vernal, Utah; *The Choirboys* (1977), *Videodrome* (1983), *Salvador* (1986), *Best Seller* (1987), *Cop* (1988), *The Boost* (1988), *The Getaway* (1994), *Nixon* (1995), *Contact* (1997).

**Woodward, Joanne** (1930– ) American, born Thomasville, Georgia; *Three Faces of Eve* (1957), *No Down Payment* (1957), *The Long Hot Summer* (1958), *The Stripper* (1963), *A Big Hand for the Little Lady* (1966), *Rachel, Rachel* (1968), *Summer Wishes, Winter Dreams* (1973), *The Glass Menagerie* (1987), *Mr and Mrs Bridge* (1990), *Philadelphia* (1993), *Breathing Lessons* (TV 1994).

**York, Michael** (1942– ) British, born Fulmer; *Accident* (1967), *Romeo and Juliet* (1968), *Cabaret* (1972), *Lost Horizon* (1973), *The Three Musketeers* (1973), *The Four Musketeers* (1974), *Jesus of Nazareth* (TV 1977), *The Island of Dr Moreau* (1977), *The White Lions* (1980), *Space* (TV 1985), *The Far Country* (TV 1986), *Sword of Gideon* (TV 1986), *Return of the Musketeers* (1989), *The Four Minute Mile* (1992), *The Ring* (1996).

**Young, Sean** (1959– ) American, born Louisville, Kentucky; *Blade Runner* (1982), *Dune* (1984), *Baby ... Secret of the Lost Legend* (1985), *Wall Street* (1987), *The Boost* (1988), *Cousins* (1989), *Wings of the Apache* (1990), *Hold Me Thrill Me Kiss Me* (1993), *Ace Ventura Pet Detective* (1994), *Special Delivery* (1999).

## Motion picture academy awards

| | Best film | Best actor | Best actress |
|---|---|---|---|
| 1970 | *Patton* (Franklin J Schaffner) | George C Scott *Patton* | Glenda Jackson *Women in Love* |
| 1971 | *The French Connection* (William Friedkin) | Gene Hackman *The French Connection* | Jane Fonda *Klute* |
| 1972 | *The Godfather* (Francis Ford Coppola) | Marlon Brando *The Godfather* | Liza Minnelli *Cabaret* |
| 1973 | *The Sting* (George Roy Hill) | Jack Lemmon *Save the Tiger* | Glenda Jackson *A Touch of Class* |
| 1974 | *The Godfather, Part II* (Francis Ford Coppola) | Art Carney *Harry and Tonto* | Ellen Burstyn *Alice Doesn't Live Here Anymore* |
| 1975 | *One Flew Over the Cuckoo's Nest* (Miloš Forman) | Jack Nicholson *One Flew Over the Cuckoo's Nest* | Louise Fletcher *One Flew Over the Cuckoo's Nest* |
| 1976 | *Rocky* (John G Avildsen) | Peter Finch *Network* | Faye Dunaway *Network* |
| 1977 | *Annie Hall* (Woody Allen) | Richard Dreyfuss *The Goodbye Girl* | Diane Keaton *Annie Hall* |
| 1978 | *The Deer Hunter* (Michael Cimino) | Jon Voight *Coming Home* | Jane Fonda *Coming Home* |
| 1979 | *Kramer vs Kramer* (Robert Beaton) | Dustin Hoffman *Kramer vs Kramer* | Sally Field *Norma Rae* |
| 1980 | *Ordinary People* (Robert Redford) | Robert de Niro *Raging Bull* | Sissy Spacek *Coal Miner's Daughter* |
| 1981 | *Chariots of Fire* (Hugh Hudson) | Henry Fonda *On Golden Pond* | Katharine Hepburn *On Golden Pond* |
| 1982 | *Gandhi* (Richard Attenborough) | Ben Kingsley *Gandhi* | Meryl Streep *Sophie's Choice* |
| 1983 | *Terms of Endearment* (James L Brooks) | Robert Duval *Tender Mercies* | Shirley MacLaine *Terms of Endearment* |
| 1984 | *Amadeus* (Miloš Forman) | F Murray Abraham *Amadeus* | Sally Field *Places in the Heart* |
| 1985 | *Out of Africa* (Sydney Pollack) | William Hurt *Kiss of the Spider Woman* | Geraldine Page *The Trip to Bountiful* |
| 1986 | *Platoon* (Oliver Stone) | Paul Newman *The Color of Money* | Marlee Matlin *Children of a Lesser God* |
| 1987 | *The Last Emperor* (Bernardo Bertolucci) | Michael Douglas *Wall Street* | Cher *Moonstruck* |
| 1988 | *Rain Man* (Barry Levinson) | Dustin Hoffman *Rain Man* | Jodie Foster *The Accused* |
| 1989 | *Driving Miss Daisy* (Bruce Beresford) | Daniel Day-Lewis *My Left Foot* | Jessica Tandy *Driving Miss Daisy* |
| 1990 | *Dances with Wolves* (Kevin Costner) | Jeremy Irons *Reversal of Fortune* | Kathy Bates *Misery* |
| 1991 | *The Silence of the Lambs* (Jonathan Demme) | Anthony Hopkins *The Silence of the Lambs* | Jodie Foster *The Silence of the Lambs* |
| 1992 | *Unforgiven* (Clint Eastwood) | Al Pacino *Scent of a Woman* | Emma Thompson *Howards End* |
| 1993 | *Schindler's List* (Steven Spielberg) | Tom Hanks *Philadelphia* | Holly Hunter *The Piano* |
| 1994 | *Forrest Gump* (Robert Zemeckis) | Tom Hanks *Forrest Gump* | Jessica Lange *Blue Sky* |
| 1995 | *Braveheart* (Mel Gibson) | Nicolas Cage *Leaving Las Vegas* | Susan Sarandon *Dead Man Walking* |
| 1996 | *The English Patient* (Anthony Minghella) | Geoffrey Rush *Shine* | Frances McDormand *Fargo* |
| 1997 | *Titanic* (James Cameron) | Jack Nicholson *As Good as it Gets* | Helen Hunt *As Good as it Gets* |
| 1998 | *Shakespeare in Love* (Guy Madden) | Roberto Benigni *Life is Beautiful* | Gwyneth Paltrow *Shakespeare in Love* |
| 1999 | *American Beauty* (Sam Mendes) | Kevin Spacey *American Beauty* | Hilary Swank *Boys Don't Cry* |
| 2000 | *Gladiator* (Ridley Scott) | Russell Crowe *Gladiator* | Julia Roberts *Erin Brockovich* |

## Film directors

Selected films are listed.

**Aldrich, Robert** (1918–83) American, born Cranston, Rhode Island; *Apache* (1954), *Vera Cruz* (1954), *Kiss Me Deadly* (1955), *Attack!* (1957), *What Ever Happened to Baby Jane?* (1962), *The Dirty Dozen* (1967).

**Allen, Woody (Allen Stewart Konigsberg)** (1935– ) American, born Brooklyn, New York City; *What's Up, Tiger Lily?* (1966), *Bananas* (1971), *Everything You Wanted to Know About Sex, But Were Afraid to Ask* (1972), *Play it Again, Sam* (1972), *Sleeper* (1973), *Love and Death* (1975), *Annie Hall* (1977), *Interiors* (1978), *Manhattan* (1979), *Stardust Memories* (1980), *A Midsummer Night's Sex Comedy* (1982), *Broadway Danny Rose* (1984), *The Purple Rose of Cairo* (1985), *Hannah and Her Sisters* (1986), *Radio Days* (1987), *Crimes and Misdemeanors* (1990), *Alice* (1991), *Shadows and Fog* (1992), *Husbands and Wives* (1992), *Manhattan Murder Mystery* (1993), *Bullets Over Broadway* (1994), *Mighty Aphrodite* (1996), *Deconstructing Harry* (1997).

**Almodóvar, Pedro** (1951– ) Spanish, born Calzada de Calatrava; *Dark Habits* (1983), *Law of Desire* (1987), *Women on the Verge of a Nervous Breakdown* (1988), *Tie Me Up! Tie Me Down!* (1990), *High Heels* (1991), *Kika* (1993), *Live Flesh* (1997).

**Altman, Robert** (1925– ) American, born Kansas City, Missouri; *The James Dean Story* (1957), *M*A*S*H* (1970), *McCabe and Mrs Miller* (1971), *The Long Goodbye* (1973), *Nashville* (1975), *A Wedding* (1978), *Popeye* (1980), *Come Back to the 5 & Dime Jimmy Dean Jimmy Dean* (1982), *Streamers* (1983), *Fool for Love* (1985), *Aria* (1987), *Vincent and Theo* (1990), *The Player* (1992), *Short Cuts* (1993), *Prêt-À-Porter* (1994), *The Gingerbread Man* (1998).

**Antonioni, Michelangelo** (1912– ) Italian, born Ferrara; *L'Avventura* (1959), *La Notte* (1960), *L'Eclisse* (1962), *Blow-Up* (1966), *The Passenger* (1975).

**Asquith, Anthony** (1902–68) British, born London; *Shooting Stars* (1928), *Underground* (1930), *Pygmalion* (1937), *French without Tears* (1939), *Quiet Wedding* (1940), *The Demi-Paradise* (1943), *Fanny by Gaslight* (1944), *The Way to the Stars* (1945), *The Browning Version* (1950), *The Importance of Being Earnest* (1952), *Orders to Kill* (1958), *The VIPs* (1963).

**Attenborough, Richard Samuel Attenborough, Baron** (1923– ) British, born Cambridge; *Oh! What a Lovely War* (1968), *A Bridge Too Far* (1977), *Gandhi* (1982), *A Chorus Line* (1985), *Cry Freedom* (1987), *Chaplin* (1992), *Shadowlands* (1993), *In Love and War* (1996).

**Badham, John** (1939– ) American, born Luton, England; *The Law* (TV 1974), *Saturday Night Fever* (1977), *Whose Life is it Anyway?* (1981), *Blue Thunder* (1982), *War Games* (1983), *American Flyers* (1984), *Short Circuit* (1986), *Stakeout* (1987), *Bird on a Wire* (1989), *The Assassin* (1992), *Another Stakeout* (1993), *Floating Away* (1998).

**Beatty, Warren (Henry Warren Beaty)** (1937– ) American, born Richmond, Virginia; *Heaven Can Wait* (1978), *Reds* (1981), *Dick Tracy* (1990), *Bulworth* (1998).

**Bergman, (Ernst) Ingmar** (1918– ) Swedish, born Uppsala; *Crisis* (1945), *Prison* (1948), *Sawdust and Tinsel* (1953), *The Face* (1955), *Smiles of a Summer Night* (1955), *The Seventh Seal* (1957), *Wild Strawberries* (1957), *The Virgin Spring* (1959), *Through a Glass Darkly* (1961), *The Silence* (1963), *Cries and Whispers* (1972), *The Magic Flute* (1974), *Autumn Sonata* (1978), *Fanny and Alexander* (1983).

**Bertolucci, Bernardo** (1940– ) Italian, born Parma; *Love and Anger* (1969), *The Conformist* (1970), *Last Tango in Paris* (1972), *1900* (1976), *The Last Emperor* (1987), *The Sheltering Sky* (1990), *Little Buddha* (1993).

**Besson, Luc** (1959– ) French, born Paris; *The Last Battle* (1983), *Subway* (1985), *The Big Blue* (1988), *Nikita* (1990), *Leon* (1994), *The Fifth Element* (1997).

**Bogdanovich, Peter** (1939– ) American, born Kingston, New York; *Targets* (1967), *The Last Picture Show* (1971), *Paper Moon* (1973), *What's Up, Doc?* (1972), *Nickelodeon* (1976), *Mask* (1985), *Illegally Yours* (1987), *Texasville* (1990), *Noises Off* (1992), *The Thing Called Love* (1993).

**Boorman, John** (1933– ) English, born Epsom, Surrey; *Point Blank* (1967), *Hell in the Pacific* (1969), *Deliverance* (1972), *Zardoz* (1974), *Exorcist II: The Heretic* (1977), *Excalibur* (1981), *The Emerald Forest* (1984), *Hope and Glory* (1987), *Where the Heart Is* (1990), *Beyond Rangoon* (1995), *The General* (1998).

**Bresson, Robert** (1901–99) French, born Bromont-Lamothe; *Les Dames du Bois de Boulogne* (1946), *Journal d'un Curé de Campagne* (1950), *Pickpocket* (1959), *Au hasard, Balthazar* (1966), *Une Femme douce* (1969), *L'Argent* (1983).

**Brook, Peter (Stephen Paul)** (1925– ) British, born London; *Lord of the Flies* (1963), *King Lear* (1971), *Carmen* (1983).

**Brooks, Mel (Melvin Kaminski)** (1926– ) American, born Brooklyn, New York City; *The Producers* (1966), *Blazing Saddles* (1974), *Young Frankenstein* (1974), *High Anxiety* (1978), *History of the World Part One* (1981), *Spaceballs* (1987), *Life Stinks* (1991), *Robin Hood: Men in Tights* (1993), *Dracula: Dead and Loving It* (1995).

**Buñuel, Luis** (1900–83) Spanish, born Calanda; *Un Chien Andalou* (with Salvador Dalí) (1928), *L'Âge d'Or* (1930), *Los Olvidados* (1950), *Robinson Crusoe* (1952), *El* (1953), *Nazarin* (1958), *Viridiana* (1961), *The Exterminating Angel* (1962), *Belle de Jour* (1967), *The Discreet Charm of the Bourgeoisie* (1972), *The Phantom of the Liberty* (1974), *That Obscure Object of Desire* (1977).

**Burton, Tim** (1958– ) American, born Burbank, California; *Peewee's Big Adventure* (1985), *Beetlejuice*

(1988), *Batman* (1989), *Edward Scissorhands* (1990), *Batman Returns* (1992), *Ed Wood* (1994), *Mars Attacks!* (1996), *Sleepy Hollow* (1999).

**Capra, Frank** (1897–1991) Italian–American, born Bisacquino, Sicily; *Platinum Blonde* (1932), *American Madness* (1932), *Lady for a Day* (1933), *It Happened One Night* (1934), *Mr Deeds Goes to Town* (1936), *Lost Horizon* (1937), *You Can't Take It With You* (1938), *Mr Smith Goes to Washington* (1939), *Meet John Doe* (1941), *Arsenic and Old Lace* (1944), *It's a Wonderful Life* (1946).

**Carpenter, John** (1948– ) American, born Carthage, New York; *Dark Star* (1974), *Assault on Precinct 13* (1976), *Halloween* (1978), *Elvis – the Movie* (TV 1979), *The Fog* (1979), *Escape from New York* (1981), *The Thing* (1982), *Christine* (1983), *Starman* (1984), *Big Trouble in Little China* (1986), *Prince of Darkness* (1987), *Memoirs of an Invisible Man* (1992), *Escape From LA* (1996), *Vampires* (1998).

**Carné, Marcel** (1909–96) French, born Batignolles, Paris; *Quai des Brumes* (1938), *Le Jour se lève* (1939), *Les Enfants du Paradis* (1944).

**Chabrol, Claude** (1930– ) French, born Paris; *Beau Serge* (1958), *Les Cousins* (1959), *Les Biches* (1968), *La Femme Infidèle* (1969), *Le Boucher* (1969), *Les Noces rouges* (1973), *Masques* (1987), *Une Affaire des Femmes* (1989), *The Swindle* (1997).

**Clair, René (René Lucien Chomette)** (1891–1981) French, born Paris; *An Italian Straw Hat* (1927), *Sous Les Toits de Paris* (1929), *Le Million* (1931), *À Nous la liberté* (1931), *I Married a Witch* (1942), *It Happened Tomorrow* (1944), *And Then There Were None* (1945), *Les Belles de Nuit* (1952), *Porte des Lila* (1956), *Tout l'or du Monde* (1961).

**Cocteau, Jean** (1889–1963) French, born Maisons-Lafitte; *Le Sang d'un poète* (1930), *La Belle et La Bête* (1946), *Orphée* (1950), *Le Testament d'Orphée* (1959).

**Coen, Ethan** (1958– ) and **Joel** (1955– ) American, both born St Louis Park, Minnesota; *Blood Simple* (1984), *Raising Arizona* (1987), *Miller's Crossing* (1990), *Barton Fink* (1991), *The Hudsucker Proxy* (1994), *Fargo* (1995), *The Big Lebowski* (1998), *O Brother, Where Art Thou?* (2000).

**Coppola, Francis Ford** (1939– ) American, born Detroit, Michigan; *The Godfather* (1972), *The Godfather, Part II* (1974), *Apocalypse Now* (1979), *One from the Heart* (1982), *The Outsiders* (1983), *Rumble Fish* (1983), *The Cotton Club* (1984), *Peggy Sue Got Married* (1987), *Gardens of Stone* (1987), *Tucker: The Man and His Dream* (1988), *The Godfather, Part III* (1991), *Dracula* (1992).

**Corman, Roger** (1926– ) American, born Detroit, Michigan; *Not of This Earth* (1957), *Bucket of Blood* (1960), *Fall of the House of Usher* (1960), *The Little Shop of Horrors* (1960), *The Intruder* (1961), *The Raven* (1963), *The Man with the X-ray Eyes* (1963), *The Masque of the Red Death* (1964), *Frankenstein Unbound* (1990), *The Pit and the Pendulum* (1990).

**Cronenberg, David** (1943– ) Canadian, born Toronto, Ontario; *Shivers* (1976), *Rabid* (1977), *The Brood* (1978), *Scanners* (1980), *Videodrome* (1983), *The Dead Zone* (1983), *The Fly* (1985), *Dead Ringers* (1988), *Naked Lunch* (1991), *M Butterfly* (1992), *Crash* (1996).

**Curtiz, Michael (Mihály Kertész)** (1888–1962) American–Hungarian, born Budapest, Hungary; *Noah's Ark* (1929), *Mammy* (1930), *Doctor X* (1932), *The Mystery of the Wax Museum* (1933), *British Agent* (1934), *Black Fury* (1935), *Captain Blood* (1935), *Charge of the Light Brigade* (1936), *The Adventures of Robin Hood* (1938), *Angels with Dirty Faces* (1938), *The Sea Hawk* (1940), *The Sea Wolf* (1941), *Yankee Doodle Dandy* (1942), *Casablanca* (1943), *Mildred Pierce* (1945), *White Christmas* (1954), *We're No Angels* (1955), *King Creole* (1958).

**Dante, Joe** (1946– ) American, born Moristown, New Jersey; *Piranha* (1978), *The Howling* (1980), *Gremlins* (1984), *Explorers* (1985), *Innerspace* (1987), *Amazon Women on the Moon* (1987), *Gremlins 2: The New Batch* (1990), *Small Soldiers* (1998).

**de Mille, Cecil B(lount)** (1881–1959) American, born Ashfield, Massachusetts; *Male and Female* (1919), *King of Kings* (1927), *The Ten Commandments* (1923 & 1956), *The Greatest Show on Earth* (1952).

**Demme, Jonathan** (1944– ) American, born Long Island, New York; *Citizen Band* (1977), *Something Wild* (1987), *Swimming to Cambodia* (1987), *Married to the Mob* (1988), *The Silence of the Lambs* (1991), *Philadelphia* (1993), *Beloved* (1998).

**de Palma, Brian** (1940– ) American, born Newark, New Jersey; *Greetings* (1968), *Carrie* (1976), *The Fury* (1978), *Dressed to Kill* (1980), *Blow Out* (1981), *Scarface* (1983), *Body Double* (1984), *The Untouchables* (1987), *Casualties of War* (1989), *Bonfire of the Vanities* (1990), *Carlito's Way* (1993), *Mission: Impossible* (1996).

**Donner, Richard** (1930– ) American; *The Omen* (1976), *Superman* (1978), *Inside Moves* (1980), *The Final Conflict* (1981), *Ladyhawke* (1984), *The Goonies* (1985), *Lethal Weapon* (1987), *Scrooged* (1988), *Lethal Weapon 2* (1989), *Lethal Weapon 3* (1992), *Maverick* (1994), *Lethal Weapon 4* (1998).

**Eastwood, Clint** (1930– ) American, born San Francisco, California; *Play Misty for Me* (1971), *The Outlaw Josey Wales* (1976), *Pale Rider* (1985), *Birdy* (1988), *Unforgiven* (1992), *The Bridges of Madison County* (1995), *True Crime* (1999).

**Eisenstein, Sergei Mikhailovich** (1898–1948) Russian, born Riga; *Stride* (1924), *Battleship Potemkin* (1925), *Alexander Nevsky* (1938), *Ten Days that Shook the World* (1928), *The Magic Seed* (1941), *Ivan the Terrible* (1942–6).

**Fassbinder, Rainer Werner** (1946–82) German, born Bad Wörishofen; *Warnung von einer heiligen Nutte* (1971), *Satan's Brew* (1976).

**Fellini, Federico** (1920–93) Italian, born Rimini; *I Vitelloni* (1953), *La Strada* (1954), *La Dolce Vita* (1960), *8½* (1963), *Satyricon* (1969), *Fellini's Rome* (1972), *Casanova* (1976), *Orchestra Rehearsal* (1979), *City of Women* (1981), *The Ship Sails On* (1983), *Ginger and Fred* (1986).

**Fleming, Victor** (1883–1949) American, born Pasadena, California; *Mantrap* (1926), *The Virginian* (1929), *The Wet Parade* (1932), *Red Dust* (1932), *Treasure Island* (1934), *Test Pilot* (1938), *Gone with the Wind* (1939), *The Wizard of Oz* (1939), *Dr Jekyll and Mr Hyde* (1941), *A Guy Named Joe* (1943).

**Forbes, Bryan (John Theobold Clarke)** (1926– ) British, born London; *The Angry Silence* (1960), *The Slipper and the Rose* (1976), *International Velvet* (1978).

**Ford, John** (1895–73) American, born Cape Elizabeth, Maine; *The Tornado* (1917), *The Iron Horse* (1924), *Arrowsmith* (1931), *The Informer* (1935), *Stagecoach* (1939), *Young Mr Lincoln* (1939), *The Grapes of Wrath* (1940), *My Darling Clementine* (1946), *The Quiet Man* (1952), *The Searchers* (1956), *The Man Who Shot Liberty Valance* (1962).

**Forman, Miloš** (1932– ) Czech, born Kaslov; *The Fireman's Ball* (1967), *Taking Off* (1971), *One Flew Over the Cuckoo's Nest* (1975), *Amadeus* (1984), *The People vs Larry Flynt* (1996).

**Frears, Stephen** (1941– ) British, born Leicester; *Gumshoe* (1971), *The Hit* (1984), *My Beautiful Laundrette* (1985), *Prick Up Your Ears* (1987), *Sammy and Rosie Get Laid* (1987), *Dangerous Liaisons* (1988), *The Grifters* (1990), *The Snapper* (1993), *Mary Reilly* (1995), *High Fidelity* (2000).

**Friedkin, William** (1939– ) American, born Chicago; *The French Connection* (1971), *The Exorcist* (1973), *The Guardian* (1990).

**Gilliam, Terry** (1940– ) American, born Minneapolis, Minnesota; *Jabberwocky* (1977), *Time Bandits* (1980), *Brazil* (1985), *The Adventures of Baron Munchausen* (1988), *The Fisher King* (1991), *Twelve Monkeys* (1995).

**Godard, Jean-Luc** (1930– ) French, born Paris; *À Bout de Souffle* (1960), *Alphaville* (1965), *Le Plus Vieux Métier du Monde* (1967), *Sauve Qui Peut La Vie* (1980), *Hail Mary* (1985), *Nouvelle Vague* (1990).

**Greenaway, Peter** (1942– ) British, born London; *The Draughtman's Contract* (1982), *The Belly of an Architect* (1987), *Drowning by Numbers* (1988), *The Cook, The Thief, His Wife and Her Lover* (1989), *Prospero's Books* (1991), *The Baby of Macon* (1993), *The Pillow Book* (1995).

**Griffith, D(avid) W(ark)** (1875–1948) American, born La Grange, Kentucky; *Judith of Bethulia* (1913), *The Birth of a Nation* (1915), *Intolerance* (1916), *Hearts of the World* (1918), *Broken Blossoms* (1919), *Orphans of the Storm* (1922).

**Hall, Sir Peter (Reginald Frederick)** (1930– ) British, born Bury St Edmunds, Suffolk; *Work is a Four Letter Word* (1968), *Perfect Friday* (1971), *Akenfield* (1974), *Never Talk to Strangers* (1995).

**Hawks, Howard Winchester** (1896–1977) American, born Goshen, Indiana; *The Dawn Patrol* (1930), *Scarface* (1932), *Twentieth Century* (1934), *Barbary Coast* (1935), *Bringing Up Baby* (1938), *His Girl Friday* (1940), *To Have and Have Not* (1944), *The Big Sleep* (1946), *Red River* (1948), *Gentlemen Prefer Blondes* (1953), *Rio Bravo* (1959).

**Hill, George Roy** (1921– ) American, born Minneapolis, Minnesota; *The World of Henry Orient* (1964), *Thoroughly Modern Millie* (1967), *Butch Cassidy and the Sundance Kid* (1969), *Slaughterhouse 5* (1972), *The Sting* (1973), *The World According to Garp* (1982).

**Hitchcock, Sir Alfred Joseph** (1899–1980) British, born Leytonstone, London; *The Lodger* (1926), *Blackmail* (1929), *Murder* (1930), *The Thirty-Nine Steps* (1935), *The Lady Vanishes* (1938), *Rebecca* (1940), *Lifeboat* (1944), *Spellbound* (1945), *Notorious* (1946), *The Paradine Case* (1947), *Strangers on a Train* (1951), *Dial M for Murder* (1955), *Vertigo* (1958), *North by Northwest* (1959), *Psycho* (1960), *The Birds* (1963), *Marnie* (1964), *Frenzy* (1972), *Alfred Hitchcock Presents* (TV 1955–61).

**Huston, John Marcellus** (1906–87) Irish–American, born Nevada, Missouri; *Murders in the Rue Morgue* (1932), *Juarez* (1939), *High Sierra* (1941), *The Maltese Falcon* (1941), *Key Largo* (1948), *The Treasure of the Sierra Madre* (1948), *The Asphalt Jungle* (1950), *The African Queen* (1951), *Moulin Rouge* (1952), *The Misfits* (1960), *Freud* (1962), *Night of the Iguana* (1964), *Casino Royale* (1967), *Fat City* (1972), *The Man Who Would Be King* (1975), *Annie* (1982), *Prizzi's Honor* (1985), *The Dead* (1987).

**Ivory, James Francis** (1928– ) American, born Berkeley, California; *Shakespeare Wallah* (1965), *Heat and Dust* (1982), *The Bostonians* (1984), *A Room with a View* (1985), *Maurice* (1987), *Mr and Mrs Bridge* (1990), *Howards End* (1992), *The Remains of the Day* (1993), *Jefferson in Paris* (1995), *Surviving Picasso* (1996).

**Jarman, (Michael) Derek** (1942–94) British, born Northwood, Middlesex; *Sebastiane* (1976), *Jubilee* (1977), *The Tempest* (1979), *Caravaggio* (1985), *The Last of England* (1987), *The Garden* (1990), *Edward II* (1991), *Wittgenstein* (1993).

**Jordan, Neil** (1950– ) Irish, born Sligo; *Angel* (1982), *The Company of Wolves* (1984), *Mona Lisa* (1986), *High Spirits* (1988), *The Crying Game* (1992), *Interview with the Vampire* (1994), *Michael Collins* (1996), *The Butcher Boy* (1997).

**Kasdan, Lawrence** (1949– ) American, born Miami Beach, Florida; *Body Heat* (1981), *The Big Chill* (1983), *Silverado* (1985), *The Accidental Tourist* (1989), *Love You to Death* (1990), *Grand Canyon* (1991), *Wyatt Earp* (1994), *French Kiss* (1995).

**Kaufman, Philip** (1936– ) American, born Chicago; *Invasion of the Body Snatchers* (1978), *The Wanderers* (1979), *The Right Stuff* (1983), *The Unbearable Lightness of Being* (1988), *Henry and June* (1990), *Quills* (2000).

**Kazan, Elia (Elia Kazanjoglou)** (1909– ) American, born Istanbul, Turkey; *Boomerang* (1947), *Gentleman's Agreement* (1947), *Pink* (1949), *A Streetcar Named Desire* (1951), *Viva Zapata* (1952), *On the Waterfront* (1954), *East of Eden* (1955), *Baby Doll* (1956), *A Face in the Crowd* (1957), *Splendor in the Grass* (1962), *America, America* (1963), *The Arrangement* (1969), *The Visitors* (1972), *The Last Tycoon* (1976).

**Kieslowski, Krzystof** (1941–96) Polish, born Warsaw; *The Scar* (1976), *Camera Buff* (1979), *No End* (1984), *A Short Film About Killing* (1988), *The Double Life of Veronique* (1991), *Three Colours: Blue* (1993), *White* (1993), *Red* (1994).

**Kubrick, Stanley** (1928–99) American, born The Bronx, New York City; *The Killing* (1956), *Paths of Glory* (1957), *Spartacus* (1960), *Lolita* (1962), *Dr Strangelove* (1964), *2001: A Space Odyssey* (1968), *A Clockwork Orange* (1971), *Barry Lyndon* (1975), *The Shining* (1980), *Full Metal Jacket* (1987), *Eyes Wide Shut* (1999).

**Kurosawa, Akira** (1910–98) Japanese, born Tokyo; *Rashomon* (1950), *The Idiot* (1951), *Living* (1952), *The Seven Samurai* (1954), *Throne of Blood* (1957), *The Lower Depths* (1957), *The Hidden Fortress* (1958), *Dersu Uzala* (1975), *The Shadow Warrior* (1981), *Ran* (1985), *Dreams* (1990), *Rhapsody in August* (1991).

**Landis, John** (1950– ) American, born Chicago; *Schlock* (1971), *Kentucky Fried Movie* (1977), *Animal House* (1978), *The Blues Brothers* (1980), *An American Werewolf in London* (1981), *Twilight Zone* (1983), *Trading Places* (1983), *Into the Night* (1985), *Spies Like Us* (1985), *The Three Amigos* (1986), *Coming to America* (1988), *Oscar* (1991), *Beverly Hills Cop III* (1994), *Blues Brothers 2000* (1998).

**Lang, Fritz** (1890–1976) German, born Vienna, Austria; *Destiny* (1921), *Dr Mabuse the Gambler* (1922), *Siegfried* (1923), *Metropolis* (1926), *Spies* (1927), *M* (1931), *The Testament of Dr Mabuse* (1932), *You Only Live Once* (1937), *The Return of Frank James* (1940), *The Woman in the Window* (1944), *The Big Heat* (1953), *Beyond a Reasonable Doubt* (1956), *While the City Sleeps* (1955).

**Lean, Sir David** (1908–91) English, born Croydon; *Pygmalion* (1938), *In Which We Serve* (1942), *Blithe Spirit* (1945), *Brief Encounter* (1946), *Great Expectations* (1946), *The Sound Barrier* (1952), *Hobson's Choice* (1954), *Summer Madness* (1955), *Bridge on the River Kwai* (1957), *Lawrence of Arabia* (1962), *Doctor Zhivago* (1965), *Ryan's Daughter* (1970), *A Passage to India* (1984).

**Lee, Spike (Shelton Jackson Lee)** (1957– ) American, born Atlanta, Georgia; *She's Gotta Have It* (1986), *School Daze* (1988), *Do the Right Thing* (1989), *Mo' Better Blues* (1990), *Jungle Fever* (1991), *Malcolm X* (1992), *Crooklyn* (1994), *Clockers* (1995), *Girl 6* (1996), *He Got Game* (1998).

**Leigh, Mike** (1943– ) British, born Salford; *Bleak Moments* (1971), *Nuts in May* (1976), *Abigail's Party* (1977), *High Hopes* (1988), *Life is Sweet* (1990), *Naked* (1993), *Secrets and Lies* (1996), *Career Girls* (1997), *Topsy-Turvy* (1999).

**Levinson, Barry** (1942– ) American, born Baltimore, Maryland; *Diner* (1982), *The Natural* (1984), *The Young Sherlock Holmes* (1985), *Tin Men* (1987), *Good Morning Vietnam* (1987), *Rain Man* (1988), *Avalon* (1990), *Bugsy* (1991), *Toys* (1992), *Disclosure* (1994), *Sleepers* (1996), *Sphere* (1998).

**Lucas, George** (1944– ) American, born Modesto, California; *THX-1138: 4EB/Electronic Labyrinth* (1965), *American Graffiti* (1973), *Star Wars* (1977), *Star Wars Episode 1: The Phantom Menace* (1999).

**Lynch, David K** (1946– ) American, born Missoula, Montana; *Eraserhead* (1976), *The Elephant Man* (1980), *Dune* (1984), *Blue Velvet* (1986), *Wild at Heart* (1990), *Twin Peaks* (TV 1990–1), *Twin Peaks: Fire Walk With Me* (1992), *Lost Highway* (1997).

**McBride, Jim** (1941– ) American, born New York City; *Breathless* (1983), *The Big Easy* (1986), *Great Balls of Fire* (1989), *The Wrong Man* (1992).

**Mankiewicz, Joseph Leo** (1909–93) American, born Wilkes-Barre, Pennsylvania; *All About Eve* (1950), *The Barefoot Contessa* (1954), *Guys and Dolls* (1954), *Suddenly Last Summer* (1959), *Sleuth* (1972).

**Miller, George** (1945– ) Australian, born Brisbane; *Mad Max* (1979), *Mad Max 2: The Road Warrior* (1982), *Mad Max Beyond Thunderdome* (1985), *The Witches of Eastwick* (1987), *Lorenzo's Oil* (1992).

**Miller, Jonathan Wolfe** (1934– ) British, born London; *The Magic Flute* (1986), *The Tempest* (1988).

**Minnelli, Vincente** (1913–86) American, born Chicago; *Ziegfeld Follies* (1946), *An American in Paris* (1951), *Lust for Life* (1956), *Gigi* (1958).

**Nichols, Mike (Michael Igor Peschkowsky)** (1931– ) American–German, born Berlin, Germany; *Who's Afraid of Virginia Woolf?* (1966), *The Graduate* (1967), *Catch-22* (1970), *Working Girl* (1988), *Postcards from the Edge* (1990), *Wolf* (1994), *The Birdcage* (1996), *Primary Colors* (1998).

**Olivier, Laurence Kerr Olivier, Baron** (1907–89) British, born Dorking, Surrey; *Henry V* (1944), *Hamlet* (1948), *Richard III* (1956), *The Prince and the Showgirl* (1958), *The Entertainer* (1960).

**Parker, Alan** (1944– ) British, born London; *Bugsy Malone* (1976), *Midnight Express* (1978), *Shoot the Moon* (1981), *Pink Floyd: The Wall* (1982), *Birdy* (1985), *Angel Heart* (1987), *Mississippi Burning* (1988), *Come See the Paradise* (1990), *The Commitments* (1991), *Evita* (1996), *Angels's Ashes* (1999).

**Pasolini, Pier Paolo** (1922–75) Italian, born Bologna; *Accatone!* (1961), *The Gospel According to St Matthew* (1964), *Oedipus Rex* (1967), *Medea* (1970).

**Polanski, Roman** (1933– ) Polish, born Paris; *Knife in the Water* (1962), *Repulsion* (1965), *Cul-de-Sac* (1966), *Rosemary's Baby* (1968), *Macbeth* (1971), *Chinatown* (1974), *Tess* (1979), *Frantic* (1988), *Bitter Moon* (1992), *Death and the Maiden* (1994).

**Pollack, Sydney** (1934– ) American, born South Bend, Indiana; *They Shoot Horses Don't They?* (1969), *The Electric Horseman* (1979), *Absence of Malice* (1981), *Tootsie* (1982), *Out of Africa* (1985), *Havana* (1990), *The Firm* (1993), *Random Hearts* (1999).

**Powell, Michael Latham** (1905–90) British, born Bekesbourne, near Canterbury; with **Emeric Pressburger** (1902–88) Hungarian–British, born

Miskolc, Hungary; *The Spy in Black* (1939), *The Thief of Baghdad* (1940), *The Life and Death of Colonel Blimp* (1943), *Black Narcissus* (1946), *The Red Shoes* (1948), *A Matter of Life and Death* (1946), *Peeping Tom* (1959).

**Redford, (Charles) Robert** (1937– ) American, born Santa Monica, California; *Ordinary People* (1980), *The Milagro Beanfield War* (1987), *A River Runs Through It* (1992), *Quiz Show* (1994), *The Horse Whisperer* (1998).

**Reed, Sir Carol** (1906–76) British, born London; *The Young Mr Pitt* (1942), *The Way Ahead* (1944), *The Fallen Idol* (1948), *The Third Man* (1949), *An Outcast of the Islands* (1952), *The Man Between* (1953), *Our Man in Havana* (1959), *Oliver!* (1968).

**Reiner, Carl** (1922– ) American, born The Bronx, New York City; *Oh God* (1977), *The Jerk* (1979), *Dead Men Don't Wear Plaid* (1982), *The Man with Two Brains* (1983), *Summer School* (1987).

**Reiner, Rob** (1945– ) American, born The Bronx, New York City; *This is Spinal Tap* (1984), *Stand by Me* (1987), *The Princess Bride* (1988), *When Harry Met Sally ...* (1989), *Misery* (1990), *A Few Good Men* (1992), *North* (1994), *The American President* (1995).

**Renoir, Jean** (1894–1979) French, born Paris; *Une Partie de Campagne* (1936), *La Règle du Jeu* (1939), *The Southerner* (1945).

**Robbins, Tim (Timothy Francis)** (1958– ) American, born West Covina, California; *No Small Affair* (1984), *Bob Roberts* (1992), *Dead Man Walking* (1995), *The Cradle Will Rock* (1999).

**Roeg, Nicolas Jack** (1928– ) British, born London; *Performance* (1970), *Walkabout* (1971), *Don't Look Now* (1973), *The Man Who Fell to Earth* (1976), *Bad Timing* (1979), *Eureka* (1983), *Insignificance* (1985), *Castaway* (1986), *Black Widow* (1988), *Track 29* (1988), *The Witches* (1990), *Heart of Darkness* (1994).

**Rossellini, Roberto** (1906–77) Italian, born Rome; *The White Ship* (1940), *Rome, Open City* (1945), *Paisan* (1946), *Germany, Year Zero* (1947), *Stromboli* (1950), *General Della Rovera* (1959).

**Russell, Ken (Henry Kenneth Alfred Russell)** (1927– ) British, born Southampton; *Women in Love* (1969), *The Music Lovers* (1970), *The Devils* (1971), *Crimes of Passion* (1984), *Gothic* (1987), *Lair of the White Worm* (1989), *The Rainbow* (1989), *Whore* (1991), *Tales of Erotica* (1996).

**Schlesinger, John Richard** (1926– ) British, born London; *A Kind of Loving* (1962), *Billy Liar!* (1963), *Midnight Cowboy* (1969), *Sunday, Bloody Sunday* (1971), *Marathon Man* (1976), *Honky Tonk Freeway* (1981), *An Englishman Abroad* (TV 1982), *Madame Sousatzka* (1988), *Pacific Heights* (1990), *The Innocent* (1993), *The Next Best Thing* (2000).

**Scorsese, Martin** (1942– ) American, born Queens, New York; *Boxcar Bertha* (1972), *Mean Streets* (1973), *Alice Doesn't Live Here Any More* (1974), *Taxi Driver* (1976), *Raging Bull* (1980), *King of Comedy* (1982), *After Hours* (1985), *The Mission* (1986), *The Color of Money* (1986), *The Last Temptation of Christ* (1988), *Goodfellas* (1990), *Cape Fear* (1991), *Age of Innocence* (1992), *Casino* (1995), *Kundun* (1997).

**Scott, Ridley** (1937– ) British, born South Shields; *Alien* (1979), *Blade Runner* (1982), *No Way Out* (1989), *Thelma and Louise* (1991), *1492* (1992), *Gladiator* (2000), *Hannibal* (2001).

**Siegel, Don** (1912–91) American, born Chicago; *Riot in Cell Block 11* (1954), *Invasion of the Body Snatchers* (1956), *Baby Face Nelson* (1957), *Coogan's Bluff* (1968), *Two Mules for Sister Sara* (1969), *Dirty Harry* (1971), *Charley Varrick* (1973), *Telefon* (1977), *Escape from Alcatraz* (1979).

**Spielberg, Steven** (1946– ) American, born Cincinnati, Ohio; *Duel* (TV 1972), *Sugarland Express* (1973), *Jaws* (1975), *1941* (1979), *Close Encounters of the Third Kind* (1977), *Raiders of the Lost Ark* (1981), *ET* (1982), *Twilight Zone* (1983), *The Color Purple* (1985), *Indiana Jones and the Temple of Doom* (1984), *Empire of the Sun* (1987), *Indiana Jones and the Last Crusade* (1989), *Hook* (1992), *Jurassic Park* (1993), *Schindler's List* (1993), *The Lost World: Jurassic Park* (1997), *Saving Private Ryan* (1998).

**Stevenson, Robert** (1905–86) British, born Buxton, Derbyshire; *King Solomon's Mines* (1937), *Mary Poppins* (1964), *The Love Bug* (1968), *Bedknobs and Broomsticks* (1971).

**Stone, Oliver** (1946– ) American, born New York City; *Platoon* (1987), *Wall Street* (1987), *Born on the Fourth of July* (1989), *The Doors* (1991), *JFK* (1991), *Heaven and Earth* (1993), *Natural Born Killers* (1994), *Nixon* (1995), *Any Given Sunday* (1999).

**Tarantino, Quentin** (1963– ) American, born Knoxville, Tennessee; *Reservoir Dogs* (1993), *Pulp Fiction* (1994), *Four Rooms* (co-director, 1995), *Jackie Brown* (1998), *40 Lashes* (2000).

**Tati, Jacques (Jacques Tatischeff)** (1908–82) French, born Le Pecq; *Jour de fête* (1947), *Monsieur Hulot's Holiday* (1952), *Mon Oncle* (1958), *Playtime* (1968), *Traffic* (1981).

**Tavernier, Bertrand** (1941– ) French, born Lyons; *L'Horloger de Saint-Paul* (1973), *Dimanche à la Campagne* (1984), *La Mort en direct* (1979), *La Vie et rien d'autre* (1989), *Daddy Nostalgie* (1990), *L 627* (1992), *Capitaine Conan* (1996).

**Truffaut, François** (1932–84) French, born Paris; *Jules et Jim* (1961), *The Bride Wore Black* (1967), *Baisers volés* (1968), *L'Enfant Sauvage* (1969), *Day for Night* (1973), *The Last Metro* (1980).

**Visconti, Luchino (Count Don Luchino Visconti Di Morone)** (1906–76) Italian, born Milan; *The Leopard* (1963), *Ossessione* (1942), *The Damned* (1969), *Death in Venice* (1971).

**Weir, Peter** (1944– ) Australian, born Sydney; *The Cars That Ate Paris* (1974), *Picnic at Hanging Rock* (1975), *Gallipoli* (1981), *The Year of Living Dangerously* (1982), *Witness* (1985), *Mosquito Coast* (1986), *Dead Poets Society* (1989), *Green Card* (1990), *Fearless* (1993), *The Truman Show* (1998).

**Welles, (George) Orson** (1915–85) American, born Kenosha, Wisconsin; *Citizen Kane* (1941), *The Magnificent Ambersons* (1942), *Jane Eyre* (1943), *Macbeth* (1948), *Othello* (1951), *Touch of Evil* (1958), *The Trial* (1962), *Chimes at Midnight* (1966).

**Wenders, Wim** (1945– ) German, born Düsseldorf; *Summer in the City* (1970), *Alice in the Cities* (1974), *Kings of the Road* (1976), *Paris, Texas* (1984), *Wings of Desire* (1987), *Until the End of the World* (1991), *Faraway, So Close* (1993), *Beyond the Clouds* (co-director 1995), *The End of Violence* (1997).

**Wilder, Billy** (1906– ) Austrian–American, born Sucha, Austria; *Double Indemnity* (1944), *The Lost Weekend* (1945), *Sunset Boulevard* (1950), *The Seven Year Itch* (1955), *Some Like It Hot* (1959), *The Apartment* (1960), *Avanti!* (1972), *Buddy Buddy* (1981).

**Wise, Robert** (1914– ) American, born Winchester, Indiana; *The Body Snatcher* (1945), *The Day the Earth Stood Still* (1951), *West Side Story* (1961), *The Sound of Music* (1965), *Star Trek: The Motion Picture* (1979).

**Zeffirelli, Franco (Gianfranco Corsi)** (1922– ) Italian, born Florence; *The Taming of the Shrew* (1966), *Romeo and Juliet* (1968), *Brother Sun, Sister Moon* (1973), *Jesus of Nazareth* (TV 1977), *The Champ* (1979), *Endless Love* (1981), *La Traviata* (1982), *Otello* (1986), *Hamlet* (1990), *Jane Eyre* (TV 1995), *Tea With Mussolini* (1999).

**Zemeckis, Robert** (1951– ) American, born Chicago; *I Wanna Hold Your Hand* (1978), *Romancing The Stone* (1984), *Back to the Future* (1985), *Who Framed Roger Rabbit?* (1988), *Back to the Future II* (1989), *Back to the Future III* (1990), *Death Becomes Her* (1992), *Forrest Gump* (1994).

**Zinnemann, Fred** (1907–97) Austrian–American, born Vienna, Austria; *High Noon* (1952), *From Here to Eternity* (1953), *A Man for All Seasons* (1966), *Five Days One Summer* (1982).

## Composers

Selected works are listed.

**Adams, John Coolidge** (1947– ) American, born Worcester, Massachusetts; works include opera (eg *Nixon in China*) and compositions for chorus and orchestra (eg *Harmonium*).

**Albéniz, Isaac** (1860–1909) Spanish, born Camprodón, Catalonia; works include operas and works for piano based on Spanish folk music (eg *Iberia*).

**Arnold, Sir Malcolm Henry** (1921– ) English, born Northampton; works include concertos, ballets, operas, vocal, choral, chamber and orchestral music (eg *Tam O'Shanter*) and film scores (eg *Bridge over the River Kwai*).

**Bach, Johann Sebastian** (1685–1750) German, born Eisenach; prolific composer, works include over 190 cantatas and oratorios, concertos, chamber music, keyboard music, and orchestral works (eg *Toccata and Fugue in D minor, The Well-tempered Clavier, Six Brandenburg Concertos, St Matthew Passion, Mass in B minor, Goldberg Variations, The Musical Offering, The Art of Fugue*).

**Bartók, Béla** (1881–1945) Hungarian, born Nagyszentmiklós; works include six string quartets, *Sonata for 2 pianos and percussion*, concertos (for piano, violin, viola and notably the *Concerto for Orchestra*), opera (*Duke Bluebeard's Castle*), two ballets (*The Wooden Prince, The Miraculous Mandarin*), songs, choruses, folksong arrangements.

**Beethoven, Ludwig van** (1770–1827) German, born Bonn; works include 33 piano sonatas (eg the 'Pathétique', 'Moonlight', *Waldstein, Appassionata*), nine symphonies (eg *Eroica*, 'Pastoral', *Choral Symphony No.9*), string quartets, concertos, *Lebewohl* and the opera *Fidelio*.

**Berg, Alban** (1885–1935) Austrian, born Vienna; works include songs (*Four Songs*), operas (*Wozzeck, Lulu*, unfinished), a violin concerto and a string quartet (*Lyric Suite*).

**Berio, Luciano** (1925– ) Italian, born Oneglia; works include compositions using tapes and electronic music (eg *Mutazioni, Omaggio a James Joyce*), works for solo instruments (*Sequenzas*), stage works (eg *Laborintus II, Opera*) and symphonies (*Synfonia*).

**Berlioz, (Louis) Hector** (1803–69) French, born Côte St André, near Grenoble; works include the overture *Le carnival romain*, the cantata (*La Damnation de Faust*), symphonies (eg *Symphonie Fantastique, Romeo et Juliette*) and operas (eg *Béatrice et Bénédict, Les Toyens*).

**Bernstein, Leonard** (1918–90) American, born Laurence, Massachusetts; works include ballets (*Jeremiah, The Age of Anxiety, Kaddish*), symphonies (eg *Fancy Free, The Dybbuk*), and musicals, (eg *Candide, West Side Story, On The Town, Songfest, Halil*).

**Birtwistle, Sir Harrison** (1934– ) English, born Accrington, Lancashire; works include operas (eg *The Mask of Orpheus*), 'dramatic pastorals' (eg *Down by the Greenwood Side*) and orchestral pieces (eg *The Triumph of Time*).

**Bizet, Georges** (1838–75) French, born Paris; works include opera (eg *Carmen, Les Pêcheurs de Perles, La Jolie Fille de Perth*), incidental music to Daudet's play *L'Arlésienne* and a symphony.

**Boulez, Pierre** (1925– ) French, born Montbrison; works include three piano sonatas, and works for piano and flute (eg *Sonatine*).

**Brahms, Johannes** (1833–97) German, born Hamburg; works include songs, four symphonies, two piano concertos, choral work (eg *German Requiem*), orchestral work (eg *Variations on a Theme of Haydn*), programme work (eg *Tragic Overture*), also the *Academic Festival Overture* and *Hungarian Dances*.

**Bruckner, Anton** (1824–96) Austrian, born Ansfelden; works include nine symphonies, a string

quartet, choral-orchestral Masses and other church music (eg *Te Deum*).

**Cage, John** (1912–92) American, born Los Angeles; works include unorthodox modern compositions, eg *Sonatas and Interludes for the Prepared Piano*.

**Carter, Elliott Cook, Jr** (1908– ) American, born New York City; works include quartets, symphonies, concertos, songs and chamber music.

**Chabrier, Emmanuel** (1841–94) French, born Ambert; works include operas (*Gwendoline, Le Roi malgré lui, Briséis*) and an orchestral rhapsody (*España*).

**Chausson, Ernest** (1855–99) French, born Paris; works include songs and orchestral works (eg *Poème*).

**Chopin, Frédéric François** (1810–49) Polish, born Zelazowa Wola, near Warsaw; wrote almost exclusively for piano — nocturnes, polonaises, mazurkas, preludes, concertos, and a funeral march.

**Copland, Aaron** (1900–90) American, born Brooklyn, New York City; ballets (eg *Billy The Kid, Appalachian Spring*), film scores (eg *Our Town, The Hucis*), symphonies (eg *Symphonie Ode, Connotations, Clarinet Concerto*).

**Corelli, Arcangelo** (1653–1713) Italian, born Fusignano, near Bologna; works include 12 concertos (eg *Concerto for Christmas Night*), and solo and trio sonatas for violin.

**Couperin, François** (1668–1733) French, born Paris; works include chamber music, four books containing 240 harpsichord pieces, motets and other church music.

**Debussy, Claude Achille** (1862–1918) French, born St Germaine-en-Laye, near Paris; songs (eg the cantata *L'Enfant prodigue*), opera (*Pelléas et Mélisande*), orchestral works (eg *Prélude à l'après-midi d'un faune, La Mer*), chamber and piano music (eg *Feux d'artifice, La Cathédrale engloutie*).

**Delius, Frederick** (1862–1934) English (of German Scandinavian descent), born Bradford; works include songs (eg *A Song of Summer, Idyll, Songs of Farewell*), concertos, operas (eg *Koanga, A Village Romeo and Juliette*), chamber music and orchestral variations (eg *Appalachia, Sea Drift, A Mass of Life*).

**Dukas, Paul** (1865–1935) French, born Paris; works include a symphonic poem (*L'Apprenti sorcier*) and opera (*Ariane et Barbe-Bleue*).

**Dutilleux, Henri** (1916– ) French, born Angers; works include a piano sonata, two symphonies, a violin concerto, a string quartet (*Ainsi la nuit*), compositions for two pianos and other orchestral works.

**Dvořák, Antonin Leopold** (1841–1904) Czech, born near Prague; works include songs, concertos, choral (eg *Hymnus*) and chamber music, symphonies (notably 'From the New World'), operas (eg *Rusalka, Armida, Slavonic Dances*).

**Elgar, Sir Edward (William)** (1857–1934) English, born Broadheath, near Worcester; works include chamber music, two symphonies, oratorios (eg *The Dream of Gerontius, The Apostles, The Kingdom*), and the orchestral work *Enigma Variations*.

**Falla, Manuel de** (1876–1946) Spanish, born Cádiz; works include opera (eg *La Vida Breve, Master Peter's Puppet Show*), ballet (eg *The Three-Cornered Hat, Love the Magician*) and orchestral suites (eg *Nights in the Gardens of Spain*).

**Fauré, Gabriel Urbain** (1845–1924) French, born Pamiers; works include songs (eg *Après un rêve*), chamber music, choral music (eg the *Requiem*), operas and orchestral music (eg *Masques et bergamasques*).

**Franck, César Auguste** (1822–90) naturalized French, born Liège, Belgium; works include tone-poems, (eg *Les Béatitudes*), sonatas for violin and piano, *Symphony in D minor* and *Variations symphoniques* for piano and orchestra.

**Gershwin, George** (1898–1937) American, born Brooklyn, New York City; Broadway musicals (eg *Lady Be Good, Of Thee I Sing*), symphonies, songs (notably 'I Got Rhythm', 'The Man I Love'), operas (eg *Porgy and Bess*), and concert works (eg *Rhapsody in Blue, Concerto in F, An American in Paris*).

**Glass, Philip** (1937– ) American, born Baltimore, Maryland; works include stage pieces (eg *Einstein on the Beach*), film scores (eg *Hamburger Hill*) and the opera *Orphee*.

**Grainger, Percy Aldridge** (1882–1961) Australian, born Melbourne; works include songs, piano and chamber music (eg *Molly on the Shore, Mock Morris, Shepherd's Hey*).

**Grieg, Edvard Hagerup** (1843–1907) Norwegian, born Bergen; works include songs, a piano concerto, orchestral suites, violin sonatas, choral music, and incidental music for *Peer Gynt* and *Sigurd Jorsalfar*.

**Handel, George Friederic** (1685–1759) naturalized English, born Halle, Saxony; prolific output including over 27 operas (eg *Almira, Rinaldo*), 20 oratorios (eg *The Messiah, Saul, Israel in Egypt, Samson, Jephthah*), orchestral suites (eg the *Water Music* and *Music for the Royal Fireworks*), organ concertos and chamber music.

**Haydn, (Franz) Joseph** (1732–1809) Austrian, born Rohrau, Lower Austria; prolific output including 104 symphonies (eg the 'Salomon' or 'London' Symphonies), string quartets and oratorios (notably *The Creation, The Seasons*).

**Holst, Gustav Theodore** (originally **von Holst**) (1874–1934) English of Swedish origin, born Cheltenham; works include choral and ballet music, operas (eg *The Perfect Fool, At the Boar's Head*), orchestral suites (eg *The Planets, St Paul's Suite for Strings*), choral music (eg *The Hymn of Jesus, Ode to Death*), and *Concerto for Two Violins*.

**Honegger, Arthur** (1892–1955) French, born Le Havre; works include five symphonies and dramatic oratorios (*King David, Joan of Arc at the Stake*).

**Ireland, John Nicholson** (1879–1962) English, born Bowden, Cheshire; works include sonatas (eg Violin Sonata in A), piano music, songs (eg 'Sea

Fever'), the rhapsody *Mai-dun* and orchestral works (eg *The Forgotten Rite, These Things Shall Be*).

**Ives, Charles** (1874–1954) American, born Danbury, Connecticut; works include five symphonies, chamber music (eg *Concord Sonata*) and many songs.

**Janáček, Leoš** (1854–1928) Czech, born Hukvaldy, Moravia; works include chamber, orchestral and choral music (eg the song cycle *The Diary of One Who Has Vanished*), operas (eg *Janufa, The Cunning Little Vixen, The Excursions of Mr Brouček, From the House of the Dead*), two string quartets and a mass.

**Lalo, (Victor Antoine) Édouard** (1823–92) French, born Lille. Works include compositions for violin (eg *Symphonie espagnole*), opera (eg *Le Roi d'Ys*) and ballet (*Namouna*).

**Ligeti, Györgi Sándor** (1923– ) Hungarian, born Dicsöszentmárton; works include orchestral compositions (eg *Apparitions, Lontano, Double Concerto*), choral works (eg *Requiem*) and music for harpsichord, organ and wind and string ensembles.

**Liszt, Franz** (1811–86) Hungarian, born Raiding; 400 original compositions including symphonic poems, piano music and masses (eg *The Legend of St Elizabeth, Christus*).

**Lloyd-Webber, Andrew Lloyd Webber, Baron** (1948– ) English, born London; works include the 'rock opera' *Jesus Christ Superstar* and the musicals *Cats, Evita* and *Aspects of Love*.

**Mahler, Gustav** (1860–1911) Austrian, born Kalist, Bohemia; works include 10 symphonies, songs, the cantata *Das klagende Lied*, and the song-symphony *Das Lied von der Erde* (The Song of the Earth).

**Mendelssohn, (Jacob Ludwig) Felix** (1809–47) German, born Hamburg; prolific output, including concerto overtures (eg *Fingal's Cave, A Midsummer Night's Dream, Hebrides*), symphonies (*Symphony in C minor, Scottish, Italian*), quartets (B minor Quartet), operas (eg *Camacho's Wedding*), and oratorios (eg *Elijah*).

**Messiaen, Olivier Eugène Prosper Charles** (1908–92) French, born Avignon; works include compositions for piano (*Vingt regards sur l'enfant Jésus, Catalogue d'oiseaux*), the symphony *Turangalila*, an oratorio (*La Transfiguration de Notre Seigneur Jésus-Christ*) and an opera (*St François d'Assisi*).

**Milhaud, Darius** (1892–1974) French, born Aix-en-Provence; works include several operas, incidental music for plays, ballets (eg the jazz ballet *La Création du monde*), symphonies and orchestral, choral and chamber works.

**Monteverdi, Claudio (Giovanni Antonio)** (1567–1643) Italian, born Cremona; works include masses (eg *Mass* and *Vespers* of the Virgin), cantatas and operas (eg *Orfeo, Il Ritorno d'Ulisse, L'Incoronazione di Poppea*).

**Mozart, (Johann Chrysostom) Wolfgang Amadeus** (1756–91) Austrian, born Salzburg; 600 compositions including symphonies (eg 'Jupiter', *Linz, Prague*), concertos, string quartets, sonatas, operas (eg *Marriage of Figaro, Don Giovanni, Così fan tutte*) and the Singspiels *The Abductions from the Seraglio, Die Zauberflöte*.

**Mussorgsky, Modeste** (1839–81) Russian, born Karevo; works include operas (eg *Boris Godunov*), song cycles and instrumental works (eg *Pictures from an Exhibition, Night on the Bare Mountain*).

**Nielsen, Carl August** (1865–1931) Danish, born Furen; works include operas (eg *Saul and David, Masquerade*), symphonies (eg 'The Four Temperaments'), string quartets, choral and piano music.

**Palestrina, Giovanni Pierluigi da** (c.1525–1594) Italian, born Palestrina, near Rome; works include chamber music and the organ work *Commotion*, masses, choral music (eg *Song of Songs*), madrigals.

**Penderecki, Krzysztof** (1933– ) Polish, born Debica; works include compositions for strings (eg *Trenofiarom Hiroszimy*), operas (eg *Die schwarze Maske*) and concertos (eg *Flute Concerto*).

**Prokofiev, Sergei** (1891–1953) Russian, born Sontsovka, Ukraine; works include 11 operas (eg *The Gambler, The Love for Three Oranges, The Fiery Angels, Semyon Kotko, Betrothal in a Monastery, War and Peace, The Story of a Real Man*), ballets (eg *Romeo and Juliet, Cinderella*), concertos, sonatas, cantatas (eg *We are Seven, Hail to Stalin*), film scores (eg *Alexander Nevsky*), and the 'children's piece' *Peter and the Wolf*.

**Puccini, Giacomo (Antonio Domenico Michele Secondo Maria)** (1858–1924) Italian, born Lucca; 12 operas (eg *Manon Lescaut, La Bohème, Tosca, Madama Butterfly, Turandot*).

**Purcell, Henry** (1659–95) English, born London; works include songs (eg 'Nymphs and Shepherds', 'Arise, ye Subterranean Winds'), sonatas, string fantasies, church music and opera (eg *Dido and Aeneas*).

**Rachmaninov, Sergei Vasilyevich** (1873–1943) Russian, born Nizhny Novgorod; works include operas, three symphonies, four piano concertos (eg *Prelude in C Sharp Minor*), the tone-poem *The Isle of the Dead*, and *Rhapsody on a Theme of Paganini* for piano and orchestra.

**Rameau, Jean Philippe** (1683–1764) French, born Dijon; works include over 30 ballets and operas (eg *Hippolyte et Aricie, Castor et Pollux*) and harpsichord pieces.

**Ravel, Maurice** (1875–1937) French, born Ciboure; works include piano compositions (eg *Sonatina, Miroirs, Ma Mère L'Oye, Gaspard de la nuit*), string quartets, operas (eg *L'Heure espagnol, L'Enfant et les sortilèges*), ballets (eg *Daphnis and Chloé*), the 'choreographic poem' *La Valse* and the miniature ballet *Boléro*.

**Rimsky-Korsakov, Nikolai Andreyevich** (1844–1908) Russian, born Tikhvin, Novgorod; works include orchestral music (eg the symphonic suite *Sheherazade, Capriccio Espagnol, Easter Festival*) and 15 operas (eg *Sadko, The Snow Maiden, The Tsar*

*Sultan, The Invisible City of Kitesh, The Golden Cockerel*).

**Rossini, Gioacchino Antonio** (1792–1868) Italian, born Pesaro; works include many operas (eg *Il Barbiere de Seviglia, Otella, Guillaume Tell*) and a number of vocal and piano pieces.

**Roussel, Albert** (1869–1937) French, born Tourcoing; works include four symphonies, numerous choral works (eg *Évocations*), ballets (eg *Bacchus and Ariane, Le Festin de l'araignée*) and an opera (*Padmâvati*).

**Saint-Saëns, (Charles) Camille** (1835–1921) French, born Paris; works include four symphonic poems (eg *Danse macabre*), piano (*Le Rouet d'Omphale, Phaëton, La Jeunesse d'Hercule*), violin and cello concertos, symphonies, the opera *Samson et Dalila*, church music (eg *Messe solennelle*), and *Carnival des animaux* for two pianos and orchestra.

**Satie, Erik Alfred Leslie** (1866–1925) French, born Hornfleur; works include ballets (eg *Parade*), lyric dramas and whimsical pieces.

**Scarlatti, (Guiseppe) Domenico** (1685–1757) Italian, born Naples; works include over 600 harpsichord sonatas.

**Schönberg, Arnold** (1874–1951) naturalized American, born Vienna, Austria; works include chamber music (eg *Chamber Symphony*), concertos (eg *Piano Concerto*), and symphonic poems (eg *Pelleas and Melisande*), the choral-orchestral *Gurrelieder*, string quartets, the oratorio *Die Jacobsiter*, and opera (*Von Heute auf Morgen, Moses und Aaron*).

**Schubert, Franz Peter** (1797–1828) Austrian, born Vienna; prolific output, works include symphonies, piano sonatas, string quartets and songs (eg *Gretchen am Spinnrade, Erlkönig, Die schöne Müllerin, Winterreise, Who is Sylvia?, Hark, Hark the Lark, Schwanengesang*).

**Schumann, Robert Alexander** (1810–56) German, born Zwickau, Saxony; works include piano music (eg *Fantasiestücke*), songs (eg The Fool's Song in *Twelfth Night*, the Chamisso songs *Frauenliebe und Leben* or 'Woman's Love and Life'), chamber music, and four symphonies (eg the *Rhenish*).

**Scriabin, Alexander** (1872–1915) Russian, born Moscow; works include a piano concerto, three symphonies, two tone-poems (eg *Poem of Ecstasy*), 10 sonatas, studies and preludes.

**Shostakovich, Dmitri** (1906–75) Russian, born St Petersburg; works include 15 symphonies, operas (eg *The Nose, A Lady Macbeth of Mtensk*), concertos, string quartets and film music.

**Sibelius, Jean** (1865–1957) Finnish, born Tavastehus; works include symphonic poems (eg *Swan of Tuonela, En Saga*), songs, a violin concerto, and seven symphonies.

**Simpson, Robert Wilfred Levick** (1921–97) English, born Leamington Spa, Warwickshire; works include 11 symphonies; concertos for violin, piano, flute and cello; 15 string quartets; other chamber pieces; brass band music and two choral compositions; also wrote on music, eg *The Essence of Bruckner* (1966).

**Stockhausen, Karlheinz** (1928– ) German, born Mödrath, near Cologne; works include orchestral music (eg *Gruppen*), choral and instrumental compositions.

**Strauss, Johann, (the Younger)** (1825–99) Austrian, born Vienna; works include over 400 waltzes (eg *The Blue Danube, Wine, Women, and Song, Perpetuum Mobile, Artist's Life, Tales from the Vienna Woods, Voices from Spring, The Emperor*), and operettas (eg *Die Fledermaus, A Night in Venice*).

**Strauss, Richard** (1864–1949) German, born Munich; works include symphonic poems (eg *Don Juan, Till Eulenspiegels lustige Streiche, Also Sprach Zarathustra, Tod und Verklärung* ('Death and Transfiguration'), *Don Quixote, Ein Heldenleben*) and operas (eg *Der Rosenkavalier, Ariadne auf Naxos, Capriccio*).

**Stravinsky, Igor** (1882–1971) Russian, born Oranienbaum, near St Petersburg (naturalized French, then American); works include operas (eg *The Rake's Progress*), oratorios (eg *Oedipus Rex, Symphony of Psalms*), concertos, ballets (eg *The Firebird, The Rite of Spring, Petrushka, Pulcinella, Apollo Musogetes, The Card Game, Orpheus, Agon*), and a musical play *Elegy for JFK* for voice and clarinets.

**Tchaikovsky, Piotr Ilyich** (1840–93) Russian, born Kamsko-Votkinsk; works include 10 operas (eg *Eugene Onegin, The Queen of Spades*), a violin concerto, six symphonies, two piano concertos, three ballets (*The Nutcracker, Swan Lake, The Sleeping Beauty*) and tone-poems (eg *Romeo and Juliet, Italian Capriccio*).

**Telemann, George Philipp** (1681–1767) German, born Magdeburg; prolific composer, works include 600 overtures, 40 operas, 200 concertos, sonatas, suites, and overtures (eg *Der Tag des Gerichts, Die Tageszeiten*).

**Tippett, Sir Michael Kemp** (1905–98) English, born London; works include operas (eg *The Midsummer Marriage, King Priam, The Knot Garden, The Ice Break*), concertos, symphonies, cantatas and oratorios (eg *A Child of Our Time, The Vision of St Augustine*).

**Varèse, Edgard** (1883–1965) American, born Paris; works are almost entirely orchestral (eg *Metal, Ionization, Hyperprism*).

**Vaughan Williams, Ralph** (1872–1958) English, born Down Ampney, Gloucestershire; works include songs, symphonies (eg *London Symphony, Pastoral Symphony*), choral-orchestral works (eg *Sea Symphony, Magnificat*), operas (eg *Hugh the Drover, The Pilgrim's Progress*), a ballet *Job*, and film music (eg *Scott of the Antarctic*).

**Verdi, Giuseppe** (1813–1901) Italian, born le Roncole, near Busseto; works include church music (eg *Requiem*) and operas (eg *Oberto, Nabucco, Rigoletto, Il Trovatore, La Traviata, Un Ballo in Maschera, La Forza del Destino, Aïda, Otello, Falstaff*).

**Vivaldi, Antonio** (1678–1741) Italian, born Venice; prolific output, works include over 400 concertos (eg *L'Estro Armonico, The Four Seasons*), 40 operas and an oratorio, *Juditha triumphans*.

**Wagner, (Wilhelm) Richard** (1813–83) German, born Leipzig; operas include *Lohengrin*, *Rienzi*, the *Ring* cycle (*Das Rheingold*, *Die Walküre*, *Siegfried*, *Götterdämmerung*), *Die Meistersinger*, *Tristan und Isolde*, *Parsifal*.

**Walton, Sir William Turner** (1902–83) English, born Oldham; works include concertos, operas (*Troilus and Cressida*, *The Bear*), a cantata (*Belshazzar's Feast*), ballet music for *The Wise Virgins*, a song-cycle (*Anon in Love*) and film music.

**Weber, Carl Maria Friedrich von** (1786–1826) German, born Eutin, near Lübeck; works include operas (eg *Oberon*, *Euryanthe*, *Silvana*), concertos, symphonies, sonatas, scenas, cantatas (eg *Kampf und Sieg*) and songs.

**Webern, Anton Friedrich Wilhelm von** (1883–1945) Austrian, born Vienna; works include a symphony, three cantatas, *Four Pieces for Violin and Pianoforte*, *Five Pieces for Orchestra*, and a concerto for nine instruments and songs.

**Whitehead, Gillian** (1941– ) New Zealand, born Whangerei; works include compostitions for choir and chamber orchestra (eg *Inner Harbour*), for soprano and instrumental ensemble (eg *Hotspur*) for opera (eg *Eleanor of Aquitaine*) and for strings (eg *Pakuru*).

**Xenakis, Iannis** (1922–2001) French, born Romania; works include compositions for piano and orchestra (eg *Erikhthon*), *Shaar* for strings, *Tetras* for string quartet and solo pieces (eg *Nomos Alpha* for cello, *Herma* for piano), and *Pithoprakta* for 50 instruments.

## Songwriters

A selection of songs is listed. Original and full names of songwriters are given in parentheses.

**Arlen, Harold (Hyman Arluck)** (1905–86) American, born Buffalo, New York; over 500 songs, including 'Between the Devil and the Deep Blue Sea', 'Stormy Weather', 'Get Happy' (lyrics by Ted Koehler), *A Star is Born* (1953) ('The Man that Got Away') (lyrics by Ira Gershwin); *The Wizard of Oz* (1939) ('Over the Rainbow') (lyrics by E Y Harburg, 1896–1981).

**Berlin, Irving** (originally **Israel Baline**) (1888–1989) American, born Temus, Siberia; composer; *Annie Get Your Gun* (1946), *Call Me Madam* (1950); over 900 songs, including 'There's No Business Like Show Business', 'White Christmas', 'God Bless America', 'Oh, How I Hate to Get Up in the Morning'.

**Bernstein, Leonard** (1918–90) American, born Laurence, Massachusetts; composer of opera, symphonies, songs; *West Side Story* (1958) (lyrics by Stephen Sondheim); songs include 'You Got Me', 'New York, New York'.

**Britten, Baron (Edward) Benjamin, of Aldeburgh** (1913–76) English, born Lowestoft; composer of choral symphonic works, opera, song cycles, eg *Our Hunting Fathers*, *On This Island* (text by W H Auden).

**Brown, Nacio Herb** (1896–1954) American, born Deming, New Mexico; composer; *Broadway Melody* (lyrics by Arthur Field, 1894–1973); *Singin' in the Rain* (1952); songs include 'You were Meant for Me'.

**Cahn, Sammy (Samuel)** (1913–93) American lyricist, born New York; 'I've Heard That Song Before', 'I'll Walk Alone', 'It's Magic' (with Julie Styne); 'All the Way', 'High Hopes' (with Jimmy van Heusen).

**Carmichael, Hoagy (Hoagland Howard)** (1899–1981) American songwriter and pianist, born Bloomington Indiana; wrote many popular and enduring songs, eg 'Riverboat Shuffle', 'Stardust', 'Georgia on My Mind', 'Lazy River', 'I Get Along Without You Very Well', 'Lamplighter's Serenade' (Frank Sinatra's first recording).

**Cohan, George M(ichael)** (1878–1942) American composer, lyricist, born Providence, Rhode Island; *Little Johnny Jones* (1904) ('Give My Regards to Broadway'); 'The Talk of the Town' (1907).

**Coward, Sir Noël Pierce** (1899–1973) English composer, lyricist, playwright, born Teddington; *Words and Music* (revue) (1932) ('Mad Dogs and Englishmen', 'Someday I'll Find You').

**Dylan, Bob (Robert Allen Zimmerman)** (1941– ) American songwriter, musician, born Duluth, Minnesota; 'Blowin' in the Wind', 'With God on Our Side', 'The Times They are A-Changin'', 'It's Alright Ma', I'm Only Bleeding', 'Mr Tambourine Man', 'Subterranean Homesick Blues', 'Like a Rolling Stone', 'Leopard-Skin Pill-Box Hat', 'Knockin' on Heaven's Door'.

**Ellington, (Edward Kennedy) 'Duke'** (1899–1974) American pianist, composer, bandleader, born Washington, DC; 2 000 works, including songs, instrumentals, film music; 'It Don't Mean a Thing if it Ain't Got That Swing' (lyrics Irving Mills), 'Best Wishes' (lyrics Ted Koehler), 'Creole Love Call' (vocal, no lyrics).

**Fields, Dorothy** (1905–74) American lyricist, born Allenhurst, New Jersey; 'I Can't Give You Anything But Love' (with Jimmy McHugh, from *Blackbirds*, 1928), 'On the Sunny Side of the Street' (with Jimmy McHugh), 'Exactly Like You', 'Lovely to Look At' and 'The Way You Look Tonight' (with Jerome Kern); *Stars in Your Eyes* (1939) (with Arthur Schwartz); *Sweet Charity* (1966) ('Big Spender') (with Cy Coleman).

**Gershwin, George** (originally **Jacob Gershvin**) (1898–1937) American composer, born Brooklyn, New York City; and **Ira Gershwin** (originally **Israel Gershvin**) (1896–1983) American lyricist, born New York City; *Lady, Be Good!* ('The Man I Love', 'How Long Has This Been Going On?'), *Girl Crazy*, *Porgy and Bess* ('Summertime') (lyrics by Ira Gershwin and Du Bose Heyward); songs include 'You Can't Take That Away from Me', 'Nice Work if You Can Get It', 'Love Walked In', 'They All Laughed'.

**Gilbert, Sir William Schwenck** (1836–1911) English librettist, born London, and **Sir Arthur Seymour**

**Sullivan** (1842–1900) English composer, born London; operettas and songs include *HMS Pinafore* (1878), *The Mikado* (1885), *The Gondoliers* (1889).

**Herman, Jerry** (1932– ) American composer, lyricist, born New York City; *Hello Dolly!* (1964), *Mame* (1966).

**Kern, Jerome (David)** (1885–1945) American composer, born New York City; 'The Way You Look Tonight' (lyrics Dorothy Fields); 'Ol' Man River', 'They Didn't Believe Me' (lyrics Herbert Reynold); *Show Boat* (1927) (lyrics Oscar Hammerstein II (1895–1960) American lyricist, born New York City).

**Lennon, John Winston** (1940–80) English songwriter, musician, born Liverpool, and **(James) Paul McCartney** (1942– ) English songwriter, musician, born Liverpool; 'Please Please Me', 'Yesterday', 'All You Need is Love', 'Strawberry Fields Forever', 'I Want to Hold Your Hand', 'Michelle', 'Eleanor Rigby', 'Ticket to Ride', 'Dear Prudence', 'Help'.

**Livingston, Jay** (1915–2001) American composer, lyricist, born McDonald, Pennsylvania; and **Ray Evans** (1915– ) American lyricist, born Salamanca, New York; 'The Cat and the Canary', 'Mona Lisa', 'Whatever Will Be, Will Be (Que Sera Sera)', 'Dear Heart'.

**Lloyd-Webber, Andrew Lloyd Webber, Baron** (1948– ) English composer, born London, with **Tim Rice** (1944– ) English lyricist, born Amersham, Buckinghamshire; *Joseph and the Amazing Technicolor Dreamcoat* (1968) ('Any Dream Will Do'); *Jesus Christ Superstar* (1970) ('Jesus Christ Superstar', 'I Don't Know How to Love Him'), *Evita* (1978) ('Don't Cry for Me, Argentina'); *Cats* (1981) (libretto T S Eliot), *Phantom of the Opera* (1986), *Aspects of Love* (1989).

**Loesser, Frank (Henry)** (1910–69) American composer, lyricist, born New York City; *Guys and Dolls* (1950) ('I've Never Been in Love Before', 'Luck Be a Lady'); *The Perils of Pauline* (1947) (words and music); lyrics for 'The Boys in the Back Room' (music by Frederick Hollander); lyrics for 'The Lady's in Love with You' and 'Some Like it Hot', from the film *Some Like it Hot* (1959).

**McHugh, Jimmy (James Frances McHugh)** (1896–1969) American composer, born Boston, Massachusetts; with Dorothy Fields, as above; 'I'm Shooting High' (with Ted Koehler); 'Exactly Like You' (with Al Dubin).

**Mancini, Henry** (1924–94) American composer of songs and film music, born Cleveland, Ohio; over 80 films, eg *Breakfast at Tiffany's* (1961); songs include 'Moon River' (lyrics Johnny Mercer), 'Days of Wine and Roses', 'Charade'.

**Mercer, Johnny H** (1909–76) American lyricist, born Savannah, Georgia; 1 500 songs for over 70 films and seven Broadway musicals; songs with Henry Mancini, as above; 'Blues in the Night' (music by Harold Arlen), 'That Old Black Magic' (music by Harold Arlen), 'Jeepers Creepers' (music by Henry Warren); lyrics for *Seven Brides for Seven Brothers*.

**Porter, Cole** (1891–1964) American composer, lyricist, born Peru, Indiana; *Gay Divorcee* (1932), *Anything Goes* (1934), *Du Barry Was a Lady* ('Well, Did You Evah!') (1939), *Kiss Me Kate* (1948) ('So in Love'); songs include 'I'm in Love Again', 'Let's Do It, Let's Fall in Love', 'Just One of Those Things'.

**Rodgers, Richard** (1902–79) American composer, born Long Island, New York; with **Lorenz Hart** (1895–1943) American lyricist, born New York City; *The Girl Friend* (1926), *Babes in Arms* (1937), 'Manhattan'; with **Oscar Hammerstein II** (1895–1960) American lyricist, born New York City; *Oklahoma!* (1943) ('Oh, What a Beautiful Morning'), *South Pacific* (1949), *The King and I* (1959) ('Shall We Dance?'), *The Sound of Music* (1959) ('Do-Re-Mi', 'Edelweiss').

**Romberg, Sigmund** (1887–1951) American composer, born Nagykanizsa, Hungary; *The Desert Song* (1926), *The New Moon* (1928), ('Lover Come Back to Me'), *The Student Prince* (1924), *Girl of the Golden West* (1938).

**Schubert, Franz (Peter)** (1797–1828) Austrian composer, born Vienna; works include 145 songs, texts by Schiller and Goethe, among others.

**Schumann, Robert (Alexander)** (1810–56) German composer, born Zwickau; songs to texts by Heine, among others.

**Simon, Paul** (1942– ) American songwriter, musician, born Newark, New Jersey; 'I am a Rock', 'Bridge over Troubled Water', 'Mrs Robinson', 'Cecilia', 'Keep the Customer Satisfied', 'Homeward Bound', 'The Boxer', 'The Sound of Silence'.

**Sondheim, Stephen (Joshua)** (1930– ) American composer, lyricist, born New York City; lyrics for Bernstein's *West Side Story* (1958), *A Funny Thing Happened on the Way to the Forum* (1962), *A Little Night Music* (1973) ('Send in the Clowns') (lyrics and music).

**Styne, Jule** (1905–94) American composer, born London, England; 'There Goes That Song Again', 'I'll Walk Alone', 'It's Magic' (with Sammy Cahn); *Gentlemen Prefer Blondes* (1949) ('Diamonds are a Girl's Best Friend') with Leo Robin.

**Warren, Harry** (1893–1981) American composer of songs, film scores, born Brooklyn, New York City; 'You're My Everything', 'We're in the Money', 'Chattanooga Choo-Choo', 'Jeepers Creepers' (with Johnny H Mercer); with **Al Dubin** (1891–1945) American lyricist, born Zurich, Switzerland; *42nd Street* (1932), 'The Boulevard of Broken Dreams', 'I Only Have Eyes for You'.

**Weill, Kurt** (1900–50) German composer, born Dessau; songs, opera, with **(Eugen) Bertolt Friedrich Brecht** (1898–1956) Germany lyricist, playwright, born Augsburg; *Threepenny Opera* (1928) ('Mack the Knife'); *Lady in the Dark* (1941) (lyrics Ira Gershwin), *Street Scene* (1947) (lyrics Langston Hughes), *Lost in the Stars* (1949) (lyrics Maxwell Anderson).

## Operas and operettas

| Name | Composer | Date |
|---|---|---|
| Aïda | Verdi | 1871 |
| Akhnaten | Philip Glass | 1984 |
| Albert Herring | Britten | 1947 |
| Alceste | Gluck | 1767 |
| Andrea Chénier | Umberto Giordano | 1896 |
| Ariadne auf Naxos | Richard Strauss | 1916 |
| Armide et Rénaud | Lully | 1686 |
| Un Ballo in Maschera | Verdi | 1859 |
| The Barber of Seville | Rossini | 1816 |
| The Bartered Bride | Smetana | 1866 |
| Béatrice et Bénédict | Berlioz | 1862 |
| The Beggar's Opera | Pepusch | 1728 |
| Billy Budd | Britten | 1951 |
| La Bohème | Puccini | 1896 |
| Boris Godunov | Mussorgsky | 1874 |
| Capriccio | Richard Strauss | 1942 |
| Carmen | Bizet | 1875 |
| Cavalleria Rusticana | Mascagni | 1890 |
| La Cenerentola (Cinderella) | Rossini | 1817 |
| La Clemenza di Tito | Mozart | 1791 |
| The Consul | Gian-Carlo Menotti | 1950 |
| Così Fan Tutte | Mozart | 1790 |
| The Cunning Little Vixen | Janáček | 1924 |
| The Damnation of Faust | Berlioz | 1846 |
| Death in Venice | Britten | 1973 |
| Dido and Aeneas | Purcell | 1689 |
| Don Carlos | Verdi | 1867 |
| Don Giovanni | Mozart | 1787 |
| Don Pasquale | Donizetti | 1843 |
| Duke Bluebeard's Castle | Bartók | 1918 |
| The Egyptian Helen | Richard Strauss | 1928 |
| Einstein on the Beach | Philip Glass | 1976 |
| Elegy for Young Lovers | Hans Werner Henze | 1961 |
| Elektra | Richard Strauss | 1909 |
| Eugene Onegin | Tchaikovsky | 1879 |
| The Fair Maid of Perth | Bizet | 1867 |
| Falstaff | Verdi | 1893 |
| Faust | Gounod | 1859 |
| La Fille du Régiment | Donizetti | 1840 |
| Fidelio | Beethoven | 1814 |
| Die Fledermaus | Johann Strauss | 1874 |
| The Flying Dutchman | Wagner | 1843 |
| La Gioconda | Amilcare Ponchielli | 1876 |
| The Golden Cockerel | Rimsky-Korsakov | 1909 |
| The Gondoliers | Gilbert and Sullivan | 1889 |
| Le Grand Macabre | Ligeti | 1978 |
| Hansel and Gretel | Humperdinck | 1893 |
| HMS Pinafore | Gilbert and Sullivan | 1878 |
| Hugh the Drover | Vaughan Williams | 1924 |
| The Ice Break | Tippett | 1977 |
| Idomeneo | Mozart | 1781 |
| L'Incoronazione di Poppea | Monteverdi | 1642 |
| Iphigénie en Tauride | Gluck | 1779 |
| Jenufa | Janáček | 1904 |
| Katya Kabanova | Janáček | 1921 |
| King Priam | Tippett | 1962 |
| Lady Macbeth of Mtsensk | Shostakovich | 1934 |
| Lohengrin | Wagner | 1850 |
| The Love of the Three Oranges | Prokofiev | 1920 |
| Lucia di Lammermoor | Donizetti | 1835 |
| Lucrezia Borgia | Donizetti | 1833 |
| Lulu | Berg | 1937 |
| Macbeth | Verdi | 1847 |
| Madama Butterfly | Puccini | 1904 |
| The Magic Flute | Mozart | 1791 |
| Les Mamelles de Tirésias | Poulenc | 1947 |
| Manon | Massenet | 1884 |
| Manon Lescaut | Puccini | 1893 |
| The Marriage of Figaro | Mozart | 1786 |
| Maskarade | Nielsen | 1906 |
| Mask of Orpheus | Harrison Birtwistle | 1986 |
| Der Meistersinger von Nürnberg | Wagner | 1868 |
| The Merry Wives of Windsor | Otto Nicolai | 1849 |
| The Midsummer Marriage | Tippett | 1955 |
| The Mikado | Gilbert and Sullivan | 1885 |
| Moses und Aron | Schönberg | 1954 |
| Nabucco | Verdi | 1842 |
| Nixon in China | Peter Adams | 1990 |
| Norma | Bellini | 1831 |
| Noye's Fludde | Britten | 1958 |
| Oedipus Rex | Stravinsky | 1927 |
| Orfeo ed Euridice | Gluck | 1762 |
| Orpheus in the Underworld | Offenbach | 1858 |
| Otello | Verdi | 1887 |
| Pagliacci | Leoncavallo | 1892 |
| Parsifal | Wagner | 1882 |
| The Pearl Fishers | Bizet | 1863 |
| Pelléas et Mélisande | Debussy | 1902 |
| Peter Grimes | Britten | 1945 |
| Porgy and Bess | Gershwin | 1935 |
| Punch and Judy | Harrison Birtwistle | 1968 |
| I Puritani | Bellini | 1835 |
| The Rake's Progress | Stravinsky | 1951 |
| The Rape of Lucretia | Britten | 1946 |
| Rigoletto | Verdi | 1851 |
| The Ring | Wagner | 1876 |
| Der Rosenkavalier | Richard Strauss | 1911 |
| Le Rossignol | Stravinsky | 1914 |
| Salome | Richard Strauss | 1911 |
| Samson et Dalila | Saint-Saëns | 1877 |
| Semele | Handel | 1744 |
| Simon Boccanegra | Verdi | 1857 |
| La Sonnambula | Bellini | 1831 |
| The Tales of Hoffman | Offenbach | 1881 |
| Tannhäuser | Wagner | 1845 |
| The Threepenny Opera | Weill | 1928 |
| Tosca | Puccini | 1900 |
| La Traviata | Verdi | 1853 |

| Name | Composer | Date | Name | Composer | Date |
|---|---|---|---|---|---|
| Tristan und Isolde | Wagner | 1865 | I Vespri Siciliani | Verdi | 1855 |
| The Trojans | Berlioz | 1863 | Werther | Massenet | 1892 |
| Il Trovatore | Verdi | 1853 | Where the Wild Things Are | Oliver Knussen | 1980 |
| Turandot | Puccini | 1926 | William Tell | Rossini | 1829 |
| The Turn of the Screw | Britten | 1954 | Wozzeck | Berg | 1925 |

## Opera singers

**Allen, Sir Thomas (Boaz)** (1944– ) English baritone, born Seaham.
**Anderson, Marian** (1902–93) American contralto, born South Philadelphia.
**Austral, Florence** (originally **Florence Wilson**) (1892–1968) Australian soprano, born Richmond, West Melbourne.
**Bailey, Norman (Stanley)** (1933– ) English baritone, born Birmingham.
**Baker, Dame Janet (Abbott)** (1933– ) English mezzo-soprano, born Hatfield, Yorkshire.
**Barstow, Dame Josephine (Clare)** (1940– ) English soprano, born Sheffield.
**Battistini, Mattia** (1856–1928) Italian baritone, born Rome.
**Berganza, Teresa** (1935– ) Spanish mezzo-soprano, born Madrid.
**Bonci, Alessandro** (1870–1940) Italian tenor, born Cesena.
**Brannigan, Owen** (1908–73) English, bass baritone, born Annitsford, Northumberland.
**Butt, Dame Clara** (1872–1936) English contralto, born Southwick, Sussex.
**Caballé, Montserrat** (1933– ) Spanish soprano, born Barcelona.
**Callas, Maria** (originally **Maria Anna Sofia Cecilia Kalogeropoulos**) (1923–77) American soprano of Greek parents, born New York City.
**Carden, Joan Maralyn** (1937– ) Australian soprano, born Melbourne.
**Carreras, José** (1947– ) Spanish tenor, born Barcelona.
**Caruso, Enrico** (1873–1921) Italian tenor, born Naples.
**Charles, Craig** (1922– ) English tenor, born London.
**Collier, Maria** (1926–71) Australian soprano, born Ballarat.
**Crossley, Ada (Jessica)** (1874–1929) Australian mezzo-soprano, born Tarraville, Gippsland.
**Davies, Arthur** (1950– ) Welsh tenor, born Wrexham.
**Davies, Ryland** (1943– ) Welsh tenor, born Cwym, Ebbw Vale.
**de Luca, Giuseppe** (1876–1950) Italian baritone, born Rome.
**De Lucia, Fernando** (1860–1925) Italian tenor, born Naples.
**de Reszke, Jean** (originally **Jan Mieczislaw**) (1850–1925) Polish tenor, born Warsaw.
**Del Monaco, Mario** (1915–82) Italian tenor, born Florence.
**Domingo, Placido** (1941– ) Spanish tenor, born Madrid.
**Evans, Sir Geraint (Llewellyn)** (1922–92) Welsh baritone, born Pontypridd, South Wales.
**Farrar, Geraldine** (1882–1967) American soprano, born Melrose, Massachusetts.
**Farrell, Eileen** (1920– ) American soprano, born Willimantic, Connecticut.
**Ferrier, Kathleen** (1912–53) English contralto, born Higher Walton, Lancashire.
**Field, Helen** (1951– ) Welsh soprano, born Awyd, North Wales.
**Fischer-Dieskau, Dietrich** (1925– ) German baritone, born Zehlendorf, Berlin.
**Flagstad, Kirsten** (1895–1962) Norwegian soprano, born Hamar.
**Forrester, Maureen** (1930– ) Canadian contralto, born Montreal.
**Fremstad, Olive** (1871–1951) American soprano, born Stockholm.
**Freni, Mirella** (1936– ) Italian soprano, born Modena.
**Galli-Curci, Amelita** (1882–1963) Italian soprano, born Milan.
**Galli-Marie, Celestine** (1840–1905) French mezzo-soprano, born Paris.
**Gigli, Beniamino** (1890–1957) Italian tenor, born Recanati.
**Harper, Heather** (1930– ) Northern Irish soprano, born Belfast.
**Jurinac, Sena** (1921– ) Yugoslav soprano, born Travnik.
**Lehmann, Lilli** (1848–1929) German soprano, born Würzburg.

**Lehmann, Lotte** (1888–1976) German soprano, born Perleberg.

**Lind, Jenny ('the Swedish Nightingale')** (1820–87) Swedish soprano, born Stockholm.

**Los Angeles, Victora de** (originally **Victora Gómez Cima**) (1923– ) Spanish soprano, born Barcelona.

**Ludwig, Christa (Deiber)** (1928– ) German mezzo-soprano, born Berlin.

**Major, Dame Malvina Lorraine** (1943– ) New Zealand soprano, born Hamilton.

**Mangin, Noel** (1931–95) New Zealand bass, born Wellington.

**Martinelli, Giovanni** (1885–1969) Italian tenor, born Montagnana.

**Meier, Johanna** (1938– ) American soprano, born Chicago.

**Melba, Dame Nellie** (originally **Helen Mitchell**) (1861–1931) Australian soprano, born Burnle, near Richmond, Melbourne.

**Melchior, Lauritz** (1890–1973) Danish tenor, born Copenhagen.

**Nash, Heddle** (1896–1961) English tenor, born London.

**Nilsson, Birgit** (1918– ) Swedish soprano, born near Karup.

**Norman, Jessye** (1945– ) American soprano, born Augusta, Georgia.

**Patti, Adelina (Adela Juana Maria)** (1843–1919) Italian soprano, born Madrid.

**Pavarotti, Luciano** (1935– ) Italian tenor, born Modena.

**Pears, Sir Peter** (1910–86) English tenor, born Farnham, Surrey.

**Pinza, Ezio** (1892–1957) Italian bass, born Rome.

**Popp, Lucia** (1939– ) Czech soprano, born Llhorsaká.

**Price, (Mary Violet) Leontyne** (1927– ) American soprano, born Laurel, Mississippi.

**Schumann, Elisabeth** (1889–1952) American soprano, born Merseburg, Germany.

**Schwarzkopf, Dame Elisabeth** (1915– ) Austrian–British soprano, born Jarotschin, near Poznan, Poland.

**Siepi, Cesare** (1923– ) Italian bass, born Milan.

**Smirnov, Dimitri** (1882–1944) Russian tenor, born Moscow.

**Söderström, Elisabeth** (1927– ) Swedish soprano, born Stockholm.

**Sutherland, Dame Joan** (1926– ) Australian soprano, born Sydney.

**Tear, Robert** (1939– ) Welsh tenor, born Barry, South Wales.

**Te Kanawa, Dame Kiri** (1944– ) New Zealand soprano, born Gisborne.

**Tetrazzini, Luisa** (1871–1940) Italian soprano, born Florence.

**Tibbett, Lawrence Mervil** (1896–1960) American baritone, born Bakersfield, California.

**Vickers, Jon(athan) Stewart** (1926– ) Canadian tenor, born Prince Albert.

**Wiener, Otto** (1911–2000) Austrian baritone, born Vienna.

## Orchestras

| Name | Date founded | Location |
|---|---|---|
| Academy of Ancient Music | 1973 | UK (London) |
| Academy of St Martin-in-the-Fields | 1959 | UK (London) |
| BBC Philharmonic | 1934 | UK (Manchester) |
| BBC Scottish Symphony | 1935 | UK (Glasgow) |
| BBC Symphony | 1930 | UK (London) |
| BBC Welsh Symphony | 1935 | UK (Cardiff) |
| Berliner Philharmonic | 1882 | Germany |
| Boston Symphony | 1881 | USA |
| Chicago Symphony | 1891 | USA |
| Cleveland Symphony | 1918 | USA |
| Concertgebouw | 1888 | Netherlands (Amsterdam) |
| Detroit Symphony | 1914 | USA |
| English Chamber | 1948 | UK (London) |
| Hallé | 1858 | UK (Manchester) |
| Israel Philharmonic | 1936 | Israel (Tel Aviv) |
| London Philharmonic | 1904 | UK |
| London Symphony | 1904 | UK |

| Name | Date founded | Location |
|---|---|---|
| Los Angeles Philharmonic | 1904 | USA |
| Melbourne Symphony | 1906 | Australia |
| Milan La Scala | 1778 | Italy |
| National Symphony | 1931 | USA (Washington DC) |
| NBC Symphony | 1937–54 | USA (New York) |
| New Orleans Philharmonic Symphony | 1936 | USA |
| New York Philharmonic | 1842 | USA |
| New York Symphony | 1878 | USA |
| Orchestre Symphonique de Montréal | 1842 | Canada |
| Oslo Philharmonic | 1919 | Norway |
| Philadelphia | 1900 | USA |
| The Philharmonia | 1945 | UK (London) |
| Pittsburgh Symphony | 1926 | USA |
| Royal Philharmonic | 1946 | UK (London) |
| Royal Scottish National | 1891 | UK (Glasgow) |
| St Petersburg Philharmonic | 1921 | Russia |
| San Francisco Symphony | 1911 | USA |
| Santa Cecelia Academy | 1895 | Italy (Rome) |
| Scottish Chamber | 1974 | UK (Edinburgh) |
| Seattle Symphony | 1903 | USA |
| Staatskapelle | 1923 | Germany (Dresden) |
| Sydney Symphony | 1934 | Australia |
| Ulster | 1966 | UK (Belfast) |
| Vienna Philharmonic | 1842 | Austria |
| Vienna Symphony | 1900 | Austria |

## Layout of an orchestra

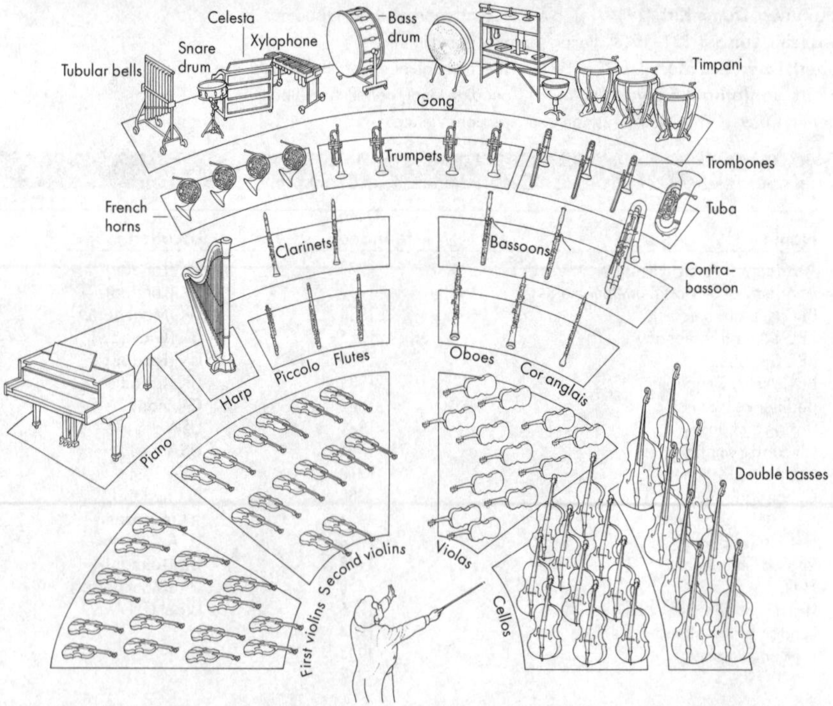

## Pop and rock musicians and singers

Selected singles and albums are listed.

**Abba** Swedish group, 1970s to early 1980s; members include Bjorn Ulvaeus (1945– ) singer, guitarist, born Gothenburg; Agnetha Faltskog (1950– ) singer, born Jankoping; Anni-Frid Lyngstad (1945– ) singer, born Narvik, Norway; Benny Andersson (1946– ) singer, keyboardist, born Stockholm; *Waterloo* (1974), *Arrival* (1976), *Voulez-Vous* (1979), *Super Trouper* (1980), *The Visitors* (1981).

**AC/DC** Australian heavy metal group, mid-1970s to present; members include Bon Scott (originally Ronald Belford Scott) (1946–80) vocalist, born Kirriemuir, Scotland; Brian Johnson (1947– ) vocalist, born North Shields, England; Angus Young (1959– ) guitarist, born Glasgow, Scotland; Malcolm Young (1953– ) guitarist, born Glasgow, Scotland; Phil Rudd (1954– ) drummer, born Melbourne, Australia; *High Voltage* (1976), *If you want blood, you've got it* (1978), *Highway to Hell* (1979), *Dirty Deeds Done Dirt Cheap* (1981), *For Those About to Rock* (1981), *Blow Up Your Video* (1988), *Stiff Upper Lip* (2000).

**Adams, Bryan** (1959– ) Canadian singer, guitarist, songwriter, born Vancouver, British Columbia; 'Everything I do', *Cuts Like A Knife* (1983), *You Want It, You Got It* (1984), *Reckless* (1985), *Into The Fire* (1987), *Waking Up The Neighbours* (1991), *So Far So Good* (1993), *LIVE! LIVE! LIVE!* (1994), *18 'Til I Die* (1997).

**Aerosmith** American group, 1970s to present; members include Steve Tyler (1948– ) vocalist, born New York City; Joe Perry (1950– ) guitarist, born Boston, Massachusetts; Tom Hamilton (1951– ) bassist, born Colorado Springs; Joey Kramer (1950– ) drummer, born New York City; 'Come Together', 'Dream On', 'Angel', 'Dude Looks Like a Lady', 'Rag Doll', 'Love in an Elevator', 'Jamie's got a Gun', *Aerosmith* (1973), *Toys in the Attic* (1975), *Permanent Vacation* (1987), *Pump* (1989), *Get a Grip* (1993), *Big Ones* (1994).

**The Animals** British group, 1960s; split up in 1960s, reformed 1983; members include Eric Burdon (1941– ) vocalist, born Newcastle upon Tyne; Alan Price (1942– ) keyboardist, born Fairfield, County Durham; 'House of the Rising Sun', 'We've Gotta Get Out Of This Place', *Animals* (1964), *Ark* (1983), *Rip It To Shreds – The Animals Greatest Hits Live* (1995).

**Armatrading, Joan** (1950– ) British singer, guitarist, born St Kitts Island, Caribbean; *Joan Armatrading* (1976), *To the Limit* (1978), *Walk Under Ladders* (1981), *The Key* (1983), *Sleight of Hand* (1986), *The Shouting Stage* (1988), *Hearts and Flowers* (1990), *Square The Circle* (1992), *What's Inside* (1995).

**Baez, Joan** (1941– ) American singer, guitarist, born Staten Island, New York; 'The Night They Drove Ol' Dixie Down' (1972), *Any Day Now* (1968), *Farewell, Anjelica* (1975), *Diamonds and Rust* (1975), *Recently* (1987), *Gone from Danger* (1997).

**Bassey, Dame Shirley** (1937– ) British singer, born Tiger Bay, Cardiff, Wales; 'Goldfinger', 'Big Spender', 'Diamonds are Forever', *The Birthday Concert* (1998).

**The Beach Boys** American group, 1960s to present; members include Brian (1942– ) bassist, vocalist; Dennis (1944–83) drummer, vocalist; and Carl (1946–98) Wilson guitarist, vocalist; all born Hawthorne, California; Mike Love (1941– ) vocalist; 'Surfin' USA', 'Help Me Rhonda', 'Barbara Ann', 'Good Vibrations', 'Fun, Fun, Fun', 'I Get Around', 'California Girls', 'Little Deuce Coupe', 'God Only Knows', 'Wouldn't It Be Nice'.

**The Beatles** British group, 1960s; John (Winston) Lennon (1940–80) singer/songwriter, guitarist; (James) Paul McCartney (1942– ) singer/songwriter, guitarist; George Harrison (1943–2001) singer/songwriter, guitarist; Ringo Starr (originally Richard Starkey) (1940– ) singer/songwriter, drummer; all born Liverpool; 'Love Me Do', 'She Loves You', 'From Me to You', 'I Want to Hold your Hand', 'Yesterday', 'Day Tripper', 'Paperback Writer', 'You've Got to Hide Your Love Away', 'Penny Lane', 'Strawberry Fields Forever', 'Hey Jude', *Please Please Me* (1963), *With the Beatles* (1963), *A Hard Day's Night* (1964), *Beatles for Sale* (1964), *Help!* (1965), *Rubber Soul* (1965), *Revolver* (1966), *Sergeant Pepper's Lonely Hearts Club Band* (1967), *Magical Mystery Tour* (1967), *Yellow Submarine* (1968), *The White Album* (1968), *Abbey Road* (1969), *Let it Be* (1970).

**The Bee Gees** Anglo-Australian group; members include Barry (1946– ), Robin (1949– ), and Maurice (1949– ) Gibb; all born Isle of Man; 'Massachusetts', 'Jive Talkin'', 'How Deep is Your Love?', 'Staying Alive', 'Night Fever', *Children of the World* (1976), *ESP* (1987), *Size Isn't Everything* (1993), *Still Waters* (1997).

**Berry, Chuck** (originally **Charles Edward Anderson Berry**) (1926– ) American singer/songwriter, guitarist; born St Louis, Missouri; 'Maybelline', 'Sweet Little Sixteen', 'Too Much Monkey Business', 'Rock and Roll Music', 'School Days', 'No Particular Place to Go', 'Johnny B Goode', 'Nadine', 'My Ding a Ling'.

**B52s** American group, 1970s to 1990s; members include Cindy Wilson (1957– ) vocalist; Ricky Wilson (1953–85) guitarist; Keith Strickland (1953– ) drummer; all born Athens, Georgia; Fred Schneider (1954– ) vocalist, born Newark, Georgia; Kate Pierson (1948– ) vocalist, keyboardist, born Weehawken, New Jersey; 'Rock Lobster', 'Love Shack', 'Roam', 'Deadbeat Club', *Wild Planet* (1980), *Mesopotamia* (1982), *Whammy* (1983), *Bouncing off the Satellites* (1986), *Cosmic Thing* (1989), *Good Stuff* (1992).

**Black Sabbath** British heavy rock group, 1970s to present; members include Ozzy Osbourne (1948– ) vocalist; Tony Iommi (1948– ) guitarist; both born

Birmingham; *Paranoid* (1971), *Sabbath Bloody Sabbath* (1973), *Dehumanizer* (1992), *Cross Purposes* (1994), *Forbidden* (1995), *Reunion* (1998).

**Blondie** American group, 1970s to present; members include Deborah Harry (1945– ) vocalist, born Miami, Florida (solo 'Island of Lost Souls', 'French Kissin' in the USA', 'Free to Fall', 'I Want That Man'); Chris Stein (1950– ) guitarist, born Brooklyn, New York City; 'Denis', 'Heart of Glass', 'Union City Blue', 'Call Me', 'The Tide is High', *Blondie* (1976), *Plastic Letters* (1977), *Parallel Lines* (1978), *Auto American* (1980), *The Hunter* (1982), *No Exit* (1999).

**Blur** British group, formed Colchester, late 1980s to present; members include Damon Albarn (1968– ) singer; Graham Coxon (1969– ) guitarist; Alex James (1968– ) bassist, vocalist; Dave Rowntree (1963– ) drummer; 'Parklife', 'For Tomorrow', 'Beetlebum', *Leisure* (1991), *Modern Life is Rubbish* (1993), *Parklife* (1994), *The Great Escape* (1995), *Blur* (1997), *13* (1999).

**Bolan, Marc (and T Rex)** (originally **Mark Feld**) (1947–77) British singer/songwriter, guitarist, born London; 'Get It On', 'Metal Guru', 'Children of the Revolution', 'Jeepster', *Unicorn* (1970).

**Bon Jovi, Jon** (originally **John Francis Bongiovi**) (1962– ) American lead singer and guitarist of Bon Jovi, 1980s to present; group members include David Bryan (1962– ) keyboardist; Richie Sambora (1959– ) lead guitarist; Alec John Such (1956– ) bassist; Tico 'Tour Monster' Torres (1953– ) drummer; *Bon Jovi* (1984), *Slippery When Wet* (1986), *New Jersey* (1988), *Keep The Faith* (1992), *These Days* (1995), *Destination Anywhere* (1997).

**Booker T and the MGs** American group, 1960s; Booker T Jones (1944– ) vocalist, organist, born Memphis, Tennessee; Donald 'Duck' Dunn (1941– ) bassist, born Memphis; Steve Cropper (1941– ) guitarist, born Willow Springs, Missouri; 'To be a Lover', *Green Onions* (1962).

**Bowie, David** (originally **David Robert Jones**) (1947– ) British singer/songwriter, guitarist, born Brixton, London; 'The Laughing Gnome', 'Space Oddity', 'Life on Mars', 'Jean Genie', 'Andy Warhol', 'Rebel Rebel', 'Ashes to Ashes', 'Blue Jean', 'China Girl', 'Let's Dance', 'Modern Love', *The Man who Sold the World* (1970), *Hunky Dory* (1971), *The Rise and Fall of Ziggy Stardust and the Spiders from Mars* (1972), *Diamond Dogs* (1974), *Heroes* (1977), *Scary Monsters* (1980), *Let's Dance* (1983), *Tonight* (1984), *Never Let Me Down* (1987), *Black Tie White Noise* (1993), *Earthling* (1997), *Hours* (1999).

**Brown, James** (1928– ) American singer/songwriter, drummer, pianist, born Barnwell, South Carolina; 'Papa's Got a Brand New Bag', 'It's a Man's Man's Man's World', 'Ain't It Funky Now', 'Sex Machine', 'Get Up Offa That Thing'.

**Bush, Kate** (1958– ) British singer/songwriter, keyboardist, born Plumstead; 'Wuthering Heights', 'The Man with the Child in His Eyes', 'Wow', 'Running Up That Hill', *Never Forever* (1980), *The Dreaming* (1982), *Hounds of Love* (1986), *The Sensual World* (1989), *The Red Shoes* (1993).

**The Byrds** American group, 1960s to present; Roger McGuinn (1942– ) guitarist, born Chicago; Chris Hillman (1942– ) bassist, mandolin player, vocalist, born Los Angeles; David Crosby (1941– ) vocalist, guitarist; Michael Clarke (1943– ) drummer, born New York City; 'Mr Tambourine Man', 'Eight Miles High', *Mr Tambourine Man* (1965), *Turn, Turn, Turn* (1966), *Fifth Dimension* (1966).

**Carey, Mariah** (1969– ) American singer, born New York City; *Mariah Carey* (1990), *Emotions* (1991), *MTV Unplugged EP* (1992), *Music Box* (1993), *Merry Christmas* (1994), *Daydream* (1995), *Butterfly* (1997).

**The Carpenters** American group, 1970s to 1980s; members include Karen Carpenter (1950–83) vocalist, drummer; Richard Carpenter (1946– ) vocalist, keyboardist; both born New Haven, Connecticut; *Close to You* (1970), *Yesterday Once More* (1974), *Voice of the Heart* (1983), *Only Yesterday* (1990), *Interpretations* (tribute album) (1994).

**Cash, Johnny** (1932– ) American singer/songwriter, guitarist, born Kingsland, Arkansas; 'Don't Take Your Guns to Town', 'Rings of Fire', 'A Boy Named Sue', 'The Man in Black', 'A Thing Called Love', *The Man In Black – The Definitive Collection* (1994).

**Charles, Ray** (originally **Ray Charles Robinson**) (1930– ) American singer/songwriter, pianist, born Albany, Georgia; 'I Got a Woman', 'Lonely Avenue', 'You Are My Sunshine', 'Crying Time', 'Hit the Road, Jack', *The Genius of Ray Charles* (1959), *Heart to Heart – 20 Hot Hits* (1980), *The Collection* (1990).

**Cher** (originally **Cherilyn Sarkasian La Pierre**) (1946– ) American singer/songwriter, born El Centro, California; (with Sonny Bono) 'I Got You Babe', 'Just You', 'All I Ever Need Is You'; 'Gypsys, Tramps and Thieves', 'Half Breed', 'The Shoop Shoop Song', *Love Hurts* (1991), *It's a Man's World* (1995).

**Clapton, Eric** (1945– ) British singer/songwriter, guitarist, born Ripley, Surrey (was in 1960s groups The Yardbirds and Cream); 'Layla', 'Lay Down Sally', 'Wonderful Tonight', 'I shot the Sheriff', 'Tulsa Time', 'Cocaine', 'I've Got a Rock 'n Roll Heart', *Derek and the Dominos* (with Duane Allman) (1970); *461 Ocean Boulevard* (1974), *Slowhand* (1977), *Just One Night* (1980), *Money and Cigarettes* (1983), *August* (1986), *Journey Man* (1989), *24 Nights* (1991), *Unplugged* (1992), *From The Cradle* (1994).

**The Clash** British group, late 1970s to 1980s; members include Joe Strummer (originally John Mellors) (1952– ) guitarist, vocalist, born Ankara, Turkey; Mick Jones (1955– ) guitarist, vocalist, born London; Paul Simonon (1956– ) bassist, born London; 'Topper' Headon (1956– ) drummer, born Dover; 'I Fought the Law', 'Rock the Casbah', 'Should I Stay or Should I Go', *The Clash* (1977), *Cost of Living* (1979), *London Calling* (1979), *Combat Rock* (1982), *Cut the Crap* (1985).

**Cochran, Eddie** (1938–60) American singer, guitarist,

born Oklahoma City; 'Three Steps to Heaven', 'Summertime Blues', 'C'mon Everybody', 'Something Else'.

**Cocker, Joe** (1944– ) British singer/songwriter, born Sheffield; 'With a Little Help from My Friends', 'You Are So Beautiful', 'Up Where We Belong' (with Jennifer Warnes), *Mad Dogs and Englishmen* (1970), *I Can Stand a Little Rain* (1974), *Unchain My Heart* (1987), *Night Calls* (1992), *Have a Little Faith* (1997).

**Cohen, Leonard** (1934– ) Canadian singer/songwriter, guitarist, born Montreal, Quebec; 'Suzanne', 'Famous Blue Raincoat', *Songs of Leonard Cohen* (1968), *Songs of Love and Hate* (1970), *Various Positions* (1984), *I'm Your Man* (1988), *The Future* (1992), *Cohen Live* (1994).

**Cooke, Sam** (originally **Sam Cook**) (1935–64) American singer/songwriter, born Chicago, Illinois; 'You Send Me', 'A Change Is Gonna Come', 'Wonderful World', *Sam Cooke at the Copa* (1964).

**Cooper, Alice** (originally **Vincent Furnier**) (1948– ) American singer/songwriter, born Detroit, Michigan; 'School's Out', 'Poison', 'Hey Stoopid', *Love it to Death* (1971), *School's Out* (1972), *Trash* (1989), *Hey Stoopid* (1991), *The Last Temptation* (1994).

**Cope, Julian** (1957– ) British singer/songwriter, born Bargoed, Wales; (with The Teardrop Explodes) 'Reward', 'Treason', 'Kilimanjaro' (1980); 'Trampoline', 'Beautiful World', 'World Shut Your Mouth', *World Shut Your Mouth* (1984), *St Julian* (1987), *Peggy Suicide* (1991), *Jehovakill* (1992), *Autogeddon* (1994), *Julian Cope Presents 20 Mothers* (1995).

**Costello, Elvis** (originally **Declan Patrick McManus**) (1955– ) British singer/songwriter, guitarist, born Paddington, London; 'Watching the Detectives', '(I Don't Want To Go To) Chelsea', 'Accidents Will Happen', 'Alison', 'Shipbuilding', 'Every Day I Write the Book', 'Don't Let Me Be Misunderstood', *My Aim is True* (1977), *This Year's Model* (with The Attractions) (1978), *Armed Forces* (1979), *Almost Blue* (1981), *Imperial Bedroom* (1982), *Punch the Clock* (1983), *Goodbye Cruel World* (1984), *King of America* (1986), *Spike* (1989), *Mighty Like a Rose* (1991), *Brutal* (1994), *Kojak Variety* (1994).

**Cray, Robert** (1953– ) American singer, blues guitarist, born Columbus, Georgia; 'Phone Booth', *False Accusations* (1985), *Showdown!* (1985), *Midnight Stroll* (1990), *Shame and Sin* (1993), *Some Rainy Morning* (1995).

**Cream** British group, late 1960s; members include Eric Clapton (1945– ) singer, guitarist; Jack Bruce singer, bassist; Ginger Baker drummer; 'I Feel Free', 'Sunshine of Your Love', 'Strange Brew', 'Badge', 'Crossroads', *Fresh Cream* (1966), *Disraeli Gears* (1967), *Wheels of Fire* (1968), *Goodbye* (1969).

**Creedence Clearwater Revival** American group, late 1960s to early 1970s; members include John Cameron Fogerty (1945– ) (solo 'Rockin' All Over the World', *Centerfield* (1985)), Tom Fogerty (1941–90), both guitarists and vocalists, born Berkeley, California; Doug Clifford (1945– ) drummer, born Palo Alto; Stu Cook (1945– ) bassist, born Oakland; 'Susie Q', 'Proud Mary', 'Bad Moon Risin'', 'Green River', 'Born on the Bayou', 'Down on the Corner', 'I Heard it through the Grapevine', 'Fortunate Son', 'Travellin' Band', 'Up, around the Bend', *Creedence Clearwater Revival* (1968), *Pendulum* (1970), *Mardi Gras* (1972).

**Crosby, Bing** (originally **Harry Lillis**) (1903–77) American singer, born Spokane, Washington; 'Swingin' on a Star', 'White Christmas', 'True Love' (with Grace Kelly).

**Crosby, Stills, Nash and Young** American group, late 1960s to present; David Crosby (originally David van Cortland) (1941– ) guitarist, vocalist, born Los Angeles; Graham Nash (1942– ) vocalist, born Blackpool, England; Stephen Stills (1945– ) guitarist, vocalist, pianist; Neil Young (1945– ) guitarist, vocalist, pianist; 'Ohio', *Déjà vu* (1970), *Four Way Street* (1971), *Allies* (1983).

**Crow, Sheryl** (1962– ) US singer/songwriter, born Kennett, Missouri; 'Every Day is a Winding Road', 'All I Wanna Do', *Tuesday Night Music Club* (1993), *Sheryl Crow* (1996).

**Culture Club** British group, 1980s to 1990s; members include Boy George (originally George O'Dowd) (1961– ) vocalist, born Eltham; Jon Moss (1957– ) drummer, born London; 'Karma Chameleon', *Colour By Numbers* (1983), *Don't Mind if I Do* (1999).

**The Cure** British group, mid 1970s to present; members include Robert Smith (1957– ) guitarist, singer/songwriter, born Crawley, Sussex; Laurence Tolhurst drummer, keyboardist; 'Killing an Arab', 'Boys Don't Cry', 'Love Cats', 'The Caterpillar', 'Close to Me', 'Standing on the Beach', 'In Between Days', *Boy's Don't Cry* (1980), *Faith* (1981), *Pornography* (1982), *The Head on the Door* (1985), *Disintegration* (1989), *Mixed Up* (1990), *Entreat* (1991), *Wish* (1992), *Paris* (1993), *Bloodflowers* (2000).

**Davis, Sammy, Jr** (1925–90) American singer, born New York City; 'Something's Gotta Give', 'That Old Black Magic', 'Candy Man', *Starring Sammy Davis Jr* (1955), *Just for Lovers* (1955), *The Wham of Sam* (1960).

**The Dead Kennedys** American group, late 1970s to 1980s; members include Jello Biafra vocalist; East Bay Ray (aka Ray Valium) guitarist; Klaüs Flouride bassist; Ted drummer; 'California Über Alles', 'Kill the Poor', 'Too Drunk to Fuck', 'Holiday in Cambodia', *Fresh Fruit for Rotten Vegetables* (1980), *Plastic Surgery Disaster* (1982), *Frankenchrist* (1985).

**Deep Purple** British heavy rock group, late 1960s to present; members include Ian Gillan (1945– ) vocalist, born Hounslow; David Coverdale (1951– ) vocalist, born Saltburn; Ritchie Blackmore (1945– ) guitarist, born Weston-super-Mare; Jon Lord (1941– ) keyboardist, born Leicester; Roger Glover (1945– ) bassist; Ian Paice (1948– ) drummer; 'Black Night',

'Smoke on the Water', *Shades of Deep Purple* (1968), *Deep Purple* (1969), *Deep Purple In Rock* (1970), *Machine Head* (1972), *Made in Japan* (1972), *Perfect Strangers* (1984), *The House of Blue Light* (1987), *The Battle Rages On* (1993), *Abandon* (1998).

**Def Leppard** British heavy metal group, 1980s to present; members include Joe Elliott (1960– ) vocalist; Rick Savage bassist; Pete Willis guitar, replaced by Phil Collen; Steve Clark (d.1991) guitarist; Rick Allen (1963– ) drummer; 'Photograph', 'Foolin'', 'Rock of Ages', 'Animal', 'Women', 'Pour Some Sugar on Me', *On Through the Night* (1980), *High and Dry* (1981), *Pyromania* (1983), *Hysteria* (1987), *Adrenalize* (1992), *Retroactive* (1993).

**Denver, John** (originally **John Henry Deutschendorf**) (1943–97) American singer/songwriter, born New Mexico; 'Take Me Home Country Roads', 'Annie's Song', 'I'm Sorry', *Back Home Again* (1974), *An Evening With John Denver* (1975), *Perhaps Love* (1981), *One World* (1986).

**Depeche Mode** British group, 1980s to present; Andy Fletcher (1961– ); Martin Gore (1961– ); Vince Clark; Alan Wilder (1963– ) keyboardist; *Speak and Spell* (1981), *Black Celebration* (1986), *Music for the Masses* (1987), *Violator* (1990), *Songs of Faith and Devotion* (1993).

**Devo** American group, 1970s to 1980s; Jerry Casale bassist, singer/songwriter; Bob Casale and Mark Mothersbaugh keyboardists, guitarists, vocalists; Bob Mothersbaugh guitarist, vocalist; Alan Myers drummer; 'Satisfaction', 'Whip It', *Q: Are We Not Men? A: We Are Devo!* (1978), *Shout* (1984).

**Diamond, Neil (Leslie)** (1941– ) American singer/songwriter, guitarist, born Coney Island, New York; 'Song Sung Blue', 'You Don't Bring Me Flowers' (with Barbra Streisand), 'Love on the Rocks', *Beautiful Noise* (1976), *The Jazz Singer* (1980), *Heartlight* (1982), *Headed for the Future* (1986), *Lovescape* (1991), *Up On The Roof – Songs From The Brill Building* (1993).

**Diddley, Bo** (originally **Ellas McDaniel**) (1928– ) American singer, guitarist, born McComb, Mississippi; 'Bo Diddley'/'I'm a Man', 'Road Runner', 'Do Wah Diddy Diddy', *Got My Own Bag of Tricks* (1971).

**Dire Straits** British group, late 1970s to 1990s; members include Mark Knopfler (1949– ) singer/songwriter, guitarist, born Glasgow (solo soundtrack *Local Hero*); David Knopfler guitarist replaced by Hal Lindes; John Illsley (1949– ) bassist, born London; Pick Withers drummer; Alan Clark keyboardist; 'Romeo and Juliet', 'Tunnel of Love', 'So Far Away', 'Money for Nothing', 'Walk of Life', *Dire Straits* (1978), *Communiqué* (1979), *Making Movies* (1981), *Love Over Gold* (1983), *Alchemy* (1984), *Brothers in Arms* (1985), *Money for Nothing* (1988), *On Every Street* (1991), *On The Night* (1993).

**Domino, Fats** (originally **Antoine Domino**) (1928– ) American singer, pianist, born New Orleans, Louisiana; 'Every Night About This Time', 'It's Midnight', 'Ain't That a Shame', 'Blue Monday', 'Blueberry Hill'.

**Donovan** (originally **Donovan Philips Leitch**) (1946– ) British singer/songwriter, guitarist, born Glasgow; 'Mellow Yellow', 'Sunshine Superman', *The Universal Soldier* (1966), *Cosmic Wheels* (1973).

**The Doobie Brothers** American group, 1970s; John Hartman (1950– ) drummer, born Falls Church, Virginia; Tom Johnston vocalist, guitarist, born Visalia, California; Tiran Porter bassist, born San Francisco; Patrick Simmons (1950– ) vocalist, guitarist, born Aberdeen, Washington; Michael Hossack (1950– ) drummer, born Paterson, New York replaced by Keith Knudson (1952– ) born Ames, Iowa; Jeff 'Skunk' Baxter (1948– ) guitarist, born Washington, DC; Michael McDonald keyboardist, vocalist, born St Louis (solo *Sweet Freedom*, 1986); 'Listen to the Music', 'Black Water', 'Fool', *What Were Once Vices Are Now Habits* (1974), *One Step Closer* (1980).

**The Doors** American group, late 1960s to early 1970s; members include Jim Morrison (1943–71), singer/songwriter, born Melbourne, Florida; Ray Manzarek (1939– ) keyboardist, born Chicago; Robby Krieger (1946– ) guitarist, born Los Angeles; John Densmore (1945– ) drummer, born Los Angeles; 'Light My Fire', 'The End', 'When the Music's Over', 'LA Woman', 'Hello, I Love You', 'Five To One', 'Touch Me', 'Riders on the Storm', *The Doors* (1967), *Strange Days* (1967), *Waiting for the Sun* (1968), *LA Woman* (1970), *An American Prayer* (1978), *Alive, She Cried* (1983), *Live At The Hollywood Bowl* (1987), *The Doors* (1991) (film soundtrack), *In Concert* (1991).

**Duran Duran** British group, 1980s to present; members include Simon Le Bon (1958– ) vocalist, born Watford, Hertfordshire; Nick Rhodes (originally Nicholas Bates) (1962– ) keyboardist, born Birmingham; John Taylor (1960– ) bassist, born Birmingham; Roger Taylor drummer; Andy Taylor guitarist; 'Planet Earth', 'Hungry Like the Wolf', 'Save a Prayer', 'Rio', 'Wild Boys', *Duran Duran* (1981), *Rio* (1982), *Seven and the Ragged Tiger* (1983), *Arena* (1984), *Notorious* (1986), *Decade* (1989), *Liberty* (1990), *Thankyou* (1995), *Pop Trash* (2000).

**Dury, Ian** (1942–2000) British singer/songwriter, born Upminster, Essex; (with the Blockheads) 'Sex & Drugs & Rock 'n' Roll', 'Hit Me with your Rhythm Stick', *New Boots and Panties* (1977), *Do It Yourself* (1979), *Laughter* (1980), *Mr Love Pants* (1998).

**Dylan, Bob** (originally **Robert Allen Zimmerman**) (1941– ) American singer/songwriter, guitarist, born Duluth, Minnesota; 'Blowin' in the Wind', 'Mr Tambourine Man', 'Desolation Row', 'Like a Rolling Stone', 'Maggie's Farm', 'All Along the Watchtower', 'Lay Lady Lay', *The Freewheelin' Bob Dylan* (1963), *The Times They Are A-Changin'* (1963), *Another Side of Bob Dylan* (1964), *Bringing It All Back Home* (1965), *Blonde on Blonde* (1966), *John Wesley Harding* (1968), *Nashville Skyline* (1969), *Blood on the Tracks* (1974), *The Basement Tapes* (1975), *Slow Train Coming* (1979), *Infidels* (1983), *World Gone Wrong* (1993), *Time Out of Mind* (1997).

**The Eagles** American group, 1970s; members include Glenn Frey (1948– ) singer, guitarist, born Detroit,

Michigan; Don Henley (1947– ) singer, drummer, born Texas (solo 'Dirty Laundry', 'Boys of Summer', *Building the Perfect Beast* (1984)); Bernie Leadon (1947– ) guitarist replaced by Joe Walsh (1947– ) guitarist, singer/songwriter, born Wichita, Kansas (solo 'Life's Been Good', *But Seriously Folks* (1976), *Got Any Gum?* (1987); Randy Meisner (1946– ) bassist, born Nebraska; 'Best of My Love', 'Lyin' Eyes', 'New Kid in Town', 'Heartache Tonight', *Eagles* (1972), *Desperado* (1973), *One of these Nights* (1975), *Hotel California* (1976), *The Long Run* (1979), *Eagles Live* (1980), *Hell Freezes Over* (1994).

**Earth, Wind and Fire** American group, 1970s to present; Maurice White (1941– ) vocalist, drummer, born Memphis, Tennessee; Verdine White (1951– ) bassist; Philip Bailey (1951– ) vocalist, born Denver, Colorado; Larry Dunn (1953– ) keyboardist, born Colorado; Johnny Graham (1951– ) guitarist, born Kentucky; Al McKay (1948– ) guitarist, born Louisiana; Andre Woolfolk (1950– ) reeds, born Texas; Ralph Johnson (1951– ) drummer, born California; 'Shining Star', 'Got to Get you into My Life', *Open Our Eyes* (1974), *That's The Way of the World* (1975), *In the Name of Love* (1997).

**Easton, Sheena** (originally **Sheena Orr**) (1959– ) British singer, born Belshill, Glasgow; 'Morning Train', 'For Your Eyes Only', 'Sugar Walls', *Best Kept Secret* (1983), *The Lover In Me* (1989).

**Electric Light Orchestra** British group, 1970s to 1980s; members include Jeff Lynne (1947– ) guitarist, vocalist; Roy Wood (1946– ) guitarist, vocalist; Bev Bevan (1946– ) drummer; all born Birmingham; 'Roll Over Beethoven', 'Evil Woman', 'Hold On Tight', 'Mr Blue Sky', 'Last Train to London', 'Calling America', *Xanadu* (1980), *Balance Of Power* (1986).

**Eno, Brian** (1948– ) British singer/songwriter, keyboardist, born Woodbridge, Suffolk (was in early 1970s Roxy Music line-up); *My Life In the Bush Of Ghosts* (with David Byrne) (1981), *Wah Wah* (1994), *Spinner* (1995), *Sonora Portraits* (1999).

**Eurythmics** British group, 1980s to present; members include David Allan Stewart (1952– ) songwriter, keyboardist, guitarist, born Sunderland, England; Annie Lennox (1954– ) singer/songwriter, born Aberdeen, Scotland; 'Love is a Stranger', 'Who's that Girl?', 'Here Comes the Rain Again', 'Sexcrime', 'Thorn in My Side', 'It's Alright (Baby's Coming Back)', 'Sisters are Doin' it for Themselves' (with Aretha Franklin), 'When Tomorrow Comes', *Sweet Dreams are Made of This* (1982), *Touch* (1983), *1984* (1984), *Be Yourself Tonight* (1985), *Revenge* (1986), *Savage* (1987), *We Too are One* (1989), *Peace* (1999).

**The Everly Brothers** American group; Don (1937– ), Phil (1939– ), born Brownie, Kentucky; 'Bye Bye Love', 'Little Susie', 'Dream', *EB 84* (1984).

**Fairport Convention** British group, mid 1960s to 1970s; members include Ashley Hutchings (1945– ), Simon Nicol (1950– ), Richard Thompson singer/songwriter, guitarist; Martin Lamble (1949–69) drummer; Judy Dyble (1948– ) singer/songwriter replaced by Sandy Denny (1941–78); Dave Swarbrick (1941– ) fiddler, all born London; Ian Matthews (1946– ) born Scunthorpe; 'Meet on a Ledge', 'A Sailor's Life', *Rosie* (1973), *Fairport 9* (1973), *Red and Gold* (1989).

**Ferry, Bryan** (1945– ) British singer, born Washington, County Durham (was founder-member of Roxy Music, 1970); 'Tokyo Joe', 'The Price of Love', 'Slave to Love', 'Don't Stop the Dance', *Boys and Girls* (1985), *Bête Noire* (1987), *Taxi* (1993), *Mamouna* (1994).

**Flack, Roberta** (1939– ) American singer/songwriter, pianist; 'Killing Me Softly With His Song', 'Back Together Again', 'Tonight I Celebrate My Love', *And Donny Hathaway* (1972), *Killing Me Softly* (1973), *Born To Love* (1983).

**Fleetwood Mac** Anglo-American group, late 1960s to present; members include Peter Green (originally Peter Greenbaum) (1946– ) singer/songwriter, guitarist, born London; Mick Fleetwood (1942– ) drummer; John McVie (1945– ) bassist; Christine McVie singer, keyboardist; Lindsey Buckingham (1947– ) singer, guitarist, born Palo Alto, California; Stevie (Stephanie) Nicks (1948– ) singer/songwriter, born Phoenix, Arizona (solo *Bella Donna* (1982), *The Wild Heart* (1983), *Rock A Little* (1985)); 'Albatross', 'Oh Well', 'Big Love', 'Little Lies', *Fleetwood Mac* (1975), *Rumours* (1977), *Mirage* (1982), *Tango in the Night* (1987), *Behind The Mask* (1990), *Time* (1995), *The Dance* (1997).

**Frankie Goes to Hollywood** British group, early 1980s; Holly Johnson (1960– ) and Paul Rutherford (1959– ) vocalists; Mark O'Toole (1964– ) bassist; Peter Gill (1960– ) drummer; Brian Nash (1963– ) guitarist; 'Relax!', 'Two Tribes', 'The Power of Love', 'Ferry Across the Mersey', *Welcome to the Pleasure Dome* (1984).

**Franklin, Aretha** (1942– ) American singer, born Memphis, Tennessee; 'Think', 'Respect', *I Never Loved A Man The Way I Love You* (1967), *Lady Soul* (1968), *Amazing Grace* (1972), *Everything I Feel in Me* (1974), *Almighty Fire* (1978), *Love All The Hurt Away* (1981), *Get It Right* (1983), *Aretha* (1986), *Through The Storm* (1989).

**Gaye, Marvin (Pentz)** (1939–84) American singer/songwriter, pianist, drummer, born Washington, DC; 'Hitch Hike', 'Can I Get a Witness', 'I Heard it through the Grapevine', 'What's Goin' On', 'Sexual Healing', *What's Goin' On* (1971), *Let's Get it On* (1973), *Here My Dear* (1979), *In Our Lifetime* (1981), *Midnight Love* (1982).

**Genesis** British group, late 1960s to present; members include (at various times) Peter Gabriel (1950– ) singer/songwriter, born Cobham, Surrey (solo 'Games without Frontiers', 'Sledgehammer', *So* (1986)); Phil Collins (1951– ) singer/songwriter, drummer, born London (solo 'You Can't Hurry Love', 'One More Night', *Face Value* (1981), *No Jacket Required* (1985)); Tony Banks (1950– ) keyboardist; Michael Rutherford (1951– ) guitarist, bassist, vocalist; *Selling England by the Pound* (1973), *Nursery*

*Cryme* (1971), *The Lamb Lies Down on Broadway* (1974), *Duke* (1980), *Abacab* (1981), *Genesis* (1983), *Invisible Touch* (1986), *We Can't Dance* (1991), *Calling All Stations* (1997).

**The Grateful Dead** American group, late 1960s to present; members include Jerry Garcia (originally Jerome Garcia) (1942–95) guitarist, born San Francisco, California; 'Dark Star', *Live Dead* (1970), *Europe* (1972), *Blues for Allah* (1975), *In the Dark* (1987), *Dylan and the Dead* (with Bob Dylan) (1988).

**Guns 'n' Roses** American group, late 1980s to present; W Axl Rose singer; Slash guitarist; Matt Sorum drummer; 'Sweet Child O' Mine', 'Welcome to the Jungle', 'Night Train', 'Patience', 'You Could Be Mine', *Appetite for Destruction* (1987), *G 'N' R Lies* (1988), *The Spaghetti Incident?* (1993).

**Haley, Bill** (1925–81) American singer/songwriter, guitarist, born Highland Park, Michigan; (with The Comets) 'Crazy Man Crazy', 'Shake Rattle and Roll', 'Rock Around the Clock', 'See You Later, Alligator', 'Rudy's Rock'.

**Harrison, George** (1943–2001) British singer/songwriter, guitarist, born Liverpool; 'My Sweet Lord', 'All Those Years Ago', 'Got My Mind Set On You', 'When We Was Fab', *All Things Must Pass* (1970), *Cloud Nine* (1987).

**Hendrix, Jimi** (originally **James Marshall Hendrix**) (1942–70) American singer/songwriter, guitarist, born Seattle, Washington; (with the Experience) 'Voodoo Chile', 'Hey Joe', 'Purple Haze', 'The Wind Cries Mary', 'Crosstown Traffic', 'All Along the Watchtower', *Are You Experienced?* (1967), *Electric Ladyland* (1968), *Axis: Bold As Love* (1968).

**Herman's Hermits** British group, 1960s; members include Peter 'Herman' Noone (1947– ) singer, pianist, guitarist, born Manchester; Karl Green (1947– ) guitarist, harmonica player, born Salford; Keith Hopwood (1946– ) guitarist, born Manchester; Derek 'Lek' Leckenby (1945– ) guitarist, born Leeds; Barry Whitwan (1946– ) drummer, born Manchester; 'I'm Into Something Good', 'Mrs Brown, You've Got a Lovely Daughter', 'I'm Henry VIII, I Am'.

**The Hollies** British group, 1960s to present; members include Allan Clarke (1942– ) vocalist, born Salford; Graham Nash (1942– ) guitarist, vocalist, born Blackpool replaced by Terry Sylvester (1945– ) born Liverpool; Tony Hicks (1943– ) guitarist, born Nelson; Eric Haydock (1943– ) bassist, born Stockport replaced by Bernie Calvert (1943– ) born Burnley; Bobby Elliott (1943– ) drummer, born Burnley; 'Searchin'', 'Just One Look', 'He Ain't Heavy, He's My Brother', 'The Air That I Breathe', 'Stop In the Name of Love'.

**Holly, Buddy** (originally **Charles Hardin Holley**) (1936–59) American singer/songwriter, guitarist, violinist, born Lubbock, Texas; (with The Crickets) 'That'll Be the Day', 'Oh Boy!', 'Not Fade Away', 'Peggy Sue', 'Every Day', 'Rave On', 'Peggy Sue Got Married'.

**Houston, Whitney** (1963– ) American singer, born Newark, New Jersey; 'Saving All My Love For You', 'How Will I Know', 'Greatest Love', 'I Wanna Dance With Somebody (Who Loves Me)', 'Where Do Broken Hearts Go', 'My Name is Not Sue', *Whitney Houston* (1985), *Whitney* (1987), *I'm Your Baby Tonight* (1990), *The Bodyguard* (1992) (soundtrack), *The Preacher's Wife* (1996) (soundtrack), *My Love is Your Love* (1998).

**The Human League** British group, late 1970s to present; members include Philip Oakey (1955– ) singer; Susanne Sully (1963– ) singer; Joanne Catherall (1962– ) singer; Ian Burden (1957– ) bassist; Jo Callis (1951– ) guitarist; 'Don't You Want Me' (1981), '(Keep Feeling) Fascination', 'Mirror Man', 'Louise', *Dare* (1981), *Crash* (1986), *Romantic?* (1990), *Octopus* (1995).

**INXS** Australian group, 1980s to present; Michael Hutchence (1960–97) singer, born Sydney; Andrew Farriss keyboardist; John Farriss drummer; Tim Farriss guitarist; Kirk Pengilly guitarist, saxophonist; Garry Beers drummer; 'Original Sin', 'This Time', 'Never Tear Us Apart', 'Need You Tonight', *Shabooh Shoobah* (1982), *Listen Like Thieves* (1985), *Kick* (1987), *X* (1990), *Live Baby Live* (1991), *Welcome To Wherever You Are* (1992), *Full Moon, Dirty Hearts* (1993).

**Iron Maiden** British heavy metal group, mid 1970s to present; members include Steve Harris (1957– ) bassist, born Leytonstone, London; Dave Murray (1958– ) guitarist, born Clapham, London; Adrian Smith (1957– ) guitarist, born London; Paul Di'Anno (1959– ) singer, born Chingford, Essex replaced by Bruce Dickinson (1958– ) born Sheffield; Nicko McBain (1954– ) drummer, born London; 'Running Free', 'Run to the Hills', *Iron Maiden* (1980), *The Number of the Beast* (1982), *Power Slave* (1984), *Live After Death* (1985), *Somewhere In Time* (1986), *Seventh Son of a Seventh Son* (1988), *Running Free/Sanctuary* (1990), *The X Factor* (1995).

**The Isley Brothers** American group; Kelly (originally O'Kelly) (1937–86), Rudolph (1939– ), Ronald (1941– ) Isley; all born Cincinnati, Ohio; 'Shout', 'Twist and Shout', 'This Old Heart of Mine (Is Weak For You)', *Harvest for the World* (1976).

**Jackson, Janet** (1966– ) American singer/songwriter, born Gary, Indiana; 'When I Think Of You', *Control* (1986), *Rhythm Nation 1814* (1989).

**Jackson, Michael (Joe)** (1958– ) American singer/songwriter, born Gary, Indiana; (was in The Jacksons, American group, 1960s to 1970s); 'Billy Jean', 'Beat It', 'The Girl is Mine', 'Say Say Say' (with Paul McCartney); 'I Can't Stop Loving You' (with Siedah Garrett), *Ben* (1972), *Off the Wall* (1979), *Thriller* (1982), *Bad* (1987), *Dangerous* (1991), *History – Past Present and Future Book 1* (1995), *Invincible* (2001)

**The Jam** British group, mid 1970s to early 1980s; members include Paul Weller (1958– ) singer/songwriter, guitarist, born Woking, Surrey (solo *Stanley Road* (1995), *Heliocentric* (2000); Bruce Foxton (1955– ) bassist, born Woking; Rick Butler

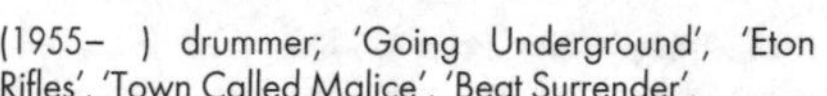




(1955– ) drummer; 'Going Underground', 'Eton Rifles', 'Town Called Malice', 'Beat Surrender'.

**Jarre, Jean-Michel** (1949– ) French keyboardist, composer, born Lyons; *Oxygène* (1977), *Equinoxe* (1978), *Magnetic Fields* (1981), *The Concerts In China* (1982), *Rendez Vous* (1986), *Revolutions* (1988), *Waiting For Cousteau* (1990), *Chronologie* (1993), *Chronologie Part 6* (1994).

**The Jefferson Airplane/Jefferson Starship/ Starship** American group, mid 1960s to present; many different members, often changing, include Grace Slick (originally Grace Wing) (1939– ) singer/songwriter, born Chicago, Illinois; 'White Rabbit', 'We Built this City', 'Sara', 'Nothing's Gonna Stop Us Now', *Surrealistic Pillow* (1967), *Crown of Creation* (1968), *Red Octopus* (1975), *Spitfire* (1976), *Knee Deep in Hoopla* (1986), *No Protection* (1987).

**Joel, Billy** (originally **William Martin Joel**) (1949– ) American singer/songwriter, pianist, born Hicksville, Long Island, New York; 'Say Goodbye to Hollywood', 'Just The Way You Are', 'My Life', 'It's Still Rock 'n' Roll to Me', 'Tell Her About it', 'Uptown Girl', 'We Didn't Start the Fire', *The Stranger* (1977), *52nd Street* (1978), *Glass House* (1980), *The Nylon Curtain* (1982), *An Innocent Man* (1983), *The Bridge* (1986), *Storm Front* (1989), *River of Dreams* (1993).

**John, Sir Elton** (originally **Reginald Kenneth Dwight**) (1947– ) British singer/songwriter, pianist, born Pinner, Middlesex; 'Your Song', 'Crocodile Rock', 'Don't Go Breakin' My Heart' (with Kiki Dee), 'Little Jeannie', 'Candle In The Wind', 'Wrap Her Up', 'Nikita', 'Sacrifice', 'Candle In The Wind' (rewritten version for the late Princess Diana's funeral), *Tumbleweed Connection* (1970), *Don't Shoot Me, I'm Only The Piano Player* (1973), *Good Bye Yellow Brick Road* (1973), *A Single Man* (1979), *Too Low for Zero*, *Ice on Fire* (1985), *Sleeping With The Past* (1989), *The One* (1992), *Duets* (1993), *Made In England* (1995), *One Night Only* (2000).

**Jones, Grace** (1952– ) Jamaican singer/songwriter, born Jamaica, West Indies; 'Private Life', 'Love is the Drug', 'Pull up to the Bumper', 'Slave to the Rhythm', *Island Life* (1983), *Inside Story* (1986).

**Jones, Tom** (originally **Thomas Jones Woodward**) (1940– ) British singer, drummer, born Pontypridd, S Wales; 'It's Not Unusual', 'What's New, Pussycat?', 'Green Green Grass of Home', 'Delilah', *After Dark* (1989), *Carrying a Torch* (1991), *The Lead and How To Swing It* (1994), *Reload* (1999).

**Joplin, Janis** (1943–70) American singer/songwriter, born Port Arthur, Texas; 'Piece of My Heart', *Cheap Thrills* (1968), *I Got Dem Ol' Kozmic Blues Again, Mama!* (1969), *Pearl* (1971).

**Joy Division/New Order** British group, late 1970s to mid 1980s; members include Ian Curtis (1957–80) vocalist, born Macclesfield; changed to New Order in 1981; members include Bernard Sumner (originally Barney Albrecht) (1956– ) vocalist, guitarist, born Salford, Lancashire; Peter Hook (1956– ) bassist; Stephen Morris (1957– ) drummer; (as Joy Division) 'Transmission', 'Love Will Tear Us Apart', *Unknown Pleasures* (1979); (as New Order) 'Blue Monday', 'Shellshock', *Movement* (1981), *Low Life* (1985).

**Khan, Chaka** (originally **Yvette Marie Stevens**) (1953– ) American singer/songwriter, born Great Lakes, Illinois; (with Rufus) *Rags to Rufus* (1974); *Chaka* (1978), *I Feel For You* (1984), *Destiny* (1986), *Life is a Dance – The Remix Project* (1989).

**King, B B** (originally **Riley B King**) (1925– ) American guitarist, singer/songwriter, born Itta Bena, near Indianola, Mississippi; *Live at the Regal* (1965), *Confessin' the Blues* (1966), *Blues Is King* (1967), *Indianola Mississippi Seeds* (1970), *Live in Stock County Jail* (1971), *There Must Be A Better World Somewhere* (1981), *Six Silver Strings* (1985).

**King, Ben E** (originally **Benjamin Earl Nelson**) (1938– ) singer, born Henderson, North Carolina; 'Stand By Me'.

**King, Carole** (originally **Carole Klein**) (1942– ) American singer/songwriter; 'It Might As Well Rain Until September', 'It's Too Late', 'You've Got A Friend', 'Will You Love Me Tomorrow', *Tapestry* (1971), *Wrap Around Joy* (1974), *Pearls* (1980).

**The Kinks** British group, 1960s to 1980s; Ray Davies (1944– ) singer/songwriter, guitarist (solo 'A Quiet Life'); Dave Davies (1947– ) singer, guitarist; both born Muswell Hill, London; Mike Avory (1944– ) drummer, born Hampton, Middlesex; Peter Quaife (1943– ) bassist, born Tavistock, Devon; 'You Really Got Me', 'All Day and All of the Night', 'Dedicated Follower of Fashion', 'Sunny Afternoon', 'Waterloo Sunset', 'Autumn Almanac', 'Lola', 'Come Dancing', 'Don't Forget to Dance', *Village Green Preservation Society* (1968), *Lola vs Powerman & The Moneyground Pt 1* (1970), *State of Confusion* (1983).

**Kiss** American group, 1970s to present; members include Paul Stanley (originally Paul Stanley Eisen) (1952– ) guitarist, born New York City; Gene Simmons (originally Gene Klein) (1949– ) bassist, born Haffa, Israel; Peter Criss (originally Peter Crisscoula) (1947– ) drummer, born New York City; Ace (Paul) Frehley (1951– ) guitarist, born New York City; 'Rock and Roll All Nite', 'Beth', 'I was Made for Lovin' You', 'Tears are Fallin'', *Dressed to Kill* (1975), *Double Platinum* (1978), *Lick It Up* (1983), *Crazy Nights* (1987), *Revenge* (1992), *Alive* (1993).

**Knight, Gladys** (1944– ) American singer, bandleader (The Pips, American group, late 1960s), born Atlanta, Georgia; (with The Pips) 'I Heard It Through The Grapevine', 'Help Me Make It Through The Night', 'Midnight Train To Georgia', 'On And On', *Imagination* (1973), *Visions* (1983), *Life* (1985).

**Kraftwerk** German group, 1970s to present; Ralph Hutter and Florian Schneider; 'Radio Activity', 'The Model', 'Trans Europe Express', 'Computer Love', 'Tour de France', *Autobahn* (1975), *Man Machine* (1978), *Computer World* (1981), *Trans Europe Express* (1982), *The Mix* (1991).

**lang, k d (Katheryn Dawn)** (1962– ) Canadian singer, born Alberta; *A Truly Western Experience* (1983); *Shadowland* (1988); *Absolute Torch and Twang* (1989), *Ingenue* (1992), *Even Cowgirls Get The Blues* (1993, soundtrack), *All You Can Eat* (1995), *Drag* (1997).

**Lauper, Cyndi** (1954– ) American singer, born New York City; 'Time After Time', 'Girls Just Want To Have Fun', 'All Through The Night', 'She Bop', *She's So Unusual* (1983), *True Colors* (1986), *A Night To Remember* (1989), *Hat Full of Stars* (1993).

**Led Zeppelin** British group, late 1960s to 1980s; members include Jimmy Page (1944– ) guitarist, born Heston, London; Robert Plant (1948– ) vocalist, born Bromwich, Staffordshire; John Paul Jones (originally John Baldwin) (1946– ) bassist, born Sidcup; John Bonham (1948–80) drummer, born Redditch; *Led Zeppelin I* (1969), *Led Zeppelin II* (1970), *Led Zeppelin III* (1970), *Led Zeppelin IV* (1971), *Houses of the Holy* (1973), *Physical Graffiti* (1975), *In Through The Out Door* (1979), *Coda* (1982), *Remasters* (1990), *BBC Sessions* (1997).

**Lee, Peggy** (originally **Norma Delores Egstrom**) (1920–2002) American singer, born Jamestown, North Dakota; 'Manana', 'Fever'.

**Lennon, John Winston** (1940–80) British singer/songwriter, guitarist, keyboardist, born Liverpool; 'Give Peace A Chance', 'Working Class Hero', 'Jealous Guy', 'Merry Xmas (War Is Over)', 'Whatever Gets You Through The Night', *Imagine* (1971), *Rock 'n' Roll* (1975), *Double Fantasy* (1980).

**Lewis, Jerry Lee** (1935– ) American pianist, singer, born Ferriday, Louisiana; 'Great Balls of Fire', 'Whole Lotta Shakin' Goin' On', 'High School Confidential', 'Breathless'.

**Little Richard** (originally **Richard Wayne Penniman**) (1935– ) American singer/songwriter, pianist, born Macon, Georgia; 'Tutti Frutti', 'Long Tall Sally', 'Rip It Up', 'The Girl Can't Help It', 'Lucille', 'Jenny, Jenny', 'Good Golly, Miss Molly', 'Lawdy Miss Clawdy', *Life Time Friend* (1986).

**The Lovin' Spoonful** American group, 1960s to 1970s; John Sebastian (1944– ) vocalist, guitarist; Zal Yanovsky (1944– ) guitarist; Steve Boone (1943– ) bassist; Joe Butler (1944– ) drummer; 'Daydream', 'Summer In The City', *Daydream* (1966), *Coal Miner's Daughter* (1971).

**Lulu** (originally **Marie McDonald McLaughlin Lawrie**) (1948– ) British singer, born Glasgow; (with The Luvvers) 'Shout', 'Leave A Little Love'; 'To Sir With Love', 'Boom Bang-A-Bang', 'The Man Who Sold The World' (with David Bowie), *Independence* (1993).

**Lynyrd Skynyrd** American group, 1970s; members include Ronnie Van Zandt (1949–77) vocalist, born McCombe, Minnesota; 'Sweet Home Alabama', 'Freebird', *Pronounced Leh-nerd Skin-nerd* (1973), *Second Helping* (1974), *Street Survivors* (1977), *Gold and Platinum* (1979), *Edge of Forever* (1999).

**McCartney, Sir Paul** (1942– ) British singer/songwriter, guitarist, born Liverpool; 'Wonderful Christmastime', 'Coming Up', 'Ebony and Ivory' (with Stevie Wonder), 'No More Lonely Nights', *Tug of War* (1982), *Pipes of Peace* (1983), *Give My Regards To Broad Street* (1984), *Flowers In The Dirt* (1989), *Off The Ground* (1993), *Flaming Pie* (1997).

**McLean, Don** (1945– ) American singer/songwriter, born New Rochelle, New York; 'And I Love You So', 'Vincent', 'Castles in the Air', *American Pie* (1971), *Chain Lightning* (1981), *Dominion* (1983).

**Madness** British group, late 1970s to 1990s; members include Graham 'Suggs' McPherson (1961– ) vocalist, born Hastings, Sussex; Mike Barson (1958– ) keyboardist, Lee Thompson (1957– ) saxophonist; Chris Foreman (1958– ) guitarist; Mark Bedford (1961– ) bassist; Daniel 'Woody' Woodgate (1960– ) drummer; Chas Smash (originally Carl Smith) (1959– ) vocalist, trumpeter; 'House Of Fun', 'Our House', 'Baggy Trousers', 'Ghost Train', *One Step Beyond* (1979), *Complete Madness* (1982), *Mad Not Mad* (1985), *Utter Madness* (1986).

**Madonna** (originally **Madonna Louise Veronica Ciccone**) (1958– ) American singer/songwriter, born Rochester, Michigan; 'Holiday', 'Crazy For You', 'Gambler', 'Into The Groove', 'Live To Tell', 'Vogue', *Madonna* (1983), *Like a Virgin* (1984), *True Blue* (1986), *Who's that Girl?* (1987), *Like a Prayer* (1989), *The Immaculate Collection* (1990), *Erotica* (1992), *Bedtime Stories* (1994), *Something to Remember* (1995), *Ray of Light* (1998).

**The Mamas and the Papas** American group, late 1960s; members include John Philips (1935–2001) singer/songwriter, guitarist, born Parris Island, South Carolina; Dennis Doherty (1941– ) born Halifax, Nova Scotia; Michelle Phillips (originally Holly Michelle Gilliam) (1944– ) born Long Beach, California; Cass Elliot (originally Ellen Naomi Cohen) (1943–74) vocalist, born Baltimore, Maryland; 'California Dreamin', 'Monday, Monday', 'Dedicated to the One I Love', 'San Francisco'.

**Manfred Mann** British group, 1960s to 1980s; members include Manfred Mann (originally Michael Lubowitz) (1940– ) keyboardist, born Johannesburg, South Africa; Paul Jones (originally Paul Pond) (1942– ) vocalist, harmonica player, born Portsmouth; '5-4-3-2-1', 'Do Wah Diddy Diddy', 'If You Gotta Go, Go Now', 'The Mighty Quinn', 'Pretty Flamingo', 'Blinded By The Light', *The Roaring Silence* (1986), *Ages of Mann* (1993).

**Manilow, Barry** (originally **Barry Alan Pinkus**) (1946– ) American singer/songwriter, pianist, born Brooklyn, New York City; 'Mandy', 'I Write the Songs', 'Looks Like We Made It', 'Copacabana (At the Copa)', *Barry Manilow* (1974), *Barry Manilow II* (1975), *Barry Manilow Live* (1977), *Even Now* (1978), *A Touch More Magic* (1983), *Showstoppers* (1991).

**Marley, Bob** (originally **Robert Nesta Marley**) (1945–81) Jamaican singer/songwriter, guitarist, born Rhoden Hall, St Ann's Parish, Jamaica; (with The

Wailers) 'No Woman, No Cry', 'I Shot the Sheriff', 'Exodus', 'Buffalo Soldier', *Catch a Fire* (1972), *Rastaman Vibration* (1976), *Uprising* (1980).

**Mayall, John** (1933– ) British singer/songwriter, guitarist, harmonica player, born Macclesfield; *Bluesbreakers – John Mayall with Eric Clapton* (1965), *Crusader* (1967), *A Hard Road* (1967), *The Turning Point* (1970), *Wake Up Call* (1993).

**Michael, George** (originally **Yorgos Kyriatou Panayiotou**) (1963– ) British singer/songwriter (was in Wham!, British 1980s group), born Finchley, London; 'Careless Whisper', 'Different Corner', 'I Want Your Sex', *Faith* (1987), *Listen Without Prejudice Vol 1* (1990), *Older* (1996).

**Midler, Bette** (1945– ) American singer, born Honolulu, Hawaii; 'From A Distance', *The Divine Miss M* (1972), *The Rose* (1979), *No Frills* (1983), *Bette of Roses* (1995).

**Miller, Steve** (1943– ) American singer/songwriter, guitarist, born Milwaukee, Wisconsin; 'Rock'n' Me', *The Joker* (1973), *Fly Like An Eagle* (1976), *Abracadabra* (1982), *Living In The 20th Century* (1986).

**Minogue, Kylie** (1968– ) Australian singer, born Melbourne; 'I Should Be So Lucky', *Kylie* (1987), *Enjoy Yourself* (1989), *Rhythm of Love* (1990), *Kylie Minogue* (1994), *Light Years* (2000).

**Mitchell, Joni** (originally **Roberta Joan Anderson**) (1943– ) Canadian singer/songwriter, guitarist, born McLeod, Alberta; 'Big Yellow Taxi', 'Help Me', *Joni Mitchell* (1968), *Clouds* (1969), *Ladies of the Canyon* (1970), *Blue* (1971), *Dog Eat Dog* (1986), *Chalk Mark in a Rain Storm* (1988), *Night Ride Home* (1991), *Turbulent Indigo* (1994).

**The Monkees** American group, late 1960s; members include Mickey Dolenz (1945– ) vocalist, drummer, born Los Angeles; Davy Jones (1946– ) vocalist, born Manchester, England; Peter Tork (originally Peter Torkelson) (1944– ) bassist, born Washington, DC; Mike Nesmith (1942– ) guitarist; 'I'm a Believer', 'Daydream Believer', *Pool It* (1987).

**The Moody Blues** British group, mid 1960s to 1990s; members include Justin Hayward guitarist, John Lodge bassist; Mike Pindar keyboardist; Graeme Edge drummer; Ray Thomas flautist, saxophonist, vocalist; 'Nights in White Satin', *Days of Future Passed* (1967), *Keys To The Kingdom* (1991).

**Morrison, Van** (originally **George Ivan Morrison**) (1945– ) Northern Irish singer/songwriter, guitarist, born Belfast; (with Them Irish group, 1960s) 'Baby Please Don't Go', 'Brown Eyed Girl', *Blowin' Your Mind* (1967); *Enlightenment* (1990), *Hymns To The Silence* (1991), *Too Long in Exile* (1993), *Days Like This* (1995).

**Motörhead** British heavy metal group, late 1970s to present; members include Lemmy (originally Ian Kilminster) (1945– ) vocalist, born Stoke-on-Trent; *Overkill* (1979), *Bomber* (1979), *Ace of Spades* (1980), *No Sleep Till Hammersmith* (1981), *Orgasmatron* (1986), *No Sleep At All* (1988), *1916* (1991), *March or Die* (1992), *Everything Louder than Everyone Else* (1999).

**Moyet, Alison 'Alf'** (1961– ) British singer, born Basildon; 'All Cried Out', 'That Ole Devil Called Love', 'Weak In The Presence Of Beauty', *Alf* (1984), *Chasing Rain* (1987), *Rain Dancing* (1987), *Essex* (1994).

**Nelson, Ricky** (originally **Eric Hilliard Nelson**) (1940–85) American singer, guitarist, born Teaneck, New Jersey; 'Travelin' Man', 'Hello Mary Lou', *Garden Party* (1972).

**The Neville Brothers** American group; Arthur Lanon Neville (1937– ) keyboardist, vocalist, percussionist; Charles Neville (1938– ) saxophonist, flautist, percussionist; Aaron Neville (1941– ) keyboardist, vocalist; Cyril Neville (1948– ) vocalist, percussionist; all born New Orleans, Louisiana; *Yellow Moon* (1989), *Brother's Keeper* (1990).

**Newman, Randy** (originally **Randolph Newman**) (1944– ) American singer/songwriter, pianist, born Los Angeles; 'I Love LA', 'Gone Dead Train', *Sail Away* (1972), *Trouble In Paradise* (1983), *The Natural* (1984) (soundtrack), *Parenthood* (1990) (soundtrack), *Awakenings* (1991) (soundtrack), *Toy Story* (1996) (soundtrack).

**Nirvana** US group, late 1980s to mid 1990s; members include Kurt Cobain (1967–94) vocalist, guitarist, born Aberdeen, Washington; Krist Novoseli (1965– ) bassist, born Croatia; Dave Grohl (1969– ) drummer, born Warren, Ohio; 'Smells Like Teen Spirit', *Nevermind* (1991), *In Utero* (1993), *Unplugged in New York* (1994).

**Oasis** British group, formed Manchester 1992 as Rain; members include Liam Gallagher (1972– ) vocalist; Noel Gallagher (1967– ) guitarist; Paul 'Bonehead' Arthurs (1965– ) guitarist; Paul McGuigan (1971– ) guitarist; Tony McCarroll drummer; *Definitely Maybe* (1994), *(What's The Story) Morning Glory* (1995), *Be Here Now* (1997).

**Oldfield, Mike** (1953– ) British multi-instrumentalist, composer, born Reading, Berkshire; 'Blue Peter', 'Moonlight Shadow', *Tubular Bells* (1973), *Hergest Ridge* (1974), *Ommadawn* (1975), *Killing Fields* (1984), *Islands* (1987), *The Songs of Distant Earth* (1994), *Voyager* (1996).

**Orbison, Roy** (1936–88) American singer/songwriter, guitarist, born Vernon, Texas; 'Only the Lonely', 'Crying', 'Dream Baby', '(Oh) Pretty Woman', 'In Dreams', 'Blue Bayou'.

**The Osmonds** American group, 1970s; members include Alan (1949– ), Wayne (1951– ), Merrill (1953– ), Jay (1955– ), Donny (originally Donald Clark Osmond) (1957– ), and Marie Osmond (1959– ); all born Ogden, Utah; Jimmy (1963– ) born Canoga Park, California, 'Crazy Horses'.

**Palmer, Robert** (1949– ) British singer, born W Yorkshire, England; 'Every Kinda People', 'Bad Case Of Loving You (Doctor Doctor)', 'Some Guys Have All The Luck', 'Addicted To Love', 'She Makes My Day', *Riptide* (1985).

**Peter, Paul and Mary** American trio, 1960s to present; Peter Yarrow (1938– ) guitarist, vocalist, born New York City; Paul Stookey (1937– ) guitarist, vocalist, born Baltimore, Maryland; Mary Travers (1937– ) vocalist, born Louisville, Kentucky; 'If I Had A Hammer', 'Blowing' In The Wind', 'Puff The Magic Dragon', 'Leavin' On A Jet Plane', *Peter, Paul & Mary* (1962), *In The Wind* (1963), *Peter, Paul & Mommy* (1969), *No Easy Walk To Freedom* (1986).

**Pickett, Wilson** (1941– ) American singer, born Prattville, Alabama; 'In The Midnight Hour', '634-5789', 'Hey Jude'.

**Pink Floyd** British group, late 1960s to present; members include 'Syd' (Roger Keith) Barrett (1946– ) singer/songwriter, guitarist; Roger Waters (1944– ) singer/songwriter; David Gilmour (1944– ) singer/songwriter, guitarist; all born Cambridge; *The Piper at the Gates of Dawn* (1967), *A Saucerful of Secrets* (1968), *Ummagumma* (1969), *Meddle* (1971), *Dark Side of the Moon* (1973), *Wish You Were Here* (1975), *The Wall* (1979), *The Final Cut* (1983), *A Momentary Lapse of Reason* (1987), *A Delicate Sound of Thunder* (1988), *The Division Bell* (1994), *Pulse* (1995).

**Pitney, Gene** (1941– ) American singer, born Hartford, Connecticut; 'The Man Who Shot Liberty Valance', '24 Hours From Tulsa'.

**The Pogues** Anglo-Irish group, 1980s to present; members include Shane MacGowan vocalist, Philip Chevron (originally Philip Ryan) (1957– ) guitarist, born Dublin; James Fearnley (1954– ) accordionist, born Manchester; Andrew Ranken (1953– ) drummer, born London; Jem Finer (originally Jeremy Max Finer) (1955– ) banjo player, born Dublin; Spider Stacy (originally Peter Richard Stacy) (1958– ) tin whistle player, born Eastbourne; 'Dirty Old Town', 'Sally Maclennane', 'A Pair of Brown Eyes', 'Irish Rover' (with the Dubliners), *Red Roses For Me* (1984), *Rum, Sodomy & The Lash* (1985), *If I Should Fall From Grace With God* (1988), *Peace and Love* (1989), *Hell's Ditch* (1990), *Waiting For Herb* (1993).

**The Pointer Sisters** American group, 1970s to 1980s; Ruth (1946– ), Anita (1948– ), Bonnie (1950– ), June (1954– ) Pointer; all born Oakland, California; 'Fairy Tale', 'Fire', 'Slow Hand', 'Jump (For My Love)', 'Automatic', 'Neutron Dance', *So Excited!* (1982), *Break Out* (1983), *Serious Slammin'* (1988).

**The Police** British group, late 1970s to 1980s; members include Sting (originally Gordon Sumner) (1951– ), singer/songwriter, bassist, born Wallsend, Northumberland (solo 'Set Them Free', 'Russians', *The Dream of the Blue Turtles* (1985), *Nothing Like The Sun* (1987), *Brand New Day* (1999)); Stewart Copeland (1952– ) drummer, born Alexandria, Virginia; Andy Summers (1942– ) guitarist, born Lancaster; 'Can't Stand Losing You', 'Roxanne', 'Message In A Bottle', 'Walking On The Moon', 'Don't Stand So Close To Me', 'Every Little Thing She Does Is Magic', 'Every Breath You Take', *Outlandos d'Amour* (1978), *Regatta de Blanc* (1979), *Zenyatta Mondatta* (1980), *Synchronicity* (1983).

**Pop, Iggy** (originally **James Newell Osterburg**) (1947– ) American singer/songwriter, drummer, born Ypsilanti, Michigan; 'I Wanna Be Your Dog', *The Stooges* (1969), *Raw Power* (1973) (with the Stooges); 'Nightclubbing', 'The Passenger', 'Real Wild Child', 'Well Did You Evah' (with Deborah Harry), *The Idiot* (1976), *Lust for Life* (1977), *Blah Blah Blah* (1986), *Instinct* (1988), *Brick By Brick* (1990), *American Caesar* (1993), *A Damned Stooge With A Pistol* (1997).

**Presley, Elvis (Aaron)** (1935–77) American singer, guitarist, born Tupelo, Mississippi; 'Heartbreak Hotel', 'Hound Dog', 'Love Me Tender', 'All Shook Up', 'Jailhouse Rock', 'One Night', 'A Fool Such as I', 'It's Now or Never', 'Are You Lonesone Tonight', *G I Blues* (1961), *Blue Hawaii* (1961), *Roustabout* (1964), *From Elvis in Memphis* (1969).

**The Pretenders** British group, late 1970s to present; members include Chrissie Hynde (1951– ) singer/songwriter, guitarist, born Akron, Ohio; 'Back on the Chain Gang', 'Brass in Pocket', *Pretenders* (1979), *Single Records* (1988), *Packed!* (1990), *Last Independents* (1994), *The Isle Of View* (1995).

**Prince** (originally **Prince Rogers Nelson**) (1958– ) American singer/songwriter, guitarist, keyboardist, drummer, born Minneapolis, Minnesota; 'Little Red Corvette', 'Delirious', 'When Doves Cry', 'Let's Go Crazy', 'Raspberry Beret', 'Kiss', *Prince* (1979), *Dirty Mind* (1980), *Controversy* (1981), *1999* (1982), *Purple Rain* (with The Revolution) (1984), *Parade* (1986), *Sign o' the Times* (1987), *Love Sexy* (1988), *Diamonds and Pearls* (1991), *Symbol* (1992), *Come* (1994), *The Gold Experience* (1995).

**Public Enemy** US group, 1980s to present; members include Chuck D (originally Carlton Ridenhour) (1960– ) vocalist; Flavor Flav (originally William Drayton) (1959– ) vocalist, instrumentalist; Terminator X (originally Norman Rogers) (1966– ) DJ; Professor Griff (originally Richard Griffin) (1960– ) vocalist; *Yo! Bum Rush the Show* (1987), *Fear of a Black Planet* (1990), *He Got Game* (soundtrack) (1998).

**Public Image Limited (PIL)** British group, late 1970s to present; members include John Lyndon; 'This Is Not A Love Song', 'Rise', *Flowers Of Romance* (1981), *The Greatest Hits So Far* (1990), *That What Is Not* (1992).

**Pulp** British group, formed Sheffield 1981 as Arabacus Pulp; members include Jarvis Cocker (1962– ) vocalist, guitarist, pianist; Simon Hinkler, keyboardist; Peter Broam, bassist; David Hinkler, keyboardist; Gary Wilson, trombonist; guest vocalists Saskia Cocker and Gill Taylor; guest keyboardist Tim Allcard; 'Common People', 'Underwear', 'Disco 2000', *IT* (1983), *Freaks* (1987), *Separations* (1991), *His 'n' Hers* (1994), *Different Class* (1995).

**Queen** British group, 1970s to present; members include Freddie Mercury (originally Frederick Bulsara) (1946–91) singer/songwriter, born Zanzibar; Brian May (1947– ) guitarist, born Hampton, Middlesex; John Deacon (1951– ) bassist, born Leicester; Roger Taylor (originally Roger Meadows-Taylor) (1949– ) drummer, born Norfolk; 'Seven Seas of Rhye', 'Killer

Queen', 'Bohemian Rhapsody', 'We are the Champions', 'Somebody to Love', 'Another one Bites the Dust', 'Crazy Little Thing Called Love', 'Under Pressure' (with David Bowie), 'Radio Ga-Ga', *Queen II* (1974), *Sheer Heart Attack* (1974), *A Night at the Opera* (1975), *A Day at the Races* (1976), *The Game* (1980), *Hot Space* (1982), *The Works* (1984), *A Kind of Magic* (1986), *The Miracle* (1989), *Innuendo* (1991), *Made In Heaven* (1995).

**Radiohead** British group, formed Oxford 1988; members include Thom Yorke, vocalist, guitarist; Ed O'Brien, guitarist, vocalist; Jon Greenwood, guitarist; Colin Greenwood, bassist; Phil Selway, drummer; *The Bends* (1995), *OK Computer* (1997).

**Ray, Johnnie** (1927–90) American singer, born Rosebud, Oregon; 'Cry'/'The Little White Cloud That Cried', 'Walkin' My Baby Back Home', 'Just Walking In The Rain', 'You Don't Owe Me A Thing', 'I'll Never Fall In Love Again', *The Big Beat* (1957).

**Redding, Otis** (1941–67) American singer/songwriter, born Dawson, Georgia; 'I've Been Loving You Too Long', 'Try a Little Tenderness', 'Mr Pitiful', 'Satisfaction', '(Sittin' On The) Dock of the Bay', 'Respect', *The Otis Redding Story* (1968).

**Reed, Lou** (originally **Louis Firbank**) (1944– ) American singer/songwriter, born Long Island, New York (was founder-member of The Velvet Underground in 1965) 'Walk On The Wild Side', 'I Love You Suzanne', *Lou Reed* (1972), *Transformer* (1972), *Rock 'n' Roll Animal* (1974), *Coney Island Baby* (1976), *Street Hassle* (1978), *New Sensations* (1984), *New York* (1989), *Magic and Loss* (1992), *The Best of Lou Reed and The Velvet Underground* (1995), *Ecstasy* (2000).

**Martha Reeves and The Vandellas** American group, 1960s; members include Martha Reeves (1941– ) singer; Rosalind Ashford (1943– ) singer; Betty Kelly (1944– ) singer; all born Detroit, Michigan; 'Nowhere To Run', 'I'm Ready For Love', 'Jimmy Mack', 'Dancing In The Street'.

**REM** American group, 1980s to present; members include Michael Stipe (1960– ) vocalist; Peter Buck (1956– ) guitarist; Michael Mills (1958– ) bassist; Bill Berry (1958– ) drummer; 'World Leader Pretend', 'The One I Love', 'Stand', 'Superman', 'Orange Crush', 'Losing my Religion', 'Shiny Happy People', *Murmur* (1983), *Reckoning* (1984), *Life's Rich Pageant* (1986), *Number 5: Document* (1987), *Green* (1989), *Out of Time* (1991), *Automatic For The People* (1992), *Monster* (1994).

**Richard, Sir Cliff** (originally **Harry Rodger Webb**) (1940– ) British singer/songwriter, guitarist, born Lucknow, India; over 100 hits including 'Livin' Doll', 'The Young Ones', 'Summer Holiday', 'Congratulations', *21 Today* (1961), *Rock & Roll Juvenile* (1971), *Love Songs* (1981), *Wired For Sound* (1981), *Now You See Me, Now You Don't* (1982), *Dressed For The Occasion* (1983), *Always Guaranteed* (1987), *Private Collection* (1988), *The Album* (1993), *Songs From Heathcliff* (1995).

**Richie, Lionel** (originally **Lionel Brockman Richie, Jr**) (1949– ) American singer/songwriter, pianist, born Tuskegee, Alabama; 'All Night Long', 'Say You', *Can't Slow Down* (1983), *Dancing On The Ceiling* (1986), *Back To Front* (1992), *Renaissance* (2001).

**The Righteous Brothers** American duo, 1960s to 1970s; Bobby Hatfield (1940– ) singer, born Beaver Dam, Wisconsin; Bill Medley (1940– ) singer, born Los Angeles; 'You've Lost That Lovin' Feelin'', 'Just Once In My Life', 'Unchained Melody', 'Ebb Tide', 'Rock And Roll Heaven'.

**Robinson, Smokey** (originally **William Robinson, Jr**) (1940– ) American singer/songwriter, born Detroit, Michigan; (with The Miracles, American group, 1960s) 'Shop Around', 'The Tracks Of My Tears', 'I Second That Emotion'; 'Being With You', *Where There's Smoke* (1979), *Smoke Signals* (1986).

**The Rolling Stones** British group, 1960s to present; members include 'Mick' (Michael Philip) Jagger (1943– ) vocalist, harmonica-player, born Dartford, Kent (solo 'Just Another Night', 'Dancing In The Street' (with David Bowie), *She's The Boss* (1985)); Keith Richards (1943– ) guitarist, born Dartford, Kent; Bill Wyman (originally William Perks) (1936– ) bassist, born Penge, London; Charlie Watts (1941– ) drummer, born Neasden, London; Brian Jones (originally Lewis Brian Hopkin-Jones) (1942–69) guitarist, born Cheltenham replaced by Mick Taylor (1948– ) born Hertfordshire replaced by Ron Wood (1947– ) born Hillingdon, Middlesex; Ian Stewart (1938–85) keyboardist; 'It's All Over Now', 'Little Red Rooster, 'The Last Time', '(I Can't Get No) Satisfaction', 'Get Off My Cloud', '19th Nervous Breakdown', 'Paint It Black', 'Mother's Little Helper', 'Let's Spend The Night Together', 'Jumpin' Jack Flash', 'Sympathy For The Devil', 'Honky Tonk Women', 'You Can't Always Get What You Want', 'Brown Sugar', 'Miss You', *The Rolling Stones* (1964), *Aftermath* (1966), *Beggar's Banquet* (1968), *Let it Bleed* (1969), *Get Yer Ya-Ya's Out* (1970), *Sticky Fingers* (1971), *Exile on Main Street* (1972), *Goat's Head Soup* (1973), *Some Girls* (1978), *Emotional Rescue* (1980), *Tattoo You* (1981), *Undercover* (1983), *Dirty Work* (1986), *Steel Wheels* (1989), *Flashpoint* (1990), *Voodoo Lounge* (1994), *Stripped* (1995).

**Ross, Diana** (1944– ) American singer, born Detroit, Michigan; with the Supremes, 1960s group; 'Ain't No Mountain High Enough', 'Baby Love', 'Stop! In the Name of Love', 'You Can't Hurry Love', 'You Keep Me Hangin' On', 'Where Did Our Love Go', 'I'm Gonna Make You Love Me'; with Lionel Richie: 'Endless Love'; 'Upside Down', 'I'm Coming Out', 'My Old Piano', 'Chain Reaction', *Diana* (1980), *Eaten Alive* (1985) *Red Hot Rhythm 'n' Blues* (1987), *The Force Behind The Power* (1991), *Take Me Higher* (1995).

**Roxy Music** British group, 1970s to early 1980s; members include Bryan Ferry (1945– ) singer, born Washington, County Durham; Brian Eno (1948– ) songwriter, keyboardist, born Woodbridge, Suffolk; Phil Manzanera (originally Philip Targett-Adams) (1941– ) guitarist, born London; Andy Mackay

(1946– ) saxophonist; 'Virginia Plain', 'Do The Strand', 'Street Life', 'Love is the Drug', 'Dance Away', 'Angel Eyes', 'Jealous Guy', 'My Only Love', *Roxy Music* (1972), *Stranded* (1973), *Siren* (1975), *Manifesto* (1980), *Avalon* (1982).

**Rush** Canadian heavy metal group, 1970s to present; members include Geddy Lee (1953– ) vocalist, bassist, born Willowdale; Alex Lifeson (1953– ) guitarist, born Fernie, British Columbia; Neil Peart (1952– ) drummer, born Hamilton, Ontario; *2112* (1976), *All The World's A Stage* (1976), *Moving Pictures* (1981), *Power Windows* (1985), *Hold Your Fire* (1987), *Roll The Bones* (1991), *Counterparts* (1993).

**Sade** (originally **Helen Folasade Adu**) Anglo-Nigerian singer/songwriter, born Ibadan, Nigeria; 'Smooth Operator', 'Paradise', *Diamond Life* (1984), *Promise* (1985), *Stronger than Pride* (1988), *Love Deluxe* (1992).

**Santana, Carlos** (1947– ) Mexican guitarist, vocalist, born Autlan de Novarra, Jalisco, Mexico; (with band Santana, late 1960s to present) 'Black Magic Woman', *Santana* (1969), *Abraxas* (1970), *Amigos* (1976), *Moonflower* (1977), *Zebop!* (1981), *Freedom* (1987), *Supernatural* (1999).

**Sedaka, Neil** (1939– ) American singer/songwriter; 'Breaking Up Is Hard To Do', 'Laughter In The Rain', 'Bad Blood', *Laughter And Tears: Best of Neil Sedaka Today* (1976).

**The Sex Pistols** British punk group, 1970s; members include Johnny Rotten (originally John Lydon) (1956– ) vocalist; Steve Jones (1955– ) guitarist; Paul Cook (1956– ) drummer; Sid Vicious (originally John Simon Ritchie) (1958–79) singer, bassist; 'Anarchy in the UK', 'God Save The Queen', 'Pretty Vacant', 'Holidays In The Sun', 'My Way', 'Something Else', 'C'mon Everybody', 'Silly Thing', *Never Mind the Bollocks – Here's The Sex Pistols* (1977), *Some Product* (1978), *Flogging a Dead Horse* (1979), *The Great Rock 'n' Roll Swindle* (1980), *Kiss This* (1992).

**The Shadows** British group, late 1950s to present; members include Hank Marvin (originally Brian Rankin) (1941– ) guitarist, born Newcastle upon Tyne; Bruce Welch (1941– ) guitarist, born Newcastle upon Tyne; Jet Harris (originally Terry Harris) (1939– ) bassist, born London; Tony Meehan (1943– ) drummer, born London; 'Apache', 'Kon Tiki', 'Wonderful Land', 'Dance On', 'Foot Tapper', 'Don't Cry For Me Argentina', *Moonlight Shadows* (1986), *Reflection* (1990), *Shadows In The Night* (1993).

**The Shangri-las** American group, mid 1960s; Betty Weiss singer; Mary Weiss; Marge and Mary Ann Ganser; 'Leader Of The Pack', 'Past, Present, And Future'.

**Shannon, Del** (1939–90) American singer, born Coopersville, Michigan; 'Runaway', *Little Town Flirt* (1963), *Drop Down And Get Me* (1983).

**Shaw, Sandie** (originally **Sandra Goodrich**) (1947– ) British singer, born Dagenham, Essex; 'There's Always Something There To Remind Me', 'Long Live Love', 'Puppet on a String', 'Hand In Glove', 'Are You Ready To Be Heartbroken?', *Nothing Less Than Brilliant* (1994).

**Simon, Carly** (1945– ) American singer/songwriter, born New York City; 'You're So Vain', 'Nobody Does It Better', 'Coming Round Again', 'Let The River Run', *No Secrets* (1972).

**Simon, Paul** (1941– ) American singer/songwriter, guitarist, born Newark, New Jersey; with Art Garfunkel (1942– ) singer, born Forest Hills, New York; 'The Sound of Silence', 'Mrs Robinson', 'Bridge over Troubled Water', 'The Boxer', 'Scarborough Fair', 'Homeward Bound', *Bridge over Troubled Water* (1970); 'You Can Call Me Al', *Paul Simon* (1972), *Graceland* (1986), *Rhythm of the Saints* (1990), *Greatest Hits: Shining Like a National Guitar* (2000).

**Simone, Nina** (originally **Eunice Waymon**) (1933– ) American singer, born Tryon, N Carolina; 'I Loves You, Porgy', 'My Baby Just Cares For Me', 'Mississippi Goddam'.

**Simple Minds** British group, late 1970s to present; members include Jim Kerr singer, born Glasgow; Charlie Burchill guitarist; Mel Gaynor drummer; Derek Forbes bassist replaced by John Giblin; Mick McNeil keyboardist; Duncan Barnwell guitarist; 'Don't You (Forget about Me)', 'Belfast Child', *New Gold Dream* (1982), *Sparkle In The Rain* (1984), *Once upon a Time* (1985), *Live in the City of Light* (1987), *Street Fighting Years* (1989), *Real Life* (1991), *Glittering Prize 81/92* (1992), *Good News From The Next World* (1995).

**Simply Red** British group, 1980s; members include Mick Hucknall singer/songwriter; Tony Bowers bassist; Chris Joyce drummer; Fritz McIntyre keyboardist; Sylvan Richardson guitarist; 'Money's Too Tight To Mention', 'Holding Back The Years', *Picture Book* (1985), *Men And Women* (1987), *A New Flame* (1989), *Stars* (1991), *Life* (1995), *Blue* (1998).

**Sinatra, Frank (Francis Albert)** (1915–98) American singer, born Hoboken, New Jersey; 'I've Got You Under My Skin', 'Strangers In The Night', 'The Lady Is A Tramp', 'Theme From New York, New York', 'My Way', *Songs For Swingin' Lovers* (1956), *Come Fly with Me* (1962).

**Siouxsie and the Banshees** British group, late 1970s to present; members include Siouxsie Sioux (originally Susan Janet Dallion) (1957– ) singer/songwriter, born London; Steve Severin (originally Steve Bailey) (1955– ) bassist, born London; Budgie (originally Peter Clarke) (1957– ) drummer, born St Helens, Lancashire; 'Wheel's On Fire', *The Scream* (1979), *Kaleidoscope* (1980), *Tinderbox* (1986), *Through The Looking Glass* (1987), *Peepshow* (1988), *Superstition* (1991), *The Rapture* (1995).

**Sly and the Family Stone** American funk and soul group, 1960s to present; members include Sly Stone (originally Sylvester Stewart) (1944– ) vocalist, guitarist, keyboardist; Freddie Stone (1946– ) guitarist; Cynthia Robinson (1946– ) trumpeter; Larry Graham (1946– ) guitarist; Rosemary Stone (1945– ) vocalist, pianist; 'Dance To The Music', 'Everyday People', *Greatest Hits* (1970).

**Smith, Patti** (1946– ) American singer/songwriter, born Chicago; 'Because the Night', *Horses* (1976), *Easter* (1978), *Dream Of Life* (1988).

**The Smiths** British group, 1980s; members include (Steven Patrick) Morrissey (1959– ) singer/songwriter (solo 'Everyday Is Like Sunday', *Viva Hate* (1988)); Johnny Marr (1963– ) guitarist, songwriter; both born Manchester; 'Hand In Glove', 'Bigmouth Strikes Again', 'Boy With The Thorn In His Side', 'Panic', *The Smiths* (1984), *Meat Is Murder* (1985), *Hatful of Hollow* (1985), *The Queen Is Dead* (1986), *Strangeways, Here We Come* (1987).

**Spandau Ballet** British group, 1980s to present; members include Tony Hadley (originally Anthony Patrick Hadley) (1959– ) vocalist, born Islington; Gary Kemp (1960– ) guitarist, songwriter; Martin Kemp (1961– ) bassist; both born London; John Keeble (1959– ) drummer; Steve Norman (1960– ) guitarist; 'Gold', 'True', *Parade* (1984).

**The Spice Girls** British group, late 1990s; members include Posh Spice (Victoria Adams) (1975– ); Sporty Spice (Melanie Chisholm) (1974– ); Ginger Spice (Geri Halliwell) (1972– ); Scary Spice (Melanie Brown) (1975– ) and Baby Spice (Emma Bunton) (1976– ); 'Say You'll Be There', '2 Become 1', 'Spice Up Your Life', *Spice* (1996), *Spice World* (1997), *Forever* (2000).

**Springfield, Dusty** (originally **Mary O'Brien**) (1939–99) British singer, born Hampstead, London; 'I Only Want To Be With You', 'You Don't Have To Say You Love Me', *Dusty In Memphis* (1969), *Reputation* (1990), *A Very Fine Love* (1995).

**Springsteen, Bruce (Frederick Joseph)** (1949– ) American singer/songwriter, guitarist, born Freehold, New Jersey; 'Hungry Heart', 'Dancing In The Dark', 'Brilliant Disguise', *Greetings from Ashbury Park, NJ* (1973), *Born to Run* (1975), *Darkness on the Edge of Town* (1978), *The River* (1980), *Nebraska* (1982), *Born in the USA* (1985), *Tunnel of Love* (1987), *Human Touch* (1992), *Lucky Town* (1992), *In Concert – MTV Plugged* (1993), *The Ghost of Tom Joad* (1995).

**Squeeze** British group, mid 1970s to present; members include Glen Tilbrook (1957– ); Chris Difford (1954– ); both guitarists, vocalists, songwriters; Jools Holland (1954– ) keyboardist replaced by Paul Carrack (1951– ) born Sheffield; John Bentley (1951– ) bassist; Gilson Lavis (1951– ) drummer; 'Goodbye Girl', 'Up The Junction', *Cool For Cats* (1979), *East Side Story* (1981), *Cosi Fan Tutti Frutti* (1985), *Babylon And On* (1987), *Frank* (1989), *Play* (1991), *Some Fantastic Place* (1993), *Ridiculous* (1995).

**Status Quo** British group, 1970s to present; members include Francis Rossi (1949– ) guitarist, vocalist; Richard Parfitt (1948– ) guitarist, vocalist; Alan Lancaster (1949– ) bassist; John Coghland (1946– ) drummer; all born London; 'Down, Down', 'Caroline', 'You're in the Army Now', *Piledriver* (1973), *Hello* (1973), *On The Level* (1975), *Blue For You* (1976), *Rockin' All Over the World* (1978), *Back To Back* (1983), *In The Army Now* (1986), *Rocking All Over The Years* (1990), *Live Alive Quo* (1992), *Thirsty Work* (1994).

**Steely Dan** American group, 1970s to present; Walter Becker (1950– ) bassist, guitarist; Donald Fagen (1948– ) keyboardist; 'Reelin' In The Years', *Aja* (1977), *Gaucho* (1980), *Gold* (1982), *Alive In America* (1995).

**Stevens, Cat** (originally **Steven Demitri Georgiou**) (1947– ) British singer/songwriter, born London; 'Lady D'Arbanville', 'Wild World', 'Peace Train', 'Morning Has Broken', *Tea For The Tillerman* (1971), *Teaser & The Firecat* (1971), *Catch Bull At Four* (1972), *Foreign* (1973), *Buddha And The Chocolate Box* (1974).

**Stewart, Rod(erick David)** (1945– ) British singer/songwriter, guitarist, born London; *Long Player* (1971) (with the Faces); 'Maggie May', 'You Wear It Well', 'Sailing', 'Do Ya Think I'm Sexy?', 'I Don't Want To Talk About It', 'Passion', 'Baby Jane', 'Stay with Me', 'Young Turks', 'The Motown Song', *Every Picture Tells A Story* (1971), *Atlantic Crossing* (1975), *Blondes Have More Fun* (1978), *Tonight I'm Yours* (1981), *Body Wishes* (1983), *Every Beat Of My Heart* (1986), *Out Of Order* (1988), *Vagabond Heart* (1991), *Unplugged And Seated* (1993), *A Spanner In The Works* (1995).

**The Stranglers** British group, mid 1970s to present; members include Hugh Cornwell (1949– ) vocalist, guitarist; Jean-Jacques Burnel, vocalist, bassist; 'Peaches', 'Walk On By', 'Golden Brown', 'Always The Sun', '96 Tears', *Rattus Norvegicus* (1977), *No More Heroes* (1977), *Feline* (1983), *Aural Structure* (1984), *Dreamtime* (1986), *Ten* (1990), *Stranglers In The Night* (1992), *About Time* (1992).

**Streisand, Barbra (Joan)** (1942– ) American singer/songwriter, born Brooklyn, New York City; (with Neil Diamond) 'You Don't Bring Me Flowers'; 'Guilty', *Stoney End* (1971), *The Way We Were* (1974), *Streisand Superman* (1977), *Emotion* (1984), *One Voice* (1987), *A Love Like Ours* (1999).

**Summer, Donna** (originally **Donna Adrian Gaines**) (1948– ) American singer, born Boston, Massachusetts; 'Love To Love You Baby', 'I Feel Love', 'Last Dance', 'Hot Stuff', 'Highway Runner', 'He's A Rebel', 'Forgive Me', 'Dinner With Gershwin', *Live And More* (1978), *Bad Girls* (1979), *The Wanderer* (1980), *She Works Hard For The Money* (1983), *All Systems Go* (1987), *Another Place and Time* (1989).

**Talking Heads** American group, mid 1970s to present; members include David Byrne (1952– ) singer/songwriter, guitarist, born Dumbarton, Scotland; Chris Frantz (1951– ) drummer, born Fort Campbell, Kentucky; Martina 'Tina' Weymouth (1950– ) bassist, born Coronado, California; Jerry Harrison (1949– ) keyboardist, born Milwaukee, Wisconsin; 'Psycho Killer', 'Burning Down the House', 'Road to Nowhere', 'And She Was', *Talking Heads* (1977), *Fear of Music* (1979), *Remain in the Light* (1980), *Speaking In Tongues* (1983), *Little Creatures* (1985), *True Stories* (1986), *Naked* (1988), *Once In a Lifetime/Sand In The Vaseline* (1992).

**Taylor, James** (1948– ) American singer/songwriter, guitarist, born Boston, Massachusetts; 'You've Got A Friend', *Mud Slide Slim And The Blue Horizon* (1971), *One Man Dog* (1972), *Gorilla* (1975), *That's Why I'm Here* (1986), *Never Die Young* (1988).

**The Temptations** Black American group, 1960s to present; members have included David Ruffin (1941– ) singer; Eddie Kendricks (1939– ) singer; Dennis Edwards (1943– ) singer; Melvin Franklin (1942– ); Otis Williams (1941– ); Damon Harris (1950– ); over 80 hit singles since 1962; 'Just My Imagination (Running Away With Me)', 'Treat Her Like a Lady', 'Papa Was A Rolling Stone', *Diana Ross & The Supremes Join The Temptations* (1968), *All Directions* (1972), *Truly For You* (1984).

**Thin Lizzy** Irish heavy rock group, 1970s to mid 1980s; members include Phil Lynott (1951–86) vocalist, bassist (solo 'Yellow Pearl', 'Nineteen'); Brian Downey (1951– ) drummer; Eric Bell (1947– ) guitarist, born Belfast; Gary Moore vocalist, guitarist, born Dublin; Brian Robertson (1956– ) guitarist, born Glasgow; Scott Gorham (1951– ) guitarist, born Santa Monica, California; 'Whiskey In The Jar', 'The Boys Are Back In Town', *Jailbreak* (1976), *Live And Dangerous* (1978), *Black Rose* (1979), *China Town* (1980), *Adventures of Thin Lizzy* (1981), *Thunder and Lightning* (1983).

**Turner, Tina** (originally **Annie Mae Bullock**) (1938– ) American singer/songwriter, born Nutbush, Tennessee; (with Ike Turner 1931– ) singer, pianist, born Clarksdale, Missisipi) 'River Deep, Mountain High', 'Nutbush City Limits', *The Best of Ike and Tina Turner* (1976); 'Let's Stay Together', 'What's Love Got to Do with It', 'Better Be Good To Me', 'We Don't Need Another Hero', *Private Dancer* (1984), *Break Every Rule* (1986), *Live In Europe* (1988), *Foreign Affair* (1989), *Simply The Best* (1991), *What's Love Got To Do With It* (1993) (soundtrack).

**UB40** British group, 1980s to present; members include Ali Campbell (1959– ) singer, guitarist; Robin Campbell (1954– ) guitarist; Jim Brown (1957– ) drummer; Brian Travers (1959– ) saxophonist; Earl Falconer (1959– ) bassist; Norman Hassan (1958– ) percussionist; Mickey Virtue (1957– ) keyboardist; 'Red Red Wine', 'I Got You Babe', 'Don't Break My Heart', 'Sing Our Own Song', *Signing Off* (1982), *Labour Of Love* (1983), *Baggariddim* (1985), *Rat In The Kitchen* (1986), *Labour of Love II* (1989), *Promises and Lies* (1993).

**U2** Irish group, 1980s to present; members include Bono (originally Paul Hewson) (1960– ) vocalist, born Dublin; The Edge (originally David Evans) (1961– ) guitarist, Larry Mullen (1961– ) drummer; Adam Clayton (1960– ) bassist; 'New Year's Day', 'Pride (In The Name of Love)', 'Sunday, Bloody Sunday', 'With Or Without You', 'Desire', *War* (1983), *Live Under a Blood Red Sky* (1983), *The Unforgettable Fire* (1984), *The Joshua Tree* (1987), *Rattle and Hum* (1988), *Achtung Baby* (1991), *Zooropa* (1993), *Pop* (1997), *All That You Can't Leave Behind* (2000).

**Valens, Ritchie** (originally **Richard Valenzuela**) (1941–59) American singer/songwriter, guitarist, born Pacoima, California; 'Come On, Let's Go', 'Donna', 'La Bamba'.

**Vandross, Luther** (1951– ) American soul singer; 'Never Too Much', 'Here And Now', *Give Me The Reason* (1986), *Any Love* (1988).

**Van Halen** American group, late 1970s to present; members include David Lee Roth (1955– ) vocalist, born Bloomingdale, Indiana (solo 'California Girls', 'Yankee Rose', *Eat 'Em and Smile* (1986), *Skyscraper* (1987)); Sammy Hagar (1951– ) singer/songwriter, guitarist, born Monterey, California (solo 'I've Done Everything For You', 'You're Love is Driving Me Crazy', 'Two Sides of Love', 'I Can't Drive 55', *Three Lock Box* (1983), *Voice of America* (1984)); Eddie Van Halen guitarist; Alex Van Halen drummer; both born the Netherlands; Michael Anthony bassist; 'You Really Got Me', 'Jump', 'Panama', 'Hot For Teacher', 'Why Can't This Be Love', *Van Halen* (1978), *Van Halen II* (1979), *Women And Children First* (1980), *Fair Warning* (1981), *Diver Down* (1982), *1984* (1984), *5150* (1986), *OU812* (1988), *For Unlawful Carnal Knowledge* (1991), *Live – Right Here Now* (1993), *Balance* (1995).

**Vega, Suzanne** (1959– ) American singer/songwriter, guitarist, born Santa Monica, California; 'Marlene On The Wall', 'Small Blue Thing', 'Left Of Center', 'Luka', 'Tom's Diner', *Suzanne Vega* (1985), *Solitude Standing* (1987), *Days of Open Hand* (1990), *99.9°F* (1992).

**The Velvet Underground** American group, late 1960s; members include John Cale (1940– ) guitarist, viola player, born Garnant, Wales; Nico (originally Christa Paffgen) (d.1988) vocalist, born Cologne, Germany; Lou Reed (originally Louis Firbank) (1944– ) singer/songwriter, guitarist, born Long Island, New York; *The Velvet Underground & Nico* (1967), *White Light, White Heat* (1968), *The Velvet Underground* (1969), *VU* (1985), *Live MCMXCIII* (1993).

**The Verve** British group, formed Wigan 1991; members include Richard Ashcroft ('Mad Richard') (1971– ) vocalist; Nick McCabe, guitarist; Simon Jones, bassist; Peter Salisbury, drummer; *A Storm In Heaven* (1993), *A Northern Soul* (1995), *Urban Hymns* (1997).

**Vincent, Gene** (originally **Vincent Eugene Craddock**) (1935–71) American singer, born Norfolk, Virginia; (with the Blue Caps) 'Be-Bop-a-Lula', 'Pistol Packin' Mama', 'Bird Doggin''.

**Waits, Tom** (1949– ) American singer/songwriter, pianist, born Pamona, California; *Small Change* (1976), *Swordfishtrombone* (1983), *The Asylum Years* (1984), *Rain Dogs* (1985), *Frank's Wild Years* (1987), *Big Time* (1988), *Bone Machine* (1992), *The Black Rider* (1993).

**Warwick, Dionne** (also **Marie Dionne Warwicke**) (1940– ) American singer/songwriter, pianist, born East Orange, New Jersey; 'There Came You' (with The Spinners); (Dionne & Friends) 'That's What Friends Are For'; *Dionne* (1979), Heartbreaker (1982), *So Amazing* (1983), *Without Your Love* (1985), *Love Songs* (1990), *Christmas In Vienna II* (1994).

**Wham!** British group, 1980s; George Michael (originally Yorgos Kyriatou Panayiotou) (1963– )

singer/songwriter, born Finchley, London; Andrew Ridgely (1963– ) singer, guitarist, born Bushey, Hertsfordshire; 'Young Guns (Go For It)', 'Club Tropicana', 'Wake Me Up Before You Go-Go', 'Freedom', 'Last Christmas', 'I'm Your Man', 'Edge of Heaven', *Fantastic* (1983), *Make It Big* (1984), *The Final* (1986).

**White, Barry** (1944– ) American, born Galveston, Texas; 'Can't Get Enough Of Your Love, Babe', *Can't Get Enough* (1974), *Right Now Barry White* (1987), *The Right Night And Barry White* (1987), *The Icon Is Love* (1995).

**The Who** British group, late 1960s to 1990s; members include Pete Townshend (1945– ) singer/songwriter, guitarist (solo *Who Came First* (1972)); Roger Daltry (1944– ) vocalist, born London (solo *After The Fire* (1985)); John Entwhistle (1944– ) bassist, French horn player; Keith Moon (1947–78) drummer; all born London; 'Substitute', 'Won't Get Fooled Again', 'You Better You Bet', *My Generation* (1966), *The Who Sell Out* (1967), *Tommy* (1969), *Who's Next* (1971), *Quadrophenia* (1973), *Face Dances* (1981), *It's Hard* (1982), *Who's Last* (1984), *Who's Better Who's Best* (1988), *Join Together* (1990), *30 Years of Maximum R&B* (1994).

**Williams, Robbie** (1974– ) British singer/songwriter, born Stoke-on-Trent (with Take That, 1990s) 'It Only Takes a Minute', 'Back for Good'; (solo) 'Angels', 'She's the One', 'Millennium', *Life Thru a Lens* (1997), *Sing When You're Winning* (2000).

**Wings** British group, 1970s; members include Paul McCartney (1942– ) singer/songwriter, guitarist; 'Give Ireland Back to the Irish', 'Venus and Mars', 'Live and Let Die', 'Crossroads', 'Mull of Kintyre', *Band On The Run* (1973), *Wild Life* (1973), *Wings over America* (1976).

**Wonder, Stevie** (originally **Steveland Judkins** or **Stevland Morris**) (1950– ) American singer/songwriter, harmonica player, keyboardist, born Saginaw, Michigan; 'Fingertips', 'Superstition', 'You Are The Sunshine Of My Life', 'Isn't She Lovely', 'Master Blaster', 'Happy Birthday', 'I Just Called to Say I Love You', 'Part-Time Lover', 'Ebony and Ivory' (with Paul McCartney), *Stevie Wonder/The 12 Year Old Genius* (1961), *Music of My Mind* (1972), *Talking Book* (1972), *Innervisions* (1973), *Songs in the Key of Life* (1976), *Hotter than July* (1980), *In Square Circle* (1985), *Characters* (1987), *Jungle Fever* (1991) (soundtrack), *Conversation Peace* (1995).

**Yardbirds** British group, 1960s; members include Keith Relf (1943–76) singer, harmonica player, born Richmond, Surrey; Paul Samwell-Smith (1943– ) bassist, born Twickenham, Middlesex; Chris Dreja (1946– ) guitarist, born Surbiton, Surrey; Eric Clapton guitarist; Jeff Beck guitarist; Jimmy Page bassist, guitarist; 'Good Morning Little Schoolgirl', 'For Your Love', 'I'm A Man', 'Happening Ten Years Time Ago'.

**Yes** British group, 1970s to present; members include Jon Anderson (1944– ) vocalist, born Lancashire; Rick Wakeman (1949– ) keyboardist, born London; Steve Howe (1947– ) guitarist, born London; Chris Squire (1948– ) bassist, born London; 'Owner of a Lonely Heart', *Fragile* (1972), *Close to the Edge* (1972), *90125* (1983), *Big Generator* (1987), *Union* (1991), *Talk* (1994).

**Young, Neil** (1945– ) Canadian singer/songwriter, guitarist, born Toronto; 'Heart Of Gold', *After the Gold Rush* (1970), *Harvest* (1972), *Tonight's the Night* (1975), *Zuma* (1975), *Rust Never Sleeps* (1979), *Reactor* (1981), *Landing On Water* (1986), *Freedom* (1989), *Ragged Glory* (1990), *Harvest Moon* (1992), *Unplugged* (1993), *Sleeps With The Angels* (1994), *Mirror Ball* (1995).

**Zappa, Frank** (originally **Francis Vincent Zappa, Jr**) (1940–93) American singer/songwriter, guitarist, bandleader (The Mothers of Invention, American 1970s group), born Baltimore, Maryland; 'Valley Girl', *Apostrophe* (1974), *Joe's Garage* (1979), *Ship Arriving Too Late To Save A Drowning Witch* (1982), *The Perfect Stranger And Other Works* (1985), *Guitar* (1988).

**ZZ Top** American group, 1970s to present; Billy Gibbons vocalist, guitarist; Dusty Hill vocalist, bassist; Frank Beard drummer; 'Gimme All Your Lovin'', 'Sharp Dressed Man', 'Legs', 'Sleeping Bag', *Tres Hombres* (1973), *Tejas* (1976), *Deguello* (1979), *Eliminator* (1983), *Afterburner* (1985), *Recycler* (1990), *Antenna* (1994).

## Jazz musicians and singers

Selected songs, compositions and albums are listed.

**Adderley, 'Cannonball' (Julian Edwin)** (1928–75) American alto saxophonist, bandleader and composer, born Tampa, Florida. Played blues and funk, one of the first to electrify the saxophone; made hits out of Afro-American themes; 'Sermonette', 'This Here', 'Work Song'.

**Armstrong, Louis (Daniel) ('Satchmo')** (1900–71) American trumpeter and singer, born New Orleans. First major jazz virtuoso and exponent of 'scat' singing (vocal imitation of an instrument); appeared in more than 50 films, also very successful commercially; 'Mack the Knife', 'Blueberry Hill', 'Hello Dolly!'.

**Ayler, Albert** (1936–70) American tenor saxophonist, born Cleveland, Ohio. Influenced from youth by gospel and religious bands; début at 16 with Little Walter as sax player; developed Free Jazz style; 'Bells', 'Ghosts'.

**Baker, Chet (Chesney H)** (1929–88) American, born Yale, Oklahoma. One of the most lyrical trumpeters in jazz history, at centre of West Coast 'cool jazz' scene; had success with Gerry Mulligan's pianoless quartet with 'My Funny Valentine'.

**Barbieri, Gato (Leandro J)** (1934– ) Argentinian clarinettist, tenor saxophonist and composer, born Rosario, Argentina. Made début playing the requinto

(clarinet) in the 'milonga' bands, then developed own styles, from Free Jazz to Latin; tenor player of tropical alcoves and clubs; won Grammy for film soundtrack *Last Tango in Paris* (1972).

**Basie, 'Count' (William Allen)** (1904–84) American pianist and bandleader, born Red Bank, New Jersey. Major big band (16-piece) leader of the swing era; Kansas City style music; compositions include 'One O'Clock Jump' and 'Jumpin' at the Woodside'.

**Bechet, Sidney (Joseph)** (1897–1959) American clarinettist and soprano saxophonist, born New Orleans. Began in New Orleans style; contributed to the popularization of jazz, mingling tradition with accessible tunes; 'Les Oignons', 'Petite Fleur', 'Dans les Rues d'Antibes'; music for ballet *La Nuit est une Sorcière*.

**Beiderbecke, Bix (Leon)** (1903–31) American cornetist and pianist, born Davenport, Iowa. First great white jazz musician, characterized by his richly harmonic tone and soft, warm sonority; 'I'm comin' Virginia', 'In the Dark', 'In a Mist' (piano solo).

**Bennett, Tony (Anthony Dominick Benedetto)** (1926– ) American jazz and popular singer, born New York. Established reputation as singer in 1950s, graduating towards jazz in the 1960s; 'I Left My Heart in San Francisco'. Recorded two albums with pianist Bill Evans in the 1970s.

**Blakey, Art ('Bu') (Buhaina, Abdullah ibn)** (1919–90) American drummer and bandleader, born Pittsburgh, Pennsylvania. Leading exponent of 'hard bop' style; played in double time; studied African rhythms; leader of The Jazz Messengers; composed score for 1985 film *Des Femmes Disparaissent; Oh, By the Way, New York Scene*.

**Bley, Carla** (née **Borg**) (1938– ) American pianist, bandleader and composer, born Oakland, California. Elegant rhythm 'n' blues, blended bebop and folk; leader of own band and record company; compositions include 'Ida Lupina', 'Sing Me Softly of the Blues' and Gary Burton's masterpiece 'A Genuine Tong Funeral'.

**Broonzy, Big Bill (Conley, William Lee)** (1893–1958) American singer, musician and composer, born Scott, Mississippi. Guitar accompanist and composer to the great blues players of his generation; played in ragtime style, also encompassing folksong, rural and urban blues; 'See See Rider', 'Trouble in Mind', his own 'Texas Tornado' and 'Bossie Woman' and recordings of John Hampton's 1938–9 *Spirituals to Sing* concerts.

**Brown, Sandy (Alexander)** (1929– ) Anglo-Indian clarinettist, bandleader and composer, born Izatnagar, India. Outstanding blues player. Originally influenced by Louis Armstrong's Hot Five and the New Orleans style, then by West Indian calypso and African folk. Leader of the Fairweather All-Stars.

**Brubeck, Dave (David Warren)** (1920– ) American pianist, bandleader and composer, born Concord, California. Pupil of Schoenberg and Milhaud; uses odd rhythms, the rondo form, fugue-like passages; made popular by Paul Desmond's 'Take Five'; compositions include 'The Duke', 'In Your own Sweet Way', 'Unsquare Dance'.

**Burton, Gary** (1943– ) American vibraphonist and bandleader, born Anderson, India. Has habit of 'discovering' new talent, eg Tommy Smith. Also involved in music education and publishing. Many successful album recordings, including Carly Bley's *A Genuine Tong Funeral* and *Alone at Last*.

**Byrd, Charlie** (1925–99) American guitarist, born Chuckatuck, Virginia. Specialist on nylon string guitar; very versatile; played jazz, classical and South American in the same concerts; prolific recordings include *Jazz/Samba* with Stan Getz.

**Calloway, Cab(ell)** (1907–94) American bandleader and singer, born Rochester, New York. His band succeeded Duke Ellington's at Harlem's Cotton Club in 1931. Known for his signature tune *Minnie the Moocher* and his scat-style catchphrases.

**Carter, Betty (Lillie Mae Jones)** (1930–98) American singer, born Flint, Michigan. Sang with bebop musicians, including Charlie Parker and Dizzie Gillespie. A brilliant vocal improvisor, who was popular in the 1950s. Rediscovered in the 1970s after setting up own record label, Bet-Car.

**Charles, Ray ('The Genius') (Robinson, Ray Charles)** (1930– ) American singer, pianist and composer, born Albany, Georgia. Successful soul artist (despite blindness) with sensitive, vibrant voice and sincere, expressive preacher's tone; often accompanied by big bands; 'Sewanee River Rock', 'What'd I Say', 'Georgia on My Mind', 'Hit the Road Jack', 'I Can't Stop Loving You', film theme 'Ruby'.

**Cherry, Don(ald Eugene)** (1936–95) American trumpeter, cornetist, bandleader and composer, born Oklahoma City. Exponent of improvised music; considered himself not playing the trumpet but singing with it; came to prominence in Ornette Coleman's Free Jazz quartet and on the John Coltrane quartet album *The Avant-Garde*.

**Christian, Charlie** (1916–42) American guitarist, born Dallas, Texas. Electric guitar pioneer, establishing it as a solo instrument; helped lay basis of bebop revolution in Minton's Playhouse; played with Benny Goodman. Early death due to TB. Shared composer credit with Goodman for 'Solo Flight' and 'Seven Come Eleven'; also 'Blues in C', 'Waitin' for Benny'.

**Clarke, Kenny ('Klook') (Kenneth Spearman)** (1914–85) American drummer, bandleader and composer, born Pittsburgh, Pennsylvania. Inventor of bebop drums; father of modern percussionists; co-led Clarke–Boland big band. Compositions include 'Epistrophy' with Thelonious Monk, 'Salt Peanuts' with Dizzy Gillespie.

**Cole, Nat 'King' (Coles, Nathaniel Adams)** (1919–65) American singer, pianist and composer, born Montgomery, Alabama. Inventor of modern concept of trio, using piano, guitar and double bass. Won popularity as a singer; 'Straighten up and Fly Right', 'Too Young', 'Unforgettable', 'Answer Me, My Love', 'Ballerina', 'Stardust'.

**Coleman, Ornette** (1930– ) American alto and tenor saxophonist, trumpeter and composer, born Fort Worth, Texas. Experimented in free-form jazz and atonality to mixed acclaim; now regarded as major innovator; invented word 'harmelodic' (improvised coloration). Albums include *Something Else!* and *The Shape of Jazz to Come*.

**Coltrane, John (William)** (1926–67) American tenor and soprano saxophonist, bandleader and composer, born Hamlet, North Carolina. One of the most influential performers of the post-bebop era. Developed and experimented with improvisation, influenced by Indian ragas, African pentatonic scales and the polyphonic music of the Pygmys; 'Giant Steps', 'A Love Supreme'.

**Corea, Chick (Corea, Armando Anthony)** (1941– ) Italian–American pianist and composer, born Chelsea, Massachusetts. His taste for diversity makes him hard to classify; plays from acoustics to electronics and from Latin rhythms to bebop, Free Jazz to classical; replaced Herbie Hancock in Miles Davis's group for *In a Silent Way* and *Bitches Brew*; 'Return to Forever', 'Crystal Silence', 'Armando's Rhumba', *Now He Sings, Now He Sobs*.

**Dankworth, John (Philip William)** (1927– ) English alto saxophonist, bandleader and composer, born London. A student of the Royal Academy of Music, he later converted stables at his home to be a workshop for young musicians. Hits include novelty 'Experiments with Mice', 'African Waltz'; ballet *Lysistrata*; film score *Saturday Night and Sunday Morning*; piece for orchestra *What the Dickens*.

**Davis, Miles (Dewey III) ('Prince of Darkness')** (1926–91) American trumpeter and bandleader, born Alton, Illinois. One of the most popular and adaptable jazz musicians of all time. Recording début with 'Now's the Time', 'Billie Bounce', 'Koko'. Working with Gil Evans, he led a nonet that inspired the 'cool jazz' school. Albums include *The Birth of the Cool* (a turning point in jazz history), *Kind of Blue*; recorded music for Louis Malle's film *Ascenseur pour l'Échafaud* (1957).

**Dolphy, Eric (Allan)** (1928–64) American alto saxophonist, clarinettist, flautist and composer, born Los Angeles. Music rooted in Afro-American tradition but with birdsong-like improvisation comprising screeches, airiness and wild escapades, eg in 'Gazelloni' on *Out to Lunch* and 'Jim Crow' on *Other Aspects*.

**Dorsey, Tommy (Thomas Francis) ('The Sentimental Gentleman of Swing')** (1905–56) American trombonist and big-band leader, born Shenandoah, Pennsylvania. Characteristic sweet-toned instrumental style with seamless legato; formed Dorsey Brothers Orchestra in 1928 with brother Jimmy, one of the most popular swing dance bands. Nearly 200 hits 1935–53 including 'Treasure Island', 'Marie', 'Satan Takes a Holiday', 'Indian Summer', 'In the Blue of Evening' (with Frank Sinatra), 'Boogie Woogie'.

**Eldridge, Roy (David Roy) ('Little Jazz')** (1911–89) American trumpeter, pianist, drummer, bass player and bandleader, born Pittsburgh, Pennsylvania. Virtuoso who influenced Louis Armstrong and Dizzy Gillespie. Famous trumpet soloist, often playing in the high register; played with top bands, eg McKinney's Cotton Pickers and the Fletcher Henderson Orchestra; vocal duet hit with Anita O'Day 'Let Me Off Uptown', also countless recordings, including *Dale's Wail* with Oscar Peterson, *The Trumpet Battle* with Charlie Shavers and Lester Young.

**Elis, Don(ald Johnson)** (1934–78) American trumpeter, bandleader and composer, born Los Angeles. Worked in both jazz and contemporary music, experimenting with oriental instruments and compositions, and incorporating string quartets; music full of virtuosity collages and improvisation, but poorly represented on disc.

**Ellington, 'Duke' (Edward Kennedy)** (1899–1974) American pianist, bandleader and composer, born Washington, DC. One of the most important jazz composers and players. Produced about 2 000 works including 'Mood Indigo', 'Sophisticated Lady', 'Take the A Train', film music for *Anatomy of a Murder* (1959) and *Paris Blues* (1961).

**Evans, Bill (William John)** (1929–80) American pianist and composer, born Plainfield, New Jersey. Most influential pianist of his generation. Won several Grammies, eg for *Conversations with Myself*; 'Waltz for Debby', 'N Y C's No Lark' (for Sonny Clark).

**Evans, Gil (Green, Ian Ernst Gilmore)** (1912–88) Canadian composer, pianist and bandleader, born Toronto. Collaboration with Miles Davis led to emergence of 'cool jazz' style; one of the first modern jazz arrangers to combine electronics and rock influences with bebop and swing. Compositions include 'Boplicity' and 'Moon Dreams' for Davis's *Birth of the Cool*, 'Concierto de Aranjuez' for *Sketches of Spain*, electric album *Svengali*.

**Fitzgerald, Ella** (1917–96) American singer, born Newport News, Virginia. Talented jazz singer; famous for scat singing (vocal imitation of an instrument) and improvisation; starred in drummer Chick Webb's orchestra; sang with Duke Ellington's and Count Basie's bands; performed *Porgy and Bess* with Louis Armstrong; 'Stone Cold Dead in the Market', 'Mack the Knife', 'Party Blues'.

**Franklin, Aretha ('Lady Soul', 'Queen of Soul')** (1942– ) American singer, born Memphis, Tennessee. Daughter of Detroit preacher and gospel singer; many million-selling singles; recorded 'Respect' with Ray Charles and 'Lady Soul' with Otis Redding; masterpiece album *Amazing Grace*; *Love All the Hurt Away*, *One Lord, One Faith, One Baptism*.

**Garbarek, Jan** (1947– ) Norwegian saxophonist, born Mysen, Norway. Despite being inspired by Coltrane, his influence is very much European, drawing on the moods and haunting melodies from his Scandinavian roots; has played and recorded with George Russell's sextet and orchestra in Sweden, and with the medieval folk group the Hilliard Ensemble (*Officium*, 1996); style described as 'distilled thought'.

**Garner, Erroll** (1921–77) American pianist, born Pittsburgh, Pennsylvania. Self-taught artist with a gift for melody; combined old and new styles; his own lingering style became known as the 'Garner amble'; known for 'Play Piano Play', 'Laura', 'Misty'; awarded gold disc for *Concert by the Sea* (1958).

**Getz, Stan(ley) ('The Sound')** (1927–91) American tenor saxophonist and bandleader, born Philadelphia. Most important white jazz saxophonist for 40 years of his life. Characteristic smooth, light tone and articulate phrasing. Popularized bossa nova jazz style in the 1960s; 'Focus', 'Desafinado', 'The Girl from Ipanema'.

**Gillespie, 'Dizzy' (John Birks)** (1917–93) American trumpeter, bandleader and composer, born Cheraw, South Carolina. Great pioneering virtuoso and innovator; created bebop style (with Charlie Parker); introduced African rhythms into jazz; compositions include classics 'Night in Tunisia', 'Groovin' High', 'Dizzy Atmosphere', 'Anthropology'.

**Goodman, Benny (Benjamin David) ('The King of Swing')** (1909–86) American clarinettist, bandleader and composer, born Chicago. The first white performer to integrate black musicians into his own band; in 1962 played in first American jazz band to perform in the Soviet Union; clean, joyful style; sextet recordings include 'Six Appeal', 'Seven Come Eleven', 'Wholly Cats', 'Breakfast Feud'; 'Jersey Bounce', 'Why Don't You Do Right' (sung by Peggy Lee).

**Gordon, Dexter (Keith)** (1923–90) American tenor saxophonist, born Los Angeles. One of the first to play bop tenor; developed modern ballad style and keen harmonic tone (which Coltrane and Rollins studied); 'The Chase', 'The Duel', 'Daddy Plays the Horn', *Gotham City*; also acted in play *The Connection* and film *Round Midnight* (1986).

**Grapelli, Stephane** (1908–97) French violinist, born Paris. Founder member (with Django Reinhardt) of Quintette du Hot Club de France, which had a European influence on jazz in the 1930s. Adapted violin to jazz; master of swing-based style; recorded swing versions of the 'Marseillaise' called 'Echoes of France', and of J S Bach's *Concerto in D Minor*. Duets with Yehudi Menuhin include *Tea for Two* and *Strictly for the Birds*.

**Guy, Buddy** (1936– ) American singer and guitarist, born Lettsworth, Louisiana. Began at 13 with home-made guitar and progressed to centre of Chicago blues scene in the 1950s and 1960s; 'Stone Crazy', début album *A Man And His Blues*, compilation with other Chicago bands *In The Beginning*.

**Hampton, Lionel ('Hamp')** (1909– ) American vibraphonist, born Louisville, Kentucky. Made vibraphone a solo instrument, first recording with Louis Armstrong; played in Benny Goodman's band before forming own big band in 1940; 'Flyin' Home' (famous solo by Illinois Jacquet).

**Hancock, Herbie (Herbert Jeffrey)** (1940– ) American pianist and composer, born Chicago. Child classical musician, but dedicated to jazz; played in Miles Davis's quintet for five years, seeing developments towards jazz rock; with own band turned to electric and electronic means. Music blends rhythm 'n' blues and soul blues, or blues and swing; 'Watermelon Man', 'Rock It'; soundtrack of Bertrand's Tavernier's film *Round Midnight* (1986) won an Oscar.

**Hawkins, Coleman (Randolph) ('Bean', 'Hawk')** (1904–69) American tenor saxophonist, born St Joseph, Missouri. Elevated tenor sax to status of solo instrument, hence title 'father of the saxophone'. Abandoned staccato style to develop melodic fluid tone. Compositions include 'Queer Notions'. Hits include masterpiece 'Body and Soul', 'The Man I Love', 'Picasso'.

**Henderson, (James) Fletcher ('Smack')** (1897–1952) American bandleader, pianist and arranger, born Cuthbert, Georgia. Pioneer of the big band formation. Perfected technique of writing for separate sections and set standard for the swing era. Joined Benny Goodman's band as pianist and arranger and contributed to its success with 'King Porter Stomp' and 'Blue Skies'.

**Henderson, Joe (Joseph)** (1937–2001) American saxophonist, bandleader and composer, born Lima, Ohio. Established reputation as a sideman, most notably to Herbie Hancock. Recorded under own name for Blue Note from 1963 onwards. In the 1990s recorded a series of award-winning records for the Verve label.

**Herman, Woody (Woodrow Charles)** (1913–87) American clarinettist, saxophonist, singer, bandleader and composer, born Milwaukee, Wisconsin. A forerunner of 'cool jazz', his first band, The Band That Plays The Blues, had 1939 hit 'Woodchopper's Ball'. His first Herd band was famous: Igor Stravinsky composed *Ebony Concerto* for him; the second had 'Four Brothers' reed section and recorded 'Early Autumn', which includes Stan Getz's influential solo.

**Hines, Earl (Kenneth) ('Fatha')** (1903–83) American pianist and bandleader, born Duquesne, Pennsylvania. Often associated with trumpeter Louis Armstrong (they had an influential duet recording 'Weather Bird'), Hines's trumpet-style of piano playing was a significant development among jazz pianists. His big band had a 12-year residency at the *Grand Terrace Ballroom*. One of the first jazz pianists to play and record solo; 'Boogie Woogie on St Louis Blues', 'Jelly Jelly', 'Second Balcony Jump', 'The Earl', 'Rosetta'.

**Hodges, Johnny ('Jeep', 'Rabbit') (Hodge, Cornelius)** (1906–70) American alto and soprano saxophonist, born Cambridge, Massachusetts. Dominant in alto scene before Charlie Parker; constant member of Duke Ellington's band (except 1951–5); technically orthodox but aesthetically inimitable, known for 'I Got It Bad', 'On the Sunny Side of the Street', 'Warm Valley' and 'In a Sentimental Mood' (later recorded by Coltrane in his honour).

**Holiday, Billie ('Lady Day') (Fagan, Eleanora)** (1915–59) American singer, born Baltimore, Maryland. Talented singer with a tragic destiny;

noticed as a cabaret singer, she became famous alongside Benny Goodman and Lester Young, toured with Artie Shaw and made a film *New Orleans* with Louis Armstrong before drug addiction killed her; 'Strange Fruit', 'Lover Man', 'God Bless the Child'.

**Hooker, John Lee** (1917–2001) American singer and guitarist, born Clarksdale, Mississippi. Popular blues musician with relaxed vocal style; often sang alone and accompanied himself on guitar; began in gospel choirs and became one of the most influential of trad bluesmen; 'Boogie Chillen', 'Boogie With the Hook', 'It Serves Me Right to Suffer'; made *Hooker and Heat* with band Canned Heat; own albums include *Do the Boogie* and *Sittin' Here Thinkin'*.

**Ibrahim, Abdullah (Dollar Brand)** (1934– ) South African pianist, born Cape Town. Formed the Jazz Epistles group, recording the country's first black jazz album. Worked with Duke Ellington in America in the 1960s. Also plays cello, soprano saxophone and flute. Known for jazz interpretations of melodies and rhythms of his African childhood.

**Jackson, 'Milt' (Milton) ('Bags')** (1923–99) American vibraphonist, born Detroit, Michigan. Most important vibraphonist of the bebop era. Co-founder with John Lewis of Modern Jazz Quartet, with which his career is linked; 'La Ronde' and 'Vendome' are the MJQ's mascots.

**Jarrett, Keith** (1945– ) American pianist and composer, born Allentown, Pennsylvania. With his idiosyncratic style of playing, going wild on the keys and embellishing his solos with big 'free' lyrical passages, he became very popular; played with Miles Davis, among others; *Facing You, Sun Bear Concerts*.

**Johnson, J J (James Louis)** (1924–2001) American trombonist, pianist, baritone saxophonist and composer, born Indianapolis, Indiana. Father of the modern jazz trombone who invented bebop trombone playing, being the first slide trombonist to match the requirements of speed and articulation, as shown when he played with Charlie Parker; compositions include 'Rodeo for Quartet and Orchestra'; *All-Star Jam, The Eminent J J Johnson, The Bosses*.

**Johnson, James P(rice)** (1894–1955) American pianist and composer, born New Brunswick, New Jersey. Pioneer of stride with 'Carolina Shout'; often accompanied the great female blues singers; swinging style influential on eg Duke Ellington and Thelonious Monk; composer of symphonic works and hits 'Old Fashioned Love', 'Charleston' (with Cecil Mack).

**Johnston, Lonny (Alonzo)** (1889–1970) American guitarist, born New Orleans. Major blues figure in New Orleans, introduced guitar in its modern form as a solo instrument; invented style of playing note by note; 'Stardust', 'Confused', 'Swinging with Lonnie'.

**Jones, Elvin (Ray)** (1927– ) American drummer, born Pontiac, Michigan. Versatile, inventive, self-taught drummer who eschewed the restrictions of continuous tempo and created complicated polyrhythms, producing the river, a new tornado of sound in jazz. Played in Coltrane's quartet for six years; *Live at the Village Vanguard, Heart to Heart* (with Davis); appeared in film dedicated to him *Different Drummer*.

**Jones, Quincy (Delight)** (1933– ) American trumpeter, bandleader, composer and arranger, born Illinois. Famous as arranger and producer, but also successful solo musician. Michael Jackson's mentor and producer of the *Thriller* album; 'Killer Joe '70', 'Just Once', 'Summer in the City' (Grammy winner).

**Joplin, Scott** (1866–1917) American ragtime pianist and composer, born Texarkana, Texas. Originator and exponent of 'Ragtime' music. First score *Multiple Leaf Rag* sold more than a million copies, but he died unfulfilled; Gunther Schiller made *Treemonisha* into a Broadway hit in the 1970s; 'The Entertainer' was used in the soundtrack of the film *The Sting* (1973).

**Kenton, Stan(ley Newcomb)** (1912–79) American pianist, composer and bandleader, born Wichita, Kansas. Exponent of 1950s big band 'progressive' jazz style; later bands had unusual five-trombone sections. Music considered loud and pretentious by some, but innovative by others; won Grammy 1961 for *West Side Story*.

**Kidd, Carol** (1944– ) Scottish singer, born Glasgow. Formed permanent trio at the age of 17. Became known in London clubs in late 1970s and later appeared in radio and television. Won various awards in the 1980s.

**King, B B (Riley B)** (1925– ) American blues singer and guitarist, born Itta Bena, Mississippi. Famous as singer and influential for economical guitar style. Prolific recording success includes 'Three O'Clock Blues', 'Sweet Black Angel' and 1981 Grammy-winner *There Must be a Better World Somewhere*.

**Kirk, (Rhasaan) Roland** (1936–77) American multi-instrumentalist, born Columbus, Ohio. Music rooted in gospel and blues; polyinstrumentalist despite blindness; could play three saxophones at once, sang into his flute and played whistle, siren, bagpipes, etc.

**Krupa, Gene** (1909–73) American drummer and bandleader, born New York City. Exuberant soloist who made the drummer a solo instrumentalist; played with Benny Goodman; formed own band; had hit 'Sing Sing Sing' with Goodman small group, and 'Rockin' Chair' with trumpeter Roy Eldridge; also 'Chickery Chick', 'Bonaparte's Retreat' and compilation *World's Greatest Drummer*; appeared in several films, eg *Some Like It Hot* (1939) and *The Benny Goodman Story* (1956).

**Lacy, Steve (Lackritz, Steven)** (1934– ) American soprano saxophonist and composer, born New York City. Concentrated on soprano sax and developed own rough-edged tone; in the 1950s was sideman to the best soloists of the revival and Swing, then was partner to Cecil Taylor (*In Transition*), then to Thelonious Monk; first record in his own name, *Soprano Today*, included some of Monk's music, as did much of his work.

**Lewis, John (Aaron)** (1920–2001) American pianist and composer, born LaGrange, Illinois.

Succeeded Monk as pianist in Dizzy Gillespie's big band; influential in the first bebop era; recorded with Charlie Parker and Miles Davis; formed the Modern Jazz Quartet in 1951; uncluttered, confident yet bluesy style; celebrated Monk with version of 'Round Midnight'; also composed 'Toccata for Trumpet' which shows Bach's influence, 'Move' and 'Rouge' in Davis's *Birth of the Cool.*

**Lunceford, Jimmie (James Melvin)** (1902–47) His band, the Chickasaw Syncopaters, was a great addition to the history of big bands, playing music by Sy Oliver and having outstanding success with 'Tain't What You Do (It's The Way That You Do It)', 'Rhythm is our Business' and 'Blues in the Night'; 'Honeydripper', 'Got a Right to Cry', 'Rag Mop', 'Pink Champagne'.

**Lyttelton, Humphrey ('Humph')** (1921– ) English trumpeter and bandleader, born Eton, Berkshire. Mainstream jazz musician; celebrated 40 continuous years as bandleader in 1988; pioneer in the British revivalist movement; introduced three-saxophone section and original tunes from English and West Indian folk roots; albums include *Bad Penny Blues.*

**McLaughlin, John** (1942– ) English electric guitarist and bandleader, born Doncaster. Impressive speed and rhythm technique; music developed into synthesis of Afro-American and Indian music. Took part in birth of jazz-rock with Miles Davis; formed Mahavishnu orchestra; first album *Extrapolation;* plays one track in 1986 film soundtrack *Round Midnight.*

**Marsalis, Wynton** (1961– ) American trumpeter and bandleader, born New Orleans. Classical soloist and jazz performer; played Haydn's *Concerto for Trumpet* at age 14; joined Art Blakey's Jazz Messengers at 18; first recording was with the 'giants' Herbie Hancock, Ron Carter and Tony Williams; style combines extension of bebop with sense of swing; won Grammy 1984 as both best classical and jazz soloist. Albums include 1987 *Standard Time.*

**Metheny, Pat** (1954– ) American guitarist and composer, born Lee's Summit, Missouri. Musically open-minded, appeals to bebop, rock and Free Jazz fans; blends acoustics and electronics; composed music for John Schlesinger's *The Falcon and the Snowman* (sung by David Bowie); *Song X* (with Ornette Coleman), *Bright Side of Life, American Garage, Offramp.*

**Mezzrow, Mezz (Mesirow, Milton)** (1899–1972) American reeds player (especially clarinet), born Chicago. Began playing sax in jail; played as a professional musician with eg Eddie Condon, Sidney Bechet; *Paris* and two volumes of *The King Jazz Story* with Bechet.

**Miller, (Alton) Glenn** (1904–44) American bandleader and trombonist, born Clarinda, Iowa. Very popular as dance band leader, especially during war years. Characteristic style was produced by doubling the lead tenor with a clarinet; 'In the Mood', 'Moonlight Serenade'.

**Mingus, Charles (Jr)** (1922–79) American double bassist, pianist, composer and bandleader, born Nogales, Arizona. One of the most important composers in 20th-century black music; 'Pussy Cat Dues', 'Boogie Stop Shuffle', 'Jelly Roll', 'Goodbye Pork Pie Hat', *Tijuana Moods.*

**Monk, Thelonious (Sphere)** (1917–82) American pianist and composer, born Rocky Mount, North Carolina. Famous 'Prophet' or 'High Priest' of bebop, with which he experimented at Minton's Playhouse in Harlem. Leading composer in jazz history; 'Round Midnight' and 'Straight No Chaser' are classics.

**Montgomery, Wes (John Lesley)** (1923–68) American guitarist, born Indianapolis, Indiana. Influential, innovative and versatile self-taught guitarist; worked with Lionel Hampton; mellow sound due to plucking strings with thumb instead of plectrum; *The Incredible Jazz Guitar of Wes Montgomery.*

**Morton, Jelly Roll (LaMenthe, Ferdinand-Joseph)** (1890–1941) American bandleader, composer and pianist, born New Orleans. First great composer in jazz, and a link between ragtime and jazz; formed successful band the Red Hot Peppers, who may have been the first to combine arranged ensemble pieces with improvisation; 'Georgia Stomp', 'Grandpa's Spells', 'Wolverine Blues', 'King Porter Stomp'.

**Mulligan, Gerry (Gerald Joseph) ('Jeru')** (1927–96) American baritone saxophonist, born New York City. Talented arranger and popular musician who made the baritone saxophone a solo instrument; wrote 'Jeru', 'Boplicity', 'Venus de Milo' and 'Godchild' for Davis's *Birth of the Cool.*

**Oliver, King (Joseph)** (1885–1938) American cornettist and bandleader, born New Orleans. By the collective improvisation of Oliver's 'Dippermouth Blues', jazz was freed from the polyphonic concept of the New Orleans style; the Chicago style developed which retained swing but had many elements (marches, melodies, polkas, etc). Oliver thus one of the 'fathers' of jazz; innovative cornet player, using newly invented mute; 'landmark' hits include 'West End Blues', 'Canal Street Blues' and 'Doctor Jazz'.

**Ørsted Pedersen, Niels-Henning** (1946– ) Danish pianist and bassist, born Osted. Established reputation as one of the top jazz bassists in the world. Flexible in style, he could play mainsteam to avant-garde. Much in demand with touring soloists. Has played extensively with pianist Oscar Peterson.

**Ory, Kid (Edward)** (1886–1973) American trombonist, singer, bandleader and composer, born La Prince, Louisiana. A master of New Orleans 'tailgate' trumpet style, playing rhythmic bass as well as solo; led and played in various successful bands, eg Kid Ory's Sunshine Orchestra, the first black jazz band to record, and Louis Armstrong's Hot Five. From 1942 he was active in the New Orleans Revival, though he'd been there from the start. Compositions include 'Muskrat Ramble'; appeared as bandleader in *The Benny Goodman Story* (1956); albums include *Kid Ory's Creole Jazz Band 1944–45.*

**Parker, Charlie (Charles Christopher) ('Bird', 'Yardbird')** (1920–55) American alto saxophonist,

bandleader and composer, born Kansas City, Missouri. Influential modern jazz performer in post-1940s, whose ideas formed the basis of the bebop style; innovative association with trumpeter Dizzy Gillespie in bebop quintets; compositions include 'Now's the Time' and 'Ornithology'.

**Pass, Joe (Passalaqua, Giuseppe)** (1929–94) American guitarist. Most influential swing guitarist since Wes Montgomery, comparable to pianist Oscar Peterson in speed and vigour; world-famous as sideman with eg Peterson, Count Basie, Ella Fitzgerald, Duke Ellington; own albums include *Virtuoso* and *University of Akron Concert*.

**Peterson, Oscar (Emmanuel)** (1925– ) Canadian pianist and composer, born Montreal. Reliable accompanist and flamboyant soloist; permanent member of Jazz at the Philharmonic; also performed with double-bass player Niels-Henning Ørsted Pedersen and guitarist Joe Pass; solo albums include *My Favourite Instrument, At Salle Playel, Affinity* and *Jazz Portrait of Frank Sinatra*.

**Pine, Courtney** (1964– ) English tenor and soprano saxophonist and bass clarinettist, bandleader and composer, born London. Originally Coltrane-inspired, this talented saxophonist of Jamaican origin has formed two bands, The Jazz Warriors and The World's First Saxophone Posse; 1986 album *Journey to the Urge Within* includes tune 'Miss Interpret'; also contributed to soundtrack of film *Angel Heart* (1987).

**Portal, Michel** (1935– ) American soprano, alto and tenor saxophonist and clarinettist, born Bayonne, New Jersey. Jazz and classical, uses different instruments for each style; a pioneer of Free Jazz in France; founded 'Unit', an open, informed group where American and European guests were welcomed; film music includes *La Cecilia* and *L'Ombre Rouge*.

**Powell, Bud (Earl)** (1924–66) American pianist and composer, born New York City. A great virtuoso, very important in bebop movement, and in jazz history generally; encouraged by Thelonious Monk in the 1940s, he made many recordings with other virtuosos and solo, including 'Cheryl', 'Dana Lee', 'Chasin' the Bird', 'Un Poco Loco', 'Passion Thoroughfare', 'Bouncing With Bud'; the character Gordon in 1986 film *Round Midnight* is based on Powell.

**Reinhardt, Django (Jean-Baptiste)** (1910–53) Belgian guitarist, born Liverchies, Belgium. Self-taught musician of gypsy background and the first European to have an influence on swing-style American guitarists, despite losing two fingers in a caravan fire; joined with Stephane Grapelli (1908–97) to form the Quintette du Hot Club de France, which inaugurated a French-style jazz; toured with the Duke Ellington orchestra, changing from acoustic to electric guitar; produced swing version of Bach's *First Movement of the Concerto in D Minor*; compositions include 'Love's Melody' and 'Improvisation', also (with Grapelli) 'HQC Strut', 'Daphne', 'Djangology'.

**Roach, Max(well)** (1924– ) American drummer, bandleader and composer, born New York City. Key member of bebop movement and a 'giant' of modern jazz; being the first to 'swing' on the drums and use them for 'melody', he created the very influential legato rhythmic feeling; *The Freedom Suite* (waltzes), *We Insist – Freedom Now Suite, Money Jungle* (with Duke Ellington), *Drums Unlimited*.

**Rollins, Sonny (Theodore Walter) ('Newk')** (1930– ) American tenor saxophonist and composer, born New York City. Powerful improviser and important voice in the 'hard bop' movement, joining Clifford Brown and Max Roach; used Caribbean calypso eg in 'Saint Thomas' and 'Don't Stop the Carnival'; 'Tenor Madness', 'Olea', 'Airegin', *Saxophone Colossus*.

**Shaw, Artie (Arshawsky, Arthur Jacob)** (1910– ) American clarinettist, bandleader and composer, born Norwalk, Connecticut. Like Benny Goodman in tone and innovation, he was also one of the first to present a mixed black and white band, which had a 'cooler' atmosphere due to its reliance on strings; 'Begin the Beguine', 'Summit Ridge Drive', 'Frenesi', 'Dancing in the Dark'.

**Shepp, Archie** (1937– ) American saxophonist, pianist, singer and bandleader, born Fort Lauderdale, Florida. Created formula of three horns, bass and drums which became the Free Jazz standard; developed frantic solo style in orchestral context; jazz for him was 'Great Black Music'; faithful to blues and gospel traditions and embraced West African trends eg in *Mama Too Tight* and *Magic of Ju-Ju*; also *Four for Trane* and *Ascension* with Coltrane.

**Shorter, Wayne** (1933– ) American tenor and soprano saxophonist, bandleader and composer, born Newark, New Jersey. Played in Art Blakey's Jazz Messengers and Miles Davis's quintet (whose development towards jazz rock he helped); formed own group Weather Report, then continued in electric jazz style; the ethereal 'Mysterious Traveller' and dance-like 'Heavy Weather' contributed to *Round Midnight* (1986) film soundtrack.

**Silver, Horace (Ward Martin Tavares)** (1928– ) American pianist, bandleader and composer, born Norwalk, Connecticut. Leading figure, with Art Blakey, of the hard bop style, and main exponent of funky jazz; first pianist and musical director of The Jazz Messengers; compositions have flavour of blues and gospel; 'Doodlin', 'The Preacher', 'Señor Blues' and 'Opus de Funk'.

**Simone, Nina (Wayman, Eunice)** (1933– ) American singer, pianist and composer, born North Carolina. Performance varied from gospel through blues and soul to modern jazz, excelling in all registers; repertoire included Gershwin; best known composition 'To Be Young, Gifted and Black'; 'I Loves You Porgy', 'Mississippi Goddam', 'Central Park Blues', 'My Baby Just Cares For Me'.

**Smith, Bessie** (1894–1937) American singer, born Chattanooga, Tennessee. Advertised as 'The Empress

of the Blues'; hers was a blues-based repertoire including recordings accompanied by leading musicians (eg Louis Armstrong). Realistic songs depict poverty and love pains often flavoured by angry feminism, eg 'Downhearted Blues'; made short film *St Louis Blues* (1929).

**Smith, Tommy** (1967– ) Scottish saxophonist and composer, born Luton, Bedfordshire. Cosmopolitan musician with broad ideas and lavish tonality; disciple of John Coltrane, with a 'European' feeling for textures and moods in his playing; in his first album *Step By Step* he plays his own compositions, with John Scofield and Jack De Johnette; also *Peeping Tom*.

**Solal, Martial** (1927– ) Algerian pianist, composer and bandleader, born Algiers. Improviser with boundless imagination who defies classification, and who can render standard pieces unrecognizable by his artistry; compositions include *Suite in D Flat* for jazz quartet, and for the film *À Bout De Souffle*.

**Sun Ra (Blount, Herman** or **Lee, Sonny)** (1914–93) American pianist, composer and bandleader, born Birmingham, Alabama. Pioneer of electronic music, little is known of him before the 1950s; his influential Arkestra functioned as a cooperative, and combined the traditions of the swing era with the freedom of improvisation and the rhythmic agility of bop; dedicated his music 'to the Creator of the Universe'.

**Surman, John** (1944– ) English multi-instrumentalist, composer and bandleader, born Tavistock, Devon. Emerging from a classical background with folk, ethnic and church music roots. He was sideman of French-born bluesman Alexis Korner before becoming world famous as soloist; *The Trio, The Amazing Adventures of Simon Simon*.

**Taylor, Cecil (Percival)** (1933– ) American pianist, bandleader and composer, born New York City. An exponent of the avant-garde due to his powerful free style of improvisation; very energetic and fast player who treats his piano like a percussion instrument; worked with saxophonist Jimmy Lyons for many years; *Conquistador, Unit Structures, For Olim*.

**Teagarden, Jack ('Mr T')** (1905–64) American trombonist and bandleader, born Texas. Great classical jazz figure with warm, natural tone; inventor of jazz trombone; also sang with Louis Armstrong; 'That's an Awful Serious Thing', 'I'm Gonna Stomp Mr Henry Lee' (with Eddie Condon), 'You Rascal You', 'Chances Are', 'Someone Stole Gabriel's Horn', 'A Hundred Years From Today'.

**Tatum, Art(hur, Jr)** (1909–56) American pianist, born Toledo, Ohio. The most influential of the swing-style pianists, and considered unequalled; despite near-blindness from birth his technique was astonishing and he became famous as the greatest in the history of jazz; 'Body and Soul', 'Tea For Two', 'Tiger Rag'.

**Thielemans, 'Toots' (Jean-Baptiste)** (1922– ) Belgian guitarist and harmonica player, born Brussels. Converted from the accordian to the guitar and harmonica by Django Reinhardt, he also played with Benny Goodman, Lester Young, Count Basie and Stan Getz in America and Europe; Quincy Jones's favourite soloist; played film soundtrack *Midnight Cowboy* (1969); successes include album *Affinity*, and 'Bluesette', a composition which followed an evening improvising with Stephane Grapelli.

**Tracey, Stan** (1926– ) English pianist, bandleader and composer, born London. Important contributor to European jazz scene; being self-taught meant an unconventional and individual technique; percussive piano style; compositions include jazz suites *Under Milk Wood, The Bracknell Connection, Genesis*, also for album *We Love You Madly*.

**Tristano, Lennie (Leonard Joseph)** (1919–78) American pianist and composer, born Chicago. Blind by age 11; 'Pianist of the Year' 1948; great jazz teacher and 'father confessor to all the avant-garde musicians in the city (Chicago)'; anticipated the 1960s Free Jazz movement in eg 'Intuition', 'Digression', 'Yesteryear'.

**Tyner, McCoy (Alfred)** (1938– ) American pianist and composer, born Philadelphia, Pennsylvania. Part of epochal Coltrane quartet, where the calmness of his playing was a background to the furious solos; later joined Ike and Tina Turner for *Sahara*; 1973 best record prize for *Enlightenment*; *Double Trios* includes revived standard and classic bebop numbers, eg 'Lover Man'.

**Vaughan, Sarah (Lois) ('Sassy', 'The Divine One')** (1924–90) American singer, born Newark, New Jersey. Encouraged by Ella Fitzgerald, she began her career in Earl Hines's and Billy Eckstein's bands; wide vocal range, keen sense of improvisation; attracted by new bebop, she recorded with its inventors, eg Dizzy Gillespie and Charlie Parker; 'Things Must Change', 'Make Yourself Comfortable', 'Whatever Lola Wants', 'Broken-Hearted Melody'.

**Walker, T-Bone (Aaron Thibeaux)** (1910–75) American guitarist, singer and songwriter, born Linden, Texas. One who achieved perfect cohesion between voice and electric sound; teenage friends with Charlie Christian (both were influential in guitar-playing field); made name as blues player with 'T-Bone Blues' in 1939; 'Call It Stormy Monday'; won Grammy 1968 for *Good Feelin'*.

**Waller, Fats (Thomas Wright)** (1904–43) American pianist, singer, bandleader and composer, born New York City. Professional musician at 15 and master of the New York 'Stride' piano style; talented musician but popular for singing and humour; prolific composer; 'Honeysuckle Rose', 'Ain't Misbehavin'', 'Black and Blue', 'I'm Crazy Bout My Baby', 'Two Sleepy People'; appeared in films eg, *Stormy Weather* (1943).

**Washington, Dinah (Jones, Ruth Lee)** (1924–63) American singer, born Tuscaloosa, Alabama. Originally 'discovered' by Lionel Hampton, she became the 'Queen of the Blues' whose vibrato voice expressed the aspirations and disappointments of the Black community; 'Baby, Get Lost', 'This Bitter Earth', 'What a Difference a Day Makes', 'Baby (You've Got What It Takes)', 'It Could Happen To You'.

**Waters, Ethel** (1900–77) American singer, born Chester, Pennsylvania. Began in blues style and became a highly regarded 1930s pop singer; also worked in cabaret and film; 'Stormy Weather', 'A Hundred Years From Today' (with Benny Goodman and Jack Teagarden), 'Come Up and See Me Sometime' (from Mae West film).

**Waters, Muddy (Morganfield, McKinley)** (1915–83) American singer, guitarist, bandleader and composer, born Rolling Fork, Mississippi. Popular blues player from 1943; sang with passionate gravelly voice; achieved fame worldwide and his pupils too are many of the 'greats' in jazz; 'Rolling Stone', 'I've Got My Mojo Working', 'Hoochie Coochie Man', 'She's 19 Years Old'.

**Weber, Eberhard** (1940– ) German bass player, bandleader and composer, born Stuttgart. Exponent of European (rather than American) music. Plays with five-string 'electro-bass', having made it a front-line instrument for rhythm to melody and improvisation; eschews American blues roots and, like Jan Garbarek, blends romanticism with evocative or moody sounds; successful first album *The Colours of Chloe*.

**Webster, Ben(jamin Francis)** (1909–1973) American saxophonist, born Kansas City, Missouri. Leading instrumentalist of the swing era. Worked with many of leading musicians of the period including Duke Ellington. Went on to become much sought after soloist.

**Williams, Tony** (1945–97) American drummer and composer, born Chicago. Contributed to evolution of jazz-rock; percussionist in Miles Davis's quartet; made fame as 1970s symbol of modern drumming; drummer for Eric Dolphy's *Out to Lunch* and Davis's *Filles de Kilimanjaro*; now plays modern jazz and jazz fusion; *Spring, Lifetime, Emergency, Turn It Over, The Joy of Flying*.

**Winding, Kai** (1922–83) Danish–American trombonist, born Aarhus, Denmark. Played with many of the jazz 'greats', eg co-leading quintet with J J Johnson, restoring trombone to important position; toured with Gillespie, Monk and Hampton; played on Davis's *Birth of the Cool;* had hit with 'More' (*Mondo Cane* (1963) film theme), also *More Brass, Betwixt And Between Jazz Showcase*.

**Young, Lester (Willis) ('Prez')** (1909–59) American tenor saxophonist, born Woodville, Mississippi. A forerunner of 'cool jazz', which was the opposite of the 1930s saxophone style (eg Coleman Hawkins); pioneer of linear improvisation (J J Johnson); eschewed accepted concepts of melody, rhythm and swing; made reputation with Count Basie's Band; recordings with them include 'Tickle Toe', 'Every Tub', 'One O'Clock Jump'; also 'Lady Be Good', 'Taxi War Dance', 'Rock-A-Bye Basie'.

## Ballet dancers

**Ashley, Merrill (Linda Michelle Merrill)** (1950– ) American, born St Paul, Minnesota.
**Barishnikov, Mikhail (Nikolaievich)** (1948– ) Russian, born Riga.
**Bessmertnova, Natalia** (1941– ) Russian, born Moscow.
**Bujones, Fernando** (1955– ) American, born Florida.
**Camargo, Maria Anna de** (1710–70) French, born Brussels.
**Chauviré, Yvette** (1917– ) French, born Paris.
**Danilova, Alexandra (Dionysievna)** (1903–97) Russian–American, born Peterhof.
**Dolin, Sir Anton (Sydney Francis Patrick Chippendall Healey-Kay)** (1904–83) English, born Slinfold, Sussex.
**Dowell, Sir Anthony** (1943– ) English, born London.
**Duncan, Isadora** (1878–1927) American, born San Francisco.
**Dunham, Katherine** (1912– ) American, born Chicago.
**Dupond, Patrick** (1959– ) French, born Paris.
**Eglevsky, André** (1917–77) Russian–American, born Moscow.
**Elssler, Fanny (Franziska Elsller)** (1810–84) Austrian, born Gumpendorf.
**Farrell, Suzanne** (1945– ) American, born Cincinnati, Ohio.
**Fonteyn, Dame Margot (Peggy Hookham)** (1919–91) English, born Reigate, Surrey.
**Fracci, Carla** (1936– ) Italian, born Milan.
**Genée, Dame Adelin (Anina Jensen)** (1878–1970) Danish, born Hinnerup.
**Gilpin, John** (1930– ) English, born Southsea.
**Gopal, Ram** (1920– ) Indian, born Bangalore.
**Gore, Walter** (1910–79) Scottish, born Waterside.
**Gorsky, Alexander Alexeivich** (1871–1924) Russian, born St Petersburg.
**Graham, Martha** (1894–1991) American, born Pittsburgh.

**Gregory, Cynthia** (1946– ) American, born Los Angeles.
**Grey, Dame Beryl (Beryl Svenson)** (1927– ) English, born London.
**Grisi, Carlotta** (1819–99) Italian, born Visinada.
**Hamilton, Gordon** (1918–59) Australian, born Sydney.
**Haydée, Marcia (Marcia Haydee Salaverry Pereira de Silva)** (1937– ) Brazilian, born Niteroi.
**Helpmann, Sir Robert** (1909–86) Australian, born Mount Gambier.
**Jasinski, Roman (Roman Czeslaw)** (1912– ) Polish–American, born Warsaw.
**Kain, Karen** (1951– ) Canadian, born Hamilton, Ontario.
**Karsavina, Tamara Platonovna** (1885–1978) Russian–British, born St Petersburg.
**Kaye, Nora (Nora Koreff)** (1920–87) American, born New York.
**Kent, Allegra** (1938– ) American, born Los Angeles.
**Kirkland, Gelsey** (1952– ) American, born Bethlehem, Pennsylvania.
**LeClerq, Tanaquil** (1929– ) American, born Paris.
**Lichine, David (David Lichenstein)** (1910–72) Russian–American, born Rostov-na-Donu.
**Makarova, Natalia** (1940– ) Russian, born St Petersburg.
**Markova, Dame Alicia (Lilian Alicia Marks)** (1910– ) English, born London.
**Martins, Peter** (1946– ) Danish, born Copenhagen.
**Mauri, Rosita** (1849–1923) Spanish, born Tarragona.
**Neary, Patricia** (1942– ) American, born Miami, Florida.
**Nemchinova, Vera (Nicolayevna)** (1899–1984) Russian, born Moscow.
**Nijinsky, Vaslav Fomich** (1889–1950) Russian, born Kiev.
**Nureyev, Rudolf Hametovich** (1938–93) Russian–British, born on a train between Lake Baikal and Irkutsk, Siberia.
**Page, Ruth** (1899–1991) American, born Indianapolis.
**Panov, Valeri (Matvevich)** (1938– ) Russian, born Vitebsk.
**Panova, Galina** (1949– ) Russian, born Archangel.
**Petipa, Lucien** (1815–98) French, born Marseilles.
**Petipa, Marie (Mariusovna II)** (1857–1930) Russian, born St Petersburg.
**Plisetskaya, Maya Mikailovna** (1925– ) Russian, born Moscow.
**Rambert, Dame Marie (Cyvia Rambam**, then **Miriam Ramberg)** (1888–1982) Polish–British, born Warsaw.
**Riabochinska, Tatiana** (1917–2000) Russian–American, born Moscow.
**Rubinstein, Ida Lvovna** (1885–1960) Russian, born St Petersburg.
**Seymour, Lynn (Lynn Springbett)** (1939– ) Canadian, born Wainwright.
**Shearer, Moira (Moira King)** (1926– ) Scottish, born Dunfermline.
**Shearer, Sybil** (1918– ) American, born Toronto.
**Sibley, Dame Antoinette** (1939– ) English, born Bromley.
**Somes, Michael** (1917–94) British, born Horsley.
**Spessivtseva, Olga Alexandrovna** (1895–1991) Russian–American, born Rostov.
**Taglioni, Marie** (1804–84) Swedish–Italian, born Stockholm.
**Tallchief, Maria** (1925– ) American, born Fairfax, Oklahoma.
**Taras, John** (1919– ) American, born New York.
**Trefilova, Vera Alexandrovna** (1875–1943) Russian, born St Petersburg.
**Ulanova, Galina (Sergeyevna)** (1910–98) Russian, born St Petersburg.
**Villella, Edward** (1936– ) American, born Bayside, New York.

## Ballet companies

| Name | Date founded | Location |
|---|---|---|
| American Ballet Theater | 1940 | New York, USA |
| The Australian Ballet | 1962 | Melbourne, Australia |
| Australian Dance Theatre | 1965 | Adelaide, Australia |
| Ballets des Champs Élysées | 1944 | Paris, France |
| Ballet Joos | 1933 | Cambridge, UK |
| Ballets de Paris | 1948 | France |
| Ballet Rambert | 1926 | London, UK |
| Ballet Russe de Monte Carlo | 1938 | Monte Carlo |
| Ballets Russes of Sergei Diaghilev (now Kirov Ballet) | 1909–29 | Paris, France and St Petersburg, Russia |
| Ballet-Théâtre Contemporain | 1968 | Amiens, France |
| Ballet du Xième Siècle | 1960 | Brussels, Belgium |
| Bolshoi Ballet | 1776 | Moscow, Russia |
| Borovansky Ballet | 1942 | Melbourne, Australia |
| Kirov Ballet | 1935 | St Petersburg, Russia |
| London Festival Ballet (originally Festival Ballet) | 1949 | UK |
| National Ballet of Canada | 1951 | Toronto |
| New York City Ballet | 1948 | USA |
| Northern Ballet (formed from part of Western Theatre Ballet) | 1969 | Manchester, UK |
| Royal Ballet (formerly Sadler's Wells Ballet) | 1936 | London, UK |
| Royal Danish Ballet | ballets from second half 16th-c | Copenhagen |
| Royal Swedish Ballet | 1st court ballet 1638 | Stockholm |
| Royal Winnipeg Ballet | 1938 | Canada |
| The San Francisco Ballet (formerly the San Francisco Opera Ballet) | 1933 | USA |
| School of American Ballet (now the American Ballet) | 1933 | New York, USA |
| Scottish Ballet (formed from part of Western Theatre Ballet) | 1969 | Glasgow, UK |
| Stanislavsky Ballet (Stanislavsky and Nemirovich-Danchenko Music Theatre Ballet) | 1929 | Moscow, Russia |
| Stuttgart Ballet | court ballets from 1609 | Germany |
| Western Theatre Ballet (divided 1969 to form Northern Ballet, Scottish Ballet) | 1957 | Bristol, UK |

## Ballets

| Ballet | Composer | Choreographer | First performance |
|---|---|---|---|
| Anastasia | Tchaikovsky, Martinu | MacMillan | 1971 |
| Apollo | Stravinsky | Balanchine | 1928 |
| L'Après-midi d'un faune | Debussy | Nijinsky | 1912 |
| La Bayadère | Minkus | Petipa | 1877 |
| Les Biches | Poulenc | Nijinska | 1924 |
| Billy the Kid | Copland | Loring | 1938 |
| Bolero | Ravel | Bejart | 1961 |
| La Boutique Fantasque | Rossini, arr. Respighi | Massine | 1919 |
| Carmen | Bizet | Petit | 1949 |
| Checkmate | Bliss | de Valois | 1937 |
| Cinderella | Prokofiev | Ashton | 1948 |

| Ballet | Composer | Choreographer | First performance |
|---|---|---|---|
| Coppélia | Delibes | St Léon | 1870 |
| Don Quixote | Minkus | Petipa | 1869 |
| Duo Concertant | Stravinsky | Balanchine | 1972 |
| Façade | Walton | Ashton | 1931 |
| Fall River Legend | Gould | de Mille | 1948 |
| Fancy Free | Bernstein | Robbins | 1944 |
| The Firebird | Stravinsky | Fokine | 1910 |
| The Four Temperaments | Hindemith | Balanchine | 1946 |
| Giselle | Adam | Coralli and Perro (later revised by Petipa) | 1841 |
| Las Hermanas | Martin | MacMillan | 1963 |
| Jewels | Fauré, Stravinsky and Tchaikovsky | Balanchine | 1967 |
| Les Noces | Stravinsky | Nijinska | 1923 |
| The Nutcracker | Tchaikovsky | Ivanov | 1892 |
| Ondine | Henze | Ashton | 1958 |
| Onegin | Tchaikovsky, arr. Stolze | Cranko | 1965 |
| Orpheus | Stravinsky | Balanchine | 1948 |
| Parade | Satie | Massine | 1917 |
| Petroushka | Stravinsky | Fokine | 1911 |
| Pineapple Poll | Sullivan, orch. Mackerras | Cranko | 1951 |
| Prince Igor | Borodin | Fokine | 1909 |
| The Prodigal Son | Prokofiev | Balanchine | 1929 |
| The Rake's Progress | Gordon | de Valois | 1935 |
| Raymonda | Glazounov | Petipa | 1898 |
| Les Rendezvous | Auber, arr. Lambert | Ashton | 1933 |
| Requiem | Fauré | MacMillan | 1976 |
| Rhapsody | Rachmaninov | Ashton | 1980 |
| The Rite of Spring | Stravinsky | MacMillan | 1962 |
| Rodeo | Copland | de Mille | 1942 |
| Romeo and Juliet | Prokofiev | Lavrovsky | 1940 |
| Le Sacré du printemps (The Rite of Spring) | Stravinsky | Nijinsky | 1913 |
| Schéhérazade | Rimsky-Korsakov | Fokine | 1910 |
| The Sleeping Beauty | Tchaikovsky | Petipa | 1890 |
| Song of the Earth | Mahler | MacMillan | 1965 |
| Spartacus | Khachaturian | Grigorovich | 1968 |
| La Spectre de la Rose | Weber | Fokine | 1911 |
| Swan Lake | Tchaikovsky | Petipa and Ivanov | 1895 |
| La Sylphide | Løvenskjold | Bournonville | 1836 |
| Les Sylphides (Chopiniana) | Chopin, variously orchestrated | Fokine | 1909 |
| Tales of Hoffman | Offenbach, arr. Lanchberg | Darrell | 1973 |
| The Three-Cornered Hat | de Falla | Massine | 1919 |
| La Ventana | Lumbye and Holm | Bournonville | 1854 |
| A Wedding Bouquet | Berners | Ashton | 1937 |

## Ballet choreographers

Selected ballets are listed.

**Ashton, Sir Frederick William Mallandaine** (1904–88) English, born Guayaquil, Ecuador; *Façade* (1931), *Les Rendezvous* (1933), *Cinderella* (1948), *Daphnis and Chloe* (1951), *Ondine* (1958), *The Two Pigeons* (1961), *The Dream* (1964), *Rhapsody* (1980).

**Balanchine, George (Georgi Balanchivadze)** (1904–83) Russian–American, born St Petersburg; *Apollo* (1928), *The Prodigal Son* (1929), *Bourrée Fantasque* (1949), *Jeu de cartes* (1937), *Agon* (1957), *The Seven Deadly Sins* (1958), *Davidsbundlertauze* (1980).

**Bournonville, August** (1805–79) Danish, born Copenhagen; *La Sylphide* (1836), *Napoli* (1842), *La Ventana* (1854).

**Cranko, John** (1927–73) South African, born Rustenburg; *Beauty and the Beast* (1949), *Pineapple Doll* (1951), *The Prince of the Pagodas* (1957), *Jeu de Cartes* (1965), *Onegin* (1965), *Taming of the Shrew* (1969), *Traces* (1973).

**Darrell, Peter** (1929–87) English, born Richmond, Surrey; *A Wedding Present* (1962), *Beauty and the Beast* (1969), *Tales of Hoffman* (1972), *Swan Lake* (1977).

**Davies, Siobhan (Susan Davies)** (1950– ) English, born London; *New Galileo* (1984), *Bridge the Distance* (1985), *Different Trains* (1990), *Winnsboro Cotton Mill Blues* (1992).

**de Mille, Agnes George** (1905–93) American, born New York City; *Three Virgins and a Devil* (1941), *Rodeo* (1942), *Fall River Legend* (1948), and for Broadway, *Oklahoma!* (1943), *Gentlemen Prefer Blondes* (1949).

**de Valois, Dame Ninette (Edris Stannus)** (1898–2001) Irish, born Baltiboys, County Wicklow; *Job* (1931), *La Création du monde* (1931), *The Rake's Progress* (1935), *Checkmate* (1937), *Don Quixote* (1950).

**Diaghilev, Sergei Pavlovich** (1872–1929) Russian, born Selistchev barracks, province of Novgorod; producer, impressario, and founder of Ballet Russes; not a choreographer himself, he fostered the talents of Balanchine, Fokine, Nijinsky.

**Fokine, Michel (Mikhail Mikhaylovich Fokine)** (1880–1942) Russian–American dancer and choreographer, born St Petersburg; *Les Sylphides* (1907), *Petroushka* (1911).

**Ivanov, Lev (Ivanovich)** (1834–1901) Russian, born Moscow; *The Enchanted Forest* (1887), *The Nutcracker* (1892), *Swan Lake* (with Petipa, 1895).

**Jooss, Kurt** (1901–79) German, born Waaseralfingen; *Petrushka* (1930), *The Green Table* (1932), *Pulcinella* (1932), *The Mirror* (1935).

**Lorring, Eugene** (1914– ) American, born Milwaukee; *Yankee Clipper* (1937), *Billy the Kid* (1938).

**Macmillan, Sir Kenneth** (1929–92) Scottish, born Dunfermline, Fife; *The Rite of Spring* (1962), *Las Hermanas* (1963), *Romeo and Juliet* (1965), *Anastasia* (1971), *The Four Seasons* (1975), *Mayerling* (1978), *Isadora* (1981).

**Massine, Léonide (Fedorovich)** (1895–1979) Russian–American, born Moscow; *Parade* (1917), *La Boutique Fantasque* (1919), *The Three-Cornered Hat* (1919), *Bachanale* (1939).

**Morris, Mark (William)** (1956– ) American, born Seattle, Washington; *Il Penseroso ed il Moderato* (1988), *Dido and Aeneas* (1989), *The Hard Nut* (1991).

**Nijinska, Bronislova (Fominitshna)** (1891–1972) Russian–Polish–American, born Minsk, Russia; *Le Renard* (1922), *Les Noces* (1923, 1966), *Les Biches* (1924, 1964), *La Valse* (1929), *The Snow Maiden* (1942).

**Perrot, Jules (Joseph)** (1810–94) French, born Lyons; *Ondine* (1843), *Les Éléments* (1847), *Faust* (1848), *Markobomba* (1854).

**Petipa, Marius** (1818–1910) French, born Marseilles; *Pharoah's Daughter* (1862), *La Bayadère* (1877), *The Sleeping Beauty* (1890), *Cinderella* (1893), *Swan Lake* (1895), *Raymonda* (1898).

**Robbins, Jerome (Jerome Rabinowitz)** (1918–98) American, born New York; *Fancy Free* (1944), *Interplay* (1945), *The Pied Piper* (1951), *Afternoon of a Fawn* (1953), *West Side Story* (1957, musical), and for Broadway, eg *The King and I* (1951).

**St-Léon, Arthur** (1821–70) French, born Paris; *Le Violon du diable* (1849), *La Fille mal gardée* (1866), *La Source* (1866), *Coppélia* (1870).

**Tudor, Antony (William Cook)** (1908–87) English, born London; *Undertow* (1945), *Lady of the Camellias* (1951), *Shadowplay* (1967), *The Tiller in the Field* (1978).

## Major painting styles

**Abstract Art** A non-representational 20th-c style developed as a means of expressing inner reality in pictorial form. Some abstract pictures bear no resemblance to reality, whereas others feature a highly subjective treatment or 'abstraction' of recognizable subjects (as in Cubism). The earliest consciously abstract paintings were by Wassily Kandinsky (1910) and Frantisek Kupka (*Amorpha: Fugue in Two Colours*, 1912), both inspired by music, the universal abstract language. Abstract art led to other movements such as Neo-Plasticism, Constructivism and American Abstract Expressionism.

**Abstract Expressionism** A term relating to the vivid, non-representational work of a group of artists in 1940s New York, who were united by their emphasis on the expression inherent in the texture and colour of the paint itself, and the interaction of artist, paint and canvas; eg work by Mark Rothko, Arshile Gorky, Franz Kline, Jackson Pollock.

**Action Painting** A form of Abstract Expressionism; the technique of creating a picture that emphasizes the physical process of painting eg by throwing, splashing, dribbling or pouring on the paint. Its early exponents included Jackson Pollock, who also used knives on his canvases, dragged things across them and rode a bicycle on them, and Willem de Kooning.

**Baroque** An extravagant, confident and highly decorative style (c.1600–1720) which inherited movement from Mannerism and a sense of grandeur and solidity from High Renaissance. It was associated with the reinvigorated Catholic Church in Europe and often expressed intense religious emotion. In secular art, such as that commissioned by Louis XIV for Versailles, it served to express the glory of royalty; eg work by Rubens.

**Buddhist** Buddhism (founded 6th-cBC, India's national religion 3rd-cBC), coupled with the patronage of such rulers as the Mauryan emperor Asoka and the Kushan ruler Kanishka, had a major influence on Indian art and architecture. From 1st-cAD Buddha, previously represented by the lotus flower, a wheel, or by his throne, could be shown in human form, which gave rise to many highly ornate statues.

**Constructivism** A term usually applied to a form of abstract art that began in Russia c.1917, using machine-age materials such as steel, glass and plastic. Leading practitioners included Vladimir Tatlin, and the brothers Antoine Pevsner and Naum Gabo. In Russia this impetus was channelled into industrial design (Soviet Constructivism). Pevsner and Gabo left Russia in the early 1920s, and their ideas subsequently influenced abstract artists in the West (International Constructivism).

**Cubism** A radical movement founded 1908 by Georges Braque and Pablo Picasso which revolutionized European painting and sculpture and continued in its purest form until the 1920s. Objects were no longer depicted from a single, fixed viewpoint, but were broken up into a multiplicity of facets, so that several different aspects of an object could be seen simultaneously; eg also work by Juan Gris, Fernand Léger, Stuart Davis.

**Dada** and **Surrealism** Two important, closely related movements in Europe and America. Both were pointedly anti-rationalist, laying emphasis on incongruous or shocking effects, but a key difference was that Dada (1916–22), arising from the mood of despair following World War I, was predominantly nihilistic, while Surrealism (1924–c.1940), which aimed to release and explore the creative powers of the subconscious mind using dreamlike effects, was much more positive in spirit; eg work by Ernst, Duchamp, Man Ray, Schwitters (Dada); Dalí, Magritte (Surrealism).

**Dutch Art, 17th-Century** The golden age in Dutch art (c.1609–70) began when the Netherlands gained its freedom from Spain; its subjects tended to celebrate the country's hard-won peace and prosperity, eg seascapes, landscapes, portraits of successful merchants, domestic scenes, and still lifes. There was little religious art because of the Protestant ethos; eg work by Frans Hals, Vermeer, Rembrandt.

**Egyptian** Painting and sculpture were mainly for decoration of tombs and temples, and figures were shown in static poses, expressing a schematic idea of their essence rather than depicting how they appeared to the eye.

**Expressionism** The communication of the internal emotional realities of a situation, rather than its external 'realistic' aspect. Traditional ideas of beauty and proportion are disregarded, so that artists can express their feelings more strongly by means of distortion, exaggeration and jarring colours. The term was first used in Germany in 1911, but the trend began with Van Gogh and Gauguin in the 1880s; eg work by the groups known as *Die Brücke* (incl Ernst Kirchner) and *Der Blaue Reiter* (incl Wassily Kandinsky) in Germany.

**Fauvism** An early 20th-c movement by a group of French painters dubbed *les Fauves* ('wild beasts'). Their work was characterized by the use of brilliant colours, distorted shapes and flat composition, without regard to realism or perspective; eg work by Matisse, André Derain, Maurice de Vlaminck.

**Feminist Art** Art not simply made by women, but exploring issues specifically relating to women's identity and experience. The movement began in the 1960s and involved reviving the reputations of neglected women artists of the past as well as promoting the work of contemporary women artists; eg Judy Chicago, Miriam Schapiro.

**Gothic** A style of Christian art (12th-c–16th-c) characterized by stylized figures wearing flowing garments.

**Greek** Greek painters and sculptors were the first to

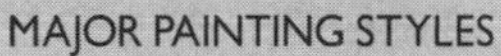



master naturalistic depiction of the human body. Most of the surviving painting is on vases or wall fragments. Greek art is broken down into four periods: Geometric (9th–8th-cBC, named after a style of vase decoration); Archaic (700–480BC); Classical (480–323BC, when Greek art reached its greatest harmony and majesty); and Hellenistic (323–27BC).

**High Renaissance** The period c.1490–1520 in Rome, Florence and Venice, during which the ideals of the Renaissance are thought to have been given most complete expression in art; eg work by Leonardo da Vinci, Michelangelo, Raphael, Titian, Andrea del Sarto.

**Impressionism** A style which aims to give a general impression of feelings and events rather than a formal or structural treatment of them. It was born in 1874 when a number of French artists who had difficulty in having their work accepted for the official Paris Salon organized their own group exhibition. Impressionist pictures are typically bright and cheerful, depicting contemporary life in a fresh and immediate way, and conveying the impression of a scene without minute detail; eg work by Monet, Manet, Pissarro, Renoir, Sisley, Degas, Cassatt.

**International Gothic** A style of art which flourished in W Europe (c.1375–c.1425), characterized by jewel-like colour, graceful shapes and realistic details. The style was seen especially in miniature paintings, drawings, and tapestries, often representing secular themes from courtly life.

**Islamic** Despite vast regional variations, there is an underlying unity in Islamic art, which reflects the main features of Islam (founded 7th-cAD): Mecca and the ornate niche in every mosque showing its direction; mosques; minarets, from which the faithful are called to prayer; and domes, symbolizing the heavens. Islamic theology forbids representation of the human figure in religious art, so decoration is abstract, eg complex geometrical patterns incorporating flowing Arabic script. However, in secular art illuminated manuscripts were produced showing hunting scenes and courtly life.

**Mannerism** A form of art and architecture prevalent in France, Spain, and especially Italy during the 16th-c. It is characterized by the playful use of Classical elements and *trompe l'oeil* effects in bizarre or dramatic compositions; eg work by Giulio Romano, Jacopa da Pontormo, Francesco Parmigianino, Giambologna.

**Medieval** The Middle Ages were dominated by Romanesque and Gothic architecture, and large-scale painting and sculpture existed mainly as adjuncts to these styles. Otherwise, painting mainly appeared as stained glass, which reached its zenith in 12th-c France.

**Neoclassicism** A movement (late 18th-c–early 19th-c) which arose partly as a reaction to Rococo and Baroque excesses in decoration, and partly from a renewed interest in the antique, especially the simplicity and grandeur of Greek and Roman art. Centred in Rome, it later spread throughout W Europe and N America. In painting, the classical themes and subjects were powerfully and dramatically represented in works by Jacques Louis David (eg *The Oath of the Horatii*, 1784).

**Neo-Expressionism** A term used to describe an international representational style which arose in the late 1970s. Works are sometimes abstract, sometimes figurative and sometimes bordering between the two, but are usually large in scale and tend to go to extremes of aggressive rawness in technique and feeling. They are characterized by a theatrical, melodramatic flavour conveyed by strong brushstrokes and colours, and distorted shapes; eg work by Julian Schnabel, Anselm Kiefer.

**Neo-Plasticism** A style of abstract painting in which geometrical patterns are formed of patches of pure flat colour enclosed by intersecting vertical and horizontal lines. It encompasses the 1920s style and theories of Dutch painter and theosophist Piet Mondrian, who tried to express an ideal of universal harmony in his austerely geometrical works.

**Pop Art** A modern art form based on the commonplace and ephemeral aspects of 20th-c urban life, such as soup cans, comics, movies and advertising. Pioneer British Pop Artists in the mid-1950s include Peter Blake, Eduardo Paolozzi, Richard Hamilton; leading American contributors in the 1960s included Jasper Johns, Andy Warhol, Roy Lichtenstein.

**Post-Impressionism** An umbrella term (coined 1910 by Roger Fry) for a number of trends in French painting that developed in the wake of Impressionism c.1880–1905. Its features included focus on structure and renewed importance of the subject; the decorative and symbolic, rather than naturalistic, use of colour and line; and emotional intensity conveyed by brilliant colour and swirling brushstrokes; eg work by Cézanne, Gauguin, Van Gogh.

**Post-Modernism** Most commonly an architectural or literary term, Post-Modernist refers to art works that blend disparate styles and make knowing use of cultural references, as in Pop Art.

**Pre-Raphaelite** A highly symbolic style characterizing the work of a group of mid-19th-c artists in London (the Pre-Raphaelite Brotherhood). Rejecting the formal academic art and neoclassicism prevalent at the time, they turned for inspiration to the brightly coloured work of Italian artists active before Raphael (1483–1520), and painted historical, literary and religious subjects with moral fervour, vivid colour, rich detail and elaborate symbolism; eg work by Holman Hunt, Dante Gabriel Rossetti, John Everett Millais.

**Primitivism** The result of the influence on modern artists of the art of the indigenous peoples of Africa, Oceania, and the Americas, which was seen to contain a sense of vitality and truth that had been polished out of western painting and sculpture; eg work by Ernst Kirchner, Modigliani, Picasso, Gauguin.

**Realism** A term which until the end of the 19th-c referred to naturalism, or the true-to-life depiction of subjects, eg late 16th-c work by Caravaggio. In

France c.1840–80 it was a specific term relating to the depiction of unidealized subject-matter taken from everyday life, deliberately chosen to make a social or political point; eg work by Gustave Courbet and Honoré Daumier. In the late 20th-c, realism may refer simply to the move away from abstract art towards a more representational style, though it may also refer to the kind of abstract art that opposes superficial appearances and focuses on inner truth as 'reality'.

**Renaissance** A style prevalent in Europe (14th-c–16th-c) reflecting classical Greek and Roman styles. Little Roman painting had survived to be copied, but the ancient artists' fidelity to nature became a basic tenet of the Renaissance style; eg work by Masaccio (the first to master perspective), Albrecht Dürer, Pieter Brueghel.

**Rococo** A florid European style born in France (c.1700). Partly a development from Baroque art and partly a reaction against it, Rococo art is characterized by elaborate ornamental details and asymmetrical patterns, and was most successful as a style of interior decoration. Whereas Baroque art is sometimes sombre and often religious, it is much lighter (often intentionally playful) in spirit and usually secular. It flourished until the 1760s in France and the late-18th-c elsewhere; eg work by Watteau, Boucher and Fragonard.

**Romanticism** An intellectual trend (late 18th-c–mid 19th-c) that regarded the emotions and self-expression, rather than beauty of form or structure, as the basis of composition. Typical themes were wild or mysterious landscapes and dramatic scenes from literature; there was also interest in dreams and nightmares and in extremes of feelings and behaviour; eg work by Delacroix, Caspar David Friedrich, J M W Turner, Goya.

## Artists

Selected paintings are listed.

**Altdorfer, Albrecht** (c.1480–1538) German, born Regensburg; *Danube Landscape* (1520), *Alexander's Victory* (1529).

**Andrea del Sarto** (properly **Andrea d'Agnolo di Francesco**) (1486–1530) Italian, born Florence; *Miracles of S Filippo Benizzi* (1509–10), *Madonna del Saeco* (1525).

**Angelico, Fra** (real name **Guido di Pietro**) (c.1400–55) Italian, born Vicchio, Tuscany; *Coronation of the Virgin* (1430–5), *San Marco altarpiece* (c.1440).

**Auerbach, Frank** (1931– ) Anglo-German, born Berlin; *Mornington Crescent* (1967), *Jake* (1990).

**Bacon, Francis** (1909–92) British, born Dublin; *Three Figures at the Base of a Crucifixion* (1945), *Two Figures with a Monkey* (1973), *Triptych Inspired by the Oresteia of Aeschylus* (1981).

**Beardsley, Aubrey (Vincent)** (1872–98) British, born Brighton; illustrations to Malory's *Morte d'Arthur* (1893), Wilde's *Salome* (1894).

**Bell, Vanessa** (1879–1961) British, born Kensington, London; *Still Life on Corner of a Mantlepiece* (1914).

**Bellini, Gentile** (c.1429–1507) Italian, born Venice; *Procession of the Relic of the True Cross* (1496), *Miracle at Ponte di Lorenzo* (1500).

**Blackadder, Elizabeth** (1931– ) British, born Falkirk; *Interior with Self-Portrait* (1972), *White Anemones* (1983), *Texas Flame* (1986).

**Blake, Peter** (1932– ) British, born Dartford, Kent; *On the Balcony* (1955–7), design for the Beatles' album *Sergeant Pepper's Lonely Hearts Club Band* (1967), *The Meeting* (1981).

**Blake, William** (1757–1827) British, born London; illustrations for his own *Songs of Innocence and Experience* (1794), *Newton* (1795), illustrations for the *Book of Job* (1826).

**Böcklin, Arnold** (1827–1901) Swiss, born Basel; *Pan in the Reeds* (1857), *The Island of the Dead* (1880).

**Bomberg, David** (1890–1957) British, born Birmingham; *In the Hold* (1913–14), *The Mud Bath* (1913–14).

**Bonnard, Pierre** (1867–1947) French, born Paris; *Young Woman in Lamplight* (1900), *Dining Room in the Country* (1913), *Seascape of the Mediterranean* (1941).

**Bosch, Hieronymus** (real name **Jerome van Aken**) (c.1460–1516) Dutch, born 's-Hertogenbosch, Brabant; *The Temptation of St Anthony*, *The Garden of Earthly Delights* (work undated).

**Botticelli, Sandro** (originally **Alessandro di Mariano Filipepi**) (1444–1510) Italian, born Florence; *Primavera* (c.1478), *The Birth of Venus* (c.1485), *Mystic Nativity* (1500).

**Boucher, François** (1703–70) French, born Paris; *Reclining Girl* (1751), *The Rising* and *The Setting of the Sun* (1753).

**Braque, Georges** (1882–1963) French, born Argenteuil-sur-Seine; *Still Life with Violin* (1910), *The Portuguese* (1911), *Blue Wash-Basin* (1942).

**Brueghel, Pieter, (the Elder)** (c.1525–69) Dutch, born Bruegel, near Breda; *Road to Calvary* (1564), *Massacre of the Innocents* (c.1566), *The Blind Leading the Blind* (1568), *The Peasant Wedding* (1568), *The Peasant Dance* (1568).

**Burne-Jones, Sir Edward (Coley)** (1833–98) British, born Birmingham; *The Beguiling of Merlin* (1874), *The Arming of Perseus* (1877), *King Cophetea and the Beggar Maid* (1880–4).

**Burra, Edward** (1905–76) British, born London; *Dancing Skeletons* (1934), *Soldiers* (1942), *Scene in Harlem (Simply Heavenly)* (1952).

**Canaletto** (properly **Giovanni Antonio Canal**) (1697–1768) Italian, born Venice; *Stone Mason's Yard* (c.1730).

**Caravaggio** (properly **Michelangelo Merisi da Caravaggio**) (1573–1610) Italian, born Caravaggio, near Burgamo; *The Supper at Emmaus* (c.1598–1600), *Martyrdom of St Matthew* (1599–1600), *The Death of the Virgin* (1605–6).

**Cassatt, Mary** (1844–1926) American, born Pittsburgh, Pennsylvania; *The Blue Room* (1878), *Lady at the Tea Table* (1885), *Morning Toilette* (1886), *The Tramway* (1891), *The Bath* (1892).

**Cézanne, Paul** (1839–1906) French, born Aix-en-Provence; *The Black Marble Clock* (c.1869–70), *Maison du Pendu* (c.1873), *Bathing Women* (1900–5), *Le Jardinier* (1906).

**Chagall, Marc** (1887–1985) Russian–French, born Vitebsk; *The Musician* (1912–13), *Bouquet of Flying Lovers* (1947).

**Chicago, Judy**, originally **Judy Gerowitz** (1939– ) American, born Chicago; *The Dinner Party* (1974–9).

**Chirico, Giorgio de** (1888–1978) Italian, born Volos, Greece; *Portrait of Guillaume Apollinaire* (1914), *The Jewish Angel* (1916), *The Return of Ulysses* (1968).

**Christo** (originally **Christo Javacheff**) (1935– ) American, born Gabovra, Bulgaria; *Surrounded Islands* (1980–3), *Wrapped Reichstag* (1995).

**Cimabue** (originally **Bencivieni di Pepo**) (c.1240–c.1302) Italian, born Florence; *Crucifix* (date unknown), *Saint John the Evangelist* (1302).

**Claude Lorraine** (in full **Claude Le Lorrain**) (real name **Claude Gêllée**) (1600–82) French, born near Nancy; *The Mill* (1631), *The Embarkation of St Ursula* (1641), *Ascanius Shooting the Stag of Silvia* (1682).

**Constable, John** (1776–1837) British, born East Bergholt, Suffolk; *A Country Lane* (c.1810), *The White Horse* (1819), *The Hay Wain* (1821), *Stonehenge* (1835).

**Corot, Jean Baptiste Camille** (1796–1875) French, born Paris; *Bridge at Narni* (1827), *Souvenir de Marcoussis* (1869), *Woman Reading in a Landscape* (1869).

**Correggio (Antonio Allegri da)** (c.1494–1534) Italian, born Corregio; *The Agony in the Garden* (c.1528).

**Courbet, (Jean Désiré) Gustave** (1819–77) French, born Ornans; *The After-Dinner at Ornans* (1848–9), *The Bathers* (1853), *The Painter's Studio* (1855), *The Stormy Sea* (1869).

**Cranach, Lucas, (the Elder)** (1472–1553) German, born Kronach, near Bamberg; *The Crucifixion* (1503), *The Fountain of Youth* (1550).

**Dalí, Salvador (Felipe Jacinto)** (1904–89) Spanish, born Figueras, Gerona; *The Persistence of Memory* (1931), *The Transformation of Narcissus* (1934), *Christ of St John of the Cross* (1951).

**Daumier, Honoré** (1808–78) French, born Marseilles; many caricatures and lithographs; *The Legislative Paunch* (1834), *The Third Class Carriage* (1840s), paintings on the theme of *Don Quixote*.

**David, Jacques Louis** (1748–1825) French, born Paris; *Death of Socrates* (1788), *The Death of Marat* (1793), *The Rape of the Sabines* (1799), *Madame Récamier* (1800).

**Davis, Stuart** (1894–1964) American, born Philadelphia; *The President* (1917), *House and Street* (1931), *Visa* (1951), *Premiere* (1957).

**Degas, (Hilaire Germain) Edgar** (1834–1917) French, born Paris; *Cotton-brokers Office* (1873), *L'Absinthe* (1875–6), *Little Fourteen-year-old Dancer* (sculpture) (1881), *Dancer at the Bar* (c.1900).

**de Kooning, Willem** (1904–97) American, born Rotterdam, the Netherlands; *Woman I-V* (1952–3), *Montauk Highway* (1958), *Pastorale* (1963).

**Delacroix, (Ferdinand Victor) Eugène** (1798–1863) French, born St-Maurice-Charenton; *Dante and Virgil in Hell* (1822), *Liberty Guiding the People* (1831), *Jacob and the Angel* (1853–61).

**Delvaux, Paul** (1897–1994) Belgian, born Antheit, near Huys; *Vénus endormie* (1932), *Phases of the Moon* (1939), *In Praise of Melancholy* (1951).

**Derain, André Louis** (1880–1954) French, born Chatou; *Mountains at Collioure* (1905), *Westminster Bridge* (1907), *The Bagpiper* (1910–11).

**Doré, (Louis Auguste) Gustave** (1832–83) French, born Strasbourg; Illustrations to Dante's *Inferno* (1861), Milton's *Paradise Lost* (1866).

**Duccio di Buoninsegna** (c.1260–c.1320) Italian; *Maestà* (Siena Cathedral altarpiece) (1308–11).

**Duchamp, (Henri Robert) Marcel** (1887–1968) French–American, born Blainville, Normandy; *Nude Descending a Staircase* (1912), *The Bride Stripped Bare by Her Bachelors Even* (1915–23).

**Dufy, Raoul** (1877–1953) French, born Le Havre; *Posters at Trouville* (1906), illustrations to Guillaume Apollinaire's *Bestiary* (1911), *Riders in the Wood* (1931).

**Dürer, Albrecht** (1471–1528) German, born Nuremberg; *Adam and Eve* (1507), *Adoration of the Magi* (1504), *Adoration of the Trinity* (1511).

**Eardley, Joan** (1921–63) British, born Warnham, Sussex; *Winter Sea IV* (1958), *Two Children* (1962).

**Ernst, Max(imillian)** (1891–1976) German–American–French, born Brühl, near Cologne, Germany; *Europe After the Rain* (1940–2), *The Elephant Célébes* (1921), *Moonmad* (1944) (sculpture), *The King Playing with the Queen* (1959) (sculpture).

**Eyck, Jan van** (c.1389–1441) Dutch, born Maaseyck, near Maastricht; *The Adoration of the Holy Lamb* (Ghent altarpiece) (1432), *Man in a Red Turban* (1433), *Arnolfni Marriage Portrait* (1434), *Madonna by the Fountain* (1439).

**Fini, Léonor** (1908–96) Italian–Argentinian, born Buenos Aires; *The End of the World* (1944).

**Fragonard, Jean Honoré** (1732–1806) French, born Grasse; *Coroesus Sacrificing Himself to Save Callirhoe* (1765), *The Swing* (c.1766), four canvases for Mme du Barry entitled *The Progress of Love* (1771–3).

**Freud, Lucian** (1922– ) German–British, born Berlin; *Woman with a Daffodil* (1945), *Interior in Paddington* (1951), *Hotel Room* (1953–4).

**Friedrich, Caspar David** (1774–1840) German, born Pomerania; *The Cross in the Mountains* (1807–8).

**Fuseli, Henri** (originally **Johann Heinrich Füssli**) (1741–1825) Anglo-Swiss, born Zurich; *The Nightmare* (1781), *Appearance of the Ghost* (1796).

**Gainsborough, Thomas** (1727–88) British, born Sudbury, Suffolk; *Peasant Girl Gathering Sticks* (1782), *The Watering Place* (1777).

**Gauguin, (Eugène Henri) Paul** (1848–1903) French, born Paris; *The Vision After the Sermon* (1888), *Still Life with Three Puppies* (1888), *The White Horse* (1898), *Women of Tahiti* (1891), *Tahitian Landscape* (1891), *Where Do We Come From? What Are We? Where Are We Going?* (1897–8), *Golden Bodies* (1901).

**Géricault, Théodore** (1791–1824) French, born Rouen; *Officer of Light Horse* (c.1812), *Raft of the Medusa* (1819).

**Ghirlandaio, Domenico** (properly **Domenico di Tommaso Bigordi**) (1449–94) Italian, born Florence; *Virgin of Mercy* (1472), *St Jerome* (1480), *Nativity* (1485).

**Giorgione (da Castelfranco)** or **Giorgio Barbarelli** (c.1478–1511) Italian, born Castelfranco; *The Tempest* (c.1508), *Three Philosophers* (c.1508), *Portrait of a Man* (1510).

**Giotto (di Bondone)** (c.1266–1337) Italian, born near Florence; frescoes in *Arena Chapel*, Padua (1304–12), *Ognissanti Madonna* (1311–12).

**Goes, Hugo van der** (c.1440–82) Dutch, born probably Ghent; *Portinari Altarpiece* (1475).

**Gorky, Arshile** (originally **Vosdanig Manoog Adoian**) (1905–48) American, born Khorkom Vari, Turkish Armenia; *The Artist and His Mother* (c.1926–36), series *Image in Xhorkam* (from 1936), *The Liver is the Cock's Comb* (1944), *The Betrothal II* (1947).

**Goya (y Lucientes), Francisco (José) de** (1746–1828) Spanish, born Fuendetotos; *Family of Charles IV* (1799), *Los Desastres de la Guerra* (1810–14), *Black Paintings* (1820s).

**Greco, El** (properly **Domenico Theotocopoulos**) (1541–1614) Greek, born Candia, Crete; *Lady in Fur Wrap* (c.1577–8), *El Espolio* ('The Disrobing of Christ') (1577–9), *The Saviour of the World* (1600), *Portrait of Brother Hortensio Felix Paravicino* (1609), *Toledo Landscape* (c.1610).

**Gris, Juan** (pseudonym of **José Victoriano González**) (1887–1927) Spanish, born Madrid; *Sunblind* (1914), *Still Life with Dice* (1922), *Violin and Fruit Dish* (1924).

**Grünewald, Matthias** (originally **Mathis Nithardt** or **Gothardt**) (c.1480–1528) German, born probably Würzburg; *Isenheim Altarpiece* (1515).

**Hals, Frans** (c.1580–1666) Dutch, born Antwerp; *The Laughing Cavalier* (1624), *Banquet of the Company of St Adrian* (1627), *Gypsy Girl* (c.1628–30), *Man in a Slouch Hat* (c.1660–6).

**Hamilton, Richard** (1922– ) British, born London; *Hommage à Chrysler Corp* (1952), *Just what is it that makes today's homes so different, so appealing?* (1956), *Study of Hugh Gaitskell as a Famous Monster of Film Land* (1964).

**Hilliard, Nicholas** (c.1547–1619) British, born Exeter; miniature of *Queen Elizabeth I* (1572), *Henry Wriothesley* (1594).

**Hirst, Damien** (1965– ) British, born Bristol; *The Physical Impossibilty of Death in the Mind of Someone Living* (1991), *The Asthmatic Escaped* (1991), *Mother and Child, Divided* (1993).

**Hockney, David** (1937– ) British, born Bradford, Yorkshire; *We Two Boys Together Clinging* (1961), *The Rake's Progress* (1963), *A Bigger Splash* (1967), *Invented Man Revealing a Still Life* (1975), *Dancer* (1980).

**Hogarth, William** (1697–1764) British, born Smithfield, London; *Before and After* (1731), *A Rake's Progress* (1733–5).

**Hokusai, Katsushika** (1760–1849) Japanese, born Tokyo; *Tametomo and the Demon* (1811), *Mangwa* (1814–19), *Hundred Views of Mount Fuji* (1835).

**Holbein, Hans, (the Younger)** (1497–1543) German, born Augsburg; *Bonifacius Amerbach* (1519), *Solothurn Madonna* (1522), *Anne of Cleves* (1539).

**Hundertwasser, Friedensreich (Friedrich Stowasser)** (1928–2000) Austrian, born Vienna; *Many Transparent Heads* (1949–50), *The End of Greece* (1963), *The Court of Sulaiman* (1967).

**Hunt, (William) Holman** (1827–1910) British, born London; *Our English Coasts* (1852), *Claudio and Isabella* (1853), *The Light of the World* (1854), *Isabella and the Pot of Basil* (1867).

**Ingres, Jean August Dominique** (1780–1867) French, born Montauban; *Gilbert* (1805), *La Source* (1807–59), *Bather* (1808), *Turkish Bath* (1863).

**John, Augustus (Edwin)** (1878–1961) British, born Tenby; *The Smiling Woman* (1908), *Portrait of a Lady in Black* (1917).

**John, Gwen** (1876–1939) British, born Haverfordwest, Pembrokeshire; *Girl with Bare Shoulders* (1909–10).

**Johns, Jasper** (1930– ) American, born Allendale, South Carolina; *Target with Four Faces* (1955), *Beer Cans* (1961) (sculpture).

**Kandinsky, Wassily** (1866–1944) Russian–French, born Moscow; *Kossacks* (1910–11), *Swinging* (1925), *Two Green Points* (1935), *Sky Blue* (1940).

**Kiefer, Anselm** (1945– ) German, born Donaueschingen, Baden; *Parsifal III* (1973), *Innenraum* (1982), *Lilith* (1989).

**Kirchner, Ernst Ludwig** (1880–1938) German, born Aschaffenburg; *Recumbent Blue Nude with Straw Hat* (1908–9), *The Drinker* (1915), *Die Amselfluh* (1923).

**Kitaj, R(onald) B(rooks)** (1932– ) American, born Cleveland, Ohio; *The Ohio Gang* (1964), *If Not, Not* (1975–6).

**Klee, Paul** (1879–1940) Swiss, born Münchenbuchsee, near Berne; *Der Vollmond* (1919), *Rosegarden* (1920), *Twittering Machine* (1922), *A Tiny Tale of a Tiny Dwarf* (1925), *Fire in the Evening* (1929).

**Klimt, Gustav** (1862–1918) Austrian, born Baumgarten, near Vienna; *Music* (1895), *The Kiss* (1907–8), *Judith II (Salome)* (1909).

**Kline, Franz Joseph** (1910–62) American, born Wilkes-Barre, Pennsylvania; *Orange and Black Wall* (1939), *Chief* (1950), *Mahoning* (1956).

**Kokoschka, Oskar** (1886–1980) Anglo-Austrian, born Pöchlarn; *The Dreaming Boys* (1908).

**Kupka, Frantisek** (1871–1957) Czech, born in Opocno, East Bohemia; *Girl with a Ball* (1908), *Amorpha: Fugue in Two Colours* (1912), *Working Steel* (1921–9).

**Landseer, Sir Edwin (Henry)** (1803–73) British, born London; *The Old Shepherd's Chief Mourner* (1837), *The Monarch of the Glen* (1850).

**La Tour, Georges (Dumesnil) de** (1593–1652) French, born Vic-sur-Seille, Lorraine; *St Jerome Reading* (1620s), *The Denial of St Peter* (1650).

**Léger, Fernand** (1881–1955) French, born Argentan; *Contrast of Forms* (1913), *Black Profile* (1928), *The Great Parade* (1954).

**Lely, Sir Peter** (originally **Pietar van der Faes**) (1618–80) Anglo-Dutch, born Soest, Westphalia; *The Windsor Beauties* (1668), *Admirals* series (1666–7).

**Leonardo da Vinci (Leonardo di Ser Piero da Vince)** (1452–1519) Italian, born Vinci; *The Last Supper* (1495–7), *Madonna and Child with St Anne* (begun 1503), *Mona Lisa* (1500–6), *The Virgin of the Rocks* (c.1508).

**Lichtenstein, Roy** (1923–97) American, born New York City; *Whaam!* (1963), *As I Opened Fire* (1964).

**Lippi, Fra Filippo**, called **Lippo** (c.1406–69) Italian, born Florence; *Tarquinia Madonna* (1437), *Barbadori Altarpiece* (begun 1437).

**Lochner, Stefan** (c.1400–51) German, born Meersburg am Bodenese; *The Adoration of the Magi* (c.1448), triptych in Cologne Cathedral.

**Macke, August** (1887–1914) German, born Meschede; *Greeting* (1912), *The Zoo* (1912), *Girls Under Trees* (1914).

**Magritte, René (François Ghislain)** (1898–1967) Belgian, born Lessines, Hainault; *The Menaced Assassin* (1926), *Loving Perspective* (1935), *Presence of Mind* (1960).

**Manet, Édouard** (1932–83) French, born Paris; *Le Déjeuner sur l'herbe* (1863), *La Brioche* (1870), *A Bar at the Folies-Bergères* (1882).

**Mantegna, Andrea** (1431–1506) Italian, born Vicenza; *Madonna of Victory* (altarpiece), *San Zeno Altarpiece* (1457–9), *Triumphs of Caesar* (c.1486–94).

**Martin, John** (1789–1854) British, born Haydon Bridge; *Joshua Commanding the Sun to Stand Still* (1816), *The Last Judgement* (1851–4).

**Martini** or **Memmi, Simone** (c.1284–1344) Italian, born Siena; *S Caterina Polyptych* (1319), *Annunciation* (1333).

**Masaccio** (real name **Tommaso di Giovanni di Simone Guidi**) (1401–28) Italian, born Castel San Giovanni di Val d'Arno; *polyptych* for the *Carmelite Church* in Pisa (1426), frescoes in *Sta Maria del Carmine*, Florence (1424–7).

**Masson, André (Aimé René)** (1896–1987) French, born Balgny, Oise; *Massacres* (1933), *The Labyrinth* (1939).

**Matisse, Henri (Emile Benoît)** (1869–1954) French, born Le Cateau-Cambrésis; *La Desserte* (1908), *Notre Dame* (1914), *The Large Red Studio* (1948), *L'Escargot* (1953).

**Michelangelo** (in full **Michelangelo di Lodovico Buonarroti**) (1475–1564) Italian, born Caprese, Tuscany; *The Pietà* (1497) (sculpture), *David* (1501–4) (sculpture), *Madonna* (c.1502), ceiling of the *Sistine Chapel*, Rome (1508–12), *The Last Judgement* (begun 1537).

**Millais, Sir John Everett** (1829–96) British, born Southampton; *Ophelia* (1851–2), *The Bridesmaid* (1851), *Tennyson* (1881), *Bubbles* (1886).

**Millet, Jean-François** (1814–75) French, born Grouchy; *Sower* (1850), *The Gleaners* (1857).

**Miró, Joán** (1893–1983) Spanish, born Montroig; *Catalan Landscape* (1923–4), *Maternity* (1924).

**Modigliani, Amedeo** (1884–1920) Italian, born Leghorn (Livorno), Tuscany; *The Jewess* (1908), *Moise Kisling* (1915), *Reclining Nude* (c.1919), *Jeanne Hébuterne* (1919).

**Mondrian, Piet** (properly **Pieter Cornelis Mondriaan**) (1872–1944) Dutch, born Amersfoot; *Still Life with Gingerpot II* (1911), *Composition with Red, Black, Blue, Yellow, and Grey* (1920), *Broadway Boogie-Woogie* (1942–3).

**Monet, Claude** (1840–1926) French, born Paris; *Impression: Sunrise* (1872), *Haystacks* (1890–1), *Rouen Cathedral* (1892–5), *Waterlilies* (1899 onwards).

**Moreau, Gustave** (1826–98) French, born Paris; *Oedipus and the Sphinx* (1864), *Apparition* (1876), *Jupiter and Semele* (1889–95).

**Morisot, Berthe (Marie Pauline)** (1841–95) French, born Bourges; *The Harbour at Cherbourg* (1874), *In the Dining Room* (1886).

**Morris, William** (1834–96) British, born Walthamstow, London; *Queen Guinevere* (1858).

**Motherwell, Robert (Burns)** (1915–91) American, born Aberdeen, Washington; *Gauloises* (1967), *Opens* (1968–72).

**Munch, Edvard** (1863–1944) Norwegian, born Löten; *The Scream* (1893), *Mother and Daughter* (c.1897), *Self-Portrait between the Clock and the Bed* (1940–2).

**Nash, Paul** (1899–1946) British, born London; *We Are Making a New World* (1918), *Menin Road* (1919).

**Newman, Barnett** (1905–70) American, born New York; *The Moment* (1946), *Onement I* (1948), *Vir Heroicus Sublimis* (1950–1).

**Nicholson, Ben** (1894–1982) British, born Denham, London; *White Relief* (1935), *November 11, 1947* (1947).

**Nicholson, Winifred** (1893–1981) British, born Oxford; *Honeysuckle and Sweet Peas* (1950), *The Copper and Capari* (1967), *The Gate to the Isles* (1980).

**Nolde, Emil** (pseudonym of **Emil Hansen**) (1867–1956) German, born Nolde; *The Missionary* (1912), *Candle Dancers* (1912).

**Oliver, Isaac** (c.1560–1617) Anglo-French, born Rouen; *Self-Portrait* (c.1590), *Henry, Prince of Wales* (c.1612).

**Palmer, Samuel** (1805–81) British, born London; *Repose of the Holy Family* (1824), *The Magic Apple Tree* (1830), *Opening the Fold* (1880).

**Parmigiano** or **Parmigianino** (properly **Girolamo Francesco Maria Mazzola**) (1503–40) Italian, born Parma; frescoes in *S Giovanni Evangelista*, Parma (c.1522), *Self-Portrait in a Convex Mirror* (1524), *Vision of St Jerome* (1526–7), *Madonna Altarpiece*, Bologna (c.1528–30), *The Madonna of the Long Neck* (c.1535).

**Pasmore, (Edwin John) Victor** (1908–98) British, born Chelsham, Surrey; *The Evening Star* (1945–7), *Black Symphony – the Pistol Shot* (1977).

**Peploe, S(amuel) J(ohn)** (1871–1935) British, born Edinburgh; one of the 'Scottish colourists'; *Boats of Royan* (1910).

**Perugino** (properly **Pietro di Cristoforo Vannucci**) (c.1450–1523) Italian, born Città della Pieve, Umbria; *Christ Giving the Keys to Peter* (fresco in the Sistine Chapel) (c.1483).

**Pevsner, Antoine** (1886–1962) French, born Orël, Russia; *Torso* (1924–6), *Development Column* (1942).

**Picabia, Francis (Marie)** (1879–1953) French, born Paris; *I See Again in Memory My Dear Undine* (1913), *The Kiss* (1924).

**Picasso, Pablo (Ruiz)** (1881–1973) Spanish, born Malaga; *Mother and Child* (1921), *Three Dances* (1925), *Guernica* (1937), *The Charnel House* (1945), *The Artist and His Model* (1968).

**Piero della Francesca** (c.1420–92) Italian, born Borgo san Sepolcro; *Madonna of the Misericordia* (1445–8), *Resurrection* (c.1450).

**Piper, John** (1903–92) British, born Epsom; *Windsor Castle* watercolours (1941–2), *Council Chamber, House of Commons* (1941); also stage designs and illustrated publications.

**Pissarro, Camille (Jacob)** (1830–1903) French, born St Thomas, West Indies; *Landscape at Chaponval* (1880), *The Boieldieu Bridge at Rouen* (1896), *Boulevard Montmartre* (1897).

**Pollock, (Paul) Jackson** (1912–56) American, born Cody, Wyoming; *No 14* (1948), *Guardians of the Secret* (1943).

**Pontormo, Jacopo da** (1494–1552) Italian; frescoes eg of the *Passion* (1522–5), *Deposition* (c.1525).

**Poussin, Nicolas** (1594–1665) French, born Les Andelys, Normandy; *The Adoration of the Golden Calf* (1624), *Inspiration of the Poet* (c.1628), *Seven Sacraments* (1644–8), *Self-Portrait* (1650).

**Raeburn, Sir Henry** (1756–1823) British, born Edinburgh; *Rev Robert Walker Skating* (1784), *Isabella McLeod, Mrs James Gregory* (c.1798).

**Ramsay, Allan** (1713–84) British, born Edinburgh; *The Artist's Wife* (1754–5).

**Raphael** (properly **Raffaello Santi** or **Sanzio**) (1483–1520) Italian, born Urbino; *Assumption of the Virgin* (1504), *Madonna of the Meadow* (1505–6), *Transfiguration* (1518–20).

**Redon, Odilon** (1840–1916) French, born Bordeaux; *Woman with Outstretched Arms* (c.1910–14).

**Redpath, Anne** (1895–1965) British, born Galashiels; *Pinks* (1947).

**Rembrandt** (properly **Rembrandt Harmensz van Rijn**) (1606–69) Dutch, born Leiden; *Anatomy Lesson of Dr Tulp* (1632), *Blinding of Samson* (1636), *The Night Watch* (1642), *The Conspiracy of Claudius* (1661–2).

**Renoir, (Jean Pierre) Auguste** (1841–1919) French, born Limoges; *Woman in Blue* (1874), *Woman Reading* (1876), *The Bathers* (1887).

**Reynolds, Sir Joshua** (1723–92) British, born Plympton Earls, near Plymouth; *Portrait of Miss Bowles with Her Dog* (1775), *Master Henry Hoare* (1788).

**Riley, Bridget (Louise)** (1931– ) British, born London; *Pink Landscapes* (1959–60), *Zig-Zag* (1961), *Fall* (1963), *Apprehend* (1970).

**Rosa, Salvator** (1615–73) Italian, born Arenella, near Naples; *Self-Portrait with a Skull* (1656), *Humana Fragilitas* (c.1657).

**Rossetti, Dante Gabriel** (1828–82) British, born London; *Beat Beatrix* (1849–50), *Ecce Ancilla Domini!* (1850), *Astarte Syriaca* (1877).

**Rothko, Mark (Marcus Rothkovitch)** (1903–70) Latvian–American, born Dvinsk; *The Omen of the Eagle* (1942), *Red on Maroon* (1959).

**Rousseau, Henri (Julien Félix)**, known as **Le Douanier** (1844–1910) French, born Laval; *Monsieur et Madame Stevene* (1884), *Sleeping Gipsy* (1897), *Portrait of Joseph Brunner* (1909).

**Rubens, Sir Peter Paul** (1577–1640) Flemish, born Siegen, Westphalia; *Marchesa Brigida Spinola-Doria* (1606), *Hélène Fourment with Two of Her Children* (c.1637).

**Sargent, John Singer** (1856–1925) American, born Florence; *Madame X* (1884), *Lady Agnew* (1893), *Gassel* (1918).

**Schiele, Egon** (1890–1918) Austrian, born Tulln; *Autumn Tree* (1909), *Pregnant Woman and Death* (1911), *Edith Seated* (1917–18).

**Schnabel, Julian** (1951– ) American, born New York City; *The Unexpected Death of Blinky Palermo in the Tropics* (1981), *Humanity Asleep* (1982).

**Seurat, Georges (Pierre)** (1859–91) French, born Paris; *Bathers at Asnières* (1884), *Sunday on the Island of La Grande Jatte* (1885–6), *Le Cirque* (1891).

**Sickert, Walter (Richard)** (1860–1942) British, born Munich; *La Hollandaise* (1905–6), *Ennui* (c.1914).

**Sisley, Alfred** (1839–99) French, born Paris; *Avenue of Chestnut Trees near La Celle Saint-Cloud* (1868), *Mosley Weir, Hampton Court* (1874).

**Spencer, Sir Stanley** (1891–1959) British, born Cookham-on-Thames, Berkshire; *The Resurrection* (1927), *The Leg of Mutton Nude* (1937).

**Steen, Jan (Havicksz)** (1627–79) Dutch, born Leiden; *A Woman at Her Toilet* (1663), *The World Upside Down* (1663).

**Stubbs, George** (1724–1806) British, born Liverpool; *James Stanley* (1755), *Anatomy of the Horse* (1766), *Hambletonian, Rubbing Town* (1799).

**Sutherland, Graham (Vivian)** (1903–80) British, born London; *Entrance to a Lane* (1939), *Crucifixion* (1946), *A Bestiary and some Correspondences* (1968).

**Tanguy, Yves** (1900–55) French–American, born Paris; *He Did What He Wanted* (1927), *The Invisibles* (1951).

**Tatlin, Vladimir Yevgrafovich** (1885–1953) Russian, born Moscow; painted reliefs, relief constructions, corner reliefs (all 1914 onwards); design for *Monument to the Third International* (1920).

**Tintoretto** (properly **Jacopo Robusti**) (1518–94) Italian, born probably Venice; *The Miracle of the Slave* (1548), *St George and the Dragon* (c.1558), *The Golden Calf* (c.1560).

**Titian** (properly **Tiziano Veccellio**) (c.1488–1576) Italian, born Pieve di Cadore; *The Assumption of the Virgin* (1516–18), *Bacchus and Ariadne* (1522–3), *Pesaro Madonna* (1519–26), *Crowning with Thorns* (c.1570).

**Toulouse-Lautrec, Henri (Marie Raymond de)** (1864–1901) French, born Albi; *The Jockey* (1899), *At the Moulin Rouge* (1895), *The Modiste* (1900).

**Turner, Joseph Mallord William** (1775–1851) British, born London; *Frosty Morning* (1813), *The Shipwreck* (1805), *Crossing the Brook* (1815), *The Fighting Téméraire* (1839), *Rain, Steam and Speed* (1844).

**Uccelo, Paolo** (originally **Paolo di Dono**) (c.1396–1475) Italian, born Pratovecchio; *The Flood* (c.1445), *The Rout of San Romano* (1454–7).

**Utamaro, Kitagawa** (1753–1806) Japanese, born Edo (modern Tokyo); *Ohisa* (c.1788), *The Twelve Hours of the Green Houses* (c.1795).

**Van Dyck, Sir Anthony** (1599–1641) Flemish, born Antwerp; *Marchesa Elena Grimaldi* (c.1625), *The Deposition* (1634–5), *Le Roi à la chasse* (c.1638).

**Van Gogh, Vincent (Willem)** (1853–90) Dutch, born Groot-Zundert, near Breda; *The Potato Eaters* (1885), *Self-Portrait with Bandaged Ear* (1888), *The Harvest* (1888), *The Sunflowers* (1888), *Starry Night* (1889), *Cornfields with Flight of Birds* (1890).

**Velázquez, Diego (Rodríguez de Silva y)** (1599–1660) Spanish, born Seville; *The Immaculate Conception* (c.1618), *The Waterseller of Seville* (c.1620), *The Surrender of Breda* (1634–5), *Pope Innocent X* (1650), *Las Meninas* (c.1656).

**Vermeer, Jan (Johannes)** (1632–75) Dutch, born Delft; *The Astronomer* (1668), *Christ in the House of Mary and Martha* (date unknown), *A Lady with a Gentleman at the Virginals* (c.1665), *The Lacemaker* (date unknown).

**Veronese** (pseudonym of **Paolo Caliari**) (1528–88) Italian, born Verona; *The Feast in the House of Levi* (1573), *Marriage at Cana* (1573), *Triumph of Venice* (c.1585).

**Verrocchio, Andrea del** (properly **Andrea del 'Cioni**) (c.1435–c.1488) Italian, born Florence; *Baptism of Christ* (c.1470), *David* (c.1475) (sculpture).

**Vlaminck, Maurice de** (1876–1958) French, born Paris; *The Red Trees* (1906), *Tugboat at Chatou* (1906).

**Warhol, Andy** (originally **Andrew Warhola**) (1928–87) American, born McKeesport, Pennsylvania; *Marilyn* (1962), *Electric Chair* (1963).

**Watteau, (Jean) Antoine** (1684–1721) French, born Valenciennes; *The Pilgrimage to the Island of Cythera* (1717), *L'Enseigne de Gersaint* (1721).

**Whistler, James (Abbott) McNeill** (1834–1903) American, born Lowell, Massachusetts; *The Artist's Mother* (1871), *Nocturne in Blue and Silver: Old Battersea Bridge* (1872–5), *Falling Rocket* (1875).

**Wilkie, Sir David** (1785–1841) British, born Cults, Fife; *The Village Politicians* (1806), *Chelsea Pensioners Reading the Waterloo Despatch* (1822).

**Wood, Grant** (1891–1942) American, born Iowa; *American Gothic* (1930), *Spring Turning* (1936).

**Wright, Joseph, (of Derby)** (1734–97) British, born Derby; *Experiment with an Air Pump* (1766), *The Alchemist in Search of the Philosopher's Stone Discovers Phosphorous* (1795).

**Wyeth, Andrew (Newell)** (1917– ) American, born Chadds Ford, Pennsylvania; *Christina's World* (1948).

## Turner prize

The Turner Prize was founded in 1984 by the Patrons of New Art. It is an award of £20 000 given to contemporary British artists under the age of 50 for an outstanding exhibition of work in the past 12 months.

| Year | Winners | Year | Winners |
|---|---|---|---|
| 1984 | Malcolm Morley (1931– ), painter | 1993 | Rachel Whiteread (1963– ), sculptor |
| 1985 | Sir Howard Hodgkin (1932– ), painter | 1994 | Antony Gormley (1950– ), sculptor |
| 1986 | Gilbert and George; Gilbert Proesch (1943– ) and George Passmore (1944– ), performance artists | 1995 | Damien Hirst (1965– ), painter and conceptual and installation artist |
| 1987 | Richard Deacon (1949– ), sculptor | 1996 | Douglas Gordon (1966– ), video artist |
| 1988 | Tony Cragg (1949– ), sculptor | 1997 | Gillian Wearing (1963– ), photographer and video artist |
| 1989 | Richard Long (1945– ), land artist | 1998 | Chris Ofili (1968– ), painter |
| 1990 | no prize awarded | 1999 | Steve McQueen (1969– ), video artist |
| 1991 | Anish Kapoor (1954– ), sculptor | 2000 | Wolfgang Tillmans (1968– ), photographer |
| 1992 | Grenville Davey (1961– ), sculptor | 2001 | Martin Creed (1968– ), sculptor and conceptual artist |

## Major architectural styles

**Art Nouveau** A deliberately new style, c.1890–1910, uninfluenced by past art, characterized mainly by undulating plant-like forms (particularly as surface decoration) and coloured materials; eg *Glasgow School of Art* by Charles Rennie Mackintosh.

**Baroque** The dominant European style of the 17th-c and early 18th-c, typically bold and exuberant, using Renaissance forms with a new freedom; eg gardens, fountains and palace at *Versailles,* France; Early Baroque: façade for *St Peter's* by Carlo Moderno; High Baroque: work by Gian Lorenzo Bernini and Francesco Borromini in Italy; Late Baroque: work by Balthasar Neumann and Johann Bernhard Fischer von Erlach.

**Brutalism** A reaction in the 1950s against the sleek sophistication of the International Modern style, characterized by chunky forms and exposed concrete; eg *Chandigarh,* the new capital of the Punjab, India, by Le Corbusier.

**Byzantine** The style of the Byzantine empire, which flourished 4th-c–15th-c, its capital being Constantinople (originally Byzantium, now Istanbul). It blends Roman and eastern influences and its most typical form is the large domed church, lavishly decorated with mosaics; eg *Hagia Sophia,* Istanbul.

**Gothic** The style that succeeded Romanesque throughout Europe, characterized most obviously by the use of pointed arches and also by rib vaults, flying buttresses and elaborate window tracery. It began in France in the 1140s and flourished in many places into the 16th-c, windows generally becoming an increasingly prominent feature; eg *Cathedrals* of *Lincoln* and *Salisbury,* England; *Cathedral of Chartres,* France.

**Gothic Revival** A revival of the Gothic style of the Middle Ages, beginning in the 18th-c and flourishing in the 19th-c, particularly in Britain; it was used in buildings of all kinds — religious, civil, commercial and domestic; eg *Houses of Parliament*, London, by Sir Charles Barry and August W N Pugin; *Grace Church,* New York City, by James Renwick.

**Greek** The style charlacteristic of ancient Greece and its Mediterranean colonies from the 7th-cBC, when stone building was revived, to the 1st-cBC, when Greece was absorbed into the Roman Empire. The most important Greek buildings were temples, and the beautifully proportioned columns that became typical of them were immensely influential on Roman and on much subsequent European architecture; eg *Parthenon,* Athens.

**High Tech** An approach popular since the 1970s in which architects stress the technological aspects of a building, typically by giving dramatic visual expression to structural elements or services (pipes, air ducts and so on) that are usually hidden from view; eg *Pompidou Centre,* Paris, and the *Lloyds* building, London both by Richard Rogers.

**International Modern** or **International Style** A sleek, functional style that dominated progressive architecture in Europe and America in the 1930s and 1940s; eg *Bauhaus,* Dessau, Germany, by Walter Gropius; *Falling Water,* Mill Run, Pennsylvania by Frank Lloyd Wright.

**Neoclassicism** A revival of the styles of ancient Greece and Rome in the late 18th-c and early 19th-c; eg *Charlotte Square,* Edinburgh, by Robert Adam; *Hôtel Dieu*, Lyons, by Jacques Soufflot.

**Post Modernism** A trend, beginning in the 1970s, in which the cool rationalism of International Modern style was abandoned in favour of stylistic eclecticism; eg *Brant-Johnson House* in Vail, Colorado, by Robert Venturi; *Piazza d'Italia,* New Orleans, by Charles Willard Moore.

**Renaissance** A revival or 'rebirth' of the classical art of ancient Rome, beginning in Italy in the early 15th-c and spreading over Europe until the advent of Baroque; eg the circular *Tempietto of S Pietro,* Montoria, Rome, by Donato Bramante.

**Rococo** A style that emerged from Baroque in the early 18th-c; like Baroque, it tended to make vigorous use of curved forms, but it was lighter and more playful; eg *Residenztheater,* Munich, by François de Cuvilliés.

**Roman** The style of the ancient Romans, which spread over their empire, at its peak 1st-c–4th-c AD; the Romans took much of the 'vocabulary' of classical architecture from the Greeks (particularly the systematic use of columns), but added many features of their own, and excelled in the sheer size of their buildings and engineering projects; eg *Pantheon,* Rome; *Colosseum,* Rome.

**Romanesque** The style prevailing in most of Europe in the 11th-c and 12th-c, characterized by massive strength of construction, and the use of round-headed arches and windows (as opposed to the pointed arches of the Gothic style that succeeded it); eg *San Miniato al Monte,* Florence.

## Architects

Selected works are listed.

**Aalto, (Hugo) Alvar (Henrik)** (1898–1976) Finnish, born Kuortane; *Convalescent Home,* Paimio, near Turku (1929–30), *Town Hall,* Saynatsab (1950–2), *Finlandia Concert Hall,* Helsinki (1971).

**Adam, Robert** (1728–92) Scottish, born Kirkcaldy; *Adelphi,* London (1769–71, demolished 1936), *General Register House* (begun 1774), *Charlotte Square* (1791), *University of Edinburgh, Old College* (1789–94), all Edinburgh; *Culzean Castle,* Ayrshire (1772–92).

**Adam, William** (1689–1748) Scottish, born Maryburgh; *Hopetoun House,* near Edinburgh (1721).

**Alberti, Leon Battista** (1404–72) Italian, born Genoa; façade of the *Palazzo Recellai,* Florence (1460), *San Andrea,* Mantua (1470).

**Anthemias of Tralles** (dates unknown) Greek, born Tralles, Lydia; *Hagia Sophia,* Constantinople (now Istanbul) (532–7).

**Apollodorus of Damascus** (dates unknown) Greek, born Syria; *Trajan's Forum,* Rome, *The Baths of Trajan,* Rome.

**Arnolfo di Cambio** (1232–1302) Italian, born Colle di Val d'Elsa, Tuscany; *Florence Cathedral* (1299–1310).

**Asplund, Erik Gunnar** (1885–1940) Swedish, born Stockholm; *Stockholm City Library* (1924–7), *Law Courts,* Gothenburg (1934–7).

**Baker, Sir Herbert** (1862–1946) English, born Kent; *Groote Schuur,* near Cape Town (1892–1902), *Union Government Buildings,* Pretoria (1907).

**Barry, Sir Charles** (1795–1860) English, born London; *Royal Institution of the Arts,* Manchester (1824), *Houses of Parliament,* London (opened 1852).

**Behrens, Peter** (1868–1940) German, born Hamburg; *Turbine Assembly Works,* Berlin (1909), *German Embassy,* St Petersburg (1912).

**Berlage, Hendrick Petrus** (1856–1934) Dutch, born Amsterdam; *Amsterdam Bourse* (1903), *Holland House,* London (1914), *Gemeente Museum,* The Hague (1934).

**Bernini, Gian Lorenzo** (1598–1680) Italian, born Naples; *St Peter's Baldacchino* (1625), *Cornaro Chapel* in the Church of Santa Maria della Vittoria (1645–52), both Rome.

**Borromini, Francesco** (1599–1667) Italian, born Bissone, on Lake Lugano; *S Carlo alle Quattro Fontane* (1637–41), *S Ivo della Sapienza* (1642–61), both Rome.

**Boullée, Étienne-Louis** (1728–99) French, born Paris; *Hôtel de Brunoy,* Paris (1772), *Monument to Isaac Newton* (never built) (1794).

**Bramante, Donato** (originally **Donato di Pascuccio d'Antonio**) (1444–1514) Italian, born near Urbino; *San Maria presso S Satiro,* Milan (begun 1482), *Tempietto of S Pietro,* Rome (1502).

**Breuer, Marcel Lajos** (1902–81) Hungarian–American, born Pécs, Hungary; *UNESCO Building,* Paris (1953–8).

**Brosse, Salomon de** (1565–1626) French, born Verneuil-sur-Oise; *Luxembourg Palace,* Paris (1615–20), *Louis XIII's Hunting Lodge,* Versailles (1624–6).

**Brunelleschi, Filippo** (1377–1446) Italian, born Florence; *San Lorenzo,* Florence (begun 1418), Dome of *Florence Cathedral* (begun 1420), *Ospedale degli Innocenti,* Florence (1419).

**Bryce, David** (1803–76) Scottish, born Edinburgh; *Fettes College* (1863–9), *Royal Infirmary* (begun 1870), both Edinburgh.

**Burnham, David Hudson** (1846–1912) American, born Henderson, New York; *Reliance Building,* Chicago (1890–5), *Monadnock Building,* Chicago (1890–1), *Selfridge Building,* London (1908).

**Burton, Decimus** (1800–81) English, born London; *Regent's Park Colosseum* (1823), *Arch at Hyde Park Corner* (1825), both London.

**Butterfield, William** (1814–1900) English, born London; *Keble College,* Oxford (1866–86), *St Augustine's College,* Canterbury (1844–73), *All Saints',* Margaret Street, London (1849–59).

**Campen, Jacob van** (1595–1657) Dutch, born Haarlem; *Maurithuis*, The Hague (1633), *Amsterdam Theatre* (1637), *Amsterdam Town Hall* (1647–55).

**Candela, Felix** (1910–97) Spanish–Mexican, born Madrid; *Sports Palace* for Olympic Games, Mexico City (1968).

**Chambers, Sir William** (1726–96) Scottish, born Stockholm; *Somerset House* (1776), pagoda in *Kew Gardens* (1757), both London.

**Chermayeff, Serge** (1900–96) American, born the Caucasus Mountains, Russia; *De La Warr Pavilion*, Bexhill (1933–5).

**Churriguera, Don José** (1650–1725) Spanish, born Salamanca; *Salamanca Cathedral* (1692–4).

**Coates, Wells Wintemute** (1895–1958) English, born Tokyo; *BBC Studios* (1932), *EKCO Laboratories* (1936), *Cinema*, Festival of Great Britain Exhibition (1951).

**Cockerell, Charles Robert** (1788–1863) English, born London; *Taylorian Institute*, Oxford (1841–5), *Fitzwilliam Museum*, Cambridge (1837–40).

**Cortona, Pietro Berrettini da** (1596–1669) Italian, born Cortona; *Villa Sacchetti*, Castel Fusano (1626–7), *San Firenze*, Florence (1645).

**Cuvilliés, François de** (1695–1768) Bavarian, born Belgium; *Amelienburg Pavilion* at Schloss Nymphenburg, near Munich (1734–9), *Residenztheater*, Munich (1750–3).

**Dance, George, (the Elder)** (1700–68) English, born London; *Mansion House*, London (1739).

**Dance, George, (the Younger)** (1741–1825) English, born London; rebuilt *Newgate Prison* (1770–83).

**Delorme, Philibert** (c.1510–70) French, born Lyons; *Tuileries* (1565–70), *Châteaux of Anet, Meudon, Saint Germain-en-Laye* (1547–55).

**Doesburg, Theo van** (originally **Christian Emil Marie Kupper**) (1883–1931) Dutch, born Utrecht; *L'Art Nouveau Shop*, Paris (1896), *Keller und Reiner Art Gallery*, Berlin (1898).

**Doshi, Balkrishna Vithaldas** (1927– ) Indian, born Poona; *City Hall*, Toronto (1958), *Indian Institute of Management*, Ahmedabad (1951–7).

**Dudok, Willem Marinus** (1884–1974) Dutch, born Amsterdam; *Hilversum Town Hall* (1928–30), *Bijenkorf Department Store*, Rotterdam (1929).

**Engel, Johann Carl Ludwig** (1778–1840) Finnish, born Berlin; layout of Helsinki (1818–26).

**Erickson, Arthur Charles** (1924– ) Canadian, born Vancouver; *Simon Fraser University Buildings*, British Columbia (1963), *Lethbridge University*, Alberta (1971).

**Fischer von Erlach, Johann Bernard** (1656–1723) Austrian, born Graz; *Karlskirche*, Vienna (1716), *Hofbibliotek*, Vienna (1723), *Kollegienkirche*, Salzburg (1707).

**Foster, Norman Foster, Baron** (1935– ) English, born Manchester; *Willis Faber Dumas Building*, Ipswich (1975), *Sainsbury Centre*, University of East Anglia (1978), *Hong Kong and Shanghai Bank*, Hong Kong (1979–85).

**Francesco di Giorgio** (1439–1501/2) Italian, born Siena; *Church of San Bernardino all'Osservanza*, Siena (1474–84), *Palazzo Ducale*, Gubbio (1476–82).

**Gabriel, Ange-Jacques** (1698–1782) French, born Paris; *Pavillon de Pompadour*, Fontainebleau (begun 1749), Paris; layout of *Place de la Concorde*, Paris (1753), *Petit Trianon*, Versailles (1761–8).

**Garnier, Tony (Antoine)** (1869–1948) French, born Lyons; *Grange Blanche Hospital*, Lyons (1911–27), *Stadium*, Lyons (1913–18), *Hôtel de Ville*, Boulogne-Bilancourt (1931–3).

**Gaudí (i Cornet), Antoni** (1852–1926) Spanish, born Reus, Tarragona; *Casa Vicens* (1878–80), *Sagrada Familia* (1884 onwards), *Casa Batlló* (1904–17), *Casa Milá* (1905–9), all Barcelona.

**Geddes, Sir Patrick** (1854–1932) Scottish, born Perth; *Ramsay Garden*, Edinburgh (1892), *Edinburgh Zoo* (1913), *Scots College*, Montpelier, France (1924).

**Gibbs, James** (1682–1754) Scottish, born Aberdeen; *St-Martin-in-the-Fields*, London (1722–6), *King's College Fellows' Building*, Cambridge (1724–49).

**Gilbert, Cass** (1859–1934) American, born Zanesville, Ohio; *Woolworth Building*, New York City (1913).

**Gilly, Friedrich** (1772–1800) German, born Berlin; *Funerary Precinct and Temple* to Frederick II, the Great of Prussia (1796), *Prussian National Theatre*, Berlin (1798).

**Giotto (di Bondone)** (c.1266–1337) Italian, born Vespignano, near Florence; *Campanile*, Florence Cathedral (from 1334).

**Giulio Romano** (properly **Giulio Pippi de' Gianuzzi**) (c.1492–1546) Italian, born Rome; *Palazzo del Tè*, Mantua (1526), *Church of S Petronio* façade, Bologna (1546).

**Greenway, Francis Howard** (1777–1837) Anglo-Australian, born Bristol; *Macquarie Lighthouse*, Sydney Harbour (1818), *St James' Church*, Sydney (1824).

**Gropius, Walter** (1883–1969) German–American, born Berlin; *Fagus Shoe Factory*, Alfeld (1911), *The Bauhaus*, Dessau (1925), both Germany; *Harvard University Graduate Centre* (1950), Massachusetts.

**Guarini, Guarino** (originally **Camillo**) (1624–83) Italian, born Modena; *San Lorenzo church*, Turin (1668–80), *Capella della SS Sindone* church, Turin (1668), *Palazzo Carignano*, Racconigi (1679).

**Hamilton, Thomas** (1784–1858) Scottish, born Glasgow; *Royal High School* (1825–9), *Royal College of Physicians Hall* (1844–5), *George IV Bridge* (1827–34), all Edinburgh.

**Haussmann, Georges Eugène** (1809–91) French, born Paris; layout of *Bois de Boulogne*, *Bois de Vincennes*, Paris (1853–70).

**Hawksmoor, Nicholas** (1661–1736) English, born Nottinghamshire; *St Mary Woolnoth Church* (1716–24), *St George's*, Bloomsbury (1716–30), both London.

**Hildebrandt, Johann Lukas von** (1668–1745) Austrian, born Genoa; *Lower and Upper Belvedere*, Vienna, (1714–15, 1720–3).

**Hoffmann, Josef** (1870–1956) Austrian, born Pirnitz; *Purkersdorf Sanatorium* (1903–5), *Stociet House*, Brussels (1905–11).

**Holland, Henry** (1746–1806) English, born London; *Carlton House*, London (1783–96), *Brighton Pavilion* (1787).

**Howard, Sir Ebenezer** (1850–1928) English, born London; *Letchworth Garden City* (1903).

**Itkinos** and **Callicrates** (dates and place of birth unknown) Greek; *The Parthenon*, Athens (447/6–438BC).

**Jacobsen, Arne** (1902–71) Danish, born Copenhagen; *Town Hall of Aarhus* (with Erik Moller, 1938–42), *Town Hall of Rodovre* (1955–6), *SAS Tower*, Copenhagen (1960), all Denmark; new *St Catherine's College*, Oxford (1959).

**Jefferson, Thomas** (1743–1826) American, born Shadwell, Virginia; *Monticello*, Albemarle County (1769), *Virginia State Capitol* (1796).

**Johnson, Philip Cortelyou** (1906– ) American, born Cleveland, Ohio; *Glass House*, New Canaan, Connecticut (1949–50), *Seagram Building*, New York City (1945), *Amon Carter Museum of Western Art*, Texas (1961), *New York State Theater*, Lincoln Center (1964).

**Jones, Inigo** (1573–1652) English, born London; *The Queen's House*, Greenwich (1616–18, 1629–35), *Banqueting House*, Whitehall, London (1619–22).

**Kahn, Louis Isadore** (1901–74) American architect, born Osel (now Saaremaa), Estonia; *Richards Medical Research Building*, Pennsylvania (1957–61), *City Tower Municipal Building*, Philadelphia (1952–7).

**Kent, William** (1685–1748) English, born Bridlington, *Holkham Hall* (begun 1734).

**Labrouste, (Pierre François) Henri** (1801–75) French, born Paris; *Bibliothèque Sainte Geneviève* (1838–50), *Bibliothèque Nationale* reading room (1860–7), both Paris.

**Lasdun, Sir Denys Louis** (1914–2001) English, born London; *Royal College of Musicians* (1958–64), *National Theatre* (1965–76), both London.

**Le Corbusier** (pseudonym of **Charles Édouard Jeanneret**) (1887–1965) French, born La Chaux-de-Fonds, Switzerland; *Salvation Army Hostel*, Paris (begun 1929), *Chapel of Ronchamp*, near Belfort (1950–4), *Chandigarh*, Punjab (1951–6), *Museum of Modern Art*, Tokyo (1957).

**Ledoux, Claude Nicolas** (1736–1806) French, born Dormans, Champagne; *Château*, Louveciennes (1771–3), *Theatre*, Besançon (1771–3).

**Leonardo da Vinci** (1452–1519) Italian, born Vinci; *Mariolo de Guiscardi House*, Milan (1497), *La Veruca Fortress*, near Pisa (1504), *Villa Melzi*, Vaprio, Milan (1513).

**Lescot, Pierre** (c.1510–78) French, born Paris; rebuilt one wing of the *Louvre*, Paris (1546), screen of *St Germain l'Auxerrois* (1541–4).

**Lethaby, William Richard** (1857–1931) English, born Barnstaple; *Avon Tyrell*, Christchurch, Hampshire (1891–2), *Eagle Insurance Buildings*, Birmingham (1899–1900).

**Le Vau** or **Levau, Louis** (1612–70) French, born Paris; *Hôtel Lambert*, Paris (1640–4), part of *Palace of Versailles* (from 1661), *Collège des Quatre Nations*, Paris (1661).

**Loos, Adolf** (1870–1933) Austrian, born Bruno, Moravia; *Steiner House*, Vienna (1910).

**Lorimer, Sir Robert Stodart** (1864–1929) Scottish, born Edinburgh; *Thistle Chapel, St Giles*, Edinburgh (1909–11), *Scottish National War Memorial*, Edinburgh Castle (1923–8).

**Lutyens, Sir Edwin Landseer** (1869–1944) English, born London; *Cenotaph*, Whitehall, London (1919–20), *Liverpool Roman Catholic Cathedral* (1929–c.1941), *Viceroy's House*, New Delhi (1921–5).

**Mackintosh, Charles Rennie** (1868–1928) Scottish, born Glasgow; *Glasgow School of Art* (1897–9), *Hill House*, Helensburgh (1902–3).

**Mackmurdo, Arthur Heygate** (1851–1942) English, born London; *Gordon Institute for Boys*, St Helens (1890).

**Maderna** or **Maderno, Carlo** (1556–1629) Italian, born Capalago; façade of *St Peter's* (1606–12), *S Susanna* (1597–1603), *Palazzo Barberini* (1628–38), all Rome.

**Mansard** or **Mansart, François** (1598–1666) French, born Paris; north wing of *Château de Blois* (1635), *Sainte-Marie de la Visitation*, Paris (1632).

**Mansard** or **Mansart, Jules Hardouin** (1645–1708) French, born Paris; *Grand Trianon, Palace of Versailles* (1678–89).

**Mendelsohn, Eric** (1887–1953) German, born Allenstein; *De La Warr Pavilion*, Bexhill (1933–5), *Anglo-Palestine Bank*, Jerusalem (1938).

**Michelozzo di Bartolommeo** (1396–1472) Italian, born Florence; *Villa Medici*, Fiesole (1458–61), *San Marco*, Florence (begun 1437).

**Mies van der Rohe, Ludwig** (1886–1969) German–American, born Aachen; *Seagram Building*, New York City (1956–8), *Public Library*, Washington (1967).

**Moore, Charles Willard** (1925–93) American, born Benton Harbor, Michigan; *Sea Ranch Condominium Estate*, Glendale, California (1965), *Kresge College*, Santa Cruz, California (1974), *Piazza d'Italia*, New Orleans (1975–8), *Civic Center*, Beverly Hills, California (1990).

**Nash, John** (1752–1835) English, born London; layout of *Regent's Park* and *Regent Street*, London (1811 onwards), *Brighton Pavilion* (1815).

**Nervi, Pier Luigi** (1891–1979) Italian, born Sondrio; *Berta Stadium*, Florence (1930–2), *Olympic Stadia*, Rome (1960), *San Francisco Cathedral* (1970).

**Neumann, (Johann) Balthasar** (1687–1753) German, born Eger; *Würzburg Palace* (1730–43), *Schloss Bruchsal* (1738–53).

**Niemeyer, Oscar** (1907– ) Brazilian, born Rio de Janeiro; *Church of St Francis of Assisi*, Pampúlha, Belo Horizonte, Brazil (1942–4), *Niemeyer House*, Rio de Janeiro (1953).

**Oud, Jacobus Johann Pieter** (1890–1963) Dutch, born Purmerend; *Alida Hartog-Ond House*, Purmerend (1906), *Café de Unie*, Rotterdam (1924), *Convention Centre*, The Hague (1957–63).

**Palladio, Andrea** (1508–80) Italian, born Padua; *Godi-Porto* (villa at Lonedo) (1540), *La Malcontenta* (villa near Padua) (1560), *San Giorgio Maggiore*, Venice (begun 1566).

**Paxton, Sir Joseph** (1801–65) English, born Milton-Bryant, near Woburn; building for *Great Exhibition* of 1851, later re-erected as the *Crystal Palace*, Sydenham (1852–4).

**Pei, Ieoh Meng** (1917– ) Chinese–American, born Canton; *Mile High Center*, Denver (1954–9), *John Hancock Tower*, Boston (1973), *Glass Pyramids*, the Louvre, Paris (1983–9).

**Perret, Auguste** (1874–1954) French, born Brussels; *Théâtre des Champs Élysées*, Paris (1911–13), *Musée des travaux publics*, Paris (1936).

**Piranesi, Giambattista** (1720–78) Italian, born Venice; *Santa Maria Arentina*, Rome (1764–6).

**Pisano, Nicola** (c.1225–c.1284) Italian, born Tuscany; *Pisa Baptistry* (1260), façade renovation of *Pisa Cathedral* (1260–70).

**Playfair, William Henry** (1789–1857) Scottish, born London; *National Gallery of Scotland* (1850–7), *Royal Scottish Academy* (1832–5), *Surgeon's Hall* (1829–32), all Edinburgh.

**Poelzig, Hans** (1869–1936) German, born Berlin; *Exhibition Hall*, Posen (1910–11), *Salzburg Festival Theatre* (1920–2).

**Pugin, Augustus Welby Northmore** (1812–52) English, born London; drawings, decorations and sculpture for the *Houses of Parliament*, London (1836–7), *Birmingham Cathedral* (1839–41).

**Renwick, James** (1818–95) American, born New York; *Smithsonian Institution*, Washington (1844–55), *Grace Church*, New York (1846), *St Patrick's Cathedral*, New York (1858–79).

**Rietveld, Gerrit Thomas** (1888–1964) Dutch, born Utrecht; *Schröder House*, Utrecht (1924), *Van Gogh Museum*, Amsterdam (1963–4).

**Rogers, Richard George Rogers, Baron** (1933– ) English, born Florence; *Pompidou Centre*, Paris (1971–9), *Lloyds*, London (1979–85), *Millennium Dome*, London (1996–9).

**Saarinen, (Gottlieb) Eliel** (1873–1950) Finnish–American, born Rantasalmi; *Cranbrook Academy of Art*, Michigan (1934–40).

**Saarinen, Eero** (1910–61) Finnish–American, born Kirkknonummi; *Jefferson Memorial Arch*, St Louis (1948–64), *American Embassy*, London (1955–60).

**Sanmichele, Michele** (c.1484–1559) Italian, born Verona; *Capella Pelegrini*, Verona (1527–57), *Palazzo Grimani*, Venice (1551–9).

**Sansovino, Jacopo** (1486–1570) Italian, born Florence; *Library* and *Mint*, Venice.

**Schinkel, Karl Friederich** (1781–1841) German, born Neurippen, Brandenburg; *Old Museum*, Berlin (1823–30), *War Memorial on the Kreuzberg* (1818).

**Scott, Sir George Gilbert** (1811–78) English, born Gawcott, Buckinghamshire; *Albert Memorial*, London (1862–3), *St Pancras station and hotel*, London (1865), *Glasgow University* (1865).

**Serlio, Sebastiano** (1475–1554) Italian, born Bologna; *Grand Ferrare*, Fontainebleau (1541–8), *Château*, Ancy-le-Franc, Tonnerre (from 1546).

**Shaw, (Richard) Norman** (1831–1912) English, born Edinburgh; *Old Swan House*, Chelsea (1876), *New Scotland Yard*, London (1888).

**Smirke, Sir Robert** (1781–1867) English, born London; *Covent Garden Theatre*, London (1809), *British Museum*, London (1823–47).

**Smythson, Robert** (c.1535–1614) English, place of birth unknown; *Wollaton Hall*, Nottingham (1580–8), *Hardwick Hall*, Derbyshire (1591–7).

**Soane, Sir John** (1753–1837) English, born near Reading; altered interior of *Bank of England* (1788–1833), *Dulwich College Art Gallery* (1811–14).

**Sottsass, Ettore, Jr** (1917– ) Italian, born Innsbruck; *Apartment Building*, Turin (1934), *Galleria del Cavalliro*, Venice (1956).

**Soufflot, Jacques Germain** (1713–80) French, born Irancy; *Hôtel Dieu*, Lyons (1741), *St Geneviève* (Panthéon), Paris (begun 1757).

**Spence, Sir Basil Urwin** (1907–76) Scottish, born India; Pavilions for Festival of Britain (1951), *Coventry Cathedral* (1951).

**Stirling, Sir James** (1926–92) Scottish, born Glasgow; *Department of Engineering*, Leicester University (1959–63) (with James Gowan), *History Faculty*, Cambridge (1965–8), *Florey Building*, Queen's College, Oxford (1966), *Neue Staatsgalerie*, Stuttgart (1980–4).

**Street, George Edmund** (1824–81) English, born Woodford, Essex; *London Law Courts* (1870–81).

**Stuart, James** (1713–88) English, born London; rebuilt interior of *Chapel of Greenwich Hospital* (1779).

**Sullivan, Louis Henry** (1856–1924) American, born Boston, Massachusetts; *Wainwright Building*, St Louis (1890), *Carson, Pirie and Scott Store*, Chicago (1899–1904).

**Tange, Kenzo** (1913– ) Japanese, born Tokyo; *Hiroshima Peace Centre* (1949–55), *Shizoka Press and Broadcasting Centre*, Tokyo (1966–7).

**Utzon, Jørn** (1918– ) Danish, born Copenhagen; *Sydney Opera House* (1956–68), *Kuwait House of Parliament* (begun 1972).

**Vanbrugh, Sir John** (1664–1726) English, born London; *Castle Howard* (1699–1726), *Blenheim Palace* (1705–20).

**Velde, Henri Clemens van de** (1863–1957) Belgian, born Antwerp; *Werkbund Theatre*, Cologne (1914), *Museum Kröller-Muller*, Otterloo (1937–54).

**Venturi, Robert Charles** (1925– ) American, born Philadelphia, Pennsylvania; *Brant-Johnson House*, Vail, Colorado (1976), *Sainsbury Wing* of the National Gallery, London (1986–91).

**Vignola, Giacomo Barozzi da** (1507–73) Italian, born Vignola; *Villa di Papa Giulio* (1550–5), church of the *Il Gesu*, Rome (1586–73).

**Viollet-le-Duc, Eugène Emmanuel** (1814–79) French, born Paris; restored cathedral of *Notre Dame*, Paris (1845–64), *Château de Pierrefonds* (1858–70).

**Voysey, Charles Francis Annesley** (1857–1941) English, born London; *Grove Town Houses*, Kensington (1891–2), *Sanderson's Wallpaper Factory*, Chiswick (1902).

**Wagner, Otto** (1841–1918) Austrian, born Penzing, near Vienna; stations for *Vienna Stadtbahn* (1894–7), *Post Office Savings Bank*, Vienna (1904–6).

**Waterhouse, Alfred** (1830–1905) English, born Liverpool; *Manchester Town Hall* (1867–77), *Natural History Museum*, South Kensington, London (1873–81).

**Webb, Sir Aston** (1849–1930) English, born London; eastern façade of *Buckingham Palace* (1912), *Admiralty Arch* (1903–10), *Imperial College of Science* (1906), all London.

**Webb, Philip** (1831–1915) English, born Oxford; *Red House*, Bexley (1859), *Clouds*, Wiltshire (1881–6), *Standen*, East Grinstead (1891).

**Wood, John, (the Elder)** (1704–54) English. *Queen Square*, Bath (1729–36).

**Wood, John, (the Younger)** (1728–82) English. *Royal Crescent*, Bath (1767–75), *Assembly Rooms*, Bath (1769–71).

**Wren, Sir Christopher** (1632–1723) English, born East Knoyle, Wiltshire; *Pembroke College Chapel*, Cambridge (1663–5), *The Sheldonian Theatre*, Oxford (1664), *Royal Greenwich Observatory* (1675–6), *St Paul's*, London (1675–1710), *Greenwich Hospital* (1696).

**Wright, Frank Lloyd** (1869–1959) American, born Richland Center, Wisconsin; *Larkin Building*, Buffalo (1904), *Robie House*, Chicago (1908), *Johnson Wax Factory*, Racine, Wisconsin (1936–9), *Falling Water*, Mill Run, Pennsylvania (1936), *Guggenheim Museum*, New York (begun 1942).

**Wyatt, James** (1746–1813) English, born Staffordshire; *London Pantheon* (1772), *Gothic Revival Country House*, Fonthill Abbey, Wiltshire (1796–1813).

## Sculptors

Selected works are listed.

**Andre, Carl** (1935– ) American, born Quincy, Massachusetts; *144 Magnesium Square* (1969), *Twelfth Copper Corner* (1975), *Bloody Angle* (1985).

**Armitage, Kenneth** (1916–2002) British, born Leeds; *People in a Wind* (1951), *Sprawling Woman* (1958), *Figure and Clouds* (1972), *Richmond Oak* (1985–90).

**Arp, Hans (Jean)** (1887–1966) French, born Strasbourg; *Eggboard* (1922), *Kore* (1958).

**Barlach, Ernst** (1870–1938) German, born Wedel; *Moeller-Jarke Tomb* (1901), *Have Pity!* (1919).

**Bernini, Gianlorenzo** (1598–1680) Italian, born Naples; *Neptune and Triton* (1620), *David* (1623), *Ecstasy of St Theresa* (1640s), *Fountain of the Four Rivers* (1648–51).

**Bologna, Giovanni da** (also called **Giambologna**) (1529–1608) French, born Douai; *Mercury* (1564–5), *Rape of the Sabines* (1579–83).

**Brancusi, Constantin** (1876–1957) Romanian–French, born Hobitza, Gorj; *The Kiss* (1909), *Torso of a Young Man* (1922).

**Bourgeois, Louise** (1911– ) American, born Paris; *Labyrinthine Tower* (1963), *Destruction of the Father* (1974), *Spiders* (1995).

**Calder, Alexander** (1898–1976) American, born Philadelphia, Pennsylvania; *Stabiles and Mobiles* (1932), *A Universe* (1934).

**Caro, Sir Anthony** (1924– ) British, born London; *Sailing Tonight* (1971–4), *Veduggio Sound* (1973), *Ledge Piece* (1978), *Night Movements* (1987–90).

**Cellini, Benvenuto** (1500–71) Italian, born Florence; salt cellar of *Neptune and Ceres* (1543), *Cosimo de' Medici* (1545–7), *Perseus with the Head of Medusa* (1564).

**Deacon, Richard** (1949– ) British, born Bangor, Wales; *Double Talk* (1987), *Kiss and Tell* (1989), *Never Mind* (1993).

**Donatello** (originally **Donnato di Niccolò di Betto Bardi**) (c.1386–1466) Italian, born Florence; *St Mark* (1411–12), *St George Killing the Dragon* (c.1417), *Feast of Herod* (1423–37), *David, Judith and Holofernes*, Piazza della Signoria, Florence.

**Epstein, Sir Jacob** (1880–1959) Anglo-American, born New York City; *Rima* (1925), *Genesis* (1930), *Ecce Homo* (1934–5), *Adam* (1939), *Christ in Majesty* (Llandaff Cathedral), *St Michael and the Devil* (on the façade of Coventry Cathedral) (1958–9).

**Frink, Dame Elizabeth** (1930–93) British, born Thurlow, Suffolk; *Horse Lying Down* (1975), *Running Man* (1985), *Seated Man* (1986).

**Gabo, Naum** (originally **Naum Neemia Pevsner**) (1890–1977) American, born Bryansk, Russia; *Kinetic Construction* (1920), *No.1* (1943).

**Gaudier-Brzeska, Henri** (1891–1915) French, born St Jean de Braye, near Orléans; *Red stone dancer* (1913).

**Ghiberti, Lorenzo** (c.1378–1455) Italian, born in or near Florence; *St John the Baptist* (1412–15), *St Matthew* (1419–22), *The Gates of Paradise* (1425–52).

**Giacometti, Alberto** (1901–66) Swiss, born Bogonova, near Stampa; *Head* (c.1928), *Woman with Her Throat Cut* (1932).

**Goldsworthy, Andy** (1956– ) British, born Cheshire; *Hazel Stick Throws* (1980), *Slate Cone* (1988), *The Wall* (1988–9).

**González, Julio** (1876–1942) Spanish, born Barcelona; *Angel* (1933), *Woman Combing Her Hair* (1936), *Cactus People* (1930–40).

**Gormley, Anthony** (1950– ) English, born London; *Natural Selection* (1981), *Angel of the North* (1997).

**Hepworth, Dame (Jocelyn) Barbara** (1903–75) British, born Wakefield, Yorkshire; *Figure of a Woman* (1929–30), *Large and Small Forms* (1945), *Single Form* (1963).

**Leonardo da Vinci** (1452–1519) Italian, born Vinci, between Pisa and Florence; *St John the Baptist*.

**Michelangelo** (in full **Michelangelo di Lodovico Buonarotti**) (1475–1564) Italian, born Caprese, Tuscany; *Cupid* (1495), *Bacchus* (1496), *Pieta* (1497), *David* (c.1500).

**Moore, Henry (Spencer)** (1898–1986) British, born Castleford, Yorkshire; *Recumbent Figure* (1938), *Fallen Warrior* (1956–7).

**Paolozzi, Sir Eduardo Luigi** (1924– ) British, born Leith, Edinburgh; *Krokodeel* (c.1956–7), *Japanese War God* (1958), *Medea* (1964), *Piscator* (1981), *Manuscript of Monte Cassino*, Edinburgh (1991).

**Pheidias** (c.490–c.417BC) Greek, born Athens; *Athena Promachos* (460–450BC), marble sculptures of the *Parthenon* (447–432BC).

**Pisano, Andrea** (c.1270–1349) Italian, born Pontedera; bronze doors of the *Baptistry* of Florence (1330–6).

**Pisano, Giovanni** (c.1248–c.1320) Italian, born Pisa; *Fontana Magiore*, Perugia (1278), *Duomo pulpit*, Pisa (1302–10).

**Pisano, Nicola** (c.1225–c.1284) Italian, birthplace unknown; *Baptistry* at Pisa (1260).

**Praxiteles** (5th-cBC) Greek, born probably Athens; *Hermes Carrying the Boy Dionysus* (date unknown).

**Robbia, Luca della** (in full **Luca di Simone di Marco della Robbia**) (c.1400–1482) Italian, born Florence; *Cantoria* (1432–7).

**Rodin, (François) Auguste (René)** (1840–1917) French, born Paris; *The Age of Bronze* (1875–6), *The Gates of Hell* (1880–1917), *The Burghers of Calais* (1884), *The Thinker* (1904).

**Schwitters, Kurt** (1887–1948) German, born Hannover; *Merzbau* (1920–43).

**Tinguely, Jean** (1925–91) Swiss, born Fribourg; *Baluba No 3* (1959), *Métamécanique No 9* (1959), *Homage to New York* (1960), *EOSX* (1967).

**Whiteread, Rachel** (1963– ) British, born London; *Torso* (1991), *House* (1993), *Orange Bath* (1996).

## Photographers

**Adams, Ansel (Easton)** (1902–84) American, born San Francisco. Notable for broad landscapes of western America, especially the Yosemite in the 1930s. One of the founders of Group f/64 (1932). Publications include *Taos Pueblo* (1930) and *Born Free and Equal* (1944).

**Adams, Marcus Algernon** (1875–1959) English, born Southampton. Portrait photographer who established studio in 1919 specializing in formal children's portraits with soft-focus style. His portraits of three generations of the British royal family taken from 1926 until his retirement in 1957 were published worldwide.

**Adamson, Robert** (1821–48) Scottish, born Berunside. Pioneer in photography. With David Octavius Hill applied the calotype process of making photographic prints on silver chloride paper for a commission to portray the founders of the Free Church of Scotland in 1843.

**Akiyama, Shotaru** (1920– ) Japanese, born Tokyo. Worked for a Japanese motion picture company before becoming a freelance photographer for a number of publishers in 1951. Chairman of the Japan Advertising Photographers Association since 1979.

**Anschütz, Ottomar** (1846–1907) German, born Yugoslavia. Pioneer of instantaneous photography and one of the first to make a series of pictures of moving animals and people, making a substantial contribution to the invention of the cinematograph.

**Arbus, Diane**, née **Nemerov** (1923–71) American, born New York City. After work in conventional fashion photography, sought to portray people 'without their masks'. Achieved fame in the 1960s with ironic studies of social poses and the deprived classes, but became increasingly depressed, eventually committing suicide.

**Arnold, Eve** (1913– ) American photojournalist, born Philadelphia. First woman to photograph for Magnum Photos in 1951. Famous for pictures of women, the poor and the elderly, as well as celebrities such as Marilyn Monroe.

**Atget, (Jean) Eugène (Auguste)** (1856–1927) French, born Libourne, near Bordeaux. Studied at the Conservatoire d'Art Dramatique, Paris (1879–81), before working as a stage actor, comedian and painter. His photographic work (1898–1925) was discovered in 1926 in Paris by Berenice Abbott.

**Avedon, Richard** (1923– ) American, born New York City. Studied photography at the New School for Social Research, New York and served in the photography section of the US merchant navy (1942–4). Established his own studio in New York and worked freelance for *Harper's Bazaar*, *Vogue* and *Life*. Received Photographer of the Year award from the American Society of Magazine Photographers in 1985.

**Bailey, David (Royston)** (1938– ) English, born London. Originally specialized in freelance fashion photography from 1959, later extending to portraits expressing the spirit of the 1960s and to studies of the nude. Also writes extensively on photography and has been director of television commercials and documentaries since the 1970s.

**Beaton, Sir Cecil (Walter Hardy)** (1904–80) English, born London. Outstanding photographer of fashion and celebrities, including royalty. Also designed scenery and costumes for ballet, operatic, theatrical and film productions. Publications include *My Royal Past* (1939), *The Glass of Fashion* (1959), *The Magic Image* (1975), as well as several volumes of autobiography (1961–78).

**Bischof, Werner** (1916–54) Swiss, born Zurich. Freelance graphic artist and photographer in Zurich (1932–6) and later magazine photographer for *Life*, *Picture Post* and *Paris Match*.

**Blumenfeld, Erwin** (1897–1969) American, born Berlin, Germany. Self-taught photographer, associated with Dadaist artists in Amsterdam (1918–23). Worked as a fashion photographer for *Verve* and *Vogue* in Paris before opening a studio in New York in 1943.

**Bourke-White, Margaret (White, Margaret)** (1904–71) American, born New York City. Photo-

journalist for *Fortune* magazine (1929) and later *Life* magazine from 1936, for which she covered World War II. First woman photographer to be attached to US armed forces. Also produced reports of the siege of Moscow (1941) and opening of the concentration camps in 1944, later covering troubles around the world. Books include *Eyes on Russia* (1931), *Halfway to Freedom* (1946) and an autobiography, *Portrait of Myself* (1963).

**Brady, Matthew B** (1823–96) American, born near Lake George, New York. Operated portrait studio in New York using daguerrotype from 1844, and later recorded the American Civil War with the Union armies, an effort which ruined him financially so that he died in poverty in a New York almshouse.

**Brandt, Bill** (1904–83) English, born London. Studied with Man Ray in Paris in 1929. In 1930s produced striking social records and during World War II worked for ministry of information recording conditions in London in the Blitz. Subsequently turned to landscape and studies of the nude. Collections include *The English at Home* (1936), *A Night in London* (1938), *Perspective of Nudes* (1961), *Shadows of Light* (1966).

**Brassaï (Halász, Gyula)** (1899–1984) French, born Brasso, Transylvania, Hungary (now Romania). From 1930 recorded underworld and nightlife of Paris. Refused to photograph during the German occupation, but worked in Picasso's studios, returning to photography after World War I.

**Bullock, Wynn (Percy Wingfield Bullock)** (1902–75) American, born Chicago. Studied photography at the Art Center School, Los Angeles (1938–40). Worked in commercial postcard photography and later taught at the Institute of Design at the University of California.

**Burgin, Victor** (1941– ) English, born Sheffield. Influenced by conceptual art of the 1960s. Concentrates on black-and-white images with text superimposed onto them, forcing the viewer to participate.

**Cameron, Julia Margaret**, née **Pattle** (1815–79) British, born Calcutta, India. Became outstanding amateur photographer in the 1860s, and received permanent acclaim for close-up portraits of Victorian celebrities.

**Capa, Robert (Friedmann, André)** (1913–54) American, born Budapest, Hungary. Recorded the Spanish Civil War (1935–7), China under Japanese attack (1938), World War II in Europe and subsequently the early days of the state of Israel. Killed by a land mine in the Indo-China fighting.

**Cartier-Bresson, Henri** (1908– ) French, born Paris. Presented his first photographic exhibition in 1933; later visited Mexico and America and worked as assistant to film director Jean Renoir. After World War II developed his human interest style of black-and-white photography in worldwide travels. Publications include *Images à la sauvette* (The Decisive Moment, 1952), *The Europeans* (1955).

**Chim, David Seymour (David Szymin)** (1911–56) American, born Warsaw, Poland. Freelance photographer who worked for *Vu* and *Ce Soir* in Paris, and throughout Europe and N Africa. Established his own studio in New York (1940–2) and was a co-founder of Magnum Photos, Paris and New York.

**Clergue, Lucien (Georges)** (1934– ) French, born Arles. Self-taught freelance teacher at Arles from 1960. Founder of Recontres Internationales de la Photographie, Arles (1970) and recipient of Photographer of the Year award, Photo Festival of Japan (1986).

**Coburn, Alvin Langdon** (1882–1966) British, born Boston, Massachusetts. Established a studio in New York (1901–2) and worked as an independent photographer in Boston, London, California and Wales. Associated with the Vorticist Group in London (1917–18).

**Cosindas, Marie** (1925– ) American, born Boston, Massachusetts. Attended photography workshops under Ansel Adams in Boston in 1961 and has worked as a freelance photographer since 1960. Received Guggenheim Fellowship in 1967.

**Crawford, Osbert Guy Stanhope** (1886–1957) British, born Bombay, India. Identified potential of aerial photography in archaeology, resulting in the collection *Wessex from the Air* (1928).

**Cunningham, Imogen** (1883–1976) American, born Portland, Oregon. Opened portrait studio in Seattle (1910) specializing in soft-focus sentimental-style portraits and still-life flower studies. Later converted to sharply defined images, and was still teaching at the Art Institute in San Francisco in her nineties.

**Curtis, Edward Sheriff** (1868–1952) American, born Madison, Wisconsin. From 1896 recorded the North American Indian tribes and their way of life, publishing first 20 volumes in 1907. Took around 40 000 negatives, stressing the Indians' peaceful arts and culture.

**Daguerre, Louis Jacques Mandé** (1787–1851) French, born Cormeilles. Inventor of the 'daguerrotype', a process in which a photographic image is obtained on a copper plate coated with a layer of metallic silver sensitized to light by iodine vapour.

**Davidson, Bruce** (1933– ) American, born Chicago. Studied photography at Rochester Institute of Technology and since 1958 has worked freelance for *Life*, *Queen*, *Vogue* and other magazines in New York, Paris and Los Angeles. Received Guggenheim Fellowship in 1962.

**DeCarava, Roy** (1919– ) African–American, born New York City. His work includes pictures of life in Harlem, jazz musicians and civil rights protests. Received Guggenheim Fellowship in 1952.

**Dodgson, Charles Lutwidge (Carroll, Lewis)** (1832–98) English, born Daresbury, near Warrington. Pioneer photographer, mainly interested in portrait photography.

**Doisneau, Robert** (1912–94) French, born Gentilly, Seine. Studied lithography in Paris (1926–9) and has worked as a photographer since 1930, including industrial photography and as a photojournalist. Awarded the Kodak Prize (1947) and the Niepce Prix (1956).

**Draper, Henry** (1837–82) American, born Prince Edward County, Virginia. Pioneer of astronomical photography who produced photographs of the Orion nebula and over 100 stellar spectra.

**Duclos du Hauron, Louis** (1837–1920) French, born Langon. Outlined principles of additive and subtractive colour separation in *Les Couleurs en Photographie* (1869). Described practical photographic methods which he patented in *Photographie en Couleur* (1878), and proposed the anaglyph method of viewing stereoscopic images.

**Eakins, Thomas** (1844–1916) American, born Philadelphia, Pennsylvania. Extended advances made by Muybridge in his studies of figures in motion. His composite plates inspired Duchamp's *Nude Descending the Staircase*.

**Eastman, George** (1854–1932) American, born Waterville, New York. Produced a successful roll-film (1884), the 'Kodak' box camera (1888) and pioneered experiments which made possible the moving-picture industry. Formed the Eastman Kodak Co in 1892 and produced the Brownie camera in 1900.

**Edgerton, Harold Eugene** (1903–90) American, born Fremont, Nebraska. Engineer who specialized in high-speed photography. Produced a krypton–xenon gas arc which was employed in photographing the capillaries in the white of the eye without harming the patient.

**Eisenstaedt, Alfred** (1898–1995) American, born Dirschau, West Prussia (now Tczew, Poland). One of the original photojournalists on *Life* magazine (1936–72). Voted Photographer of the Year in 1951. Publications include *Witness to Our Time* (1966), *The Eye of Eisenstaedt* (1969) and *Photojournalism* (1971).

**Evans, Walker** (1903–75) American, born St Louis, Missouri. Architectural and social photographer who recorded rural life in the Southern states and people in New York City subways. Publications include *American Photographs* (1938) and *Many Are Called* (1966).

**Feininger, Andreas (Bernhard Lyonel)** (1906–99) American, born Paris. Self-taught photographer, involved in industrial and architectural photography in Stockholm (1933–9). Worked as a freelance photographer in New York and as a war photographer for the US Office of War Information (1941–2).

**Fenton, Roger** (1819–69) English, born Lancashire. Photographed in Russia in 1852 and was a founder of the Photographic Society (later the Royal) in 1953; Queen Victoria became its patron and Fenton photographed the royal family at Balmoral and Windsor. In 1855 went to the Crimea as the world's first accredited war photographer. Later travelled in Britain producing architectural and landscape studies.

**Firth, Francis** (1822–98) English, born Chesterfield. Topographical photographer who produced the first photographic traveller's records to be seen in Britain during travel in Egypt and the Near East between 1856 and 1859. Established nationwide service of photographs of local scenes as prints in Britain, a business which survived commercially until 1971.

**Frank, Robert** (1924– ) Swiss, born Zurich. After working as a photographer in Zurich (1943–4) moved to America in 1947 and worked freelance for *Harper's Bazaar* and *Life* in New York. Later worked in film-making and received the Guggenheim Fellowship (1955).

**Genthe, Arnold** (1869–1942) American, born Berlin. Commercial portrait photographer who emigrated to America in 1896 and established a studio in San Francisco (1897–1906). Concentrated on dance and theatrical portraits.

**Gill, Sir David** (1843–1914) Scottish, born Aberdeen. Astronomer who pioneered use of photography for charting the heavens.

**Godwin, Fay Simmonds** (1931– ) English, born Berlin. Best known for landscape photography, including Welsh and Scottish scenes. Publications include *The Oldest Road* (1975, co-authored with J R C Anderson).

**Haas, Ernst** (1921–86) Austrian, born Vienna. Studied photography in Vienna and worked freelance for *Vogue* and *Life* in Paris (1948–50) before moving to America in 1950.

**Halsman, Philippe** (1906–79) American, born Riga, Latvia. Self-taught photographer who established a studio in Paris and worked for *Vogue* and *Voilà* (1931–40). Emigrated to America in 1940 and became President of the American Society of Magazine Photographers, New York (1944, 1954) and received a Life Achievement Award (1975).

**Hardy, Bert** (1913–95) English, born London. Photojournalist on staff of *Picture Post* until 1957, except for service as Army photographer from 1942 to 1946, during which he recorded concentration camps. Later assignments took him to the Korean and Vietnam wars. Became involved in advertising until his retirement in 1967.

**Hill, David Octavius** (1802–70) Scottish, born Perth. Pioneer in photography. With Robert Adamson applied the calotype process of making photographic prints on silver chloride paper for a commission to portray the founders of the Free Church of Scotland in 1843.

**Hine, Lewis W(ickes)** (1874–1940) American, born Oshkosh, Wisconsin. Expressed social concern through photographic studies of Ellis Island immigrants and child labour. During World War I documented the plight of refugees for the American Red Cross and recorded the construction of the Empire State Building in *Men at Work* (1932). Later registered the effects of the Depression for a US government project.

**Hiro (Yasuhiro Wakabayahi)** (1930– ) Japanese, born Shanghai, China. Moved to New York in 1954 and established a studio there in 1958. Worked freelance for *Harper's Bazaar* from 1958, and received the Photographer of the Year award from the American Society of Magazine Photographers.

**Karsh, Yousuf** (1908– ) Canadian, born Mardin, Turkey. Apprenticed to a Boston portraitist (1928–31) and in 1932 opened a studio in Ottawa. Appointed official portrait photographer to the Canadian government in 1935. Produced wartime studies of national leaders and has continued to portray statesmen, artists and writers throughout the world.

**Kertész, André** (1894–1985) Hungarian–American, born Budapest. Photographer with Hungarian army during World War I and later an acclaimed reporter of the 'human condition' in Paris. Worked for Condé-Nast publications and other magazines in New York in the 1930s and 1940s. After a major retrospective exhibition at the New York Museum of Modern Art in 1964 received belated official recognition.

**Lange, Dorothea**, originally **Nutzhorn** (1895–1965) American, born Hoboken, New Jersey. Established studio in San Francisco in 1919, and later recorded rural life in the south and west of America during the depression years from 1935. With her husband collaborated on the book *An American Exodus: A Record of Human Erosion* (1939). After World War II worked as a freelance reporter in Asia, South America and the Middle East.

**Lartigue, Jacques-Henri (Charles Auguste)** (1894–1986) French, born Courbvoie, Seine. Adopted informal approach to photography, elevating the snapshot into a creative art form. *Diary of a Century* is a collection recording the elegance of the inter-war years in France.

**Leibovitz, Annie** (1949– ) American, born Connecticut. Known for photographs of celebrities. Worked for *Rolling Stone* in the 1970s and has been chief photographer for *Vanity Fair* since 1983. Won Innovation in Photography Award in 1987. Published *Photographs 1970–90* in 1992, and *Women* in 1999.

**Levitt, Helen** (1913– ) American, born New York City. Known for documentation of urban life. Work published in *Time*, the *New York Post* and *Harper's Bazaar*. Also worked in film during the 1940s and 1950s.

**Lichfield, Patrick, 5th Earl of** (1939– ) English. After working as an assistant opened his own studio and since 1981 has achieved success in travel and publicity photography and royal portraits.

**Lichtsteiner, Rudolf** (1938– ) Swiss, born Winterthur. Freelance photographer in Zurich from 1972 and in Switzerland from 1987. Recipient of the Niepce Prix (1966).

**Marey, Étienne Jules** (1830–1903) French, born Beaune. Physiologist who pioneered scientific cinematography in studies of animal movement (1887–1900). Improved camera design and reduced exposure time to around 1/25 000 of a second to photograph insect flight.

**Martin, Paul** (1864–1942) Anglo-French, born Herbenville, France. Made use of a disguised camera to record working people in the streets of London and on holiday at the seaside (1888–98), recording the realities of late-Victorian everyday life in *London by Gaslight* (1896). Turned professional in 1899.

**McBean, Angus Rowland** (1904–90) Welsh, born Newbridge, Monmouth. Theatrical photographer from 1934, noted for an individualistic approach to portraiture, use of photographic montage, collage and double-exposure to achieve surrealistic effects. Later photographed in the world of pop music and withdrew from professional photography after 1969.

**McCullin, Don(ald)** (1935– ) English, born London. Studied painting (1948–50) and later became a photographic assistant in aerial reconnaissance with the RAF (1953–5). Worked abroad as freelance photographer and as staff photographer for the *Sunday Times* (1964–84).

**Miller, Lee** (1907–77) American, born Poughkeepsie, New York. Known for her documentary work and fashion photography. Photographer for *Vogue* before and after World War II. During war worked as official war correspondent for the American forces.

**Moholy-Nagy, László (Nagy, László)** (1895–1946) American, born Bucsborsod, near Mohol, south Hungary. Produced first 'photograms' (non-representational photographic images made directly without a camera) in 1923 and later became recognized as a leading avant-garde artist in Germany in the European New Photographers movement (1925–35), his work including film-making and typography integrated with photographic illustration. Moved to America in 1937.

**Mountford, Charles Percy** (1890–1976) Australian, born Hallett, South Australia. Ethnologist who wrote a series of books, illustrated with his own photographs about Aboriginal Australians and their culture. Later directed feature films on Aboriginal life from 1950.

**Muybridge, Eadweard (Muggeridge, Edward James)** (1830–1904) Anglo-American, born Kingston-on-Thames. Became professional photographer in 1866 and later chief photographer to the American government. In 1880 devised the zoopraxiscope to show picture sequences, achieving a rudimentary kind of cinematography. *Animal Locomotion* (1887) gives the results of his extensive survey of animal and human movement carried out for the University of Pennsylvania.

**Nadar (Tournachon, Gaspard-Felix)** (1820–1910) French, born Paris. Photographer, artist and journalist who produced lively portraits of distinguished literary and artistic contemporaries and the first 'photo-interview', series of photographs captioned with the sitter's replies to his questions. Proposed the use of aerial photographs for map-making and in 1858 took the first photographs from a balloon, of Paris.

**Newman, Arnold (Abner)** (1918– ) American, born New York City. Assistant portrait photographer (1938–9) and later Director of the Newman Portrait Studio, Miami Beach (1942–5). President since 1946 of Arnold Newman Studios Inc, New York, and recipient of the gold medal, Biennale Internazionale della Fotografica, Venice (1963).

**Newton, Helmut** (1920– ) Australian, born Berlin, Germany. Apprentice to a theatre and fashion photographer in Berlin (1936–40) and freelance photographer for *Elle*, *Queen*, *Marie-Claire* and *Vogue* since 1958. Received the Best Photography Award, Art Directors Club, Tokyo (1976).

**Niepce, Joseph Nicéphore** (1765–1833) French, born Chalon-sur-Saône. Chemist who succeeded in producing a photograph on metal (1826), said to be the world's first. Later cooperated with others in further research.

**Nilsson, Lennart** (1922– ) Swedish, born Rome. Freelance press photographer, acclaimed for several portraits such as *Sweden in Profiles* (1954) who later pioneered microfilm showing the anatomy of plants and animals. Perfected special lenses to film inside the human body, enabling him to produce pictures of the human foetus in the womb from conception to birth. *Ett barn blir till* (1965, The Everyday Miracle: A Child is Born) won the American National Press Association Picture of the Year Award.

**Parer, Damien** (1912–44) Australian, born Malvern, Victoria. Official cameraman with the 2nd Australian Imperial Forces. Filmed action at the siege of Tobruk in the Middle East, later working in Greece, Syria and New Guinea. His documentary film *Kokoda Front* was the first Australian film to win an Oscar. Killed while filming American troops landing at Peleliu, Caroline Islands.

**Parkinson, Norman**, originally **Parkinson Smith, Ronald William** (1913–90) English, born London. Opened studio in 1934 and became a well-known portrait and fashion photographer, his work being used widely in quality magazines. Later advertising work in the 1950s involved worldwide travel. Settled in Tobago in 1963.

**Parks, Gordon (Alexander Buchanan)** (1912– ) American, born Fort Scott, Kansas. Self-taught photographer; worked for the US Office of War Information (1943–5) and as a freelance fashion photographer in Minneapolis (1937–42). After working as a documentary film-maker in America and Saudi Arabia, became an independent photographer, film writer and director for Warner Brothers, MGM and Paramount Pictures (1962–71).

**Penn, Irving** (1917– ) American, born Plainfield, New Jersey. Served as an ambulance driver and documentary photographer in the American Field Service in Italy and India (1944–5). Later worked for *Vogue* in New York (1943–4) and as a freelance advertising photographer from 1952.

**Porter, Eliot (Furness)** (1901–90) American, born Winnetka, Illinois. Self-taught photographer who concentrated on his photographic career from 1939, in particular in landscape and wildlife photography. Received the Conservation Award from the US Department of the Interior (1967).

**Ray, Man (Rabinovich, Emanuel)** (1890–1976) American, born Philadelphia, Pennsylvania. After making a number of Surrealist films in Paris, published and exhibited many photographs and 'rayographs' (photographic images made without a camera) in the 1930s, returning to America in 1940. Awarded the gold medal at the Biennale of Photography in Venice (1961). Published his autobiography, *Self Portrait*, in 1963.

**Robinson, Henry Peach** (1830–1901) English, born Ludlow. Opened studio in Leamington Spa in 1857, but moved from formal portraiture to 'high art photography', often creating scenes using composites of several separate images of costumed models and painted settings in the mid-Victorian style. A founder member of The Linked Ring (1892), an association of photographers seeking artistic creation, which developed into the international Photo-Secession Group. Wrote *Pictorial Effect in Photography* (1869).

**Rodchenko, Alexander Mikhailovich** (1891–1956) Russian, born St Petersburg. Photographer, painter and designer whose most original photographic works were documentary photographs of the new communist society.

**Rosenblum, Walter** (1919– ) American, born New York City. After studying photography in New York, worked as a photographer for the US army in Europe (1943–5), becoming the most decorated photographer in the army. Editor of *Photo Notes* (1939–41) and chairman of the Exhibition Committee (1941–2) in New York. Awarded the Guggenheim Fellowship in 1979.

**Rothstein, Arthur** (1915–85) American, born New York City. Photo officer for the US army in India, Burma and China (1943–6) and picture editor for the Office of War Information, New York (1942–3). Founder of the American Society of Magazine Photographers (1941) and recipient of the Lifetime Arts Achievement award from the New York Council of the Arts (1985).

**Saint Joseph, John Kenneth Sinclair** (1912–94) English, born Worcestershire. Professor of aerial photographic studies at Cambridge (1948–80), developing large photographic archive with emphasis on systematic reconnaissance, and low-level oblique photography of natural landscapes and of archaeological monuments in their landscape setting. *Monastic Sites from the Air* (1952), *Medieval England: An Aerial Survey* (1958, 1979), *Roman Britain from the Air* (1983) are collections of some of the results.

**Salomon, Erich** (1886–1944) German, born Berlin. Prisoner-of-war in France (1915–18). Began freelance photographic career in 1927, working for *L'Illustration* of Paris and *Fortune* of New York. Died at Auschwitz with his wife and son.

**Sander, August** (1876–1964) German, born Herdorf am Sieg. Planned a massive photographic documentary study, *Men in the 20th Century*, but only the first part *Faces of Our Times* (1929) was published as his social realism was discouraged by the Nazi Ministry of Culture after 1934. Surviving material has provided penetrating portraits of all levels of German life in the early part of the century.

**Sheeler, Charles** (1883–1965) American, born Philadelphia, Pennsylvania. Worked as industrial photographer from 1912, producing creative industrial records, especially the skyscrapers of Manhattan in *Mannahatta* (1920). Commissioned to record the building of the Ford Motor installation at River Rouge, Michigan (1927), and staff photographer at the New York Museum of Modern Art (1942–5).

**Sielmann, Heinz** (1917– ) German, born Königsberg. Interested in animal photography, started making films in 1938, for which he won three German Oscars (1953–5). Developed techniques enabling photography in inaccessible animal lairs which have revolutionized the study of animal behaviour.

**Siskind, Aaron** (1903–91) American, born New York City. Self-taught freelance photographer from 1932. Member of Film and Photo League of New York and later photography teacher. Co-editor of the Chicago poetry and photographic magazine *Choice* (1961–70). Received Guggenheim Fellowship (1966).

**Smith, W(illiam) Eugene** (1918–78) American, born Wichita, Kansas. Staff photographer for *Newsweek* in New York (1937–8) and later freelance for magazines including *Harper's Bazaar* and *Life*. Pacific war correspondent (1942–5) and photographer for Hitachi in New York and Japan (1959–77). Received Honor Award from the American Society of Magazine Photographers (1959).

**Smythe, Francis Sydney** (1900–49) English, born Maidstone. Mountaineer whose many books, including *Kamet Conquered* (1932), *Camp Six* (1937), *Adventures of a Mountaineer* (1940), *Over Welsh Hills* (1941) contain acclaimed mountain photography.

**Snowdon, Antony Charles Robert Armstrong-Jones, 1st Earl of** (1930– ) English, born London. Freelance photographer from 1951 and artistic adviser for many publications. Famous for informal portraits of the famous, he has also recorded the plight of the handicapped and disabled and has produced documentaries for television on similar themes.

**Steichen, Edward Jean** (1879–1973) American, born Luxembourg. Practised painting and photography in Europe until 1914. Member of The Linked Ring in England and noted for his studies of the nude. A founder of the American Photo-Secession Group, he later served in the photographic division of the US army during World War I, and in the 1920s achieved success in fashion photography. Head of US Naval Film Services during World War II and director of photography at the New York Museum of Modern Art (1945–62), organizing the world-famous exhibition *The Family of Man* (1945).

**Stieglitz, Alfred** (1864–1946) American, born Hoboken, New Jersey. Studied engineering and photography in Berlin and later was a founder of the Photo-Secession Group in 1902, devoted to artistic expression in photography. Exerted great influence through his magazine *Camera Work* (1903–17) and his gallery of modern art. Other work includes studies of New York architecture, clouds and portraits.

**Strand, Paul** (1890–1976) American, born New York City. Became commercial photographer in 1912, committed to 'straight' photography of precision and clarity. Produced documentary films during the 1920s and 1930s, but from the 1940s concentrated on still photography for records of his life in many different parts of the world.

**Sutcliffe, Frank Meadow** (1853–1941) English, born near Whitby, Yorkshire. Received numerous international awards for studies of the vanishing world of English farmhands and fisher-folk in the local country and seacoast between 1881 and 1905. From late 1890s made use of new lightweight cameras to obtain natural snapshots rather than formal poses. A fully illustrated account of his work was published in 1974.

**Talbot, William Henry Fox** (1800–77) English, born Melbury, Dorset. Announced his invention of photography, a system of making photographic prints on silver chloride paper, in 1839. In 1841 patented the calotype, the first process for photographic negatives from which prints could be made and was awarded the Rumford Medal of the Royal Society in 1842. Also discovered a method of instantaneous flash photography and his *Pencil of Nature* (1844) was the first photographically illustrated book to be published.

**Van der Elskin, Ed(uard)** (1925– ) Dutch, born Amsterdam. Self-taught freelance photographer in Amsterdam (1947–50), Paris (1950–5) and Edam, the Netherlands since 1955. Also freelance film-maker.

**Weston, Edward (Henry)** (1886–1958) American, born Highland Park, Illinois. Became recognized as modernist, emphasizing sharp images and precise definition in landscapes, portraits and still-life. Member of Group f/64 in California from 1932. First photographer to receive a Guggenheim Fellowship with which he travelled widely throughout the American West. Illustrated an edition of Walt Whitman's *Leaves of Grass*.

**White, Minor (Martin)** (1908–76) American, born Minneapolis, Minnesota. Developed the realism of the photographic sequence and the abstraction of the 'equivalent', the visual metaphor in which he continued Stieglitz's symbolism of natural formations. In 1946 moved to San Francisco and worked with Ansel Adams. Founded the periodicals *Aperture* (1952) and *Image* (1953–7) and was appointed Professor of Creative Photography at the Massachusetts Institute of Technology (1965–76).

**Winogrand, Garry** (1928–84) American, born New York. Studied photography in New York from 1951. Received Guggenheim Fellowship (1964, 69 and 78).

## Fashion designers

**Amies, Sir (Edwin) Hardy** (1909– ) English, born London. Couturier and dressmaker by appointment to Queen Elizabeth II. Renowned especially for tailored suits for women. Founded his own fashion house in 1946 and started designing for men also in 1959.

**Armani, Giorgio** (1935– ) Italian, born Piacenza. Became designer for Nino Cerruti in 1961 and also freelanced before setting up the Giorgio Armani company in 1975. Designed first for men, then women, including loose-fitting jackets and blazers.

**Ashley, Laura** née **Mountney** (1925–85) Welsh, born Merthyr Tydfil. Started business with husband Bernard Ashley in 1953, manufacturing furnishing materials and wallpapers with patterns based mainly on 19th-century document sources. Later experimented with designing and making clothes, transforming the business from one shop to an international chain of boutiques.

**Balenciaga, Cristóbal** (1895–1972) Spanish, born Guetaria. Opened dressmaking and tailoring shops in Madrid and Barcelona in 1915. Moved to Paris in 1937 because of the Spanish Civil War. His clothes were noted for dramatic simplicity and elegant design.

**Balmain, Pierre Alexandre** (1914–82) French, born St Jean-de-Maurienne. Worked for Edward Molyneux and Lucien Lelong before opening his own house in 1945. Famous for elegant simplicity, his designs included evening dresses, tailored suits, sportswear and stoles. Also designed for the theatre and cinema.

**Cardin, Pierre** (1922– ) French, born Venice, Italy. Worked in fashion houses and on costume design in Paris after World War II and opened his own house in 1953. Since then has been prominent in fashion for both women and men.

**Chanel, Gabrielle**, known as **Coco** (1883–1971) French, born Saumur. Orphaned at an early age, she worked with her sister as a milliner until 1912, when she opened a shop of her own. Later opened couture houses in Deauville and Paris, producing designs combining simple elegance and comfort. Also introduced the vogue for costume jewellery and the evening scarf. Retired in 1938, but made a successful comeback in 1954.

**Claiborne, Liz** (1929– ) Belgian–American, born Brussels. Designed for Youth Guild Inc, New York City, before founding own company in 1976. Her designs are targeted at the working woman. She retired in 1989, though the company continues.

**Conran, Jasper** (1959– ) English, born London. Son of Sir Terence Conran, he trained in art and design in New York before joining Fiorucci briefly as a designer in 1977. Produced his first collection of easy-to-wear, quality clothes in London in 1978.

**Courrèges, André** (1923– ) French, born Pau. Trained by Balenciaga from 1952 to 1960, he opened his own house in 1961. Famous for stark, futuristic, 'Space Age' designs, he introduced the miniskirt (1964) and has featured white boots and trouser suits for women.

**De la Renta, Oscar** (1932– ) American, born Santo Domingo, Dominican Republic. Worked at Balenciaga's couture house in Madrid, joined the house of Lanvin-Castillo in Paris (1961) then Elizabeth Arden in New York (1963), before starting his own company in 1965. Has reputation for opulent, ornately trimmed clothes, particularly evening dresses, but also designs daywear and accessories.

**Dior, Christian** (1905–57) French, born Granville, Normandy. Began designing clothes in 1935, and founded his own Paris house in 1947. Achieved worldwide fame with his long-skirted 'New Look' and subsequently the 'A-line' and 'the Sack'.

**Farhi, Nicole** (1946– ) Anglo-French, born Nice, France. Started working in London on French Connection and the Stephen Marks label. Launched own company in 1983 and became well known for simple, comfortable, but elegant clothing.

**Galliano, John**, originally **Galliano, Juan Carlos** (1960– ) Gibraltan, born Gibralta. Graduated from St Martin's School of Art and Design, London in 1984. Inspired by a range of cultural and historical references. Became designer-in-chief at Givenchy in 1995. Left in 1996 to become designer-in-chief at the House of Dior.

**Garavani, Valentino** (1933– ) Italian, born Rome. Studied fashion in Milan and Paris, then worked for Dessès and Guy Laroche in Paris. Opened his own house in Rome in 1959, and achieved worldwide recognition with his 1962 show in Florence.

**Gaultier, Jean-Paul** (1952– ) French, born Paris. Worked with Cardin for two years (1969–71), then at Patou. In 1976, began working as a freelance designer, drawing inspiration from the London street-scene, which he glamorized for the Paris market. He is now one of the most influential Paris designers.

**Givenchy, Hubert James Marcel Taffin de** (1927– ) French, born Beauvais. After training and working with a number of well-known designers, opened his own house in 1952. His Bettina blouse in white cotton became internationally famous, and his clothes are noted for their elegance and quality.

**Hamnett, Katherine** (1952– ) English, born Gravesend, Kent. After studying fashion at St Martin's School of Art and Design in London, worked as a freelance designer, setting up a short-lived company (1969–74) and then her own business in 1979. Draws inspiration for designs from workwear and from movements such as the peace movement.

**Hartnell, Sir Norman (Bishop)** (1901–78) English, born Honiton, Devon. Started his own couturier business in 1923, receiving the Royal Warrant in 1940. Produced costumes for leading actresses, wartime 'utility' dresses, the WRAC uniform and Princess Elizabeth's wedding and coronation gowns.

**Hulanicki, Barbara** (1936– ) Born Palestine of Polish parents. Launched Biba's Postal Boutique in 1963. Opened three stores in London which became fashion mecca of the 1960s. Biba closed in 1973.

**Karan, Donna** (1948– ) American, born Donna Faske, New York. Became Director of Design at Anne Klein in 1974. Launched Donna Karan Company in 1984, which became Donna Karan International in 1996.

**Kenzo Takada** (1940– ) Japanese, born Kyoto. After studying art, worked in Japan before producing freelance collections in Paris from 1964. Started a shop called Jungle Jap in 1970. Creates clothes with both oriental and western influences, and is a trendsetter in the field of knitwear.

**Klein, Anne Hannah**, née **Hannah Golofski** (1921–74) American, born New York City. Started as sketcher on Seventh Avenue in 1938, and established Anne Klein & Co in 1968. Designed practical sportswear for women.

**Klein, Calvin Richard** (1942– ) American, born New York City. Graduated from New York's Fashion Institute of Technology in 1962, and set up his own firm in 1968. Quickly achieved recognition and is known for understatement and the simple but sophisticated style of his clothes, including 'designer jeans'.

**Lacroix, Christian** (1951– ) French couturier, born Arles, Provence. After studying fashion history, worked for a leather firm with Guy Paulin, a ready-to-wear designer. In 1981 joined Jean Patou; in 1987 opened the House of Lacroix in Paris. Made his name with ornate and frivolous clothes.

**Lagerfeld, Karl** (1938– ) German, born Hamburg. Won an International Wool Secretariat competition in 1954 and worked with Balmain in Paris. After three years he left to begin freelance work with a number of design houses, including Chloe, Ballantyne, Fendi and Valentino. His talents lie particularly in meticulous cut, extravagant beading, furs and knitwear. He is renowned for his flamboyant fashion shows.

**Lang, Helmut** (1956– ) Austrian, born Vienna. From 1979 has owned made-to-measure shop in Vienna. Launched his first ready-to-wear collection in 1984. Won Council of American Fashion Designers of the Year Award in 1996.

**Laroche, Guy** (1923–89) French, born La Rochelle, near Bordeaux. Worked in millinery, first in Paris then on Seventh Avenue, New York, before returning to Paris where he worked for Dessès for eight years; started his own business in 1957, achieving a reputation for skilful cutting. From 1966 his designs included menswear.

**Lauren, Ralph**, originally **Ralph Lipschitz** (1939– ) American, born The Bronx, New York City. In 1967 joined Beau Brummel Neckwear and created the Polo range for men, later including womenswear. Famous for his American styles, such as the 'prairie look' and 'frontier fashions'.

**McQueen, Alexander** (1970– ) British, born London. Showed final collection at St Martin's School of Art and Design, London in 1992. Since 1996 has been Chief Designer at Givenchy. In 1996 won Designer of the Year, London Fashion Awards.

**Mainbocher**, originally **Main Rousseau Bocher** (1891–1976) American, born Chicago. After service in World War I stayed on in Paris, eventually becoming a fashion artist with *Harper's Bazaar* and later editor of French *Vogue* until 1929. Started his couture house in Paris in 1930; created the Duchess of Windsor's wedding dress (1937).

**Missoni, Tai Otavio** (1921– ) Italian, born Yugoslavia. Founded the Missoni company in Milan with his wife, Rosita, in 1953. At first manufactured knitwear to be sold under other labels, but later created, under their own label, innovative knitwear notable for its sophistication and distinctive colours and patterns.

**Miyake, Issey** (1938– ) Japanese, born Hiroshima. Spent six years in Paris and New York fashion houses before showing his first collection in Tokyo in 1963. Distinctive style combines eastern and western influences in garments which have an almost theatrical quality, frequently in subdued colours.

**Molyneux, Edward Henry** (1891–1974) English, born London. After studying art, worked for Lucile. Opened his own couture house in Paris in 1919 with branches in London, Monte Carlo, Cannes and Biarritz, and became famous for the elegant simplicity of tailored suits with pleated skirts, and evening wear.

**Montana, Claude** (1949– ) French, born Paris. Began designing jewellery in London, and then moved to leather and knitwear companies. Designed his first ready-to-wear collection in 1976. Has been designer at the House of Lanvin since 1989.

**Mortensen, Erik** (1926– ) Danish. Since 1948, attached to the Balmain fashion house in Paris, becoming artistic director in 1960 and taking over the management after the death of Pierre Balmain in 1982. Awarded the Golden Thimble of the French Haute Couture in 1983 and 1987.

**Muir, Jean Elizabeth** (1928–95) English, born London. Started as sales assistant with Liberty's in London, then moved to Jaeger in 1956. In 1961 started on her own as Jane & Jane and in 1966 established her company Jean Muir. Her clothes are noted for their classic shapes, softness and fluidity.

**Oldfield, Bruce** (1950– ) English, born London. As a freelance designer sold sketches to Yves Saint Laurent and designed for Bendel's store in New York. Showed his first collection in 1975 in London. His designs include evening dresses for royalty and screen stars and ready-to-wear clothes.

**Ozbeck, Rifat** (1953– ) Turkish, born Istanbul. Beginning with small collections, now has multi-million pound business. Awarded Designer of the Year twice (1989 and 1992). His designs cover many styles and display cross-cultural references.

**Patou, Jean** (1880–1936) French, born Normandy. In 1912 opened Maison Parry in Paris and in 1913 sold his collection outright to an American buyer. After war service he successfully opened again as couturier in

1919. Noted for his designs for sports stars and actresses and for his perfume 'Joy'.

**Poiret, Paul** (1879–1944) French, born Paris. Worked for Jacques Doucet and Worth before opening his own fashion house in 1904. Influenced by the exotic oriental costumes of the Ballets Russes, his designs featured turbans and harem pants and he became a leader of fashion rather than a designer for individual clients. After World War I did not re-establish his prominence and died in poverty.

**Pucci, Emilio, Marchese di Barsento** (1914–92) Italian, born Naples, Member of Italy's Olympic ski team (1933–4) and later member of the Italian parliament (1963–72), he started designing ski clothes in 1947 and in 1950 opened his own couture house, creating print dresses for women. Became renowned for use of bold patterns and brilliant colour.

**Quant, Mary** (1934– ) English, born London. Began fashion design when she opened a small boutique in Chelsea in 1955. Her clothes became extremely fashionable in the 1960s when the geometric simplicity of her designs and the originality of her colours became an essential feature of the 'swinging Britain' era.

**Rhodes, Zandra** (1940– ) English, born Chatham, Kent. After studying art, designed and printed textiles and, with others, opened The Fulham Road Clothes Shop, afterwards setting up on her own. Showed her first dress collection in 1969, and is noted for distinctive, exotic designs in chiffons and silks.

**Saint Laurent, Yves**, originally **Henri Donat Mathieu** (1936– ) French, born Oran, Algeria. Employed by Christian Dior in 1955 after winning an International Wool Secretariat design competition. Took over the house on Dior's death in 1957. In 1962 opened his own house and launched the first of his 160 Rive Gauche boutiques in 1966, selling ready-to-wear clothes, a trend which many other designers were to follow.

**Schiaparelli, Elsa** (1890–1973) Italian–French, born Rome. After living in America, moved to Paris and started business in 1929. Her designs were inventive and sensational, and she was noted for her use of bright colour and traditional fabrics, featuring zippers and buttons, and outrageous hats. Opened a salon in New York in 1949, and retired in 1954.

**Ungaro, Emanuel Maffeolti** (1933– ) French, born Aix-en-Provence. Worked for small Paris tailoring firm and later with Balenciaga, before opening his own house in 1965, with Sonia Knapp designing his fabrics. Initially featured rigid lines, but later produced softer styles. Produced his first ready-to-wear lines in 1968.

**Versace, Gianni** (1946–97) Italian, born Calabria. Launched first women's wear collection in 1978. Opened boutique and designed first menswear collection in 1979. Has designed for various ballet productions. Won many awards including the CDFA in 1992 and the Golden Eye in 1982, 1984 and 1997. Was shot dead outside American home.

**Westwood, Vivienne** (1941– ) English, born London. Began clothes design on meeting Malcolm McLaren, manager of The Sex Pistols. They established a shop in London and became known as the leading creators of punk clothing. Since her split from McLaren in 1983, has become accepted by the mainstream, and was Designer of the Year in 1990 and 1991.

**Worth, Charles Frederick** (1825–95) Anglo-French, born Bourn, Lincolnshire. Achieved success as a fashion designer in Paris, gaining the patronage of the Empress Eugénie. His establishment in the Rue de la Paix became the centre of the fashion world.

**Yamamoto, Yohji** (1943– ) Japanese, born Tokyo. Started his own company in 1972 producing his first collection in 1976 in Tokyo. After some time in Paris, opened a new headquarters in London in 1987. Designs loose, functional clothes for men and women, which conceal rather than emphasize the body.

## Philosophers

**Anaxagoras** (500–428BC) Greek, born Clazomenae. Believed that matter is infinitely divisible into particles containing a mixture of all qualities and that mind is a pervasive formative agency in the creation of material objects.

**Anaximander** (611–547BC) Greek, born Miletus. Proposed that basic matter is the *apeiron*, the infinite or indefinite. Speculated that the Earth is unsupported at the centre of the Universe and that human beings developed from another species.

**Aquinas, St Thomas** (1225–74) Italian, born Roccasecca, near Aquino. Combined Christian doctrine with the teachings of Aristotle. Wrote on principles of natural religion in *Summa contra Gentiles* (1259–64) and on proving the existence of God in *Summa Theologiae* (1266–73). Had considerable influence on theological thought of following ages.

**Aristotle** (384–322BC) Greek, born Stagira, Macedonia. One of the most important philosophers and scientists in the history of Western thought, writing extensively on logic, metaphysics, ethics, politics, rhetoric, poetry, biology, zoology, physics and psychology. Best-known works include the *Metaphysics, Nicomachean Ethics, Politics, Poetics,* the *De Anima*, the *Organon*.

**Augustine of Hippo, St** (354–430) Italian, born North Africa. One of the most influential Christian theologians, he was influenced primarily by Manicheanism, then neoplatonism, before converting

to Christianity in 386. Famous works are the *Confessions* (400), *The City of God* (412–27).

**Austin, John L(angshaw)** (1911–60) English, born Lancaster. Professor at Oxford University and leading figure in 'Oxford Philosophy' movement. Examined ordinary linguistic usage to resolve philosophical perplexities. Best-known works: *Philosophical Papers* (1961), *Sense and Sensibilia* (1962), *How to do Things with Words* (1962).

**Averroës, Ibn Rushd** (1126–98) Muslim, born Cordova, Spain. Famous medieval Islamic philosopher who also wrote on jurisprudence and medicine. Most important works were the *Commentaries on Aristotle* which offered a partial synthesis of Greek and Arabic philosophical traditions.

**Ayer, Sir Alfred (Jules)** (1910–89) English, born London. Professor at London and Oxford Universities. *Language, Truth and Logic* (1936) gives an account of the logical positivist, anti-metaphysical doctrines with which he became involved in the 1930s, and aroused great hostility when published. Later publications include *The Problem of Knowledge* (1956), *The Central Questions of Philosophy* (1972). Knighted in 1970.

**Bacon, Francis, Viscount St Albans** (1561–1626) English, born London. Important philosopher and statesman, knighted in 1603. Abandoned deductive logic of Aristotle and stressed the importance of experiment in interpretation of nature. Philosophical works include *The Advancement of Learning* (1605), *De Augmentis Scientiarum* (1623), *Novum Organum* (1620). He also wrote many religious and professional works.

**Bacon, Roger** (c.1214–92) English, born probably Ilchester, Somerset. Philosopher, scientist and Franciscan monk with reputation for unconventional learning in magic and alchemy, and imprisoned for heresy. Also published many works on mathematics, philosophy, and logic whose importance was recognized in later centuries.

**Bentham, Jeremy** (1748–1832)English, born London. Philosopher, jurist and social reformer: advocated utilitarianism in *A Fragment on Government* (1776) and *Introduction to the Principles of Morals and Legislation* (1789). Published many works on penal and social reform, economics and politics.

**Berkeley, Bishop George** (1685–1753) Irish, born near Kilkenny. Developed the belief that the contents of the material world are 'ideas' that only exist when perceived by a mind in *Essay towards a New Theory of Vision* (1709), *A Treatise concerning the Principles of Human Knowledge* (1710), *Three Dialogues between Hyals and Philonous* (1713). Expressed concern about social corruption and national decadence and wrote on social reform and religion.

**Berlin, Sir Isaiah** (1909–97) British, born Riga, Russia. Oxford professor whose philosophical works include *Karl Marx* (1939), *Historical Inevitability* (1954), *Two Concepts of Liberty* (1953), *Vico and Herder* (1976) and four volumes of essays.

**Boethius, Anicius Manlius Severinus** (c.475–524) Roman, born probably Rome. Produced translations of and commentaries on Aristotle. During a period of imprisonment for treason for which he was later executed, he wrote *De Consolatione Philosophiae*, which explains the mutability of all earthly fortune and demonstrates that happiness can only be attained by virtue.

**Buber, Martin** (1878–1965) Jewish, born Vienna. Published many works on social and ethical problems and is best known for the religious philosophy expounded in *Ich und Du* (1922), contrasting personal relationships of mutuality and reciprocity with utilitarian or objective relationships.

**Burke, Edmund** (1729–87) Irish, born Dublin. Statesman and philosopher whose political thought has become the philosophy of modern Conservatism. Works include *Observations on the Present State of the Nation* (1769), *On the Causes of the Present Discontents* (1770).

**Carnap, Rudolf** (1891–1970) German–American, born Wuppertal. Leading member of the 'Vienna Circle' of logical positivists who dismissed most traditional metaphysics as a source of meaningless answers to pseudo-problems. Works include *Der logische Aufbau der Welt* (1928), *Logische Syntax der Sprache* (1934), *Meaning and Necessity* (1947), *The Logical Foundations of Probability* (1950).

**Comte, Auguste** (1798–1857) French, born Montpelier. Usually regarded as the founder of sociology. His 'positivism' sought to expound the laws of social evolution, to describe the organization of all branches of human knowledge, and to establish a science of society as a basis for social planning. Works include *Cours de Philosophie positive* (1830–42), *Système de Politique positive* (1851–4).

**Confucius (K'ung Fu-tse, 'the Master K'ung')** (551–479BC) Chinese, born state of Lu (modern Shantung). Moral teacher who tried to replace old religious observances with moral values as the basis of social and political order, emphasizing the importance of respect and benevolence. 'Confucianism' became, and remained until recently, the state religion of China. His teachings are recorded in the *Analects*, written by his pupils after his death.

**Copleston, Frederick (Charles)** (1907–93) English, born near Taunton, Somerset. Catholic philosopher; published many critical studies of philosophers and wrote *A History of Philosophy* (1946–66).

**Cousin, Victor** (1792–1867) French, born Paris. An eclectic in philosophy; published many historical studies and commentaries on other philosophers. Most original work is *Du Vrai, du Beau, et du Bien* (1854).

**Croce, Benedetto** (1866–1952) Italian, born Pescasserolli. Developed phenomenology of the mind in which four principle activities, art and philosophy (theoretical), political economy and ethics (practical), complement each other. His theory of aesthetics is described in *Lo Spirito* and his opposition to totalitarianism is expressed in *History as the Story of Liberty* (1941).

**Cudworth, Ralph** (1617–88) English, born Aller, Somerset. Leading member of the Cambridge Platonists. *The True Intellectual System of the Universe* (1678) aimed to refute determinism and materialism and to establish the reality of a supreme divine intelligence; *Treatise concerning Eternal and Immutable Morality* is a posthumous publication discussing ethics.

**Davidson, Donald Herbert** (1917– ) American, born Springfield, Massachusetts. One of the most influential recent analytical philosophers, who has made contributions to the philosophy of language, mind and action in *Essays on Action and Events* (1980) and *Structure and Content of Truth* (1990).

**de Beauvoir, Simone** (1908–80) French, born Paris. Sorbonne professor, novelist and feminist who contributed substantially to the existentialist movement. Works include *Le Deuxième Sexe* (1949), translated as *The Second Sex* (1953).

**Democritus** (c.460–370BC) Greek, born Abdera, Thrace. Prolific ancient philosopher publishing works on ethics, physics, mathematics, cosmology and music, although only fragments of his writings remain. Best known for physical speculations, in particular the belief that the world consists of an infinite number of minute particles whose different combinations account for different properties.

**Derrida, Jacques** (1930– ) French, born El Biar, Algeria. Work spans literary criticism, psychoanalysis, linguistics and philosophy. Founded the school of criticism known as 'deconstruction'.

**Descartes, René** (1596–1650) French, born La Haye, near Tours. Usually regarded as the founder of modern philosophy. *Discourse de la Méthode* (1637), *Meditationes de Prima Philosophia* (1641) and *Principia Philosophiae* (1644) set out his ideas on philosophical methods, propositions and religious beliefs. Famous for the dictum, 'I think, therefore I am' (cogito ergo sum) and for his dualism of mind and body, he also made important contributions in astronomy and mathematics.

**Dewey, John** (1859–1952) American, born Burlington, Vermont. Exponent of pragmatism whose philosophy stressed the instrumental function of ideas and judgements in problem solving. Also published widely on psychology and education. Works include *The School and Society* (1899), *Reconstruction in Philosophy* (1920), *Experience and Nature* (1925), *The Quest for Certainty* (1929), *Experience and Education* (1938).

**Diogenes** (412–323BC) Greek, born Sinope, Pontus. Continued the pre-Socratic tradition of speculation about the primary constituent of the world, which he identified as air, operating as an active and intelligent life-force.

**Duns Scotus, John** (c.1266–1308) Scottish, born probably Duns, Berwickshire. Philosopher whose beliefs represented a strong reaction against Aristotle and Aquinas; he propounded the primacy of the individual and the freedom of the individual will. His writings were mainly commentaries on the Bible and other philosophers.

**Empedocles** (490–430BC) Greek, born Acragas, Sicily. Philosopher, poet, doctor, statesman and soothsayer who described a cosmic cycle in which earth, air, fire and water periodically combine and separate under the forces of Love and Hate as well as beliefs on the transmigration and redemption of souls.

**Epicurus** (341–270BC) Greek, born Samos. Advocated a philosophy designed to promote detachment, serenity and freedom from fear, and the belief that pleasure is the only good and the only goal of morality.

**Erasmus, Desiderius** (1466–1536) Dutch, born Rotterdam. Influential Renaissance humanist and scholar who published many popular works including *Adagia* (Adages, 1500, 1508), *Enchiridion Militis Christiani* (*Handbook of a Christian Soldier*, 1503) and Encomium Moriae (*In Praise of Folly*, 1509).

**Feuerbach, Ludwig (Andreas)** (1804–72) German, born Landshut, Bavaria. Attacked conventional Christianity in *Das Wesen des Christentums* (1847), translated as *The Essence of Christianity*, arguing that God is the projection of human ideals and human nature.

**Fichte, Johann Gottlieb** (1762–1814) German, born Rammenau, Saxony. Posited the Ego as the basic reality, affirming itself in the act of consciousness and constructing the external world as its field of action. He elaborates this system in *Grundlage des Naturrechts* (1796) and *System der Sittenlehre* (1798).

**Foucault, Michel** (1926–84) French, born Poitiers. Believed that prevailing social attitudes are manipulated by those in power to define such categories as insanity, illness, sexuality and criminality and these are used to identify and oppress 'deviants'. Translations of his work include *The Order of Things* (1970), *Madness and Civilization* (1971), *The Archaeology of Knowledge* (1972), *The History of Sexuality* (1984).

**Frege, (Friedrich Ludwig) Gottlob** (1848–1925) German, born Wismar. Regarded as the founder of modern mathematical logic and the philosophy of language. Main works are *Begriffschrift* (1879), *Die Grundlagen der Arithmetik* (1884) and *Die Grundgesetze der Arithmetik* (1893, 1903).

**Gödel, Kurt** (1906–78) American, born Brünn, Austria-Hungary (now Brno, Czechoslovakia). Logician and mathematician whose theorem, published in 1931, demonstrated the existence of formally undecidable elements in any formal system of arithmetic.

**Gorgias** (c.485–380BC) Greek, born Leontini, Sicily. Advocated a philosophy which was an extreme form of scepticism or nihilism; that nothing exists, that if it did it would be unknowable, that if it were knowable it would be incommunicable to others. He is portrayed in Plato's dialogue, the *Gorgias*.

**Hamilton, Sir William** (1788–1856) Scottish, born Glasgow. Philosopher whose main work *Lectures on Metaphysics and Logic*, published posthumously (1856–60), presented views on perception and knowledge. Important figure in the revival of philosophy in Britain at this time.

**Hegel, Georg Wilhelm Friedrich** (1770–1831) German, born Stuttgart. Idealist philosopher whose major works include *Phänomenologie des Geistes* (1807), *Wissenschaft der Logik* (1812, 1816), *Enclyclopädie der philosophischen Wissenschaften in Grundrisse* (1817). Although his philosophy is difficult and obscure it has remained influential until the present.

**Heidegger, Martin** (1889–1976) German, born Messkirch, Baden. Philosopher whose writings examine the nature and predicament of human existence, classify modes of 'Being' and discuss the human mode of existence characterized by participation and involvement in the world of objects. His major work is *Sein und Zeit* (*Being and Time*, 1927).

**Heraclitus** (c.540–460BC) Greek, born Ephesus. Believed that everything is in a state of flux and that fire is the ultimate constituent of the world. Only fragments remain of his book *On Nature*.

**Herbert of Cherbury, Edward, (1st Baron)** (1583–1648) English, born Eyton, Shropshire. Soldier, statesman and philosopher who argued in *De Religione Gentilum* (1645) that all religions recognize five main articles, from the acknowledgement of a supreme God to the concept that there are rewards and punishments in a future state.

**Hobbes, Thomas** (1588–1679) English, born Malmesbury. Political philosopher whose major work *Leviathan* (1651) presented and connected his thoughts on metaphysics, psychology and political philosophy. His materialistic philosophy described how the world is a mechanical system consisting of bodies in motion in which human beings are wholly selfish and enlightened self-interest explains the existence of the sovereign state and prevents 'a war of every man against every man'. He was banned from publishing in England in 1666 after being accused of being an atheist.

**Hume, David** (1711–76) Scottish, born Edinburgh. Philosopher and historian whose beliefs concerning perception, causation, personal identity, and ethics are still influential. Most important works include *A Treatise of Human Nature* (1739–40), *Essays Moral and Political* (1741, 1742), *Enquiry concerning Human Understanding* (1748), *Political Discourses* (1752), *Dialogues concerning Natural Religion* (published posthumously, 1779).

**Husserl, Edmund (Gustav Albrecht)** (1859–1938) German, born Prossnitz, Austrian Empire. Defender of philosophy as an *a priori* discipline and founder of Phenomenology: the systematic investigation of consciousness and its objects by suspending belief in the empirical world.

**James, William** (1842–1910) American, born New York City. Philosopher and psychologist who developed the pragmatist ideas of Charles Peirce; beliefs are true because they work, not vice versa. These ideas, and discussions of ethics and religion are given in *The Will to Believe* (1907), *Pragmatism* (1907), *The Varieties of Religious Experience* (1902), *The Meaning of Truth* (1909).

**Jaspers, Karl (Theodor)** (1883–1969) German, born Oldenburg. One of the founders of existentialism; his beliefs are developed in *Philosophie* (1932).

**Kant, Immanuel** (1724–1804) German, born Königsberg, Prussia. Influential scientist and philosopher, whose main interest was in the role of reason. He argued that the immediate objects of perception depend not only on our sensations but also on our perceptual equipment and that some properties we observe in objects are due to the nature of the observer. Ethics, aesthetics and politics are also discussed in *Critique of Pure Reason* (1781), *Critique of Practical Reason* (1788), *Critique of Judgement* (1790), *Perpetual Peace* (1795).

**Kierkegaard, Søren Aabye** (1813–55) Danish, born Copenhagen. A founder of existentialism who tried to reinstate the central importance of the individual and the significant choices each of us makes informing our future selves, and wrote in many works about the necessity for individual choice rather than prescribed dogma.

**Langer, Suzanne K(nauth)** (1895–1985) American, born New York City. Published important works in linguistic analysis and aesthetics; *Philosophy in a New Key* (1942), *Feeling and Form* (1953), *Problems of Art* (1957), *Mind: an Essay on Human Feeling* (1967–82).

**Leibniz, Gottfried Wilhelm** (1647–1716) German, born Leipzig. Mathematician and philosopher who believed that the world is composed of an infinity of simple immaterial 'monads' which form a hierarchy, the highest of which is God. Had greatest influence as a mathematician.

**Locke, John** (1632–1704) English, born Wrington, Somerset. Philosopher who defended natural rights, constitutional law and the liberty of the individual. *Essay concerning Human Understanding* (1690) explores the nature and scope of human reason and seeks to establish that 'all knowledge is founded on and ultimately derives from sense ... or sensation'.

**Lukacs, George** (1885–1971) Hungarian, born Budapest. Marxist philosopher who wrote prolifically on literature and aesthetics. His major work on Marxism was *History and Class Consciousness* (1923).

**Mach, Ernst** (1838–1916) Austrian, born Turas, Moravia. Physicist and philosopher whose writings laid the foundations of logical positivism.

**Maimonides, Moses (Moses ben Maimon)** (1135–1204) Jewish, born Córdoba, Spain. Physician and philosopher who tried to harmonize the thought of Aristotle and Judaism in *Guide to the Perplexed* (1190).

**Marcuse, Herbert** (1898–1979) American, born Berlin. Radical political theorist who analysed the repressions imposed by the unconscious mind in *Eros and Civilization* (1955) and condemned the 'repressive tolerance' of modern industrial society which both stimulated and satisfied superficial material desires of the masses at the cost of more fundamental needs and freedoms in *One Dimensional Man* (1964).

**Marx, Karl** (1818–83) German, born Trier. Social, political and economic philosopher in the German idealistic tradition. Founded the theory of historical materialism, and in his *Economic and Philosophical Manuscripts of 1844* (posthumously published, 1932), developed the notion of the alienation of man under capitalism. His most famous publication *Das Kapital* (Vol 1 1867, Vols 2 & 3 posthumously published 1884, 1894) was one of the most influential works of the 19th century.

**Mencius (Meng-tzu)** (c.372–c.298BC) Chinese, born Shantung. Philosopher who popularized and developed Confucian ideas and made many proposals for social and political reform; his beliefs are recorded in a book compiled after his death, *Book of Meng-tzu*.

**Merleau-Ponty, Maurice** (1908–61) French, born Rochefort-sur-mer. Philosopher who rejected extremes of both behaviouristic psychology and subjectivist accounts; the world is neither wholly 'given', nor wholly 'constructed' for the perceiving subject, but is essentially ambiguous and enigmatic. Major works are *La Structure du Comportement* (1942) and *Phénoménologie de la Perception* (1945).

**Mill, J(ohn) S(tuart)** (1806–73) English, born London. Philosopher and social reformer, leading exponent of the British empiricism and utilitarian traditions who also restored the importance of cultural values. Active in politics, he campaigned for women's suffrage and supported the Advanced Liberals. Major works include *A System of Logic* (1843), *On Liberty* (1859), *The Subjection of Women* (1869).

**Moore, George (Edward)** (1873–1958) English, born London. Cambridge professor of mental philosophy and logic who emphasized the intellectual virtues of clarity, precision and honesty, identifying as a principal task of philosophy the analysis of ordinary concepts and arguments. Works include *Principia Ethica* (1903), *Ethics* (1916).

**More, Henry, ('the Cambridge Platonist')** (1614–87) English, born Grantham, Lincolnshire. Followed the philosophies of Plato, Plotinus and Descartes and attempted to demonstrate the compatibility of reason and faith. Later became interested in occultism and mysticism. Main works: *Philosophical Poems* (1647), *An Antidote against Atheism* (1653), *The Immortality of the Soul* (1659), *Enchiridion Ethicum* (1666), *Divine Dialogues* (1668).

**Murdoch, Dame (Jean) Iris** (1919–99) Irish novelist, playwright and philosopher. Published three important philosophical works in the Platonic tradition: *The Sovereignty of the Good* (1970), *The Fire and the Sun* (1977) and *Metaphysics as a Guide to Morals* (1992). These deal with the relationships between art and philosophy, and between love, freedom, knowledge and morality.

**Nietzsche, Friedrich (Wilhelm)** (1844–1900) German, born Röcken, Saxony. Philosopher who produced many unconventional works expressing repudiation of Christian and liberal ethics, detestation of democratic ideals, the celebration of the *Übermensch* (superman) who can create and impose his own law, and the death of God. Best-known writings include *Unzeitgemässe Betrachtungen* (Untimely Meditations, 1873–6), *Die Fröliche Wissenschaft* (The Gay Science, 1882), *Also Sprach Zarathustra* (Thus Spake Zarathustra, 1883–92), *Jenseits von Gut and Böse* (Beyond Good and Evil, 1886).

**Ockham, William of** (1285–1349) English, born Ockham, Surrey. Philosopher, theologian and political writer whose controversial religious views led to disputes with the Catholic church. Defended nominalism against realism and introduced 'Ockham's razor'; the belief that a theory should not propose the existence of anything more than is needed for its explanation. Works include *Summa Logicae, Quodlibta Septem.*

**Ortega y Gasset, José** (1883–1955) Spanish, born Madrid. Argued that great philosophies demarcate the cultural horizons of their epochs. Works include *Meditaciones del Quijote* (1914), *Tema de nuestro tiempa* (1923), *La Rebelión de Las Masas* (1930).

**Parmenides** (c.515–c.445BC) Greek, born Elea, S Italy. Argued in *On Nature* for the impossibility of motion, plurality and change, and set an agenda of problems for subsequent pre-Socratic philosophers.

**Peirce, Charles (Sanders)** (1839–1914) American, born Cambridge, Massachusetts. Philosopher, logician and mathematician, best known as the founder of pragmatism.

**Philo Judeaus** (c.20BC–c.AD40) Hellenistic Jew, born Alexandria. Prolific author who attempted to synthesize Greek philosophy and Jewish scripture.

**Plato** (c.428–c.348BC) Greek, born probably Athens. One of the most important philosophers of all time. Pupil of Socrates and teacher of Aristotle, his writings consist of philosophical dialogues and letters discussing the definition of moral virtues, the theory of knowledge as recollection, the immortality of the soul, and contrasts of transient and timeless aspects of the world. The *Republic* presents Plato's political utopia.

**Plotinus** (c.205–70) Greek, born possibly Lycopolis, Egypt. Neoplatonist philosopher who advocated asceticism and the contemplative life, and greatly influenced early Christian theology.

**Popper, Sir Karl (Raimund)** (1902–94) Austrian, born Vienna. Rejected philosophical systems with totalitarian political implications from Plato to Marx and stressed the importance of 'falsifiability'; true scientific theories must specify in advance the conditions under which they could be tested and refuted. Main works include *Die Logik der Forschung* (1934, trans *The Logic of Scientific Discovery*, 1959), *The Open Society and its Enemies* (1945), *The Poverty of Historicism* (1957).

**Protagoras** (c.490–c.420BC) Greek, born Abdera. Sophist philosopher, with a sceptical or relativistic view of human knowledge; his many works are lost and most information about him comes from Plato's dialogues.

**Pythagoras** (6th-cBC) Greek, born Samos. Philosopher and mathematician whose life is surrounded in myth and legend. Emphasized moral asceticism and purification; also associated with mathematical discoveries involving musical intervals and relations of numbers. He had a profound influence on later philosophers and scientists.

**Quine, Willard Van Orman** (1908–2000) American, born Akron, Ohio. Influential professor of philosophy who challenged the standard sharp distinctions between analysis and synthetic truths and between science and metaphysics; also presented a systematic linguistic philosophy. Best-known works: *Two Dogmas of Empiricism* (1951), *From a Logical Point of View* (1953), *Word and Object* (1960), *The Roots of Reference* (1973).

**Rawls, John** (1921– ) American, born Baltimore, Maryland. Social and political philosopher concerned mainly with the question of justice in *A Theory of Justice* (1962), *Justice as Fairness* (1991), *Political Liberalism* (1993).

**Reichenbach, Hans** (1891–1953) German, born Hamburg. Made important contributions to technical probability theory and wrote widely on logic and the philosophical bases of science in *Philosophie der Raum-Zeit-Lehre* (1927–8), *Elements of Symbolic Logic* (1947), *The Rise of Scientific Philosophy* (1951).

**Ricoeur, Paul** (1913– ) French, born Valence, Drôme. Influential figure in both French and Anglo-American philosophy, covering a wide range of problems on the nature of language, interpretation, human action and will, freedom and evil. Major works include *Philosophy of the Will* (1950–60), *The Living Metaphor* (1975).

**Russell, Bertrand (Arthur William, 3rd Earl)** (1872–1970) English, born Trelleck, Monmouthshire. Philosopher, mathematician, prolific author and controversial figure, who was imprisoned in 1918 during World War I as an active pacifist and in 1961 for taking part in a sit-down demonstration in Whitehall, London. Wrote wide-ranging literature on mathematics, philosophy, politics, education and morals, such as *The Principles of Mathematics* (1903), *The Problems of Philosophy* (1912), *Theory and Practice of Bolshevism* (1919), *On Education* (1926), *Marriage and Morals* (1932).

**Ryle, Gilbert** (1900–76) English, born Brighton, Sussex. Influential exponent of linguistic philosophy. *The Concept of Mind* (1949) was directed against the traditional theory that mind and matter were distinct and problematically related. Other works: *Dilemmas* (1954), *Plato's Progress* (1966).

**Santayana, George (Jorge Augustin Nicola Ruiz de Santayana)** (1863–1952) Spanish–American, born Madrid. Naturalistic and materialistic critic of the transcendental claims of religion and German idealism, who believed that our knowledge of the external world depends on an act of 'animal faith'. Main philosophical works: *The Sense of Beauty* (1896), *The Life of Reason* (1905–6), *Scepticism and Animal Faith* (1923), *Realms of Being* (1927–40), *Platonism and the Spiritual Life* (1927).

**Sartre, Jean-Paul** (1905–80) French, born Paris. Philosopher, dramatist and novelist who developed characteristic atheistic existentialist doctrines from an early anarchistic tendency; these are expressed in the autobiographical novel *La Nausée* (1938) and in *Le Mur* (1938). Awarded, but declined to accept, the Nobel prize for literature in 1964.

**Schelling, Friedrich (Wilhelm Joseph) von** (1775–1854) German, born Leonburg. Idealist philosopher who examined the relation of the self to the objective world and argued that consciousness itself is the only immediate object of knowledge and that only in art can the mind become fully aware of itself. Works include *Ideen zur einer Philosophie der Natur* (1797), *System des transzendentalen Idealismus* (1800).

**Schlick, Moritz** (1882–1936) German, born Berlin. Leader of the 'Vienna Circle' of logical positivists who wrote on ethics, which he argued was a factual science of the causes of human actions. Main publications: *Allgemeine Erkenntnislehre* (General Theory of Knowledge, 1918), *Fragen der Ethik* (Problems of Ethics, 1930).

**Schopenhauer, Arthur** (1788–1860) German, born Danzig. Philosopher who emphasized the active role of Will as the creative but covert and irrational force in human nature and argued that art represented the sole kind of knowledge that was not subservient to the Will; his work is often characterized as a systematic philosophical pessimism. Major work: *Die Welt als Wille und Vorstellung* (The World as Will and Idea, 1819).

**Shaftesbury, Anthony Ashley Cooper, 3rd Earl of** (1671–1713) English, born London. Moral philosopher and politician who argued that we possess natural 'moral sense' and affections directed to the good of the species and in harmony with the larger cosmic order in *Characteristics of Men, Manners, Opinions, Times* (1711).

**Socrates** (469–399BC) Greek, born Athens. One of the most important philosophers in history, responsible for a decisive shift of philosophical interest from speculation about the natural world and cosmology to ethics and conceptual analysis. His reputation for eliciting contradictions in the philosophies of others may have contributed to demands for his conviction for 'impiety' and 'corrupting the youth'; he was sentenced to die by drinking hemlock.

**Spencer, Herbert** (1820–1903) British, born Derby. Philosopher with interest in evolutionary theory which he expounded in *Principles of Psychology* (1855). Also applied his evolutionary theories to ethics and sociology and became an advocate of 'Social

Darwinism', the view that societies naturally evolve in competition for resources and that the 'survival of the fittest' is therefore morally justified. Works include *System of Synthetic Philosophy* (1862–93), *Social Statistics* (1851), *Education* (1861), *The Man Versus the State* (1884).

**Spinoza, Baruch (Benedict de)** (1632–77) Dutch, born Amsterdam. Rationalist philosopher who advocated a strictly historical approach to the interpretation of biblical sources and argued that complete freedom of philosophical and scientific speculation was appropriate. His major work, the *Ethics* (1677, posthumous) described a complete, deductive metaphysical system intended to be a proof derived with mathematical certainty of what is good for human beings.

**Tarski, Alfred** (1902–83) Polish, born Warsaw. Logician and mathematician who gave a definition of 'truth' in formal logical languages in *Der Wahrheitsbetriff in den Formalisierten Sprachen* (The Concept of Truth in Formalized Languages, 1933).

**Thales** (c.620–c.555BC) Greek, born Miletus. Traditionally the founder of European philosophy. Proposed the first natural cosmology, identifying water as the original substance and the basis of the universe. Also had wide-ranging practical and scientific interests.

**Tillich, Paul (Johannes)** (1886–1965) German, born Starzeddel, Prussia. Protestant theologian and philosopher, an early critic of the Nazis whose main work *Systematic Theology* (1951–63) combines elements of existentialism and the ontological tradition in Christian thought. He explained faith as a reality transcending finite existence rather than a belief in a personal God, leading to oversimplified accusations of atheism. Popular works include *The Courage to Be* (1952), *Dynamics of Faith* (1957).

**Weil, Simone** (1909–43) French, born Paris. Combined sophisticated scholarly and philosophical interests with dedicated involvement and interest in the oppressed and exploited. Translated philosophical and spiritual works include *Gravity and Grace* (1952), *The Need for Roots* (1952), *Waiting for God* (1951), *Oppression and Liberty* (1958).

**Whitehead, A(lfred) N(orth)** (1861–1947) English, born Ramsgate. Mathematician and idealist philosopher. *Process and Reality* (1929) attempted a metaphysics comprising psychological as well as physical experience, with events as the ultimate component of reality. Other works include *Adventures of Ideas* (1933) and *Modes of Thought* (1938).

**Williams, Sir Bernard Arthur Owen** (1929– ) English, born Essex. English philosopher whose work has been wide-ranging. Particularly influential in his contributions to moral philosophy in *Morality: an introduction to Ethics* (1972), *Ethics and the Limits of Philosophy* (1985) and *Shame and Necessity* (1993).

**Wittgenstein, Ludwig (Josef Johann)** (1889–1951) Austrian, born Vienna. Philosopher who studied the nature and limits of language. *Logisch-philosophische Abhandlung* (1921) describes how meaningful language must consist in propositions that are 'pictures' of the facts of which the world is composed and therefore many claims of speculative philosophy must be rejected. *Philosophical Investigations* (1953, posthumous) comes to different conclusions, pointing to the variety and subtlety in language and exploring its functions.

**Zeno of Elea** (c.490–c.420BC) Greek, born Elea, Italy. A disciple of Parmenides who devised famous paradoxes which purported to show the impossibility of motion and spatial division.

## Literary prizes, 1980–2001

### Booker Prize (UK)

1980 William Golding, *Rites of Passage*
1981 Salman Rushdie, *Midnight's Children*
1982 Thomas Keneally, *Schindler's Ark*
1983 J M Coetzee, *Life and Times of Michael K*
1984 Anita Brookner, *Hotel du Lac*
1985 Keri Hulme, *The Bone People*
1986 Kingsley Amis, *The Old Devils*
1987 Penelope Lively, *Moon Tiger*
1988 Peter Carey, *Oscar and Lucinda*
1989 Kazuo Ishiguro, *The Remains of the Day*
1990 A S Byatt, *Possession*
1991 Ben Okri, *The Famished Road*
1992 Michael Ondaatje, *The English Patient;* Barry Unsworth, *Sacred Hunger*
1993 Roddy Doyle, *Paddy Clarke, Ha Ha Ha*
1994 James Kelman, *How late it was, how late*
1995 Pat Barker, *The Ghost Road*
1996 Graham Swift, *Last Orders*
1997 Arundhati Roy, *The God of Small Things*
1998 Ian McEwan, *Amsterdam*
1999 J M Coetzee, *Disgrace*
2000 Margaret Atwood, *The Blind Assassin*
2001 Peter Carey, *True History of the Kelly Gang*

### Orange Prize for Fiction (women writers)

1996 Helen Dunmore, *A Spell of Winter*
1997 Anne Michaels, *Fugitive Pieces*
1998 Carol Shields, *Larry's Party*
1999 Suzanne Berne, *A Crime in the Neighborhood*
2000 Linda Grant, *When I Lived in Modern Times*
2001 Kate Grenville, *The Idea of Perfection*

### Prix Goncourt (France)

1980 Yves Navarre, *Le Jardin d'acclimatation*
1981 Lucien Bodard, *Anne Marie*
1982 Dominique Fernandez, *Dans la Main de l'ange*
1983 Frédérick Tristan, *Les Égarés*
1984 Marguerite Duras, *L'Amant*
1985 Yann Queffelec, *Les Noces barbares*
1986 Michel Host, *Valet de Nuit*
1987 Tahar ben Jalloun, *La Nuit sacrée*
1988 Erik Orsenna, *L'Exposition coloniale*
1989 Jean Vautrin, *Un Grand Pas vers le Bon Dieu*
1990 Jean Rouaud, *Les Champs d'Honneur*
1991 Pierre Combescot, *Les Filles du Calvaire*
1992 Patrick Chamoiseau, *Texaco*
1993 Amin Maalouf, *Le Rocher de Tanios*
1994 Didier van Cauwelaert, *Un Aller simple*
1995 Andréï Makine, *Le Testament français*
1996 Pascale Roze, *Le Chasseur Zéro*
1997 Patrick Rambaud, *La Bataille*
1998 Paule Constant, *Confidence pour confidence*
1999 Jean Echenoz, *Je m'en vais*
2000 Jean-Jacques Schuhl, *Ingrid Caven*
2001 Jean-Christophe Rufin, *Rouge Brésil*

### Pulitzer Prize in Letters: Fiction (USA)

1980 Norman Mailer, *The Executioner's Song*
1981 John Kennedy Toole, *A Confederacy of Dunces*
1982 John Updike, *Rabbit is Rich*
1983 Alice Walker, *The Color Purple*
1984 William Kennedy, *Ironweed*
1985 Alison Lurie, *Foreign Affairs*
1986 Larry McMurtry, *Lonesome Dove*
1987 Peter Taylor, *A Summons to Memphis*
1988 Toni Morrison, *Beloved*
1989 Anne Tyler, *Breathing Lessons*
1990 Oscar Hijuelos, *The Mambo Kings Play Songs of Love*
1991 John Updike, *Rabbit at Rest*
1992 Jane Smiley, *A Thousand Acres*
1993 Robert Olen Butler, *A Good Scent From A Strange Mountain*
1994 E Annie Proulx, *The Shipping News*
1995 Carol Shields, *The Stone Diaries*
1996 Richard Ford, *Independence Day*
1997 Steven Millhauser, *Martin Dressler: The Tale of an American Dreamer*
1998 Philip Roth, *American Pastoral*
1999 Michael Cunningham, *The Hours*
2000 Jhumpa Lahiri, *Interpreter of Maladies*
2001 Michael Chabon, *The Amazing Adventures of Kavalier & Clay*

## Nobel prizes 1982–2001

| Year | Peace | Literature | Economic Science | Chemistry | Physics | Physiology/ Medicine | Year |
|---|---|---|---|---|---|---|---|
| 1982 | Alfonso García Robles<br>Alva Myrdal | Gabriel García Márquez | George J Stigler | Aaron Klug | Kenneth G Wilson | Sune K Bergström<br>Bengt I Samuelsson<br>John R Vane | 1982 |
| 1983 | Lech Wałesa | William Golding | Gerard Debreu | Henry Taube | Subrahmanyan Chandrasekhar<br>William A Fowler | Barbara McClintock | 1983 |
| 1984 | Desmond Tutu | Jaroslav Seifert | Richard Stone | Robert B Merrifield | Carlo Rubbia<br>Simon van der Meer | Niels K Jerne<br>Georges J F Köhler<br>César Milstein | 1984 |
| 1985 | International Physicians for the Prevention of Nuclear War | Claude Simon | Franco Modigliani | Herbert Hauptman<br>Jerome Karle | Klaus von Klitzing | Joseph L Goldstein<br>Michael S Brown | 1985 |
| 1986 | Elie Wiesel | Wole Soyinka | James M Buchanan | Dudley R Herschbach<br>Yuan Tseh Lee<br>John C Polanyi | Gerd Binnig<br>Heinrich Rohrer<br>Ernst Ruska | Stanley Cohen<br>Rita Levi-Montalcini | 1986 |
| 1987 | Oscar Arias Sánchez | Joseph Brodsky | Robert M Solow | Charles Pedersen<br>Donald Cram<br>Jean-Marie Lehn | George Bednorz<br>Alex Müller | Susumu Tonegawa | 1987 |
| 1988 | UN Peacekeeping Forces | Naguib Mahfouz | Maurice Allais | Johann Deisenhofer<br>Robert Huber<br>Hartmut Michel | Leon Lederman<br>Melvin Schwartz<br>Jack Steinberger | James Black<br>Gertrude Elion<br>George Hitchings | 1988 |
| 1989 | Tenzin Gyatso (Dalai Lama) | Camilo José Cela | Trygve Haavelmo | Sydney Altman<br>Thomas Cech | Hans Dehmelt<br>Wolfgang Paul<br>Norman Ramsay | J Michael Bishop<br>Harold E Varmus | 1989 |
| 1990 | Mikhail Gorbachev | Octavio Paz | Harry M Markovitz<br>Merton Miller<br>William Sharpe | Elias James Corey | Jerome Friedman<br>Henry Kendall<br>Richard Taylor | Joseph E Murray<br>E Donnall Thomas | 1990 |
| 1991 | Aung San Suu Kyi | Nadine Gordimer | Ronald Coase | Richard R Ernst | Pierre-Gilles de Gennes | Erwin Neher<br>Bert Sakmann | 1991 |

| Year | Peace | Literature | Economic Science | Chemistry | Physics | Physiology/ Medicine | Year |
|---|---|---|---|---|---|---|---|
| 1992 | Rigoberta Menchú | Derek Walcott | Gary S Becker | Rudolph A Marcus | Georges Charpak | Edmond H Fischer<br>Edwin G Krebs | 1992 |
| 1993 | Nelson Mandela<br>F W de Klerk | Toni Morrison | Robert Fugel<br>Douglas North | Kary Banks Mullis<br>Michael Smith | Russell Hulse<br>Joseph Hooton Taylor Jr | Richard Roberts<br>Phillip Allen Sharp | 1993 |
| 1994 | Yasser Arafat<br>Shimon Peres<br>Yitzhak Rabin | Kenzaburo Oë | John Nash<br>John Harsanyi<br>Reinhard Selten | George Olah | Clifford Shull<br>Bertram Brockhouse | Martin Rodbell<br>Alfred G Gilman | 1994 |
| 1995 | Joseph Rotblat<br>Pugwash Conferences on Science and World Affairs | Seamus Heaney | Robert E Lucas | F Sherwood Roland<br>Mario Molina<br>Paul Crutzen | Martin L Perl<br>Frederick Reines | Edward B Lewis<br>Eric F Wieschaus<br>Christine Nüsslein-Volhard | 1995 |
| 1996 | Carlos Filipe Ximenes Belo<br>José Ramos-Horta | Wislawa Szymborska | James Mirrlees<br>William Vickrey | Harold Kroto<br>Robert Curl<br>Richard Smalley | David Lee<br>Douglas Osheroff<br>Robert Richardson | Peter Doherty<br>Rolf M Zinkernagel | 1996 |
| 1997 | Jody Williams and the International Campaign to Ban Landmines | Dario Fo | Robert Merton<br>Myron Scholes | Jens Skou<br>John Walker<br>Paul Boyer | Steven Chu<br>William D Phillips<br>Claude Cohen-Tannoudji | Stanley Prusiner | 1997 |
| 1998 | John Hume<br>David Trimble | José Saramago | Amartya Sen | Walter Kohn<br>John A Pople | Robert B Laughlin<br>Horst L Störmer<br>Daniel C Tsui | Robert F Furchgott<br>Louis J Ignarro<br>Ferid Murad | 1998 |
| 1999 | Médecins sans Frontières | Günter Grass | Robert A Mundell | Ahmed Zewail | Gerardus 't Hooft<br>Martinus J G Veltman | Günter Blobel | 1999 |
| 2000 | Kim Dae Jung | Gao Xingjian | James Heckman<br>Daniel McFadden | Alan J Heeger<br>Alan G McDiarmid<br>Hideki Shirakawa | Zhores I Alferov<br>Herbert Kroemer<br>Jack S Kilby | Arvid Carlsson<br>Paul Greengard<br>Eric Kandel | 2000 |
| 2001 | United Nations,<br>Kofi Annan | V S Naipaul | George A Akerlof<br>A Michael Spence<br>Joseph E Stiglitz | William S Knowles<br>Ryoji Noyori<br>K Barry Sharpless | Eric A Cornell<br>Wolfgang Ketterle<br>Carl E Wieman | Leland H Hartwell<br>R Timothy Hunt<br>Sir Paul M Nurse | 2001 |

## Museums and art galleries—Europe

A selection of the most important museums and galleries is given.

**Amsterdam**, Netherlands
Anne Frank's House
Museum of Amsterdam
Rijksmuseum, Stedelijk Museum of Modern Art
Van Gogh Museum

**Ankara**, Turkey
Archaeological Museum

**Antwerp**, Belgium
Folklore Museum
Maritime Museum
Royal Museum of Fine Art
Rubens's House

**Athens**, Greece
Acropolis Museum
Byzantine Museum
Goulandris Natural History Museum
National Archaeological Museum
Museum of Decorative Arts
Museum of Modern Art

**Barcelona**, Spain
Catalan Museum of Art
Joán Miró Foundation
Museum of Costume
Picasso Museum

**Basle**, Switzerland
Basle Historical Museum
Basle Art and Contemporary Art Museum

**Berlin**, Germany
The Bauhaus Archives and Museum of Design
Berlin Museum
Memorial Museum of the German Resistance
Museum of German Ethnology
Museum of Transport and Technology
New National Gallery
Old National Gallery

**Bruges**, Belgium
Folklore Museum

**Brunswick**, Germany
Museum of Brunswick

**Brussels**, Belgium
Museum of Brussels
Museum of Modern Art
Railway Museum
Royal Museum of the Army

**Budapest**, Hungary
Hungarian National Museum

**Cologne**, Germany
Cologne Art Collective
Diocesan Museum
Museum of the City of Cologne
Schnütgen Museum

**Copenhagen**, Denmark
Copenhagen City Museum
National Museum
State Museum of Art
Theatre Museum

**Delphi**, Greece
Archaeological Museum

**Dresden**, Germany
Semper Gallery
State Gallery of Art
Grünes Gewölbe

**Dublin**, Ireland
Dublin Civic Museum
Guinness Museum
National Gallery of Ireland
National Museum of Ireland
National Transport Museum

**Essen**, Germany
Folkwang Museum

**Figueres**, Spain
Dalí Museum

**Florence**, ,Italy
Accademia Gallery
Bardini Museum
Bargello Museum
Museum of the History of Science
Uffizi Gallery

**Frankfurt**, Germany
Goethe Museum
Historical Museum
Modern Art Gallery

**Freiburg im Breisgau**, Germany
Augustiner Museum
Museum of Modern Art
Museum of Natural History

**Geneva**, Switzerland
Museum of Art and History
Voltaire Museum

**Genoa**, Italy
Gallery of Modern Art
Palazzo Bianco
Palazzo Rosso

**Hamburg**, Germany
Altona Museum
Hamburg Art Gallery
Museum of Art and History

**Helsinki**, Finland
Helsinki City Museum
Museum of Applied Arts
Museum of Finnish Architecture
Sports Museum of Finland

**Istanbul**, Turkey
Archaeological Museum
Hagia Sophia Museum
Museum of the Ancient Orient
Topkapi Palace Museum

**Leipzig**, Germany
Museum of Art

**Liège**, Belgium
Museum of Firearms

Museum of Modern Art
Museum of Walloon Life

**Lisbon**, Portugal
Calouste Gulbenkian Museum
Museum of Archaeology and Ethnology
Museum of Art
Museum of Contemporary Art
Museum of Decorative Arts

**Madrid**, Spain
Museum of Madrid
National Archaeological Museum
National Museum of Ethnology
National Museum of Decorative Arts
Palace of El Pardo
The Prado Museum
Reina Sofia

**Milan**, Italy
Castle of the Sforzas
Gallery of Modern Art
La Scala Museum of Theatre History
Leonardo da Vinci Museum of Science and Technology

**Moscow**, Russia
Armory Museum
Central Lenin Museum
Pushkin Museum of Fine Arts
Tretyakov Art Gallery

**Munich**, Germany
Bavarian National Museum
City Museum
Deutsches Museum
Folklore Museum
Residence Museum
State Collection of Minerals

**Naples**, Italy
Archaeological Museum
Palazzo Capodimonte

**Olympia**, Greece
Museum of Ancient Olympia

**Oslo**, Norway
Edvard Munch Museum
National Gallery
Norwegian Folk Museum
Ski Museum

**Paris**, France
Auguste Rodin Museum
Carnavalet Museum
The Louvre
Musée d'Orsay
Museum of Modern Art at the Pompidou Centre
Museum of Technology

**Prague**, Czech Republic
National Museum
State Jewish Museum

**Rome**, Italy
Borghese Gallery
National Gallery of Ancient Art
National Museum of Popular Art
Vatican Museums

**Rotterdam**, The Netherlands
Rotterdam Museum: The Double Palmtree
Rotterdam Museum: Schielandshuis

**St Petersburg**, Russia
Museum of the History of Religion and Atheism
Russian Museum
State Hermitage Museum

**Salzburg**, Austria
Mozart's Birthplace
Residence Gallery

**Siena**, Italy
Siena Art Gallery
Siena Museum

**Stockholm**, Sweden
National Museum of Antiquities
Nordic Museum
Stockholm City Museum

**The Hague**, The Netherlands
Netherlands Costume Museum
Sikkens Museum of Signs

**Thessaloniki**, Greece
Archaeological Museum
Macedonian Folk Art Museum

**Toledo**, Spain
El Greco Museum
Museum of the Alcazar of Toledo

**Utrecht**, The Netherlands
Catharine Convent State Museum
Netherlands Railway Museum

**Venice**, Italy
Accademia Gallery
Correr Museum
Treasury of St Mark's

**Versailles**, France
Château de Versailles
Lambinet Museum

**Vienna**, Austria
Belvedere Gallery
Museum of the History of Art
Museum of Lower Austria
Treasury of the Holy Roman Empire

**Warsaw**, Poland
National Museum

**Zürich**, Switzerland
House for Art
Swiss National Museum

## Museums and art galleries — UK

**Aberdeen**, Scotland
Aberdeen Art Gallery

**Bangor**, Wales
Museum of Welsh Antiquities
Bangor Art Gallery

**Bath**, England
Museum of East Asian Art
Victoria Art Gallery

**Belfast**, Northern Ireland
Ulster Museum

**Birmingham**, England
The Barber Institute of Fine Arts
Birmingham Museum and Art Gallery
National Motorcycle Museum

**Bristol**, England
Arnolfini Gallery
Blaise Castle House Museum
Bristol Industrial Museum
Bristol City Museums and Art Gallery

**Cambridge**, England
The Fitzwilliam Museum
Imperial War Museum
Kettle's Yard
Museum of Classical Archaeology

**Cardiff**, Wales
National Museum of Wales
Welsh Folk Museum (at St Fagans)

**Edinburgh**, Scotland
City Art Centre
Gladstone's Land
Museum of Childhood
Museum of Scotland
National Gallery of Scotland (previously the Royal Scottish Museum and the National Museum of Antiquities of Scotland)
Royal Museum of Scotland
Scottish National Gallery of Modern Art
Scottish National Portrait Gallery

**Glasgow**, Scotland
Kelvingrove Art Gallery and Museum
The Burrell Collection
Hunterian Art Gallery and Museum
Museum of Transport
People's Palace Museum

**Leeds**, England
City Art Gallery
Leeds Industrial Museum

**Leicester**, England
Leicester Gas Museum

**Liverpool**, England
Liverpool Museum
Merseyside Maritime Museum
Museum of Liverpool Life
Tate Gallery, Liverpool
Walker Art Gallery

**London**, England
The British Museum
Courtauld Gallery
Dulwich Picture Gallery
Imperial War Museum
Institute of Contemporary Arts
London Transport Museum
Museum of Instruments
Museum of London
The National Gallery
National Maritime Museum
The National Portrait Gallery
Natural History Museum
Pollock's Toy Museum
Science Museum
The Serpentine Gallery
Tate Britain
Tate Modern
Victoria and Albert Museum
The Wallace Collection
The Wellcome Museum of the History of Medicine

**Manchester**, England
Museum of Science and Industry in Manchester
Manchester City Art Gallery
Manchester Jewish Museum
The Manchester Museum
Whitworth Art Gallery

**Newcastle upon Tyne**, England
Laing Art Gallery
Museum of Antiquities
Newcastle Discovery Museum

**Oxford**, England
Ashmolean Museum of Art and Archaeology
The Bate Collection of Historical Instruments
Museum of Modern Art
Museum of the History of Science
Pitt Rivers Museum

**Reading**, England
Museum of English Rural Life

**Sheffield**, England
Abbeydale Industrial Hamlet
Kelham Island Museum
Sheffield City Museum

**Southampton**, England
Southampton Art Gallery
Southampton Maritime Museum

**Swansea**, Wales
Glynn Vivian Art Gallery
Swansea Maritime and Industrial Museum

**York**, England
National Railway Museum
York Castle Museum
York City Art Gallery
Yorkshire Museum

## Museums and art galleries — USA

**Atlanta**, Georgia
High Museum of Art

**Baltimore**, Maryland
Baltimore Museum of Art
Walters Art Gallery

**Boston**, Massachusetts
Isabella Stewart Gardner Museum
Museum of Fine Arts
Museum of Science and Hayden Planetarium

**Buffalo**, New York
Albright-Knox Art Gallery

**Cambridge**, Massachusetts
Fogg Art Museum
MIT Museum
Arthur M Sackler Museum

**Charleston**, South Carolina
Charleston Museum

**Chicago**, Illinois
Art Institute of Chicago
Museum of Contemporary Art

**Cincinnati**, Ohio
Cincinnati Art Museum
Museum Center at Union Terminal

**Cleveland**, Ohio
Cleveland Museum of Art

**Dallas**, Texas
Dallas Museum of Art

**Denver**, Colorado
Denver Art Museum
Museum of Natural History

**Des Moines**, Iowa
Living History Farms (at Urbandale)

**Detroit**, Michigan
Detroit Institute of Arts
Henry Ford Museum

**Dodge City**, Kansas
Boot Hill Museum

**Fort Lauderdale**, Florida
Museum of Discovery and Science

**Fort Myers**, Florida
Edison Winter Home

**Gainsville**, Florida
Florida State Museum

**Hartford**, Connecticut
Wadsworth Museum

**Honolulu**, Hawaii
Honolulu Academy of Arts

**Houston**, Texas
Baker Planetarium, and the Museum of Medical Science
Burke Museum of Fine Arts
The Contemporary Arts Museum
Menil Collection

**Indianapolis**, Indiana
Children's Museum
Indianapolis Museum of Art

**Jackson**, Mississippi
Mississippi Museum of Art

**Kansas City**, Missouri
The Kemper Museum of Contemporary Art and Design
Nelson Atkins Museum of Art

**Los Angeles**, California
California Museum of Science and Industry
George C Page Museum of La Brea Discoveries
Jean Paul Getty Museum (at Malibu)
Los Angeles County Museum of Art
Museum of Contemporary Art
Natural History Museum

**Memphis**, Tennessee
Memphis Brooks Museum of Art

**Minneapolis**, Minnesota
Minneapolis Institute of Arts
Walker Art Center

**New Haven**, Connecticut
The Yale Art Gallery

**New Orleans**, Louisiana
Delgado Museum of Art
Louisiana State Museum

**New York City**, New York
American Museum of the Moving Image
American Museum of Natural History
Brooklyn Museum
Frick Collection
Gallery of Modern Art
Metropolitan Museum of Art and the Cloisters
Morgan Library
Museum of Holography
Museum of Modern Art
Museum of the American Indian
Museum of the City of New York
Solomon R Guggenheim Museum
Whitney Museum of American Art

**Oklahoma City**, Oklahoma
National Cowboy Hall of Fame

**Pasadena**, California
Norton Simon Museum

**Philadelphia**, Pennsylvania
Academy of Natural Sciences
Barnes Foundation Collection (in Merion, Pennsylvania)
Franklin Institute Science Museum
Museum of American Art
Philadelphia Museum of Art
Rodin Museum
Rosenbach Museum
University Museum of Archaeology and Anthropology

**Pittsburgh**, Pennsylvania
Carnegie Museum of Art
Carnegie Museum of Natural History

**Plymouth**, Massachusetts
Plymouth Plantation

**Portland**, Oregon
Oregon Art Institute

**Reno**, Nevada
Harrah's Auto Collection

**Rochester**, New York
Rochester Memorial Art Gallery

**Salt Lake City**, Utah
The Museum of Church History and Art

**San Francisco**, California
Asian Art Museum
California Academy of Sciences
California Palace of the Legion of Honor
M H De Young Memorial Museum
San Francisco Museum of Art

**Santa Fé**, California
El Rancho de las Golondririas (at Cienega)
Museum of Indian Art and Culture
Museum of International Folk Art

**San Marino**, California
Huntington Library and Art Gallery

**Sarasota**, Florida
Ringling Museum of Art

**Seattle**, Washington
Seattle Art Museum

**Toledo**, Ohio
Toledo Museum of Art

**Tulsa**, Oklahoma
Philbrook Art Centre

**Washington**, District of Columbia
Corcoran Gallery of Art
Dumbarton Oaks Collection
Freer Gallery of Art
Museum of Modern Art of Latin America
National Air and Space Museum
National Archives
National Gallery of Art
National Museum of American Art
National Museum of American History
Smithsonian Institute
Washington Gallery of Modern Art

**Williamsburg**, Virginia
Abby Aldrich
Rockefeller Folk Art Collection
Colonial Williamsburg

**Williamstown**, Massachusetts
Sterling and Francine Clark Art Institute

# SPORTS AND GAMES

## Olympic Games

First Modern Olympic Games took place in 1896, founded by Frenchman Baron de Coubertin (1863–1937); held every four years; women first competed in 1900; first separate Winter Games celebrations in 1924.

### Venues

**Summer Games**

| | | | | | |
|---|---|---|---|---|---|
| 1896 | Athens, Greece | 1932 | Los Angeles, USA | 1976 | Montreal, Canada |
| 1900 | Paris, France | 1936 | Berlin, Germany | 1980 | Moscow, USSR |
| 1904 | St Louis, USA | 1948 | London, UK | 1984 | Los Angeles, USA |
| 1908 | London, UK | 1952 | Helsinki, Finland | 1988 | Seoul, South Korea |
| 1912 | Stockholm, Sweden | 1956 | Melbourne, Australia | 1992 | Barcelona, Spain |
| 1920 | Antwerp, Belgium | 1960 | Rome, Italy | 1996 | Atlanta, USA |
| 1924 | Paris, France | 1964 | Tokyo, Japan | 2000 | Sydney, Australia |
| 1928 | Amsterdam, Netherlands | 1968 | Mexico City, Mexico | 2004 | Athens, Greece |
| | | 1972 | Munich, W Germany | 2008 | Beijing, China |

**Winter Games**

| | | | | | |
|---|---|---|---|---|---|
| 1924 | Chamonix, France | 1952 | Oslo, Norway | 1980 | Lake Placid, New York, USA |
| 1928 | St Moritz, Switzerland | 1956 | Cortina, Italy | 1984 | Sarajevo, Yugoslavia |
| 1932 | Lake Placid, New York, USA | 1960 | Squaw Valley, California, USA | 1988 | Calgary, Canada |
| 1936 | Garmisch-Partenkirchen, Germany | 1964 | Innsbruck, Austria | 1992 | Albertville, France |
| 1948 | St Moritz, Switzerland | 1968 | Grenoble, France | 1994 | Lillehammer, Norway |
| | | 1972 | Sapporo, Japan | 1998 | Nagano, Japan |
| | | 1976 | Innsbruck, Austria | 2002 | Salt Lake City, USA |
| | | | | 2006 | Turin, Italy |

The 1956 equestrian events were held at Stockholm, Sweden, due to quarantine laws in Australia.
Olympic Games were also held in 1906 in Athens, Greece, to commemorate the tenth anniversary of the birth of the modern Games.
In 1994, the Winter Games celebrations were re-adjusted to take place every four years between the Summer Games years.

### Leading Medal Winners

**Summer Games**

| (including 2000) | Gold | Silver | Bronze | Total |
|---|---|---|---|---|
| 1 USA | 872 | 659 | 657 | 2 188 |
| 2 Russia[1] | 517 | 423 | 382 | 1 322 |
| 3 Germany[2] | 221 | 262 | 290 | 773 |
| 4 Great Britain | 188 | 243 | 232 | 663 |
| 5 France | 189 | 195 | 216 | 600 |
| 6 Italy | 179 | 144 | 155 | 478 |
| 7 Sweden | 138 | 157 | 176 | 471 |
| 8 Hungary | 150 | 134 | 158 | 442 |
| 9 East Germany | 153 | 130 | 127 | 410 |
| 10 Australia | 103 | 110 | 139 | 352 |

**Winter Games**

| (including 1998) | Gold | Silver | Bronze | Total |
|---|---|---|---|---|
| 1 Russia[1] | 108 | 77 | 74 | 259 |
| 2 Norway | 83 | 87 | 69 | 239 |
| 3 Germany[2] | 62 | 53 | 45 | 160 |
| 4 USA | 59 | 59 | 41 | 159 |
| 5 Austria | 39 | 53 | 53 | 145 |
| 6 Finland | 38 | 49 | 48 | 135 |
| 7 East Germany | 39 | 36 | 35 | 110 |
| 8 Sweden | 39 | 28 | 35 | 102 |
| 9 Switzerland | 29 | 31 | 32 | 92 |
| 10 Canada | 25 | 25 | 29 | 79 |

[1] Includes medals won by the former USSR team, and by the Unified Team (Armenia, Azerbaijan, Belarus, Georgia, Kazakhstan, Kyrgyzstan, Moldova, Russia, Tajikistan, Turkmenistan, Ukraine and Uzbekistan) in 1992.

[2] Includes medals won as West Germany 1968–88.

## Commonwealth Games

First held as the British Empire Games in 1930; take place every four years and between Olympic celebrations; became the British Empire and Commonwealth Games in 1954; current title adopted in 1970.

### Venues

| | |
|---|---|
| 1930 | Hamilton, Canada |
| 1934 | London, England |
| 1938 | Sydney, Australia |
| 1950 | Auckland, New Zealand |
| 1954 | Vancouver, Canada |
| 1958 | Cardiff, Wales |
| 1962 | Perth, Australia |
| 1966 | Kingston, Jamaica |
| 1970 | Edinburgh, Scotland |
| 1974 | Christchurch, New Zealand |
| 1978 | Edmonton, Canada |
| 1982 | Brisbane, Australia |
| 1986 | Edinburgh, Scotland |
| 1990 | Auckland, New Zealand |
| 1994 | Victoria, Canada |
| 1998 | Kuala Lumpur, Malaysia |
| 2002 | Manchester, England |
| 2006 | Melbourne, Australia |

### Leading Medal Winners

| Nation | | Gold | Silver | Bronze | Total |
|---|---|---|---|---|---|
| 1 | Australia | 564 | 489 | 424 | 1 477 |
| 2 | England | 488 | 461 | 469 | 1 418 |
| 3 | Canada | 366 | 383 | 361 | 1 110 |
| 4 | New Zealand | 107 | 142 | 203 | 452 |
| 5 | Scotland | 65 | 78 | 126 | 269 |
| 6 | South Africa | 71 | 60 | 64 | 195 |
| 7 | Wales | 40 | 51 | 74 | 165 |
| 8 | India | 50 | 57 | 46 | 153 |
| 9 | Kenya | 50 | 34 | 43 | 127 |
| 10 | Nigeria | 30 | 38 | 39 | 107 |

## Sports

**aikido** Ancient Japanese art of self-defence; combination of karate and judo deriving from ancient jujitsu; two main systems; *tomiki* and *uyeshiba*.

**American football ▸ football**

**angling** Fishing with rod, line and hook in the form of freshwater, fly, game and deep-sea fishing. Rules govern time of year when different types of fishing take place, and type and amount of bait used. Oldest fishing club is in Ellem, Scotland.

**archery** Shooting with a bow and arrow at a circular target divided into 10 scoring zones, the smallest of which is coloured gold and worth 10 points; popular as sport from 17th century. In competition, arrows are fired from 30, 50, 70 and 90 metres (men), and 30, 50, 60 and 70 metres (women).

**athletics** Tests of running, jumping, throwing and walking skills. The running or **track** events range from the 100m (328ft) sprint to the 42.2km/26.2mi marathon; jumping and throwing or **field** events consist of high jump, long jump, triple jump and pole vault, and the discus throw, shot put, javelin throw and hammer throw (men only). Multi-event competitions are the **decathlon** (10) for men and the **heptathlon** (7) for women. Athletics dates to c.3800BC Egypt; International Amateur Athletic Federation founded 1912.

**badminton** Indoor game, two or four players, played on court 13.4m/44ft long and 5.2m/17ft wide (6.1m/20ft wide for doubles), using rackets, a shuttlecock (cork or plastic half sphere with 'feathers') and a raised central net; object is to volley the shuttlecock over the net so that the opponent is unable to return it; name derives from Badminton House, the seat of the Duke of Beaufort, where game played 19th century, but it dates from China over 2 200 years ago.

**bagatelle** Restricted form of billiards, played on a table with nine numbered cups instead of pockets; takes many different forms which vary according to local conditions.

**baseball** Team game played by two sides of 25 possible players on a diamond-shaped field which has bases at the corners each 27.43m/90ft apart. Essential pieces of equipment are long cylindrical bats, the solid ball 'pitched' from the 'mound', and the glove worn by each fielder; team 'at bat' tries to score most runs by having its players circle the three bases and touch home plate before being put out by the team 'in the field'; players out if their hit is caught, if they are tagged with the ball when 'off-base', if the base is touched by the ball before they arrive at it, or if they 'strike out', ie fail to hit the ball after three pitches have been judged strikes by the umpire; 'home run' scored when player hits ball, circles all three bases and crosses home plate; game consists of nine innings; believed to have been invented in 1839 by a West Point cadet, Abner Doubleday, at Cooperstown, NY.

**basketball** Five-a-side team ball game played on a hard surface court approx 26m/84ft by 14m/45ft 9in, with a bottomless basket 3.05m/10ft above the ground at each end; object is to move the ball by a series of passing and bouncing moves and throw it through the opponent's basket; invented by James Naismith in 1891 at Springfield, Massachusetts, but similar game believed to have been played in 10th-century Mexico.

**biathlon** Combined test of cross-country skiing and rifle shooting. It is used as a form of military training, based on the old military patrol race. Men's individual competitions are over 10 and 20km (6.2 and 12.4mi), and women's over 5 and 10km (3.1 and 6.2mi). At designated points on the course, competitors have to fire either standing or prone at a fixed target.

**billiards** Indoor table game played in many different forms. The standard green baize-covered table measures 3.66m/12ft by 1.83m/6ft and has six pockets into which the players use a tapered pole or *cue* to 'pot' the one red or two white balls to score, the balls going in off another ball. Scoring also achieved by making 'cannons' (hitting the white ball so that it successively hits the two others). Originally an outdoor game, its origins are uncertain; an early reference is 1429 when Louis XI of France owned a billiard table.

**bobsledding** Propelling oneself along snow or ice on a sledge, popular as a sport since 19th century; special luge run was created at Davos, Switzerland, in 1879. Most popular competitive forms; **luge tobogganing** on a small sledge and **bobsleighing** in a steel-bodied two- or four-person toboggan down special tracks at speeds of up to 130kph/80mph; earliest known sledge dates to c.6500BC Finland.

**bowling** Delivering a rubber or plastic ball along a 18.3m/60ft wooden lane to knock down pins; in **tenpin bowling** these are often mechanically replaced; popularized by third- and fourth-century German churchgoers, who would roll a ball at a *kegel*, a club used for protection; a hit would absolve them from sin. The game of nine pins was taken to the USA by Dutch and German immigrants; when outlawed, 10th pin introduced as a way around the legislation.

**bowls** Indoor or outdoor game played as singles, pairs, triples or fours. **Lawn bowls** ('flat green') is played on a flat level rink; **crown green bowls** is played on an uneven green raised at the centre (usually singles and pairs only); object is to deliver your bowl nearest to the *jack*, a small target ball; similar game believed to have been played by the Egyptians in c.5200BC. Glasgow solicitor William Mitchell drew up rules for modern bowls in 1848.

**boxing** Fist-fighting between two people, usually men, in a roped ring 4.3–6.1m/14–20ft square. Professional championship bouts constitute 12 three-minute rounds; amateur bouts three rounds, unless one fighter is knocked out or retires, the referee halts the fight, or a fighter is disqualified. The 17 weight divisions range from straw-weight for fighters under 48kg/105 lb to heavyweight, normally over 88kg/195 lb. Boxing dates from Greek and Roman times; first known match in Britain 1681 when Duke of Albemarle organized one between his butler and butcher in New Hall, Essex. First rules drawn up 1743, when each round lasted until one fighter was knocked down; gloves and three-minute rounds introduced 1867.

**bull-fighting** National sport in Spain, where it is called *corrida de toros* and the leading *matadors* are national heroes. *Picadors* are sent into the bull ring to weaken the bull before the matador enters the arena to make the final killing.

**caber tossing** Throwing a 3–4m/10–13ft tree trunk or *caber*, often practised in Highland Games gatherings in Scotland. The competitor has the caber placed vertically in his hands; he runs with it and tosses it so that it revolves longitudinally and lands with the base as near to the 12 o'clock position from him as possible.

**canoeing** Water sport practised by one to four people in canoes, developed 1865 by the British barrister John Macgregor. Competition usually consists of a river slalom course using poles suspended between the river banks to mark out the gates. Two types of competition canoe: the *kayak*, which has a keel (the canoeist sits in the boat), and the *Canadian canoe*, which has no keel (the canoeist kneels).

**clay-pigeon shooting** or **trap shooting** Pastime and sport in which shotguns are fired at clay targets (*clays*) in the air; these simulate birds in flight and are launched by an automatic or manually operated machine.

**cricket** Bat and ball 11-a-side team game. A wicket consisting of three stumps (wooden sticks) surmounted by a pair of bails (smaller sticks) is placed at each end of a grassy pitch 20.1m/22yd in length. Each team takes it in turn to bat (with long flat-sided wooden bats) and bowl (with a solid ball), the object being to defend the two wickets while trying to score as many runs as possible. A bowler delivers an 'over' of six balls to a batsman standing in front of one of the wickets before a different bowler attacks the other wicket. If the batsman hits a ball (and in certain other circumstances), he may exchange places with the other batsman, thus scoring at least one run. A ball reaching the boundary of the field scores four runs automatically, and six if it has not bounced on the way. A batsman can be got out by being 'caught' (a fielder catches the ball before it reaches the ground), 'bowled' (the ball from the bowler knocks the bails off the stumps), 'stumped' (the wicket-keeper knocks the bails off the stumps with the ball while the defending batsman is standing outside his 'safe ground' or 'crease'), 'run out' (the bails on the wicket towards which one of the batsmen is running are knocked off before the safe ground is reached), 'leg before wicket' or 'lbw' (when the lower part of the batsman's leg prevents the ball from the bowler reaching the wicket) and 'hit wicket' (the batsman accidentally knocks the bails off the stumps). Once 10 batsmen have been dismissed, the innings comes to a close, but a team can stop its innings or 'declare' if it thinks it has made enough runs. Each team has two innings, and the one with the greater number of runs at the end of the match wins. A similar game was played in the mid-16th century; first known county match 1719; test matches usually last five days; county championship three or four, and limited-over competitions normally concluded in one day, lasting for a specific number of overs per side. Earliest known laws: 1744; Marylebone Cricket Club (MCC) founded 1787; first test match: Melbourne 1877.

**croquet** A ball-and-mallet game for two to four players, played on a lawn about 32m/35yd long and 25m/28yd wide, on which six hoops have been arranged, with a small stake in the centre of the lawn. The object is to strike your own ball (blue, red, yellow or black) through the hoops in a prescribed order, a process which can be delayed by an opponent's ball hitting your ball out of the way. The central peg marks the finish and the first to hit it with his/her ball is the winner.

**curling** Similar to bowls but played on ice using special smooth, heavy round stones fitted with handles. The object is to slide the stones, which curl in different directions depending on the twist as they are released, near to a circular target or *house* marked on the ice, the centre of which is called the *tee*. A match lasts for a certain number of *heads* or shots, or by time. Sweeping the ice in front of a stone can make it travel further.

**cycling** Bicycle riding as a sport can take several forms: *time trials* are raced against the clock; *cyclocross* is a mixture of cycling and cross-country running, carrying the bike; *track racing* takes place on purpose-built concrete or wooden velodromes; *criteriums* are races around town or city centres; *road races* are normally in excess of 150km/100mi in length, between two points or several circuits of a predetermined course; *stage races* involve many days' racing over more than 100 miles. First cycle race Paris 1868, won by James Moore of England.

**cyclocross ► cycling**

**darts** Indoor game of throwing three 13cm/5in darts from a distance of 2.4m/8ft at a circular board which has its 'bull' or centre 1.7m/5ft 8in from the floor. The standard board is divided into 20 segments numbered 1–20 (not in numerical order); each contains smaller segments which either double or treble that number's score if hit. The centre ring (the bull) is worth 50 points, and the area around it (the outer) is worth 25 points. Most popular game '501': players start at that figure and deduct all scores from it, aiming to reduce the starting score exactly to zero; final shot must consist of a double.

**decathlon** Ten-event track-and-field competition held over two days, usually for men: 100m, long jump, shot put, high jump, 400m, 110m hurdles, discus, pole vault, javelin, and 1 500m. Points are awarded in each event.

**discus throw** Athletics field event using a circular disc of wood with metal plates, weighing 2kg/4.4 lb for men and 1kg/2.2 lb for women. It is thrown with one hand from within the confines of a circle 2.5m/8ft 2in in diameter.

**diving** Jumping from an elevated rigid or sprung board into a swimming pool, often performing a variety of twists and somersaults. Style gains marks, as does successfully completing the dive, based on the level of difficulty of each attempt (which is used as a multiplying factor). Spring-board events take place from a board 3m/9ft 10in above the water; platform diving from a rigid board 10m/32ft 10in above the water.

**falconry** Sport in which birds of prey are trained to hunt animals and other birds, also known as **hawking**. Two kinds of falcon: *long-winged* birds (eg the peregrine), used in open country, which swoop on their prey from a great height, and *short-winged* birds, or accipiters, which perch on the falconer's gloved fist or tree branch until they see their prey, and then rely on speed. The birds are hooded until such time as they are ready to 'work'.

**fencing** Sword fighting, using a light *foil*, heavier *épée*, or *sabre* (curved handle, narrow blade). Different target areas exist for each weapon, and protective clothing registers hit electronically. It can be traced back to the Egyptians of c.1300BC and was popular in the Middle Ages.

**fishing ► angling**

**fives** A handball game played on a three or four-walled court (which in Rugby fives is 5.49m/18ft wide, 8.54m/28ft long, with front wall 4.57m/15ft high, back wall 1.83m/6ft high and side walls sloping) by two or four players with a hard white ball, hit with gloved hands. It is derived from the French game *jeu de paume*. First recorded game 1825 at Eton College; another variation is Winchester fives.

**football** A field team game using an inflated ball, which has developed several different forms: **1 Association football** or **soccer**. An 11-a-side team game played on a grass or synthetic pitch measuring 90–120m/100–130yd in length, and 45–90m/50–100yd wide; goal nets measure 7.3m/8yd wide by 2.4m/8ft high; object is to move the ball around using the foot or head until it can be put into the net, thus scoring a goal. Only the goalkeeper within a specific area is allowed to touch the ball with the hand while it is in play. Ancient Greeks, Chinese, Egyptians and Romans all played a form of football; it became an organized game in 19th-century Britain, in schools and universities; standard rules drawn up 1848; Football Association formed 1863; first FA Cup final played 1872; first World Cup Uruguay 1930. **2 American football**. Players wear heavy padding and helmets, and passing of the ball by hand, including forward passing, is permitted; played on a rectangular field 91m/100yd by 49m/53yd, divided gridiron-like into 4.6m/5yd segments; object is to score 'touchdowns' by moving the ball into the opposing team's 'end zone' (area behind the posts), but progress has to be made upfield by a series of 'plays': a team must make 9.1m/10yd of ground within four plays, otherwise they lose possession of the ball. Six points are awarded for a touchdown and one for an 'extra point', for kicking the ball between the posts and over the crossbar — the equivalent of a conversion in rugby. A goal kicked from anywhere on the field (a 'field goal') is worth three points. Teams consist of more than 40 members, but only 11 are allowed on the field at any one time; special units of players have different roles so they change eg when the team changes from attacking to defending. First

intercollegiate game 1869. **3 Australian Rules football**. A handling and kicking game with few rules, a cross between Association football and rugby, with 18 players on an oval pitch measuring c.165m/180yd long by c.137m/150yd wide. The object is to score by kicking the ball between the opponent's goal posts (six points). Smaller posts are positioned either side of the main goal: a ball kicked through that area scores one point; first recorded game played 1858. **4 Gaelic football**. Mixture of rugby, soccer and Australian Rules football, played by teams of 15 on a rectangular pitch 77–91m/84–100yd wide and 128–146m/140–160yd long with goals resembling rugby posts with soccer-style nets attached; points scored by either putting the ball into the goal net (three), or over the crossbar and between the uprights (one); first game resembling Gaelic football took place 1712 at Slane, Ireland. **5 rugby football** ► **rugby**.

**foxhunting** Mounted blood sport involving chasing and killing a wild fox using foxhounds (similar in shape and colour to the beagle, but slightly larger); hunt is controlled by a Master of Hounds, the hounds by the Huntsman; season lasts November to April. It developed in the UK in the late 17th century. Since 1949 there has been a movement to try to get the sport banned in the UK.

**golf** Outdoor sport played on a course 4 500–6 500m/5 000–7 000yd long, usually with 18 but sometimes 9 holes; object is to hit a small rubber-cored ball using a long-handled iron or wooden-faced club from a flat starting point or *tee* along a *fairway* to a hole positioned on an area of smooth grass or *green*; additional hazards: trees, bushes, streams, sand-filled bunkers and the *rough*, or uncut grass beside the fairway; winner completes the course using the lowest number of strokes. The *par* is the expected number of strokes a good player needs to complete a hole; one stroke above par is called a *bogey*; one stroke below par is a *birdie*; two strokes below an *eagle*; three strokes below an *albatross*; a hole completed in one stroke is a *hole in one*. A similar game was played by the Dutch c.1300, known as *kolf* or *colf*. *Gouf* was definitely played in Scotland in the 15th century; world's first club, the Gentleman Golfers of Edinburgh, formed 1744.

**greyhound racing** Spectator sport which takes place on an enclosed circular or oval track where greyhound dogs (on whose success bets are usually placed) are lured to run by a mechanical hare; invented California 1919.

**gymnastics** Physical exercises. Men compete on the parallel bars, pommel horse, high bar, rings, horse vault and floor exercise, and women on the asymmetrical bars, beam, horse vault and floor exercise. Judges award marks out of 10, looking for control, suppleness, balance and ingenuity. The ancient Greeks and Romans performed such exercises for health purposes; modern techniques date from late 18th-century Germany.

**hammer throw** Athletics field event; hammer weighing 7.6kg/16 lb is thrown using one hand from within the confines of a circle 2.13m/7ft in diameter (protected by a wire cage). Six throws are allowed, the object being to attain the greatest distance.

**handball** Indoor and outdoor game first played in Germany c.1890; resembles Association football, but played with the hands. Indoor game played seven-a-side on a court 40m/43.8yd long and 20m/21.9yd wide, with goals 2m/6ft 6in high and 3m/9ft 9in wide; outdoor game (**field handball**) played on a field with 11 on each side.

**hang gliding** Flying in a glider with a delta-shaped wing, usually having launched from a high place. The pilot is suspended by a harness from the light frame holding the wing, and controls the direction of the craft by body movement. Providing the angle of attack is maintained, lift is generated. A hang glider with a motor and wing span increased to 10m/33ft is called a *micro-light*, which typically has a speed of 90kph/55mph. Hang gliding was pioneered in the 1890s in Germany.

**harness racing** Horse race with rider seated in a small two-wheeled cart or *sulky*; horses trot or pace; races run on an oval dirt track measuring 800–1 500m/0.5–1mi in circumference; first introduced 1554 Holland, popularized mid-19th century USA.

**hawking** ► **falconry**

**heptathlon** Seven-event track-and-field competition held over two days, usually for women: 100m hurdles, shot put, high jump, 200m, long jump, javelin and 800m; replaced pentathlon in 1981.

**high jump** Athletics field event; competitors attempt to clear a bar without any aids; height increased gradually; three failed attempts means disqualification. The winner clears the greatest height, or has the least failures.

**hockey** or (US) **field hockey** Stick-and-ball game played by two teams of 11 on a pitch 91m/100yd long and 54m/60yd wide, the object being to move the ball around with the sticks until a player can score from within the semicircle of radius 14.64m/16yd in front of the opposing side's goal; game is split into two halves of 35 minutes; ancient Greeks played a similar game c.2500BC; modern hockey dates from 1875.

**horse racing** Racing of horses against one another, each ridden by a jockey. Two categories: **flat racing** for thoroughbred horses on a flat grass or dirt surface over a predetermined distance from 1 to 4km/5 furlongs to 2.5mi, and **national hunt racing** in which the horses negotiate either movable hurdles or fixed fences over a distance up to 6.5km/4.5mi. The ancient Egyptians took part in horse races in c.1200BC; popularized in 12th-century England. Most monarchs have supported the sport, hence name the 'sport of kings'. ► **harness racing**, **hurdles** and **steeplechasing**.

**hurdles** Horse race in which the horses jump hurdles of at least 106.7cm/3ft 6in in height; hurdles are easily knocked down so that horses can continue the race.

**hurdling** Athletics event in which the competitors race to clear 10 obstacles (hurdles) placed on the track; race distances: 110m and 400m for men, 100m and 400m for women; hurdle height varies: 106.7cm/3ft 6in for the 110m; 91.4cm/3ft for the 400m and 84cm/2ft 9in for the 100m.

**hurling** or **hurley** Irish 15-a-side field game played with curved sticks and a ball; object to hit ball into opposing team's goal: under the crossbar scores three points; above the crossbar but between the posts scores one; played since 1800BC; standardized in 1884 following the formation of the Gaelic Athletic Association.

**ice hockey** Fast game played by two teams of six on an ice rink 56–61m/184–200ft long and 26–30m/85–98ft wide with sticks and a small rubber *puck*; aim is to score goals by using the stick to hit the puck into the opposing team's goal; players wear ice skates and protective clothing; possibly first played 1850s Canada.

**ice skating 1 figure skating**. Artistic dancing on ice for individuals and pairs; first known skating club formed mid-18th century London; first artificial rink opened 1876 Baker Street. **2 speed skating**. Competitors race against one another on an oval ice track over distances between 500 and 10 000m/550 and 11 000yd.

**javelin throw** Athletics field event; throwing a spear-like javelin which consists of three parts: pointed metal head, shaft and grip; men's javelin is 2.6–2.7m/8ft 6in–8ft 10in in length and weighs 800g/1.8 lb; women's is 2.2–2.3m/7ft 2in–7ft 6in and weights at least 600g/1.3 lb; the competitor runs to a specified mark with the javelin in one hand, and throws it; for throw to count, metal head must touch ground before any other part; first mark made by the head is the point used for measuring the distance achieved.

**judo** Unarmed combat sport of late 19th-century Japanese origin. Contestants wear a *judogi* or loose-fitting suit and compete on a mat which breaks their falls. When one cannot break a hold, surrender is signalled by slapping the mat; ability is graded from fifth to first Kyu, and then first to 12th Dan — only Dr Jigoro Kano, who devised the sport, has been awarded 12th Dan. Different coloured belts indicate grades; eg white for novice, brown (three degrees) and black (nine degrees).

**jujitsu** Japanese art of unarmed offence and self-defence used by the Samurai; forms basis of judo, aikido and karate; thought to have been introduced early 17th century by Chinese monk, Chen Yuan-ping.

**karate** Martial art of unarmed combat, dating from 17th century; developed Japan 20th century; name adopted 1930s; aim is to be in total control of the body's muscular power, so it can be used with great force and accuracy at any instant. Experts may show their mental and physical training by eg breaking various thicknesses of wood, but in fighting an opponent, blows do not actually make contact; levels of prowess symbolized by coloured belts.

**kendo** Japanese martial art of sword fighting, now practised with *shiani*, or bamboo swords; object is to land two scoring blows on opponent's target area. *Kendokas* (participants) wear traditional dress of the Samurai period, including face masks and aprons; grades according to ability are from sixth to first Kyu, then from first to 10th Dan; earliest reference is AD789.

**kung fu** Chinese unarmed combat dating from the sixth century, when it was practised at the Shaolin Temple; best known form is *wing chun*.

**lacrosse** Stick-and-ball field game; teams of 10 (men's) or 12 (women's) play on a pitch measuring about 100–110m/110–120yd by 55–75m/60–85yd; stick measures at least 90cm/3ft and has thongs forming a triangular net at one end in which ball is caught and carried, and thrown into opponents' goal (just under 2m/6ft square); derived from Native American game of *baggataway*; stick supposedly resembled a bishop's crozier, so French settlers called it *la crosse*; played since 15th century; spread to Europe early 19th century, and to Britain 1867.

**long jump** Athletics field event; contestant runs up to the take-off mark and leaps into a sandpit; length of the jump measured from front of take-off line to nearest break in the sand made by any part of the competitor's body; also called **broad jump** in North America.

**lugeing** Travelling across ice on a toboggan sled, usually made of wood with metal runners; rider sits upright or lies back (but lies on the stomach in tobogganing). Competitors in single or two-seater luges race against time on a predetermined run of at least 1 000m/1 094yd; luge is approximately 1.5m/5ft in length, steered by the feet and a hand rope. ► **bobsledding**.

**marathon** Long-distance running race, normally on open roads, over 42km 195m/26mi 385yd (distance first used at 1908 London Olympics so competitors could finish exactly in front of the royal box); race introduced at the 1896 Olympic Games to commemorate the run of the Greek courier (according to legend, Pheidippides) who ran the c.24mi/39km from Marathon to Athens in 490BC with the news of a Greek victory over the Persian army. In the 1980s the **half marathon** over 21km/13mi 194yd also became popular.

**martial arts** ► **aikido, judo, jujitsu, karate, kendo, kung fu, taekwondo**

**moto-cross** or **scrambling** Motorcycle racing over a circuit of rough terrain, taking advantage of natural hazards eg streams and hills; uses sturdier motorcycles than those for road use; competitions usually categorized by engine size; first moto-cross race held 1924 at Camberley, Surrey.

**motorcycle racing** Speed competitions for motorcycles which for the annual season-long grand prix are categorized by the engine sizes 80cc, 125cc, 250cc, 500cc and sidecar. Other forms include speedway, moto-cross and motorcycle trials riding.

**motor racing** Racing finely-tuned motor cars, either purpose-built or modified production vehicles;

season-long (Mar–Nov) Formula One world championship involves usually 16 races at different venues worldwide; other popular forms include stock-car racing, hill-climbing, sports-car racing and rallying; first race 1894, between Paris and Rouen.

**mountaineering** Climbing a mountain aided by ropes and other accessories, which for tall peaks can take weeks; most popular form in UK is **rock climbing**; in higher places elsewhere the form is **snow and ice climbing**.

**netball** Women's seven-a-side court game invented in the USA and developed from basketball; court is 30.5m/100ft long and 15.25m/50ft wide; object is to score goals by passing the inflated ball between players and throwing it through opponent's hoop suspended on a post 3.05m/10ft high. Players must not touch each other or run with the ball.

**octopush** A form of hockey played underwater, first introduced 1960s in South Africa; teams of six; players use miniature hockey sticks and a *puck* or *squid*, which must hit the opposing team's end of the swimming pool to score a goal.

**orienteering** Cross-country running and route-finding aided by map and compass; competitors set off at intervals and have to find their way to offical check-points; devised as a sport in Sweden in 1918, based on military training techniques; became an international sport 1960s.

**paddle tennis** Bat-and-ball game for two or four people, invented USA c.1920; rules similar to lawn tennis, but court is half the size; bat wooden and ball made of sponge.

**parachuting** Jumping out of an aircraft and landing with the aid of a parachute; competitions involve landing within a specific area; participant can choose to freefall for a few thousand feet before opening the chute, normally c.750m/2 500ft.

**pelota** Generic name for various hand, glove, racket or bat-and-ball games, all developed from French *jeu de paume*; most popular form **Pelote Basque**: it uses a walled court (*trinquete*), players wear a shaped wicker basked attached to their forearm in which they catch and propel the ball. Pelota is one of the world's fastest games.

**pentathlon** 1 Five-event track-and-field competition, usually for women: 100m hurdles, shot put, high jump, long jump, and 800m; replaced by **heptathlon** in 1981. **2 modern pentathlon**. Five-sport competition based on military training, comprising cross-country riding, épée fencing, pistol shooting, swimming and cross-country running.

**point-to-point** Horse races for amateur riders over a cross-country course, normally farmland; organized by hunts; horses used are regular hunting horses; original courses went from one point to another (hence name), but are now often over circular or oval courses with mixture of artificial and natural fences.

**pole vault** Athletics field event; jumping contest for height using fibreglass pole for leverage to clear a bar, which is raised progressively; three attempts may be made to clear the height before attempting a new one.

**polo** Stick-and-ball game; played by teams of four on horseback on a pitch measuring 274m/300yd by 146m/160yd; object is to hit the ball into the opposing team's 7.3m/8yd-wide and 3m/10ft-high goal using a long-handled mallet; match lasts about an hour, divided into seven-minute *chukkas*, the number of which varies according to competition; a pony is not expected to play more than two chukkas; game derives its name from Tibetan *pulu*; first played in C Asia c.500BC.

**pool** American table game played in many forms, using 15 balls, a *cue* similar to that used in billiards and snooker, and a table half the size of a standard billiard table, with six round pockets; UK most popular form is eight-ball pool, where the object is to pot all balls of your colour and finally the black (or No. 8) ball.

**potholing** or (US) **spelunking** Exploration and study of caves and other underground features, originally to survey extent, physical history and structure, and natural history. When practised as a hobby people descend through access points (potholes) to follow courses of underground rivers and streams; scientific term: **speleology**.

**powerboat racing** Inshore and offshore racing of boats fitted with high-powered and finely-tuned engines; first race of note Calais to Dover 1903.

**quoits** Outdoor game demanding great accuracy; metal ring is thrown at a peg; became popular mid-14th-century England; horseshoe pitching developed from quoits.

**rackets** or (US) **raquets** Racket-and-ball game; played by two or four players on walled court; probably forerunner to many racket-and-ball games; thought to have originated Middle Ages, and to have developed 18th century at the Fleet debtors' prison, London.

**rallying** Motor racing on open roads and in forests, sometimes lasting several days; driver and navigator require skill and endurance; uses modified production cars.

**real tennis** Indoor racket-and-ball game similar to rackets; played on walled court with specifically designed hazards; derivation of the 11th-century *jeu de paume*; racket developed 16th century and the game became very popular in the 17th; also known as 'royal' or 'court' tennis, and a minority sport today.

**rodeo** US sport; mainly competitive riding and a range of skills deriving from cowboy ranching practices; events include bronco riding with and without saddle (where the cowboy must stay on a wild bucking horse for a set time holding on with only one hand, points being awarded for style to the horse and rider), bull riding, steer wrestling, calf roping and team roping.

**roller skating** First seen 1760 in Liège, Belgium; developed as a sport late 19th century, following invention of the modern four-wheeled skate in 1863. Competitions exist as for ice skating;

individual, pairs, dancing and speed skating on a track.

**rounders** Outdoor bat-and-ball game; baseball may derive from it; teams of nine players; object, after hitting the ball, which is bowled from the centre of the pitch, is to score a rounder by running around the outside of the four posts without being put out (by the ball being caught, the batter being tagged between posts, or the post ahead of the batter being 'stopped' by a fielder touching it with the hand holding the ball); first reference to rounders 1774.

**rowing** Propulsion of a boat by oars; involves two or more rowers, each with an oar, and often with a coxswain; **sculling** involves one rower with two oars; rowing as an organized sport dates from 1715 (first rowing of the Doggetts Coat and Badge race on the R Thames, London).

**rugby football** Team ball game played with oval ball on a pitch 68.62m/75yd wide and 100m/110yd long; developed 1823 from football (when William Webb Ellis of Rugby school picked up the ball and ran with it); H-shaped goalposts at each end of field are 5.6m/18ft 6in wide, with a crossbar 3m/10ft above the ground; object is to score a *try* by grounding ball in opposing team's scoring area behind goal line. The 15-a-side **Rugby Union** game and 13-a-side **Rugby League** are now both professional games, with some rule differences: eg the scoring (League in brackets): try 5 (4), conversion 2 (2), penalty 3 (2), dropped goal 3 (1). Rugby League was formed by the breakaway Northern Union after a dispute with the Rugby Football Union about pay in 1895.

**sailing** Travelling over water in a suitable craft, usually a small single or double-sided dinghy, often with outboard motor or auxiliary engine for use in no wind; **yachting** involves racing small, light sailing vessels with crews of one, two or three; large ocean-going yachts may be 25m/80ft or more in length; several classes of racing yacht in Olympic and international competitions — eg the Admiral's Cup and Americas Cup.

**scrambling ▸ motocross**

**sculling ▸ rowing**

**sepek takrow** Three-a-side court game played on badminton court with ball made from rattan palm; ball is propelled over centre net (lower than in badminton) by players using any part of the body other than arms or hands; popular in SE Asia, particularly Philippines, Malaysia (as 'kick') and Thailand (as 'rattan ball').

**shinty** Twelve-a-side stick-and-ball game originating in Ireland more than 1 500 years ago, now popular in the Scottish Highlands; played on pitch up to 155m/170yd long and 73m/80yd wide; aim is to score goals by propelling the leather-covered cork and worsted ball, using curved sticks or *camans*, into the opposing team's goal or *hail*.

**shooting** Competitive shooting takes many forms and uses different types of weapon; most popular weapons: the standard pistol, small bore rifle, full bore rifle, air rifle and air pistol. All events involve shooting at still or moving targets (▸ **clay pigeon shooting**). Using firearms for sport developed in 15th century. Hunting for game, eg grouse or pheasant shooting, has specifically defined seasons.

**shot put** Athletics field event; the shot is a brass or iron sphere weighing 7.26kg/16 lb for men and 4kg/8 lb 13oz for women. It is propelled, using only one hand, from a starting position under the chin. The thrower must not leave the 2.1m/7ft diameter throwing circle. In competition six throws are allowed.

**skiing** Propelling oneself along snow while standing on skis, aided by poles; named from Norwegian *ski*, 'snowshoe'; two forms of competition skiing: **alpine skiing**, consisting of the downhill, slalom (zigzag courses through markers) and ski-jumping, and **Nordic skiing** or **langlaufing** (on narrower skis to which only the toe is attached), incorporating cross-country skiing and the **biathlon**. Other forms: **ski-flying** (ski-jumping from a high take-off point), **skijoring** (being towed behind a vehicle or horse), hang gliding on skis and parapenting on skis.

**skydiving** or **freefalling** Jumping from an aircraft and freefalling, often performing a wide range of stunts or forming patterns by holding hands with other skydivers, to a height of 600m/2 000ft, when the parachute must be opened.

**snooker** Indoor game played on a standard billiard table by two (or occasionally four) players; aim is to 'pot' the 21 colours balls (arranged on the table at the start) by hitting them with the white ball, itself hit using a tapered pole or *cue*. Fifteen of the balls are red; these must be potted alternately with the coloured ones. This sequence is called a *break* and continues until a mistake is made; reds remain in pockets but coloureds are returned to the table until no reds are left, when they are potted in ascending order; game ends when the black is finally potted. Points 1–7 relate to colours, in order: red, yellow, green, brown, blue, pink, black.

**soccer ▸ football**

**softball** Smaller version of **baseball**, played on diamond-shaped pitch of sides measuring 18.3m/60ft; ball is larger as well as softer; teams of nine; game lasts for nine innings per team, each innings lasting until a team has three players out; object is to complete a circuit of the diamond without being put out, eg by being caught out, struck out, or tagged between bases by a player with the ball. Pitching is underarm in softball, overarm in baseball; two forms: *fast pitch* and *slow pitch*; in the latter the bowler must deliver ball in arc at least 2.4m/8ft high.

**speedway** Motorcycle racing on machines with no brakes and only one gear, usually on an oval track and involving four riders at once. Other forms include *long track* racing and *ice speedway*.

**squash** or **squash rackets** Strenuous indoor racket-and-ball game played (in English singles) on an enclosed court measuring 9.75m/32ft long by 6.4m/21ft wide; small rubber ball is hit alternately by players against the front wall, so that it cannot be returned; developed 1817 from **rackets** at Harrow school.

**steeplechase** **1** National hunt horse racing; horses negotiate fixed fences normally 0.9–1.2m/3–4ft high; first one in Ireland in 1752; most famous is Grand National. ► **horse racing**. **2** Track race, usually for men, run over 3 000m and comprising 28 0.9m/3ft hurdles and seven waterjumps.

**stock-car racing** Motor racing; in USA highly supercharged production cars race around a concreted track; in UK 'bangers' (old cars) race on a round or oval track; the aim is to be the last car still moving at the end of the race; some 'rough' tactics are allowed to try to eliminate other drivers.

**street hockey** Hockey played on roller skates, popular in USA and Europe; five members to each team play on an enclosed rink.

**sumo wrestling** A Japanese national sport; competition takes place in a 3.66m/12ft diameter circle; object is to force opponent out of ring or to ground; sumo wrestlers are very heavy and eat vast amounts of food to increase weight and body size.

**surfing** Riding waves, either with the body alone, or with the aid of a board; object is to ride along the face of a wave before it breaks; board is usually about 1.8m/6ft long, but a longer one is used for competition; originated in Oceania, developed in Hawaii and has flourished in modern times there and in California and Australia.

**swimming** Propelling oneself through water without mechanical aids. Four strokes: *breast stroke*, the slowest stroke, developed in the 16th century; *front crawl* or *freestyle*, the fastest stroke; *backstroke*; and *butterfly*, developed in the USA in the 20th century. In competitions there are also relays, involving four swimmers, and medley races, combining all four strokes. Olympic-size pool is 50m/55yd long, with eight lanes; race lengths from 50m/55yd to 1 500m/1 640yd; earliest reference to swimming as a sport is 36BC Japan.

**table tennis** or **ping pong** Indoor bat-and-ball game played by two or four players; uses small wooden bats covered in rubber or sponge and a hollow plastic ball; table measures 2.75m/9ft by 1.52m/5ft and has a 15.25cm/6in-high net across it; ball must be hit over the net and into opposing half of table, to be returned without volleying; object is to play unreturnable shots; in doubles, players must hit ball alternately; winner is first to reach 21 points with at least a two-point lead; thought to have been first played 1880s.

**taekwondo** Martial art developed in Korea by General Choi Hong Hi; officially part of Korean tradition and culture since 1955, now popular as a sport.

**tenpin bowling** ► **bowling**

**tennis, lawn** Racket-and-ball game for two or four players; court measures 23.77m/78ft long by 8.23m/27ft wide (singles), or 10.97m/36ft wide (doubles); net 0.9m/3ft high is stretched across centre; rackets have oval heads strung with nylon or gut; playing surface can be grass, clay, shale, concrete, wood, or other man-made materials; object is to play unreturnable strokes, thus scoring points; progression of scoring is 15, 30, 40, deuce if both reach 40, and game; set won by winning six games with a two-game lead (or one in a 'short' set); a very close match can be decided using a tie-break. In doubles, players may hit the ball in any order, but must serve in rotation. 'Field tennis' was played 18th century but game similar to modern game was invented 1873 as *sphairstike* in Wales by Walter Wingfield.

**tobogganing** ► **bobsledding** and **lugeing**

**trampolining** Performing acrobatics on a sprung canvas sheet stretched across a frame, first used at turn of 20th century as a circus attraction; developed as a sport following design of modern trampoline in 1936. In competition, marks gained for performing difficult manoeuvres; popular forms are synchronized trampolining and tumbling.

**trap shooting** ► **clay pigeon shooting**

**triple jump** Athletics field event; takes place in same place as long jump, governed by same rules. After the run-up, competitors must take off and hop on the same foot; second phase is a step onto the other foot, followed by a jump; previously called the *hop, step and jump*.

**tug of war** Athletics event of strength; two teams (normally eight men) pull against each other from opposite ends of a long thick rope; aim is to pull the opponents over a predetermined mark. Ancient Chinese and Egyptians participated in similar events; first rules drawn up 1879.

**volleyball** Indoor court game; two teams of six play on a court measuring 18m/59ft by 9m/29ft which has a raised net stretched across the centre; aim is to score points by grounding the inflated ball on opponent's side after hitting it over net with the arms or hands; ball may not be hit more than three times on one team's side of the net.

**walking** Either a leisurely pursuit (eg **fell walking**) or a competitive sport on roads or tracks which has strict rules; eg raised foot must touch ground before the other leaves it.

**water polo** Sport played by two seven-a-side teams in a swimming pool; aim is to score by propelling inflated ball into opposing team's goal at end of the pool, without touching the bottom; developed in Britain in 1869; originally called 'football in water'.

**water skiing** Being towed by a motor boat on one or two skis, using a 23m/75ft-long rope. Competitions held for jumping, slalom and acrobatics.

**weightlifting** Test of strength by lifting weights attached to both ends of a metal pole or *barbell*. Competitors have to make two successful lifts: the *snatch*, taking the bar to an outstretched position above the head in one movement (held for two seconds), and the *clean and jerk* or *jerk*

which is achieved in two movements, first onto the chest, then above the head with outstretched arms; aggregate weight of the two lifts gives a competitor's total, and the weights are gradually increased. Another form is *powerlifting*, which calls for sheer strength rather than technique, and takes three forms: the *squat*, *dead lift* and *bench press*. Weightlifting was part of Ancient Olympic Games; introduced as sport c.1850.

**wrestling** Fighting person to person without using fists; aim is to throw opponent to the ground; most popular forms are *freestyle*, where the legs can be used to hold and trip, and *Graeco-Roman* where holds below the waist are not allowed. Ten weight divisions: light-flyweight (under 48kg) to super-heavyweight (over 100kg). Other forms: *sumo*, the national sport in Japan; *Sambo* in Russia; *Kushti* in Iran; *Glima* in Iceland; *Schwingen* in Switzerland; and *Yagli*, the national sport in Turkey; also UK variations *Devon and Cornwall* and *Cumberland and Westmoreland*.

**yachting ► sailing**

## 100 Champions in Sport

**Aaron, Hank (Henry Lewis)** (1934– )US baseball player, born Mobile, Alabama. Regarded as one of the greatest batters ever, he set almost every batting record in his 23-season career with the Milwaukee Braves and the Milwaukee Brewers: 2 297 runs batted in, 1 477 extra-base hits, and 755 home runs (he broke **Babe Ruth**'s long-standing record of 714 in 1974). Named the Most Valuable Player in 1957, he led the Braves to the World Series Championship.

**Ali, Muhammad**, formerly **Cassius Marcellus Clay** (1942– ) US boxer, born Louisville, Kentucky. Won Olympic amateur light-heavyweight title in Rome (1960); turned professional and won world heavyweight title (1964). Stripped of title 1967 for refusing military service on religious grounds, but returned 1970. Made history by regaining the world heavyweight title twice — lost 1971, regained 1974; lost 1978, regained later 1978.

**Anquetil, Jacques** (1934–87) French racing cyclist, born Normandy. Winner of Tour de France five times (1957, 1961–4); see also **Bernard Hinault**, **Miguel Indurain** and **Eddy Merckx**; also won Tour of Spain (1963) and of Italy (1964).

**Aouita, Said** (1960– ) Moroccan athlete, born Rabat. Set world records at 1 500m and 5 000m in 1985 — the first man for 30 years to hold both records. Later broke world records at 2 miles, 2 000m, and 3 000m. Also Olympic champion (1984), overall Grand Prix winner (1986) and world 5 000m champion (1987).

**Beamon, Bob (Robert)** (1946– ) US athlete, born New York City. Broke world long jump record by 55cm ($21\frac{1}{2}$ins) at the 1968 Olympic Games in Mexico City, with a jump of 8.90m (29ft $2\frac{1}{2}$ins). His record held until broken by Mike Powell in Tokyo (1991).

**Beckenbauer, Franz**, nicknamed **Kaiser Franz** (1945– ) German footballer, coach, manager and administrator, born Munich. European Footballer of the Year in 1972, he captained the West German national side to success in the European Nations Cup (1972) and in the World Cup (1974); he also won three successive European Cup winner's medals with Bayern Munich (1974–6). After retiring from playing in 1983, he coached the West German team (1984–90) and as manager of West Germany from 1986 took them to consecutive World Cup finals — as runners up in 1986 and then as winners (for Germany) in 1990.

**Best, George** (1946– ) Northern Irish footballer, born Belfast. Northern Ireland's greatest individual footballing talent; leading scorer for Manchester United in the Football League First Division (1967–8), and in 1968 winner of a European Cup medal and the title of European Footballer of the Year. Immense career success dwindled early due to pressures of top-class football.

**Biondi, Matt(hew)** (1965– ) US swimmer, born Morego, California. Winner of record seven medals at the 1986 world championships, including three golds; of seven medals at the 1988 Olympics, including five golds; and a silver in the 50m freestyle at the 1992 Olympics. Set 100m freestyle world record of 48.74 seconds in Orlando, Florida (1986).

**Border, Allan** (1955– ) Australian cricketer, born Cremorne, Sydney. Made Test debut for Australia in 1978; team captain 1984–94. World record holder for most Test match and one-day international appearances, and for runs scored in Test matches when his career total reached 10 161 (1993). Played county cricket in England for Gloucestershire and Essex.

**Borg, Björn Rune** (1956– ) Swedish tennis player. Swedish Davis Cup team member aged 15, and Wimbledon junior champion aged 16. Winner of five consecutive Wimbledon singles titles (1976–80), two Italian championship titles and six French Open titles (1974–5, 1978–81).

**Botham, Ian Terence** (1955– ) English cricketer, born Heswall, Merseyside. Played for England in 102 Test matches, took 383 wickets, and scored 5 200 runs. Held record number of Test wickets (373 wickets at an average of 27.86 runs) until overtaken by **Richard Hadlee**, and four times took 10 wickets in a match. Played county cricket in England for Somerset (1974–87), Worcestershire (1987–91) and Durham (1992–3).

**Bradman, Don (Sir Donald George)** (1908–2001) Australian cricketer, born Cootamundra, New South Wales, regarded as one of the greatest batsmen ever. Played for Australia from 1928 to 1948 (captain 1936–48); made highest aggregate and largest number of centuries in Tests against England, and holds record

for the highest Australian Test score against England (334 at Leeds in 1930); batting average in Test matches was 99.94 runs per innings.

**Bubka, Sergei** (1963– ) Ukrainian field athlete, born Donetsk. Won gold medal for pole-vaulting at the 1983 world championship, retaining title 1987, 1991, 1993 and 1995; also won gold at the 1988 Olympics. He has broken 35 world records and in 1994 took the world pole-vault record to 6.14m.

**Carson, Willie (William Hunter Fisher)** (1942– ) Scottish jockey, born Stirling. Has ridden 17 Classic winners and is third in the all-time winners table. First Classic success was on High Top in the 2 000 Guineas (1972); recorded a notable royal double for Queen Elizabeth II by winning the Oaks and the St Leger on Dunfermline (1977); won Derby first on Troy (1979), then Henbit (1980).

**Charlton, Bobby (Sir Robert)** (1937– ) English footballer, born Ashington, Northumberland. He played with Manchester United (1954–73), winning three League championship medals (1956–7, 1964–5, 1966–7) and a FA Cup winner's medal (1963), and captained Manchester United to victory in the 1968 European Cup. Also played 106 games for England between 1957 and 1973, scoring a record 49 goals, and was a member of the victorious World Cup team (1966). In all he played 754 games, scoring 245 goals.

**Clark, Jim (James)** (1936–68) Scottish racing driver, born Berwickshire. Won first motor race in 1956; Scottish Speed Champion 1958–9. Joined Lotus team as a Formula One driver 1960, and won world championship 1963, 1965; also in 1965 became the first non-American since 1916 to win the Indianapolis 500. Won 25 of his 72 Grand Prix races, breaking **Juan Fangio**'s record, and took pole position 33 times.

**Cobb, Ty(rus Raymond)**, nicknamed **the Georgia Peach** (1886–1961) US baseball player, born Narrows, Georgia. Regarded as outstanding offensive player of all time; played for the Detroit Tigers (1905–26) and the Philadelphia Athletics (1926–8), and until Pete Rose in 1985 was the only player with more than 4 000 hits in major league baseball. Career batting average was .367, (ie he had a hit more than once every three times at bat).

**Coe, Sebastian** (1956– ) English athlete, born Chiswick, London. Winner of 1 500m Olympic gold medal and 800m silver medal at both Moscow (1980) and Los Angeles (1984). Broke world record for the 800m, 1 000m and the mile in 1981. Between Sep 1976 and June 1983 he did not lose the final of any race over 1 500m or a mile.

**Comaneci, Nadia** (1961– ) Romanian gymnast, born Onesti, Moldavia. Winner at the 1976 Olympic Games (aged 14) of gold medals in the parallel bars and beam disciplines and a bronze in the floor, becoming the first to obtain a perfect score of 10 for performance on the bars and beam; also won gold medals in the beam at the 1978 world championships and in the beam and the floor exercise at the 1980 Olympics.

**Connors, Jimmy (James Scott)** (1952– ) US tennis player, born East St Louis, Illinois. Winner of the men's singles competition at Wimbledon (1974, 1982), the Australian Open (1974), and the US Open (1974, 1976, 1978, 1982–3). With Ilie Nastase, he won the men's doubles at Wimbledon (1973) and the US Open men's doubles (1975). He was World Championship Tennis champion (1977, 1980), Masters champion (1978), and a US team member in the Davis Cup (1976; 1981 victory).

**Court, Margaret Jean Smith**, née **Smith** (1942– ) Australian tennis player, born Albury, New South Wales. Winner of more Grand Slam events (66) than any other player: 10 Wimbledon titles (including the singles — the first Australian to do so — in 1963, 1965, 1970), 22 US titles (singles in 1962, 1965, 1968–70, 1973), 13 French (singles 1962, 1964, 1969–70, 1973), and 21 Australian (singles 1960–66, 1969–71, 1973). In 1970 she became the second woman (after Maureen Connolly) to win all four major titles in one year.

**Davis, Joe** (1901–78) English billiards and snooker champion, born Whitwell, near Chesterfield. Made first break of 100 aged 12. World professional snooker champion (1927–46), and billiards champion (1928–33). Attained maximum snooker break of 147 in 1955, later officially recognized as the world record.

**Davis, Steve** (1957– ) English snooker player, born London. World's leading player during the 1980s, and world champion six times (1981, 1983–4, 1987–9).

**DiMaggio, Joe (Joseph Paul)**, nicknamed **Joltin' Joe** and **the Yankee Clipper** (1914–99) US baseball player, born Martinez, California. Played entire career (1936–51) with the New York Yankees. Greatest achievement was hitting safely (recording a hit) at least once in 56 consecutive games in the 1941 season. Was the American League's Most Valuable Player three times and winner of the batting championship twice (1939, 1940). Career total was 361 home runs, with a batting average of .325.

**Eddery, Pat(rick James John)** (1952– ) Irish jockey, born Newbridge, Kildare. Champion jockey nine times between 1974 and 1993; Classics victories include the Derby (1975, 1982, 1990), the Oaks (1979, 1996), the St Leger (1986, 1991, 1994, 1997), 1 000 Guineas (1996), 2 000 Guineas (1983–4, 1993); also had four Prix de l'Arc de Triomphe wins (1980, 1985–7).

**Edwards, Gareth Owen** (1947– ) Welsh rugby player, born Gwaun-cae-Gurwen, near Swansea. First capped for Wales aged 19 (1967), and became their youngest-ever captain (1968). His 53 consecutive caps are a Welsh record; also played in 10 Lions Tests.

**Evert, Chris(tine) Marie** (1954– ) US tennis player, born Fort Lauderdale, Florida. Winner of 157 professional titles, and undefeated on clay from Aug 1973 to May 1979. Her 18 singles Grand Slam titles

were: the Australian Open (1982, 1984), the French Open (1974–5, 1979–80, 1983, 1985–6), the All-England Championship at Wimbledon (1974, 1976, 1981) and the US Open (1975–78, 1980, 1982).

**Faldo, Nick (Nicholas Alexander)** (1957– ) English golfer, born Welwyn Garden City, Hertfordshire. Early in career won the Professional Golfers' Association (PGA) championships (1978, 1980–1). Reworked swing and then won the Open championship (1987, 1990, 1996) and the Masters (1989, 1990, 1996). Ryder Cup team member since 1977.

**Fangio, Juan Manuel** (1911–95) Argentine racing driver, born Balcarce. World champion 1951, 1954–7. His record of 24 Grand Prix wins was broken by **Jim Clark**.

**Fischer, Bobby (Robert James)** (1943– ) US chess player, born Chicago. Winner of both US junior and senior chess titles aged 14; later world champion (1972–5). He won the title from Boris Spassky in 1972, but was stripped of it in 1975 for failing to agree conditions to defend it against **Anatoliy Karpov**. He achieved the highest results rating (Elo 2 785) in the history of chess.

**Fitzpatrick, Sean (Brian Thomas)** (1963– ) New Zealand rugby union player, born Auckland. New Zealand's most capped player, and the world's most capped hooker. Holds world record of 63 consecutive caps (1986–95). Captained New Zealand from 1992 and played 33 caps as captain (1992–5).

**Gavaskar, Sunil Manohar**, nicknamed **the Little Master** (1949– ) Indian cricketer, born Bombay. One of the most prolific run-scorers in Test cricket history. Played for India in 125 Test matches from 1971 to 1997, scoring 10 122 runs, including 34 test centuries. He was the first player to score more than 10 000 Test runs. The perfection of his style as well as his short stature earned him his nickname.

**Girardelli, Marc** (1963– ) Luxembourg skier, born Laustenau, Austria. Winner of overall World Cup title more times than any other skier; also 11 world championship medals (four gold, four silver, three bronze) and two Olympic silver medals.

**Gooch, Graham** (1953– ) English cricketer, born Leytonstone, London. Made debut for Essex 1973, first capped for England 1975; has played in over 100 Test matches, recording sixth-highest score of 333 runs (against India, 1990). Captained England 34 times, but resigned July 1993. Has scored over 100 centuries, and overtook David Gower (Aug 1993) to become England's highest-scoring Test player with career total of 8 293 runs.

**Grace, W(illiam) G(ilbert)** (1848–1915) English cricketer, born Downend, near Bristol. Made first-class debut with Gloucestershire aged 16 (1864) and remained in first-class cricket until 1908, making 126 centuries, scoring 54 896 runs and taking 2 864 wickets, becoming a national hero. He scored 2 739 runs in a season in 1871, 344 runs in an innings in 1876 for MCC, and 100 first-class centuries by 1895.

**Graf, Steffi** (1969– ) German tennis player, born Bruehl. In 1988 she won a Golden Grand Slam — the US, French, Australian and Wimbledon singles titles — as well as the gold medal at the Seoul Olympics. Singles wins include the French Open (1987–8, 1993, 1995–6, 1999), the Australian Open (1988–90, 1994), the US Open (1988–9, 1993, 1995–6) and the All-England championship at Wimbledon (1988–9, 1991–3, 1995–6).

**Green, Lucinda**, née **Prior-Palmer** (1953– ) English three-day eventer, born London. She won the Badminton Horse Trials a record six times (1973, 1976–7, 1979, 1983–4) and the Burghley Horse Trials twice (1977, 1981). In the European championships she won an individual gold medal (1975, 1977), a team gold (1977, 1985, 1987), and an individual and team silver (1983). In 1982 she was world champion and won another team gold.

**Gretzky, Wayne** (1961– ) Canadian ice-hockey player, born Brantford, Ontario. Played for the Edmonton Oilers (1978–88), the Los Angeles Kings (1988–96), the St Louis Blues briefly and the New York Rangers (1996–9). His numerous records include the most goals scored in a season (92 in 1981–2) and most career points (he scored his 2 500th point in 1995 and retired with a total of 2 857). National Hockey League's Most Valuable Player nine times (1980–7, 1989).

**Griffith-Joyner, Florence**, known as **Flo-Jo** (1959–98) US track and field sprinter, born Los Angeles, California. Winner of National Collegiate Athletic Association 200m title (1982), an Olympic silver medal in the 200m (1984), and three Olympic gold medals (1988): for the 100m and 200m — setting world records of 10.54 seconds for the former and 21.34 seconds for the latter — and for the 4 × 400m relay; also recipient of 1988 Sullivan award as top amateur athlete in the USA and 1988 Associated Press Female Athlete of the Year award.

**Hagen, Walter Charles**, nicknamed **the Haig** (1892–1969) US golfer, born Rochester, New York State. First US-born winner and four-times winner of the British Open championship (1922, 1924, 1928–9); also won the US Open (1914, 1919), the US Professional Golfers' Association (PGA) a record five times (1921, 1924–7), and captained the first six US Ryder Cup teams (1927–37), which won in 1927, 1931, 1935 and 1937.

**Hastings, (Andrew) Gavin** (1962– ) Scottish rugby player, born Edinburgh. Made debut for Scotland 1986 and played full-back in the 1987, 1991 and 1995 World Cups, and in the team which won the Grand Slam in 1990; Scotland captain for the first time in 1992–3 season. He also played three times for the British Lions and captained the 1993 New Zealand tour.

**Hendry, Stephen** (1969– ) Scottish snooker player, born Edinburgh. Professional from age 16, became youngest-ever winner of a professional title at the Rothmans Grand Prix (1987). Gained several titles in

1989, including the British Open and, with Mike Hallett, the Fosters World Doubles. Winner of Embassy world championship (1990, 1992–6, 1999).

**Hinault, Bernard**, known as **Le Blaireau (the badger)** (1954– ) French cyclist, born Yffiniac. Winner of the Tour de France five times (1978–9, 1981–2, 1985). (Only Hinault, **Jacques Anquetil Miguel Indurain** and **Eddy Merckx** have won five times.) Won Tour of Italy three times and Tour of Spain twice.

**Holyfield, Evander** (1962– ) US boxer, born Alabama. Undisputed heavyweight world champion in 1990–2, 1993–4 and 1996–7.

**Hutton, Len (Sir Leonard)** (1916–90) English cricketer, born Fulneck, Yorkshire. Played for Yorkshire; made debut for England 1937, scoring a century in his first Test against Australia (1938), and in the Oval Test against Australia (also 1938) scored a world record of 364 runs, which stood for 20 years until it was exceeded by one run by **Gary Sobers**. He made 129 first-class centuries, and captained England in 23 Test matches after World War II.

**Indurain, Miguel** (1964– ) Spanish cyclist, born Villava, Navarre. He is the fourth cyclist to win five Tours de France (1991–5); see **Jacques Anquetil**, **Bernard Hinault** and **Eddy Merckx**.

**Johnson, Magic (Earvin)** (1959– ) US basketball player, born Lansing, Michigan. Played with the Los Angeles Lakers (1979–91 as a guard, 1996 as a forward), when they won five National Basketball Association (NBA) championships (1980, 1982, 1985, 1987–8), and in the 1992 gold medal-winning US Olympic basketball team ('Dream Team'). A member of the NBA All-Star team (1980, 1982–92), he was named NBA Most Valuable Player in 1987, 1989 and 1990.

**Johnson, Michael** (1967– ) US track athlete, born Dallas. He won world championship races in the 200m (1991, 1995) and in the 400m (1993, 1995, 1997, 1999), and at the 1996 Olympics in Atlanta won gold medals in both 200m and 400m events, the first man ever to do so; he also set a new world 200m record.

**Jones, Bobby (Robert Tyre)** (1902–71) US amateur golfer, born Atlanta, Georgia. He won the US Open four times (1923, 1926, 1929, 1930), the British Open three times (1926, 1927, 1930), the US Amateur championship five times and the British Amateur championship once. In 1930 he won the Grand Slam of the US and British Open and Amateur championships. Later he was responsible for the founding of the US Masters in Augusta.

**Jordan, Michael Jeffrey** (1963– ) US basketball player, born Brooklyn, New York City. Played for Chicago Bulls (1984–93, 1995–8), and set many records, including most consecutive seasons leading the league in scoring (1986–7 to 1992–3); also played in US Olympic gold medal-winning basketball teams (1984, 1992). As member of National Basketball Association (NBA) All-Star team (1985–93, 1996–8), was NBA Most Valuable Player in 1988, 1991, 1992, 1996 and 1998. Holds NBA highest career scoring average, 31.5 points per game.

**Kapil Dev, (Nihanj)** (1959– ) Indian cricketer, born Chandigarh, Punjab. Made first-class debut for Haryana aged 16, and played county cricket in England for Northamptonshire and Worcestershire. Led India to victory in the 1983 World Cup, and set a competition record score of 175 not out against Zimbabwe. In 1983 became youngest player (at 24 years 68 days) to perform a Test double of 2 000 runs and 200 wickets (surpassing **Ian Botham**). In Feb 1994 he set a then world record of 432 Test wickets, surpassing **Richard Hadlee**'s 431.

**Karpov, Anatoliy Yevgenevich** (1951– ) Soviet chess player, born Zlatoust, in the Urals. Became world champion by default in 1975 after **Bobby Fischer** refused to defend his title; defeated 1985 by **Garry Kasparov** , but won title back 1993. In 1994 he won FIDE (Fédération Internationale des Échecs) world championship, but lost his title to Alexander Khalifman in 1999.

**Kasparov, Garry Kimovich**, originally **Gary Weinstein** (1963– ) Soviet chess player, born Baku, Azerbaijan. He won the USSR under-18 championship aged 12 and became world junior champion at 16. He was world champion from 1985, when he defeated **Anatoliy Karpov**, until 1993, when Karpov won the title back. In 1994 he won the Professional Chess Association world championship, losing the title to Vladimir Kramnick in 2000.

**Khan, Jahangir** (1963– ) Pakistani squash player, born Karachi. Winner of three world amateur titles (1979, 1983, 1985), a record six World Open titles (1981–5, 1988), and nine consecutive British Open titles (1982–90). He was undefeated from Apr 1981 until the World Open final in Nov 1986.

**Killy, Jean-Claude** (1943– ) French ski racer, born St-Cloud. Winner of the downhill and combined gold medals at the world championship in Chile (1966), and of three gold medals for slalom, giant slalom and downhill at the Winter Olympics (1968).

**King, Billie Jean**, née **Moffitt** (1943– ) US tennis player, born Long Beach, California. She won the ladies doubles title at Wimbledon in 1961 (with Karen Hantze) at her first attempt, and between 1961 and 1979 won a record 20 Wimbledon titles, including the singles in 1966–8, 1972–3 and 1975, and four mixed doubles. She also won 13 US titles (including four singles in 1967, 1971–2, 1974), four French titles (one singles in 1972), and two Australian titles (one singles in 1968).

**Klammer, Franz** (1953– ) Austrian alpine skier, born Mooswald. Olympic downhill champion (1976), and World Cup downhill champion five times (1975–78, 1983). Between 1974 and 1984 he won a record 25 World Cup downhill races.

**Koch, Marita** (1957– ) German athlete, born Wismar. She won the Olympic 400m title in 1980 and the European title three times, remaining undefeated over 400m between 1977 and 1981. In the 200m race, she won three indoor European championship titles and

a World Student Games title. She set 16 world records, including the 400m seven times (which still stands) and the 200m four times.

**Korbut, Olga Valentinovna** (1956– ) Soviet gymnast, born Grodno, Belorussia. In the 1972 Olympic Games she won a gold medal as a member of the winning Soviet team, as well as individual golds in the beam and floor exercises and silver for the parallel bars.

**Leonard, Sugar Ray** (1956– ) US boxer, born South Carolina. In 1976 he won an Olympic gold, starting a professional career in which he fought 12 world title fights at various weights and won world titles in each weight. In 35 fights (1977–87) he was beaten once (by Roberto Duran, welterweight title 1980). He became undisputed world welterweight champion again in 1981.

**Lewis, Carl** (1961– ) US track and field athlete, born Birmingham, Alabama. He won four gold medals at the 1984 Olympics (100m, 200m, 4 × 100m relay and long jump), emulating **Jesse Owens**'s achievement of 1936. In 1988 he won an Olympic gold in the long jump and was awarded the 100m gold after Ben Johnson was stripped of the title. In 1992 he won two more Olympic golds in the long jump and the 4 × 100m relay, and in 1996 he earned his ninth and final Olympic gold medal in the long jump.

**Louis, Joe**, professional name of **Joseph Louis Barrow** (1914–81) US boxer, born Lexington, Alabama. He won the US amateur light-heavyweight title in 1934 and turned professional. He won the world championship in 1937, and held it for a record 12 years, defending his title 25 times. In all he won 68 of his 71 professional fights.

**McBride, Willie (William) John** (1940– ) Irish rugby player, born Toomebridge, County Antrim. He played mostly with the Ballymena team from 1962. A lock forward, he won 45 caps, made a record 17 appearances for the British Lions on five tours, and played for Ireland 63 times.

**McEnroe, John Patrick** (1959– ) US tennis player, born Wiesbaden, Germany. He won the Wimbledon singles title three times (1981, 1983–4), the US Open singles four times (1979–81, 1984), and eight Grand Slam doubles events, seven of them with Peter Fleming, and one at Wimbledon in 1992, with Michael Stich. He was Grand Prix winner in 1979 and 1984–5, and world championship winner in 1979, 1981 and 1983–4.

**Maradona, Diego** (1960– ) Argentine footballer, born Lanús. One of the best players of his generation, he won over 80 international caps. He played in the 1982 World Cup in Spain, and captained the Argentine side to World Cup victory in 1986. He played for Boca Juniors, Barcelona, then Naples (1984–91), leading them to their first-ever Italian championship (1987). After leaving Naples, he played for Seville, Argentina and Boca Juniors again.

**Marciano, Rocky**, originally **Rocco Francis Marchegiano** (1923–69) US boxer, born Brockton, Massachusetts. Made his name in 1951 by defeating former world champion **Joe Louis** and won world title from Jersey Joe Walcott in 1952; on retiring in 1956 he was undefeated as world champion with a professional record of 49 bouts and 49 victories.

**Matthews, Sir Stanley** (1915–2000) English footballer, born Hanley. Joined Stoke City as a winger 1931, made debut for England aged 20, and over 22 years won 54 international caps. He played for Blackpool (1947–61), winning a FA Cup winner's medal in 1953, then returned to Stoke (1961), playing First Division football until after the age of 50. He was Footballer of the Year twice (1948, 1963), and the inaugural winner of the European Footballer of the Year award (1956).

**Merckx, Eddy**, known as **the Cannibal** (1945– ) Belgian racing cyclist, born Woluwe St Pierre, near Brussels. In the 1969 Tour de France he won the major prize in all three sections — overall, points classification and King of the Mountains. He won the Tour de France five times (1969–72, 1974, now sharing the record with **Jacques Anquetil**, **Bernard Hinault** and **Miguel Indurain**); also won Tour of Italy five times, and all the major classics, including the Milan–San Remo race seven times. World professional road race champion three times, he won more races (445) and more classics than any other rider. Retired 1978.

**Montana, Joe** (1956– ) US American football player, born New Eagle, Pennsylvania. Played as quarterback with San Francisco 49ers (1979–93), then Kansas City Chiefs (1993–5). Member of victorious San Francisco 49ers Super Bowl teams in 1982, 1985, 1989, and 1990; Most Valuable Player in 1982, 1985 and 1990.

**Moore, Bobby (Robert)** (1941–93) English footballer, born Barking, Essex. With West Ham (1958–74) and later Fulham (1974–7), he played 1 000 matches at senior level, winning a FA Cup winner's medal in 1964 and a European Cup winner's medal in 1965. He was capped a record 108 times (107 in succession), 90 of them as captain. He played in the World Cup finals in Chile in 1962 and captained the victorious England side in the 1966 World Cup.

**Moser-Pröll, Annemarie**, née **Pröll** (1953– ) Austrian alpine skier, born Kleinarl. Winner of a women's record 62 World Cup races (1970–9), she was overall champion (1979), downhill champion (1978, 1979), Olympic downhill champion (1980), world combined champion (1972, 1978), and world downhill champion (1974, 1978, 1980). Retired 1980.

**Moses, Ed(win Corley)** (1955– ) US track athlete, born Dayton, Ohio. The greatest 400m hurdler ever, he was unbeaten from Aug 1977 to June 1987, was Olympic champion twice (1976, 1984) and four times world record holder. Missed 1980 Moscow Olympics due to US boycott.

**Navratilova, Martina** (1956– ) US tennis player, born Prague, Czechoslovakia (Czech Republic). In 1975 she defected to the USA and turned professional. She won a record nine singles titles at Wimbledon (1978–9, 1982–7, 1990) and the US Open four times

(1983–4, 1986–7). Her 100-plus tournament wins include two Golden Grand Slams. She retired from regular competitive singles play after reaching the Wimbledon final in 1994.

**Nicklaus, Jack**, known as **the Golden Bear** (1940– ) US golfer, born Columbus, Ohio. His first professional victory was the US Open (1962), which he also won 1967, 1972 and 1980. Of the other Majors, he won the Masters a record six times (1963, 1965–6, 1972, 1975, 1986); the Open championship three times (1966, 1970, 1978); and the US Professional Golfers' Association (PGA) a record-equalling five times (1963, 1971, 1973, 1975, 1980). His total of 20 Major victories (including two US Amateurs pre-1962) is also a record.

**Nurmi, Paavo Johannes**, known as **the Flying Finn** (1897–1973) Finnish athlete, born Turku. He won nine gold medals at three Olympic Games (1920, 1924, 1928). From 1922 to 1926 he set four world records at 3 000m, bringing the time down to 8 minutes 20.4 seconds. He also established world records at six miles (1921, 29:7.1), one mile (1923, 4:10.4) and two miles (1931, 8:59.5).

**Oerter, Al(fred)** (1936– ) US athlete and discus-thrower, born Astoria, New York State. An outstanding Olympic competitor, he won four consecutive gold medals for the discus, at Melbourne (1956), Rome (1960), Tokyo (1964) and Mexico (1968), breaking the Olympic record each time.

**Owens, Jesse James Cleveland** (1913–80) US athlete, born Danville, Alabama; considered the greatest sprinter of his generation. In 1935, while in Ohio State University team, he set three world records and equalled another, including the long jump (26ft 8¼in/8.13m), which lasted 25 years. In 1936 he won four Olympic gold medals (100m, 200m, long jump, and 4 × 100m relay).

**Palmer, Arnold** (1929– ) US golfer, born Youngstown, Pennsylvania. After a brilliant amateur career he turned professional 1955, but won only eight Majors: the US Amateur (1954), US Masters (1958, 1960, 1962, 1964), US Open (1960) and the Open championship (1961, 1962). He was twice captain of the American Ryder Cup team.

**Payton, Walter**, nicknamed **Sweetness** (1954–99) US American football player, born Columbia, Mississippi. He played with the Chicago Bears as a running back (1975–87), establishing a National Football League rushing record of 16 726 yards (15 294m), scoring 125 touchdowns, and winning the Super Bowl in 1986. In one game (1977) he rushed for a record 275 yards (251m).

**Pelé**, pseudonym of **Edson Arantes do Nascimento** (1940– ) Brazilian footballer, born Três Corações, Minas Gerais. He made his international debut for Brazil aged 16, played in four World Cup competitions (1958–70), and led Brazil to victory in 1958, 1962 and 1970. For most of his senior career he played for Santos. Regarded as one of the finest inside-forwards in football history, he attained 1 000 goals in first-class football (Nov 1969); his career total was 1 281 in 1 363 games.

**Perry, Fred(erick John)** (1909–95) English tennis player, born Stockport, Cheshire. World singles table tennis champion in 1929, he took up lawn tennis aged 19. He won the Wimbledon singles three times (1934–6), the US Open singles three times (1933–4, 1936), and the Australian (1934) and French (1935) championships, and helped to keep the Davis Cup in Great Britain for four years (1933–6). He was the first man to win all four major titles.

**Piggott, Lester Keith** (1935– ) English jockey, born Wantage. Rode his first winner in 1948, was champion jockey in England on 11 occasions, and in all rode 30 Classic winners, including the Derby nine times. Retired 1995.

**Player, Gary** (1935– ) South African golfer, born Johannesburg. He won the British Open three times (1959, 1968, 1974), the US Masters three times (1961, 1974, 1978), the US Open once (1965), and the US Professional Golfers' Association (PGA) title twice (1962, 1972). He also won the South African Open 13 times, and the Australian Open seven times.

**Prost, Alain** (1955– ) French racing driver, born St Chamond. Won his first Grand Prix in 1981, was world champion four times (1985, 1986, 1989 and 1993), and Runner-Up four times (1983, 1984, 1988, 1990). Surpassed **Jackie Stewart**'s record of 27 Grand Prix wins in 1987, becoming the most successful driver in the history of the sport. Retired 1994.

**Redgrave, Steve (Sir Steven Geoffrey)** (1962– ) English oarsman and sculler, born Marlow, Oxfordshire. He has won five successive Olympic gold medals (coxed four 1984, coxless pairs 1988, 1992, 1996, coxless four 2000). Nine times world champion, he also won a record three gold medals in the 1986 Commonwealth Games. Together he and Matthew Pinsent (1970– ) have been world coxless pairs champions (1991, 1992, 1994, 1995), world coxless four champions (1997, 1998, 1999), and Olympic champions (1992, 1996, 2000).

**Ruth, Babe**, properly **George Herman Ruth** (1895–1948) US baseball player, born Baltimore. Started career as a left-handed pitcher with the Boston Red Sox (1914–19), and became famous for his powerful hitting with the New York Yankees (1920–34); also played for Boston Braves (1935). Considered the greatest all-rounder in baseball history, he scored a record 60 home runs in 1927. In all he played in 10 World Series, and hit 714 home runs, a record that stood unsurpassed until **Hank Aaron** broke it in 1974.

**Sampras, Pete** (1971– ) US tennis player, born Wash-ington DC. Four times winner of the US Open singles title (1990, 1993, 1995–96) and seven times winner of All-England singles title at Wimbledon (1993–95, 1997–2000).

**Sella, Philippe** (1962– ) French rugby union player, born Clairac. First capped aged 20, he succeeded Serge Blanco in 1993–4 as the most capped international player of all time with a record

111 caps. During the period 1982–95 he scored 30 international test tries and was France's most capped centre. In 1995 he joined English rugby club Saracens.

**Shoemaker, Willie (William Lee)** (1931– ) US jockey, born Fabens, Texas. In the USA his major successes included four Kentucky Derbies, five Belmont Stakes, and two Preakness event wins at Baltimore; later, he was successful in Europe too. In 1953 he rode a record 485 winners in a season. The first jockey to saddle more than 8 000 winners, he was one of the most successful in racing history and retired in 1990 with 8 833 wins.

**Smetanina, Raisa Petrovna** (1952– ) Soviet cross-country skier, born Mokhcha. She won 23 medals between 1974 and 1992, including a record 10 Olympic skiing medals: four gold, five silver and one bronze.

**Sobers, Gary**, properly **Sir Garfield St Auburn Sobers** (1936– ) West Indian cricketer, born Bridgetown, Barbados. In 93 Test matches for the West Indies (captain 1965–74), he scored more than 8 000 runs (including 26 centuries), and took 235 wickets and 110 catches. In county cricket he played for Nottinghamshire (captain 1968–74), and in 1968 scored the maximum of 36 runs (six sixes) off one over against Glamorgan at Swansea, a feat equalled by Ravi Shastri in the 1984–5 season.

**Spitz, Mark (Andrew)** (1950– ) US swimmer, born Modesto, California. Winner of seven gold medals at the 1972 Olympics, achieving a world record time in each event, and of two golds in the 1968 Games. He set 26 world records between 1967 and 1972.

**Stenmark, Ingemar** (1956– ) Swedish champion skier, born Tärnaby. In the 1974–5 World Cup he won the slalom and was second overall; he then won the World Cup (1976–8) and became the most successful competitor ever in slalom and grand slalom. He was World Master in 1978 and 1982 and won the Olympic gold medal at Lake Placid in 1980. The first man to win three consecutive slalom titles (1980–2), he won a record 86 World Cup races between 1974 and 1989, when he retired.

**Stewart, Jackie (John Young)** (1939– ) Scottish racing driver, born Dunbartonshire. World champion in 1969, 1971 and 1973, he won the Dutch, German and US Grand Prix in 1986.

**Thompson, Daley (Frances Morgan)** (1958– ) English athlete, born London. He won Olympic gold medals for decathlon (1980, 1984) and won the world championship (1983), also breaking the world record four times between 1980 and 1984. Retired 1992.

**Tyson, Mike (Michael Gerald)** (1966– ) US boxer, born New York City. Professional from 1985, he knocked out 15 of his first 25 opponents in the first round. In 1986 he beat Trevor Berbick in the World Boxing Council (WBC) world heavyweight contest, becoming the youngest heavyweight champion (20 yrs 145 days). In 1987 he defeated James Smith to gain the World Boxing Association title, and then beat Tony Tucker to become world champion. He held the title until defeated by James 'Buster' Douglas in Feb 1990. In 1996 he beat Frank Bruno to reclaim the WBC title, but later gave it up, and in 1997 was disqualified in his WBA world heavyweight fight against Evander Holyfield for biting his opponent's ear.

**Underwood, Rory** (1963– ) English rugby union player, born Middlesbrough. England's most-capped player, and most-capped wing, with 85 caps from 1985 to 1996. His 49 tries in 85 matches is also a record. Toured Australia (1989) and New Zealand (1993) with the British Lions. At club level he has represented Middlesbrough, Durham, Leicester, Newcastle and Bedford.

**Watson, Tom (Thomas Sturges)** (1949– ) US golfer, born Kansas City, Missouri. Through the mid-1970s and early 1980s he and **Jack Nicklaus** dominated world golf; Watson won the US Open, two Masters tournaments and five British Opens. He was the US Player of the Year six times and in 1993 captained the US Ryder Cup team to victory.

**Zatopek, Emil** (1922–2000) Czech athlete and middle-distance runner, born Moravia, Czechoslovakia (Czech Republic). He won an Olympic gold medal for the 10 000m in the 1948 Olympics and over the next six years broke 13 world records. In the 1952 Olympics he achieved a remarkable golden treble: he retained his gold medal in the 10 000m, and also won the 5 000m and the marathon.

**Zurbriggen, Pirmin** (1963– ) Swiss skier, born Saas Almagell. Winner of a record number of victories in the downhill during the 1980s, and a total of 39 World Cup victories. Only **Marc Girardelli** has beaten his four overall world champion titles. In the 1987 World Cup at Crans-Montana he won two gold medals (giant slalom and super G) and two silver medals (downhill and combined) within five days, and in the 1988 Winter Olympics he won a gold in the downhill and a bronze in the giant slalom.

# Champions 1987–2001

Some early 2002 results are listed where available. For 1992 Summer Olympic events the designation (UT) is given for members of the Unified Team (Armenia, Azerbaijan, Belarus, Georgia, Kazakhstan, Kyrgyzstan, Moldova, Russia, Tajikistan, Turkmenistan, Ukraine and Uzbekistan).

## Angling

### ❑ World Fresh Water Championship

First held in 1957; takes place annually.

*Individual*

| | |
|---|---|
| 1987 | Clive Branson (Wales) |
| 1988 | Jean-Pierre Fouquet (France) |
| 1989 | Tom Pickering (England) |
| 1990 | Bob Nudd (England) |
| 1991 | Bob Nudd (England) |
| 1992 | David Wesson (Australia) |
| 1993 | Mario Barras (Portugal) |
| 1994 | Bob Nudd (England) |
| 1995 | Pierre Jean (France) |
| 1996 | Alan Scotthorne (England) |
| 1997 | Alan Scotthorne (England) |
| 1998 | Alan Scotthorne (England) |
| 1999 | Bob Nudd (England) |
| 2000 | Jacob Falsini (Italy) |
| 2001 | Umberto Ballabeni (Italy) |

*Team*

| | |
|---|---|
| 1987 | England |
| 1988 | England |
| 1989 | Wales |
| 1990 | France |
| 1991 | England |
| 1992 | Italy |
| 1993 | Italy |
| 1994 | England |
| 1995 | France |
| 1996 | Italy |
| 1997 | Italy |
| 1998 | England |
| 1999 | Spain |
| 2000 | Italy |
| 2001 | England |

*Most wins*: Individual (4) Bob Nudd (England), as above. Team (13), France 1959, 1963–4, 1966, 1968, 1972, 1974–5, 1978–9, 1981, 1990, 1995.

### ❑ World Fly Fishing Championship

First held in 1981; takes place annually.

*Individual*

| | |
|---|---|
| 1987 | Brian Leadbetter (England) |
| 1988 | John Pawson (England) |
| 1989 | Wladyslaw Trzebuinia (Poland) |
| 1990 | Franciszek Szajnik (Poland) |
| 1991 | Brian Leadbetter (England) |
| 1992 | Pierluigi Cocito (Italy) |
| 1993 | Russell Owen (Wales) |
| 1994 | Pascal Cognard (France) |
| 1995 | Jeremy Herrmann (England) |
| 1996 | Pierluigi Cocito (Italy) |
| 1997 | Pascal Cognard (France) |
| 1998 | Tomas Starychfojtu (Czech Republic) |
| 1999 | Ross Stewart (Australia) |
| 2000 | Pascal Cognard (France) |
| 2001 | Vladimir Sedivy (Czech Republic) |

*Team*

| | |
|---|---|
| 1987 | England |
| 1988 | England |
| 1989 | Poland |
| 1990 | Czechoslovakia |
| 1991 | New Zealand |
| 1992 | Italy |
| 1993 | England |
| 1994 | Czech Republic |
| 1995 | England |
| 1996 | Czech Republic |
| 1997 | France |
| 1998 | Czech Republic |
| 1999 | Australia |
| 2000 | France |
| 2001 | France |

*Most wins*: Individual (3), Pascal Cognard (France), as above. Team (5), Italy 1982–4, 1986, 1992.

## Archery

### ❑ World Championships

First held in 1931; took place annually until 1959; since then, every two years.

*Individual (Men)*

| | |
|---|---|
| 1987 | Vladimir Yesheyev (USSR) |
| 1989 | Stanislav Zabrodsky (USSR) |
| 1991 | Simon Fairweather (Australia) |
| 1993 | Kyung-Mo Park (South Korea) |
| 1995 | Kyung-Chul Lee (South Korea) |
| 1997 | Kim Kyung-Ho (South Korea) |
| 1999 | Hong Sung-Chil (South Korea) |
| 2001 | Jung Ki Yeon (South Korea) |

*Team (Men)*

| | |
|---|---|
| 1987 | South Korea |
| 1989 | USSR |
| 1991 | South Korea |
| 1993 | France |
| 1995 | South Korea |
| 1997 | South Korea |
| 1999 | Italy |
| 2001 | South Korea |

*Most wins*: Individual (4), Hans Deutgen (Sweden) 1947–50. Team (13), USA 1957, 1959–83.

*Individual (Women)*

| | |
|---|---|
| 1987 | Ma Xiaojun (China) |
| 1989 | Kim Soo-Nyung (South Korea) |
| 1991 | Kim Soo-Nyung (South Korea) |
| 1993 | Kim Hyo-Jung (South Korea) |
| 1995 | Natalia Valeyeva (Moldova) |
| 1997 | Kim Du-Ri (South Korea) |
| 1999 | Lee Eun-Kyung (South Korea) |
| 2001 | Sung Hyun Park (South Korea) |

*Team (Women)*

| | |
|---|---|
| 1987 | USSR |
| 1989 | South Korea |
| 1991 | South Korea |
| 1993 | South Korea |
| 1995 | South Korea |
| 1997 | South Korea |
| 1999 | Italy |
| 2001 | China |

*Most wins*: Individual (7), Janina Kurkowska (Poland) 1931–4, 1936, 1939, 1947. Team (8), USA 1952, 1957–9, 1961, 1963, 1965, 1977.

## Athletics

### ❑ World Championships

First held in Helsinki, Finland in 1983, then in Rome, Italy in 1987; since 1995 every two years.

| *Event (Men)* | *Winners* |
|---|---|
| **1995** | |
| 100m | Donovan Bailey (Canada) |
| 200m | Michael Johnson (USA) |
| 400m | Michael Johnson (USA) |
| 800m | Wilson Kipketer (Denmark) |
| 1 500m | Noureddine Morceli (Algeria) |
| 5 000m | Ismael Kirui (Kenya) |
| 10 000m | Haile Gebrselassie (Ethiopia) |
| Marathon | Martin Fiz (Spain) |
| 3 000m steeplechase | Moses Kiptanui (Kenya) |
| 110m hurdles | Allen Johnson (USA) |
| 400m hurdles | Derrick Adkins (USA) |
| 20km walk | Michele Didoni (Italy) |
| 50km walk | Valentin Kononen (Finland) |
| 4 × 100m relay | Canada |
| 4 × 400m relay | USA |
| High jump | Troy Kemp (Bahamas) |
| Long jump | Ivan Pedroso (Cuba) |
| Triple jump | Jonathan Edwards (Great Britain) |
| Pole vault | Sergei Bubka (Ukraine) |
| Shot | John Godina (USA) |
| Discus | Lars Riedel (Germany) |
| Hammer | Andrei Abduvaliyev (Tajikistan) |
| Javelin | Jan Zelezny (Czech Republic) |
| Decathlon | Dan O'Brien (USA) |
| **1997** | |
| 100m | Maurice Greene (USA) |
| 200m | Ato Boldon (Trinidad) |
| 400m | Michael Johnson (USA) |
| 800m | Wilson Kipketer (Denmark) |
| 1 500m | Hicham El Guerrouj (Morocco) |
| 5 000m | Daniel Komen (Kenya) |
| 10 000m | Haile Gebrselassie (Ethiopia) |
| Marathon | Abel Anton (Spain) |
| 3 000m steeplechase | Wilson Kipketer (Denmark) |
| 110m hurdles | Allen Johnson (USA) |
| 400m hurdles | Stephane Diagana (France) |
| 20km walk | Daniel Garcia (Mexico) |
| 50km walk | Robert Korzeniowski (Poland) |
| 4 × 100m relay | Canada |
| 4 × 400m relay | USA |
| High jump | Javier Sotomayor (Cuba) |
| Long jump | Ivan Pedroso (Cuba) |
| Triple jump | Yoelvis Quesada (Cuba) |
| Pole vault | Sergei Bubka (Ukraine) |
| Shot | Aleksandr Bagach [1] (Ukraine) |
| Discus | Lars Riedel (Germany) |
| Hammer | Heinz Weis (Germany) |
| Javelin | Marius Corbett (South Africa) |
| Decathlon | Dan O'Brien (USA) |
| **1999** | |
| 100m | Maurice Greene (USA) |
| 200m | Maurice Greene (USA) |
| 400m | Michael Johnson (USA) |
| 800m | Wilson Kipketer (Denmark) |
| 1 500m | Hicham El Guerrouj (Morocco) |
| 5 000m | Salah Hissou (Morocco) |
| 10 000m | Haile Gebreselassie (Ethiopia) |
| Marathon | Abel Antón (Spain) |
| 3 000m steeplechase | Christopher Koskei (Kenya) |
| 110m hurdles | Colin Jackson (Great Britain) |
| 400m hurdles | Fabrizio Mori (Italy) |
| 20km walk | Ilya Markov (Russia) |
| 50km walk | German Skurygin (Russia) |
| 4 × 100m relay | USA |
| 4 × 400m relay | USA |
| Long jump | Ivan Pedroso (Cuba) |
| High jump | Vyacheslav Voronin (Russia) |
| Triple jump | Charles Michael Friedek (Germany) |
| Pole vault | Maksim Tarasov (Russia) |
| Shot | C J Hunter (USA) |
| Discus | Anthony Washington (USA) |
| Hammer | Karsten Kobs (Germany) |
| Javelin | Aki Parviainen (Finland) |
| Decathlon | Tomás Dvorák (Czech Republic) |
| **2001** | |
| 100m | Maurice Greene (USA) |
| 200m | Konstantinos Kederis (Greece) |
| 400m | Avard Moncur (Bahamas) |
| 800m | André Bucher (Switzerland) |
| 1 500m | Hicham El Guerrouj (Morocco) |
| 5 000m | Richard Limo (Kenya) |
| 10 000m | Charles Kamathi (Kenya) |
| Marathon | Gezahegne Abera (Ethiopia) |
| 3 000m steeple chase | Reuben Kosgei (Kenya) |
| 110m hurdles | Allen Johnson (USA) |
| 400m hurdles | Felix Sanchez (Dominican Republic) |
| 20km walk | Roman Rasskazov (Russia) |

| | |
|---|---|
| 50km walk | Robert Korzeniowski (Poland) |
| 4 × 100m relay | USA |
| 4 × 400m relay | Jamaica |
| High jump | Buss Martin (Germany) |
| Long jump | Ivan Pedroso (Cuba) |
| Triple jump | Jonathan Edwards (Great Britain) |
| Pole vault | Dmitry Markov (Russia) |
| Shot | John Godina (USA) |
| Discus | Lars Riedel (Germany) |
| Hammer | Szymon Ziólkowski (Poland) |
| Javelin | Jan Zelezný (Czech Republic) |
| Decathlon | Tomás Dvorák (Czech Republic) |

[1] Stripped of gold medal following positive drugs test; medal awarded to John Godina (USA).

| *Event (Women)* | *Winners* |
|---|---|
| **1995** | |
| 100m | Gwen Torrence (USA) |
| 200m | Merlene Ottey (Jamaica) |
| 400m | Marie-José Pérec (France) |
| 800m | Ann Quirot (Cuba) |
| 1 500m | Hassiba Boulmerka (Algeria) |
| 5 000m | Sonia O'Sullivan (Ireland) |
| 10 000m | Fernanda Ribeiro (Portugal) |
| Marathon | Manuela Machado (Portugal) |
| 100m hurdles | Gail Devers (USA) |
| 400m hurdles | Kim Batten (USA) |
| 10km walk | Irina Stankina (Russia) |
| 4 × 100m relay | USA |
| 4 × 400m relay | USA |
| High jump | Stefka Kostadinova (Bulgaria) |
| Long jump | Fiona May (Italy) |
| Shot | Astrid Kumbernuss (Germany) |
| Discus | Ellina Zvereva (Belarus) |
| Javelin | Natalya Shikolenko (Belarus) |
| Heptathlon | Natalya Shikolenko (Belarus) |
| **1997** | |
| 100m | Marion Jones (USA) |
| 200m | Zhanna Pintussevich (Ukraine) |
| 400m | Cathy Freeman (Australia) |
| 800m | Ana Fidelia Quirot (Cuba) |
| 1 500m | Carla Sacramento (Portugal) |
| 5 000m | Gabriela Szabo (Romania) |
| 10 000m | Sally Barsosio (Kenya) |
| Marathon | Hiromi Suzuki (Japan) |
| 100m hurdles | Ludmila Engquist (Sweden) |
| 400m hurdles | Nezha Bidouane (Morocco) |
| 10km walk | Annarita Sidoti (Italy) |
| 4 × 100m relay | USA |
| 4 × 400m relay | Germany |
| High jump | Hanne Haugland (Norway) |
| Long jump | Lyudmila Galkina (Russia) |
| Triple jump | Sarka Kasparkova (Czech Republic) |
| Shot put | Astrid Kumbernuss (Germany) |
| Discus | Beatrice Faumuina (New Zealand) |
| Javelin | Trine Hattestad (Norway) |
| Heptathlon | Sabina Braun (Germany) |
| **1999** | |
| 100m | Marion Jones (USA) |
| 200m | Inger Miller (USA) |
| 400m | Cathy Freeman (Australia) |
| 800m | Ludmilla Formanova (Czech Republic) |
| 1 500m | Svetlana Masterkova (Russia) |
| 5 000m | Gabriela Szabo (Romania) |
| 10 000m | Gete Wami (Ethiopia) |
| Marathon | Jong Song-Ok (North Korea) |
| 100m hurdles | Gail Devers (USA) |
| 400m hurdles | Daimi Pernia (Cuba) |
| 20km walk | Liu Hongyu (China) |
| 4 × 100m relay | Bahamas |
| 4 × 400m relay | Russia |
| High jump | Inga Babakova (Ukraine) |
| Long jump | Niurka Montalvo (Spain) |
| Triple jump | Paraskevi Tsiamita (Greece) |
| Pole vault | Stacy Draglia (USA) |
| Shot | Astrid Kumbernuss (Germany) |
| Discus | Franka Dietzsch (Germany) |
| Hammer | Michaela Melinte (Romania) |
| Javelin | Mirela Manjani-Tzelili (Greece) |
| Heptathlon | Eunice Barber (France) |
| **2001** | |
| 100m | Zhanna Pintusevich-Block (Ukraine) |
| 200m | Marion Jones (USA) |
| 400m | Amy Mbacke Thiam (Senegal) |
| 800m | Maria Mutola (Mozambique) |
| 1 500m | Gabriela Szabo (Romania) |
| 5 000m | Olga Yegorova (Russia) |
| 10 000m | Derartu Tulu (Ethiopia) |
| Marathon | Lidia Simon (Romania) |
| 100m hurdles | Anjanette Kirkland (USA) |
| 400m hurdles | Nezha Bidouane (Morocco) |
| 20km walk | Olimpiada Ivanova (Russia) |
| 4 × 100m relay | USA |
| 4 × 400m relay | USA |
| High jump | Hestrie Cloete (South Africa) |
| Triple jump | Tatyana Lebedeva (Russia) |
| Long jump | Fiona May (Italy) |
| Shot | Yanina Korolchik (Belarus) |
| Discus | Natalya Sadova (Russia) |
| Javelin | Osleidys Menéndez (Cuba) |
| Pole vault | Stacy Dragila (USA) |
| Hammer | Yipsi Moreno (Cuba) |
| Heptathlon | Yelena Prokhorova (Russia) |

## Badminton

### ❑ World Championships

First held in 1977; initially took place every three years; since 1983 every two years.

*Men*

| | |
|---|---|
| 1987 | Yang Yang (China) |
| 1989 | Yang Yang (China) |
| 1991 | Zhao Jianhua (China) |
| 1993 | Joko Suprianto (Indonesia) |
| 1995 | Heryanto Arbi (Indonesia) |
| 1997 | Peter Rasmussen (Denmark) |
| 1999 | Sun Jun (China) |
| 2001 | Hendrawan (Indonesia) |

*Women*

1987 Han Aiping (China)
1989 Li Lingwei (China)
1991 Tang Jiuhong (China)
1993 Susi Susanti (Indonesia)
1995 Ye Zhaoying (China)
1997 Ye Zhaoying (China)
1999 Camilla Martin (Denmark)
2001 Gong Ruina (China)

*Most titles*: (3), Han Aiping (China) singles 1985–7, women's doubles 1985

### ❑ Thomas Cup

An international team event for men's teams; inaugurated 1949, now held every two years.

1988 China
1990 China
1992 Malaysia
1994 Indonesia
1996 Indonesia
1998 Indonesia
2000 Indonesia

*Most wins*: (12) Indonesia 1958–61, 1964, 1970–9, 1984, 1994–2000.

### ❑ Uber Cup

An international event for women's teams; first held in 1957; now held every two years.

1988 China
1990 China
1992 China
1994 Indonesia
1996 Indonesia
1998 China
2000 China

*Most wins*: (7), China 1984–92, 1998–2000.

### ❑ All-England Championship

Badminton's premier event prior to the inauguration of the World Championships; first held in 1899.

*Men*

1987 Morten Frost (Denmark)
1988 Ib Frederikson (Denmark)
1989 Yang Yang (China)
1990 Zhao Jianhua (China)
1991 Ardi Wiranata (Indonesia)
1992 Liu Jun (China)
1993 Heryanto Arbi (Indonesia)
1994 Heryanto Arbi (Indonesia)
1995 Poul-Erik Hoyer-Larsen (Denmark)
1996 Poul-Erik Hoyer-Larsen (Denmark)
1997 Dong Jiong (China)
1998 Sun Jun (China)
1999 Peter Gade Christensen (Denmark)
2000 Xia Xuanze (China)
2001 Pulella Gopichand (India)

*Women*

1987 Kirsten Larsen (Denmark)
1988 Gu Jiaming (China)
1989 Li Lingwei (China)
1990 Susi Susanti (Indonesia)
1991 Susi Susanti (Indonesia)
1992 Tang Jiuhong (China)
1993 Susi Susanti (Indonesia)
1994 Susi Susanti (Indonesia)
1995 Lim Xiao Qing (Sweden)
1996 Bang Soo Hyun (South Korea)
1997 Ye Zhaoying (China)
1998 Ye Zhaoying (China)
1999 Ye Zhaoying (China)
2000 Zichao Gong (China)
2001 Zichao Gong (China)

*Most titles*: (21: 4 singles, 9 men's doubles, 8 mixed doubles), George Thomas (England) 1903–28.

## Baseball

### ❑ World Series

First held in 1903; takes place each October, the best of seven matches; professional baseball's leading event, the end-of-season meeting between the winners of the two major baseball leagues in the USA, the National League (NL) and American League (AL).

1987 Minnesota Twins (AL)
1988 Los Angeles Dodgers (NL)
1989 Oakland Athletics (AL)
1990 Cincinatti Reds (NL)
1991 Minnesota Twins (AL)
1992 Toronto Blue Jays (AL)
1993 Toronto Blue Jays (AL)
1994 *not held*
1995 Atlanta Braves (NL)
1996 New York Yankees (AL)
1997 Florida Marlins (NL)
1998 New York Yankees (AL)
1999 New York Yankees (AL)
2000 New York Yankees (AL)
2001 Arizona Diamondbacks (NL)

*Most wins*: (26), New York Yankees 1923, 1927–8, 1932, 1936–9, 1941, 1943, 1947, 1949–53, 1956, 1958, 1961–2, 1977–8, 1996, 1998–2000.

### ❑ World Amateur Championship

Instituted in 1938; since 1990 held every four years.

1988 Cuba
1990 Cuba
1994 Cuba
1998 Cuba

*Most wins*: (22), Cuba 1939–40, 1942–3, 1950, 1952–3, 1961, 1969–73, 1976–80, 1984–6, 1988–98.

## Basketball

### ❑ World Championship

First held 1950 for men, 1953 for women; takes place approximately every four years.

*Men*

1990 Yugoslavia
1994 USA
1998 Yugoslavia

*Most wins*: (4), Yugoslavia 1970, 1978, 1990, 1998.

*Women*

1987 USA
1991 USA
1994 Brazil
1998 USA

*Most wins*: (6), USSR 1959, 1964, 1967, 1971, 1975, 1983.

### ❑ National Basketball Association Championship

First held in 1947; the major competition in professional basketball in the USA, end-of-season NBA Play-off involving the champion teams from the Eastern (EC) Conference and Western Conference (WC).

1987 Los Angeles Lakers (WC)
1988 Los Angeles Lakers (WC)
1989 Detroit Pistons (EC)
1990 Detroit Pistons (EC)
1991 Chicago Bulls (EC)
1992 Chicago Bulls (EC)
1993 Chicago Bulls (EC)
1994 Houston Rockets (WC)
1995 Houston Rockets (WC)
1996 Chicago Bulls (EC)
1997 Chicago Bulls (EC)
1998 Chicago Bulls (EC)
1999 San Antonio Spurs (WC)
2000 Los Angeles Lakers (WC)
2001 Los Angeles Lakers (WC)

*Most wins*: (16), Boston Celtics 1957, 1959–66, 1968–9, 1974, 1976, 1981, 1984, 1986.

## Biathlon

### ❑ World Championships

First held in 1958; take place annually; the Olympic champion is the automatic world champion in Olympic years; women's championship first held in 1984.

*Men*

*10km* )

1987 Frank-Peter Rötsch (East Germany)
1988 Frank-Peter Rötsch (East Germany)
1989 Frank Luck (East Germany)
1990 Mark Kirchner (East Germany)
1991 Mark Kirchner (Germany)
1992 Mark Kirchner (Germany)
1993 Mark Kirchner (Germany)
1994 Serguei Tchepikov (Russia)
1995 Patrice Bailly-Salins (France)
1996 Vladimir Dratchev (Russia)
1997 Wilfried Pallhuber (Italy)
1998 Ole Einar Bjoerndalen (Norway)
1999 Frank Luck (Germany)
2000 Frode Andresen (Norway)
2001 Paul Rostovtsev (Russia)

*20km*

1987 Frank-Peter Rötsch (East Germany)
1988 Frank-Peter Rötsch (East Germany)
1989 Eiric Kvalfoss (Norway)
1990 Valeriy Medvetsev (USSR)
1991 Mark Kirchner (Germany)
1992 Yevgeny Redkine (CIS)
1993 Franz Zingerle (Austria)
1994 Sergei Tarasov (Russia)
1995 Tomaz Sikora (Poland)
1996 Sergei Tarasov (Russia)
1997 Ricco Gross (Germany)
1998 Halvard Hanevold (Norway)
1999 Ricco Gross (Germany)
2000 Wolfgang Rottman (Austria)
2001 Paavo Puurunen (Finland)

*Most individual titles*: (6), Frank Ullrich (East Germany) 10km 1978–81, 20km 1982–3.

*Women*

*7.5km*

1987 Yelena Golovina (USSR)
1988 Petra Schaaf (West Germany)
1989 Anne-Elinor Elvebakk (Norway)
1990 Anne-Elinor Elvebakk (Norway)
1991 Ingeborg Nykelmo (Norway)
1992 Anfissa Restzova (CIS)
1993 Myriam Bedard (Canada)
1994 Myriam Bedard (Canada)
1995 Anne Briand (France)
1996 Olga Romansko (Russia)
1997 Olga Romansko (Russia)
1998 Galina Koukleva (Russia)
1999 Martina Zellner (Germany)
2000 Liv Grete Skjelbreid (Norway)
2001 Kati Wilhelm (Germany)

*15km*

1987 Sanna Gronlid (Norway)
1988 Anne-Elinor Elvebakk (Norway)
1989 Petra Schaaf (West Germany)
1990 Svetlana Davydova (USSR)
1991 Petra Schaaf (Germany)
1992 Antje Misersky (Germany)
1993 Petra Schaaf (Germany)
1994 Myriam Bedard (Canada)
1995 Corrine Miogret (France)
1996 Emmanuelle Claret (France)
1997 Magdalena Forsberg (Sweden)
1998 Yekaterina Dafovska (Bulgaria)
1999 Olena Zubrilova (Ukraine)
2000 Corinne Niogret (France)
2001 Magdalena Forsberg (Sweden)

*Most individual titles*: (4), Petra Schaaf (Germany), as above.

## Billiards

### ❑ World Professional Championship

First held in 1870, organized on a challenge basis; became a knockout event in 1909; discontinued in 1934; revived in 1951 as a challenge system; reverted to a knockout event in 1980.

1987 Norman Dagley (England)
1988 Norman Dagley (England)
1989 Mike Russell (England)
1990 *not held*

| | |
|---|---|
| 1991 | Mike Russell (England) |
| 1992 | Geet Sethi (India) |
| 1993 | Geet Sethi (India) |
| 1994 | Peter Gilchrist (England) |
| 1995 | Geet Sethi (India) |
| 1996 | Mike Russell (England) |
| 1997 | *not held* |
| 1998 | Geet Sethi (India) |
| 1999 | Mike Russell (England) |
| 2000 | Mike Russell (England) |
| 2001 | Peter Gilchrest (England) |

*Most wins*: (knockout) (6), Tom Newman (England) 1921–2, 1924–7; (challenge) (8), John Roberts, Jr (England) 1870–85.

## Bobsleighing and tobogganing

### ❑ World Championships

First held in 1930 (four-man) and in 1931 (two-man); Olympic champions automatically become world champions.

*Two-man*

1987 Ralf Pichler/Celest Poltera (Switzerland)
1988 Janis Kipurs/Vladimir Kozlov (USSR)
1989 Wolfgang Hoppe/Bogdan Musiol (East Germany)
1990 Gustav Weder/Bruno Gerber (Switzerland)
1991 Rudi Lochner/Markus Zimmermann (Germany)
1992 Gustav Weder/Donat Acklin (Switzerland)
1993 Christoph Langen/Peer Joechel (Germany)
1994 Gustav Weder/Donat Acklin (Switzerland)
1995 Christoph Langen/Olaf Hampel (Germany)
1996 Christoph Langen/Markus Zimmermann (Germany)
1997 Reto Goetschi/Guido Acklin (Switzerland)
1998 Guenther Huber/Antonio Tartaglia (Italy)
1999 Guenther Huber/Ubaldo Ranzi (Italy)
2000 Christoph Langen/Markus Zimmerman (Germany)
2001 Christoph Langan/Marco Jacobs (Germany)

*Four-man*

1987 Switzerland
1988 Switzerland
1989 Switzerland
1990 Switzerland
1991 Germany
1992 Austria
1993 Switzerland
1994 Germany
1995 Germany
1996 Germany
1997 Germany
1998 Germany
1999 France
2000 Germany
2001 Germany

*Most wins*: (Two-man) (8), Eugenio Monti (Italy) 1957–61, 1963, 1966, 1968. (Four-man) (16), Switzerland 1939, 1947, 1954–5, 1957, 1971, 1973, 1975, 1982–3, 1986–90, 1993.

### ❑ Luge World Championships

First held in 1955; annually until 1981, then every two years until 1989, then annually. Not held in Olympic years.

*Men's single-seater*

1987 Markus Prock (Austria)
1989 Georg Hackl (West Germany)
1990 Georg Hackl (West Germany)
1991 Arnold Huber (Italy)
1993 Werdel Suckow (USA)
1995 Armin Zoeggeler (Italy)
1996 Jana Bode (Germany)
1997 Georg Hackl (Germany)
1999 Armin Zoeggeler (Italy)
2000 Jens Müller (Germany)
2001 Armin Zoeggeler (Itlay)

*Most wins*: (3), Georg Hackl, as above; (3), Armin Zoeggeler, as above.

*Women's single-seater*

1987 Cerstin Schmidt (East Germany)
1988 Susi Erdmann (East Germany)
1989 Susi Erdmann (East Germany)
1990 Gabriele Kohlisch (East Germany)
1993 Gerda Weissensteiner (Italy)
1995 Gabriele Kohlisch (Germany)
1996 Susi Erdmann (Germany)
1997 Susi Erdmann (Germany)
1999 Sonja Wiedemann (Germany)
2000 Sylke Otto (Germany)
2001 Sylke Otto (Germany)

*Most wins*: (5), Margrit Schumann (East Germany) 1973–7.

## Bowls

### ❑ World Outdoor Championships

Instituted for men in 1966 and for women in 1969; held every four years.

*Men's Singles*

| | |
|---|---|
| 1988 | David Bryant (England) |
| 1992 | Tony Allcock (England) |
| 1996 | Tony Allcock (England) |
| 2000 | Jeremy Henry (Ireland) |

*Men's Pairs*

| | |
|---|---|
| 1988 | New Zealand |
| 1992 | Scotland |
| 1996 | Ireland |
| 2000 | Scotland |

*Men's Triples*

| | |
|---|---|
| 1988 | New Zealand |
| 1992 | Israel |
| 1996 | Scotland |
| 2000 | New Zealand |

*Men's Fours*

| | |
|---|---|
| 1988 | Ireland |
| 1992 | Scotland |
| 1996 | England |
| 2000 | Wales |

**❑ Leonard Trophy**

Team award, given to the nation with the best overall performances in the men's world championship.

| | |
|---|---|
| 1988 | England |
| 1992 | Scotland |
| 1996 | Scotland |
| 2000 | Australia |

*Most wins*: (5), David Bryant (Singles 1966, 1980, 1988. Team 1980, and Triples 1988).

*Women's Singles*

| | |
|---|---|
| 1988 [1] | Janet Ackland (Wales) |
| 1992 | Margaret Johnston (Ireland) |
| 1996 | Carmen Anderson (Norfolk Is) |
| 2000 | Margaret Johnston (Ireland) |

*Women's Pairs*

| | |
|---|---|
| 1988 [1] | Ireland |
| 1992 | Ireland |
| 1996 | Ireland |
| 2000 | Scotland |

*Women's Triples*

| | |
|---|---|
| 1988 [1] | Australia |
| 1992 | Scotland |
| 1996 | South Africa |
| 2000 | New Zealand |

*Women's Fours*

| | |
|---|---|
| 1988 [1] | Australia |
| 1992 | Scotland |
| 1996 | Australia |
| 2000 | New Zealand |

*Women's Team*

| | |
|---|---|
| 1988 [1] | England |
| 1992 | Scotland |
| 1996 | South Africa |
| 2000 | England |

*Most wins*: (3), Merle Richardson (Fours 1977; Singles and Pairs 1985).

[1] The women's event was advanced to Dec 1988 (Australia).

**❑ World Indoor Championships**

First held in 1979; take place annually.

*Men's singles*

| | |
|---|---|
| 1987 | Tony Allcock (England) |
| 1988 | Hugh Duff (Scotland) |
| 1989 | Richard Corsie (Scotland) |
| 1990 | John Price (Wales) |
| 1991 | Richard Corsie (Scotland) |
| 1992 | Ian Schuback (Australia) |
| 1993 | Richard Corsie (Scotland) |
| 1994 | Andy Thomson (England) |
| 1995 | Andy Thomson (England) |
| 1996 | David Gourlay, Jr (Scotland) |
| 1997 | Hugh Duff (Scotland) |
| 1998 | Paul Foster (Scotland) |
| 1999 | Alex Marshall (Scotland) |
| 2000 | Robert Weale (Wales) |
| 2001 | Darren Burnett (Scotland) |
| 2002 | Tony Allcock (England) |

*Most wins*: (3), David Bryant (England) 1979–81, Richard Corsie (Scotland), as above, Tony Allcock (England) 1986–7, 2002.

**❑ Waterloo Handicap**

First held in 1907 and annually at Blackpool's Waterloo Hotel; the premier event of Crown Green Bowling.

| | |
|---|---|
| 1987 | Brian Duncan |
| 1988 | Ingham Gregory |
| 1989 | Brian Duncan |
| 1990 | John Bancroft |
| 1991 | John Eccles |
| 1992 | Brian Duncan |
| 1993 | Alan Broadhurst |
| 1994 | Bill Hilton |
| 1995 | Ken Strutt |
| 1996 | Lee Heaton |
| 1997 | Andrew Cairns |
| 1998 | Michael Jagger |
| 1999 | Ivan Smout |
| 2000 | Carl Armitage |
| 2001 | Glynn Cookson |

*Most wins*: (5), Brian Duncan 1979, 1986–7, 1989, 1992.

## Boxing

**❑ World Heavyweight Champions**

The first world heavyweight champion under Queensbury Rules with gloves was James J Corbett in 1892.

| | | Recognizing Body |
|---|---|---|
| 1987 | Tony Tucker (USA) | IBF |
| 1987 | Mike Tyson (USA) | WBA/WBC |
| 1987 | Mike Tyson (USA) | UND |
| 1989 | Francesco Damiani (Italy) | WBO |
| 1990 | James (Buster) Douglas (USA) | WBA/WBC/IBF |
| 1990 | Evander Holyfield (USA) | WBA/WBC/IBF |
| 1991 | Ray Mercer (USA) | WBO |
| 1992 | Riddick Bowe (USA) [1] | WBA/WBC/IBF |
| 1992 | Michael Moorer (USA) | WBO |
| 1993 | Evander Holyfield (USA) | WBA/IBF |
| 1993 | Lennox Lewis (UK) | WBC |
| 1993 | Tommy Morrison (USA) | WBO |
| 1993 | Michael Bentt (USA) | WBO |
| 1994 | Herbie Hide (UK) | WBO |
| 1994 | Michael Moorer (USA) | WBA/IBF |
| 1994 | Oliver McCall (USA) | WBC |
| 1994 | George Foreman (USA) [2,3] | WBA/IBF |
| 1995 | Riddick Bowe (USA) | WBO |
| 1995 | Bruce Seldon (USA) | WBA |
| 1995 | Frank Bruno (UK) | WBC |
| 1995 | Frans Botha (South Africa) [4] | IBF |
| 1996 | Mike Tyson (USA) [5] | WBA/WBC |
| 1996 | Henry Akinwande (UK) | WBO |
| 1996 | Michael Moorer (USA) | IBF |
| 1996 | Evander Holyfield (USA) | WBA |
| 1997 | Evander Holyfield (USA) | WBA/IBF |
| 1997 | Lennox Lewis (UK) | WBC |
| 1997 | Herbie Hide (UK) | WBO |
| 1999 | Vitali Klitschko (Ukraine) | WBO |
| 1999 | Lennox Lewis (UK) [6] | UND (WBA/WBC/IBF) |
| 2000 | Chris Byrd (USA) | WBO |

| | |
|---|---|
| 2000 Evander Holyfield (USA) | WBA |
| 2000 Lennox Lewis (UK) | WBC, IBF |
| 2001 John Ruiz (USA) | WBA |
| 2001 Wladimir Klitschko (Ukraine) | WBO |
| 2001 Hasim Rahman (USA) | WBC, IBF |
| 2001 Lennox Lewis (UK) | WBC, IBF |
| 2001 John Ruiz (USA) | WBA |

[1] stripped of WBC title in 1992;

[2] gave up IBF title in 1995;

[3] stripped of WBA title in 1995;

[4] stripped of IBF title in 1996;

[5] gave up WBC title in 1996;

[6] stripped of WBA title in 2000;

UND = Undisputed Champion; WBC = World Boxing Council; WBA = World Boxing Association; IBF = International Boxing Federation; WBO = World Boxing Organization.

## Canoeing

### ❑ Olympic Games

The most prestigious competition in the canoeing calendar, included at every Olympic celebration since 1936; the Blue Riband event in the men's competition is the Kayak Singles over 1 000 metres, and in the women's the Kayak Singles over 500 metres.

*Single kayak (Men)*

| | |
|---|---|
| 1988 | Greg Barton (USA) |
| 1992 | Clint Robinson (Australia) |
| 1996 | Knut Holman (Norway) |
| 2000 | Knut Holman (Norway) |

*Single kayak (Women)*

| | |
|---|---|
| 1988 | Vania Guecheva (USSR) |
| 1992 | Birgit Schmidt (Germany) |
| 1996 | Rita Koban (Hungary) |
| 2000 | Josefa Guerrini (Italy) |

*Most wins*: Men (3), Gert Fredriksson 1948–56. No woman has won more than one title.

## Chess

### ❑ World Champions

World Champions have been recognized since 1886. The first international tournament was held in London in 1851, and won by Adolf Anderssen (Germany); first women's champion recognized in 1927. Takes place annually since 2000.

*Men*

| | |
|---|---|
| 1985–93 | Garry Kasparov (USSR) |
| 1993–8 | Anatoliy Karpov (Russia) |
| 1999–2000 | Alexander Khalifman (Russia) |
| 2000 | Vishwanathan Anand (India) |
| 2001 | Janis Klovans (Latvia) |

*Longest reigning champion*: 27 years, Emanuel Lasker (Germany) 1894–1921.

*Women*

| | |
|---|---|
| 1978–91 | Maya Chiburdanidze (USSR) |
| 1991–6 | Xie Jun (China) |
| 1996–8 | Zsuzsa Polgar (Hungary) |
| 1999–2000 | Xye Jun (China) |
| 2001 | Elena Fatalibekova (Russia) |

*Longest reigning champion*: 17 years, Vera Menchik-Stevenson (UK), 1927–44.

## Contract bridge

### ❑ World Team Championship

The game's biggest championship; men's contest (The Bermuda Bowl) first held in 1950, and now takes place every two years, with the exception of 1999; women's contest (The Venice Cup) first held in 1974, and since 1985 has been concurrent with the men's event.

*Men*

| | |
|---|---|
| 1987 | USA |
| 1989 | Brazil |
| 1991 | Iceland |
| 1993 | Netherlands |
| 1995 | USA |
| 1997 | France |
| 2000 | USA |
| 2001 | USA II |

*Most wins*: (13), Italy 1957–9, 1961–3, 1965–7, 1969, 1973–5.

*Women*

| | |
|---|---|
| 1987 | Italy |
| 1989 | USA |
| 1991 | USA |
| 1993 | USA |
| 1995 | Germany |
| 1997 | USA |
| 2000 | Netherlands |
| 2001 | Germany |

*Most wins*: (7), USA 1974, 1976, 1978, 1989, 1991, 1993, 1997.

### ❑ World Team Olympiad

First held in 1960; since then, every four years.

*Men*

| | |
|---|---|
| 1988 | USA |
| 1992 | France |
| 1996 | France |
| 2000 | Italy |

*Women*

| | |
|---|---|
| 1988 | Denmark |
| 1992 | Austria |
| 1996 | USA |
| 2000 | USA |

*Most wins*: Men (4), France 1960, 1980, 1992–6. Women (4), USA 1980–4, 1996–2000.

## Cricket

### ❑ World Cup

First played in England in 1975; usually held every four years; the 1987 competition, held in India and Pakistan, was the first to be played outside England.

1987 Australia
1992 Pakistan
1996 Sri Lanka
1999 Australia

*Most wins*: (2), West Indies 1975, 1979; Australia 1987, 1999.

### ❑ County Championship

The oldest cricket competition in the world; first won by Sussex in 1827; not officially recognized until 1890, when a proper points system was introduced.

1987 Nottinghamshire
1988 Worcestershire
1989 Worcestershire
1990 Middlesex
1991 Essex
1992 Essex
1993 Middlesex
1994 Warwickshire
1995 Warwickshire
1996 Leicestershire
1997 Glamorgan
1998 Leicestershire
1999 Surrey
2000 Surrey
2001 Yorkshire

*Most outright wins*: (30), Yorkshire 1893, 1896, 1898, 1900–2, 1905, 1908, 1912, 1919, 1922–5, 1931–3, 1935, 1937–9, 1946, 1959–60, 1962–3, 1966–8, 2001.

### ❑ Norwich Union League

First held in 1969; known as the John Player League until 1987, the Refuge Assurance League until 1991, the Axa Equity and Law League until 1999 and the CGU League until 2000.

1987 Worcestershire
1988 Worcestershire
1989 Lancashire
1990 Derbyshire
1991 Nottinghamshire
1992 Middlesex
1993 Glamorgan
1994 Warwickshire
1995 Kent
1996 Surrey
1997 Warwickshire
1998 Lancashire
1999 Lancashire
2000 Gloucestershire
2001 Kent

*Most wins*: (5), Kent 1972–3, 1976, 1995, 2001.

### ❑ Cheltenham & Gloucester Trophy

First held in 1963; known as the Gillette Cup until 1981 and the NatWest Bank Trophy until 2000.

1987 Nottinghamshire
1988 Middlesex
1989 Warwickshire
1990 Lancashire
1991 Hampshire
1992 Northamptonshire
1993 Warwickshire
1994 Worcestershire
1995 Warwickshire
1996 Lancashire
1997 Essex
1998 Lancashire
1999 Gloucestershire
2000 Gloucestershire
2001 Somerset

*Most wins*: (7), Lancashire 1970–2, 1975, 1990, 1996, 1998.

### ❑ Benson and Hedges Cup

First held in 1972.

1987 Yorkshire
1988 Hampshire
1989 Nottinghamshire
1990 Lancashire
1991 Worcestershire
1992 Hampshire
1993 Derbyshire
1994 Warwickshire
1995 Lancashire
1996 Lancashire
1997 Surrey
1998 Essex
1999 Gloucestershire
2000 Gloucestershire
2001 Surrey

*Most wins*: (4), Lancashire 1984, 1990, 1995–6.

### ❑ Pura Mik Cup

Australia's leading domestic competition; contested inter-state since 1891–2; known as the Sheffield Shield until 1999.

1987 Western Australia
1988 Western Australia
1989 Western Australia
1990 New South Wales
1991 Victoria
1992 Western Australia
1993 New South Wales
1994 New South Wales
1995 Queensland
1996 South Australia
1997 Queensland
1998 Western Australia
1999 Queensland
2000 Queensland
2001 Queensland

*Most wins*: (42), New South Wales 1896–7, 1900, 1902–7, 1909, 1911–12, 1914, 1920–1, 1923, 1926, 1929, 1932–3, 1938, 1940, 1949–50, 1952, 1954–62, 1965–6, 1983, 1985–6, 1990, 1993–4.

## Croquet

### ❑ MacRobertson Shield

Croquet's leading tournament; held spasmodically since 1925; contested by teams from Great Britain, New Zealand, Australia and, since 1993, the USA.

1990 Great Britain
1993 Great Britain
1996 Great Britain
2000 Great Britain

*Most wins*: (11), Great Britain 1925, 1937, 1956, 1963, 1969, 1974, 1982, 1990, 1993, 1996, 2000.

## Cross country running

### ❑ World Championships

First international championship held in 1903, but only included runners from England, Ireland, Scotland and Wales; recognized as an official world championship from 1973; first women's race in 1967.

*Individual (Men)*

| | |
|---|---|
| 1987 | John Ngugi (Kenya) |
| 1988 | John Ngugi (Kenya) |
| 1989 | John Ngugi (Kenya) |
| 1990 | Khalid Skah (Morocco) |
| 1991 | Khalid Skah (Morocco) |
| 1992 | John Ngugi (Kenya) |
| 1993 | William Sigei (Kenya) |
| 1994 | William Sigei (Kenya) |
| 1995 | Paul Tergat (Kenya) |
| 1996 | Paul Tergat (Kenya) |
| 1997 | Paul Tergat (Kenya) |
| 1998 | Paul Tergat (Kenya) |
| 1999 | Paul Tergat (Kenya) |
| 2000 | Mohammed Mourhit (Belgium) |
| 2001 | Mohammed Mourhit (Belgium) |

*Team (Men)*

| | |
|---|---|
| 1987 | Kenya |
| 1988 | Kenya |
| 1989 | Kenya |
| 1990 | Kenya |
| 1991 | Kenya |
| 1992 | Kenya |
| 1993 | Kenya |
| 1994 | Kenya |
| 1995 | Kenya |
| 1996 | Kenya |
| 1997 | Kenya |
| 1998 | Kenya |
| 1999 | Kenya |
| 2000 | Kenya |
| 2001 | Kenya |

*Most wins*: Individual (5), John Ngugi, 1986 and as above; Paul Tergat, as above. Team (44), England, between 1903 and 1980.

*Individual (Women)*

| | |
|---|---|
| 1987 | Annette Sergent (France) |
| 1988 | Ingrid Kristiansen (Norway) |
| 1989 | Annette Sergent (France) |
| 1990 | Lynn Jennings (USA) |
| 1991 | Lynn Jennings (USA) |
| 1992 | Lynn Jennings (USA) |
| 1993 | Albertina Dias (Portugal) |
| 1994 | Helen Chepngeno (Kenya) |
| 1995 | Derartu Tulu (Ethiopia) |
| 1996 | Gete Wami (Ethiopia) |
| 1997 | Derartu Tulu (Ethiopia) |
| 1998 | Sonia O'Sullivan (Ireland) |
| 1999 | Gete Wami (Ethiopia) |
| 2000 | Deratu Tulu (Ethiopia) |
| 2001 | Paula Radcliffe (England) |

*Team (Women)*

| | |
|---|---|
| 1987 | USA |
| 1988 | USSR |
| 1989 | USSR |
| 1990 | USSR |
| 1991 | Ethiopia and Kenya (shared) |
| 1992 | Kenya |
| 1993 | Kenya |
| 1994 | Portugal |
| 1995 | Kenya |
| 1996 | Kenya |
| 1997 | Ethiopia |
| 1998 | Kenya |
| 1999 | France |
| 2000 | Ethiopia |
| 2001 | Kenya |

*Most wins*: Individual (5), Doris Brown (USA) 1967–71; Grete Waitz (Norway) 1978–81, 1983. Team (8), USA 1968–9, 1975, 1979, 1983–5, 1987.

## Curling

### ❑ World Championships

First men's championship held in 1959; first women's championship in 1979; takes place annually.

*Men*

| | |
|---|---|
| 1987 | Canada |
| 1988 | Norway |
| 1989 | Canada |
| 1990 | Canada |
| 1991 | Scotland |
| 1992 | Switzerland |
| 1993 | Canada |
| 1994 | Canada |
| 1995 | Canada |
| 1996 | Canada |
| 1997 | Sweden |
| 1998 | Canada |
| 1999 | Scotland |
| 2000 | Canada |
| 2001 | Sweden |

*Women*

| | |
|---|---|
| 1987 | Canada |
| 1988 | West Germany |
| 1989 | Canada |
| 1990 | Norway |
| 1991 | Norway |
| 1992 | Sweden |
| 1993 | Canada |
| 1994 | Canada |
| 1995 | Sweden |
| 1996 | Canada |
| 1997 | Canada |
| 1998 | Sweden |
| 1999 | Sweden |

| | |
|---|---|
| 2000 | Canada |
| 2001 | Canada |

*Most wins*: Men (26), Canada 1959–64, 1966, 1968–72, 1980, 1982–3, 1985–7, 1989–90, 1993–6, 1998, 2000. Women (12), Canada 1980, 1984–7, 1989, 1993–4, 1996–7, 2000–2001.

## Cycling

### ❑ Tour de France

World's premier cycling event; first held in 1903.

| | |
|---|---|
| 1987 | Stephen Roche (Ireland) |
| 1988 | Pedro Delgado (Spain) |
| 1989 | Greg LeMond (USA) |
| 1990 | Greg LeMond (USA) |
| 1991 | Miguel Indurain (Spain) |
| 1992 | Miguel Indurain (Spain) |
| 1993 | Miguel Indurain (Spain) |
| 1994 | Miguel Indurain (Spain) |
| 1995 | Miguel Indurain (Spain) |
| 1996 | Bjarne Riis (Denmark) |
| 1997 | Jan Ullrich (Germany) |
| 1998 | Marco Pantani (Italy) |
| 1999 | Lance Armstrong (USA |
| 2000 | Lance Armstrong (USA) |
| 2001 | Lance Armstrong (USA) |

*Most wins*: (5), Jacques Anquetil (France) 1957, 1961–4; Eddy Merckx (Belgium) 1969–72, 1974; Bernard Hinault (France) 1978–9, 1981–2, 1985, Miguel Indurain (Spain), as above.

### ❑ World Road Race Championships

Men's race first held in 1927; first women's race in 1958; takes place annually.

*Professional Men*

| | |
|---|---|
| 1987 | Stephen Roche (Ireland) |
| 1988 | Maurizio Fondriest (Italy) |
| 1989 | Greg LeMond (USA) |
| 1990 | Rudy Dhaenens (Belgium) |
| 1991 | Gianni Bugno (Italy) |
| 1992 | Gianni Bugno (Italy) |
| 1993 | Lance Armstrong (USA) |
| 1994 | Luc Leblanc (France) |
| 1995 | Abraham Olano (Spain) |
| 1996 | Johan Museeuw (Belgium) |
| 1997 | Laurent Brochard (France) |
| 1998 | Oskar Camenzind (Switzerland) |
| 1999 | Oscar Freire Gomez (Spain) |
| 2000 | Romans Vainsteins (Latvia) |
| 2001 | Oscar Freire Gomez (Spain) |

*Women*

| | |
|---|---|
| 1987 | Jeannie Longo (France) |
| 1988 | Jeannie Longo (France) |
| 1989 | Jeannie Longo (France) |
| 1990 | Catherine Marsal (France) |
| 1991 | Leontien van Moorsel (Holland) |
| 1992 | Kathryn Watt (Australia) |
| 1993 | Leontien van Moorsel (Holland) |
| 1994 | Monica Valvik (Norway) |
| 1995 | Jeannie Longo (France) |
| 1996 | Barbara Heeb (Switzerland) |
| 1997 | Alessandra Cappellotto (Italy) |
| 1998 | Diana Ziliute (Lithuania) |
| 1999 | Edita Pucinskaite (Lithuania) |
| 2000 | Zinaida Stahurskaia (Belarus) |
| 2001 | Rasa Polikeviciute (Lithuania) |

*Most wins*: Men (3), Alfredo Binda (Italy) 1927, 1930, 1932; Rik Van Steenbergen (Belgium) 1949, 1956–7; Eddy Merckx (Belgium) 1967, 1971, 1974. Women (6), Jeannie Longo, 1985–6 and as above.

## Cyclo-cross

### ❑ World Championships

First held in 1950 as an open event; separate professional and amateur events from 1967 to 1993. Since 1994 held as an open event.

*Professional*

| | |
|---|---|
| 1987 | Klaus-Peter Thaler (West Germany) |
| 1988 | Pascal Richard (Switzerland) |
| 1989 | Danny De Bie (Belgium) |
| 1990 | Henk Baars (Holland) |
| 1991 | Radomir Simunek (Czechoslovakia) |
| 1992 | Mike Kluge (Germany) |
| 1993 | Dominique Arnould (France) |

*Amateur*

| | |
|---|---|
| 1987 | Mike Kluge (West Germany) |
| 1988 | Karol Camrola (Czechoslovakia) |
| 1989 | Ondrej Glaja (Czechoslovakia) |
| 1990 | Andreas Buesser (Switzerland) |
| 1991 | Thomas Frischknecht (Switzerland) |
| 1992 | Daniele Pontoni (Italy) |
| 1993 | Henrik Djernis (Denmark) |

*Open*

| | |
|---|---|
| 1994 | Paul Herijgers (Belgium) |
| 1995 | Dieter Runkel (Switzerland) |
| 1996 | Adri van der Poel (Netherlands) |
| 1997 | Daniele Pontoni (Italy) |
| 1998 | Mario de Clerq (Belgium) |
| 1999 | Mario de Clerq (Belgium) |
| 2000 | Richard Groenendaal (Netherlands) |
| 2001 | Erwin Vervecken (Belgium) |

*Most wins*: Professional (7), Eric de Vlaeminck (Belgium) 1966, 1968–73. Amateur (5), Robert Vermiere (Belgium) 1970–1, 1974–5, 1977.

## Darts

### ❑ Embassy World Professional Championship

Run by the British Darts Organisation and first held at Nottingham in 1978.

| | |
|---|---|
| 1987 | John Lowe (England) |
| 1988 | Bob Anderson (England) |
| 1989 | Jocky Wilson (Scotland) |
| 1990 | Phil Taylor (England) |
| 1991 | Dennis Priestley (England) |
| 1992 | Phil Taylor (England) |
| 1993 | John Lowe (England) |

| | |
|---|---|
| 1994 | John Part (Canada) |
| 1995 | Richie Burnett (Wales) |
| 1996 | Steve Beaton (England) |
| 1997 | Les Wallace (Scotland) |
| 1998 | Raymond Barneveld (Netherlands) |
| 1999 | Raymond Barneveld (Netherlands) |
| 2000 | Ted Hankey (England) |
| 2001 | John Walton (England) |
| 2002 | Tony David (Australia) |

*Most wins*: (5), Eric Bristow 1980, 1981, 1984–6.

### ❑ World Cup

A team competition first held at Wembley in 1977; takes place every two years.

*Team (Men)*

| | |
|---|---|
| 1987 | England |
| 1989 | England |
| 1991 | England |
| 1993 | England |
| 1995 | England |
| 1997 | Wales |
| 1999 | England |
| 2001 | England |

*Individual (Men)*

| | |
|---|---|
| 1987 | Eric Bristow (England) |
| 1989 | Eric Bristow (England) |
| 1991 | John Lowe (England) |
| 1993 | Roland Schollen (Denmark) |
| 1995 | Martin Addams (England) |
| 1997 | Raymond Barneveld (Netherlands) |
| 1999 | Raymond Barneveld (Netherlands) |
| 2001 | Martin Adams (England) |

*Most wins*: Team (11), England 1979–95, 1999–2001. Individual (4), Eric Bristow (England) 1983–9.

### ❑ World Championship

Run by the World Darts Council (now Professional Darts Corporation) since 1994.

| | |
|---|---|
| 1994 | Dennis Priestley (England) |
| 1995 | Phil Taylor (England) |
| 1996 | Phil Taylor (England) |
| 1997 | Phil Taylor (England) |
| 1998 | Phil Taylor (England) |
| 1999 | Phil Taylor (England) |
| 2000 | Phil Taylor (England) |
| 2001 | Phil Taylor (England) |

*Most wins*: (7), Phil Taylor (England), as above.

## Draughts

### ❑ World Championship

Held on a challenge basis.

| | |
|---|---|
| 1979–90 | M Tinsley (USA) |
| 1991–4 | D E Oldbury (Great Britain) |
| 1994– | R King (Barbados) |

### ❑ British Open Championship

The leading championship in Britain; first held in 1926; now takes place every two years.)

| | |
|---|---|
| 1988 | D E Oldbury (Great Britain) |
| 1990 | T Watson (Great Britain) |
| 1992 | H Devlin (Great Britain) |
| 1994 | W J Edwards (Great Britain) |
| 1996 | J Francis (Barbados) |
| 1998 | Pat McCarthy (Republic of Ireland) |
| 2000 | William Docherty (Scotland) |

## Equestrian events

### ❑ World Championships

Show Jumping championships first held in 1953 (for men) and 1965 (for women); since 1978 they have competed together and on equal terms; team competition introduced in 1978; Three Day Event and Dressage championships introduced in 1966; all three now held every four years. Renamed the World Equestrian Games in 1990.

*Show Jumping (Individual)*

| | |
|---|---|
| 1990 | Eric Navet (France) |
| 1994 | Franke Sloothaak (Germany) |
| 1998 | Rodrigo Pessoa (Brazil) |

*Show Jumping (Team)*

| | |
|---|---|
| 1990 | France |
| 1994 | Germany |
| 1998 | Germany |

*Three Day Event (Individual)*

| | |
|---|---|
| 1990 | Blyth Tait (New Zealand) |
| 1994 | Vaughn Jefferis (New Zealand) |
| 1998 | Blyth Tait (New Zealand) |

*Three Day Event (Team)*

| | |
|---|---|
| 1990 | New Zealand |
| 1994 | Great Britain |
| 1998 | New Zealand |

*Dressage (Individual)*

| | |
|---|---|
| 1990 | Nicole Uphoff (West Germany) |
| 1994 | Anky van Grunsven (Netherlands) |
| 1998 | Isabell Werth (Germany) |

*Dressage (Team)*

| | |
|---|---|
| 1990 | West Germany |
| 1994 | Germany |
| 1998 | Germany |

## Fencing

### ❑ World Championships

Held annually since 1921 (between 1921–35, known as European Championships). Not held in Olympic years.

*Foil Individual (Men)*

| | |
|---|---|
| 1987 | Mathias Gey (West Germany) |
| 1989 | Alexander Koch (West Germany) |
| 1990 | Philippe Omnès (France) |
| 1991 | Ingo Weissenborn (Germany) |
| 1993 | Alexander Koch (Germany) |

| | |
|---|---|
| 1994 | Rolando Tuckers (Cuba) |
| 1995 | Dimitriy Chevtchenko (Russia) |
| 1997 | Sergei Golubitsky (Ukraine) |
| 1998 | Sergei Golubitsky (Ukraine) |
| 1999 | Sergei Golubitsky (Ukraine) |
| 2001 | Salvatore Sanzo (Italy) |

*Foil Team (Men)*

| | |
|---|---|
| 1987 | USSR |
| 1989 | USSR |
| 1990 | Italy |
| 1991 | Cuba |
| 1993 | Germany |
| 1994 | Italy |
| 1995 | Cuba |
| 1997 | France |
| 1998 | Poland |
| 1999 | France |
| 2001 | Italy |

*Most wins*: Individual (5), Alexander Romankov (USSR) 1974, 1977, 1979, 1982–3; Team (15), USSR (between 1959 and 1989).

*Foil Individual (Women)*

| | |
|---|---|
| 1987 | Elisabeta Tufan (Romania) |
| 1989 | Olga Velitchko (USSR) |
| 1990 | Anja Fichtel (West Germany) |
| 1991 | Giovanna Trillini (Italy) |
| 1993 | Francesca Bortolozzi (Italy) |
| 1994 | Reka Szabo-Lazar (Romania) |
| 1995 | Laura Badea (Romania) |
| 1997 | Giovanna Trillini (Italy) |
| 1998 | Sabine Bau (Germany) |
| 1999 | Valentina Vezzali (Italy) |
| 2001 | Valentina Vezzali (Italy) |

*Foil Team (Women)*

| | |
|---|---|
| 1987 | Hungary |
| 1989 | West Germany |
| 1990 | Italy |
| 1991 | Hungary |
| 1993 | Germany |
| 1994 | Romania |
| 1995 | Italy |
| 1997 | Italy |
| 1998 | Italy |
| 1999 | Germany |
| 2001 | Japan |

*Most wins*: Individual (3), Helène Mayer (Germany) 1929, 1931, 1937; Ilona Elek (Hungary) 1934–5, 1951; Ellen Müller-Preiss (Austria) 1947, 1949, 1950; Cornelia Hanisch (West Germany) 1979, 1981, 1985. Team (15), USSR (between 1956 and 1986).

*Épée Individual (Men)*

| | |
|---|---|
| 1987 | Volker Fischer (West Germany) |
| 1989 | Manuel Pereira (Spain) |
| 1990 | Thomas Gerull (West Germany) |
| 1991 | Andrei Shovalov (USSR) |
| 1993 | Pavel Kolobkov (Russia) |
| 1994 | Pavel Kolobkov (Russia) |
| 1995 | Eric Srecki (France) |
| 1997 | Eric Srecki (France) |
| 1998 | Hughes Obry (France) |
| 1999 | Arnd Schmitt (Germany) |
| 2001 | Paulo Milanoli (Italy) |

*Épée Team (Men)*

| | |
|---|---|
| 1987 | West Germany |
| 1989 | Italy |
| 1990 | Italy |
| 1991 | USSR |
| 1993 | Italy |
| 1994 | France |
| 1995 | Germany |
| 1997 | Cuba |
| 1998 | Hungary |
| 1999 | France |
| 2001 | Switzerland |

*Most wins*: Individual (3), Georges Buchard (France) 1927, 1931, 1933; Alexei Nikanchikov (USSR) 1966–7, 1970. Team (15), Italy (between 1931 and 1958, also 1989–90, 1993, 1996).

*Épée Individual (Women)*

| | |
|---|---|
| 1989 | Anja Straub (Switzerland) |
| 1990 | Taime Chappe (Cuba) |
| 1991 | Mariann Horvath (Hungary) |
| 1993 | Oksana Jermakova (Estonia) |
| 1994 | Laura Chiesa (Hungary) |
| 1995 | Joanna Jakimiuk (Poland) |
| 1997 | Miraide Garcia-Soto (Cuba) |
| 1998 | Laura Flessel (France) |
| 1999 | Laura Flessel-Colovic (France) |
| 2001 | Claudia Bokel (Germany) |

*Épée Team (Women)*

| | |
|---|---|
| 1989 | Hungary |
| 1990 | West Germany |
| 1991 | Hungary |
| 1993 | Hungary |
| 1994 | Spain |
| 1995 | Hungary |
| 1997 | Hungary |
| 1998 | France |
| 1999 | Hungary |
| 2001 | Estonia |

*Sabre Individual (Men)*

| | |
|---|---|
| 1987 | Jean-François Lamour (France) |
| 1989 | Grigory Kirienko (USSR) |
| 1990 | György Nebald (Hungary) |
| 1991 | Grigory Kirienko (USSR) |
| 1993 | Grigory Kirienko (Russia) |
| 1994 | Felix Becker (Germany) |
| 1995 | Grigory Kirienko (Russia) |
| 1997 | Stanislav Pozdniakov (Russia) |
| 1998 | Luigi Tarantino (Italy) |
| 1999 | Damien Touya (France) |

| | |
|---|---|
| 2001 | Stanislav Pozdniakov (Russia) |

*Sabre Team (Men)*

| | |
|---|---|
| 1987 | USSR |
| 1989 | USSR |
| 1990 | USSR |
| 1991 | Hungary |
| 1993 | Hungary |
| 1994 | Russia |
| 1995 | Italy |
| 1997 | France |
| 1998 | Hungary |
| 1999 | France |
| 2001 | Ukraine |

*Most wins*: Individual (4), Grigory Kirienko (Russia), as above. Team (20), Hungary (between 1930 and 1982, also 1991, 1993, 1998).

## Football, American

### ❑ Super Bowl

First held in 1967; takes place each January; an end-of-season meeting between the champions of the two major US leagues, the National Football Conference (NFC) and the American Football Conference (AFC).

| | |
|---|---|
| 1987 | New York Giants (NFC) |
| 1988 | Washington Redskins (NFC) |
| 1989 | San Francisco 49ers (NFC) |
| 1990 | San Francisco 49ers (NFC) |
| 1991 | New York Giants (NFC) |
| 1992 | Washington Redskins (NFC) |
| 1993 | Dallas Cowboys (NFC) |
| 1994 | Dallas Cowboys (NFC) |
| 1995 | San Francisco 49ers (NFC) |
| 1996 | Dallas Cowboys (NFC) |
| 1997 | Green Bay Packers (NFC) |
| 1998 | Denver Broncos (AFC) |
| 1999 | Denver Broncos (AFC) |
| 2000 | St Louis Rams (NFC) |
| 2001 | Baltimore Ravens (AFC) |

*Most wins*: (5), San Francisco 49ers 1982, 1985, 1989–90, 1995; Dallas Cowboys 1972, 1978, 1993–4, 1996.

## Football, Association

### ❑ FIFA World Cup

Association Football's premier event; first contested for the Jules Rimet Trophy in 1930; Brazil won it outright after winning for the third time in 1970; since then teams have competed for the FIFA (*Féderation Internationale de Football Association*) World Cup; held every four years.

*Post-war winners*

| | |
|---|---|
| 1950 | Uruguay |
| 1954 | West Germany |
| 1958 | Brazil |
| 1962 | Brazil |
| 1966 | England |
| 1970 | Brazil |
| 1974 | West Germany |
| 1978 | Argentina |
| 1982 | Italy |
| 1986 | Argentina |
| 1990 | West Germany |
| 1994 | Brazil |
| 1998 | France |

*Most wins*: (4), Brazil, as above.

### ❑ European Championship

Held every four years since 1960; qualifying group matches held over the two years preceding the final.

*All winners*

| | |
|---|---|
| 1960 | USSR |
| 1964 | Spain |
| 1968 | Italy |
| 1972 | West Germany |
| 1976 | Czechoslovakia |
| 1980 | West Germany |
| 1984 | France |
| 1988 | Netherlands |
| 1992 | Denmark |
| 1996 | Germany |

*Most wins*: (3), Germany, as above.

### ❑ South American Championship

Known as Copa de América; first held in 1916, for South American national sides; there were two tournaments in 1959, won by Argentina and Uruguay; discontinued in 1967, but revived eight years later; now played every two years.

| | |
|---|---|
| 1987 | Uruguay |
| 1989 | Brazil |
| 1991 | Argentina |
| 1993 | Argentina |
| 1995 | Uruguay |
| 1997 | Brazil |
| 1999 | Brazi |
| 2001 | Columbia |

*Most wins*: (14), Uruguay 1916–17, 1920, 1923–4, 1926, 1935, 1942, 1956, 1959, 1967, 1983, 1987, 1995.

### ❑ European Champions Cup

The leading club competition in Europe; open to the League champions of countries affiliated to UEFA (Union of European Football Associations); commonly known as the 'European Cup'; inaugurated in the 1955–6 season; played annually.

| | |
|---|---|
| 1987 | FC Porto (Portugal) |
| 1988 | PSV Eindhoven (Holland) |
| 1989 | AC Milan (Italy) |
| 1990 | AC Milan (Italy) |
| 1991 | Red Star Belgrade (Yugoslavia) |
| 1992 | Barcelona (Spain) |
| 1993 | Olympique Marseille (France) |
| 1994 | AC Milan (Italy) |
| 1995 | Ajax Amsterdam (Holland) |
| 1996 | Juventus (Italy) |
| 1997 | Borussia Dortmund (Germany) |
| 1998 | Real Madrid (Spain) |

| | |
|---|---|
| 1999 | Manchester United (UK) |
| 2000 | Real Madrid (Spain) |
| 2001 | Bayern Munich (Germany) |

*Most wins*: (8), Real Madrid (Spain) 1956–60, 1966, 1998, 2000.

### ❑ Football Association Challenge Cup (FA Cup)

The world's oldest club knockout competition (the 'FA cup'), held annually; first contested in the 1871–2 season; first final at the Kennington Oval on 16 March 1872; first winners were The Wanderers.

| | |
|---|---|
| 1987 | Coventry City |
| 1988 | Wimbledon |
| 1989 | Liverpool |
| 1990 | Manchester United |
| 1991 | Tottenham Hotspur |
| 1992 | Liverpool |
| 1993 | Arsenal |
| 1994 | Manchester United |
| 1995 | Everton |
| 1996 | Manchester United |
| 1997 | Chelsea |
| 1998 | Arsenal |
| 1999 | Manchester United |
| 2000 | Chelsea |
| 2001 | Liverpool |

*Most wins*: (10), Manchester United 1909, 1948, 1963, 1977, 1983, 1985, 1990, 1994, 1996, 1999.

### ❑ Football League (Premier League)

The oldest league in the world, and regarded as the toughest; founded in 1888; consists of four divisions; the current complement of 92 teams achieved in 1950.

| | |
|---|---|
| 1986–7 | Everton |
| 1987–8 | Liverpool |
| 1988–9 | Arsenal |
| 1989–90 | Liverpool |
| 1990–1 | Arsenal |
| 1991–2 | Leeds United |
| 1992–3 | Manchester United |
| 1993–4 | Manchester United |
| 1994–5 | Blackburn Rovers |
| 1995–6 | Manchester United |
| 1996–7 | Manchester United |
| 1997–8 | Arsenal |
| 1998–9 | Manchester United |
| 1999–2000 | Manchester United |
| 2000–1 | Manchester United |

*Most wins*: (18) Liverpool 1901, 1906, 1922–3, 1947, 1964, 1966, 1973, 1976–7, 1979–80, 1982–4, 1986, 1988, 1990.

## Football, Australian Rules

### ❑ Australian Football League Trophy

The top prize is the Australian Football League Trophy (Victoria Football League 1897–1989); inaugural winners in 1897 were Essendon.

| | |
|---|---|
| 1987 | Carlton |
| 1988 | Hawthorn |
| 1989 | Hawthorn |
| 1990 | Collingwood |
| 1991 | Hawthorn |
| 1992 | West Coast |
| 1993 | Essendon |
| 1994 | West Coast |
| 1995 | Carlton |
| 1996 | North Melbourne |
| 1997 | Adelaide |
| 1998 | North Melbourne |
| 1999 | North Melbourne |
| 2000 | Essendon |
| 2001 | Brisbane |

*Most wins*: (16), Carlton 1906–8, 1914–15, 1938, 1945, 1947, 1968, 1970, 1972, 1981–2, 1987, 1995.

## Football, Gaelic

### ❑ All-Ireland Championship

First held in 1887; takes place in Dublin on the third Sunday in September each year.

| | |
|---|---|
| 1987 | Meath |
| 1988 | Meath |
| 1989 | Cork |
| 1990 | Cork |
| 1991 | Down |
| 1992 | Donegal |
| 1993 | Derry |
| 1994 | Down |
| 1995 | Dublin |
| 1996 | Meath |
| 1997 | Kerry |
| 1998 | Galway |
| 1999 | Meath |
| 2000 | Kerry |
| 2001 | Galway |

*Most wins:* (32), Kerry, 1903–4, 1909, 1913–14, 1924, 1926, 1929–32, 1937, 1939–41, 1946, 1953, 1955, 1959, 1962, 1969–70, 1975, 1978–81, 1984–6, 1997, 2000.

## Gliding

### ❑ World Championships

First held in 1937; current classes are Open, Standard and 15metres; the Open class is the principal event, held every two years until 1978 and again since 1981.

| | |
|---|---|
| 1987 | Ingo Renner (Australia) |
| 1989 | Robin May (Great Britain) |
| 1991 | Janusz Centka (Poland) |
| 1993 | Andy Davis (Great Britain) |
| 1995 | Raymond Lynskey (New Zealand) |
| 1997 | Gerard Lherm (France) |
| 1999 | Holger Karow (Germany) |
| 2001 | Oscar Goudriaan (South Africa) |

*Most wins*: (3), George Lee (Great Britain) 1976, 1978, 1981; Ingo Renner (Australia) 1983, 1985, 1987.

## Golf

### ❑ British Open

First held at Prestwick in 1860, and won by Willie Park; takes place annually; regarded as the world's leading golf tournament.

| | |
|---|---|
| 1987 | Nick Faldo (Great Britain) |
| 1988 | Severiano Ballesteros (Spain) |
| 1989 | Mark Calcavecchia (USA) |
| 1990 | Nick Faldo (Great Britain) |
| 1991 | Ian Baker-Finch (Australia) |
| 1992 | Nick Faldo (Great Britain) |
| 1993 | Greg Norman (Australia) |
| 1994 | Nick Price (Zimbabwe) |
| 1995 | John Daly (USA) |
| 1996 | Tom Lehman (USA) |
| 1997 | Justin Leonard (USA) |
| 1998 | Mark O'Meara (USA) |
| 1999 | Paul Lawrie (Great Britain) |
| 2000 | Tiger Woods (USA) |
| 2001 | David Duval (USA) |

*Most wins*: (6), Harry Vardon (Great Britain) 1896, 1898–9, 1903, 1911, 1914.

### ❑ United States Open

First Held at Newport, Rhode Island, in 1895, and won by Horace Rawlins; takes place annually.

| | |
|---|---|
| 1987 | Scott Simpson (USA) |
| 1988 | Curtis Strange (USA) |
| 1989 | Curtis Strange (USA) |
| 1990 | Hale Irwin (USA) |
| 1991 | Payne Stewart (USA) |
| 1992 | Tom Kite (USA) |
| 1993 | Lee Janzen (USA) |
| 1994 | Ernie Els (South Africa) |
| 1995 | Corey Pavin (USA) |
| 1996 | Steve Jones (USA) |
| 1997 | Ernie Els (South Africa) |
| 1998 | Lee Janzen (USA) |
| 1999 | Payne Stewart (USA) |
| 2000 | Tiger Woods (USA) |
| 1986 | Retief Goosen (South Africa) |

*Most wins*: (4), Willie Anderson (USA) 1901, 1903–5; Bobby Jones (USA) 1923, 1926, 1929–30; Ben Hogan (USA) 1948, 1950–1, 1953; Jack Nicklaus (USA) 1962, 1967, 1972, 1980.

### ❑ US Masters

First held in 1934; takes place at the Augusta National course in Georgia every April.

| | |
|---|---|
| 1987 | Larry Mize (USA) |
| 1988 | Sandy Lyle (Great Britain) |
| 1989 | Nick Faldo (Great Britain) |
| 1990 | Nick Faldo (Great Britain) |
| 1991 | Ian Woosnam (Great Britain) |
| 1992 | Fred Couples (USA) |
| 1993 | Bernhard Langer (Germany) |
| 1994 | José-María Olazábal (Spain) |
| 1995 | Ben Crenshaw (USA) |
| 1996 | Nick Faldo (Great Britain) |
| 1997 | Tiger Woods (USA) |
| 1998 | Mark O'Meara (USA) |
| 1999 | José-María Olazábal (Spain) |
| 2000 | Vijay Singh (Fiji) |
| 2001 | Tiger Woods (USA) |

*Most wins*: (6), Jack Nicklaus (USA) 1963, 1965–6, 1972, 1975, 1986.

### ❑ United States PGA Championship

The last of the season's four 'Majors'; first held in 1916, and a match-play event until 1958; takes place annually.

| | |
|---|---|
| 1987 | Larry Nelson (USA) |
| 1988 | Jeff Sluman (USA) |
| 1989 | Payne Stewart (USA) |
| 1990 | Wayne Grady (Australia) |
| 1991 | John Daly (USA) |
| 1992 | Nick Price (Zimbabwe) |
| 1993 | Paul Azinger (USA) |
| 1994 | Nick Price (Zimbabwe) |
| 1995 | Steve Elkington (Australia) |
| 1996 | Mark Brooks (USA) |
| 1997 | Davis Love III (USA) |
| 1998 | Vijay Singh (Fiji) |
| 1999 | Tiger Woods (USA) |
| 2000 | Tiger Woods (USA) |
| 2001 | David Toms (USA) |

*Most wins*: (5), Walter Hagen (USA) 1921, 1924–7; Jack Nicklaus (USA) 1963, 1971, 1973, 1975, 1980.

### ❑ Ryder Cup

The leading international team tournament; first held at Worcester, Massachusetts in 1927; takes place every two years between teams from the USA and Europe (Great Britain 1927–71; Great Britain and Ireland 1973–7).

| | | |
|---|---|---|
| 1987 | Europe | 15–13 |
| 1989 | Drawn | 14–14 |
| 1991 | USA | $14\frac{1}{2}$–$13\frac{1}{2}$ |
| 1993 | USA | 15–13 |
| 1995 | Europe | $14\frac{1}{2}$–$13\frac{1}{2}$ |
| 1997 | Europe | $14\frac{1}{2}$–$13\frac{1}{2}$ |
| 1999 | USA | $14\frac{1}{2}$–$13\frac{1}{2}$ |

*Wins*: (24), USA 1927, 1931, 1935–7, 1947–55, 1959–67, 1971–83, 1991–3, 1999. (3), Great Britain 1929, 1933, 1957. (4), Europe 1985, 1987, 1995, 1997. *Drawn:* (2), 1969, 1989.

## Greyhound racing

### ❑ Greyhound Derby

The top race of the British season, first held in 1927; run at the White City every year (except 1940) until its closure in 1985; since then all races run at Wimbledon.

| | |
|---|---|
| 1987 | Signal Spark |
| 1988 | Hit the Lid |
| 1989 | Lartigue Note |
| 1990 | Slippy Blue |
| 1991 | Ballinderry Ash |
| 1992 | Farloe Melody |
| 1993 | Ringa Hustle |

| | |
|---|---|
| 1994 | Moral Standards |
| 1995 | Moaning Lad |
| 1996 | Shanless Slippy |
| 1997 | Some Picture |
| 1998 | Tom's the Best |
| 1999 | Chart King |
| 2000 | Rapid Ranger |
| 2001 | Rapid Ranger |

*Most wins*: (2), Mick the Miller 1929–30; Patricia's Hope 1972–3; Rapid Ranger, as above.

## Gymnastics

### ❑ World Championships

First held in 1903; took place every four years, 1922–78; since 1979, usually every two years.

*Individual (Men)*

| | |
|---|---|
| 1987 | Dmitri Belozerchev (USSR) |
| 1989 | Igor Korobichensky (USSR) |
| 1991 | Vitaly Scherbo (USSR) |
| 1993 | Vitaly Scherbo (Belarus) |
| 1994 | Ivan Ivankov (Belarus) |
| 1995 | Li Xianoshuang (China) |
| 1997 | Ivan Ivankov (Belarus) |
| 1999 | Nikolay Krukov (Russia) |
| 2001 | Jing Feng (China) |

*Team (Men)*

| | |
|---|---|
| 1987 | USSR |
| 1989 | USSR |
| 1991 | USSR |
| 1993 | *no team prize* |
| 1994 | China |
| 1995 | China |
| 1997 | China |
| 1999 | China |
| 2001 | Belarus |

*Most wins*: Individual (2), Marco Torrès (France) 1909, 1913; Peter Sumi (Yugoslavia) 1922, 1926; Yuri Korolev 1981, 1985; Dmitri Belozerchev 1983, 1987; Vitaly Scherbo, as above; Ivan Ivankov (Belarus), as above. Team (8), USSR 1954, 1958, 1979–81, 1985–91.

*Individual (Women)*

| | |
|---|---|
| 1987 | Aurelia Dobre (Romania) |
| 1989 | Svetlana Boginskaya (USSR) |
| 1991 | Kim Zmeskal (USA) |
| 1993 | Shannon Miller (USA) |
| 1994 | Shannon Miller (USA) |
| 1995 | Lilia Podkopayeva (Ukraine) |
| 1997 | Svetlana Khorkina (Russia) |
| 1999 | Maria Olaru (Romania) |
| 2001 | Svetlana Khorkina (Russia) |

*Team (Women)*

| | |
|---|---|
| 1987 | Romania |
| 1989 | USSR |
| 1991 | USSR |
| 1993 | *no team prize* |
| 1994 | Romania |
| 1995 | Romania |
| 1997 | Romania |
| 1999 | Romania |
| 2001 | Romania |

*Most wins*: Individual (2), Vlasta Dekanová (Czechoslovakia) 1934, 1938; Larissa Latynina (USSR) 1958, 1962; Ludmila Tourischeva 1970, 1974; Shannon Miller, as above. Team (11), USSR, 1954, 1958, 1962, 1970, 1974, 1978, 1981, 1983, 1985, 1989, 1991.

## Handball

### ❑ World Championships

First men's championships held in 1938, both indoors and outdoors (latter discontinued in 1966); first women's outdoor championships in 1949 (discontinued in 1960); first women's indoor championships in 1957.

*Men*

| | |
|---|---|
| 1990 | Sweden |
| 1993 | Russia |
| 1995 | France |
| 1997 | Russia |
| 1999 | Sweden |
| 2001 | France |

*Most wins*: Indoors (4), Romania 1961, 1964, 1970, 1974. Outdoors (5), West Germany (including once as combined East/West German team).

*Women*

| | |
|---|---|
| 1990 | USSR |
| 1993 | Germany |
| 1995 | Germany |
| 1997 | Denmark |
| 1999 | Norway |
| 2001 | Russia |

*Most wins*: Indoors (3), East Germany 1971, 1975, 1979, USSR 1982, 1986, 1990. Outdoors (2), Romania.

## Hang gliding

### ❑ World Championships

First held officially in 1976; since 1979, take place every two years.

*Individual: Class 1*

| | |
|---|---|
| 1987 | Rich Duncan (Australia) |
| 1989 | Robert Whittall (Great Britain) |
| 1991 | Tomás Suchanek (Czechoslovakia) |
| 1993 | Tomás Suchanek (Czech Republic) |
| 1995 | Tomás Suchanek (Czech Republic) |
| 1997 | John Pendry (Great Britain) |
| 1999 | Manfred Ruhmer (Austria) |
| 2001 | Manfred Ruhmer (Austria) |

*Team*

| | |
|---|---|
| 1987 | Australia |
| 1989 | Great Britain |
| 1991 | Great Britain |
| 1993 | USA |
| 1995 | Australia |
| 1997 | Switzerland |

| | |
|---|---|
| 1999 | Brazil |
| 2001 | Austria |

*Most wins*: Individual (3), Tomás Suchanek (Czech Republic), as above. Team (4), Great Britain 1981, 1985, 1989, 1991.

## Hockey

### ❑ World Cup

Men's tournament first held in 1971, and every four years since 1978; women's tournament first held in 1974, and now takes place every three or four years.

*Men*

| | |
|---|---|
| 1990 | Netherlands |
| 1994 | Pakistan |
| 1998 | Netherlands |

*Most wins*: (4), Pakistan 1971, 1978, 1982, 1994.

*Women*

| | |
|---|---|
| 1990 | Netherlands |
| 1994 | Australia |
| 1998 | Australia |

*Most wins*: (5), Netherlands 1974, 1978, 1983, 1986, 1990.

### ❑ Olympic Games

Regarded as hockey's leading competition; first held in 1908; included at every celebration since 1928; women's competition first held in 1980.

*Men*

| | |
|---|---|
| 1988 | Great Britain |
| 1992 | Germany |
| 1996 | Netherlands |
| 2000 | Netherlands |

*Women*

| | |
|---|---|
| 1988 | Australia |
| 1992 | Spain |
| 1996 | Australia |
| 2000 | Australia |

*Most wins*: Men (8), India 1928, 1932, 1936, 1948, 1952, 1956, 1964, 1980. Women (3), Australia, as above.

## Horse racing

### ❑ The Derby

The 'Blue Riband' of the Turf; run at Epsom over $1\frac{1}{2}$ miles; first run in 1780.

| | *Horse (Jockey)* |
|---|---|
| 1987 | Reference Point (Steve Cauthen) |
| 1988 | Kahyasi (Ray Cochrane) |
| 1989 | Nashwan (Willie Carson) |
| 1990 | Quest For Fame (Pat Eddery) |
| 1991 | Generous (Alan Munro) |
| 1992 | Dr Devious (John Reid) |
| 1993 | Commander in Chief (Michael Kinane) |
| 1994 | Erhaab (Willie Carson) |
| 1995 | Lammtarra (Walter Swinburn) |
| 1996 | Shaamit (Michael Hills) |
| 1997 | Benny the Dip (Willie Ryan) |
| 1998 | High Rise (Olivier Peslier) |
| 1999 | Oath (Kieren Fallon) |
| 2000 | Sinndar (John Murtagh) |
| 2001 | Galileo (Michael Kinane) |

*Most wins*: Jockey (9), Lester Piggott 1954, 1957, 1960, 1968, 1970, 1972, 1976–7, 1983.

### ❑ The Oaks

Raced at Epsom over $1\frac{1}{2}$ miles; for fillies only; first run in 1779.

| | *Horse (Jockey)* |
|---|---|
| 1987 | Unite (Walter Swinburn) |
| 1988 | Diminuendo (Steve Cauthen) |
| 1989 | Aliysa (Walter Swinburn) |
| 1990 | Salsabil (Willie Carson) |
| 1991 | Jet Ski Lady (Christy Roche) |
| 1992 | User Friendly (George Duffield) |
| 1993 | Intrepidity (Michael Roberts) |
| 1994 | Balanchine (Frankie Dettori) |
| 1995 | Moonshell (Frankie Dettori |
| 1996 | Lady Carla (Pat Eddery) |
| 1997 | Reams of Verse (Kieren Fallon) |
| 1998 | Shahtoush (Michael Kinane) |
| 1999 | Ramruma (Kieren Fallon) |
| 2000 | Love Divine (Richard Quinn) |
| 2001 | Imagine (Michael Kinane) |

*Most wins*: Jockey (9), Frank Buckle 1797–9, 1802–3, 1805, 1817–18, 1823.

### ❑ One Thousand Guineas

Run over 1 mile at Newmarket; for fillies only; first run in 1814.

| | *Horse (Jockey)* |
|---|---|
| 1987 | Miesque (Freddy Head) |
| 1988 | Ravinella (Gary Moore) |
| 1989 | Musical Bliss (Walter Swinburn) |
| 1990 | Salsabil (Willie Carson) |
| 1991 | Shadayid (Willie Carson) |
| 1992 | Hatoof (Walter Swinburn) |
| 1993 | Sayyedati (Walter Swinburn) |
| 1994 | Las Meninas (John Reid) |
| 1995 | Harayir (Richard Hills) |
| 1996 | Bosra Sham (Pat Eddery) |
| 1997 | Sleepytime (Kieren Fallon) |
| 1998 | Cape Verdi (Frankie Dettori) |
| 1999 | Wince (Kieren Fallon) |
| 2000 | Lahan (Richard Hills) |
| 2001 | Ameerat (Philip Robinson) |

*Most wins*: Jockey (7), George Fordham 1859, 1861, 1865, 1868–9, 1881, 1883.

### ❑ Two Thousand Guineas

Run at Newmarket over 1 mile; first run in 1809.

| | *Horse (Jockey)* |
|---|---|
| 1987 | Don't Forget Me (Willie Carson) |
| 1988 | Doyoun (Walter Swinburn) |

| | |
|---|---|
| 1989 | Nashwan (Willie Carson) |
| 1990 | Tirol (Michael Kinane) |
| 1991 | Mystiko (Michael Roberts) |
| 1992 | Rodrigo de Traiano (Lester Piggott) |
| 1993 | Zafonic (Pat Eddery) |
| 1994 | Mister Baileys (Jason Weaver) |
| 1995 | Pennekamp (Thierry Jarnet) |
| 1996 | Mark of Esteem (Frankie Dettori) |
| 1997 | Entrepreneur (Michael Kinane) |
| 1998 | King of Kings (Michael Kinane) |
| 1999 | Island Sands (Frankie Dettori) |
| 2000 | King's Best (Kieren Fallon) |
| 2001 | Golan (Kieren Fallon) |

*Most wins*: Jockey (9), Jem Robinson 1825, 1828, 1831, 1833–6, 1847–8.

### ❑ St Leger

The oldest of the five English classics; first run in 1776; raced at Doncaster annually over 1 mile 6 furlongs 127 yards.

| | *Horse (Jockey)* |
|---|---|
| 1987 | Reference Point (Steve Cauthen) |
| 1988 | Minster Son (Willie Carson) |
| 1989 | Michelozzo (Steve Cauthen) |
| 1990 | Snurge (Richard Quinn) |
| 1991 | Toulon (Pat Eddery) |
| 1992 | User Friendly (George Duffield) |
| 1993 | Bob's Return (Philip Robinson) |
| 1994 | Moonax (Pat Eddery) |
| 1995 | Classic Cliche (Frankie Dettori) |
| 1996 | Shantou (Frankie Dettori) |
| 1997 | Silver Patriarch (Pat Eddery) |
| 1998 | Nedawi (John Reid) |
| 1999 | Mutafaweq (Richard Hills) |
| 2000 | Millenary (Richard Quinn) |
| 2001 | Milan (Michael Kinane) |

*Most wins*: Jockey (9), Bill Scott 1821, 1825, 1828–9, 1838–41, 1846.

### ❑ Grand National

Steeplechasing's most famous race; first run at Maghull in 1836; at Aintree since 1839; war-time races at Gatwick 1916–18.

| | *Horse (Jockey)* |
|---|---|
| 1987 | Maori Venture (Steve Knight) |
| 1988 | Rhyme 'N' Reason (Brendan Powell) |
| 1989 | Little Polveir (Jimmy Frost) |
| 1990 | Mr Frisk (Marcus Armytage) |
| 1991 | Seagram (Nigel Hawke) |
| 1992 | Party Politics (Carl Llewellyn) |
| 1993 | *race declared void* Esha Ness (John White) first past the post |
| 1994 | Minnehoma (Richard Dunwoody) |
| 1995 | Royal Athlete (Jason Titley) |
| 1996 | Rough Quest (Mick Fitzgerald) |
| 1997 | Lord Gyllene (Tony Dobbin) |
| 1998 | Earth Summit (Carl Llewelyn) |
| 1999 | Bobbyjo (Paul Carberry) |
| 2000 | Papillon (Ruby Walsh) |
| 2001 | Red Marauder (Richard Guest) |

*Most wins*: Jockey (5), George Stevens 1856, 1863–4, 1869–70. Horse (3), Red Rum 1973–4, 1977.

### ❑ Prix de l'Arc de Triomphe

The leading end of season race in Europe; raced over 2 400 metres at Longchamp; first run in 1920.

| | *Horse (Jockey)* |
|---|---|
| 1987 | Trempolino (Pat Eddery) |
| 1988 | Tony Bin (John Reid) |
| 1989 | Caroll House (Michael Kinane) |
| 1990 | Suamarez (Gerard Mosse) |
| 1991 | Suave Dancer (Cash Asmussen) |
| 1992 | Subotica (Thierry Jarnet) |
| 1993 | Urban Sea (Eric Saint-Martin) |
| 1994 | Carnegie (Thierry Jarnet) |
| 1995 | Lammtarra (Frankie Dettori) |
| 1996 | Helissio (Olivier Peslier) |
| 1997 | Peintre Celebre (Olivier Peslier) |
| 1998 | Sagamix (Olivier Peslier) |
| 1999 | Montjeu (Michael Kinane) |
| 2000 | Sinndar (John Murtagh) |
| 2001 | Sakhee (Frankie Dettori) |

*Most wins*: Jockey (4), Jacko Doyasbère 1942, 1944, 1950–1; Freddy Head 1966, 1972, 1976, 1979; Yves Saint-Martin 1970, 1974, 1982, 1984; Pat Eddery 1980, 1985–7. Horse (2), Ksar 1921–2; Motrico 1930, 1932; Corrrida 1936–7; Tantième 1950–1; Ribot 1955–6; Alleged 1977–8.

## Hurling

### ❑ All-Ireland Championship

First contested in 1887; played on the first Sunday in September each year.

| | |
|---|---|
| 1987 | Galway |
| 1988 | Galway |
| 1989 | Tipperary |
| 1990 | Cork |
| 1991 | Tipperary |
| 1992 | Limerick |
| 1993 | Kilkenny |
| 1994 | Offaly |
| 1995 | Clare |
| 1996 | Wexford |
| 1997 | Clare |
| 1998 | Offaly |
| 1999 | Cork |
| 2000 | Kilkenny |
| 2001 | Tipperary |

*Most wins*: (28), Cork 1890, 1892–4, 1902–3, 1919, 1926, 1928–9, 1931, 1941–4, 1946, 1952–4, 1966, 1970, 1976–8, 1984, 1986, 1990, 1999.

## Ice hockey

### ❑ World Championship

First held in 1930; takes place annually (except 1980); up to 1968 Olympic champions also regarded as world champions.

| | |
|---|---|
| 1987 | Sweden |
| 1988 | USSR |
| 1989 | USSR |

| | |
|---|---|
| 1990 | USSR |
| 1991 | Sweden |
| 1992 | Sweden |
| 1993 | Russia |
| 1994 | Canada |
| 1995 | Finland |
| 1996 | Czech Republic |
| 1997 | Canada |
| 1998 | Sweden |
| 1999 | Czech Republic |
| 2000 | Czech Republic |
| 2001 | Czech Republic |

*Most wins*: (24), USSR 1954, 1956, 1963–71, 1973–5, 1978–9, 1981–4, 1986, 1988–90.

### ❑ Stanley Cup

The most sought-after trophy at club level; the end-of-season meeting between the winners of the two conferences in the National Hockey League in the USA and Canada.

| | |
|---|---|
| 1987 | Edmonton Oilers |
| 1988 | Edmonton Oilers |
| 1989 | Calgary Flames |
| 1990 | Edmonton Oilers |
| 1991 | Pittsburgh Penguins |
| 1992 | Pittsburgh Penguins |
| 1993 | Montreal Canadiens |
| 1994 | New York Rangers |
| 1995 | New Jersey Devils |
| 1996 | Colorado Avalanche |
| 1997 | Detroit Red Wings |
| 1998 | Detroit Red Wings |
| 1999 | Dallas Stars |
| 2000 | New Jersey Devils |
| 2001 | Colorado Avalanche |

*Most wins*: (24), Montreal Canadiens 1916, 1924, 1930–1, 1944, 1946, 1953, 1956–60, 1965–6, 1968–9, 1971, 1976–9, 1986, 1993.

## Ice skating

### ❑ World Championships

First men's championships in 1896; first women's event in 1906; pairs first contested in 1908; Ice Dance officially recognized in 1952.

*Men*

| | |
|---|---|
| 1987 | Brian Orser (Canada) |
| 1988 | Brian Boitano (USA) |
| 1989 | Kurt Browning (Canada) |
| 1990 | Kurt Browning (Canada) |
| 1991 | Kurt Browning (Canada) |
| 1992 | Viktor Petrenko (CIS) |
| 1993 | Kurt Browning (Canada) |
| 1994 | Elvis Stojko (Canada) |
| 1995 | Elvis Stojko (Canada) |
| 1996 | Todd Eldredge (USA) |
| 1997 | Elvis Stojko (Canada) |
| 1998 | Alexei Yagudin (Russia) |
| 1999 | Alexei Yagudin (Russia) |
| 2000 | Alexei Yagudin (Russia) |
| 2001 | Evgeny Plushento (Russia) |

*Most wins*: (10), Ulrich Salchow (Sweden) 1901–5, 1907–11.

*Women*

| | |
|---|---|
| 1987 | Katarina Witt (East Germany) |
| 1988 | Katarina Witt (East Germany) |
| 1989 | Midori Ito (Japan) |
| 1990 | Jill Trenary (USA) |
| 1991 | Kristi Yamaguchi (USA) |
| 1992 | Kristi Yamaguchi (USA) |
| 1993 | Oksana Baiul (Ukraine) |
| 1994 | Yuka Sato (Japan) |
| 1995 | Lu Chen (China) |
| 1996 | Michelle Kwan (USA) |
| 1997 | Tara Lipinski (USA) |
| 1998 | Michelle Kwan (USA) |
| 1999 | Maria Butyrskaya (Russia) |
| 2000 | Michelle Kwan (USA) |
| 2001 | Michelle Kwan (USA) |

*Most wins*: (10), Sonja Henie (Norway) 1927–36.

*Pairs*

| | |
|---|---|
| 1987 | Sergei Grinkov/Yekaterina Gordeeva (USSR) |
| 1988 | Oleg Vasiliev/Yelena Valova (USSR) |
| 1989 | Sergei Grinkov/Yekaterina Gordeeva (USSR) |
| 1990 | Sergei Grinkov/Yekaterina Gordeeva (USSR) |
| 1991 | Artur Dmtriev/Natalya Mishkutienok (USSR) |
| 1992 | Artur Dmtriev/Natalya Mishkutienok (USSR) |
| 1993 | Lloyd Eisler/Isabelle Brasseur (Canada) |
| 1994 | Vadim Naumov/Evgenia Shiskova (Russia) |
| 1995 | Rene Novotny/Radka Kovarikova (Czech Republic) |
| 1996 | Andrei Bushkov/Marina Eltsova (Russia) |
| 1997 | Ingo Steuer/Mandy Woetzel (Germany) |
| 1998 | Anton Sikharulidze/Elena Berezhnaya (Russia) |
| 1999 | Anton Sikharulidze/Elena Berezhnaya (Russia) |
| 2000 | Alexei Tikhonov/Maria Petrova (Russia) |
| 2001 | David Pelletier/Jamie Sale (Canada) |

*Most wins*: (10), Irina Rodnina (USSR) 1969–72 (with Aleksey Ulanov), 1973–8 (with Aleksander Zaitsev).

*Ice Dance*

| | |
|---|---|
| 1987 | Andrei Bukin/Natalya Bestemianova (USSR) |
| 1988 | Andrei Bukin/Natalya Bestemianova (USSR) |
| 1989 | Sergei Ponomarenko/Marina Klimova (USSR) |
| 1990 | Sergei Ponomarenko/Marina Klimova (USSR) |
| 1991 | Isabelle and Paul Duchesnay (France) |
| 1992 | Sergei Ponomarenko/Marina Klimova (CIS) |
| 1993 | Alesandr Zhulin/Maia Usova (Russia) |

| | |
|---|---|
| 1994 | Yevgeni Platov/Oksana Gritschuk (Russia) |
| 1995 | Yevgeni Platov/Oksana Gritschuk (Russia) |
| 1996 | Yevgeni Platov/Oksana Gritschuk (Russia) |
| 1997 | Yevgeni Platov/Oksana Gritschuk (Russia) |
| 1998 | Oleg Ovsyannikov/Anjelika Krylova (Russia) |
| 1999 | Oleg Ovsyannikov/Anjelika Krylova (Russia) |
| 2000 | Gwendal Peizerat/Marina Anissina (France) |
| 2001 | Maurizio Margaglio/Barbara Fusar-Poli (Italy) |

*Most wins*: (6), Aleksander Gorshkov and Lyudmila Pakhomova (USSR) 1970–4, 1976.

## Judo

### ❑ World Championships

First held in 1956, now contested every two years; current weight categories established in 1999; women's championship instituted in 1980.

*Men*

*Open Class*

| | |
|---|---|
| 1987 | Naoya Ogawa (Japan) |
| 1989 | Naoya Ogawa (Japan) |
| 1991 | Naoya Ogawa (Japan) |
| 1993 | Rafael Kubacki (Poland) |
| 1995 | David Douillet (France) |
| 1997 | Rafael Kubacki (Poland) |
| 1999 | Shinichi Shinohara (Japan) |
| 2001 | Alexandre Mikhaylin (Russia) |

*Over 100kg*

| | |
|---|---|
| 1987 | Grigori Vertichev (USSR) |
| 1989 | Naoya Ogawa (Japan) |
| 1991 | Sergey Kosorotov (USSR) |
| 1993 | David Douillet (France) |
| 1995 | David Douillet (France) |
| 1997 | David Douillet (France) |
| 1999 | Shinichi Shinohara (Japan) |
| 2001 | Alexandre Mikhaylin (Russia) |

*Under 100kg*

| | |
|---|---|
| 1987 | Hitoshi Sugai (Japan) |
| 1989 | Koba Kurtanidze (Japan) |
| 1991 | Stephane Traineau (France) |
| 1993 | Antal Kovacs (Hungary) |
| 1995 | Pawel Nastula (Poland) |
| 1997 | Pawel Nastula (Poland) |
| 1999 | Kosei Inoue (Japan) |
| 2000 | Kosei Inoue (Japan) |

*Under 90kg*

| | |
|---|---|
| 1987 | Fabien Canu (France) |
| 1989 | Fabien Canu (France) |
| 1991 | Hirotaka Okada (Japan) |
| 1993 | Yoshoi Nakamura (Japan) |
| 1995 | Chun Ki Young (South Korea) |
| 1997 | Ki Young (South Korea) |
| 1999 | Hidehiko Yoshida (Japan) |
| 2001 | Frederic Demoutfaucon (France) |

*Under 81kg*

| | |
|---|---|
| 1987 | Hirotaka Okada (Japan) |
| 1989 | Byung-ju Kim (South Korea) |
| 1991 | Daniel Lascau (Germany) |
| 1993 | Chun Ki Young (South Korea) |
| 1995 | Toshihiko Koga (Japan) |
| 1997 | Chul Cho In (South Korea) |
| 1999 | Graeme Randall (Great Britain) |
| 2001 | Chul Cho In (South Korea) |

*Under 73kg*

| | |
|---|---|
| 1987 | Mike Swain (USA) |
| 1989 | Toshihiko Koga (Japan) |
| 1991 | Toshihiko Koga (Japan) |
| 1993 | Yung Chung Hoon (South Korea) |
| 1995 | Daisuke Hideshima (Japan) |
| 1997 | Kenzo Nakamura (Japan) |
| 1999 | Jimmy Pedro (USA) |
| 2001 | Vital Makarov (Russia) |

*Under 66kg*

| | |
|---|---|
| 1987 | Yosuke Yamamoto (Japan) |
| 1989 | Drago Becanovic (Yugoslavia) |
| 1991 | Udo Quellmalz (Germany) |
| 1993 | Yukimasa Nakamura (Japan) |
| 1995 | Udo Quellmalz (Germany) |
| 1997 | Hyuk Kim (Korea) |
| 1999 | Larbi Benboudaoud (France) |
| 2001 | Arashi Miresmaeli (Iran) |

*Under 60kg*

| | |
|---|---|
| 1987 | Kim Jae-Yup (South Korea) |
| 1989 | Amiran Totikashvili (USSR) |
| 1991 | Tadanori Koshino (Japan) |
| 1993 | Ryudi Sanoda (Japan) |
| 1995 | Nikolai Ojeguine (Russia) |
| 1997 | Tadahiro Nomura (Japan) |
| 1999 | Manuelo Poulot (Cuba) |
| 2001 | Anis Lounifi (Tunisia) |

*Most titles*: (4), David Douillet (France) 1995 (Open), 1993–7 (over 95kg); Yashiro Yamashita (Japan) 1981 (Open), 1979, 1981, 1983 (over 95kg); Shozo Fujii (Japan) 1971, 1973, 1975 (under 80kg), 1979 (under 78kg); Naoya Ogawa (Japan) 1987–91 (Open), 1989 (over 95kg).

*Women*

*Open Class*

| | |
|---|---|
| 1987 | Fenglian Gao (China) |
| 1989 | Estela Rodriguez (Cuba) |
| 1991 | Zhuang Xiaoyan (China) |
| 1993 | Beata Maksymow (Poland) |
| 1995 | Monique van der Lee (Netherlands) |
| 1997 | Daina Beltran (Cuba) |
| 1999 | Daina Beltran (Cuba) |
| 2001 | Celine Lebrun (France) |

*Over 78kg*

| | |
|---|---|
| 1987 | Gao Fengliang (China) |
| 1989 | Gao Fengliang (China) |
| 1991 | Moon Ji-Yoon (South Korea) |
| 1993 | Johanna Hagen (Germany) |
| 1995 | Angelique Seriese (Netherlands) |
| 1997 | Christine Cicot (France) |
| 1999 | Beata Maksymow (Poland) |
| 2001 | Yuan Hua (China) |

*Under 78kg*

| | |
|---|---|
| 1987 | Irene de Kok (Netherlands) |
| 1989 | Ingrid Berghmans (Belgium) |
| 1991 | Kim Mi-Jeong (South Korea) |
| 1993 | Chun Huileng (China) |
| 1995 | Castellano Luna (Cuba) |
| 1997 | Noriko Anno (Japan) |
| 1999 | Noriko Anno (Japan) |
| 2001 | Noriko Anno (Japan) |

*Under 70kg*

| | |
|---|---|
| 1987 | Alexandra Schreiber (West Germany) |
| 1989 | Emanuela Pierantozzi (Italy) |
| 1991 | Emanuela Pierantozzi (Italy) |
| 1993 | Cho Min Sun (South Korea) |
| 1995 | Cho Min Sun (South Korea) |
| 1997 | Kate Howey (Great Britain) |
| 1999 | Sibelis Veranes (Cuba) |
| 2001 | Masae Ueno (Japan) |

*Under 63kg*

| | |
|---|---|
| 1987 | Diane Bell (Great Britain) |
| 1989 | Catherina Fleury (France) |
| 1991 | Frauke Eickhoff (Germany) |
| 1993 | Gella van de Cayeve (Belgium) |
| 1995 | Jung Sung Sook (South Korea) |
| 1997 | Servenr Vandenhende (France) |
| 1999 | Keiko Maedo (Japan) |
| 2001 | Gella van de Cayeve (Belgium) |

*Under 57kg*

| | |
|---|---|
| 1987 | Catherine Arnaud (France) |
| 1989 | Catherine Arnaud (France) |
| 1991 | Miriam Blasco (Spain) |
| 1993 | Nicola Fairbrother (Great Britain) |
| 1995 | Driulis González (Cuba) |
| 1997 | Isabel Fernandez (Spain) |
| 1999 | Driulis González (Cuba) |
| 2001 | Yourisledes Lupety (Cuba) |

*Under 52kg*

| | |
|---|---|
| 1987 | Sharon Rendle (Great Britain) |
| 1989 | Sharon Rendle (Great Britain) |
| 1991 | Alessandra Giungi (Italy) |
| 1993 | Rodriguez Verdecia (Cuba) |
| 1995 | Marie-Claire Restoux (France) |
| 1997 | Marie-Claire Restoux (France) |
| 1999 | Noriko Narasaki (Japan) |
| 2001 | Sun-Hui Kye (North Korea) |

*Under 48kg (Women))*

| | |
|---|---|
| 1987 | Zangyun Li (China) |
| 1989 | Karen Briggs (Great Britain) |
| 1991 | Cécille Nowak (France) |
| 1993 | Ryoko Tamura (Japan) |
| 1995 | Ryoko Tamura (Japan) |
| 1997 | Ryoko Tamura (Japan) |
| 1999 | Ryoko Tamura (Japan) |
| 2001 | Ryoko Tamura (Japan) |

*Most titles*: (6), Ingrid Berghmans (Belgium) 1980, 1982, 1984, 1986 (Open), 1984, 1989 (both under 72kg).

## Karate

### ❑ World Championships

First held in Tokyo in 1970; taken place every two years since 1980, when women first competed; there is a team competition plus individual competitions at Kumite (seven weight categories for men and three for women) and Kata. Since 1992 there have been separate men's and women's teams.

*Kumite*

| *Men* | | *Women* | |
|---|---|---|---|
| 1992 | Spain | 1992 | Great Britain |
| 1994 | France | 1994 | Spain |
| 1996 | France | 1996 | Great Britain |
| 1998 | France | 1998 | Turkey |
| 2000 | France | 2000 | France |

*Kata*

| *Men* | | *Women* | |
|---|---|---|---|
| 1992 | Japan | 1992 | Japan |
| 1994 | Japan | 1994 | Japan |
| 1996 | Japan | 1996 | Japan |
| 1998 | Japan | 1998 | Japan |
| 2000 | Japan | 2000 | France |

## Lacrosse

### ❑ World Championships

First held for men in 1967; for women in 1969; taken place every four years since 1974; since 1982 the women's event has been called the World Cup.

*Men*

| | |
|---|---|
| 1990 | USA |
| 1994 | USA |
| 1998 | USA |

*Most wins*: (7), USA 1967, 1974, 1982–98.

*Women*

| | |
|---|---|
| 1990 | USA |
| 1993 | USA |
| 1997 | USA |
| 2001 | USA |

*Most wins*: (6), USA 1974, 1982, 1990, 1993, 1997, 2001.

### ❑ Iroquois Cup

The sport's best known trophy; contested by English club sides annually since 1890.

| | |
|---|---|
| 1987 | Stockport |
| 1988 | Mellor |
| 1989 | Stockport |
| 1990 | Cheadle |
| 1991 | Cheadle |
| 1992 | Cheadle |
| 1993 | Heaton Mersey |
| 1994 | Cheadle |
| 1995 | Cheadle |
| 1996 | Stockport |
| 1997 | Mellor |
| 1998 | *not held* |
| 1999 | *not held* |
| 2000 | Cheadle |
| 2001 | *not held* |

*Most wins*: (18), Stockport 1897–1901, 1903, 1905, 1911–13, 1923–4, 1926, 1928, 1934, 1987, 1989, 1996.

## Modern Pentathlon

### ❑ World Championships

Held annually since 1949 with the exception of Olympic years, when the Olympic champions automatically become world champions.

*Individual*

| | |
|---|---|
| 1987 | Joel Bouzou (France) |
| 1988 | Janos Martinek (Hungary) |
| 1989 | Laszlo Fabien (Hungary) |
| 1990 | Gianluca Tiberti (Italy) |
| 1991 | Arkadiusz Skrzypaszek (Poland) |
| 1992 | Arkadiusz Skrzypaszek (Poland) |
| 1993 | Richard Phelps (Great Britain) |
| 1994 | Dmitri Svatovski (Russia) |
| 1995 | Dmitri Svatovski (Russia) |
| 1996 | Alexander Parygin (Kazakhstan) |
| 1997 | Sebastien Deleigne (France) |
| 1998 | Sebastien Deleigne (France) |
| 1999 | Gabor Balogh (Hungary) |
| 2000 | Dmitri Svatovski (Russia) |
| 2001 | Gabor Balogh (Hungary) |

*Team*

| | |
|---|---|
| 1987 | Hungary |
| 1988 | Hungary |
| 1989 | Hungary |
| 1990 | USSR |
| 1991 | USSR |
| 1992 | Poland |
| 1993 | Hungary |
| 1994 | France |
| 1995 | Poland |
| 1996 | Poland |
| 1997 | Hungary |
| 1998 | Mexico |
| 1999 | Hungary |
| 2000 | *not held* |
| 2001 | Hungary |

*Most wins*: Individual (6), Andras Balczo (Hungary) 1963, 1965–9, 1972. Team (18), USSR 1956–9, 1961–2, 1964, 1969, 1971–4, 1980, 1982–3, 1985, 1990–1.

## Motor cycling

### ❑ World Championships

First organized in 1949; current titles for 500cc, 250cc, 125cc, 80cc and Sidecar; Formula One and Endurance world championships also held annually; the most prestigious title is the 500cc category.

*500cc*

| | |
|---|---|
| 1987 | Wayne Gardner (Australia) |
| 1988 | Eddie Lawson (USA) |
| 1989 | Eddie Lawson (USA) |
| 1990 | Wayne Rainey (USA) |
| 1991 | Wayne Rainey (USA) |
| 1992 | Wayne Rainey (USA) |
| 1993 | Kevin Schwantz (USA) |
| 1994 | Michael Doohan (Australia) |
| 1995 | Michael Doohan (Australia) |
| 1996 | Michael Doohan (Australia) |
| 1997 | Michael Doohan (Australia) |
| 1998 | Michael Doohan (Australia) |
| 1999 | Alex Criville (Spain) |
| 2000 | Kenny Roberts (USA) |
| 2001 | Valentino Rossi (Italy) |

*Most wins*: (8), Giacomo Agostini (Italy) 1966–72, 1975.

*Most world titles*: (15), Giacomo Agostini, 500cc as above; 350cc 1968–74.

### ❑ Isle of Man TT Races

The most famous of all motor cycle races; take place each June; first held 1907; principal race is the Senior TT.

*Senior TT*

| | |
|---|---|
| 1987 | Joey Dunlop (Ireland) |
| 1988 | Joey Dunlop (Ireland) |
| 1989 | Steve Hislop (Great Britain) |
| 1990 | Carl Fogarty (Great Britain) |
| 1991 | Steve Hislop (Great Britain) |
| 1992 | Steve Hislop (Great Britain) |
| 1993 | Phil McCallen (Ireland) |
| 1994 | Steve Hislop (Great Britain) |
| 1995 | Joey Dunlop (Ireland) |
| 1996 | Phil McCallen (Ireland) |
| 1997 | Phil McCallen (Ireland) |
| 1998 | Ian Simpson (Great Britain) |
| 1999 | David Jefferies (Great Britain) |
| 2000 | David Jeffries (Great Britain) |
| 2001 | *not held* |

*Most Senior TT wins*: (7), Mike Hailwood (Great Britain) 1961, 1963–7, 1979.

## Motor Racing

### ❑ World Championship

A Formula One drivers' world championship instituted in 1950; constructor's championship instituted in 1958.

| | | |
|---|---|---|
| 1987 | Nelson Piquet (Brazil) | *Williams* |
| 1988 | Ayrton Senna (Brazil) | *McLaren* |
| 1989 | Alain Prost (France) | *McLaren* |
| 1990 | Ayrton Senna (Brazil) | *McLaren* |
| 1991 | Ayrton Senna (Brazil) | *McLaren* |
| 1992 | Nigel Mansell (Great Britain) | *Williams* |
| 1993 | Alain Prost (France) | *Williams* |
| 1994 | Michael Schumacher (Germany) | *Benetton* |
| 1995 | Michael Schumacher (Germany) | *Benetton* |
| 1996 | Damon Hill (Great Britain) | *Williams* |
| 1997 | Jacques Villeneuve (Canada) | *Williams* |
| 1998 | Mika Hakkinen (Finland) | *McLaren* |
| 1999 | Mika Hakkinen (Finland) | *McLaren* |
| 2000 | Michael Schumacher (Germany) | *Ferrari* |
| 2001 | Michael Schumacher (Germany) | *Ferrari* |

*Most wins*: Driver (5), Juan Manuel Fangio (Argentina) 1951, 1954–7.

### ❑ Le Mans 24-Hour Race

The greatest of all endurance races; first held in 1923.

| | |
|---|---|
| 1987 | Hans Stück (West Germany)<br>Derek Bell (Great Britain)<br>Al Holbert (USA) |
| 1988 | Jan Lammers (Netherlands)<br>Johnny Dumfries (Great Britain)<br>Andy Wallace (Great Britain) |
| 1989 | Jochen Mass (West Germany)<br>Manuel Reuter (West Germany)<br>Stanley Dickens (Sweden) |
| 1990 | John Nielsen (Denmark)<br>Price Cobb (USA)<br>Martin Brundle (Great Britain) |
| 1991 | Volker Weidler (Germany)<br>Johnny Herbert (Great Britain)<br>Bertrand Gachot (Belgium) |
| 1992 | Derek Warwick (Great Britain)<br>Mark Blundell (Great Britain)<br>Yannick Dalmas (France) |
| 1993 | Geoff Brabham (Australia)<br>Christophe Bouchut (France)<br>Eric Helary (France) |
| 1994 | Yannick Dalmas (France)<br>Hurley Haywood (USA)<br>Mauro Baldi (Italy) |
| 1995 | Yannick Dalmas (France)<br>J J Lehto (Finland)<br>Masanori Sekiya (Japan) |
| 1996 | Manuel Reuter (Germany)<br>Davy Jones (USA)<br>Alexander Würz (Austria) |
| 1997 | Michele Alboreto (Italy)<br>Stefan Johansson (Sweden)<br>Tom Kristensen (Denmark) |
| 1998 | Allan McNish (Great Britain)<br>Laurent Aiello (France)<br>Stephane Ortelli (France) |
| 1999 | Pierluigi Martini (Italy)<br>Joachim Winkelhock (Germany)<br>Yannick Dalmas (France) |
| 2000 | Franck Biela (Germany)<br>Tom Kristensen (Denmark)<br>Emanuele Pirro (Italy) |
| 2001 | Franck Biela (Germany)<br>Tom Kristensen (Denmark)<br>Emanuele Pirro (Italy) |

*Most wins*: (6), Jacky Ickx (Belgium) 1969, 1975–7, 1981–2.

### ❑ Indianapolis 500

First held in 1911; raced over the Indianapolis Raceway as part of the Memorial Day celebrations at the end of May each year.

| | |
|---|---|
| 1987 | Al Unser (USA) |
| 1988 | Rick Mears (USA) |
| 1989 | Emerson Fittipaldi (Brazil) |
| 1990 | Arie Luyendyk (Netherlands) |
| 1991 | Rick Mears (USA) |
| 1992 | Al Unser (USA) |
| 1993 | Emerson Fittipaldi (Brazil) |
| 1994 | Al Unser (USA) |
| 1995 | Jacques Villeneuve (Canada) |
| 1996 | Buddy Lazier (USA) |
| 1997 | Arie Luyendyk (Netherlands) |
| 1998 | Eddie Cheever (USA) |
| 1999 | Kenny Brack (USA) |
| 2000 | Juan Montoya (Columbia) |
| 2001 | Helio Castroneves (Brazil) |

*Most wins*: (6), Al Unser (USA) 1970–1, 1978, 1987, 1992, 1994.

### ❑ Monte Carlo Rally

The world's leading rally; first held in 1911.

| | |
|---|---|
| 1987 | Miki Biasion (Italy)<br>Tiziano Siviero (Italy) |
| 1988 | Bruno Saby (France)<br>Jean-François Fauchille (France) |
| 1989 | Miki Biasion (Italy)<br>Tiziano Siviero (Italy) |
| 1990 | Didier Auriol (France)<br>Bernard Occelli (France) |
| 1991 | Carlos Sainz (Spain)<br>Luis Moya (Spain) |
| 1992 | Didier Auriol (France)<br>Bernard Occelli (France) |
| 1993 | Didier Auriol (France)<br>Bernard Occelli (France) |
| 1994 | François Delecour (France)<br>Daniel Grataloup (France) |
| 1995 | Carlos Sainz (Spain)<br>Luis Moya (Spain) |
| 1996 | Patrick Bernardini (France)<br>Bernard Occelli (France) |
| 1997 | Piero Liatti (Italy)<br>Fabrizia Pons (Italy) |

| | |
|---|---|
| 1998 | Carlos Sainz (Spain) |
| | Luis Moya (Spain) |
| 1999 | Tommi Mäkinen (Finland) |
| | Risto Mannisemäki (Finland) |
| 2000 | Tommi Mäkinen (Finland) |
| | Risto Mannisemäki (Finland) |
| 2001 | Tommi Mäkinen (Finland) |
| | Risto Mannisemäki (Finland) |

*Most wins*: (4), Sandro Munari (Italy) 1972, 1975–7; Walter Röhrl (West Germany) 1980, 1982–4. Co-drivers: (4) Christian Geistdörfery (West Germany) 1980, 1982–4; Bernard Occelli (France) 1990, 1992–3, 1996.

## Netball

### ❑ World Championships

First held in 1963, then every four years.

| | |
|---|---|
| 1987 | New Zealand |
| 1991 | Australia |
| 1995 | Australia |
| 1999 | Australia |

*Most wins*: (8), Australia 1963, 1971, 1975, 1979, 1983, 1991, 1995, 1999.

## Orienteering

### ❑ World Championships

First held in 1966; takes place every two years (to 1978, and since 1979).

*Individual (Men)*

| | |
|---|---|
| 1987 | Kent Olsson (Sweden) |
| 1989 | Peter Thoresen (Norway) |
| 1991 | Jörgen Mårtensson (Sweden) |
| 1993 | Alan Mogensen (Denmark) |
| 1995 | Jörgen Mårtensson (Sweden) |
| 1997 | Peter Thoresen (Denmark) |
| 1999 | Bjornar Valstad (Norway) |
| 2001 | Jörgen Rostup (Finland) |

*Individual (Women)*

| | |
|---|---|
| 1987 | Arja Hannus (Sweden) |
| 1989 | Marita Skogum (Sweden) |
| 1991 | Katalin Olah (Hungary) |
| 1993 | Marita Skogum (Sweden) |
| 1995 | Katalin Olah (Hungary) |
| 1997 | Hanne Staff (Norway) |
| 1999 | Kirsi Bostrom (Finland) |
| 2001 | Simone Luder (Switzerland) |

*Most wins*: Men (2), Age Hadler (Norway) 1966, 1972; Egil Johansen (Norway) 1976–8; Oyvin Thon (Norway) 1979–81; Jörgen Mårtensson (Sweden), as above; Peter Thoresen (Norway), as above. Women (3) Annichen Kringstad Svensson (Norway), 1981–5.

*Relay (Men)*

| | |
|---|---|
| 1987 | Norway |
| 1989 | Norway |
| 1991 | Switzerland |
| 1993 | Switzerland |
| 1995 | Switzerland |
| 1997 | Denmark |
| 1999 | Norway |
| 2001 | Finland |

*Relay (Women)*

| | |
|---|---|
| 1987 | Norway |
| 1989 | Sweden |
| 1991 | Sweden |
| 1993 | Sweden |
| 1995 | Finland |
| 1997 | Sweden |
| 1999 | Norway |
| 2001 | Finland |

*Most wins*: Men (8), Norway 1970, 1978, 1981–9, 1999. Women (11), Sweden 1966, 1970, 1974–6, 1981–5, 1989–93, 1997.

## Polo

### ❑ Cowdray Park Gold Cup

First held in 1956, replacing the Champion Cup; the British Open Championship for club sides; so named because played at Cowdray Park, Sussex.

| | |
|---|---|
| 1987 | Tramontona |
| 1988 | Tramontona |
| 1989 | Tramontona |
| 1990 | Tramontona |
| 1991 | Tramontona |
| 1992 | Black Bears |
| 1993 | Alcatel |
| 1994 | Ellerston Blacks |
| 1995 | Ellerston Whites |
| 1996 | C S Brooks |
| 1997 | Labegorce |
| 1998 | Ellerston |
| 1999 | Pommery |
| 2000 | Geebung |
| 2001 | Dubai |

*Most wins*: (6), Tramontona 1986–91.

## Powerboat racing

### ❑ World Championships

Instituted in 1982; held in many categories, with Formula One and Formula Two being the principal competitions; Formula One was not held between 1987 and 1989; Formula Two was discontinued in 1989 and revived for one year in 1997.

*Formula One*

| | |
|---|---|
| 1990 | John Hill (Great Britain) |
| 1991 | Jonathan Jones (Great Britain) |
| 1992 | Fabrizio Bocca (Italy) |
| 1993 | Guido Cappellini (Italy) |
| 1994 | Guido Cappellini (Italy) |
| 1995 | Guido Cappellini (Italy) |
| 1996 | Guido Cappellini (Italy) |
| 1997 | Scott Gilman (USA) |
| 1998 | Jonathan Jones (Great Britain) |
| 1999 | Guido Cappellini (Italy) |

| | |
|---|---|
| 2000 | Scott Gilman (USA) |
| 2001 | Guido Cappellini (Italy) |

*Most wins*: (6) Guido Cappellini (Italy), as above.

*Formula Two*

| | |
|---|---|
| 1985 | John Hill (Great Britain) |
| 1986 | Jonathan Jones (Great Britain) and Buck Thornton (USA) (*shared*) |
| 1987 | Bill Seebold (USA) |
| 1988 | Chris Bush (USA) |
| 1989 | Jonathan Jones (Great Britain) |
| 1997 | Mark Rolls (Great Britain) |

*Most wins*: (2), John Hill (Great Britain) 1984–5; Jonathan Jones (Great Britain), as above.

## Rackets

### ❑ World Championship

Organized on a challenge basis, the first champion in 1820 was Robert Mackay (Great Britain).

| | |
|---|---|
| 1986–8 | John Prenn (Great Britain) |
| 1988–9 | James Male (Great Britain) |
| 1990 | Neil Smith (USA) |
| 1991 | James Male (Great Britain) |
| 1992 | Shannon Hazel (USA) |
| 1993–4 | Neil Smith (USA) |
| 1995–9 | James Male (Great Britain) |
| 1999–2001 | Neil Smith (USA) |
| 2001– | James Male (Great Britain) |

*Longest reigning champion*: (18 years), Geoffrey Atkins 1954–72.

## Real tennis

### ❑ World Championship

Organized on a challenge basis; the first world champion was M Clerge (France) c.1740, regarded as the first world champion of any sport.

| | |
|---|---|
| 1981–7 | Chris Ronaldson (Great Britain) |
| 1987–94 | Wayne Davies (Australia) |
| 1994– | Robert Fahey (Australia) |

*Longest reigning champion*: (33 years), Edmond Barre (France) 1829–62.

## Roller skating

### ❑ World Championships

Figure skating world championships were first organized in 1947.

*Men Combined*

| | |
|---|---|
| 1987 | Kevin Carroll (USA) |
| 1988 | Sandro Guerra (Italy) |
| 1989 | Sandro Guerra (Italy) |
| 1990 | Samo Kokorovec (Italy) |
| 1991 | Sandro Guerra (Italy) |
| 1992 | Sandro Guerra (Italy) |
| 1993 | Samo Kokorovec (Italy) |
| 1994 | Steven Findlay (USA) |
| 1995 | Jason Sutcliffe (Australia) |
| 1996 | Francesco Ceresola (Italy) |
| 1997 | Mauro Mazzoni (Italy) |
| 1998 | Daniel Tofani (Italy) |
| 1999 | Adrian Stolzenberg (Germany) |
| 2000 | Adrian Stolzenberg (Germany) |
| 2001 | Leonardo Pancani (Italy) |

*Women Combined*

| | |
|---|---|
| 1987 | Chiara Sartori (Italy) |
| 1988 | Rafaela Del Vinaccio (Italy) |
| 1989 | Rafaela Del Vinaccio (Italy) |
| 1990 | Rafaela Del Vinaccio (Italy) |
| 1991 | Rafaela Del Vinaccio (Italy) |
| 1992 | Rafaela Del Vinaccio (Italy) |
| 1993 | Letitia Tinghi (Italy) |
| 1994 | April Dayney (USA) |
| 1995 | Letitia Tinghi (Italy) |
| 1996 | Giusy Loncani (Italy) |
| 1997 | Sabrina Tomasini (Italy) |
| 1998 | Elke Dederichs (Germany) |
| 1999 | Elisa Facciotti (Italy) |
| 2000 | Elisa Facciotti (Italy) |
| 2001 | Elisa Facciotti (Italy) |

*Pairs*

| | |
|---|---|
| 1987 | Fabio Trevisani/Monica Mezzardi (Italy) |
| 1988 | Fabio Trevisani/Monica Mezzardi (Italy) |
| 1989 | David De Motte/Nicky Armstrong (USA) |
| 1990 | Larry McGrew/Tammy Jeru (USA) |
| 1991 | Larry McGrew/Tammy Jeru (USA) |
| 1992 | Patrick Venerucci/Maura Ferri (Italy) |
| 1993 | Patrick Venerucci/Maura Ferri (Italy) |
| 1994 | Patrick Venerucci/Beatrice Pallazzi Rossi (Italy) |
| 1995 | Patrick Venerucci/Beatrice Pallazzi Rossi (Italy) |
| 1996 | Patrick Venerucci/Beatrice Pallazzi Rossi (Italy) |
| 1997 | Patrick Venerucci/Beatrice Pallazzi Rossi (Italy) |
| 1998 | Patrick Venerucci/Beatrice Pallazzi Rossi (Italy) |
| 1999 | Patrick Venerucci/Beatrice Pallazzi Rossi (Italy) |
| 2000 | Patrick Venerucci/Beatrice Pallazzi Rossi (Italy) |
| 2001 | Patrick Venerucci/Beatrice Pallazzi Rossi (Italy) |

*Dance*

| | |
|---|---|
| 1987 | Rob Ferendo/Lori Walsh (USA) |
| 1988 | Peter Wulf/Michela Mitzlaf (West Germany) |
| 1989 | Greg Goody/Jodee Viola (USA) |
| 1990 | Greg Goody/Jodee Viola (USA) |
| 1991 | Greg Goody/Jodee Viola (USA) |
| 1992 | Doug Wait/Deanna Monaham (USA) |
| 1993 | Doug Wait/Deanna Monaham (USA) |
| 1994 | Tim Patten/Lisa Friday (USA) |
| 1995 | Tim Patten/Lisa Friday (USA) |
| 1996 | Axel Haber/Swansi Gebauer (Germany) |

| | |
|---|---|
| 1997 | Axel Haber/Swansi Gebauer (Germany) |
| 1998 | Ronald Brenn/Candi Powderly (USA) |
| 1999 | Tim Patten/Tara Graney (USA) |
| 2000 | Adam White/Melissa Quinn (USA) |
| 2001 | Adam White/Melissa Quinn (USA) |

*Most wins*: Men Combined (5), Karl-Heinz Losch (West Germany) 1958–9, 1961–2, 1966. Women Combined (5), Rafaela Del Vinaccio (Italy), as above. Pairs (10), Patrick Venerucci (Italy) as above. Dance (3), Jane Puracchio (USA) 1973, 1975–6; Tim Patten (USA), as above; Dan Littel and Florence Arsenault (USA) 1977–9; Greg Goody and Jodee Viola (USA), as above.

## Rowing

### ❑ World Championships

First held for men in 1962 and for women in 1974; Olympic champions assume the role of world champion in Olympic years; principal event is the single sculls.

*Single Sculls (Men)*

| | |
|---|---|
| 1987 | Thomas Lange (East Germany) |
| 1988 | Thomas Lange (East Germany) |
| 1989 | Thomas Lange (East Germany) |
| 1990 | Yuri Janson (USSR) |
| 1991 | Thomas Lange (Germany) |
| 1992 | Thomas Lange (Germany) |
| 1993 | Derek Porter (Canada) |
| 1994 | Andre Wilms (Germany) |
| 1995 | Iztok Cop (Slovenia) |
| 1996 | Xeno Müller (Switzerland) |
| 1997 | Jamie Koven (USA) |
| 1998 | Rob Waddell (New Zealand) |
| 1999 | Rob Waddell (New Zealand) |
| 2000 | Rob Waddell (New Zealand) |
| 2001 | Olaf Tufte (Norway) |

*Single Sculls (Women)*

| | |
|---|---|
| 1987 | Magdelena Georgieva (Bulgaria) |
| 1988 | Jutta Behrendt (East Germany) |
| 1989 | Elisabeta Lipa (Romania) |
| 1990 | Brigit Peter (East Germany) |
| 1991 | Silke Laumann (Canada) |
| 1992 | Elisabeta Lipa (Romania) |
| 1993 | Jana Phieme (Germany) |
| 1994 | Trine Hansen (Denmark) |
| 1995 | Maria Brandin (Sweden) |
| 1996 | Yekatarina Khodotovich (Belarus) |
| 1997 | Yekatarina Khodotovich (Belarus) |
| 1998 | Irina Fedotova (Russia) |
| 1999 | Ekaterina Karsten (Belarus) |
| 2000 | Ekaterina Karsten (Belarus) |
| 2001 | Katrin Rutschow-Stomporowski (Germany) |

*Most wins*: Men (5), Thomas Lange (Germany), as above. Women (5), Christine Hahn (*née* Scheiblich) (East Germany) 1974–8.

### ❑ The Boat Race

An annual contest between the crews from the Oxford and Cambridge University rowing clubs; first contested in 1829; the current course is from Putney to Mortlake.

| | |
|---|---|
| 1987 | Oxford |
| 1988 | Oxford |
| 1989 | Oxford |
| 1990 | Oxford |
| 1991 | Oxford |
| 1992 | Oxford |
| 1993 | Cambridge |
| 1994 | Cambridge |
| 1995 | Cambridge |
| 1996 | Cambridge |
| 1997 | Cambridge |
| 1998 | Cambridge |
| 1999 | Cambridge |
| 2000 | Oxford |
| 2001 | Cambridge |

*Wins*: 76 Cambridge; 69 Oxford; 1 dead-heat (1877).

### ❑ Diamond Sculls

Highlight of Henley Royal Regatta held every July; first contested in 1884.

| | |
|---|---|
| 1987 | Peter-Michael Kolbe (West Germany) |
| 1988 | Hamish McGlashan (Australia) |
| 1989 | Vaclav Chlupa (Czechoslovakia) |
| 1990 | Erik Verdonk (New Zealand) |
| 1991 | Wim van Belleghem (Belgium) |
| 1992 | Rorie Henderson (Great Britain) |
| 1993 | Thomas Lange (Germany) |
| 1994 | Xeno Müller (Switzerland) |
| 1995 | Juri Jaanson (Estonia) |
| 1996 | Merlin Vervoorn (Netherlands) |
| 1997 | Greg Searle (Great Britain) |
| 1998 | Jamie Koven (USA) |
| 1999 | Marcel Hacker (Germany) |
| 2000 | Aquil Abdullah (USA) |
| 2001 | Duncan Free (Australia) |

*Most wins*: (6), Guy Nickalls (Great Britain) 1888–91, 1893–4; Stuart Mackenzie (Great Britain) 1957–62.

## Rugby league

### ❑ Challenge Cup Final

First contested in 1897 and won by Batley; first final at Wembley Stadium in 1929.

| | |
|---|---|
| 1987 | Halifax |
| 1988 | Wigan |
| 1989 | Wigan |
| 1990 | Wigan |
| 1991 | Wigan |
| 1992 | Wigan |
| 1993 | Wigan |
| 1994 | Wigan |
| 1995 | Wigan |
| 1996 | St Helens |
| 1997 | St Helens |
| 1998 | Sheffield |
| 1999 | Leeds |
| 2000 | Bradford |
| 2001 | St Helens |

*Most wins*: (16), Wigan 1924, 1929, 1948, 1951, 1958–9, 1965, 1985, 1988–95.

### ❑ Premiership Trophy

End-of-season knockout competition involving the top eight teams in the first division; first contested at the end of the 1974–5 season; discontinued in 1997.

| | |
|---|---|
| 1987 | Wigan |
| 1988 | Widnes |
| 1989 | Widnes |
| 1990 | Widnes |
| 1991 | Hull |
| 1992 | Wigan |
| 1993 | St Helens |
| 1994 | Wigan |
| 1995 | Wigan |
| 1996 | Wigan |
| 1997 | Wigan |

*Most wins*: (6), Widnes 1980, 1982–3, 1988–90; Wigan, as above.

### ❑ Regal Trophy

A knockout competition, first held in 1971–2. Known as the John Player Special Trophy until 1989–90; discontinued in 1996.

| | |
|---|---|
| 1987 | Wigan |
| 1988 | St Helens |
| 1989 | Wigan |
| 1990 | Wigan |
| 1991 | Warrington |
| 1992 | Widnes |
| 1993 | Wigan |
| 1994 | Castleford |
| 1995 | Wigan |
| 1996 | Wigan |

*Most wins*: (8), Wigan 1983, 1986–7, 1989–90, 1993, 1995–6.

## Rugby union

### ❑ World Cup

The first Rugby Union World Cup was staged in 1987.

| | |
|---|---|
| 1987 | New Zealand |
| 1991 | Australia |
| 1995 | South Africa |
| 1999 | Australia |

*Most wins*: (2), Australia 1991, 1999.

### ❑ Six Nations' Championship

A round robin competition involving England, Ireland, Scotland, Wales, France, and from 2000, Italy; first contested in 1884.

| | |
|---|---|
| 1987 | France |
| 1988 | France and Wales |
| 1989 | France |
| 1990 | Scotland |
| 1991 | England |
| 1992 | England |
| 1993 | France |
| 1994 | Wales |
| 1995 | England |
| 1996 | England |
| 1997 | France |
| 1998 | France |
| 1999 | Scotland |
| 2000 | England |
| 2001 | England |

*Most outright wins*: (24), England 1883–4, 1892, 1910, 1913–14, 1921, 1923–4, 1928, 1930, 1934, 1937, 1953, 1957–8, 1963, 1980, 1991–2, 1995–6, 2000–1.

### ❑ County Championship

First held in 1889.

| | |
|---|---|
| 1987 | Yorkshire |
| 1988 | Lancashire |
| 1989 | Durham |
| 1990 | Lancashire |
| 1991 | Cornwall |
| 1992 | Lancashire |
| 1993 | Lancashire |
| 1994 | Yorkshire |
| 1995 | Warwickshire |
| 1996 | Gloucestershire |
| 1997 | Cumbria |
| 1998 | Cheshire |
| 1999 | Cornwall |
| 2000 | Yorkshire |
| 2001 | Yorkshire |

*Most wins*: (16), Gloucestershire 1910, 1913, 1920–2, 1930–2, 1937, 1972, 1974–6, 1983–4, 1996.

### ❑ Tetley's Bitter Cup

An annual knockout competition for English Club sides; first held in the 1971–2 season; known as the John Player Special Cup until 1988, and the Pilkington Cup until 1998.

| | |
|---|---|
| 1987 | Bath |
| 1988 | Harlequins |
| 1989 | Bath |
| 1990 | Bath |
| 1991 | Harlequins |
| 1992 | Bath |
| 1993 | Leicester |
| 1994 | Bath |
| 1995 | Bath |
| 1996 | Bath |
| 1997 | Leicester |
| 1998 | Saracens |
| 1999 | Wasps |
| 2000 | Wasps |
| 2001 | Newcastle Falcons |

*Most wins*: (10), Bath 1984–7, 1989–90, 1992, 1994–6.

### ❑ Principality Cup

The knockout tournament for Welsh clubs; first held in 1971–2; formerly known as the Schweppes Welsh Cup and the Swalec Cup.

| | |
|---|---|
| 1987 | Cardiff |
| 1988 | Llanelli |
| 1989 | Neath |
| 1990 | Neath |
| 1991 | Llanelli |

1992 Llanelli
1993 Llanelli
1994 Cardiff
1995 Swansea
1996 Pontypridd
1997 Cardiff
1998 Llanelli
1999 Swansea
2000 Llanelli
2001 Newport

*Most wins*: (11), Llanelli 1973–6, 1985, 1988, 1991–3, 1998, 2000.

## Shinty

### ❑ Camanachd Cup

The sport's principal trophy, it was first held in 1896 and won by Kingussie. Shinty is the popular name for the original game of Camanachd.

1987 Kingussie
1988 Kingussie
1989 Kingussie
1990 Skye
1991 Kingussie
1992 Fort William
1993 Kingussie
1994 Kyles Athletic
1995 Kingussie
1996 Oban
1997 Kingussie
1998 Kingussie
1999 Kingussie
2000 Kingussie
2001 Kingussie

*Most wins*: (28), Newtonmore, between 1907 and 1986.

## Shooting

### ❑ Olympic Games

The Olympic competition is the highlight of the shooting calendar; winners since 1988 are given below.

*Free Pistol (Men)*

1988 Sorin Babil (Romania)
1992 Konstantine Loukachik (UT)
1996 Boris Kokorev (Russia)
2000 Tanyu Kiriakov (Bulgaria)

*Rapid Fire Pistol (Men)*

1988 Afanasi Kouzmine (USSR)
1992 Ralf Schumann (Germany)
1996 Ralf Schumann (Germany)
2000 Sergei Alifirenko (Russia)

*Small Bore Rifle (Three Position) (Men)*

1988 Malcolm Cooper (Great Britain)
1992 Grachya Petikiane (UT)
1996 Jean-Pierre Amat (France)
2000 Rajmond Debevec (Slovenia)

*Running Game Target (Men)*

1988 Tor Heiestad (Norway)
1992 Michael Jakosits (Germany)
1996 Yang Ling (China)
2000 Yang Ling (China)

*Trap (Men)*

1988 Dmitri Monakov (USSR)
1992 Petr Hrdlicka (Czechoslovakia)
1996 Michael Diamond (Australia)
2000 Michael Diamond (Australia)

*Skeet (Men)*

1988 Axel Wegner (East Germany)
1992 Zhang Shan (China)
1996 Ennio Falco (Italy)
2000 Mykola Milchev (Ukraine)

*Small Bore Rifle (Prone) (Men)*

1988 Miroslav Varga (Czechoslovakia)
1992 Lee Eun-chul (South Korea)
1996 Christian Klees (Germany)
2000 Jonas Edmans (Sweden)

*Air Rifle (Men)*

1988 Goran Maksimovic (Yugoslavia)
1992 Yuri Fedkin (UT)
1996 Artem Khadzhibekov (Russia)
2000 Yalin Cai (China)

*Air Pistol (Men)*

1988 Tariou Kiriakov (USSR)
1992 Wang Yifu (China)
1996 Roberto di Donna (Italy)
2000 Franck Dumoulin (France)

*Sport Pistol (Women)*

1988 Nino Saloukvadze (USSR)
1992 Marina Logvinenko (UT)
1996 Li Duihong (China)
2000 Maria Grozdeva (Bulgaria)

*Air Rifle (Women)*

1988 Irina Chilova (USSR)
1992 Yeo Kab Soon (South Korea)
1996 Renata Mauer (Poland)
2000 Nancy Johnson (USA)

*Small Bore Rifle (Women)*

1988 Silvia Sperber (West Germany)
1992 Launa Meili (USA)
1996 Alexandra Ivosev (Yugoslavia)
2000 Renata Mauer-Rozanska (Poland)

*Air Pistol (Women)*

1988 Jasna Sekuric (Yugoslavia)
1992 Marina Logvinenko (UT)
1996 Olga Klochneva (Russia)
2000 Luna Tao (China)

## Skiing

### ❑ World Cup

A season-long competition first organized in 1967; champions are declared in downhill, slalom, giant slalom and super-giant slalom, as well as the overall

champion; points are obtained for performances in each category.

*Overall winners*

*Men*

| | |
|---|---|
| 1987 | Pirmin Zurbriggen (Switzerland) |
| 1988 | Pirmin Zurbriggen (Switzerland) |
| 1989 | Marc Girardelli (Luxembourg) |
| 1990 | Pirmin Zurbriggen (Switzerland) |
| 1991 | Marc Girardelli (Luxembourg) |
| 1992 | Paul Accola (Switzerland) |
| 1993 | Marc Girardelli (Luxembourg) |
| 1994 | Kjetil-Andre Aamodt (Norway) |
| 1995 | Alberto Tomba (Italy) |
| 1996 | Lasse Kjus (Norway) |
| 1997 | Luc Alphand (France) |
| 1998 | Hermann Maier (Austria) |
| 1999 | Lasse Kjus (Norway) |
| 2000 | Hermann Maier (Austria) |
| 2001 | Hermann Maier (Austria) |

*Women*

| | |
|---|---|
| 1987 | Maria Walliser (Switzerland) |
| 1988 | Michela Figini (Switzerland) |
| 1989 | Vreni Schneider (Switzerland) |
| 1990 | Petra Kronberger (Austria) |
| 1991 | Petra Kronberger (Austria) |
| 1992 | Petra Kronberger (Austria) |
| 1993 | Anita Wachter (Austria) |
| 1994 | Vreni Schneider (Switzerland) |
| 1995 | Vreni Schneider (Switzerland) |
| 1996 | Katja Seizinger (Germany) |
| 1997 | Pernilla Wiberg (Sweden) |
| 1998 | Katja Seizinger (Germany) |
| 1999 | Alexandra Meissnitzer (Austria) |
| 2000 | Michaela Dorfmeister (Austria) |
| 2001 | Janica Kostelic (Croatia) |

*Most wins*: Men (5), Marc Girardelli, as above. Women (6), Annemarie Moser-Pröll (Austria) 1971–5, 1979.

## Snooker

### ❑ World Professional Championship

Instituted in the 1926–7 season; a knockout competition open to professional players who are members of the World Professional Billiards and Snooker Association; played at the Crucible Theatre, Sheffield.

| | |
|---|---|
| 1987 | Steve Davis (England) |
| 1988 | Steve Davis (England) |
| 1989 | Steve Davis (England) |
| 1990 | Stephen Hendry (Scotland) |
| 1991 | John Parrott (England) |
| 1992 | Stephen Hendry (Scotland) |
| 1993 | Stephen Hendry (Scotland) |
| 1994 | Stephen Hendry (Scotland) |
| 1995 | Stephen Hendry (Scotland) |
| 1996 | Stephen Hendry (Scotland) |
| 1997 | Ken Doherty (Ireland) |
| 1998 | John Higgins (Scotland) |
| 1999 | Stephen Hendry (Scotland) |
| 2000 | Mark Williams (Wales) |
| 2001 | Ronnie O'Sullivan (England) |

*Most wins*: (15), Joe Davis (England) 1927–40, 1946.

### ❑ World Doubles

First played in 1982; discontinued after 1987.

*All winners*

| | |
|---|---|
| 1982 | Steve Davis (England)/Tony Meo (England) |
| 1983 | Steve Davis (England)/Tony Meo (England) |
| 1984 | Alex Higgins (Ireland)/Jimmy White (England) |
| 1985 | Steve Davis (England)/Tony Meo (England) |
| 1986 | Steve Davis (England)/Tony Meo (England) |
| 1987 | Mike Hallett (England)/Stephen Hendry (Scotland) |

*Most wins*: (4), Steve Davis and Tony Meo (England), as above.

### ❑ World Team Championship

Also known as the World Cup; first held in 1979.

| | |
|---|---|
| 1987 | Ireland 'A' |
| 1988 | England |
| 1989 | England |
| 1990 | Canada |
| 1991 | *not held* |
| 1992 | *not held* |
| 1993 | *not held* |
| 1994 | *not held* |
| 1995 | *not held* |
| 1996 | Scotland |
| 1997 | *not held* |
| 1998 | *not held* |
| 1999 | *not held* |

*Most wins*: (4), England 1981, 1983, 1988–9.

### ❑ World Amateur Championship

First held in 1963; originally took place every two years, but annual since 1984.

| | |
|---|---|
| 1987 | Darren Morgan (Wales) |
| 1988 | James Wattana (Thailand) |
| 1989 | Ken Doherty (Republic of Ireland) |
| 1990 | Stephen O'Connor (Republic of Ireland) |
| 1991 | Noppodol Noppajorn (Thailand) |
| 1992 | Neil Mosley (England) |
| 1993 | Chuchat Triratanapradit (Thailand) |
| 1994 | Mohamed Yusuf (Pakistan) |
| 1995 | Sakchai Sim-Nhan (Thailand) |
| 1996 | Stuart Bingham (England) |
| 1997 | Marco Fu (China/Hong Kong) |
| 1998 | Luke Simmonds (England) |
| 1999 | Ian Preece (Wales) |
| 2000 | Stephen Maguire (Scotland) |
| 2001 | *not held* |

*Most wins*: (2), Gary Owen (England) 1963, 1966; Ray Edmonds (England) 1972, 1974; Paul Mifsud (England) 1985–6.

## Softball

### ❑ World Championships

First held for women in 1965 and for men the following year; now held every four years.

*Men*

1988 USA
1992 Canada
1996 New Zealand
2000 New Zealand

*Most wins*: (5), USA 1966, 1968, 1976, 1980, 1988.

*Women*

1986 USA
1990 USA
1994 USA
1998 USA

*Most wins*: (6), USA 1970, 1974, 1986–98.

## Speedway

### ❑ World Championships

Individual championships inaugurated in 1936; team championship instituted in 1960; first official pairs world championship in 1970 (threes since 1991); became World Team Cup in 1994.

*Individual*

1987 Hans Nielsen (Denmark)
1988 Erik Gundersen (Denmark)
1989 Hans Nielsen (Denmark)
1990 Per Jonsson (Sweden)
1991 Jan Pedersen (Denmark)
1992 Gary Havelock (England)
1993 Sam Ermolenko (USA)
1994 Tony Rickardsson (Sweden)
1995 Hans Nielsen (Denmark)
1996 Billy Hamill (USA)
1997 Greg Hancock (USA)
1998 Tony Rickardsson (Sweden)
1999 Tony Rickardsson (Sweden)
2000 Mark Loram (England)
2001 Tony Rickardsson (Sweden)

*Most wins*: (6), Ivan Mauger (New Zealand) 1968–70, 1972, 1977, 1979.

*Pairs/Threes*

1987 Erik Gundersen/Hans Nielsen (Denmark)
1988 Erik Gundersen/Hans Nielsen (Denmark)
1989 Jeremy Doncaster/Paul Thorp (Great Britain)
1990 Sam Ermolenko/Rick Miller (USA)
1991 Hans Nielsen/Jan Pedersen/Tommy Knudsen (Denmark)
1992 Greg Hancock/Sam Ermolenko/Ronnie Correy (USA)
1993 Greg Hancock/Sam Ermolenko (USA)

### ❑ World Team Cup

1994 Per Gustaffson/Tony Rickardsson/Michael Karlsson (Sweden)
1995 Hans Nielsen/Tommy Knudsen/Brian Carger (Denmark)
1996 Tomasz Gollob/ Piotr Protasiewicz/Slawomir Drabik (Poland)
1997 Hans Neilsen/Tommy Knudsen/Jesper Jensen (Denmark)
1998 Greg Hancock/Sam Ermolenko/Billy Hamill (USA)
1999 Jason Crump/Jason Lyons/Leigh Adams/Ryan Sullivan/Todd Wiltshire (Australia)
2000 Tony Rickardsson/Mikael Karlsson/Henrik Gustafsson/Peter Karlsson/Niklas Klingberg (Sweden)
2001 Jason Crump/Leigh Adams/Ryan Sullivan/Todd Wiltshire/Craig Boyce (Australia)

*Most wins*: (9), Hans Nielsen 1979, 1986–91, 1995, 1997; Team (10) Denmark 1981, 1983–8, 1991, 1995, 1997.

## Squash

### ❑ World Open Championship

First held in 1976; takes place annually for men and women; every two years for women 1976–89.

*Men*

1987 Jansher Khan (Pakistan)
1988 Jahangir Khan (Pakistan)
1989 Jansher Khan (Pakistan)
1990 Jansher Khan (Pakistan)
1991 Rodney Martin (Australia)
1992 Jansher Khan (Pakistan)
1993 Jansher Khan (Pakistan)
1994 Jansher Khan (Pakistan)
1995 Jansher Khan (Pakistan)
1996 Jansher Khan (Pakistan)
1997 Rodney Eyles (Australia)
1998 Jonathon Power (Canada)
1999 Peter Nicol (Great Britain)
2000 *not held*
2001 *postponed*

*Women*

1987 Sue Devoy (New Zealand)
1989 Martine Le Moignan (Great Britain)
1990 Sue Devoy (New Zealand)
1991 *not held*
1992 Sue Devoy (New Zealand)
1993 Michelle Martin (Australia)
1994 Michelle Martin (Australia)
1995 Michelle Martin (Australia)
1996 Sarah Fitz-Gerald (Australia)
1997 Sarah Fitz-Gerald (Australia)
1998 Sarah Fitz-Gerald (Australia)
1999 Cassie Campion (Great Britain)
2000 Carol Owens (Australia)
2001 Sarah Fitz-Gerald (Australia)

*Most wins*: Men (8), Jansher Khan (Pakistan), as above. Women (4), Sue Devoy (New Zealand), 1985 and as above.

## Surfing

### ❑ World Professional Championship

A season-long series of Grand Prix events; first held in 1970.

*Men*

| | |
|---|---|
| 1987 | Damien Hardman (Australia) |
| 1988 | Barton Lynch (Australia) |
| 1989 | Martin Potter (Great Britain) |
| 1990 | Tommy Curren (USA) |
| 1991 | Damien Hardman (Australia) |
| 1992 | Kelly Slater (USA) |
| 1993 | Derek Ho (Hawaii) |
| 1994 | Kelly Slater (USA) |
| 1995 | Kelly Slater (USA) |
| 1996 | Kelly Slater (USA) |
| 1997 | Kelly Slater (USA) |
| 1998 | Kelly Slater (USA) |
| 1999 | Mark Occhilupo (Australia) |
| 2000 | Sunny Garcia (USA) |
| 2001 | C J Hobgood (USA) |

*Women*

| | |
|---|---|
| 1987 | Wendy Botha (South Africa) |
| 1988 | Frieda Zamba (USA) |
| 1989 | Wendy Botha (South Africa) |
| 1990 | Pam Burridge (Australia) |
| 1991 | Wendy Botha (Australia) |
| 1992 | Wendy Botha (Australia) |
| 1993 | Pauline Menczer (Australia) |
| 1994 | Lisa Andersen (USA) |
| 1995 | Lisa Andersen (USA) |
| 1996 | Lisa Andersen (USA) |
| 1997 | Lisa Andersen (USA) |
| 1998 | Layne Beachley (Australia) |
| 1999 | Layne Beachley (Australia) |
| 2000 | Layne Beachley (Australia) |
| 2001 | Layne Beachley (Australia) |

*Most wins*: Men (6), Kelly Slater (USA), as above. Women (4), Wendy Botha (South Africa), as above; Lisa Andersen (USA), as above; Layne Beachley (Australia), as above.

## Swimming and diving

### ❑ World Championships

First held in 1973 and again in 1975; since 1978 take place approximately every four years; the complete list of 2001 world champions is given below.

*Men*

| | |
|---|---|
| 50metres freestyle | Anthony Ervin (USA) |
| 100metres freestyle | Anthony Ervin (USA) |
| 200metres freestyle | Ian Thorpe (Australia) |
| 400metres freestyle | Ian Thorpe (Australia) |
| 1 500metres freestyle | Grant Hackett (Australia) |
| 100metres backstroke | Matt Welsh (Australia) |
| 200metres backstroke | Aaron Peirsol (USA) |
| 100metres breaststroke | Roman Sloudnov (Russia) |
| 200metres breaststroke | Brendan Hansen (USA) |
| 100metres butterfly | Lars Frolander (Sweden) |
| 200metres butterfly | Michael Phelps (USA) |
| 200metres individual medley | Massimiliano Rosolini (Italy) |
| 400metres individual medley | Alessio Boggiatto (Italy) |
| 4 × 100metres freestyle relay | Australia |
| 4 × 200metres freestyle relay | Australia |
| 4 × 100metres medley relay | Australia |
| 3metre springboard diving | Dimitry Saoutine (Russia) |
| 1metre springboard diving | Feng Wang (China) |

*Women*

| | |
|---|---|
| 50metres freestyle | Inge de Bruijn (Netherlands) |
| 100metres freestyle | Inge de Bruijn (Netherlands) |
| 200metres freestyle | Giaan Rooney (Australia) |
| 400metres freestyle | Yana Klochova (Ukraine) |
| 800metres freestyle | Hannah Stockbauer (Germany) |
| 100metres backstroke | Natalie Coughlin (USA) |
| 200metres backstroke | Diana Iuliana Mocanu (Romania) |
| 100metres breaststroke | Xuejuan Luo (China) |
| 200metres breaststroke | Agnes Kovacs (Hungary) |
| 100metres butterfly | Petria Thomas (Australia) |
| 200metres butterfly | Petria Thomas (Australia) |
| 200metres individual medley | Martha Bowen (USA) |
| 400metres individual medley | Yana Klochova (Ukraine) |
| 4 × 100metres freestyle relay | Germany |
| 4 × 200metres freestyle relay | Great Britain |
| 4 × 100metres medley relay | Australia |
| 1metre springboard diving | Blythe Hartley (Canada) |
| 3metre springboard diving | Mian Xu (China) |
| Synchronized swimming | |
| Solo | Olga Brusnikina (Russia) |
| Duet | Japan |
| Team | Russia |

## Table tennis

### ❑ World Championships

First held in 1926 and every two years since 1957.

*Swaythling Cup (Men's Team)*

| | |
|---|---|
| 1989 | Sweden |
| 1991 | Sweden |
| 1993 | Sweden |
| 1995 | China |
| 1997 | China |
| 1999 | *not held* |
| 2000 | Sweden |
| 2001 | China |

*Corbillon Cup (Women's Team)*

| | |
|---|---|
| 1987 | China |
| 1989 | China |
| 1991 | Unified Korea |
| 1993 | China |
| 1995 | China |
| 1997 | China |
| 1999 | *not held* |
| 2000 | China |
| 2001 | China |

*Most wins*: Swaythling Cup (12), Hungary 1926, 1928–31, 1933 (twice), 1935, 1938, 1949, 1952, 1979. Corbillon Cup (14), China 1965, 1975, 1977, 1979, 1981, 1983, 1985, 1987, 1989, 1993, 1995, 1997, 2000–2001.

*Men's Singles*

| | |
|---|---|
| 1987 | Jiang Jialiang (China) |
| 1989 | Jan-Ove Waldner (Sweden) |
| 1991 | Jorgen Persson (Sweden) |
| 1993 | Jean-Philippe Gatien (France) |
| 1995 | Kong Linghui (China) |
| 1997 | Jan-Ove Waldner (Sweden) |
| 1999 | Liu Guoliang (China) |
| 2001 | Wang Liqin (China) |

*Women's Singles*

| | |
|---|---|
| 1987 | He Zhili (China) |
| 1989 | Qiao Hong (China) |
| 1991 | Deng Yaping (China) |
| 1993 | Hyun Jung-Hwa (South Korea) |
| 1995 | Deng Yaping (China) |
| 1997 | Deng Yaping (China) |
| 1999 | Wang Nan (China) |
| 2001 | Wang Nan (China) |

*Men's Doubles*

| | |
|---|---|
| 1987 | Chen Longcan/Wei Quinguang (China) |
| 1989 | Jaerg Rosskopf/Stefen Fetzner (West Germany) |
| 1991 | Peter Karlsson/Tomas von Scheele (Sweden) |
| 1993 | Wang Tao/Lu Lin (China |
| 1995 | Wang Tao/Lu Lin (China) |
| 1997 | Jan-Ove Waldner/Jorgen Persson (Sweden) |
| 1999 | Liu Guoliang/Kong Linghui (China) |
| 2001 | Liu Guoliang/Kong Linghui (China) |

*Women's Doubles*

| | |
|---|---|
| 1987 | Yang Young-Ja/Hyun Jung-Hwa (Korea) |
| 1989 | Qiao Hong/Deng Yaping (China) |
| 1991 | Chen Zhie/Gao Jun (China) |
| 1993 | Liu Wei/Qiao Yunping (China) |
| 1995 | Qiao Hong/Deng Yaping (China) |
| 1997 | Wang Nan/Li Ju (China) |
| 1999 | Wang Nan/Li Ju (China) |
| 2001 | Wang Nan/Li Ju (China) |

*Mixed Doubles*

| | |
|---|---|
| 1987 | Hui Jun/Geng Lijuan (China) |
| 1989 | Yoo Nam-Kyu/Hyun Jung-Hwa (South Korea) |
| 1991 | Wang Tao/Liu Wei (China) |
| 1993 | Wang Tao/Liu Wei (China) |
| 1995 | Wang Tao/Liu Wei (China) |
| 1997 | Kong Linghui/Deng Yaping (China) |
| 1999 | Zhang Yingying/Ma Lin (China) |
| 2001 | Qin Zhijian/Yang Yin (China) |

*Most wins*: Men's singles (5), Viktor Barna (Hungary) 1930, 1932–5. Women's singles (6), Angelica Rozeanu (Romania) 1950–5. Men's doubles (8), Viktor Barna (Hungary/England) 1929–33 (won two titles 1933), 1935, 1939. Women's doubles (7), Maria Mednyanszky (Hungary) 1928, 1930–5. Mixed doubles (6), Maria Mednyanszky (Hungary) 1927–8, 1930–1, 1933 (two titles).

## Tennis (lawn)

### ❑ All-England Championships at Wimbledon

The All-England Championships at Wimbledon are Lawn Tennis's most prestigious championships; first held in 1877.

*Men's Singles*

| | |
|---|---|
| 1987 | Pat Cash (Australia) |
| 1988 | Stefan Edberg (Sweden) |
| 1989 | Boris Becker (West Germany) |
| 1990 | Stefan Edberg (Sweden) |
| 1991 | Michael Stich (Germany) |
| 1992 | André Agassi (USA) |
| 1993 | Pete Sampras (USA) |
| 1994 | Pete Sampras (USA) |
| 1995 | Pete Sampras (USA) |
| 1996 | Richard Krajicek (Netherlands) |
| 1997 | Pete Sampras (USA) |
| 1998 | Pete Sampras (USA) |
| 1999 | Pete Sampras (USA) |
| 2000 | Pete Sampras (USA) |
| 2001 | Goran Ivanisevic (Croatia) |

*Women's Singles*

| | |
|---|---|
| 1987 | Martina Navratilova (USA) |
| 1988 | Steffi Graf (West Germany) |
| 1989 | Steffi Graf (West Germany) |
| 1990 | Martina Navratilova (USA) |
| 1991 | Steffi Graf (Germany) |
| 1992 | Steffi Graf (Germany) |
| 1993 | Steffi Graf (Germany) |
| 1994 | Conchita Martínez (Spain) |
| 1995 | Steffi Graf (Germany) |
| 1996 | Steffi Graf (Germany) |
| 1997 | Martina Hingis (Switzerland) |
| 1998 | Jana Novotna (Czech Republic) |
| 1999 | Lindsay Davenport (USA) |
| 2000 | Venus Williams (USA) |
| 2001 | Venus Williams (USA) |

*Men's Doubles*

| | |
|---|---|
| 1987 | Ken Flach/Robert Seguso (USA) |
| 1988 | Ken Flach/Robert Seguso (USA) |
| 1989 | John Fitzgerald (Australia)/Anders Jarryd (Sweden) |

| | |
|---|---|
| 1990 | Rick Leach/Jim Pugh (USA) |
| 1991 | John Fitzgerald (Australia)/Anders Jarryd (Sweden) |
| 1992 | John McEnroe (USA)/Michael Stich (Germany) |
| 1993 | Todd Woodbridge/Mark Woodforde (Australia) |
| 1994 | Todd Woodbridge/Mark Woodforde (Australia) |
| 1995 | Todd Woodbridge/Mark Woodforde (Australia) |
| 1996 | Todd Woodbridge/Mark Woodforde (Australia) |
| 1997 | Todd Woodbridge/Mark Woodforde (Australia) |
| 1998 | Jacco Eltingh/Paul Haarhuis (Netherlands) |
| 1999 | Mahesh Bhupathi/Leander Paes (India) |
| 2000 | Todd Woodbridge/Mark Woodforde (Australia) |
| 2001 | Donald Johnson/Jared Palmer (USA) |

*Women's Doubles*

| | |
|---|---|
| 1987 | Claudia Kohde-Kilsch (West Germany)/ Helena Sukova (Czechoslovakia) |
| 1988 | Steffi Graf (West Germany)/Gabriela Sabatini (Argentina) |
| 1989 | Jana Novotna/Helena Sukova (Czechoslovakia) |
| 1990 | Jana Novotna/Helena Sukova (Czechoslovakia) |
| 1991 | Natalya Zvereva/Larissa Savchenko (USSR) |
| 1992 | Gigi Fernandez (USA)/Natalya Zvereva (CIS) |
| 1993 | Gigi Fernandez (USA)/Natalya Zvereva (CIS) |
| 1994 | Gigi Fernandez (USA)/Natalya Zvereva (CIS) |
| 1995 | Arantxa Sanchez Vicario (Spain)/Jana Novotna (Czech Republic) |
| 1996 | Helena Sukova (Czech Republic)/ Martina Hingis (Switzerland) |
| 1997 | Gigi Fernandez (USA)/Natalya Zvereva (Belarus) |
| 1998 | Jana Novotna (Czech Republic) Martina Hingis (Switzerland) |
| 1999 | Lindsay Davenport/Corina Morariu (USA) |
| 2000 | Serena Williams/Venus Williams (USA) |
| 2001 | Lisa Raymond (USA)/Rennae Stubbs (Australia) |

*Mixed Doubles*

| | |
|---|---|
| 1987 | Jo Durie/Jeremy Bates (Great Britain) |
| 1988 | Zina Garrison/Sherwood Stewart (USA) |
| 1989 | Jana Novotna (Czechoslovakia)/Jim Pugh (USA) |
| 1990 | Zina Garrison/Rick Leach (USA) |
| 1991 | Elizabeth Smylie/John Fitzgerald (Australia) |
| 1992 | Larissa Savchenko-Neiland (Latvia)/ Cyril Suk (Czechoslovakia) |
| 1993 | Martina Navratilova (USA)/Mark Woodforde (Australia) |
| 1994 | Helena Sukova (Czech Republic)/Todd Woodbridge (Australia) |
| 1995 | Martina Navratilova/Jonathan Stark (USA) |
| 1996 | Helena Sukova/Cyril Suk (Czech Republic) |
| 1997 | Helena Sukova/Cyril Suk (Czech Republic) |
| 1998 | Serena Williams (USA)/Max Mirnyi (Belarus) |
| 1999 | Lisa Raymond (USA)/Leander Paes (India) |
| 2000 | Kimberly Po/ Donald Johnson (USA) |
| 2001 | Daniela Hantuchova (Slovakia)/ Leos Friedl (Czech Republic) |

*Most wins*: Men's singles (7), William Renshaw (Great Britain) 1881–6, 1889, Pete Sampras, as above. Women's singles (9), Martina Navratilova (Czechoslovakia/USA) 1978, 1982–7, 1990. Men's doubles (8), Lawrence Doherty/Reg Doherty (Great Britain) 1897–1901, 1903–5. Women's doubles (12), Elizabeth Ryan (USA) 1914, 1919–23, 1925–7, 1930, 1933–4. Mixed doubles (7), Elizabeth Ryan (USA) 1919, 1921, 1923, 1927–8, 1930, 1932.

### ❑ United States Open

First held in 1891 as the United States Championship; became the United States Open in 1968.

*Men's Singles*

| | |
|---|---|
| 1987 | Ivan Lendl (Czechoslovakia) |
| 1988 | Mats Wilander (Sweden) |
| 1989 | Boris Becker (West Germany) |
| 1990 | Pete Sampras (USA) |
| 1991 | Stefan Edberg (Sweden) |
| 1992 | Stefan Edberg (Sweden) |
| 1993 | Pete Sampras (USA) |
| 1994 | Andre Agassi (USA) |
| 1995 | Pete Sampras (USA) |
| 1996 | Pete Sampras (USA) |
| 1997 | Pat Rafter (Australia) |
| 1998 | Pat Rafter (Australia) |
| 1999 | Andre Agassi (USA) |
| 2000 | Marat Safin (Russia) |
| 2001 | Lleyton Hewitt (Australia) |

*Women's Singles*

| | |
|---|---|
| 1987 | Martina Navratilova (USA) |
| 1988 | Steffi Graf (West Germany) |
| 1989 | Steffi Graf (West Germany) |
| 1990 | Gabriela Sabatini (Argentina) |
| 1991 | Monica Seles (Yugoslavia) |
| 1992 | Monica Seles (Yugoslavia) |
| 1993 | Steffi Graf (Germany) |
| 1994 | Arantxa Sanchez Vicario (Spain) |
| 1995 | Steffi Graf (Germany) |
| 1996 | Steffi Graf (Germany) |

| | |
|---|---|
| 1997 | Martina Hingis (Switzerland) |
| 1998 | Lindsay Davenport (USA) |
| 1999 | Serena Williams (USA) |
| 2000 | Venus Williams (USA) |
| 2001 | Venus Williams (USA) |

*Most wins*: Men (7), Richard Sears (USA) 1881–7; Bill Larned (USA) 1901–2, 1907–11; Bill Tilden (USA) 1920–5, 1929. Women (7), Molla Mallory (*née* Bjurstedt) (USA) 1915–16, 1918, 1920–2, 1926; Helen Wills-Moody (USA), 1923–5, 1927–9, 1931.

### ❑ Davis Cup

International team competition organized on a knockout basis; first held in 1900; contested on a challenge basis until 1972.

| | |
|---|---|
| 1987 | Sweden |
| 1988 | West Germany |
| 1989 | West Germany |
| 1990 | USA |
| 1991 | France |
| 1992 | USA |
| 1993 | Germany |
| 1994 | Sweden |
| 1995 | USA |
| 1996 | France |
| 1997 | Sweden |
| 1998 | Sweden |
| 1999 | Australia |
| 2000 | Spain |
| 2001 | France |

*Most wins*: (31), USA 1900, 1902, 1913, 1920–6, 1937–8, 1946–9, 1954, 1958, 1963, 1968–72, 1978–9, 1981–2, 1990, 1992, 1995.

## Tenpin bowling

### ❑ World Championships

First held in 1923 by the International Bowling Association; since 1954 organized by the Fédération Internationale des Quillieurs (FIQ); since 1963, when women first competed, held every four years.

*Men*

| | |
|---|---|
| 1987 | Rolland Patrick (France) |
| 1991 | Jon Juneau (USA) |
| 1995 | Marc Doi (Canada) |
| 1999 | Gery Verbuggen (Belgium) |

*Women*

| | |
|---|---|
| 1987 | Edda Piccini (Italy) |
| 1991 | Asa Larsson (Sweden) |
| 1995 | Debby Ship (Canada) |
| 1999 | Kelly Kulick (USA) |

*Most wins*: No one has won more than once.

## Trampolining

### ❑ World Championships

First held in 1964 and annually until 1968; since then, every two years.

*Men*

| | |
|---|---|
| 1988 | Vadim Krasnoshapka (USSR) |
| 1990 | Aleksandr Moskalenko (USSR) |
| 1992 | Aleksandr Moskalenko (Russia) |
| 1994 | Aleksandr Moskalenko (Russia) |
| 1996 | Dimitri Poliarauch (Belarus) |
| 1998 | German Khanytchve (Russia) |
| 1999 | Alexandre Moskalenko (Russia) |

*Women*

| | |
|---|---|
| 1988 | Rusadan Khoperia (USSR) |
| 1990 | Elena Merkulova (USSR) |
| 1992 | Elena Merkulova (Russia) |
| 1994 | Irina Karavaeva (Russia) |
| 1996 | Tatyana Kovaleva (Russia) |
| 1998 | Irina Karavaeva (Russia) |
| 1999 | Irina Karavaeva (Russia) |

*Most wins*: Men (3), Aleksandr Moskalenko (Russia), as above. Women (5), Judy Wills (USA) 1964–8.

## Tug of war

### ❑ World Outdoor Championships

Instituted in 1975, now usually held every two years; contested at 560kg from 1982.

| | 720kg | 640kg | 560kg |
|---|---|---|---|
| 1988 | Ireland | England | England |
| 1990 | Ireland | Ireland | Switzerland |
| 1992 | Switzerland | Switzerland | Spain |
| 1994 | Switzerland | Switzerland | Spain |
| 1996 | Netherlands | Switzerland | Ireland |
| 1998 | Netherlands | England | Spain |
| 2000 | Switzerland | Switzerland | Switzerland |

## Volleyball

### ❑ World Championships

Inaugurated in 1949; first women's championships in 1952; now held every four years, but Olympic champions are also world champions in Olympic years.

*Men*

| | |
|---|---|
| 1988 | USA |
| 1990 | Italy |
| 1992 | Brazil |
| 1994 | Italy |
| 1996 | Netherlands |
| 1998 | Italy |
| 2000 | Yugoslavia |

*Women*

| | |
|---|---|
| 1988 | USSR |
| 1992 | Cuba |
| 1994 | Cuba |
| 1996 | Cuba |
| 1998 | Cuba |
| 2000 | Cuba |

*Most wins*: Men (9), USSR 1949, 1952, 1960, 1962, 1964, 1968, 1978, 1980, 1982. Women (8), USSR 1952, 1956, 1960, 1968, 1970, 1972, 1980, 1988.

## Walking

### ❑ Lugano Trophy

The principal Road Walking trophy; contested every two years by men's national teams; first held in 1961.

| | |
|---|---|
| 1987 | USSR |
| 1989 | USSR |
| 1991 | Italy |
| 1993 | Mexico |
| 1995 | Mexico |
| 1997 | Russia |
| 1999 | Russia |
| 2001 | *not held* |

*Most wins*: (5), East Germany 1965, 1967, 1970, 1973, 1985.

### ❑ Eschborn Cup

The women's equivalent of the Lugano Trophy; first held in 1979; takes place every two years.

| | |
|---|---|
| 1987 | USSR |
| 1989 | USSR |
| 1991 | USSR |
| 1993 | Italy |
| 1995 | China |
| 1997 | Russia |
| 1999 | China |
| 2001 | *not held* |

*Most wins*: (5), USSR/Russia 1981, 1987–91, 1997.

## Water polo

### ❑ World Championships

First held in 1973, and sporadically since 1978; formerly included in the World Swimming Championships, now held separately; first women's event in 1986.

*Men*

| | |
|---|---|
| 1990 | Italy |
| 1994 | Italy |
| 1998 | Spain |
| 2001 | Spain |

*Women*

| | |
|---|---|
| 1990 | USSR |
| 1994 | Hungary |
| 1998 | Italy |
| 2001 | Italy |

### ❑ World Cup

Inaugurated in 1979 and held every two years. Women's event unofficial until 1989.

*Men*

| | |
|---|---|
| 1987 | Yugoslavia |
| 1989 | Yugoslavia |
| 1991 | USA |
| 1993 | Italy |
| 1995 | Hungary |
| 1997 | United States |
| 1999 | Hungary |
| 2001 | Spain |

*Women*

| | |
|---|---|
| 1988 | Netherlands |
| 1989 | Netherlands |
| 1991 | Netherlands |
| 1993 | Netherlands |
| 1995 | Australia |
| 1997 | Netherlands |
| 1999 | Netherlands |
| 2001 | Italy |

*Most wins*: Men (3), Hungary 1979, 1995, 1999; USA 1991, 1997; Yugoslavia 1987–9. Women (6), Netherlands, as above.

## Water skiing

### ❑ World Championships

First held in 1949; take place every two years; competitions for Slalom, Tricks, Jumps, and the Overall Individual title.

*Overall (Men)*

| | |
|---|---|
| 1987 | Sammy Duvall (USA) |
| 1989 | Patrice Martin (France) |
| 1991 | Patrice Martin (France) |
| 1993 | Patrice Martin (France) |
| 1995 | Patrice Martin (France) |
| 1997 | Patrice Martin (France) |
| 1999 | Patrice Martin (France) |
| 2001 | Jaret Llewellyn (Canada) |

*Overall (Women)*

| | |
|---|---|
| 1987 | Deena Brush (USA) |
| 1989 | Deena Mapple (née Brush) (USA) |
| 1991 | Karen Neville (Australia) |
| 1993 | Natalia Rumiantseva (Russia) |
| 1995 | Judy Messer (Canada) |
| 1997 | Elena Milakova (Russia) |
| 1999 | Elena Milakova (Russia) |
| 2001 | Elena Milakova (Russia) |

*Most wins*: Men (6), Patrice Martin (France), as above. Women (3), Willa McGuire (*née* Worthington) (USA) 1949–50, 1955; Liz Allan-Shetter (USA) 1965, 1969, 1975, Elena Milakova (Russia), as above.

## Weightlifting

### ❑ World Championships

First held in 1898; 11 weight divisions; the most prestigious is the 110kg-plus category (formerly known as Super Heavyweight); Olympic champions are automatically world champions in Olympic years.

*108kg-plus*

| | |
|---|---|
| 1987 | Aleksandr Kurlovich (USSR) |
| 1988 | Aleksandr Kurlovich (USSR) |
| 1989 | Stefan Botev (Bulgaria) |
| 1990 | Stefan Botev (Bulgaria) |
| 1991 | Aleksandr Kurlovich (USSR) |
| 1992 | Aleksandr Kurlovich (UT) |
| 1993 | Ronnie Weller (Germany) |
| 1994 | Aleksandr Kurlovich (Belarus) |
| 1995 | Andrey Chemerkin (Russia) |

| | |
|---|---|
| 1996 | Andrey Chemerkin (Russia) |
| 1997 | Andrey Chemerkin (Russia) |
| 1998 | Andrey Chemerkin (Russia) |
| 1999 | Andrey Chemerkin (Russia) |
| 2000 | Hossein Rezazadeh (Iran) |
| 2001 | Saeed Salem Jaber (Qatar) |

*Most titles (all categories)*: (8), John Davies (USA) 82.5kg 1938; over 82.5kg 1946–50; over 90kg 1951–2; Tommy Kono (USA) 67.5kg 1952; 75kg 1953, 1957–9; 82.5kg 1954–6; Vasiliy Alexseyev (USSR) over 110kg 1970–7.

## Wrestling

### ❑ World Championships

Graeco-Roman world championships first held in 1921; first freestyle championships in 1951; each style contests 10 weight divisions, the heaviest being the 130kg (formerly over 100kg) category; Olympic champions become world champions in Olympic years.

*Super-heavyweight/130kg*

*Freestyle*

| | |
|---|---|
| 1987 | Aslam Khadartsev (USSR) |
| 1988 | David Gobedzhishvilli (USSR) |
| 1989 | Ali Reiza Soleimani (Iran) |
| 1990 | David Gobedzhishvilli (USSR) |
| 1991 | Andreas Schroder (Germany) |
| 1992 | Bruce Baumgartner (USA) |
| 1993 | Bruce Baumgartner (USA) |
| 1994 | Mahmut Demir (Turkey) |
| 1995 | Bruce Baumgartner (USA) |
| 1996 | Mahmut Demir (Turkey) |
| 1997 | Zekeriya Güglü (Turkey) |
| 1998 | Alexis Rodriguez (Cuba) |
| 1999 | Stephen Neal (USA) |
| 2000 | David Moussoulbes (Russia) |
| 2001 | David Moussoulbes (Russia) |

*Graeco-Roman*

| | |
|---|---|
| 1987 | Igor Rostozotskiy (USSR) |
| 1988 | Aleksandr Karelin (USSR) |
| 1989 | Aleksandr Karelin (USSR) |
| 1990 | Aleksandr Karelin (USSR) |
| 1991 | Aleksandr Karelin (USSR) |
| 1992 | Aleksandr Karelin (UT) |
| 1993 | Aleksandr Karelin (Russia) |
| 1994 | Aleksandr Karelin (Russia) |
| 1995 | Aleksandr Karelin (Russia) |
| 1996 | Aleksandr Karelin (Russia) |
| 1997 | Aleksandr Karelin (Russia) |
| 1998 | Aleksandr Karelin (Russia) |
| 1999 | Aleksandr Karelin (Russia) |
| 2000 | Rulon Gardner (USA) |
| 2001 | Rulon Gardner (USA) |

*Most titles (all weight divisions)*: Freestyle (12), Aleksander Medved (USSR) 90kg 1962–4, 1966; 100kg 1967–8, Over 100kg 1969–72. Graeco-Roman (12), Aleksandr Karelin (Russia), as above.

## Yachting

### ❑ America's Cup

One of sport's famous trophies; first won by the schooner Magic in 1870; now held approximately every four years, when challengers compete in a series of races to find which of them races against the holder; all 25 winners up to 1983 were from the USA.

*Winning Yacht (Skipper)*

| | |
|---|---|
| 1987 | Stars & Stripes (USA) (Dennis Conner) |
| 1988 | Stars & Stripes (USA) (Dennis Conner) [1] |
| 1992 | America (USA) (Bill Koch) |
| 1995 | Black Magic (New Zealand) (Russell Coutts) |
| 2000 | Black Magic (New Zealand) (Russell Coutts) |

[1] Stars and Stripes (USA) skippered by Dennis Conner won a special challenge match but on appeal the race was awarded to the New Zealand boat. However the decision was reversed by the New York Appeals court in 1989.

*Most wins*: (Skipper) (3), Charlie Barr (USA) 1899, 1901, 1903; Harold Vanderbilt (USA) 1930, 1934, 1937; Dennis Conner (USA) 1980, 1987, 1988.

### ❑ Admiral's Cup

A two-yearly series of races, originally held in the English Channel, around Fastnet rock and at Cowes; originally four national teams of three boats per team, now nine teams of three boats per team; first held in 1957.

| | |
|---|---|
| 1987 | New Zealand |
| 1989 | Great Britain |
| 1991 | France |
| 1993 | Germany |
| 1995 | Italy |
| 1997 | USA |
| 1999 | Netherlands |
| 2001 | *not held* |

*Most wins*: (9), Great Britain 1957, 1959, 1963, 1965, 1971, 1975, 1977, 1981, 1989.

## Card, board and other indoor games

**baccarat** Casino card game; most popular version **baccarat banque**, in which bank plays against players; in another, **chemin de fer**, all players take turns to hold the bank; object is to assemble, either with two or three cards, a points value of nine: picture cards and the 10 = 0; ace = one; other cards face value; if total is a double figure then the first figure is ignored, eg 18 would count as 8. Of 15th-century derivation, thought to have been introduced into France from Italy during reign of Charles VIII.

**backgammon** Board game for two players; each has 15 round counters which are moved around the *outer* and *inner tables* on the throw of two dice; aim is to be first to return one's pieces home to inner table and remove them from the board. Equipment similar to backgammon was found in Tutankhamen's tomb; introduced to Britain by the Crusaders; known as backgammon from c.1750.

**bézique** Card game played with at least two players; each has a pack but with 2s, 3s, 4s, 5s and 6s taken out; object is to win tricks (rounds of play) and score points on the basis of the cards won. Believed to have originated in Spain and brought to England in 1861; first rules drawn up 1861; a variation is **rubicon bézique**.

**blackjack** Casino card game with object of accumulating score of 21 (with two cards this is a *blackjack*). Ace = one or 11; picture cards = 10; others according to face value. Normally four packs of cards are shuffled together and dealt from a wooden 'shoe' by a banker; bets placed before first card is dealt; all cards dealt face up.

**bridge** Card game developed from whist, using full set of 52 playing cards, played by two pairs of players; thought to have originated in either Greece or India, introduced into Britain in 1880. Most popular forms: **auction bridge** and **contract bridge**. In the former, trumps are decided by preliminary bid or auction. In contract bridge, the most widely played form, trumps are nominated by the highest bidder. Scoring uses chart designed by US inventor, Harold Stirling Vanderbilt, based on tricks (rounds of play) contracted for and won.

**canasta** Card game similar to rummy, where cards are picked up and discarded; uses two packs, including four jokers; object is to collect as many of same denomination as possible. All have points value, but jokers and deuces (2s) are 'wild' (can take any value). Originated in Uruguay in the 1940s, the name deriving from the Spanish word *canasta* ('basket'), probably referring to tray where cards were discarded.

**checkers** ► **draughts**

**chemin de fer** or **'chemmy'** Casino card game; variant of **baccarat banque**, played by up to nine players; object is to obtain total near as possible to nine with two or three cards; if total is a double figure then the first figure is ignored; 16 would count as 6. Ace = 1; picture cards = 10; others face value.

**chess** Game of strategy for two players using chequered board of 64 squares. Each player has 16 pieces: eight pawns, two castles or rooks, two knights, two bishops, queen and king; object is to capture or *checkmate* opponent's king; all pieces have set moves, queen is most versatile. Played in ancient India as *chaturanga*; earliest reference c.600AD; current pieces have existed in standard form for over 500 years.

**Cluedo®** Board game where board is divided into 'rooms' and the players, who are each dealt a few person, place, and implement cards, are characters who must find out the facts concerning a murder (ie murderer, implement used and scene of the crime), which are on cards seen by no-one and hidden in an envelope at the start. Detective work is done by deduction, arranging meetings in the rooms and asking the other character involved to reveal his or her relevant cards.

**contract bridge** ► **bridge**

**craps** Casino dice game of American origin, adapted from game 'hazard' in 1813. Using two dice, a player loses throwing 2, 3, and 12, but wins with 7 or 11.

**cribbage** Card game played with two, three or four people with pack of 52 cards and a holed board, the *peg board*, used for scoring. Number of cards dealt to each player is five, six or seven, depending on number of players; cards are discarded into a dummy hand, which each player has in turn; points are scored according to cards dropped (ie for playing a card that makes a pair, a run of three or more, etc); cards are discarded in each round until total of 31 is reached; play continues until the players have discarded all their cards; value of hand then calculated.

**dominoes** Indoor game, various forms, played by two or more players; dominoes are either wooden or plastic rectangular blocks, with the face of each divided into two halves, each half containing a number of spots, no two identical. In a double-six set of dominoes, every combination between 6–6 and 0–0 is marked on the 28 dominoes. Object of basic game is to lay out sequence or 'line' of dominoes, each player in turn having to put down a domino of the same value as the one at either end of the line.

**draughts** or (US) **checkers** (Game played on chess board by two players, each with 12 small, flat, round counters or *pieces*, which are lined up on alternate squares on the first three rows at either side of the board; object is to remove opponent's pieces from board by jumping over them into a vacant diagonal square, having got in a position to do so by moving only forward (until a piece reaches back row of opponent's 'territory', thus becoming a two-piece *king* and permitted to move backwards and

forwards) and always on squares of the same colour; believed to have been played in ancient Egypt; first book about draughts published Spain 1547.

**gin rummy** ► **rummy**

**go** National game of Japan; first played China c.1500BC; board game for two players played on grid of 19 vertical and 19 horizontal lines (361 intersections); each player has supply of counters and play alternates beginning with black; object is to conquer territory by both encircling vacant intersections and surrounding opponent's counters which are then removed from board; handicapping system exists.

**hazard** Card game for four players in pairs; similar to **solo**, but to make 25 cards, all cards with face value of two to eight are discarded, and joker is added.

**mah-jong** Chinese game, originally played with cards, introduced to the West under its present name after World War I; usually played by four people using 144 small tiles divided into six suits. (Sets containing 136 tiles and five suits are also used.) Aim is to collect sequences of tiles. Name means 'sparrow', a bird of mythical great intelligence, which appears on one tile.

**Monopoly**® Board game for two or more players; aim is acquisition of property; players move a counter each around a board which has some of a capital city's streets, stations and public utility companies on it, which can be bought, built upon, mortgaged etc and for which rent must be paid (using Monopoly money) when landed on as a non-owner. Game ends when all but one player are bankrupt.

**pinochle** Card game derived from **bézique**; uses two packs of 24 cards, all cards from two to eight having been discarded; object is to win tricks, as in whist, and to score points according to cards won: ace = 11; ten = 10; king = 4; queen = 3; jack = 2; nine = 0.

**poker** Gambling card game for two to eight players; object is to get a better hand than opponents (or convince them that you have one). Hands are ranked: best hand is *royal flush* ie 10, Jack, Queen, King, Ace, all of the same suit. Most popular varieties: five-card draw, five-card stud and seven-card stud. Poker started in 19th-century USA.

**pontoon** or **vingt-et-un** Card game; a variation of **blackjack**, played by any number of players, but ideally six. Object is to try to obtain a total of 21. A *royal pontoon* consists of a picture card and an ace (ace = 11 or 1). Bets are placed and bank held by any player (usually latest royal pontoon winner).

**roulette** Casino game played with ball and spinning wheel, which is divided into 37 alternately either red or black segments numbered 0 to 36, but not in numerical order. Bets are placed (before the wheel is spun) on where ball will come to rest, and can take several forms — on a single number, any two numbers, or any three numbers etc, and on whether winning one will be odd or even.

**rummy** Domestic card game; possibly derived from **mah-jong**; cards picked up and discarded with object of forming two *hands* of three and four cards, or one of seven; hand obtained must consist of cards of same denomination, or sequence in same suit. A variation is **gin rummy**, where hands are laid face upwards and can be added to by any player during the game. Points are obtained for each card dropped according to its face value, and deducted according to cards remaining in hand when one player wins game by disposing of all his or her cards.

**Scrabble**® Word game on special board for two to four players; points scored by placing letter tiles of different values crossword-fashion to form interlocking words; each player has choice of seven tiles until none remain. Scores can be doubled or trebled by making use of premium squares on the board.

**shogi** Japanese form of **chess**, believed to have originated in India; played on square board with pieces (of which each player has 20) of different powers; object is to *checkmate* king.

**solo** Card game; a form of **whist**, and similar to **bridge**; players must declare how many tricks they will win before each game; tricks won as in whist.

**Trivial Pursuit**® Board game in which players make progress by giving correct answers to general knowledge questions on eg art and literature, entertainment, geography, history, science and nature, and sport and leisure, which are written on special cards. Coloured wedges corresponding to all topics have to be won and the middle space reached to win the game.

**whist** Non-gambling card game; normally played with four people in pairs; each player receives 13 cards; object is to win more *tricks*, or rounds of play, than the opposing pair; trumps (suit of which cards can win against any card of any other suit) are decided before each game; at *whist drives* trumps are normally played in the following order: hearts, clubs, diamonds, spades; a round of 'no trumps' (where all suits have equal power) is also common.

## Hobbies and pastimes

**abseiling** Descending a steep slope or mountainside; used in mountaineering but now recognized as pursuit in itself. A rope is attached either around the body or through *karabiners* (steel links with spring clips in one side) and is secured from above so that speed of downwards climb can be safely controlled.

**aerobics** System of exercises which are designed to increase oxygen consumption and speed blood circulation, thereby increasing fitness.

**ballooning ▸ hot-air ballooning**

**batik** Ancient folk art of fabric design using a basic wax-resist technique; warm wax is painted onto light-coloured fabric, according to a chosen design, and then dipped into a solution of dye and water — only unwaxed fabric takes dye so when wax is removed design appears against coloured background.

**bell-ringing** or **campanology** Ringing church bells; two popular forms; *change ringing* (handpulled method) and *carillon* (uses keyboard connected to the clapper of the bells).

**birdwatching** or **ornithology** Study and observation of birds in their natural habitat; may involve recording details concerning bird anatomy, behaviour, song and flight patterns.

**brass-rubbing** Duplicating designs on ornamental brass plate, such as is found in churches; brass is covered with paper and then rubbed over with coloured crayons or chalk until copy is produced.

**bungee-jumping** Leaping from river-crossing bridges; practised most commonly in USA, Australia and New Zealand; person's legs are tied together, covered with protective material, and then clipped with a strong elastic (bungee) rope (adapted to their weight and height), and secured firmly to the bridge; the jumper 'dives for the horizon' from a platform on top of the bridge and freefalls, before hanging suspended by the elastic rope, experiencing a series of bouncing movements.

**butterfly-collecting** or **lepidoptery** Obtaining butterflies either by catching them in their natural environment or purchasing them already preserved; insects are identified and mounted, usually in a glass display unit.

**calligraphy** Penmanship, or writing at its most formal; a major art form in many countries of E Asia and in Arabic-speaking countries; revival of interest in Europe and America since the 19th century; special pen nibs, brushes, ink and paper usually required.

**campanology ▸ bell-ringing**

**candle-making** Producing candles by repeatedly dipping a prepared wick into wax, pouring wax over a wick or pouring wax into moulds; paraffin wax is most often used; candles can be created in any colour, shape, size or fragrance.

**climbing** Generally refers to scaling anything from a 15m/50ft wall to an assault on the Himalayas, although there should be some level of difficulty in reaching highest point; as well as the physical aspect, climbing also involves psychological thrills of discovery, exploration and avoidance of danger.

**coin-collecting ▸ numismatics**

**cookery** Preparing and cooking food; may involve production of exotic and speciality dishes and creation of new recipes.

**crochet** Making a variety of textile items; uses a special hook to loop yarn in a number of different stitches according to pattern requirements.

**dancing** The following are just a few of the many forms that dancing takes: **1 ballroom** Social dance form; developed early 20th century, revealing strong influence of American ragtime, syncopated rhythms producing the foxtrot, quickstep and tango; also popular were animal dances (eg Turkey Trot, Bunny Hug) and Latin-American dances (cha-cha-cha and samba). **2 country** Historic social dances began to spread across Europe in the 17th century, taught by travelling dancing masters, adding 19th-century forms such as the waltz, quadrille and polka; emphasis on spatial design, with couples in long or circular sets, using simple walking steps. **Traditional dance** In *England*, began 16th century; lines, circles, and square sets are common patterns; steps based on simple walking and skipping. In *Ireland*, early forms share the European history of country and court dance; jigs and reels typical, resembling English and Scottish stepping; competitive high stepping form is a 20th-century creation; arms are held stiffly to the sides; body is erect; there is rapid, complex rhythmic use of the feet; and the knees are sharply lifted. In *Scotland* some country dances are commonly known as **Scottish reels**, but strictly, the reel is an indigenous form of stepping dance performed to bagpipes and showing French aristocratic connections; originally performed in circles as in 'round reels' (threesome, foursome, eightsome etc) and later in lines, 'longwise forms'; feet are in balletic positions with the weight on the balls of the feet; typical steps include slip step, pas de basque, strathspey, and schottische; men's costume is the kilt; women wear dresses with a tartan sash. Other country dances in Scotland also progress in two long lines of male/female couples, and there are square dances (eg quadrille), and circle dances (eg Circassian circle); dances take place to traditional tunes, formerly played on the fiddle, and now also on the accordion; nowadays reels danced to these instruments too. In *Wales*, due to former religious disapproval, there are few traces of traditional dance, but there are some reels and country dances similar to those in England. **3 disco** Popular form of dance mainly for young people, originating 1960s; accompanying music is usually contemporary, often loud, with a rhythmic beat. Definite fashions eg new romantic style, soul, punk, break dancing, robotics, and gothic style. It takes account of Black music, particularly rapping, and

heavy rock. **4 jazz** N American form of vernacular dancing performed to jazz rhythms; a style that swings, owing its origins to African and Caribbean forms of dance, blended with European influences; also used in musical shows on Broadway and in the UK (eg *Cats*). **5 Morris** Ceremonial form of traditional dance found in England. Distinctive features: stamping and hopping; files of performers usually dressed in white and always carrying a stick, handkerchief or garland; some wear bells; accordion or concertina with brass drum accompaniment. Originally exclusively a male domain, women can now take part. **6 step** Social and often competitive form of dance relying on rhythmically complex footwork using parts of the foot, heel, and toe beats, often performed in clogs; maintained through folk festivals both as social and exhibition dance; structure in performance is part fixed and part improvised.

**dressmaking** Pastime usually undertaken to make low-cost clothes, using a bought tissue-paper pattern and a length of material, but also a creative hobby lending itself to sophisticated fashion design.

**electronic games** Games programmed and controlled by a small microprocessor; most connected to visual display unit and known as **video games**; many have war themes, others simulate sports; some board games (eg Monopoly®, Scrabble®, Trivial Pursuit®) are available in electronic form; all operated either by using a computer keyboard or a joystick plugged into home computer. Larger versions are produced for use in eg amusement arcades.

**embroidery** Ornamentation of fabric with decorative stitching; dates from very early times, when designs were sewn on to a base fabric by hand; became highly developed eg for rich garments and furnishings, and church vestments in the Middle East, India and Europe; famous example is 11th-century Bayeux tapestry. Hand embroidery still exists as a craft, but today computer-controlled sewing machines are also used.

**fell-walking** Trekking on hills or moorland, wearing specialized walking boots and using map and compass to find direction in otherwise desolate tracts of land.

**gardening** Laying out and cultivating plants on a piece of ground for ornamental purposes, rather than for economic gain; type of garden depends not only on gardener's tastes and space available, but also on soil type and fertility, climate, air pollution, and shelter from wind and sun, provided by eg existing trees and rocks. Some special garden types and techniques are: **1 espalier** Technique involving the training of trees on a lattice-work of wood flat against a wall; tree is carefully tied to the trellis and pruned to control its shape, often creating a decorative effect in limited space. **2 herb garden** Usually includes shrubs as well as herbs, all mostly perennial. The herbs are used primarily for cooking, either fresh or dried (see pp76–8). **3 Japanese style garden** Maximum use is made of evergreen plants, the only colour being eg spring-flowering azaleas, and autumn berries; features include stone lanterns, walkways, natural or simulated streams and waterfalls, and occasional stones; **bonsai** technique is associated with Japanese style, though it originated in China; involves dwarfing plants by shallow planting in containers, starvation, root and soil pruning, and the twisting of new shoots with wire to give plants gnarled, aged appearance; pine, fir and maple trees often used. **4 rock garden** or **rockery** Man-made or natural heap of soil and rock fragments in a garden for growing rock plants, usually flowering, hardy perennials, and dwarf trees; rock gardens are often terraced to prevent the topsoil being washed away by rain. **5 water garden** Plants arranged in and around natural or artificial pools and streams, eg water lilies and marsh marigolds. **6 wild-flower garden** Often includes native marsh or bog plants as well as forest-floor wild flowers; usually requires a rich, acid soil.

**go-kart racing** Driving and racing small, single-seated, motorized vehicles around outdoor tracks; originated USA; has gained a popular following in the UK.

**hatha yoga ▸ yoga**

**horse-riding** Involves acquirement of specialized skills learned in order to control the horse from a seated position on its back. Commands are signalled by hand, leg and voice instruction, sometimes reinforced by the use of whip and spurs.

**hot-air ballooning** Being carried as a passenger through the air by hot-air balloon; may involve navigating the balloon, the mechanics of getting the balloon airborne, and following the balloon in road vehicles.

**ikebana** Formal Japanese style of flower arrangement; a few blooms or leaves are selected and placed in very careful relationship to one another; popular 1950s and 1960s pastime in W Europe.

**kite-flying** Flying a light frame covered with paper, cloth or plastic at the end of a length of string, usually requiring windy conditions. Kites can be brightly coloured and of various different shapes; simplest form has only one string, but with two strings, one attached to each side, it can be more easily controlled from the ground and made to do complicated loops and dives in the air.

**knitting** Ancient craft used for making fabric; loops of yarn are linked together using two or three hand-held needles; machines are now used to produce complex knitted garments and fabrics of many kinds, but they cannot create all the intricate designs commonly produced by skilled hand knitters.

**lace-making** Most popular method (especially in Europe) of lace production is *bobbin* or *pillow* lace. As many as 1 100 bobbins are wound with thread and hung on pins which are inserted, according to the design required, into the small holes on a piece of stiff

paper attached to a pillow, cushion or polystyrene base; bobbins then looped, plaited and twisted following pattern instructions until the desired item is produced.

**lepidoptery** ▸ **butterfly-collecting**

**macramé** Making a type of coarse lace by knotting and plaiting; widespread revival in mid-19th century; used to make decorative fringed borders for costumes as well as furnishings eg window blinds, antimacassars, and cushions.

**model-making** Mainly the construction of cars, ships, trains and aeroplanes by gluing together preshaped plastic or wooden parts from specialized kits. Some enthusiasts design and produce the parts for their own models.

**numismatics** Studying and collecting coins, notes and other similar objects, eg medals; dates from Italian Renaissance; 17th-century collectors were first to catalogue their collections.

**ornithology** ▸ **bird-watching**

**origami** Making models of animals or other objects by folding sheets of paper into shapes, with minimum use of scissors or other implements; often used as an educational aid for young children; originated 10th-century Japan.

**paintball** Simulation of military combat; involves firing paint pellets which splatter on contact with clothing to indicate a hit; played by two or more teams; popular in the USA, UK and parts of Europe; believed to be beneficial in the reduction of stress.

**panelology** Carving thin, wooden panels which may be either framed or lodged between other upright and cross pieces normally stretching across the surface of a wall; pictures are often painted onto these panels; most effective results achieved on panels made from chestnut, oak or white poplar.

**paragliding** Being towed through the air by a plane whilst wearing an adapted parachute and then being separated in order to glide to the ground.

**philately** Collecting stamps; one of the world's most popular hobbies; often involves documentation in special books or albums; stamps issued and stamped by the post office on their first day of issue (*first-day covers*) increasingly popular; first philatelist said to have been John Tomlinson, who started collecting the day after the issue of the first postage stamp (the *penny black*) in 1840.

**pigeon-fancying** Breeding pigeons to exhibit or race, popular in the USA, UK and France.

**pigeon racing** Pigeons are taken from their loft and released at a starting point that may be hundreds of miles away; their homing instinct takes them back to their loft where a special clock times their arrival, thus establishing the fastest pigeon.

**pottery** or **potting** Forming clay objects; moist clay is shaped and then dried, usually by *firing* in a *kiln* or oven. Shaping by hand may be aided by using a *potter's wheel*, on which a lump of clay is rotated so it can be *thrown* by the potter's hands; moulding may involve either pressing soft clay into a mould and allowing it to dry, or *slip moulding*, where liquid clay or *slip* is poured into a mould that absorbs the moisture; shaped or moulded objects can be decorated by etching and painted with a colour *glaze*. Pottery tends to be porous and so is protected by a second glaze, which may be transparent or opaque and also gives shiny decorative appearance. Glaze is applied after first firing (when the pottery is called *biscuit*); then object is placed in kiln a second time at a lower temperature.

**scuba diving** Underwater swimming with the aid of *scuba* (self-contained underwater breathing apparatus) or *aqualung*, first developed in 1942 by Jacques Cousteau and Émil Gagnan; equipment consists of air tank(s), face mask, air regulator, depth gauge, weight belt and buoyancy compensator; diver propels himself with his legs, wearing large *fins* or *flippers*.

**shuffleboard** or **shovelboard** Deck game played aboard ship; a larger version of the popular shove-halfpenny; wooden discs, usually c.15cm/6in in diameter, are pushed along deck with long-handled drivers into scoring area.

**skateboarding** Riding on a single flexible board, longer and wider than the foot, fixed with four small wheels on the underside; speeds of over 100kph/60mph are possible and difficult jumps performed; developed as a way of experiencing surfing thrills on land; became popular in 1960s USA and in UK in 1970s and again in late 1980s.

**skin-diving** Underwater swimming, popularized in the 1930s. Skin-divers use only goggles, face mask, flippers, and short breathing tube or *snorkel*.

**skipping** Making jumps over a rope, the ends of which are held in each hand so that it can be twirled over the head and under the feet; often thought of as a child's pastime; recognized as good form of exercise and keep-fit.

**skittles** Game played in several different forms; object is to knock down nine pins with a ball. **Alley skittles** is played in long alleys and **table skittles** is played indoors on a specially constructed table with a swivelled ball attached to a mast by means of a chain; pins are much smaller than those used in tenpin bowling, and are replaced manually, rather than mechanically.

**spinning** Converting fibres into yarns, originally using distaff and later the spinning wheel, and now often using methods such as friction and rotor spinning; two types of yarn traditionally produced were *woollen* (fibres are randomly arranged), and *worsted* (fibres lie parallel to the length of the yarn).

**stamp-collecting** ▸ **philately**

**tapestry** Creation of decorative textiles, originally hand woven, with multi-coloured pictorial designs, made by passing coloured threads among fixed warp threads; Oriental in origin, used for wall hangings, furniture and floor coverings.

**taxidermy** Preparation and practice of creating lifelike replicas of animals and birds from their treated skins and the careful use of celluloids and other plastics.

**train-spotting** Identifying locomotives by their numbers or names and ticking them off in special, collectable notebooks.

**video games** ► **electronic games**

**weaving** Ancient fabric-producing craft; warp (lengthwise) and weft (crosswise) threads are interlaced on machines called *looms*; hand looms known from very early times; modern industry uses modern weaving looms which have dispensed with shuttles — 'bullets', 'rapiers', water jets and air jets now carry the weft across the warp, with 1 500 picks per minute being possible on some machines.

**yoga** In Indian religious tradition, any of various physical and contemplative techniques designed to free the superior, conscious element in a person from involvement with the inferior material world. **Hatha yoga** most common form in W Hemisphere; importance of physical exercises and positions and breathing-control is stressed in promoting physical and mental well-being.

# THOUGHT AND BELIEF

## Greek gods of mythology

| | |
|---|---|
| **Adonis** | God of vegetation and rebirth |
| **Aeolus** | God of the winds |
| **Alphito** | Barley goddess of Argos |
| **Aphrodite** | Goddess of love and beauty |
| **Apollo** | God of prophecy, music, youth, archery and healing |
| **Ares** | God of war |
| **Arethusa** | Goddess of springs and fountains |
| **Artemis** | Goddess of fertility, chastity and hunting |
| **Asclepius** | God of healing |
| **Athene** | Goddess of prudence and wise council; protectress of Athens |
| **Atlas** | A Titan who bears up the earth |
| **Attis** | God of vegetation |
| **Boreas** | God of the north wind |
| **Cronus** | Father of Zeus |
| **Cybele** | Goddess of the earth |
| **Demeter** | Goddess of the harvest |
| **Dionysus** | God of wine, vegetation and ecstasy |
| **Eos** | Goddess of the dawn |
| **Eros** | God of love |
| **Gaia** | Goddess of the earth |
| **Ganymede** | God of rain |
| **Hades** | God of the underworld |
| **Hebe** | Goddess of youth |
| **Hecate** | Goddess of the moon |
| **Helios** | God of the sun |
| **Hephaestus** | God of fire |
| **Hera** | Goddess of marriage and childbirth; queen of heaven |
| **Hermes** | Messenger of the gods |
| **Hestia** | Goddess of the hearth |
| **Hypnos** | God of sleep |
| **Iris** | Goddess of the rainbow |
| **Morpheus** | God of dreams |
| **Nemesis** | God of destiny |
| **Nereus** | God of the sea |
| **Nike** | Goddess of victory |
| **Oceanus** | God of the river Oceanus |
| **Pan** | God of male sexuality and of herds |
| **Persephone** | Goddess of the underworld and of corn |
| **Poseidon** | God of the sea |
| **Rhea** | The original mother goddess; wife of Cronus |
| **Selene** | Goddess of the moon |
| **Thanatos** | God of death |
| **Zeus** | Overlord of the Olympian gods and goddesses; god of the sky and all its properties |

## Roman gods of mythology

| | |
|---|---|
| **Apollo** | God of the sun |
| **Bacchus** | God of wine and ecstasy |
| **Bellona** | Goddess of war |
| **Ceres** | Goddess of corn |
| **Consus** | God of seed sowing |
| **Cupid** | God of love |
| **Diana** | Goddess of fertility and hunting |
| **Egreria** | Goddess of fountains and childbirth |
| **Epona** | Goddess of horses |
| **Fauna** | Goddess of fertility |
| **Faunus** | God of crops and herbs |
| **Feronia** | Goddess of spring flowers |
| **Fides** | God of honesty |
| **Flora** | Goddess of fruitfulness and flowers |
| **Fortuna** | Goddess of chance and fate |
| **Genius** | Protective god of individuals, groups and the state |
| **Janus** | God of entrances, travel, the dawn |
| **Juno** | Goddess of marriage, childbirth, light |
| **Jupiter** | God of the sky and its attributes (sun, moon, thunder, rain, etc) |
| **Lares** | Gods of the house |
| **Liber Pater** | God of agricultural and human fertility |
| **Libitina** | Goddess of funeral rites |
| **Luna** | Goddess of the moon |
| **Maia** | Goddess of fertility |
| **Mars** | God of war |
| **Mercury** | Messenger of the gods; also god of merchants |
| **Minerva** | Goddess of war, craftsmen, education and the arts |
| **Mithras** | The sun god; god of regeneration |
| **Neptune** | God of the sea |
| **Ops** | Goddess of the harvest |
| **Orcus** | God of death |
| **Pales** | Goddess of flocks |
| **Penates** | Gods of food and drink |
| **Picus** | God of woods |
| **Pluto** | God of the underworld |
| **Pomona** | Goddess of fruit trees |

| | |
|---|---|
| **Portunus** | God of husbands |
| **Proserpina** | Goddess of the underworld |
| **Rumina** | Goddess of nursing mothers |
| **Saturn** | God of fertility and agriculture |
| **Silvanus** | God of trees and forests |
| **Venus** | Goddess of spring, gardens and love |
| **Vertumnus** | God of fertility |
| **Vesta** | Goddess of the hearth |
| **Victoria** | Goddess of victory |
| **Vulcan** | God of fire |

## Norse gods of mythology

| | |
|---|---|
| **Aegir** | God of the sea |
| **Aesir** | Race of warlike gods, including Odin, Thor, Tyr |
| **Alcis** | Twin gods of the sky |
| **Balder** | Son of Odin and favourite of the gods |
| **Bor** | Father of Odin |
| **Bragi** | God of poetry |
| **Fafnir** | Dragon god |
| **Fjorgynn** | Mother of Thor |
| **Frey** | God of fertility |
| **Freyja** | Goddess of libido |
| **Frigg** | Goddess of fertility; wife of Odin |
| **Gefion** | Goddess who received virgins after death |
| **Heimdall** | Guardian of the bridge Bifrost |
| **Hel** | Goddess of death; Queen of Niflheim, the land of mists |
| **Hermod** | Son of Odin |
| **Hoder** | Blind god who killed Balder |
| **Hoenir** | Companion to Odin and Loki |
| **Idunn** | Guardian goddess of the golden apples of youth; wife of Bragi |
| **Kvasir** | God of wise utterances |
| **Logi** | Fire god |
| **Loki** | God of mischief |
| **Mimir** | God of wisdom |
| **Nanna** | Goddess wife of Balder |
| **Nehallenia** | Goddess of plenty |
| **Nerthus** | Goddess of earth |
| **Njord** | God of ships and the sea |
| **Norns** | Goddesses of destiny |
| **Odin (Woden, Wotan)** | Chief of the Aesir family of gods, the 'father' god; the god of battle, death, inspiration |
| **Otr** | Otter god |
| **Ran** | Goddess of the sea |
| **Sif** | Goddess wife of Thor |
| **Sigyn** | Goddess wife of Loki |
| **Thor (Donar)** | God of thunder and sky; good crops |
| **Tyr** | God of battle |
| **Ull** | Stepson of Thor, an enchanter |
| **Valkyries** | Female helpers of the gods of war |
| **Vanir** | Race of benevolent gods, including Njord, Frey, Freyja |
| **Vidar** | Slayer of the wolf, Fenrir |
| **Weland (Volundr, Wayland, Weiland)** | Craftsman god |

## Egyptian gods of mythology

| | |
|---|---|
| **Amun-Re** | Universal god |
| **Anubis** | God of funerals |
| **Apis** | God of fertility |
| **Aten** | Unique god |
| **Geb** | God of the earth |
| **Hathor** | Goddess of love |
| **Horus** | God of light |
| **Isis** | Goddess of magic |
| **Khnum** | Goddess of creation |
| **Khonsou** | Son of Amun-Re |
| **Maat** | Goddess of order |
| **Nephthys** | Goddess of funerals |
| **Nut** | God of the sky |
| **Osiris** | God of vegetation |
| **Ptah** | God of creation |
| **Sekhmet** | Goddess of might |
| **Seth** | God of evil |
| **Thoth** | Supreme scribe |

## Figures of myth and legend

**Bold** type indicates that a figure of mythology is described elsewhere in the list.

**Achilles** Greek hero; son of **Peleus** and the goddess **Thetis**; his body invulnerable to injury, except his ankle, due to being held by the ankles when he was dipped in the R Styx (in another version **Cheiron** replaced his ankle bone with one taken from the fast-running giant Damysos); killed with an arrow in the heel by **Paris** or **Apollo**.

**Actaeon** Greek hero; a hunter who came upon **Artemis**, the goddess of chastity, while she was bathing and therefore naked; she threw water at him, changing him into a stag, so that he was pursued and then killed by his own hounds.

**Adad** Mesopotamian god of storms; known throughout the area of Babylonian influence; the Assyrians called him **Hadad**, and in the Bible he is Rimmon, the god of thunder; helped to cause the Great Flood in Gilgamesh; his symbol was the lightning held in his hand and his animal the bull.

**Adapa** Akkadian hero; one of the seven Apkallu, beings of great brilliance and genius, and envoy of the god **Ea**, the divine creator of Man, who lost the opportunity of immortality due to disagreements between Ea and **Anu**, the god of heaven.

**Aditi** Indian goddess; mother of the gods and all beings, and the guardian of childbirth; outwith the divine world, she represented *everything* at the same time, being the total, the beginning, the end and the opposites; adopted by Buddhist tradition.

**Adonis** God of Phoenician origin; son of Myrrha, the daughter of the king of Syria who had been turned into a tree; spent one third of the year with **Persephone**, goddess of hell, and two thirds with **Aphrodite** after a decision by **Zeus**; mortally wounded by a wild boar in a battle.

**Aegir** Norse god of the sea; a giant, who collected dead sailors in his hall on the island of Hlesey; here also he sometimes gave banquets to the gods.

**Aegisthus** Greek hero; son of **Thyestes**; while **Agamemnon** was absent at Troy he became the lover of **Clytemnestra**; together they killed Agamemnon on his return to Argo; later killed by **Orestes**.

**Aeneas** Greek hero; son of **Aphrodite**, and bravest of the Trojans after **Hector** whose command he replaced in the fight against the Greeks; sailed to coast of Italy and is said to have given Rome its divine origin; subject of the *Aeneid* by Virgil.

**Aeolus** Greek god of the winds; in the *Odyssey*, Aeolus lived on an island, and gave **Odysseus** the winds tied in a bag so that his ship would not be blown off course; the ship had nearly reached Ithaca when Odysseus's men opened the bag, thinking it contained treasure; as a result, the ship was blown far away.

**Aesculapius ► Asclepius**

**Agamemnon** Greek king of Argos; commander of the Greek army in the Trojan War; Homer calls him 'king of men'; on his return he was murdered by his wife **Clytemnestra**.

**Agni** Indian god of fire; immortal god, regarded as the guide and protector of men; had two faces, one calm, one terrible, and gave both life and death.

**Ahura Mazda** Indo-Iranian god; had the form of the sun and nine wives; creator of other living beings and formed the world by his thought; his powers made plants grow and allowed fire to give its heat, water to quench thirst, animals to reproduce and armies to be victorious.

**Ajax** Two Greek heroes of the Trojan War; one was the son of Telamon, king of Salamis, therefore known as Telamonian Ajax and was proverbial for his size and strength; in all the worst situations he 'stood like a tower'; when the armour of the dead **Achilles** was not given to him, he went mad and killed himself. The second was the son of Oileus, king of Locris; returning from Troy, he provoked the anger of the gods, and was killed by **Poseidon** as he reached the shore of Greece.

**Alcestis** Greek heroine; she saved her husband, Admetus, who was doomed to die, by offering to die in his place; the action so impressed **Heracles** that he wrestled with the messenger of death and brought her back to life.

**Alcmaeon** Greek hero; to avenge the death of his father, Amphiaros, he killed his mother, and was pursued by the **Erinyes** until he came to a land which had not seen the sun at the time of his mother's death; he found this recently emerged land at the mouth of the R Achelous; **Apollo** commanded him to lead the expedition of the **Epigoni** against Thebes.

**Alcyone ► Halcyone**

**Alexander ► Paris**

**Amaterasu** Japanese goddess of the sun and light; considered to be the divine origin of the imperial dynasty; shut herself in a cave after a conflict with her brother Susa-no-o, plunging the world into darkness; returned light to the world when the gods managed to tempt her out.

**Amazons** Warrior-women of Greek myth; people of the Amazon state, where men were only tolerated for work of a servile nature; removed one breast so that they would not be restricted in the practice of archery and spear-throwing; said to be descendants of the god of war, **Ares**, and the **Nymph**, Harmony; crushed the Atlantians, occupied Gorgon and the greater part of Libya, fought with **Priam** during the Trojan war and invaded Attica; their leader, Hippolyta, married **Theseus**.

**Amen ► Amun-Re**

**Amitabha** The divine buddha; one of five 'meditation buddhas' sent by Adi buddha, the original buddha; wished to gather together all those who would pray to him with faith, to enjoy perfect happiness until they entered nirvana.

**Amma** Dogon god; origin of all creation; with the earth gave birth to twins who were sacrificed to make the earth fertile, then brought back to life in the form of a human couple; created the sun and divided the world into two domains; his myth led to the practice of male circumcision.

**Ammon, Amon ► Amun-Re**

**Amphitrite** Greek goddess of the sea; married to **Poseidon**; the mother of **Triton** and other minor deities.

**Amphitryon** In Greek mythology, the husband of Alcmene; in his absence, **Zeus** took his shape and so became the father of **Heracles**.

**Amun-Re (Amen, Ammon, Amon)** Egyptian god; Amun was the local god of Thebes, considered as the god of air or fertility, who had the form of a man, but sometimes also the head of a ram; was likened to the sun-god Re, thus becoming Amun-Re; the pharaohs developed his cult.

**Anahita** Persian goddess of dawn and fertility; became a spirit of prosperity, collaborating in the work of creation, fighting for justice and initiating men into religious rites.

**Anchises** In Roman mythology, the Trojan father of **Aeneas**; the *Aeneid* gives an account of Aeneas's piety in carrying Anchises on his shoulders out of the blazing city of Troy.

**Androcles** Roman slave; escaped from his master, met a lion, and extracted a thorn from its paw; when recaptured, he was made to confront a lion in the arena, and found it was the same animal, so that his life was spared.

**Andromache** In Greek mythology, the wife of **Hector**, the hero of Troy; after the fall of the city she became the slave of **Neoptolemus**.

**Andromeda** In Greek mythology, the daughter of Cepheus, king of the Ethiopians; to appease **Poseidon**, she was fastened to a rock by the seashore as an offering to a sea-monster; rescued by **Perseus**, who used the **Gorgon**'s head to change the monster to stone; the persons named in the story were all turned into constellations.

**Angels** Messengers of God; nine choirs were divided into three ranks; the seraphim, cherubim and thrones; the dominions, powers and virtues; and the principalities, archangels and angels. The first class was to praise and worship God, and the last was to assist the course of the stars, nations and people; angels or lesser gods would pass on messages, give orders or bring help to men.

**Angra Mainyu** Persian **demon**; creator of darkness and of evil things; belonged to death, filth and rottenness, inspiring disgust.

**Anna Perenna** Roman goddess; represented as an old woman, and worshipped in a sacred wood situated north of Rome; named Perenna, meaning eternity, when she became a **Nymph**; approached by Mars (► **Ares**) when she was old and asked to be an intermediary between himself and Minerva (► **Athene**); realizing this was impossible, she substituted herself for the chaste goddess and made fun of Mars.

**Antigone** Greek heroine; the guardian of the family; defied the dictator **Creon** to follow the wishes of the gods to fulfil the rite of burial for warriors considered as traitors, and for this was buried alive by Creon in the family tomb, where she hanged herself.

**Anu** Sumerian god of heaven; earthly royalty was descended from him, and as the god of Uruk, he gave back the city to Rim-Sin of the Larsa dynasty, who later conquered the neighbouring cities by Anu's strength.

**Anubis** Egyptian god; guide of souls to the world beyond; often represented with a human body and the head of a jackal or dog.

**Aphrodite (Venus)** Greek goddess of love who reigned over the hearts and senses of men; a proud and cruel goddess who punished all those who would not succumb to her; as a bribe, offered **Paris** the most beautiful mortal, **Helen**, causing the Trojan war; her worship was assimilated by the Romans with that of Venus, a goddess of ancient Italy.

**Apis** Egyptian god of strength and fecundity; represented as a bull for whom divine honours were reserved; Menes, the first Egyptian pharaoh, was said to have started the cult of Apis about 3000BC.

**Apollo** Greek and Roman god; son of **Zeus**; young and handsome, seer, poet and musician, he was said to be the most powerful of the gods; often identified with the sun, his nature also had a terrifying side and even his friends were afraid of him; said to have been responsible for the death of **Achilles**.

**Arachne** In Greek mythology, a weaver from Lydia; challenged **Athene** to a contest; when Arachne's work was seen to be superior, Athene destroyed the web and Arachne hanged herself; Athene saved her, but changed her into a spider.

**Ares (Mars)** Greek god of war; a supreme fighter who cared little for the interests he defended, and delighted in bloody massacres; fought with **Athene**, the sons of **Poseidon** and **Heracles**; identified with the Roman god Mars, said to be the father of **Romulus**, the founder of Rome.

**Arethusa** Greek **Nymph**; pursued by the river-god Alpheus from Arcadia in Greece to Ortygia in Sicily; the myth attempts to account for the freshwater fountain which appears in the harbour of Syracuse and is believed to have flowed under the Ionian Sea.

**Argonauts** Greek heroes; sailed in the *Argo* to find the Golden Fleece; under **Jason**'s leadership they sailed through the Symplegades (presumably the Dardanelles) and along the Black Sea coast to Colchis; their return is variously described, and may have included a river-passage to the North Sea.

**Argus** Greek watchman with a hundred eyes, appointed by **Hera** to watch over **Io**; after Argus was killed by **Hermes**, the eyes were placed in the tail of the peacock; also the name of **Odysseus**'s dog.

**Ariadne** In Greek mythology, the daughter of King **Minos** of Crete; enabled **Theseus** to escape from the labyrinth by giving him a ball of thread; he fled with her, but deserted her on the island of Naxos; there she eventually became the wife of **Dionysus**.

**Aristaeus** Greek god of the countryside; a minor deity who introduced bee-keeping, vines, and olives; pursued **Eurydice**, the wife of **Orpheus**, who trod on a snake and died; in revenge her sister **dryads** killed his bees; **Proteus** told him to sacrifice cattle to appease the dryads, and in nine days he found bees generated in the carcasses.

**Arjuna** Indian hero; in the *Bhagavadgita*, a poem in the *Mahabharata*, he hesitates before entering the battle, knowing the killing which will ensue; his charioteer, Krishna, urges him to fulfil the action which is his duty as a warrior, explaining that the whole universe needs the fulfilment of actions which advance God's will.

**Artemis (Diana)** Greek goddess; daughter of **Zeus** and sister of **Apollo**; defender of virginity and modesty, and warrior who turned against anyone who attempted to force her against her will; also the protectress of women in labour and newborn children; identified with the Roman goddess Diana, a huntress.

**Arthur** Celtic medieval hero; brought up by **Merlin**

and crowned king of Britain, King Arthur; armed with his magical sword Excalibur, he rid his country of monsters and giants, drove out the invaders, conquered the continent to reach Rome and in some stories as far as Palestine, from where he brought back the Cross of Christ.

**Asclepius (Aesculapius)** Greek and Roman god of the earth; son of **Apollo**, he acquired the magic powers to cure and revitalize from **Cheiron** the **Centaur**; used his powers to serve mortals, curing the sick and bringing the dead back to life; became a god when killed by **Zeus**, who was enraged that Asclepius had upset the natural order by restoring **Hippolytus** to life.

**Astarte ▸ Ishtar**

**Atalanta** Greek heroine; nurtured by a she-bear and grew up to be a strong huntress; refused to marry any man who would not take part in a foot-race with her; those who lost were killed; eventually Hippomenes (or Milanion) threw three golden apples of the **Hesperides** at her feet, so that her attention was diverted and she lost.

**Aten** Egyptian god; showed himself to mankind in the form of the solar disc, gave life, was the creator of all things, and all things depended on him; had no connection with the other, numerous gods.

**Athene (Minerva)** Greek goddess of restraint and forethought; daughter of **Zeus**, virgin and warrior, whose protégés were **Odysseus**, **Heracles** and **Achilles**; fought with the Achaeans in the Trojan war, and enemy of **Ares**; in competition with **Poseidon**, won the possession of Attica, beginning the era of civilization for the city of Athens; identified with the Roman god Minerva.

**Atlas** Greek **Titan**; made to hold up the heavens with his hands, as a punishment for taking part in the revolt against the Olympians; when books of maps came to be published, he was often portrayed as a frontispiece, hence the term atlas.

**Atreus** Greek king of Argos; quarrelled with his brother **Thyestes**, and placed the flesh of Thyestes' children before him at a banquet; the father of **Agamemnon** and **Menelaus**.

**Atropos ▸ Moerae**

**Attis (Atys)** Greek god of vegetation; connected with the Asiatic cult of **Cybele**; died after castrating himself, and was resurrected; the story was later associated with the spring festival.

**Aurora ▸ Eos**

**Autolycus** In Greek mythology, the maternal grandfather of **Odysseus**, who surpassed all men in thieving; he was said to be a son of **Hermes**.

**Baal** Phoenician god of fertility and fecundity; known as king of the gods, and with his sister Anat was responsible for the universal prosperity of people and animals; his victory over the god of the sea gave sailors the courage to set their boats on water.

**Bacchus ▸ Dionysus**

**Balder** Norse god of sovereignty and power; son of **Odin** and **Frigg**; unlike the other power gods, he was kind and pleasant; a jealous god **Loki** conspired to kill him, and on death he went to the home of Hel, the terrible; the goddess of hell agreed to free him on condition that every creature would weep for him; all did, except an old woman (Loki in disguise), so that Balder would have to remain in hell until the battle (*Ragnarok*) which will bring about the end of the world.

**Basilisk (Cockatrice)** Greek monster; a small dragon-like creature combining features of the snake and the cockerel; its eye could freeze and kill, hence the expression: 'If looks could kill'; equivalent to the Cockatrice, which was hatched by a serpent from the egg of a cock.

**Bellerophon** Greek hero; sent to Lycia with a letter telling the king to put him to death; the king set him impossible adventures, notably the killing of the **Chimera**; in later accounts it is said that **Athene** helped him to tame **Pegasus**.

**Berserker** Norse warrior; fought in a 'bear-shirt' in such a frenzy that he was impervious to wounds; the name is the origin of the phrase 'to go berserk'.

**Bes** Egyptian god; depicted as a bandy-legged dwarf who was horrific in appearance, but congenial in temperament; the protector in childbirth, and guardian of the family.

**Bladud** Legendary king of Britain; discovered the hot spring at Bath and founded the city; one story is that he was a leper who found that the mud cured him.

**Brahma** Indian god; the creator; divided himself into two to make a couple bringing **Sarasvati**, feminine energy, into existence; he then developed four heads so that he could always see Sarasvati as she constantly circled him; he was also given four arms to show his power; organized the world, and laid down the rules of *karma*, the standard of reward for one's actions.

**Bran** Celtic hero; known as Bendigeid Vran, the son of Llyr; invaded Ireland to help his sister, and died there; his seven followers cut off his head and buried it on the site of the Tower of London, from where it protects the whole island of Britain. In another legend, he was an Irish voyager who set out to find the Other World with 27 companions; on their return, as they approached the shore, people asked who they were, and said that the only Bran they knew was the hero of the ancient tale of *The Voyages of Bran*, so Bran wandered away forever.

**Brigit (Brighid)** Irish goddess of fire and the hearth; also of poetry and handicrafts; in the Christian era a number of her attributes were taken over by St Brigid.

**Brunhild (Brunhilde, Brynhild)** Norse **Valkyrie** who has assumed human form; **Odin** places her behind a wall of flame where she lies in an enchanted sleep; she is woken by **Sigurd**, who is able to leap the barrier on his horse Grani; tricked into marrying Gunnar, she finally kills herself on Sigurd's funeral pyre; in the similar Nibelungen legend, she is the wife of Gunther.

**Buddha** Founder of Buddhism; in legend, Siddhartha Gautama was born around 560BC into a noble family, and spent his childhood in a palace of luxury, protected from the sorrow and suffering outside; one day he discovered this and decided to save humanity from its evils; became the Buddha when he discovered the four 'noble truths', and attained awakening and enlightenment. Spent the rest of his life teaching, and died at the age of 80.

**Bunyip** In Australian aboriginal mythology, the source of evil; not to be thought of as a spirit or as a human; the **Rainbow Snake**, the mother of life, confined Bunyip to a waterhole; it haunts dark and gloomy places.

**Cadmus** Greek hero; son of Agenor, king of Tyre; set off in pursuit of his sister **Europa**, arrived in Greece, and founded the city of Thebes, teaching the natives to write; sowed dragon's teeth, from which armed men sprang up.

**Calchas** Greek seer; advised that **Iphigeneia** should be sacrificed at Aulis; at Troy he told **Agamemnon** to return Chryseis, the daughter of the priest of **Apollo**, to stop the plague; died in a combat of 'seeing'.

**Calliope** Greek **Muse** of epic poetry; sometimes said to be the mother of **Orpheus**.

**Callisto** Arcadian **Nymph**; attendant upon **Artemis**; loved by **Zeus**, she became pregnant, and was sent away from the virgin band; **Hera** changed her into a she-bear and after 15 years had passed, her son tried to spear her; taking pity on them, Zeus changed her into the constellation Ursa Major.

**Cassandra** Greek heroine; daughter of **Priam**, king of Troy; favoured by **Apollo**, who gave her the gift of prophecy; because she did not return his love, he decreed that while she would always tell the truth, she would never be believed; at the fall of Troy she was allotted to **Agamemnon**, and murdered on her arrival in Argos.

**Castor** and **Pollux** Greek heroes; twin sons of **Leda**; Pollux the son of **Zeus** and Castor the son of Tyndareus, king of Sparta, but both born at the same time; Castor was a good fighter and Pollux a skilled boxer, and the twins were inseparable; during their search for the Golden Fleece with the **Argonauts**, they saved the ship, the *Argos*, from a storm; when Castor was killed in a fight, Zeus agreed to Pollux's pleas for Castor to share his immortality so that he would not be separated from his brother.

**Cecrops (Kekrops)** Greek ancestor and first king of the Athenians; born from the earth, and formed with snakelike appendages instead of legs; during his reign, **Athene** and **Poseidon** fought for the possession of Athens; buried in the Erechtheum.

**Centaurs** Mythical Greek monsters; half man, half horse, aggressive and unintelligent with reputations for raping and kidnapping, with two exceptions: **Cheiron**, tutor of **Apollo**, **Jason** and **Achilles**, and Pholus, friend of **Heracles**, who were kindly Centaurs.

**Cerberus** Greek dog; guards the entrance to the underworld; originally fifty-headed, later with three heads; any living souls visiting hell gave 'a sop to Cerberus', ie a honey-cake, to quieten him; **Heracles** carried him off as one of his labours.

**Ceres** ► **Demeter**

**Cernunnos** Celtic god of plenty; represented with the ears and antlers of a stag, often accompanied by a serpent with the head of a ram; master of wild, earthly and aquatic animals.

**Chac** Mayan rain-god; characterized by two wide eyes, a long turned-up nose and two curved fangs; in the East he was red, in the North, white, in the West, black and in the South, yellow; made thunder and rain and was regarded as beneficent and friend of man.

**Charon** Greek ferryman of the underworld; carried the shades or souls of the dead across the R Styx; sometimes other rivers are substituted in literature, such as Acheron and Lethe; the Greeks placed a small coin in the mouth of a corpse as Charon's fee.

**Chimera (Chimaera)** Greek monster; had the head of a lion, the body of a goat (the name means 'she-goat'), and the tail of a serpent, which breathed fire.

**Cheiron** Greek **Centaur**; son of **Cronus** and Philyra the **Oceanid**, who kept a school for princes in Thessaly; educated **Asclepius** in the art of medicine and music, **Jason** the **Argonaut**, **Odysseus** and **Achilles**; wounded by one of **Heracles**'s poisoned arrows, he gladly gave up his immortality to be rid of pain.

**Circe** Greek enchantress; in the *Odyssey*, detained **Odysseus** and his followers on the island of Aeaea; her house was full of wild beasts; transformed Odysseus's men into swine with a magic drink, but he was able to defeat her charms through the protection of the herb moly.

**Clio** Greek **Muse** of history and lyre-playing.

**Clotho** ► **Moerae**

**Clytemnestra (Clytemestra)** In Greek mythology, the twin sister of **Helen** and the wife of **Agamemnon**; murdered her husband on his return from Troy, assisted by her lover, **Aegisthus**; killed in revenge by her son, **Orestes**.

**Cockatrice** ► **Basilisk**

**Consentes Dii (Di)** Twelve Roman gods; their statues, grouped in male/female pairs, stood in the Forum; probably Jupiter/Juno, Neptune/Minerva, Mars/Venus, Apollo/Diana, Volcanus/Vesta and Mercury/Ceres (► **Zeus/Hera**, **Poseidon/Athene**, **Ares/Aphrodite**, **Apollo/Artemis**, **Hephaestus/Vesta** and **Hermes/Demeter**).

**Creon (Kreon)** Greek kings; the name (meaning 'ruler') is applied especially to the brother of **Jocasta**, regent of Thebes, who awarded the throne to **Oedipus**; later, after the siege of the city by the seven Champions, he commanded that **Polynices** should not be buried, and condemned **Antigone** for disobedience.

**Cressida** In medieval accounts of the Trojan War, the daughter of Calchas, a Trojan priest; beloved by **Troilus**, a Trojan prince, she deserted him for **Diomedes** when transferred to the Greek camp.

**Cronus (Kronos)** Greek ruler of the universe (the second ruler); a **Titan**, the youngest son of **Uranus**, who rebelled against his father; during his rule people lived in the Golden Age; probably a pre-Greek deity, he is incorrectly, but popularly, confused with Chronos 'Time', because he too devoured his children.

**Cú Chulainn** Irish hero and supreme warrior; halted the progress of enemies united against his country; finally killed by Lugaid, the son of one of his victims.

**Cupid ► Eros**

**Cybele** Phrygian goddess of the earth; made through the mutilation of a hermaphrodite monster by the gods, she lived in forests and mountains.

**Cyclopes** Greek mythological monsters; one-eyed giants who worked as smiths and were associated with volcanic activity; the Cyclops **Polyphemus** was outwitted and blinded by **Odysseus**.

**Daedalus** Athenian inventor; worked for King **Minos** in Crete and constructed the labyrinth; later he escaped to Sicily with wings he had made for himself and **Icarus**; there he made the golden honeycomb kept at Mt Eryx; any archaic work of skill was ascribed to him, and he was a patron saint of craftsmen in Ancient Greece.

**Danaans (Danaoi)** Collectively, the Greeks who joined together in the expedition to Troy.

**Danae** Greek heroine; daughter of King Acrisius of Argos; when an oracle prophesied that her son would kill his grandfather, Acrisius imprisoned her in a bronze tower, where **Zeus** visited her in the form of a golden shower; gave birth to a son, **Perseus**, who accidentally killed Acrisius with a discus.

**Danaoi ► Danaans**

**Danu** Celtic mother-goddess; associated with hills and the earth.

**Daphne** Greek heroine; daughter of a river-god, Ladon (or, in another story, Peneios); pursued by the god **Apollo**, she was saved by being turned into a laurel, which became Apollo's sacred tree.

**Daphnis** Sicilian shepherd; half-brother of **Pan**, who was loved by a **Nymph**; he did not return her love, so she blinded him; became the inventor of pastoral poetry; in another story he would love nobody; when he died, all the beings of the island mourned him.

**Deirdre** In Irish legends, a girl destined to cause evil; grew up to be the most beautiful girl in Ireland; although intended for King Conchobhar, she was abducted by Naoise, a young king, and lived with him for seven years; when Naoise was killed by treachery, she was forced to marry Conchobhar, and killed herself.

**Demeter (Ceres)** Greek goddess of corn; presided over the interplay between life and death, and provided food; forced a compromise after **Hades** imprisoned her daughter **Persephone** in the underworld allowing her to return to the world above between spring and autumn; identified with the Roman goddess Ceres.

**demons** Evil celestial beings who force men to do evil and also do harm to men themselves, taking on the appearance of foreign gods, led by Satan; invisible and innumerable, they originally preferred to live in isolated and unclean places like deserts and ruins, and were greatly feared, especially at night; exorcisms are religious rites to remove demonic influences when a demon is thought to inhabit the body of a person, stripping him or her of self control and moral awareness.

**Deucalion** Greek hero; son of **Prometheus**; when **Zeus** flooded the world, Deucalion and his wife Pyrrha built an 'ark' which grounded on the top of Parnassus; as the only survivors, they asked how the human race was to be restored; an oracle told them 'to throw the bones of their mother over their shoulders'; they correctly interpreted this oracle, and threw stones (the bones of their mother Earth) which turned into human beings.

**Diana ► Artemis**

**Dido** Greek heroine; in the *Aeneid*, the daughter of the king of Tyre, who founded Carthage; **Aeneas** was diverted to Africa by storms, and told her his story; they fell in love, but when Aeneas deserted her she committed suicide by throwing herself upon a pyre.

**Diomedes (Diomede)** Greek hero; fought in the Trojan War, even taking on the gods in battle; also a wise counsellor, the partner of **Odysseus** in various schemes; in the medieval version of the story, he became the lover of **Cressida**.

**Dionysus (Bacchus)** Greek god of wine and the vine; lord of exuberance and drunkenness, he upset everything that got in his way, did not respect laws or customs and wandered about in caves; said to have made his followers coarse and vulgar, taught them to drink wine and caused madness.

**Dragons** Legendary animals present in Chinese, Greek and Indian mythology, and medieval Christian legends; had the claws of a lion, the wings of an eagle, a powerful serpent's tail and breathed fire; sometimes represented as the guardian of treasure, eg guarding the Golden Fleece, as an incarnation of Satan, as a primordial principle and as the symbol of the power of the emperor of China.

**Dryads** Greek mythological **Nymphs**; originally connected with oak-trees, but more usually referring to a wood-nymph, living in or among the trees; were usually friendly, but could frighten travellers.

**Durga** Indian goddess; wife of **Shiva** and his feminine part, and both the creator and destroyer of the world; a force for leading astray as well as for salvation, and a warrior who enjoyed battle and bloodshed.

**Ea ► Enki**

**Echidna** Greek monster; half-woman and half-snake, and the mother of various other monsters, eg **Hydra**.

**Echo** Greek **Nymph**; in one legend, beloved by **Pan**, and torn to pieces, only her voice surviving; in another story, punished by **Hera** so that she could only repeat the last words of another speaker; loved **Narcissus**, who rejected her, so that she wasted away to a voice.

**Electra** Heroine of Greek tragedies (but not in Homer); daughter of **Agamemnon** and **Clytemnestra**, who assisted her brother **Orestes** when he came to Argos to avenge his father, and who later married his friend Pylades; her personality is developed in different ways by the playwrights.

**Endymion** Greek shepherd of Mt Latmos; loved by the moon-goddess **Selene**; **Zeus** put him to sleep, while Selene looked after his flocks, and visited him every night; one of the mythological figures who was said to have founded the Olympic Games, as king of Elis.

**Enki (Ea)** Sumerian god who organized life on earth and developed the world; invented man and made a mould from him so that he could be reproduced, and created plants and livestock.

**Enlil** Sumerian god and keeper of sovereign power who maintained the order of the world; originally ruled over proletarian gods who became exhausted by their work and rebelled; it was agreed that man should be created to take over a part of the labours necessary for the maintenance of the world; later the prosperity and din of mankind, whose number was steadily increasing, irritated Enlil, who sent epidemics, suffering, death and worldwide flood.

**Eos (Aurora)** Greek goddess of the dawn; daughter of **Helios**, mother of **Memnon**; abducted various mortals; when she took the mortal Tithonus, **Zeus** granted her request that he should be made immortal, but she forgot to ask for perpetual youth, so he grew older and older, finally shrinking to no more than a voice or, possibly, the cicada insect.

**Epigoni** Greek heroes; collectively, the 'next generation'; after the failure of the **Seven against Thebes**, their sons made another expedition and succeeded; this was shortly before the Trojan War.

**Epona** Gallic goddess and guardian of horses; patron of civil and military horsemen, travellers and those on their way to the Great Beyond; sometimes seen as a goddess of fertility and also identified with **Rhiannon**.

**Erato** Greek **Muse** of lyric poetry and hymns.

**Erechtheus** Greek king of Athens; born from the earth and nurtured by **Athene**; sacrificed his daughter Chthonia to secure victory over the Eleusinians, but was killed by **Poseidon**; the Erechtheum, a temple on the Acropolis, is probably on the site of his palace.

**Erinyes (Furies)** Greek goddesses; inhabitants of hell who were responsible for punishing bloody crimes; named Alecto, Tisiphone and Megara, they were represented as winged spirits who had long hair entwined with snakes, and carried whips and torches; tortured their victims and drove them mad.

**Eris** Greek heroine; daughter of Night and the sister of **Ares**; a late story tells how she was present at the wedding of **Peleus** and **Thetis** and threw a golden apple 'for the fairest'; this brought **Hera**, **Athene**, and **Aphrodite** into contention, and was the first cause of the Trojan War; the name means 'strife' in Greek.

**Eros (Cupid)** Greek god, responsible for keeping the world together and for the continuation of the species; his power to inspire sexual desires could make people lose their reason and paralyse their will power; became Cupid for the Romans.

**Eteocles** Greek hero; elder of **Oedipus**'s two sons, whom he cursed; became king of Thebes after his father's death, and refused to share power with his brother **Polynices**; the **Seven against Thebes** attacked the city, and Eteocles was killed by Polynices.

**Eumenides** A euphemistic name given to the **Erinyes** after being domesticated at Athens in Aeschylus' play of the same name; the name means 'the kindly ones'.

**Europa (Europe)** Greek heroine; daughter of Agenor, king of Tyre, who was abducted by **Zeus** in the shape of a bull, and swam with her on his back to Crete; her children were **Minos** and **Rhadamanthus**.

**Eurydice** Greek **Dryad**; wife of **Orpheus**; after her death, Orpheus went down to the underworld and persuaded **Hades** to let her go by the power of his music; the condition was that she should follow him, and that he should not look at her until they reached the light; not hearing her footsteps, he looked back, and she disappeared back into the underworld.

**Euterpe** Greek **Muse** of flute-playing.

**Fates ► Moerae**

**Faunus** Roman god of agriculture; responsible for the fertility of plants and the energy of living nature; reproduced himself in fauns, **satyrs** who were half man, half goat.

**Finn mac Cumhal** Irish hero; warrior and magician who avenged his father who was killed in battle and reorganized his elite troops, whose qualities were intelligence, cunning, faithfulness, a hatred of money and respect for women; possessed the gift of receiving visions when he bit his thumb.

**Flora** Roman goddess of flowers and flowering plants; appears with the spring; given a temple in 238BC; her games were celebrated on 28 April.

**Fortuna** Roman goddess of fortune; introduced by King Servius Tullius (578–534BC); in the Middle Ages was highly revered as a divine and moral figure, redressing human pride; her wheel is frequently referred to and depicted, as at St Etienne in Beauvais, where figures can be seen climbing and falling off.

**Freyja** Norse goddess of love, fertility, fecundity, victory and peace, and sister of **Freyr**; took on the form of a falcon to travel between one world and the other.

**Freyr (Frey)** Norse god of fertility and fecundity and brother of **Freyja**; presided over love, wealth and orgies, brought sun and rain to make crops grow; mainly worshipped by women.

**Frigg (Frigga)** Norse goddess of married love; wife of **Odin** (often confused with **Freyja**).

**Furies ► Erinyes**

**Gaea (Gaia, Ge, Tellus)** Greek goddess; 'the earth' personified, and later the goddess of the whole earth (not a particular piece of land); came into being after Chaos, and was the wife of **Uranus**, producing numerous children; the Romans identified her with Tellus.

**Galahad, Sir** One of King **Arthur**'s knights; son of **Lancelot** and Elaine; distinguished for his purity, he alone was able to succeed in the adventures of the Siege Perilous and the Holy Grail.

**Galatea** Greek **Nymph**; a sea-nymph, wooed by **Polyphemus** the **Cyclops** with uncouth love-songs; in some versions Polyphemus destroys his rival Acis with a rock; in other versions he happily marries Galatea; probably a Sicilian story.

**Ganesha** Indian god; master of intelligence and the patron of artists and writers who was given by **Brahma** the task of copying the *Mahabharata*; represented with the head of an elephant; a popular god, he put obstacles in the way of those who neglected him, and spared others.

**Ganymede** In Greek mythology, the son of Tros, a Trojan prince; **Zeus** sent a storm-wind, or (later and more usually) an eagle, who carried Ganymede up to Olympus, where he became the cup-bearer; in return his father was given a stud of exceptional horses.

**Gawain (Gawayne)** One of King **Arthur**'s knights; son of King Lot of Orkney, whose character varies in different accounts; in the medieval *Sir Gawayn and the Grene Knight*, he is a noble hero undergoing a test of faith; in other stories he is a jeering attacker of reputations, especially that of **Lancelot**.

**Gawayne ► Gawain**

**Genii** Spirits of mythology throughout the world; their forces were less beneficent than those of **angels**, but less wicked than those of **demons**; regarded as the doubles of objects, beings and events.

**Giants** Large, strong and often stupid beings from mythology throughout the world; in the Bible, the product of an unnatural union between fallen angels and the daughters of men; taught men the rudiments of the knowledge they had from being able to see from high up; for the Greeks, sons of the earth representing youth, strength and virility, who could only be killed by a god and a man together.

**Gigantes** Greek giants; sons of earth and Tartaros, with snake-like legs; made war on the Olympian gods, were defeated, and are buried under various volcanic islands; the Gigantomachy ('war of the giants') was the subject of large-scale sculpture, as at Pergamum; a sub-group, the Aloadi, piled Mt Pelion upon Mt Ossa.

**Gilgamesh** Sumerian hero; tyrannical king of Uruk and intrepid adventurer; began an adventure to search for immortality, but failed, and returned to Uruk to accept his fate and resume his former life.

**Gorboduc** Legendary king of Britain; first heard about in Geoffrey of Monmouth's *History*; when he grew senile, his two sons Ferret and Porrex quarrelled over the inheritance; he was the subject of an early Elizabethan tragedy in the Senecan style, written by Norton and Sackville (1561).

**Gorgons** Three mythical Greek monsters; represented with hair made of angry serpents, tusks like a boar's, hands of bronze and golden wings; anyone who looked at them was turned to stone; Euryale represented sexual excess, Stheno, social perversion, and **Medusa**, vanity; Medusa's head was cut off by **Perseus**, and the children of **Poseidon** emerged from the wound.

**Graces** In Greek mythology, three daughters of **Zeus** and **Hera**; embodied beauty and social accomplishments; sometimes called Aglaia, Euphrosyne and Thalia.

**Graiae** In Greek mythology, three sisters with the characteristics of extreme old age; had one eye and one tooth between them; **Perseus** took the eye and made them tell the route to the **Gorgons**, who were their sisters.

**Griffin (Gryphon)** Greek monster; originated in tales of the Arimaspians, who hunted the creature for its gold; had a lion's body, and an eagle's head, wings, and claws; collected fragments of gold to build its nest, and, instead of an egg, laid an agate.

**Gryphon ► Griffin**

**Guan Di (Kuan Ti)** Chinese god of war; based on a historical person who died in the 3rd-cAD; made a god in 1594, and greatly revered.

**Gudrun** Norse heroine; wife of **Sigurd** the Volsung; after his death she married Atli (the legendary Attila) who put her brothers to death; in revenge she served up his sons in a dish, and then destroyed him by fire; in the similar German story she is known as Kriemhild.

**Guinevere** King **Arthur**'s queen; originally Guanhamara in Geoffrey of Monmouth's *History*, and there are other spellings; in later romances, much is made of her affair with Sir **Lancelot** (an example of courtly love); in Malory's epic poem she survives Arthur's death and enters a nunnery.

**Hadad** Assyrian god of storms, known as **Adad** by the Mesopotamians; invoked in curses when begged to send torrential rain to the lands of enemies, but also brought agricultural fertility.

**Hades (Pluto)** Greek god of hell; brother of **Zeus** and **Poseidon**; invisible god who ruled the dead, assisted by **demons**; forbade his subjects to leave

his domain and became enraged when anyone tried to steal his prey; the most hated of the gods among mortals; identified by the Romans as Pluto.

**Halcyone (Alcyone)** In Greek mythology, daughter of **Aeolus**, who married Ceyx, son of the morning star; either for impiety, or because she mourned his death at sea, both were changed into seabirds (halcyons, or kingfishers, who are fabled to calm the sea); sometimes described instead as one of the **Pleiades**.

**Hamadryads** Greek **Nymphs**; tree-nymphs who were offended or died when the trees containing them were harmed.

**Hanuman** Indian monkey god, son of the god of the winds, Vayu; as soon as he was born, he rushed towards the sun believing it to be a ripe fruit, crashing into all the planets on the way; as protector, he destroyed the death rays emitted by the planets and was known as the god of athletes and gymnasts.

**Harpies** Greek genii/spirits; represented as three women with wings or birds with the heads of women; seized children and souls and tortured their victims.

**Harpocrates ► Horus**

**Hathor** Egyptian goddess; portrayed as a woman bearing the sun between two cow's horns representing the intoxication of pleasure, love and fertility; identified by the Greeks with **Aphrodite**.

**Hebe** Greek goddess of youth and youthful beauty; daughter of **Zeus** and **Hera**; became cup-bearer to the Olympians, and was married to **Heracles** after he was deified.

**Hecabe ► Hecuba**

**Hecate** Greek goddess of witchcraft, spooks, and magic; not in Homer, she appears in Hesiod, and seems to represent the powerful mother-goddess of Asia Minor; worshipped with offerings at places where three roads cross, and so given three bodies in sculpture.

**Hector** Hero of Greek mythology; the bravest Trojan, who led out their army to battle; the son of **Priam**, and married to **Andromache**; **Achilles** killed him and dragged his body behind his chariot; Priam ransomed it at the end of the *Iliad*.

**Hecuba (Hecabe)** Greek heroine; wife of **Priam**, king of Troy, and mother of 18 children, including **Hector** and **Cassandra**; after the Greeks took Troy, she saw her sons and her husband killed, and was sent into slavery.

**Heimdallr** Norse god; born of nine mothers, he could see everything and never closed his eyes; the guardian of the gods' abode; at the moment of the end of the world, it was said that he would blow his trumpet to call all the gods to hold a council.

**Hel (Hela)** In Norse mythology, the youngest child of **Loki**; half her body was living human flesh, the other half decayed; assigned by **Odin** to rule Helheim (the underworld) and to receive the spirits of the dead who do not die in battle.

**Helen** Greek heroine; daughter of **Zeus** and **Leda**, sister to **Clytemnestra**, **Castor** and **Pollux**; the most beautiful of women who captivated all men, and as a result was the cause of the Trojan War when she was abducted by **Paris**; granted immortality by Zeus and **Apollo**.

**Helios** Greek god of the sun; represented as a charioteer with four horses; in early times Helios was not worshipped, except at Rhodes; in the late classical period, there was an Imperial cult of the sun, Sol Invictus.

**Hellen** In ancient Greek genealogies, the eldest son of **Deucalion**; father of Doros, Xuthos and Aiolos, who were the progenitors of the Dorian, Ionian, and Aeolic branches of the Greek race; the Greeks (or Hellenes) were named after him.

**Hephaestus (Volcanus, Vulcan)** Greek god of fire; son of **Zeus** and **Hera**; lame (either because his mother dropped him from Olympus when she realized how ugly he was, or because Zeus threw him down onto the island when he took his mother's side in a marital dispute); volcanoes were his workshops and the **Cyclopes** his assistants in his work as a blacksmith and jeweller; identified by the Romans as Vulcan.

**Hera (Juno)** Greek goddess; married her brother **Zeus**; conceived some of her sons without any male assistance by hitting the ground with her hand or eating a lettuce; pursued with a vengeance Zeus's mistresses and their children, putting enormous snakes into **Heracles**'s cradle forcing Zeus to hide his illegitimate children by transforming them into animals or enclosing them in the earth; identified by the Romans as Juno; her name means 'lady'.

**Heracles (Hercules)** Greek hero; demonstrated amazing strength from birth, choking the serpents sent to him by the jealous **Hera**; many achievements are attributed to him including the 12 labours of Eurystheus; he delivered Troy from a monster but came back to wreak havoc on the city because it did not pay his salary; succeeded in injuring **Hades** and **Hera** with his arrows and won immortality; identified by the Romans as Hercules.

**Hercules ► Heracles**

**Hermaphroditus** Greek god; a minor god with bisexual characteristics, the son of **Hermes** and **Aphrodite**; the **Nymph** Salmacis, unloved by him, prayed to be united with him; this was granted by combining them in one body.

**Hermes (Mercury)** Greek god of the spoken word and son of **Zeus**; intermediary who went from men to Olympus and Olympus to **Hades**; as the god of commerce, the only person to achieve immortality as a result of a contract; identified by the Romans as Mercury.

**Hero** and **Leander** Greek lovers; lived on opposite sides of the Hellespont; Hero was the priestess of **Aphrodite** at Sestos, and Leander, who lived at Abydos, swam across each night guided by her light; when this was extinguished in a storm, he was

drowned, and Hero committed suicide by throwing herself into the sea.

**Hesperides** In Greek mythology, the daughters of the evening star (Hesper); guarded the Golden Apples together with the dragon, Ladon; sang as they circled the tree, which was given by **Gaia** to **Hera** as a wedding-present; when **Heracles** had to fetch the apples, he either killed the dragon, or sent it to sleep, or, more usually, persuaded **Atlas** to get them for him while he took over Atlas' function of holding up the sky.

**Hestia (Vesta)** Greek goddess of hearth and home; sister of **Zeus** and **Hera**; never intervened in the stormy history of the gods and became the central point, the meeting place; identified by the Romans as Vesta.

**Hiawatha** Native American hero; appeared in *The Song of Hiawatha*, which retells Native American legends in the manner and metre of the Finnish *Kalevala*; Hiawatha is educated by his grandmother Nokomis, and marries Minnehaha.

**Hippolytus** Greek hero; son of **Theseus** and Hippolyta, leader of the **Amazons**; Theseus' new wife, **Phaedra**, made advances to Hippolytus, which were refused, so she falsely accused Hippolytus of rape; Theseus invoked a curse, **Poseidon** sent a frightening sea-monster, and Hippolytus was thrown from his chariot and killed.

**Horae** In Greek mythology, 'the seasons'; implied the right or fitting time for something to happen; given various names either connected with fertility or peace.

**Horatii** and **Curiatii** Early Roman legend used to justify appeals; under Tullus Hostilius there was war between Rome and Alba; two groups of three brothers were selected from Rome (the Horatii) and Alba (the Curiatii) to fight, the winners to decide the battle; all were killed except one, Horatius; when his sister, who was betrothed to a Curiatius, abused him, he murdered her, but was acquitted after appealing to the Roman people.

**Horus (Harpocrates)** Egyptian god; husband of **Hathor**, brother of **Seth** and ancestor of the dynasties of the pharaohs; had a falcon's head and ruled the air, his eyes being the sun and the moon; became universal king of the earth after defeating Seth, who had seized power after murdering Horus's father.

**Huang-ti** Chinese cultural hero; legendary emperor, patron of alchemists, doctors and seers, and one of the fathers of Taoism; born miraculously after his mother was made pregnant by lightning from the Great Bear; invented chariots, ships and houses, and understood that every activity in the world had to be preceded by putting the individual body in order; discovered the way of the Tao in a dream and searched for ways of attaining immortality.

**Huitzilopochtli** Aztec god of war and protector of the city; symbolized in the midday sun and represented with hummingbird feathers on his head and left leg, a black face and brandishing a serpent of turquoise or fire; massacred all his brothers and sisters immediately after he was born, as they planned to kill his mother; as a soothsayer he communed with the priests at night and as a cruel god, tore out the hearts of those who disobeyed him.

**Hydra** Greek monster; many-headed child of **Typhon** and **Echidna**, which lived in a swamp at Lerna; since the heads grew again when struck off, **Heracles** could kill it only with the assistance of Iolaos, who cauterized the places where the heads grew; the name means 'water-snake'.

**Hygeia** Greek goddess; the daughter of **Asclepius**; a minor deity, her name was a personification of the word for 'health'.

**Hymen** Greek god of marriage; in Ancient Greece and Rome, the cry of 'O Hymen Hymenaie' at weddings (later a marriage song) led to the invention of a being called Hymen of Hymenaeus, who was assumed to have been happily married, and therefore suitable for invocation as a god of marriage; depicted as a youth with a torch.

**Hyperboreans** Greek unvisited people of fabled virtue and prosperity; lived in the land 'beyond the North Wind'; in Herodotus they worshipped **Apollo** and sent offerings to Delos; could refer to a lost Greek colony in what is now Romania, or even to the Swedes at the end of the trans-European amber route.

**Hyperion** Greek **Titan**; son of **Uranus** and **Gaia**, and father of **Eos** (the Dawn), **Helios** (the sun), and **Selene** (the moon); later, as in Shakespeare and Keats, identified with the sun.

**Iapetus** Greek **Titan**; father of **Prometheus** and **Atlas**; grandfather of **Deucalion**; the close resemblance to Japhet may indicate borrowing from near Eastern sources.

**Icarus** In Greek mythology, the son of **Daedalus**; his father made him wings to escape from Crete, but he flew too near the sun; the wax holding the wings melted and he fell into the Aegean at a point now known as the Icarian Sea.

**Idomeneus** Leader of the Cretans; a descendant of **Minos** who assisted the Greeks at Troy; caught in a storm at sea, he vowed to sacrifice the first thing he met on his safe return; this was his own son; after carrying out the sacrifice he was driven into exile.

**Inanna** Sumerian goddess of love and war; stole the *me* (meaning everything that makes up civilization) from **Enki** to give to her city, Uruk; attempted to seize power of the underworld from her sister but failed; in rage at her husband's lack of sympathy for her resulting predicament, she ordered the **demons** to torture him and imprison him in hell.

**Indra** Indian god; an athlete and exemplary warrior who gave life and light, created the ox and the horse, gave the cow milk and made all women fertile; crushed the evil **demon** Vrtra, allowing the dawn and the sunrise to be created.

**Io** Greek heroine; beloved by **Zeus**, who turned her into a heifer to save her from **Hera**'s jealousy; Hera kept her under the gaze of the **Argus**; but she escaped with **Hermes**'s help; was then punished with a gad-fly which drove her through the world until she arrived in Egypt; there Zeus changed her back into human shape, and she gave birth to Epaphos, ancestor of many peoples.

**Iphigeneia** Greek priestess; daughter of **Agamemnon** and **Clytemnestra**; was about to be sacrificed at Aulis as the fleet could not sail to Troy, because the winds were against it, but at the last moment was saved by **Artemis**, who made her a priestess in the country of the Tauri (the Crimea); finally her brother **Orestes** saved her.

**Irene** In Greek mythology, a personification of 'peace'; one of the **Horae**.

**Iris** Greek goddess of the rainbow; became the messenger of the gods, especially of **Zeus** in Homer, and of **Hera** in later writers; depicted sitting under Hera's throne.

**Ishtar (Astarte)** Mesopotamian goddess; as the star of the morning, personified war, and as the star of the evening, personified love; came to the aid of the sexually impotent and was cruel and determined as a hostile warrior; established the fame of Assyria and was responsible for the cruelty of its kings.

**Isis** Egyptian goddess; mother of **Horus**; wore a solar disc and the horns of a cow, and was known as the protectress of love and mistress of destiny; obtained her powers by trickery and as a magician, cured her son who had been bitten by a snake.

**Isolde** ► **Tristan** and **Isolde**

**Itzamma** Mayan god of heaven; the creator and civilizer of mankind, with the appearance of an old toothless man with sunken cheeks and a prominent nose, he gave places their names and distributed land between the different tribes; sometimes depicted as an enormous serpent which represented the sky.

**Iuppiter** ► **Zeus**

**Ixion** Greek king of Thessaly; the first murderer; also the father of the **Centaurs**; for attempting to rape **Hera** he was bound to a wheel of fire, usually located in the underworld.

**Izanagi no Mikoto** and **Izanami no Mikoto** Japanese male and female gods; in the creation myth these were the first beings who created islands in the water and the other gods; Izanami died when she gave birth to fire; Izanagi followed her to the land of the dead (Yomi), but she turned against him and pursued him; finally he had to block the exit from Yomi with a large rock and Izanami then became the goddess of the underworld.

**Janus** Roman god of beginnings; a two-faced god who personified clearsightedness; protected **Saturn** when he was being hunted by Jupiter (► **Zeus**); invented money, the cultivation of soil and legislation.

**Jason** Greek hero; son of the king of Iolcus, who was deposed by his half-brother, Pelias; Jason claimed the power from Pelias, who challenged him to demonstrate his worthiness of the crown by bringing back the Golden Fleece, guarded by an ever-wakeful dragon, hoping that Jason would never return from such an impossible mission; a ship, the *Argo*, was built for the mission, and Jason overcame many obstacles to return with the Golden Fleece; the king did not keep his promise, and weary of war, Jason stole the fleece and left.

**Jimmu Tenno** First emperor of Japan in the Shinto religion; said to be descended from Amaterasu, and to have reigned between 660 and 585BC, dying at the age of 127; probably a real person, subsequently deified.

**Jocasta** In Greek legend, the wife of King Laius of Thebes and mother of **Oedipus**; later unwittingly became the wife of her son; she is called Epikaste in Homer; bore Oedipus four children: **Eteocles**, **Polynices**, **Antigone**, and Ismene; killed herself when she discovered her incest.

**Julunggul** ► **Rainbow Snake**

**Juno** ► **Hera**

**Jupiter** ► **Zeus**

**Kama** Indian god of love; represented with a bow and arrow; as soon as he was born, looked around him and asked who he was going to set on fire; always ready to initiate love in men or in the gods.

**Kami** Japanese spirits; manifestations of natural forces and superior to men; there were 80 million kami, to personify anything big or inexplicable at a time when animals, rivers, lakes and seas were objects of veneration; the drink saké was the offering preferred by the kami.

**Kane** ► **Tane**

**Kekrops** ► **Cecrops**

**Kreon** ► **Creon**

**Krishna** Indian god; a lovable child and merciless warrior; endowed with exceptional strength and intelligence, he killed the monster Baku who had taken the form of a crane, and fought with Kaliya, the king of serpents; his life with 16 000 wives and 180 000 children was interspersed with numerous battles against **demons**; has become the only god in many Hindu sects.

**Kronos** ► **Cronus**

**Kuan Ti** ► **Guan Di**

**Kumarbi** Hurrian god; deposed from the divine throne by the storm-god, **Teshub**; became the father of an enormous stone man in the hope that this son could overthrow the storm-god, but this was prevented by the other gods.

**Lachesis** ► **Moerae**

**Laius** Greek king of Thebes; father of **Oedipus**; he married **Jocasta**, and was warned by an oracle that their son would destroy him; this happened when Oedipus, assumed to be dead, returned from Corinth and accidentally killed Laius during a quarrel on the road.

**Lakshmi** Indian goddess of happiness, beauty and prosperity; the wife of **Vishnu**, she was the incarnation of the great god's power.

**Lancelot, Sir (Launcelot du Lac)** The most famous of King **Arthur**'s knights, though he is a relatively late addition to the legend; the son of King Ban of Benwick, the courtly lover of **Guinevere**, and the father of **Galahad** by Elaine; in spite of his near-perfection as a knight, he was unable to achieve the Grail adventure; he arrived too late to help Arthur in the last battle.

**Laocoon** Trojan prince; a priest of **Apollo**, who objected to the plan to bring the Wooden Horse into Troy; two serpents came out of the sea and killed him, together with his two sons.

**Lapiths** In Greek mythology, a people of Thessaly; Perithous, king of the Lapiths, invited the **Centaurs** to his wedding with Hippodameia; a terrible fight took place between the two groups, in which the Centaurs were defeated.

**Lares** Roman gods; protectors of inhabited places; depicted as two boys accompanied by a dog; divided into two groups; *lares compitales* were found in the country, at crossroads and in meeting places; *lares familiares* were guardians of the family home.

**Latinus** Roman ancestor and eponymous king of the Latins; descended from **Circe** (according to Hesiod) or from **Faunus** (according to Virgil); in the *Aeneid*, Latinus gives his daughter Lavinia to **Aeneas**.

**Latona** ► **Leto**

**Launcelot du Lac** ► **Lancelot, Sir**

**Leander** ► **Hero** and **Leander**

**Lear** Legendary king of Britain; son of **Bladud**, who reigned for 60 years; in his old age two of his daughters, Goneril and Regan, conspired against him, but the third daughter, Cordelia, saved him and became queen after his death (the story is changed by Shakespeare, so that she died before his eyes); Leicester is named after him.

**Leda** In Greek mythology, the wife of Tyndareus, king of Sparta, and mother, either by him or **Zeus**, of **Castor** and **Pollux**, **Helen**, and **Clytemnestra**; a frequent subject in art is Zeus courting Leda in the form of a swan; Helen was believed to have been hatched from an egg, preserved at Sparta into historic times.

**Lemminkäinen** Finnish hero; in the *Kalevala*, has to undertake impossible tasks, such as shooting the swan of Tuonela; this causes his death, and his mother has to reanimate him; his ride through a land of horrors inspired Sibelius.

**Lemures** Roman ghosts; wandered about outside the house on 9, 11, and 13 May (the Lemuria).

**Leto (Latona)** Greek **Titan**; mother by **Zeus** of the twins **Apollo** and **Artemis**; they were born at Delos, because in her jealousy **Hera** would allow no land to harbour Leto; luckily, at that time Delos was a floating island.

**Leviathan** Phoenician monster; personification of evil, believed to have come out of the primal chaos; sparks of fire shot from his mouth and smoke poured from his nostrils; always present, hidden in each individual.

**Lif** and **Lifthrasir** In Norse mythology, the mother and father of the new race of human beings after Ragnarok (the last battle); the names presumably mean 'life' and 'strong life'.

**Lilith** In Jewish legend, the first wife of Adam; or, more generally, a **demon** woman.

**Lohengrin** In Germanic legend, the son of Parsifal (► **Perceval, Sir**); left the temple of the Grail and was carried to Antwerp in a boat drawn by swans; there he saved Princess Elsa of Brabant, and intended to marry her; however, she asked forbidden questions about his origin, and he was forced to leave her, the swan-boat taking him back to the Grail temple.

**Loki** Norse god; represented deceit, disorder, malevolence and perversity; fathered horrible monsters and put obstacles in the way of happiness; as a magician, had the power to transform himself into different animals and insulted and offended the other gods.

**Lotus-eaters (Lotophagi)** People encountered by **Odysseus**; lived on 'a flowery food' which makes those who eat it forget their own country, and wish to live always in a dreamy state; Odysseus had to force his men to move on.

**Lucretia (Lucrece)** Roman wife of Collatinus; raped by Sextus, son of Tarquinius Superbus; after telling her story, she committed suicide; the incident led to the expulsion of the Tarquins from Rome.

**Lud** Legendary king of Britain; first walled the principal city, from that time called Kaerlud after him, and eventually London; buried near Ludgate, which preserves his name.

**Lug** Irish god; skilled in many arts and fulfilled the office of all gods; proclaimed by the king to be the wisest of the wise and given the task of organizing the battle which conquered the Fomoiri, evil beings who occupied Ireland and oppressed its inhabitants.

**Lycurgus** Greek king of Thrace; opposed **Dionysus** and was blinded; his name is shared by the founder of the Spartan constitution, with its military caste-system (the date when this originated has been much disputed, and is now thought to be c.600BC, much too late for the legendary Lycurgus to have participated).

**Maat** Egyptian goddess; represented the social and cosmic order and the guardian of ethics and rites; there at the beginning of the universe, she maintained order in heaven as on earth, and was responsible for the seasons, night and day, the movement of the stars and rainfall.

**Maenads** Greek 'mad women'; followed **Dionysus** on his journeys; dressed in animal-skins and so strong that they could uproot trees and kill wild animals, eating the flesh raw; also known as Bacchae or Bacchantes.

**Manes** In Roman religion, 'the dead'; the concept developed from the spirits of the dead in general, to the gods of the underworld, Di Manes, the ancestors of the family, and the spirits of individuals in gravestone inscriptions.

**Marduk** Babylonian god; represented life, civilization and progress; created the winds and raised the tempest, distressing the first-born gods who declared war on him but were defeated; Marduk created heaven, earth and man; when the god of death succeeded by a ruse in making him rise from his seat, the sun stopped shining, the roads became infested with brigands, and man ate man until Marduk took his place again.

**Mars ▸ Ares**

**Marsyas** Greek **satyr**; challenged **Apollo** to a flute-contest; defeated and flayed alive by the god, his blood or tears formed a river of the same name.

**Medea** Greek witch; daughter of Aeetes, the king of Colchis, who assisted **Jason** in obtaining the Golden Fleece; on their return to Iolcos, she renewed the youth of Aeson, and tricked the daughters of Pelias into performing a similar ritual, so that they destroyed their own father; when deserted by Jason at Corinth, she fled in her aerial chariot after killing her children.

**Medusa** Greek **Gorgon**; depicted with staring eyes and snakes for hair.

**Meleager** Greek hero; at his birth the **Moerae** appeared and prophesied that he would die when the brand then on the fire had burnt away; his mother, Althaea, removed it and kept it; when the quarrel over the Calydonian boar took place and her brothers were killed, she threw the brand onto the fire, so that he died.

**Melias ▸ Nymphs**

**Melpomene** Greek **Muse** of tragedy.

**Memnon** In Greek mythology, a prince from Ethiopia; son of **Eos**; killed at Troy by **Achilles**; the Greeks thought that one of the gigantic statues at Thebes represented him; it gave out a musical sound at sunrise.

**Menelaus** King of Sparta; younger brother of **Agamemnon**, who married **Helen**; took part in the Trojan War and was delayed in Egypt on his return; finally settled down at Sparta with Helen again.

**Mercury ▸ Hermes**

**Merlin** Good wizard or sage whose magic was used to help King **Arthur**; son of an incubus and a mortal woman, and therefore indestructible, but was finally entrapped by Vivien, the Lady of the Lake, and bound under a rock for ever; famous for his prophecies.

**Mermaid** Legendary sea-creature; had the body of a woman and the tail of a fish, a fiction possibly based on early encounters with seals or sea-cows; in stories their singing attracts mortal men to love them; their male counterparts were mermen.

**Midas** King of Phrygia; as a reward for helping the **Satyr** Silenus, **Dionysus** gave Midas a wish, and he asked that anything he touched should turn to gold; however, this caused so many difficulties (eg in eating and drinking) that he asked to be released; he was told to bathe in the River Pactolus, which thereafter had golden sands.

**Minerva ▸ Athene**

**Minos** Greek hero; son of **Zeus**, who took the form of a bull in order to impregnate Europe; claimed power as king of Crete and took part in military expeditions to avenge the murder of his son and to force Athens to provide men and women to feed to the **Minotaur**, the monster born from a bull given to Minos by **Poseidon**; became a judge in hell after being drowned in his bath.

**Minotaur** Greek monster; son of **Pasiphae** and a bull from the sea, half bull and half human; the name means **Minos**'s bull; kept in a labyrinth made by **Daedalus**, and killed by **Theseus** with the help of **Ariadne**.

**Mithra** Indo-European god; represented friendship, benevolence, non-hostility and compromise; depicted as a 'killer of the bull', plunging a sword into a dying bull's body, from which all herbs and beneficial plants were born; closely associated with the sun.

**Mnemosyne** Greek **Titan**; daughter of earth and heaven, and mother of all the **Muses**; her name means 'Memory'.

**Modimo** African god; originally from Zimbabwe, and considered to be the creator; when appearing in the east, he distributed good things and belonged to the element water; appearing in the west, he was a destroyer, responsible for drought, cyclones and earthquakes, and represented the element fire; his name was taboo and spoken only by priests or seers, and he could only be reached by imperfect beings.

**Moerae (Fates, Parcae)** Three Greek goddesses; named Atropos, Clotho and Lachesis, daughters of **Zeus**; the first spun a thread which signified birth, the second unravelled the thread, symbolizing the unravelling of life, and the third cut the thread, signifying death; they were the personification of inflexible law, representing destiny and the limits which could not be overstepped; in Rome assimilated to the Parcae, who were originally birth **demons**.

**Moloch** Biblical god of the Canaanites and other peoples; in his cult children were sacrificed by fire; a rebel angel in Milton's *Paradise Lost*, his name is used for any excessive and cruel religion.

**Monsters** Wild, unmanageable forces which appear as enemies in all mythologies; in general, a mixture of living creatures (eg horse and man for **Centaurs** and fish and woman for **Sirens**); signified irrational forces, the death necessary for new life and the anarchical energy which preceded and produced creation and order.

**Morgan le Fay** Legendary enchantress; 'Morgan the Fairy', King **Arthur**'s sister, and generally hostile towards him; one of the three queens who received him at his death.

**Morpheus** Roman god of sleep; one of the sons of Somnus ('sleep') who sent or impersonated images of

people in the dreamer's mind; later, as in Spenser, the god of sleep.

**Muses** Nine Greek goddesses; daughters of **Zeus**, each with the vocation to promote an area of the arts: epic poetry, mime, history, the flute, dance, lyric poetry, tragedy, comedy, astronomy; they favoured communication, delighted the gods and inspired poets; ► **Calliope**, **Polyhymnia**, **Clio**, **Euterpe**, **Terpsichore**, **Erato**, **Melpomene**, **Thalia**, **Urania**.

**Myrmidons** Greek band of warriors from Thessaly; went to the Trojan War with **Achilles**.

**Naiads** Greek **Nymphs**; inhabited springs, rivers, and lakes.

**Narcissus** Greek hero; the symbol of self-love, he was told by a seer that he would live to a ripe old age as long as he never looked at himself; caring for no one but himself, he drove his friends and those who fell in love with him to despair; the goddess **Nemesis** decided to avenge his victims by leading him to a spring in which he saw his own reflection, which he immediately fell in love with, and moving towards it, he fell into the spring and drowned; from his body was born the flower which bears his name.

**Nausicaa** Greek heroine; in Homer's *Odyssey*, the daughter of King Alcinous; when **Odysseus** landed in Phaeacia, alone and naked, she was doing the laundry by the sea-shore; she took him home to her father's palace.

**Nemesis** Greek goddess of moderation; ruled over the distribution of wealth, taking revenge on arrogance and punishing excess; said to have prevented the Persians from seizing the city of Athens.

**Neoptolemus** Greek warrior; son of **Achilles**, his original name being Pyrrhus; went with **Odysseus** to persuade **Philoctetes** to come to Troy; at the end of the war he killed **Priam** and enslaved **Andromache**; for this, **Apollo** prevented him from reaching his home, and he was killed in a dispute at Delphi.

**Nephthys** Egyptian goddess; wife of **Seth**; cared for and protected the dead; took sides with her husband's enemies and when he was vanquished, killed and torn to pieces, helped to find the fragments of his body and put them back together, bringing him to life; Nephthys and her sister were the guardians of the tomb.

**Neptune** ► **Poseidon**

**Nereids** Greek **Nymphs**; 50 or (in some accounts) 100 daughters of **Nereus**; lived with their father in the depths of the sea.

**Nereus** Greek god of the sea; the wise old man of the sea who always told the truth; Heracles had to wrestle with him to find the location of the Golden Apples.

**Nergal** Babylonian god of death; son of the god of heaven, he loved catastrophes, epidemics and war, and made death his personal territory; later acquired the power of the ruler of the underworld; tricked **Marduk** into rising up from his seat, resulting in chaos throughout the world, until Marduk regained his position.

**Nessus** Greek **Centaur**; attacked **Heracles**'s wife, Deinira; Heracles shot him, and the dying Centaur told Deinira that his blood would be a cure for infidelity; later, through jealousy, she put the blood on a shirt, or made Heracles wear Nessus' shirt; this coated him with poison, so that he died.

**Nestor** A Greek leader in the Trojan War; in the *Iliad*, Homer portrays him as a long-winded sage, whose advice is often not taken; in the *Odyssey*, he is still living at Pylos, where a Mycenaean palace was discovered in the 1930s.

**Nibelungen** Medieval German race of dwarfs; lived in Norway and possessed a famous treasure; the *Nibelungenlied* recounts how Siegfried obtained the treasure and his later misfortunes; Wagner conflated this with other legends for his opera cycle.

**Nike (Victoria)** Greek goddess of victory, either in war or in an an athletic contest; the frequent subject of sculpture, often shown as a winged figure; identified by the Romans as Victoria.

**Ninurta** Sumerian god of war; chosen by the gods to fight against Anzu, who had stolen the tablets of destiny; on victory, he became champion of the gods.

**Niobe** Greek heroine; proud of having seven sons and seven daughters, she insulted mothers who had few children; her insults to **Leto** earned the revenge of Leto's son and daughter, **Apollo** and **Artemis**, and their father, **Zeus**, who murdered Niobe's children, left them without burial for nine days and turned her to stone on Mt Sipylus.

**Nix (Nixie)** European water-sprite; occasionally entrapped people in her pool; not to be confused with the deity **Nyx** in Greek mythology.

**Njord** Norse god; father of **Freyr** and **Freyja**; succeeded **Odin** as sovereign and maintained peace and prosperity.

**Norns** Three Norse goddesses; Urdr represented the past, Verdandi, the present, and Skuld, the future; decided the fates of men and gods without reason or interest, dealing out as much good as evil.

**Nox, Nux** ► **Nyx**

**Nymphs** Greek goddesses; symbolized the beauty and charm of nature; for the most part, Nymphs were daughters of **Zeus** with lives lasting several centuries; dark formidable powers, whose beauty could lead to madness, and provoked sudden terror at midday; grouped into **Melias**, **Naiads**, **Nereids**, **Oreads**, **Dryads** and **Oceanids**.

**Nyx (Nox, Nux)** Greek goddess; a very ancient deity ('Night'), born of Chaos, and mother of Aither and Day, the **Hesperides**, and the **Moerae**; in the Orphic religion, Night was the original first principle; she laid an egg from which sprang other gods.

**Oberon** European king of the fairies; appears in European literature such as Shakespeare's *A Midsummer Night's Dream* and Wieland's *Oberon*.

**Oceanids** Greek **Nymphs**; inhabited the ocean and other watery places; daughters of **Oceanus** and Tethys.

**Oceanus** Greek **Titan**; son of **Uranus** and **Gaia**; a benign god who personified the stream of Ocean which was assumed to surround the world, as known to the Greeks.

**Odin (Woden, Wotan)** Norse god; keeper of all knowledge, represented as an old one-eyed bearded man wearing a multicoloured robe and a wide-brimmed hat; his horse had eight legs and galloped through the air, on the ocean as well as on ground; a cruel sovereign, he inspired deceit and was fond of human sacrifices; preserved the head of the decapitated giant Mimir, who was famous for his knowledge, and consulted it whenever he had some mystery to unravel.

**Odysseus (Ulysses)** Greek hero; a leader of the Achaeans in the Trojan War; returning to Greece, he became separated by a windstorm from his companions and overcame **Cyclopes**, **Sirens**, gods and magicians to return; his adventures are described in Homer's *Odyssey*.

**Oedipus** Greek hero; afflicted from birth by the curse that he would kill his father, marry his mother and be at the root of an endless series of misfortunes which would lead to the ruin of his family; because of this, his father abandoned him, and he was adopted by King Polybus; when the child was older and learned of the curse, he became frightened for the king, whom he believed to be his father and went into voluntary exile; he later killed his father in a fight when they met coincidentally; after being crowned king, he unknowingly married his mother, widowed by the death of his father.

**Ogmios** Celtic god; an old wrinkled man who wore a lion's skin and carried a club, a bow and a quiver; could draw or tow men attached by their ears to a gold chain, the end of which passed through the god's pierced tongue; attracted his followers by magic.

**Olympians** Greek gods and goddesses; collectively, the major gods and goddesses who were thought to live on Mt Olympus, the highest mountain in Ancient Greece, situated in a range between Macedonia and Thessaly.

**Ops** Roman goddess of plenty, the consort of **Saturn**, identified with **Rhea**.

**Oreads ► Nymphs**

**Orestes** In Greek legend, the son of **Agamemnon** and **Clytemnestra**; after his father's murder he went into exile, but returned to kill **Aegisthus** and his mother, for which he was pursued by the **Erinyes**.

**Orion** Greek gigantic hunter; beloved by **Eos** and killed by **Artemis**; changed into a constellation, and this generated further astronomical stories, for example, that he pursues the **Pleiades**.

**Orpheus** Greek hero; a musician and poet, he had the power to enchant gods, men, animals and inanimate objects who followed him under his spell; married the **Nymph Eurydice** who was taken to hell after dying from the bite of a serpent; Orpheus charmed the rulers of hell who agreed to release Eurydice on the condition that Orpheus did not turn round to look at her as she followed him out of hell; his doubts that she was following made him eventually turn round, to see Eurydice disappear into the underworld forever.

**Osiris** Egyptian god of vegetation; provided laws and customs and gave the fruits of the earth; his jealous brother **Seth** conspired to kill him by trapping him in a wooden chest and sinking it in a river; his wife **Isis** recovered the body and managed to make Osiris father a son, to take vengeance on her enemies.

**Ouranus ► Uranus**

**Pan** Greek god of animal instinct; half man, half goat with a long wrinkled face and two horns on his head; son of **Hermes** he lived in hills and woods; constantly pursued by **Nymphs** and those who became possessed by him took on his characteristics.

**Pandarus** Trojan prince; in Homer's *Iliad*, was killed by **Diomedes**; in later developments of the story of **Troilus** and **Cressida**, he became her uncle and their 'go-between' (hence 'pander').

**Pandora** Greek heroine; the first woman on earth, who led men to their downfall by seduction and entrapment; a gift from **Zeus** to man, made in the form of the immortal goddesses, Pandora was divine in appearance but human in reality; with her she brought a box which she had been forbidden to open; overcome with curiosity, she opened the box and let out all the evils of the world, such as disease, death, lies and theft, which spread throughout nature.

**Pan Gu** Chinese first being of creation; broke open the primal egg from within, held up the sky, and prevented it from bearing down upon the earth; the world was then made from parts of him, so that his body became the mountains, his hair the stars, and his eyes the sun and moon.

**Parasurama** Indian hero; united the religious purity of a Brahman with the impurity of a warrior; cut off his mother's head as requested by his father, who believed her to have produced the racial impurity; in 21 battles, freed the world of the kshatriya warriors.

**Parcae ► Moerae**

**Paris (Alexander)** Greek hero; a prince of Troy, the son of **Priam**; because of a prophecy, he was exposed at birth on Mt Ida, where he was loved by Oenone, a **Nymph**; there he also chose **Aphrodite** as the fairest of three goddesses; she offered him the most beautiful woman in the world; he abducted **Helen**, causing the Trojan war; wounded by **Philoctetes**, and in his death-agony asked Oenone for help, which she refused.

**Parsifal ► Perceval, Sir**

**Pasiphae** In Greek mythology, the daughter of **Helios**; wife of **Minos**, king of Crete; loved a bull sent by **Poseidon**, and became the mother of the **Minotaur**.

**Patroclus** Greek warrior; faithful follower of **Achilles** at Troy; went into battle wearing Achilles's armour, but was cut down by **Hector**; his death made Achilles return to the battle.

**Pegasus** Greek winged horse; sprang from the body of the **Medusa** after her death; **Bellerophon** caught it with **Athene**'s assistance; various fountains sprang from the touch of its foot, such as Hippocrene on Mt Helicon; finally it was placed in the sky as a constellation.

**Peleus** Greek king of Phythia in Thessaly; had to capture Thetis, a **Nereid**, before he could marry her; the gods attended the wedding feast; the father of **Achilles**.

**Pelops** Greek hero; protégé of **Poseidon**; eaten unknowingly by **Demeter** at birth as a result of his father's attempt to test the keenness of the gods; the other gods resurrected him to restore their reputation; protected by Poseidon on Olympus until his father led him to steal the nectar and ambrosia of the gods to give to mortals, for which he was forced to return to earth; drove his chariot drawn by winged horses to win the chance to marry Hippodameia; one of the mythological figures said to have founded the Olympic Games, in memory of his victory.

**Penates** Roman guardians of the storeroom; '**Lares** and Penates' were the household gods; the *penates publici* were the 'luck' of the Roman state, originally brought by **Aeneas** from Troy and kept at Lavinium.

**Penelope** In Greek legend, the wife of **Odysseus**; faithfully waited 20 years for his return from Troy; tricked her insistent suitors by weaving her web (a shroud for Odysseus' father, Laertes, which had to be finished before she could marry), and undoing her work every night.

**Pentheus** In Greek mythology, the king of Thebes; did not welcome **Dionysus**; disguising himself as a woman, he tried to spy on the orgiastic rites of the **Maenads**, who tore him to pieces, his mother leading them on.

**Perceval, Sir (Parsifal)** One of King **Arthur**'s knights; went in quest of the Holy Grail; in the German version (Parzival) his bashfulness prevented him from asking the right questions of the warden of the Grail castle, so that the Fisher King was not healed.

**Peri** Persian good fairy or genie; Peri-Banou, for example, was the name of a beautiful fairy in the *Arabian Nights*.

**Persephone (Proserpine)** Greek goddess of the underworld; daughter of **Demeter** and **Zeus**, originally called Kore ('maiden'); while gathering flowers at Enna in Sicily was abducted by **Hades** and made queen of the underworld; there she ate the seeds of the pomegranate, which meant (in fairy lore) that she was bound to stay; however, a compromise was arranged so that she could return for half of every year (an allegory of the return of spring).

**Perseus** Greek hero; shut in a chest and thrown into the sea by his grandfather; washed up on the island of Seriphos; after he grew up, the island's tyrant demanded that he bring him the gift of the head of a **Gorgon**; with the help of **Hermes** and the **Nymphs**, he slayed **Medusa** and returned with her head; married **Andromeda** after freeing her from the sea-monster to whom she was promised; unknowingly killed his grandfather, fulfilling an oracle which predicted this.

**Perun** Slavic god of rain and fertility; represented as a human being with a silver head and golden moustache; controlled the seasons and destroyed the countries of wicked men with hail.

**Phaedra** Greek heroine; daughter of **Minos** and the second wife of **Theseus**; while he was away she fell in love with her step-son **Hippolytus**; he rejected her, so she killed herself, but left a note accusing him of trying to rape her; Theseus called on **Poseidon** to grant a promised favour, and punish Hippolytus with death.

**Phaethon** Greek hero; son of **Helios**; challenged to prove his ancestry by his friends, he asked to drive his father's chariot for a day; as he was inexperienced in this, the horses bolted, the chariot veered off its route and everything in their path was set on fire; the earth complained to the king of Olympus, and **Zeus** struck down the charioteer.

**Phenix ▸ Phoenix**

**Philemon** and **Baucis** Greek old man and wife; the only ones to entertain the Greek gods **Zeus** and **Hermes** when they visited the earth to test people's hospitality; in return they were saved from a flood, made priest and priestess, and allowed to die at the same time, when they were changed into trees.

**Philoctetes** Greek hero; son of Poeas, who inherited the bow of **Heracles** and its poisoned arrows; on the way to Troy was bitten by a snake, and the wound stank, so that he was left behind on the island of Lemnos; it was prophesied that only with the arrows of Heracles could Troy be taken, so **Diomedes** and **Odysseus** came to find Philoctetes; his wound was healed and he entered the battle, killing **Paris**.

**Philomela (Philomel)** and **Procne (Progne)** In Greek mythology, daughters of Pandion, king of Athens; Procne married Tereus, king of Thrace, who raped Philomela and removed her tongue; but she was able to tell Procne by a message in her embroidery; Procne served up her son Itys, or Itylos, in a meal to his father; while pursuing the sisters, the gods changed Tereus into the hoopoe, Philomela into the swallow, and Procne into the nightingale; in Latin legend, the birds of the sisters are reversed.

**Phoebe** Greek **Titan**, identified with the moon; later she was confused with **Artemis**.

**Phoenix (Phenix)** Legendary bird; lived for a long time; killed itself on a funeral pyre, but was then reborn from the ashes.

**Pleiades** In Greek mythology, the seven daughters of **Atlas** and **Pleione**; Maia, Taygete, Elektra, Alkyone,

Asterope, Kelaino and Merope; after their deaths they were transformed into the star-cluster of the same name.

**Pluto** ► **Hades**

**Pollux** ► **Castor** and **Pollux**

**Polyhymnia** Greek **Muse** of dance, mime and acting.

**Polynices (Polyneices)** Greek hero; second son of **Oedipus**, who led the **Seven against Thebes**; **Creon**'s refusal to bury him led eventually to the death of **Antigone**.

**Polyphemus** Greek **Cyclops**; imprisoned **Odysseus** and some of his companions in his cave; Odysseus blinded Polyphemus's one eye, and told him that 'No one' had hurt him; as a result, when he called on the other Cyclopes for help, and they asked who had attacked him, they did not understand his answer; Odysseus's band escaped by hiding under the sheep when they were let out of the cave to graze.

**Pomona** Roman goddess of fruit-trees and their fruit, especially apples and pears.

**Poseidon (Neptune)** Greek god of the sea; represented wielding a trident and being pulled by monsters in a chariot; could evoke storms and set fire to rocks; took part in the construction of the walls of Troy, then called up a monster to devastate the area when he did not receive payment; Neptune was a Roman water god who was later associated with Poseidon.

**Prajapati** Indian god; master of creatures and posterity, he was born aged a thousand years from a primordial egg; created the gods, the evil spirits, man, melodies and the sun, then wasted away, exhausted by his tasks.

**Priam** In Greek legend, the king of Troy; son of Laomedon, and husband of **Hecuba**; presented in the *Iliad* as an old man; when **Hector** was killed, went secretly to **Achilles** to beg his son's body for burial; at the sack of Troy, he was killed by **Neoptolemus**.

**Priapus** Greek god; represented as a small bearded man with an oversized penis; in some traditions, the son of **Zeus** and **Aphrodite**; Zeus's jealous wife **Hera** made sure that the child was born with the extraordinary deformity to which he owes his name; Aphrodite abandoned him in the mountains; the guard of the orchard, he scared off thieves and threatened females with sexual violence.

**Procrustes** Thief of Attica; in the legend of **Theseus**, made travellers lie on his bed, and either cut or lengthened them to fit it; his name means 'the stretcher'; Theseus gave him the same treatment, and killed him.

**Prometheus** Greek hero; symbolized the revolt of man against the gods and brought to humanity all the good things refused it by the gods; punished for this when **Zeus** sent mankind the gift of **Pandora**, who spread evils throughout the world; became immortal after exchanging death for immortality with **Cheiron** the **Centaur**.

**Proserpine** ► **Persephone**

**Proteus** Greek god of the sea; associated with seals, and a shape-changer; he gave answers to questions after a wrestling match; was sometimes to be found on the island of Pharos, in Egypt, where **Menelaus** wrestled with him.

**Psyche** Greek personification of 'the soul'; usually represented by a butterfly; in the story told by Apuleius, was beloved by Cupid ( ► **Eros**), who hid her in an enchanted palace, and visited her at night, forbidding her to look at him; her sisters persuaded her to light a lamp; she saw Cupid, but was separated from him, and given impossible tasks by Venus ( ► **Aphrodite**), who impeded her search for him.

**Ptah** Egyptian god; principal god of the city of Memphis, known as the creator and master of craftsmen; subsequently regarded as a healing god in the form of a flat-headed dwarf and as a protective spirit.

**Purusha** Primordial being of India; thought to be a gigantic man who covered the earth and went beyond it; heaven made up three-quarters of his being, and the fourth quarter consisted of all mortal creatures.

**Pwyll** Celtic hero; wise prince of Dyfed who as a service to the king of Annwn killed the king's permanent enemy; courteous and powerful, he emerged victorious from a thousand trials.

**Pygmalion** In Greek mythology, a king of Cyprus; made a statue of a beautiful woman; he prayed to **Aphrodite**, and the sculptured figure came to life.

**Pyramus** and **Thisbe** Two lovers; kept apart by their parents, they conversed through a crack in the wall between their houses, and agreed to meet at Ninus's tomb outside the city of Babylon; finding Thisbe's blood-stained cloak, Pyramus thought she had been killed by a lion, and committed suicide; when she found him, Thisbe killed herself on his sword; incorporated into Shakespeare's *A Midsummer Night's Dream*.

**Python** Greek monster; lived at Delphi and was killed by **Apollo** when he took over the shrine; the name Pythia continued in use, and the Pythian games were celebrated there.

**Qat** Hero of Oceania; born from a rock which had been hollowed out in the centre to allow his birth; organizer of life, he created man and then death to allow renewal; initiated day and night; canoed away to a far country, taking with him the hopes of mankind.

**Querinus** Roman god; initially a god of the city who watched over the material well being of the community; also likened to **Ares** by the Greeks, and to **Romulus**, founder of Rome.

**Quetzalcoatl** Aztec god of vegetation and wind; depicted as a bearded man wearing a mask,

earrings and a conical hat; son of the sun-god and one of the five goddesses of the moon; created mankind from the bones of the ancient dead; taught measurement of time and how to discover the movement of the stars.

**Ra** ► **Re**

**Rainbow Snake (Julunggul)** Australian Aboriginal fertility spirit; both male and female, creator and destroyer, known as Julunggul; associated with streams and waterholes, from which it emerges in the creation story and leaves special markings on the ground.

**Rama** Indian hero; incarnation of the god **Vishnu** on earth; was taught magic spells to allow him to conquer the rakasa, the **demons**; saved his wife from abduction and was made king; after his wife had been swallowed up by the earth, gave up his royal status, and went to the river Sarayu to be carried off to heaven.

**Re (Ra)** Egyptian god; the ancient sun-god of Heliopolis; as the creator, he emerged from the primeval waters at the beginning of time; depicted as a falcon with the sun's disc on his head; at night he appears as a ram-headed god who sails through the underworld.

**Rhadamanthus (Rhadamanthys)** In Greek mythology, a Cretan, son of **Zeus** and **Europa**; did not die but was taken to Elisium, where he became the just judge of the dead.

**Rhea (Rheia)** Greek **Titan**; sister and wife of **Cronus**, and mother of **Zeus** and other Olympian gods; when Cronus consumed his children, Rhea gave him a stone instead of Zeus, who was saved and later rebelled against his father.

**Rhiannon** Celtic heroine; mistress of horses and horsemen; refused all her suitors out of love for **Pwyll**, who prepared to marry her; Pwyll, however, agreed to grant a supplicant, Gnawl, any wish, and he claimed Rhiannon; Pwyll later set her free from Gnawl through trickery and became her husband; accused of infanticide after her son mysteriously disappeared, but the child later reappeared.

**Roc** Arabian mythical creature; an enormous bird encountered by travellers in the Indian ocean, capable of carrying off an elephant.

**Rod** Slavic god; initially the god of husbandmen but also a universal god, the god of heaven, the thunderbolt and rain; responsible for the nation's increase and closely linked with the worship of ancestors; later dethroned by **Perun**.

**Romulus** and **Remus** In Roman legend, the twin sons of Mars (► **Ares**) and the Vestal Virgin Rhea Silvia; an example of an invented myth, to explain the name of the city; thrown into the Tiber, which carried them to the Palatine, where they were suckled by a she-wolf; in building the wall of Rome, Remus made fun of the work and was killed by Romulus or one of his followers; having founded Rome, Romulus was later carried off in a thunderstorm.

**Rosmerta** Gallo-Roman goddess; represented as a woman standing draped in a long robe, holding a cornucopia and a patera; invoked to obtain fertility, fruitfulness and everything essential for a better life.

**Rudra** Indian god; a being with a thousand eyes and a thousand feet, with plaited hair, a black belly, a red back and armed with a bow and arrows; the great destroyer, he cast evil spells over men and beasts, and spread terror and illness.

**Sakhmet** ► **Sekhmet**

**Sarapis** ► **Serapis**

**Sarasvati** Indian goddess; wife of **Brahma**; personification of the word of the god Veda; carried the book of Veda, a musical instrument and a rosary composed of the letters of the alphabet; mother of the scriptures, the sciences and the arts; also associated with water.

**Sarpedon** Warrior of Greek mythology; in the *Iliad*, a son of **Zeus**, who led the Lycian troops on the Trojan side, and made an important speech on the duties of a warrior; killed by **Patroclus**, and carried off by Sleep and Death to Lycia.

**Saturn** Roman god; master of agriculture who invented the dressing of the vine, taught man agricultural methods and provided the first laws; depicted as being armed with a scythe; associated with the Golden Age, synonymous with religious festivals and feasts.

**Satyr** Greek god; a minor deity associated with **Dionysus**; usually depicted with goat-like ears, tail, and legs; rural, wild and lustful, the satyrs were said to be the brothers of the **Nymphs**.

**Scylla** Greek sea-monster; usually located in the Straits of Messina opposite to Charybdis; originally a woman, she was changed by **Circe** or **Amphitrite** into a snake with six heads; in the *Odyssey* she snatched six men from **Odysseus**'s ships.

**Sekhmet (Sakmet, Sakhmet, Sekmet)** Egyptian goddess; wife of the god **Ptah**; depicted with the head of a lioness and the body of a woman; a terrible bloodthirsty goddess, responsible for epidemics, death, carnage and war; also had the power of healing.

**Selene** Greek goddess of the moon; depicted as a charioteer (the head of one of her horses may be seen among the Elgin Marbles).

**Semele** In Greek mythology, the daughter of Cadmus, and mother by **Zeus** of **Dionysus**; asked Zeus to appear in his glory before her, and was consumed in fire, but it made her son immortal.

**Semiramis** In Greek mythology, a queen of Assyria; founded many cities, including Nineveh and Babylon.

**Serapis (Sarapis)** Egyptian god; a compound deity, combining the names and aspects of two Egyptian gods, **Osiris** and **Apis**, to which were further added features of major Greek gods, such as **Zeus** and **Dionysus**; introduced to Alexandria by Ptolemy I in an attempt to unite Greeks and Egyptians in common worship.

**Sesostris** Egyptian king; alleged to have conquered vast areas of Europe, Asia and N Africa; probably a compound of the three Egyptian pharaohs (c.20th–19th-cBC) and Rameses II (13th-cBC).

**Seth** Egyptian god; depicted as a strange being with a forked tail, a long gaunt body, huge ears and protruding eyes; represented all evils and caused all disasters; fought the **demon** Apopis every morning and every evening and as a result of this permanent conflict, the equilibrium of forces and universal harmony were born.

**Seven against Thebes** Seven Greek Champions; attacked Thebes to deprive **Eteocles** of his kingship; led by his brother **Polynices**; the names of the other six were Tydeus, Adrastus (or Eteoklos), Capaneus, Hippomedon, Parthenopaeus and Amphiarus; defeated by another seven champions at the seven gates of Thebes; all were killed in battle, except for Amphiarus, whom the earth swallowed alive, and Adrastus, who escaped; later the sons of the Seven, the **Epigoni**, led by Adrastus, succeeded in destroying the city.

**Seven Sleepers of Ephesus** In medieval legend, seven persecuted Christians who fled into a cave at the time of the Emperor Decius (AD250); slept for 200 years, emerging in 447 at the time of Theodosius II; the story was thought to confirm the resurrection of Christ.

**Shamash** Babylonian god; depicted bearing a head-dress with four rows of horns and a large beard, wearing a long robe and holding a staff and a hoop; symbolized by a solar disc rising between two mountains or by a spoked wheel; god of light and justice, he gave light to the world and distributed punishment and reward.

**Shango** African god of thunder; dispensed justice using the thunderbolt which was regarded as the god's punishment; the victim of his punishment was compelled to pay heavy fines and to appease him by means of sacrifices; originally a cruel king whose subjects drove him away; he hanged himself from a tree leaving a hole from which emerged an iron chain; finding the tree without the body, his supporters concluded that he had become a god.

**Shiva** Indian god; representing darkness, his three eyes were filled with snakes; had four arms and a girdle made of skulls; danced amid devils on cremation sites, representing the world's constructive and destructive periods; withdrew to the mountains after the suicide of his wife but later came back to produce a son to kill a **demon** which threatened the world; carried out many heroic deeds and was regarded as a beneficent force.

**Sibyl (Sibylla)** Roman prophetess; uttered mysterious wisdom; **Aeneas** met the Cumaean Sibyl, who was inspired by **Apollo** and whose prophecies were written on leaves; she had been given 1 000 years of life, and eventually shrank to a tiny creature hung up in a bottle; later there were said to be 10 Sibyls; the Sibylline Books were nine books of prophecy offered by the Sibyl to Tarquinus Priscus, who refused to pay her price; she destroyed three, and came again, with the same result; she destroyed three more, and then Tarquin bought the remainder for the price originally asked.

**Sigurd** In Norse mythology, the son of Sigmund the Volsung; killed Fafnir the dragon and won **Brunhild**; married **Gudrun**, having forgotten Brunhild, and was killed by Gudrun's brother Gutthorn; virtually the same story is told of Siegfried in German legends.

**Sileni** Greek followers of **Dionysus**; depicted with horse ears, tail and legs, or as old men in need of support (Papposileni); could give good advice to humans if captured; plural form of **Silenus**.

**Silenus** Greek demi-god; fostered and educated **Dionysus**; represented as a festive old man, usually quite drunk.

**Silvanus (Sylvanus)** Roman god of uncultivated land, especially woodland; he was therefore strange, and dangerous, like **Pan**.

**Sin** Sumerian god; represented the moon; depicted seated on a throne, with a long beard, holding an axe, a sceptre and a staff; his predictions were binding on the gods and man, and an eclipse was his most formidable sign, announcing catastrophe.

**Sirens** Three Greek demonesses; became half woman, half bird when they asked the gods for wings, to look for **Persephone** who had been taken to the underworld by **Hades**; one held a lyre, the second sang and the third played the flute; devoured sailors lured to their island by their enchanting sounds.

**Sisyphus** In Greek mythology, a Corinthian king who was a famous trickster; in one story he caught and bound Thanatos (Death); in the underworld was condemned to roll a large stone up a hill from which it always rolled down again.

**Sita** Indian heroine; emerged from a furrow in a ploughed field; married **Rama** and was abducted by Ravana; on reunion with her husband, was tested by fire and exiled as he believed she had been unfaithful; requested the earth to open up and swallow her forever.

**Skanda** Indian hero; son of **Shiva** and chief of the divine armies; killed the **demon** Taraka who threatened the world.

**Skyamsen ▸ Thunderbird**

**Soma** Indian moon-god; marked the rhythm of the days and months and was the nectar of immortality, a divine drink essential to the gods.

**Sucellus** Gallic god; depicted with a tunic, cowl and boots, holding a club or sceptre and a vase, indicating that he was a sovereign and the dispenser of food; married to the river goddess.

**Svarog** Slavic god of fire; dispenser of all wealth, and judge and protector of monogamy; also a magician and soothsayer.

**Sventovit** Slavic god of war; depicted holding a trumpet and a bow; also the god of fertility, fruitfulness and destiny; his horse had the gift of divination, and its movement could reveal the meaning of oracles it wished to communicate.

**Sylvanus** ► **Silvanus**

**Syrinx** Greek **Nymph**; pursued by **Pan**, she called on the earth to help, and so sank down into it and became a reed-bed; Pan cut some of the reeds, and made the panpipes.

**Tammuz (Thammuz)** Babylonian god of vegetation; beloved by **Ishtar** (in Assyria by Astarte); returned from the dead and died again each year.

**Tane (Kane)** Divinity from the Pacific Islands; kept heaven and earth apart, permitting the world to exist; misfortune and death were born from his destructive war with his enemy, the god Tangaroa.

**Tantalus** In Greek mythology, a king of Sisyphos in Lydia; committed terrible crimes; stole the food of the gods, so becoming immortal, and served them his son **Pelops** in a dish; for this he was punished in the underworld; he sits in a pool which recedes when he bends to drink, and the grapes over his head elude his grasp.

**Taranis** Gallic god; master of the universe, who inspired fear by sending thunder and lightning; at the same time, brought the gentle rain which fed the earth and made crops grow; demanded human sacrifices; his victims were shut in wooden cages which were set alight, and severed heads were offered to him.

**Tarpeia** Roman woman who betrayed the Capitol to the Sabines, in return for 'what they wore on their left arms' (meaning gold rings); in their disgust, they threw their shields on her and crushed her to death.

**Telemachus** Greek hero; in the *Odyssey*, the son of **Odysseus** and **Penelope**; set out to find his father, visiting **Nestor** and **Menelaus**; later helped Odysseus fight Penelope's suitors.

**Tellus** ► **Gaea**

**Tengri** Mongol god of heaven; imposed the order of the natural world, the organization and movements of the stars and the government of the Mongol empire; distributed good luck and wealth and showed his anger by sending thunderstorms.

**Terminus** Roman god of boundary marks; his statue or bust was sometimes placed there; his stone on the Capitol was within the temple of Jupiter Optimus Maximus (► **Zeus**), but was not allowed to be covered in.

**Terpsichore** Greek **Muse** of dance and lyric poetry.

**Teshub** Hurrian god of the thunderstorm; depicted holding an axe and thunderclouds; dethroned the king of heaven to become the supreme god and battled victoriously against the deposed king who sought his revenge.

**Teutates** Gallic god; a warrior god, sometimes compared to Mars (► **Ares**) and Mercury (► **Hermes**); depicted beside a serpent with a ram's head; a cruel god who demanded human sacrifices; the victims were drowned in a vat of water.

**Tezcatlipoca** Aztec god; depicted in human form with a stripe of black paint across his face and a mirror replacing one of his feet; said to have been mutilated by the mythical crocodile on which the earth was supposed to rest; reigned over the four worlds destroyed prior to the creation of the present one; with his mirror could see everything and was aware of both human actions and thoughts; a malevolent wizard who brought the custom of human sacrifice to Mexico.

**Thalia (Thaleia)** Greek **Muse** of comedy and idyllic poetry.

**Thammuz** ► **Tammuz**

**Themis** Greek goddess of established law and justice; a consort of **Zeus**, she was the mother of the **Horae** and the **Moerae**.

**Theseus** Greek hero; set out for Athens to find his father, the king, and slayed many monsters on the way; fought those who tried to depose his father and killed the **Minotaur**; assumed power and defended Attica against the **Amazons** who almost won but in the end were forced to sign a peace treaty (he married their leader, Hippolyta); later became powerless and was forced into exile before being killed when thrown into a ravine.

**Thetis** Greek goddess; mother of **Achilles**; saved **Zeus** from a conspiracy to remove his power; an oracle predicted that her son would be more powerful than his father, and fearing this, Zeus forced her to marry a mortal; an unhappy goddess, she failed in her determined attempts to make her children immortal.

**Thor** Nordic god; son of **Odin**; armed with a hammer which returned automatically to the hand of the one who hurled it, and doubled his strength by wearing a magic belt; fond of tricks and practical jokes; killed the serpent of Midgard, but was himself killed by its venom.

**Thoth (Hermes)** Egyptian god; skilled at calculation, secretary to the gods and master of effective speech; also a magician and capable of providing cures; identified by the Greeks as Hermes.

**Thunderbird (Skyamsen)** Totem figure of NW Native American religion; lightning flashed from its eye and it fed on killer whales; the chief of the Thunderbirds was Golden Eagle (Keneun).

**Thyestes** In Greek mythology, a son of **Pelops**; inherited the curse upon that house; his brother **Atreus** set before him a dish made of the flesh of Thyestes's children; later became the father of **Aegisthus**.

**Tiamat** Akkadian goddess; a primordial divinity who represented salt water; became angry after an old god was murdered by a younger one; decided to create monsters as gods, and in the resulting confrontation was killed by **Marduk**; from one half of her corpse, heaven was created, and from the other half, Marduk formed dry land.

**Tiresias** In Greek mythology, a blind Theban prophet; takes a prominent part in Sophocles's plays

about **Oedipus** and **Antigone**; later legends account for his wisdom by saying that he had experienced the life of both sexes.

**Titania** Greek female **Titan**; identified with the moon; in Shakespeare's *A Midsummer Night's Dream* she is the queen of the fairies, who is tricked into falling in love with Bottom the Weaver.

**Titans** Greek gods; members of the older generation of gods, the children of **Uranus** and **Gaia**; after **Zeus** and the Olympians took power, the Titans made war on them; but they were defeated and imprisoned in Tartarus; one or two, notably **Prometheus**, helped Zeus; may represent memories of pre-Greek Mediterranean gods.

**Tlaloc** Aztec god of mountains, rain and springs; represented as a man painted black with huge round eyes with circles or serpents around them, and long fangs; ordered the distribution of rain and hurricanes; sometimes killed by means of a thunderbolt; his victims were buried with a piece of dry wood which would come back to life in Tlaloc's paradise.

**Tlazolteotl** Aztec goddess of lust; represented as a young girl wearing a rubber mask and a crescent-shaped ornament in her nose; responsible for conjugal infidelities and at the same time the granter of pardon; also the goddess of renewal.

**Triglav** Slavic god; had three heads and a golden veil which covered his eyes and mouth, signifying his desire to disregard human faults; a soothsayer, priest, warrior and nourisher.

**Tristan** and **Isolde** Celtic heroes; Tristan was a master harp-player and huntsman; Isolde was the daughter of the king of Ireland, who was to marry Mark the king of Cornwall, and become queen; through a misunderstanding, Tristan and Isolde drank from the same love potion and became bound by an indissoluble love; discovered to be meeting secretly, Tristan and the queen were condemned to be burned alive, and both fled; King Mark searched for them, and finding them asleep, became seized with pity, leaving his sword between them and replacing a ring on Isolde's finger; moved by his generosity, the lovers returned to the court, where Isolde was accepted, but Tristan was sent into exile.

**Triton** In Greek mythology, the son of **Poseidon** and **Amphitrite**; depicted in art as a fish from the waist down, and blowing a conch-shell; beings of similar form (mermen) who serve Poseidon are often referred to as Tritons.

**Troilus** In Greek legend, a prince of Troy; son of **Priam** and **Hecuba**, who was killed by **Achilles**; in medieval stories, the lover of **Cressida**.

**Tuatha de Danann** Irish race of wise beings; came to Ireland in c.1500BC, and became the ancient gods of the Irish; the name means 'the people of the goddess Danu'; conquered by the Milesians, and retreated into tumuli near the R Boyne.

**Tyche** Greek goddess of chance or luck; prominent in the Hellenistic period; depicted as blind, or, with a wall, as the luck of a city.

**Typhoeus ► Typhon**

**Typhon (Typhoeus)** Greek monster; had 100 heads and was brought forth by **Gaea**; a serious challenge to **Zeus**, who hurled his thunderbolts and thrust him down into Tartarus; in another story, said to be buried under Etna.

**Tyr** Nordic god; courageous and bold, he guaranteed right and justice; lost one arm in the courageous act of restraining the horrible wolf Fenrir.

**Ulysses ► Odysseus**

**Unicorn** Creature of medieval legend; a horse with a single horn on its forehead; probably based on stories of the rhinoceros; could be captured only by a virgin putting its head in her lap.

**Urania** Greek **Muse** of astronomy.

**Uranus (Ouranus)** Greek god of the sky; father of the Titans; a very abstract figure, not the subject of worship or of art, he was displaced by **Cronus**; equivalent to Roman Caelus, 'the heavens'.

**Uther Pendragon** Legendary king of Britain; father of King **Arthur** by Ygerna, the wife of Duke Gorlois of Cornwall.

**Vahagn** Armenian deity; born of water and fire, and married to the goddess of the stars; god of victory and destroyer of obstacles; created the Milky Way when he stole some straw one night and fled in haste across the sky, leaving wisps of straw across his path.

**Väinämöinen** Finnish sage, shaman and bard; dominates the epic *Kalevala*; sought the sampo, the magic cauldron of plenty, and invented the kantele or harp.

**Valkyries** Nordic goddesses; goddesses of fertility and the angels of battle; 40 are recorded as magicians and combat goddesses who selected those who were doomed to die, apportioning death not as a punishment, but as a reward.

**Varuna** Indian god and guardian of world order; ordered nature and supervised sacrificial rites; his domain consisted of darkness and the waters, and the stars were his thousand eyes; also producing evil, he caused earthquakes and sent disease, but possessed and provided the remedies.

**Venus ► Aphrodite**

**Vesta ► Hestia**

**Vesta** Roman goddess of the hearth; particularly known for the cult dedicated to her; her temple in the Roman Forum was served by virgins who were walled up alive at the Colline Gate if they failed to remain chaste; a fire was kept lit in her honour all year round.

**Viracocha** Incan god; the creator and civilizer, he created the first men, but disappointed by them, he changed some into stone statues and destroyed the others by fire; recreated humanity, accompanied by the sun and moon, then provided mountains, rivers and farmland to permit them to live in a civilized

way; after this mission, disappeared over the horizon, and his return is still awaited; protector of the emperor of the Incas.

**Vishnu** Indian god; originally a dwarf who wanted to secure dominion over the world, he became the god of space, who gave the world its stability; the origin of the fertility of both nature and man; appeared in the form of heroes and animals each time the world needed him.

**Visvamitra** Indian hero; tried to equal the Brahman Vasistha by leading a life of increasing rigid asceticism; finally achieved his aim by stopping eating and breathing for a number of years.

**Volcanus ► Hephaestus**

**Vulcan ► Hephaestus**

**Wak** Ethiopian god; kept heaven at a distance from the earth and covered it with stars; created man on the flat earth, then buried him for seven years while he made fire rain down to create the mountains; when after this, man sprang back to life, he said that he had slept only for a brief moment; this was said to be why man is awake for most of the day; later created woman.

**Weyland** Norse, German, and Old English legendary inventor; known as Weyland the Smith; lame, having been maimed by King Nidud; many heroes carry swords made by him; his 'Smithy', is a dolmen on the Berkshire Downs, UK.

**Woden, Wotan ► Odin**

**Xipe Totec** Aztec god of springtime, renewal and nocturnal rain; inspired Mexican ceremonies with human sacrifices and mock battles; during the ceremonies the priests flayed the sacrifices and wore their skins.

**Xiuhtecuhtli** Aztec god of the hearth, fire, the sun and volcanoes; also associated with peppers and the pine, the tree from which torches were made.

**Yama** The first Indian man; the first mortal who on death became king of the dead; came to look for those who had used up their lifetimes; produced excessive increases of the human population when one day he became distracted and did not make a single man die.

**Yggdrasil** In Norse mythology, a giant ash; the World-Tree, which supported the sky, held the different realms of gods and men in its branches, and had its roots in the underworld.

**Yu the Great** Chinese hero; a thin, ill man who hopped about on one foot; dug out the mountains and allowed waters to flow from a catastrophic flood, working for 13 years without returning home; became a god and travelled the world to plan it; first emperor of the Hsia Dynasty.

**Zanhary** Madagascan god; creator god and father of heaven; terrifying, and spoke in thunder and lightning; a double god, the Zanhary from below created man and Zanhary from above gave him life; the two gods disagreed over women and became enemies, separating the worlds above and below forever.

**Zeus (Jupiter, Iuppiter)** Greek god of all gods; god of light and weather, and arbiter among gods and among men; had many wives and affairs with mortal women to whom he appeared in various guises, eg as a shower of gold, a bull or a swan; hanged his jealous wife **Hera** from Olympus with anvils fastened to her ankles.

## Baha'i

**Founded** 1863 in Persia.

**Founder** Mirza Husayn Ali (1817–92), known as Baha'u'llah (Glory of God). He declared himself the prophet foretold by Mirza ali Mohammed (1819–50), a direct descendant of Mohammed, who proclaimed himself to be the Bab ('gate' or 'door').

**Sacred texts** Most Holy Book, The Seven Valleys, The Hidden Words and the Bayan.

**Beliefs** Baha'i teaches the oneness of God, the unity of all faiths, the inevitable unification of humankind, the harmony of all people, universal education, and obedience to government. It does not predict an end to this world or any intervention by God but believes there will be a change within man and society.

**Organization** There is a network of elected local and national level bodies, and an elected international governing body. Although there is little formal ritual (most assemblies are simply gatherings of the faithful), there are ceremonies for marriages and funerals, and there are shrines and temples.

## Buddhism

**Founded** c.500BC in India.

**Founder** Prince Siddhartha Gautama (c.560–c.480BC) who became Buddha ('the enlightened') through meditation.

**Sacred texts** The Pali Canon or Tripitaka made up of the Vinaya Pitaka (monastic discipline), Sutta Pitaka (discourses of the Buddha) and the Abhidhamma Pitaka (analysis of doctrines). Other texts: the Mahayana Sutras, the Milindapanha (Questions of Milinda) and the Bardo Thodol (Tibetan Book of the Dead).

**Beliefs** Buddha's teaching is summarized in the Four Noble Truths; suffering is always present in life; desire is the cause of suffering; freedom from life

can be achieved by Nirvana (perfect peace and bliss); the Eightfold Path leads to Nirvana. Karma, by which good and evil deeds result in appropriate reward or punishment, and the cycle of rebirth can be broken by taking the Eightfold Path. All Buddhas are revered but particularly Gautama.

**Organization** There is a monastic system which aims to create favourable conditions for spiritual development. This involves meditation, personal discipline and spiritual exercises in the hope of liberation from self. Buddhism has proved very flexible in adapting its organization, ceremony and pattern of belief to different cultural and social conditions. There are numerous festivals and ceremonies, and pilgrimage is of great spiritual value.

**Divisions** There are two main traditions in Buddhism. Theravada Buddhism adheres to the teachings of the earliest Buddhist writings; salvation can be attained only by the few who accept the severe discipline and effort necessary to achieve it. Mahayana Buddhism developed later and is more flexible and creative, embracing popular piety. It teaches that salvation is possible for everyone and introduced the doctrine of the bodhisattva (one who attains enlightenment but out of compassion forestalls passing into Nirvana to help others achieve enlightenment). As Buddhism spread, other schools sprang up including Zen, Lamaism, Tendai, Nichiren and Soka Gakkai.

## Major Buddhist festivals

Weekly Uposatha Days, Buddha's Birth, Enlightenment, First Sermon and Death are observed in the different countries where Buddhism is practised but often on different dates. In some of these countries there are additional festivals in honour of Buddha.

## Christianity

**Founded** 1st-cAD.

**Founder** Jesus Christ 'the Son of God' (c.4BC–c.30AD).

**Sacred texts** The Bible consisting of the Old and New Testaments. The New Testament written between AD30 and 150 consists of the Gospels, the Acts of the Apostles, the Epistles, and the Apocalypse.

**Beliefs** A monotheistic world religion, centred on the life and works of Jesus of Nazareth in Judaea, who proclaimed the most important rules of life to be love of God, followed by love of one's neighbour. Christians believe that Jesus was the Son of God who was put to death by crucifixion as a sacrifice in order to save humanity from the consequences of sin and death, and was raised from the dead; he makes forgiveness and reconciliation with God possible, and ensures eternal life for the repentant believer. The earliest followers of Jesus were Jews who believed him to be the Messiah or 'Saviour' promised by the prophets in the Old Testament. Christians believe he will come again to inaugurate the 'Kingdom of God'.

**Organization** Jesus Christ appointed 12 men to be his disciples:

1 Peter (brother of Andrew)
2 Andrew (brother of Peter)
3 James, son of Zebedee (brother of John)
4 John (brother of James)
5 Philip
6 Bartholomew
7 Thomas
8 Matthew
9 James of Alphaeus
10 Simon the Canaanite (in Matthew and Mark) or Simon 'the Zealot' (in Luke and the Acts)
11 Judas Iscariot

(Thaddeus in the book of Matthew and Mark is the twelfth disciple, while in Luke and the Acts the twelfth is Judas or James. Matthias succeeded to Judas's place.) Soon after the resurrection the disciples gathered for the festival of Pentecost and received special signs of the power of God, the Holy Spirit. The disciples became a defined new body, the Church. Through the witness of the Apostles and their successors, the Christian faith quickly spread and in AD315 became the official religion of the Roman Empire. It survived the 'Dark Ages' to become the basis of civilization in the Middle Ages in Europe.

**Divisions** Major divisions — separated as a result of differences of doctrine and practice — are the Orthodox or Eastern Church, the Roman Catholic Church, acknowledging the Bishop of Rome as head, and the Protestant Churches stemming from the split with the Roman Church in the 16th-c. All Christians recognize the authority of the Bible, read at public worship, which takes place at least every Sunday, to celebrate the resurrection of Jesus Christ. Most Churches recognize at least two sacraments (Baptism and the Eucharist, Mass, or Lord's Supper) as essential.

## Major Christian Denominations

**Denomination and Origins**

**Baptists** In radical Reformation objections to infant baptism, demands for church–state separation; John Smyth, English Separatist in 1609; Roger Williams, 1638, Providence, Rhode Island.

**Church of England** Henry VIII separated the English Catholic Church from Rome, 1534, for political reasons.

**Lutherans** Martin Luther (1483–1546) in Wittenberg, Germany, 1517, objected to Catholic doctrine of salvation by merit and sale of indulgences; break complete by 1519.

**Methodists** John Wesley (1703–91) began movement, 1738, within Church of England.

**Orthodox** Original Christian proselytizing in 1st-c; broke with Rome, 1054, after centuries of doctrinal disputes and diverging traditions.

**Denomination and Origins**

**Pentecostal** ► **Pentecostalism** on p653.

**Presbyterians** In Calvinist Reformation in 1500s; differed with Lutherans over sacraments, and church government. John Knox (c.1513–1572) founded Scottish Presbyterian Church about 1560.

**Roman Catholic** Traditionally in the naming of St Peter as the first vicar by Jesus; historically, in early Christian proselytizing and the conversion of imperial Rome in the 4th-c.

**United Church of Christ** Union of the Congregational and Christian Churches with the Evangelical and Reformed Church. An ecumenical Protestant Church, it allows for variation in organization and interpretation of doctrine but reflects its Reformed theological background.

## The Ten Commandments

- I I am the Lord your God, who brought you out of the land of Egypt, out of the house of bondage. You shall have no other gods before me.
- II You shall not make for yourself a graven image. You shall not bow down to them or serve them.
- III You shall not take the name of the Lord your God in vain.
- IV Remember the sabbath day, to keep it holy.
- V Honour your father and your mother.
- VI You shall not kill.
- VII You shall not commit adultery.
- VIII You shall not steal.
- IX You shall not bear false witness against your neighbour.
- X You shall not covet.

The Ten Commandments appear in two different places in the Bible — Exodus 20:17 and Deuteronomy 5:6-21. Most Protestant, Anglican and Orthodox Christians enumerate the Commandments differently from Roman Catholics and Lutherans.

## Major immovable Christian feasts

For Saints' days ► pp644–7

|  |  |
|---|---|
| 1 Jan | Solemnity of Mary, Mother of God |
| 6 Jan | Epiphany |
| 7 Jan | Christmas Day (*Eastern Orthodox*) [1] |
| 11 Jan | Baptism of Jesus |
| 25 Jan | Conversion of Apostle Paul |
| 2 Feb | Presentation of Jesus (*Candelmas Day*) |
| 22 Feb | The Chair of Peter, Apostle |
| 25 Mar | Annunciation of the Virgin Mary |
| 24 Jun | Birth of John the Baptist |
| 6 Aug | Transfiguration |
| 15 Aug | Assumption of the Virgin Mary |
| 22 Aug | Queenship of Mary |
| 8 Sep | Birthday of the Virgin Mary |
| 14 Sep | Exaltation of the Holy Cross |
| 2 Oct | Guardian Angels |
| 1 Nov | All Saints |
| 2 Nov | All Souls |
| 9 Nov | Dedication of the Lateran Basilica |
| 21 Nov | Presentation of the Virgin Mary |
| 8 Dec | Immaculate Conception |
| 25 Dec | Christmas Day |
| 28 Dec | Holy Innocents |

[1] Fixed feasts in the Julian Calendar fall 13 days later than the Gregorian Calendar date.

## Movable Christian feasts 1995–2010

| Year | Ash Wednesday | Easter | Ascension | Whit Sunday (Pentecost) | Trinity Sunday | Sundays after Trinity | Corpus Christi | First Sunday in Advent |
|---|---|---|---|---|---|---|---|---|
| 1995 | 1 Mar | 16 Apr | 25 May | 4 Jun | 11 Jun | 24 | 15 Jun | 3 Dec |
| 1996 | 21 Feb | 7 Apr | 16 May | 26 May | 2 Jun | 25 | 6 Jun | 1 Dec |
| 1997 | 12 Feb | 30 Mar | 8 May | 18 May | 25 May | 26 | 29 May | 30 Nov |
| 1998 | 25 Feb | 12 Apr | 21 May | 31 May | 7 Jun | 24 | 11 Jun | 29 Nov |
| 1999 | 17 Feb | 4 Apr | 13 May | 23 May | 30 May | 25 | 3 Jun | 28 Nov |
| 2000 | 8 Mar | 23 Apr | 1 Jun | 11 Jun | 18 Jun | 23 | 22 Jun | 3 Dec |
| 2001 | 28 Feb | 15 Apr | 24 May | 3 Jun | 10 Jun | 24 | 14 Jun | 2 Dec |
| 2002 | 13 Feb | 31 Mar | 9 May | 19 May | 26 May | 26 | 30 May | 1 Dec |
| 2003 | 5 Mar | 20 Apr | 29 May | 8 Jun | 15 Jun | 23 | 19 Jun | 30 Nov |
| 2004 | 25 Feb | 11 Apr | 20 May | 30 May | 6 Jun | 24 | 10 Jun | 28 Nov |
| 2005 | 9 Feb | 27 Mar | 5 May | 15 May | 22 May | 26 | 26 Jun | 27 Nov |
| 2006 | 1 Mar | 16 Apr | 25 May | 4 Jun | 11 Jun | 24 | 15 Jun | 3 Dec |
| 2007 | 21 Feb | 8 Apr | 17 May | 27 May | 3 Jun | 25 | 7 Jun | 2 Dec |
| 2008 | 6 Feb | 23 Mar | 1 May | 11 May | 18 May | 27 | 22 May | 30 Nov |
| 2009 | 25 Feb | 12 Apr | 21 May | 31 May | 7 Jun | 24 | 11 Jun | 29 Nov |
| 2010 | 17 Feb | 4 Apr | 13 May | 23 May | 30 May | 25 | 3 Jun | 28 Nov |

Ash Wednesday, the first day of Lent, can fall at the earliest on 4 February and at the latest on 10 March.

Palm (Passion) Sunday is the Sunday before Easter; Good Friday is the Friday before Easter; Holy Saturday (often referred to as Easter Saturday) is the Saturday before Easter; Easter Saturday, in traditional usage, is the Saturday following Easter.

Easter Day can fall at the earliest on 22 March and at the latest on 25 April. Ascension Day can fall at the earliest on 30 April and at the latest on 3 June. Whit Sunday can fall at the earliest on 10 May and at the latest on 13 June. There are not fewer than 22 and not more than 27 Sundays after Trinity. The first Sunday of Advent is the Sunday nearest to 30 November.

## Saints' days

The official recognition of Saints, and the choice of a Saint's Day, varies greatly between different branches of Christianity, calendars and localities. Only major variations are included below, using the following abbreviations:

C Coptic *E* Eastern G Greek *W* Western

### ❑ January

1 Basil (*E*), Fulgentius, Telemachus
2 Basil and Gregory of Nazianzus (*W*), Macarius of Alexandria, Seraphim of Sarov
3 Geneviève
4 Angela of Foligno
5 Simeon Stylites (*W*)
7 Cedda, Lucian of Antioch (*W*), Raymond of Penyafort
8 Atticus (*E*), Gudule, Severinus
9 Hadrian the African
10 Agatho, Marcian
12 Ailred, Benedict Biscop
13 Hilary of Poitiers
14 Kentigern
15 Macarius of Egypt, Maurus, Paul of Thebes
16 Honoratus
17 Antony of Egypt
19 Wulfstan
20 Euthymius, Fabian, Sebastian
21 Agnes, Fructuosus, Maximus (*E*), Meinrad
22 Timothy (*G*), Vincent
23 Ildefonsus
24 Babylas (*W*), Francis de Sales
25 Gregory of Nazianzus (*E*)
26 Paula, Timothy and Titus, Xenophon (*E*)
27 Angela Merici
28 Ephraem Syrus (*E*), Paulinus of Nola, Thomas Aquinas
29 Gildas
31 John Bosco, Marcella

### ❑ February

1 Brigid, Pionius
3 Anskar, Blaise (*W*), Werburga, Simeon (*E*)
4 Gilbert of Sempringham, Isidore of Pelusium, Phileas
5 Agatha, Avitus
6 Dorothy, Paul Miki and companions, Vedast
8 Theodore (*G*), Jerome Emiliani
9 Teilo
10 Scholastica

11 Benedict of Aniane, Blaise (*E*), Caedmon, Gregory II
12 Meletius
13 Agabus (*W*), Catherine dei Ricci, Priscilla (*E*)
14 Cyril and Methodius (*W*), Valentine (*W*)
16 Flavian (*E*), Pamphilus (*E*), Valentine (*G*)
18 Bernadette (*France*), Colman, Flavian (*W*), Leo I (*E*)
20 Wulfric
21 Peter Damian
23 Polycarp
25 Ethelbert, Tarasius, Walburga
26 Alexander (*W*), Porphyrius
27 Leander
28 Oswald of York

**❑ March**

1 David
2 Chad, Simplicius
3 Ailred
4 Casimir
6 Chrodegang
7 Perpetua and Felicity
8 Felix, John of God, Pontius
9 Frances of Rome, Gregory of Nyssa, Pacian
10 John Ogilvie, Macarius of Jerusalem, Simplicius
11 Constantine, Oengus, Sophronius
12 Gregory (the Great)
13 Nicephorus
14 Benedict (*E*)
15 Clement Hofbauer
17 Gertrude, Joseph of Arimathea (*W*), Patrick
18 Anselm of Lucca, Cyril of Jerusalem, Edward
19 Joseph
20 Cuthbert, John of Parma, Martin of Braga
21 Serapion of Thmuis
22 Catherine of Sweden, Nicholas of Fluë
23 Turibius de Mongrovejo
30 John Climacus

**❑ April**

1 Hugh of Grenoble, Mary of Egypt (*E*), Melito
2 Francis of Paola, Mary of Egypt (*W*)
3 Richard of Chichester
4 Isidore of Seville
5 Juliana of Liège, Vincent Ferrer
7 Hegesippus, John Baptist de la Salle
8 Agabus (*E*)
10 Fulbert
11 Gemma Galgani, Guthlac, Stanislaus
12 Julius I, Zeno
13 Martin I
15 Aristarchus, Pudus (*E*), Trophimus of Ephesus
17 Agapetus (*E*), Stephen Harding
18 Mme Acarie
19 Alphege, Leo IX
21 Anastasius (*E*), Anselm, Beuno, Januarius (*E*)
22 Alexander (*C*)
23 George
24 Egbert, Fidelis of Sigmaringen, Mellitus
25 Mark, Phaebadius
27 Zita
28 Peter Chanel, Vitalis and Valeria
29 Catherine of Siena, Hugh of Cluny, Peter Martyr, Robert
30 James (the Great) (*E*), Pius V

**❑ May**

1 Asaph, Joseph the Worker, Walburga
2 Athanasius
3 Philip and James (the Less) (*W*)
4 Gotthard
5 Hilary of Arles
7 John of Beverley
8 John (*E*), Peter of Tarantaise
10 Antoninus, Comgall, John of Avila, Simon (*E*)
11 Cyril and Methodius (*E*), Mamertus
12 Epiphanius, Nereus and Achilleus, Pancras
14 Matthias (*W*)
16 Brendan, John of Nepomuk, Simon Stock
17 Robert Bellarmine, Paschal Baylon
18 John I
19 Dunstan, Ivo, Pudens (*W*), Pudentiana (*W*)
20 Bernardino of Siena
21 Helena (*E*)
22 Rita of Cascia
23 Ivo of Chartres
24 Vincent of Lérins
25 Aldhelm, Bede, Gregory VII, Mary Magdalene de Pazzi
26 Philip Neri, Quadratus
27 Augustine of Canterbury
30 Joan of Arc

**❑ June**

1 Justin Martyr, Pamphilus
2 Erasmus, Marcellinus and Peter, Nicephorus (*G*), Pothinus
3 Charles Lwanga and companions, Clotilde, Kevin
4 Optatus, Petrock
5 Boniface
6 Martha (*E*), Norbert
7 Paul of Constantinople (*W*), Willibald
8 William of York
9 Columba, Cyril of Alexandria (*E*), Ephraem (*W*)
11 Barnabas, Bartholomew (*E*)
12 Leo III
13 Anthony of Padua
15 Orsisius, Vitus
17 Alban, Botulph
19 Gervasius and Protasius, Jude (*E*), Romuald
20 Alban
21 Alban of Mainz, Aloysius Gonzaga
22 John Fisher and Thomas More, Niceta, Pantaenus (*C*), Paulinus of Nola
23 Etheldreda
24 Birth of John the Baptist
25 Prosper of Aquitaine
27 Cyril of Alexandria (*W*), Ladislaus
28 Irenaeus
29 Peter and Paul
30 First Martyrs of the Church of Rome

**❑ July**

1 Cosmas and Damian (*E*), Oliver Plunket
3 Anatolius, Thomas

4 Andrew of Crete (*E*), Elizabeth of Portugal, Ulrich
5 Anthony Zaccaria
6 Maria Goretti
7 Palladius, Pantaenus
8 Kilian, Aquila and Prisca (*W*)
11 Benedict (*W*), Pius I
12 John Gualbert, Veronica
13 Henry II, Mildred, Silas
14 Camillus of Lellis, Deusdedit, Nicholas of the Holy Mountain (*E*)
15 Bonaventure, Jacob of Nisibis, Swithin, Vladimir
16 Eustathius, Our Lady of Mt Carmel
17 Ennodius, Leo IV, Marcellina, Margaret (*E*), Scillitan Martyrs
18 Arnulf, Philastrius
19 Macrina, Symmachus
20 Aurelius, Margaret (*W*)
21 Lawrence of Brindisi, Praxedes
22 Mary Magdalene
23 Apollinaris, Bridget of Sweden
25 Anne and Joachim (*E*), Christopher, James (the Great) (*W*)
26 Anne and Joachim (*W*)
27 Pantaleon
28 Innocent I, Samson, Victor I
29 Lupus, Martha (*W*), Olave
30 Peter Chrysologus, Silas (*G*)
31 Giovanni Colombini, Germanus, Joseph of Arimathea (*E*), Ignatius of Loyola

❑ **August**

1 Alphonsus Liguori, Ethelwold
2 Eusebius of Vercelli, Stephen I
4 Jean-Baptiste Vianney
6 Hormisdas
7 Cajetan, Sixtus II and companions
8 Dominic
9 Matthias (*G*)
10 Laurence, Oswald of Northumbria
11 Clare, Susanna
13 Maximus (*W*), Pontian and Hippolytus, Radegunde
14 Maximilian Kolbe
15 Arnulf, Tarsicius
16 Roch, Simplicianus, Stephen of Hungary
17 Hyacinth
19 John Eudes, Sebaldus
20 Bernard, Oswin, Philibert
21 Jane Frances de Chantal, Pius X
23 Rose of Lima, Sidonius Apollinaris
24 Bartholomew (*W*), Ouen
25 Joseph Calasanctius, Louis IX, Menas of Constantinople
26 Blessed Dominic of the Mother of God, Zephyrinus
27 Caesarius, Monica
28 Augustine of Hippo
29 Beheading of John the Baptist, Sabina
30 Pammachius
31 Aidan, Paulinus of Trier

❑ **September**

1 Giles, Simeon Stylites (*E*)
2 John the Faster (*E*)
3 Gregory (the Great)
4 Babylas (*E*), Boniface I
5 Zacharias (*E*)
9 Peter Claver, Sergius of Antioch
10 Finnian, Nicholas of Tolentino, Pulcheria
11 Deiniol, Ethelburga, Paphnutius
13 John Chrysostom (*W*)
15 Catherine of Genoa, Our Lady of Sorrows
16 Cornelius, Cyprian of Carthage, Euphemia, Ninian
17 Robert Bellarmine, Hildegard, Lambert, Satyrus
19 Januarius (*W*), Theodore of Tarsus
20 Agapetus or Eustace (*W*)
21 Matthew (*W*)
23 Adamnan, Linus
25 Sergius of Rostov
26 Cosmas and Damian (*W*), Cyprian of Antioch, John (*E*)
27 Frumentius (*W*), Vincent de Paul
28 Exuperius, Wenceslaus
29 Michael (*Michaelmas Day*), Gabriel and Raphael
30 Jerome, Otto

❑ **October**

1 Remigius, Romanos, Teresa of the Child Jesus
2 Leodegar (Leger)
3 Teresa of Lisieux, Thomas de Cantilupe
4 Ammon, Francis of Assisi, Petronius
6 Bruno, Thomas (*G*)
9 Demetrius (*W*), Denis and companions, Dionysius of Paris, James (the Less) (*E*), John Leonardi
10 Francis Borgia, Paulinus of York
11 Atticus (*E*), Bruno, Nectarius
12 Wilfrid
13 Edward the Confessor
14 Callistus I, Cosmas Melodus (*E*)
15 Lucian of Antioch (*E*), Teresa of Avila
16 Gall, Hedwig, Lullus, Margaret Mary Alacoque
17 Ignatius of Antioch, Victor
18 Luke
19 John de Bréboeuf and Isaac Jogues and companions, Paul of the Cross, Peter of Alcántara
21 Hilarion, Ursula
22 Abercius
23 John of Capistrano
24 Anthony Claret
25 Crispin and Crispinian, Forty Martyrs of England and Wales, Gaudentius
26 Demetrius (*E*)
28 Firmilian (*E*), Simon and Jude
30 Serapion of Antioch
31 Wolfgang

❑ **November**

1 All Saints, Cosmas and Damian (*E*)
2 Eustace (*E*), Victorinus
3 Hubert, Malachy, Martin de Porres, Pirminius, Winifred

4 Charles Borromeo, Vitalis and Agricola
5 Elizabeth (*W*)
6 Illtyd, Leonard, Paul of Constantinople (*E*)
7 Willibrord
8 Elizabeth (*E*), Willehad
9 Simeon Metaphrastes (*E*)
10 Justus, Leo I (*W*)
11 Martin of Tours (*W*), Menas of Egypt, Theodore of Studios
12 Josaphat, Martin of Tours (*E*), Nilus the Ascetic
13 Abbo, John Chrysostom (*E*), Nicholas I
14 Dubricius, Gregory Palamas (*E*)
15 Albert the Great, Machutus
16 Edmund of Abingdon, Eucherius, Gertrude (the Great), Margaret of Scotland, Matthew (*E*)
17 Elizabeth of Hungary, Gregory Thaumaturgus, Gregory of Tours, Hugh of Lincoln
18 Odo, Romanus
19 Mechthild, Nerses
20 Edmund the Martyr
21 Gelasius
22 Cecilia
23 Amphilochius, Clement I (*W*), Columban, Felicity, Gregory of Agrigentum
25 Clement I (*E*), Mercurius, Mesrob
26 Siricius
27 Barlam and Josaphat
28 Simeon Metaphrastes
29 Cuthbert Mayne
30 Andrew, Frumentius (*G*)

❑ **December**

1 Eligius
2 Chromatius
3 Francis Xavier
4 Barbara, John Damascene, Osmund
5 Clement of Alexandria, Sabas
6 Nicholas
7 Ambrose
10 Miltiades
11 Damasus, Daniel
12 Jane Frances de Chantal, Spyridon (*E*), Vicelin
13 Lucy, Odilia
14 John of the Cross, Spyridon (*W*)
16 Eusebius
18 Frumentius (*C*)
20 Ignatius of Antioch (*G*)
21 Peter Canisius, Thomas
22 Anastasia (*E*), Chrysogonus (*E*)
23 John of Kanty
26 Stephen (*W*)
27 John (*W*), Fabiola, Stephen (*E*)
29 Thomas à Becket, Trophimus of Arles
31 Sylvester

## Confucianism

**Founded** 6th-cBC in China.

**Founder** K'ung Fu-tse (Confucius) (c.551–479BC).

**Sacred texts** Shih Ching, Li Ching, Shu Ching, Chu'un Ch'iu, I Ching.

**Beliefs** The oldest school of Chinese thought, Confucianism did not begin as a religion. Confucius was concerned with the best way to behave and live in this world and was not concerned with the afterlife. He emerges as a great moral teacher who tried to replace the old religious observances with moral values as the basis of social and political order. He laid particular emphasis on the family as the basic unit in society and the foundation of the whole community. He believed that government was a matter of moral responsibility, not just manipulation of power.

**Organization** Confucianism is not an institution and has no church or clergy. However ancestor-worship and veneration of the sky have their sources in Confucian texts. Weddings and funerals follow a tradition handed down by Confucian scholars. Social life is ritualized and colour and patterns of clothes have a sacred meaning.

**Divisions** There are two ethical strands in Confucianism. One, associated with Confucius and Hsun Tzu (c.298–238BC), is conventionalistic: we ought to follow the traditional codes of behaviour for their own sake. The other, associated with Mencius (c.371–289BC) and medieval neo-Confucians, is intuitionistic: we ought to do as our moral natures dictate.

## Major Chinese festivals

| | |
|---|---|
| January/February | Chinese New Year |
| February/March | Lantern Festival |
| March/April | Festival of Pure Brightness |
| May/June | Dragon Boat Festival |
| July/August | Herd Boy and Weaving Maid Festival |
| August | All Souls' Festival |
| September | Mid-Autumn Festival |
| September/October | Double Ninth Festival |
| November/December | Winter Solstice |

## Hinduism

**Founded** c.1500BC by Aryan invaders of India with their Vedic religion.

**Sacred texts** The Vedas ('knowledge'), including the Upanishads which contain much that is esoteric and mystical. Also included are the epic poems the Ramayana and the Mahabharata. Best known of all is the Bhagavad Gita, part of the Mahabharata.

**Beliefs** Hinduism emphasizes the right way of living (dharma) and embraces many diverse religious beliefs and practices rather than a set of doctrines. It acknowledges many gods who are seen as manifestations of an underlying reality. Devout Hindus aim to become one with the 'absolute reality' or Brahman. Only after a completely pure life will the soul be released from the cycle of rebirth. Until then the soul will be repeatedly reborn. Samsara refers to the cycle of birth and rebirth. Karma is the law by which consequences of actions within one life are carried over into the next.

**Organization** There is very little formal structure. Hinduism is concerned with the realization of religious values in every part of life, yet there is a great emphasis on the performance of complex demanding rituals under the supervision of a Brahman priest and teacher. There are three categories of worship: temple, domestic and congregational. The most common ceremony is prayer (puja). Many pilgrimages take place and there is an annual cycle of festivals.

**Divisions** As there is no concept of orthodoxy in Hinduism, there are many different sects worshipping different gods. The three most important gods are Brahman, the primeval god, Vishnu, the preserver, and Shiva, both destroyer and creator of life. The three major living traditions are those devoted to Vishnu, Shiva and the goddess Shakti. Folk beliefs and practices exist together with sophisticated philosophical schools.

## Major Hindu festivals

*S* = Sukla ('waxing fortnight') *K* = Krishna ('waning fortnight')

| | |
|---|---|
| Chaitra S 9 | Ramanavami (Birthday of Lord Rama) |
| Asadha S 2 | Rathayatra (Pilgrimage of the Jagannatha Chariot at Puri) |
| Sravana S 11–15 | Jhulanayatra (Swinging the Lord Krishna) |
| Sravana S 15 | Rakshabandhana (Tying on Lucky Threads) |
| Bhadrapada K 8 | Janamashtami (Birthday of Lord Krishna) |
| Asvina S 7–10 | Durga-puja (Homage to Goddess Durga) (*Bengal*) |
| Asvina S 1–10 | Navaratri (Festival of Nine Nights) |
| Asvina S 15 | Lakshmi-puja (Homage to Goddess Lakshmi) |
| Asvina K 15 | Diwali, Dipavali (String of Lights) |
| Kartikka S 15 | Guru Nanak Jananti (Birthday of Guru Nanak) |
| Magha K 5 | Sarasvati-puja (Homage to Goddess Sarasvati) |
| Magha K 13 | Maha-sivaratri (Great Night of Lord Shiva) |
| Phalguna S 14 | Holi (Festival of Fire) |
| Phalguna S 15 | Dolayatra (Swing Festival) (*Bengal*) |

## Islam

**Founded** 7th-cAD.

**Founder** Mohammed (c.570–c.632).

**Sacred texts** The Koran, the word of God as revealed to Mohammed, and the Hadith, a collection of the prophet's sayings.

**Beliefs** A monotheistic religion, God is the creator of all things and holds absolute power over man. All persons should devote themselves to lives of grateful and praise-giving obedience to God as they will be judged on the Day of Resurrection. It is acknowledged that Satan often misleads humankind but those who have obeyed God or have repented of their sins will dwell in paradise. Those sinners who are unrepentant will go to hell. Muslims accept the Old Testament and acknowledge Jesus Christ as an important prophet, but they believe the perfect word of God was revealed to Mohammed. Islam imposes five pillars of faith on its followers: belief in one God and his prophet, Mohammed; salat, formal prayer preceded by ritual cleansing five times a day, facing Mecca; saum, fasting during the month of Ramadan; Hajj, pilgrimage to Mecca at least once; zakat, a religious tax on the rich to provide for the poor.

**Organization** There is no organized priesthood but great respect is accorded to descendants of Mohammed and holy men, scholars and teachers such as mullahs and ayatollahs. The Shari'a is the Islamic law and applies to all aspects of life, not just religious practices.

**Divisions** There are two main groups within Islam. The Sunni are the majority and the more orthodox. They recognize the succession from Mohammed to Abu Bakr, his father-in-law, and to the next three caliphs. The Shiites are followers of Ali, Mohammed's nephew and son-in-law. They believe in 12 imams, perfect teachers, who still guide the faithful from paradise. Shi'ah practice tends towards the ecstatic. There are many other subsects including the Sufis, the Ismailis and the Wahhabis.

## Major Islamic festivals

| | |
|---|---|
| 1 Muharram | New Year's Day; starts on the day which celebrates Mohammed's departure from Mecca to Medina in AD622. |
| 12 Rabi I | Birthday of Mohammed (Mawlid al-Nabi) AD572; celebrated throughout month of Rabi I. |
| 27 Rajab | 'Night of Ascent' (Laylat al-Miraj) of Mohammed to Heaven. |
| 1 Ramadan | Beginning of month of fasting during daylight hours. |
| 27 Ramadan | 'Night of Power' (Laylat al-Qadr); sending down of the Koran to Mohammed. |
| 1 Shawwal | 'Feast of Breaking the Fast' (Id al-Fitr); marks the end of Ramadan. |
| 8–13 Dhu-I -Hijja | Annual pilgrimage ceremonies at and around Mecca; month during which the great pilgrimage (Hajj) should be made. |
| 10 Dhu-I-Hijja | Feast of the Sacrifice (Id al-Adha). |

## Jainism

**Founded** 6th-cBC in India.

**Founder** Vardhamana Mahavira (c.540–468BC).

**Sacred texts** Svetambara canon of scripture and Digambara texts.

**Beliefs** Jainism is derived from the ancient jinas ('those who overcome'). They believe that salvation consists in conquering material existence through adhering to a strict ascetic discipline, thus freeing the 'soul' from the working of karma for eternal, all-knowing bliss. Liberation requires detachment from worldly existence, an essential part of which is Ahimsa, non-injury to living beings. Jains are also strict vegetarians.

**Organization** Like Buddhists, the Jains are dedicated to the quest for liberation and the life of the ascetic. However, rather than congregating in monastic centres, Jain monks and nuns have developed a strong relationship with lay people. There are temple rituals resembling Hindu puja. There is also a series of lesser vows and specific religious practices that give the lay person an identifiable religious career.

**Divisions** There are two categories of religious and philosophical literature. The Svetambara have a canon of scripture consisting of 45 texts, including a group of 11 texts in which the sermons and dialogues of Mahavira himself are collected. The Digambara hold that the original teachings of Mahavira have been lost but that their texts preserve accurately the substance of the original message. This disagreement over scriptures has not led to fundamental doctrinal differences.

## Judaism

**Founded** c.2000BC.

**Founder** Abraham (c.2000 –1650BC), with whom God made a covenant, and Moses (15th–13th-cBC), who gave the Israelites the law.

**Sacred texts** The Hebrew Bible, consisting of 24 books, the most important of which are the Torah or Pentateuch — the first five books. Also the Talmud made up of the Mishna, the oral law, and the Gemara, an extensive commentary.

**Beliefs** A monotheistic religion, the Jews believe God is the creator of the world, delivered the Israelites out of bondage in Egypt, revealed his law to them, and chose them to be a light to all human-kind. However varied their communities, Jews see themselves as members of a community whose origins lie in the patriarchal period. Ritual is very important and the family is the basic unit of ritual.

**Organization** Originally a theocracy, the basic institution is now the synagogue, operated by the congregation and led by a rabbi of their choice. The chief rabbis in France and Britain have authority over those who accept it; in Israel the two chief rabbis have civil authority in family law. The synagogue is the centre for community worship and study. Its main feature is the 'ark' (a cupboard) containing the handwritten scrolls of the Pentateuch. Daily life is governed by a number of practices and observances: male children are circumcised, the Sabbath is observed, and food has to be correctly prepared. The most important festival is the Passover, which celebrates the liberation of the Israelites from Egypt.

**Divisions** Today most Jews are descendants of either the Ashkenazim or the Sephardim, each with marked cultural differences. There are also several religious branches of Judaism from ultra-liberal to ultra-conservative, reflecting different points of view regarding the binding character of the prohibitions and duties prescribed for Jews.

## Major Jewish festivals

For Gregorian calendar equivalents, see p64

| | |
|---|---|
| 1–2 Tishri | Rosh Hashana (New Year) |
| 3 Tishri | Tzom Gedaliahu (Fast of Gedaliah) |
| 10 Tishri | Yom Kippur (Day of Atonement) |
| 15–21 Tishri | Sukkot (Feast of Tabernacles) |
| 22 Tishri | Shemini Atzeret (8th Day of the Solemn Assembly) |
| 23 Tishri | Simchat Torah (Rejoicing of the Law) |
| 25 Kislev to 2–3 Tevet | Hanukkah (Feast of Dedication) |
| 10 Tevet | Asara be-Tevet (Fast of 10th Tevet) |
| 13 Adar | Taanit Esther (Fast of Esther) |
| 14–15 Adar | Purim (Feast of Lots) |
| 15–22 Nisan | Pesach (Passover) |
| 5 Iyar | Israel Independence Day |
| 6–7 Sivan | Shavuot (Feast of Weeks) |
| 17 Tammuz | Shiva Asar be-Tammuz (Fast of 17th Tammuz) |
| 9 Av | Tisha be-Av (Fast of 9th Av) |

## Shintoism

**Founded** 8th-cAD in Japan.

**Sacred texts** Kojiki and Nihon Shoki.

**Beliefs** Shinto 'the teaching' or 'way of the gods', came into existence independently from Buddhism which was coming to the mainland of Japan at that time. It subsequently incorporated many features of Buddhism. Founded on the nature-worship of Japanese folk religions, it is made up of many elements; animism, veneration of nature and ancestor-worship. Its gods are known as kami and there are many ceremonies appealing to these kami for benevolent treatment and protection. Great stress is laid on the harmony between humans, their kami and nature. Moral and physical purity is a basic law. Death and other pollutions are to be avoided. Shinto is primarily concerned with life and this world and the good of the group. Followers must show devotion and sincerity but aberrations can be erased by purification procedures.

**Organization** As a set of prehistoric agricultural ceremonies, Shinto was never supported by a body of philosophical or moralistic literature. Shamans originally performed the ceremonies and tended the shrines, then gradually a particular tribe took over the ceremonies. In the 8th-c Shinto became political when the imperial family were ascribed divine origins and state Shintoism was established.

**Divisions** In the 19th-c Shinto was divided into Shrine (jinga) Shinto and Sectarian (kyoko) Shinto. Jinga became a state cult and it remained the national religion until 1945.

## Major Japanese festivals

Public holidays in Japan are listed on p70. In addition, the following festivals should be noted:

| | |
|---|---|
| 1–3 Jan | Oshogatsu (New Year) |
| 3 Mar | Ohinamatsuri (Doll's or Girls' Festival) |
| 5 May | Tango no Sekku (Boys' Festival) |
| 7 Jul | Hoshi matsuri *or* Tanabata (Star Festival) |
| 13–31 Jul | Obon (Buddhist All Souls) |

## Sikhism

**Founded** 15th-c in India.

**Founder** Guru Nanak (1469–1539).

**Sacred text** Adi Granth.

**Beliefs** Nanak preached tolerance and devotion to one God before whom everyone is equal. Sikh is the Sanskrit word for disciple. Nanak's doctrine sought a fusion of Brahmanism and Islam on the grounds that both were montheistic. God is the true Guru and his divine word has come to humanity through the 10 historical gurus. The line ended in 1708, since when the Sikh community has been called guru.

**Organization** There is no priestly caste and all Sikhs are empowered to perform rituals connected with births, marriages, and deaths. Sikhs worship in their own temples but they evolved distinct features like the langar, 'kitchen', a communal meal where people of any religion or caste could eat. Rest houses for travellers were also provided. The tenth guru instituted an initiation ceremony, the Khalsa. Initiates wear the Five Ks (uncut hair, steel bangle, comb, shorts, ceremonial sword) and a turban. Members of the Khalsa add the name Singh (lion) to their name and have to lead pure lives and follow a code of discipline. Sikhs generally rise before dawn, bathe and recite the japji, a morning prayer. Hindu festivals from northern India are observed.

**Divisions** There are several religious orders of Sikhs based either on disputes over the succession of gurus or points of ritual and tradition. The most important current issue is the number of Khalsa Sikhs cutting off their hair and beards and relapsing into Hinduism.

## Taoism

**Founded** 600BC in China.

**Founder** Lao-tzu (6th-cBC).

**Sacred texts** Chuang-tzu, Lao-tzu (Tao-te-ching).

**Beliefs** Taoism is Chinese for 'the school of the tao' and the 'Taoist religion'. Tao ('the way') is central in both Confucianism and Taoism. The former stresses the tao of humanity, the latter the tao of nature, harmony with which ensures appropriate conduct. Taoist religion developed later and was probably influenced by Buddhist beliefs. The doctrine emphasizes that good and evil action decide the fate of the soul. The Taoists believe that the sky, the earth and water are deities; that Lao-tzu is supreme master; that the disciple masters his body and puts evil spirits to flight with charms; that body and spirit are purified through meditation and by taking the pill of immortality to gain eternal life; and that the way is handed down from master to disciple. Religious Taoism incorporated ideas and images from philosophical Taoist texts, especially the Tao-te-ching but also the theory of Yin-Yang, the quest for immortality, mental and physical discipline, interior hygiene, internal alchemy, healing and exorcism, a pantheon of gods and spirits, and ideals of theocratic states. The Immortals are meant to live in the mountains far from the tumult of the world.

**Organization** This is similar to Buddhism in the matter of clergy and temple. The jiao is a ceremony to purify the ground. Zhon-gyual is the only important religious festival, when the hungry dead appear to the living and Taoist priests free the souls of the dead from suffering.

**Divisions** Religious Taoism emerged from many sects. These sects proliferated between 618 and 1126AD and were described collectively as Spirit Cloud Taoists. They form the majority of Taoist priests in Taiwan, where they are called 'Masters of Methods' or Red-headed Taoists. The more orthodox priests are called 'Tao Masters' or Black-headed Taoists.

## Sacred texts of world religions

**Religion and Texts**

**Baha'i** Most Holy Book, The Seven Valleys, The Hidden Words, the Bayan

**Buddhism** Tripitaka, Mahayana Sutras, Milinda-panha, Bardo Thodol

**Christianity** Old Testament: Genesis, Exodus, Leviticus, Numbers, Deuteronomy, Joshua, Judges, Ruth, 1 Samuel, 2 Samuel, 1 Kings, 2 Kings, 1 Chronicles, 2 Chronicles, Ezra, Nehemiah, Esther, Job, Psalms, Proverbs, Ecclesiastes, Song of Solomon, Isaiah, Jeremiah, Lamentations, Ezekiel, Daniel, Hosea, Joel, Amos, Obadiah, Jonah, Micah, Nahum, Habakkuk, Zephaniah, Haggai, Zechariah, Malachi. New Testament: Matthew, Mark, Luke, John, Acts of the Apostles, Romans, 1 Corinthians, 2 Corinthians, Galatians, Ephesians, Philippians, Colossians, 1 Thessalonians, 2 Thessalonians, 1 Timothy, 2 Timothy, Titus, Philemon, Hebrews, James, 1 Peter, 2 Peter, 1 John, 2 John, 3 John, Jude, Revelation. Apocrypha (Revised standard version 1957): 1 Esdras, 2 Esdras, Tobit, Judith, Additions to Esther, Wisdom of Solomon, Ecclesiasticus, Epistle of Jeremiah, Baruch, Prayer of Azariah and the Song of the Three Young Men, (History of) Susanna, Bel and the Dragon, Prayer of Manasseh, 1 Maccabees, 2 Maccabees. (The Authorized version incorporates Jeremiah into Baruch; The prayer of Azariah is simply called the Song of the Three Holy Children. The Roman Catholic Church includes Tobit, Judith, all of Esther, Maccabees 1 and 2, Wisdom of Solomon, Ecclesiasticus, and Baruch in its canon.)

**Confucianism** Shih ching, Li ching, Shu ching, Chu'un Ch'iu, I Ching

**Hinduism** The Vedas (including the Upanishads), Ramayana, Mahabharata and the Bhagavad Gita

**Islam** The Koran, the Hadith

**Jainism** Svetambara canon, Digambara texts

**Judaism** The Hebrew Bible: Torah (Pentateuch): Genesis, Exodus, Leviticus, Numbers, Deuteronomy. Also the books of the Prophets, Psalms, Chronicles and Proverbs. The Talmud including the Mishna and Gemara. The Zohar (Book of Splendour) is a famous Cabalistic book.

**Shintoism** Kojiki, Nihon Shoki

**Sikhism** Adi Granth

**Taoism** Chuang-tzu, Lao-tzu (Tao-te-ching)

## Other religions, sects and religious movements

**Adventist** A member of one of the many Christian groups which believe the second coming of Christ will happen very soon. ► **Seventh Day Adventists**

**anthroposophy** A modern spiritual movement founded in Switzerland in 1912 by Rudolf Steiner (1861–1925). *Anthropos* (meaning 'man') suggests it is more human-centred than God-centred; fundamental to anthroposophy is the aim to develop the whole human being — socially, intellectually and spiritually — and to restore the innate human capacity for spiritual perception, which has been dulled by materialism. Anthroposophy has influenced many areas of activity, particularly the foundation of special schools around the world.

**charismatic movement** A modern international, transdenominational Christian movement of spiritual renewal, which has its roots in the Pentecostal Church. Taking a variety of forms in Roman Catholic, Protestant, and Eastern Orthodox churches, it emphasizes the present reality and work of the Holy Spirit in the life of the Church and the individual. It may be characterized by the practice of speaking in tongues (glossolalia), prophecy and healing.

**Christadelphians** A Christian sect, founded in 1848 in the USA by John Thomas (1805–71). They claim that Christ will soon come again to establish a theocracy lasting for a millennium and based in Jerusalem. They are congregational in organization and have no ordained ministers. They believe in the complete accuracy of the Bible, and claim that only true believers will go on to life after death and that adult followers must be baptized to attain full salvation.

**ecumenism** A movement seeking to unify the different churches and denominations within Christianity. Modern ecumenism stems from the Edinburgh Missionary Conference (1910) and led to the formation in 1948 of the World Council of Churches. It encourages dialogue between churches, unions where possible, joint acts of worship, and joint service in the community.

**evangelicalism** A term (from Greek 'to announce the good news') which since the Reformation has been applied to the Protestant Churches due to their principles of justification through faith alone, and the supreme authority accorded to Scripture (ie not to church tradition or institutional figures). Although the term goes beyond denominational divisions, and has featured throughout the history of the Christian Church, in later years it has been applied more narrowly to Protestant Churches which emphasize biblical authority, and personal experience of conversion, commitment and ongoing relationship with Jesus Christ. Evangelicals believe in and are inspired by the necessity of carrying the Christian faith to those not already within the community of the Christian Church.

**Freemasonry** An international, secretive adult male fraternity who meet in clubs called lodges for social enjoyment and mutual assistance, united by their belief in a supreme being and in the immortal soul. The organization comes under attack for the secrecy concerning its activities, both towards outsiders and between the different levels of freemasons. Modern Freemasonry in the UK began in the early 18th-c, and is known for its rituals and signs of recognition that date back to ancient non-Christian religions and to the practices of the medieval craft guild of the stonemasons (in England).

**Fundamentalism** A conservative theological movement seeking to preserve the essential doctrines of the Christian faith, eg the Virgin birth and the resurrection of Christ. Its roots lie in the 19th-c when traditional assumptions began to be challenged by the concept of evolution and the growth of biblical criticism. The term dates from a 1920s Protestant movement in the USA, which was characterized by a literal interpretation of the Bible, and revived to describe some Christian and Muslim movements in the late 20th-c.

**Hare Krishna** Popular name for a Hindu cult founded in the USA in 1965 by His Divine Grace A C Bhaktivedanta Swami Prabhupada as The International Society for Krishna Consciousness. It focuses on love for Krishna (an incarnation of the god Vishnu) and promotes wellbeing through consciousness of God based on the ancient Vedic texts of India, eg the *Bhagavad Gita*. Its saffron-robed devotees are sometimes seen gathered in town centres chanting the mantra 'Hare Krishna'; they are vegetarians, avoid intoxicants and gambling, and are celibate apart from procreation within marriage.

**Jehovah's Witnesses** A millenarian movement organized in the USA in 1884 by Charles Taze Russell (1852–1916), then by Joseph Franklin Rutherford (1869–1942). They have their own translation of the Bible, which they interpret literally, and view themselves as entirely distinct from orthodox Christianity. They believe in the imminent second coming of Christ, and that their place in heaven depends on their obedience to God. Expected to 'witness' through house-to-house visiting, they avoid worldly involvement, and refuse to obey laws which they view as a contradiction of the law of God (eg taking oaths and military service). Their newspaper is called *The Watchtower* and their churches 'Kingdom Halls'.

**Mormons** The members of a religious sect called The Church of Jesus Christ of Latter-Day Saints, which since 1847 has been based in Salt Lake City, Utah. The sect was founded in 1830 by Joseph Smith (d.1844) and was polygamous until 1890. They base their beliefs on *The Book of Mormon* and on Smith's own revelations, *Doctrine and Covenants* and *The Pearl of Great Price*; these texts tell of the coming of a millennium when Christ will rule from a New Jerusalem established in America. Smith claimed to have received visions of the Angel Moroni and a new revelation of the prophet Mormon

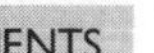



on golden tablets which he translated as *The Book of Mormon*. Mormons believe that God was a physical being like them, that humans progress from a spiritual state with God, to mortality and then on to an afterlife, that they too can become gods, and that the incarnation of Jesus was unique only because it was the first.

**New Age** A modern cultural trend encompassing a wide range of concepts concerned with the union of mind, body, and spirit. New Age expresses itself in an interest in a variety of beliefs and disciplines such as mysticism, meditation, astrology, and holistic medicine, including the pseudoscientific application of the 'healing powers' of crystals. Many adherents of New Age anticipate the dawning of an astrological or spiritual age in which humans will realize a 'higher' existence and experience true peace and harmony, and were therefore keenly aware of the dawn of the year 2000.

**Pentecostalism** A Christian renewal movement which began in the early 1900s in the USA — in Topeka, Kansas (1901) and Los Angeles (1906) — inspired by the coming of the Holy Spirit upon the disciples (Acts 2) and in reaction to the loss of evangelical fervour among Methodists and other denominations. Pentecostals believe in the blessing and empowering of Christians through the gifts of the Holy Spirit, eg speaking in tongues, prophecy and healing, and in the literal interpretation of the Bible. Their churches are characterized by missionary zeal, informal worship, enthusiastic singing, and the practice of spiritual gifts.

**Plymouth Brethren** A fundamentalist Christian sect founded in 1827 by a group of evangelicals in Dublin, Ireland, under John Nelson Darby (1800–82). It spread to England in 1832 and met in Plymouth. Millenarian in outlook, the sect is characterized by a simplicity of belief, practice and style of life based on the New Testament. There are no ordained priests and no maintained church buildings since meetings are held in members' homes.

**Quakers**, properly **The Society of Friends** A Christian sect rooted in radical Puritanism, founded in England by George Fox (1624–91). A colony for persecuted Quakers was founded in Pennsylvania in 1682 by William Penn (1644–1718). Belief in the 'inner light', a living contact with the divine Spirit, is the basis of its meetings for worship, where Friends gather in silence until moved by the Spirit to speak. Many meetings now have programmed orders of worship. Quakers are often actively involved in promoting tolerance, justice and peace.

**Scientology** A movement developed in the USA in the 1950s by L Ron Hubbard (1911–86). Based on his *Dianetics: The Modern Science of Mental Health*, which outlines a type of counselling for curing emotional illnesses and for enhancing life, it strives to open the minds of adherents to all great truths and to self-determination. The Church of Scientology (founded 1954) has made several controversial religious and scientific claims.

**Seventh Day Adventists** A section of the American Adventist movement of 1831 that stemmed from the preaching of William Miller (1782–1849). Many followers left the movement when Miller's prophecy that Christ would return to earth in 1843 or 1844 did not materialize. Some turned to the teaching of Ellen Gould White (1827–1915), particularly the importance of honouring the Sabbath (Friday evening to Saturday evening), and formed the Seventh Day Adventists (1863). They believe Christ's second coming is imminent, but delayed until the Adventist message is preached worldwide. They also observe Old Testament dietary laws, abstain from alcohol, and practise adult baptism by total immersion.

**transcendental meditation** or **TM** A meditation technique based in part on Hindu meditation, but with no doctrinal content and practised by both religious and non-religious people. Rediscovered by Guru Dev, it came to prominence after 1958 through Dev's disciple Maharishi Mahesh Yogi, who travelled widely teaching TM. Practitioners are taught to meditate for 20 minutes twice a day, sometimes repeating a silent mantra, as a means of reducing stress, achieving relaxation and gaining self understanding. The ultimate goal is 'god-realization'.

**Zoroastrianism** An ancient religion of Persian origin founded or reformed by Zoroaster, which teaches the existence of two equally opposed divine beings, one good and the other evil. It was forced out of Persia by the expansion of Islam. Zoroastrians believe that the spirit of evil, Ahriman, will finally be overcome by Ahura Mazda ('Wise Lord') or God, only if individuals play their part in saving the world. Their body of scripture is known as the *Avesta*, and rites of worship are performed by priests.

## Population distribution of major beliefs

Figures have been compiled from the most accurate recent available information and are in most cases correct to the nearest 1%.
Where possible within Islam the relative proportion of Sunnis and Shiites is indicated.
No precise information was available for the following: Armenia, Azerbaijan, Belarus, Cyprus, Estonia, Georgia, Hong Kong, Kazakhstan, Kyrgyzstan, Latvia, Lebanon, Lithuania, Macedonia, Micronesia, Moldova, Mongolia, Nauru, Russia, Slovenia, Tajikistan, Turkmenistan, Ukraine, Uzbekistan.

❑ **Baha'i**

| | |
|---|---|
| Bolivia | 3% |
| Kiribati | 3% |
| Panama | 1% |
| Tuvalu | 1% |

❑ **Buddhism**

| | |
|---|---|
| Bhutan | 73% |
| Brunei | 12% |
| Cambodia | 95% |
| China | 6% |
| France | 1% |
| India | 1% |
| Indonesia | 1% |
| Japan | 38% |
| Korea, Democratic People's Republic of (North Korea) | 2% |
| Korea, Republic of (South Korea) | 47% |
| Laos | 76% |
| Malaysia | 17% |
| Myanmar (Burma) | 89% |
| Nepal | 5% |
| Singapore | 28% |
| Sri Lanka | 69% |
| Taiwan | 42% |
| Thailand | 95% |
| Vietnam | 55% |

❑ **Chinese folk religion**

| | |
|---|---|
| China | 20% |
| Laos | 1% |
| Malaysia | 12% |
| Taiwan | 45% |

❑ **Christianity**

◇ *Protestantism* (includes all non-Roman Catholic denominations and forms of Christianity)

| | |
|---|---|
| Albania | 8% |
| Andorra | 1% |
| Angola | 12% |
| Antigua and Barbuda | 87% |
| Argentina | 2% |
| Australia | 47% |
| Austria | 7% |
| Bahamas, The | 74% |
| Barbados | 67% |
| Belgium | 10% |
| Belize | 30% |
| Benin | 3% |
| Bermuda | 73% |
| Bolivia | 5% |
| Botswana | 41% |
| Bosnia-Herzegovina | 35% |
| Brazil | 7% |
| Brunei | 8% |
| Bulgaria | 80% |
| Burkina Faso | 1% |
| Burundi | 7% |
| Cameroon | 18% |
| Canada | 42% |
| Central African Republic | 25% |
| Chad | 5% |
| Chile | 8% |
| Congo, Democratic Republic of | 15% |
| Côte d'Ivoire | 7% |
| Croatia | 11% |
| Cuba | 3% |
| Czech Republic | 8% |
| Denmark | 92% |
| Djibouti | 2% |
| Dominica | 16% |
| Ecuador | 2% |
| Egypt | 6% |
| El Salvador | 20% |
| Eritrea | 50% |
| Ethiopia | 42% |
| Fiji | 37% |
| Finland | 90% |
| France | 4% |
| Gabon | 30% |
| Germany | 39% |
| Ghana | 32% |
| Greece | 98% |
| Grenada | 38% |
| Guatemala | 22% |
| Guinea | 8% |
| Guinea-Bissau | 6% |
| Guyana | 36% |
| Haiti | 15% |
| Honduras | 3% |
| Hungary | 25% |
| Iceland | 93% |
| India | 2% |
| Indonesia | 6% |
| Iraq | 3% |
| Ireland | 3% |
| Israel | 2% |
| Jamaica | 55% |
| Jordan | 6% |
| Kenya | 38% |
| Kiribati | 38% |
| Korea, Democratic People's Republic of (North Korea) | 1% |
| Korea, Republic of (South Korea) | 39% |
| Laos | 1% |
| Lesotho | 49% |
| Liberia | 68% |
| Liechtenstein | 8% |
| Luxembourg | 2% |
| Madagascar | 18% |
| Malawi | 50% |
| Malaysia | 6% |
| Mali | 1% |
| Malta | 1% |
| Marshall Islands | 90% |
| Mauritius | 2% |
| Mexico | 3% |
| Monaco | 5% |
| Morocco | 1% |
| Mozambique | 3% |
| Myanmar (Burma) | 6% |
| Namibia | 66% |
| Netherlands, The | 27% |
| New Zealand | 52% |
| Nicaragua | 5% |
| Niger | 5% |
| Nigeria | 28% |
| Norway | 88% |
| Pakistan | 1% |
| Panama | 5% |
| Papua New Guinea | 44% |
| Paraguay | 9% |
| Peru | 5% |
| Philippines | 9% |
| Poland | 3% |
| Portugal | 2% |
| Romania | 88% |
| Rwanda | 9% |
| St Kitts and Nevis | 71% |
| St Lucia | 10% |
| St Vincent and the Grenadines | 62% |
| Samoa | 78% |
| São Tomé and Príncipe | 10% |
| Seychelles | 8% |
| Sierra Leone | 6% |
| Slovakia | 10% |
| Solomon Islands | 72% |
| Somalia | 2% |
| South Africa | 54% |
| Sri Lanka | 8% |
| Sudan, The | 7% |
| Suriname | 25% |
| Swaziland | 52% |
| Sweden | 91% |
| Switzerland | 40% |
| Syria | 10% |
| Taiwan | 5% |
| Tanzania | 35% |
| Togo | 7% |
| Tonga | 63% |
| Trinidad and Tobago | 28% |
| Tunisia | 1% |
| Tuvalu | 98% |
| Uganda | 33% |
| UK | 65% |
| Uruguay | 3% |
| USA | 56% |
| Vanuatu | 67% |
| Yugoslavia | 66% |
| Zambia | 41% |
| Zimbabwe | 33% |

◇ *Roman Catholicism*

| | |
|---|---|
| Albania | 4% |
| Andorra | 94% |
| Angola | 69% |
| Antigua and Barbuda | 9% |
| Argentina | 90% |
| Australia | 26% |
| Austria | 77% |
| Bahamas, The | 21% |
| Barbados | 4% |
| Belgium | 75% |
| Belize | 62% |
| Benin | 19% |
| Bermuda | 14% |
| Bolivia | 92% |
| Bosnia-Herzegovina | 15% |
| Botswana | 9% |
| Brazil | 87% |
| Burkina Faso | 10% |
| Burundi | 63% |
| Cameroon | 35% |
| Canada | 47% |
| Cape Verde | 98% |
| Central African Republic | 25% |

Chad 20%
Chile 80%
Colombia 95%
Comoros 14%
Congo 50%
Congo, Democratic Republic of 45%
Costa Rica 85%
Côte d'Ivoire 18%
Croatia 77%
Cuba 40%
Czech Republic 40%
Denmark 1%
Djibouti 4%
Dominica 77%
Dominican Republic 92%
Ecuador 94%
El Salvador 77%
Equatorial Guinea 89%
Fiji 9%
Finland 1%
France 80%
Gabon 65%
Germany 37%
Ghana 18%
Grenada 52%
Guatemala 73%
Guyana 19%
Haiti 80%
Honduras 94%
Hungary 64%
Iceland 1%
Indonesia 3%
Ireland 88%
Italy 85%
Jamaica 6%
Kenya 28%
Kiribati 53%
Korea, Republic of (South Korea) 12%
Laos 1%
Lesotho 45%
Liechtenstein 80%
Luxembourg 97%
Madagascar 24%
Malawi 20%
Malta 97%
Marshall Islands 7%
Mauritius 26%
Mexico 93%
Monaco 90%
Mozambique 25%
Namibia 24%
Netherlands, The 36%
New Zealand 15%
Nicaragua 95%
Nigeria 12%
Norway 1%
Palau 66%
Panama 84%
Papua New Guinea 22%
Paraguay 90%
Peru 93%
Philippines 83%
Poland 93%
Portugal 94%
Romania 6%
Rwanda 65%
St Kitts and Nevis 7%
St Lucia 90%
St Vincent and the Grenadines 19%
Samoa 22%
San Marino 93%
São Tomé and Príncipe 80%
Senegal 2%
Seychelles 90%
Sierra Leone 3%
Slovakia 59%
Solomon Islands 19%
South Africa 8%
Spain 97%
Suriname 23%
Swaziland 8%
Sweden 2%
Switzerland 46%
Togo 23%
Tonga 16%
Trinidad and Tobago 32%
Uganda 33%
UK 14%
Uruguay 60%
USA 28%
Vanuatu 15%
Vatican 100%
Venezuela 92%
Vietnam 7%
Yugoslavia 4%
Zambia 28%
Zimbabwe 12%

### ❑ Druze

Israel 2%

### ❑ Hinduism

Bangladesh 12%
Bhutan 22%
Fiji 38%
Guyana 35%
India 82%
Indonesia 2%
Kuwait 2%
Malaysia 7%
Mauritius 52%
Myanmar (Burma) 1%
Nepal 90%
Oman 13%
Pakistan 2%
Qatar 1%
Seychelles 1%
Singapore 5%
South Africa 2%
Sri Lanka 15%
Suriname 27%
Trinidad and Tobago 24%
UK 1%

### ❑ Islam

Afghanistan 99% (Shiite 25%, Sunni 74%)
Albania (Sunni) 60%
Algeria (Sunni) 99%
Austria 2%
Bahrain 95% (Shiite 73%, Sunni 22%)
Bangladesh 87%
Belgium 2%
Benin 17%
Bhutan 5%
Bosnia-Herzegovina (Sunni) 40%
Brunei 65%
Bulgaria 13%
Burkina Faso 44%
Burundi 1%
Cambodia 2%
Cameroon 22%
Central African Republic 14%
Chad 50%
China 2%
Comoros (Sunni) 86%
Congo 2%
Congo, Democratic Republic of 10%
Côte d'Ivoire 45%
Croatia 1%
Djibouti (Sunni) 94%
Egypt (Sunni) 94%
Equatorial Guinea 1%
Eritrea 50%
Ethiopia 40%
Fiji 8%
France 6%
Gabon 1%
Gambia, The 95%
Germany 3%
Ghana 10%
Greece 1%
Guinea 85%
Guinea-Bissau 42%
Guyana 9%
India 12%
Indonesia 87%
Iran 99% (Shiite 91%, Sunni 8%)
Iraq 96% (Shiite 54%, Sunni 42%)
Israel 14%
Jordan (Sunni) 94%
Kenya 7%
Kuwait 85% (Shiite 40%, Sunni 45%)
Laos 1%
Liberia 14%
Libya (Sunni) 97%
Madagascar 6%
Malawi 21%
Malaysia 53%
Maldives (Sunni) 100%
Mali 85%
Mauritania 99%
Mauritius 17%
Morocco (mostly Sunni) 99%
Mozambique 17%
Myanmar (Burma) 4%
Nepal 3%
Netherlands, The 3%
Niger (Sunni) 80%
Nigeria 50%
Oman 86%
Pakistan 97% (Shiite 20%, Sunni 77%)
Panama 5%
Philippines 5%
Qatar (mostly Sunni) 95%
Romania 1%
Rwanda 1%
Saudi Arabia (mostly Sunni) 99%
Senegal (Sunni) 92%
Sierra Leone (Sunni) 39%
Singapore 16%
Somalia (Sunni) 98%
South Africa 1%
Sri Lanka 8%
Sudan, The 70%
Suriname 21%
Sweden 1%
Switzerland 2%
Syria (mostly Sunni) 90%
Taiwan 1%
Tanzania 33%
Thailand 4%
Togo 15%
Trinidad and Tobago 6%
Tunisia (Sunni) 98%
Turkey (Sunni) 99%
Uganda 16%
UK 3%
United Arab Emirates 96% (Shiite 16%, Sunni 80%)
USA 2%
Yemen 97% (Shiite 56%, Sunni 41%)
Yugoslavia 19%
Zimbabwe 1%

**❑ Jainism**

| | |
|---|---|
| India | 1% |

**❑ Judaism**

| | |
|---|---|
| Argentina | 2% |
| Bulgaria | 1% |
| France | 1% |
| Hungary | 1% |
| Israel | 82% |
| Luxembourg | 1% |
| UK | 2% |
| Uruguay | 2% |
| USA | 2% |

**❑ Non-religious belief/unaffiliated**

| | |
|---|---|
| Albania | 28% |
| Andorra | 5% |
| Antigua and Barbuda | 1% |
| Australia | 17% |
| Austria | 8% |
| Bahamas, The | 3% |
| Barbados | 17% |
| Belgium | 10% |
| Belize | 2% |
| Bermuda | 8% |
| Bosnia-Herzegovina | 1% |
| Brazil | 3% |
| Bulgaria | 5% |
| Canada | 8% |
| Cape Verde | 1% |
| Central African Republic | 1% |
| Chile | 11% |
| China | 59% |
| Cuba | 55% |
| Czech Republic | 40% |
| Denmark | 2% |
| Dominican Republic | 1% |
| Equatorial Guinea | 4% |
| Finland | 9% |
| France | 8% |
| Germany | 15% |
| Haiti | 1% |
| Hungary | 8% |
| Iceland | 6% |
| Ireland | 5% |
| Italy | 14% |
| Jamaica | 18% |
| Korea, Democratic People's Republic of (North Korea) | 67% |
| Malta | 1% |
| Mexico | 1% |
| Netherlands, The | 32% |
| New Zealand | 16% |
| Norway | 6% |
| Poland | 2% |
| Portugal | 3% |
| Romania | 4% |
| San Marino | 3% |
| Singapore | 17% |
| Slovakia | 31% |
| Sweden | 6% |
| Switzerland | 9% |
| Trinidad and Tobago | 5% |
| UK | 14% |
| Uruguay | 35% |
| USA | 10% |
| Vanuatu | 1% |
| Vietnam | 15% |

**❑ Rastafarianism**

| | |
|---|---|
| Antigua and Barbuda | 1% |
| Jamaica | 6% |

**❑ Shintoism**

| | |
|---|---|
| Japan | 40% |

**❑ Sikhism**

| | |
|---|---|
| Fiji | 1% |
| India | 2% |
| UK | 1% |

**❑ Taoism**

| | |
|---|---|
| Singapore | 13% |

**❑ Traditional beliefs**

| | |
|---|---|
| Angola | 19% |
| Benin | 61% |
| Botswana | 50% |
| Brunei | 15% |
| Burkina Faso | 45% |
| Burundi | 29% |
| Cameroon | 25% |
| Central African Republic | 22% |
| Chad | 25% |
| Congo | 48% |
| Congo, Democratic Republic of | 30% |
| Côte d'Ivoire | 30% |
| Cuba | 2% |
| Equatorial Guinea | 4% |
| Ethiopia | 14% |
| Gabon | 4% |
| Gambia, The | 1% |
| Ghana | 34% |
| Guatemala | 5% |
| Guinea | 7% |
| Guinea-Bissau | 52% |
| Kenya | 26% |
| Korea, Democratic People's Republic of (North Korea) | 30% |
| Korea, Republic of (South Korea) | 2% |
| Laos | 20% |
| Lesotho | 6% |
| Liberia | 10% |
| Madagascar | 52% |
| Malawi | 9% |
| Mali | 14% |
| Mozambique | 55% |
| Namibia | 10% |
| Niger | 15% |
| Nigeria | 10% |
| Palau | 34% |
| Papua New Guinea | 34% |
| Rwanda | 25% |
| Senegal | 6% |
| Sierra Leone | 52% |
| Singapore | 21% |
| South Africa | 35% |
| Sudan, The | 23% |
| Suriname | 4% |
| Swaziland | 40% |
| Tanzania | 30% |
| Togo | 55% |
| Uganda | 18% |
| Vanuatu | 8% |
| Zambia | 31% |
| Zimbabwe | 40% |

**❑ Unspecified/others**

| | |
|---|---|
| Afghanistan | 1% |
| Algeria | 1% |
| Antigua and Barbuda | 2% |
| Argentina | 6% |
| Australia | 10% |
| Austria | 6% |
| Bahamas, The | 2% |
| Bahrain | 5% |
| Bangladesh | 1% |
| Barbados | 12% |
| Belgium | 3% |
| Belize | 6% |
| Bosnia-Herzegovina | 9% |
| Brazil | 3% |
| Bulgaria | 1% |
| Cambodia | 3% |
| Canada | 3% |
| Cape Verde | 1% |
| Central African Republic | 13% |
| Chile | 1% |
| China | 13% |
| Colombia | 5% |
| Costa Rica | 15% |
| Croatia | 11% |
| Czech Republic | 12% |
| Denmark | 5% |
| Dominica | 7% |
| Dominican Republic | 7% |
| Ecuador | 4% |
| El Salvador | 3% |
| Ethiopia | 4% |
| Fiji | 7% |
| Gambia, The | 4% |
| Germany | 6% |
| Ghana | 6% |
| Greece | 1% |
| Grenada | 10% |
| Guyana | 1% |
| Haiti | 4% |
| Honduras | 3% |
| Hungary | 2% |
| Indonesia | 1% |
| Iran | 1% |
| Iraq | 1% |
| Ireland | 4% |
| Italy | 1% |
| Jamaica | 15% |
| Japan | 4% |
| Kenya | 1% |
| Kiribati | 6% |
| Kuwait | 13% |
| Liberia | 8% |
| Libya | 3% |
| Liechtenstein | 12% |
| Malaysia | 5% |
| Malta | 1% |
| Marshall Islands | 3% |
| Mauritania | 1% |
| Mauritius | 3% |
| Mexico | 3% |
| Monaco | 5% |
| Nepal | 2% |
| Netherlands, The | 2% |
| New Zealand | 17% |
| Norway | 5% |
| Oman | 1% |
| Panama | 5% |
| Paraguay | 1% |
| Peru | 2% |
| Philippines | 3% |
| Poland | 2% |
| Portugal | 1% |
| Qatar | 5% |
| Romania | 1% |
| St Kitts and Nevis | 22% |
| St Vincent and the Grenadines | 19% |
| San Marino | 4% |
| São Tomé and Príncipe | 10% |
| Saudi Arabia | 1% |
| Seychelles | 1% |
| Soloman Islands | 9% |
| Spain | 3% |
| Switzerland | 3% |
| Taiwan | 7% |
| Tanzania | 2% |
| Thailand | 1% |
| Tonga | 21% |
| Trinidad and Tobago | 5% |
| Tunisia | 1% |
| Turkey | 1% |
| Tuvalu | 1% |
| United Arab Emirates | 4% |
| USA | 2% |
| Vietnam | 23% |
| Yemen | 3% |
| Yugoslavia | 1% |
| Zambia | 1% |
| Zimbabwe | 14% |

## Religious symbols

**The Trinity**

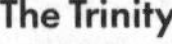

Equilateral triangle

Triangle in circle

Circle within triangle

**God**

**Father**

All-seeing eye

**Son**

Fish

**Holy Spirit**

Sevenfold flame

Seven branch candlestick The Menorah

Abraham

Pentateuch (The Law)

Doorposts and lintel (Passover)

Twelve tribes of Israel

Star of David

### Crosses

Barbée

Trefly

Canterbury

Celtic

Cercelée

Cross crosslet

Crux ansata

Globical

Graded (Calvary)

Greek

Iona

Jerusalem

Latin

Maltese

Millvine

Papal

Patée

Patée formée

Patriarchal (or Lorraine)

Potent

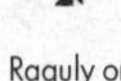
Raguly or Rarulée

Russian Orthodox

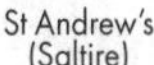
St Andrew's (Saltire)

St Peter's

Tau (St Anthony's)

Ankh (Egyptian)

Yin-yang (Taoism; symbol of harmony)

Torii (Shinto)

Om (Hinduism, Buddhism, Jainism; sacred syllable)

Ik-onkar (Sikhism; symbol of God)

Swastika (traditional; symbol of wellbeing)

Yantra, Sri Cakra (wheel of fortune)

## Signs of the zodiac

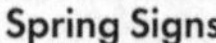

### Spring Signs

Aries, the Ram
*21 Mar–19 Apr*

Gemini, the Twins
*21 May–21 Jun*

Taurus, the Bull
*20 Apr–20 May*

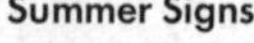

### Summer Signs

Cancer, the Crab
*22 Jun–22 July*

Leo, the Lion
*23 July–22 Aug*

Virgo, the Virgin
*23 Aug–22 Sep*

### Autumn Signs

Libra, the Balance
*23 Sep–23 Oct*

Scorpio, the Scorpion
*24 Oct–21 Nov*

Sagittarius, the Archer
*22 Nov–21 Dec*

### Winter Signs

Capricorn, the Goat
*22 Dec–19 Jan*

Aquarius, the Water Bearer
*20 Jan–18 Feb*

Pisces, the Fishes
*19 Feb–20 Mar*

# INDEX